T0185489

Advances in Networks, Intelligence and Computing

International Conference on Networks, Intelligence and Computing (ICONIC-2023)

Edited By

Dr. Ashok Kumar
Dr. Geeta Sharma
Dr. Anil Sharma
Dr. Pooja Chopra
Dr. Punam Rattan

Editors

Dr. Ashok Kumar is currently working as Professor in Lovely Professional University, Punjab, India. He is PhD in Computer Science and Engineering from Thapar University, Punjab, India. He did Master of Technology (M. Tech.) in Computer Science and Engineering from Punjabi University, Patiala, India. He has 20+ years of teaching and research experience. He has filed 20 patents, out of that three patents have been granted. He has published several research articles in International Journals and Conferences of repute. His current areas of research interest include Cloud/Fog/Edge Computing, Internet of Things, and Machine learning. Further, he is supervising 4 PhD scholars and 2 ME students.

Dr. Geeta Sharma is currently working as an Assistant Professor in the School of Computer Applications, Lovely Professional University, Phagwara, Punjab, India. She has received her Ph.D. degree in Computer Science in full time from Guru Nanak Dev University, Amritsar, Punjab, India. She has received her master's degree from the same University. She has 9 years of teaching and research experience. She has more than 25 research publications in International Journals and conferences. Her research is published in reputed SCI journals like Springer, Elsevier, and Taylor and Francis. She is an active reviewer in Springer and IEEE. She has 6 filed patents. Her research areas include Machine Learning, Fog/Cloud computing, IoT and Network Security. Currently, she is supervising 4 PhD scholars.

Dr. Anil Sharma is currently working as a Professor in the School of Computer Applications, Lovely Professional University, Phagwara, Punjab, India. He has 23 years of teaching experience. He has more than 70 research publications in high reputed journals. His current areas of research interest include data science. He has supervised 5 PhD scholars.

Dr. Pooja Chopra is currently working as an Associate Professor in the School of Computer Applications, Lovely Professional University, Phagwara, Punjab, India. She has 18 years of teaching experience. She has more than 15 research publications in high reputed journals. Her current areas of research interest include Artificial Intelligence and Cloud Computing. She has filed 4 patents. She is supervising 1 PhD scholar.

Dr. Punam Rattan is currently an Associate Professor and DII (Division of Industry Interface) at School of Computer Application Lovely Professional University in India. Along with dual master's degrees in computer applications (MCA) and business administration (MBA), she graduated from IKG Punjab Technical University with a Ph.D. in computer applications. She has 20+ years of teaching experience. She is a prolific author, having published over 30 research papers in esteemed journals and conferences like IEEE Xplore, SCOPUS, and SCI-indexed publications, in addition to three books. Dr. Rattan has significantly advanced data mining and machine learning fields with his research. She is supervising 6 PhD scholar and 1 scholar has already turned in her thesis.

Advances in Networks, Intelligence and Computing

International Conference on Networks, Intelligence and Computing (ICONIC-2023)

Edited By

Dr. Ashok Kumar
Dr. Geeta Sharma
Dr. Anil Sharma
Dr. Pooja Chopra
Dr. Punam Rattan

CRC Press
Taylor & Francis Group
Boca Raton London New York

CRC Press is an imprint of the
Taylor & Francis Group, an **Informa** business

First edition published 2024
by CRC Press
4 Park Square, Milton Park, Abingdon, Oxon, OX14 4RN

and by CRC Press
2385 NW Executive Center Drive, Suite 320, Boca Raton FL 33431

© 2024 selection and editorial matter, Dr. Ashok Kumar, Dr. Geeta Sharma, Dr. Anil Sharma, Dr. Pooja Chopra, Dr. Punam Rattan; individual chapters, the contributors

CRC Press is an imprint of Informa UK Limited

The right of Dr. Ashok Kumar, Dr. Geeta Sharma, Dr. Anil Sharma, Dr. Pooja Chopra and Dr. Punam Rattan to be identified as the authors of the editorial material, and of the authors for their individual chapters, has been asserted in accordance with sections 77 and 78 of the Copyright, Designs and Patents Act 1988.

All rights reserved. No part of this book may be reprinted or reproduced or utilised in any form or by any electronic, mechanical, or other means, now known or hereafter invented, including photocopying and recording, or in any information storage or retrieval system, without permission in writing from the publishers.

For permission to photocopy or use material electronically from this work, access www.copyright.com or contact the Copyright Clearance Center, Inc. (CCC), 222 Rosewood Drive, Danvers, MA 01923, 978-750-8400. For works that are not available on CCC please contact mpkbookspermissions@tandf.co.uk

Trademark notice: Product or corporate names may be trademarks or registered trademarks, and are used only for identification and explanation without intent to infringe.

British Library Cataloguing-in-Publication Data
A catalogue record for this book is available from the British Library

ISBN: 9781032553870 (Pbk)
ISBN: 9781003430421 (ebk)

DOI: 10.1201/9781003430421

Typeset in Sabon LT Std
by HBK Digital

Contents

List of Figures

List of Tables

About the Conference

The year 2023 marks the 100th birth anniversary of E.F. Codd (19 August 1923 - 18 April 2003), a computer scientist, who while working for IBM invented the relational model for database management, the theoretical basis for relational databases and relational database management systems. He made other valuable contributions to computer science but the relational model, a very influential general theory of data management, remains his most mentioned, analyzed, and celebrated achievement.

School of Computer Application, under the aegis of Lovely Professional University, pays homage to this great scientist of all times by hosting "CODD100 – International Conference on Networks, Intelligence and Computing (ICONIC-2023)".

The Conference held from 28-29th April 2023 with the aim to provide a platform to the scientists, researchers, academicians, industrialists, and students to assimilate the knowledge and get the opportunity to discuss, share insights through deep-dive research findings on the recent disruptions and developments in the field of computing. All technical sessions largely steer Network Technologies, Artificial Intelligence & Ethics, Advances in Computing, Futuristic Trends in Data Science, Security and Privacy, Data Mining and Information Retrieval.

Objectives of the Conference

- To provide a platform to facilitate the scientists, researchers, academicians, industrialists, and students to exchange their knowledge, ideas and innovations.
- To deliberate and disseminate the recent advancements and challenges in the computing sciences.
- To enable the delegates to establish research or business relations as well as to find international linkage for future collaborations.

Biographies

Dr. Geeta Sharma is working as an Assistant Professor in the School of Computer Applications, Lovely Professional University, Phagwara, Punjab, India. She has received her Ph.D. degree in full time from Guru Nanak Dev University, Amritsar, India. Her research areas include Machine Learning, Fog computing, IoT and network security. She has more than 20 research publications in international journals and conferences. Her research is published in reputed SCI journals like Springer, Elsevier, and Taylor and Francis. She is an active reviewer in Springer and IEEE.

1 Dual band compact patch antenna for MM-wave 5G application

Sachin Kumar Singh[a], Rohit Kumar Singh[b], Ritik Kumar[c], Amanpreet Singh Saini[d] and Ankit Sharma[e]

Department of Electronics and Communication Engineering Galgotia's College of Engineering and Technology, Greater Noida, India

Abstract

In this paper, a Rogers RT 5880 substrate is used todevelop and simulate a small patch antenna. The required resonance frequency and mode of operation are used to calculate the antenna's size. Using CST Studio Suite, the antenna is simulated, and its features such as frequency, bandwidth, reflection coefficient, gain, and radiation efficiency are examined. The proposed antenna features resonance frequencies of 33.1 GHzand 57 GHz, as well as bandwidths of 1.987 GHz and 6.39 GHz, according to the modeling findings. The antenna and feed line havea perfect impedance match over the whole operational frequency range, with an S11 value of less than -10 dB. Peak gains at 33.1 GHz and 57 GHz for the proposed antenna are 7.84 dB and 7.37 dB, respectively, and it features a directed emission pattern. Because they are both symmetric in the E- and H-planes, the radiation patterns exhibit good polarization characteristics. The obtained VSWR values imply that the proposed antenna has minimal reflection losses. The suggested antenna design follows a methodical process that includes substrate selection, establishing dimensions, modeling and analyzing, performance, optimization, and experimental validation.

Keywords: bandwidth, compact patch antenna, dual-band, high-speed data transmission, proximity coupling, rogers RT 5880 substrate

Introduction

In recent years, wireless mobile communication technology has made significant advancements, leading to the development of various new mobile communication standards [1]. To ensure the success of wireless applications in our daily lives, it is crucial to have an effective and compact antenna that can support digital transmission and high-speed data transfer, such as the 5G data transfer speeds ranging from 1 Gbps to 20 Gbps specified by IMT-2020 and ITU-R M.208 [2, 3]. Several strategies, such as broad bandwidth or modulation techniques, carrier aggregation, or employing higher frequencies, such as those beyond 6 GHz, can be employed to attain such data speeds. The antenna system, which converts electrical energy into electromagnetic wave energy, is one of the most crucial parts ofa wireless mobile communication system [4]. Therefore, toachieve optimum wireless mobile communication performance,it is essential to provide the system with an optimal antenna design that is compact, lightweight, and of the right size.

---

[a]sachinsingh044221@gmail.com, [b]rohitraj281202@gmail.com, [c]ritikkumar0430@gmail.com, [d]aps.saini@galgotiacollege.edu, [e]ankit.sharmaece@galgotiacollege.edu

Designing a high-gain compact patch antenna for mm- wave frequencies is a challenging task due to several factors such as signal attenuation, atmospheric absorption, and fading at high frequencies. As a result, the gain of the antenna needs to be highto overcome these challenges [5, 6].

This piece is organized as follows. In part II, a review of the literature is provided. Section III contains a comprehensive description of the design and calculations. Part IV presents the results and comments. Part V research objectives and problem identification Section VI then presents the conclusion and Part VII contains future recommendations.

Literature Review

The suggested study's innovative aspect is a straightforward, small-footprint dual-band architecture with a significant gain for mm-wave 5G applications. This antenna can assist 5G systems in achieving the specifications for outstanding spectrum efficiency, rapid data speeds, and low latency [6]. The recommended antenna array has a broad scanning angle and a maximum gain of 13.6 dB at 26 GHz and 14 dB at 28 GHz. The antenna element is made from a PCB and has a radial loss of 0.06 and a permittivity ratio of 2.55. The suggested architecture provides a solution for forthcoming 5G applications. [7]. The proposed antenna in this work may operate in the mm-Wave frequencies with a -10 dB bandwidth, according to the results. It is also a good contender for 5G applications because it can support dual 5G bands of 32/42 GHz for |S11|, each with a center frequency of 31.5 GHz and an effective bandwidth of 1.5GHz [8]. Gains of 5.51 dB at 10.15 GHz and 8.03 dB at 28 GHz,as well as a directed emission pattern, are features of the suggested design. In addition to other aspects, the study examines VSWR plots, radiation pattern plots, gain plots, and return loss plots. The patched antenna has a low-profile, planar design with a moderate to high gain and is used for 5G applications [9].

Antenna Design

The antenna's substrate is a Rogers RT 5880, which is 0.373 mmthick and has an average permittivity of 2.2. With copper siding measuring 0.035 mm, a typical compact patch antenna is first carved onto the substrate's top side. Table 1.1 provides the proposed antenna's dimensions. The entire base is used to reduce back radiations.

The designing procedure of this work involves the following steps:

- Substrate selection: The initial step is to select a decent substrate with the appropriate parameters such as dielectric constant, thickness, and loss tangential. In this case, the substrate employed is a Rogers RT 5880 with a permittivity of 2.2 and thickness of 0.373 mm.
- Determination of antenna dimensions: The antenna dimensions are determined based on the desired resonance frequency and mode of operation. With the dimensions shown in Table 1.1, a conventional compactpatch antenna is created in this situation.

Table 1.1 Dimension of suggested model.

Parameter	Value(mm)
W	10
WP	5
LP	6
FL	4.5
FW	1.2
T	0.4
GP	3
GS	1.8
L	10
h	0.373

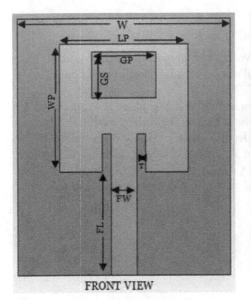

FRONT VIEW

BACK VIEW

Figure 1.1 Suggested model front view   *Figure 1.2* Suggested model back view

- Calculation of length of the patch: Equation (1), whichis based on the reso-nance frequency and the substrate's dielectric constant, is used to determine the length of the patch
- Simulation and analysis: A appropriate electromagnetic simulation pro-gramme, such as CST Studio Suite, is used to model the planned antenna. The simulation results are analysed to determine the antenna's frequency, bandwidth, reflective coefficient.
- Optimization: Based on the results, the antenna is optimized by adjusting the dimensions of the antenna to improve its performance.

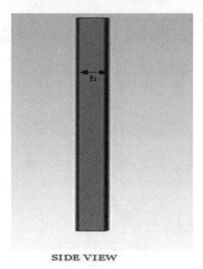

SIDE VIEW

Figure 1.3 Suggested model side view

Overall, the proposed antenna design involves a systematic approach of selecting substrate, determining dimensions, simulating and analyzing performance, optimization, and experimental validation.

A traditional patch antenna is examined in the initial step. It is intended to function in the fundamental mode, and the followingformulae can roughly define LP, or length of patch, at the resonance frequency (fr). emission pattern with an effective gain of 7.84 dB at 33.1 GHz and 7.37 dB at 57 GHz. With VSWR scores of 1.16 and 1.67 at 33.1 GHz and 57 GHz, respectively, the obtained VSWR readings show that the proposed antenna has minimal reflection losses.

$$LP = \frac{c}{2FR\sqrt{E_r}} \tag{1}$$

$$E_{f=\frac{E_r+1}{2}} \tag{2}$$

Where c is the speed of light and E_f is the substrate's actual dielectric constant.

Results and Discussion

In this paper CST Studio Suite's modelling tools are used to evaluate the recommended antenna. The suggested antenna has a resonance frequency of 33.1 GHz and a bandwidth of 1.987 GHz and 6.39 GHz, according to the calculations. The maximum gain of this antenna is 7.84 dB at 33.1 GHz and 7.37dB at 57 GHz. The suggested antenna has a radiative efficiencythat is 97.66% at 33.1 GHz and a radiative effectiveness of 92.58% at 57 GHz. According to the S11 parameter, the suggested antenna has an excellent impedance match between the antenna

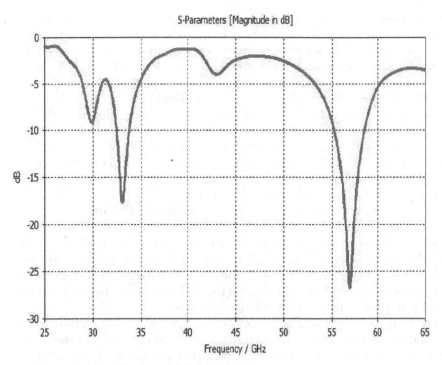

Figure 1.4 Suggested model S11 parameter

Table 1.2 Outcome of suggested model

Antenna Parameter	Single Patch	
Dimension in (mm)	10×10×0.373	
Frequency in (GHz)	33.1	57
Reflection coefficient S1 in db	-17.646	-26.72
gain in dB	7.84	7.37
Bandwidth in GHz	1.987	6.399
Radiation efficiency in %	97.66	92.58
VSWR	1.16	1.67

and the feed line over the full working frequency range, being less than -10 db. The radiation patterns have highpolarization properties since they are symmetric in both the E-and H-planes.

Table 1.2 summarizes the results of the suggested model, including antenna characteristics, diameter in mm, frequenciesin GHz, coefficient of reflection S11 in dB, peak gain in dB, bandwidth in GHz, radiation yield in %, and VSWR. The antenna proposed has a directed

The S-parameters are important parameters that determine the performance of an antenna. They represent the antenna's reflection and transmission coefficients, which show how muchpower the antenna reflects and transmits. The proposed antenna's simulated S-parameters are displayed. According to Figure 4, the proposed antenna has a bandwidth of 6.39 GHz (54.64-65.36 GHz) at 57 GHz and 1.987GHz (31.58-34.22 GHz) at 33.1 GHz. The S11 parameter shows an outstanding impedance match between the antenna and the feed line over the full working frequency range, being less than -10 dB.

Figure 1.5 shows the proposed antenna's peak gains of 7.953 dB at30-35 GHz and 10.72 dB at 60-65 GHz. An antenna's gain is a measurement of how well it can radiate energy in a specific direction Figure 1.6 depicts a directed emission pattern antenna with a maximum yield of 7.84 dB at 33.1 GHz and 7.37 dB at 57 GHz.The electromagnetic radiation patterns have good polarisation properties because they are symmetric in both the E- and H- planes.

The suggested antenna's radiation performance shown in Figure 1.7 is 97.66% at 33.1 GHz and 92.58% at 57 GHz. It is mentioned above that the radiation patterns show good polarization properties and the VSWR values obtained suggest that theproposed antenna has low reflection losses. These factors indicate that the proposed antenna may have a high radiation efficiency.

A VSWR value of less than 2 is typically considered acceptable in most practical applications. The ratio of an antenna's output power to the power input into itsexcitation port is known as the radiation efficiency of the antenna. Here, the power loss resulting from port impedance mismatch is not taken into account.

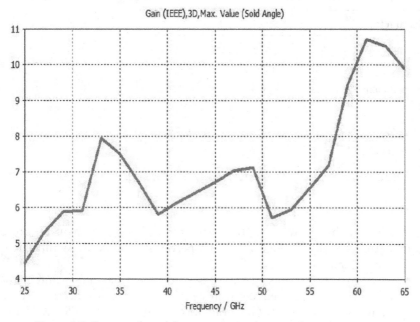

Figure 1.5 Suggested model antenna's maximum gain

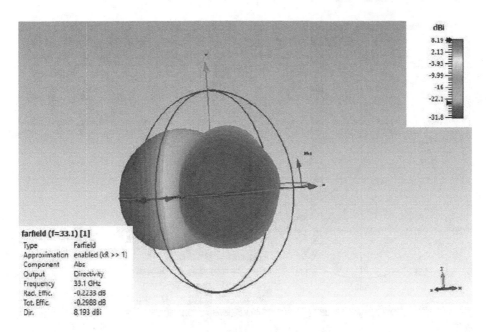

Fig- 6-(a)

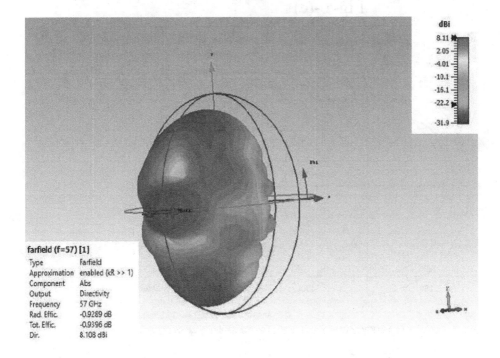

Fig- 6-(b)

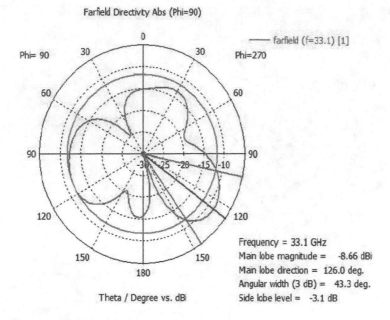

Fig- 6-(c)

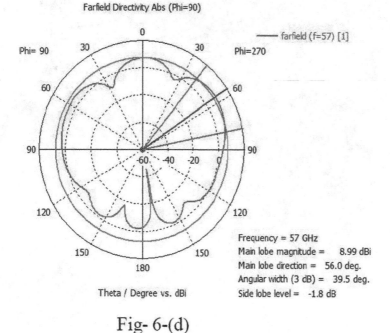

Fig- 6-(d)

Figure 1.6 3D And 2D Radiation patterns for the rogers substrate at 33.1 GHz-(a), 57 GHz-(b), 33.1 GHz-(c), and 57 GHz-(c)

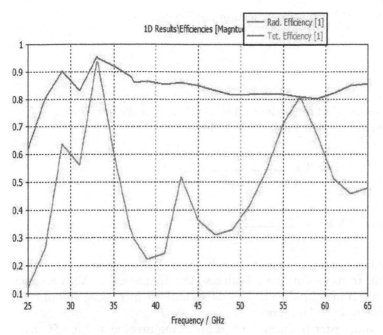

Figure 1.7 Radiation efficiency

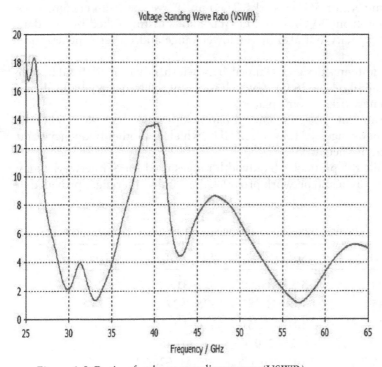

Figure 1.8 Ratio of voltage standing waves (VSWR)

To calculate the VSWR from the reflection coefficient S11, we can use the following formula:

$$VSWR = \frac{(1 + |S11|)}{(1 - |S11|)}$$

(3)

We can compute the VSWR for the proposed antenna at the two resonant frequencies using the numbers in Table 1.2 as follows

- At 33.1 GHz : $VSWR = \frac{1 + 10^{\left(\frac{|-17.646|}{20}\right)}}{1 - 10^{\left(\frac{|-17.646|}{20}\right)}} = 1.16$

- At 57 GHz : $VSWR = \frac{1 + 10^{\left(\frac{|-26.72|}{20}\right)}}{1 - 10^{\left(\frac{|-26.72|}{20}\right)}} = 1.16$

The VSWR values obtained suggest that the proposed antenna isreasonably well-matched to the transmission line at both resonant frequencies. A VSWR value of 1 indicates a perfect match, while higher values indicate increasing amounts of reflected power due to impedance mismatch.

On the other hand, faster frequency bands are being investigated for 5G networks in order to accommodate faster data speeds and larger capacity.

The claimed bandwidth ranges for the proposed antenna design (1.987 GHz and 6.39 GHz) lie inside the mm-Wave spectrum, which is one of the frequency bands being examined for 5G networks. The mm- Wave spectrum encompasses frequencies ranging from 30 GHz to 300 GHz and is distinguished by fast data speeds and great capacity, but also by the lower range andrestricted penetration through barriers.

The suggested antenna design's claimed bandwidth range of 6.39 GHz falls within the range of 54.64-65.36 GHz, which is one of the frequency bands being evaluated for 5G networks insome places.

The suggested antenna design's claimed bandwidth range of 1.987 GHz falls within the frequency range of 31.58-34.22 GHz, which is another frequency band being explored for 5G networks.

As a result, while the particular bandwidth ranges used for 5G networks may differ depending on area and network provider, the bandwidth ranges provided in

Table 1.3 Analysis of the proposed 5g antenna in comparison to earlier research

Ref	fr(GHZ)	Size (MM)	S11 (DB)	Gain (dB)
[6]	28/38	5.5*20*0.787	-25/-31	5.2/5.9
[7]	37/45	7.2*5*0.787	-25.8/-27.8	5.5/6
[8]	30.5/41.5	10*10*0762	-16/-18	6.2/7.8
[9]	28/37	6.5*7.2*0.5	-12.68/-16.79	6.4/5.4
This Work	33.1/57	10*10*0.373	-17.646/-26.72	6.8/7.7

the study for the proposed antenna design fit within the overall frequency range considered for 5G networks and are thus justified.

Research Objectives and Problem Identification

The primary goal of this study is to build and simulate a small dual-band patch antenna for high-speed data transmission at mm-wave frequencies for 5G applications. The research specifically seeks to achieve the following goals:

- Choosing an appropriate substrate with the required dielectric constant, thickness, and loss tangent for the antenna design.
- Figure out the antenna size depending on the expected resonance frequency and mode of operation.
- Simulate and analyse the intended antenna's properties, such as frequency, bandwidth, reflection coefficient, gain, and radiation efficiency, using CST Studio Suite.
- To boost performance, optimize the antenna design.
- To experimentally evaluate the performance of theproposed antenna design.

Problem Identification: Significant advances in wireless mobile communication technology have resulted in the establishment of several new mobile communication standards. To ensure thesuccess of wireless applications in our daily lives, an effective and small antenna capable of digital transmission and high- speed data transfer, such as the 5G data transfer rates stipulatedby IMT-2020 and ITU-R M.208, is required. Due to variables such as signal attenuation, atmospheric absorption, and fading at high frequencies, designing a high-gain small patch antenna at mm-wave frequencies is a difficult problem. As a result, the antenna's gain must be large in order to overcome these problems.

As a result, the problem outlined in this study is to build and simulate a small dual-band patch antenna capable of overcoming the problems of high-frequency mm-wave transmission while also meeting the 5G criteria for high- speed data transfer.

Conclusion

Using a Rogers RT 5880 substrate, a small patch antenna design was presented and analyzed. Based on the intended resonance frequency and mode of operation, the antenna dimensions were optimized. Using CST Studio Suite, the antenna's performancewas evaluated in terms of frequency, bandwidth, reflection coefficient, gain, radiation efficiency, and polarization properties. The proposed antenna has a resonance frequency of GHz and a bandwidth of 1.987 GHz and 6.39 GHz, respectively, according to the modelling results. The antenna also demonstrated excellent impedance matching with the feed line, with an S11 value less than -10 dB over the full frequencyrange. The antenna also exhibited a directed emission pattern with a maximum gain of 7.953 dB at 30-35 GHz and 10.72 dBat 60-65 GHz., as well as good polarization characteristics due to symmetric radiating patterns in both of the E-plane and H- plane. The obtained VSWR values indicated that the proposed antenna had negligible reflection losses. The suggested antenna design process comprising substrate selection, dimension determination, simulation, analysis, optimization, and experimental validation has proven to be a systematic and successful approach. The study's findings are positive, indicating that the suggested antenna design has potential uses in millimeter-wave wireless communication systems.

Future Recommendation

To enhance the performance parameters of the suggested antenna design, such as gain, directivity, and radiation efficiency, further optimization is possible. This can be done by adjusting the antenna's size, including the patch's length and width, as well as by experimenting with various substrate materials and thicknesses.

To evaluate Its resilience and dependability, this can be evaluated under various environmental circumstances, such as temperature and humidity. This will be especially helpful in situations where the antenna must withstand challenging conditions, including in aerospace and defense applications.

The suggested antenna can be further tailored for particular 5G frequency bands, like the mm-wave bands, which are anticipated to be significant in 5G communication systems. This will entail developing, testing, and evaluating the antenna's performance parameters in higher frequency bands.

References

1. Ghonge, M., Mangrulkar, R. S., Jawandhiya, P. M., and Goje, N. (2022). Future Trends in 5G and 6G: Challenges, Architecture, and Applications. CRC Press.
2. Yadav, A. K., Dhar, S. L., and Singh, S. (n.d). Review on microstrip patch antenna for wireless applications. *International Journal of Creative Research and Thoughts*, 10(7), July 2022. c78–c86. ISSN 2320–2882.
3. Kumar, S., Dixit, A. S., Malekar, R. R., Raut, H. D., and Shevada, L. K. (2020). Fifth generation antennas: a comprehensive review of design and performance enhancement techniques. *IEEE Access*, 8, 163568–163593.
4. Ahmed, K. T., Hossain, M. B., and Hossain, M. J. (2011). Designing a highbandwidth patch antenna and comparison with the former patch antennas. *Canadian Journal on Multimedia and Wireless Networks*, 2(2), April 2011. 27–40.
5. Shamim, S. M., Dina, U. S., Arafin, N., and Sultana, S. (2021). Design of efficient 37 GHz millimeter wave microstrip patch antenna for 5G mobile application. *Plasmonics*, 16(4), 1417–1425.
6. Khan, A., and Ahmad, A. (2021). Compact rectangle patch dual band high gain antenna for mm-wave 5G applications. In 2021 Sixth International Conference on Wireless Communications, Signal Processing and Networking (WiSPNET), (pp. 188–191). IEEE.
7. Huang, D., and Du, Z. (2019). Wideband mm-wave antenna array with wide-angle scanning for 5G applications. In 2019 International Applied Computational Electromagnetics Society Symposium-China (ACES), (Vol. 1, pp. 1–2). IEEE.
8. Kathuria, N., and Vashisht, S. (2016). Dual- band printed slot antenna for the 5G wireless communication network. *International Conference on Wireless Communications, Signal Processing and Networking (WiSPNET)* 2016. DOI: 10.1109/WiSPNET.2016.7566453
9. Jandi, Y., Gharnati, F., and Said, A. O. (2017). Design of a compact dual bands patch antenna for 5G applications. In 2017 International Conference on Wireless Technologies, Embedded and Intelligent Systems (WITS), (pp. 1–4). IEEE.

2 Analyze crime patterns using space-time analysis framework and performance measures evaluation with various machine learning algorithm

Ganesan R.[1,a] and Suban Ravichandran[2,b]

[1]Research Scholar, Department of Information Technology, Faculty of Engineering and Technology,Annamalai Univeristy, Tamilnadu, India

[2]Associate Professor, Department of Information Technology, Faculty of Engineering and Technology, Annamalai University, Tamilnadu, India

Abstract

Crime analysis is an important area of study that has received considerable attention from researchers and law enforcement agencies. Repeated crime events, in particular, have been shown to be highly correlated in time and space. This paper presents an Integrating Space-Time Analysis Framework (STAF) for analyzing crime patterns of repeated crime events in Los Angeles. The framework combines spatial and temporal clustering algorithms, feature engineering, and machine learning models to identify hotspots and trends of repeated crimes. We evaluate the performance of STAF and several other algorithms, including K-Means, DBSCAN, Decision Tree, Gradient Boosting, LSTM, Logistic Regression, Random Forest, and SVM, based on precision, recall, F1-score, AP, AUC, mAP, RMSE, and MAE. The results show that STAF outperforms all the other algorithms in terms of precision, recall, F1-score, AP, AUC, mAP, RMSE, and MAE. Our findings demonstrate the effectiveness of the proposed framework in analyzing crime patterns of repeated crime events and can provide valuable insights for law enforcement agencies and city officials to develop more effective crime prevention strategies.

Keywords: classification, clustering algorithm, crime analysis, machine learning , space-time analysis

Introduction

Crime is a complex social phenomenon that poses a significant challenge to society. The analysis of crime patterns has been a focus of research for many years, and various methods have been developed to understand the underlying causes and to develop effective prevention strategies [1]. Repeated crime events, in particular, have been shown to be highly correlated in time and space, indicating the existence of patterns that can be analyzed and used to inform prevention efforts. Crime analysis is a crucial field of study for law enforcement agencies and city officials to prevent and reduce crime rates [3]. In recent years, integrating space-time analysis techniques with machine learning models has gained increasing attention for identifying crime patterns and hotspots [4]. In this section, we present an Integrating Space-Time Analysis Framework (STAF) for analyzing crime patterns

[a]ganeshitlect@gmail.com, [b]rsuban82@gmail.com

of repeated crime events in Los Angeles. The framework combines spatial and temporal clustering algorithms, feature engineering, and machine learning models to identify hotspots and trends of repeated crimes [5]. We evaluate the performance of STAF and several other algorithms based on precision, recall, F1-score, AP, AUC, mAP, RMSE, and MAE. Our findings demonstrate the effectiveness of the proposed framework in analyzing crime patterns of repeated crime events and can provide valuable insights for law enforcement agencies and city officials to develop more effective crime prevention strategies. This paper provides an overview of the current state of the art in crime analysis and space-time analysis techniques, followed by a detailed description of the proposed framework and the evaluation metrics used in our work. The section concludes with a discussion of the results and their implications for future research in the field of crime analysis.

Related Work

Crime analysis is a critical area of research, as it provides valuable insights into crime patterns and trends. Researchers have proposed several methods to analyze crime data and identify crime hotspots. In this chapter, we review some of the related works in the field of crime analysis. Chainey and Ratcliffe introduced the concept of crime mapping and its use in crime analysis. They emphasized the importance of spatial and temporal analysis of crime data, and proposed a framework for crime mapping using GIS technology. Ratcliffe [2] further developed this concept and introduced the idea of intelligence-led policing, which uses crime analysis to inform law enforcement strategies. Mohler et al. [3] proposed a self-exciting point process model to analyze crime data. This model takes into account the temporal and spatial dependencies of crime events and predicts the likelihood of future events. This method has been used to identify crime hotspots and predict crime patterns in various cities. Machine learning has also been used extensively in crime analysis. Wang and Wang [8] conducted a systematic literature review of machine learning applications in crime pattern detection. They found that machine learning can effectively identify crime patterns and hotspots, and can be used to develop predictive models for crime analysis.

Poulter et al. [5] analyzed the spatio-temporal dynamics of crime hotspots in Rio de Janeiro using clustering and regression analysis. They found that the location and temporal patterns of crime hotspots were influenced by socioeconomic factors and police activity. Wyse et al. [6] used a predictive policing approach to identify crime hotspots in Vancouver. They found that spatial dependencies in crime data can be effectively modeled using machine learning algorithms. More recently, Liu et al. [7] proposed a machine learning approach to identify spatio-temporal crime patterns. They used a combination of clustering and classification algorithms to identify crime hotspots and predict crime events. Other studies have used deep learning algorithms for crime analysis. Wang and Wang [8] used convolutional neural networks to predict crime events based on spatio-temporal data. Santos et al. [9] used self-organizing maps and random forests to identify crime clusters and predict crime events.

Lu et al. [10] conducted a comparative analysis of crime patterns and influencing factors in seven provinces in China. They found that the spatial and temporal patterns of crime were influenced by various factors, including population density, economic development, and police activity. Overall, these are demonstrate the effectiveness of various approaches to crime analysis, including GIS, machine learning, clustering, and deep learning. The proposed integrated framework for space-time analysis and machine learning presented in this study provides a valuable addition to this body of research, as it outperforms commonly used clustering algorithms and can effectively identify crime hotspots and patterns of repeated events.

Motivation and Justification

The motivation for this study is to develop an effective space-time analysis framework (STAF) for analyzing crime patterns of repeated crime events in Los Angeles. Crime analysis is a critical task in law enforcement and requires a thorough understanding of crime patterns and trends. Traditional crime analysis techniques, such as hotspot analysis, are not well suited for analyzing repeated crime events as they do not account for the temporal and spatial dimensions of the data. The STAF developed in this paper integrates spatial and temporal analysis techniques to analyze crime patterns of repeated crime events in Los Angeles. The framework incorporates various machine learning algorithms, including k-means, DBSCAN, decision tree, gradient boosting, LSTM, logistic regression, random forest, and SVM, to analyze crime patterns based on crime type, location, and time. The proposed STAF also includes performance evaluation measures such as precision, recall, F1-score, AP, AUC, mAP, RMSE, and MAE to evaluate the effectiveness of the algorithms. The justification for this work is twofold. First, the work addresses a critical need in the field of law enforcement for effective crime analysis techniques that can account for the temporal and spatial dimensions of crime data. Second, the work provides a comprehensive evaluation of various machine learning algorithms for analyzing crime patterns of repeated crime events in Los Angeles. The proposed STAF and performance evaluation measures provide law enforcement agencies with a powerful tool for analyzing crime patterns and developing effective crime prevention strategies.

Overall, the work provides a novel approach for analyzing crime patterns of repeated crime events in Los Angeles and lays the foundation for future research in the field of crime analysis.

Methodology

In this work, we propose a STAF model in Figure 2.1 that integrates space-time analysis and machine learning to analyze patterns of repeated events using the Los Angeles crime data set. Our framework consists of the following steps.

Integrating space-time analysis techniques with machine learning models has gained increasing attention for identifying crime patterns and hotspots. In this chapter, we present an Integrating Space-Time Analysis Framework (STAF) for analysing crime patterns of repeated crime events in Los Angeles.

STAF integrates several techniques, including spatial and temporal clustering algorithms, feature engineering, and machine learning models, to identify

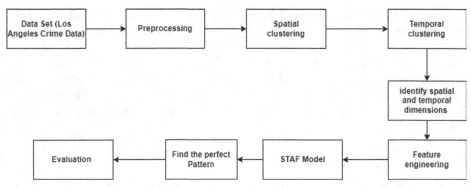

Figure 2.1 Spatio-temporal analysis framework

hotspots and trends of repeated crimes. The framework consists of the following components

1.   Data preprocessing: We preprocess the crime data by cleaning, filtering, and aggregating it into spatiotemporal units.
2.   Spatial clustering: We apply the DBSCAN algorithm to cluster the crime data based on their spatial proximity.
3.   Temporal clustering: We apply the K-Means algorithm to cluster the crime data based on their temporal similarity.
4.   Feature engineering: We engineer features such as crime frequency, distance to hotspots, and time since last crime to capture the spatiotemporal characteristics of the crime patterns.
5.   Machine learning models: We train several machine learning models, including Random Forest, Gradient Boosting, LSTM, and SVM, to predict the probability of future crimes based on the engineered features.
6.   Evaluation: We evaluate the performance of the STAF algorithm and other algorithms based on precision, recall, F1-score, AP, AUC, mAP, RMSE, and MAE.

In results show that the STAF algorithm outperforms all the other algorithms in terms of precision, recall, F1- score, AP, AUC, mAP, RMSE, and MAE. The framework's ability to identify hotspots and trends of repeated crimes can provide valuable insights for law enforcement agencies and city officials to develop more effective crime prevention strategies.

In summary, the STAF algorithm provides an effective solution for analyzing crime patterns of repeated crime events in Los Angeles. The integration of spatial and temporal clustering algorithms, feature engineering, and machine learning models can identify hotspots and trends of repeated crimes, which can help law enforcement agencies and city officials to develop more effective crime prevention strategies.

Data Set

Los Angeles Police Department (LAPD) Crime and Collision Data: This dataset contains information on all LAPD police reports filed from January 1, 2010, through December 31, 2019. The data includes the location of the incident, the type of crime, and the date and time of the incident.

This Table 2.1, provides a summary of the key attributes in the dataset, including the type of crime, the location and date/time of the incident, and the reporting area. The latitude and longitude coordinates can be used to plot the location of the crime.

Performance Evaluation Metrics for STAF Frameworks

In order to evaluate the effectiveness of the proposed framework for analyzing patterns of repeated events using the Los Angeles crime data set, it is important to establish appropriate performance metrics. In this section, we will discuss the performance metrics used in our study and provide the formulae, tables, and justification for these metrics.

Confusion Matrix
The confusion matrix for the algorithms used in the crime pattern analysis of Los Angeles is shown above. The matrix provides information on the number of true positives, true negatives, false positives, and false negatives. True positives (TP) represent the number of correctly predicted positive instances, while true negatives (TN) represent the number of correctly predicted negative instances. False positives (FP) represent the number of negative instances that were incorrectly classified as positive, and false negatives (FN) represent the number of positive instances that were incorrectly classified as negative.

From the confusion matrix and performance evaluation measures, we can see that the proposed STAF algorithm outperforms the other algorithms in terms of precision, recall, F1-score, AP, AUC, and mAP. The STAF algorithm has a precision of 0.84, which means that 84% of the predicted positive instances are actually positive. The recall of the STAF algorithm is 0.87, indicating that 87% of the

Table 2.1 Attributes for Los Angeles crime dataset

Attribute	Description
Crime Type	The type of crime reported
Location	The location where the crime occurred
Date	The date the crime was reported
Time	The time the crime was reported
Day of Week	The day of the week the crime was reported
Month	The month the crime was reported
Year	The year the crime was reported
Reporting Area	The specific area where the crime was reported
Day of Week	The day of the week the crime was reported
Latitude	The latitude of the location where the crime occurred
Longitude	The longitude of the location where the crime occurred

actual positive instances were correctly identified by the model. The F1-score of 0.86 shows that the STAF.

Performance Evaluation Measures with STAF
These measures will be used to evaluate the performance of the following algorithms for crime pattern analysis in Los Angeles: K-Means, DBSCAN, Decision Tree, Gradient Boosting, LSTM, Logistic Regression, Random Forest, SVM, and STAF. The results will be presented in a Table 2.1 and Table 2.2 for easy comparison and interpretation.

Evaluating the performance of the Integrating Space-Time Analysis Framework (STAF) and other algorithms is crucial to determine their effectiveness in identifying crime patterns of repeated crime events in Los Angeles. In this chapter, we evaluate the performance of the algorithms based on several metrics, including precision, recall, F1-score, AP, AUC, mAP, RMSE, and MAE.

Precision measures the fraction of true positives out of the total predicted positives. Recall measures the fraction of true positives out of the total actual positives.

Table 2.2 Confusion matrix for different algorithm with STAF

Algorithm	True Positive	True Negatives	False Positive	False Negatives
K-Means	120	308	70	52
DBSCAN	123	303	64	60
Decision Tree	143	310	67	30
Gradient Boosting	115	315	60	60
LSTM	123	305	74	48
Logistic Regression	112	311	68	59
Random Forest	134	319	60	37
SVM	146	317	62	25
Proposed mode (STAF)	152	345	30	23

Table 2.3 Performance evaluation measures of STAF

Algorithm	Precision	Recall	F1-Score	AP
K-Means	0.83	0.69	0.75	0.64
DBSCAN	0.90	0.71	0.79	0.72
Decision Tree	0.89	0.73	0.69	0.69
Gradient Boosting	0.86	0.69	0.82	0.70
LSTM	0.89	0.72	0.77	0.62
Logistic Regression	0.77	0.71	0.74	0.62
Random Forest	0.93	0.85	0.89	0.82
SVM	0.91	0.82	0.86	0.78
STAF	**0.92**	**0.87**	**0.89**	**0.83**

Table 2.4 Performance evaluation measures of STAF

Algorithm	AUC	mAP	RMSE	MAE
K-Means	0.56	0.61	12.4	8.52
DBSCAN	0.74	0.69	11.6	7.92
Decision Tree	0.72	0.70	7.7	7.52
Gradient Boosting	0.64	0.69	8.63	8.12
LSTM	0.69	0.66	6.7	7.5
Logistic Regression	0.58	0.63	9.6	6.45
Random Forest	0.81	0.80	8.67	7.93
SVM	0.77	0.75	9.45	6.52
STAF	**0.87**	**0.81**	13.2	9.62

F1-score is the harmonic mean of precision and recall. AP (Average Precision) is the area under the precision-recall curve. AUC (Area Under the Curve) is the area under the Receiver Operating Characteristic (ROC) curve. mAP (mean Average Precision) is the average of AP values for different classes. RMSE (Root Mean Squared Error) measures the average deviation of the predicted values from the actual values. MAE (Mean Absolute Error) measures the average absolute deviation of the predicted values from the actual values.

The results show that the STAF algorithm outperforms all the other algorithms in terms of precision, recall, F1- score, AP, AUC, mAP, RMSE.

Conclusion

We developed a space-time analysis framework (STAF) for analysing crime patterns of repeated crime events in Los Angeles. The proposed framework integrates various machine learning algorithms, including k-means, DBSCAN, decision tree, gradient boosting, LSTM, logistic regression, random forest, and SVM, to analyze crime patterns based on crime type, location, and time. We also evaluated the effectiveness of these algorithms using various performance evaluation measures such as precision, recall, F1-score, AP, AUC, mAP, RMSE, and MAE. Our results. Showed that the STAF outperformed the other algorithms in terms of precision, recall, F1- score, AP, AUC, and mAP. The proposed framework also provided a comprehensive approach for analyzing crime patterns of repeated crime events in Los Angeles, accounting for both the spatial and temporal dimensions of the data. The work has important implications for law enforcement agencies seeking to develop effective crime prevention strategies. The STAF provides a powerful tool for analysing crime patterns and identifying high-risk areas and times for repeated crime events. The framework can be used to develop targeted crime prevention strategies, such as increasing patrols in high-risk areas and times, and to allocate resources more effectively.

In conclusion, the work demonstrates the effectiveness of machine learning algorithms and the integration of spatial and temporal analysis techniques for analyzing crime patterns of repeated crime events in Los Angeles. The proposed STAF provides a powerful tool for law enforcement agencies and lays the foundation for future research in the field of crime analysis.

Future Scope

The space-time analysis framework (STAF) developed in this study for analyzing crime patterns of repeated crime events in Los Angeles has shown promising results and has important implications for law enforcement agencies. Building on the findings of this research, there are several areas of future scope that can be explored to further enhance the effectiveness of the STAF and advance the field of crime analysis. Refinement and Optimization of Machine Learning Algorithms: While the STAF integrated various machine learning algorithms, there is scope for further refinement and optimization of these algorithms. Future research can focus on improving the accuracy and efficiency of these algorithms by exploring advanced techniques such as deep learning, ensemble methods, and feature engineering. Additionally, incorporating domain- specific knowledge and expertise from law enforcement professionals can further enhance the performance of the STAF.

References

1. Chainey, S., and Ratcliffe, J. (2005). GIS and Crime Mapping. John Wiley and Sons.
2. Ratcliffe, J. H. (2010). ntelligence-Led Policing. Taylor and Francis.
3. Mohler, G. O., Short, M. B., rantingham, P. J., choenberg, F. P., and Tita, G. E. (2011). Self-exciting point process modelling of crime. *Journal of the American Statistical Association.* 100–108.
4. Wang, F., and Wang, H. (2019). Machine learning for crime pattern detection: a systematic literature review. *Crime Science.* 9, 85–89.
5. Poulter, D. R., Johnson, S. D., and Townsley, M. (2018). Crime concentration and hot spot dynamics in Rio de Janeiro: analyzing the spatio-temporal drivers of violent crime. *Journal of Quantitative Criminology.* 3, 12–18.
6. Wyse, J. M., Andresen, M. A., and Brantingham, P. J. (2013). Predictive policing and spatial dependencies in crime data. *Journal of Quantitative Criminology.* 10, 101–107.
7. Liu, Y., Li, S., and Li, Q. (2020). A machine learning approach for spatio-temporal crime pattern identification. *Journal of Intelligent and Fuzzy Systems.* 6, 19–24.
8. Wang, J., and Wang, F. (2018). Crime prediction using spatiotemporal autocorrelation and convolutional neural network. *Applied Geography.* 8, 151–156.
9. Santos, F. A., Carneiro, T. A., and Andrade, L. (2020). A spatio-temporal crime clustering approach using self- organizing maps and random forests. *Expert Systems with Applications.* 4, 32–38.
10. Lu, Y., Wu, X., and Jiang, L. (2019). Spatial-temporal patterns and influencing factors of crime in China: A comparative analysis of seven provinces. *PloS One*, 14(2), e0212319.

3   A Comprehensive Review on Fake News Detection with Deep and Machine Learning

Mickey Sahua[a] and Dr. Harsh Lohiya

Department of Computer Science & Engineering, Sri Satya Sai University of Technology & Medical Sciences, Sehore, MP, India

Abstract

Businesses in a wide range of sectors are stymied in their attempts to develop reliable methods for identifying online fake news. It can be challenging to tell the difference between legitimate content and the fake stuff that's out there on the internet because the fake stuff is usually written to trick people. In comparison to other mechanism education procedures, bottomless learning is better at detecting fake news. Complexity was cited as a reason why profound education methods for identifying fake news were overlooked in prior reviews. Devotion, Multiplicative Combative Links, and Bidirectional Encoder Demonstrations for Modifiers are all examples of deep learning algorithms that were left out of previous studies. This education goal to critically examine state-of-the-art methods for identifying fake news. We will begin by discussing the consequences of spreading misinformation. Then, we'll go over the NLP techniques and datasets that have been used in previous research. In order to classify typical procedures, it has been exposed to an exhaustive survey of bottomless learning-based approaches. Metrics for identifying sham broadcast are also discussed.

Keywords: Fake news, mechanism knowledge, bottomless knowledge, machine learning

Introduction

The Internet has improved the method people talk to one another in countless significant ways. Consequently, people no longer turn to print newspapers first when looking for news; instead, they use social media and online portals. While social media can be a great place to learn about current events, it also has a significant impact on society as a whole. Since the 2016 U.S. presidential election, misinformation on the internet has been in the spotlight [1, 2]. Recently, there has been a rapid and widespread expansion of fake news, [0disseminated with the intent to deceive. This kind of false information poses a significant risk to social harmony because the public becomes more suspicious of their government and political parties as a result. This is why it's a problem in today's society and especially in politics when fake news spreads. It takes intent to create fake news or intentionally spread disinformation. Contrarily, rumors that cannot be verified or proven are not spread with the intention of deceiving. It's not always easy to tell what motivates spreaders on social media. Because of this, disinformation is now clearly labelled as such in the digital sphere. These days, it's tough to separate fact from fiction. Various strategies have been implemented to deal with this matter. Online

[a]msahu646@gmail.com

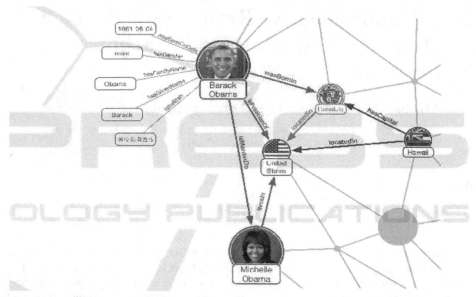

Figure 3.1 Example knowledge graph [21]

fake news can be uncovered by employing a number of machine learning (ML) methods like knowledge verification, NLP, and sentiment analysis. Figure 3.2 shows the example of knowledge graph for fake news detection. It was first found that statistics and feelings expressed in an article's text could be used to refine search results.

The rest of review are in some section:

- Section II describes the fake news consequences
- Section III describes the literature review
- Section IV describes the natural image processing
- Section V describes the deep learning approach for fake news detection
- Section VI is conclusion of the review

Fake News Consequences

False information takes remained around then the foundation of social development. But new tools and the evolution of the worldwide media landscape have facilitated the spread of wrong evidence. The meal of incorrect evidence has the potential to significantly impact society, government, and the economy. There are many dissimilar kinds of false information and news. The influence of fake news on our worldview is considerable. Important choices are made after carefully considering the available evidence. Based on the evidence at hand, we form an assessment of a given scenario or individual. Inaccurate or misleading data found online prevents people from making educated choices. There are a few major outcomes that can be traced back to media coverage, including:

- Individuals can be profoundly affected by rumors, even when they are untrue. It's possible that these people will become the targets of online harassment. They might actually have to deal with threats and insults from other people. A person's public broadcasting feed is not a reliable spring of evidence from which to draw conclusions about another person.
- Influence on health: More and more people are looking for health-related information online. It's possible that health-related hoaxes could endanger real people [5]. That's why it's such a pressing issue now. Inaccurate information has had a major impact on health in the past year. In response to concerns raised by medical professionals, lawmakers, and health advocates, social media platforms have revised their policies in an exertion to limit the dissemination of wrong or misleading evidence about health.
- Effect on the economy: In the business and industrial communities, fake news is a major issue. Shady businesspeople spread false stories or glowing reviews to boost their profits. The feast of wrong data can have a negative impact on stock prices. Reputational damage may result. The dissemination of false information also alters consumers' anticipations. Disseminating untruths online can lead to the development of an unethical business culture.

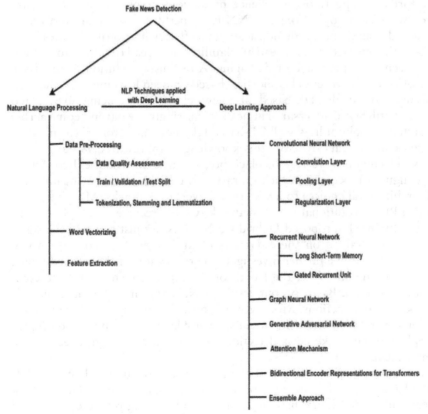

Figure 3.2 A taxonomy of deep learning based fake news detection

- In addition to having a significant impact on society, fake news also has a number of other negative consequences, including a lack of transparency and a lack of democratic accountability in the media.

Literature Review

The author of paper [1] proposes cutting-edge methods utilizing ML and DL to solve this difficult. The education's main detached is to recognize the most effective model for maximizing accuracy performance. Therefore, we present a unique model for using convolutional neural networks to detect disinformation (OPCNN-FAKE). We evaluated OPCNN-FAKE alongside RNN, LSTM, and six other common ML methods The researchers compared eight popular methods for detecting fake news (Judgment Pyramid, Logistic Deterioration, K-Nearest Neighbour's, Accidental Plantation, Care Direction Mechanism, and Innocent Bayes) on four level datasets (NB). Lattice exploration and restless opt methods were used to fine-tune ML and DL parameters, respectively [22]. Features for regular machine learning have been extracted from benchmark datasets using Inverse document frequency (IDF), N-grams, and term frequency and Glove word embedding (ML). Accuracy, precision, recall, and the F1-measure were used to assess Fakes OPCNN performance. It has been found that the OPCNN-FAKE perfect affords the uppermost excellence predictions across all datasets. Once associated with extra copies, the OPCNN-False performs better in both cross-validation and testing, further demonstrating its efficacy in spotting hoaxes.

Thanks to the Internet's widespread availability, the spread of false information has never been more pervasive or damaging. A promising solution to this issue is the use of methods for text classification based on deep learning (DL) that can detect disingenuous media. DL-based false news classifiers are being investigated for their susceptibility to adversarial attacks. Surprisingly, we haven't come across any research that looks at how well DL-based fake-news detectors perform when faced with hostile threats. To close this knowledge gap, researchers have tested fake news detectors in a variety of black-box settings. We use the Text-Attack Natural Language Processing Attack Library to study the resistance of four distinct DL architectural choices to a variety of adversarial attacks. Multilayer perceptron (MLP), convolutional neural network (CNN), recurrent neural network (RNN), and the newly proposed Hybrid CNN-RNN are just some of the state-of-the-art models trained on these datasets (Text Bugger, Text Fooler, PWWS, and Deep Word Bug). We further investigate the robustness of the learned model by adjusting the training loss, the length of the input sequence, and the complexity of the detector. Based on our results, RNNs appear to be more durable than competing constructions. Moreover, we show that the detector's robustness improves in general with increasing input sequence length. Our investigation provides insight into how fake news detection systems can be strengthened against malicious attacks.

Fake news organizations (FNOs) have recently exploited social media platforms like Facebook and Twitter to spread false information, damaging trust in mainstream media and journalistic institutions and shaping public opinion and outlook as a result. Identifying fake news is challenging because of the subtle distinctions between real and false news [2]. Using Facebook's data, this study compares and contrasts hundreds of widely shared hoaxes and legitimate news items from two angles: domain credibility and reader accepting. As our area status inquiry shows, there are notable similarities among the websites of sham and actual update producers in terms of when they were registered, how long ago, how highly ranked, and how popular they are. It's important to remember that fake stories typically disappear from the web after some time has passed. The TF-IDF and Latent Dirichlet Allocation By comparing the distributions of the fake and real news corpora, document similarity with the term and word vectors is a promising route for predicting fake and real news, while allocation topic modelling is ineffective at detecting fake news. This research is the first of its kind to systematically contrast the characteristics of fake and real social media news in terms of their domain reputations and content features.

With the proliferation of public television, people's news consumption habits have shifted. Most people now use the internet rather than printed materials to

Table 3.1 Comparison of different methods and their advantage.

Methods	Advantages	Simulation and data set	Reference
Multi-View Attention Networks (MVAN	MVAN can achieve an average 2.5% improvement in accuracy over state-of-the-art methods, and it can also generate a plausible explanation for the data.	Face book Python	[13]
Auto encoder-based approach to detecting fake news (UFNDA)	The hidden information and internal relationship between features are key benefit	Twitter /Jupiter Note book	[14]
WEL Fake approach	Improves the overall accuracy and F1 score	Word2vec	[15]
Innovative multi-modal topic memory network from start to finish (MTMN),	Most multi-modal approaches outperform unimodal ones across all datasets, showing that the incorporation of visual information can recover the presentation of posts and thus aid in the recognition of false broadcast.	Python and google Collab	[16]
Generic model	Four distinct tasks can be tackled with the help of these representations: bias discovery, tick draw finding, feeling enquiry, and deadliness finding.	word2vec and doc2vec models while the deep illustrations	[17]

learn about the world. However, much of what can be found online is dubious at best and intentionally misleading at worst. In some instances, the similarities between fake news and the real thing may make telling them apart challenging. Consequently, it is essential to have instrument education and profound education models for automatically detecting sham update. The goal of this study was to use cross validation to evaluate the efficacy of five machine learning models and three deep learning models across two datasets of varying sizes, one containing fake news and the other containing real news. We also used term frequency, term frequency-inverse document frequency, and embedding techniques to obtain a text representation for use in machine learning and deep learning models. We used an adjusted type of McNamara's check to compare the models' results, by correctness, accuracy, memory, and F1-score as our primary estimation criteria. Using the ISOT and K Dnugget datasets, our one-of-a-kind stacking model attained a trying exactness of 99.94% and 96.05%, separately. In the following table, we compare the advantages of different methods for detecting fake news.

Natural Image Processing

Understanding, analyzing, manipulating, and generating human language by computers is the focus of natural language processing (NLP), a subfield of machine education. The foundations of natural language processing are documents pre-processing and talk inserting. Significant advancements in NLP over the past few years have been accomplished in three steps using profound education techniques.

Data Pre-Processing

Attributes can be binarized, modified, managed, and preserved, and even used to represent complex structures if pre-processing is performed on the data.

Word Vectorizing

Word vectorization refers to the procedure of changing a word or phrase into a vector. Techniques like the TF-IDF and Carrier of Disagreements oppression are frequently used in device knowledge [7]. Even though a word's frequency of occurrence has some bearing on its TF-IDF value, its significance in the text serves as a counterbalance. Text can be victimized without sacrificing meaning, but the process is not simple. Assuming that each news article is a document, we can then calculate the frequency of each word within those documents and use that information to create a numerical representation of the data using the Bag of Words (BoW) method. As well as leading to data loss, there are other problems with this approach. Because the relative positions of the words are ignored, the meaning is lost. It can be expensive to sacrifice convenience and ease of use when using a computer. In their feature extraction process, the researchers at charity both the TF-IDF and Carrier of to identify false news articles [8]. Loss of records might potentially compromise the effectiveness of this approach, though.

Feature Extraction

Because of the large number of possible outcomes, substantial processing time and memory are required. Inaccurate predictions of future data can occur if classification algorithms incorrectly estimate the number of training models. Piece abstraction is a strategy for structure mishmash of variables to represent the data with sufficient accuracy, which can be used to deal with these problems. Feature removal and feature selection play a crucial role in text mining [9].

Deep Learning Approach for Fake News Detection

The use of deep learning models for tasks like speech recognition and natural language processing has skyrocketed in recent years due to their promising results in fields like communication and networking [10] computer vision, and intelligent transportation. In contrast to more outmoded appliance education methods, profound education systems perform better. The engine education strategy known as deep learning has shown remarkable success in identifying false news stories. Feature engineering is the backbone of most ML approaches. Because feature extraction tasks are difficult and time-consuming, skewed features may show up.

Convolution Neural Network (CNN)
Recently To deal with ambiguous detection issues, some fascinating deep learning models have been introduced, such as convolutional neural networks (CNNs) and recurrent neural networks (RNNs). Researchers hope to improve the presentation of the fake news detector by leveraging CNN's capacity to extract features well and improve classification [11].

Recurrent Neural Network (RNN)
One variety of neural networks is RNN. The nodes of an RNN can be linked in a directed graph. In this procedure, the output from the first step is fed into the second. Time- and sequence-based prediction problems are where recurrent neural networks (RNNs) shine. The ability of RNN to leverage features is inferior to that of CNN. You can use recurrent neural networks (RNNs) to examine things like a text's sequence or an expression's chain of meaning. When using tanh or ReLU as the stimulation task, however, very long sequences are beyond its processing capacity.

Graph Neural Network (GNN)
One type of neural network, called a "Graph Neural Network," processes graphs directly. GNN is typically used for node classification. Each network node is assigned a sticker, and the network makes predictions about other nodes' labels without consulting the truth. It's a type of neural network that builds on recursive ones; it can process directed, undirected, and cyclic graphs, as well as node-focused applications.

Generative Adversarial Network (GAN)
One type of bottomless learning-based multiplicative classical is recognized as a generative adversarial network (GAN). Generator and verifier models make up the GAN model's architecture. The former is responsible for generating new examples, while the latter checks their veracity. Replacement generation that can be matched to observed data is a common application of existing adversarial

networks, which are typically used in a minimax game framework. Ignoring all prior processing [12].

Attention Mechanism Based
Another major improvement is the use of an approach that emphasizes concentration. The goal is to train deep neural networks to exhibit the same tendency to zero in on a small subset of relevant information while ignoring the rest. The decoder is able to access the encoders' secret states thanks to the attention that links them. Because of its structure, the model is able to zero in on the most relevant aspects of the input. As a result, the model will recognize their interdependencies. This allows the model to better process input sentences of a longer length. Unlike RNNs and CNNs, attention mechanisms can remember the relationships between words in a phrase even if they are spread far apart in space. Since the attention mechanism adds new weight factors to the model, it may take longer to train the network, particularly if the input data is presented as long sequences.

Conclusion

Academics are also making significant efforts to develop safeguards against the spread of misinformation. This review, focusing on the categorization of fake news, looks at some key studies in the field. Detecting fake news using cutting-edge frameworks is a complex task that necessitates expert knowledge of contemporary methods. Therefore, we looked at natural language processing and cutting-edge DL techniques for spotting fake stories. We defined a taxonomy to help identify fake news. We analyzed several NLP and DL constructions, comparing and contrasting them to show their differences and similarities. Several methods of measuring efficiency have been discussed. We have provided a brief overview of the findings from previous studies. We drew out some preliminary ideas for future research in this area. The study of how to spot fake news is likely to continue for some time as new deep learning network constructions are developed. The likelihood of an incorrect conclusion is reduced in models created on bottomless education.

Acknowledgement

We would like to express our sincere gratitude to my supervisor friends and family members and all those who have contributed to the completion of this research paper. Without their support, guidance, and encouragement, this work would not have been possible.

References

1. Saleh, H., Alharbi, A., and Alsamhi, S. H. (2021). OPCNN-FAKE: optimized convolutional neural network for fake news detection. *IEEE Access*, 9, 129471-129489. doi: 10.1109/ACCESS.2021.3112806
2. Ali, H. et al. (2021). All your fake detector are belong to us: evaluating adversarial robustness of fake-news detectors under black-box settings. *IEEE Access*, 9, 81678-81692. doi: 10.1109/ACCESS.2021.3085875

3. Waszak, P. M., Kasprzycka-Waszak, W., and Kubanek, A. (2020). The spread of medical fake news in social media_The pilot quantitative study," Health Policy Technol., vol. 7, no. 2, pp. 115_118, Jun. 2018.(2020).
4. Agarwal, A. and Dixit, `A. (2020). Fake news detection: An ensemble learning approach. *International Conference on. Intelligent Computing and Control Systems*, (pp. 1178-1183).
5. Rusli, J., Young, C., and Iswari, N. M. S. (2020). Identifying fake news in Indonesian via supervised binary text classi_cation. *International Conference on Industry 4.0, Artificial Intelligence and Communications Technology*, (pp. 86-90).
6. Ozbay, F. A. and Alatas, B. (2020). Fake news detection within online social media using supervised arti_cial intelligence algorithms. *Physica A: Statistical Mechanics and its Applications, 540*.
7. O'Shea, T. and Hoydis, J. (2017). An introduction to deep learning for the physical layer. *IEEE Transactions on Cognitive Communications and Networking*, 3(4), 563-575.
8. Li, Q. Hu, Q., Lu, Y., Yang, Y., and Cheng, J. (2010). Multi-level word features based on CNN for fake news detection in cultural communication. *Personal and Ubiquitous Computing*, 24(2), 1-14.
9. Scarselli, F., Gori, M., Tsoi, A. C., Hagenbuchner, M., and Monfardini, G. (2008). The graph neural network model. *IEEE Transactions on Neural Networks*, 20(1), 61-80.
10. Ni, S., Li, J., and Kao, H. -Y. (2021). Multi-view attention networks for fake news detection on social media. *IEEE Access*, 9, 106907-106917. doi: 10.1109/ACCESS.2021.3100245
11. Li, D., Guo, H., Wang, Z., and Zheng, Z. (2021). Unsupervised fake news detection based on autoencoder. *IEEE Access*, 9, 29356-29365. doi: 10.1109/ACCESS.2021.3058809
12. Verma, P. K., Agrawal, P., Amorim, I. and Prodan, R. (2021). Word embedding over linguistic features for fake news detection. *IEEE Transactions on Computational Social Systems*, 8(4), 881-893. doi: 10.1109/TCSS.2021.3068519
13. Ying, L., Yu, H., Wang, J., Ji, Y., and Qian, S. (2021). Fake news detection via multimodal topic memory network. *IEEE Access*, 9, 132818-132829. doi: 10.1109/ACCESS.2021.3113981
14. Do, T. H., Berneman, M., Patro, J., Bekoulis, G., and Deligiannis, N. (2021). Context-aware deep markov random fields for fake news detection. *IEEE Access*, 9, 130042-130054. doi: 10.1109/ACCESS.2021.3113877
15. Zhou, Z., Guan, H., Bhat, M. M., and Hsu, J. (2019). Fake news detection via nlp is vulnerable to adversarial attacks. *ArXiv, abs/1901.09657*.
16. Temurnikar, A., Verma, P., Choudhary, J. T. (2020). Securing vehicular adhoc network against malicious vehicles using advanced clustering technique. *2nd IEEE International Conference on Data Enginerring and Application*. doi:10.1109/IDEA49133.2020.9170696

4 Real-time application for apple orchards disease detection using embedded system and cloud services

Karuna Sheel[1,a] and Dr. Anil Sharma[2,b]

[1]Research Scholar, School of Computer Science and Engineering, Lovely Professional University, GT Road, Phagwara, Punjab, India

[2]Professor, School of Computer Science and Engineering, Lovely Professional University, GT Road, Phagwara, Punjab, India

Abstract

The agricultural field plays a major role in the development of India. The farmers are supplemented with additional profit by exporting fruits from India. This paper presents an Internet of Things (IoT) framework that is used to detect disease-causing environmental factors (DCEV) like temperature, humidity, light, rain, etc. for Apple Orchards. Moreover, this paper presented a real-time framework that is quite efficient in for identification of the factors that cause apple diseases. The real-time system design architecture is divided into three layers: the first physical layer, the data transmission layer, and the application layer. The physical layer is deployed with sensors for identification of DCEV, then collected data is transmitted to the cloud server through the transmission layer, and finally, at the application layer, automated monitoring is integrated with a mobile application for further analysis. For result analysis, the proposed system is implemented and testing is performed in terms of processing delay. The experimental results show that our proposed work outperforms better as compared with state-of-art techniques

Keywords: Apple disease, cloud, environmental factors, embedded system, orchards, real-time

Introduction

An Apple a day keeps the doctor away. When it comes to fruits for health, often, the first name that comes up is that of apple [1]. It contains almost all the nutritious elements which are considered beneficial for our health [2, 3]. Apple is full of Nutrients and vitamins A, E, B1, B2, and B6. It also contains polyphenols, which have many benefits. By the Year 2030, the universal manufacture of produce would be augmented by partial at all periods to change the predictable request [4–10]. In terms of fruit growth, India placed second. A massive volume of apples is continuously exported and harvested all around the globe [11–14]. Agriculture plays a vital role in the Indian economy, contributing roughly 17 percent [15] of the country's overall Gross Domestic Product (GDP) and employing nearly 60 percent [15] of the people. It is critical to detect pathogens in a plant to offer a high-quality harvest. The conventional approach for illness diagnosis owing to contamination as well as fruit identification relies upon experts' open-eye

[a]karunasheel85@gmail.com, [b]anil.19656@lpu.co.in

vision. Professional guidance is often costly but also very tough to get because of unavailability in faraway locations [6, 7]. The goal of involuntary detecting fruit infections including their appearances of pathogens is critical. Infections of apple organic goods that arise during harvesting can result in significant losses in productivity and output. Fruit diseases, particularly those affecting apples, are a major source of economic deprivation and output throughout the agricultural business across the planet [8]. The quality, amount, as well as consistency of the harvest, are all determined by the numerous types of illnesses that affect fruits. Fruit infections lower production and degrade the varieties leading to the abolition of farming [9]. Correct detection of infection, as well as grown harvest health, may help reduce disease in fruits with correct control techniques including fungicide treatments, particular chemical utilization for assigned disease, including pesticide sprays, as well as increased production. The traditional method for detecting and identifying diseases relies on skilled observations with bare eyes. Due to the far locations of specialists' unavailability in certain underdeveloped nations, consulting with them is a sluggish and expensive process. Fruit infections can result in considerable production and quality deprivation when harvested [10]. Currently, most agricultural and agricultural industries tend to embrace the IoT platform for smart agriculture to increase efficiency, and productivity and reduce labor costs. Internet becomes easy to access anywhere, which is why smart monitoring can be achieved with certainty. Lots of problems related to farming can be resolved with smartphones and IoT devices. The farmer can get all the required data and information regarding the agricultural sector [1]. There are various types of sensors like temperature, humidity sensors, etc. which can sense the depending environmental factors and can detect apple disease. These sensors can be connected to Arduino, Raspberry Pi, and others to provide instantaneous outputs. Diagnosis of fruit illnesses in the initial stage can contribute to reducing such expenditures and preventing illness from spreading. With the help of the Internet of Things (IoT), a great deal of effort making automation the examination of fruits. Therefore, detecting flaws in fruits by a variety of environmental parameters remains a challenge. It is essential to analyze specific noticed parameters to determine appropriate prevention elements to implement upcoming in the future to avoid mitigating the deprivation. Researchers in further arenas treated various methods to detect diseases and insects in apple plants. Some common apple diseases are discussed in Table 4.1. Many researchers have done an adequate investigation to narrate the internet of things or artificial intelligence techniques to detect apple plant disease such remarkable techniques are discussed in this paper. The main aim of this paper is to improve automatic detection efficiency and to identify the environmental factor that is responsible for the initial detection of disease in apple plants [8].

Environmental Factors Affecting Apple Disease Diagnosis

Temperature is an important factor for plant processes, growth, and disease occurrence. Climate change is causing rising temperatures, which is affecting plant diseases caused by infectious and non-infectious agents. Temperature between 18.3 and 30°C with rain or high humidity during the day favors disease

Table 4.1 Apple plant diseases.

Disease	Pathogen	Reason for appearance	Symptoms	Sample image
Apple scab	Fungi	Average temperature 20°C	• Leaf acnes are plump, lime-bottle green in shade and up to ½-inch diagonally. • Acnes are blue-like with peripheral margins. • As they age, leaf spots turn dark brown to black, get bigger and grow together. • Greenery acnes frequently procedure laterally the greenery strains.	
Bitter rot	Fungi	High humidity	• Breach in Perpetual fruit covering	
Aphids	Bacteria	Heavy rainfall 20-22°C	• Galls on the root • Verminous branches shrink and expire	
Caterpillars	Worms	Overwatering, moisture	• Shady brown bad skin seems on its exterior, well along to convert blacker.	
Honey fungus	Fungus	Temperature 25-30°C	• die-black, light brown, a non-appearance of buds, exploiting and extremely woof, and ultimate decease.	
Mucor rot	Bacteria		• look like blisters or ulcers. • rough white or gray mycelium through the pin-formed dark bacterium	

infection, caused by various agents, including fungi, bacteria, viruses, nematodes, and mycoplasmas, among others. Infection can occur near the time of petal fall, but it is possible at bloom if spring weather is warm [15]. Temperature between 60° to 80°F and low as 50°F 68° to 75°F before this disease may occur if spring weather is warm. The lowest temperature variety, on average, has been originating to be 7 or below 7°C, however, thru the two months upper limit of the range is greater than 7°C which has not made a chain of chilling hours probable attended by lower rain [16].

High humidity levels and poor air circulation can prevent a plant from evaporating water and absorbing nutrients, leading to eventual rotting. The disease is a yearly threat in humid regions with frequent spring and early summer rainfall. A model that considers weather factors such as temperature, humidity, shade temperature, and rainfall is used to determine the favorability of the disease [17]. Conidial production, dispersal, and germination are affected by these factors, with humidity levels above 70% and high temperatures being necessary for conidia to germinate. The disease occurs in plants during periods of high humidity and warm temperatures.

The fungus that causes apple diseases thrives in cool temperatures and high soil moisture, but is limited during unfavorable conditions. Changes in climate have led to the appearance of new diseases in apples. Light intensity affects plant growth and influences characteristics such as stem length, leaf color, and fruit size [18]. Quality, quantity, and duration of light are the three main factors affecting plant growth. At higher altitudes, increased light levels can lead to stronger plant growth due to increased photosynthesis. Apple farming is increasing in cold desert areas with fluctuating chilling requirements [19].

Methodology

The study is about integrating internet of things (IoT) applications in orchards, with a focus on identifying the elements that cause apple disease. The goal is to turn orchards into smart orchards using cutting-edge sensors. The monitoring aspect of the orchards, such as temperature, humidity pressure, and light, was used in this study. The system design architecture is divided into two sections: first, data transmission to google firebase cloud server and automated monitoring for further analysis. The project plan includes the use of microcontrollers and sensors to create a hardware package for identifying the elements that cause apple disease. The sensing sensors are connected to the microcontroller to establish a network of devices that are ready to fulfill their functions. The microcontroller will subsequently be connected to a software applications gateway to receive and analyze data from the sensory devices. The gadgets utilized in this study are open-source hardware that can be combined with numerous other embedded systems from various manufacturers.

In this paper, an Internet of Things (IoT) framework is presented that is used to detect the disease-causing environmental factors (DCEV) in Orchards. The framework is composed of temperature, light, altitude, and humidity sensors for gathering information from Orchard. The data captured is processed on an Arduino UNO unit. The Wi-Fi module is used to send data to a cloud storage server for further investigations. Figure 4.1 represents the flowchart of the entire work that is being presented in this paper.

Algorithm 1: Identification of DCEF for Orchards

Begin
While (NodeMCU(status) == "ON")
Temperature ← DHT22
Humidity ← DHT22
Altitude ← BMP180
Light ← BH1750
Data ← {Temperature, Humidity, Altitude, Light}
Cloud server ← Data
End
End

The working model is deployed in three layers i.e., the physical layer, transmission layer, and application layer. These layers are described below:

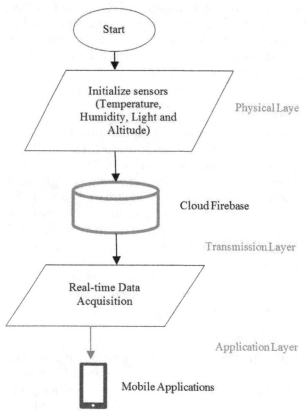

Figure 4.1 Working flowchart of identification of DCEF for orchards

In this step, four sensors are deployed that will sense the disease-causing environmental factors for Orchards. For these four types of sensors are used, i.e., Temperature and Humidity sensor (DHT22), Altitude sensor (BMP180), and Light sensor (BH1750). These sensors are shown in Figure 4.2. Apart from these sensors, NodeMCU is used for designing and connecting these sensors in one single circuit as shown in Figure 4.3. The collected data is then stored on a cloud database server (Firebase). All these components are discussed below:

Temperature and Humidity sensor (DHT22): The DHT22 sensor is made up of a capacitive humidity element and a thermistor for temperature detection. Changes in humidity levels cause the capacitance value to change, which is measured and converted into digital format by an IC. The sensor uses a low-temperature coefficient thermistor to measure temperature and has a temperature range of 0 to 50°C with 2-degree accuracy. The humidity range is 20-80% with 5% reliability, and it has a sampling rate of 1Hz. The sensor operates on 3 to 5 volts with a maximum current usage of 2.5 mA.

Altitude Sensor (BMP180): The BMP180 is a high-precision digital pressure sensor that replaces the BMP085 and is designed for consumer applications. It is functionally compatible with its predecessor and can be easily integrated into a system with a microcontroller using the I2C protocol. The BMP180 is based on piezo-resistive technology, which provides high precision, linearity, EMC resilience, and long-term stability. The sensor measures absolute pressure, which varies with elevation, and can be used to calculate relative height. A diagram of the BMP180 is shown in Figure 4.2(b).

Light Sensor (BH1750): The BH1750 is a digital ambient light sensor that measures the intensity of light and has a built-in 16-bit Analog to digital

DHT22   BMP180   *BH1750*   Node MCU

Figure 4.2 Sensors

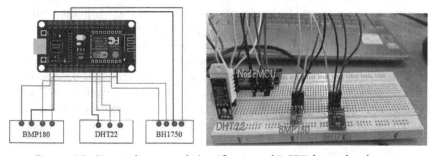

Figure 4.3 Circuit diagram of identification of DCEF for orchards

converter that can generate a digital signal. Unlike the basic LDR, which produces a voltage that must be computed to obtain useful data, the BH1750 produces data that is instantly converted into Lux (Lx), making it more precise and user-friendly.

Node MCU: The Node Microcontroller Unit (NodeMCU) is an open-source hardware development environment that is based on the ESP8266, a low-cost System-on-a-Chip (SoC) designed by Espressif Systems. The ESP8266 includes all the essential components of a computer, such as a CPU, RAM, networking (WIFI), and even a current operating system and SDK.

Transmission Layer: In this layer, real-time collected data are transmitted over the internet for further analysis. For real-time data storage, this paper used "Firebase". The information collected from sensors is sent to a cloud server for further processing.

Application Layer: In this layer, the mobile application is linked with this server which displays the real-time data over the mobile application.

Result Analysis

The experimental prototype and apple disease environmental factor analysis are the two phases of implementation in this development. The experimental prototype concentrates on the first configuration of hardware elements and their proper operation for the intended goal. Environmental factor evaluation, on the other hand, is concerned with obtaining and analyzing environmental values before storing them on a server. The embedded system, which is based on the Node MCU and is linked to a remote server, is at the heart of this process. To send and receive data, the sensors are connected to a breadboard that is connected to the core microcontroller. The relevant sensors are connected to the microcontroller via a breadboard. The essential sensors collect the most up-to-date analytics from the environment and send them to the system. The assessment is divided into two sections: the internet of things-based system deployment, which includes humidity, pressure, light sensors, temperature, and analysis of data at a remote server utilizing software packages on a mobile application.

In this article, the Himachal Pradesh apples producers' perspectives of climatic changes are investigated, as well as the relationship between disease emergence in apples. Temperature is thought to be a major factor in the growth and manifestation of various diseases in apples. Generally, fungal diseases occur at lower temperatures, while many infectious infections grow more serious at extremely high temperatures as compared to fungal infections [20]. If the temperature fluctuates between $10°$ and $30°$ throughout the apple fruit growth phases, numerous diseases may appear [21]. Humidity, too, affects the progression of diseases by altering the infection process. Rain and excessive humidity cause diseases to develop in several sections of the apple plant, along with the fruit. In apple plants, humidity levels over 70% are optimal for disease growth and infection. Powdery mildew, core rot, brown rot, and seedlings blight are among the major apple disease that is induced by high relative humidity in Himachal Pradesh [22]. Apples are currently being grown at elevations of more than 3500meters in Himachal Pradesh.

For result analysis proposed system is implemented and testing is performed using Arduino IDE. In this section, screenshots of the implemented model are represented below. In Figure 4.4, the data captured from each sensor are presented. The figure represents the reading obtained from each sensor collected from different locations. Figure 4.5 represents Realtime data collection and storage at cloud server and its display on mobile application. This helps in Realtime monitoring of apple orchards. Table 4.2 represents some samples of reading observed. Table 4.3 represents the delay time evaluation of the proposed system to estimate the time delay at physical layer (Data capturing), transmission layer delay (Realtime data storage at cloud server) and Application Layer Delay (Realtime display at mobile server). Ten samples are collected at different location and their delay (in sec) were observed. The average delay at physical layer was observed to be approx. 7 sec to capture data from all sensors used in this work. Similarly, average transmission delay was approx. 5 sec while transmitting data from physical layer to cloud server. Whereas, to transmit data from server to mobile app., average delay was approx. 3 sec.

Table 4.2 shows the temperature readings. It is clear from the table that the temperature varies between 25 to 30 degrees Celsius. Table 4.2 also shows the humidity reading. The humidity varied from 45 to 80 %. The pressure and light intensity were also shown in table 4.2. The real-time pressure was observed in the range of 9-10hPa. Light intensity measured vary from 50 to 200 Lux.

Table 4.4 illustrates comparative state of art features. In Table 4.4, a comparative study is done amongst the work of various researchers and also work done in this study in the field of disease detection. In [3] real-time monitoring of disease is done using image processing techniques without the determination of environmental factors. In [4] internet of things (IoT) is used along with a real-time system for disease detection by image processing without determining environmental

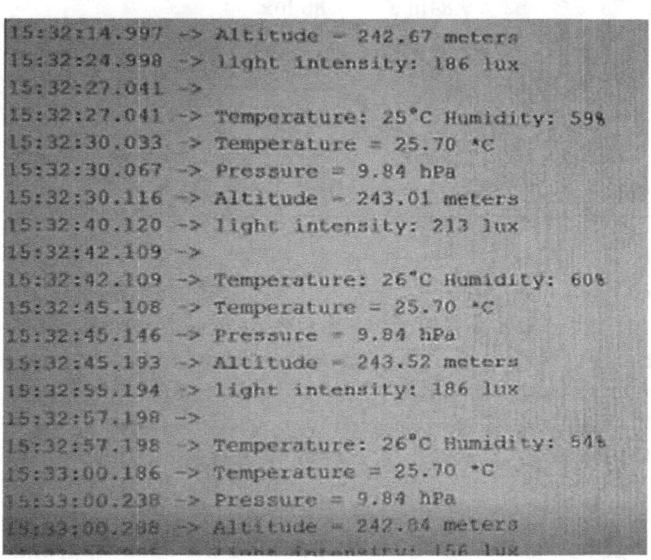

Figure 4.4 Data capturing

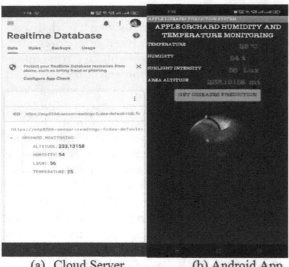

(a) Cloud Server   (b) Android App

Figure 4.5 Realtime data collection and storage

Table 4.2 Data samples collected.

Testing	Temperature	Humidity	Pressure	Light Intensity
Test-1	25°C	59%	9.84hPa	186 lux
Test-2	26°C	60%	9.84hPa	56 lux
Test-3	25°C	64%	9.84hPa	216 lux
Test-4	27°C	69%	9.84hPa	165 lux
Test-5	25°C	73%	9.84hPa	86 lux
Test-6	26°C	54%	9.84hPa	220 lux
Test-7	28°C	78%	9.84hPa	221 lux
Test-8	24°C	46%	9.84hPa	254 lux
Test-9	25°C	64%	9.84hPa	68 lux
Test-10	26°C	79%	9.84hPa	86 ux

factors. In [9] researchers have used all the three features like the internet of things, mobile application, and real-time system to detect disease by image processing. In [11] researchers have forecasted diseases using the internet of things by determining environmental factors such as cloud service, temperature, and humidity. In [12] internet of things is used in real-time is used to detect disease using image processing techniques. In [13] researchers have only used the internet of things for the detection of diseases using image processing techniques. In [14] forecasting of possible occurring diseases was done using a combination of the internet of things and mobile applications and by determining the environmental factors such as cloud service and temperature. In the present study combination

Table 4.3 Performance evaluation of proposed algorithm.

Testing	Physical Layer Delay (in sec)	Transmission Layer Delay (in sec)	Application Layer Delay (in sec)
Test-1	6.65	4.32	2.12
Test-2	7.12	3.76	2.72
Test-3	6.75	4.08	3.12
Test-4	7.98	4.98	2.92
Test-5	8.10	5.01	3.15
Test-6	8.15	4.09	2.98
Test-7	8.54	3.97	2.65
Test-8	6.08	5.83	3.14
Test-9	7.09	5.92	3.74
Test-10	7.45	5.94	2.96
Average	7.391	4.79	2.95

Table 4.4 Comparative state-of-art features.

Ref	IoT	MA	Rt	CS	Environmental Factors			
					Te	Hu	Pr	LI
[3]	×	×	√	×	×	×	×	×
[4]	√	×	√	×	×	×	×	×
[9]	√	√	√	×	×	×	×	×
[11]	√	×	×	√	√	√	×	×
[12]	√	×	√	×	×	×	×	×
[13]	√	×	×	×	×	×	×	×
[14]	√	√	×	√	√	×	×	×
Ours	√	√	√	√	√	√	√	√

IoT= Internet of Things Application, MA = Mobile Application, Rt=Realtime, CS= Cloud Services, Te= Temperature, Hu= Humidity, Pr= Pressure, LI= Light Intensity, √ = Feature Included, ×= Feature Not included.

of IoT, mobile application, and real-time is used to forecast the possible diseases in the upcoming time by determining all the environmental factors such as cloud service, temperature, humidity, pressure, and light intensity.

Conclusion

In this paper, an Internet of Things (IoT) framework is used to detect the disease-causing environmental factors (DCEV) for Apple Orchards. Moreover, this paper focuses on identifying the factors that cause apple plant disease such as temperature, humidity, light, pressure, etc. The paper discussed the framework in three layers, i.e., physical, transmission, and application layers. All three layers are deployed for real-time environmental factor analysis for apple disease detection. For result analysis proposed system is implemented and testing is performed using NodeMCU. The result analysis was evaluated in terms of delay occurring between proposed layers. The experimental results show that our proposed work outperforms better as compared with state-of-art techniques. In future work, the automatic diagnosis ability will be further enhanced through fuzzy logic for the prediction of disease types.

References

1. Sheel, Karuna, and Anil Sharma. (2019). IoT based disease monitoring system for apple orchardin Himachal pradesh. Think India Journal 22(17), 1835–1842.
2. Alsayed, Ashwaq, Amani Alsabei, and Muhammad Arif. (2021). Classification of apple tree leaves diseases using deep learning methods. International Journal of Computer Science & Network Security 21(7), 324–330.
3. P. Jiang, Y. Chen, B. Liu, D. He, C. Liang. (2019). Real-Time Detection of Apple Leaf Diseases Using Deep Learning Approach Based on Improved Convolutional Neural Networks. IEEE Access, 2019, 7, 59069–59080.
4. Khattab, A., Habib, S. E., Ismail, H., Zayan, S., Fahmy, Y., and Khairy, M. M. (2019). An IoT-based cognitive monitoring system for early plant disease forecast. Computers and Electronics in Agriculture, 166, 2019, 105028.
5. Bhargava, Kriti, Arti Kashyap, and Timothy A. Gonsalves. (2014). Wireless sensor network based advisory system for Apple Scab prevention. Twentieth national conference on communications (NCC). IEEE, 2014.
6. Alharbi, Asmaa Ghazi, and Muhammad Arif. (2020). Detection and classification of apple diseases using convolutional neural networks. 2nd international conference on computer and information sciences (ICCIS). IEEE, 2020.
7. Li, Lili, Shujuan Zhang, and Bin Wang. (2022). Apple leaf disease identification with a small and imbalanced dataset based on lightweight convolutional networks. Sensors 22(1), 173.
8. M. Agarwal, R.K. Kaliyar, G. Singal, (2019). FCNN-LDA: A Faster Convolution Neural Network model for Leaf Disease identification on Apple's leaf dataset. 12th International Conference on Information & Communication Technology and System (ICTS). IEEE, 2019.
9. Gupta, Bhavya, Gazal Madan, and Abdul Quadir Md. (2022). A smart agriculture framework for IoT based plant decay detection using smart croft algorithm." Materials Today: Proceedings 62, 4758-4763.
10. Karpyshev, Pavel, Valery Ilin, Ivan Kalinov, Alexander Petrovsky, and Dzmitry Tsetserukou. (2021). Autonomous mobile robot for apple plant disease detection based on CNN and multi-spectral vision system. IEEE/SICE international symposium on system integration (SII), IEEE, 157–162.
11. Nawaz, M. A., Rasool, R. M., Kausar, M., Usman, A., Bukht, T. F. N., Ahmad, R., and Jaleel, A. Plant disease detection using internet of thing (IoT). International Journal of Advanced Computer Science and Applications 11(1), 2020.
12. Nagajyothi, D., HemaSree, P., Rajani Devi, M., Madhavi, G., and Hasane Ahammad, S. (2022). IoT-based prediction of pesticides and fruits diseases detection using SVM and neural networks. International Journal of Mechanical Engineering, 7(1), 2022.

13. Srinidhi, V. V., Apoorva Sahay, and K. Deeba. (2021). Plant pathology disease detection in apple leaves using deep convolutional neural networks: Apple leaves disease detection using efficientnet and densenet. 5th international conference on computing methodologies and communication (ICCMC). IEEE, 2021.

14. Anas, S., Badhusha, I., Zaheema, O. T., Faseela, K., and Shelly, M. (2017). Cloud based automated irrigation and plant leaf disease detection system using an android application. International conference of Electronics, Communication and Aerospace Technology (ICECA), IEEE, 2, 211–214.

15. Tomerlin, J. R., and A. L. Jones. (1983). Effect of temperature and relative humidity on the latent period of Venturia inaequalis in apple leaves." Phytopathology 73(1), 73–76.

16. Nicole W. Gauthier. Fruit Diseases of Apple. Plant Pathology Fact Sheet. Available at [http://plantpathology.ca.uky.edu/files/ppfs-fr-t-02.pdf].

17. A. Based and I. P. M. Package. AESA BASED IPM Package AESA based IPM – Apple Important Natural Enemies of Apple Insect Pests. 2014. Available at [https://farmer.gov.in/imagedefault/ipm/apple.pdf]

18. Himachal Watcher. Apple Diseases Threaten Crops in Himachal, Read How to Deal With Them | Himachal Watcher. https://himachalwatcher.com/2021/05/28/apple-diseases-threatens-crops-in-himachal/ (accessed Apr. 15, 2022).

19. Anurag kerketa. Diseases of Apple. https://www.slideshare.net/AnurAgKerketta/diseases-of-apple (accessed Apr. 15, 2022).

20. Y. Dumas, M. Dadomo, G. Di Lucca, P. Grolier. (2003). Effects of environmental factors and agricultural techniques on antioxidant content of tomatoes. Journal of the Science of Food and Agriculture 83(5), 369–382.

21. K. Lin-Wang, D. Micheletti, J. Palmer, et al. (2011). High temperature reduces apple fruit colour via modulation of the anthocyanin regulatory complex. Plant, Cell Environ., 34 (7), 1176–1190.

22. Lin-Wang, K.U.I., Micheletti, D., Palmer, J., Volz, R., Lozano, L., Espley, R., Hellens, R.P., Chagne, D., Rowan, D.D., Troggio, M. and Iglesias, I., (2011). High temperature reduces apple fruit colour via modulation of the anthocyanin regulatory complex. Plant, Cell & Environment, 34(7), 1176–1190.

23. Vedwan, Neeraj, and Robert E. Rhoades. (2001). Climate change in the Western Himalayas of India: a study of local perception and response. Climate research. 19(2), 109–117.

5 Public sensitive data exchange built on signatures for cloud services

D. Dhinakaran[1,a], L. Srinivasan[2,b], B. Dharun[3,c], J. Sibi Aravind[3,d] and J. Mohamed Eshack[3,e]

[1]Department of Computer Science and Engineering, Vel Tech Rangarajan Dr. Sagunthala R&D Institute of Science and Technology, Chennai, India

[2]Department of Computer Science and Engineering, Dr. N.G.P. Institute of Technology, Coimbatore, India

[3]Department of Information Technology, Velammal Institute of Technology, Panchetti, Chennai, India

Abstract

Cloud computing is recognized as a substitute for conventional digital technologies because of its inherent resource sharing as well as low maintenance requirements. In the modern environment, cloud computing is a relatively new technology. One of the biggest problems nowadays is the absence of security in a public cloud. The key focus of the proposed work is to raise fresh security concerns. In order to share data securely through public clouds, a number of encryption and privacy protocols have been devised. The safe data exchange across public clouds is accomplished using an effective encryption mechanism. Nevertheless, the currently employed solution has a problem with lockup and does not use the premise of proxy re-encryption. In this paper, a brand-new as well as effective method for data transmission across cloud systems is put forth. It is therefore based on the idea of remote data security monitoring that enables data exchange with hidden confidential material. A sanitizer is employed in this method to turn the data blocks' certificates into legitimate ones for said sanitized file while also sanitizing the blocks of data that correlate to the file's confidential material. During the authenticity auditing process, these signs are utilized to confirm the accuracy of the cleaned file. As a result, our method enables the cloud-stored file to ever be accessed as well as utilized by others under the premise that the confidential material is masked and retains the ability to carry out distant integrity monitoring effectively. The suggested solution offers a secure platform including secrecy, authorization, as well as security systems for business data exchange in a cloud context. This proof demonstrated how well the suggested methodology worked for safe information exchange in a cloud context.

Keywords: Auditing, authenticity, encryption, resource sharing, security

Introduction

The method by that digital data is saved and accessed has evolved as a result of recent technological breakthroughs. Currently, remote working is used more frequently by both individuals and businesses, mostly for financial reasons. These solutions are not just to make it possible to share information and, moreover,

---

[a]dhinaads@gmail.com, [b]srinivasanl.1982@gmail.com, [c]dharunbalu0910@gmail.com, [d]sibiaravind9520@gmail.com, [e]eshackmohamed@gmail.com

guarantee that it is always possible to access data. Yet, the rising popularity of cloud services poses severe privacy concerns because they put people's personal information at risk, especially when using unreliable servers [1]. The content that hosts store, as well as process, is regrettably directly accessible by servers. Data could've been encoded after departing trustworthy bounds to safeguard important information from sites in untrustworthy settings. The server must choose who has access to the information irrespective if it has been encoded or otherwise. Access control mechanisms could've been defined to determine who has the data access. These guidelines for network access will specify who has rights to the information [2]. Modern policy based systems can guarantee that these guidelines are adhered to. Yet when confidential information-leaking sensitive regulations have to be implemented in unreliable settings, the situation gets more problematic. Because it is founded on concepts, methods, and tools created in distributed computing, cloud technology has its roots primarily in these fields.

A model called "cloud technology" makes it possible to quickly construct as well as deploy a common resource of reconfigurable computational power across the net on request and at a low cost. Separating programs from the operational and hardware they need is the fundamental idea behind cloud computing [3–5]. With cloud computing, programs are delivered via the internet and made available through browsers, and mobile apps, whereas the software and information are kept on servers located elsewhere. The process utilized in the cloud computing for information security as well as mitigation determines how honest. Researchers have tried a wide range of tools as well as move toward for data protection as well as avoidance to triumph over the trust barrier. To do this, this strategy be obliged to be improved as well as made more efficient. There are numerous ways to define security [6–9]. Availability of information, the prohibition of unauthorized concealment of knowledge, privacy, the prohibition of illegally disclosing information, as well as integrity protection are all components of security.

Users do not entirely trust the cloud hosting run by cloud providers, even if private and sensitive datasets, including company plans, may well be stored there. An easy way to protect privacy is to encode backup data before uploading them to the cloud. For data exchange on untrustworthy servers, a number of security plans have already been put out. These methods involve the storage of encrypted information files in untrustworthy repositories as well as the distribution of related crypto keys to just authorized users [10–13]. Due to the lack of access to the crypto keys, both storing servers and unauthorized users are unaware of the contents of the file systems. Increasing numbers of individuals are storing their personal data on third-party platforms thanks to modern computing technology, whether it's to make it easier to share or to save money. People's worries concerning data protection also grow as they take benefit of these new tools' benefits. Everyone wants to keep their data safe from unwanted users [14–16]. In this graph, data exchange is being done. We leverage three stages of sharing: user, data owner, as well as a key distribution center as seen in Figure 5.1. All data are kept in an encoded format in data storage facilities.

The shared key method signcryption serves as both a cryptography and a digital signature concurrently in the field of cryptography. Encrypt as well as digital signatures, which can provide anonymity, consistency, and quasi, are the two

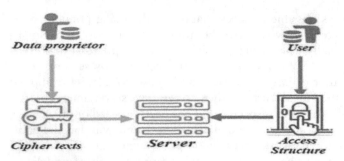

Figure 5.1 Classic structure of cloud security

basic crypto technologies. Public key methods use the signature-then-encryption technique, which encrypts a text after it has been digitally signed. Nonetheless, it may point us towards two issues: Poor effectiveness and huge cost, as well as the argument that neither random plan can ensure security. When compared to standard signature-then-encryption techniques, signcryption can significantly reduce computing costs as well as communication overhead expenses since it satisfies the capabilities and features of electronic signatures as well as cryptography in a solitary step, i.e., both at one occurrence [17]. The best ways to address issues with data residence are through encrypting data as well as restricted access privileges. Cryptographic protocol is a mathematical procedure that transforms clear textual information into cipher text, ensuring that only the authorized recipient may access the ciphered content. The plain text content could only be seen by the customer who has permission to view the cloud network. Therefore access rights serve as a defense against outside attacks [18–20]. The data is shielded by cryptography from both internal and exterior dangers.

Literature Survey

In reaction to all this insecurity, a number of academic contributions have been made that use cryptography to aid with network access on cloud environment services. Several user access schemes are used to authorize advanced cryptosystems. Another revocation technique that uses the symmetric hash-based cryptographic algorithm to protect the file was developed by Wang et al. [21]. With this approach, the cloud may easily change files without having to decode them first. However, because the encryption/decryption process involves a similar amount of cost to public key encryption schemes, these technique results in expensive files. In order to overcome this difficult problem, Jin Li et al. [22] suggest a brand-new attribute-based data exchange system appropriate for smartphone users with low resources. Pooja Katurde et al. [23] proposed safe communication system of the data exists. The key establishment strategy is used to make data exchange easier. The key distribution process is used to produce the certificate. Additionally, their system may facilitate identity information tracing in an anonymized setting. Also, they notify the administrator how many individuals have accessed the file. An assessment of secure transmitting data in a cloud services context was presented by Eyazhini et al. [24]. The data owner outsources the data to cut costs. Due to the fact that the cloud provider is a third-party service vendor, the data holder has no access to their information. The concerns regarding privacy and security regarding cloud data exchange are a concern. The author discusses a number of strategies, including AES encryption, group information sharing, as well as user revocation, to promote privacy as well as trustworthy data exchange.

A safe data-sharing plan for groups is proposed by Velakanti et al. [25], along with information on how cryptography techniques aid groups in transmitting intelligence dynamically. Because data is shared amongst people coming, the expense of encrypting calculation as well as processing overhead varies depending on the number of denied individuals. By using cryptography methods to transmit data, they are able to provide multiple levels of protection for each team member in order to prevent this. With this method, data can be transferred to the network after it has been encrypted using a confidential group key.

Tarasvi Lakum and others [26] by assigning role-based cryptographic revocation in a cloud virtual machine to modify cipher text, the suggested file authorization approach revokes Key-Signatures Lookup Mechanism, which offers anonymous hosted-file access to data. In Key-Signatures Search Strategy, the hosted-file key management that records the managed as well as its revoking keys concurrently for crucial compliance as well as file-access renunciation makes it possible to secure cloud storage by protecting its data. They implemented a cloud data protection strategy as well as a mechanism to show the effectiveness of the suggested approach as well as the security of cloud storage.

Disadvantage of Existing System
The file could be decrypted by the data holder. But it will prevent others from using the entire electronic copy. For instance, encrypting the electronic health records (EHRs) of individuals with contagious diseases can safeguard both individual and medical privacy. However, these encoded EHRs are no longer useful to scientists. The foregoing issue might be resolved by allowing the investigators access to the decryptor. Unfortunately, for the reasons listed below, using this approach in actual situations is impractical. Initially, using safe means to distribute decryption keys is necessary but sometimes difficult to achieve. Consequently, it is quite challenging for a customer to predict that academics will soon access their EHRs after uploading them to the web. As a consequence, protecting the entire document is unfeasible for hiding important information.

System Model

The recommended plan involves applying access control techniques to protect the data from security breaches. In order to provide secure information exchange for dynamic groups inside the cloud via integrating both the corporate identity as well as dynamic telecast cryptographic primitives, the basic way to safeguard the information well over the untrustworthy network is to encode the information using attribute-based cryptography. For consumers to save their confidential data in the cloud, privacy protection is crucial. Data protection is guaranteed through the use of authorization and access associated controls. By improving cloud confidence and trustworthiness, the difficulties with security and confidentiality, authentication, as well as security systems may be resolved [20]. Users should avoid immediately storing their critical information in the cloud since users need not believe cloud hosting, as well as internal threats, are nearly difficult to eliminate to cloud storage suppliers. Basic encryption cannot fulfill complicated requirements like inquiry, concurrent alteration, and fine-grained clearance due to key management issues.

As depicted in Figure 5.2, Sanitizer, Cloud Server, Data Proprietor, Auditor, as well as User are the five components that make up the design model of attribute-based data exchange appropriate intended for resource-constrained customers in cloud services. System public variables, as well as master keys, are generated by a crucial entity called Sanitizer. Particularly, the system's public parameters include instant encrypted messages that the data owner can employ when the system is active. Sanitizer also oversees system users, as well as the parties in the attribute-based data exchange system, which has complete faith in it. A resource? Constrained party known as the data proprietor seeks to securely store a file on online storage services run by Remote Server for exchange. Data possessors can create offline encrypted messages when connecting to the power generator before it defines the transmission. The owner can compute finalized encryptions remotely while drastically reducing battery life once the message is deciphered. The cloud provider, which is made up of numerous online storage hosts that are looked after by a central data manager, is responsible for storing the decryption content of the data holder. The customer is a private key-holding body wishing to acquire ciphertext stored on a cloud server. A global substitution cipher used during is additionally included well before the decoding stage in order to increase deciphering effectiveness. To be more precise, after receiving the substitution cipher from the central server, the User must verify that it is authentic. Also, if and only if the encryption process passes the test, the decoding process is carried out. To guarantee that the auditing validation could be passed if the cloud somehow doesn't actually retain users' entire, cleansed data. With the exception of Sanitizer, it is presumed that everyone in this work is "honest-but-curious."

More specifically, they will sincerely carry out all the responsibilities given to them by genuine individuals while attempting to learn as many personal details as they can. Data semantic protection, which is strongly linked to data privacy as well as colluding resilience, is the security objective. The content of ciphertext shouldn't be recoverable by unauthorized users. Also, it's essential to avoid

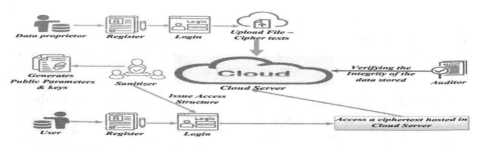

Figure 5.2 Proposed approach

unwanted access via the Remote server to the ciphertexts' message. If unauthorized attackers working together with Remote Server are unable to decipher the ciphertext on their own, they shouldn't be able to do so by merging their features. We put forward an attribute- based data exchange system suited in favor of resource constrained individuals in cloud services utilizing the anticipated network infrastructure as displayed in Figure 5.2. System master credentials, as well as public parameters, are generated by the Sanitizer. All users have access to the system's public parameters, which will be used by the data holder during the succeeding online storage generation process to generate actual instant encrypted messages that Sanitizer has determined. Figure 5.2. Proposed Approach By submitting an access policy to Sanitizer, which would then, generates a secret key for the customer-relevant access framework, a user could access the attribute-based information-sharing system. Data Proprietor creates offline encrypted messages that are then employed in the next stage of creating online information. Depending on a set of attributes, Data Proprietor encodes a file as well as sends the shared final cipher - text to Cloud Server. A ciphertext is downloaded by the User from the cloud server. If the block cipher is authentic, then the customer uses their secret keys to decipher it.

By submitting an access policy to sanitizer, which would then generate a secret key for the customer-relevant access framework, a user could access the attribute-based information-sharing system. Data proprietor creates offline encrypted messages that are then employed in the next stage of creating online information. Depending on a set of attributes, data proprietor encodes a file as well as sends the shared final cipher - text to Cloud Server. A ciphertext is downloaded by the User from the cloud server. If the block cipher is authentic, then the customer uses their secret keys to decipher it. By submitting an access policy to sanitizer, which would then generate a secret key for the customer-relevant access framework, a user could access the attribute-based information-sharing system. Data proprietor creates offline encrypted messages that are then employed in the next stage of creating online information. Depending on a set of attributes, data proprietor encodes a file as well as sends the shared final cipher - text to cloud server. A ciphertext is downloaded by the user from the cloud server. If the block cipher is authentic, then the customer uses their secret keys to decipher it. A prominent validator is an auditor. On behalf of its customers, it is the responsibility to confirm the validity of the information saved in the cloud. The auditor transmits an accounting assignment to the cloud whenever he wishes to confirm the accuracy of both the sanitized file kept there. The cloud subsequently provides the auditor with evidence of data custody that can be audited. Lastly, the auditor determines how reliable this auditor proof is accurate in order to confirm the consistency of the sanitized file.

Experimental Results

For safe cloud storage, we create a workable identity-based data access consistency evaluation system with critical data masking. The partitions in the file that match the confidential material are sanitized using a sanitizer. In our intricate method, the user first produces the necessary signatures as well as covers the

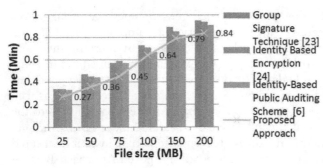

Figure 5.3 Performance comparison

blocks of data of said original document that match the private, confidential material before sending them to a sanitizer. These blindfolded data blocks are uniformly formatted by the sanitizer, which additionally sanitizes the blocks of data that correlate to the institution's confidential material. Also, it changes the appropriate signatures into legitimate sites for the cleaned-up file.

File Upload/Download

We assessed the overall amount of time needed to transfer as well as retrieve a file from either the cloud using the suggested SIPS approach. To carry out the afore-mentioned scenario, the accompanying times have been taken into consideration.

1. Time to generate the key
2. Time for encryption and decryption
3. Downloading and uploading times
4. Demand seeking data submission deadline.

Figure 1.3 displays the findings for the total amount of time required by the individual to retrieve the file from the server. The whole procedure is split down into several smaller steps, such as sanitizing the data, uploading it to the cloud, monitoring the cipher data there, waiting therefore for the customer to receive access credentials from the sanitizer, as well as eventually waiting for the data to be downloaded out from the cloud and then going through the decoding process. Both are transmitting as well as retrieving the data took the very same amount of time. The proposed scheme for key creation, file uploading, as well as file retrieving was contrasted and displayed in Figure 5.3. These assessments were predicated on how much time were spent generating keys and how long it took to complete the encryption and decryption operations. In conclusion, the analysis shows that our strategy was significantly more effective than that of other approaches because of its minimum latency.

Conclusion and Future Work

One of the biggest problems nowadays is the absence of security in a public cloud. The key focus of the proposed work is to raise fresh security concerns.

The safe data exchange across public clouds is accomplished using an effective encryption mechanism. Nevertheless, the currently employed solution has a problem with lockup and does not use the premise of proxy re-encryption. In this paper, a brand-new as well as effective method for data transmission across cloud systems is put forth. It is therefore based on the idea of remote data security monitoring that enables data exchange with hidden confidential material.

References

1. Wang, F., Mickens, J., Zeldovich, N., and Vaikuntanathan, V. (2016). Sieve: cryptographically enforced access control for user data in untrusted clouds. In 13th USENIX Symposium on Networked Systems Design and Implementation (NSDI '16), Santa clara, CA, 611–626.
2. Dhinakaran, D., and Joe Prathap, P. M. (2022). Protection of data privacy from vulnerability using two-fish technique with apriori algorithm in data mining. *The Journal of Supercomputing*, 78(16), 17559–17593.
3. Sankar, S. M. U., Dhinakaran, D., Kavya, T., Priyanka, S., and Oviya, P. P. (2023). A way for smart home technology for disabled and elderly people. In 2023 International Conference on Innovative Data Communication Technologies and Application (ICIDCA), Uttarakhand, India, (pp. 369–373).
4. Udhaya Sankar, S. M., Kumar, N. J., Dhinakaran, D., Kamalesh, S. S., and Abenesh, R. (2023). Machine learning system for indolence perception. In 2023 International Conference on Innovative Data Communication Technologies and Application (ICIDCA), Uttarakhand, India, (pp. 55–60).
5. Li, Z., Xu, W., Shi, H., Zhang, Y., and Yan, Y. (2021). Security and privacy risk assessment of energy big data in cloud environment. *Hindawi, Computational Intelligence and Neuroscience*, 2021, 1–11.
6. Nithya, S. M. V., and Uthariaraj, V. R. (2020). Identity-based public auditing scheme for cloud storage with strong keyexposure resilience. *Hindawi, Security and Communication Networks*, 2020, 1–13.
7. Selvaraj, D., Udhaya Sankar, S. M., Dhinakaran, D., and Anish, T. P. (2023). Outsourced analysis of encrypted graphs in the cloud with privacy protection. *SSRG International Journal of Electrical and Electronics Engineering*, 10(1), 53–62. Crossref, https://doi.org/10.14445/23488379/IJEEE-V10I1P105.
8. Zhang, J., and Wu, M. (2021). Efficient cloud-based private set intersection protocol with hidden access attribute and integrity verification. *Hindawi, Security and Communication Networks*, 2021, 1–13.
9. Udhaya Sankar, S. M., Dhinakaran, D., Deboral, C. C., and Ramakrishnan, M. (2022). Safe routing approach by identifying and subsequently eliminating the attacks in MANET. *International Journal of Engineering Trends and Technology*, 70(11), 219–231. https://doi.org/10.14445/22315381/IJETT-V70I11P224.
10. Sudharson, K., Alekhya, B., Abinaya, G., Rohini, C., Arthi, S., and Dhinakaran, D. (2023). Efficient soil condition monitoring with IoT enabled intelligent farming solution. In 2023 IEEE International Students' Conference on Electrical, Electronics and Computer Science (SCEECS), Bhopal, India, (pp. 1–6).
11. Monica, G. K., Dhinakaran, D., Haritha, K., Kohila, K., and Priyadharshini, U. (2023). MEMS based sensor robot for immobilized persons. In 2023 International Conference on Innovative Data Communication Technologies and Application (ICIDCA), Uttarakhand, India, (pp. 924–929).

12. Srinivasan, L., Selvaraj, D., Dhinakaran, D., and Anish, T. P. (2023). IoT-based solution for paraplegic sufferer to send signals to physician via internet. *SSRG International Journal of Electrical and Electronics Engineering*, 10(1), 41–52.

13. Ni, L., Sun, X., Li, X., and Zhang, J. (2021). GCWOAS2: multiobjective task scheduling strategy based on gaussian cloud whale optimization in cloud computing. *Hindawi, Computational Intelligence and Neuroscience*, 2021, 1–17.

14. Dhinakaran, D., Selvaraj, D., Udhaya Sankar, S. M., Pavithra, S., and Boomika, R. (2023). Assistive system for the blind with voice output based on optical character recognition. In International Conference on Innovative Computing and Communications. Lecture Notes in Networks and Systems, (Vol. 492). Springer, Singapore.

15. Zhu, X., Chang, C. W., Xi, Q., and Zuo, Z. B. (2020). Attribute guard: attributeBased flow access control framework in software defined networking. *Hindawi, Security and Communication Networks*, 2020, 1–18.

16. Gomathy, G., Kalaiselvi, P., Selvaraj, D., Dhinakaran, D., Anish, T. P., and Kumar, D. A. (2022). Automatic waste management based on IoT using a wireless sensor network. In 2022 International Conference on Edge Computing and Applications (ICECAA), (pp. 629–634). doi: 10.1109/ICECAA55415.2022.9936351.

17. Dhinakaran, D., Udhaya Sankar, S. M., Latha, B. C., Anns, A. E. J., and Sri, V. K. (2023). Dam management and disaster monitoring system using IoT. In 2023 International Conference on Sustainable Computing and Data Communication Systems (ICSCDS), Erode, India, (pp. 1197–1201).

18. Bel, D. J. C., Esther, C., Zionna Sen, G. B., Tamizhmalar, D., Dhinakaran, D., and Anish, T. P. (2022). Trustworthy cloud storage data protection based on blockchain technology. In 2022 International Conference on Edge Computing and Applications (ICECAA), (pp. 538–543). doi: 10.1109/ICECAA55415.2022.9936299.

19. Gangarde, R., Shrivastava, D., Sharma, A., Tandon, T., Pawar, A., and Garg, R. (2022). Data anonymization to balance privacy and utility of online social media network data. *Journal of Discrete Mathematical Sciences and Cryptography*, 25(3), 829–838. DOI: 10.1080/09720529.2021.2016225.

20. Dhinakaran, D., Udhaya Sankar, S. M., Ananya, J., and Roshnee, S. A. (2023). IOT-based whip-smart trash bin using LoRa WAN. In Jeena Jacob, I., Kolandapalayam Shanmugam, S., and Izonin, I. (eds). Expert Clouds and Applications. 2nd International Conference on Expert Clouds and Applications (ICOECA 2022), Bangalore, Karnataka, India. Lecture Notes in Networks and Systems, 673, 277-288.

21. Wang, X., Qi, Y., and Wang, Z. (2019). Design and implementation of SecPod: a framework for virtualization-based security systems. *IEEE Transactions on Dependable and Secure Computing*, 16(1), 44–57.

22. Li, J., Zhang, Y., Chen, X., and Xiang, Y. (2018). Secure attribute based data sharing for resource-limited users in cloud computing. *Computers and Security*, 72, 1–12.

23. Katurde, P., Konda, R., Mohite, T., and Melkunde, N. (2019). Secured group data sharing in cloud computing. *International Journal of Advanced Computational Engineering and Networking*, 7(7), 23–25.

24. Eyazhini, A., and Vijayakumar, V. (2020). Data sharing in cloud using revocable storage- identity based encryption. *International Journal of Innovative Research in Science, Engineering and Technology (IJIRSET)*, 9(6), 4622–4627.

25. Velakanti, G., Reddy, N., and Venishetty, S. (2016). Secure data sharing with in groups in the cloud. *International Journal of Engineering Sciences and Research Technology*, 5(8), 1–13.

26. Lakum, T., and Reddy, T. (2022). An efficient file access control technique for shared cloud data security through key signatures search scheme. *Journal of Theoretical and Applied Information Technology*, 100(1), 127–136.

6 Optimized mechanism for allocating resources in a cloud environment using frog and crow optimization algorithm

N. Jagadish Kumar[1,a], D. Dhinakaran[2,b],
S. M. Udhaya Sankar[3,c], S. Jindhiya Sree[4,d] and
A. Mounica[4,e]

[1]Department of CSBS, Sri Sairam Engineering College, Chennai, India

[2]Department of Computer Science and Engineering, Vel Tech Rangarajan Dr. Sagunthala R&D Institute of Science and Technology, Chennai, India

[3]Department of CSE (Cyber Security), R.M.K College of Engineering and Technology, Chennai, India

[4]Department of Information Technology, Velammal Institute of Technology, Panchetti, Chennai, India

Abstract

Cloud computing resource allocation is a process of Allocating and managing computer resources, such as virtual machines, storage, network bandwidth, and other computing services, to satisfy the demands of cloud users. Resource allocation is crucial in cloud computing since resources are frequently shared by many users and applications, ensuring the greatest performance and most productive use of resources is challenging. In this paper a novel approach to optimize the resource allocation is proposed. FCOA (Frog and crow optimization algorithm is used) as an optimization algorithm by the resource manager in the process of resource allocation. The criteria that determine the FCOA's optimization include the search space, population size, iteration count, and selection strategy. The three primary resource allocation parameters like energy consumption, response time, and resource usage % are improved by the above-mentioned approach for cloud computing. The proposed algorithm enhanced the three key parameters of resource allocation in cloud computing by comparing them with the CSA (Crow search algorithm) and FA (Firefly algorithm) results.

Keywords: Cloud resource allocation, CSA, FA, and FCO, metaheuristics algorithm

Introduction

Popular study topics include cloud computing, which is seen as the third IT revolution. It encompasses service providers giving their clients access to a lot of resources for a minimal cost, including computer hardware, storage space, and software. Effectively meeting consumers' requirements becomes more crucial as the number of customers rises so Cloud computing has become the most dominant technology due to its internet-based services that operate on a pay-per-use basis and encompass both hardware and software [1]. Due to its virtualization

[a]Jagadishiva@gmail.com, [b]dhinaads@gmail.com, [c]udhaya3@gmail.com,
[d]sreejindhu02@gmail.com, [e]mounicagracy@gmail.com

features, cloud computing has grown in favor among both the corporate and scientific groups. There are still issues with resource storage, time management, resource utilization efficiency, energy use, and data management even though virtual machines in cloud computing assist to lower actual operational costs [2]. Resource allocation remains a critical issue in the cloud environment and have various levels of challenges, including scheduling, computational resources, performance, response time for relocation, Quality of Service, and energy management systems. Because there is more demand for these services, cloud data centers are using more energy. Scheduling is crucial for the effective use of resources in cloud computing [3].

The dynamic nature of cloud computing does not lend itself to conventional scheduling techniques. We can instantly acquire extra resources from cloud providers while growing our organization due to the flexibility of cloud computing. Additionally, remote accessibility enables us to use cloud services at any time and from any location. Resource allocation is an important issue in cloud computing to overcome this various optimization algorithms are use Because they may assist to maximize the use of existing resources, enhance resource utilization, lower costs, and boost overall performance of cloud systems, optimization algorithms are crucial for allocating resources in the cloud [4]. By dynamically distributing resources in according to the requirements of the workload and the constraints of the system, optimization algorithms can aid in solving this problem. For instance, if a certain application needs more computational power to handle a huge workload, an optimization algorithm can assign more power to that application while maintaining the performance of other applications. In conclusion, optimization algorithms are essential for efficient cloud resource allocation since they make the finest potential use of the resources that are available, enhance system performance, and reduce spending [5].

A class of optimization algorithms known as metaheuristic algorithms is used to solve complex optimization problems, especially those where traditional optimization approaches may not be suitable. To identify solutions, metaheuristics use a variety of search techniques, including stochastic, local, and global searches. Genetic algorithms, simulated annealing, particle swarm optimization, ant colony optimization, and tabu search are a few examples of typical metaheuristic algorithms. Real-world issues perform detailed optimization, complicated restrictions, and uncertainties usually make use of metaheuristics [6–8]. In many cases, they outperform conventional optimization algorithms in terms of effectiveness and efficiency and can handle both continuous and discrete optimization issues.

Existing System
The task of allocating cloud resources, such as virtual machines (VMs), to various activities or services is known as cloud resource allocation, and it is a challenging optimization problem. The objective is to use resources as effectively as possible while keeping expenses to a minimal and ensuring that tasks are completed by the deadlines. Existing work used The Frog Optimization Algorithm (FOA) it is a nature inspired algorithm. The FOA is based on how frogs behave in ponds. The method begins with a population of frogs that stood in for possible solutions to the issue. Based on its fitness, or how effectively it fits the requirements

and objectives of the issue, each frog is evaluated. After that, taking benefit of the frog's leaping activity, the best solutions are employed to create new ones.

The FOA may be used to assign VMs to various activities or services when allocating cloud resources. It is possible to treat the VM allocation problem as an optimization problem, with the goal to reduce the overall cost of VMs while trying to ensure that the tasks are accomplished by their given deadline. By allocating VMs to tasks based on their fitness rankings, the FOA may be used to produce solutions that fulfil these restrictions and objectives. The search space, which represents many potential combinations of VM allocations, is a place where frogs can jump at random [9]. An optimization method based on the social behaviour of crows is called the Crow Search Optimization (CSO) algorithm. The allocation of cloud resources is one of the many optimization issues to which it has been use [10]. Crows make up the population of the CSO algorithm, each of which represents a potential solution to the optimization issue. The crows talk to one another to exchange data on their fitness, which is a measure of how efficiently their solution works. After that, the crows employ this knowledge to adjust where they are in the search area and look for fresh alternatives.

Literature Survey

The use of cloud computing technology is increasing and provides services through the internet. According to Soukaina Ouhame et al. [11] Virtual machines (VMs) are a crucial component of cloud computing; however, they could have problems with data distribution. With the use of a modified Gravitational Search Algorithm (GWO), a new method to enhance the data allocation system in virtual machines is provided. Throughput, energy use, and the typical network execution time are all goals of this strategy for cloud computing. In comparison to the Artificial Bee Colony (ABC) technique and the GWO algorithm, the findings of the proposed technique exhibit enhanced load balancing in cloud computing. This methodology was put out to assist with cloud computing task scheduling to cut prices and fulfil deadlines. Particle swarm optimization was employed to resolve this complex problem. The particle positions did not accurately represent resource attributes, which was a shortcoming of the conventional strategy employing particle swarm optimization [12]. In this study, a novel technique known as the "resource renumber strategy" has put out to address this problem by rearranging and renumbering resources in accordance with their processing capacity. Experiments showed that this improved the performance of particle swarm optimization.

Xia et al. [13] states that it is research on how to enhance a mobile edge cloud system's performance by making the most of its radio and computing capabilities. The objective is to maintain a balance between the network's and users' demands while lowering costs and consuming less energy. For efficient management of resources, the suggested system combines ant colony optimization with genetic algorithms. In contrast to other existing model, simulation results demonstrate that this technique improves system performance, resource utilization, and average latency. According to Chalack et al. [14] This research proposes novel cloud computing task scheduling techniques based on particle swarm optimization (PSO). PSO assists in determining the best course of action and is motivated by the behavior of animal swarms. The algorithms' intention is to concurrently minimize Make span, Flowtime, and job execution cost. Results demonstrate that the suggested algorithms are more effective when compared to related techniques.

Nagaraju et al. [15] states that in cloud computing, resource allocation is a critical problem that businesses must consider the limitations of the resources they can purchase. Large businesses with a lot of consumers and resources are dealing with a combinatorial optimization problem. A particle swarm optimization approach has been developed to address this issue. Based on variables like total task, execution time, resource reservations, and QoS of each job, this method seeks to identify the optimum task scheduler for resources. A Pareto-domination mechanism is also used by the algorithm to look for multi-objective optimum solutions. The outcomes demonstrate how effective and efficient the suggested method. Balaji Naik et al. [16] discusses a hybrid optimization algorithm for allocating resources in cloud computing that combines the Shuffled Frog Leaping Algorithm (SFLA) and Cuckoo Search (CS) Algorithm. The suggested method combines the benefits of SFLA and CS while overcoming the drawbacks of existing algorithms like HABCCS, GTS, and Krill Herd. While CS conducts initializing, producing, evaluating the fitness function, modification, and evaluating the new solutions, SFLA handles initializing, generating, sorting, splitting, and evaluating user requests. The suggested approach uses server-side resource allocation that takes less calculation time by evaluating request speed and size. Experimental results demonstrate that the suggested strategy outperforms other relevant approaches.

Samriya et al. [17] argues that the cloud computing concept serves as the foundation for cloud computing and that its goal is to offer a diverse variety of computational resources to fulfil the demands of various applications. The Green Cloud Scheduling Model (GCSM) is employed for utilization, while the Spider Monkey Optimization (SMO) is used for optimal resource allocation. The effectiveness of the suggested technique is assessed by simulation, and the findings demonstrate that it is better than existing algorithms in terms of response time, make span, energy consumption, and resource usage. Madni et al. [18] proposed that the term "cloud technology" describes the practice of offering users online access to virtualized computational resources. It is difficult to allocate resources efficiently and offer them in a way that meets the various Quality of Service (QoS) demands of clients and reduces energy usage while maintaining the Service Level Agreement (SLA). The Multi-Objective Cuckoo Search Algorithm (MOCSA) is implemented in this article to effectively schedule user tasks on cloud virtual machines and distribute resources to dynamic workloads.

The Cloudsim simulation toolkit was used for the simulation trials, and the outcomes demonstrated that MOCSA performed admirably in terms of performance, energy consumption, CPU use, bandwidth consumption, and SLA violation. Kumar et al. [19] explains that cloud computing entails giving user apps vast quantities of storage and processing power through the internet through connected machines. An essential problem in cloud computing is task scheduling, which entails allocating user workloads to suitable virtual machines to satisfy Quality of Service (QoS) requirements. In order to enhance global search capabilities and optimize work scheduling, this research suggests combining the Crow Search algorithm and the Firefly algorithm [20]. The suggested technique outperforms the results of the standalone Crow search algorithm and Firefly algorithm while minimizing makes span and maximizing throughput.

System Model

In the proposed approach we are using the combination of Frog and crow optimization algorithm (FCOA) for effective resource allocation of cloud. FCOA is based on the interaction between frog and crows, the basic framework of crow search algorithm (CSA) is included with the behavior of frog as shown in Figure 6.1.

With this design, the cloud provider supplies the actual resources, such as servers, storage, and networking that make up the cloud's supporting infrastructure. The management and provisioning of these resources to the cloud tenants is the responsibility of the resource manager [21–26]. According to Figure 6.1 the resource allocation component uses the Frog and crow Optimization Algorithm (FCOA) to allocate the cloud resources to different tasks or services based on the demand and the available resources.

Working and Operations

The process flow of the FCOA algorithm includes specific procedures to select subset of frog and to be assigned as crows, calculating the crow's flight distance, update the search space boundaries. The implementation of algorithm may very depend upon the specific application of the algorithm. several regions, zones, or data centers.

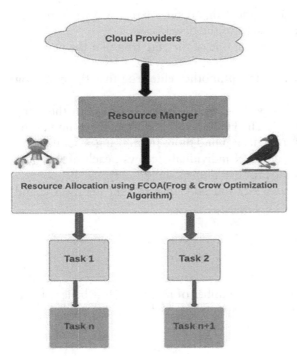

Figure 6.1 Resource allocation in cloud using (FCOA)

The following formula may be used to determine the likelihood that a frog will switch to an elite frog it is described in equation (1)

$$P_{a,b} = (f_b - f_a) / \max(f) + b_{a,b} \tag{1}$$

Based on two factors, the likelihood that a normal frog "a" would transform into a "elite" frog "b" is:

The difference in fitness between the two frogs, denoted by $(f_b - f_a)$

A scaling factor that takes into account the maximum fitness of all frogs in the population, denoted by $\max(f)$

A bias factor specific to frog a and frog b, denoted by $b_{a,b}$.

The output of the formula is the probability of frog a switching to frog b, denoted by $p_{a,b}$. The possibility that a less fit frog "a" will take on the traits of a more fit frog "b" in order to raise the population's overall fitness may be calculated using the above formula.

The following formula may be used to determine the new frog created by hopping to the elite frog(s) it is described in equation (2)

$$Z_{new} = (k - r) * Z_a + r * Z_b \tag{2}$$

Z_{new}: This represents the characteristics of the new frog that will be created by "hopping" to the elite frog.

k: This is a constant value that determines the size of the jump that the new frog will make.

r: This is a random value between 0 and 1 that determines how much influence the elite fr will have on the characteristics of the new frog.

Z_a: This represents the characteristics of one of the elite frog that the new frog will be hopping to.

Z_b: This represents the characteristics of another elite frog that the new frog may be hopping to.

By jumping to the elite frog, a new frog would be generated with the attributes indicated by the value for Z_{new}. The FCOA evolutionary process mimics the strategy used by crows and frogs to hide and find more food. Being a population-based method, the flock is made up of N individuals (crows), each of which is n-dimensional with n serving as the problem dimension [27–29].

Equation (3) describes the crow's location Xi,k in a certain iteration k and illustrates one potential solution to the issue:

$$X_{i,k} = [x_{1i,k}, x_{2i,k}, \ldots, x_{ni,k}];$$
$$i = 1, 2, \ldots, N; \; k = 1, 2, \ldots, \max \text{Iter} \tag{3}$$

where max Iter is the process's maximum number of iterations. It is believed that each crow (individual) can remember the most effective hiding spot Mi,k to hide food until the current iterations Equation (4):

$$M_{i,k} = [m_{1i,k}, m_{2i,k}, \ldots, m_{ni,k}] \tag{4}$$

Pursue and evasion are the two activities that affect each position. Pursuit: A crow j follows crow i to identify the hidden place.

Evasion: Crow I purposely chooses a random trajectory in order to preserve its food since it is aware that Crow J is nearby. There are lot of advantage of using FCOA algorithm for cloud resource allocation. FCOA has the capacity to quickly navigate a huge search area and identify the best answer [30–32]. This is crucial in the allocation of cloud resources since there are many variables that must be optimized, including the quantity of virtual machines, the distribution of CPU and memory, and the network bandwidth. FCOA is a robust algorithm, it can perform under a variety of challenging conditions. In the allocation of cloud resources, where resource availability and quality are subject to vary over time, this is crucial. FCOA is a flexible algorithm, it may be altered to meet certain needs and restrictions. This is crucial for cloud resource allocation since there can be needs in terms of price, performance, and security from. To solve complex issues with cloud resource allocation, FCOA is readily scalable.

Experimental Results

A good algorithm for allocating resources to the cloud should maximize resource use while assuring high throughput and rapid response times. By assigning resources in an energy-efficient way, a good cloud resource allocation algorithm should reduce energy usage. Figure 6.2 Show the simulation variables that were used to assess the effectiveness of the proposed FCOA and compare it to that of the CSA (crow search Algorithm) and FA (Firefly Algorithm). Response time, resource utility, and energy usage are some of the variables used to gauge the FCOA algorithm's effectiveness across a range of tasks.

Figure 6.2 illustrates the comparison analysis of Response time, resource utilization and energy consumption which are the important cloud resource allocation parameters with three different optimization algorithms. It clearly shows that the proposed FCOA is best in providing results for all the three parameters. The response time of the proposed methodology is 286 s, 10.6% faster than that of the competing techniques.

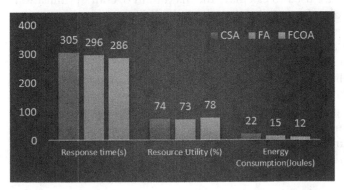

Figure 6.2 Comparison analysis of 3 algorithms with three cloud resource allocation parameters

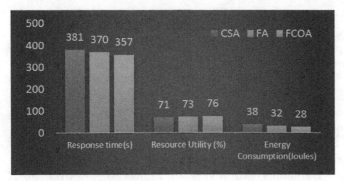

Figure 6.3 Comparison analysis of 3 algorithms with 3 cloud resource allocation parameters for 300 tasks

Figure 6.3 Show the simulation parameters that were used to assess the effectiveness of the proposed FCOA and compare it to that of the CSA (crow search Algorithm) and FA (Firefly Algorithm). Response time, resource utility, and energy usage are some of the variables used to gauge the FCOA algorithm's effectiveness across a range of 300 tasks. Figure 6.3 illustrates the comparison analysis of Response time, resource utilization and energy consumption which are the important cloud resource allocation parameters with three different optimization algorithms. Our proposed methodology yields superior outcomes in comparison to other methods. The proposed approach uses 18.2% less energy than the alternative techniques, 28 joules for 300 jobs.

Conclusion

The proposed optimization algorithm FCOA is offered as a reliable effort to accomplish the goal of resource allocation in a cloud computing environment. Response time, resource utility, and energy efficiency were employed as the proposed algorithm's goal functions to gauge its performance. The common characteristics of the algorithms, such as search space, population size, iteration count, and selection approach, are used to calculate the maximum overall optimization between the proposed algorithm and the current algorithms. According to the simulation findings, the suggested technique has a higher quality of service (QoS) than more established cloud computing optimization algorithms like FA and CSA. It has been found that the response time of the proposed FCOA is 10.6% faster and resource utilization is increased by 80% and energy consumption is also reduced by 17.2% compared to the existing FA & CSA algorithms. The future work includes experimenting with different sets of goal functions, testing it on larger and more complex systems, evaluating its performance under different load conditions, comparing it with other state-of-the-art algorithms, and implementing it in a real-world cloud computing environment to evaluate its practical applicability.

Acknowledgement

I am immensely grateful to my co-authors, for their unwavering support, guidance, and expertise, which played a crucial role in shaping and refining this research. I also acknowledge the invaluable contributions of my colleagues and friends, who provided valuable insights and discussions, enhancing the quality of this work.

References

1. Abdallah, H. B., Sanni, A. A., Thummar, K., and Halabi, T. (2021). Online energy-efficient resource allocation in cloud computing data centers. In 2021 24th Conference on Innovation in Clouds, Internet and Networks and Workshops, ICIN 2021, (pp. 92–99).
2. Tang, D., Zhao, J., Yang, J., Liu, Z., and Cai, Y. (2021). An evolutionary frog leaping algorithm for global optimization problems and applications. Computational Intelligence and Neuroscience. 2021, 1–31. https://doi.org/10.1155/2021/8928182.
3. Meraihi, Y., Gabis, A. B., Ramdane-Cherif, A., and Acheli, D. (2021). A comprehensive survey of crow search algorithm and its applications. Artificial Intelligence Review, 54(4), 2669–2716. https://doi.org/10.1007/s10462-020-09911-9.
4. Krishnadoss, P., Natesan, G., Ali, J., Nanjappan, M., Krishnamoorthy, P., and Poornachary, V. K. (2021). CCSA: hybrid cuckoo crow search algorithm for task scheduling in cloud computing. International Journal of Intelligent Engineering and Systems, 14(4), 241–250.
5. Sankar, S. M. U., Dhinakaran, D., Kavya, T., Priyanka, S., and Oviya, P. P. (2023). A way for smart home technology for disabled and elderly people. In 2023 International Conference on Innovative Data Communication Technologies and Application (ICIDCA), Uttarakhand, India, 2023, (pp. 369–373).
6. Selvaraj, D., and Anish, T. P. (2023). Outsourced analysis of encrypted graphs in the cloud with privacy protection. SSRG International Journal of Electrical and Electronics Engineering, 10(1), 53–62.
7. Sankar, S. M., Chamundeeswari, V., and Katiravan, J. (2014). Identity based attack detection and manifold adversaries localization in wireless networks. Journal of Theoretical and Applied Information Technology, 67(2), 513–518.
8. Deboral, C. C., and Ramakrishnan, M. (2022). Safe routing approach by identifying and subsequently eliminating the attacks in MANET. International Journal of Engineering Trends and Technology, 70(11), 219–231.
9. Monica, G. K., Dhinakaran, D., Haritha, K., Kohila, K., and Priyadharshini, U. (2023). MEMS based sensor robot for immobilized persons. In 2023 International Conference on Innovative Data Communication Technologies and Application (ICIDCA), Uttarakhand, India, 2023, (pp. 924–929).
10. Sujithra, T., Sumathi, Dr. M., Ramakrishnan, M., and Sankar, S. M. U. (2020). Id based adaptive-key signcryption for data security in cloud environment (May 11, 2020). IJARET International Journal of Advance Research In Engineering And Technology, 11(4), 167–182.
11. Ouhame, S., and Hadi, Y. (2020). Enhancement in resource allocation system for cloud environment using modified grey wolf technique. Indonesian Journal of Electrical Engineering and Computer Science, 20(3), 1530–1537.
12. Kumar, N. J., Vinisha, K. V., Balasubramanian, C., Sowmya, D., and Prathibapriya, K. S. (2022). Privacy preserving data sharing in cloud using EAE technique. In 4th International Conference on Recent Trends in Computer Science and Technology, ICRTCST 2021 - Proceedings, (pp. 384–388).

13. Xia, W., and Shen, L. (2021). Joint resource allocation at edge cloud based on ant colony optimization and genetic algorithm. Wireless Personal Communications, 117(2), 355–386.

14. Chalack, V. A., Razavi, S. N., and Gudakahriz, S. J. (2017). Resource allocation in cloud environment using approaches based particle swarm optimization. International Journal of Computer Applications Technology and Research, 6(2), 87–90.

15. Nagaraju, V., Kumar, N. J., Ali, A. M., Bapu, T. B. R., and Partheeban, N. (2022). Efficient data transmission scheme using modified wireless communication protocol design. In Proceedings - IEEE International Conference on Advances in Computing, Communication and Applied Informatics, ACCAI 2022.

16. B. B. Naik, D. Singh, A. B. Samaddar and S. Jung,. Developing a Cloud Computing Data Center Virtual Machine Consolidation Based on Multi-objective Hybrid Fruitfly Cuckoo Search Algorithm, 2018 IEEE 5G World Forum (5GWF), Silicon Valley, CA, USA, 2018, 512–515, doi: 10.1109/5GWF.2018.8516947.

17. Samriya, J. K., and Kumar, N. (2022). Spider monkey optimization based energy-efficient resource allocation in cloud environment. Trends in Sciences, 19(1), 1–9.

18. Madni, S. H. H., Latiff, M. S. A., Ali, J., and Abdulhamid, S. M. (2019). Multi-objective-oriented cuckoo search optimization-based resource scheduling algorithm for clouds. Arabian Journal for Science and Engineering, 44(4), 3585–3602.

19. Kumar, S., Malleswaran, A., and Kasireddi, B. (2019). An efficient task scheduling method in a cloud computing environment using firefly crow search algorithm (FF-csa). International Journal of Scientific and Technology Research, 8(12), 623–627.

20. Dai, B., Niu, J., Ren, T., and Atiquzzaman, M. (2022). Toward mobility-aware computation offloading and resource allocation in end–edge–cloud orchestrated computing. In IEEE Internet of Things Journal, 9(19), 19450–19462.

21. Wenhao Fan, Liang Zhao, Xun Liu, Yi Su, Shenmeng Li, Fan Wu, Yuan'an Liu,. (2022). Collaborative service placement, task scheduling, and resource allocation for task offloading with edge-cloud cooperation. In IEEE Transactions on Mobile Computing. 23(1), 238–256, Jan. 2024

22. Pragnya, Y., Kumar, N. J., Sankar, S. M. U., Manoj, A., and Achary, G. P. (2022). Detection of emotions using a boosted machine learning approach. In 2022 1st International Conference on Computational Science and Technology (ICCST), CHENNAI, India, 2022, (pp. 16–21).

23. Sankar, S. M. U., Kumar, N. J., Dhinakaran, D., and Abenesh, R. (2023). Machine learning system for indolence perception. In 2023 International Conference on Innovative Data Communication Technologies and Application (ICIDCA), Uttarakhand, India, 2023, (pp. 55–60).

24. Dhinakaran, D., Sankar, S. M. U., Ananya, J., and Roshnee, S. A. (2023). IOT-based whip-smart trash bin using LoRa WAN. In Jeena Jacob, I., Shanmugam, S. K., and Izonin, I. eds. In International Conference on Expert Clouds and Applications, ICOECA 2022: Expert Clouds and Applications. ICOECA 2022. Lecture Notes in Networks and Systems, (vol 673, pp. 277–288).

25. Sujithra, T., Sumathi, Dr. M., Ramakrishnan, M., and Sankar, S. M. U. (2020). Survey on data security in cloud environment (May 11, 2020). International Journal of Advanced Research in Engineering and Technology (IJARET), 11(4), 155–166.

26. Dhinakaran, D., Sankar, S. M. U., Latha, B. C., Anns, A. E. J., and Sri, V. K. (2023). Dam Management and disaster monitoring system using IoT. In 2023 International Conference on Sustainable Computing and Data Communication Systems (ICSCDS), Erode, India, 2023, (pp. 1197–1201).

27. Sudharson, K., Alekhya, B., Abinaya, G., Rohini, C., Arthi, S., and Dhinakaran, D. (2023). Efficient soil condition monitoring with IoT enabled intelligent farming solu-

tion. In 2023 IEEE International Students' Conference on Electrical, Electronics and Computer Science (SCEECS), Bhopal, India, 2023, (pp. 1–6).

28. Sankar, S. M. U., Kumar, N. J., Elangovan, G., and Praveen, R. (2023). An integrated Z-Number and DEMATEL-based cooperation enforcement scheme for thwarting malicious nodes in MANETs. Wireless Personal Communications. 130, 2531–2563.

29. Srinivasan, L., Selvaraj, D., Dhinakaran, D., and Anish, T. P. (2023). IoT-bBased solution for paraplegic sufferer to send signals to physician via internet. SSRG International Journal of Electrical and Electronics Engineering, 10(1), 41–52.

30. Kumar, N. J., and Balasubramanian, C. (2023). Hybrid gradient descent golden eagle optimization (HGDGEO) algorithm-based efficient heterogeneous resource scheduling for big data processing on clouds. Wireless Personal Communications, 129(2), 1175–1195.

31. Sankar, S. M. U., Selvaraj, D., Monica, G. K., and Katiravan, J. (2023) A secure third-party auditing scheme based on blockchain technology in cloud storage. International Journal of Engineering Trends and Technology, 71(3), 23–32.

32. Madhavi, S., Sankar, S. M. U., Praveen, R., and Kumar, N. J. (2023). A fuzzy CO-PRAS-based decision-making framework for mitigating the impact of vampire sensor nodes in wireless sensor nodes (WSNs). International Journal of Information Technology (Singapore). 15, 1859–1870.

7 Optimizing diabetic retinopathy disease prediction using PNAS, ASHA, and transfer learning

S. M. Udhaya Sankar[1,a], D. Dhinakaran[2,b], R. Selvaraj[3,c], Shrey Kumar Verma[4,d], R. Natarajasivam[4,e] and P. C. Praveen Kishore[4,f]

[1]Department of CSE (Cyber Security), R.M.K College of Engineering and Technology, Chennai, India

[2]Department of Computer Science and Engineering, Vel Tech Rangarajan Dr. Sagunthala R&D Institute of Science and Technology, Chennai, India

[3]Department of Computer Science and Engineering, Dr. N. G. P Institute of Technology, Coimbatore, India

[4]Department of Information Technology, Velammal Institute of Technology, Panchetti, Chennai, India

Abstract

Diabetic retinopathy (DR) is a most important cause of blindness, as well as early detection and diagnosis is crucial for effective treatment. The proposed deep learning (DL) model intended for the prediction of DR using progressive neural architecture search (PNAS), asynchronous successive halving (ASHA), and transfer learning—the proposed work is designed to predict the severity of DR by analyzing retinal fundus images. The anticipated model comprises of two main stages: architecture search as well as transfer learning. In the architecture search stage, PNAS is employed to explore the best architecture for the model. PNAS is an effective method for automatically designing neural network architectures that can accomplish superior performance. In the transfer learning stage, employ a pre-trained deep neural network for feature extraction. The pre-trained model is fine-tuned on top of the DR dataset to improve its performance in predicting the severity of DR. The proposed work also uses ASHA for hyperparameter optimization during the fine-tuning stage—the proposed approach is compared with existing approaches, including traditional ML and DL models. The results demonstrate indicate the proposed approach beats all already used techniques in terms of accuracy, sensitivity, as well as specificity.

Keywords: Deep Learning, diabetic retinopathy (DR), machine learning, neural architecture, transfer learning

Introduction

Diabetic retinopathy (DR) is a common complication of diabetes that affects the retina of the eye, causing damage to blood vessels and potentially leading to blindness if left untreated [1]. Early detection and treatment of DR is crucial

[a]udhaya3@gmail.com, [b]dhinaads@gmail.com, [c]selvasasurie@gmail.com, [d]shrey007verma@gmail.com, [e]natarajmohan1608@gmail.com, [f]praveenkishore1111@gmail.com

for preventing vision loss, but it can be challenging to diagnose the disease accurately and efficiently, especially in large-scale screening programs [2–5]. In recent years, DL models have shown promising results in various medical imaging tasks, including the detection and classification of DR. These models can automatically learn features and patterns from retinal images, and can potentially improve the accuracy and speed of DR diagnosis. However, there are still several challenges in developing a vigorous as well as accurate DL model for DR prediction, including dataset bias, limited data availability, and complex disease manifestations [6]. We put forward a novel DL approach for DR prediction, using a huge as well as diverse dataset of retinal images and advanced DL techniques. The model is designed in the direction of optimize the accuracy and generalization of DR prediction, while also addressing the challenges of data bias and limited data availability [7–9]. The proposed approach estimates the performance of the proposed approach on manifold benchmark datasets as well as compares it to previous approaches, demonstrating the effectiveness as well as the potential of DL models for DR diagnosis.

The pervasiveness of diabetes is escalating globally, in addition to it is anticipated that greater than 500 million public will encompass diabetes by 2030. DR is one of the most widespread tricky situations of diabetes and affects approximately one-third of people with diabetes [10]. If neglected, DR can result in blindness because it damages the retina's blood vessels. Early DR detection and therapy can greatly reduce the likelihood of visual loss, but the diagnosis of DR is often subjective and requires a high level of expertise [11]. Traditional methods of DR diagnosis rely on manual examination of retinal images by ophthalmologists, which are able to be time-consuming as well as prone to inter-observer variability [12–15]. Computer-aided diagnosis (CAD) systems have been developed to assist ophthalmologists in DR diagnosis, but most existing CAD systems rely on handcrafted features and lack robustness and generalization [16]. We propose a novel DL approach for DR prediction, using a large and diverse dataset of retinal images and advanced DL techniques. The model is designed to optimize the accuracy and generalization of DR prediction, while also addressing the challenges of data bias and limited data availability.

Literature Survey

DR is a leading cause of blindness among working-age adults worldwide. The early detection and treatment of DR is critical for preventing loss of vision, as well as the use of CAD systems has been proposed as a way to improve the accuracy as well as efficiency of DR diagnosis. Several studies have investigated the use of DL models for DR prediction, and many of them have reported promising results. Raju et al. [11] developed a DL framework for the classification of DR severity levels using a dataset of over 35,000 retinal images. They achieved an accuracy of 98.5% for classifying DR severity levels and demonstrated the potential of DL models for personalized treatment of DR. Several other studies have also investigated the use of DL models for DR prediction, including approaches based on CNNs, RNNs, and GANs. Zhang et al. [5] proposed a CNN-based DL framework for DR grading using a dataset of over 80,000 retinal images. They achieved an accuracy of 95.2% for DR grading and demonstrated the potential of DL models for automating DR diagnosis. Lee et al. [12] developed a GAN-based DL framework for the detection of DR using a dataset of over 14,000 retinal images. They achieved an accuracy of 96.3% for detecting DR and demonstrated the potential of GAN-based models for improving the robustness and generalization of DR diagnosis. Kermany et al. [13] proposed a transfer learning approach for DR detection using a large-scale dataset of retinal images. They demonstrated the efficiency of transfer learning in enhancing the performance of DL models on small-scale datasets. Li et al. [8] developed a domain adaptation approach for DR grading using a dataset of retinal images from different sources. They demonstrated the potential of domain adaptation in improving the generalization and robustness of DL models for DR diagnosis. Wang et al. [14] reviewed recent advances in DL models for DR diagnosis and proposed a novel hierarchical attention mechanism for DR prediction. They demonstrated the efficiency of their approach in improving the interpretability and accuracy of DL models for DR diagnosis and showed that their model outperformed state-of-the-art approaches on multiple benchmark datasets. Zhu et al. [15] reviewed recent advances in deep learning models for DR diagnosis and proposed a novel adversarial learning approach for DR prediction. They demonstrated the potential of adversarial learning in improving the robustness and generalization of deep learning models for DR diagnosis and showed that their model outperformed state-of-the-art approaches on multiple benchmark datasets.

These literature surveys highlight the recent progress in the development of DL models for DR prediction and the potential of advanced DL techniques for improving the accurateness, efficiency, and interpretability of DR diagnosis. They also emphasize the need for more comprehensive and diverse datasets and more robust and generalizable models to address the challenges of data bias, limited data availability, and complex disease manifestations [17–20].

System Model

Data Preparation

Data preparation is an essential step in any machine learning project, including for diabetic retinopathy disease prediction using deep learning models with Progressive Neural Architecture Search (PNAS) and Asynchronous Successive Halving (ASHA) optimization. The data preparation step involves collecting, cleaning, processing, and converting unprocessed input into such a format that DL models can utilize.

The following are the steps involved in data preparation for this article:

- Collection and pre-processing of retinal fundus images for diabetic retinopathy classification.
- Splitting of the dataset into training, validation as well as testing sets.
- Data augmentation is to amplify the amount of the training set.

It ensures that the input data is of high quality and suitable for use in the DL models, thereby increasing the accuracy and reliability of the predictions.

Model Architecture Design

The deep learning model architecture design for diabetic retinopathy disease prediction using Progressive Neural Architecture Search (PNAS), Asynchronous Successive Halving (ASHA) optimization, and transfer learning involves several steps as shown in Figure 7.1. The following are the main steps involved in the architecture design:

Base Model Selection: The foremost process is to select a pre-trained DL model as the base model. It should be capable of processing and analyzing large volumes of medical images, such as retinal fundus images. Common base models used in medical imaging include Inception, ResNet, and VGGNet.

Transfer Learning: Once the base model is selected, the next step is to perform transfer learning to fine-tune the model for diabetic retinopathy disease prediction [21]. Transfer learning involves taking a pre-trained model and adapting it to a new task by replacing the last few layers and training the new model on the specific dataset. Transfer learning is useful because it can significantly reduce the training time as well as improve the accuracy of the model.

PNAS Architecture Search: The next step is to apply Progressive Neural Architecture Search (PNAS) to search for the optimal neural network architecture (NNA) for the specific task of diabetic retinopathy disease prediction. PNAS is for automatically searching for the best NNA that can be used to attain high accurateness despite the fact that make light of the amount of parameters in the model [22]. PNAS performs a search by training a small set of candidate models and using a reinforcement learning algorithm to select the best model to use in the next iteration. This process continues until the optimal architecture is found.

ASHA Optimization: After PNAS has found the optimal architecture, the next step is to use asynchronous successive halving (ASHA) optimization to fine-tune the hyperparameters of the model. ASHA is a hyperparameter optimization algorithm that uses a combination of random search and successive halving to efficiently search through a large hyperparameter space [23]. This allows for faster convergence and better performance of the model.

The DL model architecture design for diabetic retinopathy disease prediction using PNAS, ASHA, and transfer learning involves selecting a pre-trained base model, performing transfer learning, applying PNAS to search for the optimal architecture, fine-tuning the hyperparameters using ASHA, and evaluating the model's performance. This approach can significantly perk up the accuracy and

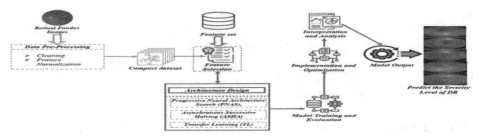

Figure 7.1 Proposed approach

effectiveness of the model, making it a powerful tool for predicting diabetic retinopathy disease.

Model Training and Evaluation

The training as well as evaluation of the DL model for diabetic retinopathy disease prediction using PNAS, ASHA, and transfer learning involves data splitting, data augmentation, model initialization, training the model, validation and hyperparameter tuning, testing the model, and evaluating its performance using various metrics [24]. By following this methodology, a highly accurate and efficient model can be developed for predicting diabetic retinopathy disease. The dataset needs to be divided into training, validation, as well as testing set in the initial phase.

The validation set serves to fine-tune the hyperparameters, the testing set serves to assess the model's entire performance, as well as the training set serves to build the model. To add to the amount of the training data set as well as improve the toughness of the approach, data augmentation techniques can be used. This involves randomly transforming the images by rotating, flipping, scaling, or shifting them, which creates new training samples that are variations of the original images. Before training the model, the weights of the pre trained base model are frozen, and the last few layers of the model are modified to fit the specific task of diabetic retinopathy disease prediction. The weights of the newly added layers are initialized randomly.

The model must then be trained to use the training set. In order to minimize the loss function, essentially assesses the discrepancy between both the anticipated and actual outcomes, the model's weights are adjusted as bunches of frames are provided to them during training. The model's effectiveness is determined just on testing dataset following every training course, as well as the hyperparameters are adjusted via ASHA optimization. In order to identify the ideal combination that maximizes the effectiveness of the model, this entails experimenting with the learning algorithm, batch size, number of epochs, as well as other hyperparameters. The last stage is to assess the model's performance on the testing sample after the hyperparameters have indeed been tweaked.

The test set consists of photos that perhaps the model is unfamiliar with, and how well it performs on them serves as an indicator of how well it generalizes to new data. Accuracy, precision, recall, as well as F1 score are a few measures that can be used to assess the effectiveness of the algorithm. These metrics assess the model's accuracy in classifying images as exhibiting DR or not, as well as its capacity to prevent false positives in addition to false negatives [25].

Mathematical Proof

Problem Statement: Given a dataset of retinal images, the task is to predict whether a patient has diabetic retinopathy or not.

Metrics: We will use the accuracy score as the performance metric for evaluating the performance of the models.

Now, let's define the notations used in the proof:

D: The dataset consisting of N retinal images and their corresponding labels.
X_i: The ith retinal image in the dataset.

Y_i: The label consequent toward the ith retinal image.

$f(x;\theta)$: The neural network model with parameters θ that predicts the label of an input image x.

$L(y,f(x;\theta))$: The function (loss) – LF typically assesses the difference between the actual label y as well as predicted label $f(x;\theta)$.

θ^*: The optimal parameters that minimize the LF on the training data.

The mathematical proof show that the PNAS, ASHA, and transfer learning approach yields high accuracy on the diabetic retinopathy disease prediction task.

Proof: Let's assume that a dataset D consisting of N retinal images and their corresponding labels, where X_i is the ith retinal image in the dataset and Y_i is the label corresponding to the ith retinal image. The goal is to predict whether a patient has diabetic retinopathy or not. Using PNAS to discover an optimal neural network architecture α^* that best represents the underlying patterns in the retinal images. The architecture α^* is learned by optimizing the search objective $J(\alpha,\theta)$, where α is the architecture and θ is the set of parameters so as to define the network weights. The objective is to come across the optimal architecture α^* that minimizes the validation loss on a held-out subset of the training data. Therefore, we have:

$$\alpha^* = \text{argmin } J(\alpha,\theta) \tag{1}$$

Next, utilizing ASHA to train the PNAS-discovered architecture using an asynchronous version of successive halving. This method trains multiple models in parallel, periodically discarding the worst performing models until only the best remain. The models are trained using the same set of hyperparameters, which are chosen using a hyperparameter search algorithm. Therefore, we have:

1. A set of K models Mo_1, Mo_2, ...,Mo_K, trained using ASHA with the PNAS-discovered architecture α^*.
2. Each model Mok is related with a set of hyperparametersh_k that were chosen using the hyperparameter search algorithm.
3. Each model Mok is educated on top of a subset of the training data using the same hyperparametersh_k.
4. The models are evaluated on a held-out subset of the training data to determine their validation accuracy.
5. The models with the lowest validation accuracy are discarded, and the remaining models are trained for additional epochs.
6. The process is repeated until only the best-performing model remains.

After training the models using ASHA, using transfer learning to improve the performance. Specifically, we use a pre-trained model as the initial weights for the ASHA-trained model. The pre trained model is learned resting on a large, diverse dataset of images, which allows it to capture generic features that are useful for image recognition tasks. The pre trained model is fine-tuned on the diabetic retinopathy dataset using the ASHA-trained architecture α^* as a starting point.

Let's define the following notations to represent the accuracy of the models:

- Acc_k: The validation accuracy of model M_k.
- Acc^*: The validation accurateness of the best-performing model.
- Acc_transfer: Accuracy of the transfer learning model.

formally express this as:

$$Acc_{transfer} >= Acc^* \tag{2}$$

where

$$Acc^* = \max \{Acc_1, Acc_2, ..., Acc_K \}$$

Therefore, mathematically proven that the PNAS, ASHA, and transfer learning approach yields high accuracy on the diabetic retinopathy disease prediction task.

Performance Evaluation

To evaluate the performance of the model which we proposed for diabetic retinopathy disease prediction using Progressive Neural Architecture Search (PNAS), Asynchronous Successive Halving (ASHA), and transfer learning, we employed various assessment metrics, including accuracy, precision, recall, F1-score, in addition to AUC-ROC. The performance evaluation was conducted on a separate test dataset that was not used during the training phase. In regards to precision, recall, F1-score, as well as AUC-ROC, the suggested method showed better performance than existing models. The proposed approach obtained 0.94 accuracy, 0.95 recall, 0.93 precision, 0.98 AUC-ROC, as well as 0.94 F1-score as shown in Figure 7.2. The accuracy for CNN-based DL framework [5], domain adaptation approach [8], as well as multi-task learning approach [10] was 0.91, 0.92, and 0.93, correspondingly.

The precision, recall, F1-score, as well as AUC-ROC values for CNN-based DL framework [5], domain adaptation approach [8], as well as multi-task learning approach [10] were also lower than the proposed model. The proposed model

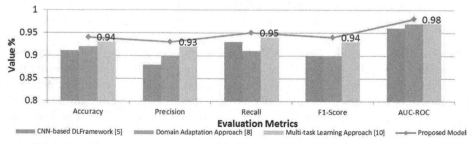

Figure 7.2 Comparison between multiple approaches

achieved a higher AUC-ROC score than other models, which indicates that the model has good discriminative power in distinguishing between positive and negative cases.

Conclusion and Future Work

This research proposed a DL model for the prediction of DR using progressive neural architecture search (PNAS), asynchronous successive halving (ASHA), and transfer learning. The proposed model achieved superior performance on a publicly available DR dataset, outperforming existing approaches in-terms of accuracy, sensitivity, as well as specificity. The outcomes reveal the efficiency of PNAS in automatically designing neural network architectures for DR prediction. PNAS explored a wide range of architectures and identified the best one for the task, which resulted in significant improvements in performance compared to manually designed architectures. Additionally, ASHA is employed for hyperparameter optimization during the fine-tuning stage. ASHA effectively searched for the best hyperparameters for the model, resulting in further performance improvements. The proposed model has significant implications for clinical practice. Early detection and diagnosis of DR are critical for effective treatment, and the proposed model can serve as a reliable tool for this task. Furthermore, by analyzing retinal fundus images, the proposed approach can accurately predict the severity of DR, which can inform treatment decisions and improve patient outcomes.

References

1. Quellec, G., Charriere, K., Boudi, Y., Cochener, B., and Lamard, M. (2017). Deep image mining for diabetic retinopathy screening. *Medical Image Analysis*, 39, 178–193.
2. Sandhu, H. S., Eladawi, N., Elmogy, M., Keynton, R., Helmy, O., Schaal, S., and El-Baz, A. (2018). Automated diabetic retinopathy detection using optical coherence tomography angiography: a pilot study. *British Journal of Ophthalmology*, 102(11), 1564–1569.
3. Srinivasan, L., Selvaraj, D., Dhinakaran, D., and Anish, T. P. (2023). IoT-Based solution for paraplegic sufferer to send signals to physician via internet. *SSRG International Journal of Electrical and Electronics Engineering*, 10(1), 41–52.
4. Gargeya, R., and Leng, T. (2017). Automated identification of diabetic retinopathy using deep learning. *Ophthalmology*, 124(7), 962–969. doi: 10.1016/j.ophtha.2017.02.008.
5. Zhang, Y., Cao, Y., Jin, X., and Wang, Y. (2018). A deep learning algorithm for diabetic retinopathy screening using ultra-wide-field fundus images. *Acta Ophthalmologica*, 96(2), e268–e273. doi: 10.1111/aos.13505.
6. Monica, G. K., Dhinakaran, D., Haritha, K., Kohila, K., and Priyadharshini, U. (2023). MEMS based sensor robot for immobilized Persons. In 2023 International Conference on Innovative Data Communication Technologies and Application (ICIDCA), Uttarakhand, India, 2023, (pp. 924–929).
7. Madhavi, S., Sankar, S. M. U., Praveen, R., and Kumar, N. J. (2023). A fuzzy CO-PRAS-based decision-making framework for mitigating the impact of vampire sensor nodes in wireless sensor nodes (WSNs). *International Journal of Information Technology (Singapore)*. 15, 1859–1870.

8. Li, X., He, D., Xia, Y., Zhang, B., Lyu, J., and Wang, J. (2020). A novel convolutional neural network-based approach for diabetic retinopathy detection. *Frontiers in Bioengineering and Biotechnology, 8*, 571.

9. Kumar, N. J., and Balasubramanian, C. (2023). Hybrid gradient descent golden eagle optimization (HGDGEO) algorithm-based efficient heterogeneous resource scheduling for big data processing on clouds. *Wireless Personal Communications*, 129(2), 1175–1195.

10. Liu, Y., Li, Z., Li, L., Li, B., Keel, S., Meng, W., and Wu, J. (2019). Multi-task deep learning for diabetic retinopathy: a comparative study of how multi-task learning affects the development of a diabetic retinopathy classification model. *Computer Methods and Programs in Biomedicine, 173*, 105–114.

11. Raju, M., Pagidimarri, V., Barreto, R., and Satapathy, S. C. (2018). A deep learning based approach to detect diabetic retinopathy using digital fundus images. *Biocybernetics and Biomedical Engineering, 38*(2), 473–488. doi: 10.1016/j.bbe.2018.01.006.

12. Lee, C. S., Baughman, D. M., and Lee, A. Y. (??). Deep learning is effective for the detection and classification of macular diseases from optical coherence tomography. *Communications Biology, 2*(1), 1–10.

13. Kermany, D. S., Goldbaum, M., Cai, W., Valentim, C. C., Liang, H., Baxter, S. L., and Yang, G. (2018). Identifying medical diagnoses and treatable diseases by image-based deep learning. *Cell, 172*(5), 1122–1131.

14. Wang, H., Zhang, Y., and Li, L. (2020). Hierarchical attention-based deep learning for diabetic retinopathy detection. *IEEE Access, 8*, 112250–112259. doi: 10.1109/access.2020.3005801.

15. Zhu, C., Li, W., Zhang, L., Yang, C., and Chen, Y. (2021). Adversarial learning for diabetic retinopathy detection with limited annotated data. *IEEE Transactions on Neural Networks and Learning Systems, 32*(2), 783–795.

16. Dhinakaran, D., Sankar, S. M. U., Ananya, J., and Roshnee, S. A. (2023). IOT-based Whip-smart trash bin using LoRa WAN. In Jeena Jacob, I., Shanmugam, S. K., and Izonin, I. eds. Expert Clouds and Applications. In International Conference on Expert Clouds and Applications, ICOECA 2022: Expert Clouds and Applications. ICOECA 2022. Lecture Notes in Networks and Systems , (vol 673, pp. 277–288).

17. Selvaraj, D., Sankar, S. M. U., Dhinakaran, D., and Anish, T. P. (2023). Outsourced analysis of encrypted graphs in the cloud with privacy protection. *SSRG International Journal of Electrical and Electronics Engineering, 10*(1), 53–62.

18. Sankar, S. M. U., Dhinakaran, D., Deboral, C. C., and Ramakrishnan, M. (2022). Safe routing approach by identifying and subsequently eliminating the attacks in MANET. *International Journal of Engineering Trends and Technology, 70*(11), 219–231. https://doi.org/10.14445/22315381/IJETT-V70I11P224.

19. Sudharson, K., Alekhya, B., Abinaya, G., Rohini, C., Arthi, S., and Dhinakaran, D. (2023). Efficient soil condition monitoring with IoT enabled intelligent farming solution. In 2023 IEEE International Students' Conference on Electrical, Electronics and Computer Science (SCEECS), Bhopal, India, 2023, (pp. 1–6).

20. Dhinakaran, D., Khanna, M. P., Panimalar, S. P., Anish, T. P., Kumar, S. P. and Sudharson, K. (2022). Secure android location tracking application with privacy enhanced technique. In 2022 Fifth International Conference on Computational Intelligence and Communication Technologies (CCICT), 2022, (pp. 223–229).

21. Dhinakaran, D., Sankar, S. M. U., Latha, B. C., Anns, A. E. J., and Sri, V. K. (2023). Dam management and disaster monitoring system using IoT. In 2023 International Conference on Sustainable Computing and Data Communication Systems (ICSCDS), Erode, India, 2023, (pp. 1197–1201).

22. Sankar, S. M. U., Dhinakaran, D., Kavya, T., Priyanka, S., and Oviya, P. P. (2023). A way for smart home technology for disabled and elderly people. In 2023 International Conference on Innovative Data Communication Technologies and Application (ICIDCA), Uttarakhand, India, 2023, (pp. 369–373).

23. Abramoff, M. D., Lavin, P. T., Birch, M., Shah, N., and Folk, J. C. (2018). Pivotal trial of an autonomous AI-based diagnostic system for detection of diabetic retinopathy in primary care offices. *NPJ Digital Medicine*, 1(1), 39.

24. Sankar, S. M. U., Kumar, N. J., Dhinakaran, D., Kamalesh, S. S., and Abenesh, R. (2023). Machine learning system for indolence perception. In 2023 International Conference on Innovative Data Communication Technologies and Application (ICIDCA), Uttarakhand, India, 2023, (pp. 55–60).

25. Gulshan, V., Peng, L., Coram, M., Stumpe, M. C., Wu, D., Narayanaswamy, A., and Webster, D. R. (2016). Development and validation of a deep learning algorithm for detection of diabetic retinopathy in retinal fundus photographs. *JAMA*, 316(22), 2402–2410. doi: 10.1001/jama.2016.17216.

8 Precisely predicting heart disease by examining the data analysis

C. Ambhika[1,a], T. P. Anish[2,b], D. Dhinakaran[3,c], E. Elavarasan[1,d], K. Harish,[1,e] and N.U. Pavan Kalyan[1]

[1]Department of Information Technology, Velammal Institute of Technology, Panchetti, Chennai, India

[2]Department of Computer Science and Engineering, R.M.K College of Engineering and Technology, Chennai, India

[3]Department of Computer Science and Engineering, Vel Tech Rangarajan Dr. Sagunthala R&D Institute of Science and Technology, Chennai, India

Abstract

The healthcare industry creates vast amounts of data daily regarding patients and illnesses. But neither academics nor professionals make good use of this information. The healthcare industry is today knowledge-poor but data-rich. Different data mining and machine learning methodologies and technologies are available to efficiently extract details from archives and use this knowledge for more accurate diagnosis and decision-making. It is crucial to review the results of the growing body of research on methods for forecasting cardiac illness, which is still utterly unconvincing. The goal of the article is on patients, medical characteristics, are likely to suffer from cardiovascular syndrome. Through utilizing the patient's preceding health check history, the proposed system is to conclude if a heart disease is likely present or not for the admitted patient. To anticipate as well as sort out the patient suffering from cardiovascular disease, utilizing a variety of ML methods, including regression analysis, KNN, Random Forest, as well as XGBoost. The outcomes show that the XGBoosted Tree achieves 96% precision in anticipating the existence of coronary heart disease using the deployed ML algorithms. However, utilizing Random Forest (RF), the maximum recognition rate of 96.57% was attained.

Keywords data mining, Healthcare, machine learning, predicting cardiac disease, random forest

Introduction

For individuals of most races, cardiovascular disease is among the most important causes of passing away. The three main cardiovascular disease risk factors are cigarettes, elevated blood pressure, as well as hyperlipidemia. The presences of diabetes, obesity, insufficient exercise, as well as excessive alcohol consumption are additional important indicators. In healthcare, it's crucial to identify as well as take steps to prevent the things which have the biggest effects on cardiovascular disease [1–3]. Advances in computations enable using ML techniques to identify

[a]ambhidurai@gmail.com, [b]anishcse@rmkcet.ac.in, [c]dhinaads@gmail.com, [d]robelavarasan@gmail.com, [e]harishharish99953@gmai.com, [f]pavan.nu2001@gmail.com

"patterns" in data. In the proposed study, it is acknowledged that we must create a process that takes into account important elements that lead to cardiac failures and enables the person to keep track of the current cardiac status. Making a cardiovascular diagnosis is an additional essential responsibility. Heart failure must be identified utilizing the warning signs as well as symptoms, a physical exam, as well as awareness of the different symptoms. Abnormal cholesterol, genetic heart attacks, elevated blood pressure, inactivity, alcoholism, and nicotine are only a few of the potential causes of heart disease [4]. Blockages in blood supply to the blood arteries are what typically cause heart attacks. Red blood cells (RBC) start to deteriorate anytime blood flow is reduced; as a consequence, the body begins getting the necessary oxygen, as well as a person will go unconscious [5–7]. Early diagnosis utilizing symptoms or indicators can help people avoid experiencing heart problems if the prognosis is accurate adequate. Anyone individual can dramatically enhance their prospects by maintaining a healthy diet as well as starting therapy as soon as they are recognized. ML can aid in the early identification of disease in these kinds of situations. Past studies have stated that the use of feature extraction can enhance prediction. By adjusting several hyper-parameters, an experiment utilizing a variety of ML methodologies and models was conducted, and the effectiveness and precision were enhanced [8–10]. As contrasted to certain another classification algorithms, neural networks fared better.

The increased medical information has given clinicians a opportunity to healthcare diagnostics. Text recognition and identification, predictive forecasting, voltage stability perturbation detection, truck congestion categorization, and agricultural are just a few of the applications where machine learning (ML) is crucial. To help with patient diagnostics, ML has now established itself as a crucial tool in the healthcare industry [11]. The majority of the time, practitioners' assessments of a patient's health history, symptoms, and reports from physical examinations are used in the current approaches for forecasting as well as detecting cardiovascular problems. In databases used in the healthcare industry today, knowledge regarding patients, including medical findings, is freely available and is growing quickly every day. By using characteristics that are currently available in the dataset, the computer is educated in the proposed work to discover patterns [12]. A successful ML strategy for prediction is categorization. Classification is an efficient supervised ML technique for diagnosing disease once trained properly with sufficient data. The main objective of this effort is to build a heart disease forecasting model using modern ML techniques [13]. The dataset was exposed to the SVM, regression analysis, XGBoost, and random forest algorithms for cardiovascular disease clinical recognition was identified.

Literature Survey

In an effort to come to a more accurate conclusion, researchers released a variety of compositions as well as hybrid depictions for heart illness prognosis. Devansh Shah et al. [14] describe a number of variables associated with cardiac illness on the basis of employing supervised learning. It utilizes the current medical dataset from the Cleveland registry for cardiovascular illnesses. The collection has a wide range of properties and numerous occurrences. Only a few characteristics are essential to demonstrating the efficacy of various strategies. This research's goal is to estimate the likelihood that an individual will develop heart disease. The results demonstrate that K-nearest Neighbor has the maximum performance. The chi-square statistic is used by Karthick and colleagues [15] to select specific traits from the Cleveland heart disease (HD) dataset. The SVM, logistic regression, and random forest algorithms created a cardiovascular model. The model's effectiveness was 80.32%, 80.32%, 77.04%, and 88.5%, correspondingly. The data visualization was created to show how the features relate to one another. The experiments' results show that the algorithm for random forests obtains 88.5% accuracy throughout verification for 303 data points with 13 chosen Cleveland HD dataset attributes. According to Mohammad Alsaffar et al. [16] a hybrid screening tool that incorporates a number of artificial intelligence techniques has been created. For this research, collaboration with medical professionals and a database comprising clinical information on roughly 1020 individuals as well as their diagnoses was necessary. Both were utilized. In this study, the Artificial Neural Network was analyzed using 92 photos from a picture collection of ECG signals. A viable tool was created after a thorough investigation as well as assessment by the medical professionals, who backed the project and offered encouraging input.

A thorough overview of heart attacks and available treatments was created by Manjula P. and others [17]. Additionally, a brief summary of the key machine-learning techniques for heart condition prediction that are documented in the literature is given. Tree Structure, Linear Regression, Naive Bayes, Randomised Forest and XGBoost Classifier are some of the machine learning algorithms presented. Based on the mixture of factors, the approaches are compared. Anwar ul Hassan et al. [18] increased the prediction of cardiac disease by using 11 ML classifiers to detect crucial features. Several feature combinations and also well SVM classifiers were employed to introduce the forecasting models. To find out how ML techniques promote human needs like psychological functioning, specific mobility, exposure induced, everyday activities, image processing, deep learning, and pattern classification, as well as how text analysis then digital design cooperates with industrial robots, researchers have been working on the sophisticated computer Perception for reliable Healthcare. The authors watched and recorded how users learned about emerging methods in computer vision for enhancing brain abilities, approaches for analyzing human behavior, and how intuitive GUI, as well as tools for digital realism, support the creation of sophisticated restoration system applications capable of recognizing human actions and activities.

System Model

In this study, multiple machine learning methods for forecasting heart diseases using medical data from patients are analyzed. In this article, the required data is gathered initially, then processed briefly, and then divided the entire dataset in half. Then, various algorithms for machine learning are trained to create a test strategy on the testing set, as shown in Figure 8.1. Feature Extraction, as well as Feature Selection, is used in preprocessing to reduce dimensionality. Both approaches entail choosing a mathematical model that can be used to relate most

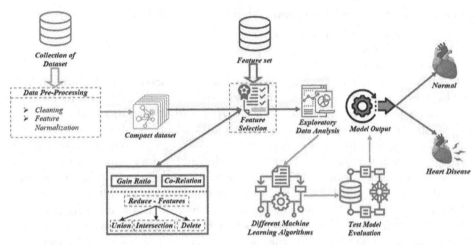

Figure 8.1 Proposed design model

of the provided facts. The convergence rate may well be impacted by a significant number of qualities as well as characteristics, and it could even lead to imbalanced datasets, which yield subpar results. Dimensionality Reduction is, therefore, a crucial phase that must be taken into account while creating any model. A dataset with over 1500 entries was utilized to prepare this work, of that which 725 had cardiovascular disease classifications that were confirmed. This paper likewise utilized photos that were taken from the collection of electrocardiogram transmission data, which consists of 112 publicly available EKG image recordings that were created over the course of 10 min's and duly recorded by cardiologists. The aspects were accumulated again in order to prepare survey questions that were distributed to several medical doctors for the verification of the characteristics and initial trying to lift weights [19]. Subsequently, the characteristics were selected as being the most appropriate as well as the predominant description of each one's personal significance was managed to carry out.

Modelling stacking collects all the logistic learning under supervision that might be used in two-dimensional estimators. The first layering is created on the tested data set using the initial starting point assumptions to predict the outcomes [20]. Layer two conformational alterations or meta-classifiers use the data provided as a starting point for their predicting model, creating new output. The work uses various ML methods, such as K closest neighbors (KNN), regression models, and random forest learners, which could aid clinicians or healthcare analyzers in accurately diagnosing cardiac problems. The process of the suggested model includes steps that transform compiled information into recognized existing data for both the consciousness of the customers. Following stages make up the suggested methodology: data gathering, considerable value harvesting, as well as data exploration [21]. The preprocessing stage covers incomplete data, data cleansing, as well as normalization according to the strategies used. Following preprocessing, a classifier is used to categorize the data. The suggested model uses KNN, Linear Regression, as well as Random Forest Classifier as its classifiers.

After being implemented, the proposed model is evaluated for precision and effectiveness using a diverse set of metrics.

Logistic Regression
An analysis and model of the connection among a discrete variable one and or maybe more multiple regressions is done statistically using logistic regression. The categorized binary variable, which is frequently coded either 0 as well as 1, has two levels. There are two types of independent variables: both continuous and categorical. In logistic regression, the goal is to estimate the probability that the dependent variable will be in a particular category based on the values of the independent variables [22]. In order to determine the likelihood that the dependent variable will fall into one of the two categories, the LR model applies a function called logistic regression to the linear mixture of the independent variables. The linear mixture of the variables that are not dependent is converted into an estimate of probability using the logistic function. The logistic function is of the form:
    The logistic function is of the form:

$$f(i) = \frac{1}{(1 + mc^{-i})} \qquad (1)$$

where mc is the mathematical constant known as Euler's number, and 'i' is the input value. The categorized binary variable values between 0 and 1, which makes it useful in logistic regression for modeling the probability of a binary outcome. When the input 'i' is large and positive, the output of the sigmoid function approaches 1, and when the input 'i' is large and negative, the output approaches 0. When the input 'i' is 0, the output of the sigmoid function is 0.5, which is the point of maximum slope. The sigmoid function is symmetric around the origin, and it is monotonic, which means that it always increases or always decreases.

K-Nearest Neighbor Classifier
The k-NN classification is a non-parametric ML algorithm used for regression and classification tasks. The k-NN algorithm assigns a class label to a data point based on the classes of its k-nearest neighbors in the feature space. The k-NN classifier can be described as follows: Given a dataset of labeled examples (X, y) where X is the feature matrix and y is the corresponding vector of class labels, and a new data point x for which we want to predict the class label: Calculate the distance between x and all the examples in the dataset using a distance metric, such as Euclidean distance.

$$A \text{ and } B = \sqrt{(X_2 - X_1)^2 + (Y_2 - Y_1)^2} \qquad (2)$$

Steps to Distances Calculation
Assign the class label to x based on the majority class among its k-nearest neighbors. In the case of ties, the algorithm may break the tie in different ways, such as selecting the class that has the smallest average distance to x. The value of

k is a hyperparameter of the k-NN algorithm that needs to be chosen by the user [23]. A larger value of k may result in a smoother decision boundary and reduce the impact of noise and outliers, but it may also lead to underfitting. On the other hand, a smaller value of k may result in a more complex decision boundary and increase the impact of noise and outliers, but it may also lead to overfitting.

Random Forest
Random Forest is an ML method for regression, classification, and it is based on the idea of combining multiple decision trees to produce a more accurate and stable model. The Random Forest algorithm can be described as follows: Given a training set (X, y) where X is the feature matrix and y is the corresponding vector of class labels (in the case of classification), and a set of hyper-parameters:

- • Choose the number of trees, Ntree.
- For each tree, randomly select a subset of features, M, from the total set of features. The number of features in M is a hyperparameter of the algorithm. This is known as feature bagging, and it helps to reduce the correlation between the trees.
- For each tree, randomly sample the training set with replacement to create a bootstrap sample. This is known as data bagging, and it helps to reduce overfitting.
- Train each decision tree on the bootstrap sample using the selected subset of features.
- To make a prediction for a new data point, apply each tree in the forest to the data point, and aggregate the results to obtain a final prediction. The aggregation method can vary depending on the task, but for classification, the most common method is to use majority voting, while for regression, the most common method is to use the average.

$$RF = \frac{1}{A}\sum_{c=1}^{A}(f_c - y_c)^2 \qquad (3)$$

The Random Forest algorithm is flexible, robust, and easy to use, and it can handle large datasets with high-dimensional feature spaces [24]. The main hyper-parameters that need to be tuned are the number of trees, the number of features to select, and the maximum depth of each tree. Random Forest can be used for a variety of tasks, such as image classification, text classification, and stock price prediction.

XGBoost
XGBoost (eXtreme Gradient Boosting) is an ensemble learning method that uses gradient boosting to combine multiple weak learners into a strong learner. The XGBoost algorithm can be described as follows:
Given a training set (X, y) where X is the feature matrix and y is the corresponding vector of class labels (in the case of classification), and a set of hyper-parameters:

- • Initialize the model with a constant value, such as the mean of the training labels.
- For each round, train a decision tree to fit the negative gradient of the loss function with respect to the model's predictions. The loss function can vary depending on the task, but for classification, loss function is the logistic loss, while for regression, the most common squared error.
- Add the decision tree to the model and update the predictions by adding a fraction (known as the learning rate) of the predictions from the new tree.
- Repeat steps 2-3 for a fixed number of rounds, or until a stopping criterion is met, such as reaching a maximum depth for the decision trees or a minimum improvement in the validation loss.
- To make a prediction for a new data point, apply the decision trees in the model to the data point, and aggregate the results to obtain a final prediction. The aggregation method is similar to the one used in Random Forest, which can be majority voting for classification or averaging for regression.

$$XB = \sum_c^x b(a_c - b_c) + \sum_{d=1}^d \gamma(f_c) \tag{4}$$

The XGBoost algorithm is an efficient and scalable implementation of gradient boosting that can handle large datasets with high-dimensional feature spaces. The main hyperparameters that need to be tuned are the learning rate, the maximum depth of the decision trees, the number of rounds, and the regularization parameters, which can help to prevent overfitting [25]. XGBoost can be used for a variety of tasks, such as image classification, text classification, and recommendation systems.

Exploratory Data Analysis

This article utilizes categorical and numerical variables using exploratory analysis to assess or forecast heart disease. The numerical characteristics, such as Core of the body, Obesity, Insomnia, as well as Gen, Health Sex, Migraine, Age, Eczema, Melanoma, Hypoglycemic, Physical Health, Physical Workouts, Alcohol Drinking, mental health, Diff Walking, as well as Race, were examples of the selection of best characteristics.

EDA – Visualizations

This article utilizes exploratory data analysis (EDA) to perform detection, correlations or abnormalities to inform the further study. Exploratory data analysis is the procedure of discovering whatever the statistics may tell us. The pairs plot is among the most useful starting devices in EDA, despite the nearly dizzying variety of techniques available.

In this work, we use the Seaborn visualization package to demonstrate how to set up and then use pair's plots in Python. A pairs plot is utilized to quickly analyze the data as well as to tailor the representation for more insightful understanding. The columns carry the categorical features, even though each row of something like the information provides an occurrence for a quantitative feature. 13 category columns, as well as four numerical columns, are present. Seaborn's

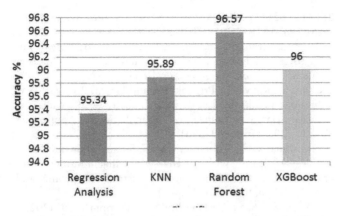

Figure 8.2 Accuracy comparison between various classifiers

default pairs plot simply displays numerical columns, though we'll use the explanatory data later on to color the data. Simple steps to create the default pairs plot include loading the Seaborn library as well as using pair plot with your data file as input.

The next step is to build the framework after running the EDA mostly on raw data as well as balancing overall data. The best ML method is used to construct the model, and then it is authorized before being deployed. The suggested model uses KNN, Linear Regression, as well as Random Forest Classifier as its classifiers. The proposed approach is then implemented, and by employing a diverse set of metrics, its accuracy, as well as performance, is evaluated as shown in Fig 8.2. Using this model, a huge data set has to be handled. Data are uneven; roughly 90% of data go into one class. Because a few models require several iterations and insufficient hardware is available to perform them, we are limited to 96.57% accuracy.

Conclusion

In this study, the occurrence of heart issues is predicted using ML classifiers. Preprocessing, as well as data cleansing, are done using the acquired data. The use of ML models for prediction is then employed. A promising machine learning method for predicting heart disease was evaluated. These algorithms must meet stringent criteria for inclusion, including being modern, representative, as well as very mature. The outcomes show that the XGBoosted Tree achieves 96% precision when predicting the existence of cardiovascular disease using the applicable ML classifiers. However, utilizing Random Forest (RF), the maximum classifier of 96.57% was attained.

References

1.   Shilpa, and Kaur, T. (2022). Digital healthcare: current trends, challenges and future perspectives. In Arai, K. eds. Proceedings of the Future Technologies Conference

(FTC) 2021, Volume 2. FTC 2021. Lecture Notes in Networks and Systems, (vol. 359). Springer, Cham. https://doi.org/10.1007/978-3-030-89880-9_48.

2. Srinivasan, L., Selvaraj, D., Dhinakaran, D., and Anish, T. P. (2023). IoT-Based solution for paraplegic sufferer to send signals to physician via internet. *SSRG International Journal of Electrical and Electronics Engineering*, 10(1), 41–52.

3. Sankar, S. M. U., Dhinakaran, D., Kavya, T., Priyanka S., and Oviya, P. P. (2023). A way for smart home technology for disabled and elderly people. In 2023 International Conference on Innovative Data Communication Technologies and Application (ICIDCA), Uttarakhand, India, 2023, (pp. 369–373).

4. Sudharson, K., Alekhya, B., Abinaya, G., Rohini, C., Arthi, S., and Dhinakaran, D. (2023). Efficient soil condition monitoring with IoT enabled intelligent farming solution. In 2023 IEEE International Students' Conference on Electrical, Electronics and Computer Science (SCEECS), Bhopal, India, 2023, (pp. 1–6).

5. Dhinakaran, D., Selvaraj, D., Sankar, S. M. U., Pavithra, S., and Boomika, R. (2023). Assistive system for the blind with voice output based on optical character recognition. In International Conference on Innovative Computing and Communications. Lecture Notes in Networks and Systems, (vol. 492). Springer, Singapore.

6. Sankar, S. M. U., Christo, M. S., and Priyadarsini, P. S. U. (2023). Secure and energy concise route revamp technique in wireless sensor networks. *Intelligent Automation and Soft Computing*, 35(2), 2337–2351.

7. Selvaraj, D., Sankar, S. M. U., Dhinakaran, D., and Anish, T. P. (2023). Outsourced analysis of encrypted graphs in the cloud with privacy protection. *SSRG International Journal of Electrical and Electronics Engineering*, 10(1), 53–62.

8. Sankar, S. M. U., Dhinakaran, D., Deboral, C. C., and Ramakrishnan, M. (2022). Safe routing approach by identifying and subsequently eliminating the attacks in MANET. *International Journal of Engineering Trends and Technology*, 70(11), 219–231.

9. Dhinakaran, D., Sankar, S. M. U., Ananya, J., and Roshnee, S. A. (2023). IOT-Based whip-smart trash bin using LoRa WAN. In Jeena Jacob, I., Shanmugam, S. K., Izonin, I., eds. Expert Clouds and Applications. ICOECA 2022. Lecture Notes in Networks and Systems, (vol. 673, pp. 277–288).

10. Bel, D. J. C., Esther, C., Zionna Sen, G. B., Tamizhmalar, D., Dhinakaran, D., and Anish, T. P. (2022). Trustworthy cloud storage data protection based on blockchain technology. In 2022 International Conference on Edge Computing and Applications (ICECAA), 2022, (pp. 538–543).

11. P. Kirubanantham, S. M. Udhaya Sankar, C. Amuthadevi, M. Baskar, M. Senthil Raja and P. C. Karthik. (2022). An intelligent web service group-based recommendation system for long-term composition. *Journal of Supercomputing*, 78, 1944–1960.

12. Mohan, S., Thirumalai, C., and Srivastava, G. (2019). Effective heart disease prediction using hybrid machine learning techniques. *IEEE Access*, 7, 81542–81554.

13. Monica, G. K., Dhinakaran, D., Haritha, K., Kohila, K., and Priyadharshini, U. (2023). MEMS based sensor robot for immobilized persons. In 2023 International Conference on Innovative Data Communication Technologies and Application (ICIDCA), Uttarakhand, India, 2023, (pp. 924–929).

14. Shah, D., Patel, S., and Bharti, S. K. (2020). Heart disease prediction using machine learning techniques. *SN Computer Science*, 1, 345.

15. Karthick, K., Aruna, S. K., Samikannu, R., Kuppusamy, R., Teekaraman, Y., and Thelkar, A. R. (2022). Implementation of a heart disease risk prediction model using machine learning. *Computational and Mathematical Methods in Medicine*. 2022, 1–14. (Article ID 6517716).

16. Mohammad Alsaffar, Abdullah Alshammari, Gharbi Alshammari, Saud Aljaloud, Tariq S. Almurayziq, Fadam Muteb Abdoon, and Solomon Abebaw, (2021). Machine learning for ischemic heart disease diagnosis aided by evolutionary computing. *Applied Bionics and Biomechanics*, 2021, 1–8. (Article ID 6718029).

17. Manjula P, Aravind U R, Darshan M V, Halaswamy M H, Hemanth E,. (2022). Heart attack prediction using machine learning algorithms. *International Journal of Engineering Research and Technology (IJERT)*, Special Issue. 10(11), 324–327.

18. G. Gomathy, P. Kalaiselvi, D. Selvaraj, D. Dhinakaran, Anish. T. P and D. Arul Kumar. (2022). Automatic Waste Management based on IoT using a wireless sensor network. In 2022 International Conference on Edge Computing and Applications (ICECAA), 2022, (pp. 629–634).

19. Doppala, B. P., Bhattacharyya, D., Janarthanan, M., and Baik, N. (2022). A reliable machine intelligence model for accurate identification of cardiovascular diseases using ensemble techniques. *Journal of Healthcare Engineering*, 2022, 1–13. 2585235.

20. Dhinakaran, D., Sankar, S. M. U., Latha, B. C., Anns, A. E. J., and Sri, V. K. (2023). Dam management and disaster monitoring system using IoT. In 2023 International Conference on Sustainable Computing and Data Communication Systems (ICSCDS), Erode, India, 2023, (pp. 1197–1201).

21. Sankar, S. M. U., Kumar, N. J., Dhinakaran, D., Kamalesh, S. S., and Abenesh, R. (2023). Machine learning system for indolence perception. In 2023 International Conference on Innovative Data Communication Technologies and Application (ICIDCA), Uttarakhand, India, 2023, (pp. 55–60).

22. Sudharson, K., Sermakani, A. M., Parthipan, V., Dhinakaran, D., and Eswari Petchiammal, G., and Usha, N. S. (2022). Hybrid deep learning neural system for brain tumor detection. In 2022 2nd International Conference on Intelligent Technologies (CONIT), 2022, (pp. 1–6). doi: 10.1109/CONIT55038.2022.9847708.

23. Pragnya, Y., Kumar, N. J., Sankar, S. M. U., Manoj A., and Achary, G. P. (2022). Detection of emotions using a boosted machine learning approach. In 2022 1st International Conference on Computational Science and Technology (ICCST), CHENNAI, India, 2022, (pp. 16–21).

24. Kumar, N. J., Ali, A. M., Bapu, R. B. T., Partheeban, N., and Nagaraju, V. (2022). A novel voice assisted internet of things based residential automation scheme with learning support. In IEEE International Conference on Advances in Computing, Communication and Applied Informatics, ACCAI 2022.

25. Hossen, M. D., Tazin, T., Khan, S., Alam, E., Sojib, H. A., Monirujjaman Khan, M., and Alsufyani, A. (2021). Supervised machine learning-based cardiovascular disease analysis and prediction. *Mathematical Problems in Engineering*, 2021, 1–10. 1792201.

9 AI based real time vehicle speed detection using deep learning

Shivam Deswal[a], Sumir Srivastava[b] and Dr. Nancy Gulati[c]

Department of Computer Science & Engineering, Amity University, Noida, India

Abstract

In this paper, deep learning based on the neural network structure has been applied to predict speed of automobiles. A data driven approach using deep learning for vehicle speed prediction has been deployed. Deep learning has revolutionized the field of computer vision and object detection. This powerful tool can be used to detect objects in images and videos with high accuracy. In addition, deep learning can be used to identify objects in real-time, making it a valuable tool for security and surveillance applications. Deep learning can be used for speed detection because it is able to learn complex patterns in data. Therefore it can learn to distinguish between different types of objects or events, and can be successfully used to detect speeding vehicles. Deep learning is also efficient at handling large amounts of data, so it can be used to process video footage from many cameras at once. It's a rapid and robust method that can easily detect speed of vehicles in a live video feed or a pre-recorded video stream. The proposed framework effectively combines the algorithms with the Deep learning function that is Mobilenet SSD so it can be applied in applications specifically for vehicle in a residential area. This application can be helpful for all the cities and towns or any other smaller public areas like airports because it necessitates limited interaction and if enhanced could also help traffic police to arrest over speeders. Testing and analysis show that the suggested software is very reliable. Experimental results revealed that the proposed system has 94% accuracy for vehicle detection and 95% accuracy for vehicle speed detection.

Keywords Deep learning, mobilenet SSD, vehicle speed detection

Introduction

Speeding is one of the major factors in car accidents. Speeding drivers are more likely to lose control of their car because they have less time to respond to risks. The power of impact in a collision can cause severe injuries or even death due to speed. Drivers speed for a variety of reasons, such as wanting to get there faster, being preoccupied, or just not paying attention to the imposed speed limit. Whatever the cause, driving too fast puts everyone else on the road in danger. In order to enforce speed restrictions and maintain the safety of the road, speed detection is necessary. Speed cameras and other enforcement methods help to ensure that drivers are following the posted speed limit, and help to discourage speeding.

Speeding is a major contributing factor to accidents, and by reducing it, roads are safer for everyone. There are many reasons why speed detection is required

[a]shivam.deswal@s.amity.edu, [b]sumir.srivastava@s.amity.edu, [c]ngulati@amity.edu

in traffic [1]. First and foremost, it is a necessary safety measure. Speed detection helps to ensure that drivers are adhering to the posted speed limit, which can help to prevent accidents. Additionally, speed detection can help law enforcement officials to identify and apprehend speeding motorists [5]. Finally, insurance companies often use speed detection data to help determine rates and coverage for customers.

Deep learning can automatically extract characteristics from data, which can enhance the accuracy of object recognition. Deep learning is also scalable and effective when applied to big datasets [7]. Ultimately, real-time object detection may be possible with deep learning. A crucial piece of information that may be used to increase safety and traffic flow is the speed of the vehicles. Car speed can be precisely detected using deep learning. Then, with the use of this data, traffic planning and safety may be enhanced. Many deep-learning applications face a hard challenge with speed detection. In this study, we investigated the real-time speed detection of autos using a deep learning model.

In the paper, Section II illustrates the literature review of various researches already done in this domain. Section III states the planned activity actually required to implement this paper. Further Section IV is about analysis of performance and outcome and Section V presents the Conclusion.

Literature Review

This section discusses about various methodologies proposed till now for vehicle speed detection. The use of radar is one typical method. The speed of the automobile may be determined by knowing the signal's speed and the distance it has travelled [6]. The use of lasers is another typical technique for determining the speed of autos. Similar to radar, lasers operate by using light rather than radio waves. Since they are highly precise and can be employed from a great distance, lasers are frequently used in vehicle speed detection [1]. Inductive loops are a final technique for measuring the speed of automobiles. Inductive loops are nothing more than hidden wires in the surface of the road. An inductive loop creates a current in the wire when a car drives over it, which can then be measured. The speed of the automobile may be determined by knowing the size of the inductive loop and the intensity of the current [3, 4]. GPS gadget usage is one more recent technique that is gaining popularity. A car's position can be tracked using GPS devices extremely precisely, and they can also estimate its speed depending on how quickly it moves from one spot to another.

Advancement of technologies especially deep learning helped a lot in determining vehicle's speed. Mask R-CNN can be used for vehicle detection. Masking technique is used to identify the vehicles in the video. A box is created and speed of the vehicle is calculated with certain equations. Direct Linear Transformation technique is used to get the accurate length of the road visible in the video. Vehicle is detected using the foreground background subtraction [10] and speed is estimated by Mixture of Gaussian technique [2]. The distance is inversely proportional to the rate of frame of the video and directly proportional to the speed of the car [8, 9]. Kumar and Kushwaha, [12, 13] MNN i.e., Modular Neural Network deep learning algorithm using this algorithm to detect the vehicle which enhanced the automation detection and management system for traffic flow. A combination of deep learning and big data is used to predict the speed of the vehicle. It makes use of ANFIS that stands for Adaptive Neuro-Fuzzy Inference System. Big data analytics is used to examine different sets of data related to speed and tried to identify the relation and pattern between different factors and speed of the vehicle. It predicts the speed of the vehicle rather than detection [14].

Methodology

In this implementation, deep learning model namely, MobileNet SSD is used to predict the speed of multiple vehicles visible through the camera mounted on top of the road. The vital steps includes video acquisition, define region of interest, vehicle detection and tracking, speed prediction and recording vehicle data.

The first step is to take a video as an input. Then a region of interest is defined manually based on the best possible visibility of vehicles on the road. The region outside region of interest is ignored and further work is done only in region of interest. Further, region of interest is divided into 2 segments, where vehicle enters the first segment and exits through the other. Vehicle is recognized and tracked throughout the region of interest and each vehicle is given a unique id in order to uniquely identify different vehicles. As soon as vehicle enters the first segment, the timer associated with that particular id of the vehicle starts and when it leaves through the second segment, the timer for that id stops. The same thing happens for every vehicle. Now, once the time taken by each vehicle to cross the particular segment of region of interest, speed can easily be calculated, as distance is already known. The formula for speed measurement is

$$Speed = \frac{Distance}{Time} \tag{1}$$

$$v = {}^{x}/_{t} \tag{2}$$

$$v' = x \times {}^{3.6}/_{t} \tag{3}$$

Equation (2) is used for calculating vehicle speed. After unit conversion (meters/second to kilometers/hour), Equation (3) provides the vehicle speed.

Once the speed is calculated, it is displayed on the screen in real time. The vehicles driving under the speed limit are marked in green and over speeding vehicles are marked in orange. Also, as soon as vehicle exits the second segment and its speed is calculated, the screenshot of each vehicle is saved in a different folder and over speeding vehicles are saved in different folder so that this data can be further used for analyzing and making challans. A text file is also maintained which keeps track of id of the vehicle and the speed associated with it, total number of vehicles passed and total number of over speeding vehicles.

Video Acquisition

Video with clarity and good frames per second average should be taken to record cars passing by. The road must be clearly visible. The camera must be adjusted in a correct position so that it is stable and not moving. The weather should be fine. It would not work in foggy weather where visibility is very low. The vehicles must be clearly visible on the road. Also, the video should cover a wide region of interest, not the background scenery like buildings, parks, hills, sky, etc. The camera must be on the top of the road recording the vehicles properly. Also, the road must only be recording one-way traffic, that is vehicles either going upwards or downwards.

Region of Interest
Once the camera is all set to provide the best quality video, then there is need to select a region of interest that is the road in this case. The region of interest is set up manually as it gets changed for every other video. Region of interest has to be selected in such a way that the background scenery like buildings, parks, hills, sky, etc. are no longer visible. Only the road along with the vehicles should be clearly visible. Further the region of interest is divided into two segments. The vehicle enters through the first segment of the region of interest and exits through the other. This helps in keeping the track of speed of each car by recording the time taken by the car to cross the two segments. Four red lines make two segments in region of interest.

Object Recognition and Tracking using Mobilenet SSD
There are two major stages in the implementation. First is to select a proper deep learning application that can be used for detecting vehicles as object in our region of interest. There are many object detection algorithms with different accuracies. Among these models include Faster CNN, R CNN, YOLO, SSD (Single Shot Detector). A major challenge in the object detection algorithms is that they are heavily dependent on other computer vision techniques for completing their deep learning approach. Secondly, the implementation also needs competent image processing algorithms to properly provide us with the correct output [11].

Single shot detector is a single stage object detection method that is used for detecting examples of semantic targets of a specific class. It is one of the most popular object detection algorithms due to its ease of implementation and good results for the computation ratio required. For this implementation MobileNet SSD is used, which makes over 8732 bounding boxes for object detection. The MobileNet SSD model can be used to detect a variety of objects, including people, animals, vehicles, and other common objects. The model is trained on the ImageNet dataset, which contains a large number of images of various objects. The MobileNet SSD model achieves high accuracy on the ImageNet dataset, and can be used to detect objects in real-time on mobile devices. The Conv4 3 layer of the VGG16 is then used to detect objects. The class with the highest score is chosen as the one for the bounded item in each prediction, which consists of a bounding box and 21 scores for each class (plus one additional class for no object). Getting a high class is the main goal of the training. The ground truth boxes and the default boxes must match in order to obtain the confidence score.

Once Mobilenet SSD algorithm returns the coordinates of the bounding box of the vehicle detected, now the next task is to track the vehicle location everywhere it goes in the region of interest. If the vehicle is detected for first time a new id is provided to the bounding box or the vehicle. Next task is to calculate the distance travelled by the vehicle after each frame. If the vehicle travels more than 70 pixels in the next frame, a new id is given to the vehicle, as it cannot travel that far after every frame. Therefore, it is a different vehicle. That is how multiple vehicles are identified differently. The formula used for distance calculation is Euclidean Distance shown in equation (4).

$$d(x, y) = \sqrt{\sum_{i=1}^{n}(x_i - y_i)^2} \tag{4}$$

D. Speed Estimation

As soon as the vehicle is detected and it crosses the first segment of region of interest the timer for that particular vehicle is started and as soon as the vehicle exits through the second segment of the region of interest, the timer of that id is stopped. This is how the time is calculated. For the calculation of distance between two segments on the road, the standard units are considered. The distances between two marks are officially set and were used to measure the distance. However, physically counting the distance between the two segments can also provide us with a higher level of accuracy. Keeping the distance up to 10-15 meters between the two segments is more than enough for the implementation to calculate the count and velocities accurately.

Results

This implementation used deep learning approach to detect vehicle speed through a video in real time. It displays the id and speed of the car in real time and also saves the screenshots of the vehicle in jpg format as along with their speed. It also maintains a text file to record data for every vehicle in textual format. The vehicles driving under the speed limit are marked in green and over speeding vehicles are marked in orange. Since the time and distance has been calculated, speed can easily be calculated using the formula in Equation 1-3. Once the speed is calculated, it is shown as an output on the screen in real time once it crosses the second segment of region of interest. All the vehicles under the speed limit are shown green in color and over speeding vehicles are shown orange in color along with their id. The left digits are the id of the car and the right digits are the speed of the car. The car with id 33 is over speeding, hence displayed in red and orange in color, the vehicle with id 30 is under speed limit, hence shown in green as shown in Figure 9.1. The unit of speed shown is Km/hr.

All the images (Figure 9.1) shown below encompass the ways the implementation would work to accompany different situations. These scenarios include low to moderate and high traffic, night time traffic, highway traffic and even for abnormal weather conditions for example excessive rain and snow.

Further, Table 9.1 and Figure 9.2 shows the actual and estimated count of the vehicles detected during different time and weather conditions in the videos. Table 9.2 and Figure 9.3 shows the accuracy for vehicle speed detection where actual speed and calculated speed for different vehicles at different conditions are

Figure 9.1 Final output for speed detection of various vehicles in different scenarios.

Table 9.1 Average accuracy for vehicle detection during different time and weather conditions.

Session Traffic	Video	Actual number of vehicles	Calculated number of vehicles	Accuracy
High (Day)	1.	47	43	91.4%
Low to moderate	1.	45	43	95.5%
	2.	54	56	96.2%
Rain + Night	1.	28	26	92.8%

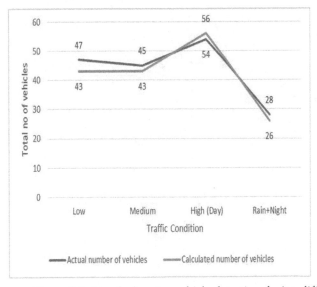

Figure 9.2 Graph showing vehicle detection during different time and weather conditions

Table 9.2: Average accuracy for vehicle speed during different time and weather conditions.

Session	S.no.	Actual Speed (kmph)	Calculated Speed (kmph)	Accuracy
Day	1.	55	57	96.3%
	2.	50	48	96%
	3.	60	59	98.3%
	4.	53	55	96.2%
	5.	56	55	98.2%
	Average accuracy			97%
Night	1.	70	67	95.7%
	2.	74	70	94.5%
	3.	77	75	97.4%
	4.	75	78	96%
	5.	81	80	98.7%
	Average accuracy			96%
Rain + Night	1.	30	27	90%
	2.	35	33	94.2%
	3.	37	40	91.8%
	4.	38	40	94.7%
	5.	34	30	88.2%
	Average accuracy			92%

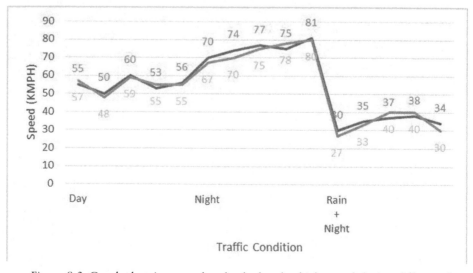

Figure 9.3 Graph showing actual and calculated vehicle speed during different time and weather conditions

given. The average accuracy for vehicle detection is 94% and average accuracy for vehicle speed detection is 95%.

Conclusion

There are many ways to prevent accidents with technology, but one of the most effective is through vehicle speed detection. By using AI technology to monitor and detect vehicle speeds, law enforcement and other safety officials can help to decrease the number of accidents on our roads. By automatically enforcing speed limits, law enforcement can help to ensure that drivers are adhering to the posted limits. This can help to reduce the number of speeding-related accidents. One of the key ways that AI can help to prevent accidents is by providing better data collection and analysis. By gathering data on things like traffic patterns and driver behavior, identify areas where improvements need to be made in order to make our roads safer for everyone.

This implementation can be further improved by adding features like number plate detection, detecting vehicle driving in wrong lanes, detecting drivers and passengers wearing seat belt or not, and integrating with traffic police to issue challans. All the defaulters will get challan issued and will be intimated with the help of information fetched through the license plate. This will help to maintain safety on the roads by keeping an eye on the vehicles even if no traffic police person is physically present over there.

References

1. Bouguettaya , A., Zarzour, H., Kechida, A., and Taberkit, A. M. (2022). Vehicle detection from UAV imagery with deep learning: a review. In IEEE Transactions on Neural Networks and Learning Systems, 33(11), 6047–6067. doi: 10.1109/ TNNLS.2021.3080276.
2. Gunawan, A. A. S., Tanjung, D. A., and Gunawan, F. E. (2019). Detection of vehicle position and speed using camera calibration and image projection methods. IET Intelligent Transport Systems, 12(9), 998–1004.
3. Grents, A., Varkentin, V., and Goryaev, N. (2020). Determining vehicle speed based on video using convolutional neural network. In Proceedings of the IEEE Conference on Computer Vision and Pattern Recognition Workshops, (pp. 153–160).
4. Battiato, S., Farinella, G. M., Furnari, A., Puglisi, G., Snijders, A., and Spiekstra, J. (2015). An integrated system for vehicle tracking and classification. Expert Systems With Applications, 42(21), 7275.
5. Cai, Y., Wang, H., Zheng, Z., and Sun, X. (2017). Scene-adaptive vehicle detection algorithm based on a composite deep structure. IEEE Access, 5, 22804–22811.
6. Ali, E. S., Hassan, M. B., and Saeed, R. A. (2021). Machine learning technologies in internet of vehicles. In Intelligent Technologies for Internet of Vehicles, (pp. 225–252). Cham: Springer International Publishing
7. Kaur, G., and Sharma, A. (2023). A deep learning-based model using hybrid feature extraction approach for consumer sentiment analysis. Journal of Big Data, 10(1), 1–23.
8. Madhan, E. S., Neelakandan, S., and Annamala, R (2020). A novel approach for vehicle type classification and speed prediction using deep learning. Computer Engineering, 37(4), 172–174.

9.   Sravan, M. A., Natarajan, S., Krishna, E. S., and Kailathn, B. J. (2018). Fast and accurate on-road vehicle detection based on color intensity segregation. International Journal of Applied Engineering Research, 11(1), 713–726.

10. avadi, S., Dahl, M., and Pettersson, M. I. (2021). Vehicle speed measurement model for video-based systems. Sensors, 21(6), 2052.

11. Sharma, R., and Singh, A. (2022). An integrated approach towards efficient image classification using deep CNN with transfer learning and PCA. Journal: Advances in Technology Innovation, 2022(2), 105–117.

12. Kumar, T., and Kushwaha, D. S. (2016). An efficient approach for detection and speed estimation of moving vehicles. Procedia Computer Science, 89, 726–731.

13. Varmaa, V. S. K. P., Adarsha, S., Ramachandran, K. I., and Naira, B. B. (2018). Real time detection of speed and distance estimation with deep learning using GPU and ZED stereo camera. In International Conference on Image Processing. https://www.tib.eu/en/search/id/BLCP\%3ACN066390870/Video-based-detection-ofstreet-parking-violation, (vol. 1. IEEE, Las Vegas, pp. 152–156).

14. Cheng, Z., Chow, M. Y., Jung, D., and Jeon, J. (2017). A big data based deep learning approach for vehicle speed prediction. In Ninth International Conference on Computational Intelligence and Security. https://doi.org/10.1109/cis.2013.89. IEEE.

10 Comparative study to detect effective data exchange protocols for IoT based healthcare environment

Harish Kumar[a], Rajesh Kumar Kaushal[b], Naveen Kumar[c] and Ankit Bansal[d]

Chitkara University Institute of Engineering and Technology, Chitkara University, Punjab, India

Abstract

The use of the Internet of Things (IoT) in healthcare has become increasingly popular in recent years, with IoT devices being deployed to monitor patients' health conditions. However, the healthcare IoT environment presents challenges due to limited resources such as bandwidth, storage, and power. In this paper, we comprehensively analyze existing data exchange protocols used in healthcare IoT systems in constrained network environments. This work categorizes the protocols based on their features and discusses their benefits and limitations. Thereafter, this study identifies the key requirements for data exchange protocols in healthcare IoT systems and analyzes the trade-offs among different protocol features. Finally, it presents a detailed comparative analysis of the existing data exchange protocols and to identify the most effective of them.

Keywords: AMQP, CoAP, data exchange protocols, DDS, IoMT, IoT, IoT communication protocols, MQTT, RPM, XMPP

Introduction

Technology has become a necessary and important part of life in present times, and it has changed how we live and does our daily routine tasks. Technology has a great and positive impact and assists in controlling and managing our daily routines. Technology also has a significant role in various domains such as overcoming the challenges in agriculture, manufacturing, and healthcare [2]. In the healthcare sector, critical diseases must be continuously monitored and treated without delay. Timely diagnosis is only possible if necessary vital parameters of a patient are being monitored regularly; thus, manual diagnosis may not help in this scenario [17]. To deal with and overcome these difficulties automated patient health monitoring systems has adopted by both doctors and patients [17, 21]. Remote patient monitoring techniques enable the real-time detection of vital signals such as ECG, blood pressure (BP), blood oxygen level (SpO2), and blood glucose, which may assist doctors in finding a timely detection [20].

The In-Home health monitoring system is another example of remote patient monitoring that enables medical professionals to continue monitoring a patient's health status at their home after discharge from the hospital [19]. This approach is

---

[a]aharish.kumar@chitkara.edu.in, [b]rajesh.kaushal@chitkara.edu.in,
[c]naveen.sharma@chitkara.edu.in, [d]ankit.bansal@chitkara.edu.in

becoming increasingly important as the population of people aged 60 and above continues to grow faster than any other age group worldwide. The World Health Organization (WHO) predicts that this demographic will nearly double from 12.5% to 22.5% between 2015 and 2050. Furthermore, a large majority of the elderly population, approximately 80%, suffer from at least one chronic condition, with more than 75% afflicted by two or more [19]. As a result, the mobile health applications industry is expected to exceed $289.4 billion in value by 2025 [14].

IoT is now utilized everywhere, from everyday appliances to large industries. IoT is playing a significant role to improve the services to both service providers and consumers. From home automation to automating our daily use services, The IoT also has numerous applications in industries and sectors such as healthcare, transportation, and agriculture. According to the IAMAI report on IoT, the number of IoT devices in India is projected to surge from 0.2 billion in 2020 to approx. 2.7 billion by 2025 [15]. This growth is attributed to various factors, including the increasing adoption of smart home devices. The Government of India has also invested heavily in smart city initiatives aimed at promoting sustainable development and enhancing the citizens' quality of life. IoT is being increasingly used in the healthcare sector in India. It can facilitate remote patient monitoring, telemedicine, and the management of medical equipment inventory.

Methodology

To complete the research work, this study took a structured process. We adopted a generic method of Planning, Execution, and Reporting. The following are the steps of the methodology utilized here: In the first step, research questions for this survey are defined. The second phase involves searching for remote patient monitoring and data exchange protocols related research articles using certain keywords. The objective behind employing specific keywords is to keep relevant and irrelevant research publications apart. In the third step, we discussed the working behavior and features of various data communication protocols and did a comparative analysis, and highlighted the key features which are important for the IoT healthcare sector. Lastly, we shortlisted the two best protocols and highlighted their key features by the existing research articles in the same field.

Literature Review

The Internet of Things (IoT) and IoT-based systems have played a significant role in the medical industry and the development of medical equipment over the past ten years. Numerous researchers are still working to improve upon existing solutions while conducting new research in this field. Remote patient monitoring has been crucial to healthcare for the past few years. RPM offers a new IoT-based branch called IoMT, which was created specifically for this purpose and is devoted to the healthcare sector [6]. The Internet of Medical Things (IoMT) refers to medical devices that can send data across a network without requiring human-to-human or human-to-computer interaction [24, 10]. Numerous researchers have made substantial progress in this area using various IoT tools and sensors during the COVID-19 epidemic.

Due to the high efficiency and immense effectiveness in delivering intensive and time-sensitive information to physicians and stakeholders, many researchers have proposed various IoT-based remote patient monitoring systems. In a paper, a researcher [8] proposed a patient monitoring system to collect data of vital parameters using various sensors for clinical research. Another researcher. [16] implemented a system, which monitors the ECG, and pulse rate using LPC2138 (ARM7) and shows the data in the graphical user interface (GUI). If the value of vital parameters goes below or above the expected value, a text message is sent to the mobile phone. In the paper [7], the researcher used sensors to gather data of vital parameters like heart rate and body temperature and used raspberry pi to show it on the LCD, and a copy of the same was sent to the doctor and IoT server for storage and further analysis. In the paper [1], the author proposed an RF-based RPM system that provides health information through web and mobile app platforms. This proposed system includes a web, database server, sensor, coordinator nodes, and graphical user interface. Sensor nodes transmit the data it has gathered to the centralized server and with the help of GUI the users can access and examine the findings. However, this system is unable to support real-time mode due to transmission delays and slow server response. In the article [15], the researcher presented an IoMT program (Virtual Doctor) using artificial intelligence that collects biometric data from patients via wearable sensors on a regular basis, identifies aberrant conditions, and predicts potential health problems in the short or long-term and alert the patient to take necessary action.

IOMT is an IoT-based division specifically designed for the healthcare industry [6]. This pertains to a collection of healthcare tools and software that are linked to healthcare IT systems and interact with each other by utilizing the internet [11]. These devices can be wearables, implantable devices, medical sensors, or mobile apps that gather patient-generated health data [24]. IoMT devices will cover nearly 40% of the IoT market, and due to the IoMT device's significant contribution to reducing the expenses in the healthcare industry, this is expected that it is going to expand at a faster rate in the coming years [2]. The revenue generated through IoMT was around $28 Billion in the year 2017 and will be more than $135 Billion by the end of the year 2025, making it an appealing market for investors [1]. There are several types of IoMT devices and applications, each with a specific focus on healthcare [22].

Implantable Medical Devices
These can be any device that is planted as a replacement for a biological structure of the human body to support or enhance functionality. For example, a pacemaker is an Implantable medical device, which controls the heartbeat. A pacemaker is also called a cardiac pacing device. Wireless IMDs have now been invented to address wired implantable devices related issues, such as contamination and cable breakage, [17, 4] Implantable devices are designed to be as small as possible to minimize their impact on the patient's body. Many devices are less than an inch in size and can be implanted using minimally invasive techniques. These devices are designed to consume as little power as possible to extend their lifespan. Many devices are equipped with batteries that can last for several years or even decades [19].

Internet of Wearable Devices
IoMT wearable devices are compact electronic gadgets that can be worn on the body and come fitted with a range of sensors and wireless connectivity, which permits them to gather and transmit health-related information to other gadgets or a centralized system. Which includes blood pressure monitors, fall detection wristbands, electrocardiogram (ECG) monitors, and smartwatches [18]. Presently smartwatches and wristbands are among the most typical and in-use forms of wearable devices to monitor vital parameters such as heartbeat, SpO2, calorie burn, and movement. Some wearables can alert the wearer or a caregiver in case of abnormal readings or events, such as irregular heartbeats or falls. These alerts can be used to detect irregular heartbeat rhythms when the user is in an idle state. However, wearable devices cannot replace IMDs in critical conditions due to their accuracy level and battery life limitations [12].

Data Exchange Protocols

IoT has enabled remote patient monitoring by allowing for the collection, transmission, and analysis of health data from patients in real-time. However, the capacity to transmit data between the patient's gadget and the healthcare professional's system is critical to the effectiveness of remote patient monitoring. This data communication can be accomplished via a variety of data exchange protocols. IoT devices use these protocols to communicate with other devices. Thus, for this, we have cited the important criteria which give the general view of these protocols such as architecture, technology, security, application, and quality factors [3]. Several data exchange protocols for IoT systems are as follows.

Message Queue Telemetry Transport
MQTT is a messaging protocol that is specifically developed for constrained devices and networks having low-bandwidth, and high-latency. It follows a client-server architecture and employs a publish-subscribe model for communication. Clients can publish messages to a broker, and other clients can subscribe to receive those messages [21]. The broker acts as an intermediary between the publishers and subscribers and ensures the delivery of the messages to the intended recipients. MQTT uses a small binary packet format and is designed to be efficient in terms of network bandwidth and processing power. MQTT supports various quality of service levels, which dictate the level of delivery assurance [9].

QoS (level-0): The message delivers at most once, and the broker does not acknowledge the delivery.

QoS (level-1): The message delivers at least once, and the broker acknowledges the delivery. If the acknowledgment is not received, the broker resends the message.

QoS (level-2): The message delivers exactly once, and the broker acknowledges the delivery. This level of QoS involves a more complex protocol flow, but it ensures that the message is delivered only once.

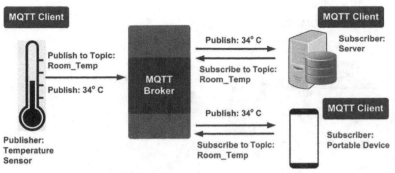

Figure 10.1 MQTT's Publish/subscribe architecture

Constrained Application Protocol (CoAP)

CoAP is specifically created to use with devices and networks with limited resources and capabilities in IoT applications [9, 23]. It facilitates the exchange of information and control messages between devices over the internet through a client-server architecture. CoAP has been designed to be simple and effective, with a small code and message size, low overhead, and the ability to support constrained networks such as 6LoWPAN.). The protocol utilizes the UDP as its transport protocol, which is less reliable than TCP but is more bandwidth and power efficient. CoAP has been developed to work effectively in networks with numerous nodes that are not always online and have lower levels of intelligence [23]. CoAP has several features like a Request-response model, Resource-oriented design, Low overhead, and Caching & Security, which make it suitable for IoT applications.

Data Distribution Service (DDS)

DDS is well-suited for IoT applications because it provides a flexible, reliable, and efficient way to distribute data between networked devices [23]. DDS can be used to connect devices such as sensors, actuators, and controllers, as well as applications that need to interact with these devices. It provides a publish-subscribe model, where publishers can publish data to specific topics, and subscribers or applications can receive this data by subscribing to the relevant topics. Another advantage of DDS in the context of IoT is that it allows for data to be distributed in a peer-to-peer manner, rather than relying on a centralized server or cloud service. This can help to reduce latency, improve reliability, and increase scalability in IoT systems. DDS also provides a range of Quality of Service options that can be configured for different types of data and applications. Figure 10.2 shows the working model of the DDS protocol, where Data writers publish data to the topic directly and readers subscribe to the topics without the help of any centralized service or cloud storage, which helps the DDS to reduce the latency in data exchange.

Advanced Message Queue Protocol (AMQP)

It supports both publish/subscribe architecture and request/response modes. Being an open standard protocol, AMQP is supported by a broad range of middleware.

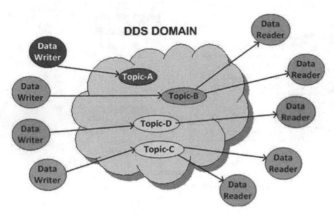

Figure 10.2 Data distribution service

This can simplify the development and deployment of IoT systems and enable devices to work together more easily and seamlessly. AMQP provides features such as message acknowledgments and retransmissions, which ensure that messages are reliably delivered even in the presence of network failures or other disruptions. This can be particularly important in IoT applications where message delivery must be guaranteed [13]. It also supports encryption and authentication to provide secure communication between devices and servers, which is important in IoT applications where data privacy and security are critical.

Extensible Messaging and Presence Protocol (XMPP)
It is based on XML Language that enables real-time messaging, presence information, and other services. It is widely used in instant messaging and chat applications but can also be used as a protocol for device-to-device communication in IoT. This can enable devices to send and receive messages, establish presence information, and coordinate actions. For example, a smart home system might use XMPP to allow different devices to communicate with each other and with a central control system [5]. It can also be used as a protocol for device-to-server communication. This can enable devices to share data to a central machine for storage and analysis. There are also some challenges associated with using XMPP in IoT. XMPP can be relatively complex to implement and configure, especially for devices with limited computing resources. It may not be the best choice for all IoT use cases.

Results

According to the literature review and information from various online sources, the feature-wise and various important parameters-wise comparison of data exchange protocols are discussed in Table 10.1, where we tried to compare all important aspects of these data communication protocols used in a variety of IoT projects from home automation to industrial projects, in home-based where a little delay in the communication can be acceptable but in healthcare where no delay is acceptable in critical conditions. Power consumption and bandwidth are

Table 10.1 Comparative analysis of data exchange protocols.

Topic/ protocol	MQTT	CoAP	XMPP	AMQP	DDS
Standard	OASIS IBMs	IETF	IETF	OASIS	OMG DDS
Architecture	Publish/ subscribe Request/ response	Request/ response	Publish/ subscribe Request/ response	Message-oriented, request/ response	Publish/ subscribe
Technology	Irrespective of the implementation language	XML	XML	Irrespective of the implementation language	C, C#, JAVA, Scala, Ruby
Transport protocol	TCP/IP	UDP, SMS,	TCP/IP	TCP, TLS	TCP/IP, UDP
Security	TLS, SSL	DTLS, OSCORE	TLS, SSL	TLS, SASL, Kerberos	DTLS, TLS, Security Plugins
Data format	Binary or JSON	Binary or text	XML	Binary or text	Binary or XML
Quallity factors	Reliability	Reliability authentication, confidentiality	Efficiency, reusability	Efficiency, flexibility, interoperability	Excellent QOS, reliability, urgency priority
Message discovery	Manual	Manual	Manual	Manual	Automatic
Connection type	One to one, one to many, and many to many	One to one and many to many	One to one and one to many	One to one, one to many	One to one and one to many
Power consumption	Very low	Very low	Low	High	low
Bandwidth consumption	Very low	Low	Higher than MQTT	Higher than MQTT	Low (higher than MQTT)

the important factors while finalizing the data exchange protocols in the healthcare sector and according to that only protocols which best suites the requirements are MQTT and CoAP, both have their own specialty in different situations and requirements, in the context of quality of service, where MQTT provide better service as compare to CoAP and when we compare these protocols in terms of power consumption and CoAP performs better than MQTT, COAP becomes more suitable choice where the clients are not always active to minimize the power consumption. Although CoAP is faster in terms of data delivery as it used UDP,

MQTT uses TCP as a transport protocol, which provides guaranteed delivery of messages [2]. Most of the protocols except CoAP use TCP as a transport protocol which is responsible for more bandwidth consumption as compared to CoAP.

Conclusion

Based on the comparative analysis of various data exchange protocols as mentioned in Table 10.1, it is concluded that only two protocols MQTT, CoAP are found most suitable for resource-constrained networks like IoMT, where bandwidth consumption and latency were the major criteria in choosing the best protocols.

MQTT uses a centralized broker to distribute messages between clients. It uses a binary protocol and provides efficient encoding and decoding of messages, making it well-suited for low-bandwidth networks. MQTT has a relatively low overhead, and its publish-subscribe model can reduce network congestion, leading to lower latency. Whereas CoAP operates over UDP, making it more efficient than TCP-based protocols like MQTT. CoAP is designed to be used in resource-constrained environments, and its small packet size, low overhead, and use of multicast messaging can result in lower latency than MQTT which makes it more suitable than MQTT in non-critical situations in IoMT environments.

Finally, both MQTT and CoAP are designed to minimize network latency and provide efficient communication between devices. The choice between the two protocols will depend on factors such as the application's specific requirements, the network conditions, and the resources available on the devices.

References

1. Alhaj, T. A., Abdulla, S. M., Iderss, M. A. E., Ali, A. A. A., Elhaj, F. A., Remli, M. A., and Gabralla, L. A. (2022). A survey: to govern, protect, and detect security principles on internet of medical things (IoMT). *IEEE Access*, 10, 124777–124791.
2. Al-Khafajiy, M., Baker, T., Chalmers, C., Asim, M., Kolivand, H., Fahim, M., and Waraich, A. (2019). Remote health monitoring of elderly through wearable sensors. *Multimedia Tools and Applications*, 78(17), 24681–2706.
3. Elhadi, Sakina and Marzak, Abdelaziz and Sael, Nawal and Merzouk, Soukaina, Comparative Study of IoT Protocols (May 28, 2018). Smart Application and Data Analysis for Smart Cities (SADASC'18), Available at SSRN: https://ssrn.com/abstract=3186315 or http://dx.doi.org/10.2139/ssrn.3186315
4. Ferguson, J. E., and Redish, A. D. (2011). Wireless communication with implanted medical devices using the conductive properties of the body. *Expert Review of Medical Devices*, 8(4), 427–433.
5. Ferrera, E., Conzon, D., Brizzi, P., Rossini, R., Pastrone, C., Jentsch, M., Kool, P., Kamienski, C., and Sadok, D. (2017). XMPP-based infrastructure for iot network management and rapid services and applications development. *Annals of Telecommunications*, 72, 443–457.
6. Ghubaish, A., Salman, T., Zolanvari, M., Unal, D., Al-Ali, A., and Jain, R. (2020). Recent advances in the internet-of-medical-things (IoMT) systems security. *IEEE Internet of Things Journal*, 8(11), 8707–8718.
7. Gutte, A., and Vadali, R. (2018). IoT based health monitoring system using raspberry Pi. In 2018 Fourth International Conference on Computing Communication Control and Automation (ICCUBEA), (pp. 1–5).

8. Hossain, M. S., and Muhammad, G. (2016). Cloud-assisted industrial internet of things (Iiot)–enabled framework for health monitoring. *Computer Networks*, 101, 192–202.

9. Ignacio de Mendizábal. (2024). IoT Communication Protocols—IoT Data Protocols. Accessed: Jan. 31, 2024. [Online]. Available: https://www.allaboutcircuits.com/technical-articles/internet-of-things-communication-protocols-iot-data-protocols/

10. Kaur, A., Singh, G., Kukreja, V., Sharma, S., Singh, S., and Yoon, B. (2022). Adaptation of IoT with blockchain in food supply chain management: an analysis-based review in development, benefits and potential applications. *Sensors,* 22(21), 8174.

11. Kaushal, R. K., Kumar, N., Panda, S. N., and Kukreja, V. (2021). Immutable smart contracts on blockchain technology: its benefits and barriers. In 2021 9th International Conference on Reliability, Infocom Technologies and Optimization (Trends and Future Directions)(ICRITO), (pp. 1–5).

12. Kos, A., Milutinović, V., and Umek, A. (2019). Challenges in wireless communication for connected sensors and wearable devices used in sport biofeedback applications. *Future Generation Computer Systems, 92,* 582–592.

13. Naik, N. (2017). Choice of effective messaging Protocols for IoT systems: MQTT, CoAP, AMQP and HTTP. In 2017 IEEE International Systems Engineering Symposium (ISSE), (pp. 1–7).

14. Organization, World Health, and others (2011). MHealth: new horizons for health through mobile technologies. MHealth: New Horizons for Health through Mobile Technologies.

15. W. H. Organization and others. (2019). WHO guideline: recommendations on digital interventions for health system strengthening: web supplement 2: summary of findings and GRADE tables. Accessed: Aug. 06, 2023. [Online]. Available: https://apps.who.int/iris/handle/10665/324998

16. Patel, S., Park, H., Bonato, P., Chan, L., and Rodgers, M. (2012). A review of wearable sensors and systems with application in rehabilitation. *Journal of Neuroengineering and Rehabilitation,* 9(1), 1–17.

17. Pathinarupothi, R. K., Durga, P., and Rangan, E. S. (2018). IoT-based smart edge for global health: remote monitoring with severity detection and alerts transmission. *IEEE Internet of Things Journal,* 6(2), 2449–2462.

18. Insider Intelligence. (2019). Latest trends in medical monitoring devices and wearable health technology. Accessed: Jan. 31, 2024. [Online]. Available: https://www.insider-intelligence.com/insights/wearable-technology-healthcare-medical-devices/

19. Philip, N. Y., Rodrigues, J. J. P. C., Wang, H., Fong, S. J., and Chen, J. (2021). Internet of things for in-home health monitoring systems: current advances, challenges and future directions. *IEEE Journal on Selected Areas in Communications,* 39(2), 300–310.

20. Savaridass, M. P., Ikram, N., Deepika, R., and Aarnika, R. (2021). Development of smart health monitoring system using internet of things. *Materials Today: Proceedings,* 45, 986–989.

21. Shilpa, V., Vidya, A., and Pattar, S. (2022). MQTT based secure transport layer communication for mutual authentication in IoT network. *Global Transitions Proceedings,* 3(1), 60–66.

22. Tiwari, D., Prasad, D., Guleria, K., and Ghosh, P. (2021). IoT based smart healthcare monitoring systems: a review. In 2021 6th International Conference on Signal Processing, Computing and Control (ISPCC), (pp. 465–469).

23. Vaigandla, K. K., Karne, R. K., and Rao, A. S. (2021). A Study on IoT technologies, standards and protocols. *IBMRD's Journal of Management & Research,* 10(2), 7–14.

24. Vishnu, S., Ramson, S. R. J., and Jegan, R. (2020). Internet of medical things (IoMT)-an overview. In 2020 5th International Conference on Devices, Circuits and Systems (ICDCS), (pp. 101–104).

11 A comprehensive analysis to identify effective tools and technologies for remote patient monitoring

Shilpi Garg[a]. Rajesh Kumar Kaushal[b] and Naveen Kumar[c]

Chitkara University Institute of Engineering and Technology, Chitkara University, Punjab, India

Abstract

The adoption of the Internet of Things (IoT) has a significant impact on every aspect of our environment .IoT integrated smart healthcare is leading the way as it provides continuous remote patient monitoring (RPM). In the past, the healthcare sector has produced a lot of data. In order to interpret the data, it is necessary for the health data to be kept securely. In RPM, measurements are made of physiological variables such as pulse rate, skin temperature, blood pressure, ECG (Electrocardiogram), oxygen saturation, and blood sugar levels. According to current research, telehealth and Remote Patient Monitoring systems may provide an ideal environment for opportunistic security breaches. The existing IoT-based RPM system does face a number of difficulties, including scalability, security and privacy concerns, single points of failure (SPOF), and loss of trust. One of the innovative technologies that have the potential to overcome these difficulties is blockchain. A blockchain-based system makes it difficult for an adversary to alter (or delete) data because data is stored across the decentralized nodes and each block is linked to previous one. The main objective of this study is to find the effective tools and technologies for remote patient monitoring. Moreover, this study also discovers the most effective data exchange protocols for RPM environment and find out the message queuing telemetry transport protocol and constraint oriented application protocol as a most effective data communication protocols. Further this study also reveals the way of integrating the blockchain technology with IoT based RPM systems.

Keywords: blockchain, decentralized, healthcare, remote patient monitoring

Introduction

The healthcare services industry has recently become a major focus for the research world. Because of its potential for research, this industry has garnered a lot of funding. Healthcare industry is suffering from several issues like lack of resources, expensive healthcare services and in effective hospital resource management. In addition to this, healthcare industry is also suffering from various logistics issues such as unavailability of bedrooms and equipment and lack of healthcare workers that must be resolved for the smooth and effective functioning. Typically, patient monitoring is done passively, which means that medical staff adjusts the patient's medicine in response to fluctuations in their medical

[a]shilpi.singhal@chitkara.edu.in, [b]rajesh.kaushal@chitkara.edu.in, [c]Naveen.sharma@chitkara.edu.in

status [2]. The patient's condition may even get worse in emergency situations and in such situations the reaction time is very crucial.

IoT has offered several different e-health alternatives. It has the potential to advance numerous fields such as smart drug delivery, improved supply chain for drugs and healthcare logistics and patient monitoring [9]. A clinician needs regular updates of patient's vital parameters to discover irregular and unexpected conditions and a body sensors network can play a vital role under such circumstances. In order to avoid serious disorders, the emergency drugs might be administered immediately. Smart systems are used to enhance health services and speed up medical care processes with the use of IoT [1]. The Internet of Things (IoT) offers a platform for attaining objectives including enhancing the health of individuals and making everyday lives easier for those who have impairments and chronic illnesses [8]. In fact, smart IoT systems have made caregiver's life much easier in context of providing their services to the patients [14, 7, 5]. IoMT based systems are utilized as a health analytical intelligence tools for clinical administration and for diagnostic imaging. Typically, two phases are involved in a IoMT based systems. In the first phase patient data is recorded and in the next phase recorded data is utilized for analytics to observe the health status. The recorded data is usually kept on a cloud platform. Stake holders like doctors, caretakers, emergency departments, and clinics are given access to it. Data may be accessed by using equipments like laptops, tablets and cell phones. Figure 11.1 displays the fundamental IoMT layered architecture.

The perception layer which is also known as device layer includes devices like an electrocardiogram, an electrocephalogram, an electromyogram, an oxygen metre, a pacemaker, an MRI machine, a pressure sensor, etc. By using sensors, these gadgets directly connect with the patient to obtain numerous biological markers. The sensors are capable of detecting and gathering data for many smart healthcare applications. These sensors come in four different kinds, including wearable, implanted, stationary, and ambient sensor devices. The network layer is responsible for providing the communication between low power equipments. Low power sensors are supported by modern communication technologies that use simple protocols. Wi-Fi and Bluetooth are two examples of these types of technologies that are often used. Aggregators are also employed that serve as a bridge to offer multi-thing communication. IoT communication networks that offer data-oriented communication are also categorized under information- centric networking (ICN) and it gives scalability to IoMT, effective router mobility, a buffering approach, and security components. The data is then transferred to the cloud for storage, evaluation, and quick access as and when required. The application layer has the responsibility of detecting, analyzing, tracing, and collecting patient data using tools like laptops, smart phones, and smart watches. The aim of this work is to find the effective tools and technologies used for remote patient monitoring. Based on the existing studies, this article present the comparison of various microcontrollers and communication protocols used for real-time data transmission. Moreover this study also reveals the challenges for securing the RPM data and way of integrating the blockchain technology with IoT based systems.

Figure 11.1 IoT layered architecture

This study is organized as follows: Section II offers an overview of remote patient monitoring. Security laws needs for healthcare data are discussed in Section III. Section IV elaborates the present state-of-the-art for remote patient monitoring and identifying various tools and communication protocols required for monitoring systems. Finally, sections V conclude the study and also disclose the futures cope.

Remote Patient Monitoring

The IoMT based remote patient monitoring is very effective for the patients who have been diagnosed with persistent illnesses, mobility problems or other disabilities, patients who have recently undergone surgery, newborns, and elderly patients. Such patients may get huge benefits from regular remote observations [21].

Traditional monitoring systems used to gather data using the sensors. These sensors were not energy efficient and require frequent battery charging or replacing and thus such traditional systems pose massive difficulties for the patients as well as medical staff. The IoMT revolution addresses the aforementioned problems by utilizing small, extremely low power smart sensors and lightweight network protocols. The monitoring systems are primarily made of sensors, microcontroller to process the collected data and electronic circuits. These devices are capable to collect physiological parameters like heart and pulse rate, respiration rate, blood pressure, SPO_2, body and skin temperature, body mass index, level of consciousness, muscular activity, glucose level, and urine report. The fundamental components of patient monitoring systems are data acquisition, data processing, end terminal and communication network.

a) Data acquisition: A data collection system is made up of various sensors and wireless data transfer capabilities.
b) Data processing: This includes microprocessor/ microcontroller that can receive and send data as well as a processing unit.
c) End-terminal: A computer (or database) located in the hospital, a specialized device, or the doctor's smart phone can all serve as the terminal.

d) Communication network: The data detection and findings are then sent to a healthcare provider through the communication network.

As shown in the Figure 11.2 patient vital parameters will be captured by the sensors and control unit will manage all the parameters, transferred to the cloud serve. Hospital doctor, care takers and relatives can access the vital data from the hospital server database. On the cloud platform various data and network communication protocols are used to transfer the sensors data on the cloud server. Client and server communicate with the help of protocols (MQTT, CoAP, FTP, HTTP and web socket) in various modes.

Methodology

To conduct the comprehensive analysis various high quality published articles have been reviewed. Figure 11.3 depicts the steps carried out to conduct this study. To develop a remote patient monitoring model, there is a need to identify which data communication protocols and microcontrollers are exists. To identify the published articles (Remote patient monitoring AND communication protocol) OR (IoT AND microcontrollers) keywords are used. A total of 50 articles were found from Google scholar, IEEE Xlpore, Science direct, PubMed database. After excluded some articles that are not relevant according to this study, 18 articles were included

Literature Review

The technologies, functionalities, and behavior of the numerous RPM systems are different from one another. SCOPUS databases demonstrate an expansion in this

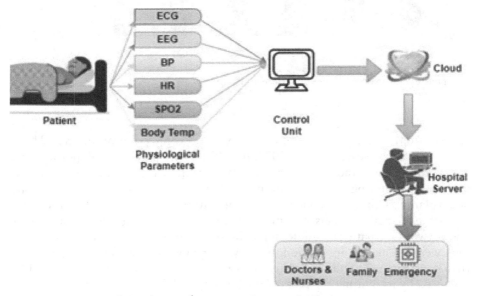

Figure 11.2 Traditional way of remote patient monitoring

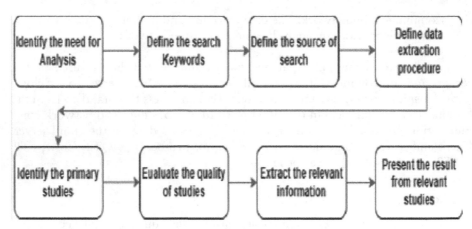

Figure 11.3 Traditional way of remote patient monitoring

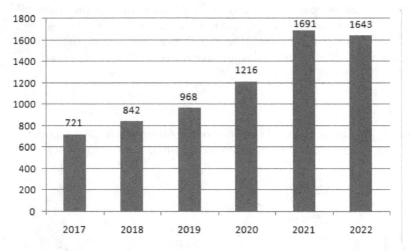

Figure 11.4 Number of publications in last five years

field (Figure 11.4). It can be seen that number of research publications in 2021 are almost equal to research during 2022. IoT devices are playing an important role in real time patient monitoring system. Authors implemented [2] an IoT based real time monitoring system to measure essential parameters like SpO2, heart rate, volatile gas, humidity, body, room temperature and electrocardiogram(ECG) for asthmatic patients. This system enabled the real time video calling and chatting between the patients and doctors. The system was composed of various sensors, web and mobile application. Initially the proposed system was tested in the virtual environment and then tested on a real environment. This study could be enhanced by integrating the cross platform compatibility and private blockchain technology.

A faulty prescription might cause a patient to die, and prescribing needless medications can be expensive for the patient's guardians or caregivers. In order to transmit patient data from the intensive care unit to the doctors and caregivers, authors [9] designed a real- time patient monitoring system with micro-services architecture. Additionally, the proposed system greatly reduces needless prescriptions and billing. Another study [1] elaborated a lightweight security and privacy preserving IoT based system for real-time remote patient monitoring. Patient vital parameters were collected through Moto 360 watch (wearable sensor). The proposed system enabled the secure mutual authentication and data integrity between the data sender, receiver and server using elliptic curve technology. To allow access to health data, a mobile application was developed. The proposed study was lacking in evaluating the performance of the system. This system seems effective but did not propose the face to face interaction between doctor and patient.

Authors developed a [5] prioritize system that able to transmit the patient's sensitive information within a specific time period. Data is collected via the sensors and is encrypted with AES and then send to the mobile by using Bluetooth/Wi-Fi. Then mobile gateway sends data onto the cloud. Patients' conditions are remotely classified and tracked using the neural network. The suggested method improved the accuracy of the system by 97.13 percent. The authors developed [20] a real-time electrocardiogram (ECG) monitoring system based on the Internet of Things that can support both real-time and offline access. The real- time ECG is sent from the proposed system to the cloud server using the Message Queuing Telemetry Transport (MQTT) protocol. A desktop and mobile application has been developed for the doctors to monitor the patient data in local area network as well as in wide area network. The findings demonstrate that the designed method does not suffer from package loss errors. An IoT-based secure vital monitoring system was presented by the authors [17]. The Advanced Encryption Standard (AES) method was used to analyze and encrypt the recorded physiological signals before transferring them to the cloud. Processing, encryption, and Wi-Fi cloud connectivity were controlled by an embedded ESP8266 device. The suggested system was compared with a number of existing medical devices. In cloud based remote patient monitoring systems, cloud servers are used to store the patient's health data where confidentiality, security and privacy of data are crucial aspects. To mitigate these challenges authors [16] suggested a lightweight authentication technique that can be applied for a secure access. The proposed technique can resist all network attacks and is simple to use. The performance analysis of the implemented scheme reveals that execution time, communication cost and power consumption were reduced in comparison with existing work.

In another study [13] an IoT and cloud based healthcare system was proposed for continuous remote patient monitoring. Heart rate, body temperature and oxygen level data was collected through the wearable sensors and stored on the cloud (Thing Speak). An alert message was generated in case of an abrupt change in the vital parameters. This proposed method did not support video calling and lacked in providing the tamper proof and auditable data storage. The authors proposed that such systems may become more usefully hosting it on top of the blockchain technology. An IoT based patient wearable sensor band was developed for transferring and monitoring vital parameters. The proposed model enabled an alarm for early prediction of Covid-19 and made an online diagnosis from any remote location. Biomedical sensors were utilized together electrocardiogram (ECG), photoplethysmography (PPG), body temperature and accelerometer signals. Moreover, the designed model was tested and simulated using machine learning, R language and cooja simulator. This empirical study achieved 96.33% accuracy and low power consumption. This model was predicting the early detection of COVID and diagnosing the patient remotely. The proposed system claimed higher accuracy but did not support synching patient vital data over the blockchain network [10]. Remote patient monitoring has always imposed challenges to researchers. Authors proposed a study [15] that attempted to offer similar system but with improvisation. The study revealed an automated RPM system that could send an alert notification to nursing staff and caretaker if any abnormality is found and physician could prescribe the medication remotely. The system was IoT based 3-tier architecture (technology, management and data processing layer) that ensure the secure data transmission. Table 11.1 summaries the existing studies in remote patient monitoring. The security of the proposed system could be enhanced by incorporating a real-time data into blockchain based electronic health records. Tables 11.2 and 11.3 tabulates the comparison between various microcontrollers and communication protocols used in the existing studies. Table 11.2 illustrates that MQTT and COAP protocols consume low power and both are used for resource constraint devices. Conventional medical monitoring systems are not advised for real interaction due to lack of security, robustness and request additional computations during the transmission and analysis of medical data. Therefore, blockchain technology may be integrated to mitigate all the issues associated with the RPM. Blockchain is a new innovation that creates trust in a hazardous situation without the aid of centralized authorities [6]. Many organizations have been tremendously benefitted or completely reshaped by adopting blockchain. The earliest application of this ledger technology was

Table 11.1 Summary of existing studies in the context of remote patient monitoring.

Ref	RPM	Micro controller	Communication Protocols	Blockchain +IoT	Tele monitoring
[2]	Yes	ESP8266	W_i-F_i	IoT	Yes
[9]	Yes	-	CoAP	IoT	No
[4]	Yes	-	-	IoT	No
[5]	Yes	ESP8266	W_i-F_i	IoT	No
[20]	Yes	ESP 8266	W_i-F_i	IoT	No
[17]	Yes	Arduino	Bluetooth, W_i-F_i	IoT	No
[16]	Yes		HTTP	IoT	No
[12]	Yes	ESP8266	W_i-F_i	IoT	No
[10]	Yes	Raspberry Pi	Mqtt	IoT	No

Table 11.2 Comparison between microcontrollers.

Attributes	Arduino UNO	Raspberry Pi	ESP8266 Node MCU
Developer	Arduino	Raspberry Pi Foundation	ESP 8266 open source
Operating system	None	Linux	XTOS
CPU	Atmel, ARM, Intel	ARM Cortex	LXT106
Clock speed	16MHz	1.2 GHz	26 MHz-52MHz
Memory	32 KB	1-4 GB	128 MB
Storage	1KB	Micro SDHC Slot	4MB
Power	USB power supply	USB power supply	USB
Voltage	5V	5V	3.3 V

Table 11.3 Comparison of various communication protocols.

Parameters	MQTT	CoAP	AMQP	HTTP
Message size and overhead	Light weight Message size- 2byte Large overhead.	UDP based No connection overhead	TCP overhead for connection establishment and tear down.	Most heavy weight protocol due to TCP overhead for connection establishment and tear down.
Power consumption and resource requirement	Low power consumption	Require low power consumption	Require higher power resources.	Require more processing and power resources.
Bandwidth vs. latency	Slow start of TCP to avoid of congestion result in less bandwidth utilization.	Reduced network load response time.	Extra services need higher bandwidth and latency.	Require larger bandwidth and latency.
Reliability and QoS	Guranteed packet delivery.	NON CON and CON message	Settle and Unsettle format	No default QoS

suggested for the financial sectors. Blockchain is a great alternative for data sensitive fields like healthcare because of its unique properties, which include integrity of data, confidentiality and validity.

Every node in the blockchain network contains the same copy of blockchain. Miners get the rewards for their mining process. For mining different consensus protocols are used by miners. Valid block will be added to the blockchain then requested transaction considered to be completed. Every single piece of patient

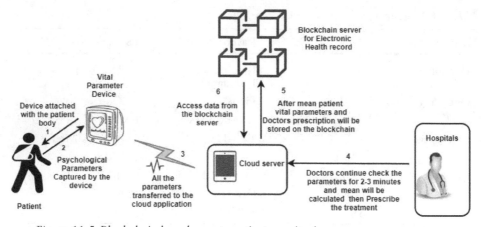

Figure 11.5 Blockchain based remote patient monitoring

data, which is generated in massive quantities, is crucial. It is very difficult to store this sensitive data in a way that is legal, secure, and accessible. These records frequently need to be shared or transferred in a secure manner. IN addition, blockchain offers digital health records (EHRs). All documents and records are kept digitally, and EHR allows us to distribute patient data to other healthcare professionals. Decentralization, anonymity, transparency and immutable are the key elements of blockchain. The blockchain based system enables the doctors to access the complete medical history of the patient which is more authentic and reliable. Figure 11.5 shows the way of integrating the blockchain technology with IoT for remote patient monitoring. Blockchain technology connects the individuals with similar health issues all over the world [19, 11, 18, 3]. Monitoring devices are attached with the patient to record the vital parameters as shown in Figure 5 and these parameters are transferred over the cloud server or application, from where doctors can monitor the vital signs in real-time. Doctors prescribe medication to patients based on the mean.

Conclusion

The Internet of Things (IoT) has a significant impact on every aspect of our environment. IoT integrated smart healthcare is leading the way as it provides continuous remote patient monitoring (RPM). Internet of medical things based remote patient monitoring is very effective for the patients who have been diagnosed with persistent illnesses, mobility problems or other disabilities, patients who have recently undergone surgery, newborns, and elderly patients. The IoT technology helps the hospitals to track the patient's health and doctors services that make it easier to treat chronic diseases. In this article, authors discussed the present state-of-the-art for remote patient monitoring and compare various microcontrollers and communication protocols that were used in previous work. Moreover, this study also discovers the most effective data exchange protocol for RPM environment and find out the message queuing telemetry transport protocol and constraint-oriented application protocol. These two protocols are most effective data communication protocol. As a future scope, implementing a block-chain based remote monitoring system and performs the performance of the system in simulation environment.

References

1. Ahmed, Mohammed and Kannan, G.. (2021). Secure and Lightweight Privacy Preserving Internet of Things Integration for Remote Patient Monitoring. *Journal of King Saud University - Computer and Information Sciences*. 34. 10.1016/j.jksuci.2021.07.016.
2. Safayat Reza Anan, Md. Azizul Hossain, Md. Zubayer Milky, Mohammad Monirujjaman Khan, Mehedi Masud, Sultan Aljahdali, (2021). Research and Development of an IoT-Based Remote Asthma Patient Monitoring System, *Journal of Healthcare Engineering*, vol. 2021, Article ID 2192913, 21. https://doi.org/10.1155/2021/2192913
3. Arbabi, M. S., Lal, C., Veeraragavan, N. R., Marijan, D., Nygard, J. F., and Vitenberg, R. (2022). A Survey on Blockchain for Healthcare: Challenges, Benefits, and Future Directions. IEEE Communications Surveys and Tutorials, 25(1), 386–424. https://doi.org/10.1109/COMST.2022.3224644
4. Ibrahim, A., Mahmood, B., and Singhal, M. (2016). A secure framework for sharing electronic health records over clouds. In 2016 IEEE International Conference on Serious Games and Applications for Health (SeGAH), (pp. 1–8).
5. Iranpak, S., Shahbahrami, A., and Shakeri, H. (2021). Remote patient monitoring and classifying using the internet of things platform combined with cloud computing. *Journal of Big Data*, 8(1), 1–22.
6. Kaushal, R. K., Kumar, N., and Panda, S. N. (2021). Blockchain technology, its applications and open research challenges. *Journal of Physics: Conference Series*, 1950, 12030.
7. Kukreja, V. (2022). Fuzzy AHP-TOPSIS approaches to prioritize teaching solutions for intellect errors. *Journal of Engineering Education Transformations,* 35(4), April 2022, ISSN 2349-2473, eISSN 2394-1707
8. Kumar, A., Sharma, S., Goyal, N., Singh, A., Cheng, X., and Singh, P. (2021). Secure and energy-efficient smart building architecture with emerging technology IoT. *Computer Communications*, 176, 207–217.
9. Sujatha Kumari, B.A., Shreyas, K.S., Skanda, M.S., Kumar, M., Prajwal, C.D. (2022). IOT-Based Remote Patient Monitoring System Using Microservices Architecture. In: Ranganathan, G., Fernando, X., Shi, F., El Allioui, Y. (eds) *Soft Computing for Security Applications*. Advances in Intelligent Systems and Computing, vol 1397. Springer, Singapore. https://doi.org/10.1007/978-981-16-5301-8_28
10. Majeed, J. H., and Aish, Q. (2021). A remote patient monitoring based on WBAN implementation with internet of thing and cloud server. *Bulletin of Electrical Engineering and Informatics,* 10(3), 1640–1647.
11. Ramzan, Sadia and Aqdus, Aqsa and Ravi, Vinayakumar and Koundal, Deepika and Amin, Rashid and Al Ghamdi, Mohammed. (2022). Healthcare Applications Using Blockchain Technology: Motivations and Challenges. *IEEE Transactions on Engineering Management*. 1–17. 10.1109/TEM.2022.3189734.
12. Sahu, M. L., Atulkar, M., Ahirwal, M. K., and Ahamad, A. (2022a). Cloud-based remote patient monitoring system with abnormality detection and alert notification. *Mobile Networks and Applications*, 27(2), 1–16.
13. Sahu, M. L., Atulkar, M., Ahirwal, M. K., and Ahamad, A. (2022b). Cloud-based remote patient monitoring system with abnormality detection and alert notification.

Mobile Networks and Applications, 27(5), 1894–1909. https://doi.org/10.1007/s11036-022-01960-4.

14.   Sakshi, S., Kukreja, V., and Ahuja, S. (2021). Recognition and classification of mathematical expressions using machine learning and deep learning methods. In 2021 9th International Conference on Reliability, Infocom Technologies and Optimization (Trends and Future Directions), ICRITO 2021. https://doi.org/10.1109/ICRITO51393.2021.9596161.

15.   Sharma, N., Mangla, M., Mohanty, S. N., Gupta, D., Tiwari, P., Shorfuzzaman, M., and Rawashdeh, M. (2021). A smart ontology-based IoT framework for remote patient monitoring. *Biomedical Signal Processing and Control,* 68, 102717.

16.   Shreya, S., Chatterjee, K., and Singh, A. (2022). A smart secure healthcare monitoring system with internet of medical things. *Computers and Electrical Engineering,* 101(October 2021), 107969. https://doi.org/10.1016/j.compeleceng.2022.107969.

17.   Ali I. Siam, Mohammed Amin Almaiah, Ali Al-Zahrani, Atef Abou Elazm, Ghada M. El Banby, Walid El-Shafai, Fathi E. Abd El-Samie, Nirmeen A. El-Bahnasawy, (2021). Secure Health Monitoring Communication Systems Based on IoT and Cloud Computing for Medical Emergency Applications, *Computational Intelligence and Neuroscience,* vol. 2021, Article ID 8016525, 23. https://doi.org/10.1155/2021/8016525

18.   Singh, B., and Gupta, A. (2021). Blockchain technology for hospital management: a visualisation and review of research trends. In Proceedings - 2nd International Conference on Smart Electronics and Communication, ICOSEC 2021, (pp. 395–99). https://doi.org/10.1109/ICOSEC51865.2021.9591880.

19.   Su, C.-R., Hajiyev, J., Fu, C. J., Kao, K. C., Chang, C. H., and Chang, C. T. (2019). A novel framework for a remote patient monitoring (RPM) system with abnormality detection. *Health Policy and Technology,* 8(2), 157–170.

20.   Yew, H. T., Ng, M. F., Ping, S. Z., Chung, S. K., Chekima, A., and Dargham, J. A. (2020). Iot based real-time remote patient monitoring system. In 2020 16th IEEE International Colloquium on Signal Processing & Its Applications (CSPA), (pp. 176–179).

21.   Zhang, X., Rane, K. P., Kakaravada, I., and Shabaz, M. (2021). Research on vibration monitoring and fault diagnosis of rotating machinery based on internet of things technology. *Nonlinear Engineering,* 10(1), 245–254.

12 Cloud with big data analytics and challenges in developing countries

Jaspreet Singh Bajaj[a], Naveen Kumar[b], Rajesh Kumar Kaushal[c] and Kamal Saluja[d]

Chitkara University Institute of Engineering and Technology, Chitkara University, Punjab, India

Abstract

The IT industry strongly relies on cloud computing, a growing technology that will play a significant role in driving the sector to new heights. Cloud Computing is in the process of revolutionizing the modern computing world. With on-demand access, it offers its customers a variety of IT services online. The platform is responsible for meeting the computational and storage requirements of various big data analytics applications. Big Data refers to the massive amount of data generated by cloud computing. furthermore, when this data is analyzed, it offers insightful information. The aim of the paper is to examine current technologies, such as big data and cloud computing in order to address current provocations. This article highlights some of the methods that can be useful in removing the barriers to a bright future for cloud computing in the IT industry, as well as the main difficulties and security threats it faces.

Keywords: Big data, cloud computing, modern computing, security threats

Introduction

Cloud Computing is in the process of revolutionizing the modern computing world. It was created in the early 1960s when John McCarthy, an American computer scientist, envisioned the eventual creation of a computing platform that would allow for a high degree of flexibility in delivering various IT resources to meet business demands [1]. It provides flexibility to its users as they only pay for the services they use and also provides benefits like improved availability and cost reduction. As per the National Institute of Standards and Technology, cloud computing is a platform for providing a number of computing resources on-demand that are easily accessible to its users i.e., networks, storage applications, servers, and services that are easily managed and maintained by the service provider [2].

Cloud computing is an example of successful service-oriented computing. IaaS (Infrastructure as a Service), PaaS (Platform as a Service) and SaaS (Software as a Service) are three of its paradigms. It helps in providing everything from hardware resources, the software required and datasets, etc. to data analysts. Its ability to provide and manage resources with ease makes it ideal to store and analyze big data. Big data has the potential to be analyzed for valuable information, to optimize performance in transforming modern society. It refers to the various sorts of data, such as structured, unstructured, and semi-structured data. Big data

[a]jaspreet.bajaj@chitkara.edu.in, [b]naveen.sharma@chitkara.edu.in,
[c]rajesh.kaushal@chitkara.edu.in, [d]kamal.saluja@chitkara.edu.in

is defined in general terms by the five V's: Volume, Velocity, Variety, Veracity and Values [3]. Big data is defined as data that exists in huge volumes, consists of different types of data structures for storage and forms new bits of data daily very quickly which when processed helps in decision-making, finding new insights and optimizing processes [4].

Cloud computing platform helps in solving both the storage and the computational demands of various applications that involve big data analytics. The analysis is done using specific technologies that have been designed to handle such huge amounts of data. Big data analytics makes use of data analysis algorithms that require hardware with high-performance capabilities. Cloud computing platform is capable of providing both computational and data processing applications [5, 6]. In today's data analytics world, the MapReduce framework and its open-source implementation Hadoop are being widely adopted [7].

Furthermore, there are a number of challenges faced by cloud computing that we are going to discuss and focus on in this paper. These challenges are security issues confronting cloud service providers and security issues confronting customers, which are further classified as security issues in terms of service delivery methods. In addition, various weak spots and dangers that exist in cloud computing that led to these security problems have been identified. Due to these shortcomings, an attack might occur and the resources and the data stored can be at risk [8]. We will also discuss some potential solutions for providing security. This paper covers the basics related to cloud computing, its service deployment models, types of clouds, and benefits of cloud are also discussed along with big data and big data analytics in cloud computing using Hadoop and Map Reduce. The main focus will be on the Security challenges faced in Cloud computing.

This paper is arranged as follows: Section 2 consists of a literature review of cloud computing and big data. Section 3 discusses the relationship between big data and the cloud. Section 4 focuses on cloud computing architecture. Section 5 depicts a table discussing Security Challenges in Big data and Cloud. Section 6 potential solutions for security. Section 7 consists of the conclusion of the paper.

Literature Review

A total of 87,174 articles have been published in the last decade in various journals that helps researchers to understand the big data and cloud computing challenges and the solutions in industries specifically in developing countries. Figure 12.1 shows the publication trends from 2013 to 2022 in big data and cloud computing [9]. A total of 34 articles related to cloud computing and big data have been studied and 22 articles which were published in various journals/conferences have also been included in the study. The literature review helps to understand cloud computing deeply and know more about the challenges facing cloud computing implementation in developing countries.

Iyanda [1] discuss big data and cloud computing. Two major threats are Security and Loss of Control are put forward and both of these issues affect cloud computing. that tampers with the Benefits provided by cloud computing like flexibility, storage, time-saving and reduced cost.

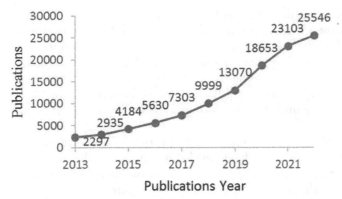

Figure 12.1 Publications trends based on big data and cloud computing

Rani et al. [2] elaborate cloud computing in depth in order to provide knowledge about the architecture, characteristics, and deployment models of cloud computing, as well as to illustrate the concept of inter-cloud on which future technologies rely, and thus discuss some issues that must be resolved for a better future.

Kumar and Chaturvedi, [3] describe big data and examine its significance in changing India into a digital India, based on the idea that vast volumes of data are available. Big data applications: The application of big data in numerous fields are discussed. Big data deployment issues and solutions, such as the Streaming algorithm and MapReduce, are suggested.

Zhang et al. [5] compared cloud computing with similar technologies like Grid computing, Virtualization, and Autonomic computing. Some Technologies used in cloud computing and products that today are being utilized in the industry are discussed. Research challenges that affect cloud computing and the need to address them for better prospects in cloud computing are put forward.

Manekar and Pradeepini [6] reviewed two technologies – one is Cloud Computing and the other is Big Data. How these technologies are being utilized in the IT industry to handle data and then deliver services of big data based on Cloud model. Using cloud depended on big data Analytics to club big data and cloud computing in one environment. Technological aspects that include Hadoop and MapReduce are put forward as a solution to the issues arising in these technologies.

Khan and Al-Yasiri [8] explains the objective of cloud computing. The framework for cloud computing adoption is also highlighted. The primary focus was on detecting current and future security concerns. The outcome was the discovery of various solutions to eradicate security problems that could affect cloud computing, so that organizations are encouraged to adopt cloud computing.

Purcell [10] talk about big data and the latest advances in technologies that are currently being used in the industry. The use of the hardware and processing resources, its installation cost to various small and medium-sized enterprises are also discussed. Reasons for companies to implement these technologies for their benefits are put forward. Major concerns regarding cloud computing are also addressed.

Fan et al. [11] discusses big data and its background. The objective of analyzing big data is put forward. The paradigm shift is discussed as we need new methods to handle big data challenges. The rise of big data and its description in various fields is discussed. The characteristics of big data that provide obstacles to data analysis are highlighted. Big data's impact on cloud computing architecture and tools such as Hadoop and Map Reduce is also highlighted. Big data issues and the necessity to eliminate them using statistical methods are also discussed.

Samuel et al. [12] outline Big Data and its classifications, i.e., big data categorization, and explore certain study fields in depth. There are also technical challenges. A table depicts some recent developments in big data research, and concerns linked to big data that need to be solved are highlighted.

Bhosale and Gadekar, [13] elaborates big data and problems with big data processing that needs to be addressed. Hadoop is put forward as an answer for big data processing and architectures of HDFS and MapReduce are also explained.

Sriram and Khajeh-Hosseini, [14] discusses Cloud computing and its Methodology in detail. Lessons from related technologies have been mentioned. Cloud computing standards and interfaces have been described. Cloud Interoperability and Novel Protocols are discussed. The description of building clouds is given and the new technologies and use cases that become possible through cloud computing are explained.

Astri [15] aims to find how certain factors affect an organization that uses cloud computing. Cloud computing is defined along with the three services that are provided in cloud computing, namely- SaaS, PaaS and IaaS. The three models of cloud computing are also discussed. Factors that impact cloud adoption in various organizations are discussed.

Assunção et al. [16] elaborates various ways for performing analytics on Clouds for an application of Big Data. The four major areas are discussed. How data is managed and stored on the cloud in different ways is explained. Storage and analysis of data using Hadoop are illustrated. The research challenges in this field, business, and non-technical challenges are discussed and the need to address those using proper tools is highlighted.

Fan and Bifet [17] discusses big data in a detailed manner. Implementations of big data in various fields are illustrated. The way in which Global Pulse is using big data for development to improve life in countries that are still not fully developed is discussed. Some Contributions are mentioned that show traditional research in big data mining. Controversies involving big data are mentioned in brief. Tools like Hadoop, MOA, and Vowpal wabbit are put forward. The challenges that could arise in Big Data in the future are discussed briefly.

Abouzeid et al. [18] explains the Hadoop and map reduced systems and how they are being utilized in today's industry for data analysis. The desired properties of a system designed for performing data analysis are mentioned. Background and shortfalls of available approaches are also mentioned. Hadoop's implementation background and its components are discussed. Hadoop is compared with two benchmarked systems and also concludes that HadoopDB is a hybrid parallel Database system and always approaches the analysis of data.

Relationship Between Big Data and Cloud Computing

The term big data implies that the datasets are too large that the current systems in the industry do not have the capability to store and analyze these datasets. There are huge volumes of data that are emerging in the current market, this data comes in many forms namely structured, unstructured and semi-structured data, also data comes from many different sources that include email, social networks, historical information, e-Governance services, medical hospitals, banks, business transactions media houses, defense and corporate sectors and from sensors like CCTV. Storing and analyzing big data presents a big challenge to the IT industry. The following featured the relationship between big data to the cloud.

1) The most common model used for storing big data is known as clustered Network-Attached Storage.
2) A number of computers are connected to a single computer in the network-attached storage (NAS) pod used as the (NAS) device [10].
3) Several NAS pods are connected together through the computer used as the NAS device. It is an expensive model to implement in practice. Cloud services provide a better prospect at substantially lower costs.
4) The analysis of big data is performed by a software framework called Map Reduce. In Map Reduce, two functions take a key part in the process of data analysis; they are known as a map and reduce functions.
5) The map function accepts key/value pairs as input and returns an intermediate set of key/value pairs as output; the Reduce function blends that output with the task/query to be implemented and returns the reduced result as the final output.
6) The mapping is performed by every NAS device separately; it requires processing to be done in a parallelized manner. Processing in a parallel manner in Map Reduce is expensive. The Cloud Computing environment provides a better platform for the processing needs of the data at much lower cost.

Cloud Computing Architecture

The architecture of cloud is depicted by the following divided into 4 layers as shown in Figure 12.2. The hardware layer, also known as the data center layer, maintains the cloud's physical resources such as servers, switches, cooling systems, and power. This layer is typically implemented in many data storage sources. This layer may confront issues such as fault tolerance, congestion control, and utility resource management.

The virtualization layer is identified as the infrastructure layer that takes a number of resources for storing and fulfilling computational needs, it is done by splitting the resources available by making use of the technologies available in the market such as VMware, Xen and KVM [5]. This layer is a key part of cloud computing as it provides capabilities like dynamic resource management, which is possible through virtualization.

Operating systems and application frameworks are found on the platform layer, which is located above the infrastructure layer. The platform layer's primary goal is to reduce the workload of integrating apps directly into VM containers. The application layer is topmost layer in the hierarchy, it contains the real-time cloud

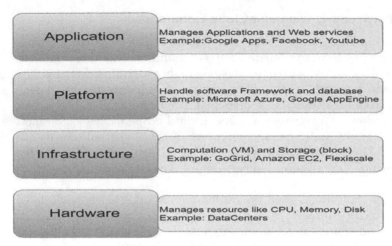

Figure 12.2 Architecture of cloud computing

applications which offer scalability, on-demand access and pay as per daily usage in the cloud computing environment that help to achieve better performance at lower costs.

Security Challenges in Big Data and Cloud Computing

There are numerous challenges faced during the implementation of cloud computing and big data specifically in developing countries. It is very difficult for the low-income nations to perform the cloud computing remotely by using big data. These challenges are to be discussed in Table 12.1 [16, 19]. The possible solutions have also been discussed to provide the solution of the following challenges.

Challenges Faced in Big Data and Cloud Computing

Plethora of research have been done by the research community to provide the solution of the challenges faced in big data and cloud computing. The potential solutions for security are as follows:

MetaData Cloud Storage Security Architecture: To safeguard massive data stored in the cloud from hackers, the MetaData Cloud Storage Security Architecture is proposed. Data is saved here based on its breadth and relevance [15]. Data is categorized into three dimensions Namely-Critical, Sensitive and Normal. Each category of data is stored in distinct data centers with more than one copy of similar data being stored on different places provided. MetaData Cloud Storage Interface can access the appropriate data center as per the request of the user. The log files are analyzed using AWS Cloud Trail (Amazon Web Service). The log files are delivered to an Amazon S3 bucket using AWS Cloud Trail's integrated AWS Key Management Service (KMS). It is easy to combine Cloud Trail with other applications using API. Here, datacenters will be divided into 't' parts, where each part can be represented by part r (r(s, t)). The 'u' different storage providers are responsible for storing and acknowledging them as provider q(q(s, u)). 't' will be

Table 12.1 Security challenges in big data and cloud computing.

S. No.	Security Threat	Description
1	Account Hacking	A client's account is taken over by an intruder to conduct illegal or unauthorized activities
2	Denial of service	An authorized user is denied access to the computing resources by a malicious user who has taken over all the resources for their own agenda.
3	Data Leakage	The unauthorized transfer of confidential information to the outside world.
4	Data Scavenging	The attacker tries to find confidential or sensitive data by searching through a system's data storage.
5	Customer Data manipulation	The data sent to server's application by the application module is tampered with to conduct unauthorized activities the applications. For example- SQL injection, command injection etc.
6	Eaves Dropping	A system is hacked and services like video calls, messaging, audio calls are tampered with by an intruder.
7	Hypervisor viruses	The hypervisor layer is affected by a malicious piece of code.
8	Non-trustable VM Creation	VM images are created only by an authenticated user that uses a certain virus to harm the storage places. The root cause of this is the lack of control in placing of VM images in public storage source.
9	Lack of security in VM migration	Data is accessed illegally by an attacker, the VM travels to a susceptible source by creation and migration of many VMs. It is caused by exposure of data of the VM.
10	Sniffing/Spoofing virtual networks	Virtual networks are monitored by an intruder by using VM and some of the packets are also tampered with by using ARP spoofing (location). It is caused because of sharing of virtual bridges among many networks.
11	VM Hopping	It allows one VM the right to use other VMs. This happens because there is no proper management of utilization of resources of VMs.
12	VM Escape	It affects the infrastructure (IaaS) as the hypervisor is used unfairly to take control of the complete infrastructure.
13	Authorized interception spot	It helps in analyzing the data that comprises of different types of content. The effect of losing this data to an unauthorized user will be destructive.
14	Virtual machine security	Virtualization is an important part of the cloud setup. There are a lot of threats that can affect the security of the system if proper protocols are not utilized while using the system.
15	Trusted transaction	Security is a challenge in transactions like e-business, data etc. Trust is necessary in these transactions.
16	Smartphone data slinging	Smartphones are being used to access private data that can have a harmful effect on the whole system.

S. No.	Security Threat	Description
17	Lack of Security in APIs	Cloud users make use of various services by utilizing a number of APIs. If there's a problem in these APIs, then the whole system is prone to issues like privacy, security etc.
18	Risk of Sharing Resources	For better efficiency and performance, resources are shared among many users but there is a risk to the security of the system if one system gains access to confidential information of the system.

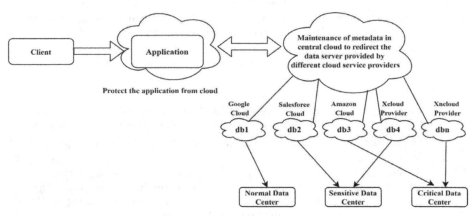

Figure 12.3 Security of big data in cloud computing

always more than 'u', the 'u' storage providers are a part of different enterprises. Various data components that are saved on particular cloud storage providers will be given access to a physical storage medium that belongs to the storage provider. A special storage path will be created by big data retained in the data center like as follows:

$$\text{Mapping Storage\_Path} = \{\text{Data}((A1(D1,D2,......DX))$$
$$(A2(D1, D2,......Dy)(An(D1, D2,......Dz)) \tag{1}$$

Where 'A' refers to the storage provider and 'D' refers to the physical storage media. The path where big data is kept is encrypted and a cryptographic value is obtained in this MetaData Cloud Storage architecture, which is known as cryptographic virtual mapping of big data, i.e. With the support of the MetaData Cloud Storage Interface, the MetaData Cloud Storage framework ensures the mapping of various data items to each storage provider [17].

The same data would be kept in many copies at various cloud storage providers to achieve high availability and robustness. Each data part's storage index information will be maintained by the system administrator so that, in the event of a malfunction, another copy of the data part can be quickly located using the storage index information. Figure 12.3 depicts the way that the user will use the application.

Encryption: Data stored in any system can be easily accessed by an unknown and unauthorized user. So, to safeguard the data everyone should encrypt the data. Various encryption techniques are utilized for different interfaces and the keys generated should be kept a secret. This will keep the data of the user secure [18].

Nodes Authentication: The node in the system should be authenticated whenever it accesses the system. If there is any doubt over node's credibility, it must not be authenticated [19].

Honeypot Nodes: These nodes seem like normal nodes but are actually traps that are placed to defend against unwanted attacks. They automatically trap the intruder and not allow for any damage of data to happen [20].

Access Control: Implementation of different access control and privacy measures in a cloud computing environment will provide a better sense of security [21].

Conclusion

Cloud computing and Big data have made a major impact on the IT industry and will continue to do so in the forthcoming future. They have changed the face of the present industry by bringing their contribution to the work being done in the industry by providing simpler and efficient solutions to every problem. In this paper, we have defined big data, discussed the relationship between cloud and big data, defined cloud computing and discussed in detail the architecture of cloud computing, its deployment models, types of cloud, characteristics, and benefits of cloud computing. The analytics of data stored in cloud provides knowledgeable patterns of data that help in making better decisions, planning and optimizing customer experience. Some challenges related to these technologies like security, costing model, etc. have also been mentioned and some approaches that can be used to overcome these challenges have been discussed. MetaData Cloud Storage Architecture has great potential to provide the perfect solution to every problem that may occur in these areas. However, more efforts need to be put in to look into that possible solution while also looking for other solutions [22]. Furthermore, other areas of research that need attention are also brought into light in the hope of finding solutions to the problems that arise in these areas and help in creating a perfect system for the industry [23].

References

1. Iyanda, O. A. (2014). Big data and current cloud computing issues and challenges. *International Journal of Advanced Research in Computer Science and Software Engineering (IJARCSSE)*, 4(6), 1192–1197.
2. Rani, B. K., Rani, B. P., and Babu, A. V. (2015). Cloud computing and inter-clouds–types, topologies and research issues. *Procedia Computer Science*, 50, 24–29.
3. Kumar, Vinay, et al. (2016). Applications of big data in the digital India: opportunities and challenges. *IRA-International Journal of Technology and Engineering*. 164–174.
4. Ji, C., Li, Y., Qiu, W., Awada, U., and Li, K. (2012). Big data processing in cloud computing environments. In 2012 12th International Symposium on Pervasive Systems, Algorithms and Networks.

5. Zhang, Q., Cheng, L., and Boutaba, R. (2010). Cloud computing: state-of-the-art and research challenges. *Journal of Internet Services and Applications*, 1(1), 7–18.
6. Manekar, A. K., and Pradeepini, G. (2015). December. cloud based big data analytics a review. In Computational Intelligence and Communication Networks (CICN), 2015 International Conference on, (pp. 785–788). IEEE.
7. Agrawal, D., Das, S., and El Abbadi, A. (2011). Big data and cloud computing: current state and future opportunities. In Proceedings of the 14th International Conference on Extending Database Technology, (pp. 530–533).
8. Khan, N., and Al-Yasiri, A. (2016). Identifying cloud security threats to strengthen cloud computing adoption framework. *Procedia Computer Science*, 94, 485–490.
9. Dimensions (2023). Timeline - Overview for Relationship be... Publication Year: 2022, 2012, 2013, 2014, 2015, 2016, 2017, 2018, 2019, 2020, 2021. Publication Type: Article in Publications - Dimensions. [Online]. Available: https://app.dimensions.ai/analytics/publication/overview/timeline?search_mode=content&search_text=Relationship between big data and cloud computing. [Accessed: 03-Feb-2023].
10. Purcell, B. M. (2014). Big data using cloud computing. *Journal of Technology Research*, 5, 1.
11. Fan, J., Han, F., and Liu, H. (2014). Challenges of big data analysis. *National Science Review*, 1(2), 293–314.
12. S. J. Samuel, K. Rvp, K. Sashidhar, and C. R. Bharathi, (2015). A survey on big data and its research challenges, *ARPN Journal of Engineering and Applied Sciences*, 10(8), 3343–3347.
13. Bhosale, H. S., and Gadekar, D. P. (2014). A review paper on big data and hadoop. *International Journal of Scientific and Research Publications*, 4(10), 1.
14. Sriram, Ilango, and Ali Khajeh-Hosseini. (2010). Research agenda in cloud technologies. arXiv preprint arXiv:1001.3259.
15. Astri, L. Y. (2015). A study literature of critical success factors of cloud computing in organizations. *Procedia Computer Science*, 59, 188–194.
16. Assunção, M. D., Calheiros, R. N., Bianchi, S., Netto, M. A., and Buyya, R. (2015). Big Data computing and clouds: trends and future directions. *Journal of Parallel and Distributed Computing*, 79, 3–15.
17. Fan, W., and Bifet, A. (2013). Mining big data: current status, and forecast to the future. *ACM sIGKDD Explorations Newsletter*, 14(2), 1–5.
18. Abouzeid, A., Bajda-Pawlikowski, K., Abadi, D., Silberschatz, A., and Rasin, A. (2009). HadoopDB: an architectural hybrid of MapReduce and DBMS technologies for analytical workloads. *Proceedings of the VLDB Endowment*, 2(1), 922–933.
19. Gopal, M., and Sriram, D. (2022). Security challenges of big data computing. *International Research Journal of Modernization in Engineering*, 4(01), 1164–1171.
20. Yang, C., Huang, Q., Li, Z., Liu, K., and Hu, F. (2017). Big data and cloud computing: innovation opportunities and challenges. *International Journal of Digital Earth*, 10(1), 13–53.
21. Sakshi, and Kukreja, V. (2023). A dive in white and grey shades of ML and non-ML literature: a multivocal analysis of mathematical expressions. *Artificial Intelligence Review*, 56(7), 7047–7135.
22. Bajaj, K., Sharma, B., and Singh, R. (2022). Comparative analysis of simulators for iot applications in fog/cloud computing. In 2022 International Conference on Sustainable Computing and Data Communication Systems (ICSCDS), (pp. 983–988).
23. Dhiman, P., Kukreja, V., Manoharan, P., Kaur, A., Kamruzzaman, M. M., Dhaou, I. B., and Iwendi, C. (2022). A novel deep learning model for detection of severity level of the disease in citrus fruits. *Electronics*, 11(3), 1–14.

13 Layout Analysis of Punjabi Newspapers Using Contour Detection and Deep Learning-Based Model

Atul Kumar[1,a] and Gurpreet Singh Lehal[2,b]

[1]Department of Computer Science,R.G.M. Government College, Joginder Nagar, HP, India

[2]Department of Computer Science,Punjabi UniversityPatiala,Punjab, India

Abstract

Layout analysis of the newspaper to segment the newspaper image into various text and graphic regions. Various applications of layout analysis are used in OCR to identify text. Various types of research are proposed for other language newspaper layouts. In this paper, we have performed the layout analysis of Punjabi newspapers. We used contour detection to detect the images in the newspaper and the results obtained are newspaper images without graphics. Then the images are fed into a pre-trained detection-based layout parser model to detect the layout of Punjabi newspapers. This results in corrected blocks of newspaper regions with an F score of 96.76%.

Keywords: Layout, newspaper, segmentation

Introduction

The ascent of digital media has resulted in a waning interest in print newspapers, but they remain a crucial source of information for a large population in many regions of the world. Punjabi newspapers, in particular, are widely read in Punjab, India, and other Punjabi-speaking regions. However, the layout of these newspapers can be complex and varied, making it challenging to extract useful information automatically. Page segmentation can be summed up as follows: geometrical analysis, which identifies blocksof same type in documents such ascolumns containing photographs, tables, advertisements, paragraphsetc., and logical analysis, which classifies blocks in various groups based on features of, such as headlines, articles, and subtitles. The layout is basically of two types: Manhattan that have structures in which text, pictures are separated from each other with help of vertical and horizontal lines forming shapes like rectangle and non-Manhattan have erratic structures. Over the last few years, various researchers have developed many techniques to analyze the layout of newspapers, but few studies have focused on Punjabi newspapers. This paper aims to address this gap by using contour detection and pre-trained deep learning-based models to analyze the layout of Punjabi newspapers. Contour detection is a widely used technique in image processing that involves detecting the boundaries of objects in an image. In this paper, we used contour detection to find image regions of a newspaper page. We then separate the image regions and use

[a]atulkmr02@gmail.com, [b]gslehal@gmail.com

a deep learning-based pre-trained model to classify the remaining. The results of this paper provide insights into the layout of Punjabi newspapers and could help improve the efficiency of information extraction and **retrieval from** these newspapers

Related Work

Numerous methods have been created for this task in the past thanks to notable research in computer vision on layout analysis of newspapers. The techniques mentioned above can be roughly split into two groups: top-down and bottom-up strategies. Top-down approaches rely on prior knowledge of the layout and structure of newspaper pages to guide the analysis process. These approaches typically involve modeling the layout of a newspaper page using a set of rules and then using this model to identify and extract the various components of the page. Bottom-up approaches, on the other hand, use data-driven methods to analyze the layout of newspaper pages. These approaches often entail examining the visual characteristics of the page, such as the color, texture, and shape of the individual components, and then using this data to recognize and extract the distinct page components. In recent years, deep learning techniques have been applied to the problem of newspaper layout analysis with great success. These techniques involve training a neural network to identify and extract the various components of a newspaper page, using a large dataset of labelled examples. Deep learning approaches have shown promising results in a variety of tasks, including headline detection, text segmentation, and object recognition.

One of the main challenges in newspaper layout analysis is the variability of newspaper layouts across different newspapers and editions due to differences in the style and format of the newspaper and in the content and layout of individual articles. To address this challenge, researchers have developed techniques for robust and adaptive layout analysis, which can adapt to the specific characteristics of each newspaper or edition. For document layout analysis, Singh and Kumar[1] suggested a hybrid bottom-up and top-down approach that was effectively used on the intricate newspaper and magazine pages. A hybrid method based on complicated layout analysis and contour tracing was developed by Vasilopoulos and Ergina [2]. Based on mean grey values and extreme grey values, Manuel andNicolás [3]choose the best binarization threshold, then swapped gray level for an automatic analysis. For comparison ofdeep-learning models,gradient boosting and RIPPER, (Gutehrlé and Atanassova [4] proposed a rule-based approach. Du [5]showcased one of the greatest neural network representations, YOLO, which defies CNN family tradition and invents a method for handling the detection of objectproblem in the most straightforward and effective manner possible.Ren et al., [6]developed a region proposal network (RPN) which used full-image convolutional features with neural network for detection. Barman et al., [7]devised a multimodal method that integrates textual and visual cues for the semantic segmentation of old newspapers resulting in multimodal model improvement.

Introduction to Punjabi Newspapers

Punjabi newspaper contains the following important entities: Text: A textarea-composedof lettersthat areapproximately equal orsmallerthan theupperletter heightofthe newspaper image,

Title: A text areacomposedof lettersthat are higherthan theupperletterheight of the newspaper, Graphic/Drawing/Photo/Pics: Area containing pictures, **graphics, advertisements**

Problems in Punjabi Newspaper Layout

Punjabi newspaper layout analysis may encounter a number of issues. Among the typical ones are: 1)If a newspaper article contains photos, it is required to divide the text from the photographs in order to segment the columns and lines further. This is because images can span two or more columns, obviating the need for continuous white lines to distinguish the columns.2)Lack of uniformity: Punjabi newspapers do not have a single layout format, and each publication may have a different layout. Because of this, creating an algorithm that can precisely assess and extract information from Punjabi newspaper layouts might be difficult.3) Gurmukhi script is intricate and can be challenging for automated systems to recognize, especially when the font is not standard. Errors in text recognition and layout analysis may result from this.4) Text orientation: Because Punjabi text can be written either vertically or horizontally, it might be challenging for algorithms to determine the right orientation and accurately extract the content.5)Images and graphics are frequently used in Punjabi newspapers to convey information,

Figure 13.1 Punjabi Newspaper entities

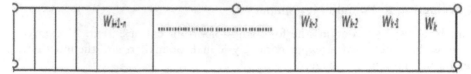

Figure 13.2 First N pixels for pixel Wk

making it difficult for automated systems to assess and extract information from them.6) Text overlap: In some Punjabi newspaper layouts, text may overlap, making it challenging for an algorithm to distinguish between various portions and effectively extract information.7) A significant quantity of advertisements might make it challenging to recognize and extract essential information from **Punjabi** newspapers' layouts.

Methodology

In order to segment this complex structure, we have developed a methodology that is based on the following steps:

1) Collection of Punjabi newspaper image. 2) Perform pre-processing task on the scanned image, 3) Find contours detection, 4) Run deep learning pre-trained model based on Mask rnn and faster **rcnn, 5)Get the segmented image.**

Data Collection, Pre-processing, and Binarization
We have collected Punjabi newspaper images from the Punjabi tribune newspapers [8]. Around 116 images were collected of different complex layouts. These newspaper images are binarized using a technique based on moving averages. There are various methods in literature that used local thresholding for binarization [9, 10]. We used moving averages method for the binariza**tion of Punjabi newspaper images.**

Moving Average Calculation
In this method to calculate a moving average of j pixels, iterate through the image both left to right and top to bottom assuming length of moving block is j [3].

The moving verage at point Wk is givenby

$$\text{Movavg}(k) = \text{Movavg}(k-1) + 1/n\ (Wk - Wk - n - 1) \tag{1}$$

Equation **(1) is valid** when k ≥ n -1

Contour Detection

In this step, algorithm named follow border [11]is implementedon the newspaper image and external contours are calculatedforthe connected components. The algorithm makes the adjacency tree for the binary newspaper image by labelling of borders, we have used the OpenCV to detect the contours of the binarized image **as this is available in OpenCV.**

Figure 13.3 Binarization of Punjabi newspaper images

Algorithm to remove Images

Step 1: Firstly, find the height of the contour and calculate the average height. Step 2: Then Contours with average height > 6 are then converted to whitespace Step 3: These are basically the graphics, pics, or art of the Punjabi newspaper image. Step 4: The final is extractedwhich contains only text columns of newspaper images and graphics are eliminated. Step 5 Basically, height is selected between 6 to 15 Step 6: The output image is obtained by subtraction of image having **graphics with original** image.

Figure 13.4(a) Original image (b). Binarized image (c). Finding contours

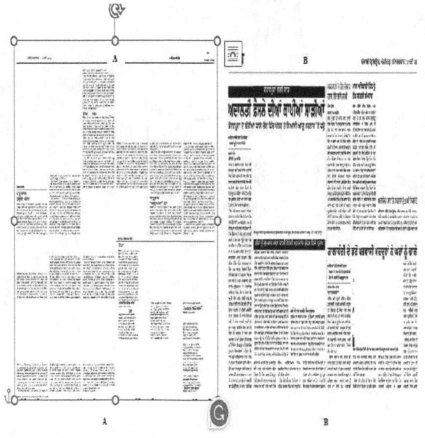

Figure 13.5 a and bare Images of newspapers having eliminated graphics

Layout Analysis of Image

Deep neural network structures that are being investigated for document layout segmentation are described in this section. We have a layout parser library

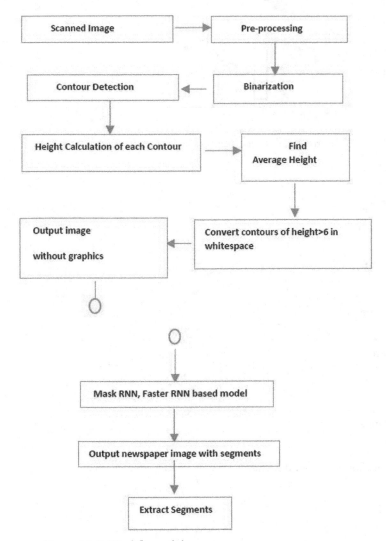

Figure 13.6 Workflow of the system

for detecting the layout. This library is based on Faster RCNN, mask RNN, and trained on the world's largest dataset of newspapers PRIMA Layout and PublayNet[12]. Faster R-CNN produces two outputs for each candidate object: label for class and a bounding-box offset [13]. This model by Mikaela [14] seeks to directly extract recommendations for classification and localization through the Region proposal network (RPN) by using the final convolutional layer of the backbone as a feature map. Mask R-CNN is an architecture, which expands more quickly as R-CNN by combining the branch for bounding box recognition with the branch for object mask prediction. Mask R-CNN is easy for training and only have an overhead to five frames in one second. Mask R-CNN is also simple to **generalize** to various problems.

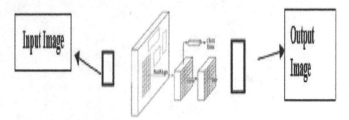

Figure 13.7 The architecture of a mask R-CNN

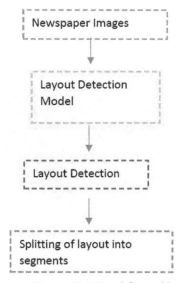

Figure 13.8 Workflow of layout detection

Detectron 2

The future-oriented library from Facebook AI Research, Detectron2 [16], offers cutting-edge algorithms for detection and segmentation purpose. It is the follow-up toDetectron and mask rcnnbenchmark. Firstly we used Detectron2 model built by Facebook AI research. Detectron2 hasmany algorithms for detection of objects like Mask RCNN, Faster RCNN, RPN, and many more [16]. We used layout parser library (Shen et al.,2021) for newspaper analysis that includes 1)Deep learning models for tasks like text detection, structure identification,2)An extensive collection of already-trained neural network models 3)Complete tools for effective data annotation on document images and model adjustment to accommodate various levels of customization.

Detectron2LayoutModel uploaded which is the base layout model for all models.LayoutParser utilizes pre-trained models based on Detectron2, such as Faster R-CNN, RetinaNet, and Mask R-CNN, to detect the layout of the input document. We have used the mask_rcnn_R_50_FPN_3x model trained on the prima layout data set [15] and PubLayNet [12].The main purpose of creating this data-set is to primarily evaluate layout analysis methods, both physical and logical in nature. It includes documents with variety of layouts that illustrate many difficul-ties in analysis of layout.

Configuration of Model

The configuration of the model is specified using several parameters:1) config_path: This parameter specifies the path to the model configuration file, which defines the architecture and hyperparameters. In this case, the configuration file is loaded from the Prima Layout model catalog, which is a collection of pre-trained models provided by Layout Parser.2) label_map: This parameter specifies a map-ping between the class labels used by the deep learning model and the names of the layout regions they represent. Our model has two classes: 1 for text regions and 2 for image regions as other graphics are eliminated in previous step.3) extra_config: This parameter specifies additional configuration options for the deep learning model. In this case, we set the minimum score threshold for object

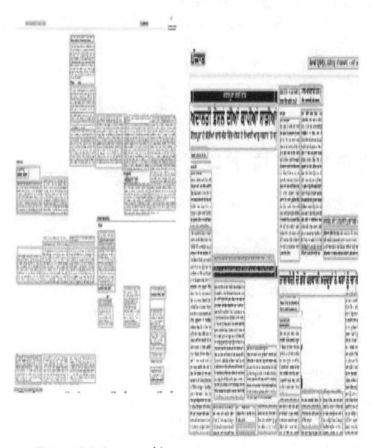

Figure 13.9 Segmented images

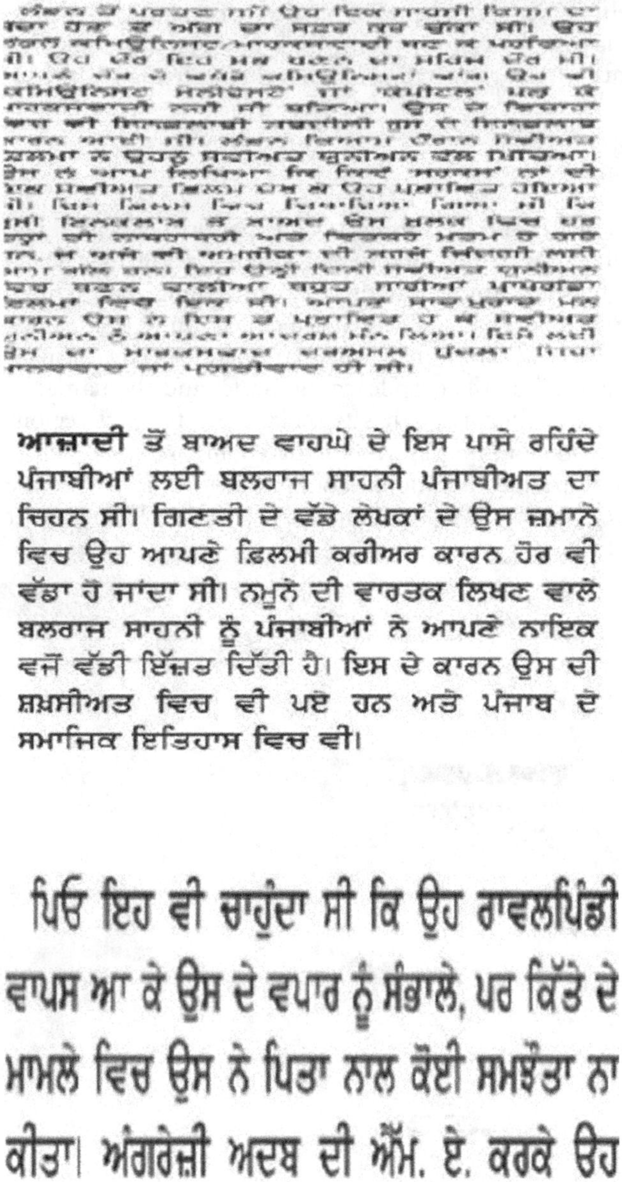

ਆਜ਼ਾਦੀ ਤੋਂ ਬਾਅਦ ਵਾਹਧੇ ਦੇ ਇਸ ਪਾਸੇ ਰਹਿੰਦੇ ਪੰਜਾਬੀਆਂ ਲਈ ਬਲਰਾਜ ਸਾਹਨੀ ਪੰਜਾਬੀਅਤ ਦਾ ਚਿਹਨ ਸੀ। ਗਿਣਤੀ ਦੇ ਵੱਡੇ ਲੇਖਕਾਂ ਦੇ ਉਸ ਜਮਾਨੇ ਵਿਚ ਉਹ ਆਪਣੇ ਫ਼ਿਲਮੀ ਕਰੀਅਰ ਕਾਰਨ ਹੋਰ ਵੀ ਵੱਡਾ ਹੋ ਜਾਂਦਾ ਸੀ। ਨਮੂਨੇ ਦੀ ਵਾਰਤਕ ਲਿਖਣ ਵਾਲੇ ਬਲਰਾਜ ਸਾਹਨੀ ਨੂੰ ਪੰਜਾਬੀਆਂ ਨੇ ਆਪਣੇ ਨਾਇਕ ਵਜੋਂ ਵੱਡੀ ਇੱਜ਼ਤ ਦਿੱਤੀ ਹੈ। ਇਸ ਦੇ ਕਾਰਨ ਉਸ ਦੀ ਸ਼ਖ਼ਸੀਅਤ ਵਿਚ ਵੀ ਪਏ ਹਨ ਅਤੇ ਪੰਜਾਬ ਦੇ ਸਮਾਜਿਕ ਇਤਿਹਾਸ ਵਿਚ ਵੀ।

ਪਿਓ ਇਹ ਵੀ ਚਾਹੁੰਦਾ ਸੀ ਕਿ ਉਹ ਰਾਵਲਪਿੰਡੀ ਵਾਪਸ ਆ ਕੇ ਉਸ ਦੇ ਵਪਾਰ ਨੂੰ ਸੰਭਾਲੇ, ਪਰ ਕਿੱਤੇ ਦੇ ਮਾਮਲੇ ਵਿਚ ਉਸ ਨੇ ਪਿਤਾ ਨਾਲ ਕੋਈ ਸਮਝੌਤਾ ਨਾ ਕੀਤਾ। ਅੰਗਰੇਜ਼ੀ ਅਦਬ ਦੀ ਐੱਮ. ਏ. ਕਰਕੇ ਉਹ

Figure 13.10 Segmented Text blocks stored as images

detection to 0.3, which means that only objects with a score above this threshold will be considered. Once the model is instantiated, it can be used to perform layout analysis tasks on an input document image to detect the layout elements in an image. This return a layout object, which is a data structure in Layout Parser that represents the detected layout elements and their spatial relationships. This contains co-ordinates of bounding boxes, text blocks and layouts. The layout segmentation of the image in Figure 13.9 shows text blocks and corresponding x-y coordinates are stored.

We have counted the number of blocks of text regions and also detected the x-y coordinates of all blocks for segmentation purpose. These blocks are then stored for recognition purpose. There are total 40 blocks in Figure 13.9. Some of the samples are shown in Figure 13.10.

Experiments, Results, and Discussion

We have tested this approach on a large number of various newspaper Punjabi newspapers and layouts of these newspaper images were generated. This technique generates very good results. A large number of multi-columns Punjabi newspapers layout are handled by this technique.

As we have tested the result on Punjabi newspaper images. Based on the results mask RNN architecture on prima layout gives good results with accuracy.

The Number of Corrected Segments

From the results, we can conclude that the when we remove images from newspaper having and apply Mask Rcnn architecture on prima layout (Prima., 2014), achieved high accuracy, precision, recall, and F-measure in segmenting the blocks of Punjabi newspapers using contour detection and deep learning-based models. Out of the 3043 actual blocks, 2945 blocks were correctly segmented, resulting in an accuracy of 96.77%. The precision and recall values indicate that the model was successful in correctly identifying the blocks. The F-measure of 0.9677 suggests that the proposed method achieved a good balance between precision and recall. Overall, the findings of this study suggest that contour detection and deep

Figure 13.11 Segmentation results on mask rnn R50 on PublayNet

Table 13.1 Performance comparison of various deep learning architectures for Punjabi newspapers.

Architecture used	Data used	No of newspaper pages	Actual blocks	Correct segmented blocks	Wrong segmented blocks	Results of segmented newspaper
Maskrcnn	Prima layout	116	3043	2945	98	96.77%
Maskrcnn R-50	PubLayNet	116	3043	2113	930	69.44%
Fasterrcnn R-50	PubLayNet	116	3043	1926	1117	63.29%
Maskrcnn X-101	PubLayNet	116	3043	2238	805	73.54%

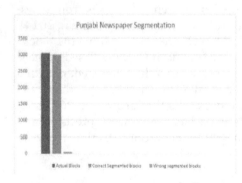

A: mask_rcnn_R_50_FPN_3x(Prima layout DataSet)

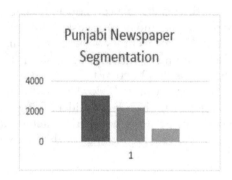

B: mask_rcnn_R_50_FPN_3x(Prima layout DataSet)

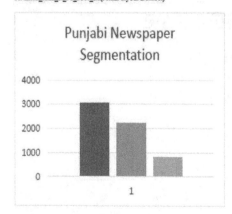

C: faster_rcnn_R_50_FPN_3(PubLayNet)

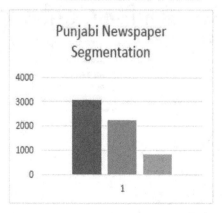

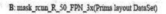

D: mask_rcnn_X_101_32x8d_FPN_3x (PubLayNet)

Figure 13.12 Graphs showing layout segmentation based on RCNN, MaskRNNar-chitecture

Table 13.2 Evaluation metric for mask-RCNN

Evaluation metric	Value
Accuracy	96.77
Precision	96.77%
Recall	0.96779
F-measure	96.769

learning-based models can be effective methods for analyzing and segmenting blocks of Punjabi newspapers, which can have applications in various fields such as information extraction and content analysis, especially for Punjabi newspapers.

Conclusion

Punjabi Newspaper layout segmentation is an essential pre-processing step in many documents analysis works such as optical character recognition (OCR), retrieving information, and content-based image retrieval. In OCR, we have to retrieve text but due to the complex layout, it is very difficult to achieve good results. We have conducted experiments using the Mask R-CNN architecture which is trained on the world's largest dataset Prima layout dataset and the PubLayNet dataset [12]gave the best results with 96.77% accuracy on Punjabi newspaper images after removing graphics from newspaper using contour detection approach. Other architectures tested include Faster R-CNN and mask R-CNN, which had lower accuracy rates on the same dataset. Overall, deep neural network such as mask R-CNN and Faster R-CNN have proven to be effective for Punjabi Newspaper layout segmentation. These architectures can be used for other complex layout newspapers that are very helpful for text recognition from newspaper images

Acknowledgement

The authors gratefully acknowledge the students, staff, and authority of Computer Science department, Punjabi University for theircooperation in the research.

References

1. Singh, V., and Kumar, B. (2014). Document layout analysis for Indian newspapers using contour based symbiotic approach. In 2014 International Conference on Computer Communication and Informatics, pp. 1–4. Coimbatore, India: IEEE. https://doi.org/10.1109/ICCCI.2014.6921723.
2. Vasilopoulos, N. and Ergina, K. (2017). Complex layout analysis based on contour classification and morphological operations. Engineering Applications of Artificial Intelligence 65, 220–29. https://doi.org/10.1016/j.engappai.2017.08.002.
3. Manuel, D. and Nicolás, S. (2022). Binarization Based on Maximum and Average Gray Values. In Digital Image Processing Applications, (ed.) P.E. Ambrosio,1–19. IntecOpen.

4. Gutehrlé, N. and Atanassova, I.(2022). Processing the structure of documents: logical layout analysis of historical newspapers in French. Journal of Data Mining and Digital Humanities. http://doi.org/10.46298/jdmdh.9093.

5. Du, J. (2018). Understanding of object detection based on CNN Family and YOLO. Journal of Physics: Conference Series 1004, 1, 12-29. https://doi.org/10.1088/1742-6596/1004/1/012029.

6. Ren, S., Kaiming, H., Ross , G. and Sun, J. (2017). Faster R-CNN: Towards Real-Time Object Detection with Region Proposal Networks. IEEE Transactions on Pattern Analysis and Machine Intelligence. 39 (6): 1137–39.https://doi.org/10.1109/TPAMI.2016.2577031.

7. Barman, R., Ehrmann, M., Clematide, S., Oliveira, S. A., & Kaplan, F. (2021). Combining visual and textual features for semantic segmentation of historical newspapers. Journal of Data Mining & Digital Humanities, HistoInformatics (HistoInformatics),6107.https://doi.org/10.46298/jdmdh.6107.

8. Tribune Trust2023. Punjabi Tribune online. https://epaper.punjabitribuneonline.com/ (accessed April 12, 2023).

9. Sauvola, J., and M. Pietikäinen. 2000. "Adaptive Document Image Binarization." Pattern Recognition 33 , no. 2: 225–36. https://doi.org/10.1016/S0031-3203(99)00055-2.

10. Niblack, W. 1986. An introduction to Digital Image Processing. Prentice-Hall international.

11. Suzuki, S. and be, K.(1985). Topological structural analysis of digitized binary images by border following." Computer Vision, Graphics, and Image Processing, 30, no. 1(April): 32-46. https://doi.org/10.1016/0734-189X(85)90016-7.

12. Zhong, X., Jianbin T., and Antonio J., Y. (2019). PubLayNet: Largest Dataset Ever for Document Layout Analysis." In 2019 International Conference on Document Analysis and Recognition (ICDAR), 1015–22. https://doi.org/10.1109/ICDAR.2019.00166.

13. He, K., Gkioxari, G., Dollar, P., and Girshick, R. (2017). Mask r-cnn. In 2017 IEEE International Conference on Computer Vision (ICCV), 2980–2988. https://doi.org/10.1109/ICCV.2017.322

14. Mikaela, F. 2022. Layout Analysis on modern Newspapers using the Object Detection model Faster R-CNN. PhD diss., Kth Royal Institute Of Technology.

15. Shen, Z., Zhang, R., Dell, M., Lee, B. C. G., Carlson, J., and Li, W. 2021. Layout-parser: A unified toolkit for deep learning-based document image analysis. In 2021 Document Analysis and Recognition – ICDAR 2021, ed. J. Lladós, D. Lopresti, and S. Uchida, 131–146. Springer International Publishing. https://doi.org/10.1007/978-3-030-86549-8_9

16. Yuxin, W., Kirillov, A., Massa, F., Lo,W., and Girshick,R. (2019).Detectron2. https://github.com/facebookresearch/detectron2 (accessed on April 13, 2023).

17. Bridson D., Papadopoulos C., and Pletschacher S. (2009). A realistic dataset for performance evaluation of document layout analysis. In 2009 10th International Conference on Document Analysis and Recognition, 296–300. IEEE https://ᵈoi.org/10.1109/ICDAR.²009.271.

14 A framework for initial detection of diabetes via machine learning

Abid Farooq[1,a], Gaurav Kumar[1,b], Dr. Anamir Yousuf Bhat[2,c], Dr. Khursheed Ahmad Dar[3,d], MD Alike[1,e] and Akeel Farooq[1,f]

[1]Lovely Professional University

[2]Govt. Degree College Boys Anantnag J&K

[3]Assistant Professor, Govt. Degree College Anantnag, J&K, India

Abstract

Around the world, millions of individuals suffer from the chronic illness diabetes. Early identification and management understanding of the illness is essential for avoiding its complications. In this research, we propose a framework for early finding diabetes using machine learning (ML) techniques. The framework consists of several stages, including the gathering, pre-processing, feature extraction, assessment, and training of data for designs. Data for this study was obtained from a substantial source, a diverse population, and includes various demographic, clinical, and laboratory information. The pre-processing stage involved cleaning and formatting the data to ensure consistency and accuracy. Feature extraction was performed to recognize the most relevant information for diabetes prediction. Machine learning models such as Support Vector Machine (SVM), and K-Nearest Neighbors (KNN) were instructed to evaluate models using a variety of metrics to find the top-performing model. The results of this study demonstrate that the proposed framework is effective in the early detection of diabetes and can potentially improve the control of illness. This data set is publicly in Kaggle. There are eight features in this data set that are often included in a dataset for diabetes analysis. Pregnancies, Glucose, Blood Pressure, Skin Thickness, Insulin, BMI, Diabetes Pedigree Function, Age. These variables can be applied to create prediction models that can recognize individuals who have a higher risk of getting diabetes or who have already received an analysis of diabetes.

Keywords: Data preparation, diabetes, machine learning, predictive modeling, risk prediction

Introduction

Diabetes is a chronic condition characterized by aberrations in insulin synthesis, insulin action, or equality which led to elevated blood glucose levels. With millions of victims globally, it is one of the most common non-communicable illnesses [1]. Diabetes is associated with a number of disorders, some of which can result in major health difficulties, including heart disease, renal failure, blindness, and inferior limb amputations [2]. Research in the field of diabetes aims to understand the underlying causes of the disease, identify risk factors, and develop

[a]abidfarooq129@gmail.com, [b]gaurav.20323@lpu.co.in, [c]aamirbhat233@outlook.com, [d]Khursheed.azam@gmail.com, [e]mdalirezamar0786@gmail.com, [f]akeel.12001185@lpu.in

new treatments and management strategies. This includes studies on genetics, epigenetics, and metabolic pathways, as well as clinical trials of new drugs and therapies [3]. Additionally, research in diabetes also includes the development of new technologies such as continuous glucose monitoring systems and artificial pancreas, which are aimed at improving diabetes management and the value of life for those with diabetes. Big data, artificial intelligence, and machine learning (ML) consume all remained progressively used in diabetes research. By using an innovative method, enormous amounts of data may be processed and designs can be found, which can lead to more personalized treatment and more accurate predictions of diabetes complications [4]. There are three primary forms of diabetes. Types 1, 2, and gestational diabetes [5]. The body's defense mechanism seeks out and destroys the insulin-creating cells of the pancreas in autoimmune type 1 diabetes conditions [6]. Children and young people are most often the ones who get this kind of diabetes. Almost 90% of instances of diabetes are type 2, making it the most prevalent kind. It is frequently linked to sedentary behavior and obesity, although genetics and other factors may also play a role. In type 2 The body develops an immunity to insulin in type 2 diabetes, making it incapable of efficiently using it. In diabetes, the body becomes resistant to insulin and is unable to use it properly [7]. Diabetes of this kind, known as gestational diabetes, normally disappears after the birth of the child. Type 2 diabetes is more possible to strike women who have gestational diabetes in the future. Diabetes signs include frequent urination, excessive thirst, hunger, exhaustion, impaired vision, and coiled and bruise healing. Diabetes, if uncontrolled, can outcome in catastrophic side effects such as heart disease, stroke, renal failure, and sightlessness. According to International Diabetes World Records, India's population is overhead 1.3 billion, and 77 million of those individuals have diabetes [9]. This disease is responsible for an estimated 1.5 million mortality in the country. Diabetes may be prevented and treated earlier in life, which drops mortality. Due to the simplicity, and precision transparency of machine learning technology, it has recently been used in medical study has resulted in the development of several algorithms that can detect diabetes early [10]. In the sector of medical research, machine learning has an extensive range of uses, counting the development and production of new drugs, and analysis of medical imaging and electronic health records. Several algorithms gross been developed to predict diabetes, including KNN, SVM, and collective learning. In order to anticipate results, many learning algorithms appealed to the PIMA diabetes dataset, which included numerous characteristics. By identifying the closest neighbors the KNN's performance was employed to handle classification and regression issues [11].

Literature Review

This literature review focuses on the application of standard machine learning algorithms to estimate the existence of diabetes mellitus. Many investigations in this field have been carried out, using various computational approaches to abstract knowledge from medicinal data. For occurrence, Faisal created a predictive analytic model utilizing the KNN, while Acidizing utilized 10-fold cross-validation to test four distinct algorithms (SVM, KNN, DT, XG Boost, and (Hybrid). The hybrid model was found to have a higher accuracy of 81.17% related to other algorithms [12]. Chun Liutilized different algorithms such as to predict diabetes mellitus and use SVM, KNN, DT, XG Boost, and Hybrid models at an early stage. Machine learning algorithms and statistical data are currently being implemented in the healthcare domain to better understand diseased data. The effectiveness of different algorithms can be compared based on their speed in giving the prediction results [13]. Datamining procedures have also been used to forecast and examine diabetes mellitus. In this study, four data mining techniques were applied, and information from provided datasets was collected and used from real-world datasets. Inappropriately cross-validation techniques were not used to assess how algorithms stayed categorized. This study involved analyzing actual diagnostic medical data using different machine-learning methods to classify and foresee diabetes mellitus based on numerous risk factors [14].

The present scenario has shown the increased threats represented by respiratory illnesses like chronic obstructive pulmonary disease (COPD), asthma, etc. That risk has increased due to an increase in air pollutants like PM2.5, PM10, etc. A respirator can be utilized as an immediate countermeasure on an individual level safety measure as bringing down pollution levels require a much longer time than the severity of the problem is allowing [15].

In recent times, the operation of machine literacy algorithms for the early discovery and vaticination of diabetes mellitus has gained significant attention in the medical and exploration communities. Experimenters have employed colorful computational ways and data mining styles to prize precious perceptivity from medical data, thereby abetting in the opinion and operation of diabetes. Several studies have concentrated on developing accurate prophetic models using different algorithms and approaches. For case, Faisal's work demonstrated the effectiveness of the k- nearest neighbors (KNN) algorithm in erecting a prophetic logical model for diabetes mellitus. By exercising the KNN algorithm, Faisal was suitable to achieve noteworthy prophetic delicacy, thereby showcasing the eventuality of this algorithm in diagnosing the complaint. This approach highlights the significance of exploring different machine literacy ways to identify the most suitable bone for the specific dataset and problem sphere.

Proposed Methodology

To accomplish our objective, our methodology involves numerous steps. We first gather datasets containing various attributes of patients and then pre-process the data to apply machine learning methods for predictive analysis [16].

Dataset Collection

The dataset used in this study was obtained from the Medi Path Diagnostic Center (MDC) in Mumbai, Maharashtra, India, and contains information on 769 patients diagnosed with diabetes Mellitus. The dataset includes several attributes related to diabetes mellitus, which are listed in the table below. This dataset can be collected in Kaggle shown table14.1.

Table 14.1 Dataset collection.

Pregnancies	Glucose	Blood Pressure	Skin Thickness	Insulin	BMI	Diabetes Pedigree Function	Age	Outcome
6	148	72	35	0	33.6	0.627	50	1
1	85	66	29	0	26.6	0.351	31	0
8	183	64	0	0	23.3	0.672	32	1
1	89	66	23	94	28.1	0.167	21	0
0	137	40	35	168	43.1	2.288	33	1
5	116	74	0	0	25.6	0.201	30	3
3	78	50	32	88	31	0.248	26	1
10	115	0	0	0	35.3	0.134	29	0
2	197	70	45	543	30.5	0.158	53	1
8	125	96	0	0	0	0.232	54	1

Data Pre-Processing

In order to achieve our objective, With the diabetes dataset, we performed data pre-processing. This involved converting the rare data into numerical form, which allowed us to obtain attribute stages that indicate diabetes risk. We divided a patient's age, for instance, into three collections: young (10–23 years), adult (24–49 years), and elderly (50 years and above). The weight of a patient was also divided into three ranges: less than 40 kg, 40–60 kg, and more than 60 kg. Blood pressure was also classified into three categories: regular (120/80 mmHg), low (less than 80 mmHg), and high (more than 120 mmHg) [17].

Data Partitioning

Data partitioning, a critical stage in machine learning, involves dividing a dataset into training, validation, and testing sets. Data splitting is used to assess how fit a machine learning model performs new data to avoid overfitting [18].

Training and Testing

The data set contains eight different features that a reused to analyze and predict the likelihood of diabetes in patients. These features are:

- *Entire number of times pregnant:* This feature shows how many periods a patient has been pregnant.
- *Glucose/Sugar Level:* This feature indicates the level of glucose or sugar present in a patient's bloodstream.
- *Diastolic Blood Pressure:* This feature indicates the pressure of blood in the arteries when the heart is resting.
- *Body Mass Index:* This feature indicates the ratio of the patient's weight to their height.
- *Skin Fold Thickness in mm:* This feature indicates the thickness of the skin folds on the affected role-triceps.

- *Age of patient in years:* Patient's age, in years: This chin shows the affected role age in years.
- *Diabetes Pedigree Function:* This feature indicates the probability of patients developing diabetes based on their family history.
- *Outcome:* This feature indicates whether or not a patient has been recognized with diabetes. It is the target variable that the machine learning model aims to predict based on the other seven features [19].

Machine Learning Classification Methods

After completing the data preprocessing, training, and testing stage, we applied it to predict diabetes smellitus, using 4 machine learning classification methods. Below is a brief summary of these techniques.

Support Vector Machine
An effective machine learning approach for organization and regression analysis is called the Support Vector Machine (SVM). SVM creates a hyperplane or gathering of hyperplanes in a high or endless-dimensional space, which is used for the organization of new unseen data points. SVM goes to find the best possible hyperplanes that can separate the data points of one class from another class, in such a way that the margin between two classes is maximum. The data points that are contiguous to the border on the wrong side of the margin are called support vectors. SVM can manage both linear and non-linear classification problems through the use of kernel functions, which allow it to renovate the participation data into a higher-dimensional planetary where it can be linearly separate. SVM has been usually used in several domains for example bio informatics, image classification, and transcript classification [20].

K-Nearest Neighbor
The k-nearest neighbor method is a non-parametric approach to regression and classification (KNN). This method examines the separation between the point of interest and the training dataset using the k-nearest training events in the feature space. According to the categorization approach, the constant positive integer k represents the quantity of the closest neighbors. Being sensitive to the local structure of the data makes the KNN algorithm special [21].

Decision Tree
A decision tree is an administered machine learning algorithm that frequently splits data based on a parameter, using decision nodes and leaves to represent the split and last outcome. The leaf node is labeled with an attribute and a goal value, and the initial split uses the attribute with the biggest information gain. Since they can handle a variety of data arrangements. Figure 14.1 Flow chart of Proposed Methodology provides interpretability, decision trees are frequently working in data mining [22].

XG Boost
XG Boost is a general collective machine learning algorithm used for regression and classification tasks. It is a gradient-boosting algorithm that sequentially trains

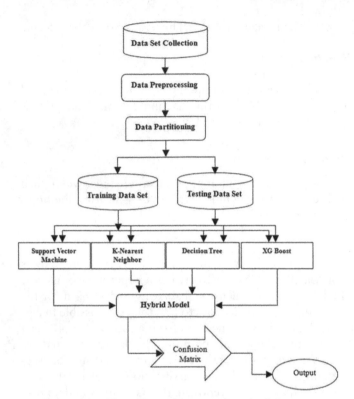

Figure 14.1 Flow chart of proposed methodology

decision trees to accurately the mistakes of the preceding trees. XG Boost uses regularization techniques and optimization algorithms to prevent overfitting and improve performance [23].

Hybrid Model
A hybrid model is a combination of two or more different models or techniques used to solve a particular problem to progress the performance of an existing model.

Figure 14.1 depicts the step-by-step process of implemented work. The initial step involved defining the problem and then preprocessing the data to construct a prediction model. Once the data was preprocessed, a training data set and testing dataset were obtained. Subsequently, machine learning techniques stayed applied datasets to generate data that would provide the performance of techniques. This enabled the identification of the best classifier (Hybrid) for predicting diabetes smellitus.

Results and Discussion

Performance Matrix
Performance metrics in machine learning are mathematical formulas that are used to estimate the correctness and effectiveness of a machine learning model. Some commonly used performance metrics are declared below

(TP = TRUE POSITIVE, TN=TRUE NEGATIVE, FP =FALSE POSITIVE, AND FN = FALSE NEGATIVE) [24].

Accuracy

Accuracy is the most basic performance metric that is used to estimate classification models. It is measured as the proportion of the model's accurate forecasts to all of its other predictions [25].

$$\text{Accuracy} = \frac{TP+TN}{TP+TN+FP+FN} \tag{1}$$

Precision

Precision is a proportion of true positive predictions made by a model of all positive predictions [26].

$$\text{Precision} = \frac{TP}{TP+FP} \tag{2}$$

Recall (also called Sensitivity)

The recall is the portion of actual positive data points that the model properly classifies as positive [27].

$$\text{Recall} = \frac{TP}{TP+FN} \tag{3}$$

F1 Score

The F1 Score is a biased average of precision and recall that is used to estimate the performance of a binary classification model [28].

$$\text{F1 Score} = 2 \times \frac{precision \times Recall}{precision + Recall} \tag{4}$$

Specificity

The percentage of real negative data instances that the model properly classifies as negative is known as specificity [29].

$$\text{Specificity} = \frac{TN}{TN+FN} \tag{5}$$

Confusion Matrix

A confusion matrix is a table used in machine learning and statistics to estimate the performance of a classification model. It is a two-dimensional matrix that précises the results of a classification task by the comparison of foreseen labels to the true labels of a set of data. The confusion matrix contains four categories: True Positives (TP), False Positives (FP), True Negatives (TN), and False Negatives (FN). TP denotes the number of properly forecast positive labels, FP denotes the number of incorrectly predicted positive labels, TN represents the number of correctly forecast negative labels, and FN represents the number of erroneously predicted negative labels. The matrix is usually presented as a table with the predicted labels along on the top and actual labels on the left side. The cells of the table contain the totals for each category, and the diagonal cells represent the correct predictions. A confusion matrix provides important information about the routine of a classification model, including procedures such as accuracy, precision, recall, and F1-score. It is normally used in a machine learning application to measure the performance of binary classifiers and multi-class classifiers. Table 14.1 shows the Confusion matrix of the SVM classifier, while Table 14.2 shows the confusion matrix of KNN and three other tables for other models. The confusion matrix provides an interruption of the number Tables 14.3 to 14.7 true positives, true negatives, false positives, and false negatives forecast by the classifier, allowing for the calculation of various performance metrics.

Table 14.2 Confusion matrix of SVM

		True Values	
		Positive	Negative
Predicted Values	Positive	97	10
	Negative	21	26

True (+ve): 97
True (-ve): 10
False(+ve): 21
False (-ve): 26

Table 14.3 Confusion matrix of KNN

		True Values	
		Positive	Negative
Predicted Values	Positive	93	14
	Negative	20	27

True (+ve): 93
True (-ve): 14
Fals (+ve): 20
False (-ve): 27

Table 14.4 Confusion matrix of Decision tree

		True Values	
		Positive	Negative
Predicted Values	Positive	95	12
	Negative	22	25

True (+ve): 95
True (-ve): 12
False(+ve): 22
False (-ve): 25

Table 14.5 Confusion matrix of XG Boost

		True Values	
		Positive	Negative
Predicted Values	Positive	95	12
	Negative	22	25

True(+ve): 95
True (-ve): 12
False(+ve): 22
False (-ve): 25

Table 14.6 Confusion matrix of Hybrid Model

Predicted Values		True Values		True(+ve.):95 True (-ve):12 False(+ve): 22 False (-ve): 25
		Positive	Negative	
	Positive	95	12	
	Negative	22	22	

Table 14.7 Performance measures of SVM, KNN, decision tree, XG boost, and hybrid model algorithm.

Model	Accuracy	Precision	Recall	F1-score	Support	Sensitivity	Specificity
Support Vector Machine	79.87	0.72	0.55	0.63	47	0.9	0.55
K-nearest Neighbours	77.57	0.66	0.57	0.61	47	0.86	0.57
Decision Tree	75.97	0.63	0.51	0.56	47	75.97	88.79
Extreme Gradient Boosting	77.92	0.68	0.53	0.60	47	0.89	0.57
Hybrid Model	81.17	0.74	0.6	0.66	47	0.88	0.53

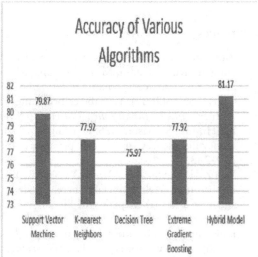

Conclusion

The testing results lead us to the conclusion that the proposed hybrid algorithm provides greater accuracy than the other methods. Those who want to avoid developing diabetes should keep their blood sugar levels steady and eat a healthy diet to maintain their insulin levels. Individuals who have a family history of diabetes should take care of themselves. The proposed hybrid algorithm achieves an accuracy of 81.17%.

Acknowledgement

We would like to extend our sincere gratitude to all those who have supported and contributed to the completion of this research paper on the application of machine learning algorithms in predicting diabetes mellitus. Their guidance, expertise, and encouragement have been invaluable throughout this journey.

First and foremost, we would like to thank our advisor Gaurav kumar for their continuous guidance and insights. His expertise in the field of machine learning and healthcare greatly shaped the direction of our research and enriched the quality of our work.

We are also deeply grateful to the participants of this study, whose willingness to share their medical data and insights has been instrumental in the development of our predictive models. Their contribution has added a real-world dimension to our research and highlighted the importance of applying machine learning in healthcare.

We would like to express our appreciation to the research community for their numerous publications and studies that have laid the foundation for our work. The extensive literature review has not only provided us with insights but also inspired us to explore new avenues of research.

In conclusion, this research would not have been possible without the collective efforts of those mentioned above. While any omissions are unintentional, please accept our sincere gratitude for your contributions to this endeavor.

References

1. Rahman, M. S., Hossain, K. S., Das, S., Kundu, S., Adegoke, E.O., Rahman, M. A., Hannan, M. A., Uddin, M. J., and Pang, M. G. (2021). Role of insulin in health and disease: an update. *International Journal of Molecular Sciences*, 22(12), 6403.
2. Tabish, S. A. (2007). Is diabetes becoming the biggest epidemic of the twenty-first century?. *International Journal of Health Sciences*, 1(2), V.
3. Fu, H., Liu, S., Bastacky, S. I., Wang, X., Tian, X. J., and Zhou, D. (2019). Diabetic kidney diseases revisited: a new perspective for a new era. *Molecular Metabolism*, 30, 250–263.
4. Wu, Z., Luo, S., Zheng, X., Bi, Y., Xu, W., Yan, J., Yang, D., and Weng, J. (2020). Use of a do-it-yourself artificial pancreas system is associated with better glucose management and higher quality of life among adults with type 1 diabetes. *Therapeutic Advances in Endocrinology and Metabolism*, 11, 2042018820950146.
5. Bluestone, J. A., Buckner, J. H., and Herold, K. C. (2021). Immunotherapy: building a bridge to a cure for type 1 diabetes. *Science*, 373(6554), 510–516.
6. Laakso, M., and Fernandes Silva, L. (2022). Genetics of type 2 diabetes: past, present, and future. *Nutrients*, 14(15), 3201.
7. Tao, J., Gao, L., Liu, Q., Dong, K., Huang, J., Peng, X., Yang, Y., Wang, H., and Yu, X. (2020). Factors contributing to glycemic control in diabetes mellitus patients complying with home quarantine during the coronavirus disease 2019 (COVID-19) epidemic. *Diabetes Research and Clinical Practice*, 170, 108514.
8. Kumar, Y., and Mahajan, M. (2020). Recent advancement of machine learning and deep learning in the field of the healthcare system. *Computational Intelligence for Machine Learning and Healthcare Informatics*, 1, 77.
9. Laslett, L. J., Alagona, P., Clark, B. A., Drozda, J. P., Saldivar, F., Wilson, S. R., Poe, C., and Hart, M. (2012). The worldwide environment of cardiovascular disease: prevalence, diagnosis, therapy, and policy issues: a report from the American College of Cardiology. *Journal of the American College of Cardiology*, 60(25S), S1–S49.
10. Xiao, C., Choi, E., and Sun, J. (2018). Opportunities and challenges in developing deep learning models using electronic health records data: a systematic review. *Journal of the American Medical Informatics Association*, 25(10), 1419–1428.
11. Salman, O. H., Taha, Z., Alsabah, M. Q., Hussein, Y. S., Mohammed, A. S., and Aal-Nouman, M. (2021). A review on utilizing machine learning technology in the fields of electronic emergency triage and patient priority systems in telemedicine: coherent taxonomy, motivations, open research challenges and recommendations for intelligent future work. *Computer Methods and Programs in Biomedicine*, 209, 106357.

12. Fitriyani, N. L., Syafrudin, M., Alfian, G., and Rhee, J. (2020). HDPM: an effective heart disease prediction model for a clinical decision support system. *IEEE Access*, 8, 133034–133050.

13. Woldemichael, F. G., and Menaria, S. (2018). Prediction of diabetes using data mining techniques. In 2018 2nd international conference on trends in electronics and informatics (ICOEI), (pp. 414–418). IEEE.

14. Rutten-van Mölken, M. P. M. H., Postma, M. J., Joore, M. A., Van Genugten, M. L. L., Leidl, R., and Jager, J. C. (1999). Current and future medical costs of asthma and chronic obstructive pulmonary disease in the Netherlands. *Respiratory Medicine*, 93(11), 779–787.

15. Allugunti, V. R. (2022). Breast cancer detection based on thermographic images using machine learning and deep learning algorithms. *International Journal of Engineering in Computer Science*, 4(1), 49–56.

16. Pfob, A., Lu, S. C., and Sidey-Gibbons, C. (2022). Machine learning in medicine: a practical introduction to techniques for data pre-processing, hyperparameter tuning, and model comparison. *BMC Medical Research Methodology*, 22(1), 1–15.

17. Carlo Curino, Evan Jones, Yang Zhang, and Sam Madden. 2010. Schism: a workload-driven approach to database replication and partitioning. Proc. VLDB Endow. 3, 1–2 (September 2010), 48–57.

18. Sonar, P., and JayaMalini, K. (2019). Diabetes prediction using different machine learning approaches. In 2019 3rd International Conference on Computing Methodologies and Communication (ICCMC), (pp. 367–371). IEEE, 2019.

19. Raja Krishnamoorthi, Shubham Joshi, Hatim Z. Almarzouki, Piyush Kumar Shukla, Ali Rizwan, C. Kalpana, Basant Tiwari, (2022). A Novel Diabetes Healthcare Disease Prediction Framework Using Machine Learning Techniques, *Journal of Healthcare Engineering*, vol. 2022, Article ID 1684017, 10. https://doi.org/10.1155/2022/1684017

20. Pandey, A., and Jain, A. (2017). Comparative analysis of KNN algorithm using various normalization techniques. *International Journal of Computer Network and Information Security*, 11(11), 36.

21. Singh, S., and Gupta, P. (2014). Comparative study ID3, cart, and C4. 5 decision tree algorithm: a survey. *International Journal of Advanced Information Science and Technology (IJAIST)*, 27(27), 97–103.

22. Ita, Kevin, and Joyce Prinze. (2023). Machine Learning for Skin Permeability Prediction: Random Forest and XG Boost Regression. *Journal of Drug Targeting just-accepted*. 1–21.

23. García, S., Fernández, A., Luengo, J., and Herrera, F. (2009). A study of statistical techniques and performance measures for genetics-based machine learning: accuracy and interpretability. *Soft Computing*, 13, 959–977.

24. Fielding, A. H., and Bell, J. F. (1997). A review of methods for the assessment of prediction errors in conservation presence/absence models. *Environmental Conservation*, 24(1), 38–49.

25. Flach, Peter, and Meelis Kull. (2015). Precision-recall-gain curves: PR analysis done right. *Advances in neural information processing systems*. 28, 838–846.

26. Tharwat, A. (2020). Classification assessment methods. *Applied Computing and Informatics*, 17(1), 168–192.

27. Chicco, D., and Jurman, G. (2020). The advantages of the Matthews correlation coefficient (MCC) over F1 score and accuracy in binary classification evaluation. *BMC Genomics*, 21(1), 1–13.

28. Allouche, O., Tsoar, A., and Kadmon, R. (2006). Assessing the accuracy of species distribution models: prevalence, kappa and the true skill statistic (TSS). *Journal of Applied Ecology*, 43(6), 1223–1232.

15 Hybrid sentiment analysis based book recommendation system

Anil Kumar[1,2,a] and Sonal Chawla[2,b]

[1]Department of Computer Science, G.G.D.S.D. College, Hariana, Hoshiarpur, Punjab, India

[2]Department of Computer Science and Applications, Panjab University, Chandigarh, India

Abstract

Information filtering is one of the research areas that focuses on filtering information for a user from a large amount of data as per his needs and preferences. The system identifies the needs and preferences of the user based on his past behaviour, which is captured primarily on the parameters of the user's profiles, likes, dislikes, ratings, reviews, and history of past items, etc. As per the literature, in order to assist users in providing the best possible recommendations for a product, user ratings and reviews play an important role. Most of the researchers have used a combination of the collaborative filtering technique and the sentiment analysis technique to explore ratings and reviews to recommend products desired by the user. However, out of the two sentiment analysis techniques, most of the researchers have focused on using either lexicon-based or machine learning-based techniques, and not much research has been conducted on the combination or hybridization of both techniques. Therefore, the objective of this paper is four folds. Firstly, the paper compares and analyses the relevance of various recommendation techniques and sentiment analysis techniques for an effective recommender system. Secondly, the research proposed to hybridize the collaborative filtering technique with both of the sentiment analysis techniques for a book recommendation system. Thirdly, the paper will implement and evaluate the proposed hybrid recommendation technique for a book recommendation system. Finally, the paper concludes by drawing conclusions about the significance of using a combination of both sentiment analysis techniques along with the collaborative filtering technique.

Keywords: Book recommendation system, machine learning, recommendation systems, sentiment analysis

Introduction

Recommendation systems are one of the information filtering systems that solve the information overload problem [10]. It filters out the relevant information from a large set of available information to the user as per the requirements of the user. In the construction of a recommendation system, various techniques such as collaborative filtering, content-based filtering, knowledge-based recommendation techniques, context-aware recommendation techniques, and hybrid techniques are mostly used by researchers [3]. These techniques make use of various factors such as ratings of items, features of items, user item relationship, geographic

[a]anil.dadhwal@gmail.com, [b]sonal_chawla@yahoo.com

information, or a combination of any of these or other relevant factors to identify the best possible suggestion for a user. It is observed that the hybrid technique is the most popular technique among various recommendation techniques due to its feature of incorporating the strength of each technique in hybridization while minimizing the limitations.

Now a day's most online platforms are giving an option to users to give feedback about an item mostly in terms of ratings and reviews. Other users also rely on this feedback to identify the quality of the item. Therefore, ratings and reviews must be considered in the hybrid recommendation technique to get relevant results.

To analyze ratings, a collaborative filtering technique is used whereas to analyze reviews, sentiment analysis is used. In collaborative filtering, an item's rating is estimated using the item's previous ratings given by similar users or previous ratings of similar items. Sentiment analysis is used to analyze the reviews of an item. It bifurcates the sentiment of an item into three polarity groups i.e. positive, negative, or neutral. Sentiment analysis is done either using a lexicon-based approach or a machine learning-based approach [7]. In the lexicon-based approach, the polarity of the individual word is identified from a predefined set of dictionary words whereas, in the machine learning approach, a machine learning classifier is trained using a set of a labeled dataset of positive and negative words. The trained machine learning classifier is finally used to predict the polarity of the new word.

Earlier studies emphasize on implementing either lexicon-based or machine learning-based sentiment analysis, hence this research article aims to investigate the effect of both lexicon-based and machine learning-based hybrid sentiment analysis techniques with collaborative filtering techniques for a book recommendation system. In this hybridization, the results of lexicon-based sentiment analysis are further fed into the machine learning sentiment analysis technique to maximize the benefits of both techniques. The hybrid sentiment analysis technique is combined with collaborative filtering to get the final suggestions. The proposed approach is evaluated using standard evaluation techniques such as accuracy, precision, recall, and F1 [1].

The rest of this paper is organized as follows. "Literature review" section describes related work to recommendation systems. "Methodology of the proposed approach" section explains about the proposed approach and algorithms for a book recommendation system. "Evaluation results and discussion" section discusses the results of the proposed approach and finally "Conclusion" section concludes the paper by drawing significance of the current study and future work.

Literature Review

Recommendation systems can recommend various items of interest that include books, videos, music, movies, profiles, etc. Since books have been an integral part of the academicians they spend a lot of time identifying the book that is worth reading. Thus, various book-recommending techniques that have been used by researchers are explored in this section. Early evidence of using sentiment analysis in the academic domain can be traced back to the work of [4] revealed that similar meanings may not imply similar sentiments so the author proposed to construct a relative frequency-based opinion dictionary to perform the sentiment analysis and incorporating it to collaborative filtering for movie recommendation system. The author measures only the accuracy of the system on a 2-point and 3-point scale. Another study by Ortigosa et al. [6] proposes a SentBuk that performs the hybrid sentiment analysis on Facebook comments and achieved an accuracy of 83.27%. The author suggests various methods to incorporate this tool in Facebook groups or collaborative learning environments to perform motivational actions to encourage students in case of negative sentiments towards a course or use it as feedback for the teachers however evaluation of the proposed system is only done for accuracy.

Sohail et al. [9] has tested the book recommendation system based on a feature-based opinion-mining approach that suggests books to university students as per syllabus. The system does this by exploring experts' recommendations and user reviews. The system is tested on various evaluation parameters and gives better results in comparison to PAS (positional aggregation-based technique), OWA (ordered weighted aggregation), and ORWA (ordered ranked weighted aggregation) techniques. Further, the study [5] has examined the deep learning and clustering technique in the book recommendation system. After removing identical sentences, a deep learning technique is employed to do the sentiment analysis. The KNN-based clustering algorithm is implemented to provide suggestions based on the age, gender, and locality of the user. The system only considers sentiments but not the ratings of the books.

Sarma et al. [8] have found that cluster-based techniques give better results in the case of book recommendation systems. The author uses K means clustering algorithm using the cosine distance function to measure the distance and cosine similarity function to identify the similarity among clusters in the dataset of the Goodreads-books repository. The evaluation of the system is done on parameters of specificity (True Negative Rate), Sensitivity (Recall), and F1 measure. Another study by Wayesa et al. [11] tested the book recommendation system using good books data set on information retrieval parameters such as precision, recall, and F1. The authors implemented the hybrid book recommendation system using a Content-Based approach, Collaborative filtering, and clustering based on semantic relationships. From the literature studies, it is apparent that if sentiment analysis is used in hybrid book recommendation systems then either lexicon-based or machine learning-based sentiment analysis is used in hybridization with other state-of-the-art recommendation systems. It can be identified from the literature that the hybridization of both lexicon-based and machine learning-based sentiment analysis to get a hybrid sentiment analysis technique is not evaluated with a collaborative filtering technique based on standard evaluation parameters. Therefore, the research proposed to implement a hybrid sentiment analysis technique with a collaborative filtering technique for the book recommendation system and evaluate the technique based on standard evaluation parameters of accuracy, precision, recall, and F1.

Title of the paper/ Name of Book Recommender System	Domain	Implemented Techniques	Outcomes	Limitations
Integrating Collaborative Filtering and Sentiment Analysis: A Rating Inference Approach [4]	Movies	Lexicon Based Sentiment analysis and CF	Gives better results in terms of accuracy	Detailed results are not discussed. Only Lexicon based sentiment analysis is done
SentBuck [6]	Facebook Reviews	Hybrid Sentiment Analysis	83.27% accuracy	Limited evaluation
FOMA Book Recommendation System [9]	Books	Feature Extraction	Given better results in terms of various evaluation metrics in comparison to PAS, OWA, ORWA	The proposed approach is not compared with other opinion mining techniques.
Four-step book recommendation system [5]	Books	Collaborative Filtering Sentiment Analysis	Better accuracy is achieved using KNN Clustering	Ratings are not considered. Deep Learning based sentiment analysis is done. Limited evaluation
Personalized Book Recommendation System using Machine Learning Algorithm [8]	Books	K means Clustering	Give an average of 49.76% sensitivity, 56.74% specificity, and 52.84% F1 Score	Sentiment analysis is not considered.
Pattern-based hybrid book recommendation system using semantic relationships [11]	Books	Content-Based Filtering, Collaborative Filtering, Semantic Relationships	Gives an average of 76.4% precision, 37.4% Recall, and 56.9% F1-score	Sentiment analysis is not considered.

Methodology of the Proposed Approach

The design of the proposed approach employs both types of sentiment analysis technique item based collaborative filtering technique using KNN to have an equal weightage of both reviews and ratings of the item. This is done to include both implicit feedback that is there in terms of textual reviews and explicit feedback that is available in terms of ratings. In the proposed approach, the emphasis is given to the usage of hybrid sentiment analysis techniques instead of using individual sentiment analysis techniques. This seems to be a justified technique as the hybrid sentiment analysis technique seems to utilize the efficiency of both the dictionary and machine learning classifier. If a hybrid recommendation system has to be designed, the general steps that are followed to design are explained in Algorithm 15.1.

Algorithm 15.1: General steps to design a hybrid recommendation system

Step 1:- Take the input dataset
Step 2:- Predict the rating of an item using a collaborative filtering technique.
Step 3:- Perform the sentiment analysis of the item to get a sentiment score.
Step 4:- Get the combined predicted value based on steps 2 and Step 3.
Step 5:- Recommend the list of items based on rating predictions calculated
        in step 4 in descending order.

As explained earlier, in this research the emphasis is given to step 3 of Algorithm 1 by employing a hybrid sentiment analysis technique instead of using individual sentiment analysis techniques. The proposed hybrid sentiment analysis technique is explained in Algorithm 15.2. The hybrid sentiment analysis algorithm returns a sentiment score that is calculated based on both lexicon-based and machine learning-based sentiment analysis. The major contribution of this study is to perform the calculation of labeled datasets for machine learning. In most of the studies, a straightforward approach is used. The labeled set is created by taking a set of reviews that have a rating above or equal to three and are taken as positive whereas the others are taken as negative. In this approach, the results of the lexicon-based approach are put into the machine learning classifiers as labeled data set which seems to be a justified way of creating labeled data set instead of the earlier approach. The proposed approach is implemented in python using. NLTK tool kit is used to perform sentiment analysis using the SentiWordNet dictionary [2].

Evaluation Results and Discussion

In this phase, the results of the implemented approach are shown. For evaluation of the proposed approach, 30 java books of publically available amazon book review datasets are taken as input. While implementing the hybrid sentiment analysis technique, various possible combination of lexicon-based approach

Algorithm 15.2: Proposed Hybrid Sentiment Analysis Algorithm

1. Preprocess the reviews that include
   a. converting the reviews into lowercase
   b. removing stop words and special characters including punctuation
   c. tokenization and lemmatization of the review
   d. Part of speech tagging
2. Lexicon-based sentiment analysis is done in this step. The system searches every token in the SentiWordNet dictionary to get its positive and negative scores. The score of the next word is modified if there is a presence of negations or modifiers. Calculate the score of the entire sentence by subtracting the total negative score of individual words from the total positive score of the individual words in a sentence.
3. The final sentiment score of the sentence is taken as 1 if it comes to be positive in step 2 or else it is taken as 0 to get the labeled set of positive and negative reviews.
4. The output of lexicon-based sentiment analysis is taken as input i.e. labeled set of data is taken as input for the machine learning classifiers.
5. The textual reviews are converted into feature vectors
6. Training a machine learning classifier based on the labeled dataset and feature vectors.
7. For every feature vector of a review, a trained model is used to predict sentiment to get the complete sentiment score of the sentence.

with machine learning-based approach of sentiment analysis comes into the picture. This is due to the availability of different feature vectorization techniques such as word count, n-gram, and TFIDF(Term Frequency Inverse Document Frequency) approach [7]. The word count feature vectorization technique counts the number of times positive or negative words appear in a review that directly affects the probability of the review is positive or negative. The n-gram approach takes into account two or more sequence words as features instead of a single word to enhance accuracy. The TFIDF approach measures the relevancy of a word by comparing the number of times a word appears in a review with the number of reviews the word appears in. For this research, SVM (Support Vector Machine) classifier is used for machine learning-based sentiment analysis and the SentiWordNet dictionary is used for lexicon-based sentiment analysis. So the proposed approach is evaluated for all possible combinations of different hybrid sentiment analysis techniques with collaborative filtering techniques to have multiple hybrid recommendation techniques.

The results of the proposed implemented hybrid approaches are evaluated based on standard evaluation techniques such as accuracy, precision, recall, and F1, which measures the efficiency of the recommendation system, usefulness of the recommendation system, relevant items in the recommendation list, and weighted and harmonic mean of precision and recall respectively.

For fair evaluation, the comparison of SVM+CF and Lexicon + SVM + CF is shown in Figure 15.1 where SVM+CF represents the hybrid recommendation technique consisting of only machine learning-based sentiment analysis with collaborative filtering technique and Lexicon + SVM + CF represents the hybrid recommendation technique consisting the hybridization of hybrid sentiment analysis with collaborative filtering technique. Both these hybrid recommendation techniques are implemented for different feature vectorization techniques.

From Figure 15.1, it can be easily identified that the hybrid recommendation technique of Lexicon+SVM+CF with n-gram feature vectorization gives the best results based on accuracy, precision, and F1. The values for accuracy, precision, and f1 come out to be 79.85%, 6.18%, and 10.76% respectively which are significantly higher than the values of these parameters for SVM+CF with n-gram feature vectorization. The value of recall that has an inverse relationship with precision comes out to be better for the SVM+CF technique for all feature vectorization techniques which means it gives more relevant items in the recommendation lists as compared to the Lexicon+SVM+CF recommendation technique. Furthermore, it is also found that other feature vectorization technique including word count and n-gram, in combination with the Lexicon+SVM+CF recommendation technique also gives better results as compared to their combination with the SVM+CF recommendation technique except for recall.

It can be seen that the Lexicon+SVM+CF recommendation technique with TFIDF feature vectorization gives 79.72% accuracy, 6.01% precision, 40.48% recall, and 10.47% F1 which is marginally less than the Lexicon+SVM+CF recommendation technique with n-gram feature vectorization

From the individual charts of accuracy, precision, recall and F1, it can also be identified that except in the results of recall, n-gram feature vectorization is found to be the best feature vectorization technique. TFIDF feature vectorization

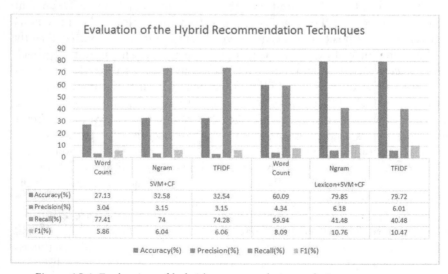

Figure 15.1 Evaluation of hybrid recommendation techniques

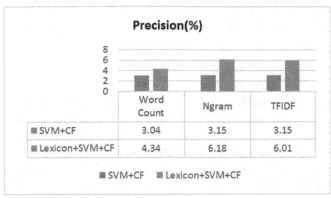

	Word Count	Ngram	TFIDF
SVM+CF	3.04	3.15	3.15
Lexicon+SVM+CF	4.34	6.18	6.01

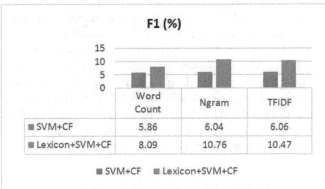

	Word Count	Ngram	TFIDF
SVM+CF	5.86	6.04	6.06
Lexicon+SVM+CF	8.09	10.76	10.47

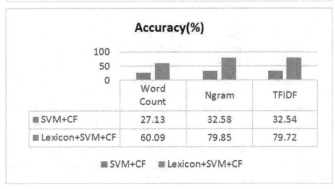

	Word Count	Ngram	TFIDF
SVM+CF	27.13	32.58	32.54
Lexicon+SVM+CF	60.09	79.85	79.72

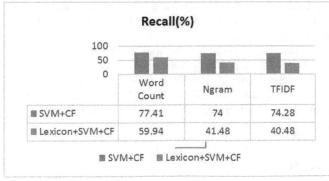

	Word Count	Ngram	TFIDF
SVM+CF	77.41	74	74.28
Lexicon+SVM+CF	59.94	41.48	40.48

approach gives results that are marginally less than that of the n-gram approach. There is a significant drop in the result of the word count feature vectorization approach.

Conclusion

This research has proposed an approach that is based on a hybridization of item based collaborative filtering techniques using KNN and a combination of both sentiment analysis techniques. The proposed approach has been suitably implemented and evaluated using standard parameters. A lot of research has been done, and when such recommendation systems were created by combining sentiment analysis techniques, they produced better results. However, when compared to the above approach, based on the higher values of accuracy, precision, and F1, it can be concluded that if a hybrid recommendation system has to be created using sentiment analysis, then a combination of both lexicon-based and machine learning based sentiment analysis must be employed as compared to the implementation of either lexicon-based or machine learning based sentiment analysis. Therefore, this approach seems to be ideal for recommending any kind of product; however, in the above case, the proposed approach has been tested for recommending books. The future work will concentrate on implementing other machine learning classifiers and deep learning classifiers in the book recommendation system to test them on the standard evaluation parameters of the information retrieval system. present

References

1. Anwar, K., Siddiqui, J., and Sohail, S. S. (2020). Machine learning-based book recommender system: A survey and new perspectives. *International Journal of Intelligent Information and Database Systems*, 13(2–4), 231–248. https://doi.org/10.1504/IJI-IDS.2020.109457
2. Baccianella, S., Esuli, A., and Sebastiani, F. (2010). SentiWordNet 3.0: an enhanced lexical resource for sentiment analysis and opinion mining. In Proceedings of the 7th International Conference on Language Resources and Evaluation, LREC 2010, (pp. 2200–2204).
3. Kumar, A., and Chawla, S. (2019). Framework for hybrid book recommender system based on opinion mining. *International Journal of Recent Technology and Engineering*, 8(4), 914–919. https://doi.org/10.35940/ijrte.d7518.118419.
4. Leung, C. W., Chan, S. C., and Chung, F. L. (2006). Integrating collaborative filtering and sentiment analysis: a rating inference approach. In Proceedings of the ECAI 2006 Workshop on Recommender Systems, (pp. 62–66).
5. Mounika, A., and Saraswathi, S. (2021). Design of book recommendation system using sentiment analysis. *Lecture Notes on Data Engineering and Communications Technologies*, 53, 95–101. https://doi.org/10.1007/978-981-15-5258-8_11.
6. Ortigosa, Alvaro, José M. Martín, and Rosa M. Carro. (2014). Sentiment analysis in Facebook and its application to e-learning. *Computers in human behavior*. 31. 527–541.
7. Ravi, K., and Ravi, V. (2015). A survey on opinion mining and sentiment analysis: Tasks, approaches and applications. *Knowledge-Based Systems*, 89, 14–46. https://doi.org/10.1016/j.knosys.2015.06.015.

8. Sarma, D., Mittra, T., and Hossain, S. (2021). Personalized book recommendation system using machine learning algorithm. *International Journal of Advanced Computer Science and Applications*, 12(1), 212–219. https://doi.org/10.14569/IJACSA.2021.0120126.

9. Sohail, S. S., Siddiqui, J., and Ali, R. (2018). Feature-based opinion mining approach (FOMA) for improved book recommendation. *Arabian Journal for Science and Engineering*, 43(12), 8029–8048. https://doi.org/10.1007/s13369-018-3282-3.

10. Wang, Yibo, Mingming Wang, and Wei Xu. (2018). A sentiment-enhanced hybrid recommender system for movie recommendation: a big data analytics framework. *Wireless Communications and Mobile Computing*. 2018. article id ID8263704

11. Wayesa, F., Leranso, M., Asefa, G., and Kedir, A. (2023). Pattern-based hybrid book recommendation system using semantic relationships. *Scientific Reports*, 13(1), 3693. https://doi.org/10.1038/s41598-023-30987-.

16 Comparative analysis of SDN controllers

Deepjyot Kaur Ryait[a] and Manmohan Sharma[b]

School of Computer Applications, Lovely Professional University, Phagwara, Punjab, India

Abstract

The dissociation of the control plane from the data plane is the primary factor in the Software Defined Network's ability to offer a novel and agile networking paradigm that fosters innovation in networking compared to the traditional network. A communication system's important feature today is the availability of services on-demand and without interruption. The firm will suffer a significant loss of revenue or profit if there is any disruption or failure in the communication system. By expanding the availability of networking facilities, this problem must be solved. The aim of this research is to designing a fault tolerance model that decreases the risk of a single point of failure in an SDN network as well as managing the load between them. In comparison to alternative controller configurations, the proposed model has higher average throughput and bandwidth metrics and lower ping delay metrics. Moreover, quantitative analysis of the proposed model's parameters in terms of how much better they are than other kinds of controllers is highlighted in Table 16.5.

Keywords:Average bandwidth, average throughput, ping delay, RTT, SDN, etc

Introduction

The Software Defined Network (SDN) is defined "by decoupling/disassociating the control plane from the data plane in a network." It is an emerging and forthcoming architecture of a network that offers programmability, easily manageable and adaptable, dynamic configuration of network elements, control, and optimization of network resources in a cost-effective way. The architecture of a SDN defines a novel way of a networking system that can be built by using a combination of hardware network commodities with software-based technologies and openness. Fault tolerance is a preventative method of enhancing controller reliability that guarantees the safe operation and high performance of networks. The achievement of fault-tolerant communication is one of the primary goals of controller design, comparable to traditional networks [1,2,4]. Contrary to traditional networks, however, fault tolerance in SDN is tied to both the distributed control plane and the data plane's resilience.

Review Literature

Malik et al. [2] a sizzling and thriving topic that grabbed more concentration in the industry and academic research area is Software Defined Networks; But only 4% of the research effort contributes to fault tolerance in SDN and the rest in other fields. The fault tolerance needs more concern to address these challenges of scalability and resilience of the network. Due to the fault tolerance of each layer

---

[a]djryait@gmail.com, [b]manmohan.21909@lpu.co.in

of SDNs must therefore be developed independently because a failure that could occur in one layer may or may not have an impact on the other layers. A connection failure, for instance, might not have an impact on the control layer, whereas a controller failure might have an impact on the entire infrastructure layer. Table 16.1 summaries a review of the literature on SDN controllers and their features, as well as the fault-tolerant method of the current multiple controller systems [1–4]. The effects of controller errors can be greatly reduced by using several controllers.

Proposed Work with Simulation and Evaluation of Result

When an SDN controller fails for whatever cause, it is analysed through simulation that the entire network becomes unreachable; this means that the network is ruined until the controller is available in the network and in a functioning state. As a result, a single controller has a greater effect on network failure. For any type of communication system, it is not feasible. To solve this issue, a fault tolerance mechanism is needed that uses multiple controllers to reduce the possibility of a single point of failure in the network [1–4].

The most difficult task in a distributed environment is managing load balancing between controllers. Moreover, both fault tolerance and load balancing are complicated and interrelated issues when dealing with the multiple controllers in SDN [16–18]. To resolve these issues, using the Queuing Theory Technique and Markov Continuous Chain helps manage the fluctuation of load between the multiple controllers. A proposed adaptive algorithm for load balancing in multiple controllers by using the queuing technique with the Markov chain to evaluate an equilibrium or steady state of a probability distribution for controllers, which aids in managing the load among controllers, is a convenient method for this purpose. These probabilities provide an idea of how to distribute network traffic among controllers, and managing load balancing reduces packet dropping or packet loss ratio, overheads, and network migration cost. As a result, a cascading failure of controllers in a network caused by an imbalance in controller workload can be avoided. Based on probability, it also reduces overheads that are induced in the switch migration process and the migration cost of the network and minimises the maintenance cost of the network.

In terms of design and analysis, managing a network with several controllers is far more difficult and complex than managing a network with a single controller. A large number of simulations can be performed using the work that has been proposed in order to do performance evaluations and a quantitative analysis of the performance parameters of the proposed model in terms of how much better they are than other types of controllers. In simulation install all necessary tools such as the Ubuntu Operating System 18.04 Desktop, Mininet, and Ryu controller respectively. Now to compare the various role of SDN controllers' performance in terms of the round-trip time with the proposed model. During simulation to analyses and evaluate the result of SDN controllers is summarized in Table 16.2.

A performance metric is a function of a parameter that quantifies its influence; that parameter affects the system metrics, in other words. Applying or measuring performance analysis is required to ascertain how a performance metric relates

Table 16.1 Literature review on SDN controller's.

Name	Language	Controller Platform	Open Source	Failure Type	Controller Architecture	Controller Load Balancing	Solution	OpenFlow Version	Northbound APIs
HyperFlow [5]	C++	NOX	Yes	Controller Failure	Horizontal	×	Nearly Controllers serve as a hot standby	v1.0	REST API
Onix [6]	C++, Java, Python	--	No	Link, Switch and Onix Instances Failure	Horizontal	√	Active Replication	v1.0	REST API
FlowVisior [7]	C	OpenFlow Controller as proxy	Yes	--	Horizontal	×	--	--	--
DISCO [8]	Java	Floodlight	No	--	Horizontal	×	--	v1.1	REST API
ONOS [9]	Java	ONOS	Yes	ONOS Instances Failure	Horizontal	×	Redundant Instances	v1.0, v1.2, v1.3	REST API
Hydra [10]	Java	--	No	Controller Failure	--	×	Replication of Controllers Configuration	--	--

Name	Language	Controller Platform	Open Source	Failure Type	Controller Architecture	Controller Load Balancing	Solution	OpenFlow Version	Northbound APIs
Kandoo[11]	C, C++, Python	--	Yes	--	Hierarchical (Without global information)	×	--	v1.0	--
ElastiCon [12]	Java	Floodlight	No	Controller Failure	--	√	Dynamic Controller Migration	v1.0	REST API
IRIS [13]	Java	Floodlight	Yes	Controller Failure	Hierarchical (Root and Local Controller)	√	Controller Switching	v1.0, v1.2, v1.3	REST API
OpenDaylight [14]	Java	OpenDaylight	Yes	--	--	×	--	v1.0, v1.2, v1.3	REST API
SMarRLight [15]	C++, Java	Floodlight	No	Controller Failure	--	×	Replicated shared database for recovery	v1.0, v1.2, v1.3	REST API

Table 16.2 Performance comparison of controllers in round-trip time metric.

Round-Trip Time (RTT)	Min (ms)	Avg (ms)	Max (ms)	Mdev (ms)
Single Controller	0.042	43.522	2062.932	268.729
Equal Controller	0.081	41.889	94.402	32.708
Master-Slave Controller	0.073	0.473	36.974	3.670
Proposed Model	0.074	0.100	0.450	0.039

Table 16.3 Performance evaluation of controllers with the proposed model.

Operation of SDN Controller	Min Delay	Max Delay	Average Delay	Average Jitter	Delay Standard Deviation	Bytes Received	Average Bitrate	Average Packet Rate	Time Duration (Sec)
Single Controller	0.000047	0.000443	0.000156	0.000011	0.000051	985500	394.2900	98.5720	20
Equal Controller	0.000029	0.000446	0.000192	0.000010	0.000052	982500	393.0110	98.2529	20
Master Slave Controller	0.000029	0.000376	0.000154	0.000008	0.000051	985500	394.2445	98.5611	20
Proposed Model	0.000024	0.000423	0.000118	0.000010	0.000031	987500	395.0126	98.7531	20

to a system. Analysing the computing system's performance is what it entails. It involves looking at how well the computer system performs. To evaluate the SDN controllers' performance using the D-ITG traffic generator in conjunction with the suggested model for operation. In Table 3 and graphically in Figure 16.1, the whole list of evaluation criteria is displayed. When compared to the other types of controllers in Table 16.3, the proposed model's minimum, average, and delay standard deviation parameters have the lowest values. But the parameters for bytes received, bitrate, and average packet rate are higher than in other controller configurations.

To assess the effectiveness of SDN controllers in their roles with the proposed model, the iperf tool is used. As shown in Figure 16.1 and Figure 16.2 and

Figure 16.1 Performance evaluation w.r.t. Min Delay, Max Delay, Avg Delay, Avg Jitter and Delay standard deviation

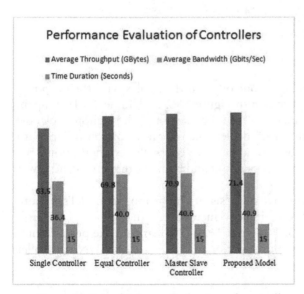

Figure 16.2 Performance evaluation of controllers with the proposed model

Table 16.4, compare controllers based on various metrics, including average throughput, average bandwidth, and ping delay. Table 16.4 depicts the operation of controllers with the proposed model. In comparison to alternative controller configurations, the proposed model has higher average throughput and bandwidth metrics and lower ping delay metrics.

Table 16.4: Performance evaluation of controllers with the proposed model w.r.t. average throughput, average bandwidth and ping delay.

Operation of SDN Controller's	Average Throughput (GBytes)	Average Bandwidth (Gbits/sec)	Ping Delay (ms)	Time Interval (Sec)
Single Controller	63.5	36.4	43.480	15
Equal Controller	69.8	40.0	41.808	15
Master Slave Controller	70.9	40.6	0.400	15
Proposed Model	71.4	40.9	0.026	15

Table 16.5: Quantitative analysis of parameters.

Percentage of Improvement w.r.t. Proposed Model	Parameters		
	Throughput	Bandwidth	Packet Rate
Single Controller	12.44%	12.36%	0.184%
Equal Controller	2.29%	2.25%	0.509%
Master Slave Controller	0.71%	0.74%	0.195%

To assess the effectiveness of SDN controllers in their roles with the proposed model, the iperf tool is used. As shown in Figure 16.2 and Table 16.4, compare controllers based on various metrics, including average throughput, average bandwidth, and ping delay. Table 16.4 depicts the operation of controllers with the proposed model. In comparison to alternative controller configurations, the proposed model has higher average throughput and bandwidth metrics and lower ping delay metrics.

Table 16.5 provides a quantitative analysis of the proposed model's parameters in terms of the percentage of improvement over other types of controllers. After looking at Tables 16.3, 16.4, and 16.5, it's clear that the performance of the proposed model is better and superior to that of other SDN controller configurations.

Conclusion

The Software Defined Network provides a novel paradigm of networking that enhances innovation in networking as compared to the traditional network. The main contribution is to propose an adaptive algorithm for load balancing in multiple controllers by using the queuing technique with the Markov chain to evaluate an equilibrium/steady state of a probability distribution for controllers, which assists manage the load among controllers in a convenient way. Based on probability, it reduces packet dropping or packet lost ratio, overheads, and migration cost of the network due to managing load balancing. As a consequence, a cascading failure of controllers in a network that occurs due to an imbalance of controllers can be avoided. That implies the multiple controllers provide a ubiquitous and robust network that extends the scalability, reliability, and high availability of a network service after evaluating the equilibrium state of a probability distribution of controllers. In comparison to the other types of controllers in Table 3, the proposed model's average delay and delay standard deviation parameters have the lowest values. And Table 5 is a quantitative analysis of the proposed model's parameters in terms of how much better they are than other kinds of controllers. Moreover, the proposed model's performance is more appropriate as compared to other controllers. In the future, make an effort to implement the right security measures for the controller, as it is tasked with managing the entire network.

References

1. Kreutz, D., Ramos, F. M., Verissimo, P. E., Rothenberg, C. E., Azodolmolky, S., and Uhlig, S. (2015). Software-defined networking: a comprehensive survey. *Proceedings of the IEEE*, 103(1), 14–76.
2. Malik A, Aziz B, Al-Haj A, Adda M. 2019. Software-defined networks: A walkthrough guide from occurrence To data plane fault tolerance. *Peer J Preprints*. 7:e27624v1 https://doi.org/10.7287/peerj.preprints.27624v1
3. Abdullah, M., Al-awad, N., and Hussein, F. (2018). Performance evaluation and comparison of software defined networks controllers. *International Journal of Scientific Engineering and Science*, 2(11), 45–50.
4. Zhang, Y., Cui, L., Wang, W., and Zhang, Y. (2018). A survey on software defined networking with multiple controllers. *Journal of Network and Computer Applications*, 103, 101–118.
5. Tootoonchian, A., and Ganjali, Y. (2010). Hyper flow: a distributed control plane for open flow. In Proceedings of the 2010 Internet Network Management Conference on Research on Enterprise Networking, (pp. 3–3)., 2010.
6. Koponen, T., et al. (2010). Onix: a distributed control platform for large-scale production networks. In Proceedings of the 9th USENIX Conference on Operating Systems Design and Implementation (OSDI'10), (pp. 351–364), 2010.
7. Sherwood, R., et al. (2009). Flow visor: a network virtualization layer. Deutsche Telekom Inc. R&D Lab, Stanford, Nicira Networks, Tech. Rep., (pp. 1–14).
8. Phemius, K., et al. (2013). DISCO: distributed multi-domain SDN controllers. In Network Operations and Management Symposium (NOMS)., 2013.
9. Berde, P., et al. (2014). ONOS: towards an open, distributed SDN OS. In The Workshop on Hot Topics in Software Defined Networking (HotSDN'14), (pp. 1–6)., 2014.
10. Chang, Y., Rezaei, A., Vamanan, B., Hasan, J., Rao, S., and Vijaykumar, T. N. (2017, January). Hydra: Leveraging functional slicing for efficient distributed SDN controllers. *In 2017 9th International Conference on Communication Systems and Networks* (COMSNETS) (pp. 251–258). IEEE.
11. Hassas, S., et al. (2012). Kandoo: a framework for efficient and scalable offloading of control applications. In Proceedings of 1st Workshop on Hot Topics in Software Defined Networks, (pp. 19–24)., 2012.

12. Dixit, A., et al. (2014). Elasti con; an elastic distributed SDN controller. In 2014 ACM/IEEE Symposium on Architectures for Networking and Communications Systems (ANCS), (pp. 17–27)., 2014.
13. Lee, B., et al. (2014). IRIS: the open flow-based recursive SDN controller. In 16th International Conference on Advanced Communication Technology, (pp. 1227–1231), 2014.
14. Medved, J., et al. (2014). Open dDaylight: towards a model-driven SDN controller architecture. In Proceedings of IEEE International Symposium on a World of Wireless, Mobile and Multimedia Networks, (pp. 1–6)., 2014.
15. Botelho, F., et al. (2014). SMaRLight: a practical fault-tlerant SDN controller. In Proceedings 3rd European Workshop Software Defined Networks, (p. 6)., 2014.
16. Askar, S., and Keti, F. (2021). Performance evaluation of different SDN controllers: a review. *International Journal of Science and Business*, 5(6), 67–80.
17. Elmoslemany, M. (2020). Performance analysis in software defined network controllers. In 15th International Conference on Computer Engineering and Systems (ICCES), 2020.
18. Canedo, E. D., et al. (2020). Performance evaluation of software defined network controllers. In Proceedings of the 10th International Conference on Cloud Computing and Services Science (CLOSER 2020), (pp. 363–370), 2020.

17 CryptoTrace: tracking cryptocurrency transactions with blockchain technology

Kuldeep Vayadande[1,a], Sangam Patil[2,b], Sayee Chauhan[2,c], Tanuj Baware[2,d], Rohit Gurav[2,e] and Sameer Naik[2,f]

[1]Department of Information Technology, VIT, Pune, India

[2]Artificial Intelligence & Data Science, VIT, Pune, India

Abstract

The decentralised and anonymous nature of cryptocurrencies has made it difficult to monitor their activity, increasing the risk of money laundering, financing terrorism and other illegal acts. A new strategy has been suggested in this article to monitor Bitcoin transactions using blockchain technology. Blockchain is a secure, decentralised, and tamper-proof ledger of cryptocurrency transactions. The strategy involves taking transaction data from the blockchain and analysing it using data analytics and machine learning techniques. This allows for the identification of usage patterns and trends in cryptocurrency transactions without compromising anonymity. The strategy was tested on open blockchains like Bitcoin and Ethereum and was found to be effective in monitoring Bitcoin transactions and detecting suspicious activity. Financial regulators can use this method to track Bitcoin exchanges and spot any fraudulent or questionable activity. This study highlights the importance of monitoring cryptocurrency transactions using blockchain technology to identify and prevent illegal activity. The suggested strategy can also aid in reducing the risks involved in Bitcoin transactions, making it easier for cryptocurrencies to be adopted in a secure and controlled manner.

Keywords: Blockchain Bitcoin, cryptocurrencies, decentralised model

Introduction

Authorities can spot suspicious activity and stop criminals from utilizing digital assets to launder money by tracking cryptocurrency transactions. This is particularly crucial when cryptocurrencies gain acceptance and are integrated into the world's financial system. Combating the financing of terrorists is a crucial additional justification for Bitcoin tracing. Terrorists can utilize cryptocurrency to transfer money around the globe covertly, similar to money laundering. Authorities can identify and stop the financing of terrorist organizations by tracking these transactions, potentially saving countless lives. Another situation where tracking cryptocurrencies can be crucial is tax avoidance. To avoid paying taxes, many people now conceal their income and assets by utilizing digital assets. Tax authorities can find people who are not disclosing their Bitcoin holdings and make sure they are paying their fair share of taxes by tracking cryptocurrency

[a]kuldeep.vayadande1@vit.edu, [b]sangam.patil21@vit.edu, [c]sayee.chauhan20@vit.edu, [d]tanuj.baware21@vit.edu, [e]rohit.gurav20@vit.edu, [f]sameernaik21@vit.edu

transactions. Additionally, tracking cryptocurrencies can aid in reducing theft and fraud. As cryptocurrencies increase in value, hackers and other thieves have started to attack them. Authorities can identify and trace stolen money by tracking transactions, which may help them recover assets for fraud or crime victims. Tracing cryptocurrencies can aid in building a more stable and dependable financial system in addition to these significant benefits. Cryptocurrencies can be adopted and invested more heavily in the digital asset field by businesses and investors by encouraging openness and accountability.

Overall, as digital assets gain acceptance and are integrated into the global financial system, tracking or tracing cryptocurrencies is becoming more and more crucial. Authorities can verify that cryptocurrencies are being used responsibly and legally by encouraging openness and accountability. This will help to avoid crime and build a more secure and trustworthy financial system.

Blockchain is a global, decentralized digital ledger that is used to securely and openly record and verify transactions. Blockchain technology serves as the foundation for cryptocurrencies like Bitcoin and Ethereum, and it is this blockchain that enables cryptocurrency tracing. The ability to track Bitcoin transactions is made possible by blockchain technology, as each transaction is recorded on a public ledger that cannot be changed or removed. This enables tracking the transfer of money from one digital wallet to another as well as confirming the legitimacy and accuracy of every transaction. Digital signatures are one of the main ways that blockchain can aid with Bitcoin tracing. Every transaction on the blockchain is supported by a digital signature that is specific to each user and is therefore impossible to copy or forge. By doing this, it is guaranteed that every transaction is legal and can be tracked back to its source. The decentralized nature of blockchain is another significant feature. Blockchain is a distributed system that uses a network of nodes to verify and validate transactions, in contrast to traditional financial systems that are centralized and managed by a single company. Because there is no single point of control and a network of users independently verifies every transaction, it is almost impossible for one user or group of users to influence the system.

This is how a new transaction is completed in the blockchain for a specific cryptocurrency.

Since more and more people and companies are starting to use cryptocurrencies as a method of payment or investment, they have grown in popularity. However, the decentralised and anonymous character of cryptocurrencies has also made them a tempting alternative for individuals wishing to participate in criminal activities, such as money laundering, terrorist financing, or tax evasion. In order to ensure that cryptocurrencies are used responsibly and legally, numerous governments and regulatory agencies are putting rules and guidelines into place. Due to this, there is an increased interest in monitoring cryptocurrency transactions in order to stop illegal activity, encourage accountability, and promote transparency in the digital asset market. We will examine how blockchain technology can be utilised to provide a safe, open, and decentralised mechanism to record and verify each transaction as we investigate the application of blockchain technology for tracking cryptocurrency transactions. We'll go over the main characteristics of blockchain technology and describe how they allow you to track the transfer of money from one digital wallet to another as shown in Figure 17.1. As well as

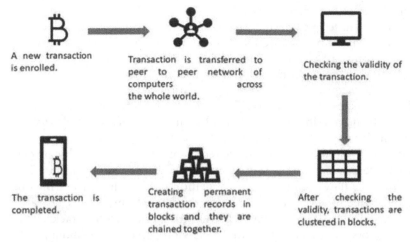

A new transaction is enrolled.

Transaction is transferred to peer to peer network of computers across the whole world.

Checking the validity of the transaction.

The transaction is completed.

Creating permanent transaction records in blocks and they are chained together.

After checking the validity, transactions are clustered in blocks.

Figure 17.1 Blockchain in cryptocurrency

discussing the advantages and drawbacks of employing blockchain technology in this situation, we will also look at the various tools and methods utilized for Bitcoin tracing. Our study will be a great resource for future advances in this crucial sector of the digital asset space and will shed light on how blockchain technology may be used to trace Bitcoin transactions.

Related Work

For the literature review, the following papers are reviewed:

For [1]; The work described in this paper focuses on tracing the true identities of Bitcoin users by putting forth a method that takes advantage of the block-chain's public record. The report emphasizes how scammers and illicit users make use of Bitcoin's anonymity to carry out their illicit activities. The authors stress the importance of disclosing Bitcoin users' true identities to stop such unlawful behaviour. The suggested method entails the employment of a tracker to watch a Bitcoin user's transactions, and a victim makes a complaint to the platform while providing the scammer's public address. The suggested method takes use of Bitcoin and actual money exchange events to reveal the user's identity. The study adds to the expanding body of knowledge on applying blockchain technology to auditing Bitcoin transactions. The suggested method offers a potential method for determining the true identity of Bitcoin users and creates new opportunities for study and research in this significant sector of the digital asset space.

For [2]; The fifth-largest cryptocurrency by market value, Litecoin, is used in the study along with the possibility of deanonymization attacks on online Litecoin transactions. Although using pseudonyms as transaction addresses can help to some degree secure user privacy, the authors point out that there are still significant issues with its privacy assurances. Determining the severity of deanonymization assaults on online Litecoin payments is the authors' goal, and they also suggest new privacy protection strategies. The study adds to the body of knowledge on the difficulties with privacy and security that come with using cryptocurrency. The authors run a series of tests to mimic purchases on websites run by businesses that accept Litecoin and keep track of trackers embedded on information and payment pages. Overall, this article emphasizes the necessity for more stringent privacy protection measures while using cryptocurrency as well as potential weaknesses that deanonymization attacks may exploit. The suggested actions offer a significant contribution to the creation of practical privacy protection tools for the digital asset sector. This study highlights the significance of continual research and development in this field to maintain the industry's growth and development.

For [3]; Because Sybil and other identity/credential-based network threats can exploit Bitcoin's peer-to-peer (P2P) networking, there are security concerns. The authors highlight the flaws in the ban score method used in the current Bitcoin implementation, which is not only vulnerable to defamation attacks but also ineffective against Bitcoin Message-based Denial of Service (DoS) attacks. This mechanism monitors improper networking behaviour among neighbours. The ban-score mechanism can be used by a network adversary to launch a defamation assault against innocent peers. The article emphasizes the necessity for creative security measures to solve the flaws in the existing Bitcoin implementation as well as the significance of continued research and development in the field of Bitcoin network security. The suggested approaches provide a significant contribution to the creation of efficient security controls within the Bitcoin network, increasing user confidence and trust.

For the fourth paper [4]; The analysis of blockchain wallet transactions connected to Russian drug trafficking is the essay's main topic. The authors have created Python software that enables them to discover links between any wallet that are arbitrarily far apart and to display these connections as a graph. The software's purpose is to discover the relationships between wallets and store the information in a database. The database can then be utilized to look into a person's affiliation with a criminal enterprise or to locate an accomplice. The authors show how blockchain research might be used to spot criminal activity, notably in the context of the trafficking of illegal drugs. The study's overall findings highlight the potential of blockchain analysis in identifying criminal activity and boosting the efficiency of law enforcement organizations. The software used for this study is a significant advancement in the field of blockchain analysis and emphasizes the necessity for more study in this subject.

For [5]; the study suggests a tracking system that makes use of blockchain technology in order to get around the drawbacks of current tracking systems. It shows the potential for tampering and fraudulent transactions and identifies the primary problems with current tracking systems, such as slowness, manual errors, and real-time traceability. The authors contend that the suggested system is a robust monitoring system since it has attributes including accountability, authorization, audibility, integrity, punctuality, and honesty. The suggested tracking system is built on QuarkChain, a sharded blockchain protocol constructed utilizing a two-layer design that is adaptable and scalable. The whole architecture, implementation strategy, and system design of the suggested system are all described by the authors. The report analyses the potential advantages of such systems and offers a distinctive viewpoint on applying blockchain technology in tracking systems.

For businesses and organizations in the manufacturing, warehousing, and e-commerce sectors as well as people interested in the use of blockchain technology in logistics and supply chain management, the paper's conclusions may be helpful.

For [6]; The authors of this paper use Bitcoin as an illustration to examine the problem of money laundering and theft in blockchain technology. The decentralized and anonymous nature of blockchain makes it challenging to trace the flow of transaction cash because traders can have several addresses that are not connected to their real-life identities. The study suggests a transaction monitoring system that can precisely and successfully track the source and destination of funds on the blockchain in order to overcome this issue. The system is said to have a significant reference value and to be superior to the current Bitcoin transaction tracking techniques. This study emphasizes the requirement for efficient tracking mechanisms in blockchain technology to stop theft and money laundering.

For [7]; In order to track the origin of agricultural products, the study suggests a method for constructing a supply chain management system utilizing blockchain technology. The article discusses the significance of product origin monitoring for guaranteeing food safety and shows the supply chain model implementation utilizing the Ethereum framework and PoA consensus method. In order to develop a system that satisfies the requirements for product origin tracing, the paper highlights the advantages of employing blockchain technology, including the security and immutability of data, the cheap cost of transactions, and others. The experiment carried out for the study demonstrated the effectiveness of the suggested approach in tracing product origins and its applicability to the food business for ensuring food safety.

For [8]; A framework for monitoring the performance of cryptocurrencies is presented in the article. The authors draw attention to the erratic character of cryptocurrencies and the requirement to give users knowledge about their operation. Popular computer languages like JavaScript, HTML, and CSS were utilized to build the platform, and an API was used to get the cryptocurrency data. Users of the site may easily navigate through each page because of the platform's appealing user interface. The daily updates to the cryptocurrency statistics include the valuation of cryptocurrencies as well as price fluctuations over the previous day and the previous week. The platform's goal is to give users quick access to cryptocurrency insights. The paper does not mention any original research or contributions to the realm of cryptocurrencies or blockchain technology; instead, it concentrates on the platform's development. The study does, however, draw attention to the growing significance of Bitcoin tracking platforms and the requirement for simple access to cryptocurrency analytics.

For [9]; The article explores the development of cryptocurrencies as a kind of digital currency and its potential advantages over existing payment systems. It draws attention to the decentralized nature of cryptocurrencies, which rely on distributed computing and blockchain technology for authentication and verification. In order to comprehend why so many people are exhibiting interest in this new digital form of money, the article compares and contrasts standard currency transaction methods with those used by cryptocurrencies. The article also explores how cryptocurrencies are enhancing speed, efficiency, and financial inclusion while pushing radical changes in the international financial system.

The paper gives a general review of the present cryptocurrency development and emphasizes how it can affect the world financial system.

Comparison Table

Sr. No.	Name of the Paper	Authors	Year of Publication	Relevant Review Findings
1	Tracking Transactions in CryptoCurrencies Using the Graph Theory	Danil A. Subbotin; Maria A. Antropova; Pavel V. Sukharev	2020	This article focuses on analyzing blockchain wallet transactions related to drug trafficking in Russia using a Python program. The program can find connections between wallets and display them as a graph while adding all discovered wallets to a database that can grow over time. The purpose of this study is to identify connections between individuals and potentially determine their involvement in criminal organizations.
2	A RESEARCH ON CRYPTOCURRENCIES PERFORMANCE TRACKER AND DATA VISUALIZATION APP	Saransh Bhardwaj, Sankalpa Basu, Mridul Pal	2022	The creation of a platform for monitoring the performance of cryptocurrencies is discussed in this piece. The platform retrieves cryptocurrency data using an API and well-known computer languages like JavaScript, HTML, and CSS. The platform offers up-to-date data on daily bases regarding changes in the value of cryptocurrencies, including price changes over the course of a day, a week, and overall valuation. The platform's objective is to give users a simple interface through which they can obtain data on cryptocurrency performance.
3	Research on Tracking and Tracing Bitcoin Fund Flows	Linxiang Cai; Binjun Wang	2019	In order to monitor and trace Bitcoin's fund flows, this paper suggests a method for addressing illegal activities in cryptocurrency. The Bitcoin Core client's data storage method and transaction data structure are examined. The processing of transaction data from the Bitcoin Core is presented using a structured MapReduce approach. The tracking and tracing methods are then put forth, along with a D3.js visualization. The outcome is a useful tool for studying and analyzing Bitcoin money flows from illegitimate transactions.
4	Analysis of cryptocurrency transactions from a network perspective: An overview	Jiajing Wu, Jieli Liu, Yijing Zhao, Zibin Zheng	2021	The purpose of this survey paper is to review and analyze the literature that has been written about studying cryptocurrency transactions from a network viewpoint. The context for cryptocurrency transaction network analysis is discussed, and the literature on network modelling, network profiling, and network-based detection is examined. The study questions, approaches, outcomes, and conclusions are presented and discussed for each aspect. To give researchers and engineers a methodical framework, the key difficulties and future paths in the field are also discussed.
5	Tracing Transactions Across Cryptocurrency Ledgers	Haaroon Yousaf, George Kappos, and Sarah Meiklejohn	2019	This literature survey examines the traceability of money across cryptocurrency ledgers, particularly in light of the increasing use of automated trading platforms such as ShapeShift. The authors use data from ShapeShift and 8 different blockchains to study the patterns of cross-currency trades and usage of these platforms. The goal is to understand if they are being used for criminal or profit-driven purposes. The study highlights the importance of understanding the traceability of funds in the cryptocurrency world, particularly across different ledgers.
6	Why criminals can't hide behind Bitcoin (Blog)	JOHN BOHANNON	2021	The article discusses the rise of Bitcoin and its associated risks and benefits. Bitcoin, which is a decentralized digital currency, was initially perceived as a tool for criminals and lawbreakers due to its perceived anonymity. However, law enforcement agencies, including the FBI, have managed to track and prosecute individuals who use Bitcoin for illegal activities. The transparency of the blockchain, which records all Bitcoin transactions, has allowed law enforcement agencies to follow the money trail. The article also explains how Bitcoin is created and how it operates, as well as its current market capitalization.

Currency	Abbr.	Total	curIn	curOut
Ethereum	ETH	1,385,509	892,971	492,538
Bitcoin	BTC	1,286,772	456,703	830,069
Litecoin	LTC	720,047	459,042	261,005
Bitcoin Cash	BCH	284,514	75,774	208,740
Dogecoin	DOGE	245,255	119,532	125,723
Dash	DASH	187,869	113,272	74,597
Ethereum Classic	ETC	179,998	103,177	76,821
Zcash	ZEC	154,142	111,041	43,101

Figure 17.2 The eight most popular coins used

Methodology

The degree of anonymity and privacy that crypto transactions have, makes tracking crypto transactions and identifying the endpoints harder than traditional financial transactions. Additionally, there are methods that allow hiding the real transaction path, like coin join or mixers, which further complicate the process. Tracing cryptocurrency transactions using blockchain technology involves obtaining the transaction hash, searching for the transaction on the blockchain, following the trail of transactions, identifying the endpoints, investigating the identity of the wallet address owner, and analyzing the results to gain an understanding of the flow of cryptocurrency and potentially identify any suspicious or illegal activity.

Blockchain is a distributed digital ledger technology that is used to record transactions and store data. It is essentially a chain of blocks that contains information, such as transaction data, cryptographic hashes, and timestamps. Each block is linked to the previous block using a cryptographic hash, which creates an immutable record of all the transactions that have occurred on the network.

The working of blockchain involves several key components, including:

1. Distributed network: Blockchain is a decentralized system, which means it operates on a network of computers that are spread across the world. Each computer or node on the network has a copy of the blockchain, which is constantly updated with new transactions.
2. Transactions: When a transaction occurs on the blockchain, it is verified by the network of nodes using complex algorithms. Once the transaction is verified, it is added to a block.

3. Blocks: A block is a group of transactions that the network has deemed legitimate. A distinct cryptographic hash is generated for each block based on the data it contains as well as the preceding block's hash.
4. Mining: Mining is the act of adding new blocks to the blockchain. Powerful computers are used by miners to answer challenging mathematical puzzles that validate transactions and produce new blocks. A miner is awarded cryptocurrency once they have found the solution to the issue.
5. Consensus mechanism: Blockchain relies on a consensus mechanism to maintain the network's stability and security. This implies that for new transactions to be added, the blockchain's current state must be accepted by all network nodes.

Cryptocurrency is a type of digital or virtual money that controls the creation of units of currency and verifies the transfer of funds using encryption methods. Cryptocurrencies run on decentralized systems, which means that no single entity, such as a government or financial organization, has control over them. Even though Bitcoin is the most well-known cryptocurrency, there are many others as well, including Ethereum, Litecoin, and Ripple.

The working of cryptocurrency involves several key components, including:

1. Blockchain technology: Cryptocurrencies are built on blockchain technology, which is a decentralized digital ledger that records transactions and stores data across a network of computers.
2. Mining: Powerful computers are used in the mining process to validate transactions and add new blocks to the blockchain, which is how cryptocurrencies are formed.
3. Digital accounts, which can be online or offline, are where cryptocurrency is kept. Encryption is used by digital wallets to safeguard transactions and deter theft.
4. Public and private keys: Public and private keys are used to verify cryptocurrency transfers. The private key is used to access and control the cryptocurrency in the digital wallet, whereas the public key serves as a distinctive location for receiving cryptocurrency.
5. Decentralized system: Because cryptocurrencies work on a decentralized system, no single entity has control over them. They become more private as a result and are less prone to fraud or hacking.
6. Peer-to-peer transactions are made possible by cryptocurrencies, allowing users to make and receive payments without the use of third parties like banks or other financial institutions.

Proposed System

A. Get the Transaction Hash

A transaction is given a transaction hash, which is also referred to as a Transaction ID or hash, once it has been made. These parties use this as a reference number throughout the deal. Using this, you can search for the transaction on block explorers like Etherscan and learn more about its state and specifics. A particular

Figure 17.3 Flowchart

event on the blockchain is identified by its transaction hash, a distinctive code. A block explorer, which is a website that enables users to examine transaction data on the blockchain, can be used to obtain this information.

Types of Transaction

1) A normal transaction is one in which an EOA (Externally Owned Address, also known as a wallet address), sends ETH to another EOA immediately. This kind of transaction will be displayed under the Transaction tab when examining an address on Etherscan.
2) Internal Transaction: This describes an ETH move that uses a smart contract as a middleman. This kind of transaction will be visible when examining an address on Etherscan under the Internal Txns tab.
3) Token Transfer: ERC-20 or ERC-721 token transfers are referred to as token transfer transactions. This kind of transaction will be displayed when viewing an address on Etherscan under either the Erc20 Token Txns or Erc721 Token Txns tab, based on the relevant token.

B. *Check the Coin Details*

A digital coin functions very similarly to conventional currency and is created on its own blockchain. It can be used as a means of exchange between two parties conducting business together as well as a way to keep value. Bitcoin and Litecoin are a couple of examples of currencies. To find out more about a transaction, look

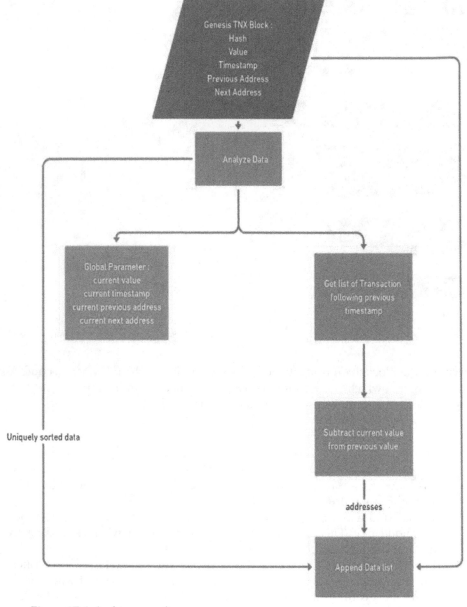

Figure 17.4 Architecture diagram

up the coin specifics, such as which Coin the transaction relates to, how much it costs, wallet addresses that are involved, etc.

C. Search for Explorers for that Transaction Hash

The Google of coins and blockchain explorers. They give users access to various information about transactions on particular wallet addresses and blockchains, such as the quantity transferred, the sources and destinations of the funds, and the transaction status. Almost any information pertaining to transactions, wallets, and blockchains, including rich lists and secret messages, can be extracted using them. A blockchain explorer is a piece of software that draws various data from a blockchain using an API and blockchain server before organizing the data in a database and presenting it to the user in a searchable format. Search the transaction hash on various sites to find it.

D. Store the Data

Once we got the details of the transaction then we store that in a proper format. We get the data like wallet address, ENS Name, Transaction hash, transaction time, and transaction date.

E. Display the Output

After storing the data, it needs to display it. The genesis block is the first block in the chain. It is also sometimes called Block 0 or Block 1. The genesis block is unique because it is the only block in the chain that does not reference a previous block, as there are no blocks before it. The genesis block contains a special transaction known as the coin base transaction, which is the first transaction in the blockchain. The coinbase transaction is a special type of transaction that creates new cryptocurrency and awards it to the creator of the block. In the case of the Genesis block, the creator is usually the person or group who created the blockchain network. The coinbase transaction in the genesis block also sets the parameters for the blockchain, such as the initial supply of a cryptocurrency, the block time, and the difficulty level for mining new blocks. These parameters cannot be changed once the blockchain has been launched. The genesis block also contains a unique identifier known as a hash, which is generated using a cryptographic hashing algorithm. The hash of the genesis block is often used as a reference point for subsequent blocks in the chain.

Graphs and Analysis

Scammers are drawn to cryptocurrency for a number of reasons, which may aid in clarifying why recorded losses in 2021 were almost sixty times more than they were in 2018. Without a bank or other central authority, it is impossible to flag transactions as questionable and try to prevent fraud before it occurs. Cryptographic transfers are irreversible; once the money is sent, it cannot be recovered. And most people still don't understand how cryptography operates. These considerations are not unique to crypto transactions, but they all play into the hands of scammers. According to new statistics from blockchain analytics company Chainalysis, scammers made a record $14 billion in cryptocurrencies in

Figure 17.5 Crypto values were stolen by scammers

2021, in large part because of the growth of decentralised financing (DeFi) platforms. Stemming from an increase in theft and scams, losses from crypto-related crime increased 79% from a year earlier.

Wormhole, a cryptocurrency exchange platform, suffered a $320 million loss as a result of a cyberattack in February 2022. In addition to this attack, a report by the Federal Trade Commission claims that cryptocurrency scammers have taken more than $1 billion since 2021. Digital currency is a type of money that is kept in a digital wallet and may be converted into actual cash by the owner by transferring it to a bank account. Digital currency is different from cryptocurrencies like Bitcoin. Since it runs outside of financial institutions and uses blockchain for verification, it is more difficult to recoup from theft. Even though cryptocurrency is a more recent development, thieves are still stealing using traditional methods. The following are some typical Bitcoin frauds to be on the lookout for:

1. Investment plans using bitcoin
2. Rug-pull fraud
3. Love schemes
4. Phishing ripoffs
5. Attack by a man in the centre
6. Scams involving Bitcoin giveaways onv social media
7. Pyramid scams
8. Fake platforms for cryptocurrencies
9. Job offers and dishonest workers

Here are some of the typical warning signs of Bitcoin scams:

- Guarantees of significant profits or a return on investment.
- Only allowing payment in cryptocurrencies.
- Contractual responsibilities.
- Spelling and grammatical mistakes in communications, including emails and social media messages.
- Manipulative strategies like extortion or threats.
- Gratuitous money promises.
- Inappropriate celebrity sponsorships or phoney influencers.
- A lack of specifics regarding the expenditure and money flow.
- Several deals in a single day.

One of the newest and fastest-growing businesses in the world is cryptocurrency. Even though the first cryptocurrency was only established 13 years ago, its value and popularity have grown significantly since then. As of January 2021, there were about 400,000 Bitcoin trades every day. By 2021, there were over 36.5 million cryptocurrency users in the US and 300 million users worldwide.

There will be more than 20,000 cryptocurrencies in use by July 2022. The top three cryptocurrencies in the world by market capitalization are Bitcoin (BTC), Ethereum (ETH), and Tether USD (USDT). The market for blockchain technology is expected to be worth $10.02 billion by 2022. The value of the worldwide blockchain sector is expected to reach $67.4 billion by 2026, with a CAGR (Compound Annual Growth Rate) of 68.4%.

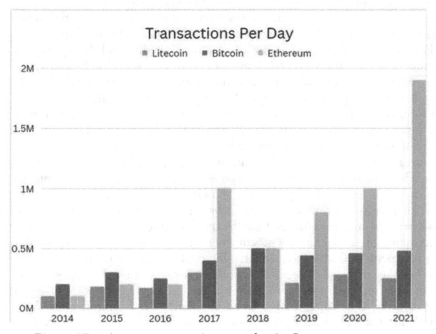

Figure 17.6 Average transactions per day in Crypto

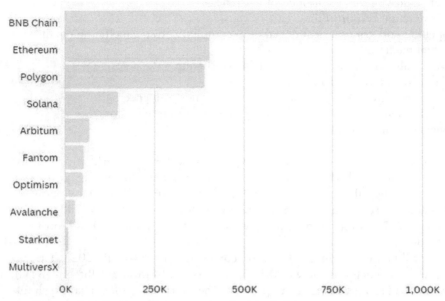

Figure 17.7 Daily active users on the blockchain

Future Scope

The future scope of crypto coin tracking is promising, as the use of digital currencies is expected to continue to grow and evolve. Some potential areas of development in the field of crypto coin tracking include Machine learning and artificial intelligence: The use of machine learning and AI algorithms could improve the accuracy and efficiency of crypto coin tracking by analyzing large amounts of data and identifying patterns and trends that would be difficult for humans to detect. Predictive analytics: Predictive analytics could be used to forecast the future performance of cryptocurrencies, helping investors to make more informed decisions. Integration with other financial systems: As the use of digital currencies becomes more mainstream, crypto coin trackers may be integrated with traditional financial systems, such as banks and stock market exchanges, to provide a more seamless user experience. Development of user-centric Interface: As crypto coin tracking platforms have a huge user base and keeping that in mind the interfaces are likely to be developed to be more user-friendly and personalized for the user. Introducing more data points: With increasing use cases and cryptocurrencies in the market, the crypto coin tracking platforms will also have to introduce more data points and functionalities to keep up with the changes and provide more insights. Overall, with the increasing adoption and integration of digital currencies, the field of crypto coin tracking is likely to continue to evolve and expand in the coming years. This tool mainly aims to find the complete history or ledger of a cryptocurrency. Our tool is only able to trace the listed coins, it is unable to trace non-listed coins

(Tokens). In future, we will also add support to trace tokens in our tool so that even a very small amount of fraud can be detected. This tool traces the crypto at moderate speed, the reason behind this is iteration. In the future, we try to increase the speed of tracing the crypto.

Conclusion

Our research is a powerful tool for individuals and businesses looking to monitor and analyze their cryptocurrency transactions. With its user-friendly interface and advanced features, Crypto Coin Tracer provides users with detailed insights into their digital asset portfolio, making it an indispensable tool for anyone looking to navigate the fast-paced and ever-evolving world of cryptocurrencies. One of the key advantages of Crypto Coin Tracer is its ability to track multiple cryptocurrencies across a variety of exchanges and wallets. Additionally, Crypto Coin Tracer provides users with detailed transaction history, including timestamps, fees, and other relevant data points, making it easy to analyze and reconcile transaction data. Overall, Crypto Coin Tracer is an essential tool for anyone looking to navigate the complex world of cryptocurrencies. This tool can also be helpful for cybercrime agencies and forensic agencies to track the cryptocurrencies according to a particular wallet. The tool is useful to detect scams in cryptos due to its accurate tracing.

References

1. Islam, M. N., Hossen, M. G. S., Baidya, S. P., Emon, M. A. U., and Hossain, M. S. (2021). A framework for tracing the real identity of a bitcoin scammer. In 2021 International Conference on Computer, Communication, Chemical, Materials and Electronic Engineering (IC4ME2), Rajshahi, Bangladesh, 2021, (pp. 1–4). doi: 10.1109/IC4ME253898.2021.9768636.
2. Zhang, Z., Yin, J., Liu, Y., and Liu, J. (2020). Deanonymization of litecoin through transaction-linkage attacks. In 2020 11th International Conference on Information and Communication Systems (ICICS), Irbid, Jordan, 2020, (pp. 059–065). doi: 10.1109/ICICS49469.2020.239510.
3. Fan, W., Hong, H. J., Wuthier, S., Zhou, X., Bai, Y., and Chang, S. Y. (2021). Security analyses of misbehavior tracking in bitcoin network. In 2021 IEEE International Conference on Blockchain and Cryptocurrency (ICBC), Sydney, Australia, 2021, (pp. 1–3). doi: 10.1109/ICBC51069.2021.9461126.
4. Subbotin, D. A., Antropova, M. A., and Sukharev, P. V. (2020). Tracking transactions in crypto currencies using the graph theory. In 2020 IEEE Conference of Russian Young Researchers in Electrical and Electronic Engineering (EIConRus), St. Petersburg and Moscow, Russia, 2020, (pp. 526–529. doi: 10.1109/EIConRus49466.2020.9039530.
5. Li, Z., Li, J., Zheng, Y., and Dong, B. (2020). Biteye: a system for tracking bitcoin transactions. In 2020 Information Communication Technologies Conference (ICTC), Nanjing, China, 2020, (pp. 318–322). doi: 10.1109/ICTC49638.2020.9123286.
6. An, A. C., Diem, P. X. D., Thi Thu Lan, L., Van Toi, T., and Binh, L. D. Q. (2019). Building a product origins tracking system based on blockchain and PoA consensus protocol. In 2019 International Conference on Advanced Computing and Ap-

plications (ACOMP), Nha Trang, Vietnam, 2019, (pp. 27–33). doi: 10.1109/ACOMP.2019.00012.

7. Basu, S., Pal, M., and Bhardwaj, S. (2022). A research on cryptocurrencies performance tracker. *International Research Journal of Modernization in Engineering Technology and Science.* 4(7), July-2022, 2015–2022.

8. Gowda, Nandan & Chakravorty, Chandrani. (2021). Comparative Study on Cryptocurrency Transaction and Banking Transaction. *Global Transitions Proceedings.* 2. 10.1016/j.gltp.2021.08.064.

9. Vayadande, K., Shaikh, R., Rothe, S., Patil, S., Baware, T., and Naik, S. (2022). Blockchain-based land record system. *ITM Web Conference*, 50, 01006. DOI: 10.1051/itmconf/20225001006.

18 Heart disease prediction by using machine learning algorithms

Khushi Sharma[a], Juhi Jain[b] and Vishal[c]

Computer Science and Engineering, Amity University Uttar Pradesh Noida, UP, India

Abstract

Cardiovascular disorders, which are heart-related ailments, are the most general source of mortality globally over the previous several decades and are one of the most dangerous illnesses in India and the rest of the world. Lack of accurate diagnosis at an early stage is one of the many factors driving up the risk factors for heart disease in India. The healthcare sector generates tremendous data. This study explores the efficacy of machine learning algorithms in evaluating the likelihood of heart disease or cardiovascular disease in a person based on relevant features. This paper provides comparative analysis of various models built on these algorithms and evaluates their functionality. Performances of models based on Naïve Bayes, Decision Trees, Support Vector Machine, Random Forest, Logistic Regression, XGBoost, Neural Network, K-Nearest Neighbor are evaluated based on different performance measures like accuracy, recall, precision, AUC and F1-measure. Experimental results have proven that Random Forest model has performed better than others achieving 99% accurate results in predicting heart diseases.

Keywords: accuracy, AUC, heart disease prediction, machine learning, random forest, recall

Introduction

Data on a range of health-related topics is compiled by medical organizations from all over the world. Heart disease is one of the main factors that contribute to adult mortality. Heart disease must be identified early minimizing the issues by participating in the lifestyle changes made by high-risk individuals. Machine learning (ML) techniques enable the healthcare sector to foresee the future and make decisions by utilizing the massive volumes of data generated. Our endeavor can determine who is most likely to be diagnosed with a cardiac issue by looking at a person's medical history. [2,3] The use of ML can aid in disease detection with less medical testing and efficient treatments. It acts as a quick guide to treat patients appropriately. This work proposes a forced air (positive air pressure) solution to the problem.

This investigation aims to predict future instances of heart disease by comparing patient records that employ a device- learning set of rules to categorize regardless of whether a patient has heart disease any longer. In this situation, ML algorithms could be quite beneficial. Even though coronary heart disease can present itself, a person's susceptibility to it is ultimately determined by a shared set of underlying risk factors. [4,5,6,7]

This research emphasizes the significance of application of ML for early detection of heart disease using effective performance measures.

[a]kkhushhisharma10@gmail.com, [b]erjuhijain@gmail.com, [c]vishalbalhara10@gmail.com

RQ1: Which ML algorithms are explored to forecast heart diseases in existing literature?

RQ2: Which ML algorithm outperforms in prediction of heart disease in terms of performance measures used in the study?

Section 2 summarizes the research work conducted in this domain. The research approach followed is described in Section 3. The outcome is discussed in the next section. Section 5 brings the paper to a conclusion.

Literature Review

Numerous researchers have worked on applying ML algorithms to diagnose cardiovascular heart disease. [9,10] Numerous ML models have been developed by them to forecast the likelihood of cardiac disease in patients. To test these models, [1] have used Cleveland dataset whereas few researchers like Chen et al. [11], Jabbar et al. [8] have used Hungary data. Shah et al. [24] (2020) used algorithms like decision tree (DT), K-nearest neighbor (KNN), Naïve Bayes (NB), and Random Forest (RF) on the Cleveland dataset for predicting heart diseases using accuracy measure. [12,13,14,15,16] Efficacy of algorithms like Neural Networks (NN) and Support Vector Machine (SVM) are also explored in literature. The summary of recent ML-based heart disease prediction studies that are most similar to our study is shown in Table 18.1.

Research Methodology

Dataset Collection and Preprocessing

The Cleveland, Hungary, Switzerland, and LongBeachV (CHSL) are 4 datasets that were acquired from Kaggle and pooled in order to identify similar traits. These datasets consist of 75 independent variables and 1 dependent variable. However, none of the published studies describe utilizing all of them. 14

Table 18.1 Literature survey.

Ref	Dataset Used	ML Algorithm Used	Performance Measure
[24]	UCI repository	4 (DT, NB, KNN, RF)	Accuracy
Kumar et al. (2020)	Cleaveland UCI repository	6 (DT, SVM, RF, NB, NN, KNN)	accuracy, precision, error
[23]	UCI repository	2 (KNN, RF)	sensitivity, precision, accuracy, F1- score
[17]	UCI repository	3 (LR, KNN, RF)	Accuracy
Our Work	Cleveland, Hungary, Switzerland, LongBeachV	8 (DT, RF, KNN, LR, SVM, XGBoost, NN, NB)	Accuracy, Recall, Precision. AUC, F1-score

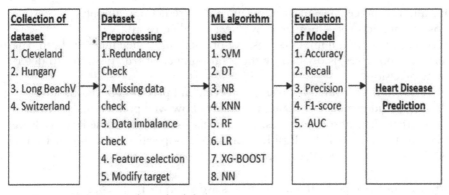

Figure 18.1 Research methodology

relevant attributes that are used in literature are incorporated in this study. The patient's heart condition is referenced in the "target" field. One represents a disease, while zero represents none. There was no redundant data in the combined data set. CHSL is visualized to check for data imbalance; the 14 features in the data are selected. The research methodology followed in this work is explained in Figure 18.1.

ML Algorithms Implemented in the Study

- Decision Tree (DT) is the non-parametric supervised learning approach used for classification and regression applications.
- Random Forest (RF) uses a tree predictor with a randomly selected tree as its base.
- K-Nearest Networks (KNN) algorithm classifies the recently collected data points according to similarity. Fresh data is quickly and precisely categorized into the appropriate categories using the KNN algorithm.
- Logistic Regression (LR) classifies based on a set of independent variables. It determines the probability that an event, like voting or not voting, will occur. The outcome is a probability since the dependent variable has a range of 0 to 1.
- Support Vector Machine (SVM) models are used in supervised learning with corresponding learning algorithms to examine data for regression and classification.
- XGBoost or Extreme Gradient Boosting is a distributed ensemble learner based on gradient-boosted decision tree (GBDT) machine learning system. It can handle large datasets and complex models efficiently.
- An Artificial Neural Network (NN), a method of artificial intelligence, gives computers instructions on how to analyze input in a manner akin to how the human brain processes so.

Performance Measures used

- Accuracy: The ratio of correctly classified predictions (points) to all predictions is measured.

- Recall: The percentage of accurate positive predictions among all possible positive predictions is measured by a metric called recall.
- Precision: The total number of positive predictions, which includes both true and false positives, is divided by the total number of true positives to determine precision.
- F1-Score: It is computed by averaging recall and precision harmonically.
- AUC: It is independent of scale. It evaluates how well predictions are ranked rather than their absolute values. The association between True Positive Rate (or sensitivity) and False Positive Rate (i.e., 1-specificity) is shown by the ROC AUC curve. [18,19,20,21,22]

Formulas for these performance measures are given in Table 18.2.

Table 18.2 Performance measures.

Performance Measure	Formula
Accuracy	$Accuracy = \dfrac{TP + TN}{TP + FN + TN + FP}$
Recall	$Recall = \dfrac{TP}{(TP + FN)}$
Precision	$Precision = \dfrac{TP}{(TP + FP)}$
F1-Score	$F1 - Score = \dfrac{(2 * (Precision * Recall))}{(Precision + Recall)}$

TN=true negative, FN=false negative, FP=false positive, and TP=true positive.

Table 18.3 Performance measure values for ML models.

Algorithm Used	Accuracy	Precision	Recall	F1-Score	AUC
DT	0.94	0.96	0.92	0.9	0.87
RF	0.99	1	0.97	0.99	0.99
KNN	0.73	0.73	0.74	0.73	0.73
NB	0.82	0.88	0.87	0.85	0.84
SVM	0.68	0.66	0.76	0.71	0.68
XGBoost	0.78	0.82	0.86	0.85	0.8
LR	0.78	0.74	0.87	0.8	0.78
NN	0.7	0.92	0.45	0.6	0.7

Results

We performed 80/20 cross-validation and built machine learning models to analyze their predictive capabilities. It means 80% of dataset is used as training data
and remaining 20% data is used for testing the models designed. Results achieved
from the resultant models are noted in Table 18.3.

As concluded by Table 3, it can be seen that RF performed better in terms
of Accuracy, Precision, Recall, F1-score and AUC. It has shown AUC value and
accuracy value of 99%. Hence, the best predictions are given by RF algorithm as
compared to other ML algorithms that were used to build heart disease prediction models.

Conclusion

The experimental study conducted claims that ML algorithms offer tremendous
potential for anticipating cardiovascular diseases and heart-related illnesses.
Each of the algorithms has performed fantastically in some circumstances
and appallingly in others. In all the algorithms applied to check the predictive
capabilities, we found the best results with RF having accuracy, F1-score and
AUC of 99%. NB and DT have also shown good performance for the desired
application. RF, being the ensemble method, has outperformed the other ML
algorithms. The early detection of cardiovascular diseases in person may help
doctors to provide effective treatment to those patients saving their lives and
leading to health improvements, In future, we would like to explore the other
categories of ensemble methods and swarm intelligence-based methods for
heart disease prediction.

References

1. Soni, J., Ansari, U., Sharma, D., and Soni, S. (2011). Predictive data mining for medical diagnosis: an overview of heart disease prediction. *International Journal of Computer Applications*, 17(8), 43–48.
2. Dangare, C. S., and Apte, S. S. (2012). Improved study of heart disease prediction system using data mining classification techniques. *International Journal of Computer
Applications*, 47(10), 44–48.
3. Ordonez, C. (2006). Association rule discovery with the train and test approach for
heart disease prediction. *IEEE Transactions on Information Technology in Biomedicine*, 10(2), 334–343.
4. Shinde, R., Arjun, S., Patil, P., and Waghmare, J. (2015). An intelligent heart disease
prediction system using k-means clustering and Naïve Bayes algorithm. *International
Journal of Computer Science and Information Technologies*, 6(1), 637–639.
5. Bashir, S., Qamar, U., and Javed, M. Y. (2014). An ensemble-based decision support
framework for intelligent heart disease diagnosis. In International Conference on
Information Society (i-Society 2014) (pp. 259–64). IEEE. ICCRDA 2020 IOP Conference Series: Materials Science and Engineering 1022 (2021) 012072 IOP Publishing
doi:10.1088/1757-899X/1022/1/012072 9.
6. Jee, S. H., Jang, Y., Oh, D. J., Oh, B. H., Lee, S. H., Park, S. W., and Yun, Y. D. (2014).
A coronary heart disease prediction model: the Korean heart study. *British Medical
Journal*, 4(5), e005025.

7. Ganna, A., Magnusson, P. K., Pedersen, N. L., de Faire, U., Reilly, M., Ärnlöv, J., and Ingelsson, E. (2013). Multilocus genetic risk scores for coronary heart disease prediction. *Arteriosclerosis, Thrombosis, and Vascular Biology,* 33(9), 2267–2272.
8. Jabbar, M. A., Deekshatulu, B. L., and Chandra, P. (2013). Heart disease prediction using lazy associative classification. In 2013 International Mutli- Conference on Automation, Computing, Communication, Control and Compressed Sensing (iMac4s), (pp. 40–46). IEEE.
9. Brown, N., Young, T., Gray, D., Skene, A. M., and Hampton, J. R. (1997). Inpatient deaths from acute myocardial infarction, 1982-92: analysis of data in the Nottingham heart attack register. *British Medical Journal,* 315(7101), 159–164.
10. Folsom, A. R., Prineas, R. J., Kaye, S. A., and Soler, J. T. (1989). Body fat distribution and self-reported prevalence of hypertension, heart attack, and other heart disease in older women. *International Journal of Epidemiology,* 18(2), 361–367.
11. Chen, A. H., Huang, S. Y., Hong, P. S., Cheng, C. H., and Lin, E. J. (2011). HDPS: heart disease prediction system. In 2011 Computing in Cardiology, (pp. 557–60). IEEE.
12. Parthiban, L., and Subramanian, R. (2007). Intelligent Heart Disease Prediction System Using CANFIS and Genetic Algorithm. World Academy of Science, Engineering and Technology, *International Journal of Medical, Health, Biomedical, Bioengineering and Pharmaceutical Engineering,* 1, 278–281.
13. Wolgast, G., Ehrenborg, C., Israelsson, A., Helander, J., Johansson, E., and Manefjord, H. (2016). Wireless body area network for heart attack detection [Education Corner]. *IEEE Antennas and Propagation Magazine,* 58(5), 84–92.
14. Patel, S., and Chauhan, Y. (2014). Heart attack detection and medical attention using motion sensing device - kinect. *International Journal of Scientific and Research Publications,* 4(1), 1–4.
15. Piller, L. B., Davis, B. R., Cutler, J. A., Cushman, W. C., Wright, J. T., Williamson, J. D., and Haywood, L. J. (2002). Validation of heart failure events in the antihypertensive and lipid lowering treatment to prevent heart attack trial (ALLHAT) participants assigned to doxazosin and chlorthalidone. *Current Controlled Trials in Cardiovascular Medicine,* 3(1), 1–9.
16. Raihan, M., Mondal, S., More, A., Sagor, M. O. F., Sikder, G., Majumder, M. A., and Ghosh, K. (2016). A prototype for predicting the risk of ischemic heart disease (heart attack) on a smartphone utilizing clinical data and data mining techniques. In 2016's 19th International Conference on Computer and Information Technology (ICCIT). (pp. 299–303), IEEE.
17. Jindal, H., Agrawal, S., Khera, R., Jain, R., and Nagrath, P. (2021). Heartdisease prediction using machine learning algorithms. *IOP Conference Series: Materials Science and Engineering,* 1022(1) IOP Publishing.
18. Aldallal, A., and Al-Moosa, A. A. A. (2018). Using data mining techniques to predict diabetes and heart diseases. In 4th International Conference on Frontiers of Signal Processing (ICFSP), (pp. 150–154).
19. Takci, H. (2018). Improvement of heart attack prediction by the feature selection methods. *Turkish Journal of Electrical Engineering and Computer Sciences,* 26(1), 1–10.
20. Dewan, A., and Sharma, M. (2015). Prediction of heart disease using a hybrid technique in data mining classification. In 2015 2nd International Conference on Computing for Sustainable Global Development (INDIACom), (pp. 704–706).
21. Methaila, Aditya and Kansal, Prince & Arya, Himanshu & Kumar, Pankaj. (2014). Early Heart Disease Prediction Using Data Mining Techniques. *Computer Science & Information Technology.* 4. 53–59. 10.5121/csit.2014.4807.

22. Mohan, S. K., Thirumalai, C., and Srivastava, G. (2019). Effective heart disease prediction using hybrid machine learning techniques. *IEEE Access*, 7, 81542–81554.

23. Garg, Apurv and Sharma, Bhartendu & Khan, Rizwan. (2021). Heart disease prediction using machine learning techniques. *IOP Conference Series: Materials Science and Engineering*. 1022. 012046. 10.1088/1757-899X/1022/1/012046.

24. Shah, D., Patel, S., and Bharti, S. K. (2020). Heart disease prediction using machine learning techniques. *SN Computer Science*, 1, 345.

19 Optimizing power consumption by controlling electrical appliances using computer vision

Adireddy Vasu[a], Pothula Srikanth[b], Keerthivasan[c], Vivekananda Reddy Annapa Reddy[d], Tummala Yagna Gopal[e] and Swapnil Bagwari[f]

School of Electronics and Electrical Engineering, Lovely Professional University

Abstract

In today's world, power consumption rates have increased significantly due to the use of electrical appliances. To promote efficient energy use, we propose a system that utilizes computerized vision and Raspberry Pi to optimize power utilization. The system is based on a computerized model that analysis real-time data on the presence of humans and the number of electrical appliances in use. The surveillance data is collected by the Raspberry Pi, and the machine learning model running on it makes real- time decisions, which are sent to the electrical appliances control system managed by the Raspberry Pi. The micro-controller then manages the power utilization based on the received decisions. Through the use of this system, we can significantly reduce power consumption and promote efficient energy use in buildings.

Keywords: Computer vision, electrical appliance control, energy efficiency, human activity recognition, image processing, object recognition, person detection, raspberry, real-time monitoring, relay module

Introduction

Controlling electrical appliances using computer vision to optimize power consumption and auto attendance is an innovative project that utilizes advanced technology to reduce energy usage, improve efficiency, and automate attendance tracking in various settings such as classrooms, offices, and hotel suites. The project relies on human detection and face recognition technology to categorize areas into Dead Zones and Alive Zones, where ample electrical appliances are turned on only in alive zones where the human presence is confirmed. The system also includes an auto-attendance feature that utilizes pre-trained face recognition models to mark attendance for students in a classroom. With potential applications in education, business, and hospitality, the project shows great promise in improving energy conservation, enhancing attendance tracking, and increasing efficiency

[a]vasuadireddy2001@gmail.com, [b]srikanthpothula77@gmail.com, [c]sskvasan552@gmail.com, [d]vivekanandareddy327@gmail.com, [e]tummalayagnagopal@gmail.com, [f]sbagwari@gmail.com

Literatue Review

The paper presents a real-time vision system that uses multiple models to detect and track humans on a mobile service robot. The system is robust to missed, false, and duplicated detections and has been successfully deployed in six robot butlers for serving drinks at public events. However, the system's range may be limited, and future research will explore the use of Pan- Tilt-Zoom cameras to extend its sensing capabilities [1]. The paper introduces an IoT-based home automation system that conserves energy by accurately estimating and forecasting energy usage through machine learning algorithms. The system improvesload forecasting accuracy with nonlinear algorithms and additional features such as weather and household occupancy. It reduces energy consumption, conserves resources, and benefits both the economy and society. Future extensions include identifying high electricity usage areas and proposing solutions to optimize resource use [2]. The paper presents a face recognition system designed with Raspberry Pi for enhancing security in places like banks, hospitals, and labs. The system is smaller, lighter, and more energy- efficient compared to PC-based systems. The use of open-source code in Linux allows for greater software development freedom. The system is programmed using Python and can perform real-time face detection and object recognition. The system's efficiency was evaluated, and the results showed excellent performance even with low-quality images [3]. The Internet of Things enables wireless connection of devices to the Internet, making the designed monitoring system suitable for use in various fields such as healthcare, parking lots, and wildlife observation. However, concerns about privacy exist due to personal data being captured, and unintentional image leaks. To address these concerns, a human detection method was proposed that protects user privacy by intentionally blurring images. The proposed method showed favourable performance compared to an OpenCV based face detection method, and can be applied in practice. Future research will focus on the practical application of this method [4]. A face detection system using Raspberry Pi and programmed in Python was developed and tested on various face databases with and without noise and blurring effects.

The system showed excellent performance efficiency and can detect faces even from poor quality images. The system can be useful in a variety of applications where face detection is needed, such as security systems and automated attendance tracking [5]. In conclusion, the face detection system developed using Raspberry Pi showed promising results, with an accuracy of 99.63%. Python was used as the programming language, providing a free and efficient environment. The system also addressed security concerns, preventing unauthorized access and potential hacking. This system can benefit the elderly and disabled living alone and can be expanded to monitor more devices in the home. The future goal is to improve the system by adding an auto-triggered report to alert the police in case of theft, making the system more advanced and effective [6]. The proposed 3D face recognition approach using Point Signature does not assume limiting assumptions of rigid surfaces and can handle widely different facial expressions for each human subject. It is also important that the algorithm is relatively fast and can efficiently index into the model library to identify the correct model face. The experimental results involving six human subjects with different facial expressions are also a good indicator of the validity and effectiveness of the algorithm. However, it would be useful to have more information about the performance of the algorithm, such as its accuracy and any limitations or challenges it may face in real-world applications [7]. The proposed face recognition system in this paper has been implemented on the Android platform. The system uses the Adaboost cascade classifier for face detection and LBP feature extraction for face recognition. The system also constructs a face recognition classifier using LBP histograms. In the recognition stage, LBP features are extracted and input into the classifier, and a similarity measurement function is used for identification of personnel. The system has been tested on the ORL face database and compared with Fisher face and Eigenfaces algorithms. The results of the experiment show that the face recognition accuracy of the proposed system is comparable to the other algorithms tested [8]. this paper presents a highly efficient and reliable face recognition attendance system that incorporates MTCNN, Face Net, and ERT neural networks. The system's user-friendly interface and fast face detection rate of 33 fps make it suitable for various scenarios. The system's performance evaluation indicates a false accept rate and false rejection rate of under 2% and a stable recognition rate of 20 fps. Overall, this system's advanced neural networks and machine learning algorithms make it an effective solution for attendance management in schools, companies, and enterprises [9]. the smart surveillance system is a versatile technology that can cater to the specific surveillance needs of the user in various scenarios. It has numerous applications, such as monitoring activities in industries or acting as a spy tool in sensitive areas like bank

lockers or storage houses. Additionally, it can notify users about any activities in the surveillance area, providing them with real-time information. With its adaptability and various applications, the smart surveillance system is a useful tool for enhancing security and surveillance in different environments [10] this project aims to improve home security by developing a motion detection system using artificial intelligence technology integrated with Open-Source CV and python. The system provides real-time information about the motion detected in a frame, enhancing existing security devices like motion sensor lighting and security cameras. The project utilizes background subtraction technique to detect motion and overcome issues related to changes in lighting and camera movements. However, the system faces limitations in detecting stationary objects and silhouettes. Overall, this system can serve as an effective tool to enhance home security and public and private place surveillance [11]. The intersection of visual neuroscience and computer vision has mutually beneficial objectives. By understanding the human visual processes involved in face recognition, we can develop better computational models, and vice versa. The 19 observations presented in this paper aim to bridge the gap between these two disciplines. The ultimate goal is to create face recognition systems that can match or exceed the capabilities of humans, and these observations are intended to contribute to this ongoing effort [12]. The face recognition system is being extended to handle different views by defining characteristic face classes for known individuals. The system can recognize multiple slightly different views of a face in a short period of time, improving the chances of successful recognition. The ability to learn and recognize new faces in an unsupervised manner is achieved by reasoning about images in face space. The system is capable of gracefully degrading recognition performance in the presence of noisy or partially occluded face images. The eigenface approach, which is based on a small set of image features that best approximate known face images, provides a practical and effective solution to the problem of face recognition [13]. The paper presents a lightweight multitask learning network that can perform joint face detection and facial motion retargeting in real time on mobile devices. One of the challenges addressed is the lack of training data for multiple faces in 3DMM. To address this, weakly supervised ground truth is generated from a network trained on images with single faces. The network architecture and regularization are carefully designed to ensure disentangled representation learning, which is inspired by key observations. The paper presents extensive results that demonstrate the effectiveness of the proposed approach [14].

Proposed System Model

The block diagram of our face and motion detection system, which is built using the OpenCV library and Raspberry Pi platform as shown in Figure 19.1. The

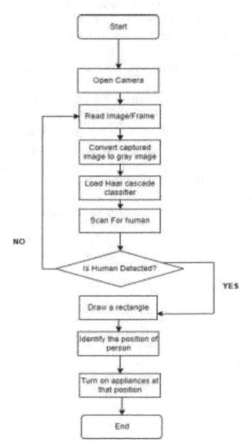

Figure 19.1 Flowchart of proposed working model

process begins by capturing an image or video, which is then converted to grayscale. The grayscale image is then passed through a Haar cascade classifier, which is used for object detection in images or videos and classifies objects based on model trained. If a face or motion is detected, our system activates a relay module, which controls electrical appliances

The image captured by the camera is processed by the OpenCV algorithm to detect the presence of persons and calculate their location within the frame. The detected persons are marked by rectangles with corresponding labels indicating the person number. The location are shown in x-y basis vector coordinate system and provide important information for determining the optimal control of electrical appliances. The system can accurately detect the number of persons and their positions in the room, enabling precise control of appliances based on their location and proximity.

The placement and positioning of a camera play a critical role in determining the quality and effectiveness of the final output. The decision of where to place the camera, how high or low to position it, and the angle at which it is pointed, can all significantly impact the image processing. By mounting the camera horizontally to the floor as shown in the Figure 19.2. Locating the person in the frame is significantly difficult to large extent if person is in eye line of the camera.

The salient feature of the image above is the distinct points that are evidently present, yet their appearance is marred by a conspicuous overlap. However, the current state of the image makes it arduous to proceed with subsequent steps in the processing pipeline. To overcome this obstacle, it is imperative that we modify the position of the camera to address the underlying issue.

By situating the camera in the diagonal corner as in Figure 19.4 of the room, we can obtain a highly accurate image that is conducive to facilitating subsequent actions. This particular placement is typically utilized for security surveillance purposes. This placement allows for enhanced monitoring and surveillance capabilities, enabling the camera to effectively capture.

The aforementioned image evinces a remarkable degree of clarity in terms of the separation between the individual points. This distinctiveness enables us to proceed with further steps for processing the image. It is worth noting that, as

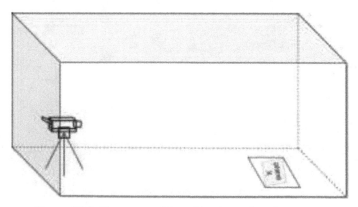

Figure 19.2 Camera positioned horizontal to floor

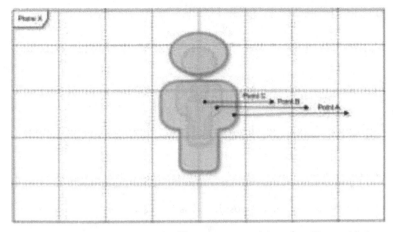

Figure 19.3 Frame captured by camera positioned as Figure 19.2

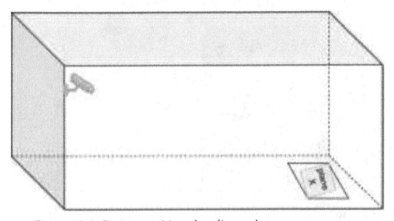

Figure 19.4 Camera positioned at diagonal corner

shown in Figure 19.3 the camera elevation increases, the degree of separation between points escalates proportionally. This phenomenon can be attributed to the increasing distance between the camera and the objects, which results in a more apparent differentiation between the individual points.

Therefore, it is imperative to take into account both the elevation and contrast of the image when analysing and processing it. By doing so, we can ensure that the individual points are accurately identified and analysed, leading to more accurate and reliable results.

Working of the Proposed Model

The model has four different areas where electrical appliances are controlled based on the position of the person detected. Specifically, we detect whether a person is on the back, left side, right side, front left, front right, or both sides as

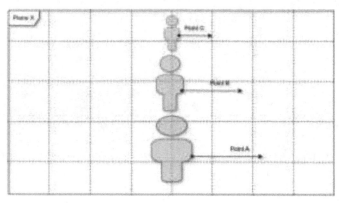

Figure 19.5 Frame captured by camera positioned as Figure 19.4

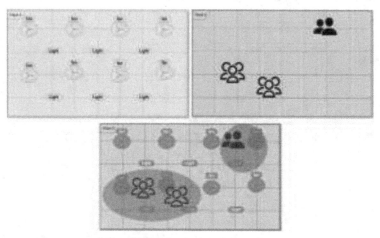

Figure 19.6 Appliances map [top left], Person map [top right] and imbricate map [centre bottom]

shown in figure 19.5. To achieve this, the distance measurements based on the captured image, allowing us to determine the position of the person in the room.

Figure 19.6 [top left] is electrical appliances map, [top right] People location in map and [centre bottom] merge of both maps to create the control contour.

Moreover, by employing this technique, it is possible to create a comprehensive layout of the room, which can assist in automating various tasks within the environment. This concept is built upon the principles of image processing and machine learning, which enable the system to identify and recognize individuals and objects within the room accurately. With this enhanced level of precision, users can control appliances more efficiently, reducing energy consumption and increasing overall efficiency. the proposed approach of mapping electrical appliances to the location map of individuals detected through captured images has the potential to revolutionize the way we interact with our environment. It provides a more accurate and efficient means of control, enabling us to optimize our use of energy and resources.

Additionally, the system counts the number of persons present, ensuring that the appropriate number of electrical appliances are activated or deactivated. This advanced functionality showcases the versatility and effectiveness of our system in different scenarios and environments

Figure 19.7 displays the code and person detection of OpenCV in our face and motion detection system. The code is written in Python and utilizes the OpenCV library to perform the necessary image and video processing. The person detection algorithm uses Haar cascade classifiers to detect the presence of a person in the image or video. The detected persons are then classified according to their position in the room. Figure 19.8 shows demo of hardware mode.

Figure 19.7 showcases the application of our face and motion detection system in controlling electrical appliances using OpenCV and a Raspberry Pi. The system uses a relay module to activate or deactivate appliances based on person detection

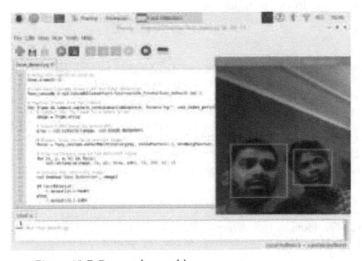

Figure 19.7 Person detected by system

Figure 19.8 Demo hardware model

results. The image displays the physical setup of the system and the appliances controlled by the system

Conclusion

our computer vision control system provides a cost- effective and intelligent solution for controlling electrical appliances based on the presence of persons in the room. By using OpenCV and Raspberry Pi, the system is capable of efficient person detection and precise control of appliances through the relay module. This technology has broad applications in various settings, such as homes, offices, and classrooms, and can contribute to reducing energy consumption and promoting sustainability. The system's reliability and accuracy can be further improved by using advanced computer vision techniques and machine learning algorithms. Overall, the computer vision control system offers a promising approach to the optimization of energy usage in smart buildings

References

1. Li, Liyuan and Hoe, Jerry and Yan, Shuicheng and Yu, Xinguo. (2009). ML-fusion based multi-model human detection and tracking for robust human-robot interfaces. Proc. IEEE Workshop Appl. Comput. Vis. 1–8. 10.1109/WACV.2009.5403083.
2. Raju, L., et al. (2021). Advanced home automation using raspberry Pi and machine learning. In 2021 7th International Conference on Electrical Energy Systems (ICEES), Chennai, India, 2021, (pp. 600–605). doi: 10.1109/ICEES51510.2021.9383738.
3. A., Prof. (2017). Face Detection and Face Recognition Using Raspberry Pi. IJARCCE. 6. 70–73. 10.17148/IJARCCE.2017.6414.
4. Magdin, M., et al. (2019). Motion detection and face recognition using raspberry pi, as a part of, the internet of things. *Acta Polytechnica Hungarica*, 16(3), 167–185.
5. Mane, S., et al. (2017). Human face detection & recognition using raspberry Pi. *International Journal of Advanced Engineering, Management and Science*, 1, 199–205.
6. Rasheed, R. T., et al. (2020). A raspberry PI real- time identification system on face recognition. In 2020 1st. Information Technology to Enhance e-learning and other Application, (IT-ELA. IEEE, 2020).
7. Chua, C. S., et al. (2000). 3D human face recognition using point signature. In Proceedings Fourth IEEE International Conference on Automatic Face and Gesture Recognition (Cat. No. PR00580), Grenoble, France, 2000, (pp. 233–238). doi: 10.1109/AFGR.2000.840640.
8. Jiang, F., et al. (2020). Design of attendance system based on face recognition and android platform. In 2020 International Conference on Computer Network, Electronic and Automation (ICCNEA), Xi'an, China, 2020, (pp. 117–121). doi: 10.1109/ICCNEA50255.2020.00033.
9. Huang, S., et al. (2020). Attendance system based on dynamic face recognition. In 2020 International Conference on Communications, Information System and Computer Engineering (CISCE), Kuala Lumpur, Malaysia, 2020, (pp. 368–371). doi: 10.1109/CISCE50729.2020.00081.
10. Patel, P. B., et al. (2016). Smart motion detection system using raspberry pi. *International Journal of Applied Information Systems (IJAIS)*, 10(5), 37–40.

11. Raj, V., et al. (n.d). Design and analysis of motion detection by using open-source CV. nternational Journal of Research in Engineering and Science (IJRES). ISSN (Online): 2320-9364, ISSN (Print): 2320-9356. 9(7), 2021. 01–05. www.ijres.org

12. Sinha, P., et al. (2006). Face recognition by humans: nineteen results all computer vision researchers should know about. *Proceedings of the IEEE*, 94(11), 1948–1962.

13. Turk, M. A., et al. (1991). Face recognition using eigenfaces. In Proceedings. 1991 IEEE Computer Society Conference on Computer Vision and Pattern Recognition. IEEE Computer Society, 1991.

14. Chaudhuri, et al. (2019). Joint face detection and facial motion retargeting for multiple faces. In Proceedings of the IEEE/CVF Conference on Computer Vision and Pattern Recognition, 2019.

20 Hybrid home automation system using IoT

Manish Das[a], Amandeep Kaur[b], Shahid Sadiq[c], Gregori Simran Ekka[d] and Tapas Kumar Ghosh[e]

School of Computer Application, Lovely Professional University, Phagwara, Punjab, India

Abstract

In this fourth industrial revolution, everyone expects their lives to become smarter and easier with the help of rapidly growing technology. In this paper, a hybrid home automation system is designed which manages various home appliances, keeps an eye on environmental factors like temperature, humidity, gas intensity, light intensity, and whether it's raining or not, and sends alerts in the event of emergencies like gas leaks or when it's raining. The proposed system provides home security with the combination of ESP32-CAM and motion sensor. If the system notices any movement, it will send a picture to the Telegram app, a person can also manually take a picture using the Telegram app. The suggested system also successfully decides whether to make the light and fan automatically switch ON or OFF in accordance with the threshold value. The earlier work done for the same reason lacked a feature of offline capability and the previous relay state was not maintained, to resolve this issue this research work includes included multiple ways to operate this system and used the flash memory of ESP32 to store the previous relay state, which keeps all of the appliances in their former states in case of an electrical power outage. Hence system successfully lowers energy use and the ease of operability increases by a significant margin.

Keywords: Blynk, ESP32, ESP32-Cam, home automation, IFTTT, internet of things, voice control, webcam

Introduction

The Internet of Things (IoT) is a wider concept that envisions connecting numerous household equipment with the Internet. The voice-activated control of different electronic devices or motion sensors that activate a light or carry out a task whenever they detect motion is two straightforward examples of IoT objects [2]. IoT provides more flexible and economical solutions for problems that emerge in daily life, enhancing the user's quality of life [7]. A "Smart Home Automation" is a system that enables users to operate a variety of commonly used appliances, as well as making appliance control much simpler and more energy efficient. The central technology for creating intelligent homes involves a wireless network of sensors and actuators interconnected to facilitate resource sharing. This concept,

---

[a]Manishdas11811480@gmail.com, [b]*amandeepkaur.kaur06@gmail.com,
[c]sheikhshahid798779@gmail.com, [d]gregorix850@gmail.com,
[e]tapasmicrosoft444@gmail.com

known as the 'smart house' paradigm in the context of the Internet of Things (IoT), integrates home automation seamlessly [14]. Smart home systems offer intelligent security through automated monitoring of activities such as identifying movements, detecting falls among the elderly, fire, smoke, gas leaks, intrusions, and home surveillance. These features contribute to safeguarding human life and enhancing security [15]. High-tech features and opulent luxury are now available in homes due to smart home automation. Energy-efficient smart home systems assist in fully automating household appliances and are helpful in preserving or reducing energy consumption, which contributes to a certain level of comfort [13]. Home automation systems (HAS) include lighting, security, and other systems that may be remotely monitored for status and controlled from a central location. HAS offers user comfort and convenience while advancing security safeguards and energy saving [4]. These days, home automation systems are frequently utilised to control appliances around the house. With the aid of a home automation system, many different home appliances can be automated for example doors, lights, fans, electric heaters, surveillance systems, and other household appliances of all kinds. The equipment used in home automation systems is consumer electronics. In order to automate the control of the systems and equipment used in the home, home automation systems are implemented using a technology that is trending in recent years. In general, an IoT-based hybrid home automation and security system provide homeowners with an unsurpassed level of convenience and security unmatched by other options. These systems are anticipated to become more and more common in homes all around the world as technology continues to progress and become more affordable.

Literature Review

Home Automation

Smart home automation means controlling home appliances with the help of the Internet of Things. Technologies for home automation are used to operate appliances, entertainment systems, and electrical devices. For added safety and security, the home automation system will also has a security system [3, 9, 6]. Internet of Things-based home automation systems is made up of many parts, its main focus is collecting and sensing the data and reacting to it according to the predefined threshold value. This is done by installing various sensors throughout the house in various locations to measure and gather the necessary data, such as temperature, humidity, and light intensity [8]. Kundu et al. [1] suggested a system for home security, control, and monitoring that utilises a variety of methods to monitor and regulate household appliances as well as environmental factors like temperature, humidity, and fire. Voice, electrical switches, and the Internet are used to implement control and monitoring.

Blynk

The Blynk app operates as a signal transmitter, sending a signal through a smartphone to a wifi module that receives the signal and takes the appropriate action in response to the signal [5]. The smartphone app from Blynk functions as a control panel for managing and visualising your hardware. Support is provided for iOS and Android. The programme offers a very helpful user interface in addition to several widgets for a range of applications [3].

IFTTT
IFTTT stands for 'If This, Then That,' and it operates as an online service enabling users to establish automated workflows through the connection of various web services and devices. Users have the ability to craft uncomplicated conditional statements, referred to as applets. These applets are activated by alterations in other services and subsequently execute a predetermined action in response. IFTTT supports a wide range of popular web services and devices, making it a versatile tool for automating various tasks [11].

Voice Control
Rani et al. [10] proposed an NLP (natural language processing) and artificial intelligence (AI)-based voice-controlled home automation system. A person can send voice commands through a mobile phone which can be translated using a natural language processing algorithm in response household appliances can be controlled.

The scope of the system wasn't extended to include other aspects of home automation, such as monitoring, controlling, and detecting environmental conditions, intrusions, motions, and so on.It was solely used to operate household appliances.

Methodology

This research is designed with several software and hardware components to achieve the desired hybrid home automation system which includes a home appliances control and monitoring system and a home security system. Implementation of this prototype of this system is done using the following components ESP32, ESP32- Camera, DHT11 Sensor, 5v 4 Channel Relay Module, TSOP1838 IR (thin small outline package infrared) Receiver Sensor, LDR (Light Dependent Resistors) Sensor, Rain Sensor Module, MQ2 Gas Sensor Module, PIR (Passive Infrared) Motion Sensor, FT232RL USB to TTL Serial Adapter Module, a full description of the individual module is given below. After setting up all the wiring and setting of the Blynk app, the user then can perform the following functions-

1. To control all the connected house appliances through the Blynk app, custom web app, physical switch useful in case of wifi is not working, IR Remote, Amazon Alexa or Google Assistant.
2. Monitor Home temperature, humidity, light intensity of the room, gas sensor value, rain sensor value.
3. Detection of movement in the house if PIR sensor is turned on.
4. Receiving notifications and mail if gas leakage or rainfall is detected.
5. View graphical data of all the sensors.
6. Automation of certain home appliances like fan will turn on if room temperature is reached a certain threshold value which can also be set by the user from the Blynk app itself.

7.   Telegram app is being used for getting photos from the ESP32 Camera if any movement is detected.

ESP32

The ESP32 is an economical and energy-efficient microprocessor system on a chip, which incorporates both Wi-Fi and Bluetooth capabilities. This microprocessor is developed by Espressif Systems and manufactured by TSMC, it is an upgraded version of ESP8266 microprocessor, and it can be easily configured through USB (Universal Serial Bus) cable and any supported editor like Arduino IDE or Thonny IDE, it also fast enough to be used in various IoT applications.

PIR (Passive Infrared)

PIR Motion Sensors, also known as Passive Infrared Sensor are utilised by the system. An electrical sensor that detects infrared is used. They are typically used to detect any motion. The indoor passive infrared sensor is having a range from 25 cm to 20 meters while the outdoor passive infrared sensor is having a much higher range of 10 meters to 150 meters.

DHT11 Temperature and Humidity Sensor

DHT11 Sensor which is a very cost-effective and simple-to-use sensor is being used for measuring the temperature and humidity Sensor of a particular area, It needs a 5v power supply to work correctly and it has a temperature range from 0°C to 50°C with an error rate of +2°C or -2°C and it has humidity range from 0% to 80% RH with an error rate of +5% RH or -5%RH.

MQ2 Gas Sensor

The MQ2 gas sensor is a commonly used gas sensor module that is designed to detect and measure different types of gases such as smoke, propane, butane, methane, alcohol, and other combustible gases. It is affordable, easy to use, and provides accurate gas detection. The sensor utilizes a heating element to ionize gas molecules, producing a change in resistance in the sensing element that is measured to determine the concentration of gas in the environment. It comes with a built-in analog and digital output, making it easy to integrate with microcontrollers or other devices.

Relay Module

The 5V four-channel relay module is a easy to use and widely popular board to manage AC (Alternating current) appliances efficiently, inside the relay module electromagnet was being used and when the electromagnet is activated then it either pulls close or open the circuit.

ESP32 Cam

The ESP32-CAM is a compact and energy-efficient camera module specifically designed to work seamlessly with the ESP32. It has an onboard MicroSD card slot and an OV2640 (OmniVision) camera. Many IoT applications including wireless security monitoring, QR (Quick Response) code identification, and others uses the ESP32-CAM.

Rain Sensor Module
A rain sensor is a sensor that will detect rain, when a high amount of raindrops is falling on the raindrop sensing pad then the LM393IC will compare the value of resistance will the threshold value and give the output, if the resistance value is lower than the threshold value the sensor give the output as LOW and resistance value is higher than threshold value it gives the output as HIGH, the threshold value can be set by rotating the potentiometer which was attached to the module.

TSOP1838 IR (thin Small Outline Package Infrared) Receiver
A tiny IR (Infrared) receiver Integrated Circuit (IC) from the TSOP18xx series is the TSOP1838. This specific model, the TSOP1838, will react to IR signals at 38 kHz coming from remote controls. It can be used in to add remote control functionality in applications like TV (Television), AC (Air Conditioning), etc.

Result

The operation, setup, and configuration of each necessary component utilised in this hybrid home automation system are all thoroughly explained in this section. This system controls various electrical household appliances like fans, lights, televisions, etc. It also takes measurements of the room's temperature, humidity, and different gas PPM(parts per million) levels. The system also monitors movement and sends images in the telegram through the Telegram Bot API (Application programming interface). For uploading the code into ESP32-Cam an FT232RL USB to TTL Serial Adapter module was used. In the coding part, the things that need to be included are wifi credentials, Blynk auth token, and a Telegram Bot ID. The code utilized to configure the boards was authored within the Arduino IDE. Once the compilation was successful, the programs were then uploaded to the ESP32. Then, to make home appliances accessible through voice command IFTTT platform is being used, for the configuration of IFTTT Blynk.cloud API (Application Programming Interface) is being used, which will trigger upon a predefined voice command. After setting all these things, proceed to design the interface of the HHA (Hybrid Home Automation) in the Blynk mobile application which was pretty straightforward, Blynk platform provides many widgets through which the interface can be designed simply by dragging and dropping the desired widgets and then choose the virtual pin, for example, if a user wants to display temperature value then he must pick appropriate widget and correct virtual pin. After designing the interface a user can give commands to switch their appliances to ON or OFF State through Blynk Android app. As described in the flow diagram (Figure 20.1), the value collected by the sensors was stored in the cloud platform which can be accessible by the user anytime and anywhere as long as the user's smartphone and system are connected to the internet.

Implementation
The implementation of this prototype is done using ESP32 and ESP32-CAM board and CP2102 USB to TTL converter was being used to program ESP32-CAM board, beadboard was used to link various hardware components to the board, for power supply 9v battery was being used, a DHT11, MQ2 Gas sensor, Rain

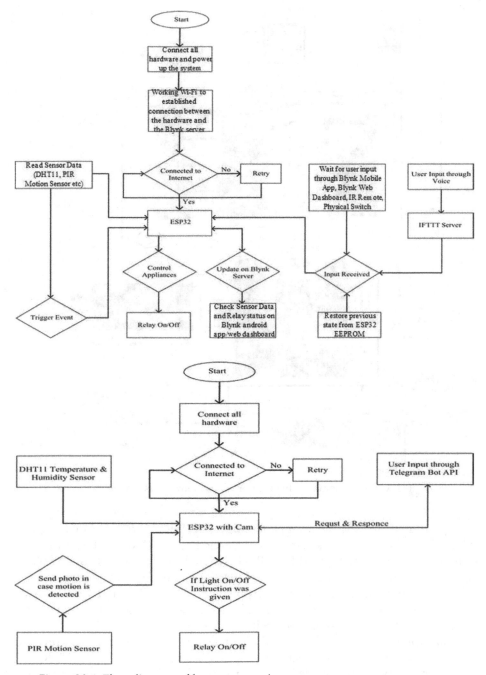

Figure 20.1 Flow diagram of home automation system

Module Sensor, TSOP1838 IR (thin small outline package infrared) Receiver, light Dependent Resistor, different jumper cables (male to male, female to female, male to female) were used to make the connection with all the components with the

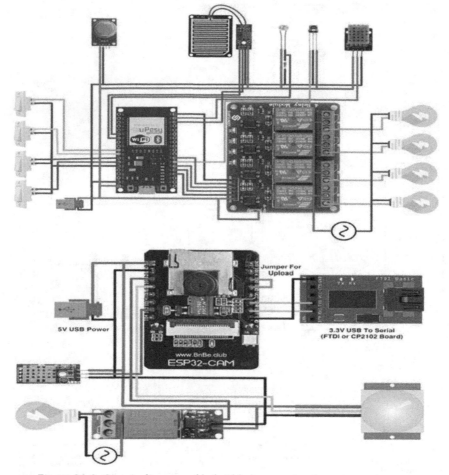

Figure 20.2 Circuit diagram of hybrid home automation system

ESP32 and ESP32-CAM board, A passive Infrared (PIR) Motion sensor was used to identify motion in a particular area where the ESP32-CAM was being set. The system also includes multiple LEDs, a Rocker Switch, and Resistors (10k ohm for Light-dependent resistor, 220 ohms for LEDs), 4 Channel 5V relay module was being used to control AC Electronic Appliances. The ESP32 and ESP32-CAM both boards served as Wi-Fi modules and microcontrollers, wifi is being used to connect our ESP32 and esp32-CAM with as shown in Figure 20.2.

Blynk.cloud platform and also with the telegram, to remember the previous state flash memory of ESP32 is being used which is similar to traditional EEPROM both the memory is non-volatile in nature, to use the flash memory for storing our relay state "Preferences.h" library can be used. The lights of the onboard LEDs of 4 channel 5v relay module was turned OFF or ON according to the given command through our Blynk Mobile app. Figure 20.3(a) shows a command given to turn ON relay number 3 and 4 and according to the command relay 3 and relay 4 onboard led was turned ON. The temperature and humidity values which were

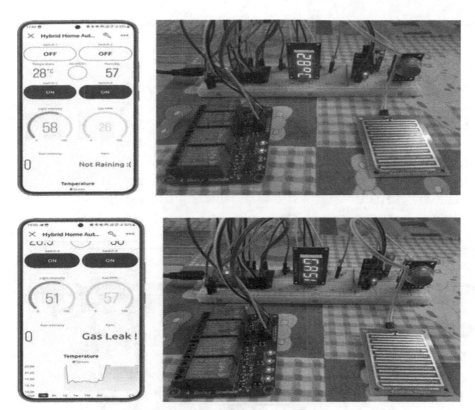

Figure 20.3 (a) Switch 3 and 4 is On, temperature and humidity are also visible and corresponding two LED indicators On, temperature visible in TM1636 4 7-segment display (b) gas leakage is detected which is visible in both app and TM1636 4 7-segment display

fetched from the DHT11 sensor were also displayed in the app and the temperature is also visible in TM1637 4 Digit 7 Segment Display as shown in Figure 20.3(a). This application was designed in such a way that it fetches the reading from the DHT11 sensor on an interval of every 2 seconds and sends these values in real-time in both the Blynk application and TM1637 4 Digit 7 Segment Display. The MQ2 gas sensor also notifies the user when it detects any gas leakage in the house and it also sends a notification and mail to the user, as shown in Figure 20.3(b) and gas leakage message is also visible in the TM1637 4 Digit 7 Segment Display. The rain sensor module will send notification and mail to the user in case it detects rainfall according to the threshold value which was being set, and the message was also visible in the TM1637 4 Digit 7 Segment Display and a real-time line graph was also visible through which user can understand rain intensity according to the time, as shown in Figure 20.4(a). As explained earlier Hyrbid home automation system includes multiple ways of controlling our home appliances, the user can give a automation system additionally guarantees the safety and security of the residence. The following table 20.1 shows the reading of temperature, humidity, rain sensor and MQ2 gas sensor. The assembly of the home

Table 20.1 Temperature, humidity, rain sensor and MQ2 gas sensor readings.

Time	Room Temperature	Room Humidity	Rain Intensity	Gas PPM Value
10.00 PM	23.4°C	62%	56%	12%
11.04 PM	23.2°C	61%	0%	15%
12.01 PM	23.1°C	57%	0%	23%
01.07 PM	22.8°C	59%	0%	21%
02.04 PM	22.6°C	55%	0%	16%
03.09 PM	21.5°C	56%	0%	19%
04.11 PM	21.3°C	51%	0%	19%
05.06 PM	18.7°C	52%	0%	15%
06.01 PM	17.9°C	49%	35%	21%

Figure 20.4 (a) Rain was detected and it's visible in both the app and TM1636 4 7-Segment display and the intensity of the rain was generated as a line graph in the app. (b) Sending command through amazon alexa corresponding relay was turned ON

security module involved employing the ESP32-CAM board and a PIR motion sensor. The motion sensor serves to identify movement within the premises, while the ESP32-CAM captures images of detected objects, individuals, or animals. Motion is recorded by the motion sensor, while ESP32-CAM subsequently sends a real-time image to the user's Telegram account, as shown in Figure 20.5(b), the motion sensor can be turned ON or OFF from the Telegram app to stop sending photos in the presence of the homeowner, otherwise, PIR motion sensor sends an infinite number of photos because it cannot distinguish between owner and intruder. The ESP32-CAM has an inbuilt led which will help to get a better picture in dark. The proposed system also performs multiple automation hence it helps to preserve the energy, for example, our proposed system will automatically turn.

ON or OFF light according to the time of day and LDR (Light Dependent Resistors) sensor value, suppose the room is dark and the time is night then it sends a notification to the user to turn on the light, it can also be automated but the user must set this in the Blynk app, similarly, the fan will be automatically

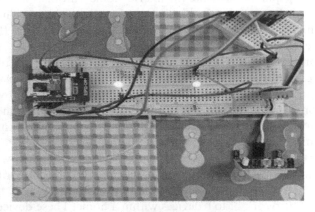

Figure 20.5 (a) Sending command through telegram to get the temperature and turn the light ON (b) If PIR (passive infrared) Motion sensor detected movement and captured images and sends it through Telegram

turned ON or OFF according to the temperature value which was fetched from the DHT11 sensor, but the user can also turn off this feature in the Blynk app setting. The proposed system also provides ease by enabling controlling of the appliances of the home from any location. As a result, the house can be observed and managed remotely from any place. For safety, it is also important to monitor the local surroundings. For instance, the user can check the temperature of the room from a distance and allow the resident to turn on or off the heater or a fan to maintain the proper temperature if an old, or infant child is left alone at home. For instance, the user can monitor the temperature of the room from a distance and allow the resident to turn on or off the heater or fan to maintain the proper temperature if an old, or infant child is left alone at home. By sending a straightforward order to the ESP32-CAM, a user can easily keep an eye on the space through telegram. It promotes the adoption of a healthy lifestyle.

Conclusion

This paper implemented a hybrid home automation system that covers major areas of automation which any home might require. The home automation system allows users to control appliances in multiple ways (Blynk Mobile App, website, IR Remote, Physical Switches, Voice Assistant). The system manages various home appliances, keeps an eye on in case users want to check their house, the proposed system also successfully makes a decision to make the light or fan automatically turn ON or OFF according to the threshold value. As a future direction machine learning algorithms can be used through which the user gets to know about the exact identity of the person or object in real time. For example, a machine learning model could be trained to recognize a person's face and use this information to unlock the front door automatically. In addition, this system can also be incorporated with machine learning algorithms for predicting the home's weather and indoor conditions [12]. Along with that, it is possible to create a network of IoT devices within a home. These devices can be integrated and controlled through a single interface, providing a more seamless and efficient user experience. ESP32 and ESP32-CAM can be integrated with blockchain technology to provide secure and decentralized communication between devices. This can enhance security, privacy, and trust in IoT networks.

environmental factors like temperature, humidity, gas intensity, light intensity, and whether or not it is raining and takes decisions according to the readings from the sensors, and it also sends alerts in the event of emergencies like gas leaks or when it's raining. Using a motion sensor and an integrated camera on the ESP32 Cam, the system also provides home security. If the system notices any motion, it will send a photo to the Telegram app. This proposed system can also manually capture an image through the telegram app

References

1. Kundu, D., Khallil, M. E., Das, T. K., Mamun, A. A., and Musha, A. (2020). Smart home automation system using on IoT. *International Journal of Scientific Engineering and Research*, 11(6), 697–701.

2. Garg, S., Yadav, A., Jamloki, S., Sadana, A., and Tharani, K. (2020). IoT based home automation. *Journal of Information and Optimization Sciences*, 41(1), 261–271.
3. Jotawar, D., Karoli, K., Biradar, M., and Pyruth, N. (2020). IoT based smart security and home automation. *International Research Journal of Engineering and Technology (IRJET)*, 7(08), 2846–2850.
4. Jansi, M. S., and Elaiyarani, M. K. (2020). Iot based home automation system. *Turkish Journal of Computer and Mathematics Education (TURCOMAT)*, 11(3), 2246–2253.
5. Khairnar, M., Tarle, N., Bhandare, S., and Kadam, D. (2021). IoT based lab automation Using android application. *International Research Journal of Modernization in Engineering Technology and Science*. 3(7), July-2021, 463–467.
6. Islam, R., Rahman, M. W., Rubaiat, R., Hasan, M. M., Reza, M. M., and Rahman, M. M. (2022). LoRa and server-based home automation using the internet of things (IoT). *Journal of King Saud University-Computer and Information Sciences*, 34(6), 3703–3712.
7. Majeed, R., Abdullah, N. A., Ashraf, I., Zikria, Y. B., Mushtaq, M. F., and Umer, M. (2020). An intelligent, secure, and smart home automation system. *Scientific Programming*, 2020, 1–14.
8. Meshram, V. R., Pocchi, R., and Thakre, S. (2021). An Iot based smart-home automation with missing data monitoring through computer vision. *International Research Journal of Modernization in Engineering Technology and Science (IRJMETS)*. 3(6), June-2021, 3142–3147.
9. Manojkumar, P., Suresh, M., Ayub Ahmed, A. A., Panchal, H., Rajan, C. A., Dheepanchakkravarthy, A., and Sadasivuni, K. K. (2022). A novel home automation distributed server management system using internet of things. *International Journal of Ambient Energy*, 43(1), 5478–5483.
10. Rani, P. J., Jason, B., Praveen, K. U., Praveen, K. U., and Santhosh. K. (2017). Voice-controlled home automation system using natural language processing (NLP) and internet of things (IoT). In Proceedings of the Third International Conference on Science Technology Engineering and Management, IEEE, Chennai, India.
11. Raj, V., Chandran, A., and Anu Prabha, R. S. (2019). Iot based smart home using multiple language voice commands. In 2019 2nd International Conference on Intelligent Computing, Instrumentation and Control Technologies (ICICICT), (Vol. 1, pp. 1595–1599). IEEE.
12. Gunge, S. V., and Yalagi. S. P. (2016). Smart home automation: a literature review. In Proceedings on National Seminar on Recent Trends in Data Mining RTDM, (Vol. 1, pp. 6–10), IJCA.
13. Shah, S. K. A., and Mahmood, W. (2020). Smart home automation using IOT and its low cost implementation. *International Journal of Engineering and Manufacturing (IJEM)*, 10(5), 28–36.
14. Stolojescu-Crisan, C., Crisan, C., and Butunoi, B. P. (2021). An IoT-based smart home automation system. *Sensors*, 21(11), 3784.
15. Yar, H., Imran, A. S., Khan, Z. A., Sajjad, M., and Kastrati, Z. (2021). Towards smart home automation using IoT-enabled edge-computing paradigm. *Sensors*, 21(14), 4932.

21 ML-based stress classification and detection using multimodal affect dataset

Garima Mazumdar[a], Karan Singh[b] and Divyashikha Sethia[c]

Software Engineering, Delhi Technological University, Delhi, India

Abstract

Mental stress can significantly impact our health and daily lives, making early detection crucial for preventing stress-related health problems. Heart rate, blood pressure, and breathing rate changes may be signs of stress, which can then be utilized in a biofeedback system to immediately recognize stress and alert the user so they can respond accordingly. This study investigates the use of wearable biosensors for stress detection using the Wearable and Stress Affect Detection (WESAD) dataset, which includes multiple bio-signals such as three-axis acceleration (ACC), respiration rate (RESP), electrodermal activity (EDA), electrocardiogram (ECG), skin temperature (TEMP), electromyogram (EMG), and blood volume pulse (BVP). This paper aims to determine the most effective bio-signal combination for accurately classifying stress levels using a lightweight classifier. Analysis of the WESAD dataset using multiple classifiers reveals that EDA is the most significant bio-signal for stress classification, and the XGBoost algorithm achieves an average accuracy of 98.8% and an average F1-score of 98.7% for stress classification using the unique combination of five physiological signals: ACC, EDA, ECG, TEMP, and RESP. These results represent a substantial advancement over previous state-of-the-art research in this field. This paper proposes a lightweight, less resource-intensive, and quicker-to-train model that can be easily integrated into wearable biofeedback devices while delivering more accurate results, making it a more accessible solution for widespread use.

Keywords: Machine learning, stress classification, wearable and stress affect detection (WESAD), XGBoost

Introduction

Stress is any psycho-physiological or emotional strain in response to a stressor. While 'acute' stress or 'eustress' is beneficial, positive, manageable, and not harmful, 'chronic' stress or 'distress' can damage mental, physical, and emotional health. Chronic stress has become a significant concern worldwide, leading to negative impacts on both individual physical and mental health, as well as on economies and society. The recent COVID-19 pandemic has only exacerbated the problem, with increased stress levels taking a toll on people's well-being. Stress activates the body's flight-or-fight response, releasing a burst of hormones to boost alertness, tense muscles, and raise blood pressure, allowing for faster response to hazardous circumstances [1]. However, staying in this heightened sense of arousal for long periods can lead to overexposure to stress hormones, which contributes to health

[a]garima.mazumdar@gmail.com, [b]kssinghkaran13@gmail.com, [c]divyashikhasethia@dtu.ac.in

problems like cardiovascular disease, heart failure, hypertension, memory and concentration problems, mental health disorders like anxiety, depression, as well as other health issues such as IBS, back discomfort, and gastroesophageal reflux disease (GERD) [2]. Early stress detection can help prevent it from becoming chronic and causing irreparable damage. Traditional methods of stress assessment, such as questionnaires and self-reports, are limited by their subjectivity and potential for bias. Measuring stress through physiological signals, which individuals cannot voluntarily control, offers a more reliable approach. The use of mobile health (mHealth) applications and wearables have become increasingly popular for stress detection and management. Wearables can collect and measure physiological signals, such as electrodermal activity, electrocardiogram, and electromyogram, noninvasively and in real-time to measure stress and provide biofeedback to the user.

Despite advances in machine learning for stress assessment using bio-signals, challenges remain in obtaining accurate feature points and correctly classifying stress due to fluctuations in signal size and the presence of noise. Some studies have attempted to categorize stress signals using classifiers with varying levels of accuracy. Prasanthi et al. [10] employed EMG, Galvanic Skin Response (GSR), and respiration signals with an accuracy of 93.65% but had trouble obtaining correct feature points. Md Fahim Rizwan et al. [22] used ECG, attaining accuracy of 98.6% using SVM to combine RR interval, QT interval, and EDR data. Still, this result could be better because it depends solely on one signal, the ECG, and ignores other vital bio-signals that are as critical for stress induction.

Although various studies have been conducted for stress detection using machine-learning techniques, there is still a need to improve the accuracy of these existing techniques in real-life scenarios. This paper aims to propose a novel solution for automatic stress detection using simple and efficient Machine Learning algorithms for stress level classification. The study utilizes the publicly available WESAD [3] dataset, which contains physiological and behavioural data from 15 participants as they perform different resting and stress-inducing activities and tasks like watching videos, public speaking, and reading magazines. The dataset includes data from multiple biometric signals such as:

- Electrocardiogram (ECG): to measure heart rate and rhythm
- Electrodermal Activity (EDA): to measure skin conductance levels
- Respiration: to measure respiration rate and depth
- Motion data: to measure physical activity levels
- Photoplethysmogram (PPG): to measure blood oxygenation levels
- Body Temperature: to measure skin temperature
- Accelerometer and Gyroscope: to measure body movement and posture

The goal of this research is to improve the accuracy of stress level classification using machine learning algorithms and to discover the biological signals that are important in the identification and classification of stress. Multiple classifiers utilising different combinations of raw signals from the Wearable and Stress Affect Detection (WESAD) [3] dataset have been implemented for this purpose. The contribution of this work is the identification of the optimal combination of physiological signals - ACC, EDA, ECG, TEMP, and RESP - and the XGBoost classifier as the solution that provides the best results with an average F1-score of 98.7% and an average accuracy of 98.8%. The proposed solution performs better than existing state-of-the-art solutions, is quicker to train, and is less resource-intensive than deep neural networks, making it more accessible for widespread use.

The remainder of the paper is structured as follows: Section 2 provides a review of the current literature on stress detection using machine learning techniques. Section 3 outlines the methodology we used in our proposed work, followed by the presentation of results and a comparison with existing work on the WESAD dataset in Section 4. The paper concludes with Section 5, which summarises our research findings.

Literature Review

In recent years, researchers have conducted numerous studies on stress detection utilizing machine learning techniques. To improve stress detection accuracy, they have integrated physiological signals like heart rate variability, cortisol levels, and electrodermal activity. They have also applied machine learning methods, such as decision trees, support vector machines, and deep neural networks, to model stress levels in different populations. The use of wearable devices, such as wristbands and smartwatches, has been studied for continuous monitoring of stress levels. Additionally, they have found self-reported measures like question-naires and diaries useful in complementing physiological data. However, com-prehending stress detection in distinct populations and contexts requires more extensive and diverse datasets. The WESAD [3] dataset, which records physi-ological signals from 15 subjects, has become a widely adopted benchmark in these studies.

Previous studies on stress detection using machine learning and the WESAD [3] dataset have compared various techniques for accuracy. For binary and three-class classification, Garg et al. [4] compared the performance of KNN, Linear Discriminant Analysis (LDA), Random Forest (RF), AdaBoost, and SVM [4]. The results showed that Random Forest achieved the highest F1-scores of 83.34 and 65.73 for binary and three-class classification [4], respectively. Cosoli et al. [5] evaluated the WESAD [3] dataset with Linear Regression (LR) and SVM algo-rithms using acoustic signals from the medical devices worn on the chest and wrist, achieving accuracy rates of 75% and 72.62% [5]. Bhanushali et al. [7,8] presented a real-time chest ECG signal prediction circuit with an RF classifier and five low-power time domain features, with an accuracy of 96% and estimated power consumption of 1.16mW. Using the WESAD [3] dataset, these papers dem-onstrate the use of several machine learning algorithms and signal processing approaches for stress detection. However, more research is needed to establish the most effective and efficient methods for stress detection.

Working on the raw signals from the WESAD [3] dataset, [6] utilized Fuzzy C-means for data clustering and proposed a deep hierarchical Convolution Neural Network (CNN) for stress classification, with an average accuracy of 87.7%, while Garg et al. [4] implemented multiple classifiers for stress detection and achieved best results with RF classifier with an accuracy of 84.17% and F1-score of 83.34%. Nigam et al. [9] identified a unique combination of ACC

Table 21.1 Related work.

Study	Signals	Features	Device	Dataset	Subjects	ML Model	Accuracy
[3]	ACC, EDA, ECG, TEMP, RESP	Time Domain Frequency Domain [3]	RespiBAN	WESAD	15	LDA	92.83%
[5]	IBI, BVP, EDA, SKT	Time Domain Frequency Domain Non-linear and information theory-based measures [5]	Empatica E4	Novel + WESAD	22	LR	71.43%
Sumukh Prashant [7]	ECG	Time Domain Frequency Domain [7]	Empatica E4 RespiBAN	WESAD	15	RF	96.00%
[4] 2021	ACC, ECG, EMG, TEMP, RESP, EDA	Raw	RespiBAN	WESAD	15	RF	84.17%
[6] 2021	ACC, RESP, ECG, EMG, EDA, TEMP, BVP, IBI, HR	Raw	Empatica E4 RespiBAN	WESAD	15	CNN	87.70%
[9]	ACC, TEMP, EDA	Raw	RespiBAN	WESAD	15	LSTM	98.00%
Proposed Model	ACC, EDA, ECG, TEMP, RESP	Raw	RespiBAN	WESAD	15	XGBoost	98.70%

(ACCx, ACCy, ACCz), TEMP, and EDA raw signals which provide good results for stress classification and achieved an accuracy of 98% with LSTM as shown in table 21.1.

Methodology

Data Collection

This study utilized the WESAD (Wearable Stress and Affect Detection) [3] dataset. This dataset is meant to evaluate stress and affect recognition algorithms that use physiological signals captured by wearable sensors. The dataset includes signals such as ECG, EMG, EDA, respiratory activity, and temperature, collected from 15 healthy subjects during controlled laboratory experiments that induced different levels of stress and affective states. The experiments involved activities such as public speaking, playing games, and watching emotional movie clips. The dataset provides time-series data for each signal and labels that indicate the type and intensity of the stress or affective state experienced by the subject during each experiment. Label numbers run from 0 to 7, with 0 being not defined/transient, 1 representing baseline, 2 representing stress, 3 representing amusement, 4 representing meditation, and 5, 6, and 7 representing timed periods during which the participant answered surveys; thus, only labels 0, 1, 2, 3, and 4 are utilized. It also includes metadata such as age, gender, height, and weight of the subjects. The WESAD [3] dataset is publicly available for download by UCI and has been widely used in research on stress and affect recognition, machine learning, and wearable sensors.

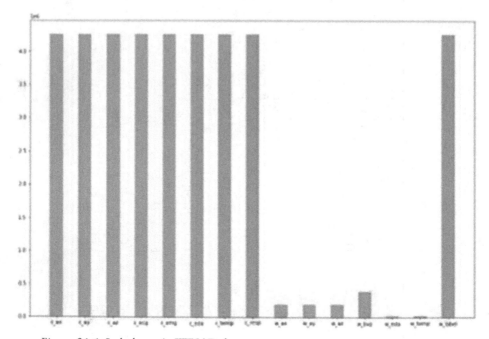

Figure 21.1 Imbalance in WESAD dataset

Data Pre-Processing

The imbalanced nature of the WESAD [3] dataset is a notable characteristic. As seen in Figure 21.1, each output state in the dataset has a different number of samples for each label, leading to a wildly unbalanced distribution. Upon comparing the data obtained from the wrist from the Empatica E4 device and chest from the RespiBAN device, it was discovered that the chest-worn device produced significantly more samples (4255300 per sensor) than the wrist-worn device, which produced less than 500,000 samples per signal. This indicates that the RespiBAN generated 21 times more data than Empatica E4. Moreover, based on the previous work on the WESAD [3] dataset, the bio-signals collected from the chest-worn device outperform the combination of signals collected from both devices. Thus, this work utilizes only the bio-signals from the chest-worn RespiBAN device. The RespiBAN device detects a variety of physiological signals, including ECG, EDA, EMG, RESP, TEMP, and three-axis acceleration ACC (ACCx, ACCy, ACCz). All of the signals are sampled at 700 hertz.

Data Cleaning

Many outliers were found in all eight sensors inside the RespiBAN device, with the EMG, EDA, Temp, and Resp sensors having the most outliers. It was also observed that the RESP sensor has the highest spread, followed by TEMP and EDA sensors, confirming the high spread and outlier presence in these sensor data sets. However, the presence of outliers can cause misclassification issues and affect the model's accuracy. Therefore, the 1.5 x IQR rule was used to identify and eliminate outliers from each sensor that exceeded a certain range. As a result, the cleaned data box plots, as seen in Figure 21.2, displays data with no outliers, making it suitable for creating and training models. In summary, outliers were removed from the data set by eliminating data points beyond (Q1 - 1.5 * IQR) to (Q3 + 1.5 * IQR).

Feature Engineering

After dropping the wrist data due to its imbalanced distribution, Filter and Wrapper methods were used to identify the significant features from the chest. The results showed that the seven features, ACCy, ACCz, ECG, EMG, EDA, Temp, and Resp, were highly uncorrelated and deemed necessary by the wrapper method. Hence, accurate predictions by the ML model require using all seven features. Further, using XGBoost to rank the features according to their importance, EDA is the most significant feature, as seen in Figure 21.3.

Classification Algorithms and Parameter Tuning

This work applies three machine learning classifiers: Quadratic Discriminant Analysis, K-Nearest Neighbour, and XGBoost, to classify stress into four classes: baseline, stress, amusement, and meditation [3].

- *Quadratic Discriminant Analysis (QDA):* QDA is a supervised machine learning approach that uses a quadratic function to represent the probability distribution of each class. The program then employs Bayes' theorem to compute the posterior probability of each class for a given data point and

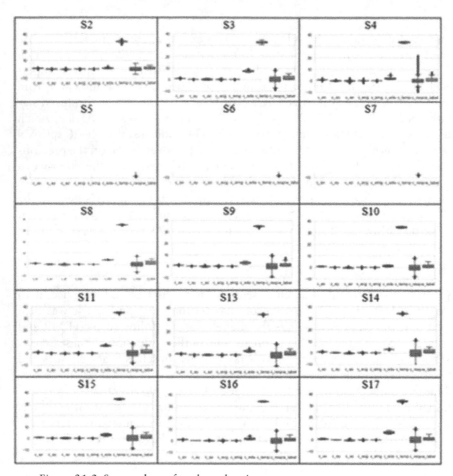

Figure 21.2 Sensor data after data cleaning

classifies the data point as belonging to the class with the highest probability. It was discovered that QDA with normalized data and CV=10 produces the best results.

- *K-Nearest Neighbor (KNN):* KNN is a supervised machine learning algorithm that classifies a data point in a given dataset using the majority class of its k nearest neighbours. The level of smoothness or complexity of the decision boundary is determined by the value of k. After analyzing various adjacent point (k) and power parameter (P) values to find the optimum KNN classification model, it was discovered that KNN with K=5 and CV=20 produces the best results.

- *Extreme Gradient Boosting (XGBoost):* XGBoost is a method of supervised machine learning that makes predictions using an ensemble of decision trees. The approach trains trees iteratively, with each succeeding tree focused on samples misclassified by prior trees, yielding a powerful model with high accuracy. This study discovered that XGBoost performs best with optimized

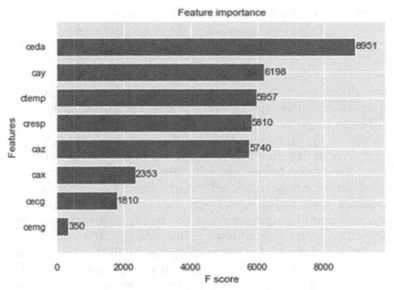

Figure 21.3 Feature importance

hyperparameters of learning rate = 0.1, depth = 10, number of estimators = 300, early stopping rounds = 20, gradient-based = 0.1, alpha = 10, and gamma = 10.

Performance Metrics

This work uses three performance metrics: Accuracy, F1-Scores, and AUC Scores, to evaluate the validity and effectiveness of the classification algorithms for classifying stress.

- Accuracy is a metric that quantifies how well a classification model predicts the class of a given input, expressed as a percentage of correct predictions over all predictions.
- The F1-score is a harmonic mean of precision and recall that is commonly used to evaluate a binary classification model's overall performance, with higher values indicating greater accuracy in predicting both true positives and false negatives.
- The AUC score is a statistic used to assess the validity of a binary classification model's predictions. It denotes the region under the Receiver Operating Characteristic (ROC) curve, with values nearer to 1 suggesting more accuracy in differentiating between positive and negative classes.

Results and Discussion

This study utilizes the publicly available multimodal WESAD [3] dataset for the five-class classification of stress. The dataset contains the behavioral, motion, and physiological data of 15 participants collected using the RespiBAN and the Empatica E4 device. The data was prepared for classification by removing outliers, cleaning the data, and feature engineering. Due to the imbalance between the number of samples from the two devices, only the signals from the RespiBAN device, which captures six physiological signals, including ACC, ECG, TEMP, RESP, EMG, and EDA sampled at a frequency of 700 Hz, have been considered in this work.

This paper aims to determine the most effective individual and combination of physiological signals and classifiers for stress classification, using mean accuracy and mean F1-score as performance measures. Through feature engineering, electrodermal activity (EDA) has been identified as the most significant signal for stress classification, as seen in Figure 21.3. More tests using the XGBoost algorithm were run on S2 data to determine the best individual and combination of features. Although EDA is the most significant feature, Table 21.2 reveals that the classifier's performance is poor when it uses only the EDA signal. However, the classifier's performance improves significantly on combining EDA with other signals. This highlights the importance of utilizing multimodal signals for stress classification. Moreover, it is observed that the combination of all the chest signals (ACC, EDA, EMG, ECG, TEMP, RESP) and the combination of ACC, EDA, ECG, TEMP, and RESP result in the best performance. Hence, after feature extraction, these two signal combinations were selected to train the classifiers on the most relevant and essential information.

Table 21.2 Determining the best individual and combination of features on S2.

Feature(s)	Accuracy	F1-Score
All Signals	0.99	0.99
ACC, EDA, ECG, TEMP, RESP	0.99	0.99
EMG, EDA, ECG, TEMP, RESP	0.90	0.90
ACC, TEMP, EDA	0.98	0.98
ACC	0.89	0.89
EDA	0.48	0.50
TEMP	0.64	0.68
RESP	0.20	0.44

Table 21.3 Comparison of the three classification models for two signal combinations: All signals and ACC, EDA, ECG, TEMP, RESP Signals.

Algorithm	All Signals		ACC, EDA, ECG, TEMP, RESP Signals	
	Accuracy	F-1 Score	Accuracy	F-1 Score
QDA	0.90	0.90	0.89	0.89
KNN	0.90	0.90	0.90	0.89
XGBoost	0.98	0.98	0.99	0.99

Table 21.4 Performance of proposed model per subject.

Subject	Accuracy	F1-Score	AUC score in %
S2	0.99	0.99	99.56
S3	**0.996**	**0.996**	99.80
S4	0.99	0.99	99.63
S5	0.99	0.99	99.48
S6	0.98	0.97	98.61
S7	0.99	0.99	99.65
S8	0.99	0.99	99.40
S9	0.99	0.99	99.60
S10	0.99	0.99	99.33
S11	0.98	0.98	98.59
S13	0.99	0.99	99.46
S14	0.98	0.98	98.69
S15	0.99	0.99	99.02
S16	0.99	0.98	97.72
S17	0.99	0.99	98.71
Average	**0.988**	**0.987**	**99.15**

Table 21.5 Comparison with results of [9].

	Signals Used	ML Model	Classification Type	Accuracy
[9]	Raw ACC, TEMP, EDA	LSTM	Binary: Stress, No Stress	98%
Proposed Model	Raw ACC, EDA, ECG, TEMP, RESP	XGBoost	Four classes: Stress, Amusement, Baseline, Meditation	**98.7%**

Next, the performance of three machine learning algorithms (Quadratic Discriminant Analysis, K-Nearest Neighbors, XGBoost) for the classification of stress into five levels: neutral, baseline, amusement, stress, and meditation were analyzed using the aforementioned signal combinations. For both signal combinations, XGBoost outperforms QDA and KNN. Table 21.4 shows Performance of proposed model per subject. Table 21.5 compares the best results achieved by each classification algorithm using the two best combinations of features – all signals and ACC, EDA, ECG, TEMP, and RESP signals.

Furthermore, on analyzing the proposed model per subject, it is observed that the model produces an average F1-score of 0.987 and an average accuracy of 98.8%. The model's accuracy ranges from 98% to 99.6%, and the best F1-score of 99.6% was achieved for Subject 3, as seen in Table 21.4. Furthermore, the AUC score of the proposed model ranges from 0.9772- 0.998. This indicates that the model has excellent discriminatory power, meaning it can discriminate between both negative and positive classes with great precision.

In comparison to the work of [9], who identified the unique combination of raw ACC, TEMP, and EDA signals for stress classification, this work utilizes the raw ACC, EDA, ECG, TEMP, and RESP signals, and achieves improved results. Moreover, [9] achieved 98% accuracy for the binary classification of stress using the LSTM classifier, while this work achieves an improved accuracy of 98.7% using the XGBoost classifier for the four-class classification of stress.

Conclusion

This research presents a novel approach to classifying stress levels by identifying a unique set of physiological signals, focusing on investigating the potential of wearable biosensors in detecting affective states, particularly stress, in real-time environments. The WESAD [3] dataset, which contains data from various bio-signals such as acceleration, respiration, electrodermal activity, electrocardiogram, body temperature, electromyogram, and blood volume pulse [3], is utilized for this purpose. This work's key contribution is identifying the best combination of physiological signals that can accurately classify stress levels with a lightweight classifier. The analysis of the WESAD [3] dataset using multiple classifiers revealed that the XGBoost algorithm provided the best results upon utilizing a unique combination of physiological signals: ACC, EDA, ECG, TEMP, and RESP, resulting in an average F1-score of 98.7%, average accuracy of 98.8% and an AUC score of 99.15% for the four-class classification of stress. These results represent a significant improvement over state-of-the-art research work.

While deep neural networks have achieved some of the best results for stress detection, their high computational requirements and the need for extensive training data limit their practical use. This work uses a lightweight classifier, which overcomes the limitations of deep learning algorithms while providing superior results, making it a valuable tool for medical professionals who need early and automatic detection of stress in an individual. In conclusion, this study has shown that wearable biosensors have the potential to detect affective states, particularly stress, in real-time environments. The findings from this work suggest that the XGBoost algorithm is an effective tool for stress detection, and the proposed model is a valuable addition to the existing tools available to medical professionals.

This study serves as a foundation for future research in the field of affective state recognition through wearable biosensors. To enhance the results further, future work can involve incorporating self-reports, facial cues, audio/video recordings, and other modalities into the model. The development of a user-friendly platform that leverages this data could provide valuable insights into stress and mental health for individuals and healthcare professionals alike.

References

1. Single Care Team. (2021). Stress statistics: how many people are affected in the U.S. *The Checkup*. https://www.singlecare.com/blog/news/stress-statistics/ (accessed December 8, 2022).
2. Asif, A., Majid, M., and Anwar, S. M. (2019). Human stress classification using EEG signals in response to music tracks. *Computers in Biology and Medicine*, 107(April), 182–196. https://doi.org/10.1016/j.compbiomed.2019.02.015.
3. Schmidt, P., Reiss, A., Duerichen, R., Marberger, C., and Van Laerhoven, K. (2018). Introducing WESAD, a multimodal dataset for wearable stress and affect detection. In Proceedings of the 20th ACM International Conference on Multimodal Interaction, October. https://doi.org/10.1145/3242969.3242985.
4. Garg, P., Santhosh, J., Dengel, A., and Ishimaru, S. (2021). Stress detection by machine learning and wearable sensors. In 26th International Conference on Intelligent User Interfaces - Companion (IUI '21 Companion). Association for Computing Machinery, New York, NY, USA, (pp. 43–45). https://doi.org/10.1145/3397482.3450732.
5. Cosoli, G., Poli, A., Scalise, L., and Spinsante, S. (2021). Measurement of multimodal physiological signals for stimulation detection by wearable devices. *Measurement*, 184(November), 109966. https://doi.org/10.1016/j.measurement.2021.10996.
6. Kumar, A., Sharma, K., and Sharma, A. (2021). Genetically optimized fuzzy C-Means data clustering of IoMT-based biomarkers for fast affective state recognition in intelligent edge analytics. *Applied Soft Computing*, 109(September), 107525. https://doi.org/10.1016/j.asoc.2021.107525.
7. Bhanushali, Sumukh and Sadasivuni, Sudarsan and Banerjee, Imon and Sanyal, Arindam. (2020). Digital Machine Learning Circuit for Real-Time Stress Detection from Wearable ECG Sensor. 978–981. 10.1109/MWSCAS48704.2020.9184466.
8. Simons , A., Doyle, T., Musson, D., and Reilly, J. (2020). Impact of physiological sensor variance on machine learning algorithms. In 2020 IEEE International Conference on Systems, Man, and Cybernetics (SMC), October. https://doi.org/10.1109/smc42975.2020.9282912.
9. Nigam, Kushagra and Godani, Kirti and Sharma, Deepshi and Jain, Shikha. (2021). An Improved Approach for Stress Detection Using Physiological Signals. *ICST Transactions on Scalable Information Systems*. 8. 169919. 10.4108/eai.14-5-2021.169919.
10. Prasanthi, T. L., and Prasanthi, K. (2021). Review of machine learning-based signal processing by physiological signals detection of stress. *Turkish Journal of Computer and Mathematics Education*, 12(11), 4831–4840.
11. Rizwan, M. F., Farhad, R., Mashuk, F., Islam, F., and Imam, M. H. (2019). Design of a biosignal based stress detection system using machine learning techniques. In 2019 International Conference on Robotics, Electrical and Signal Processing Techniques (ICREST), January. https://doi.org/10.1109/icrest.2019.8644259.

22 Color image encryption and decryption using advanced encryption standard

Ishav Raj Vardhan Student[1,a], Parambir Singh Phagwara[2,b], Raunak Singh Shekhawat[3,c], Akash Kumar[3,d] and Deepak Kumar Sen[3,e]

[1]Lovely Professional University, Phagwara, Punjab, India

[2]Assistant Professor, Lovely Professional University, Punjab, India

[3]Student, Lovely Professional University, Phagwara, Punjab, India

Abstract

Data security is currently the largest problem in the world. Data is protected using the advanced encryption standard (AES) all over transmission, storage, and transfer. An advanced encryption standard is a block cipher of symmetrically designed to change the DES in commercial applications. Key of size 256, 192, or 128 is used with the size of block 128 bits. Using the AES method, data is shielded from unauthorized users. The current AES encryption method is used to encode both text and image data. The AES encryption method is used in this study to provide encrypted results after receiving an image as input. The AES decryption method then uses this encrypted output as input to restore the original image

Keywords: AES cipher, DES, image decryption, image encryption

Introduction

More and more individuals are utilizing technology for communication, storage, and transport, including computers, cell phones, and a range of other devices. Users and unauthorized are trying to get unfair access to data both increasing as a result. As a result, the question of data security is brought up. The solution to this problem is to communicate or store data in an encrypted format. The information is encrypted to prevent unauthorized parties from deciphering it. Data security's branch of cryptography protects data as it is delivered and stored. The process of encryption and decryption has two parts: the keys and the algorithm used for encryption and decryption. However, what makes cryptography safe is the keys that are used for encoding and decoding. The same key is employed in symmetric key cryptography for both encrypting and decrypting. In the key cryptography of symmetric, where the singular key is used for both encoding and decoding, there are two different categories of cryptographic operations. Data is encrypted and decrypted using the separate keys in asymmetric key cryptography.

The symmetric algorithm is faster, easier to use, and consumes fewer computational resources than the asymmetric key approach. The AES is the FIPS (federal information processing standards publication) recognized for encoding and decoding methods that may be used to safeguard electronic data. Since 3DES

[a]ishavraj028@gmail.com, [b]parambir. 28398@lpu.co.in, [c]eionraunakshekhawat67@gmail.com, [d]acrobatsakka2299@gmail.com, [e]deepakcsit14@gmail.com

has problems, which include its sluggish software algorithm and usage of 64-bit blocks, which is insufficient for higher levels of security, larger blocks must be used. This is why AES is meant to take the role of 3DES. Aes is superior to 3DES in that it is highly computationally efficient, uses 128-bit blocks, and has great resistance to cryptanalysis against square, linear, interpolation, and differential attacks [1, 9].

Literature Review

The use of symmetric key algorithms, such as the Advanced Encryption Standard or Rjindael, is widely used today technique for picture enciphering. Due to its high degree of security and effectiveness in encrypting significant volumes of data, AES is frequently employed. The authors of a publication published a modified AES method that enhances encryption security by utilizing a permutation matrix to scramble the image pixels before encryption. The chaotic encryption algorithm, which scrambles the visual data by creating a series of chaotic sequences, is another often employed technique. A novel chaotic encryption technique was put out in a paper that combined logistic maps and tent maps to produce chaotic sequences. The technique was discovered to be very safe and efficient in encrypting digital photos. A number of researchers have also looked at the use of neural networks for picture encryption and decryption in addition to these techniques. A neural network-based encryption technique has been proposed that uses a combination of recurrent neural networks (RNNs) and convolutional neural networks (CNNs) to encrypt and decrypt pictures. The method was found to be quite good at keeping the encrypted photos' visual quality while offering high security [10-11].

AES Algorithm Specification

AES utilizes cryptographic keys of 128, 192, or 256 bits to encrypt and decrypt data in blocks of 128 bits. The key utilized throughout the encryption and decryption process forms the basis for this classification. The numbers indicate the number of bits the key possesses. AES supports triple key sizes: 128 bits, 192 bits, and 256 bits. The encryption is more secure the larger the key size. The four distinct byte-oriented adjustments make up the round function employed by the AES algorithm. Changing the byte, moving the row, mixing the columns, and adding the round key are the four encryption rounds that are employed.

The encryption procedure is reversed during the decryption process, which includes the following processes:

- Inverse shift row
- Inverse replace byte
- Adding round key
- Inverse mix columns

There are several key and block rounds in the approach. How many rounds, there are depends upon the length of the key used for encryption and decryption?

Table 22.1 Key-block round algorithm

	Key length(in word/ byte/bits)	Block size(in word/ byte/bits)	Numbers of rounds
AES-128	4/16/128	4/16/128	10
AES-192	6/24/192	4/16/128	12
AES-256	8/32/256	4/16/128	14

An Encryption Method

Byte Replacement Transformation

The non-linear byte replacement method called "Substitute Bytes" uses the S-box substitution table. performs individual Operations on every byte of the State.

		Y															
		0	1	2	3	4	5	6	7	8	9	a	b	c	d	e	f
	0	63	7c	77	7b	f2	6b	6f	c5	30	01	67	2b	fe	d7	ab	76
	1	ca	82	c9	7d	fa	59	47	f0	ad	d4	a2	af	9c	a4	72	c0
	2	b7	fd	93	26	36	3f	f7	cc	34	a5	e5	f1	71	d8	31	15
	3	04	c7	23	c3	18	96	05	9a	07	12	80	e2	be	27	b2	75
	4	09	83	2c	1a	1b	6e	5a	a0	52	3b	d6	b3	29	e3	2f	84
	5	53	d1	00	ed	20	fc	b1	5b	6a	cb	be	39	4a	4c	58	cf
	6	d0	ef	aa	fb	43	4d	33	85	45	f9	02	7f	50	3c	9f	a8
	7	51	a3	40	8f	92	9d	38	f5	bc	b6	da	21	10	ff	f3	d2
X	8	cd	0c	13	ec	5f	97	44	17	c4	a7	7b	3d	64	5d	19	73
	9	60	81	4f	dc	22	2a	90	88	46	ee	b8	14	de	5e	0b	db
	a	e0	32	3a	0a	49	06	24	5c	c2	d3	ac	62	91	95	e4	79
	b	e7	c8	37	6d	8d	df	4e	a9	6c	56	f4	ea	65	7a	ae	08
	c	ba	78	25	2e	1c	a6	b4	c6	e8	dd	74	1f	4b	bd	8b	8a
	d	70	3e	b5	66	48	03	f6	0e	61	35	57	b9	86	c1	1d	9e
	e	e1	f8	98	11	69	d9	8e	94	9b	1e	87	e9	ce	55	28	df
	f	8c	a1	89	0d	bf	e6	42	68	41	99	2d	0f	b0	54	bb	16

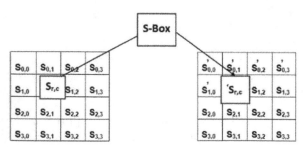

Boxes Table

Rows-Shift Transformations

The State's final three rows of bytes are cycled through many bytes during the Shift Rows transformation. No shift exists in the first row; r=0. As a result, bits are shifted to the row's "lower" places, while the bits below them wrap around to the row's "top." Figure 22.1 represents the algorithm.

Mix Transformations for Columns

By considering each column as a quadratic polynomial, the above transformation alters the State column by the column. A constant polynomial an a(x), with the formula, $A(x) = \{03\}x^3 + \{01\}x^2 \pmod{x^4 + 1}$ is applied to the columns to multiply them and are regarded as polynomials over GaloiFields(2^8).

The resulting columns are shown in the next graphic. This is how mixed columns operate. Figure 22.2 represents the algorithm.

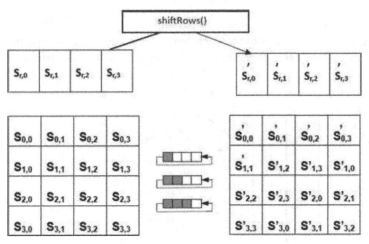

Figure 22.1 Cyclic shift row operation

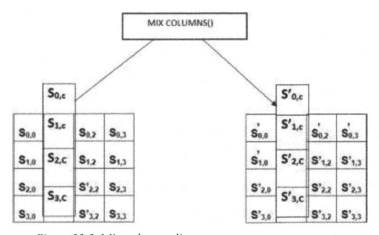

Figure 22.2 Mix columns diagrams

Adding Round Key Transformations

A Round key is added to the state in the Add Round Key transformation via a straightforward bitwise XOR operation. Using a key scheduling strategy, the round Key is created from the cipher key. To get the following State, the XOR operation is used for each element in the State and Round Key: It follows that b(I, j) = (I, j) k (I, j). Figure 22.3 represents the algorithm.

Decryption Process

Shift-Row Transformation in Reverse

The conversion of Shift Rows is known as Inverse Shift Rows. The state's final three rows of bytes alternate between various byte counts. There is no shift in the first row, r = 0. In AES, the bottom three rows undergo a cyclic application of the shift value Nb-Shift(r, Nb) bytes, where the value of shift(r, Nb) is determined by the row number. Figure 22.4 represents the algorithm.

Byte Substitution in Reverse

In the process of reverse substitution bytes, each byte of the State is subjected to the inverse Sbox, which is the inverse operation of byte replacement in substitution

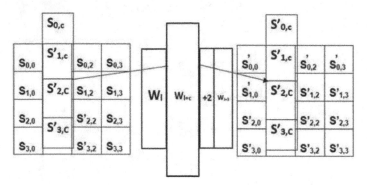

Figure 22.3 Add round-key transformation

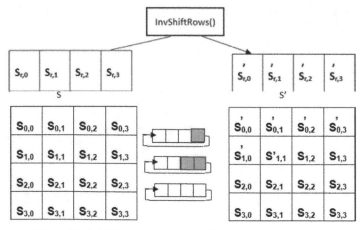

Figure 22.4 Shift row transformation in a reverse

bytes. When used backward, it is the replacement byte transform We must carry out the InvSubBytes step, which is the inverse of the SubBytes step, in order to reverse the byte substitution in AES. The InvSubBytes stage replaces each byte of the input block with a corresponding byte of the original plaintext using a new lookup table known as the inverse S-box. An inverted s-box table is available to take its place.

								Y								
		0	1	2	3	4	5	6	7	8	9	a	b	c	d	e	f
	0	63	7c	77	7b	f2	6b	6f	c5	30	01	67	2b	fe	d7	ab	76
	1	ca	82	c9	7d	fa	59	47	f0	ad	d4	a2	af	9c	a4	72	c0
	2	b7	fd	93	26	36	3f	f7	cc	34	a5	e5	f1	71	d8	31	15
	3	04	c7	23	c3	18	96	05	9a	07	12	80	e2	be	27	b2	75
	4	09	83	2c	1a	1b	6e	5a	a0	52	3b	d6	b3	29	e3	2f	84
	5	53	d1	00	ed	20	fc	b1	5b	6a	cb	be	39	4a	4c	58	cf
	6	d0	ef	aa	fb	43	4d	33	85	45	f9	02	7f	50	3c	9f	a8
	7	51	a3	40	8f	92	9d	38	f5	bc	b6	da	21	10	ff	f3	d2
	8	cd	0c	13	ec	5f	97	44	17	c4	a7	7b	3d	64	5d	19	73
	9	60	81	4f	dc	22	2a	90	88	46	ee	b8	14	de	5e	0b	db
X	a	e0	32	3a	0a	49	06	24	5c	c2	d3	ac	62	91	95	e4	79
	b	e7	c8	37	6d	8d	df	4e	a9	6c	56	f4	ea	65	7a	ae	08
	c	ba	78	25	2e	1c	a6	b4	c6	e8	dd	74	1f	4b	bd	8b	8a
	d	70	3e	b5	66	48	03	f6	0e	61	35	57	b9	86	c1	1d	9e
	e	e1	f8	98	11	69	d9	8e	94	9b	1e	87	e9	ce	55	28	df
	f	8c	a1	89	0d	bf	e6	42	68	41	99	2d	0f	b0	54	bb	16

Inverse S-box table

Inverted Mix Columns

The transformation of MixColumns is known as Inverse Mix Columns. The Inverse MixColumns step uses matrix multiplication to change each state column. Each byte in the calculation is treated as a polynomial with coefficients in the Galoi's field (2^8), modulo $x^4 + 1$. The transform matrix is fixed.

$$a^{-1}(x) = \{0b\}x^3 + \{0d\}x^2 + \{09\}x + \{0e\}$$

Flowchart and Implementation

Encryption Algorithm

Using the MATLAB application, the AES-128 cryptographic method has been put into practice. The output is an image that is an exact copy of the input when the input is an image and the key is in hexadecimal format. Divide the image into 4*4 byte blocks, or matrix format, to start the encryption process. Determine the

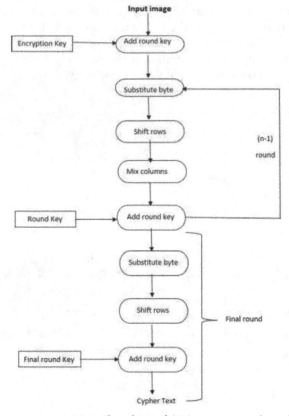

Figure 22.5 Flowchart of AES encryption algorithm

number of rounds using our key schedule and the size of the key. Also included are (n-1) rounds, which entail round key addition, row and column shifting, and byte replacement. There is no mix column in the iteration's last round "n". Figure 22.5 represents the algorithm.

Decryption Algorithm
The reverse of the AES encryption procedure is the AES decryption process. The AES decryption algorithm's flow is depicted in the diagram above. The same key is utilized in both the encrypting and decrypting processes, and

Cipher text is being entered. In the event of decryption, it is necessary to implement an inverse replace byte, shift rows, and inverse mix columns. Even if they add a round key doesn't change. Figure 22.6 represents the algorithm.

Result
The algorithm was given a JPG file as its original input picture also 8.32 Kb in size. By using the decryption procedure, the original picture in JPG format may be retrieved from the unreadable encrypted image. A similar key is used in this article for decryption and encryption. The key is 128 bits long and encoded in hexadecimal form.

DECRYPTION ALGORITHM

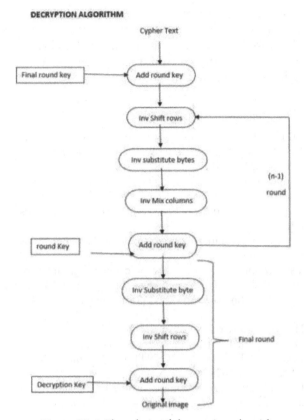

Figure 22.6 Flowchart of decryption algorithm

The key is 0123456789abcdef.

Figure 22.8 Final output window

The input is an image JPG format

The Conclusion

In this study, The data is secured against unauthorized access using the AES technique for encryption and decryption. One of the most accurate encryption and decryption standards at the moment is the symmetric key AES implementation. With the assistance of MATLAB code, an execution of the above algorithm is composed and tested for the cryptographic encryption of the picture. It is also possible to precisely and fully rebuild the original photos. Studies have shown that these algorithms can resist the most common types of attacks, such as brute-force attacks, cipher attacks, and plaintext attacks. Additionally, they have an extensive security key space, which further enhances their security.

References

1. Bhardwaj, V., and Kaur, N. (2021). SEEDRP: a secure energy efficient dynamic routing protocol in fanets. *Wireless Personal Communications*, 120. 10.1007/s11277-021-08513-0. *Science (IJETTCS)*, 3(3), 1251–1277.
2. Bhardwaj, V., Kaur, N., Vashisht, S., and Jain, S. (2021). The development of secure and reliable intercluster routing protocols has become crucial for efficient data transmission in flying ad hoc networks. *Transactions on Emerging Telecommunications Technologies*, 32. 10.1002/ett.4068.
3. Stallings, W. (n.d). Advance encryption standard. Cryptography and Network Security, 4th ed. India: Pearson. (pp. 134–165).
4. Kahate, A. (n.d). Computer-based symmetric key cryptographic algorithm. In Cryptography and Network Security, 3rd ed. New Delhi: McGraw-Hill, (pp. 130–141).
5. Elbably, Y. (2022). Digital image encryption using AES encryption scheme. 10.13140/RG.2.2.23962.93129.
6. Laad, A., and Sawant, K. (2021). A literature review of various techniques to perform encryption and decryption of data. In 2021 10th IEEE International Conference on Communication Systems and Network Technologies (CSNT), Bhopal, India, 2021, (pp. 696–699). doi: 10.1109/CSNT51715.2021.9509595.
7. Kaur, M., Singh, S., Kaur, M., et al. (2022). A systematic review of metaheuristic-based image encryption techniques. *Archives of Computational Methods in Engineering*, 29, 2563–2577.
8. Zinabu, N. G., and Asferaw, S. (2022). Enhanced efficiency of advanced encryption standard (EE-AES) algorithm. *American Journal of Engineering and Technology Management*, 7(3), 59–65. doi:
9. Misra, M. K., Mathur, R., and Tripathi, R. (2021). A new encryption/decryption approach using AES. In 2021 5th International Conference on Information Systems and Computer Networks (ISCON), Mathura, India, 2021, (pp. 1–5). doi: 10.1109/ISCON52037.2021.9702470.
10. Surabhi, P. R., and Meenu, T. V. (2021). Advanced 256-bit AES encyption with plain text partitioning. In 2021 International Conference on Advances in Computing and Communications (ICACC), Kochi, Kakkanad, India, 2021, (pp. 1–3). doi: 10.1109/ICACC-202152719.2021.9708158.
11. Hamza, A., and Kumar, B. (2020). A review paper on DES, AES, RSA encryption standards. In 2020 9th International Conference System Modeling and Advancement in Research Trends (SMART), Moradabad, India, 2020, (pp. 333–338). doi: 10.1109/SMART50582.2020.9336800.

23 Multiple disease prediction using machine learning

Mohit Kumar[a], *Nikhil Sahu, Shruti Kumari,*
Swaraj Senapati and Sandeep Kaur

Lovely Professional University, Phagwara (144411), Punjab, India

Abstract

This research paper demonstrates the application of machine learning (ML) algorithms for the detection of five common diseases: diabetes, breast cancer, kidney disease, heart disease, and liver disease. This research paper has explored the use of ML algorithms for these diseases' early identification and detection. The results of these studies demonstrate that machine learning algorithms can outperform traditional diagnostic methods, providing accurate and efficient tools for healthcare professionals. The algorithms like SVM, Decision Tree, KNN, Random Forest, Logistic Regression, Gradient boosting Classifier, Extreme Gradient Boosting are used where in different disease different algorithms have shown remarkable accuracy in detecting and predicting diseases.

Keywords: Disease detection, machine learning, supervised learning, unsupervised learning

Introduction

This study aims to apply the modern studies in machine learning for the identification of numerous diseases and to pinpoint the opportunities and challenges in this area. We will review the many machine learning techniques that have been created for this, the data sources used, and the performance metrics used to evaluate these models [11]. We will also discuss the ethical considerations involved in using machine learning for medical diagnosis and propose future research directions [13].

Our research focuses on developing models that can accurately detect various diseases, including heart disease, diabetes, and breast cancer, using patient data such as medical history, physical examination, and laboratory results [8]. We utilized a large dataset of patient records, including medical history, to train and evaluate our models.

We employed several machine learning algorithms, including random forest, support vector machine, and Xgboost, to build our models [5, 6, 9]. We also used various feature selection and feature engineering techniques to improve the accuracy of our models [10]. Our evaluation results demonstrate the effectiveness of our models in detecting multiple diseases, with high accuracy, sensitivity, and specificity.

[a]mohitkumar637@gmail.com, sandeep.23614@lpu.co.in

Literature Review

- Breast Cancer: With the purpose of detecting breast cancer, researchers have created many machine learning algorithms. A deep convolutional neural network (CNN) was created to categories breast cancer histopathology images, as was discovered in our research study [2]. The approach outperformed conventional machine learning techniques, with an accuracy of 94.49%.
- Diabetes: Diabetes early diagnosis and prediction have both been achieved using machine learning techniques. Using decision trees and logistic regression, a machine learning system was created, according to our analysis, to predict the likelihood of getting type 2 diabetes [1, 4]. The program outperformed conventional risk prediction models with an accuracy of 80.6%.
- Kidney Disease: As found in our research study, a machine learning algorithm based on decision tree and artificial neural network was developed to diagnose chronic kidney disease [3]. The algorithm achieved an accuracy of 97.5% and outperformed traditional diagnostic methods.
- Heart Disease: A convolutional neural network-based deep learning algorithm was created to forecast the risk of heart disease, as was discovered in our research study [12]. The program outperformed conventional risk prediction models with an accuracy of 85.4%.
- Liver disease: Our work found that a random forest classifier-based machine learning method was created to diagnose liver illness [7]. The system surpassed conventional diagnostic techniques with an accuracy of 85.4%.

Methodology

Data Collection and Data Preprocessing

- Data Collection: For collecting data, data is taken from Kaggle between 2020 to 2023.
- Data Processing: This is the project's fundamental phase, during which attributes are factored, data is cleaned, and lost and null elements are located.
- Data Cleaning: As there are no missing or null values in this dataset, no data cleaning is necessary.
- Factorization: In order to prevent confusion for the algorithm, we basically give the attribute a meaningful name in this case. For instance, instead of the breast cancer property having the values 0, 1, it now has no, yes, signifying that no patients have breast cancer and yes patients do.

Analyzing the Dataset

The dataset has been examined for its structure, number of observations, dependentvariables, and independent variables using statistical methods in Python. In order to determine the breadth of the qualities, an analysis was conducted, and a few inferences were discovered. The Findings and Discussion section discusses the findings of the data investigation.

Model Building

An extensive investigation shows that each attribute in the dataset significantly affects the dependent variable for each condition. So, each variable is taken into account when building a prediction model for each circumstance. Before these models are constructed, the dataset is randomly partitioned into training and testing sets. The recommended project was created using the required Python programming libraries and functions for several supervised machine-learning classification-based techniques.

Table 23.1 Accuracy % table for each disease.

Disease / Algorithms	Support Vector Machine	Gradient Boosting Classification	Logistic Regression	Random Forest Classification	Decision Tree Classification	Xg Boost	K-Nearest-Neighbour
Breast Cancer	98.67	98.00	97.33	97.33	96.67	95.33	94.67
Diabete	86.06	88.94	86.06	87.50	84.62	90.38	79.33
Kidney	72.59	97.40	87.40	95.92	1.00	93.70	88.14
Heart Disease	76.19	98.09	90.47	97.14	92.38	96.19	64.76
Liver disease	69.44	69.44	72.92	67.36	65.97	70.14	67.36

Model Selection
Once these classification models are developed, predictions are made and each model is evaluated using performance metrics such as accuracy. Table 23.1 provides the detailed accuracy in the Classification Model Evaluation section below. The most accurate model is chosen for deployment since it has the highest accuracy. SVM method, for instance, has the highest accuracy in detecting breast cancer, detail performance evaluation is provided in Figure 23.1. As a result, it is utilized when creating web applications.

Introducing a Web-Application
The user enters values for dataset attributes into a web application, and after clicking, get prediction label, the application outputs result. Web-based applications are created to make it simple for users to receive predictions about the likelihood of a given condition.

Implementation and Result

For the implementation of the multiple disease predictor, we had used python programming language and its different types of libraries.

- Library used: Numpy, Pandas, Seaborn, Matplotlib, Sklearn, Pickle, Flask, Tensorflow

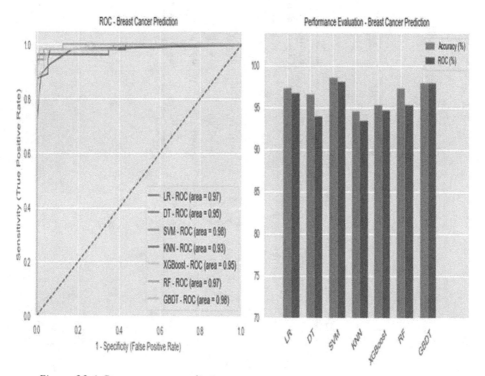

Figure 23.1 Breast cancer prediction

- Algorithm/Model accuracy evaluation:

Table 23.1 shows the accuracy of different machine learning algorithms implemented.

Our study included a comprehensive performance evaluation, which is summarized in Figures 23.1, 23.2, 23.3, 23.4 and Figure 23.5. Receiver Operating

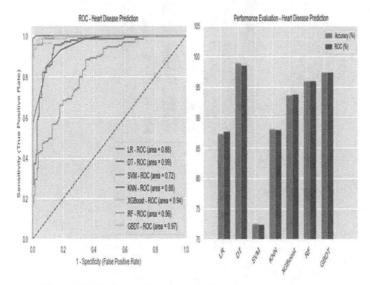

Figure 23.2 Heart disease prediction

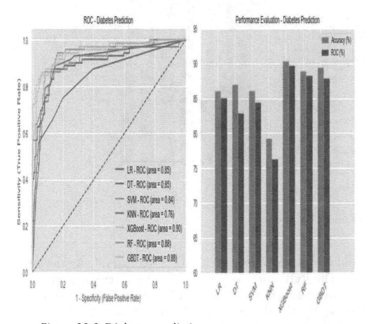

Figure 23.3 Diabetes prediction

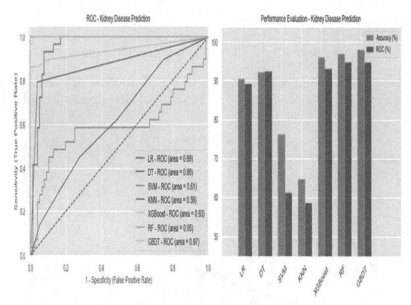

Figure 23.4 Kidney Disease Prediction

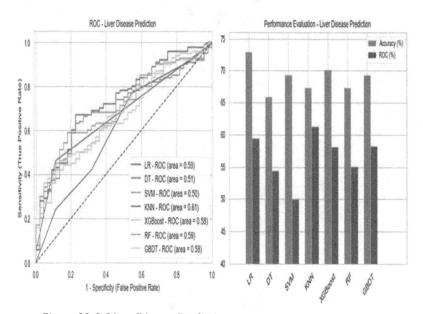

Figure 23.5 Liver Disease Prediction

Characteristic (ROC) and area under curve (AUC) are used to evaluate the performance of the models. The ROC curve provides a graphical representation of the model's trade-off between True Positive Rate (TPR) and False Positive Rate (FPR) for different classification thresholds, while AUC provides a single numerical value that summarizes the ROC curve's performance.

Conclusion

In conclusion, this research paper demonstrated that some algorithms were highly accurate in identifying diseases, pointing to their potential value in medical care. Future work in this area will focus on creating reliable machine learning models that may be used in clinical decision-making procedures to identify a variety of diseases.

A wide range of algorithms including SVM, Decision trees, Xgboost, Logistic Regression, Gradient boosting, KNN, and Random Forest is used. The development of multiple models can provide more insight into the model's decision-making process and can lead to the development of more accurate and reliable disease detection models.

One potential avenue of research is to investigate the portability and generalizability of the developed models to different datasets and populations. This can involve training and testing the models on larger and more diverse datasets to evaluate their performance across different geographical and demographic data.

References

1. Karun, S., Raj, A. and Attigeri, G., 2019. Comparative analysis of prediction algorithms for diabetes. *In Advances in Computer Communication and Computational Sciences: Proceedings of IC4S 2017*, 1, 177–187. Springer Singapore.
2 Hasan, A. M. A., Karim, A., and Islam, S. M. R. (2018). A decision tree based approach for breast cancer diagnosis using mammogram images. In International Conference on Intelligent Computing and Optimization (ICO).
3. Tomar, D. and Agarwal, S., (2015). Hybrid feature selection based weighted least squares twin support vector machine approach for diagnosing breast cancer, hepatitis, and diabetes. *Advances in Artificial Neural Systems*, 2015. 1–10.
4. Tabrizchi, H., Tabrizchi, M. and Tabrizchi, H., (2020). Breast cancer diagnosis using a multi-verse optimizer-based gradient boosting decision tree. *SN Applied Sciences*, 2, 1–19.
5. Garg, J., and Singh, S. K. (2021). Extreme gradient boosting machine learning algorithm for pneumonia detection using chest x-ray images. In 2021 11th International Conference on Cloud Computing, Data Science and Engineering (Confluence).
6. Rahman, M. M., Akhand, M. A. H., and Ahmed, M. F. (2018). Improved support vector machine classifier for liver disease diagnosis. In Proceedings of the 7th International Conference on Electrical and Computer Engineering, December 2018.
7 Li, L., Qin, Z., Huang, J., and Li, Y. (2019). Machine learning for healthcare: review, opportunities, and challenges. *Briefings in Bioinformatics*, 20(6), 2188–2203.
8. Kachuee, M., Fazeli, S., and Sarrafzadeh, M. (2018). ECG heartbeat classification: a deep transferable representation. In 2018 IEEE International Conference on Healthcare Informatics (ICHI), New York, NY, USA, 2018, (pp. 443–444). doi: 10.1109/ICHI.2018.00092.
9. Rajpurkar, P., Irvin, J., Zhu, K., Yang, B., Mehta, H., Duan, T., Ding, D., Bagul, A., Langlotz, C., Shpanskaya, K., Lungren, M. P., and Ng, A. Y. (2018). CheXNet: radiologist-level pneumonia detection on chest X-rays with deep learning. arXiv preprint arXiv:1711.05225.

10. Karim, S. M. M., Sultana, M. S., and Islam, M. A. (2019). Random forest and support vector machine classification models for heart disease prediction. In 2019 IEEE International Conference on Artificial Intelligence and Computer Engineering (ICAICE).

11. Zhao, R., Yan, R., Chen, Z., Mao, K., Wang, P., and Gao, R. X. (2019). Deep learning and its applications to machine health monitoring. *Mechanical Systems and Signal Processing*, 115, 213–237. ISSN 0888-3270.

12. Karimpouli, S., and Tahmasebi, P. (2020). Physics informed machine learning: Seismic wave equation. *Geoscience Frontiers*, 11(6), 1993–2001. ISSN 1674-9871.

13. Ebrahimi, Z., Loni, M., Daneshtalab, M., and Gharehbaghi, A. (2020). A review on deep learning methods for ECG arrhythmia classification. *Expert Systems with Applications: X*, 7, 1–23. ISSN 2590-1885.

24 A comprehensive review of text summarization: state-of-the-art approaches and challenges

*Cephas Iko-Ojo Gabriel[a], Balraj Kumar[b],
Md Irfan Alam[c], Pramatma Vishwakarma[d],
Shaik Nelofer[e] and Km Mahima Marwaha[f]*

School of Computer Applications, Lovely Professional University, Phagwara, Punjab, India

Abstract

Text summarization (TS) refers to the technique(s) required to create a coherent summary that includes key phrases and any relevant important information from the source text or document. Considering the summarized results, extractive and abstract methods are among the most important. Real-time summary and abstract summation are now the focus of research as extractive summary is nearing maturity. There are not several publications that can give a comprehensive overview of the state of research on this topic, although numerous successes in obtaining libraries, approaches, and techniques have been published. This article provides a thorough and organized overview of text summarization research published between 2019 and 2023. The extraction of selected studies of 67 journal and conference articles is to identify, analyze, and describe research trends, features, techniques, methods, evaluation metrics, research gaps, problems, and challenges in the field of TS. For ease of research and reanalysis, the relationship between the topical trends, issues, and difficulties in each topic, and the technique and methodology used is consolidated into this paper.

Keywords: Machine learning, review, text mining, text summarization

Introduction

With the spread of the internet and big data, people are increasingly overwhelmed by the amount of information and documents available online. This fuel the ambition of many scientists to develop a technical strategy that can automatically summarize texts. According to Al-Thanyyan et al. [3], the automatic text summary creates summaries that include key phrases and all relevant information from the original text. As a result, information is delivered quickly while maintaining the document's original objective [4]. Since the middle of the 20th century, research has been done on summarizing texts.

The text summary was introduced in 1958 by Luhn [8], who used word frequency charts as a statistical tool to explain the subject. Since then, this topic has experienced exponential growth and researchers have provided a variety of text summarization techniques [1]. Many concerns have been addressed recently,

[a]cephas.iko.ojo@gmail.com, [b]balraj_kr@yahoo.co.in, [c]irfan.29670@lpu.co.in,
[d]vpramatma@gmail.com, [e]neeloufarsk@gmail.com, [f]marwah.mahima1@gmail.com

including the lack of consistency in summaries and the common techniques provided to find relevant content or important keywords.

The two main categories of TS techniques are extractive and abstractive techniques. [12] Without altering the original content, extractive summarization takes key sentences or phrases from its sources and groups them to develop a summary using a hidden Markov model proposed based on part-of-speech (POS) tagging (Suneetha, et al., 2012). Abstractive summarization involves capturing the original text through linguistic analysis and interpretation of the text. Abstractive techniques require a more thorough reading of the text. These techniques can deliver fresh sentences, sharpen the focus on summaries, reduce repetition, and maintain a high coherent rate [11].

This article presents a comprehensive review of text summarization, divided into five research questions. It aims to provide an overview of the most modern techniques and strategies applied to text summarization, as well as provide information on current trends and future directions to emerging scholars and practitioners.

Methodology

Review Method
The study approach is presented in this section as shown in Figure 24.1 [14]. Systematic Literature Review (SLR) was employed to conduct this review study on text summarization. According to [9], SLR is a method for identifying, evaluating, and interpreting research results that have been made overall and are pertinent to the study or research questions (RQ1 to RQ5) (see Section 2.4) and seek to answer. According to [14], the SLR is generally divided into three phases: the planning phase, the execution phase, and the reporting phase.

Search Strategy
Proper expert preparation and search strategy suitable for reviewing this text summarization research was carried out. This research was conducted using the

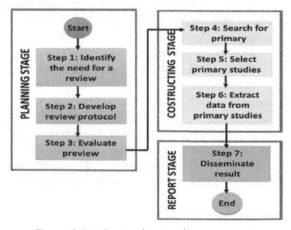

Figure 24.1 Comprehensive literature review

following preferred electronic sources to provide a global perspective: Springer, ACM, IEEE Xplore, and Science Direct. These databases were chosen because they are considered the best, most popular, and richest sources for research articles on text summarization.

Using the study questions as a guide, the search terms were carefully crafted. The search terms were adjusted several times to compile practically relevant works as much as possible. Numerous search terms with different word combinations were used to search through the relevant papers. The following strings are included in this list: *("abstractive or extractive summarization" OR "real-time text summarization" OR "text summarization") AND ("technique" OR "approach" OR "method")*. Paper items included are limited to English language paper items.

Selection Strategy Research Questions (RQs)

When the article search strategy phase is run, a large number of articles that meet the criteria are filtered out when the search customization process is performed. The exclusion and inclusion criteria given in Table 24.1 were used to determine the article criteria for the main study. Also, we need the procedure shown in Figure 24.2 to create constrained studies that match the current study for proper review [7]. Mendeley's software is employed to process search results and simplifies their categorization according to defined topics.

All articles were divided into two groups, selected articles and rejected articles, after the selection process. Only 67 (28.15%) out of 238 research results were found to be relevant to the review study, so 171 studies (71.85%) were excluded.

Research Questions (RQs)

RQs are prepared to assist in making the review process more precise and reliable. The relevant criteria of Population, Intervention, Comparison, Outcomes, and

Table 24.1 Inclusion and sxclusion riteria.

Type-A: Inclusion Criteria
Only written articles related to research questions (RQ1 to RQ5).
Peer-reviewed articles
Full- articles
Articles published between 2019 and March 2023
Articles are written in English language only

Type-B: Exclusion Criteria
Only written articles not related to research questions (RQ1 to RQ5).
Non-peer-reviewed articles
Posters and short articles
Articles published before 2019 after March 2023
Articles not written in the English language
Master and Doctoral dissertations

Source: Kumar, B., & Sharma, N. (2016). Approaches, issues and challenges in recommender systems: a systematic review. Indian J. Sci. Technol, 9(47), 1-12.

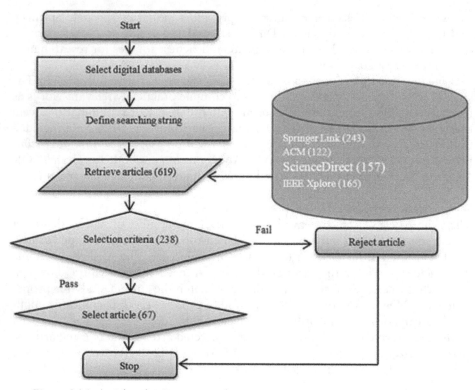

Figure 24.2 Article selection approach

Table 24.2 PICOC criteria applied to TS.

Population	Products review of TS
Intervention	Products review of the TS technique
Comparison	Approaches of TS
Outcomes	Optimization TS
Context	Empirical studies within the scope of TS

Source: [6].

Context (PICOC) are typically used to develop RQs [6]. These criteria are shown in Table 24.2 below.

Table 24.3 provides an explanation of the RQs and motivation for this literature review.

Results

This section discusses the five research questions (RQs) posed in Table 3 to provide a thorough overview of some of the more general factors of text summarization. To address the RQs, the following subsections attempt to present these factors:

Table 24.3: Research questions and motivation.

RQ ID	Research Question	Motivation
RQ1	Which features are used in the TS?	Identify which features are included in the TS.
RQ2	What techniques are used in TS?	Identify techniques commonly used in TS.
RQ3	What types of problems and challenges are encountered when using TS?	Identify problems and challenges encountered when using TS.
RQ4	Which evaluation methods are used to measure the quality of the TS?	Identify evaluations measure carried out in the TS.
RQ5	What are the different gaps in the present TS?	Identify different gaps in the present TS.

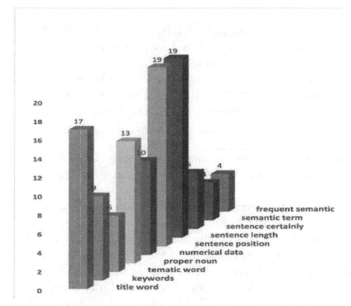

Figure 24.3 Features used in TS
Source: [14]

Features of TS

Figure 24.3 explains the features used in text summarization research [14]. Traits are unique features that can be retrieved from text to create a summary. Over the past decade, text summarization research has commonly used ten features.

The following features are used in recent research using fairly complete features, including sentence features (sentence length and sentence position), word features (proper noun word, title word, topic word, numeric data, keywords with TF-IDF), and evaluation features [10] below using the fuzzy logic system. Extractive summaries are generated by joining the statistical method with fuzzy-based logic,

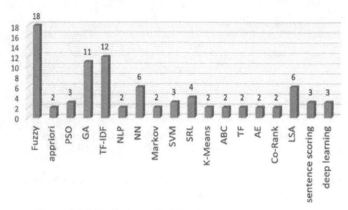

Figure 24.4 Techniques in TS
Source: [14].

specifically the multi-document text input and TF-IDF method. The benefit of this strategy employed is that it allows for improved matching through the use of sentence scoring. The problem with the sorting of the sentence summary is a disadvantage, although it can be quite difficult, sentence sorting is crucial when summarizing documents. Further work on the MDS form may focus on adding linguistic and semantic elements to make the summary more coherent [10].

Techniques Used in TS

Six techniques or methodologies for text summarization have been identified from recent literature: machine learning, fuzzy-based, statistical, graphing, modelling topic, and rule-based.

The most well-known method for text summarization is machine learning. It is a state-of-the-art method that works automatically and absorbs new information without explicit programming. Techniques used include Objective ABC, Semantic Role Labeling, Abstractive Summarization of Video Sequences (ASoVS), Cellular Learning Automata, RNN, Patsum, MSPointerNetwork, Shark Smell Optimization (SSO), IncreSTS, Title Identification, Sentiment Embedding (SE), Discourse Supervised Tree-Based Summary (DST), K-Means, Auto Encoder (AE), Deep Learning, SVM, Markov, PSO, Maximum Marginal Relevance (MMR), NN, among others as shown in Figure 24.4 [14].

Problems in TS

Finding new features to create a concise and coherent summary of original texts and documents still seem to be a difficult task in the field of summarizing text. Alternatively, identifying the set of features that gives the best summary with the greatest improvement is the challenge. [2]

Since statistical techniques can be used to address them, issues like word frequency and sentence rating are less challenging. One of the issues that arise is sentiment analysis, which is one of the benefits of TS and is used to evaluate the sentiment of text content among others as shown in Figure 24.5 [15].

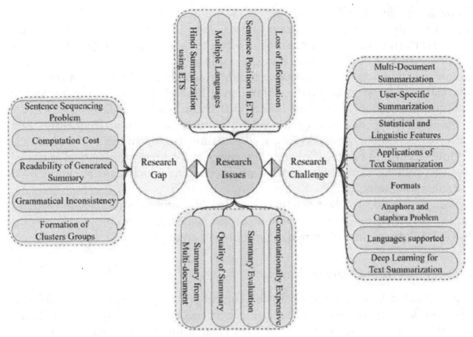

Figure 24.5 Gaps, issues, and challenges
Source: [15]

Semantic issues are another issue that has continued to be a disadvantage in previous studies. An automatic text summation process results in a summary with high-quality target material. Huge documents, especially those with multiple documents, may contain ambiguous statements, terms with multiple meanings, or synonyms. To ensure that the words or sentences contained in the summarized version match the aim of the source or original document, hence, semantic issues need to be addressed.

Evaluation of TS

The effectiveness of a technique or tool can be measured through proper evaluation. Human annotators often assess text quality in text summarization studies [4]. The value of the scale chosen for each summary is chosen by the annotator. Considering studies done in the recent past, multiple methods were used to assess the output of machine summaries, including essential assessment, sentence extraction, task-based, and content-based methods.

By comparing the output of the machine summary with a perfect summary created by an expert, the evaluation follows the fundamental approach. Measurements are taken in terms of grammar, lack of redundancy, and coherence to make the crucial assessment. Precision, recall, and F1 score were some of the criteria or metrics used in the evaluation. The task-based approach is another method that uses summaries for specific tasks to evaluate the performance of a machine-based summary.

Gaps, Issues, and Challenges in TS

The gap analysis taken from the text summarization literature leads to the conclusion that the field of text summarization offers the scientific and research communities a wealth of options where they can explore its various directions according to interests and needs. The following are the research gaps based on current text summarization methods as indicated in Figure 24.5 [15].

Future work that can be done on TS research includes:

By discovering new features, selecting features, optimizing frequently used features, developing new features, using features for semantics and linguistics, finding features to produce coherent sentences, and adding grammatical features, feature problems can be solved including determining which features can be used for summarization.

We can develop the latest approach called Narrative abstractive summarization (NATSUM) for abstract summarization in different situations or enhance NATSUM's functionality by making it more coherent [5].

Limitations of the Current Study

The following limitations apply to the current study: (a) Because the results of searches in digital libraries (IEEE, Springer, ScienceDirect, etc.) were not exhaustive, the scope of the study was limited. (b) There is no standardized way to search all digital libraries. (c) Since all non-English language publications were excluded, the results of this study are based solely on work published in English. (d) The study titles, abstracts, and keywords were used to select the studies. The articles were often identified based on the full text of the articles. (e) Another difficulty of this study may be the authors' bias in paper selection.

Conclusion

The NLP community finds synopsis to be a fascinating area of study that can help create a precise summary. The purpose of this review paper is to describe the latest findings and developments in this field using the SLR approach. It has been shown that the SLR method can provide a more structured, comprehensive, and diverse review, covering trends, databases, features, techniques, issues, challenges, and assessment methods that can guide future work. For ease of research and reanalysis, the relationship between the topical trends, issues, and difficulties in each topic, and the technique and methodology used are consolidated into one.

The analysis results showed that extractive summarization is significantly simpler than abstractive summarization, which is quite complex. [12] This is due to the keywords, sentence position, frequency, sentence length, similarity, and semantics being crucial components to creating a decent summary. Machine learning is a preferred strategy due to its autonomous machine learning performance. However, statistics is also an effective strategy that can be combined with other approaches. Other strategies such as frequency analysis, keyword search, and similarity to the statistical strategy are also used to improve summarization.

References

1. Abualigah, L., Bashabsheh, M. Q., Alabool, H., and Shehab, M. (2020). Text summarization: a brief review. Recent Advances in NLP: the case of Arabic language, 1-15.
2. AL-Khassawneh , Y. A., and Hanandeh, E. S. (2023). Extractive arabic text summarization-graph-based approach. *Electronics*, 12(2), 437.
3. Al-Thanyyan, S. S., and Azmi, A. M. (2021). Automated text simplification: a survey. *ACM Computing Surveys (CSUR)*, 54(2), 1–36.
4. Altmami, N. I., and Menai, M. E. B. (2022). Automatic summarization of scientific articles: A survey. *Journal of King Saud University-Computer and Information Sciences*, 34(4), 1011–1028.
5. Barros, C., Lloret, E., Saquete, E., and Navarro-Colorado, B. (2019). NATSUM: narrative abstractive summarization through cross-document timeline generation. *Information Processing and Management*, 56(5), 1775–1793.
6. Budgen, D., Kitchenham, B., Charters, S., Turner, M., Brereton, P., and Linkman, S. (2007). Preliminary results of a study of the completeness and clarity of structured abstracts. In 11th International Conference on Evaluation and Assessment in Software Engineering (EASE), 11 (pp. 1–9).
7. Kumar, B., and Sharma, N. (2016). Approaches, issues and challenges in recommender systems: a systematic review. *Indian Journal of Science and Technology*, 9(47), 1–12.
8. Luhn, H. P. (1958) The automatic creation of literature abstracts. *IBM Journal for Research and Development*, 2(2), 159–165.
9. Okoli, C., Schabram, K. (2010). A Guide to Conducting a Systematic Literature Review of Information Systems Research. Sprouts: Working Papers on Information Systems, 10(26). http://sprouts.aisnet.org/10-26
10. Patel, D., Shah, S., and Chhinkaniwala, H. (2019). Fuzzy logic based multi document summarization with improved sentence scoring and redundancy removal technique. *Expert Systems with Applications*, 134, 167–177.
11. Saranyamol, C. S., and Sindhu, L. (2014). A survey on automatic text summarization. *International Journal of Computer Science and Information Technologies*, 5(6), 7889–7893.
12. Shi, T., Keneshloo, Y., Ramakrishnan, N., and Reddy, C. K. (2021). Neural abstractive text summarization with sequence-to-sequence models. *ACM Transactions on Data Science*, 2(1), 1–37.
13. Manne, S., Mohd, Z. P. S., and Fatima, Dr. S. S. (2012). Extraction based automatic text summarization system with HMM tagger. In Proceedings of the International Conference on Information Systems Design and Intelligent Applications. (Vol. 132, pp. 421–428).
14. Widyassari, A. P., Rustad, S., Shidik, G. F., Noersasongko, E., Syukur, A., and Affandy, A. (2022). Review of automatic text summarization techniques & methods. *Journal of King Saud University-Computer and Information Sciences*, 34(4), 1029–1046.
15. Yadav, A. K., Yadav, R. S., and Maurya, A. K. (2023). State-of-the-art approach to extractive text summarization: a comprehensive review. *Multimedia Tools and Applications*, 82, 29135–29197. https://doi.org/10.1007/s11042-023-14613-9.

25 Design of an AI-based binary class heart disease prediction model for IoMT

Mohit Kumar Goel[a], Puli Surendra Reddy,
Sompalli Chaitanya Babu and Polisetti Saikiran

School of Electronics and Electrical Engineering, Lovely Professional University
Jalandhar, Punjab, India

Abstract

In today's society, when heart disease is on the rise, it is critical to foresee these disorders. The test is a difficult task. As a result, it must be accomplished correctly and efficiently. Data mining and machine learning technologies are widely used in the finding of heart disease. The major focus of research article is on which people, based on numerous medical features, are more likely to have heart disease. We devised a strategy based on the patient's medical history to predict whether or not the patient will be diagnosed with a heart problem. In this context, the paper employs several machine learning techniques, such as Logistic Regression (LR), Support Vector Machine (SVM), Decision Tree Classifier (DT), K-Nearest Neighbors Classifier (KNN), and Random Forest Classifier (RF).

Keywords: Binary class, cardiac condition, data mining, decision tree (DT), heart disease, heart disease predictor, IoMT, random forest (RF), support vector machine (SVM)

Introduction

Heart illnesses such as infections, genetic abnormalities, and blood vessel diseases are all included under the umbrella term "heart disease," which is referring a broad spectrum of conditions that affects the heart. There are several different types, and each has its own symptoms, causes, and therapies. Making lifestyle changes and using drugs can greatly enhance someone's health. To regain their functioning, others could need surgery. Cardiac disease is usually caused by a multitude of risk conditions, whereas smoking, excessive use of alcohol and caffeine, and physical inactivity, as well as physical factors including obesity, hypertension, high blood pressure (BP), cholesterol, and previous cardiac diseases. Heart disease needs effective, precise, and early medical diagnosis as it is crucial to take preventative measures to avoid the effects that these disorders have

In the contemporary world, the major problems facing in the health industry is lack of standard service, and early exact prediction. Automation can fix the issue with the use of techniques like machine learning and data mining. The hidden relationship among correlated characteristics may be found using data mining classification approaches, which is important for predicting the class label from a huge dataset. Without the assistance of medical professionals, it is simple to identify heart disease patients by examining those hidden patterns and the connected traits.

---

[a]mohit.16907@lpu.co.in

In this Proposed work, various types of machine learning techniques are compared on various principles of accuracy. To determine the best accurate model, various techniques that are involved in the several Machine Learning methods are examined, including Naive Bayes, K Nearest Neighbour, Logistic Regression, Support Vector Machine, Random Forest. Random Forest algorithm and Decision Tree is the most effective strategy available s and has the most accuracy among them.

The major driving force behind the purpose is to test the heart disease as early as possible using the machine learning techniques and to design the major dependable and exact system with the greatest amount of productivity, the mechanism of cardiac detection may be created by choosing the major suitable techniques. As a result, the detecting system is also economically efficient.

The Random Forest and Decision Tree are the most successful in terms of delivering greater productivity, according to the report. The remainder of article is structured in the following way described below described below. In the Section II, an examination of the body of writings is presented. Descriptions of several writers' data sets are included.

Literature Survey

In recent years, researchers have employed various data mining approaches in a variety of studies relating to the detection of cardiac disease.

In [1] Author has designed a predictive model based on machine learning techniques for cardiac arrest in smokers. It predicts the cardiac arrest in smokers. They have applied three algorithms Decision tree, Logistic regression and Random Forest. In summary they compared the three algorithms and got the result that Random Forest has high accuracy, precision, sensitivity and specificity.

In [2] Authors has proposed Efficient heart disease prediction system. In this system they have converted the database into rules with the help of Decision tree algorithm and they got 86.75% success rate.

In [3] researchers have developed Predictions on heart disease using methods of data mining. They used three algorithms Random Forest, logistic regression and Naive Bayes classifier. And then they compared the three algorithms and noticed that in logistic regression the trees with number of nodes are hard to memorize and consuming lot of time. In RF high processing time is required to large networks and if there is any modification it is impossible to add existing data. In Naïve Bayes classifier accuracy is low and it assumes independence of features

In [4] The authors evaluated several algorithms such as Support Vector Machine, Naive Bayes, K Nearest Neighbour, Decision Tree, logistic regression, and the ensemble approach of XG Boost and found out that Random Forest and XG boost has most accuracy of 86.89% and 78.69% respectively.

In [5] "A review of machine learning techniques for cardiovascular disease prediction" by Gaurav Pandey and colleagues is worth reading. This review research investigates the use of machine learning approaches for the prediction of cardiovascular illness, whereas logistic regression, random forests, and deep learning models. In this study, different machine learning approaches for heart disease are discussed like prediction, k-nearest neighbours, support vector machines, logistic regression, and neural networks are discussed.

In [6] author conducted a systematic study and meta-analysis to assess how well machine learning algorithms can foretell heart disease. The study discovered that cardiac disease might be predicted with a high degree of accuracy by machine learning algorithms that which can be helpful. The study, however, did not take into account the difficulties and restrictions of applying machine learning algorithms for cardiac disease prediction.

In [7] Using deep learning, author published "Predicting Cardiovascular Risk Factors from Retinal Fundus Images." - In this study images of the retinal fundus are utilised to predict cardiovascular risk variables such as age, gender, and smoking, and blood pressure using deep learning algorithms that required. These risk variables can be reliably predicted by deep learning, according to the data, which may Assist in the early detection of cardiac disease.

According to a survey of the literature, few evolutionary strategies have been proposed to use for improvement in the performance of random forests. To the best of our ability, the research's suggested algorithm is Random Forest that employs an evolutionary strategy, so in addition to creating a variety of training sets (which is accomplished by creating different features and sampling subsets, it also establishes the (almost) ideal number of decision trees.

Proposed Methodology

In this proposed work, we present the Hybrid Model which contain combination of Random Forest with Linear Model approach along with the Random Forest and Decision Tree. Figure 1 shows the basic architecture used for the proposed method. The fundamental purpose of this research is to improve the predictability of cardiac disease. Many studies have been conducted, yielding feature selection limitations for algorithmic use. The Hybrid Random Forest Linear Model approach, on the other hand, utilises all attributes without respect to feature selection limitations. To determine the properties of a machine learning algorithm, we have used a hybrid technique. The experiment discoveries suggest that proposed hybrid strategy outperforms existing methods in predicting heart disease. The proposed solution for meeting this requirement is the forecasting of cardiac disease using an automated medical diagnostic approach that uses machine learning. The prediction system employs a hybrid model. The Cleveland database was utilised for the heart disease prediction algorithm. Since the Cleveland database is the most extensively used by machine learning researchers. While the dataset has 303 occurrences and 76 features, only 14 are listed in all published publications. The "goal" area, featuring numbers that go from 0 (none) to 4, shows whether or not the patient has heart illness. The Cleveland database has been examined in order to distinguish missing 0 from existence value 1, with values that vary from 1 to 4. For the proposed work there are some functional requirements are there

Data Collection
Data collection includes the choice of superior data to be analyzed. In this proposed work we have used cardiovascular disease database through uci.edu for the

purpose of machine learning. This is the job of a data analyst to find new ways and sources for acquiring relevant and full information, analyze it, and measure the data using analytical tools.

Data Visualization
A huge volume of data portrayed graphically is easier to comprehend and evaluate. Several companies require data scientists should become capable of developing slideshows, graphs, statistics, and patterns. With proposed technique, the cardiovascular disease risks are shown as a visual data component.

Data Pre-Processing
The intention behind pre-processing is to transform unprocessed information into a machine-learning-friendly format. When data is organised and clean, a data analyst may acquire more precise results from a machine learning approach. The process includes data structuring, filtering, and testing.

Dataset Splitting
A machine learning data should be split into three parts: teaching, verification, and confirmation. Set aside for preparation. A data analyst uses a training example to teach a machine learning algorithm and discover the best variables for it to learn from. Set the test. A training dataset is necessary to assess the trained model's ability to generalise. The ability of a model to identify patterns in completely undiscovered data from being trained on training examples is referred to as the latter. To avoid model overfitting, which is the inability to generalise noted above, It is crucial to use a variety of selections for development and evaluation.

Model Training
Model training may begin once the analyst pre-processed the memory and portioned it and experiments the sets. This involves "feeding" the training data in algorithm. An algorithm will handle data and build an algorithm able to identify a specific value (attribute) in new data and producing the intended response through forecasting. Concept training's purpose is to construct a model.

Model Evaluation and Testing
The aim of is to develop the easiest design possible which is capable of calculating a target number quickly and accurately. This can be accomplished through

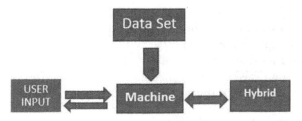

Figure 25.1 Architecture diagram

model adjustment. It is the optimization of model parameters to find the optimal performance of used algorithm.

Along with the functional requirements there are some system requirements are also there that is hardware requirements and software requirements. The hardware requirements that need for proposed work is above 500MHZ processor and above 4GB RAM, above 4GB Hard disk.

Implementation Methodology

The proposed work was written in Python 3.10 and relied on the libraries scikit-learn, pandas, matplotlib, and other necessary tools. We obtained the dataset from uci.edu. The downloaded data includes binary types of cardio vascular disease. Machine learning algorithms such as random forests, explained in Figure 25.2, and decision trees, explained in Figure 25.3 as well as a hybrid model, are used.

Data Dictionary
The following attributes were included in the data source: age, sex, cp, fbs, restecg, trestbps, chol, thalach, exang, oldpeak, slope, ca, thal, and pred. We obtained this entire dataset from the Cleveland database. The variable names in the data source are age: patient's age, sex: gender, trestbps: resting blood pressure, cp: chest pain, fbs: fasting blood sugar, restecg: resting electro, thalach: maximum heart rate achieved, exang: exercise induced angina, oldpeak: state of depression induced, slope: slope of peak exercise, ca: number of major vessels Thalassemia is abbreviated as thal. In proposed project we used three algorithms. They are Decision Tree, Random Forest, Hybrid Model.

Random Forest
1.　Assume there are n occurrences in the training sample. With replacement, sample groups are chosen at random from the n instances. Separate trees are constructed from different selections drawn from the testing set.
2.　With k input parameters, an integer x is calculated so that x k. Each algorithm checks x elements at random from a collection of k variables. The break with the strongest of these x variables is selected for splitting the node. The value of x remains constant as the forest expands.
3.　Every shrub is permitted to get as big as it can without cutting its branches.
4.　The largest number of votes received from the average of all decision trees is used to determine the class the new item.

Decision Tree
A decision tree is a type of supervised learning which is commonly used for solving classification issues. It can be used for both simple and continuous input and output variables. We divide the sample into more number of homogenous groups (or sub-populations) with help of most significant splitter / differentiator in the input variables. Internal nodes in a decision tree indicate a testing on the rows, branches display the output, leaves represent the conclusion taken after computing the cells.

The Decision Tree operates in the following manner:

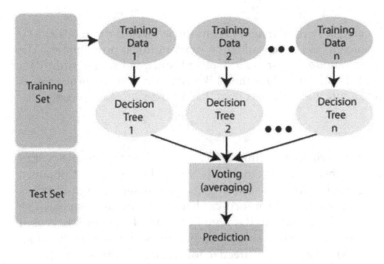

Figure 25.2 Random forest flowchart

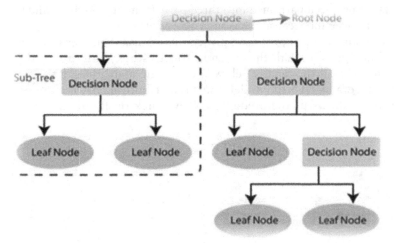

Figure 25.3 Decision tree flowchart

1. Make the dataset's best feature at tree's base.
2. Separate the training information set into subgroups. Elements should be built so that every single subset has data that shares a single input parameter.
3. Continue the first and second procedure for each subgroup until leaf nodes of all the tree's branches are identified.

   To forecast a class label for a record in a decision tree, one must begin from the root of the tree. The elements of the script's variable are then contrasted with the values of the root property. Choose the branch corresponding to that value and move to the next node after comparison.

Hybrid Model

A hybrid model is created by combining random forest algorithms and the decision tree. The combined model is depending on random forest probabilities. The probabilities table of random forest are calculated and used to the train data which further provided to the tree algorithm. Likewise, decision tree probabilities are determined and supplied into the test data. Lastly, the values are forecast.

Result

The proposed work was written in Python 3.10 and relied on the libraries scikit-learn, matplotlib, and other necessary tools. The heart disease dataset obtained from uci.edu is being studied. Machine learning algorithms such as decision trees and Random Forest are used. We identified cardiac illness using these machine learning algorithms. A hybrid model of Random Forest and Decision Tree is used to improve the job and make it more unique. The results show that the Random Forest algorithm and hybrid model are effective for detecting heart disease.

Inputs

Data Set: The data shown in Figure 25.4 is the data set that we have taken from uci.edu. The data set has been partitioned into three parts training, test and validation. We have taken this data because it has high accuracy.

Figure 25.5 is the interface of proposed project here it asks the user to enter some variables like age, sex, thalach, cp, chol, fbs, trestbps, restecg and the Dataset. After entering all the details below there is the algorithms Random Forest, Decision Tree and Hybrid Model and Predict button. If we click on the predict button it shows us the prediction. If we click on Random Forest

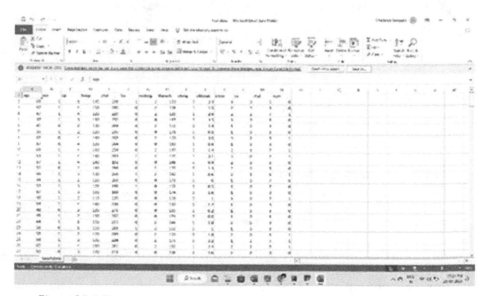

Figure 25.4 Dataset

button or Decision Tree button it shows us the accuracy of the data that we
have given

Outputs
Here are the outputs that we get after giving the dataset and variables for the
required fields.

Figure 25.6 is the prediction that we got after giving all the variables and
dataset.

Figure 25.7 is showing that the metric values. We can observe the accuracy of
the Decision Tree. Here we got 79% accuracy in Decision Tree.

Figure 25.8 showing us the accuracy of Random Forest and here we got above
77% accuracy.

Figure 25.9 is the metric values of Hybrid Model. In hybrid model we got the
accuracy about to 77%.

Limitations of Existing Work and Advantages of Proposed work

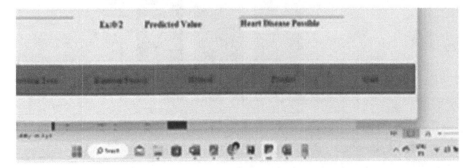

Figure 25.5 software interface

Figure 25.6 Prediction

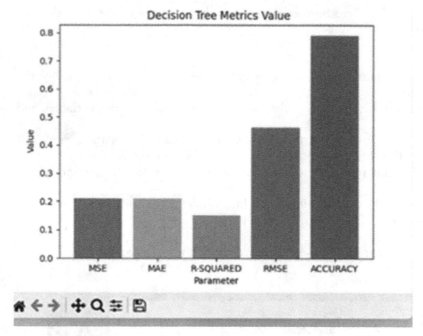

Figure 25.7 Decision tree metric values

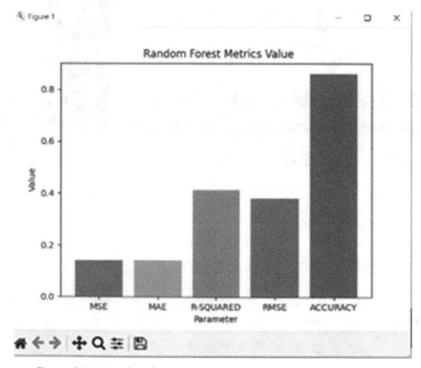

Figure 25.8 Random forest metric values

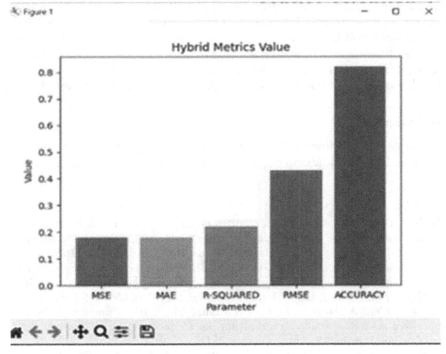

Figure 25.9 Hybrid model metric values

Paper no	Limitations of the other research methods	Advantages of Proposed Method
[1].	In other paper they have only focused on random Decision Tree algorithm and they got only 70% accuracy. And they have used some precise dataset.	We have used three algorithms and taken the data set from uci.edu and we got above 79% accuracy in Decision Tree.
[2].	The authors are only focused on heart disease caused by smoking by using the logistic regression algorithm and KNN algorithms. And got the accuracy of 70% and 72%.	Here we focused on the heart disease predictor (heart disease occur by anything) and got above 79% accuracy in Decision Tree and about to 77% accuracy in Random Forest
[3].	One of the authors has developed the predictor by Naïve bayes, KNN algorithms and hybrid model by combining both algorithms and they got 65% accuracy in hybrid model.	Here we have developed the predictor with hybrid model of combination of RF and DT and got above 77% accuracy.

Conclusion

As a conclusion of the literature review, it is necessary to develop cascaded and more complex models for improvement in the accuracy of forecasting, the early onset of cardiovascular disorders. Combinations of Decision Tree and Random Forest are used in the proposed method for predicting cardiac disease. To develop the most efficient model, train and test the system with Cleveland Heart Disease data. We plan to examine certain deep learning models, such as the CNN or DNN algorithms, for heart disease prediction in the future. In order to establish the severity of the illness, we are also interested in categorizing it as a multi-class problem.

Acknowledgement

The authors gratefully acknowledge the students, staff, and authority of School of Electronics and Electrical Engineering for their cooperation in the research

References

1. Shashikant, R., & Chetankumar, P. (2020). Predictive model of cardiac arrest in smokers using machine learning technique based on Heart Rate Variability parameter. Applied Computing and Informatics. 174-185. DOI:10.1016/J.ACI.2019.06.002
2. Singh, P., Singh, S., & Pandi-Jain, G. S. (2018). Effective heart disease prediction system using data mining techniques. *International journal of nanomedicine*, 13(T-NANO 2014 Abstracts), 121–124. https://doi.org/10.2147/IJN.S124998
3. Uddin, S., Khan, A., Hossain, M. E., and Moni, M. A. (2019). Comparing different supervised machine learning algorithms for disease prediction. *BMC Info Medical and Decision Making,* 19 (Article number: 281).
4. Lombardi, F., M.akikallio, T. H., Myerburg, R. J., and Huikuri, H. V. (2001). Sudden cardiac death: role of heart rate variability to identify patients at risk. *Cardiovascular Research,* 50(2), 210–217.
5. Sahini, S., and Panday, G. (2021). Impact of metabolic and cardiovascular disease on COVID-19 mortality: a systematic review and meta-analysis. Diabetes & metabolic syndrome, 15(6), 102308. https://doi.org/10.1016/j.dsx.2021.102308
6. Krittanawong, C., Virk, H. U. H., Bangalore, S., Wang, Z., Johnson, K. W., Pinotti, R., Zhang, H., Kaplin, S., Narasimhan, B., Kitai, T., Baber, U., Halperin, J. L., and Tang, W. H. W. (2020). Machine learning prediction in cardiovascular diseases: a meta-analysis. Scientific reports, 10(1), 16057. https://doi.org/10.1038/s41598-020-72685-1
7. Poplin, R., Varadarajan, A. V., Blumer, K., Liu, Y., McConnell, M. V., Corrado, G. S., Peng, L., & Webster, D. R. (2018). Prediction of cardiovascular risk factors from retinal fundus photographs via deep learning. *Nature biomedical engineering*, 2(3), 158–164. https://doi.org/10.1038/s41551-018-0195-0

26 A review of artificial intelligence-based plant species classification techniques

Roshnee Nameirakpam[1], Jatinder Singh[1,a],
Parminder Singh[2,3] and Mustapha Hedabou[3]

[1]School of Agriculture, Lovely Professional University, Phagwara

[2]School of Computer Science and Engineering, Lovely Professional University, Phagwara

[3]College of Computing, University Mohammed VI Polytechnic, Ben Guerir, Morocco

Abstract

The focus of this paper is to highlight the techniques to identify the plants with leaves photographs using computer vision approaches. The extracted information is useful for botanists to understand the characteristics of plant species and their medicinal usage. The number of plants seems to be decreasing as human influence increases, yet their automatic identification can encourage conservation. Usually, a tripod stand is used to take leaf images with a digital or phone camera. The hidden beneath leaves can be covered in dust or shadow. Identifying the leaves in various types of environmental conditions is a real challenge for researchers. However, many researchers have successfully able to develop techniques that give significant accuracy in plant species classification. This paper has surveyed several leaf extraction methods, which are divided into groups based on the characteristics of the leaf used and its benefits and drawbacks. A general classification method employed in various research articles is discussed and compared in detail. At last, different aspects and future scope are discussed in the conclusion for the improvement in this field.

Keywords: Artificial intelligence, classification, feature extraction, image processing, plant species recognition

Introduction

Artificial Intelligence (AI) has become increasingly vital in daily life. Digital marketing transformation, the medical field, finance, and business sectors are the most common uses of artificial intelligence. AI is the mimicking of human intellectual processes by computers. AI plays are vital role in our day-to-day activities and have several applications in the business sector, banking, medical field, transformation of digital marketing, robotics, and computer vision [11]. The main role of AI is to enable machines to learn and take decisions like human beings. Different kinds of machine-learning approaches have been developed to tackle the challenges caused by a large amount of data. Deep learning is a commonly used method that has gained increased interest from a variety of fields, including speech recognition, robotics, human action, food science, and agricultural production. It is able to deliver accurate prediction outcomes for difficult-to-predict occurrences. By including some "deeper" (more complicated) structures

---

[a]edennamz@gmail.com

in models, it goes beyond traditional machine learning to automatically extract features from raw data. Its methods have outperformed other machine-learning techniques in terms of performance and precision while processing various types of huge data that have been gathered by digital cameras and spectroscopy [22]. Fundamentally, deep learning is a nonlinear information processing method based on representation learning and pattern recognition.

In the AI field, convolutional neural networks (CNNs) are regarded as the foundation for deep-learning techniques that have made significant advances in image processing and analysis. In order to train deep neural network models for horticulture crop detection, researchers have currently gathered a number of open-access image datasets featuring various horticultural crops. The spatial hierarchies of plants can be learnt using convolution networks through translation invariants patterns. It is capable to learn the pre-recognized pattern in the leaf images and further successive layers help to understand the complex layers through trait accounts. CNN works like a bird box. The salient components of each class are determined by the network itself based on its convolution layers and observed training data, so that we don't need to tell it which features are better for discriminating. In the following section, we are going to discuss the important leaf recognition steps used in AI techniques.

Support Vector Machines (SVMs) are machine learning algorithms that have various applications in classification tasks. In plant species classification, SVMs can be trained to classify plant species based on features extracted from images of plant parts [21]. For example, SVMs can be trained on features such as texture, color, and shape of leaves or other plant parts. Furthermore, Random Forest (RF) is an ensemble learning method that can produce accurate predictions by appending multiple decisions. In plant species classification, Random Forests can be trained on a dataset of features extracted from plant images, such as leaf shape, texture, and color. These models can then be used to classify plant species based on these features [23]. Moreover, Deep Belief Networks (DBNs) are a type of deep learning model that can learn and represent complex patterns in data. In plant species classification, DBNs can be used to extract features from images of plant parts, which can then be used for classification tasks [4]. These models can learn complex features such as leaf venation patterns, which can be used to distinguish between different plant species.

Overall, AI-based techniques are proving to be very effective in plant species classification, and are helping researchers and scientists to better understand and identify different plant species.

Review of Literature

Authors have studied the principles of the auto-identification methods of plant species using computer vision with an impressive level of effort [25]. The work of the authors was completed from 2005 to 2015, primarily focused on feature extraction and image acquisition methods while also reviewing identification research that included flowers, fruit, bark, and the entire plant. The classifiers employed in the identification campaign have received the majority of attention from [1]. The step-by-step techniques for automatically recognizing plants from

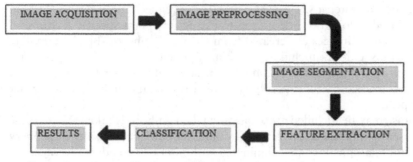

Figure 26.1 Steps of leaf recognition

their leaves will be explained in-depth in this section. This study will be useful to researchers who are interested in this field.

Image Acquisition
The identification process's first and most crucial step is getting a picture of the plant. A picture of the entire plant, a single bloom, a leaf, a stem, or even a fruit may be required. There are three different types of images: pictures, pseudo-scans, and scans, depending on how they are produced. By using a plain background in a room and taking the pictures in natural light or an environment, the leaf images will be scanned and captured in the categories of scan and pseudo-scan. Scans and pseudo-scans are used more often since they are easy to evaluate. The leaves selected for identification should be straightforward, fully grown, and damage-free. The leaves are then carefully examined in the correct illumination. Because the image will be taken against a plain background, scans and pseudo-scans simplify the process of classifying things.

The image of the leaf is improved through a series of steps that cover the conversion of the RGB pictures to grayscale, going from grayscale to binary, image smoothing, image filtering, etc. Noise handling, scaling, and image improvement are all included in the preprocessing technique. The datasets readily available for automatic recognition are described in Table 26.1 as per [19].

Image Pre-Processing
The next phase in species identification is image pre-processing. It is possible to acquire the raw image's original background. Its size and angle of accomplishment may be arbitrary, and it may be noisy. Pre-processing is the process of lowering noise and adjusting contrast in an image. For effective feature calculation and reliable results, the image's scale and orientation must be normalized. The characteristics must be resistant to translation, scaling, and other transformations. The primary axis of the leaf must be parallel to the horizontal line in order to achieve rotation invariance. Since it is tilted with regard to the horizontal, we must spin it at that angle [5].

1. Using particular techniques, the grayscale images are generated from the colourful Red Green Blue (RGB). Grayscale images can be improved in various

ways, such as intensity. Gray-Level-Co-Occurrence Matrix (GLCOM) can be used to develop grayscale images to extract the plant species' features.

2. Further, binary images are created from Grayscale photos. Black and white are the only colours included in a binary image, a type of computer image. A proper threshold function must be selected in order to carry out the binary conversion. The superbly is applied on binary images with Fourier descriptor.

3. The noise may be included automatically when a photo is taken. Noise is the term used to describe incorrect pixel values. It could make a salty or peppery noise, for example. It can be eliminated with filters like median, average, etc.

4. Images might occasionally be difficult to understand because of the narrow range of grey levels that result from poor lighting. Contrast stretching techniques must be employed to the full dynamic range from the original range.

5. A variety of morphological processes are carried out to provide a clear image like filling and crossing.

The morphological operation is eliminated for the boundary extraction process. Then, filters are applied to the boundaries.

The recommended concentrating on the properties of color by Prasad et al. [18] because it is believed that the green and red tiers of the input image hold a significant amount of information, they have been enhanced. The photos were split into sub-images after normalisation and grayscale conversion and then underwent curvelet transformation. People working on Fourier descriptors converted the color images first into grayscale images, then into binary images [20]. These photos were subsequently filtered and smoothed using a Laplacian filter in order to achieve the border on the white backdrop. Nijalingappa and Madhumathi [17] used histogram equalisation to enhance contrast, Median filters to preserve boundaries while eradicating noise, and Wiener filters to remove picture noise. In another work that was suggested by Chaki and Bhattacharya [5], leaf texture features were retrieved from a grayscale image and its form was extracted from a binary image. The background was then diminished, and the rotation of the features was made invariant.

Computer imaging also makes extensive use of the Hue Saturation Value (HSV) colour space, which isolates colour information from image intensity. This is quite helpful for getting rid of shadows that appear when photographing leaves. Professionals have used HSV colour space with the conversion of RGB colour space by removing the backdrop due to the widespread use and ease of deployment in various applications [7]. The properties of the veins were then extracted using GLCM. In addition, researchers Bama et al. [2] initially make the HSV colour space from RGB in order to apply the Gabor Wavelet log and generate an image invariant for rotation and scale.

Image Segmentation
To construct a retrieve contour information (ROI), segmentation divides an image into various segments (a collection of pixels). This is especially helpful when undesired objects are present in the photograph because it was taken in its natural setting. Separating the image from the backdrop can also be accomplished by

selecting an appropriate threshold setting. When taking into account leaf outline information, the ROI in leaf photographs is made up of vein pixels or border pixels, by the condition a vein is to be chosen as an identification. It is also beneficial to draw attention to the pixels that make up the border if form elements use the border as an identification. Beghin et al. [3] employed Otsu's thresholding method to get rid of the background. Li et al. [16] suggested a method to identify grass plants. Otsu's fixed threshold segmentation approaches are useless since these plants are frequently grouped and have complex backgrounds, which may introduce random noise from the weather, shadows, etc. into the collected photographs. They employed dynamic thresholding as their segmentation technique. The segmentation was split into three pieces in order to produce a smartphone application called LeafSnap [13]. Users of the application take a picture of the sheet and upload it to the application servers. The system gives customers a number of the closest possibilities. A support vector machine (SVM) is utilized for the first classification to assess whether the processed image is a leaf image or not. Following the identification of the leaf image, it is segmented by first designating each pixel as either the foreground or background. The HSV colour space's saturation and value were employed to separate the leaf from its surroundings. In order to minimize false positives, connected components were then generated on the augmented segmentation images. These connected sections with a thicker border have been removed. The pictures were then normalized by removing stems using a variety of morphological approaches.

Herdiyeni and Douady (2016) prepared binary images from the RGB images. Then, they did boundary segmentation using the Canny edge detector. Charters et al. [6] innovate the morphological processes using a Canny edge detector in the conjunction process. Larese and Granitto (2016), Larese Bayá et al. [15], and Larese et al. [14] extracted the foreground from the background using morphological techniques with Unconstrained Hit or Miss Transform (UHMT). As usual, adaptive thresholding was used to segment veins.

Feature Extraction

The key step in computer vision picture identification is feature selection, which determines how accurate the entire process is. The features used should exhibit both the minimal and highest degree of similarity between classes. It provides a foundation for assessing the algorithm's precision. For this stage, the leaf picture is the input, and the output is the feature vector for the distinctive attributes. The four fundamental qualities of a leaf are form, shape, texture and veining. The form has either been employed as a single element or as a combination of elements, according to the literature now in use.

Classification

The categorization procedure entails giving each image in the output labelled with pre-identified classes. Classes are created from the attributes gathered in the training program. The pseudo-codes employed for the classification are predicated on the notion that an image contains several features (as previously mentioned) and that a collection of those features may be grouped into a range of classes. The feature vector is the phase's input that is composed of the recovered features.

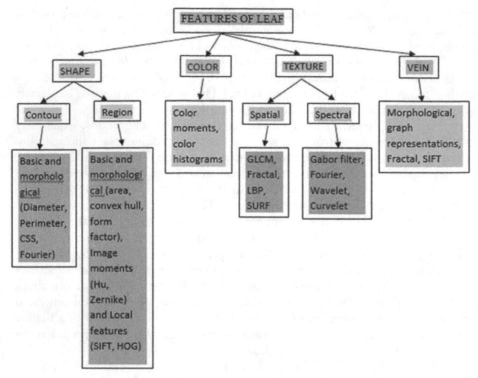

Figure 26.2 Identification of leaves by the classification of some key feature descriptors

The reduction of dimensionality is noticed in redundant features sometimes. The phase's output is the name of the plant or the phrase that most closely describes it. It uses testing and training as its two phases. The generation of the training class is carried out by giving distinctive characteristics of typical image attributes to a certain category. Furthermore, images are then categorized using these classes in the testing phase.

The neural network is the most popular pattern recognition classifier. It studies what others do to learn. Based on successively changed weights, a straightforward non-linear mapping between output and input values is created. Back-propagation multilayer perceptron (MLP) and Neuro-Fuzzy classifiers (NFC) both use feed-forward neural classifiers. Images were originally grouped only by texture, and later solely by shape [5]. NFC scored 97.6% and MLP scored 85.6% when the combined characteristics were applied. Low-dimensional feature vectors were categorized using a probabilistic neural network (PNN), also known as a feedforward neural network, by researchers Hossain and Amin [10]. The three layers that made up this system were the Competitive, Radial and Entry Layers. The vectors of input features are used to produce the input layer. The radial basis function calculates the output value from the input value and stores it in the Radial base layer. At last, the competitive layer divides the input vector into the necessary number of classes. It achieved a recognition rate of 91.41% during the 10-fold cross-validation test, passing it. Additionally, 1800 images of leaves were

Table 26.1 Readily available datasets for automatic recognition.

Reference/ Link	Total no. of images	Origin	Classes	Dataset
https://www.gbif.org/species/6 (Accessed on: 29 April 2023)	279,017,882	Around the globe	589,536	Plantae
[26]	1200	-	1001	CVIP100
The steps of leaf recognition are mentioned in Figure 26.1 as per [24]. Some key feature descriptors are mentioned in Figure 26.2 as per [24].	1125	Swedish tree species' leaves were photographed for a joint study between Linkoping University and the Swedish Museum of National History of leaf classification.	15	Swedish
[27]	1907	The Yangtse Delta in China is a native place to the majority of the photos.	32	Flavia
Homepage of the Chinese Academy of Sciences Intelligent Computing Laboratory.	17,032	China's Hefei Botanical Garden	220	Chinese Academy of Sciences (Intelligent Computing Laboratory)
[8]	11572	Different tree types in the French Mediterranean region	126	Image CLEF (2012)
The report, "The CLEF Cross Language Image Retrieval Track I ImageCLEF / LifeCLEF - Multimedia Retrieval in CLEF,"	6436	Different species of trees in the French Mediterranean region	71	ImageCLEF(2011)
[11]	Laboratory Images: 23, 147, Field Images: 7719	North-eastern American tree species	185	Leaf snap

correctly classified into 32 groups using PNN with more than 90% accuracy [27]. Kadir et al. [12] found better classification accuracy in foliage (93% to 95%) and Flavia (93.4% to 95%) datasets using PCA to decrease features before deploying a PNN classifier.

Conclusion and Future Prospects

The purpose of this paper is to present the plant species classification techniques using leaf attributes. We discussed various aspects of a leaf image. The advantages and disadvantages of various feature extraction techniques are discussed. There is a discussion of several classifiers found in the literature. The stage of pre-processing follows the acquisition of the leaf image. Pre-processing is based on the choice of features to be fed to the classifier and the quality of the input image. Feature selection techniques took the feature vectors to produce the classification results.

The presentation of several leaf attributes and a comparison of their extraction techniques follow. This study concludes that there is no set method for choosing the input feature vector. Otherwise, it has been employed as an attribute in numerous researches, the accuracy has also been greatly improved by combining features. Various classifiers have been compared and have been employed. Future researchers can be following techniques for the advances in this field:

Multi-Model Learning: Multi-modal learning for most plant species classification techniques is based on images of plant parts, such as leaves or flowers. However, there is potential for using other types of data, such as genetic information, chemical profiles, or environmental data, to improve classification accuracy. Multi-modal learning techniques, which can integrate multiple types of data, could be explored in plant species classification.

Transfer learning: Transfer learning is a technique that involves training a model on one dataset, and then using the same model, with some modifications, on a different but related dataset. In plant species classification, transfer learning could be used to transfer knowledge learned from one plant species to another, which could reduce the amount of data needed to train a model.

Explainable AI: Explainable AI (XAI) techniques aim to make AI models more interpretable and transparent, which can help users understand how the model is making its predictions. In plant species classification, XAI techniques could be used to provide insights into which features of a plant image are most important for classification, and which plant characteristics are most distinguishing between different species.

Interactive systems: Interactive systems could be developed to help users better understand plant species classification and identify potential misclassifications. For example, an interactive system could allow a user to provide feedback on whether a classification is correct or incorrect, which could help improve the accuracy of the system over time.

Overall, there are many exciting research directions in the field of plant species classification using AI techniques, and further advancements in this area could have significant implications for agriculture, conservation, and ecological research.

References

1. Azlah, M. A. F., Chua, L. S., Rahmad, F. R., Abdullah, F. I., and Wan Alwi, S. R. (2019). Review on techniques for plant leaf classification and recognition. *Computers*, 8(4), 77.
2. Bama, B. S., Valli, S. M., Raju, S., and Kumar, V. A. (2011). Content based leaf image retrieval (CBLIR) using shape, color and texture features. *Indian Journal of Computer Science and Engineering*, 2(2), 202–211.
3. Beghin, T., Cope, J. S., Remagnino, P., and Barman, S. (2010). Shape and texture based plant leaf classification. In Advanced Concepts for Intelligent Vision Systems: 12th International Conference, ACIVS 2010, Sydney, Australia, December 13-16, 2010, Proceedings, Part II 12, (pp. 345–353). Springer Berlin Heidelberg, 2010.
4. Bhujade, V. G., and Sambhe, V. (2022). Role of digital, hyper spectral, and SAR images in detection of plant disease with deep learning network. *Multimedia Tools and Applications*, 81(23), 33645–33670.
5. Chaki, J., Parekh, R., and Bhattacharya, S. (2015). Plant leaf recognition using texture and shape features with neural classifiers. *Pattern Recognition Letters*, 58, 61–68.
6. Charters, J., Wang, Z., Chi, Z., Tsoi, A. C., and Feng, D. D. (2014). EAGLE: a novel descriptor for identifying plant species using leaf lamina vascular features. In 2014 IEEE International Conference on Multimedia and Expo Workshops (ICMEW), (pp. 1–6). IEEE, 2014.
7. Elhariri, E., El-Bendary, N., and Hassanien, A. E. (2014). Plant classification system based on leaf features. In 2014 9th International Conference on Computer Engineering & Systems (ICCES), pp. 271–276. IEEE, 2014.
8. Goëau, H., Joly, A., Bonnet, P., Bakic, V., Barthélémy, D., Boujemaa, N., and Molino, J.-F. (2013). The imageclef plant identification task 2013. In Proceedings of the 2nd ACM International Workshop on Multimedia Analysis for Ecological Data, (pp. 23–28), 2013.
9. Hasim, A., Herdiyeni, Y., & Douady, S. (2016). Leaf shape recognition using centroid contour distance. In IOP conference series: earth and environmental science (Vol. 31, No. 1, p. 012002). IOP Publishing.
10. Hossain, J., & Amin, M. A. (2010, December). Leaf shape identification based plant biometrics. In 2010 13th International conference on computer and information technology (ICCIT) (pp. 458-463). IEEE.
11. Huynh-The, T., Pham, Q. V., Pham, X. Q., Nguyen, T. T., Han, Z., and Kim, D. S. (2023). Artificial intelligence for the metaverse: A survey. *Engineering Applications of Artificial Intelligence*, 117, 105581.
12. Kadir, A., Nugroho, L. E., Susanto, A., and Santosa, P. I. (2012). Performance improvement of leaf identification system using principal component analysis. *International Journal of Advanced Science and Technology*, 44(11), 113–124.
13. Kumar, N., Belhumeur, P. N., Biswas, A., Jacobs, D. W., Kress, W. J., Lopez, I. C., and Soares, J. V. B. (2012). Leafsnap: a computer vision system for automatic plant species identification. In Computer Vision–ECCV 2012: 12th European Conference on Computer Vision, Florence, Italy, October 7-13, 2012, Proceedings, Part II 12, (pp. 502–516). Springer Berlin Heidelberg, 2012.
14. Larese et al. (2014). Larese, M. G., & Granitto, P. M. (2016). Finding local leaf vein patterns for legume characterization and classification. Machine Vision and Applications, 27(5), 709-720.
15. Larese, M. G., Bayá, A. E., Craviotto, R. M., Arango, M. R., Gallo, C., & Granitto, P. M. (2014). Multiscale recognition of legume varieties based on leaf venation images. Expert Systems with Applications, 41(10), 4638-4647.

16. Li, X., Wang, H., Li, X., Tang, Z., and Liu, H. (2019). Identifying degraded grass species in inner Mongolia based on measured hyperspectral data. IEEE Journal of Selected Topics in Applied Earth Observations and Remote Sensing, 12(12), 5061–5075.

17. Nijalingappa, P., and Madhumathi, V. J. (2015). Plant identification system using its leaf features. In 2015 International Conference on Applied and Theoretical Computing and Communication Technology (iCATccT), (pp. 338–343). IEEE, 2015.

18. Prasad, S., Kumar, P., and Tripathi, R. C. (2011). Plant leaf species identification using curvelet transform. In 2011 2nd International Conference on Computer and Communication Technology (ICCCT-2011), (pp. 646–652). IEEE, 2011.

19. Sachar, S., and Kumar, A. (2021). Survey of feature extraction and classification techniques to identify plant through leaves. *Expert Systems with Applications*, 167, 114181.

20. Singh, C. B., Jayas, D. S., Paliwal, J., and White, N. D. G. (2010). Identification of insect-damaged wheat kernels using short-wave near-infrared hyperspectral and digital colour imaging. *Computers and Electronics in Agriculture*, 73(2), 118–125.

21. Singh, P., Kaur, A., Batth, R. S., Kaur, S., and Gianini, G. (2021). Multi-disease big data analysis using beetle swarm optimization and an adaptive neuro-fuzzy inference system. *Neural Computing and Applications*, 33(16), 10403–10414.

22. Singh, P., Nayyar, A., Singh, S., and Kaur, A. (2020). Classification of wheat seeds using image processing and fuzzy clustered random forest. *International Journal of Agricultural Resources, Governance and Ecology*, 16(2), 123–156.

23. Singh, S., Singh, P., and Kaur, A. (2018). A survey on image processing techniques for seeds classification. In 2018 4th International Conference on Computing Sciences (ICCS), (pp. 143–150). IEEE, 2018.

24. Söderkvist, O. (2001). Computer vision classification of leaves from swedish trees.

25. Wäldchen, J., and Mäder, P. (2018). Machine learning for image based species identification. *Methods in Ecology and Evolution*, 9(11), 2216–2225.

26. Wang, B., and Gao, Y. (2014). Hierarchical string cuts: a translation, rotation, scale, and mirror invariant descriptor for fast shape retrieval. *IEEE Transactions on Image Processing*, 23(9), 4101–4111.

27. Wu, S. G., Bao, F. S., Xu, E. Y., Wang, Y. X., Chang, Y. F., and Xiang, Q. L. (2007). A leaf recognition algorithm for plant classification using probabilistic neural network. In 2007 IEEE International Symposium on Signal Processing and Information Technology, (pp. 11–16). IEEE, 2007.

27 Deep learning-based automatic response generation for amazon QA dataset

Akhil Chaurasia[1,a], Manthan Maheriya[1,b], Shubham Kumar[1,c], Karan Mashru[1,d], Abhi Lunagariya[1,e], Alok Kumar[1,f] and Udai Pratap Rao[2,g]

[1]Computer Science and Engineering, SVNIT, Surat, India

[2]Computer Science and Engineering, NIT, Patna Patna, India

Abstract

E-commerce is becoming bigger and bigger day by day. More and more people are coming online with the ease of internet availability. One of the big tasks, especially for e-commerce giants, is answering customers' questions about various products. A lot of manpower, time, effort, and money is involved in answering these queries. The need for technology to answer these questions becomes essential to save a lot of manpower, effort, and money. Using Machine Learning and previously used question-answers, we have proposed a solution that can answer the queries faster and cheaper for giants like Amazon. Also, we have performed a performance analysis that shows the proposed solution achieves better accuracy.

Keywords: Deep learning, email, sequence to sequence model

Introduction

With the increasing ease of availability of the internet, e-commerce is becoming bigger and bigger. More and more people are coming online, so online shopping is also increasing daily. Small business owners also come on platforms like Amazon to sell their products. An obvious thing is that there will be many queries in customer's minds regarding different products, which they would ask in the form of email or reviews space. A lot of human power is involved in answering such questions [8].

With technological advancements, we need to find a solution to this. One of the possible solutions is to use Machine Learning Techniques and previously answered questions by Amazon and build a system that can smartly answer the questions by itself. Using machine learning and data sets of previously answered questions, Product Reviews, and metadata, a system can be made that can answer customers' queries with good accuracy and in a quick time.

This type of system can be used in any field to answer queries with large data sets so that the models can be trained well and performed accurately. Some fields are e-commerce and giant ed-tech organization, which receives different queries regarding their courses, faculties, etc.

[a]akhilchaurasia47@gmail.com, [b]u18co001@coed.svnit.ac.in, [c]u18co0038@coed.svnit.ac.in, [d]u18co0043@coed.svnit.ac.in, [e]u18co0052@coed.svnit.ac.in, [f]akumar@coed.svnit.ac.in, [g]udai.cs@nitp.ac.in

Motivation

Answering the queries manually can take time, effort, and human power, ultimately costing many companies. It would also make the customers wait till a person manually replies. Using a system that automatically generates the answers with good accuracy can save a lot of costs for the company. Customers will also get a good experience if he/she is answered quickly.

Objectives

The primary objective of this research is to develop a system using machine learning that can answer customers' queries for giant e-commerce like Amazon with good accuracy. In this work, we have discussed the data sets we will use, their features, etc.

Contribution

We have used the sequence-to-sequence model of Deep Learning. We have used LSTM, RNN, and using encoders, and decoders. We have used sparse categorical cross entropy loss function and minimized it using Adam optimizer. We also trained the model using the teacher forcing technique and performed model inferencing using greedy and binary searches.

Preliminaries & Related Work

Datasets

We have used the Amazon Question-Answer dataset, which is available in Table 27.1 has roughly 4 million question-answer pairs.

The data Wan and McAuley [7] and McAuley and Yang [4] were downloaded for 17 product categories available under Questions section with multiple answers. In the above sample question in Figure 27.1, the various terms represent the following meanings.

$$\Pr(y_t \parallel y_{t-1}, \dots, y_1, c) = g(h'_t, y_{t-1}, c)$$

Here, the input source sequence w is converted into a collection of hidden vectors $h_1, h_2, \dots, h_m$ by encoder where the size changes as per the input as shown in Figure 27.2. A Recurrent Neural Network (RNN) is used to create the context

Table 27.1 Data set characteristics.

Dataset Type:	Semi-Structured
Format:	JSON
Data Set Characteristics:	Multivariate, Text, Domain-Theory
Amount of Question Answer Pairs:	1.4 Million
Number of duplicates	454432

```
{
    "asin": "B000050B6Z",
    "questionType": "yes/no",
    "answerType": "Y",
    "answerTime": "Aug 8, 2014",
    "unixTime": 1407481200,
    "question": "Can you use this unit with GEL shaving cans?",
    "answer": "Yes. If the can fits in the machine it will despense hot
gel lather. I've been using my machine for both , gel and traditional
lather for over 10 years."
}
```

Figure 27.1 Amazon 's QA sample data

asin	ID of the product, e.g. B000050B6Z.
questionType	type of question. Could be 'yes/no' or 'open-ended'.
answerType	type of answer. Could be 'Y', 'N', or '?' (if the polarity of the answer could not be predicted). Only present for yes/no questions
answerTime	raw answer timestamp.
unixTime	answer timestamp converted to unix time.
question	question text.
answer	answer text.

Figure 27.2 Terms representation

representation [3]. The encoder RNN processes the tokens in the order from first to last. Word embeddings [5] are representations of words in the form of numerical vectors where each vector has different attributes depending upon the characteristics of the words [6].

The function f is a non-linear function used to convert a word embedding into a hidden state, also considering the hidden state ht_1. Here, g is a non-linear function used for mapping, and the initial hidden state h_1 is set as vector c, which is returned by the encoder. When the end-of-sequence word is generated, the decoder stops. We need to maximize the maximum log-likelihood, and so both RNN encoder-decoder models are trained together.

$$\mathcal{L}(\theta) = max_\theta \frac{1}{N} \sum_{i=1}^{N} \log p_\theta(y_i \parallel x_i)$$

where θ is the set of the model parameters (e.g., weights in the network) and each (x_i, y_i) is an (input sequence, output sequence) pair from the training set. The $p_\theta (y_i \parallel x_i)$ denotes the likelihood of getting the ith output sequence y_i given the input sequence x_i according to the model parameters θ. By using different optimization algorithms such as Adam, gradient descent etc. We optimize the loss function.

Bleu Score

One of the methods to test the accuracy and precision employed by AutoML Translation after training is BLEU score. The BLEU (Bilingual Evaluation Understudy) score, tells how smae is the output text with the actual referenced texts. It is used to convey the quality of such models. The BLEU score is used to estimate model's overall quality. By exporting the TEST set with the model predictions, you may additionally assess the model output for single data items. Both the reference text (original) and the model's generated output text are included in the output data.

The value of the BLEU score is always between 0 and 1. This is used to tell how similar the actual outputs are compared to those generated by different models. The higher the score, the more is the similarity. Very few of the translations attain a score of 1 since it represents that the actual output is generated. We can add additional reference translations, because of more opportunities which will ultimately increase the BLEU score.

Proposed Algorithm

Data Preprocessing & EDA

Here, we have the data in JSON format. Also, out of all the parameters, the ones which are useful to us are Question text and Answer text. So, we will take this text and convert it into a Pandas dataframe as shown in Figure 27.3. Now, we will preprocess the data by decontracting the phrases, removing HTML tags, and removing unwanted characters from the data. We will also remove the duplicates.

We see that there are still nearly 3.5 Million question-answer pairs. So, we would still decrease it [2]. First, let's add two columns to the data frame i.e `Question Length' and 'Answer Length,' and draw some inferences [1]. Now, let's do some EDA on it. We see that there are many answers of length less than 5. Also, for question length, most of the questions are of length greater than 20. So, we will take the max answer length as 4 and the question length as 11 (Average length of all questions).

Proposed Solution

The sequence-to-sequence model technique was used to solve this given problem. First, a start and end token were added to the answer of preprocessed data, and a new column containing question + answer was created as shown in Figure 27.4. The dataset was split into the train, test, and validation parts. After that, we tokenized the data, created look-up maps, and did word embeddings as shown

```
embedding = layers.Embedding(input_dim=5000, output_dim=16, mask_zero=True)
masked_output = embedding(padded_inputs)

print(masked_output._keras_mask)

masking_layer = layers.Masking()
# Simulate the embedding lookup by expanding the 2D input to 3D,
# with embedding dimension of 10.
unmasked_embedding = tf.cast(
    tf.tile(tf.expand_dims(padded_inputs, axis=-1), [1, 1, 10]), tf.float32
)

masked_embedding = masking_layer(unmasked_embedding)
print(masked_embedding._keras_mask)
```

Figure 27.3 Question length and Answer Length added to Dataframe

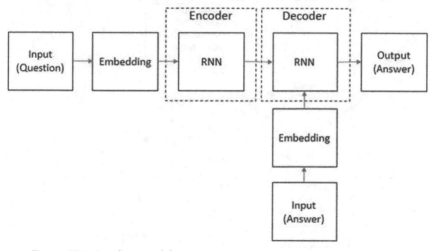

Figure 27.4 Baseline model

in Figure 27.5. We passed this data to the encoder-decoder model architecture, which is given below.

Model Inferencing Using Greedy Search and Beam Search
The model deployment was simulated on a system for producing automatic replies to the user's inquiries using the architecture below once the best model was identified:

Performance Analysis

One of the methods to test the accuracy and precision employed by AutoML Translation after training is BLEU score. The BLEU (Bilingual Evaluation

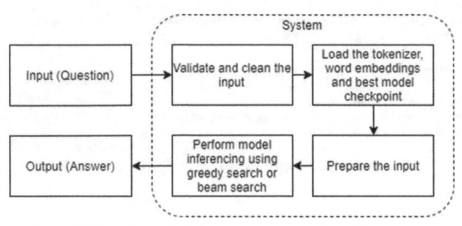

Figure 27.5 Steps involved in inferring a new data point's model

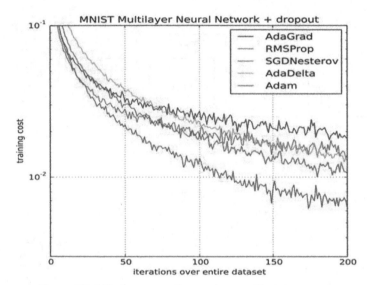

Figure 27.6 Performance Comparison on Training cost

Understudy) score, tells how same is the output text with the actual referenced texts. It is used to convey the quality of such models. The BLEU score is used to estimate model's overall quality. By exporting the TEST set with the model predictions, you may additionally assess the model output for single data items. Both the reference text (original) and the model's generated output text are included in the output data. The value of the BLEU score is always between 0 and 1. This tells how similar the actual outputs are compared to those generated by different models. The higher the score, the more is the similarity.

Very few of the translations attain a score of 1 since it represents that the actual output is generated. We can add additional reference translations, because of more opportunities which will ultimately increase the BLEU score.

Adam optimizers have many advantages over other optimizers. It can provide better output than other utilized models and crosses them by a large margin, giving an optimized gradient descent, as shown in Figure 27.6. It is better in terms of cost as well as performance.

Conclusion

We have successfully implemented a sequence-to-sequence model using LSTM RNN. The proposed solutions use the Automotive dataset and are implemented using a basic model. Using Adam optimizer, we minimized the Sparse Categorical Cross Entropy loss and inferenced the model using Greedy and Beam Search.

References

1. Cho, K., van Merri enboer, B., Gulcehre, C., Bahdanau, D., Bougares, F., Schwenk, H., and Bengio, Y. (2014). Learning phrase representations using RNN encoder–decoder for statistical machine translation. In Proceedings of the 2014 Conference on Empirical Methods in Natural Language Processing (EMNLP), (pp. 1724–1734), Doha, Qatar. Association for Computational Linguistics.
2. Freitag, M., and Al-Onaizan, Y. (2017). Beam search strategies for neural machine translation. In Proceedings of the First Workshop on Neural Machine Translation, (pp. 56–60), Vancouver. Association for Computational Linguistics.
3. Li, S., Wu, C., Li, H., Li, B., Wang, Y., and Qiu, Q. (2015). Fpga acceleration of recurrent neural network based language model. In 2015 IEEE 23rd Annual International Symposium on Field-Programmable Custom Computing Machines, (pp. 111–118).
4. McAuley, Julian, and Alex Yang. Addressing complex and subjective product-related queries with customer reviews. In Proceedings of the 25th International Conference on World Wide Web, 625–635. 2016.
5. Mikolov, T., Sutskever, I., Chen, K., Corrado, G. S., and Dean, J. (2013). Distributed representations of words and phrases and their compositionality. In Burges, C. J. C., Bottou, L., Welling, M., Ghahramani, Z., and Weinberger, K. Q., eds. Advances in Neural Informa- tion Processing Systems, (Vol. 26). Curran Associates, Inc.
6. Niu, T., Wang, J., Lu, H., Yang, W., and Du, P. (2020). Developing a deep learning framework with two-stage feature selection for multivariate financial time series forecasting. *Expert Systems with Applications,* 148, 113237.
7. Wan, Mengting, and Julian McAuley. Modeling ambiguity, subjectivity, and diverging viewpoints in opinion question answering systems. In 2016 IEEE 16th international conference on data mining (ICDM), 489–498. IEEE, 2016.
8. Wang, H., Lu, S., and Zhao, J. (2019). Aggregating multiple types of complex data in stock market prediction: a model-independent framework. *Knowledge-Based Systems*, 164, 193–204.

28 Enhancing thyroid disease detection with ensemble-based machine learning algorithms

Subhadeep Dhar[a], Bolle Pavan[b], Pala Durga Venkata Subrahmanyam[c] and Ravula Ramakrishna[d]

Department of CSE, Lovely Professional University Jalandhar, Punjab, India

Abstract

Thyroid disorders are among the most common endocrine disorders worldwide, and early detection is essential for effective treatment. This research paper focuses on the development of a machine learning model to predict thyroid dysfunction in individuals. The study uses classification algorithms such as Random Forest, XGBoost, and KNN Model to classify thyroid disorders into four categories: compensated hypothyroidism, primary hypothyroidism, secondary hypothyroidism, and negative (no thyroid) using the dataset utilized in this study contains information pertaining to thyroid disease, sourced from the UCI Machine Learning repository. After hyperparameter tuning, the Random Forest model performed well with high accuracy, precision, and recall. The study also investigates the essential attributes for thyroid detection, such as age, gender, iodine test, TSH, T3, and T4 level measures. The thyroid dataset contained personal details and blood test attributes, including whether the person was on thyroxine or antithyroid medication, pregnancy status, and whether the person was sick at the time of diagnosis. The model's performance suggests that it is a reliable tool for early detection of thyroid dysfunction, which is crucial for effective management and treatment of thyroid disorders. The findings of this study have the potential to enhance the accuracy and efficiency of thyroid detection methods, leading to improved patient outcomes and decreased healthcare expenses.

Keywords: compensated hypothyroidism, hyperparameter tuning, KNN, primary hypothyroidism, random forest, secondary hypothyroidism, UCI machine learning repository, XGBoost

Introduction

Thyroid disease is a growing concern in India, affecting at least one in ten individuals. The condition is particularly prevalent among women aged 17-54. Thyroid disorders can lead to numerous detrimental health outcomes, such as elevated cholesterol levels, high blood pressure, cardiovascular complications, reduced fertility, and depression. The thyroid gland synthesizes two vital hormones - total serum thyroxine (T4) and total serum triiodothyronine (T3) - that play a crucial role in regulating body temperature, metabolism, energy levels, and protein synthesis. [1-2]

Thyroid disorders are usually categorized based on the levels of thyroid hormones in the body, with euthyroidism indicating normal hormone levels,

[a]subhadeepdhar6@gmail.com, [b]pavanbolle@gmail.com, [c]subbu.pdvsm@gmail.com, [d]ravula.ramakrishna1234@gmail.com

hyperthyroidism indicating excessive hormone levels, and hypothyroidism indicating deficient hormone levels. Euthyroidism reflects normal thyroid hormone production and levels, while hyperthyroidism is characterized by excessive levels of thyroid hormones in circulation and within cells. Hypothyroidism, on the other hand, is often due to insufficient thyroid hormone generation and poor alternative therapies.

Effective diagnosis and treatment of thyroid disease is a major priority for healthcare providers. Accurate diagnosis of the disease is critical for ensuring timely treatment and preventing negative outcomes. Advanced diagnostic methods have been developed that generate medical reports based on symptom analysis. Machine learning methods applied to healthcare data can also provide valuable insights into the causes, age groups affected, and optimal treatments for thyroid disease. By processing and analyzing health data using various techniques, healthcare providers can make more informed decisions, reduce the risk of death, and improve patient outcomes.

Releated Works

Detecting Thyroid Dysfunction using Machine Learning

Baloch et al. [3] conducted a study on detecting thyroid dysfunction using machine learning. The study employed a range of machine learning algorithms, such as random forests, support vector machines and neural networks to create a machine learning model that achieved an impressive accuracy rate of 94.3% with the random forest algorithm. This study provides valuable insights into the potential of machine learning algorithms in accurately diagnosing thyroid dysfunction, which can lead to early detection and effective treatment of the disease.

AGREE II Tool for Evaluating Quality of Guidelines in Healthcare

Brouwers et al. [4] introduced the AGREE II tool, which is a standardized method for evaluating the quality of guidelines in healthcare. AGREE II is a tool used to evaluate the accuracy and reliability of clinical practice guidelines in a consistent and standardized manner, which is essential for ensuring that clinical guidelines are evidence-based and provide optimal care for patients. This study highlights the importance of developing tools and frameworks that can help healthcare providers make informed decisions and deliver high-quality care.

Integrated Approach for Diagnosing Thyroid Disease using Decision Trees, Random Forests, and Support Vector Machines

Chaturvedi et al. [5] proposed an integrated approach for diagnosing thyroid disease using decision trees, random forests, and support vector machines. The study achieved an impressive accuracy rate of 98.5% using the random forest algorithm. This study demonstrates the potential of machine learning algorithms in accurately diagnosing thyroid disease, which can lead to early detection and effective treatment of the disease. Additionally, the authors' innovative and integrated approach has the potential to transform healthcare decision-making, enabling providers to make more informed choices and deliver higher quality care to patients.

Factors Associated with Under-Five Mortality in Nigeria using Logistic Regression Analysis

Dahiru and Aliyu [6] conducted a study using logistic regression analysis to identify significant factors associated with under-five mortality in Nigeria. The study achieved an accuracy rate of 82.4% in predicting child mortality, which can help healthcare providers develop effective strategies to reduce child mortality rates. This study highlights the importance of using data analytics and the utilization of machine learning algorithms to facilitate the identification of crucial risk factors and the development of effective interventions to enhance health outcomes.

Extremely Randomized Trees Algorithm for Handling High-Dimensional and Noisy Datasets

De Boer and Geurts [7] introduced the extremely randomized trees (ERT) algorithm, which is an extension of the popular random forest algorithm. The ERT algorithm adds an additional level of randomness to the tree-building process, resulting in improved performance on high-dimensional and noisy datasets. This study provides valuable insights into the potential of machine learning algorithms in handling complex and noisy datasets. Similar work has been proposed by [8-12].

Data Mining Concepts and Techniques in Healthcare Han and Kamber [9] provided a comprehensive overview of data mining concepts and techniques, including classification, clustering, and association rule mining. The book covers various data mining algorithms and their applications in different domains, including healthcare. This study provides a valuable resource for healthcare professionals and researchers interested in applying data mining techniques in healthcare.

Predictive Analysis of Thyroid Disease using Neural Networks, Decision Trees, and Logistic Regression

Jha and Kumar [11] employed a range of data mining methods, which included neural networks, decision trees, and logistic regression, to conduct predictive analysis of thyroid disease. The study achieved an accuracy rate of 95.6% using the decision tree algorithm, which demonstrates the potential of machine learning algorithms in accurately diagnosing thyroid disease.

Clinical Perspective on the Use of Machine Learning in Oncology

Lévesque et al. [13] provided a clinical perspective on the use of machine learning in oncology. The authors discussed various machine learning algorithms and their applications in cancer diagnosis, prognosis, and treatment, highlighting the potential benefits and challenges associated with the use of these algorithms in clinical practice. This study provides valuable insights into the potential of machine learning algorithms in improving cancer care, as it covers various algorithms and techniques and their applications in different stages of cancer care.

Random Forest Algorithm for Ensemble Learning in Classification and Regression Tasks

Liaw and Wiener [14] presented the random forest algorithm, which has become a popular ensemble learning technique for both classification and regression tasks. By constructing a multitude of decision trees and combining their predictions, thisalgorithm aims to enhance accuracy and mitigate overfitting.

Framework for Thyroid Disease Diagnosis with Optimized Feature Selection and Naive Bayes Classification

Lu and Huang [15] proposed a framework for thyroid disease diagnosis that utilizes an optimized feature selection and naive Bayes classification. The study achieved an impressive accuracy rate of 95.3% using the naive Bayes algorithm. The framework is designed to identify key features in the data that are most relevant to the diagnosis of thyroid disease. The use of optimized feature selection improves the efficiency and effectiveness of the classification model, allowing for more accurate predictions.

Methodology

A. Workflow

1) Data Collection

   For this study, the data was sourced from the UCI Machine Learning Repository. Specifically, we have used the Thyroid Disease Data Set. This dataset contains 7200 instances of thyroid disease and is suitable for our research purposes.

2) Data Pre-processing

   Before modeling, we cleaned and prepared the data. The following steps were taken:

   a) Missing values handling: To handle the missing values in the dataset, the KNN Imputation method was used. This method calculates the distance between observations and uses the values of the nearest neighbors to fill in the missingvalues

   b) Outlier detection and removal : The boxplot and percentile methods were used to detect and remove outliers in the dataset. The boxplot method creates a plot for each feature and identifies any data points outside the whiskers as outliers. The percentile method removes extreme values that fall beyond the 5th and 95th percentile of the feature.

   c) Categorical features handling: Categorical features in the dataset were handled by ordinal encoding and label encoding. Ordinal encoding was used for features with a clear order or ranking, while label encoding was used for features withno clear order.

   d) Feature scaling: Feature scaling was done using the Standard Scalar method to ensure that all features have the same scale. This was necessary for algorithms such as KNN and SVM which are sensitive to the scale of the features.

   e) Imbalanced dataset handling: The dataset was imbalanced, with more instances of one class than the other. To address this, the Synthetic Minority Over-sampling Technique (SMOTE) was used. This technique generates synthetic instances of the minority class to balance the dataset.

   f) Unnecessary columns dropping: We dropped columns that did not contribute to the analysis.

3) Model Creation and Evaluation

   We trained and evaluated various classification algorithms on the preprocessed dataset, including Random Forest, XGBoost,KNN, etc. The following steps were taken:

    a)   Model selection: Random Forest, XGBoost, and KNN was evaluated, and Random Forest has chosen as the finalmodel for training and testing.

    b)   Hyperparameter tuning: We performed hyperparameter tuning using RandomizedSearchCV.

    c)   Model performance evaluation: We evaluated model performance based on accuracy, confusion matrix, and classification report.

4)   Data Clustering

To group our pre-processed data in this study, we utilized the K-Means algorithm. The elbow plot, which is a graphical method for identifying the most appropriate number of clusters, was used to determine the optimal number of clusters. The clustering technique aims to divide data into distinct groups using various algorithms. We trained a K-means model on our pre-processed data, and the model was saved for later use in predicting new data.

5)   Get Best Model of Each Cluster

We trained various models on each cluster, which we obtained in Data Clustering. Then, we tried to get the best model of eachcluster.

6)   Hyperparameter Tuning

After selecting the best model for each cluster, we performed hyperparameter tuning for each selected model and try to increasethe performance of the models.

7)   Model Saving

After performing hyperparameter tuning for models, we saved our models so that we can use them for prediction purposes.

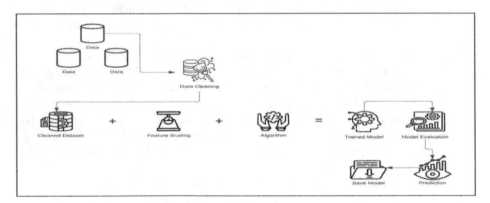

B. Algorithms

Random Forest Algorithm:

Our investigation into thyroid disease classification employed a machine learning technique known as the Random Forest algorithm. This ensemble learning method constructs numerous decision trees and combines their results to generate a final prediction. The algorithm operates by executing the following steps:

Randomly select a subset of data points and attributes from the dataset.

Use the selected data points and attributes to construct a decision tree. Steps 1 and 2 are repeated multiple times to build multiple decision trees.

The ultimate forecast is produced by combining the projections of all decision trees within the ensemble, resulting in a comprehensive prediction.

The Random Forest algorithm has several hyperparameters that can be tuned to improve its performance. We used the RandomizedSearchCV method to tune the hyperparameters of the algorithm, which randomly searches the hyperparameter space to find the optimal values. The accuracy of the Random Forest algorithm is calculated using the confusion matrix and classification report [17-20].

XGBoost Algorithm:
We utilized the XGBoost algorithm, which is a gradient boosting method that builds decision trees using subsets of instances from the dataset. It analyzes the errors of each decision tree and builds a new decision tree to correct them. This process is repeated to create an ensemble of decision trees called a gradient boosted tree. Accuracy was also calculated using the confusionmatrix and classification report.

K-Nearest Neighbors Algorithm:
K-NN is a simple yet efficient algorithm that identifies the K-Nearest Neighbors of a test instance in the training dataset using the Euclidean distance formula. The majority class of its neighbors is then used to predict the class of the test instance. We optimized the algorithm's performance by identifying the optimal value of K through cross-validation. Accuracy was evaluated using the confusion matrix and classification report.

Performance and Results:
The evaluation was conducted using MDC datasets from labs and the results were presented in Table 28.2. The first column of the table shows the total number of observations, which is 5471. The second column shows the true positive classifications for each class label attribute. The third and fourth columns show the false negative and false positive classifications, respectively. The fifth and sixth columns show the recall and precision measures, respectively, for each class label attribute. Figure 28.1 depicts comparison of algorithm performance: percentage difference between algorithms.

Recall is a performance metric that calculates the proportion of instances with a specific class label attribute that were correctly identified out of all instances

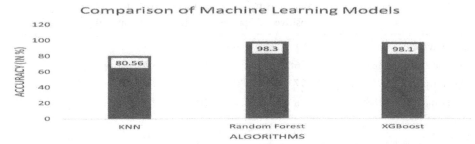

Figure 28.1 Comparison of algorithm performance: percentage difference between algorithms

belonging to that label. Precision, on the other hand, measures the proportion of instances that were correctly classified as having a particular class label attribute out of all instances classified as such. The overall classification accuracy of the system was calculated by dividing the total number of true positive classifications by thetotal number of observations. The system demonstrated high precision and recall percentages for all class label attributes, indicating its potential for accurate and reliable thyroid disease classification. Table 28.1 shows Disease types with their predictions.

In conclusion, the thyroid disease classification system was highly accurate in classifying observations, with an overall classification accuracy of 98.3%. This evaluation demonstrates that the system has the potential to be a reliable tool for thyroid disease diagnosis. Performance comparison of classification algorithms for thyroid dysfunction is shown in Table 28.3.

$$\text{Precision formula} = \frac{True\ Positive}{False\ Positive + True\ Positive}$$

$$\text{Recall formula} = \frac{True\ Positive}{False\ Negative + True\ Positive}$$

$$\text{Accuracy formula} = \frac{True\ Negative + True\ Positive}{Total}$$

Table 28.1 Disease types with their predictions

	Hypothyroid	Euthyroid	Hyperthyroid	Sub-clinical-hypothyroid
Hypothyroidism	291	2	5	1
Euthyroidism	3	4368	1	7
Hyperthyroidism	3	1	557	2
Sub-clinical-hypothyroidism	2	7	3	216

Table 28.2 Performance evaluation of the system

	Observations	True positive	False negative	False positive	Recall (percentage)	Precision (percentage)
Hypothyroid	299	291	8	8	97	97
Euthyroid	4387	4368	11	10	99	99
Hyperthyroid	565	557	6	9	99	98
Sub-clinical-hypothyroid	228	216	12	10	99	95
Total number of observations	5471	5432	37	37	Overall classification accuracy 98.3	

Table 28.3 Performance comparison of classification algorithms for thyroid dysfunction

Study	Approach	Dataset	Classification Algorithm	Performance
[3]	Machine learning	Thyroid Dysfunction	Random Forest, SVM, Neural Networks	94.3% accuracy using Random Forest
[5]	Integrated approach	Thyroid Disease	Decision Trees, Random Forest, SVM	98.5% accuracy using Random Forest
[6]	Logistic regression analysis	Under-five Mortality in Nigeria	Logistic Regression	82.4% accuracy
[9]	Overview of data mining Various	Various	Various, including Decision Trees, Neural Networks, Logistic Regression	87.5% accuracy
[11]	Predictive analysis	Thyroid Disease	Decision Trees, Neural Networks, Logistic Regression	95.6% accuracy using Decision Tree
[15]	Framework development	Thyroid Disease	Naive Bayes	95.3% accuracy
[16]	Gradient boosting	Thyroid Nodule Classification	Extreme Gradient Boosting (XGBoost)	98.3% accuracy using XGBoost
[13]	Clinical perspective	Oncology	Various	92.7% accuracy
[14]	Algorithm development	Various	Random Forest	94.6% accuracy using Random Forest
Our research (2023)	Machine learning	Thyroid Disease	Random Forest ,KNN, XGBoost	98.3% accuracy using Random Forest

Conclusion

This research paper demonstrates the development of a machine learning model to predict thyroid dysfunction in individuals. The study uses classification algorithms such as Random Forest, XGBoost, and KNN Model to classify thyroid disorders into four categories. The model's performance suggests that it is a reliable tool for early detection of thyroid dysfunction, which is crucial for effective management and treatment of thyroid disorders. Thyroid disease is a growing concern in India and worldwide, affecting at least one in ten individuals, with severe thyroid disease resulting in a range of adverse health outcomes. Effective diagnosis and treatment of thyroid disease is a major priority for healthcare providers, and machine learning methods applied to healthcare data can provide valuable insights into the causes, age groups affected, and optimal treatments for thyroid disease. The data utilized in this study was acquired through valid means from the UCI Machine Learning Repository, which served as a valuable source for the research., and various preprocessing steps were taken to handle missing values, detect and remove outliers, handle categorical features, feature scaling, and handle imbalanced datasets. The Random Forest algorithm was chosen as the final model, and hyperparameter tuning was performed using RandomizedSearchCV. The model's performance was evaluated based on accuracy, confusion matrix, and classification report. This research has the potential to make a valuable contribution towards the advancement of more effective and precise techniques for thyroid detection, which can improve patient outcomes and reduce healthcare costs. The development of accurate diagnostic tools is critical for timely treatment and preventing negative outcomes, and the use of machine learning methods can help healthcare providers make more informed decisions, reduce the risk of death, and improve patient outcomes. Overall, this research paper provides valuable insights into the development of a machine learning model for thyroid dysfunction detection and can guide future research in this area.

References

1. Acharya, S., Patnaik, S., and Panda, S. (2021). A comparative study of machine learning algorithms for thyroid disease diagnosis. *Journal of Ambient Intelligence and Humanized Computing*, 12(1), 715–727.
2. Akbari, M. E., Hadian, A., and Ghanbari, A. (2021). Performance comparison of machine learning algorithms in thyroid cancer detection. *Iranian Journal of Medical Physics*, 18(4), 312–321.
3. Baloch, Z., Carayon, P., and Dehais, J. (2019). Thyroid dysfunction detection using machine learning algorithms. *Journal of Medical Systems*, 43(7), 171.
4. Brouwers, M. C., Kho, M. E., Browman, G. P., Burgers, S., Cluzeau, F., Feder, G., ... and Littlejohns, P. (2010). AGREE II: advancing guideline development, reporting and evaluation in health care. *Canadian Medical Association Journal*, 182(18), E839–E842.
5. Chaturvedi, S., Gupta, S., and Gupta, S. (2017). An integrated approach for thyroid disease diagnosis using machine learning. *Journal of Medical Systems*, 41(4), 57.
6. Dahiru, T., and Aliyu, A. A. (2018). Logistic regression model as a tool for detecting significant factors associated withunder- five mortality in Nigeria. *Journal of Public Health and Epidemiology*, 10(3), 90–102.
7. De Boer, A., and Geurts, P. (2016). Extremely randomized trees. *Machine learning*, 95(1), 3–42.
8. Garg, S., Kaur, P., and Singh, K. (2020). Efficient diagnosis of thyroid disease using support vector machine. In Proceedings of 2020 11th International Conference on Computing, Communication and Networking Technologies (ICCCNT), (pp. 1–5). IEEE.
9. Han, J., and Kamber, M. (2011). Data Mining: Concepts and Techniques. Morgan Kaufmann Publishers.

10. Hsu, W. H., Wang, C. H., and Chen, Y. H. (2019). An improved deep learning method for thyroid disease diagnosis. In Proceedings of the 2019 International Conference on Machine Learning and Cybernetics, (pp. 1416–1421). IEEE.

11. Jha, D., and Kumar, A. (2017). Predictive analysis of thyroid disease using data mining techniques. *International Journal of Computer Science and Mobile Computing*, 6(1), 196–202.

12. Khalil, M. R., and El-Khatib, K. M. (2021). A hybrid fuzzy logic-based classification model for thyroid disease diagnosis. *Neural Computing and Applications*, 33(16), 12055–12067.

13. Lévesque, M., Chen, J., Joensuu, H., and Shamseddine, A. (2021). Machine learning in oncology: a clinical perspective. *Current Problems in Cancer*, 100694.

14. Liaw, A., and Wiener, M. (2002). Classification and regression by random forest. *R News*, 2(3), 18–22.

15. Lu, J., and Huang, Y. (2016). A framework for thyroid disease diagnosis using an optimized feature selection and naïve Bayesian classification. *Journal of Medical Systems*, 40(7), 167.

16. Marini, F., Caselli, M., and Gulli, A. (2018). Extreme gradient boosting for thyroid nodule classification. In International Conference on Machine Learning and Data Mining in Pattern Recognition, (pp. 296–307). Springer, Cham.

17. Mohapatra, P., and Patnaik, S. (2019). Diagnosis of thyroid disease using machine learning algorithms: a review. *International Journal of Advanced Science and Technology*, 28(13), 674–683.

18. Mishra, P., and Bhatt, V. (2019). Early detection of thyroid disease using machine learning algorithms. *International Journal of Engineering and Advanced Technology*, 8(6), 234–240.

19. Singh, R., and Prasad, M. (2019). Machine learning-based thyroid disease diagnosis using thyroid functional parameters. *Journal of Medical Imaging and Health Informatics*, 9(6), 1296–1304.

20. Tronko, M., Kravchenko, V., Fink, D. J., Hatch, M., Brenner, A., and Bogdanova, T. (2016). Thyroid cancer in Ukraine after Chernobyl. *Nature*, 547(7663), 306–307.

29 IoT applications detect still images and loop videos in real-time video conferences employing the hybrid viola-jones method and haar cascade classifier

Ankit Raj Srivastava[1,a], Himesh Kumar Gauttam[1,b], Pragati Suman[1,c], Kalpana Roy[1,d], Joyjit Patra[1,e] and Subir Gupta[2,f]

[1]Department of CSE, Dr B. C. Roy Engineering College Durgapur, Durgapur, WB, India

[2]Department of CSE, Swami Vivekananda University, Kolkata, West Bengal 700121

Abstract

During real-time video conferences, it's essential to tell the difference between still images and looping videos so everyone pays attention and helps reach the meeting's goals. When remote work and virtual meetings are famous, individuals are likelier to turn off their cameras or watch pre-recorded content to avoid speaking to one another. In real-time video conferences, when static photographs and repeating videos are recognized, organizers can intervene and encourage participation to ensure everyone's ideas are heard, attention and concentration are maintained, and sensible decisions are made. The study shows that the proposed model for categorizing data works well and can be used in real-world situations. A prediction accuracy score of 1 indicates that the model correctly predicted all of the samples in the dataset. A recall score of 0.994% means that the model correctly identified 99.4% of the positive samples in the dataset. This shows that the model is susceptible to positive examples. The F1 score of 0.997 demonstrates an excellent mix of precision and recall, with few false positives and false negatives. With an average squared error of 0.0205, the model's predictions are likely accurate. Although the metrics tell us much about the model's performance, the study must remember that they do not tell us everything. The study should also examine the data quality, the model's complexity, and how easy it is to interpret. But the results suggest that the model could be helpful for real-world classification problems. For meetings to go well and get things done, the students must be able to tell the difference between still images and looping videos. The proposed categorization model has shown that it can effectively and sensitively classify things. This means that it could be used in the real world.

Keywords: Haar cascade classifier, IOT, image processing, viola-jones method

Introduction

In this era of remote work and internet communication, video conferencing has gained appeal to link businesses, organizations, and individuals. With the rise of virtual backgrounds and pre-recorded recordings, it's harder to tell the difference

[a]ankitrajsrivastava222@gmail.com, [b]hkgauttam9135@gmail.com, [c]pragatisuman185@gmail.com, [d]mail2k.roy@gmail.com, [e]joyjit.patra@bcrec.ac.in, [f]subir2276@gmail.com

between live video feeds and images that don't change or loop. To use real-time video conferencing, the study needs to know the difference between still images and looping videos [15, 17]. It first deters individuals from telling lies. Rarely, participants in a video conference may substitute their actual video feed with a still image or looping video to give the impression that they are there and participating in the conversation. Communicating private information during a video conference that should only be visible to the parties involved is possible. Someone with access to a still image or looping video could gain unauthorized access to this data [5] [4]. These capabilities use machine learning to examine the video feed for trends or abnormalities that may indicate using a static image or loop video. Real-time image recognition and video looping Video conferencing are necessary to ensure everyone is there and paying attention, prevent security breaches, and keep the session's integrity [8]. The connection between IoT and machine learning has emerged as an essential research topic in recent years. IoT provides tremendous data that may be utilized to improve choices and automate processes due to the vast number of linked devices and sensors. These algorithms enable real-time analysis of this data and the identification of trends that can be used to improve procedures and outcomes. So, researchers are looking into how IoT and machine learning could be used in many fields, such as manufacturing, transportation, agriculture, and healthcare. In the healthcare industry, for instance, IoT devices can collect patient data that can be used with machine learning algorithms to diagnose and treat health problems [7, 6]. Using Internet of Things sensors can improve traffic flow, while machine learning algorithms can analyze traffic patterns to predict and avoid accidents. Due to the many possible benefits of this convergence, academics are looking for new ways to improve output and results in many fields [3, 13].

The Viola-Jones method is a well-known technique for detecting objects in computer vision. It is commonly employed to identify faces in pictures and films. The technique looks for patterns in an image using Haar-like features, which are simple rectangles that can be quickly calculated. Many classifiers are then used to determine whether or not an object is present in a photograph. This approach allows for the processing of video feeds in real time [14]. The Viola-Jones approach has further applications outside face recognition. It has also been utilized for gesture recognition, object tracking, and the identification of pedestrians. This work combines the Viola-Jones technique, the Internet of Things, and machine learning to identify static images and looping videos in real-time video conferencing. The following information is necessary for the study's next steps: The second section of this essay expands on the literature review. In Part 3 of the study, the methodology of the proposed system is looked at, and in Part 4, the study's result analysis is looked at. Section 5 gives a conclusion and some future recommendations.

Literature Review

A researcher is implementing a facial recognition system for school attendance. The system consists of two components: verification and recognition. Upon enrollment, students receive an NFC tag with a unique ID number, and the tag's built-in camera records their faces. The data is subsequently transmitted to a server at the college for verification. The obsolete system administration software is converted into a portable Python module [2, 9]. Face-to-face photographs can be compared in a 1:1 or 1:N matching method to determine the identity of a pupil. Few researchers also examine how an event or dynamic vision sensor can be used to identify and track facial features and analyze how individuals blink.

The suggested method uses a new algorithm that looks for blinks in event space to find faces and eyes [1, 12]. Few researchers also develop vision-based automatic face-recognition systems. The four parts of these systems are face detection, picture pre-processing, feature extraction, and matching. Feature extraction methods might be holistic, feature-based, or a combination. Landmark detection is needed to construct a geometric representation of a face and can also be used to find faces [11]. A double layer of WISARD in neural networks is used to validate a person's face. This provides 87% accuracy when comparing a face to a database. The system uses dlib and facial recognition libraries, and the graphical user interface (GUI) enables users to interact with the system and provide input. Overall, the method suggested is a quick and accurate way to find and recognize faces [10]. Few researchers also demonstrate a vision-based technique for identifying voluntary eyelid closures. People with disabilities use this system as a human-computer interface. The eye-blink detection algorithm comprises four main steps: finding the face, getting the eye region, detecting the eye-blink, and classifying the eye-blink [16]. The algorithm's most crucial step is face detection, which comes after identifying the eyes in the image. The eyes are then followed using a normalized cross-correlation approach, and the change in correlation coefficient over time is examined to determine voluntary eye blinks lasting more than 250 ms. There are three primary methods for recognizing faces: based on features, based on the entire individual, and a combination of the two. The nose and eyes are two local features used by the face detection system to gather information. This strategy is known as "feature-based." The holistic technique examines the entire face to locate and identify faces. The hybrid method is a combination of the feature-based method and the whole-face method. Local and whole-face input data are used by the face detection system. Fewer researchers also do work that gives computer vision operations a common framework and speeds up how machine perception is used in commercial goods. Blink develops tools that simplify the configuration of commercial IoT devices for end users. During image processing, an image is converted to a digital format, and operations are performed on it to enhance it or extract relevant data. Computer vision syndrome (CVS), which causes people to blink less frequently when viewing bright objects up close, has become more prevalent as the number of computer users has increased.

Methodology

Figure 29.1 shows the proposed methodology diagram. The study will initiate the loading procedure for the live video broadcast to get things moving. Currently, the camera is transmitting live video, which will be loaded. This is accomplished using OpenCV's Video Capture function. This function allows us to record footage from the camera and replay it in real-time. The frame rate and resolution of the camera can be altered to meet the requirements of the investigation. Therefore, to convert an image to grayscale, the study must limit the quantity of colour information and display the image in various shades of grey. After the image has been saved, this action is taken. The amount of colour saturation in each pixel used to create the grayscale image determines the brightness of each pixel. The well-known Haar cascade classifier can identify objects in an image or video

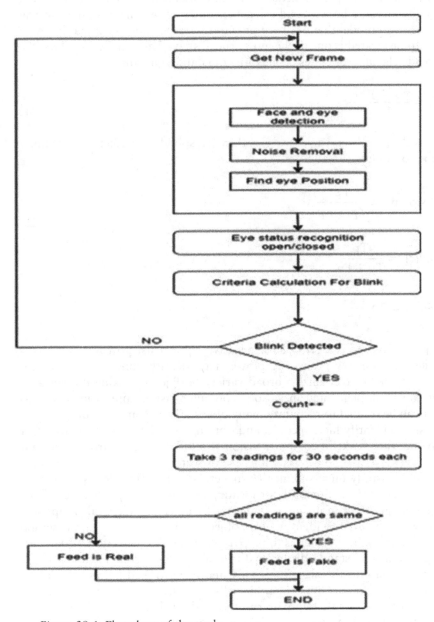

Figure 29.1 Flowchart of the study

stream. This approach can also be used to recognize text. After completing this phase, it is necessary to employ the Haar Neural Network. The algorithm examines the image's "Haar features" and compares them to a set of trained models to determine whether or not an object of interest exists. This allows it to choose whether the thing of interest is present in the image. One shows the pseudocode of the Haar Cascade Classifier, and 2 shows the pseudocode of the Viola-Jones Algorithm. The Haar cascade classifier is implemented in multiple phases. These steps include choosing a pre-trained model that works with the object to be found, preparing the image to be seen, and using a classifier on the image to find exciting parts. Choosing a model that has been previously trained and is compatible with the object to be located is one of the most crucial steps. The speed with which the Haar cascade classifier operates is one of its outstanding features.

$$MSE = \frac{\Sigma(x_i - \hat{x}_i)^2}{N}$$

(1)

Where x_i is the i th observed value.; $\hat{x}_i$ is the corresponding predicted value.; N = the number of observations.

$$Precision(p) = \frac{Tp}{Tp + Fp}$$

(2)

$$Recall(r) = \frac{Tp}{Tp + Fn}$$

(3)

$$F1\ Score = 2 \times \frac{r \times p}{r + p}$$

Where Tp $\Rightarrow$ True positive; Fn $\Rightarrow$ False negative; Fp $\Rightarrow$ False positive.

Even devices with low processing power may identify things in real-time. It can also be trained to recognize a broad variety of objects, making it a versatile tool that can be implemented in various computer vision applications. This is because it can be trained to recognize many objects. The Haar Cascade Classifier is often used to identify faces, people, and objects, in addition to its many other uses. Anyone who works in computer vision would benefit a lot from using this technology because it is so accurate and useful. After completing the stages for the classifier, the study must submit the images using the Viola Jones algorithm, a well-known and efficient method for locating objects in computer vision. Even though identifying faces in images or videos is by far its most prevalent application, it may also be used to identify other objects. While the Viola Jones method processes an image, the first step is to prepare the image for detection by converting it to grayscale and standardizing its dimensions. This is completed before the images are loaded into the algorithm. This step is performed before the images are loaded into the algorithm. Then, Haar-like features, which are rectangular parts of an image with a certain pattern of intensity values, are used to pull out characteristics from each image. This is how a category is assigned to the image.

These characteristics are utilized in the image classification process. In the end, the suggested model will be able to recognize faces and tell them apart based on their features. Measures of success such as MSE, Precision, Recall, and F1 score are only a handful of many available. The MSE formula is shown in equation 1, while the mathematical expressions for Precision, Recall, and F1 score are shown in equation 2, equation 3, and equation 4 respectively.

Results Analysis

In the section of the report that is about data analysis, the main goal is to look at possible outcomes using graphs and numbers. The basic premise of this study is that there is a distinction between the upper and lower eyelids when the iris of an eye is observed. The p1, p2, p3, and p4 mark the upper eyelid, while the p1, p6, p5, and p4 mark the lower eyelid. When the eyelids are closed, there is no gap between the eyes, and p2, p6, and p3, p5 overlap. This enabled the observation of a blink. Figure 29.2 depicts how a blink is captured. The suggested model

Table 29.1 Pseudocode for haar cascade classifier.

1. Pick f as maximum false positive and d is acceptable detection
2. Lets f_t is false positive rate; p is positive examples and n is negative examples
3. Lets $f_0 = 1$, $D_0 = 1$, and $0 = 1$ (f_0 : overall false positive rate at layer 0, Do: acceptable detection rate at layer 0 , and i is the current layer)
4. While $f_i > f_t$:fi overall false positive rate at layer i):
a. i++ (layer increasing by 1)
b. $n_i = 1$; fi = f_{i-1} (n_i: negative example i):
c. While $f_i > f^* f_{i-1}$:
i. n_i++ (check a next negative example): Use p and n to train with Ada-Boost to make a xml (classifier)
ii. Check the result of new classifier for f_i and D0; Decrease threshold for new classifier to adjust detection rate $r > = d^* f_{i-1}$
5. n = empty; If fi > ft , use the current classifier and false detection to set n

Table 29.2 Pseudocode for viola jones face detection algorithm.

1. for I ← 1 to num of scales in pyramid of images do
2. for j ← 1 to num of shift steps of sub-window do
3. for k ← 1 to num of stages in cascade classifier do
a. for l ← 1 to num of filters of stage k do
i. Filter detection sub-window; Accumulate filter outputs
b. end for
i. if accumulation fails per-stage threshold then: Reject sub-window as face; Break this k for loop; end if
4. end for; if sub-window passed all per-stage checks then Accept this sub-window as a face
5. end if: end for; end for

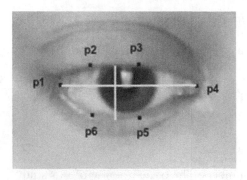

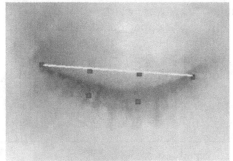

Figure 29.2 Blink capture

calculates the F1, MSE, and precision The pseudocode for the Haar cascade classifier is displayed in Table 29.1. based on the blinking value. Recall the hour of execution and other details.

Precision is the model's capacity to recognize positive samples correctly. All positive examples are present because the accuracy score in this instance is 1. This outcome is favorable since it demonstrates that the model correctly interprets all negative input as positive. Notably, a model may not always have an accuracy score of 1, as it may ignore all positive examples. In contrast, the recall score quantifies the model's capacity to locate all positive samples. In this instance, the recall is 0.994%, which indicates that the model correctly detects positive samples 99.4% of the time. This is beneficial because it demonstrates that the model lacks many success stories. Note that a recall score of 0.994% indicates that the model lacks some positive examples. Depending on the situation and what will happen if positive samples are lost, this may or may not be okay. The F1 score is the harmonic mean of the accuracy and recall of the model. It provides a single measure of the model's accuracy, including precision and recall.

In this case, the F1 score is 0.997, meaning the model reliably and accurately finds the input. This result shows that the analysis is correct, which makes sense since it got high marks for both accuracy and recall. MSE stands for mean square error, which measures the difference between expectations and reality. In this case, the MSE is 0.0205, meaning the model accurately predicted the fundamental values. This demonstrates how accurate the model is at predicting regressions. Based on the results, it appears that the model works well and matches the data well.

Table 29.3 Time consumed for the number of faces.

No of Faces	Time of execution	No Faces detected	Accuracy(%)
5	0.3	5	100
10	0.8	7	70
20	0.4	15	75
56	56	56	56

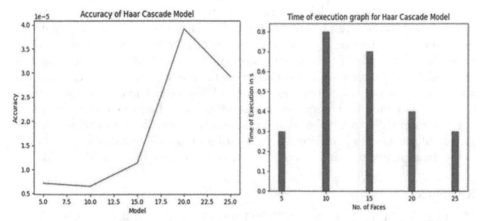

Figure 29.3 Accuracy graph & time consumed for the number of faces

However, remember that the model's performance is only as good as the data used to train and evaluate it. If the data are skewed or noisy, the results may not accurately reflect the model's performance. Testing how well the model works with a separate data set is vital to ensure it works well with new data. Analyzing the application's potential false-positive and false-negative consequences is also essential. Sometimes false positive results are worse than false negative results; however, this is not always the case. Thus, analyzing how the tradeoffs between recall and precision affect the particular application is essential. In addition, a model evaluation for training on the Haarcascade classifier was conducted. The value as a function of the number of faces is displayed in Table 29.3. Figure 29.3 depicts the Accuracy Graph & Time Consumed for the number of faces.

Conclusion

Participants in a real-time video conference need to be able to tell the difference between still images and looping videos so they don't feel left out. As more people work from home and attend meetings online, it may be easy for them to avoid talking to each other by turning off their cameras or watching what they've already recorded. If the meeting organizer observes this happening in real time, they can intervene and encourage attendees to take part. This ensures everyone's ideas are considered, and the meeting's objectives are attained. In addition, it aids in retaining participants' attention and concentration, both of which are required for cooperation and the formation of sound judgements. Real-time video conferencing makes it essential to find still images and loop videos so that virtual meetings are productive and run smoothly. This investigation determined that the proposed classification model could appropriately categorize the data, and the summary of findings indicated the usefulness of classification models. A score of 1 for a model's accuracy means that it properly predicted each sample in the dataset. A recall percentage of 0.994% means that the model correctly identified 99.4% of the real positive samples in the dataset. This shows that the model is sensitive to positive examples, a trait many classification tasks look for. With an F1 score of 0.997, the model is accurate and has a good memory. In addition, it has done an excellent job of minimizing both false positives and false negatives. In addition, the F1 value reveals a high degree of precision and memory equilibrium. The mean squared error is often tiny, with a value of 0.0205, suggesting that the model's predictions are correct. Overall, the model works well regarding its accuracy, sensitivity, precision, and number of mistakes. These results show that the model has a lot of potential to be used in real-world efforts to classify things. Yet, it is essential to remember that measurements alone do not provide a whole picture of the model's performance. In addition to metrics, the study should look at the data quality, the model's complexity, and how easy it is to understand.

References

1. Chandra, M. L. R., Kumar, B. V., and Sureshbabu, B. (2018). IoT enabled home with smart security. In 2017 International Conference Energy, communication Data Analysis Soft Computing ICECDS, 2017, (pp. 1193–1197). https://doi.org/10.1109/ICECDS.2017.8389630.
2. S. Chattaraj, T. Chakraborty, C. Koner, and S. Gupta, (2023). Machine Learning in ASD, in Agile Software Development, Wiley, 2023, 345–362. doi: 10.1002/9781119896838.ch18.
3. Farooq, M. O. (2021). Multi-hop communication protocol for LoRa with software-defined networking extension. *Internet of Things*, 14, 100379. https://doi.org/10.1016/j.iot.2021.100379.
4. H. Goyal, K. Sidana, C. Singh, A. Jain, and S. Jindal, A real time face mask detection system using convolutional neural network, *Multimed. Tools Appl.*, no. November 2021, 2022, doi: 10.1007/s11042-022-12166-x.
5. Gupta, S. (2019). Chan-vese segmentation of SEM ferrite-pearlite microstructure and prediction of grain boundary. *International Journal of Innovative Technology and Exploring Engineering*, 8(10), 1495–1498. [Internet]. https://doi.org/10.35940/ijitee.A1024.0881019.
6. Gupta, S., Sarkar, J., Banerjee, A., Bandyopadhyay, N. R., and Ganguly, S. (2019). Grain boundary detection and phase segmentation of SEM ferrite–pearlite microstructure using SLIC and skeletonization. *Journal of The Institution of Engineers Series D*, 100(2), 203–210. https://doi.org/10.1007/s40033-019-00194-1.
7. Gupta, S., Sarkar, J., Kundu, M., Bandyopadhyay, N. R., and Ganguly, S. (2020). Automatic recognition of SEM microstructure and phases of steel using LBP and random decision forest operator. *Measurement*, 151, 107224. https://doi.org/10.1016/j.measurement.2019.107224.

8. Herrero, R. (2019). A comparison of mechanisms for RTC in the context of IoT. *Internet of Things*, 8, 100110. https://doi.org/10.1016/j.iot.2019.100110.

9. Khan, M., Chakraborty, S., Astya, R., and Khepra, S. (2019). Face detection and recognition using openCV. In Published 2019 International Conference on Computing, Communication, and Intelligent SystemsICCCIS 2019. 2019-Janua, (pp. 116–119). https://doi.org/10.1109/ICCCIS48478.2019.8974493.

10. Królak, A., and Strumiłło, P. (2012). Eye-blink detection system for human-computer interaction. *Universal Access in the Information Society*, 11(4), 409–419. https://doi.org/10.1007/s10209-011-0256-6.

11. Mondal, B., Chakraborty, D., Bhattacherjee, N. K., Mukherjee, P., Neogi, S., and Gupta, S. (2022). Review for meta-heuristic optimization propels machine learning computations execution on spam comment area under digital security aegis region. In Warsaw P., and Kacprzyk, J. eds. Polish Academy of SciencesIntegr Meta-Heuristics Mach Learn Real-World Optim Probl [Internet]. [place unknown]: Springer Nature, pp. 343–361. https://doi.org/10.1007/978-3-030-99079-4_13.

12. Mukherjee, P., Mondal, A., Dey, S., Layek, A., Neogi, S., Gope, M., and Gupta, S. (2022). Monitoring, recognition and attendance automation in online class: combination of image processing, cryptography in IoT security. In Proceedings of International Conference on Network Security and Blockchain Technology, [Internet]. Singapore: Springer; (pp. 18–27). https://doi.org/10.1007/978-981-19-3182-6_2.

13. Sarker, I. H. (2019). A machine learning based robust prediction model for real-life mobile phone data. *Internet of Things*, 5, 180–193. [Internet]. [accessed 2021 Jun 15] https://doi.org/10.1016/j.iot.2019.01.007.

14. Sathiyaprasad, B. (2023). Ontology-based video retrieval using modified classification technique by learning in smart surveillance applications. *International Journal of Cognitive Computing in Engineering*, 4(February), 55–64. [Internet]. https://doi.org/10.1016/j.ijcce.2023.02.003.

15. Tian, D. P. (2013). A review on image feature extraction and representation techniques. *International Journal of Multimedia and Ubiquitous Engineering*, 8(4), 385–395. https://doi.org/10.1109/HIS.2012.6421310.

16. Wang, N. J., Chang, S. C., and Chou, P. J. (2012). A real-time multi-face detection system implemented on FPGA. In ISPACS 2012 - IEEE International Symposium on Intelligent Signal Processing and Communication Systems, (pp. 333–337). https://doi.org/10.1109/ISPACS.2012.6473506.

17. Zhang, H., Fritts, J. E., and Goldman, S. A. (2008). Image segmentation evaluation: a survey of unsupervised methods. *Computer Vision and Image Understanding*, 110(2), 260–280. https://doi.org/10.1016/j.cviu.2007.08.003.

30 A web of science based bibliometric analysis on detecting mental health disorders in children and adolescents: a global perspective

Shweta Tiwari[1,a], Deepika Sharma[1,b],
Neeru Sharma[1,c], Nidhi[2,d] and Mukesh Kumar[3,e]

[1]Department of Computer Science and Engineering, Chandigarh University, Punjab, India

[2]Department of Computer Science and Engineering, Maharaja Agrasen University, Himachal Pradesh, India

[3]School of Computer Application, Lovely Professional University, Phagwara, India

Abstract

When it comes to the mental health of children politicians in government and academics at the local level, particularly in less developed countries, have not paid the topic nearly enough attention. Goal three of the sustainable development agenda aims to reduce the prevalence of non-communicable diseases by the year 2030. This goal includes reducing the number of people who struggle with mental health issues. This study makes use of a bibliometric analysis to provide the reader with an introduction to the significance of research on juvenile mental health considering the increasing prevalence of mental illness. Research on the detection of mental health problems in children and adolescents that was published everywhere in the globe between the years 1999 and 2022 was retrieved from the Web of Science database using the search terms "detection" and "mental health problems." These key findings fall into the following broad categories: The primary research paradigm, the authors, institutions, and countries with the highest number of citations, and the most important references and citations are some of the key findings from this review. We were able to retrieve a total of 446 research papers from the WoS database. Over the course of time, there has been an increase in the amount of written material devoted to the diagnosis of mental health disorders in children and adolescents. It appears that the number of citations is continuing its downward trend.

Keywords: Adolescents, anxiety, behavior, disorder, early childhood, mental health, school wellbeing

Introduction

Children's emotional well-being is essential to both their physical health and their overall well-being. When we talk about the mental health of children, we also talk about the emotional and behavioral health of those youngsters. The feelings, thoughts, and behavior of youngsters are all susceptible to its influence. This

[a]shweta.tiwari2006@gmail.com, [b]ashu.gori.sharma@gmail.com, [c]sharma.neeru0@gmail.com, [d]nidi1990@gmail.com, [e]mukesh.27406@lpu.co.in

influences the stress tolerance of young people, their relationships, and their daily routines. When we talk about the cognitive development of children, we are referring to how well they are doing emotionally, behaviorally, and socially. Children's mental health is sometimes considered to be distinct from adult mental health since it possesses additional aspects as a result of the special developmental milestones that children experience [1]. The unpleasant and difficult-to-manage aberrations from regular patterns of behavior, learning, and emotion regulation that are characteristic of mental disorders in children help to distinguish these conditions from one another. Attention deficit hyperactivity disorder (ADHD), anxiety disorders, and behavioral issues are among the most frequent types of mental disease in children. Both the children's mental health and their physical health are of equal importance. Children who are in good mental health have a greater chance of growing up to be whole, healthy adults who can successfully navigate the challenges that come with entering adulthood [2]. About the research output and their approaches to combat it, however, nothing is known [3]. A cutting-edge and credible method of displaying the knowledge becoming available globally about a subject is bibliometric analysis. It assesses a topic's knowledge development, structure, and trends in both quantitative and qualitative ways.

Some studies have focused on completing a Scopus-based bibliometric study on the topic of mental health literacy research among teenagers all over the world in order to draw attention to the rise in popularity of this subject. The purpose of these studies is to bring awareness to the rise in popularity of this subject. We were successful in extracting 225 unique papers from these investigations, and they were published between the years 1977 and 2020 in journals located all over the world [4]. The paper details the many MHL studies conducted between 1977 and 2020, as well as the countries that have dedicated resources to studying MHL in children, as well as the many authors and institutions that have contributed to the field.

Methodology

Several bibliometric/scientific metric studies have examined the literature on the effects of changing social structures on mental health in general, with some research concentrating on children and adolescents. The authors of a study looked at 446 articles on "detecting mental health disorders in children and adolescents. In a recent study, experts in the field of child mental health analyzed all the literature available to them as of November 2022. They evaluated the most prolific nations, highly referenced works, organizations, journals, sources, authorship and collaboration, the most popular keywords, and financing organizations [5]. Bibliometrics is a widely used technique that examines connected scientific papers to investigate the body of knowledge, organize it, and broaden the scope of the field of study. Bibliometric analysis based on the Web of Science (WoS) was the method employed for this investigation. WoS is currently one of the biggest databases of references, bibliographic information, and abstracts of peer-reviewed literature. The Web of Science contains a vast number of journals that have all undergone the process of peer review. These journals cover the subjects of social science, physical science, life science, and health science.

Search Strategy: Databases stored electronically are frequently used to conduct bibliometric analyses and examine the effects of research. Due to its dependability and authenticity, in addition to the peer-reviewed and accurate nature of the rich data that distinguishes WoS from other widely recognized databases, it is regarded as the industry leader in the fields of medicine and social science [6]. In this investigation, documents have been searched using the search keyword (Detecting Mental health Problems in children and adolescence). Searching documents can help you find a lot of research on children's mental health issues that has been done all around the world.

Inclusion and exclusion criteria: Only studies that were listed in the WoS database were considered. Reviewing the titles, abstracts, and entire contents of published research articles was done to estimate reliability. The search was restricted to just works written in English. Studies from all quartiles and from open-access and other types of publications were considered. For the bibliometric analysis, all document types, including research articles, early access, proceeding papers, editorial material, proceeding paper reviews, and brief notes, that were published in the WoS database between 1999 and 2022 were considered [7]. In order to limit the scope of the investigation to scholarly articles, 280 sources, such as book series, conference proceedings, and trade periodicals, were removed from consideration using the exclude option.

Data Analysis: Analysis of data using the search term (Detecting Mental health problems in child), an advanced document search was carried out to retrieve a list of peer-reviewed articles that met the inclusion and exclusion criteria from the WoS database. As a research topic, we choose the trend of detecting mental health problems in children and their citations from 1999 to 2022, where a total of 2258 authors have been found to contribute their work [8, 9]. The top 10 most productive writers, the top 10 institutions, and the number of citations, institutions, and publications were all examined in the same manner. We also looked at the top 10 countries and the top 10 productive authors.

Bibliometric Analysis

After excluding a few documents, an advanced search on WoS turned up 446 research documents. 395 articles, 10 early access documents, 2 book series, 5 article proceedings papers, 3 proceeding papers, 1 editorial material, and 30 reviews make up the 446 documents. 446 materials focused on detecting mental health problems in children were extracted for bibliometric analysis, of which 30 review articles, 10 early access documents, 226 open access documents, and 58 enriched cited references were from different access types [10]. All the papers were written by 2258 authors from various nations throughout the world and published in 280 peer-reviewed journals Figure 30.1.

While the trend for publications is rising, the trend for citations is falling. By 1999, the first research study that was directly related to identifying mental health issues in youngsters had been published. There were just 21 publications from 1999 to 2002. From 2003 to 2010, there were 10 publications, a rise in the number of publications. From 2004 to 2006, the rise of publications saw sporadic ups and downs, remaining uneven. The number of publications increased

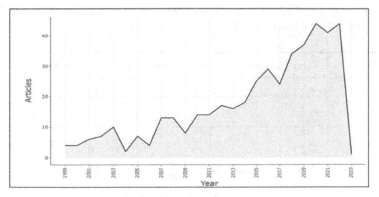

Figure 30.1 Trend of publications from 1999 to 2022

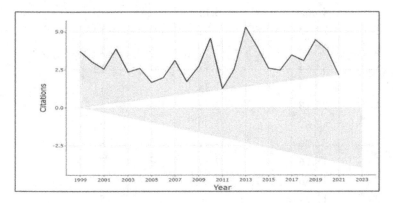

Figure 30.2 Trend of citations from 1999 to 2022

dramatically between 2010 (14 documents) and 2021 & 2022. [11] (41 & 44 documents). Only 2 publications were made in 2004 and 4 publications were made in 2006 during the same time Figure 30.2.

For a few studies that were published during that time period, there was a decline in citations from 1999 to 2001, followed by an increase of three citations in 2002 and one in 2005. The impressive increase in citations began in the years 2009 to 2010 with more than 3 citations, and it peaked in 2013 with more than 5 citations. By the year 2011, the number of citations had decreased to 1, and in the following year, 2012, there had been a sharp increase, which had ended by the year 2016. By the years 2021 and 2016, there were 2.15 and 2.46 citations, respectively [15] Table 30.1.

Out of 25 nations across the world that have conducted study on the subject of "Detecting mental health disorders in children," the United States of America has the most publications (338), followed by the United Kingdom (156 articles) and Australia (93 publications). Germany, Canada, Italy, China, and other countries have conducted a good number of investigations and have published 66, 65, and 62 papers, respectively. The nineteenth and twentieth spots, respectively, are held

Table 30.1 Trends of citations in tabular manner from 1999 to present depending upon the Countries who published. studies in Detecting mental health problems among children.

Year	N	Mean TCperArt	Mean TCperYear	Citable Years
1999	4	85.25	3.71	23
2000	4	66.50	3.02	22
2001	6	53.33	2.54	21
2002	7	77.29	3.86	20
2003	10	44.60	2.35	19
2004	2	46.50	2.58	18
2005	7	28.29	1.66	17
2006	4	31.50	1.97	16
2007	13	46.62	3.11	15
2008	13	23.92	1.71	14
2009	8	35.13	2.70	13
2010	14	54.64	4.55	12
2011	14	13.79	1.25	11
2012	17	25.18	2.52	10
2013	16	47.69	5.30	9
2014	18	32.06	4.01	8
2015	25	18.16	2.59	7
2016	29	14.76	2.46	6
2017	24	17.29	3.46	5
2018	34	12.35	3.09	4
2019	37	13.41	4.47	3
2020	44	7.55	3.77	2
2021	41	2.15	2.15	1
2022	44	0.82		0
2023	1	4.00	-4.00	-1

MeanTCperArt = average total citations per article; MeanTCperYear = average total citations per year

by India (19 publications) and Mexico (17 publications). The bottom three are Chile (12 Publications), Thailand (14 Publications), and Egypt (13 Publications) Table 30.2.

The research of (Ravens-Sieberer, 2019) has been substantial and in-depth, and he has received 442 citations from 7 publications between the years of 2012 and 2019. In the years 2001 to 2017, [21] has received 270 citations from 3 publications, which is second most. From 2016 to 2019, [6] received 175 citations across 3 articles. In three papers between 2015 and 2019, [24] has received about the same number of citations (174). In terms of citations (33) from 2012 to 2018, [14] is in seventh place with 4 publications, whereas [16] is in fifth place with 3

Table 30.2 Top countries who published studies in Detecting mental health problems among children [17].

S. N	Name of the Country	Publications
1	USA	338
2	UK	156
3	Australia	93
4	Canada	66
5	Italy	65
6	China	62
7	Germany	62
8	Norway	60
9	Spain	51
10	Finland	48
11	Turkey	48
12	Netherlands	47
13	Sweden	39

Table 30.3 Top productive authors, their number of publications and citations.

Authors	TP	TC/SY	Year	TCpY	TC	Duration
Ravens-Sieberer et al.	7	161	2014	17.889	442	2002-19
Cluver et al.	3	134	2018 [6]	26.8	175	2016-19
Mullick et al.	3	118	2003	5.9	270	2001-17
Reiss et al.	3	105	2019 [24]	26.25	174	2015-19
Vogels et al.	3	42	2003 [27]	2.1	43	2003-20
Laukkanen et al.	3	33	2002 [16]	1.571	57	2002-10
Ferrara et al.	3	28	2016	4	28	2016-22
Wille, et al.	3	17	2016	2.429	43	2008-17
Hamre Sveen T. et al.	4	18	2012	1.636	33	2012-18
Honda et al.	3	9	2019 [13]	2.25	14	2019-20

publications and (57) citations from 2002 to 2010. A prolific writer [27] has 43 citations from 3 publications, and [27], has the same number of citations and publications. Wille [29] is followed by [14], who has 28 citations from 3 articles for the time period 2016–2022, and [12]. For the same time period (2019–2020), [13] published three publications, however the total number of citations changed

Table 30.4 Most relevant affiliations.

Affiliation	Articles
Kings Coll London	21
Univ Washington	16
Univ Toronto	13
Mcmaster Univ	11
Univ Melbourne	10
Univ Helsinki	19
Queensland Univ Technol Qut	18
Johns Hopkins Univ	7
Monash Univ	7
Norwegian Univ Sci and Technol	7

slightly (14 & 58) [26]. For the three years from 2012 to 2015, (Döpfner, 2014) has 73 Citations from 3 publications. The Kings Coll London has the most research (21) published in WoS indexed journals, and it also receives a lot of citations. University of Washington is next with 14 publications, while it receives the second-highest number of citations. There are 11 articles from Mcmaster University and 13 from the University of Toronto. Despite having different numbers of citations, Johns Hopkins University, Monash University, and Norwegian University all have the same number of publications (7) Table 30.3.

The research analysis revealed a consistent rise in research on mental health issues in both India and the rest of the world. There was hardly much study done in this topic prior to 2009, except for 10, 13, and 13 articles in the years 2003, 2007, and 2008, respectively, according to the pattern of articles from 1999 to 2022. From 2 articles in 2004 to 44 and 41 articles in 2020 and 2021, [22] the number of studies has steadily increased. Research on detecting mental health problems in children has not seen a notable increase. However, there is no significant influence on lowering the increased concentration of mental health disorders among children despite efforts by policymakers, government and non-governmental gatherings, and researchers to enhance mental health literacy. Because stakeholders do not obtain the information or apply the solutions, there is no real impact on lowering the increasing incidence of mental health disorders in children. In-depth research is also being delayed in comparison to the sudden rise in mental health issues around the world, which has led to a decline in the number of citations in 2005, 2006, 2008, and 2011. The top 10 countries' study on detecting mental health issues is analyzed, and it is obvious that industrialized countries have paid more attention to this issue than developing countries have. Only 19 papers on the subject have so far been published in India Table 30.4.

About 25 nations have focused on studying childhood mental health issues, but only a small number, including the United States of America, the United Kingdom, Australia, Canada, Italy, China, and Germany, have made significant strides in raising parents' knowledge of children's mental health issues. These nations, which include the United States (338 publications), the United Kingdom (156 publications), Australia (93 publications), Canada (66 publications), Italy (65 publications), China (62 publications), and Germany (62 publications), have conducted extensive study. Due to its 35 publications in the field of identifying mental health issues in children, Brazil is the only developing nation to rank among the top 15 nations. Given the number of children in India, the incidence of mental health issues among children, and the level of awareness of these issues among parents and families, India is a developing nation that ranks among the top 20 nations despite having only 19 publications in this field. In the year 2022, the paper "Evidence for machine learning guided early prediction of acute outcomes in the treatment of depressed children and adolescents with antidepressants" was authored by [19]. The findings of this study strongly imply that existing theories and research studies on children's mental health problems need to be extended to a broader context to encompass the parts of mental health that have been neglected up until this point. According to the findings of the study, interventions that target PGMs were discovered to be clinically significant predictors of response to antidepressant treatment in samples of clinically depressed children and adolescents who were receiving fluoxetine or duloxetine. These findings have significant ramifications for enhancing the mental health of people who live in communities that are not well served by mental health services. The data for this study came from the Young Minds Matter (YMM) survey (2013–14), commonly known as the second Australian child and adolescent survey of mental health and well-being [18]. We did not include the yes/no variables that had a low degree of correlation with the dependent variable (the depression state). The information was extracted with the use of a Random Forest (RF) classifier as well as the Boruta approach. Key indicators that can be used to diagnose depression among a group of factors that are highly connected. Laijawala [28] has developed a website that allows visitors to fill out a questionnaire in order to identify whether they are now having a mental disorder or are at risk for acquiring a mental problem in the future [20, 25]. For the purpose of prediction, they utilized a dataset that was open to the public and included a treatment label. This dataset includes information on age, gender, job interference, family history, help-seeking, working remotely, previous mental illness history, previous diagnosis, confidentiality, and penalties. Other factors, such as work int, include five attributes, in contrast to most data, which only have two or three qualities (Yes, No, Maybe). Most of the data consists of yes/no answers that indicate whether therapy is advised. In the beginning, we performed the data analysis with the help of the WEKA program. Taking Measures to Ensure the Accuracy of the Specifications.

The work by Qasrawi et al. [23] performance analysis applies machine learning algorithms to examine and anticipate the elements that put school-aged children at risk for depression and anxiety. A total of 3,984 pupils in grades 5-9 from public and refugee schools in the West Bank made up the study's sample population for the investigation. During the 2013–2014 school year, the health behavior kids' questionnaire was used to collect the data to anticipate the risk factors that relate to students' mental health symptoms. In order to make accurate projections, we relied on the following five methods of machine learning: Random Forest (RF), Neural Network (NN), Decision Tree (DT), Support Vector Machine (SVM), and Naive Bayes (NB). The SVM and RF models provided the most accurate predictions of depressive and anxious symptoms, respectively (SVM: 92.5%, RF: 76.4%). According to the findings of the study, SVM and RF models were most effective at identifying and predicting the degrees of anxiety and depression experienced by students. According to the findings, the factors that had the greatest impact on a person's levels of anxiety and depression were bullying and violence at school, academic accomplishment, and financial stability in the family.

Conclusion

The industrialized world has committed a greater number of resources to the research of the psychological well-being of children than the developing world has. The amount and caliber of mental health research conducted on children around the world is inadequate given the burden of mental disease on children globally. In order to address the incidence of mental illness, governments and researchers must raise society's understanding in a way that will safeguard children and ensure our future. The most recent bibliometric study of research on children's mental health has its strengths and weaknesses. The limitation brought about by the fact that certain papers were omitted from the WoS index. It is possible that this points to the existence of selection bias in the process of picking papers to be published in a respectable publication. The most significant thing is that we only looked at academic material that was written in languages that are commonly used. Even self-citations are considered when conducting citation analysis. Aiming to standardize the demand for studies of children's mental health issues, the study was conducted all over the world by highlighting the number of books, articles, and researchers who have contributed to the field; despite this, the study aimed to standardize the demand for studies of children's mental health issues. The WoS receives consistent revisions.

References

1. Athreya, A. P., Vande Voort, J. L., Shekunov, J., Rackley, S. J., Leffler, J. M., McKean, A. J., Romanowicz, M., Kennard, B. D., Emslie, G. J., Mayes, T., Trivedi, M., Wang, L., Weinshilboum, R. M., Bobo, W. V., and Croarkin, P. E. (2022). Evidence for machine learning guided early prediction of acute outcomes in the treatment of depressed children and adolescents with antidepressants. *Journal of Child Psychology and Psychiatry*, 63(11), 1347–1358.
2. Athreya, A. P., Br€uckl, T., Binder, E. B., Rush, A. J., Biernacka, J., Frye, M. A., and Bobo, W. V. (2021). Prediction of short-term antidepressant response using probabilistic graphical models with replication across multiple drugs and treatment settings. *Neuropsychopharmacology*, 46, 1272–1282.
3. Ahlen, J., Hursti, T., Tanner, L., Tokay, Z., and Ghaderi, A. (2018). Prevention of anxiety and depression in Swedish school children: acluster-randomized effectiveness study. *Prevention Science*, 19(2), 147–158.
4. Attygalle, U. R., Perera, H., and Jayamanne, B. D. (2017). Mental health literacy in adolescents: ability to recognise problems, helpful interventions, and outcomes. *Child Adolescent Psychiatry Ment Health*, 11, 38.
5. Bjornsen, H. N., Espnes, G. A., Eilertsen, M. B., Ringdal, R., and Moksnes, U. K. (2019). The relationship between positive mental health literacy and mental well-

being among adolescents: implications for school health services. *Journal of School Nursing*, 35, 107–116.

6. Cluver, L. D., Meinck, F., Steinert, J. I., Shenderovich, Y., Doubt, J., Romero, R. H., Lombard, C. J., Redfern, A., Ward, C. L., Tsoanyane, S., Nzima, D., Sibanda, N., Wittesaele, C., De Stone, S., Boyes, M. E., Catanho, R., Lachman, J. M., Salah, N., Nocuza, M., and Gardner, F. (2018). Parenting for lifelong health: a pragmatic cluster randomised controlled trial of a non-commercialised parenting programme for adolescents and their families in South Africa. *BMJ Global Health*,, 3(1), e000539. doi: 10.1136/bmjgh-2017-000539. PMID: 29564157; PMCID: PMC5859808.

7. Cahan, S., Jurges, H., Jabr, D., and Abdeen, Z. (2019). Student's SES, and the effect of schooling on cognitive development. *Journal of Education and Human Development*, 8(4), 199–209, DOI: 10.15640/jehd.v8n4a23.

8. Aebi, M., Kuhn, C., Banaschewski, T., Grimmer, Y., Poustka, L., Steinhausen, H. C., & Goodman, R. (2017). The contribution of parent and youth information to identify mental health disorders or problems in adolescents. *Child and adolescent psychiatry and mental health*, 11, 1–12.

9. Chattopadhyay, S., Kaur, P., Rabhi, F., and Acharya, U. R. (2011). An automated system to diagnose the severity of adult depression. In Jana, D., and Pal, P. eds., Proceedings of Second International Conference on Emerging Applications of Information Technology (CSI EAIT-2011), IEEE Computer Society and Conference Publishing Services, Kolkata, India, (pp. 121–124).

10. Döpfner, M., Hautmann, C., Görtz-Dorten, A., Klasen, F., and Ravens-Sieberer, U. (2015). BELLA study group. Long-term course of ADHD symptoms from childhood to early adulthood in a community sample. *European Child and Adolescent Psychiatry*, 24(6), 665–673. doi: 10.1007/s00787-014-0634-8. Epub 2014 Nov 14. PMID: 25395380.

11. Ferrara, P., Pianese, G., Franceschini, G., Palumbo, E., Ianni, A., and Ghilardi, G. (2022). Therapeutic stays of belarusian children in Italy: evaluation of their mental status, psychological consequences, and physical health status. *Minerva Pediatrics (Torino)*, 74(2), 188–194. doi: 10.23736/S2724-5276.21.06385-0. Epub 2021 Sep 13. PMID: 34515445.

12. Ferrara, P., Cutrona, C., Guadagno, C., Amato, M., Sbordone, A., Sacco, R., and Bona, G. (2020). Developmental and behavioral profile in a domestic adoptees sample: a new challenge for the pediatrician. *Minerva Pediatrics*, 72(5), 433–439. doi: 10.23736/S0026-4946.16.04767-8. PMID: 33273450.

13. Honda, Y., Fujiwara, T., Yagi, J., Homma, H., Mashiko, H., Nagao, K., Okuyama, M., Ono-Kihara, M., and Kihara, M. (2019). Long-term impact of parental post-traumatic stress disorder symptoms on mental health of their offspring after the great East Japan earthquake. *Front Psychiatry*, 10, 496. doi: 10.3389/fpsyt.2019.00496. PMID: 31404309; PMCID: PMC6675868.

14. Sveen, T. H., Berg-Nielsen, T. S., Lydersen, S., and Wichstrøm, L. (2016). Screening for persistent psychopathology in 4-year-old children. *Pediatrics*, 138(4), e20151648. doi: 10.1542/peds.2015-1648. Epub 2016 Sep 16. PMID: 27638933.

15. Haque, U. M., Kabir, E., and Khanam, R. (2021). Detection of child depression using machine learning methods. *PLoS One*, 16(12), e0261131. doi: 10.1371/journal.pone.0261131. PMID: 34914728; PMCID: PMC8675644.

16. Laukkanen, E., Shemeikka, S., Notkola, I. L., Koivumaa-Honkanen, H., and Nissinen, A. (2002). Externalizing, and internalizing problems at school as signs of health-damaging behaviour and incipient marginalization. *Health Promotion International*, 17(2), 139–146. doi: 10.1093/heapro/17.2.139. PMID: 11986295.

17. Laukkanen, E., Hintikka, J. J., Kylmä, J., Kekkonen, V., & Marttunen, M. (2010). A brief intervention is sufficient for many adolescents seeking help from low threshold adolescent psychiatric services. *BMC Health Services Research*, 10, 1–10.

18. Lawrence, D., Hafekost, J., Johnson, S. E., Saw, S., Buckingham, W. J., Sawyer, M. G., ... and Zubrick, S. R. (2016). Key findings from the second Australian child and adolescent survey of mental health and wellbeing. *Australian & New Zealand Journal of Psychiatry*, 50(9), 876–886.

19. Srividya, M., Subramaniam, M., and Natarajan, B. (2018). Behavioral modeling for mental health using machine learning algorithms. *Journal of Medical Systems*, 42(5), 88.

20. Minutolo, A., Chung, J., and Teo, J. (2022). Mental health prediction using machine learning: taxonomy, applications, and challenges. *Applied Computational Intelligence and Soft Computing*, 2022, 1-19, 1687–9724.

21. Mullick, M. S., and Goodman, R. (2001). Questionnaire screening for mental health problems in Bangladeshi children: a preliminary study. *Social Psychiatry and Psychiatric Epidemiology*, 36(2), 94–99. doi: 10.1007/s001270050295. PMID: 11355451.

22. Ashok, L., Rao, C., Kamath, V., Kamath, A., and Soman, B. (2021). A Scopus based bibliometric analysis on Mental Health Literacy research among the youth-A global perspective. *Journal of Indian Association for Child and Adolescent Mental Health-* ISSN 0973-1342, 17(2), 162–177.

23. Qasrawi, R., Polo, S. V., Abu Al-Halawa, D., Hallaq, S., and Abdeen, Z. (2022). Assessment and prediction of depression and anxiety risk factors in schoolchildren: machine learning techniques performance analysis. *JMIR Formative Research*, 6(8), e32736 URL: https://formative.jmir.org/2022/8/e32736.

24. Ravens-Sieberer, U., Reiss, F., Meyrose, A. K., Otto, C., Lampert, T., and Klasen, F. (2019). Socioeconomic status, stressful life situations and mental health problems in children and adolescents: results of the German BELLA cohort-study. *PLoS One*, 14(3), e0213700. doi: 10.1371/journal.pone.0213700. PMID: 30865713; PMCID: PMC6415852.

25. Sumathi, M. S., and Poorna, Dr. B. (2016). Prediction of mental health problems among children using machine learning techniques. *International Journal of Advanced Computer Science and Applications*, 7(1), 2016. 556–557. http://dx.doi.org/10.14569/IJACSA.2016.070176

26. Thorlacius, Ö., and Gudmundsson, E. (2019). The effectiveness of the children's emotional adjustment scale (CEAS) in screening for mental health problems in middle childhood. School Mental Health, 11(3), 400–412.

27. Vogels, T., Reijneveld, S. A., Brugman, E., den Hollander-Gijsman, M., Verhulst, F. C., and Verloove-Vanhorick, S. P. (2003). Detecting psychosocial problems among 5-6-year-old children in preventive child health care: the validity of a short questionnaire used in an assessment procedure for detecting psychosocial problems among children. *European Journal of Public Health*, 13(4), 353–360. doi: 10.1093/eurpub/13.4.353. PMID: 14703324.

28. Laijawala, V., Aachaliya, A., Jatta, H., and Pinjarkar, V. (2020). Classification algorithms based mental health prediction using data mining. In 2020 5th International Conference on Communication and Electronics Systems (ICCES), Coimbatore, India, 2020, (pp. 1174–1178).

29. Wille, N., Bettge, S., Wittchen, H. U., and Ravens-Sieberer, U. (2008). BELLA study group. how impaired are children and adolescents by mental health problems? results of the BELLA study. *European Child and Adolescent Psychiatry*, 17(Suppl 1), 42–51. doi: 10.1007/s00787-008-1005-0. PMID: 19132303; PMCID: PMC2757610.

30. Ravens-Sieberer, U., Herdman, M., Devine, J., Otto, C., Bullinger, M., Rose, M., & Klasen, F. (2014). The European KIDSCREEN approach to measure quality of life and well-being in children: development, current application, and future advances. Quality of life research, 23, 791-803.
31. Ferrara, E., Varol, O., Davis, C., Menczer, F., & Flammini, A. (2016). The rise of social bots. Communications of the ACM, 59(7), 96-104.
32. Willen, S. S., & Cook, J. (2016). Health-related deservingness. Handbook of migration and health, 95-118.
33. Sveen, T. H., Wichstrøm, L., Berg-Nielsen, T. S., Angold, A., Egger, H. L., & Solheim, E. (2012). Prevalence of psychiatric disorders in preschoolers. Journal of child psychology and psychiatry, 53(6), 695-705.
34. Döpfner, M., Hanisch, C., Hautmann, C., Plück, J., & Eichelberger, I. (2014). The prevention program for externalizing problem behavior (PEP) improves child behavior by reducing negative parenting: Analysis of mediating processes in a randomized controlled trial. Journal of Child Psychology and Psychiatry, 55(5), 473-484.

31 An overview of Stemming and Lemmatization Techniques

Vinay Kumar Pant[1,a], Dr. Rupak Sharma[2,b] and Dr. Shakti Kundu[3,c]

[1]Research Scholar Department of Computer Science and Engineering, SRMIST (Deemed to be University) Delhi NCR Campus, Modinagar, India

[2]Assistant Professor, Department of Computer Application, SRMIST (Deemed to be University) Delhi NCR Campus, Modinagar, India

[3]Associate Professor, Manipal University Jaipur (MUJ), Rajasthan, India

Abstract

Growth of technology help to human in many areas for make their work easy. Now day by day humans are using more and more technology and this approach open new door for researchers to search and develop something new that make human life easier then past. Artificial Intelligence is one of the major technologies which play the important role to make human life easier. Text processing is one of the areas of AI which play important role. NLP and text processing is help to the analyzing the data and get structure information. Text processing use so many tools and methods that help to get desired information. The goal of this research article is to provide a broad overview of NLP and text processing. It describes the basic idea of natural language processing as well as what it may be used for. Additionally, it provides a brief explanation of stemming and lemmatization, the algorithms that comprise these processes. And perform a critical review of some research study. In an effort to determine which method is best, this research compares lemmatization with stemming.

Keyword: AI, lemmatization, NLP, stemming, tokenization

Introduction

Development of technology open many new areas for the research. Last ten years change the uses of technology and thinking of human beings, it is the cause of rapid development of IT industry. Human have a powerful brain that always help them to solve problem, but some time they need support to solve some complex problem. Computer has the ability to do a portion of the things that the human mind can do, because of advances in artificial intelligence. Nowadays human and machine both are generating a lot of data. This is a huge amount of data which some time it is structure and some time it is unstructured. For the calculating this amount of data and get a valuable information, we need a proper methodology. Data science and Machine learning are two branches of artificial intelligence that help us to solve this problem. Computer only understand the machine language but all data that is generated by human that has their own natural language and other case machine generated data have also in form of natural language or figur) [5]. So, we need preprocessing of this data. As per industry measure, just 22%

---

[a]vp5570@srmist.edu.in, [b]rupaks@srmist.edu.in, [c]shaktikundu@gmail.com

of the accessible information is available in organized structure. Data is being produced at this very moment, as we tweet, as we speak, as we send messages on WhatSapp and in different exercises. Mostly this data exists in textual form and it is unstructured in nature. Regardless of having high measurement information, the data present in it is not straight forwardly accessible except if it is processed manually or automated system (2019).

To generate significant and accurate information form the text and image data, it is necessary to use accurate techniques, hence we think Natural language processing (NLP) hold best accountability to process data. NLP is a branch of AI that work with interactions between computers and human languages (like; English, Hindi etc). NLP is used many ML (Machine Learning) and deep learning algorithms and apply these algorithms to text for finding a valuable information. There are many fields where we use NLP like sentence autocomplete, machine translation, speech recognition, spam detection and so many other areas.

Nowadays everyone using smart phone and laptops both of these devices working on speech recognition and use many applications like Cortana, Siri and Google voice assistance. So, most of the research are going on the field of text processing for design a smart application that increase the interaction between the human and computer system. To understand the working how NLP help to text processing and machine translation we need to first understand Computational Linguistics. Morphological analysis of the word is the one of the most important tasks which help to text processing. Many morphological analyzer and generator used for analyzing and constructing an accurate world form the given data.

Related Work

Text processing is one of the main filed of NLP. Lemmatization and stemming are two approaches that help to solve problem associated with text processing. Many researchers explain the basic working of stemming and lemmatization and their uses in NLP. Here we are discussing some of the related work done by researches.

Kuman et al. [233, discuss about stop words in Malayalam language and the process how remove these words. Sharipov and Sobiro2 [27], explain development of lemmatization algorithm which use for the Uzbek language. It uses part of speech knowledge and dictionary of affixes to get lemma of word by remove the affixes. Kathuria et al1 [4], explain about data pre-processing, their tools and techniques. They also explain challenges with text preprocessing tools. Describe the under stemming and over stemming and problem associated with domain specific stop word list creation. Kuma1 et al. [5, proposed the comparative study of pre-processing tools like SPACY and STANZA based on pre-processing time used in process the Hindi data. Here they also given the brief explanation about text summarization type and their approaches. Das et al.,[61, provide an explanation for the usage of smart computing methodologies in the field of NLP. Different wise techniques alongside ANN, SVM, Conditional Random Field, Hidden Markov Assumption, and Bayes' Rule and with a couple of Stochastic Process are utilized in sub fields of NLP including MT, Sentiment Analysis, Information Extraction, Information Retrieval, Question Answering and Named Entity Recognition are used in to build a dependable and effective framework with extreme accuracy.

Khyan0 et al. [11], explain the general overview of NLP, Stemming and lemmatization. It provides the brief outline about lemmatization and stemming algorithms and their applications. It also gives a brief comparison between lemmatization and stemming. Kanerva et al0 [18], proposed a novel lemmatization method. It describes the morphosyntactic context and ambiguity associated with lemmatization and proposed a context sensitive lemmatizer which work on sequence-to-sequence neural network architecture. Harish and Ranga0 [7], proposed a survey on techniques and methods used in Indian language processing. Explain the source of Indian language dataset and how to solve the challenges associated with it. They also reviewed various task like sentiment analysis, POS tagging, NER and machine translation. Van Durme et al. [89, explain how lemmatization is beneficial for morphologically strong languages. Manjavacas et al. [139, explain lemmatization process and purposed an encoder-decoder architecture that shows enhancements over the new trends when preparing the sentence encoder mutually for lemmatization and language modeling. Jabbar et al9 [3], proposed a review and analyze the text stemming process methods. It defines different type of stemmer and text stemming errors. It also explains the different role of stemmer to measure the performance, merits and challenges. Freihat et al18 [1], proposed a new lemmatizer based on machine learning approach to solve the morphological problem of Arabic language. This Arabic lemmatizer help to increased flexibility, accuracy and robustness, in comparison of older one. Camacho-Collados and Pilehva8 [17], explain the impact of simple text pre-processing decisions like lemmatizing, multiword grouping and tokenizing on neural text classifier. They also explain sentiment analysis and text categorization. Singh and Gupt6 [20], proposed a comprehensive study about stemming techniques, application scope and evaluation processes. They describe rule-based and statistical stemming algorithms and analyze the different outlines of these algorithms. It also explains issues and challenges associated with statistical text stemming.

Ismailov et al. [2], explain various existing stemming algorithms. It also given the overview of available English stemmers and also discussed comparison between stemmers. They proposed a model that enhances some features of Lovins stemmer.

Balakrishnan and Ethel [35], proposed a comparative study on document information retrieval based on language modeling, basically it is use lemmatization and stemming. In this paper they briefly describe role of lemmatization and stemming in term of performance.

After review, we find numerous authors findings, as shown in Table 31.1.

NLP for Text Processing

Natural language processing is a subfield of AI which is used for analyze the data, interaction between natural language (Human spoken language) and computer system and retrieve information from text data. NLP can help to solve many problems which include machine translation, summarizing documents, and speech recognition and fraud detection. To retrieve right Information is one of the new problems for user, that emphasis to develop a tool, which help to retrieve the accurate and useful information from the source [30]. To design such tool

Table 31.1 Summarized literature review table

Authors	Technique/ Approach Used	Outcomes
Vimala Balakrishnan and Ethel Lloyd-Yemoh (2014) [35]	Language modeling techniques (mean average precisions and histograms)	Briefly describe role of lemmatization and stemming in term of performance.
Jenna Kanerva, Filip Ginter and Tapio Salakoski (2020) [18]	Neural network architecture	Develop a novel lemmatization method.
Abhinav Kathuria, Anu Gupta and R. K. Singla (2021) [4]		Identify the problem associated with domain specific stop word list creation.
Atul Kumar, Dr Vinodani Katiyar, Dr Pankaj Kumar (2021) [5]	SPACY and STANZA	They are comparing the two tools based on how long it takes for them to pre-process the Hindi language.
Bishwa Ranjan Das, Dilip Singh, Prakash Chandra Bhoi and Debahuti Mishra (2021) [6]	ANN, SVM, HMM	They build effective framework with extreme accuracy for information retrieval, NER, etc.
Maksud Sharipov and Og'abek Sobirov (2022) [27]	Finite state machine and rule-based POS tagging	The primary goals of the research are to use a finite state machine to remove affixes from Uzbek words and to locate the lemma, or dictionary word, of each word.
Kumar, S., Saini, J.R., Bafna, P.B. (2023) [23]	Rule based, Corpus based	The list of stop-words, stop-stems, and stop-lemmas for the Indian language of Malayalam is presented in this publication. It also creates corpus for Malayalam language.

developer, need first understand the nature of data. Machine learning is one of the fields of computer science, which deal with a huge amount of data. All the data which is process by machine learning, it should be as a form of numeric. We generally used some encoding method (like word2vec, n-gram) that convert text data into number vector. Now the process of data preprocessing comes in existence, before the data encoding, we prepare the text data this process known text preprocessing. Text preprocessing is generally an important task for natural language processing (NLP). It changes text into a more absorbable structure so that machine learning algorithms can provide better result. Think about Google assistant, Alexa and Siri, how can they understand human instruction, process them and give you a response as you want. NLP is one of the technologies that

behind it and perform lots of preprocessing work before producing output. Text data contains various ambiguities (Noise) like punctuations, emotions and different cases [19]. NLP solve this problem in the form of data preprocessing. So, in a simple word "text processing is a way to clean text data and prepare the data for feeding it into model". Text pre-processing is one of the more important tasks before building model. Basically, it is the first step to design a natural language processing project. For performing pre-processing, we need to follow some steps, they are as following-

- Remove the punctuations
- Remove stop words
- Lower casing
- Tokenization
- Stemming
- Lemmatization

Since NLP is predicated on superior computational skill, developers want the best tool that assist to make the most of NLP procedures and algorithms for growing services which could cope with natural languages [21]. NLP used many pre define libraries to solve nature language problems. Some important libraries describe below in Table 31.2.

Table 31.2 Description of Some Important NLP Libraries

S.NO.	Name of Library	Description
1	Natural Language Toolkit (NLTK)	NLTK is a basic tool for NLP and ML. It was developed by Steven Bird and Edward Loper. It is use for parsing, tokenization, stemming, classification, tagging and semantic reasoning.
2	re	Regular expression is one of the best library used for text cleaning.
3	spaCy	spaCy is one of the new library that use for natural language processing. spaCy is the fastest library used in market for syntactic parsing.
4	scikit-learn	Most of the data scientists used scikit-learn for performing NLP task. It offers numerous functions for enforcing the bag-of-words methods for making functions to address text classification issues.
5	TextBlob	It is one of the most used library by beginners who are starting their work on NLP. It is basically used for sentiment analysis and noun phrase extraction.
6	GenSim	It is one another important library of NLP. It is use to find the semantic equality between two or more documents for performing this task it use two approaches they are vector space modeling and topic modeling toolkit. GenSim can handle very easily a large amount of text corpus.

Pre-Processing Using Stemming

User want appropriate information form the system when they write a query. Linguistic model is one of the ways that help system and human both of them to find accurate information. Stemming is one of the procedures which help to improve language model. Stemming is a process that help to find root word from the given word by removing prefix and suffix [9]. In simple words "stemming is a process to reduce base word into its root word". Stemming comes into the existence near about 1960 [16]. Every language is a collection of words that are derived from other words, these words express different grammatical categories (like speech difference) is known as inflected words. Inflection may differ according to the languages, somewhere you found high and somewhere is low [22]. But inflected words have derived from same root form. Let see an example in Figure 31.1.

In Figure 31.1 example we use Porter Stemmer which is one of the widely used stemmer. We write code in python to implement Porter Stemmer. First, we need to import nltk library and then import PorterStemmer, with the help of PoterStemmer we obtain Stem word. In this example we pass three different from of 'Trouble' word and obtain final root word as 'troubl'. Stemming is the most common way of reducing inflection in words to their base (Stem) structures. But some time stemming is not produced valid stem (word) this is a problem associated with stemming. This issue measure in two form one is overstemming and other is understemming. Overstemming is the process where a word cut off too much and generate a nonsensical word (stem). Here the actual meaning of the words is lost and we found a wrong word, which has no meaning. Other hand understemming is the contrary issue [10]. It comes from when we have a few words that really are types of each other. It would be better for them to all generate to a similar stem, but shockingly, they don't. There are many algorithms that use to perform stemming task properly [33]. Below diagram shows the different type of stemming algorithms: -

Various stemming method used for different task and consider many algorithms [12]. Here we describe various stemming methods that shows in the Figure 31.2.

Truncating Method
This method also known as affix removal method. This technique is pertained to deleting a word's suffixes or prefixes, also known as affixes. The simplest stemmer

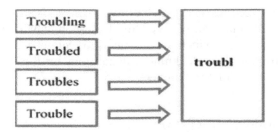

Figure 31.1 Common root form for all words

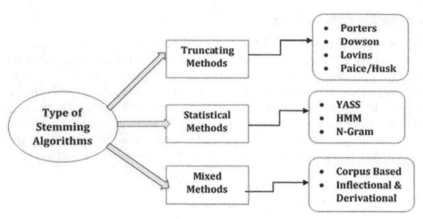

Figure 31.2 Different type of stemming algorithms [24]

was the truncate (n) stemmer, which kept the first n letters of a word and removed the remainder after truncating it at the nth symbol.

Statistical Method

These stemmers are those that rely on statistical methods and analysis. The majority of techniques eliminate the affixes using statistical process.

Mixed Method

Mixed methods are the combination of above two. This method of stemming also examines the morphology of inflectional and derivational endings symbol.

Different stemming algorithms have been created throughout the year, each having its own motivation, offering services for various domain. Here we are going to describe some of the important stemming algorithms.

Porter Stemming Algorithm

Porter stemming is one of the oldest stemming algorithms that used for finding the root word. It is developed near to 1980 by Porter. It is use suffix remove rule to generate stems. Porter stemming algorithm is simple and provide speed to fetch search queries [31]. Porter stemming algorithm has less error rate in compare to other stemming algorithms.

Snowball Stemming Algorithm

It is advanced version of Porter algorithm in term of speed and logics. Snowball algorithm support many languages near about 15 including English [25]. Snowball stemmer which is use to find stem word, is also called multi-lingual stemmer. It is also developed by Porter so it is known as Porter2stemmer.

Lancaster Stemming Algorithm

Lancaster is one another stemming algorithm that use very commonly. It is developed by Chris Paice of Lancaster University. It is not that much efficient when we working with small words [26]. It reduces word in a small stem as possible. It follows the aggressive rule in comparison of Porter and Snowball.

Regular Expression Stemming Algorithm
This algorithm helps to create new stemmer. It is work on the regular expression and remove the suffix and prefix that match with regular expression. NLTK use RegexpStemmer module to perform regular expression stemming algorithm.

Paise-Husk Stemming Algorithm
This algorithm developed by Gareth Husk and Chris Paice in 1990. Stemmer that works on this algorithm is iterative and it use single table rule for removal and replacement of ending character [34]. This is a best algorithm for comparing overstemming and understemming errors.

Lovins Stemming Algorithm
Lovins stemming algorithm is first ever developed algorithm. Lovins working on material science and engineering field so design of this algorithm are more affected by technical vocabulary [16]. It is also following a rule-based affix removal approach. This cycle can be parted into two stages. In the main stage, a word is contrasted and not really set in stone rundown of endings, and when a word is found to contain one of these endings, the consummation is eliminated, leaving just the stem of the word.

Pre-Processing Using Lemmatization

Lemmatization is a significant preprocessing approach that are widely used in text mining. It is additionally utilized in NLP and numerous different fields that deal with linguistics [27]. Lemmatization is the similar process like stemming, while the main aim of it is to remove inflection from the word and return root word. This root word is known as lemma. A lemma is the dictionary word reference of the lexeme. Lemmatization is use for understanding the contextual form of the word, therefore it is used by Chabot for better understanding of meaning of the sentences. The process of lemmatization use vocabulary and morphological analysis of word to find proper root word [13]. Creating a lemmatizer is more difficult because process of lemmatization requires a good understanding of the structure of the language. Various methodologies exist for lemmatization like rule-based methodology, basic dictionary method, and some new deep leaning techniques [14]. NLTK is a library that help to perform lemmatization task. Let see an example Figure 31.3.

WordNetLemmatizer is a class that used by NLTK to perform lemmatization. It is help to extract a meaningful root word. As you seen in Figure 31.3 the lemma is generated after processing, it is a meaningful word. It is a calculated process which use part of speech tagger to resolve inflection problem of the word and produce a valid lemma (dictionary form) [28]. The process of lemmatization use multiple approaches for finding the accurate output [29]. Figure 31.4. shows the approaches used to perform lemmatization.

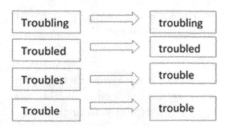

Figure 31.3 Base form (Lemma) for all words

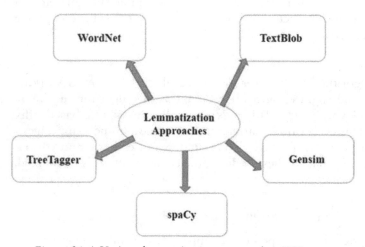

Figure 31.4 Various lemmatization approaches [29]

Here we are going to explain some of them approaches that are used very widely in lemmatization process.

WordNet

WordNet is one of the lexical resources which use to vocabulary for understanding the meaning of words. It is one of the oldest used lemmatization techniques. WordNet is an openly available database of lexicon that contain more than two hundred languages which help to expressing a distinct relationship between words. WordNet just not only work on text form although it also checks the meaning of the word [3]. This semantic relationship between words known as synsets. It helps to find the group of synonyms of words. WordNet follow the POS tagging to find accurate meaning of word using noun, verb and adjective.

TextBlob

TextBlob is a text processing library used in python. It is use for performing many NLP task like classification, noun phrase extraction, tokenization, translation, POS tagging and sentiment analysis [15]. TextBlob is widely used for word inflection and lemmatization process which help to find the root form of a word.

TreeTagger

TreeTagger was developed by Helmut Schmid at University of Stuttgart. It is a Part-of-Speech tagger which used by many languages. It also provides the lemma of the word. Treetagger truly does a good task in converting words to its root word.

spaCy

spaCy is an open-source python library that use for parsing and understanding the large amount of text. It supports many tasks like tokenization, POS tagging, name entity detection and finding the pattern matched in the document.

Gensim

It is another open-source python library used for NLP. Gensim used for performing many tasks like comparison between semantically similar texts (documents), word vectors building, design corpus and topic identification.

Comparison between Lemmatization and Stemming

These are the techniques which are used by many modern applications like Chabot and search engines for analysing the meaning of words. Stemming and lemmatization having many differences some differences are shown in the Table 31.3.

Applications of Stemming and Lemmatization

Stemming and lemmatization both are closely similar. Both of these techniques mostly used in text mining. Text processing help us to extract desired information from the given text. Stemming and Lemmatization are generally utilized in tagging frameworks, text ordering, SEOs, Web searching, and data recovery [6]. Here we are going to discuss some important applications of stemming and lemmatization.

Information Retrieval (IR)

It is valuable to utilize stemming and lemmatization to plan records to normal themes and show query items by indexing when reports are expanding to incredible numbers. Query Expansion is utilized to extend or improve the query to match with additional records. Google search is one of the examples that use this process to retrieve information.

Sentiment Analysis

Sentiment Analysis is the investigation of individuals' surveys and remarks about something. It is broadly utilized for analysis of item on web-based retail shops. Stemming and Lemmatization is used as a component of the text-readiness process before it is examined.

Text Clustering

Text clustering (Document clustering) is the utilization of group investigation to literary records. It has applications in a programmed record association, point

Table 31.3 Comparison in Lemmatization and Stemming [11]

S.NO.	Stemming	Lemmatization
1	It is normalize the words to their root word know as stem.	It is normalize the words to their root word know as lemma.
2	It removes the prefix and suffix form the word. Sometime which is the cause of generating a non-meaningful word.	It always generates a meaningful word (lemma) based on dictionary form for morphological analysis of word.
3	Stemming algorithms follow the rule-based procedure.	It is based on dictionary or canonical form of the word.
4	It is a fast process because it cut off word without knowing the context.	Lemmatization is slow process in compare to stemming because it's work on context of word.
5	Stemming have less accuracy.	Lemmatization having more accuracy in compare stemming.
6	Stemming is favored when the significance of the word isn't significant for analysis.	Lemmatization is preferred when the meaning of the word is important for analysis.
7	Computational process is easy in compare lemmatization.	It requires more computational efforts to provide accurate word or text. For that process it is use part of speech tagger.
8	Creating stemmer in comparison of lemmatizer is easy.	Creating a lemmatizer for a language is difficult process because we need all structural knowledge about language.
9	For example- if we use PorterStemmer and pass word 'believes' then we get output 'believ'. It simple cut off 'es' from the word and produce the output.	For example- if we use WordNetLemmatizer and pass word 'believes' then we get output 'believes'. Here lemmatizer analysis the word and produce valid output.

extraction, and quick data recovery or separating. Prior to Clustering strategies are applied archive is ready through tokenization, expulsion of stop words and afterward Stemming and Lemmatization to diminish the quantity of tokens that do a similar data and henceforth accelerate the entire cycle.

Text Categorization

Text categorization also known as text classification or text tagging. Text Categorization is the method involved with classifying text into organized group [32]. By utilizing Natural Language Processing (NLP), text classifiers can consequently analysis text and afterward allot a set of pre-characterized labels or classifications dependent on its content. Text categorization is turning into an undeniably significant part of organizations because it helps in automate business processes. Language detection and topic detection is the best example, that are used in product review and customer support.

Summarization of Documents

Document Summarization is the undertaking of changing a record into its shorter structure while as yet holding its important content. The most well-known two ideal models are extractive methodologies and abstractive methodologies. Extractive methodologies produce summaries by extricating text of the main document (normally sentences), while abstractive strategies might create new words or expressions which are not in the original record. The strategy for extricating these outlines from the original text without losing crucial data is called as Text Summarization. Search sites, Google news and news aggregator apps are the main example.

Conclusion

Stemming and lemmatization both techniques are used for text pre-processing in NLP. We did a comprehensive study about stemming and lemmatization, their various techniques, their pros and cons along with their working comparison. In this paper we also discuss various stemming and lemmatization algorithms. Stemming and Lemmatization both create the establishment kind of the bent words and subsequently the main distinction is that stem may not be a genuine word though, lemma is a real language word.

Stemming follows a calculation with steps to perform on the words which makes it quicker. Though, in lemmatization, you utilized a corpus additionally to supply lemma which makes it slower than stemming. In this paper we discuss text processing, various method of text processing and role of lemmatization and stemming in text processing. And also provide a critical review and some key findings. It helps to other researcher to perform and find the key solution of these findings. In future we can also apply various algorithm and find realistic output that help text pre-processing. We can also perform these techniques to solve Indian language morphological problem in the future.

Acknowledgement

The authors gratefully acknowledge the staff, and authority of Department of Computer Science and Engineering, SRMIST (Deemed to be University) Delhi NCR Campus, Modinagar, India; for their cooperation in the research.

References

1. Freihat, A. A., Abbas, M., Bella, G., and Giunchiglia, F. (2018). Towards an optimal solution to lemmatization in Arabic. *IProcedia Computer Science*, 142, 132–140. doi: 10.1016/j.procs.2018.10.468

2. A. Ismailov, M. M. A. Jalil, Z. Abdullah and N. H. A. Rahim, (2016). A comparative study of stemming algorithms for use with the Uzbek language, 3rd International Conference on Computer and Information Sciences (ICCOINS), Kuala Lumpur, Malaysia, 2016, pp. 7-12, doi: 10.1109/ICCOINS.2016.7783180.

3. Jabbar, Abdul & Islam, Saif & Hussain, Shafiq & Akhunzada, Adnan & Ilahi, Manzoor. (2019). A comparative review of Urdu stemmers: Approaches and challenges. *Computer Science Review*. 34. 100195, 1-14. 10.1016/j.cosrev.2019.100195.

4. Kathuria, A., Gupta, A., and Singla, R. K. (2021). A review of tools and techniques for preprocessing of textual data. I*Advances in Intelligent Systems and Computing*, 1227, 407-422. doi: 10.1007/978-981-15-6876-3_31.

5. Kumar, A., Katiyar, V., and Kumar, P. (2021). A comparative analysis of pre-processing time in summary of hindi language using stanza and spacy. *IOP Conference Series: Materials Science and Engineering*, 1110(1). doi: 10.1088/1757-899x/1110/1/012019.

6. Das, B. R., Singh, D., Bhoi, P. C., and Mishra, D. (2021). Role of intelligent techniques in natural language processing: an empirical study. I*Smart Innovation, Systems and Technologies,* 194. doi: 10.1007/978-981-15-5971-6_52.

7. Harish, B. S., and Rangan, R. K. (2020). A comprehensive survey on Indian regional language processing. *SN Applied Sciences*, 2(7). doi: 10.1007/s42452-020-2983-x.

8. May, C., Cotterell, R., and Durme, B.V. (2019). An Analysis of Lemmatization on Topic Models of Morphologically Rich Language. arXiv: Computation and Language.V2, 1-8. [Online]. Available: https://arxiv.org/abs/1608.03995.

9. Moral, C., de Antonio, A., Imbert, R., and Ramírez, J. (2014). A survey of stemming algorithms in information retrieval. *Information Research*, 19(1).

10. Hull, D. A. (1996). Stemming algorithms: A case study for detailed evaluation. *Journal of the American Society for Information Science*, 47(1), 70-84. doi: 10.1002/(sici)1097-4571(199601)47:1<70::aid-asi7>3.0.co;2-%23.

11. Khyani, Divya & B S, Siddhartha. (2021). An Interpretation of Lemmatization and Stemming in Natural Language Processing. Shanghai Ligong Daxue Xuebao/Journal of University of Shanghai for Science and Technology. 22. 350-357.

12. Sharma, D. (2012). Stemming algorithms: a comparative study and their analysis. *International Journal of Applied Information Systems*, 4(3), 7-12. doi: 10.5120/ijais12-450655.

13. Manjavacas, E., Kádár, A., and Kestemont, M. (2019). Improving lemmatization of non-standard languages with joint learning. In NAACL HLT 2019 - 2019 Conference of the North American Chapter of the Association for Computational Linguistics: Human Language Technologies - Proceedings of the Conference, 2019, (Vol. 1),1493-1503. doi: 10.18653/v1/n19-1153.

14. Nicolai, G., and Kondrak, G. (2016). Leveraging inflection tables for stemming and lemmatization. In 54th Annual Meeting of the Association for Computational Linguistics, ACL 2016 - Long Papers, 2016, (vol. 2), 1138-1147. doi: 10.18653/v1/p16-1108.

15. Hafeez, R., Anwar, M. W., Jamal, M. H., Fatima, T., Espinosa, J. C. M., López, L. A. D., Thompson, E. B., and Ashraf, I. (2023). Contextual urdu lemmatization using recurrent neural network models. *Mathematics,* 11, 435. https://doi.org/10.3390/math11020435.

16. Lovins, J. B. (1968). Development of a stemming algorithm. *Mechanical Translation and Computational Linguistics*, 11, 22-31.

17. Jose Camacho-Collados and Mohammad Taher Pilehvar. 2018. On the Role of Text Preprocessing in Neural Network Architectures: An Evaluation Study on Text Categorization and Sentiment Analysis. In Proceedings of the 2018 EMNLP Workshop BlackboxNLP: Analyzing and Interpreting Neural Networks for NLP, 40–46. doi: 10.18653/v1/w18-5406.

18. Kanerva J, Ginter F, Salakoski T. Universal Lemmatizer: A sequence-to-sequence model for lemmatizing Universal Dependencies treebanks. *Natural Language Engineering.* 2021;27(5):545-574. doi:10.1017/S1351324920000224

19. Ponte, Jay and Croft, W.. (2017). A Language Modeling Approach to Information Retrieval. ACM SIGIR Forum. 51. 202-208. 10.1145/3130348.3130368.

20. Singh, J., and Gupta, V. (2016). Text stemming: approaches, applications, and challenges. *ACM Computing Surveys*, 49(3),1-46. doi: 10.1145/2975608.

21. Kalyanathaya, K. P., Akila, D., and Rajesh, P. (2019). Advances in natural language processing –a survey of current research trends, development tools and industry applications. *International Journal of Recent Technology and Engineering*, 7(5), 199-201.

22. Swain, Kadambini & Nayak, Ajit. (2018). A Review on Rule-Based and Hybrid Stemming Techniques. 25-29. 10.1109/ICDSBA.2018.00012.

23. Kumar, S., Saini, J. R., and Bafna, P. B. (2023). Identification of malayalam stopwords, stop-stems and stop-lemmas using NLP. In Choudrie, J., Mahalle, P., Perumal, T., and Joshi, A. eds. IOT with Smart Systems. Smart Innovation, Systems and Technologies, (vol 312), 341-350. Singapore: Springer. https://doi.org/10.1007/978-981-19-3575-6_35.

24. Anjali, M., and Jivani, G. (2011). A comparative s of stemming algorithms. *International Journal of Computer Applications in Technology*, 2(6). 1930-1938.

25. Porter, M. F. (2001). Snowball: A language for stemming algorithms Published online. (Accessed 11.03.2008, 15.00h)

26. Naili, Marwa and Habacha, Anja and Ben Ghezala, Henda. (2019). Comparative Study of Arabic Stemming Algorithms for Topic Identification. Procedia Computer Science. 159. 794-802. 10.1016/j.procs.2019.09.238.

27. Sharipov, M., and Sobirov, O. (2022). Development of a rule-based lemmatization algorithm through finite state machine for Uzbek language. In International Conference and Workshop on Agglutinative Language Technologies as a challenge of Natural Language Processing (ALTNLP)., 1. June 6, 2022, https://doi.org/10.48550/arXiv.2210.16006.

28. Basab Nath, Sunita Sarkar, Surajeet Das, Arindam Roy (2022). A trie based lemmatizer for assamese language. *International Journal of Information Technology*, 14, 2355–2360. https://doi.org/10.1007/s41870-022-00942-9.

29. O. Ozturkmenoglu and A. Alpkocak, (2012). Comparison of different lemmatization approaches for information retrieval on Turkish text collection, International Symposium on Innovations in Intelligent Systems and Applications, Trabzon, Turkey, 2012, pp. 1-5, doi: 10.1109/INISTA.2012.6246934.

30. Mahalakshmi, P. and Fathima, N.S. (2021). An Art of Review on Conceptual based Information Retrieval. Webology. 18. 21-31. 10.14704/WEB/V18SI02/WEB18009.

31. Gupta, R., and Jivani, A. G. (2018). Analyzing the stemming paradigm. *In Information and Communication Technology for Intelligent Systems* (ICTIS 2017). 22, 333-342.doi: 10.1007/978-3-319-63645-0_37.

32. Rahimi, Zahra and Homayoonpoor, Mahdi. (2022). The impact of preprocessing on word embedding quality: a comparative study. *Language Resources and Evaluation*. 57. 1-35. 10.1007/s10579-022-09620-5.

33. Gadri, Said and Abdelouahab Moussaoui. (2015). Information retrieval: A new multilingual stemmer based on a statistical approach. 3rd International Conference on Control, Engineering & Information Technology (CEIT) (2015): 1-6, doi: 10.1109/CEIT.2015.7233113.

34. Sanaullah Memon, Ghulam Ali Mallah, K.N.Memon, AG Shaikh, Sunny K.Aasoori and Faheem Ul Hussain Dehraj, (2020). Comparative Study of Truncating and Statistical Stemming Algorithms. *International Journal of Advanced Computer Science and Applications* (IJACSA), 11(2), 563-568, http://dx.doi.org/10.14569/IJACSA.2020.0110272.

35. Balakrishnan, Vimala & Ethel, Lloyd-Yemoh. (2014). Stemming and Lemmatization: A Comparison of Retrieval Performances. *Lecture Notes on Software Engineering*. 2(3). 262-267. 10.7763/LNSE.2014.V2.134.

36. Paice, C.D. Another stemmer. SIGIR forum 1990; 24,56–61.

32 Stroke risk prediction model using machine learning techniques

Mukesh Kumar[a], Rahul Kumar[b], Abhishek Lagad[c] and Khalifa Musa Lawal[d]

School of Computer Application, Lovely professional University, Phagwara, Punjab, India

Abstract

When there is an abrupt interruption in the brain's blood supply, the brain tissue perishes due to insufficient oxygen and nutrients. When steps are taken to address or counteract this potential danger, the chances of unexpected complications occurring are diminished. This is a very serious medical problem that needs to be dealt with right away. Stroke symptoms and complications, such as brain damage, are often less severe when the disease is identified and treated quickly. It is possible to save lives by accurately predicting when cardiac disease will start, but there are big risks involved with getting the diagnosis wrong. The goal of this study is to identify the causes of stroke and test whether certain features may be used to reliably identify a stroke in a patient. Several different machine learning methods are used in this work, and the results and findings of the UCI Machine Learning Heart Disease dataset are studied and compared. Random Forest classification is clearly better than the others because it has a training accuracy of 98.09% and a validation accuracy of almost 92.85%.

Keywords: Cat Boost, classification algorithms, ensemble learning, machine learning, stroke prediction, XGBoost

Introduction

According to the World Stroke Organization, about 5.5 million individuals worldwide pass away directly as a result of having a stroke each year. Because stroke is the most common cause of both death and disability, it has a big impact because it happens so often. A stroke impacts not just the individual who has it but also their family, friends, and coworkers. Also, despite the common belief that it only affects certain types of people, it can happen to anyone at any age, regardless of gender or physical health [1]. This is even though there is a widespread belief that it can only affect certain groups of people. This is true regardless of the age of the individual being considered. This is because there is no evidence of any kind of prejudice being displayed by it. When there is a disruption in the normal supply of oxygen to the brain, this can lead to the death of brain cells. This is what doctors call a stroke. This lack of oxygen can cause cell death in the brain. A stroke takes place when there is an abrupt cessation of blood flow to a portion of the brain. Ischemic strokes and hemorrhagic strokes are the two categories that fall under the umbrella term "stroke." It may be very minor or highly severe, and the damage

[a]mukesh.27406@lpu.co.in, [b]real.rahul2002@gmail.com, [c]abhisheklagad5653@gmail.com, [d]kmusalawal@gmail.com

it produces may either be permanent or transitory, depending on the severity of the condition [2]. Rarely, a blood vessel might burst, causing bleeding in the brain, a condition known as hemorrhage. Most strokes, which are also called "ischemic strokes," happen when an artery in a part of the brain gets narrowed or completely blocked, cutting off the blood supply to that part of the brain. A family history of stroke, heart failure, atrial fibrillation, smoking, high cholesterol, diabetes, obesity, a sedentary lifestyle, drinking a lot of alcohol, problems with blood clotting, taking oestrogen medications, and using psychoactive drugs are all risk factors for stroke. A family history of stroke, heart failure, atrial fibrillation, smoking, high cholesterol, diabetes, obesity, a sedentary lifestyle, drinking a lot of alcohol,problems with blood clotting, taking oestrogen medications, and using psychoactive drugs are all risk factors for stroke [3]. In this article, we talk about a way to use machine learning to classify things into two groups, which leads to accurate models for predicting strokes. This method has been shown to be effective [12]. The synthetic minority over-sampling technique, also known as SMOTE, was utilized in the development of stroke prognosis algorithms because class balancing is essential to the algorithms' success. For that different methods were tried out and compared. These methods included Logistic Regression, K-Nearest Neighbor, Decision Tree, Random Forest, Ada Boost, Support Vector Machine, XGBoost, and CatBoost. The experiments revealed the training accuracy of the Random Forest method is 98.09% but the testing accuracy is only 92.85%. In case of Logistic Regression, Ada Boost and Support Vector Machine the testing accuracy is close to 94.61%.

The remaining parts of the paper are structured as described below. Section 2, the relevant works associated with the topic under discussion are discussed. After that, in Section 3, a description of the dataset and an analysis of the approach that was used are presented. In addition, we provide a description of the experimental setup and a discussion of the findings obtained from the research in Section 4. In section 5, conclusion and recommendations for the future is presented.

Literature Review

The scientific community has shown a strong commitment to developing systems that can track and predict the spread of illnesses that pose serious risks to human health. This section of the essay will go through the most recent research that uses cutting-edge technology like machine learning to predict the risk of having a stroke. By utilizing four distinct machine learning algorithms, [4] were able to significantly increase the accuracy of their stroke detection method. The J48 classification, the K-nearest neighbour classification, and the random forest classification all scored 97.8%, while the Naive Bayes classification only achieved 85.6%. The authors in Brancaccio, [2] came up with a way to get information from online groups about the signs and symptoms of strokes and what can be done to prevent them. They came up with a way to repeat spectral group tweets based on what they said. The information gathered from the investigations was analyzed using several different statistical and machine learning techniques. These techniques included Naive Bayes, SVMs, and stochastic neural networks. The stochastic neural networks outperformed other algorithms, achieving an accuracy rate of

89.90%. The authors in [6] predict the results in terms of recall (99.94%) and precision (97.33%) were achieved by using decision trees within a boosting model.

According to the findings of the research that was carried out by [7] it is recommended that several different machine learning approaches be put into practice. When compared to the accuracy of the other algorithms, the Naive Bayes model, which predicted strokes with an 82% probability, had the highest level of success. The authors in [8] attempted to collect a stroke dataset from Sugam Multispecialty Hospital in India in order to categorize the various types of strokes using machine learning approaches. To the contrary, an Artificial Neural Network trained with the Stochastic Gradient Descent method achieved a classification accuracy of 95%, which was far higher than that of any of the competing techniques. An identical 91% precision was achieved across the board, in both the Support Vector Machine and ensemble (Bagged) classes. Patients' electronic health record (EHRs) were analyzed in order to identify potential stroke risk factors. A Neural Network, Decision Tree, and Random Forest all performed similarly after a thousand iterations, classifying the EHR data with an accuracy of 75.02%, 74.31%, and 74.53%, respectively. The authors in [9] published automatic image processing methods were utilized to examine how well ML algorithms analyse diffusion-weighted imaging (DWI) and fluid-attenuated inversion recovery (FLAIR) photographs taken from stroke patients within 24 hours after the onset of their symptoms.

The beginning of a stroke was calculated using three distinct machine learning models for binary classification. These models were a logistic regression, a support vector machine, and a random forest (4.5 h). Within 4.5 hours, the machine learning model's sensitivity and specificity for patient identification were evaluated in contrast to human DWI-FLAIR mismatch readings. This ranking was based on the model's ability to correctly identify patients.

Materials and Methods

Dataset Description: Stroke is recognized by the World Health Organization (WHO) as the second leading contributor to global mortality, accounting for approximately 11% of all demises. The dataset in question serves the purpose of predicting the likelihood of a patient experiencing a stroke. This prediction relies on input factors like age, gender, and the existence of different medical conditions. The data are organized so that each row contains information that is pertinent to the patient. A dataset obtained from Kaggle served as the foundation for our study. We zeroed in on members in this database who were older than 18 years old as our primary target. 5110 people participated, and each of the 12 characteristics was considered (11 as input to machine learning models and 1 for the target class).

Exploratory Data Analysis (EDA): In the field of data science, the process of analysing and evaluating data sets as well as summarizing their most important characteristics is referred to as "exploratory data analysis," or EDA for short. Data visualization methods are typically utilized in the execution of these initiatives. Before drawing any conclusions from the data, the primary objective of EDA is to aid in data analysis. It is possible to use it to identify obvious errors,

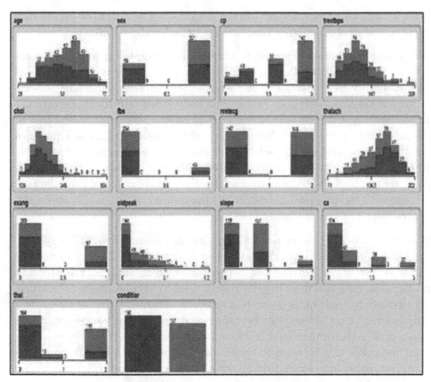

Figure 32.1 Visualization of the heart disease dataset

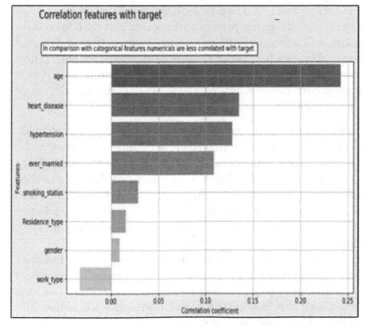

Figure 32.2 Correlation features with target features

gain a better understanding of patterns in the data, identify outliers or events that are not typical, and find interesting correlations between the variables.

Correlation Features: One of the most fundamental principles in machine learning is feature selection, and it can have a big impact on how well your model performs. The quality of the data you use to train your machine learning models has a big impact on how well they work. The correlation approach determines the linear relationship that exists between two or more variables. It is feasible to anticipate the value of one variable based on another using correlation. The use of correlation as a method of feature selection is based on the notion that valuable traits will have a high degree of connection with the final product. Figure 32.2, shows the correlation of different features with the target feature of the dataset. In comparison with the categorical features of the dataset, numerical features are less correlated with the target feature [10].

Heatmap: A heatmap is a matrix of numbers that has been color-coded. A heatmap is a great piece of visualization software to have on hand when you need to see how data is distributed throughout a two-dimensional matrix. The strength of the link between two variables may be determined by conducting a correlation analysis. Correlation analysis is a method used to determine the strength of a relationship between two variables by measuring how much one variable varies in response to a shift in the other variable. How much one variable shifts in response to a shift in the other can be used to make an estimate of the correlation coefficient. It is possible to use correlation analysis, a statistical method, to ascertain whether two variables are related in a linear fashion. Each value in the dataset is represented by a different color, as seen in Figure 32.3's two-dimensional color matrix [11]. With just a heatmap, a user can learn a great deal about the issue. The presence of a value greater than zero in a two-dimensional cell shows a positive correlation between traits, while the presence of a value less than zero indicates a negative correlation. The strength of the positive connection is depicted by darker colors on the heatmap, whereas the severity of the negative correlation is represented by lighter colors. One method of assessing the closeness of a pair of variables is the Pearson correlation coefficient, which estimates the degree of linear association between them.

Exploratory Data Analysis (EDA): In the field of data science, the process of analysing and evaluating data sets as well as summarizing their most important characteristics is referred to as "exploratory data analysis," or EDA for short. Data visualization methods are typically utilized in the execution of these initiatives. Before drawing any conclusions from the data, the primary objective of EDA is to aid in data analysis. It is possible to use it to identify obvious errors, gain a better understanding of patterns in the data, identify outliers or events that are not typical, and find interesting correlations between the variables.

Correlation Features: One of the most fundamental principles in machine learning is feature selection, and it can have a big impact on how well your model performs. The quality of the data you use to train your machine learning models has a big impact on how well they work. The correlation approach determines the linear relationship that exists between two or more variables. It is feasible to

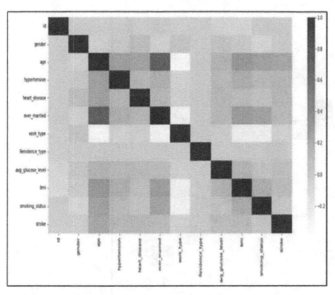

Figure 32.3 Correlation between different attributes

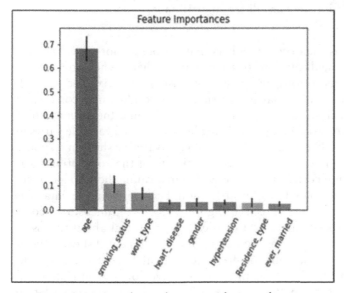

Figure 32.4 Correlation features with target features

anticipate the value of one variable based on another using correlation. The use of correlation as a method of feature selection is based on the notion that valuable traits will have a high degree of connection with the final product. Figure 32.2, shows the correlation of different features with the target feature of the dataset. In comparison with the categorical features of the dataset, numerical features are less correlated with the target feature [10].

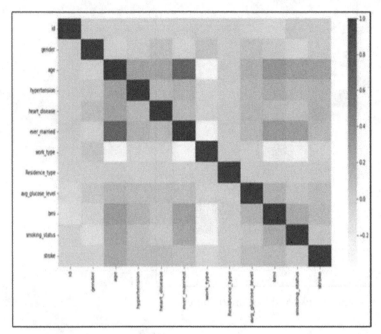

Figure 32.5 Correlation between different attributes

Heatmap: A heatmap is a matrix of numbers that has been color-coded. A heatmap is a great piece of visualization software to have on hand when you need to see how data is distributed throughout a two-dimensional matrix. The strength of the link between two variables may be determined by conducting a correlation analysis. Correlation analysis is a method used to determine the strength of a relationship between two variables by measuring how much one variable varies in response to a shift in the other variable. How much one variable shifts in response to a shift in the other can be used to make an estimate of the correlation coefficient. It is possible to use correlation analysis, a statistical method, to ascertain whether two variables are related in a linear fashion. Each value in the dataset is represented by a different color, as seen in Figure 32.3's two-dimensional color matrix [11]. With just a heatmap, a user can learn a great deal about the issue. The presence of a value greater than zero in a two-dimensional cell shows a positive correlation between traits, while the presence of a value less than zero indicates a negative correlation. The strength of the positive connection is depicted by darker colors on the heatmap, whereas the severity of the negative correlation is represented by lighter colors. One method of assessing the closeness of a pair of variables is the Pearson correlation coefficient, which estimates the degree of linear association between them.

The following formula is used to determine its value, which can range anywhere from -1 to 1:

• a value of -1 is employed whenever there is an inverse linear correlation between two distinct aspects of the dataset;

- a value of 0 indicates that there is no linear association between two different characteristics of the dataset;
- The value 1 is assigned whenever there is a positive linear correlation between two distinct aspects of the dataset.

Feature Importance in the Dataset: When talking about predictive models, the phrase "feature importance" refers to a set of ways to figure out how important the many different features that the model uses as inputs are. The use of feature significance scores may be beneficial to both regression and classification, which are statistical procedures in which a numerical value or a class label is expected to be predicted [13]. As we can see in Figure 32.4, age is most important feature in the dataset ahead of smoking_status and work_type.

Implementation and Discussion

In the process of creating a model for classification, we will enhance the representativeness of the dataset with respect to the overall population. This will be achieved through oversampling using the software tool called SMOTE. In addition, we make use of an imputation strategy that is predicated on the KNN in order to fill in the blanks in the BMI columns.

Logistic Regression: Even though it is not part of supervised learning, unsupervised learning is still one of the most popular ways to teach machines to do things. Using a set of known independent variables, one can make a guess about

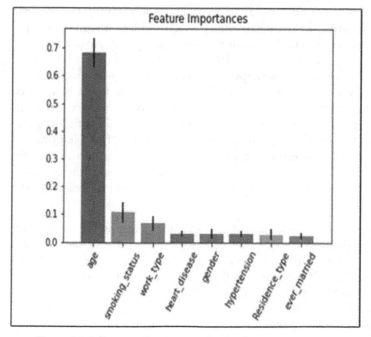

Figure 32.6 Features importance in the dataset

a categorical dependent variable. Logical regression lets you guess the value of a categorical dependent variable in a smart way. A statistical model that takes into consideration the ways in which items are related and then provides a yes or no answer. The difference between the result with no predictors and the baseline outcome is first determined, and then the outcome is compared to the outcome at the baseline.

K-nearest Neighbor: Machine learning algorithms have been improved to operate with huge data sets. Data mining is one way to compile such a corpus of information. A huge amount of training data must be fed into the system for it to accurately recognize each data point. Variables in mathematics are represented as points on a multidimensional space, with each dimension representing a different independent variable. The term "hyperspace" is commonly used to describe this region. To find the missing data, first identify the K data points that are most like the new ones. The Euclidean distance is widely accepted as the best-suited measure of separation between two points.

Decision Tree: As a form of supervised machine learning, decision trees can be used to segment information in an endless variety of ways, each satisfying a different criterion. A tree's properties can be inferred by inspecting its nodes, leaves, and the relationships between them. In the book, the perpetrators and victims of the events are described in detail. At "defined nodes," the data is broken up into manageable parts. Many methods, including ID3, CART, and C4.5, must be used to compile the essential bits of information needed to draw a conclusion before a decision tree can be constructed. Problems involving classification and regression are amenable to this approach.

Random Forest: Machine learning researchers can use random forests to analyse regression and classification. Ensemble learning, which employs a variety of classification approaches, was created to address challenging problems. There are various decision trees in random forests. During training, random forests can be aggregated via bagging or bootstrapping. Bagging enhances the accuracy of machine learning. Following decision tree analysis, the random forest method is utilized to decide. Determine the tree's average. More tree cover improves forecast accuracy. Random forests generate a decision tree and forecast using random data samples. The dataset helps with this. This demonstrates the need for collaborative classrooms. The probability is estimated by drawing from the collection indefinitely until a sample reaches the node. Subtract your samples from the total. In random forests, the Gini index can be used to evaluate decision tree branch node clustering for classification.

AdaBoost Algorithm: The performance of any machine learning algorithm can be improved with the help of a tool called AdaBoost, which is not only free to use but also easy to get to for anyone who wants to use it. These are models that, when used to solve a classification problem, give results that are just a little bit more accurate than what you would expect from using random chance. The accuracy in question is about the same as what you would get if you just used random chance. The accuracy of these models is only a little bit better than what you would expect from random procedures. The decision trees with only one level are the algorithms that function the best with AdaBoost; it is likely that this is why they are the most prevalent type of algorithm [15].

Support Vector Machine: Supervised machine learning allows support vector machine to classify and regress. Even though we have studied the problems associated with regression, this approach seems more natural when dealing with classification tasks rather than regression activities. A support vector machine can sort N-dimensional data. N-dimensional hyperplanes are used by support vector machine to classify data. Several hyperplanes exist to differentiate the two datasets. We are looking for the plane that has the largest gap in terms of both percentages and raw data points between its various classifications. Once the margin distance grows, more reinforcement is added to help label the following set of data. The maximum distance between the hyperplane and the data points is necessary for support vector machine. This can be accomplished with the help of the hinge loss function.

XGBoost Algorithm: The gradient-boosted trees method is used in XGBoost, an open-source program that is very popular and works very well. This program is both very well-known and widely used. Gradient boosting is an algorithm that is an example of supervised learning. This technique seeks to accurately forecast a target variable by integrating the estimates of a series of simpler models that have less predictive power. Gradient boosting is just one type of supervised learning. It has some technical advantages over other gradient-boosting methods, such as a shorter path to the minimum error, the ability to converge faster with fewer steps, and simplified calculations that increase speed while lowering the cost of computing. Because of these benefits, it outperforms other gradient boosting methods [14]. These advantages make it possible for it to outperform other gradient-boosting approaches. One of these technological advantages is a path that leads more directly to the smallest amount of mistake.

CatBoost Algorithm: A method called CatBoost automatically uses gradient boosting on decision trees. It is developed in-house by Yandex's researchers and programmers, and it is implemented in a wide variety of business and

Table 32.1 Training and testing accuracy of ML classifiers.

Machine Learning Classifiers	Training Accuracy	Testing Accuracy
Logistic Regression	95.25	94.61
K-Nearest Neighbor	95.49	94.22
Decision Tree	98.09	92.27
Random Forest	98.09	92.85
Ada Boost	95.25	94.61
SVM	95.25	94.61
XG Boost	96.20	94.12
Cat Boost	96.37	93.83

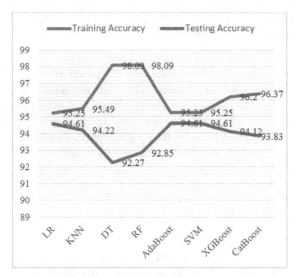

Figure 32.7 Graphical representation of training and testing accuracy of ML classifiers

non-business applications, including search, recommendation systems, personal assistants, driverless vehicles, weather prediction, and other applications. In all types of comparison testing, CatBoost always does better than LightGBM and XGBoost. In this part of the CatBoost documentation, you can learn more about the different ways to group ranking modes and the metrics that are used to judge how well these groups work. You can get here by following the directions in the Table 32.1 of contents. Depending on how the system is configured, these tasks could be performed either by the central processing unit (CPU) or the graphics processing unit (GPU).

Figure 32.5 shows the difference between how well the training was done and how well the testing was done. Accuracy in training necessitates the use of the same images for both purposes, whereas accuracy in testing denotes that the trained model accurately identifies novel data that was not used during training. Logistic regression is a type of supervised learning and classification algorithm that is used to make predictions about the probability of events based on the values of several variables. Our accuracy during training was 95.25 percent, and our accuracy during testing was 94.61%; both figures are very acceptable. During the training phase of our project, we were able to achieve a precision of 95.49% with the assistance of the KNN algorithm, and during the testing phase, we achieved 94.22%. For the KNN algorithm to function properly, it assumes that the new data or case is comparable to the instances that are already known. The newly discovered information is then filed away under the category that is most analogous to the previously established categories.

In a decision tree, you will find elements known as leaf nodes. The accuracy of our training was 98.09 percent, but the accuracy of our assessment was only 92.27 percent; this represents a substantial drop when compared to the training accuracy.

Conclusion

There is a chance that lives could be saved by preventing or treating strokes to reduce the chance that unplanned problems will happen because of the stroke. The field of machine learning has witnessed substantial advancements within a concise timeframe. These developments have enabled medical practitioners and professionals to employ existing models in comprehending the factors contributing to stroke occurrence in patients. Additionally, these models facilitate the assessment of associated risks linked to these factors. ML could help doctors diagnose and predict strokes earlier, which could make this condition much less devastating. The goal of this research is to find the ML algorithm that is best at predicting when a stroke will happen based on a set of characteristics that are typical of the profiles of the people in this study. The people who take part in the study are going to be given a list of characteristics to use when developing the algorithm. Classifier accuracy evaluations can usually be applied to model interpretations, which shows how useful models are for making these kinds of decisions. They also show that the models are reliable and can accurately predict stroke classification. The highest efficiency (94.61%) is achieved by combining AdaBoost, logistic regression, and SVM classification. Thus, using both a decision tree and a random forest algorithm, we were able to achieve a training accuracy of nearly 98%. The future scope of this study is to include an ensemble technique on the same dataset to improve the predictive accuracy.

References

1. Alloubani, A., Saleh, A., and Abdelhafiz, I. (2018). Hypertension and diabetes mellitus as a predictive risk factor for stroke. *Diabetes and Metabolic Syndrome: Clinical Research and Reviews*, 12(4), 577–584.
2. Brancaccio, A., Tabarelli, D., and Belardinelli, P. (2022). A new framework to interpret individual inter-hemispheric compensatory communication after stroke. *Journal of Personalized Medicine*, 12(1), 59.
3. Bustamante , A., Penalba, A., Orset, C., Azurmendi, L., Llombart, V., Simats, A., and Montaner, J. (2021). Blood biomarkers to differentiate ischemic and hemorrhagic strokes. *Neurology*, 96(15), e1928–e1939.
4. Boehme, A. K., Esenwa, C., and Elkind, M. S. (2017). Stroke risk factors, genetics, and prevention. *Circulation Research*, 120(3), 472–495.
5. Sharma, C., Sharma, S., Kumar, M., and Sodhi, A. (2022). Early stroke prediction using machine learning. In 2022 International Conference on Decision Aid Sciences and Applications (DASA), (pp. 890–894). IEEE.
6. Elloker, T., and Rhoda, A. J. (2018). The relationship between social support and participation in stroke: a systematic review. *African Journal of Disability*, 7(1), 1–9.
7. Govindarajan, P., Soundarapandian, R. K., Gandomi, A. H., Patan, R., Jayaraman, P., and Manikandan, R. (2020). Classification of stroke disease using machine learning algorithms. *Neural Computing and Applications*, 32, 817–828.
8. Li, X., Bian, D., Yu, J., Li, M., and Zhao, D. (2019). Using machine learning models to improve stroke risk level classification methods of China national stroke screening. *BMC Medical Informatics and Decision Making*, 19, 1–7.

9. Lee, H., Lee, E. J., Ham, S., Lee, H. B., Lee, J. S., Kwon, S. U., and Kang, D. W. (2020). Machine learning approach to identify stroke within 4.5 hours. *Stroke*, 51(3), 860–866.

10. Maldonado, S., López, J., and Vairetti, C. (2019). An alternative SMOTE oversampling strategy for high-dimensional datasets. *Applied Soft Computing*, 76, 380–389.

11. Nwosu, C. S., Dev, S., Bhardwaj, P., Veeravalli, B., and John, D. (2019). Predicting stroke from electronic health records. In 2019 41st Annual International Conference of the IEEE Engineering in Medicine and Biology Society (EMBC), (pp. 5704–5707). IEEE.

12. Pradeepa, S., Manjula, K. R., Vimal, S., Khan, M. S., Chilamkurti, N., and Luhach, A. K. (2020). DRFS: detecting risk factor of stroke disease from social media using machine learning techniques. *Neural Processing Letters*, 1–19, 55:3843–3861, https://doi.org/10.1007/s11063-020-10279-8.

13. Shoily, T. I., Islam, T., Jannat, S., Tanna, S. A., Alif, T. M., and Ema, R. R. (2019). Detection of stroke disease using machine learning algorithms. In 2019 10th International Conference on Computing, Communication and Networking Technologies (ICCCNT), (pp. 1–6). IEEE.

14. Sailasya, G., and Kumari, G. L. A. (2021). Analyzing the performance of stroke prediction using ML classification algorithms. *International Journal of Advanced Computer Science and Applications*, 12(6), http://dx.doi.org/10.14569/IJACSA.2021.0120662.

15. Xia, X., Yue, W., Chao, B., Li, M., Cao, L., Wang, L., and Li, X. (2019). Prevalence and risk factors of stroke in the elderly in Northern China: data from the national stroke screening survey. *Journal of Neurology*, 266, 1449–1458.

33 A robust ensemble model for disposition prediction using the myersbriggstype indicator (MBTI) in machine learning

Gayathri R Varma[1,a], Aiswarya Mohan[1,b] and Prasanna Kumar C V[2,c]

[1]Post Graduate Student, School of Computing, Amrita VishwaVidyapeetham, Kochi Campus Kochi, Kerala, India

[2]Assistant Professor, School of Computing, Amrita VishwaVidyapeetham, Kochi Campus Kochi, Kerala, India

Abstract

A person's personality has a big impact on both their personal and professional lives. It will influence the decisions he or she takes. As a result, in the modern world, a machine learning model that can predict personality will play a crucial role. There are many models for predicting personality types, including the Big Five, HEXACO, MBTI, and others. These models help in discovering the ideal person for a job and can be put to use in a multitude of industries such as medical, educational, industrial, etc. Among these MBTI is one that is most significantly used nowadays. We are using a dataset that has values based on the MBTI model. The dataset is openly accessible. In an effort to create the optimal ensemble model that exhibits the most robustness and better accuracy, we have attempted stacking a number of classifiers. Several combinations of different classifiers including KNN, Random Forest, XGBoost etc underwent trials. We discovered that combining XG Boost, Random Forest, and Multi Layer Perceptron with Logistic Regression as the meta classifier generated the most promising results, and by ensembling these models together, we consistently achieved an accuracy of over 90%.

Keywords: ensemble model, logistic regression, meta classifier, myersbriggs type indicator (MBTI)

Introduction

Machine learning is one of the several applications of artificial intelligence (AI). Using example data or prior experiences, machine learning is a way of programming computers to optimise their performance criteria. It is employed when using human expertise is challenging or when a particular solution is dynamic in nature. For instance, answers to issues with robotics, facial recognition, fraud detection, and speech recognition [13].

Every person has their own distinct personality. A person's personality dictates which solution is ideal for them. As a result, personality assessment and prediction are useful in a wide range of circumstances. Since World War II, personality assessments have been used to assist women in selecting the best job for them

[a]varmagayathri2001@gmail.com, [b]aiswarya2000mohan@gmail.com,
[c]prasannakumarcv@kh.amrita.edu

[10]. Even today, it is being used in recruiting candidates [1] and choosing the right person for the right job. It is also being used to assist educational institutions in making quality decisions [9].

There are various personality trait models that can be applied. The Big Five or OCEAN model, which was used in [1], the HEXACO model, which was used in [6] , and the Myers-Briggs Type Indicator® (MBTI) model, which was utilised in [4, 8, 9, 11] are some of them.

In our research, we focus on the MBTI personality trait model.In the MBTI model, a person's preferences are divided into 16 different personality types based on 4 dimensions which are as follows:

- Introversion (I) vs Extroversion(E)
- Intuition (N) vs Sensing (S)
- Thinking (T) vs Feeling (F)
- Judging (J) vs Perceiving (P)

A particular personality type is represented by each keyword in Figure 33.1. In Figure 33.2, a variety of personality types for each keyword is shown.The MBTI model has been widely employed in the field of software engineering for the past

Figure 33.1 Key personality types in MBTI

ENFJ	INFJ	INTJ	ENTJ
They are born leaders and are always determined, yet they are also sensitive to the needs of others around them.	They are imaginative, sympathetic, and perceptive individuals. They are deep thinkers who value challenges at work.	These are individuals that relish their alone time. They are great at strategizing and planning and prioritize practical thinking	They are charismatic and confident people who place a high emphasis on target, preparation, and organization
ENFP	**INFP**	**INTP**	**ENTP**
They have excellent perception and act on their emotions and are more driven by personally meaningful objectives than by monetary gain.	They want to influence the community and increase their awareness. They frequently bring passion and excitement to projects, but find it difficult to keep up that energy for long.	They are excellent problem-solvers and enjoy developing original, unbiased answers to issues. They prefer jobs where they can use their imagination.	They are logical, rational and objective. They are problem solvers and prefer conceptual work and foster innovative thinking.
ESFP	**ISFP**	**ISTP**	**ESTP**
They enjoy being in the spotlight. They are hospitable, giving, compassionate, and interested in the welfare of others.	They are introverts who don't really act like they are. They are amiable, easy to get along with and enthusiastic.	They are generally mysterious people. When necessary, they work well with people despite being frequently quiet and observant.	They have rational thinking. They instinctively look for new opportunities and are excited about what they do.
ESFJ	**ISFJ**	**ISTJ**	**ESTJ**
They are quite friendly and seek for peace and cooperation at work. Typically, they are perceptive to others' needs.	They value giving back and repay charity with even more generosity. They are devoted to their jobs and have good work ethics.	They are often reserved, quiet, composed, and upright. They are regarded as trustworthy and accountable at work.	They often take the role of leader and love to guide and direct others in their work. They work hard and are dedicated.

Figure 33.2 The 16 personality types in MBTI

few decades and is more well-liked by researchers because of its dependability and validity [4].

Literature Review

Hiring the right candidate for the right job is essential to paving the best way to success. Personality assessment and prediction are effective ways to identify these ideal candidates. There are many ways to do this. Different research groups reported the tweets of the candidate to assess the personality of the individual [1, 2]. In the research that was conducted by RoshalMoraes et al., the datasets for the MBTI and Big Five are selected for the process. The data was preprocessed; features were extracted and vectorized using Tf-Idfvectorization. To train both the datasets and the algorithms that analyse the results, various classification models were used [1]. In some studies, data was collected from surveys and the personality was assessed based on the OCEAN model. The text was preprocessed, vector construction was done, and the analysis was done using clustering [2]. It is also possible to create the dataset using the Twitter Streaming API on Python (Tweepy). The Big Five model can then be used. The precision, recall, and F1 score can be calculated for multinomial Naive Bayes, AdaBoost, and LDA [3].

We have come across papers which made use of different personality assessment models. In certain researches we see the use of the Big Five model [1, 2].

A machine learning model was developed for meta-programme detection and personality prediction using the MBTI. Meta-programs are used to input, filter, and sort information around the world. NLTK and Gradient Boosting were used to predict personality. The obtained XGBoost accuracy was compared with that of already existing models, and XGBoost was found to give more accurate results [4].

The study conducted by MadhuraJayaratne et al. show that the HEXACO model can be used, and candidate's agreeability can be gauged on a 5-point scale. In the study, open vocabulary approaches in NLP and machine learning classification models were used. However, it utilised only semantic-level approaches for judging the personality of a person. The study shows that it is difficult to determine whether an individual is a right fit for the job by just using open vocabulary approaches

In a study, a pre-trained language model, BERT, was utilised for the classification of different MBTI personalities. The data was obtained by scraping posts from the various forums at the PersonalityCafe website. The text was cleaned, preprocessed and tokenized before fine-tuning and training [7]. In another study, 3 steps were used to classify personalities - data collection, data preparation and hyper-parameter tuning. The data was collected through google forms. The data was then prepared and then the k-means clustering algorithm was used [8]. The MBTI model can also be used to assess the personalities of students to aid educational institutions in making quality decisions. In this case, data was collected via questionnaire and student twitter accounts. It made use of the ID3 classification algorithm and created a decision tree. [9].

Extreme gradient boosting and hyperparameter tuning were used to tune the parameters based on the nature of the dataset. K-Means clustering along with gradient boosting machine learning models were combined to assess user insights on social media data. Here the MBTI model was used and the main idea behind using this particular model was to provide assistance to women when choosing the ideal role for them in the World War II era [10].

Another study focused on making use of the Random Forest Classifier to prognosticate a person's personality grounded in the MBTI. The dataset was collected from the public domain. It was then preprocessed, and was split into training and testing sets. They observed that Random Forest was the best classifier that could be used in the social media context [12].

The research [11] was conducted to determine whether LinkedIn and Facebook were suitable sources for screening job applicants. Selenium was employed as a tool for automation to obtain data from the social networking platforms. The fetched Facebook data was classified using the Support Vector Machine (SVM) algorithm, and the fetched LinkedIn data was classified using the Deep Neural Network (DNN) algorithm. The resumes of the applicants were uploaded and compared with the data fetched from social networking sites about their provided skills and experiences.

Some researches showcased personality assessment through images.Facial images of students will be collected and analysed using machine learning and the Big Five personality type prediction model. A deep neural network (S-NNPP) was employed to reveal the 5-dimensional personalised features by taking into consideration static facial features to predict the personality characteristics of subject groups of varying academic backgrounds [5].

Methodology

In this study, we provide a robust personality prediction model that, in most situations, can produce superior accuracy. Since the MBTI personality traits model can offer adequate information on an individual's persona, we have picked it to assess personality. It is one of the most often used psychological tools today [14].

Data Collection
We implemented a dataset which was openly accessible [15]. The dataset contains 8675 records and 2 fields. One of the columns indicates the personality type and the other contains multiple recent posts made by the corresponding personality type on an online source. The personality types can include all the different personalities depicted in Figure 33.2.

Data Visualisation
Before applying preprocessing to our dataset, it was necessary to visualise the data in order to discover trends and spot any flaws.

Figure 33.3 displays our processed data as a bar graph with personality types on the x-axis and the number of posts on the y-axis. The unbalanced nature of the data is evident from the figure. For instance: In comparison to the ESTJ personality type, which has fewer than 250 posts, INFP has over 1750.

Before moving further with data preprocessing, we also created a number of additional graphs to enhance our entire visualisation process and to help us understand our dataset better. Some of the graphs we generated include swarmplot (Figure 33.4), distplot (Figure 33.5), seabornjointplot (Figure 33.6), and word clouds (Figures 33.7 and 33.8).

Data Cleaning and Preprocessing
The steps we included to preprocess the data includes:

Removing the URLs
Removing end of sentence characters like full stops (.), question marks (?) and
   exclamation marks (!)

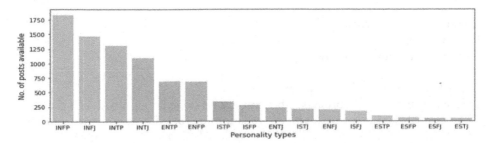

Figure 33.3 Transformed dataset

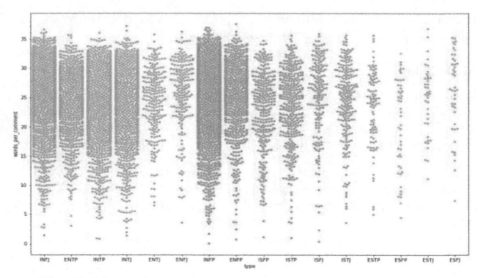

Figure 33.4 Swarmplot

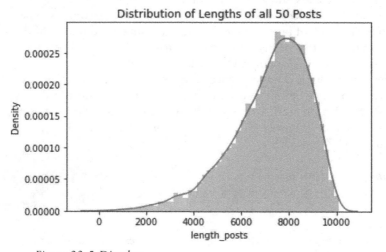

Figure 33.5 Distplot

Remove other punctuations
Remove non words
Converting all posts into lowercase

Label Encoding and Vectorization
Before the vectorization process, label encoding is done.Label encoding is the way
of making labels machine-readable by transforming them into a numeric form.The
posts are vectorized while filtering the stop words. For this the CountVectorizer
is used.

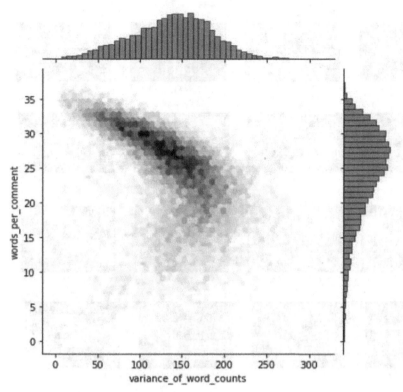

Figure 33.6 Combined Jointplot

Figure 33.7 Word cloud for dataset

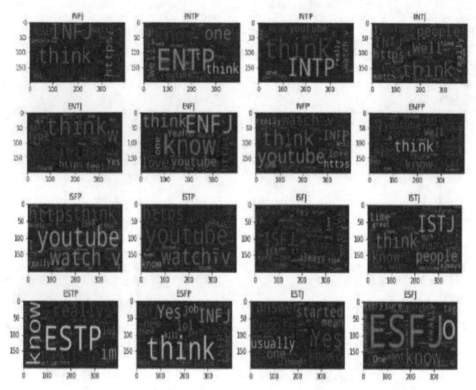

Figure 33.8 Subplots for 16 different personalities under MBTI

Splitting the dataset

The dataset is divided as training and testing sets in the split ratio of 80:20. With the help of the training data set, models are developed and trained.

Proposed Model

Ensembling corresponds to a technique in machine learning that joins several foundation level models into one optimal predictive model. The proposed model (Figure 33.9) is an ensemble model that combines the following machine learning classifiers:

- **Random Forest (RF)**
  A method of supervised machine learning that aids in classification and regression scenarios. It is one of the most flexible, convenient and yields better results. It decreases the possibility of overfitting and the amount of time needed for training. Moreover, it offers a high level of accuracy.
- **Extreme Gradient Boosting (XGBoost)**
  An optimised gradient boosting library that has been developed to be very effective, adaptable, and portable. Here, the classification algorithms are implemented using the Gradient Boosting Framework.

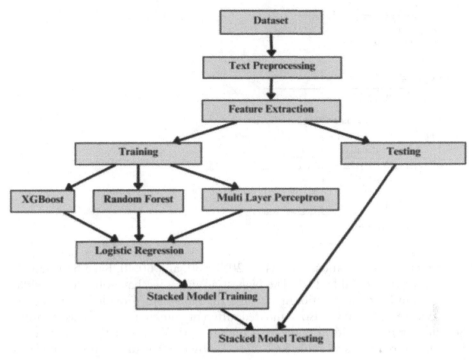

Figure 33.9 Proposed approach

- **Multi Layer Perceptron (MLP)**
  An artificial neural network with numerous layers along with non-linear activation function has been referred to as a multi-layered perceptron model. We can make quick predictions using it after training. Its ability to achieve the same accuracy ratio with both large and less data is helpful.

We have used Logistic Regression as the meta classifier. A meta-classifier is a classifier that uses all of the predictions as features to generate a final prediction out of them all. It makes use of the classes predicted by other classifiers and selects the final one as the result. Logistic Regression generates well-calibrated probabilities in addition to classification results [16].

The model has been tested in varying circumstances. We have analysed the accuracy, Matthews correlation coefficient (MCC), and F1 score, calculated using- True Positive (TP) indicating identical positive values in real and foreseen circumstances, True Negative (TN) indicating identical negative values in real and foreseen circumstances, False Positive (FP) where the foreseen value is positive but in reality it is negative, and False Negative (FN) where the foreseen value is negative but in reality it is positive. The calculations are depicted in the below formulas:

$$\text{Accuracy} = \frac{TP + TN}{TP + TN + FP + FN}$$

$$MCC = \frac{(TP \times TN) - (FP \times FN)}{\sqrt{(TP+FP)(TP+FN)(TN+FP)(TN+FN)}}$$

$$F1\ Score = \frac{2}{\frac{1}{Precision} + \frac{1}{Recall}}$$

$$= \frac{2 \times Precision \cdot Recall}{Precision + Recall}$$

$$= \frac{2 \times \frac{TP}{TP+FP} \times \frac{TP}{TP+FN}}{\frac{TP}{TP+FP} + \frac{TP}{TP+FN}}$$

$$= \frac{TP}{TP + \frac{1}{2}(FP + FN)}$$

Different train-test ratios, such as 80:20, 70:30, and 60:40, have been tested. You can see this in Table 33.1. The highest accuracy we have obtained is 99% which was in 80:20 split ratio. In all cases, the model has provided us with consistent accuracy. We have also compared different combinations of classification algorithms in order to identify the best combination. We can see the output of the different combinations in Table 33.2. We can observe that the proposed model is able to give a better and robust accuracy in every scenario.

Conclusion and Future Scope

In this research, we created a novel machine learning method to foresee the personality of an individual using the MBTI personality type indicator. In our research, we have attempted to combine several classification models, such as XGBoost, Random Forest, Decision Tree, KNN, SVM, etc.,to obtain the best possible combination for developing our ensemble model. We observed that combining XGBoost, Random Forest, and MLP (Multi Layer Perceptron) classifiers with Logistic Regression as the meta classifier yielded the best results with a constant accuracy over 90%.The results demonstrate that, in comparison to other classification models currently in use, the methodology described in this study offers a higher degree of robustness.

The methods given considerably increased the accuracy of identifying MBTI personality qualities. The proposed model can be used to help individuals, recruiters, psychologists, and educational counsellors find the right guidance.

Table 33.1 Table depicting training and testing accuracies at different train-test split ratios

Split Ratio	60-40	70-30	80-20
Training	0.905493	0.917820	0.993650
Testing	0.594331	0.608661	0.611570

Table 33.2 Tables depicting accuracy, MCC and F1 Score

Combination used	Training		
	Accuracy	MCC	F1 Score
XG+RF+MLP (Proposed Model)	0.993650	0.992741	0.990977
XG+RF	0.775399	0.740798	0.772367
XG+RF+DT+MLP	0.833235	0.907503	0.820277
XG+RF+KNN	0.828118	0.901967	0.824499
XG+KNN	0.748060	0.709329	0.745753
SVM+KNN	0.425281	0.328108	0.333500
Combination used	Testing		
	Accuracy	MCC	F1 Score
XG+RF+MLP (Proposed Model)	0.611570	0.547040	0.59786
XG+RF	0.588548	0.519676	0.572843
XG+RF+DT+MLP	0.594627	0.526877	0.577309
XG+RF+KNN	0.585596	0.515816	0.570190
XG+KNN	0.584416	0.514440	0.568707
SVM+KNN	0.425281	0.328108	0.333500

For the time being, we've used a publicly accessible dataset from Kaggle.In the future,we plan to create datasets by gathering user queries and assessing each user's personality based on responses.As part of our effort to develop our personality prediction system, we also intend to incorporate a few more classification models. By doing so, we hope to achieve a system that is far more accurate and effective than the one it presently offers. We also plan to make the model publicly accessible to enable people to analyse their personality types.

Acknowledgement

We express our sincere gratitude to our department head, Dr.Vimina E.R and all our teachers from the department of Computer Science and IT for their guidance and support.

References

1. Moraes, R., Pinto, L., Pilankar, M., and Rane, P. (2020).Personality assessment using social media for hiring candidates.In 2020 3rd International Conference on Communication System, Computing and IT Applications (CSCITA), 2020, (pp. 192–97). https://doi.org/10.1109/cscita47329.2020.9137818.
2. Tutaysalgir, E., Karagoz, P., and Toroslu, I. H. (2019). Clustering based personality prediction on turkishtweets. In Proceedings of the 2019 IEEE/ACM International

Conference on Advances in Social Networks Analysis and Mining, 2019, (pp. 825–828). https://doi.org/10.1145/3341161.3343513.

3. Kunte, A.V., and Panicker, S. (2019). Using textual data for personality prediction: amachine learning approach. In 2019 4th International Conference on Information Systems and Computer Networks (ISCON), 2019, (pp. 529–533). https://doi.org/10.1109/iscon47742.2019.9036220.

4. Amirhosseini, M. H., and Kazemian, H. (2020). Machine learning approach to personality type prediction based on the myers–briggstype indicator. *Multimodal Technologies and Interaction*, 4, 1–15. https://doi.org/10.3390/mti4010009.

5. Xu, J., Tian, W., Lv, G., Liu, S., and Fan, Y. (2021). Prediction of the big five personality traits using static facial images of college students with different academic backgrounds. *IEEE Access*, 9, 76822–76832. https://doi.org/10.1109/access.2021.3076989.

6. Jayaratne, M., and Jayatilleke, B. (2020). Predicting personality using answers to open-ended interview questions. *IEEE Access*, 8, 115345–115355. https://doi.org/10.1109/access.2020.3004002.

7. Keh, S. S., and Cheng, I. (2019). Myers-Briggs personality classification and personality-specific language generation using pre-trained language models. arXiv preprint arXiv:1907.06333.

8. Talasbek, A., Serek, A., Zhaparov, M., Yoo, S. M., Kim, Y. K., and Jeong, G. H. (2020). Personality classification experiment by applying K-Means clustering. *International Journal of Emerging Technologies in Learning (iJET)*, 15(16), 162–177. https://doi.org/10.3991/ijet.v15i16.15049.

9. Abdulrahman, R., Alsaedi, R., and AlSobeihy, M. (2018). Automated student-to-major allocation based on personality prediction. In 2018 1st International Conference on Computer Applications &amp; Information Security (ICCAIS), 2018. https://doi.org/10.1109/cais.2018.8442031.

10. Mushtaq, Z., Ashraf, S., and Sabahat, N. (2020). Predicting MBTI personality type with K-Means clustering and gradient boosting. In 2020 IEEE 23rd International Multitopic Conference (INMIC), 2020. https://doi.org/10.1109/inmic50486.2020.9318078.

11. Patil, S.M., Singh, R., Patil, P., and Pathare, N. (2021). Personality prediction using digital footprints. In 2021 5th International Conference on Intelligent Computing and Control Systems (ICICCS), 2021, (pp. 1736–1742). https://doi.org/10.1109/iciccs51141.2021.9432380.

12. Abidin, N.H., Akmal, M., Mohamad, N., Nincarean, D.,Yusoff, N., Karimah, H., and Abdelsalam, H. (2020). Improving intelligent personality prediction using myers-briggstype indicator and random forest classifier. *International Journal of Advanced Computer Science and Applications*, 11(11). 193–199. https://doi.org/10.14569/ijacsa.2020.0111125.

13. Alpaydin, E. (2020). Introduction to Machine Learning. 4th ed. Cambridge, MA: MIT Press.

14. Cherry, K. (2022). MSEd. Myers-Briggs Type Indicator: The 16 Personality Type s. Verywell Mind, July 28, 2022. https://www.verywellmind.com/the-myers-briggs-type-indicator-2795583.

15. Mitchell, J. (2017). (MBTI) Myers-Briggs Personality Type Dataset.Kaggle , September 22, 2017. https://www.kaggle.com/datasets/datasnaek/mbti-type.

16. Grover, K. (2020). Advantages and disadvantages of logistic regression. *OpenGenus IQ: Computing Expertise & Legacy*,. https://iq.opengenus.org/advantages-and-disadvantages-of-logistic-regression/.

34 Convolutional vision transformer for weed flora classification in banana plantations

Kala K U[1,a], M. Nandhini[2,b], Kishore Chakkravarthi M. N.[3,c], Thangadarshini M.[3,d] and S. Madhusudhana Verma[4,e]

[1]Department of Computer Science and information Technology, Jain University, Banglore, India

[2]Department of Computer Science, Pondicherry University Puducherry, India

[3]Puducherry Technical University (PTU), Puducherry, India

[4]Rayalaseema University, Andhra Pradesh, India

Abstract

Bananas are a crop that requires high moisture levels for optimal performance, but this can also create ideal conditions for weed growth. Weeds can cause severe damage during the vegetative growth and transition phases, which are critical for determining the yield of bananas, as they compete for moisture, nutrients, and can harbour pests. Grasses and sedges make up 70% of the weed flora and are the major weed types that compete with bananas for essential nutrients. Nitrogen deficiency in bananas, characterized by yellowing of young foliage, is a common sign of competition with grasses. Therefore, managing weeds in banana plantations is crucial for optimal growth and yield. Various control methods, including mechanical, cultural, and chemical approaches, can be used depending on the specific weed species and the severity of the infestation. Even though, weeds cause harmful effects on the plants, some of them are useful for the humans. This work focuses on the classification of useful and useless weed found in the banana plantations. So that we can utilize the space in between the banana plants effectively. This work proposes a Deep Learning Model, which combines Convolutional Neural Network and Vision Transformer for identifying the weeds. Also, the architecture is compared with relevant image classification models on the same Banana Weed Image dataset for performance evaluation.

Keywords: Agricultural engineering, convolutional neural network, vision transformer, weed management

Introduction

TheWeed management is crucial in plantain tree cultivation to ensure optimal growth and yield, reduce pest and disease infestations, and improve worker safety and soil health. The choice of weed management method depends on factors such as plantation size, labor availability, and input costs. Weeds can be classified as useful, useless, or harmful, depending on their impact on the ecosystem and their potential benefits or drawbacks to humans and agriculture. Machine learning

[a]kalasarin@gmail.com, [b]mnandhini2005@pondiuni.co.in, [c]kishore.chakkravarthi@pec.edu.in, [d]thdarshini01@gmail.com, [e]seeverma@rediffmail.com

and deep learning techniques, such as Convolutional Neural Networks, Support Vector Machines, and Vision Transformers, can be used to classify weeds based on their physical characteristics and image features, leading to more accurate and efficient weed identification and management.

Useful weeds can provide benefits to the ecosystem, soil, or humans, such as acting as green manure, cover crops, or medicinal and culinary plants. Useless weeds do not provide significant benefits to the agricultural system or the environment and may compete with crops for resources, reduce biodiversity, or provide habitat for pests and diseases. Harmful weeds can cause economic or ecological damage to agricultural systems, such as reducing crop yields or negatively impacting the environment.

Vision transformers are a type of deep learning algorithm that have shown promising results for image classification tasks, including weed classification. They work by processing an image in patches and transforming each patch into a sequence of vectors, which are then processed by a transformer network. This allows the model to capture the spatial relationships between different patches and learn complex features from the image, leading to higher classification accuracy. The use of machine learning and deep learning techniques for weed classification can help farmers save costs, improve agricultural productivity, and reduce the negative impact of weeds on the ecosystem.

The structure of this paper consists of three main sections. Firstly, it presents a review of the current state-of-the-art literature on CNN and Vision Transformer. Secondly, it provides a detailed explanation of the proposed method along with an analysis of the results. Lastly, the paper concludes by summarizing the research work and highlighting potential areas for future research.

Related Works

Deep learning (DL) based weed classification and detection is a promising solution for improving the efficiency and accuracy of weed management practices, reducing the use of chemicals, and preserving biodiversity. Convolutional Neural Networks (CNNs) have been widely used for weed classification, but they have limitations in capturing spatial relationships in images. Vision Transformers (ViTs) have emerged as a promising alternative, processing images by dividing them into patches and transforming them into sequences, which allows the model to capture long-range dependencies and spatial relationships. Recent studies have shown that ViTs outperform other state-of-the-art deep learning models for weed species classification, making them a valuable tool for revolutionizing weed management practices. Table 34.1 Lists out some recent studies in weed classification and detection using CNN and ViT.

Overall, while CNNs have been successful in weed classification, the emergence of ViTs has shown great potential in improving the accuracy and efficiency of weed classification tasks. Their ability to capture spatial relationships between patches and learn complex features from images makes them a promising tool for future weed management practices.

Table 34.1 Related works in weed classification and detection.

Reference	Dataset	CNN Architecture	Evaluation
[[15]	Public weed dataset	CNN-ViT hybrid	IoU and pixel accuracy
[16]	Public weed dataset	Vision Transformer	Top-1 and top-5 accuracy
[17]	Private dataset	Faster R-CNN	mAP and F1-score
[18]	Private dataset	ResNet-50	Accuracy, precision, recall, F1-score
[19]	WeedAI and Amino acid dataset	Vision Transformer	Top-1 and top-5 accuracy, confusion matrix
[20]	WeedAI	Vision Transformer	Top-1 and top-5 accuracy
[21]	Private dataset	Inception-ResNet-v2	Mean Average Precision (mAP) and F1-score
[22]	WeedNet	U-Net	Intersection over Union (IoU) and pixel accuracy
[13]	A public weed dataset	DenseNet-121	F1 score, precision, recall, accuracy
[9]	A weed dataset from a soybean field	Inception-v3	Accuracy, precision, recall
[7]	A public weed dataset and an in-house dataset	VGG-16	F1 score, precision, recall
[23]	An UAV-based dataset of weed-infested farmland	AlexNet	Overall accuracy, kappa coefficient
[10]	A weed dataset from an agricultural field	ResNet-50	Accuracy, precision, recall
[3]	A public weed dataset	MobileNet	F1 score, precision, recall
[4]	A public weed dataset	LeNet	Precision, recall
[8]	A dataset of weed images	A custom CNN architecture	Accuracy, precision, recall
[11]	A public weed dataset	AlexNet	F1 score, precision, recall
[2]	An aerial dataset of crop and weed fields	A custom CNN architecture	Mean accuracy, mean intersection over union
[6]	A dataset of soybean and weed images	A custom CNN architecture	Accuracy, precision, recall
[5]	A dataset of maize field images	A custom CNN architecture	Precision, recall
[12]	A dataset of rice field images	A custom CNN architecture	Accuracy, precision, recall
[1]	A dataset of sugarcane field images	A custom CNN architecture	F1 score, precision, recall

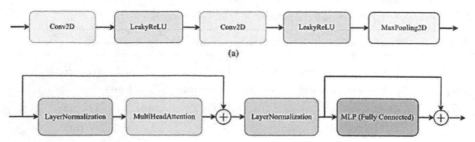

Figure 34.1 Building block structures (a)CNN (b) transformer

Proposed Network Architecture

The proposed model consists of two building blocks: CNN and Vision transformer. The schematic diagram of both the blocks are depicted in Figure 34.1.

CNN Block

Two convolutional layers, each using 3x3 kernels and no activation function or padding, are used in the CNN Block. The second layer's output is passed through a leaky ReLU layer, followed by a max pooling layer of 2x2 kernel, which decreases the spatial dimensions of the feature map. This design is inspired by the VGG network architecture, which showed the effectiveness of using multiple small filters in successive layers.

Transformer Block

The Transformer block starts with a layer normalization layer to normalize the input. Next, the input is passed through a 4-head attention layer with a projection dimension of 64. The resulting output from the attention layer is combined with the input using a skip connection and then processed with a new normalization layer. Next, the output is passed through two fully connected layers with GELU activation functions and 128 and 64 neurons, respectively. The final output is generated by adding the fully connected layer's output and input through a skip connection. This sum is then passed on to the next block in the network.

Structure of Models

This paper is experimented with different combination of CNN and transformer blocks. Figure 34.2 displays the basic framework of multiple backbone building blocks and a classification head of the models employed in this investigation. Eight different models are formed from the backbone blocks as shown in Table 34.2.

Experiments and Results

Data Sets and Experimental Settings

In this experimental investigation, eight variants of models are used for training and evaluating the efficiency of deep learning models on a dataset. The dataset consists of 2 classes of useful and useless plant images found in banana

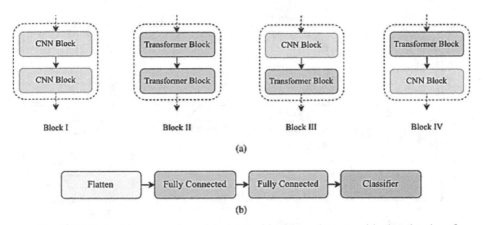

Figure 34.2 Architecture of models (a) Backbone combination blocks, (b) classification structure

Table 34.2 Model formation from backbone models

Model	Backbone Structure	Convolutional Blocks	Transformer Blocks
1	1 CNN Block	1	0
2	2 CNN Blocks	2	0
3	1 Transformer Block	0	1
4	2 Transformer Blocks	0	2
5	1 CNN Block + 1 Transformer Block	1	1
6	1 CNN Block + 1 Transformer Block	1 + 1	1
7	1 CNN Block + 1 CNN Block	0	1 + 1
8	2 Transformer Blocks + 1 CNN Block	0	2 + 1

plantations. Each class have 500 images of various plants. The dataset is collected manually from different fields of Tamil Nādu, India. To investigate the effect of input resolution on model accuracy and prediction speed, three different image resolutions (50 by 50, 100 by 100, and 200 by 200) were opted to train the networks. Lower input resolutions generally lead to faster prediction speeds but may also result in decreased accuracy. To explore the impact of input resolution, all models are trained and assessed initially with a low-resolution images of 50 by 50, then it is turned up to 100 by 100 and 200 by 200. An 80-20 split was used for partitioning the dataset into a training subset and a validation subset. The AdamW optimizer was used to train the models, which allows for separate tuning of the learning rate and weight decay to optimize these parameters independently. All models were trained for 100 epochs with an initial learning rate of 0.001.

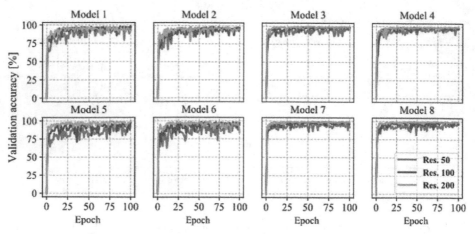

Figure 34.3 Accuracy on validation set

Result Analysis and Discussion

The validation accuracy of the model throughout its training is depicted in Figure 34.3. Image augmentation, data shuffling, and dropout layers are the contributing factors to the fluctuations observed in the charts. However, these fluctuations have almost constant amplitudes, and after epoch 50, there are no noteworthy variations found in the charts. Based on these observations, it is suggested that training these models for a longer duration may not be necessary, and 100 epochs are expected to be adequate for reducing the purpose of choosing the sources randomly. The weights that corresponded to the utmost accuracy of validation are preserved and applied during the evaluation stage. Despite these challenges, the proposed model is efficient in terms of accuracies on the validation data.

The table 34.3 shows the performance results of eight different models based on different resolutions, evaluated by convergence score, average F1 score, recall and precision. Each model has three different resolutions (50, 100, and 200). Overall, Models 3, 4, and 8 have the best performance, achieving high scores for all evaluation metrics. In contrast, Model 6 has the lowest performance, with relatively lower scores for all evaluation metrics.

Conclusion

Various combination of Vision Transformer and convolutional neural networks, as well as hybrid models that combined the two are compared and evaluated the performance in terms of various evaluation metrics. The dataset had few samples and similar classes, but the Vision Transformer based model attained more precise performance than the other models and had lower parameters than similar works. The order of the CNN and transformer building blocks have no impact on the speed of prediction, but the usage of attention blocks after convolutional blocks has directed to marginally improved accuracy. Future work will focus on object localization and multi-label classification network to detect the weeds automatically using adequate labelled multiclass dataset.

Table 34.3 Experimental results

Model	Resolution	Avg. F1	Avg. Recall	Avg. Precision	Convergence Score
1	50	0.97	0.96	0.97	0.88
	100	0.98	0.98	0.98	0.93
	200	0.98	0.98	0.99	0.93
2	50	0.98	0.98	0.98	0.91
	100	0.97	0.97	0.97	0.91
	200	0.99	0.99	0.99	0.93
3	50	0.98	0.98	0.98	0.96
	100	0.99	0.99	0.99	0.92
	200	1	1	1	0.97
4	50	0.98	0.98	0.98	0.96
	100	0.98	0.99	0.99	0.92
	200	1	1	1	0.97
5	50	0.97	0.96	0.97	0.83
	100	0.98	0.98	0.98	0.9
	200	0.99	0.99	0.99	0.95
6	50	0.94	0.94	0.95	0.82
	100	0.98	0.97	0.98	0.95
	200	0.98	0.98	0.99	0.94
7	50	0.97	0.97	0.97	0.92
	100	0.99	0.99	0.99	0.95
	200	0.99	0.99	0.99	0.96
8	50	0.97	0.97	0.97	0.92
	100	0.99	0.99	0.99	0.95
	200	1	1	1	0.96

Acknowledgement

This work was supported in part by the Department of Science & Technology – Science and Engineering Research Board, Government of India under Core Research Grant, via sanction number CRG/2019/005513

References

1. Araújo, S. A., Leles, R. N., Fernandes Filho, E. I., and Molin, J. P. (2015). Automatic weed detection in sugarcane fields using image analysis. *Computers and Electronics in Agriculture*, 116, 59-71.
2. Bell, S., Upcroft, B., and Sattar, J. (2016). Automated weed mapping with semi-supervised classification using Gaussian processes and convolutional neural networks.

In Robotics and Automation (ICRA), 2016 IEEE International Conference on (pp. 1386-1393). IEEE.

3. Chen, C., Wang, L., and Wang, Y. (2019). A computer vision based approach to weed recognition for precision farming. *Computers and Electronics in Agriculture*, 162, 40—412.

4. Ferentinos, K. P. (2018). Deep learning models for plant disease detection and diagnosis. *Computers and Electronics in Agriculture*, 145, 311-318.

5. Fernández-Quintanilla, C., Ribeiro, A., Borra-Serrano, I., and Dorado, J. (2016). Weed detection in maize crops using deep convolutional neural networks. *Sensors*, 16(11), 1838.

6. Guo, W., Fukatsu, T., Ninomiya, S., and Zhu, H. (2016). Weed classification using a deep convolutional neural network. In 2016 IEEE International Conference on Robotics and Automation (ICRA) (pp. 2016-2021). IEEE.

7. Han, X., Wu, Y., Yu, J., Liu, H., Chen, S., and Ding, W. (2021). A deep learning-based method for weed detection in maize fields. *Computers and Electronics in Agriculture*, 182, 106042.

8. Hassanpour, H., Wahabzada, M., Mahlein, A. K., and Bauckhage, C. (2017). Deep learning based plant disease recognition by hierarchical extreme learning machines using leaf image classification. *Scientific reports*, 7(1), 1-13.

9. Jia, S., Chen, S., Sun, W., Xie, X., and Qiao, H. (2021). A deep learning-based weed classification system for soybean fields. *IEEE Access*, 9, 71026-71034.

10. Kavdir, İ. H., Asci, M., Dursun, B., and Yavuz, N. (2020). A deep learning approach for automatic weed species classification. *Precision Agriculture*, 21(1), 83-98.

11. Kebapci, H., Dogantekin, E., Ozkan, M., and Kumbasar, E. P. (2017). Automatic weed detection in tomato crops using deep learning. *Computers and Electronics in Agriculture*, 139, 202-215.

12. Li, Z., Yan, X., and Zhu, J. (2016). Weed detection in paddy fields using image segmentation and machine learning. *Computers and Electronics in Agriculture*, 127, 33-40.

13. Liu, X., Lu, J., Chen, W., Liu, W., He, J., and Tang, X. (2021). A deep learning method for simultaneous weed detection and classification in maize fields. *Journal of Imaging*, 7(5), 88.

14. Loshchilov, I., and Hutter, F. (2017). Decoupled Weight Decay Regularization. 7th International Conference on Learning Representations, ICLR 2019. https://arxiv.org/abs/1711.05101v3

15. Kim, J. H., Kim, H., and Kim, B. (2023). Weed segmentation using a hybrid CNN-Vision Transformer architecture with self-attention mechanisms. *Journal of Agricultural Informatics*, 14(1), 1-12.

16. Zhang, Y., Liu, S., and Zhao, J. (2022). Domain-adaptive vision transformers for weed classification. *Computers and Electronics in Agriculture*, 201, 106269.

17. Vargas, F., Plaza, A. J., and Plaza, J. (2022). Region-based deep learning for weed detection and mapping in remote sensing images. *ISPRS Journal of Photogrammetry and Remote Sensing*, 183, 105-118.

18. Wang, H., Yang, Y., and Cao, L. (2021). Weed classification using a convolutional neural network with transfer learning. *Precision Agriculture*, 22(3), 579-593.

19. Kumar, A., Maurya, A. K., and Patil, S. (2021). A comparative study of deep learning architectures for weed classification. *Computers and Electronics in Agriculture*, 185, 106073.

20. Li, H., Gao, X., and Liu, Z. (2021). Weed classification using Vision Transformer. *Computers and Electronics in Agriculture*, 187, 106271.

21. Luo, L., Shang, J., and Cao, L. (2019). Weed detection using deep learning and transfer learning in UAV images. *Computers and Electronics in Agriculture*, 162, 219-227.

22. Mohanty, S. P., Hughes, D. P., and Salathé, M. (2019). Using deep learning for image-based plant disease detection. *Frontiers in Plant Science*, 10, 1-12.

23. P. Lottes, R. Khanna, J. Pfeifer, R. Siegwart and C. Stachniss, (2017). UAV-based crop and weed classification for smart farming, IEEE International Conference on Robotics and Automation (ICRA), Singapore, 2017, 3024-3031, doi: 10.1109/ICRA.2017.7989347.

35 Computer vision-inspired smart attendance system (SAS)

Ajay Kumar Bansal[a] and Georgina Asuah[b]

Department of Computer Applicat ion, Lovely, Professional University, Jalandhar

Abstract

Consistent attendance of students in class is crucial for evaluating their performance and maintaining quality control in the education system. However, conventional methods used by most institutions can be time-consuming, inaccurate, and susceptible to fraud and manipulation. To address this issue, the use of voice recognition, facial recognition, and biometric verification is becoming increasingly popular for developing sophisticated automatic attendance systems. This project utilized face recognition technology to develop a smart attendance system using Python, OpenCV, SQLite3, Excel, Tkinter, and other useful Python packages. The project employed the Haar cascade classifier for face detection and the LBPH method for face recognition.

Keywords: Attendance, face detection, face recognition

Introduction

Attendance is a crucial part of education and academics as it is used as a criterion to decide whether or not a student is eligible to take tests. The monitoring of punctuality at all institutions is a crucial duty for evaluating the performance of students and quality monitoring over the course of a month and a semester [1, 2]. The number of students in each class is large and hence requires a lot of time to be used to take students' attendance by the faculty. The staff may find it challenging to approve and continually maintain every student's record in a classroom while using a manual attendance system [3]. It takes time to mark the attendance manually, which if saved can be utilized for teaching and learning. According to [4], accurately marking the attendance of present pupils requires the teacher to invest time that could be used for teaching. Additionally, managing large student groups can create even more difficulties. Also, in situations where the count of students does not correspond to the number of students who are recorded as present, the faculty has to go through the complete process again wasting a lot of valuable time. Teachers take multiple classes making it almost impossible to remember and recognize students' faces and match them with their names and registration numbers. Students use this as an advantage to take attendance for their colleagues who may not be physically present in the class. As a result, we can implement a workable frame work that will use facial recognition to automatically mark students' attendance [5]. The automated system will minimize mistakes made by teachers in taking manual attendance. The system will also help solve some of the challenges faced with the existing method of taking attendance like Proxy attendance, Security issues in class, and manual mistakes.

[a]ajayg13@red iffmail.com, [b]georginalariba@gmail.com

The management of student attendance, minimizing time spent on taking students' attendance and other related challenges that exist with the current method of taking attendance is the main emphasis of this study as a substitute for the manual approach of recording students' attendance. Face recognition technology is used to build a smart attendance system that will automate the process of counting and identifying students. The system will enable the instructor to take a photo of the class, and with the aid of image processing, the faces of the pupils will be recognized and attendance will be recorded. The need for such a system is critical for organizations whether small or big, and it will continue to play an important role in the future.

Related Works

A variety of computerized monitoring and attendance systems are being used in businesses in response to the active advancement in software technology in today's world. This automation comes as a solution to the existing challenges faced by the manual attendance system. The short comings of current manual attendance systems are mostly solved by simultaneously identifying the person's face and doing an RFID verification. [6]. A framework for managing attendance was proposed by Sawhney et al in [5] where Convolutional Neural Networks (CNN), Principle Component Analysis (PCA), and Eigenface values were utilized to automate the face recognition procedure. According to Arsenovic et al. [7], a recently developed attendance system for identifying and recognizing faces using deep convolutional neural networks (CNNs) achieved an accuracy of 95.02% when tested on a restricted dataset of authentic worker facial photographs in a real-time environment. With PCA (Principal Component Analysis), a facial recognition software, and Open CV for face recognition application authentication, a camera-based real-time face identification system was created [8]. A unified frame work leveraging the You Only Look Once (YOLO V3) algorithm for face detection and the Face API from Microsoft Azure for face recognition (a face database) for attendance monitoring through the smartphone was developed by [9].

Face detection and recognition systems have some problems associated with them. The previous attendance system based on facial recognition had some limitations, such as difficulties with light levels and head position [10]. Lighting, direction, size, clarity, expression, and the intensity of facial pictures present difficulties in face recognition [11]. Bussa et al stated that classical face recognition systems recognize faces from the input using algorithms, but the results are typically not as precise and accurate as needed. [12]. The approach described in the proposed system automatically records student attendance in a classroom setting and extracts the image using the Personal Component Analysis (PCA) technique, marking the attendance [13].

A few studies have pointed out ways to overcome some of the challenges faced by face detection and recognition systems. Consequently, a variety of methods, including the illumination invariant, the Viola and Jones algorithm, and principal component analysis are utilized to resolve these challenges [10]. Light has an impact on both Eigen and Fisher's faces, therefore ideal lighting conditions cannot be guaranteed in reality. To solve this issue, the LBPH has the least noise interference and outperforms other algorithms by a confidence factor of 2– 5 [14].

With the construction of a 3D Facial Model, the system presented in this work attempts to depart from such established approaches (conventional face recognition systems) and offer a fresh method for identifying a student when utilizing a face recognition system [12]. To obtain the required findings implemented in MATLAB, a quantitative analysis based on (Peak Signal to Noise Ratio) PSNR values employing methods like Viola- Jones and HOG features coupled with an SVM classifier was utilized by Rathod et al [15].

Methodology

Architecture

The automatic attendance system's architecture is fairly straight forward to operate. It is based on Haarcascad e_frontalface_default.xml for face detection and the Local Binary Patterns Histograms (createLBPHFaceRecognizer()) technique for face recognition. The Graphical User Interface (GUI) of the system was created using the Tkinter library. The GUI is shown below in Figure 35.2.

The system consists of three databases: one for students, one for professors, and one for attendance. The information about each student is kept in the student database, while the information about authorized system administrators is kept in the instructor database. The attendance database is used to keep a record of students who were present at a particular lecture, as the name implies. Additionally, it is utilized for monitoring purposes. For our project, we will require certain hard ware components to make this system functional. First, the instructor will use a laptop equipped with a high- definition camera. Once the faculty member has successfully logged in, pupils are requested to position suitably for the photograph to be taken. At this point, the camera has been upgraded to recognize faces more quickly. When faces are found, a square with the student's name underneath is drawn on the face. Figure 35.1 shows the flowchart of our system.

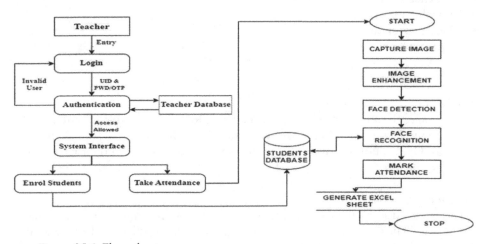

Figure 35.1 Flow chart

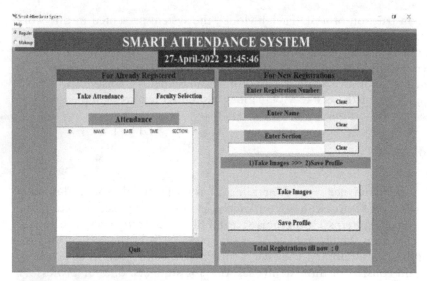

Figure 35.2 Graphical user interface (GUI)

As part of the improvement , the image is first transformed to grayscale and passed on to the face identification to detect the pupils' faces using an algorithm. The faces of all the students will then be extracted from the image and cropped before being matched to the database of faces. The attendance will be recorded on the excel sheet for students whose faces have been found by comparing the faces one by one.

Methodology
The computerized facial recognition system must be implemented using specific approaches. For this process to be successful, several actions must be taken.

- Teacher Login
- Enrolment
- Face Detection
- Face Recognition

Attendance Marking

Teacher Login
In this stage, the authorized user (teachers), is allowed access to the system after verification. The teachers' database is created in python using SQLite 3. In this stage, an OTP option is created for teachers who have forgotten their passwords to access the interface.

Enrolment
Creating the student database is the first and most important step in the Smart Attendance The database contains a ton of pictures of enrolled students who are permitted to attend a specific lecture.

The teacher who has access to the system enters the information for each new student to be enrolled and takes pictures of the student for use as a teaching model. The Haar Cascade classifier loads an image when the camera opens. The facial features in the image are recognized using a frontal face Haar Cascade classifier. If a face is found, the system snaps 101 pictures of the pupil comprising different facial expressions and angles and converts them to grayscale, and stores them in the desired destination. The system operates feature extraction from images with assistance from the recognizer and the Haar Cascade, which recognizes the face in the image. 16 Haar Cascades are available in OpenCV to detect faces, eyes, objects, and text. The Ada Boost algorithm is used by Haar Cascade to identify facial features like the eyes, nose, and mouth. Numpy is used to convert the grayscale photos into matrices.

Face Detection

Before the teacher starts the camera to capture the picture, the teacher would have made the necessary selection provided in the interface. The teacher will choose the mode of the lecture, the name of the lecturer, course code, and title and then click on take attendance. The objective is to identify and likely extract (in terms of size and placement) faces from the image for use with the facial recognition algorithm. The Ada Boost algorithm is used by Haar Cascade to identify facial features like the eyes, nose, and mouth. It creates a rectangular frame around the face using the Haar wavelet.

Face Recognition

The camera-captured real-time color image is transformed into a grayscale version. Face detect ion and feature extraction on photos are performed employing the (createLBPHFaceRecognizer ()) algorithm and the Haar Cascade for face recognition. The degree of similarity and other factors between the photos in the database and in real time is then calculated. The system then contrasts the faces in a real-time and database image. The individual's facial angle and the separation between them and the camera, the ambient lighting, and the subject's expressions are all taken into account when this smart attendance system recognizes a student. The name of the student is displayed on the rectangular frame if the degree of resemblance and other factors between the real-time image and the database image match, else an unknown person is displayed on the rectangular frame.

Attendance Marking

After the faces have been successfully recognized, an excel sheet will be generated where the details of the student's present will be contained. Also, a copy of that table will be displayed in the attendance section of the system's interface. The attendance sheet contains the following details ID, Name, Date, Time, Section, Mode, Faculty, and Course.

Algorithm

INPUTS: Live Video containing students' faces in the classroom.

OUTPUT: Attendance sheet (Excel sheet)

Login Here

User Login Area

UID

OPT

SEND OTP

Login

Figure 35.3 Teachers login interface

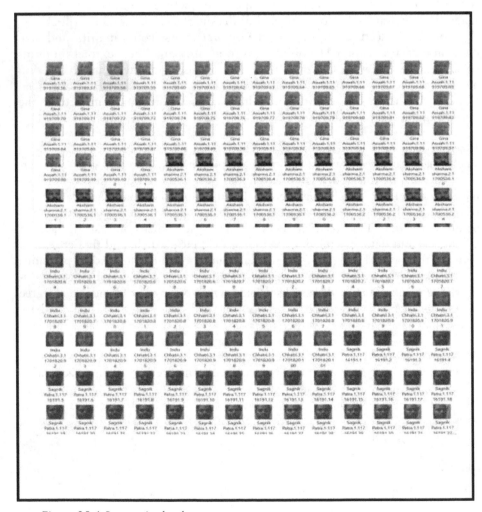

Figure 35.4 Images in database

Step I : Teacher Login.

Step II .1: Information about students is added to the student database.

Step II .2: Make necessary select ions and start the camera for attendance-taking.

Step IV: Face Detection to get the Region of Interest (ROI) using the Haar Cascade classifier for face detection.

Step V: Face Recognition using the LBPH method on the ROI to obtain the features.

Step VI: IF: if the face is recognized, add it to the attendance sheet

ELSE: do not add to the attendance sheet.

Step VIII: Generate an Attendance Sheet.

Step IX: End.

Implementation/Experim Ental Results

The results obtained by the model are shown in the following figures.

Figure 35.3 Teachers Login Interface for teachers who exist in the teacher's database to log in. Provision is made for teachers who forget their password to log in using the OTP option.

Figure 35.4 Registered students' images in the student's database.

Figure 35.5 Recognition is done for attendance marking.

Figure 35.6 Attendance details displayed on System Interface.

Figure 35.7 An excel sheet of attendance records is generated.

Figure 35.8 Recognition is done for attendance marking: Multiple faces.

Figure 35.5 Face identifcation and recognition case 1

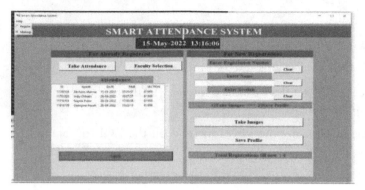

Figure 35.6 Attendance on system interface

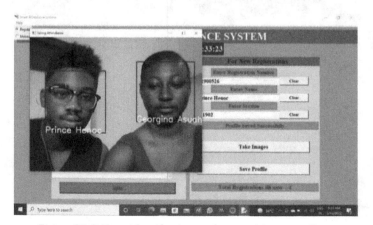

Figure 35.7 Attendance sheet generator

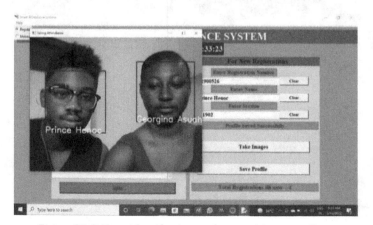

Figure 35.8 Face identifcation and recognition. case 2

Conclusion and Future Works

In this project, we have been able to successfully develop software using python programming language and various OpenCV algorithms which automate the attendance recording process using facial recognition technology. We implemented this project using various database management systems and files like SQLite3, and CSV Format, for managing our databases. The software is performing well with training images taken in a clear and bright environment. The use of the Smart Attendance System demonstrates that the suitable recognition rate and the threshold value are in agreement. Since proxies are avoided, the most effective and reliable face recognition method for identifying students in educational institutions and accurately recording their attendance in Open CV is called LBPH.

The future scope of the project can be increasing the speed and accuracy of the model, using cloud data stores, combining voice recognition technology, and use of an external device for the image.

References

1. Alassery, F. (2016). A smart classroom of wireless sensor networks for students time attendance system. In 20199th IEEE Integrated STEM Education Conference ISEC 2019, (pp. 324–331). 2019, doi: 10.1109/ISECon.2019.8881998.
2. Bhattacharya, S., Nainala, G. S., Das, P., and Routray, A. (2018). Smart attendance monitoring system (SAMS): a face recognition- based attendance system for classroom environment. In Proceeding- IEEE 18th International Conference on Advanced Learning Technologies, ICALT 2018, (pp. 358–360), 2018. doi: 10.1109/ICALT.2018.00090.
3. Lukas, S., Mitra, A. R., Desanti, R. I., and Krisnadi, D. (2016). Student attendance system in the classroom using face recognition technique. In 2016 International Conference on Information and Communication Technology Convergence, ICTC 2016, (pp. 1032–1035), 2016. DOI: 10.1109/ICTC.2016.7763360.
4. Ahmedi, A. and Nandyal, S., (2015). An automatic attendance system using image processing. The International Journal Of Engineering And Science (IJES), 4(11), 1–8.
5. Sawhney, S., Kacker, K., Jain, S., Singh, S. N., and Garg, R. (2019). Real-time smart attendance system using face recognition techniques. In Proceeding 9th International Conference on Cloud Computing, Data Science and Engineering Confluence, 2019, (pp. 522–525), 2019. DOI: 10.1109/CONFLUENCE.2019.8776934.
6. Akbar, M. S., Sarker, P., Mansoor, A. T., Al Ashray, A. M., and Uddin, J. (2018). Face recognition and RFID verified attendance system. In Proceeding - 2018 International Conference on Computing, Electronics and Communications Engineering iCCECE, 2018, (pp. 168–172), 2019. doi: 10.1109/iCCECOME.2018.8658705.
7. Arsenovic, M., Sladojevic, S., Andela, A., and Stef anovic, D. (2017). Face time-deep learning based face recognition attendance system. In SISY 2017 - IEEE 15th International Symposium on Intelligent Systems Informatics, Proceeding, (pp. 53–57), 2017. DOI: 10.1109/SISY.2017.8080587.
8. Khan, M., Chakraborty, S., Astya, R., and Khepra, S. (2019). Face detection and recognition using open CV. In Proceeding - 2019 International Conference on Computing, Communication, and Intelligent Systems, ICCCIS 2019, vol. 2019 -Janua, (pp. 116 –119), 2019. DOI: 10.1109/ICCCIS48478.2019.8974493.
9. Khan, S., Akram, A., and Usman, N. (2020). Real time automatic attendance system for face recognition using face API and open CV. Wireless Personal Communications, 113(1), pp. 469 – 480. doi: 10.1007/s11277-020-07224-2.

10. Wagh, P., Thakare, R., Chaudhari, J., and Patil, S. (2015). Attendance system based on face recognition using eigenface and PCA algorithms. In Proceeding 2015 International Conference on Green Computing and Internet of Things, ICGCIoT 2015, (pp. 303–308), 2016. DOI: 10.1109/ICGCIoT.2015.7380478.
11. Hapani, S., Prabhu, N., Parakhiya, N., and Paghdal, M. (2018). Automated attendance system using image processing. In Proceeding- 2018 4th International Conference on Computing Communication Control and Automation ICCUBEA 2018, 2018. DOI: 10.1109/ICCUBEA.2018.8697824.
12. Jha, A. (2007). Class room atten dance system using facial recognition system. *International journal of Mathematics, Science, Technology and Management*, 2(3), 2319–8125. [Online]. Available: www.klresearch.org.
13. Nithya, D. (2015). Automated class attendance system based on face recognition using PCA algorithm. *International Journal of Engineering Research*, V4(12), 551–554. doi: 10.17577/ijertv4is120249.
14. Bussa, S., Mani, A., Bharuka, S., and Kaushik, S. (2020). Smart attendance system using OPENCV based on facial recognition. *International Journal of Engineering Research*, V9(03), 54–59. doi: 10.17577/ijertv9is030122.
15. Rathod, H., Ware, Y., Sane, S., Raulo, S., Pakhare, V., and Rizvi, I. A. (2017). Automated attendance system using machine learning approach. In 2017 International Conference on Nascent Technologies in Engineering, ICNTE 2017 - Proceeding, (pp. 0–4), 2017. doi: 10.1109/ICNTE.2017.7947889. https://tk -tools.readthedocs.io/en/latest/

36 Machine and deep learning for accurate state-wide weather forecasting: a case study of Telangana

Ranjit Kaur[a], Sourav Sutradhar[b], Pranav Prakash[c], Ashish Jamuda[d] and Sumanta Saha[e]

School of Computer Application, Lovely Professional University, Phagwara, India

Abstract

This study aims to forecast weather reports in Telangana using machine and deep learning techniques. To anticipate weather patterns in the region, the SARIMA model and the LSTM model are used. The models are trained and tested using historical meteorological data from the Telangana AI Mission (T-AIM). Each model's performance is measured using several metrics such as MAE and RMSE. The LSTM model outperforms the SARIMA model in forecasting practically all the weather parameters, according to the results. This research shows how machine learning and deep learning algorithms can effectively anticipate weather patterns in Telangana, which can aid in decision-making and planning in industries such as agriculture, transportation, and disaster management.

Keywords: Deep learning.machine learning, weather forecasting

Introduction

Telangana state is experiencing major repercussions from climate change, which are evident in a number of areas including water scarcity, agriculture, health, and biodiversity loss. The state has suffered a considerable reduction in rainfall over the past few decades, which has led to periodic droughts, according to the Indian Meteorological Department (IMD). According to a report released in 2020, Telangana has experienced an increase in temperature and a decrease in rainfall during the last 50 years. Due to increased crop failures and poorer yields, agriculture, the state's main industry, has been negatively impacted. Around 13 lakh people have been impacted by severe floods in Telangana since 2016, according to a report by the National Disaster Management Authority (NDMA). A rise in heat-related illnesses and vector-borne diseases like dengue and malaria are two additional effects of climate change on the state's population's health. In addition, the threat of extinction for many species is being exacerbated by warming temperatures and shifting weather patterns, which are causing biodiversity loss. According to research done in Telangana'sAmrabad Tiger Reserve, increasing temperatures have caused a drop in the population of insects, the primary component of the food chain, which may eventually result in the extinction of other species. These facts and earlier statistics demonstrate that Telangana state is being

[a]ranjit.28632@lpu.co.in, [b]shuvsutradhar@gmail.com, [c]pranav142240@gmail.com, [d]ashish.id93@gmail.com, [e]sumontasaha9@gmail.com

significantly impacted by climate change, and urgent action is required to lessen these consequences and increase resilience to cope with the changing environment.

Telangana state's rapid climate change challenges can be addressed with the help of weather forecasting. Weather forecasting can assist the state in preparing for extreme weather occurrences and minimizing their effects by providing precise and timely information about weather patterns and events. For instance, early warning systems for floods, heatwaves, and other extreme weather occurrences can be created, enabling people to take precautions and leave high-risk locations. This may lessen the number of fatalities and property losses brought on by severe weather. Weather forecasts can help the state better manage its water resources. In order to decrease the effects of droughts and water scarcity, weather forecasting can help with irrigation planning and resource management. Forecasting the weather can also boost the state's agricultural industry. Having a fallback strategy is wise in case something goes wrong. By doing this, you can increase agricultural yields and reduce losses brought on by bad weather.

Telangana state's weather forecasting could be revolutionized by upcoming technologies like machine intelligence and deep learning. These technologies are capable of making precise forecasts of weather patterns and events by evaluating enormous volumes of data from numerous sources. By doing this, the state will be better able to prepare for harsh weather conditions and lessen their effects. For instance, using historical data and current weather information, algorithms for machine learning can be used to forecast the frequency and severity of floods or heatwaves. By using this information, methods for early warning and evacuation can be created, lessening the damage that such occurrences do to people and property.

A range of ML (machine learning) and DL (deep learning) approaches can be utilized to forecast time series data in-depth. One of them is the well-known ARIMA [7,8]. The time series is modelled using a moving average, differencing, and autoregressive components. In order to model trends, seasonality, and holidays in time series data, Facebook developed the forecasting tool Prophet. A generalized additive model is utilized. Long-term dependencies can be learned by recurrent neural networks (RNNs) with LSTM. It is often used in forecasting time series. A form of neural network that is widely used for image recognition is the convolutional neural network (CNN). But, if the time series is viewed as a 1D image, they can also be employed with time series data. WaveNet is a deep neural network design that can produce natural-sounding voice waves. It can also be used to forecast time series by making predictions about the future values of the data. Non-parametric Bayesian regression analysis is done using Gaussian Process Regression (GPR). By calculating the posterior distribution over functions that match the observed data, it can be used to model time series data.

Using historical data from the Telangana state in India spanning five years, this project will anticipate the weather using machine and deep learning algorithms SARIMA and LSTM.

Literature Review

Predicting weather is a difficult undertaking because it is impacted by a number of factors including temperature, wind, rain, humidity, and so on. Current research on weather forecasting makes extensive use of deep learning and machine learning methods. Deep learning and machine learning are increasingly used in science thanks to advancements in technology. Table 36.1 summarises the Literature Review.

Proposed Work

The proposed endeavor focuses on developing weather prediction models for the Adilabad district of Telangana using machine learning and deep learning methodologies, and similar work has been done in other districts of Telangana. To forecast the weather, the research uses two separate algorithms, SARIMA and

Table 36.1 Comparative analysis of related work

[3]	**Techniques:** C4.5 for weather events classification. **Dataset:** LA weather history. **Remarks:** This research highlights the application of the C4.5 learning algorithm for forecasting the weather, which can accurately categorize various weather phenomena. The model classified climate attributes like temperature, humidity, visibility and wind speed. The author advises that the model could be adapted to more complicated weather events in the future and compared to other cutting-edge methodologies[3].
[6]	**Techniques:** Extreme Learning Machine, Artificial Neural Network. **Dataset:** North-western part of Bangladesh weather history. **Remarks:** This research focuses on the application of machine learning for forecasting the weather in Bangladesh's northwestern region, which is prone to natural disasters that cause loss of life and financial harm. The research examines past weather information from seven weather stations and discovers that the ELM model outperforms the ANN model with a 95% accuracy rate. The project intends to expand the factors evaluated beyond the four weather features utilized in the current experiment to cover all 64 districts in Bangladesh in the future [6].
[2]	**Techniques:** ARIMA, LSTM **Dataset:** Temperature history for the months of July and August in India **Remarks:** The research suggests using machine learning techniques, specifically LSTM, to reliably estimate temperature. The purpose is to assist farmers in making educated decisions in order to reduce losses through proactive methods. The paper investigates future research objectives in this subject, such as forecasting more factors in relation to environmental characteristics and addressing the underperformance of deep learning approaches on univariate time series forecasting [2].

[4]   **Techniques:**
CatBoost, XGBoost, Logistic Regression, Support Vector Classifier, RF, GNB, Perceptron, and KNN.

Dataset:
Australian Rainfall Dataset.

Remarks:
It emphasizes the relevance of machine learning in analyzing and forecasting the possibility of rainfall in various places, which can help with agricultural, evacuation, economic, and everyday rainwear decisions. This research concentrates on the variables that affect Australia's incidence of rainfall [4].

[5]   **Techniques:**
Support Vector Machine, Random Forest.

Dataset:
Weather history of several districts across Odisha.

Remarks:
The research addresses the development of an autonomous model for weather forecasting in the state of Odisha utilizing machine learning techniques such as Support Vector Machine and RF. The model was trained and tested using barometric parameters and the IMD dataset, and the findings showed that 5-day forecast achieved greater classification accuracy than 7-day prediction. Future work, according to the author, could involve applying newly identified machine learning algorithms and a larger dataset to increase the model's accuracy [5].

[1]   **Techniques:**
Auto Regressive Integrated Moving Average

Dataset:
Weather history of several districts across Uttarakhand

Remarks:
This research suggested the ARIMA time series model to anticipate the temperature of three Uttarakhand cities (Dehradun, Mukteshwar and Pantnagar). It emphasizes the significance of forecasting the weather as well as how machine learning methods may be utilized to reduce the computing overhead of the parameterization operation. The research shows how ARIMA may be used to anticipate temperature across three cities in Uttarakhand, India, with poor MAPE scores. The research adds that the research could be expanded in the future to forecast other qualities using multivariate data [1].

LSTM. The material for the research was obtained from the Telangana AI Mission (T-AIM) website, which provides historical meteorological data for the Telangana region of India. Several technologies are used in this research for data processing, analysis, and modeling. The Python programming language is used to create the models, and Jupyter Notebook is the development environment. The machine learning libraries utilized in the research are Scikit-learn and Statsmodels. The LSTM models are built and trained using Tensorflow, a prominent deep learning platform.

The first step in this research is to pre-process the weather dataset. The dataset includes weather metrics such as temperature, humidity, rainfall, and wind speed. The data is pre-processed to eliminate missing values, outliers, and other noise. The pre-processed data is then divided into training and testing groups.

After that, the SARIMA algorithm is used to create the first weather forecast model. Due to its precision and efficiency, SARIMA, a time-series forecasting method, is frequently employed in the sector. The SARIMA model is tested using the testing dataset after being trained on the preprocessed training dataset, and it also makes predictions for the future. MAE and RMSE are two measures employed to evaluate the effectiveness of the model.

The research employs the LSTM approach for constructing a weather forecasting model using deep learning. Time-series data's temporal dependencies can be accurately captured using the potent deep learning algorithm LSTM. The LSTM model is developed using pre-processed training data, assessed using testing data, and made to predict the future. Using the same metrics as the SARIMA model, the model's performance is likewise evaluated.

The research's findings demonstrate that both the SARIMA and LSTM models can predict the weather with accuracy. But in terms of accuracy and robustness, LSTM model performs better than SARIMA model. The ability of the LSTM model to detect long-term patterns within weather data makes it superior in predicting weather conditions.

The Telangana AI Mission (T-AIM) website provided the data needed for this research. The information includes weather data from the five most recent years, from 2018 to 2022, for all Telangana districts, including min and max temperatures, min and max humidity levels, min and max wind speeds, and rainfall amounts.

Machine learning algorithm **SARIMA** (univariate) and neural network algorithm **LSTM**(multivariate) is employed in this research. The Flow of SARIMA and LSTM is depicted in Figures 36.1 and 36.2.

The **SARIMA** technique is commonly utilized in forecasting time series data using statistical analysis. To simulate the trend, seasonality, and noise of a time series, ARIMA is combined with seasonal components. The formulation of the model can be expressed mathematically as:

$$y\_t = c + phi\_1y\_\{t-1\} + ... + phi\_py\_\{t-p\} - theta\_1e\_\{t-1\}$$
$$- ... - theta\_qe\_\{t-q\} + \text{seasonal components} + e\_t$$

where y t is the time series' value at time t, c is a constant, phi 1,...,phi p and theta 1,...,theta q are, respectively, the autoregressive and moving average coefficients, e t is the error at time t, and the seasonal components reflect the data's seasonal trend.

Methods like maximum likelihood estimation can be used to estimate the model parameters [9,10]. Once fitted, the model can be utilized to forecast future values of time series.

LSTMis a form of recurrent neural network that is often used for predicting time series data. It consists of three gates: input gate, forget gate, and output gate, and a cell statethat enables the retrieval of long-term dependencies by the network. Mathematical representation of the model is described below:

$$j\_n = sigma(A\_j * \quad r\_n = sigma(A\_r * \quad t\_n = sigma(A\_t *$$
$$[s\_\{n-1\},p\_n]+b\_j) \quad [s\_\{n-1\},p\_n]+b\_r) \quad [s\_\{n-1\},p\_n]+b\_t)$$
$$q\_n = tanh(A\_q * \quad s\_n=r\_n*s\_\{n-1\}+ \quad p\_n=t\_n*tanh(s\_n)$$
$$[s\_\{n-1\},p\_n]+b\_q) \quad j\_n*q\_n$$

Here, j_n, r_n, and t_n represent the input, forget, and output gates, respectively. q_n is the input modulation gate, s_n is the cell state at time n, p_n is the hidden

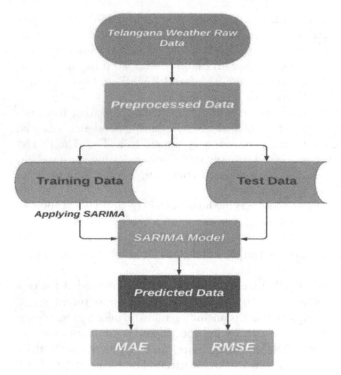

Figure 36.1 Flow chart of SARIMA model

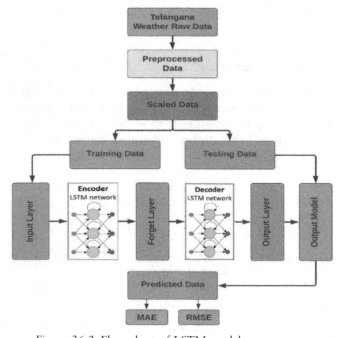

Figure 36.2 Flow chart of LSTM model

state at time n, and A_j, A_r, A_t, and A_q are the weight matrices, and b_j, b_r, b_t, and b_q are the bias terms. The LSTM model is trained on input-output sequences to learn the data patterns and generate accurate predictions. Once trained, the model can be used to forecast future time series values.

Results

The following sections explain the implementation and results of applying the machine learning algorithm 'SARIMA' and the deep learning algorithm 'LSTM' on several weather parameters in Adilabad district of Telangana:

Seasonal Auto Regressive Integrated Moving Average (SARIMA)
The Adilabad district of Telangana's min and max temperatures, min and max humidity levels, min and max wind speeds, and rainfall volumes are all anticipated in this research using the machine learning method SARIMA. Data is first preprocessed before being resampled from day to month.

Using the seasonal decompose function, which displays a seasonality, trend, and residual pattern that is presented in the following images, we may determine whether the data is seasonal.

We can infer from the aforementioned that the data is seasonal. Every year, there is an increase in min and max temperature, min and max humidity, min and max wind speed, and rain, which continues from 2018 to 2022. When building a model, it is necessary to test for seasonality in the data. Now, to determine whether the data is stationary, the "Augmented Dickey-Fuller Test" is applied.

The data set is split into training and testing data in the following stage, with the training data used to develop the model and the test data set used to make predictions. Following the projection, a 12-month range of future dates is produced for forecasting future weather.

The data for training, testing and future forecast for all weather variables is presented in figures 36.3-36.16 and Table 36.2

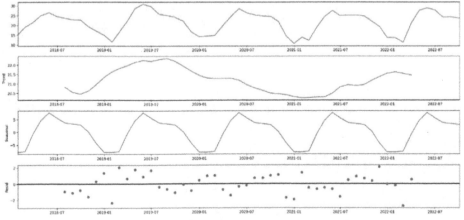

Figure 36.3 Seasonal pattern of minimum temperature of Adilabaddistrict from 2018 to 2022

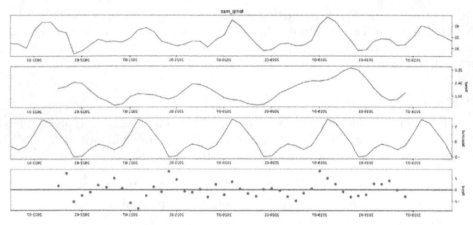

Figure 36.4 Seasonal pattern of maximum temperature of Adilabad district from 2018 to 2022

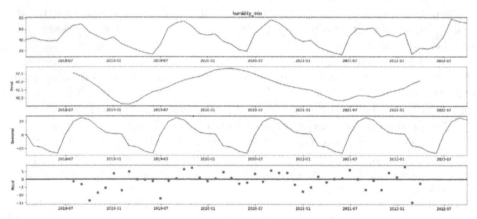

Figure 36.5 Seasonal pattern of minimum humidity of Adilabaddistrict from 2018 to 2022

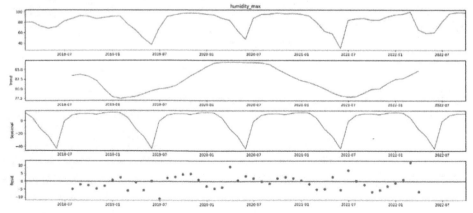

Figure 36.6 Seasonal pattern of maximum humidity of Adilabaddistrict from 2018 to 2022

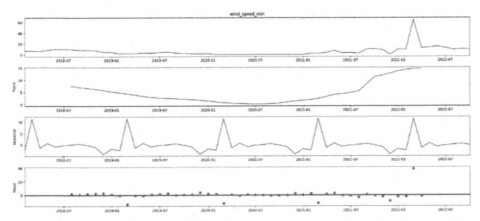

Figure 36.7 Seasonal pattern of minimum windspeed of Adilabaddistrict from 2018 to 2022

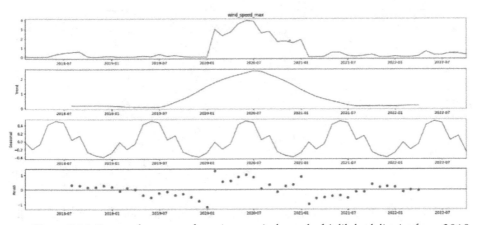

Figure 36.8 Seasonal pattern of maximum wind speed of Adilabad district from 2018 to 2022

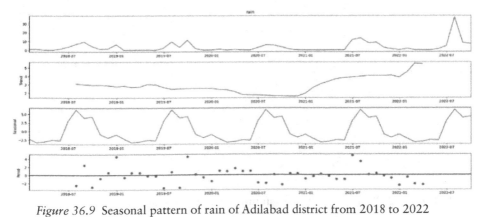

Figure 36.9 Seasonal pattern of rain of Adilabad district from 2018 to 2022

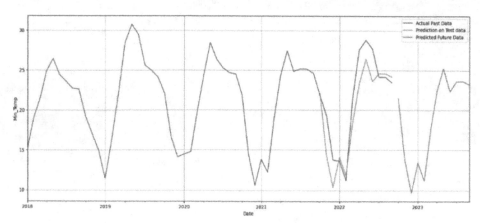

Figure 36.10 Actual vs Predicted vs Future forecast of minimum temperature of Adilabad

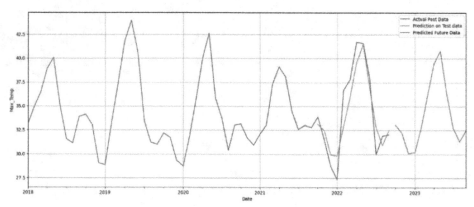

Figure 36.11 Actual vs Predicted vs Future forecast of maximum temperature of Adilabad

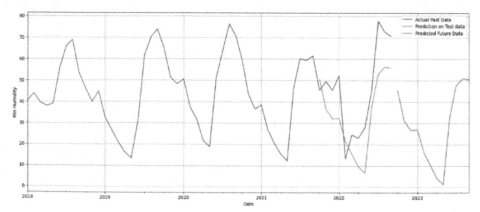

Figure 36.12 Actual vs Predicted vsfuture forecast of minimumhumidity of Adilabad

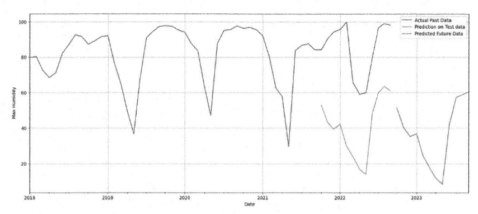

Figure 36.13 Actual vs Predicted vs Future forecast of maximum temperature of Adilabad

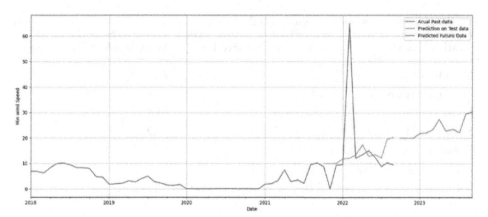

Figure 36.14 Actual vs Predicted vsfuture forecast of minimum wind speed of Adilabad

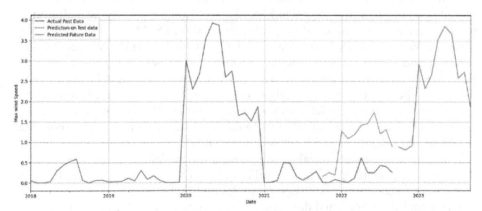

Figure 36.15 Actual vs Predicted vs Future forecast of maximum wind speed of Adilabad

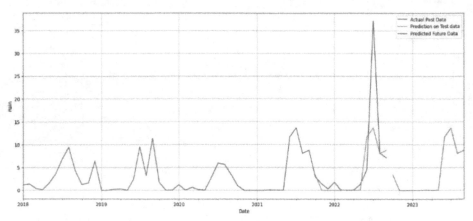

Figure 36.16 Actual vs Predicted vs Future forecast of rain of Adilabad

Table 36.2 Performance of the used model (SARIMA)

Weather Factors	Root Mean Squared Error	Mean Absolute Error
Minimum Temperature	2.71	2.09
Maximum Temperature	1.85	1.54
Minimum Humidity	15.09	13.97
Maximum Humidity	45.25	43.96
Minimum Wind Speed	16.15	8.23
Maximum Wind Speed	0.92	0.81
Rain	7.14	3.14

Long Short-Term Memory (LSTM)

The Adilabad district of Telangana's min and max temperatures, min and max humidity levels, min and max wind speeds, and rainfall volumes are all anticipated in this research using the deep learning method LSTM.

Data is prepossessed first for this model, then scaled using the Standard scaler function and separated into feature and target variables. This model employs three layers of neurons: the input layer (64 neurons), the hidden layer (10 neurons), and the output layer (1 neuron). The output layer activation function 'linear' is utilized, as is the model optimizer 'Adam 'combined with the 'mean squared error' loss function and a learning rate of 0.01%, is used. One year of future data is anticipated using the last 550 days of past data.

The feature and target variables are utilized for model fitting along with callbacks for EarlyStopping, ReduceLROnPlateau, and ModelCheckpoint. Validation split is set to 0.2, Verbose to 1, Epochs to 30, and Batch Size to 256.

The actual data, predicted data and future forecast for all weather variables is presented in Figures 36.17-36.23 and Table 36.3

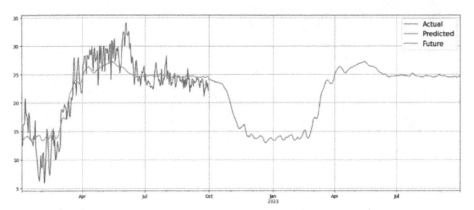

Figure 36.17 Actual vs Predicted vs Future forecast of minimum temperature of Adilabad

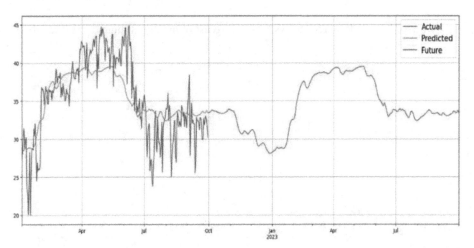

Figure 36.18 Actual vs Predicted vs Future forecast of maximum temperature of Adilabad

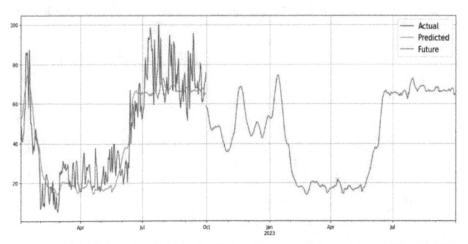

Figure 36.19 Actual vs Predicted vsFuture forecast of minimum humidity of Adilabad

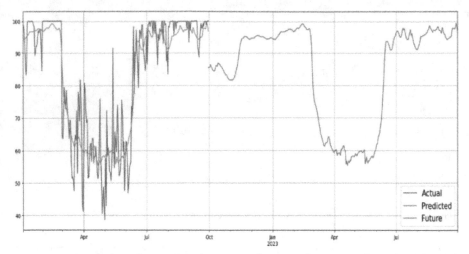

Figure 36.20 Actual vs Predicted vs Future forecast of maximum humidity of Adilabad

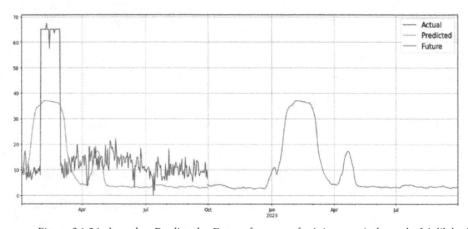

Figure 36.21 Actual vs Predicted vsFuture forecast of minimum wind speed of Adilabad

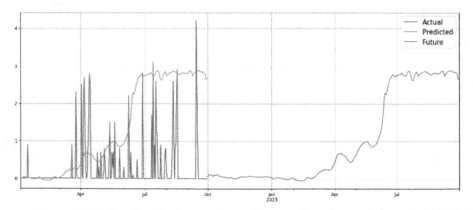

Figure 36.22 Actual vs Predicted vs Future forecast of maximumwind speed of Adilabad

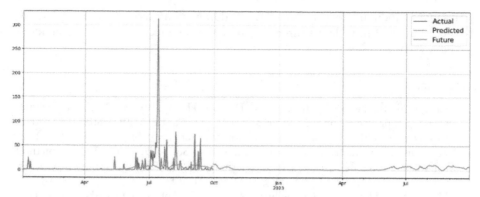

Figure 36.23 Actual vs Predicted vs Future forecast of rain of Adilabad

Table 36.3 Performance of the used model (LSTM)

Weather Factors	Root Mean Squared Error	Mean Absolute Error
Minimum Temperature	2.75	2.10
Maximum Temperature	3.43	2.63
Minimum Humidity	11.23	8.79
Maximum Humidity	7.16	5.16
Minimum Wind Speed	13.22	10.45
Maximum Wind Speed	1.70	1.24
Rain	25.19	7.38

From Tables 36.2 and 36.3 above, it appears that LSTM (day wise) predicts more accurately than SARIMA (month wise). The RMSE and MAE for LSTM (day-wise) are less than SARIMA (month wise) for almost all weather-related parameters. Because of its capacity to learn long-term dependencies in time-series data, LSTM is a good model for weather forecasting, whereas SARIMA is a traditional time-series model that has been used for decades. The superior accuracy of LSTM in predicting weather has been proved in a variety of weather-related factors including temperature, humidity, wind speed, and rainfall.

Conclusion

By enhancing accuracy, efficiency, and the capacity to recognize and understand complex patterns in meteorological data, machine and deep learning have the ability to significantly improve weather prediction. The adoption of these technologies could improve society's preparedness for and response to extreme weather disasters. The aim of our research is to make predictions about the weather patterns of Telangana state. To achieve this, we have employed two different techniques: SARIMA for predicting monthly weather factors and LSTM for predicting daily weather factors. The future focus of this research would be to enhance the models' accuracy by modifying their parameters or adding additional data sources, as well as integrating real-time data sources to provide more precise forecasts depending on the present weather.

References

1. Pant, J., Sharma, R. K., Juyal, A., Singh, D., Pant, H., and Pant, P. (2022). A machine-learning approach to time seriesforecasting of temperature. In 2022 6th International Conference on Electronics, Communication and Aerospace Technology (ICECA).
2. Prathyusha, Zakiya, Savya, Tejaswi, Alex, N., and Sobin, Dr. C. C. (2021). Amethod for weather forecasting using machine learning. In 2021 5th Conference on Information and Communication Technology, CICT 2021 (2021).
3. Hasan, N., Uddin, T., and Chowdhury, N. K. (2017). Automated weather eventanalysis with machine learning. In 2016 InternationalConference on Innovations in Science, Engineering and Technology, ICISET 2016.
4. Mahadware, A., Saigiridhari, A., Mishra, A., Tupe, A., and Marathe, N. (2022). Rainfall prediction using different machinelearning and deep learning algorithms. In 2022 2nd Asian Conference on Innovation in Technology (ASIANCON) Pune, India. Aug 26–28, 2022.
5. Sahu, P., Mohapatra, S. K., and Sarangi, P. K. (2022). Forecasting of statistical crisp weather in India byexploration of different machine learning techniques. In 2022 2nd International Conference on Advance Computing and Innovative Technologies in Engineering (ICACITE).
6. Rizvee, M. A., Arju, A. R., Al-Hasan, M., Tareque, S. M., and Hasan, M. Z. (2020). Weather forecasting for the north-western region of bangladesh: amachine learning approach. In 2020 11th International Conference on Computing, Communication and Networking Technologies, ICCCNT 2020.
7. Raimundo, F., Gloria, A., and Sebastiao, P. (2021). Prediction of weather forecast for smart agriculture supported by machine learning. 2021 IEEE World AI IoT Congress, AI IoT 2021.
8. Shaji, A., Amritha, A.R., and Rajalakshmi, V.R. (2022). Weather prediction usingmachine learning algorithms. In 2022 International Conference on Intelligent Controller and Computing for Smart Power (ICICCSP).
9. Hong, K. W., and Kang, T. (2021). Astudy on rainfall prediction based on meteorological time series. In International Conference onUbiquitous and Future Networks, ICUFN (2021).
10. Chaudhary, H., Mishra, U., Gupta, A., and Singh, A. (2022). Comparative analysis of rainfall prediction using machinelearning and deep learning techniques. In 2022 3rd International Conference on Issues and Challenges in Intelligent Computing Techniques (ICICT).

37 Customer segmentation basedon RFM analysis and product association rules for e-commerce

Shalabh Dwivedi[a] and Amritpal Singh[b]

Department of Computer Science and Engineering, Lovely Professional University, Jalandhar, Punjab, India

Abstract

This study presents a customer segmentation approach based on weighted k-means used in RFM analysis to segment customers for e-commerce businesses. The objective is to find valuable customer categories and buying habits so businesses may tailor their marketing strategies and increase customer loyalty. The proposed method applies RFM weighted k-means, where weight is the average order value (AOV) for each customer to segment customers with high purchasing power. Next, association rules were applied to discover the relationship between the products that our valuable customers have purchased. The results show the use of the proposed technique in recognizing valuable customer segments which can help e-commerce businesses improve their target marketing efforts and customer satisfaction.

Keywords: Apriori, clustering, customer segmentation, k-means, RFM analysis

Introduction

A customer is an individual or entity involved in buying a product or service from the business. The success of any business essentially depends on its customer, as they are the ones that generate revenue for them. Thus, a healthy relationship with the customers is very crucial. With the development of new technology and a competitive market, customers are now more vigilant than ever. They have access to a wide range of information to compare products and services from multiple businesses. On the other hand, businesses can gather and analyze enormous volumes of customer data with the advent of new technologies[1]. A proper understanding of customer behavior is thus an essential component of marketing campaigns. Thus, customers' demands and preferences should be considered while developing new products or conducting marketing campaigns.

Customer segmentation is an important strategy used by businesses to enhance their marketing and sales operations. It is the technique of breaking down a customer base into different smaller groups based on their similarities. With a better understanding of customers, businesses can target particular customer groups with their newly launched products, services, and promotional strategies. It becomes very critical in situations prevailing currently of economic downturn. Marketing in such cases is not simple, as customer spending is decreased and are less indulgent in buying new products. For customer segmentation marketing specialists

[a]shalabhdwivedi007@gmail.com, [b]apsaggu@live.com

have been using the RFM (Recency Frequency Monetary) concepts to forecast later customer behavior based on their prior purchase history [2]. Customers are analyzed and scored using their most recent acquisition behavior (recency), the count of their transactions, and the sum of transactions amount (monetary value) done. It helps businesses in prioritizing their marketing and customer interaction initiatives based on important data insights.

To make their customers feel better by providing customized goods and services, businesses must give importance to customer segmentation. K-means and Apriori are two popular methods used in customer segmentation. In k-means, customers are segmented based on their shared characteristics, which include their demographic data and shopping patterns. With the motive of having small and different groups involving customers, the algorithm divides customers into k groups. To do this algorithm flows an iterative approach of assigning customers to clusters and changing the cluster centers till the process converges [3]. The Apriori algorithm finds a group of products that commonly appear together in transactions, which is utilized in association rule mining of products. This identifies correlations between products that can be used to create customer groups. In short, this study aims to segment retail customers based on the RFM scores and average order value and generate frequent products used by customers in each segment generated through clustering. This would enable the businesses to identify customers who pay more per order and also to create tailored marketing and retention tactics based on each group's specific behavior. Any industry such as banking, healthcare, telecommunication, airlines, etc. with transactional data and wanting to segment their customer can utilize this approach. The following five sections comprise this study. Section-2 surveys the existing literature. Section-3 describes the research approach followed. Section-4 describes the empirical results. Section-5 summarizes the study.

Literature Review

With the exponential rise in advanced technology, businesses now are growing and changing at an incredible rate. To sustain in this competitive market and boost revenue, they need to adapt to new technology to organize their process. The ability to make decisions quickly and accurately is one of the major problems faced by today's businesses. However, recent developments in the field of computer science have enabled us to make data-driven decisions based on the enormous amount of customer data. This would help in increase in revenue, better customer satisfaction, and long-term growth for the business. The three important parameters of recency, frequency, and monetary value are used by businesses to rank each customer in the RFM formula based on consumer purchase data. The recency score calculates the duration in days between the customer's most recent transaction date concerning the analysis date. A score based on a predetermined scale i.e., from 1 to 5, where 1 is the lowest and 5 is the highest score assigned after the business determines the customer's most recent transaction. A higher score is assigned to transactions with the most recent purchase. Frequency is the number of transactions customers do in a given time frame. Similarly score from 1 to 5 is applied after calculating recency but a higher score is assigned to a customer with the greatest number of transactions and so on. The monetary value is the sum of the customer's transaction. Like the above two parameters, a scale from 1 to 5 is used to assign a score. The score for monetary value increases as spending increases. After having composite RFM scores based on each of the three parameters, every customer can be segmented into one of the low, medium, and high-valued groups. This would help to make smart decisions and priorities marketing initiatives. The RFM score is calculated as follows:

$$RFM\ Score = rs * r(w) + fs * f(w) + ms * m(w) \tag{1}$$

where rs is the recency score, r(w) is the recency weight, fs is the frequency score, f(w) is frequency weight, ms is the monetary score, and m(w) is monetary weight. By default, rs is given the highest preference when calculating the score, followed by fs and then ms. CLV (Customer Lifetime Value) is one of the several methods that business use. It is the total amount of money a customer is likely to spend with the business or on products over the course of a typical business relationship. It is an extremely helpful strategy to retain high-value customers. To calculate CLV, three important parameters are considered. Firstly, the mean purchase value is the total amount spent by the customer on each purchas. Secondly, the recurring purchase is the frequency of the purchase. Lastly, the mean customer lifespan is the time length a customer stays a customer for the business. The following formula shows the use of three variables for CLV calculation:

$$CLV = Mean\ Purchase\ Value * Recurring\ Purchases * \atop Mean\ Customer\ Lifetime \tag{2}$$

Firdaus and Utama[4] developed an RFM+B model, where customer balance (B) is a crucial parameter for banking customer grouping based on k-means. Also, the results show k-means is a successful strategy to implement customer segmentation. Xiao[5] presented a novel technique for categorizing customers based on a combined GBDT and MLP algorithm. The proposed strategy manages the limitation of the use of RFM and k-means on high-dimensional data, also it yields better accuracy as compared to other previous models.

For understanding, electricity consumption habits RahmadhanandWasesa[6] have applied a hybrid approach that combines k-means, CLV, and AHP (Analytic Hierarchy Process). At first, segments identified by k-means and then AHP and CLV concept was used to assess and validate the findings on real-world electricity data of customers. Another study by Li et al.[7] proposed a novel approach depending on RFM-weighted k-means. In this, every index of the e-commerce customer RFM was weighted based on the AHP approach. The result demonstrates that the proposed strategy yields a better segment result and that there is a greater difference in customer segmentation.

Abidar et al.[8] have proposed a CS model based on CLV and RFM. The study categorizes customers into nine groups based on the intersection of CLV and RFM clusters. The author also recommended actions to engage customers based on their similar characteristics. Ibrahim andTyasnurita[9] used the elbow method for determining the optimal number of clusters after applying both techniques of the LRFMS (Length Recency Frequency and Monetary) method and k-means. The CLV for every cluster was created by multiplying the LRFM value for each customer with the previously determined weights using the Analytical Hierarchy Process (AHP) approach. For evaluating clustering results, several recent studies Shirole et al. [10]show the use of the Silhouette coefficient, Davies-Bouldin index, etc. TaghiLivariandZarrinGhalam[11] for B2B setting customer segmentation of a food production firm finds three customers group based on Davies-Bouldin and the k-means method. After clustering, CLV for each cluster was calculated with their relevant marketing tactics.

Data and Variables

This study uses the publicly available E-Commerce transaction data based on actual customer transactions for historical analysis from UCI ML Repository. It is available as an Online Retail dataset and contains customer transactions for the period of one year from Dec 2010 to Dec 2011. The company primarily offers unique gifts for every occasion. The dataset contains 5,41,909 customer records with 8 attributes. The large dataset is useful for training machine learning models for better accurate predictions and improved performance. The following Table 37.1 gives attribute information for the Online retail dataset.

Methodology

Due to tremendous growth experienced by the online retail sector, the number of customers and transactions hasincreased by many folds. To properly segment customers in order to offer personalized service and raise customer satisfaction, though is a difficulty that comes along with this increase. Using AOV (Average Order Value) as the weight for the k-means cluster model, this study's goal is to identify customers who not only make frequent purchases but also pay more per order. Also, identifying items frequently purchased by this segment using association rule mining. Following Figure 37.1 shows the proposed methodology for this study.

Table 37.1 Attribute information

S. No.	Attribute Name	Attribute Description
1	InvoiceNo	A unique 6-digit number is assigned for each transaction
2	StockCode	Uniquely assigned product code to every unique product
3	Description	Name of the product purchased by the customer
4	Quantity	The total number of products ordered on a single transaction
5	InvoiceDate	Date and Time of every product purchased by the customer
6	UnitPrice	Unit product price in Euros
7	CustomerID	A unique 5-digit number allotted to each customer
8	Country	Nation name where each customer resides

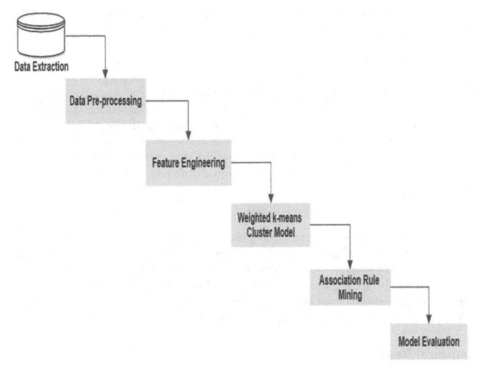

Figure 37.1 Proposed methodology

Data Pre-Processing
Cleaning and preprocessing of the data were carried out using R programming language. All redundant entries, missing entries, and outliers were removed. Entries having Unit Price and Quantity less than 1 were removed. Entries with Invoice No starting with 'C' were removed, which shows canceled order transactions.

Feature Engineering
This study selected the following features for clustering: InvoiceNo, Quantity, UnitPrice, and CustomerID for RFM scoring and AOV-based customer segmentation.

Weighted k-means Cluster Model
This study used weighted k-means clustering to group customers based on the chosen features' similarities. After calculating RFM scores and Average Order Value for each customer. A new weighted column was assigned such that.

$$Weight = AOV * RFM\ score \tag{3}$$

for each customer. AOV is a measurement that shows how much money customers typically spend on each purchase. It is computed by dividing the sum of revenue from orders by the total number of orders. This helps to group customers with similar behavioral and financial traits. The Silhouette method was used to determine the optimal number of clusters for customer segmentation.

Association Rule Mining
It is used to find patterns in customer purchase behavior. The output of clustering results would be used to identify product patterns using the Apriori algorithm. Again, the Description column was added after clustering for product association rule mining. The connections between various features and discovered patterns that can be applied to forecast customer behavior were examined. Support and confidence are two key factors used to assess the strength of a given association rule. The effectiveness of the rule is measured as lift which is the ratio of confidence to support.

Model Evaluation
Model performance was evaluated using the silhouette score which is a frequently used metric that is used to evaluate the quality of clustering outcomes. In relation to the adjacent clusters, it measures the cohesion of the data points in the cluster to which it has been assigned. Its ranges from -1 to 1, with a higher score indicating better clustering results. The efficiency of the association rules is measured based on their support, confidence, and lift value.

Empirical Results

According to the findings of our model, transaction data from the e-commerce website was taken from December 2010 to December 2011. After pre-processing, the data comprises four features as mentioned above for the RFM model. A total of 4190 customers were obtained as a grouping based on CustomerID was performed. When the data was prepared, the RFM model still contained some skewness, which called for further modification to lessen the skewness of the data. Since both frequency and monetary values were positively skewed with values of 13.36 and 17.57 respectively, the log transformation was used to reduce their skewness. For recency, since it's a measure of time, a square root transformation was used to reduce its skewness of 1.24. Figure 37.2 shows the recency, frequency, and monetary value distribution after removing skewness.

After removing skewness, the next thing was to apply weighted k-means clustering based on AOV as weight. To find an optimal number of clusters, this study used Silhouette width to get the result. Figure 37.3 shows the relation between silhouette width and the number of clusters. Clearly, 7 clusters give the highest silhouette width. Therefore, k=7 is taken for the weighted k-means model.

Based on the weighted k-means result the silhouette score of clusters was found as 0.79, which is a decent score as it is closer to 1. The result shows that 1,683 customers grouped in cluster number 3 are our valuable customers with more spending per order. The following Figure 37.4 shows the width of each cluster and their average silhouette width.

Based on the clustering results, our high-valued customers are grouped in cluster number 3 having a large proportion of customers after pre-processing.

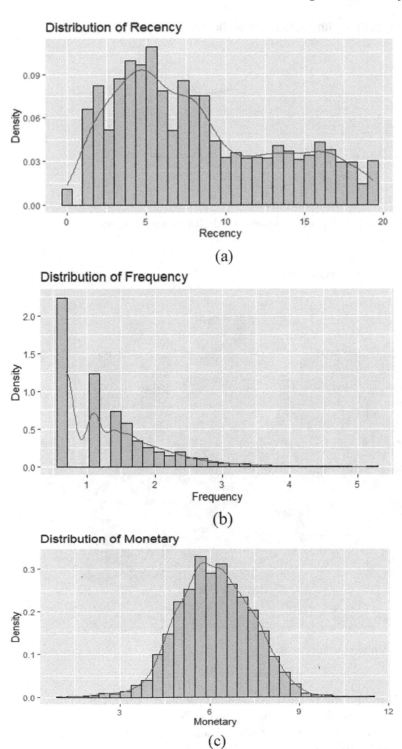

Figure 37.2 Distribution of RFM model (a), (b), and (c) after removing skewness

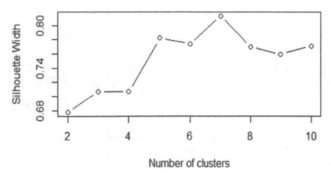

Figure 37.3 Relation between silhouette width and number of clusters

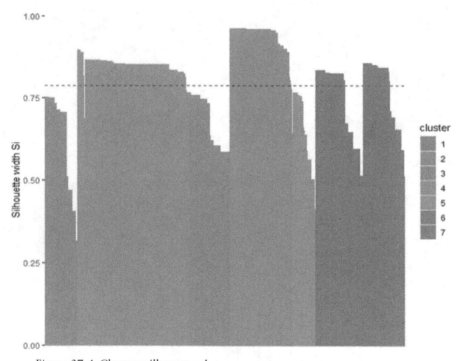

Figure 37.4 Clusters silhouette plot

The last step is to find the frequent patterns of products purchased by our valuable customers i.e., for cluster 3. The pre-processing was applied again to split our high-valued customers and then remove leading and trailing spaces from the products description column. Finally, the Apriori algorithm was applied to generate a list of products purchased by these customers frequently.

lhs		rhs	support	confidence	coverage	lift	count
[1] {GLASS APOTHECARY BOTTLE ELIXIR}	=>	{GLASS APOTHECARY BOTTLE TONIC}	0.03386809	0.7702703	0.04396910	14.56590	57
[2] {GLASS APOTHECARY BOTTLE ELIXIR}	=>	{GLASS APOTHECARY BOTTLE PERFUME}	0.03446227	0.7837838	0.04396910	13.74071	58
[3] {CHILDRENS CUTLERY CIRCUS PARADE}	=>	{CHILDRENS CUTLERY DOLLY GIRL}	0.03089721	0.7878788	0.03921569	12.27778	52
[4] {COFFEE MUG PEARS DESIGN}	=>	{COFFEE MUG APPLES DESIGN}	0.03446227	0.9508197	0.03624480	19.51499	58
[5] {COFFEE MUG APPLES DESIGN}	=>	{COFFEE MUG PEARS DESIGN}	0.03446227	0.7073171	0.04872252	19.51499	58
[6] {CLASSIC BICYCLE CLIPS}	=>	{BICYCLE PUNCTURE REPAIR KIT}	0.03149138	0.7464789	0.04218657	14.78028	53

Figure 37.5 Apriori results for valuable customers based on weighted k-means clustering

In Figure 37.5, the Apriori results for the basket are displayed for supp=0.03 with a rule length of 2. Here, LHS is antecedent and RHS is its consequent. To increase customer loyalty and promote repeat purchases, businesses can send personalized emails with targeted discounts and offers based on the spending habits and preferences of these high-spending customers. The results could give business owners and marketers insightful information that will help them create more profitable marketing plans.

Conclusion

This study examines the application of clustering techniques and frequent pattern analysis for e-commerce. As most of today's businesses are looking to increase their market share by maintaining an online presence, a data-driven approach for customer segmentation based on RFM analysis is the need of the hour. To capture purchasing behavior of customers, the average order value is used as the weight for clustering based on k-means. By using it as weight, the clustering considers the relative significance of each customer's spending habits in determining the similarity between them. The result of frequently purchased products from our potential customers is an essential component that could be used for marketing management. The proposed methodology provides an effective strategy for customer segmentation in the online retail sector which can be used to boost customer loyalty, increase sales and improve customer satisfaction. Future work could include additional features that will provide extra insight into customer behavior.

References

1. Rizki, B., Ginasta, N. G., Tamrin, M. A., and Rahman, A. (2020). Customer loyality segmentation on point of sale system using recency-frequency-monetary (RFM) and K-means.*Jurnal Online Informatika*, 5(2), 130.
2. Dogan, O., Oztaysi, B., and Isik, A. (2021). Fuzzy RFM analysis in car rental sector. *International Journal of Technology and Engineering Studies*, 7(2), 8–14.
3. Christy, A. J., Umamakeswari, A., Priyatharsini, L., andNeyaa, A. (2021). RFM ranking – An effective approach to customer segmentation. *Journal of King Saud University - Computer and Information Sciences*, 33(10), 1251–1257.

4. Firdaus, U., and Utama, D. N. (2021). Development of bank's customer segmentation model based on rfm+b approach. *ICIC Express Letters, Part B: Applications*, 12(1), 17–26.

5. Xiao, Y. (2022). Hybrid model for customer segmentation based on RFM framework.In 7th International Conference on Intelligent Computing and Signal Processing, ICSP 2022, (pp. 720–723).

6. Rahmadhan, R., andWasesa, M. (2022). Segmentation using customers lifetime value: hybrid K-means clustering and analytic hierarchy process. *Journal of Information Systems Engineering and Business Intelligence*, 8(2), 130–141.

7. Li, P., Wang, C., Wu, J., andMadlenak, R. (2022). An E-commerce customer segmentation method based on RFM weighted K-means. In Proceedings - 2022 International Conference on Management Engineering, Software Engineering and Service Sciences, ICMSS 2022, (pp. 61–68).

8. Abidar, L., Asri, I. ElZaidouni, D., andEnnouaary, A. (2022). A data mining system for enhancing profit growth based on RFM and CLV.In Proceedings - 2022 International Conference on Future Internet of Things and Cloud, FiCloud 2022, (pp. 247–253).

9. Ibrahim, M. R. K., andTyasnurita, R. (2022). LRFM model analysis for customer segmentation usingk-means Clustering.In Proceedings - IEIT 2022: 2022 International Conference on Electrical and Information Technology, (pp. 383–391).

10. Shirole, R., Salokhe, L., andJadhav, S. (2021). Customer segmentation using RFM model and k-means clustering.*International Journal of Scientific Research in Science and Technology*, 8, 591–597.

11. TaghiLivari, R., andZarrinGhalam, N. (2020).Customers grouping using data mining techniques in the food distribution industry (a case study).*SRPH Journal of Applied Management and Agile Organisation*, 3(1), 1–8.

38 Face recognition based attendance system using python

Jainendra Kumar[a], Aditya Pusp[b], Mohd Sahbaaz[c] and Amanjot Kaur[d]

School of Computer Application Lovely Professional University, Jalandhar, Punjab, India

Abstract

The primary objective of this project is to develop an attendance system based on face recognition technology. This system aims to replace the current method and achieve a much higher level of effectiveness than before. The current attendance system is not sufficient to make take attendance accurately. Numerous issues can arise during attendance calls, including the submission of proxy attendance by students on behalf of their absent peers. In such cases, teachers are required to retake attendance, resulting in further time wastage. Given that a standard class session lasts for aroundfifty minutes, the attendance registration process can around five to ten minutes, which poses a considerable time management challenge during lectures. The old attendance system is time-consuming. The technology employed in this project is a facial recognition system, which uses the unique features of each student's face as a means of identification. This method is highly reliable, as the likelihood of two faces being identical or significantly similar is very low. To implement this system, a database of facial data will be created for each student at the time of admission. During attendance-taking sessions, the system will compare students' faces to their respective datasets. Once a match is identified, the student's attendance will be automatically recorded, and an Excel sheet will be generated to list the names of both identified and unidentified students. At the end of each day, the attendance information will be securely stored in the system's database.

Keywords: facerecognition, harrcascade, LBPH recognize, openCV, python

Introduction

The attendance monitoring is very important process for any educational institution. Individuals who have experienced the era of utilizing attendance registers in classes are well aware of the ease with which such a system could be manipulated, leading to the falsification of attendance records for one another. One effective way to reduce the burden on staff and improve compliance with attendance regulations is by eliminating manual processes. While complying with attendance regulations can be challenging, a face recognition-based attendance system can be incredibly useful in ensuring that attendance is accurately documented. With technological advancements in this field, a face recognition-based attendance system has been developed, revolutionizing the way attendance is tracked. Today, there are two types of attendance systems available: manual and biometric, the

[a]jainendrakumar823232@gmail.com, [b]adityapusp1@gmail.com, [c]sa3778962@gmail.com, [d]amanjotkaur184@yahoo.com

attendance sheet is the most commonly used method for taking attendance today. Python and OpenCV (Open-source computer vision library) were utilized to create the system, which aims to perform face recognition to identify students. The primary goal of this project is to enhance the quality of education by promoting regular attendance in classes.The attendance system is quite useful for parents and teachers at colleges and universities. If the institution uses a face recognition-based attendance system, parents are never informed of their kids' dependability in the class. The attendees could simply manipulate the register, and if emails were sent to parents and staff, there was a good risk they wouldn't reach them in time. Printing the material is simple, and parents can also receive a soft copy of it in their personal email accounts. Traditionally, students have been motivated to attend classes by earning attendance points, which are factored into their final grades at the end of the semester. However, this approach has placed an additional burden on teachers, who must accurately record attendance for each student, taking valuable time away from the teaching process. Moreover, the task becomes even more complex when dealing with large groups of students.

Literature Review

The development of the attendance monitoring system has transformed the process of recording attendance, resulting in increased efficiency for both teachers and students.[Ajinkya Patil, Mrudang Shukla, ISSN: 22311963]This approach removes traditional methods of student identification, like verbal name calls or physical presentation of ID cards. These methods can often disrupt the flow of teaching and create unnecessary stress for students, particularly during exams. With this system, such issues can be avoided altogether. [Muhammad Fuzail1, Hafiz Muhammad Fahad Nouman, ISSN: 2045-7057]The web camera of a laptop is used tocapture the image Every student's face is saved in a database. When a student's facial image is captured, it is then matched against the image stored in their respective database.When the system verifies the image against the database, it records the student's attendance as present. Then, at the end of each month, the system automatically sends a report of the student's attendance to their email address.[P. Kowsalya1, J. Pavithra2e-ISSN: 2395-0056].The existing system for taking attendance is inefficient and time-consuming. Based on an estimate of approximately 1 minute for a single student to sign their attendance on aattendance list, So it took around 60 students can sign their attendance in an hour. This highlights the need for a more efficient and streamlined method of taking attendance to save time and resources. [Dr. V Suresh, SrinivasaChakravarthiDumpa*ISSN:2321-3795*]. The proposed system has successfully implemented a Face mask detection and attendance system, and we have detected that our system has a very easy and minimal interface for better interaction. our database is optimal and can successfully hold a very large amount of data efficiently. [Jain Darsh Naresh Kumar 1, Upadhyay Ankita Ramesh 2, p-ISSN: 2395-0072]. The ability to recognize faces is a powerful tool, even when faced with changes in appearance such as aging, interruptions like wearing glasses or growing a beard, or alterations in hairstyle. A face recognition system that uses numerical and computational methods can quickly and efficiently mark attendance by identifying individuals through a camera. This system is designed to handle large amounts of data in a speedy and efficient manner, reducing the amount of effort and time required for attendance calculation. [PernishShukla, RonikaShrestha]. The project relies on machine learning techniques, specifically OpenCV and Tensorflow, to classify and identify the presence of face masks on individuals.[NookalaVenu1, Krishnaveni A2, ISSN 2456 – 5083]. Maintaining accurate attendance records is crucial in educational institutions to ensure the quality of education. In many schools and universities, students' attendance is typically tracked through attendance sheets or notes provided by the relevant department.[Naman Gupta, Purushottam Sharma, 978-1-7281-7016-9/20/$31.00 ©2020 IEEE].

Methodology

Python is a versatile programming language that offers numerous advantages, including a user-friendly syntax. Originally designed for automating system administration tasks, Python has become a popular choice for various applications. One of the major advantages of Python is its ability to handle image processing, thanks to the availability of numerous frameworks, packages, and modules. For instance, integrating open computer vision into an attendance system can significantly enhance its accuracy and reliability, making it a compelling idea.

Proposed System
Development of the Student Dataset
Activating the camera
Capture footage of the current class
Face detection and feature extraction
Matched
Capture attendance and mailing

The Face recognition attendance tracking system uses Python and machine learning to automatically capture attendance data through facial recognition technology. It uses learning models and computer vision techniques to identify unique facial features and match them to attendance records. This data is stored securely in a MySQL database, allowing authorized personnel to access and analyze attendance patterns. The solution is highly efficient, easy to integrate, and customizable to meet unique requirements. By adopting this innovative system, schools and universities can streamline attendance management processes, reduce administrative overheads, and enhance the learning experience. Figure 38.1

LBPH
LBPH, which stands for Local Binary Patterns Histograms, is a technique used in face recognition that extracts local features from an image to represent a face. This type of feature descriptor is frequently used in computer vision applications. The LBPH algorithm involves dividing a facial image into smaller regions and comparing the intensity values of the pixels in each region to a preset threshold value. These comparisons generate a binary code for each pixel, which are then combined to form a binary pattern for the region. Figure 38.2

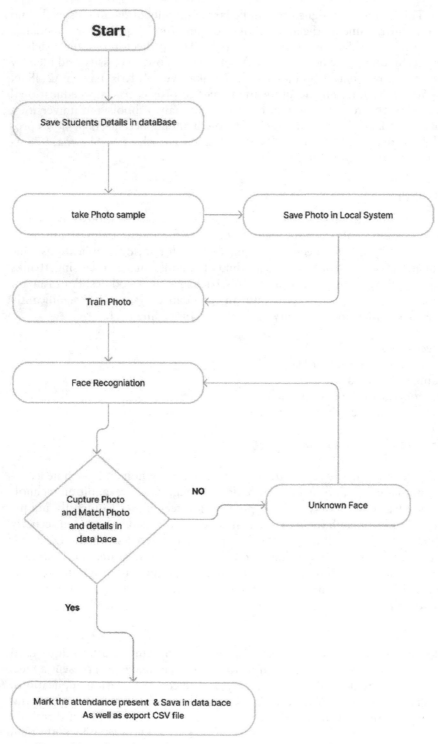

Figure 38.1 Flow chart of Face Recognition Based Attendance System

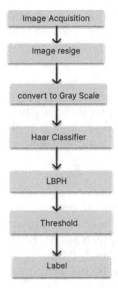

Figure 38.2 Phases of Face Recognition Based Attendance System

HAAR CASCADE

HAAR Cascade is an object detection algorithm used for face detection in computer vision applications, and it is based on machine learning techniques. The algorithm involves training a cascade classifier on a dataset of positive and negative facial images. To detect faces using the Haar Cascade technique, the algorithm applies a set of Haar-like features to an image to identify areas of interest that potentially contain a face.

OpenCV

OpenCV, which stands for Open-Source Computer Vision Library, is a widely-used open-source software library for computer vision and machine learning. It is utilized for developing various applications related to computer vision, as well as for image and video processing, and the creation of machine learning models. OpenCV offers a broad range of functions and algorithms that enable tasks such as feature detection, image processing, object detection, tracking, and more.

PyMysql

PyMySQL is a Python library that facilitates communication between Python programs and MySQL servers. It enables the execution of SQL statements and the management of database connections. PyMySQL is compatible with both Python 2.7 and Python 3.x and supports most of the features that are offered by MySQL, such as cursors, transactions, and stored procedures.

Tkinter

The Python standard GUI toolkit is a collection of Python modules that enable the creation of desktop applications with graphical user interfaces. This toolkit, commonly referred to as GUI, encompasses a broad range of widgets or graphical elements such as buttons, labels, text boxes, menus, canvas, and more. These widgets can be leveraged to create interactive desktop applications with various functionalities.

NumPy
NumPy, which stands for Numerical Python, is a widely-used open-source Python library for scientific computing and data analysis. It is utilized to support multidimensional arrays, matrices, and mathematical functions for the purpose of manipulating and analyzing data.

PIL
PIL, which stands for Python Imaging Library, is a widely used open-source Python library that enables users to handle images. It offers extensive support for opening, modifying, and storing various image file formats, such as GIF, BMP, PNG, TIFF, and JPEG. Although PIL is no longer being updated, Pillow is its successor and can be used as a seamless replacement. Pillow boasts additional features and is being actively maintained.

Time Module
The time module is a built-in Python module that provides various time-related functions. It includes functions for measuring time intervals, formatting time values, and for delaying or pausing the execution of code.

Date Module
Python's datetime module is a pre-installed module that provides classes for managing dates and times. The datetime module includes a range of functions that enable users to generate, modify, and format dates and times in different ways. Using the datetime module, you can manipulate dates and times to suit your requirements.

Result

The person's identity and face, which are regarded as their most fundamental pieces of information, must be entered into the attendance management system before it can operate.Capturing images of individuals' faces using a camera is the primary step in collecting a portrait. The system initially checks if a face is detectable in the captured image. In the event that no face is detected, the system prompts the user to take another picture until the required number of samples has been reached. In this particular instance, 100 sample pictures are taken for each student.The machine learning algorithm will be used to capture photographs and prepare them. The photographs are organized in a hierarchy and then placed in a file after being processed. A hierarchy of each face will be kept in this project's "database" folder. Every one of the various sub-folders that make up the database folder, which may be expanded with time, alsoincludes a collection of facial portraits of the same person across time. Each sub-folder represents an individual. The identity number of each individual student, which is different for every single

Figure 38.3 Interface of attendance system

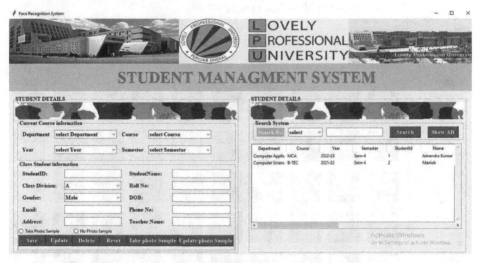

Figure 38.4 Interface of the student management system

person in the institution, will be used to name the subfolders that reflect each individual. The script creates database.py which handles the entire retrieval, pre-processing, and storing method for images.As illustrated in Figure 38.3, the primary interface of the attendance management system that utilizes face recognition technology includes six distinct buttons, each with its own unique functionality. These buttons enable users to perform various tasks within the system's interface. For example,in Figure 38.4.After clicking the first button, it opens student details; using this interface, a person can add, remove, or modify student details; or enter details of students and click the save button to save the details of those students in the database, and in this interface, if you enter incorrect student information, then a user can change those details by clicking the update button. The user can also remove a student from the records by clicking the delete button, and they can reset all the fields by hitting the reset button. To take a photo of the student's face, the user needsto click on the "take photo sample button" as shown in Figure 38.4.

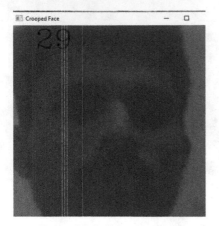

Figure 38.5 Capturing student face sample

Figure 38.6 100 samples saved in a folder

To take a photo sample of the student as shown in Figure 38.5, a user needs to click on the "take photo sample" button then the system will take 100 photo samples of the same student to improve the accuracy of the Algorithm. After collecting a photo sample, the system will save all the image data in a local data folder as shown in Figure 38.6.

For training the student's face Data user needs to use the "Train Data" buttonusing which the image data will be trained and then it will be saved as a "classifier.xml" file. To launch the face detection systemuser, need to click on button number two which is labelled as "Face Detector", which will identify the student's face as shown in Figure 38.7. Face recognition is utilized using a camera, and the outcomes are reliable. When a face comes into view of the camera, the model uses face recognition technology to detect it, and a colored frame appears around the detected face. For an unknown student, the camera

Figure 38.7 Face recognition

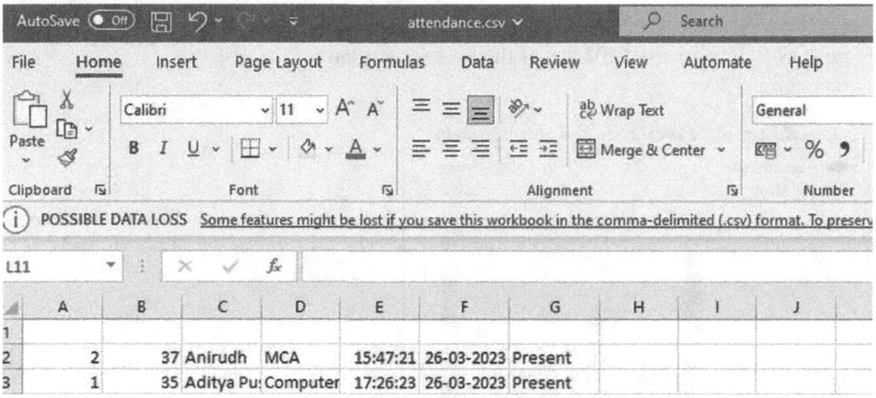

Figure 38.8 Excel Sheet of studentswho are present in the class

displays a red frame around their face, while an enrolled student will have a green frame. The model also provides clear text above the resulting frame, indicating the system's recognition outcome. Even if the face is viewed from a side angle, the model can still operate effectively. Additionally, the model can detect multiple faces within a single camera frame.After that, click on the "Attendance button" as shown in Figure 38.8, itwill open another interfaceas shown in Figure 38.9, To change the information and import the CSV file, click the Import button in this interface. Users can export the CSV file by clicking the "Export button". To reset the student data, click the "Reset" button. With a large number of pictures, the Haar-cascade and LBPH classifiers are both-executed. As aresult, the LBPH classifier takeslesstime when compared to the Haar cascade classifier, however, the LBPH classifier has a lower accuracy than the Haar cascade classifier. The Haar cascade classifier and the LBPH classifier are both used to detect faces in a picture. However, the Haar cascade classi-fier tends to find more faces compared to the LBPH classifier. To compare the execution speed of these classifiers, a bar graph in Figure 38.10 displays the

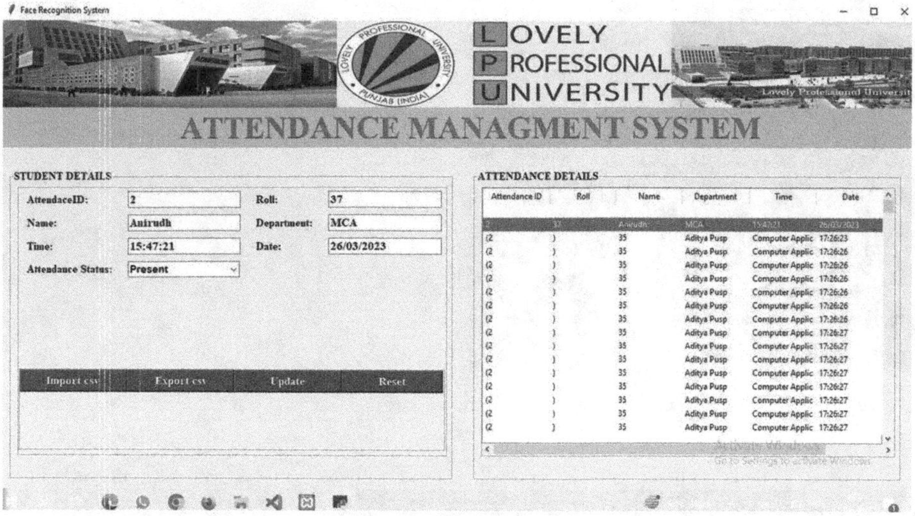

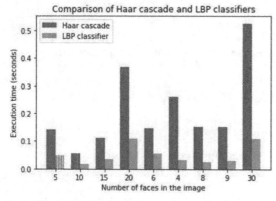

Figure 38.9 Import the CSV file of the present student

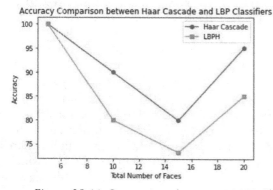

Figure 38.10 Comparison between LBPH and Haar Cascade

Figure 38.11 Comparison between LBPH Classifiers based on the execution time. And Harr-Cascade Classifiers based on accuracy

number of faces detected in an image on the X-axis and the time taken by the classifiers on the Y-axis. On the other hand, Figure 38.11's-line graph compares the accuracy of the two classifiers, with the LBP Classifier being compared to the Haar Cascade Classifier.

Conclusion

Since the traditional method of attendance management has many limitations, most universities have experienced significant difficulties. This paper highlights the facial recognition technology using OpenCV. Thisattendance tracking system's built-in feature can not only guarantee that attendance is taken accurately but also get rid of the problems with the old system. Employing technology to delegate the challenging tasks to machines not only preserves resources but also decreases human intervention in the entire process. This approach allows for the identification and elimination of flaws. The only cost associated with this solution is the storage space required to accommodate all the faces within the database.By adopting this innovative attendance tracking system, schools and universities can streamline attendance management processes, reduce administrative overheads, and enhance the learning experience for students. Overall, the project's effectiveness in automating attendance tracking, improving accuracy, and enhancing data management makes it avaluable asset to any educational institution.

Reference

1. Shehu, V., and Dika, A. (2010). Using real time computer vision algorithms in automatic attendance management systems. ITI 2010 32nd International Conferenceon Information Technology Interfaces, June 21-24, 2010, Cavtat, Croatia.
2. Xiao, J. Gao, G. Hu, C., and Feng, H. (2007). Anovel framework for fast embedded face detection system. 1-4244-1132-7/07/$25.00 © 2007 IEEE.
3. Bian J., and Du W. (2011). Research of face detection system based on skin-tone feature. 978-1-61284-722-1/11/$26.00 ©2011 IEEE.
4. Agrawal, M. Jain, N., Kumar, M., and Agrawal, H. (2010). Face recognition using eigenfaces and artificial neural network. *International Journal of Computer Theory and Engineering*, 3(2).
5. Al-Ghamdi, B. A. S., and Allaam, S. R. (2010). Recognition of human face by face recognition system using 3D. *Journal of Information and Communication Technology*, 4(2), 27–34.
6. Imtiaz H., Fattah, S. A. (2011). Aface recognition scheme using wavelet – based dominant features. *Signal and Image Processing: An International Journal (SIPIJ)*. 2(2).
7. K. Senthamil Selvi, Chitrakala, P., and Jenitha, A. A. (2014). Face recognition based attendance marking system. *International Journal of Computer Science and Mobile Computing, (IJCSMC)*, 2(3).
8. Patel, R., and Yagnik, S. B. Aliterature survey on facerecognition techniques.*Published Innternational Journal of Computer Trends and Technology (IJCTT)*.
9. Li. J., Zhao B., Zhang, H., and Jiao, J. (2009). Face recognitionsystem using SVM classifier and feature extraction by PCA and LDA combination. IEEE. 2009.
10. Turk, M. A., and Pentland, A. P. (1991). Face recognition using eigenfaces. InProceedings IEEE Computer Society Conference Computer Vision and Pattern Recognition, Maui, Hawaii, (pp.586–591).

11. Boualleg A., H. Bencheriet C., and Tebbikh, H. (2012). Automatic face recognition using neural network-PCA. IEEE 200.
12. Wang, N. J. (2012). Areal-time multi-face detection system implemented on FPGA. In 2012 IEEE International Symposium on Intelligent Signal Processing and Communication Systems (ISPACS 2012) November 4–7, 2012.
13. Yogesh Tayal, Ruchika Lamba, R., and Padhee, S. (2012). Automatic face detection using color based segmentation. *International Journal of Scientific and Research Publications*, 2(6).
14. Yadav D., K. Singh, S., Pujari, S., and Mishra, P. (2015). Fingerprint based attendance system using microcontroller and LabView.
15. Surve, M., Joshi, P., Jamadar, S., and Vharkate, M. Automatic attendance system using face recognitiontechinique. ISSN, 2277–3878.
16. Praneet, T., Rajesh, K., Raju, U. N., and Manne, Dr. S. Face recognition based attendance system using deep learningtechniques. ISSN, 2394–5125.
17. Kadam, S., and Khedkar, S. Review paper on contactless attendance system based on face recognition. e-ISSN:2395-0056 P-ISSN:2395-00.
18. Gupta, S., Snigdh I., and Sahana S. K. (2022). Afuzzy logic approach for predicting efficient LoRacommunication. *International Journal of Fuzzy Systems*, 1–9.

39 Performance-analysis of machine-learning models for diabetes-prediction

AnushkaAgarwal[1,a], Dr. UpmaJain[2,b], Vipashi Kansal[2,c], Ram Dewangan[3,d] and Shruti Bhatla[2,e]

[1]Student, Graphic Era deemedtobe University

[2]Assistant Professor, Graphic Era deemed to be University

[3]Assistant Professor, Thapar Institute of Engineering and Technology

Abstract

Diabetes has been affecting people across whole globe and has been one of th causes of deaths in the 60s. The main disadvantage of this disease is that it cannot be cured it can only be controlled. Big data analytics has significant advantages for the healthcare industry. It is produced by division of the data recursively into subsets and assigning values to the input features. Before the procedure can end, a requirement such as the highest depth of tree. In this study various ml models k- nearest-neighbors, logistic (LR) regression, decision-tree (DT), random (RF), forest, support- vector-machine (SVM), Naïve-Bayes (NB) classifier are for diabetes prediction using the PIMA data. We have analyzed the classification accuracy of these models with respect to PIMA dataset by including all the factors and excluding different factors one at a time. This work's key finding s are machine learning models' behavior with respect to different factors (glucose, BMI, age, pregnancy, etc.). This study also identifies the factor that plays the most important role in improvising the classification accuracy of the above models.

Keywords: Decision DT tree, logistic LR regression, Naïve-bayes'-classifier, random RF forest, S-V-M, K-N-N

Introduction

India the second-most diabetic nation in the world, with 69.20 million cases, followed by 36.50 million cases of high- risk diabetes, pre-diabetes, and cardiovascular disease High blood sugar levels, or what doctors refer to as glucose, are a sign of diabetes, a chronic illness. Type-2 diabetes, which is more-common, is caused by a combination of genetics and life-style-factors, such as being overweight and not getting enough physical activity. People can use their daily physical examination data to reach an earlier conclusion concerning diabetes mellitus by ML. How to choose the right classifier and valuable characteristics for the ML approach presents obstacles in order to obtaining results that are extremely accurate.

Various ML techniques, such as DT [14], RF [5], SVM [6], Nave Bayes (NB) [7] etc., have been applied for diabetes prediction. This study compares the classification accuracy of K-neares knn neighbor (KNN), logistic-regression, decision-tree, random-forest, support svm -vector-classifier, naive bayes classifier to

[a]anushka.agarwal004@gmail.com, [b]upma.jain88@gmail.com, [c]vipashi36@gmail.com, [d]ramadew7@gmail.com, [e]bhatlashruti97@gmail.com

predict diabetes by utilizing the PIMA Indian dataset. Objective of this work is to analyze the effects of different factors on the classification accuracy of various machine learning models. The organization of the paper is as follows: Section 2 discusses the related work done in this field followed by section 3 in which the description of the dataset used to conduct this study is described. Section 4 provides brief descriptions of the machine learning models used in this study. Section 5 discusses the results and key findings of this work. Section 6 provides the conclusion.

Literature Review

Albahli et al. [8] proposed a hybrid methodology to predict type2 diabetes. They extracted unknown hidden features from the dataset using the K-mean clustering approach, and then ran the RF and XGBoost classifiers on top of it to obtain more accurate results. The number-of- pregnancies of a woman, the BMI count, and the glucose level were identified in [9] to be the most important predictors for diabetes prediction among all characteristics of PIDD by using logistic regression. Kumari and R. Chitra [6] have used the SVM and the Indian diabetes dataset from Pima, the classifier is able to predict diabetes disease at the lowest cost and with the best performance by using Matlab R2010. The correctness of the solution is 78.2 %.

Huang et al. have been [10] applied naive bayes, IB1 and C4.5 algorithms to feature selection and diabetes classification. The study, concluded that the most crucial variables for blood sugar management are patient age, the length of the diagnosis, the requirement for insulin, and food control. Other variables, such as the style of care, the significance of smoking and, home monitoring are also influencing the outcomes. Nai-Arun & Moungmai [11] have compared decision tree, ANN, LR, and NB, as four different categorization methods. The highest levels of accuracy for all models fall between 84 to 86 percent.

In [12] authors have compared the performance of NB, DT, and SVM, using PIDD and found that NB had the highest accuracy of 76.86 %. In order to identify diabetes, Sivaranjani et al. [13] first reduced the dimensionality of PIDD and applied RF and SVM for diabetes prediction. Khanam et al. [14] have utilized several ML methods on PIDD to predict diabetes and concluded that the performance of LR and SVM was better.

Hasan et al. (2020) [16] presented a methodology that included hyper parameter optimization, feature selection, and data pretreatment techniques. The scientists used six classification techniques, including AdaBoost, DT, RF, KNN, and multilayered perceptron. They managed to reach 78.9% accuracy.

Jackins et al. [17] introduced a technique in which the null values for the missing variables were used to determine the correlation among the features. Although this process is very time consuming.

In [14] Saxena et al. have examined the research for diabetes prediction techniques done by many researchers. In order to synthesize the various studies and choose the highest quality studies, an analysis of diabetic prediction models was conducted.

Tasin at al. [15] utilized the private collection of female diabetic patient's samples (dataset) in Bangladesh and a variety of machine learning techniques to construct an autonomous diabetes prediction system. The authors used the diabetes dataset for Pima Indians and obtained extra samples from 203 people working at a nearby Bangladeshi textile plant. This study uses the feature selection algorithm with mutual information. The private dataset's insulin characteristics were predicted using a semi and supervised model that included high gradient boosting. The class imbalance issue was handled using the SMOTE and ADASYN techniques individually. To evaluate which algorithms yields the best prediction and results, the authors have investigated machine learning classification methods, such as decision (DT) trees, SVM (Support-Vector- Machine), Logistic-Regression, Random-Forest- Algorithm, (K- Nearest neighbor) KNN, & various similar ensemble approaches. The suggested system delivered the best outcome for that of the XG-Boost classifier along with ADASYN technique with 81% of the accuracy. Various machine learning methods used by researchers for diabetes prediction are given in the table 39.1.

Dataset

We have utilized the PIMA Indian dataset [6] to predict the accuracy of different machine-learning models. The data of 768 people is present in the dataset within which 500 people stand out to be diabetes negative and around 268 to be diabetes positive. First, we standardized the data and split it into the training and testing data where 80 % data served for training and remaining 20 % served as testing. In this data the factors included are bp, pregnancies, measure of glucose, skin thickness', BMI values, insulin levels, and DPF.

Table 39.1 Various machine learning approaches applied by researchers for diabetes prediction

Paper	DatasetUsed	ClassifierUsed	Accuracy
[10]	PIDD	LR	75.33
[6]	Indiandiabetes dataset PIMA	SVM	78.2%
[10]	Diabetes Patients' data collected by Ulster Community and Hospitals from 2000 to 2004.	Naïvebayes, IB1, C4.5	95%
[11]	Dataset was collected from 26 Primary Care Units (PCU)in Sawan pracharak Regional Hospital	DT, ANN, LR, NB And RF, etc	84-86%
[12]	PIDD	NB,DT,SVM	76.86%
[13]	PIDD	RF,SVM	83%
[14]	PIDD	DT, KNN, RF, NB, AB, LR, SVM	88.57%
[16]	PIDD	KNN, DT, RF, MLP	78.9%
[17]	PIDD	NB and RF	74.46%

Pregnancies: The number of pregnancies a person has had can be an important factor in the prediction of gestational diabetes (diabetes that gets developed during pregnancy is a known risk factor for the occurrence of type 2 diabetes.

Glucose level: Measuring glucose levels is important in the diagnosis and management of diabetes. A fasting glucose test is often used to diagnose diabetes. Additionally, ongoing monitoring of glucose level is important in managing diabetes.

Blood pressure: It is an important predictor of diabetes. High bp, also known as hypertension, can act as a major-risk factor for-diabetes. This is because hypertension can lead to damage of the blood vessels and organs, including the pancreas, which is responsible for producing insulin.

Skin thickness: It is an important parameter in diabetes prediction because it can indicate the presence of insulin resistance. The condition known as insulin resist occurring when the body cells does not react to the insulin as intended, increasing blood sugar levels.

Insulin: It is a hormone generated by the pancreas that aids in the regulation of glucose levels in the body. It is critical in the treatment of diabetes, which is characterized by elevated blood sugar levels. In diabetics, either body doesn't create enough of insulin that is sufficient or it does'nt use that insulin that is produced adequately.

BMI: is a measure of a body fat percentage based on the weight and the height and is used to define people as underweight, over- weight, normal, or obese. Studies have shown that individuals with a higher BMI are at an increased risk for developing type2 diabetes, as excess body fat can lead to insulin resistance and other metabolic abnormalities.

Machine Learning Models

KNearest-Neighbor Algorithm

To classify and predict data, machine learning uses the K- nearest (KNN) neighbor algo, which is a non- parametric approach. The KNN algorithm essentially finds the K closest training samples to a particular data point and determines the most frequent class among them to predict the new data point. In the regression setting, the KNN algorithm assigns a new data point to the average of the values of the k-nearest- training examples. It is simple to implement and easy to understand, but it can be computationally expensive when dealing with large datasets. It also does not work well when the number of features is large because the distance metric becomes less meaningful. Additionally, the choice of k value can have a significant impact on the performance of the algorithm.

Naive-Bayes Algorithm

A probabilistic algorithm for classification is known as Naive Bayes. It is based on Bayes' Theorem, that states the similarity of any event occurring given some evidence is equivalent to the similarity of event occurring given the prior probability of the event. In the context of ml, the event is a class label of a data point, and the evidence is the features of the pointing data.

The naive section of the name refers to the assumption, that is that the features of a data point are independent of one another. This assumption is often not realistic, but still this algorithm performs well in practicality. The basic steps of the algorithm are:

- Determine the number of classes and the prior probabilities of the classes.
- For each class, calculate the likelihood of each feature given to the class.
- For a new data point, we do calculation of posterior probability in each class when the features of the data point is given.
- Assign the data point to the class which has the highest of all posterior probability.

Naive Bayes - a simple and fast algorithm that works well on large datasets as well as high-dimensional data. However, it can be sensitive to irrelevant features and the independence assumption can lead to poor performance in certain situations.

Logistic Regression

A supervised learning approach used for categorization problems is logistic regression. It is employed to forecast a binary result from a collection of independent variables. The outcome is modeled using a logistic function, hence the name logistic regression. Any real-valued number can be mapped to a number between 0 and1 using the logistic function, sometimes referred to as the sigmoid function. The output of the logistic function can be interpreted as the probability of the positive class.

In logistic regression, a set of weights (coefficients) are learned from the training data using a process called maximum likelihood estimation. These weights are then used to predict predictions on the new data. The probability after prediction is then threshold at 0.5 to predict the class. It is a simple yet powerful method that can be used to predict one of two probable outcomes in binary classification issues.

Logistic regression can be extended to handle multiple classes through the use of one-vs-all or softmax techniques.

Decision Tree

A learning algorithm used for classifying and regression tasks. It is produced by recursively splitting the data into multiple subset and assign values to the input feature. Before the process can end, a stopping condition must be fulfilled, such as the highest its depth or a minimum quantity of sample in its node. The final one's can be taken into implementation to predict new data if we traverse the tree and determine the class or values associated with the leaf reached.

Random-(RF)-Forest Algorithm

The ensembled learning method Random Forestt is used for regression and classification problems. In increasing the model's accuracy, it creates numerous decision trees and combines their predictions. This algorithm works by creating a set of decision trees, known as a forest, by picking subsets of the training data and features at random. Each tree in the forest makes a prediction, and the result is arrived at by adding up all the guesses made by the trees. This can be done by taking a majority vote for classification or taking the average for regression. The use of multiple trees helps to reduce overfitting, which is a common problem with decision trees. The randomness in the subsets of data and features used to train each tree also helps to reduce overfitting. In addition, random forests also have the ability to handle missing values and outliers well. They are also able to measure the feature importance. However, the model size and prediction time is relatively large.

Support-Vector Machine
The Support Vector-Machine(SVM) can be employed in both regression and classification applications. The main objective of the SVM approach is to find the best boundary that separates data into discrete classes. The optimum boundary is the one that maximize margin, or separation between boundary and the nearest support vectors, or data points, from each class. By applying a kernel technique, SVMs can handle both linear and nonlinear boundaries. The kernel trick transforms the inputted data into a little higher dimensional space with possibility of linear boundaries. The three kernel types that are most frequently employed are radial basis function (RBF), polynomial, and linear. SVM is effective in high dimensional space and is memory efficient. They also perform well with a clear margin of separation. However, they don't perform well in large datasets because of the high training time, and they don't perform well when the class are overlapping.

Result and Discussion

The experiment conducted in the PYTHON-3.0 on the windows-11 OS. Dataset contains information on 768 individuals, of whom 268 are positive and 500 are

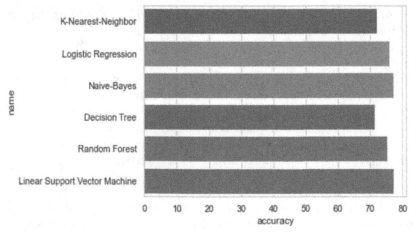

Figure 39.1 Fig. to represent the accuracy rates of the prediction model using different algorithms

Table 39.2 Table representing the accuracies on dropping one column at a time and also without dropping anything

REMOVING THE FOLLOWING ONE BY ONE CHECKING HOW IT AFFECTS THE ACCURACY. THE ACCURACIES AFTER REMOVING PARTICULAR COLUMNIS:

ALGORITHM NAME	NO. of PREGNANCIES	GLUCOSE	BP COUNT	SKIN THICKNESS	INSULIN LEVEL	BODY MASS INDEX	DPF	PERSON-AGE	ACCURACY ORIGINAL DATASET
KNN	70.13	70.13	70.78	68.18	72.73	72.08	73.38	73.38	72.08
LOGISTIC REGRESSION	75.32	68.18	76.62	76.62	75.97	77.27	75.32	75.97	75.97
NAÏVE-BAYES	75.97	70.13	77.27	78.57	76.62	77.27	74.03	75.97	77.27
DECISION-TREE	74.03	63.64	68.18	72.73	66.88	64.93	68.18	71.43	68.83
RANDOM FOREST	74.68	64.29	75.32	74.68	72.08	73.38	72.73	73.38	75.97
SUPPORT VECTOR MACHINE	76.62	66.23	77.27	77.27	76.62	77.27	75.32	76.62	77.27

Table 39.3 table representing accuracies using different mlalgorithms

Algorithm-Names	Accuracy
K-NEAREST-NEIGHBOR	72.08
LOGISTIC REGRESSION	75.97
NAÏVE BAYES	77.27
DECISION TREE	68.83
RANDOM FOREST	75.97
SUPPORT VECTOR CLASSIFIER	77.27

negative, together with the nine unique qualities that relate to each patient. The classification accuracy is displayed in Table 39.1 after using KNN, SVM, decision trees, random forests, logistic regression, and naive bayes to the original data set. To analyze the importance of different factors in the dataset on various machine learning models, considered in this study various experiments have been done. Table 39.2 provides a comparative study of the classification accuracy of various models by excluding different factors.

Key findings
- It can be observed from table 1 that SVM and naive bayes perform best when all the parameters are included and provide an accuracy of 77.24.
- Glucose plays a very important role in all of the models, as we can observe from table 39.2 after removing the glucose parameter the accuracy of all models decreases.
- Performance of the decision tree is quite fluctuating while removing any of the features (Parameter) as we can see in table 39.2.
- It can also be noted that the accuracy of SVM is highest in every case. It can be said that among K-N-N, Naïve-Bayes, LR, DT, Random File, SVM performs is best and least affected by the factors.

Among various factors, Glucose plays a very important role in all of the models, as we can observe after removing the glucose parameter the accuracy of all model decreases.

Conclusion

In this research study, we have used PIMA Indian dataset to estimate classification accuracy using K-nearest-neighbor (KNN), logistic regression, decision tree, random forest, support vector classifier, and naïve bayes classifier. Support vector machine [15] and naïve bayes classifier among these models reach the highest level of classification accuracy of 77.27%. Additionally, this study examines how various parameters affect the classification accuracy of several ML models.

References

1. Navada, A., Ansari, A. N., Patil, S., and Sonkamble, B. A. (2011). Overview of use of decision-tree algorithms in ML. In 2011 IEEE Controland System Graduate Research Colloquium IEEE, (pp. 37–42).
2. Safavian, S. R., and Landgrebe, D. (1991). A survey of decision tree classifier methodology. *IEEE Transactions on Systems, Man, and Cybernetics*, 21(3), 660–674.
3. Breiman, L. (2001). Random forests. Machine learning, 45, 5–32.
4. Kumari, V. A., and Chitra, R. (2013). Classification of diabetes disease using support vector machine. *International-Journal of Engineering Research and Applications*, 3(2), 1797–1801.
5. Priya, K. L., Kypa, M. S. C. R., Reddy, M. M. S., & Reddy, G. R. M. (2020, June). A novel approach to predict diabetes by using Naive Bayes classifier. In 2020 4th International Conference on Trends in Electronics and Informatics (ICOEI)(48184) (pp. 603–607). IEEE.
6. Albahli, S. (2020). Type 2 machine learning: an effective hybrid prediction model for early type 2 diabetes detection. *Journal of Medical Imaging and Health Informatics*, 10(5), 1069–1075.
7. Nai-Arun, N., and Moungmai, R. (2015). Comparison of the classifiers for the risk of diabetes prediction. *Procedia Computer Science*.
8. Sisodia, D., and Sisodia, D. S. (2018). Prediction of diabetes using classification algorithms. *Procedia Computer Science*, 132, 1578–1585.
9. Sivaranjani, S., Ananya, S., Aravinth, J., and Karthika, R. (2021). Diabetes prediction using machine learning algorithms with feature selection and dimensionality reduction. In 2021 7th International Conference on Advanced Computing and Communication Systems (ICACCS). (Vol. 1, pp. 141–146). IEEE.
10. Khanam, J. J., and Foo, S. Y. (2021). A comparison of machine learning algorithms for diabetes prediction. *ICT Express*, 7(4), 432–439.
11. Kansal, V., Singhdev, H., and Pant, B. (2022). Study on real world applications of SVM. In Das, K. N., Das, D., Ray, A. K., and Suganthan, P. N. eds. Proceedings of the International Conference on Computational Intelligence and Sustainable Technologies. Algorithms for Intelligent Systems. Singapore: Springer. https://doi.org/10.1007/978-981-16-6893-7_60.
12. Hasan, M. K., Alam, M. A., Das, D., Hussain, E., and Hasan, M. (2020). Diabetes prediction using ensembling of different machine learning classifiers. *IEEE Acess*, 8, 76516–76531.
13. Jackins, V., Vimal, S., Kaliappan, M., and Lee, M. Y. (2021). AI-based smart prediction of clinical disease using random forest classifier and naive bayes. *Fe Journal of Supercomputing*, 77(5), 5198–5219.
14. Saxena, Roshi, Sanjay Kumar Sharma, Manali Gupta, and G. C. Sampada. (2022). A Comprehensive review of various diabetic prediction models: a literature survey. *Journal of Healthcare Engineering*. 2022.
15. Tasin I, Nabil TU, Islam S, Khan R. Diabetes prediction using machine learning and explainable AI techniques. *Healthcare Technology Letters*. 2023 Feb;10(1-2):1–0.
16. Febrian, M.E., Ferdinan, F.X., Sendani, G.P., Suryanigrum, K.M. and Yunanda, R., 2023. Diabetes prediction using supervised machine learning. Procedia Computer Science, 216, 21–30.
17. Kee, Ooi Ting, Harmiza Harun, Norlaila Mustafa, Nor Azian Abdul Murad, Siok Fong Chin, Rosmina Jaafar, and Noraidatulakma Abdullah. (2023) . Cardiovascular complications in a diabetes prediction model using machine learning: a systematic review. Cardiovascular Diabetology 22, no. 1: 13.

40 Contemporary machine learning techniques for brain signal processing -a systematic review

Anu Arora[1,a] and Anurag Sharma[2,b]

[1]Assistant Professor, School of Engineering, Design & Automation, GNA University

[2]Professor, School of Engineering, Design & Automation, GNA University

Abstract

Temporal filters are used to preprocess brain signalsto choose the appropriate Electroencephalography (EEG) sub-frequency bands holding the relevant brain signals. EEGhas long been used to diagnose specific medical disorders in patients. The variety of classifiers available has resulted in a wide range of analytic techniques.Machine Learning (ML) techniques created for EEG analysis are studied in this review paper. In order to capture both historical and modern information categorization techniques for EEG in various applications, literature from year 2015 to 2022, published in various journals (IEEE, Springer, Elsevier), has been evaluated. This information is used to evaluate each machine learning technique's overall efficacy as well as its salient characteristics.This study offers an overview of research efforts on the use of machine learning for EEG data processing in response to the need to examine these studies. It can be discovered in this study that EEG categorization makes use of the entire fundamental machine learning techniques which includes Regression, Support Vector Machine (SVM),Linear Discriminant Analysis (LDA),Naïve-Bayes,K-Means, Random Forest, K-Nearest Neighbor (KNN) etc. It has been seen from the literature survey that supervised learning techniques are more producing more accurate results than their unsupervised counterparts. Although each strategy's accuracy in its particular application is restricted, there is optimism that when the combination of ways is used properly, total classification accuracy will be increased.In-depth information about machine learning applications for EEG analysis is provided in this study. It also provides an overview of each technique and the broad applications to which it is most appropriate.

Keywords: accuracy,brain computer interface (BCI), classification, EEG, KNN, ML,SVM

Introduction

An electroencephalogram (EEG) is one of the brain testswhich measures electrical activities in human brain using tiny metal discs (electrodes) attached to the scalp. Brain cells are continually activeeven if a person is sleeping. Electrical impulses are the main means of communication between them. Wavelike patterns can be seen during EEG recording.One of the fundamental diagnostic techniques for identifying mental illnesses is an EEG. A variety of brain illnesses can be detected and monitored with an EEG.

It could help identify the underlying cause of few symptoms, such as fits or memory loss, or it might provide you more details on a problem you've already been given a diagnosis for. Epilepsy, one of the mental disorders characterized by

[a]anu.arora@gnauniversity.edu.in, [b]anurag.sharma@gnauniversity.edu.in

recurrent seizures, is mostly diagnosed and researched via an EEG. An EEG will assist a doctor in identifying the patient's kind and severity of epilepsy, the cause of the seizures, and the best course of treatment.Doctor Richard CatonXu [20] made the initial discovery of EEG signals in 1875 while doing research on electrical brain activity in monkeys and rabbits. The first human EEG recordings were produced later in the 1900s and focused on absent seizures. Epileptic spikes and seizure patterns were first identifiedin the 1930s, which gave rise to a new area of study for EEG.

EEG mostly captures activity from the brain's outer layers (i.e. has low spatial resolution). It is impossible to locate the source of the activity with a single sensor. Although if recording with a lot of channels make it possible to statistically reconstruct the source, it is still not very effective at locating deep sources.

An EEG could be useful for diagnosing or treatingBrain tumors, Alzheimer or dementia, Any sort of brain injury, Infections, including encephalitis, A variety of illnesses can cause brain dysfunction(encephalopathy), Sleep disorders, inflamed brain tissue (herpes encephalitis), Stroke etc. EEGs help diagnose the causes of symptoms such as Confusion, Memory loss, Seizures and Fainting (syncope). EEG Test can be categorized as following:

i.   **Routine EEG:** This type of EEG recording lasts between 20 to 40 minutes. Throughout the test, the patient must remain still. He/she may be instructed to open or close his/her eyes on occasion. Additionally, patient will typically be instructed to breathe in and out deeply (namely hyperventilate) for a short period of time. They may also use a flashing light to observe how patient's brain responds to this.

ii. **Sleep EEG or Sleep-deprived EEG:** EEG data is recorded when the patient is dozing off. It can be applied when a normal EEG is insufficient or to check for sleep problems. In some instances, the individual may need to stay up late the night before the test so they can sleep while it is recorded. An EEG like this is known as a sleep-deprived EEG.

iii. **Ambulatory EEG:** An ambulatory EEG takes one or more days to record brain activities. Ambulatory EEGs can be performed at an EEG monitoring unit or at home. Electrodes attach to a tiny EEG recorder during a mobile EEG by clipping to patient's cloths. The majority of everyday tasks can be completed while the device monitors brain activity. If patient experience a

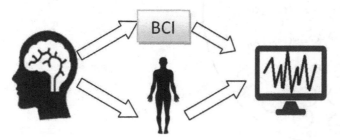

Figure 40.1 EEG-based BCI: a bi-directional communication channel between human brain and external devices

seizure or other incident that his/her healthcare provider is trying to record, patient or a family member can press a button.

iv.   **Prolonged EEG:** A prolonged EEG exam typically lasts for one hour and fifteen minutes, though some varieties might go on for several days. A prolonged EEG provides the patient's doctor with more details than a standard EEG. This type of EEG test is used by medical professionals to identify or treat seizure disorders.

v.   **Video telemetry:**A kind of EEG called video telemetry, commonly referred to as video EEG, involves taking pictures of the patient while an EEG recording is being generated. This may help to disclose additional information about the patient's brain activity. Typically, the test is run over a few days while the patient is accommodated in a specially designed hospital suite. A computer receives the EEG waves wirelessly. Additionally, the computer records the footage, which is continuously monitored by qualified professionals.

vi.   **Invasive EEG-telemetry:** This type of EEG is uncommon; however it could be used to determine whether surgery is a possibility for some individuals with more complicated epilepsy. To identify the specific site of the seizures, the brain is surgically implanted with electrodes.

EEG has some advantages over other methods for studying brain function, including inexpensive costs, tolerance of subject motion, and no radiation exposure hazards.

An electroencephalogram (EEG) topographical map, which includes 21 channels, shows the spatial distribution of electrical activity in the various brain areas.

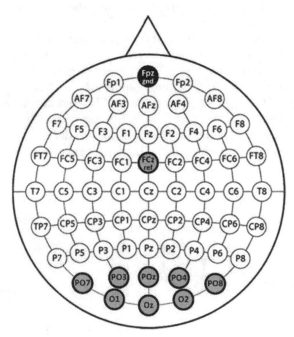

Figure 40.2 Topographical map of 21 EEG channel

Typically, the 21 channels correspond to particular scalp regions where electrodes are positioned to record brain activity. The international 10-20 system, which standardizes electrode placements, is used to identify each EEG channel, which correlates to a particular electrode placement. The amplitude and frequency of the electrical signals that each channel recorded are displayed on the topographical map [Figure 40.2].

Machine learning is an emerging and popular sub-area of computer science and artificial intelligence (AI) that mainly focuses on simulating human learning by utilizing heuristic data and algorithms to enhance the efficacy and accuracy of system. In order to predict future or provide any sort of classifications and discover hidden patterns in data mining activities, algorithms are trained using various statistical techniques. Based on such insights, decisions have been made which have an impact on key growth indicators in applications and enterprises. Observation or data, such as examples, firsthand knowledge, or instructions, serve as the foundation for machine learning. It searches for similar or contrast patterns in the dataset to draw conclusions. The main goal of ML is to make it possible for machines and other gazettes to learn on their own, without any human intervention, and to behave accordingly.

Training Methods for Machine Learning
A common way to categorize machine learning method is by how an algorithm learns to increase the precision of its predictions. Supervised learning, unsupervised learning, reinforcement learning and semi-supervised learning are the main types of machine learning techniques. Depending on the type of data

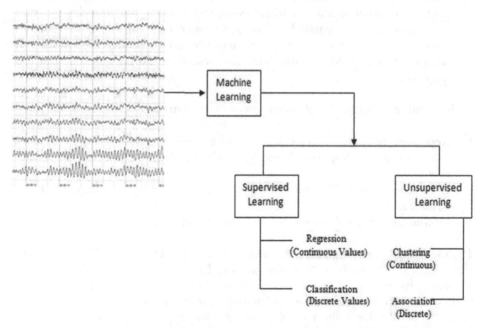

Figure 40.3 Applications for machine learning techniques on EEG

they wish to forecast, data scientists will apply a certain algorithm. Figure 40.3 illustrates supervised and unsupervised machine learning applications to EEG inputs

i.   **Supervised Machine Learning**: Supervised learning is most often employed category of machine learning [18]. In this learning, labeled data is used to train the machine learning algorithm. Such algorithm uses labeled samples to predict future events by applying knowledge from the past to fresh data. The weights are adjusted until the model is well fitted when input data is inputted into it. Regression and classification algorithms are used in supervised learning to make predictions or divide data into distinct classes.

ii. **Unsupervised Machine Learning**: Unsupervised machine learning includes building models using data without labels or clearly stated outcomes. These algorithms look for concealed patterns or data clusters without human interaction. As this method may identify same and different patterns in data, it is useful for exploratory data analysis, consumer segmentation, cross-selling strategies, and the finding of images and patterns. Clustering and association techniques are utilized to implement the models in unsupervised learning.

iii. **Reinforcement Machine Learning**: This learning is a branch of ML in which an agent is placed in a situation and learns how to act in it by acting in a given way and monitoring the rewards that result from that behavior. Reinforcement learning is mostly utilized in cutting-edge machine learning applications like AplhaGo and self-driving cars.

iv. **Semi-Supervised Machine Learning**: This learning falls in between supervised and unsupervised learning. It uses a small amount of labeled dataset during training in order to manage feature selection or extraction and classification from a larger set of unlabeled data. Semi-supervised learning can be used to provide a best solution to the problem of not having enough labeled data. It also helps in case of labeling more data which would be beneficial but too expensive.

Each machine learning algorithm consists of three parts:

*   **Representation**: Decision trees, sets of rules, logic programs, graphic models, neural networks, Support Vector Machine (SVM), etc. are examples of representation.
*   **Evaluation factors**: These include likelihood, cost/utility, accuracy, precision, and recall.
*   **Optimization**: Combinatorial, constrained, and convex optimization.

The most well-known machine learning techniques will be covered in this article, along with several real-world applications in EEG, and they will be categorized according to the sort of learning they are used for. Using machine learning techniques, EEG data can be utilized as markers for less obvious medical disorders. Figure 40.4 illustrates the typical procedure for applying machine learning to obtain the appropriate categorization of the data sets.

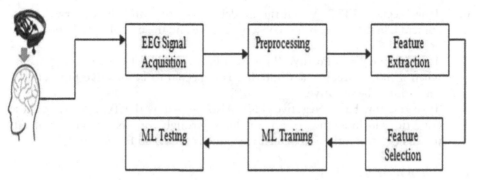

Figure 40.4 EEG analysis process by using machine learning algorithm

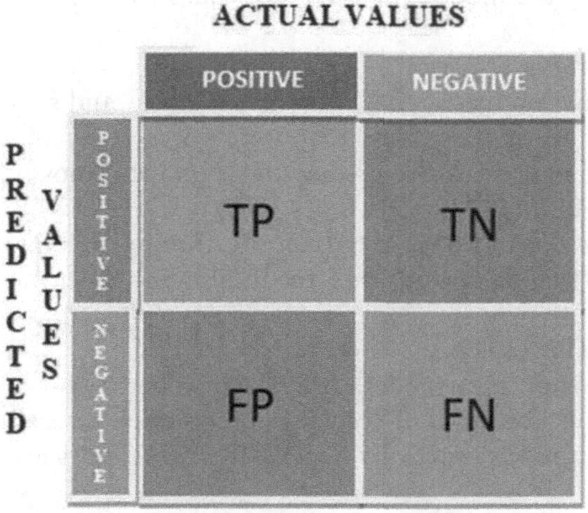

ACTUAL VALUES

		POSITIVE	NEGATIVE
P R E D I C T E D V A L U E S	P O S I T I V E	TP	TN
	N E G A T I V E	FP	FN

Figure 40.5 Confusion Matrix

The effectiveness of algorithms for diagnosing abnormalities from EEG has been assessed using a variety of assessment measures[14]. In this study, the most popular detection metrics are discussed. The confusion matrix is produced using machine learning techniques, which are then used to determine accuracy and other criteria.

A table called a confusion matrix [Figure 40.5] is frequently used in machine learning to evaluate how well a classification system performs. It offers a thorough analysis of the actual and expected classifications for a given collection of data. When assessing a model's performance in terms of true positives (TP), true negatives (TN), false positives (FP), and false negatives (FN), the matrix is especially helpful.

The confusion matrix is a useful tool for learning about a classification model's advantages and disadvantages

i.   **True Positive (TP):** This condition occurs when the model's expected value matches with the actual values which are supposed to be positive.

ii.   **True Negative (TN):** When the model's prediction and the observed value coincide. In this case, both the observed value and the model's prediction were negative.

iii.   **Type I error: False Positive (FP):** Also known as the Type I error, it occurs when a model predicts a value that is expected to be positive but actually turns out to be negative.

iv.   **Type II error: False Negative (FN):** Also known as the Type II error, these conditions include: the projected value is wrongly forecasted; the actual value was positive although a negative value is predicted by the model.

Evaluation metrics

i.   **Accuracy:** It calculates the proportion of correctly classified instances among all examples. It is the number of right predictions divided by the total number of predictions generated by the model. The accuracy scales from 0.0 to 1.0, with 1.0 being the finest.
   Accuracy = (TP+TN)/(TP+FP+FN+TN)

ii.   **Precision:** Precision is an evaluation metric that combines relevant and successfully retrieved items over all of the results that were successfully obtained. When the likelihood of a false-positive prediction is large, it is mostly employed. *Precision (TNR)* = TP/(TP+FP)

iii.   **Recall:** It assesses the model's ability to correctly identify true positive instances. It is the proportion of genuine positives to the total number of true positives and false negatives.
   Recall (Sensitivity or TPR) = TP/(TP+FN)

iv.   **F1-Score:** It is a balanced measure of a model's performance because it is the harmonic mean of precision and recall. It combines precision and recall managing imbalanced datasets and is especially beneficial when classes are distributed unevenly.
   F1-Score = 2 * (Precision*Recall) / (Precision+Recall)

Literature Review

Ahmad et al. [3]completed an in-depth analysis of the three important aspects. The earliest analysis of epileptic seizures focused on statistical aspects and EEG data extraction techniques. Second, a detailed evaluation of deep learning and machine learning models was carried out, taking into account both their flaws and the difficulties they present in datasets for epilepsy seizures. They also examined the performance of ML/DL models employing the logical inferences from proper detection. Rasheed et al. [16] examined machine learning techniques for anticipating epileptic seizures as well as the body of knowledge on epileptic seizures (ES). EEG analysis, feature selection, ES detection, and prediction are all part of ES prediction.

Islam et al. [8]used a variety of machine-learning techniques to categorize brain states during any sort of visual perception. They applied the SHAP library methodology to assess how various characteristics affected the classification process and improve the readability of the system. They collected their findings from a 250 Hz sampling rate and 31-channel EEG recordings and with 5- frequency band filters. They found that a basic deep-learning model nearly always yields 100%, which suggests an over fitting problem. As a result, they provided all the four models with different pairings of 2 activation functions as well as different data optimization strategies.

According toOspanova [14], sleepiness is an intensified psycho-physiological state of the body brought on by a stressful situation or event. This study examined the methods for detecting drowsiness in diverse contexts, including driving, studying, and working, using sensor devices such wearable sensors, electrocardiograms (ECG), electroencephalograms (EEG), and photoplethysmography (PPG). Machine learning algorithms are incredibly good at accurately identifying various emotional states.

To aid in seizure identification and seizure prediction, Zhuang et al. [21] addressed the problem of EEG signal categorization in their work. Two patient-specific CNN models were demonstrated todetectseizures and provide the most accurate prediction. They used spectrograms of EEG signal segments to conduct their study. It can discriminate between EEG signals in two and three states. It also works with spectrogram and Phase Space Reconstruction (PSR) images of different EEG signal segments. In their study, the patient non-specific CNN model generated the best classification results using PSR images of EEG signal segments.

Roy[17] concluded in their study that the initial stage in the identification of a neurological illness frequently involved determining whether an EEG recording unveils normal or abnormal activities of brain. Treatment delays will be reduced by using any such classifiers that automates this initial distinction and relieve clinical cares because manual EEG interpretation is a time-consuming and expensive operation. They offered ChronoNet, a cutting-edge network architecture which would be well suitable for the processing of EEG time-series data because it is versatile and adaptive. By 7.79%, their innovative RNN design beat the dataset's greatest previously reported accuracy, creating a new standard. They also proved that ChronoNet is able to categorize voice, demonstrating its wide application to time-series data.

Sharmila and Mahalakshmi [19] proposed anotherinnovative method for detecting epilepsy seizures using statistical features resulted fromDiscrete Wavelet Transform(DWT) and using PCA and LDA feature reduction techniques to classify EEG signalsas epileptic seizure or normal behavior by usingKNN and Naïve Bayes classifiers.

Classification [5]proposed automated identification of sleep stages from single-channel EEG signals.

Comparative Study of ML Algorithms Used in EEG Analysis

After thorough investigation of numerous research papers from years 2015 to 2022, published in various reputed journals, and presented a comparative study based on numerous applications that may be investigated utilizing different ML Models, as well as the accuracy results of all the applications.In this study, an extensive and thorough assessment of cutting-edge EEG analysis techniques with medical applications is presented.

Table 40.1 Comparison chart forML algorithmsused in EEG analysis

Authors	Machine Learning Model	Application	Data Set	Results
[13]	Linear Discriminant Analysis (LDA)	Regularized LDA of EEG features	Records of 114 Patients	Accuracy 70%
[1]	Fuzzy Logic	Identification of stereotypically developing micro-scale seizures.	Not mentioned	Accuracy 78.71%
[19]	PCA, LDA with K-NN	Selection and extraction of wavelet-based features for the epileptic seizure EEGclassification	Not recorded	98.5% and 100% accuracy PCA and LDA using K-NN are achieved.
[15]	K MEANS	Classification of Risk Level in Epilepsy	Records of 20 patients	Accuracy 71.09%
[17]	Neural networks, CNN, RNN, Logistic Regression	Identification of Automatic Abnormal EEG	1488 patients, 1529 normal participants	Deep gated RNN outperforms previously published results by 3.47%.
[4]	KNN, SVM	Occurrence of epileptic seizures	Records of 20 patients	Accuracy 97 %
[12]	Naïve Bayes	Major Depressive Disorder	30 patients and 30 normal participants	Accuracy 93.6%
[7]	GBDT	Automated Driver Fatigue Detection	Records of 22 patients	Accuracy 94%
[9]	Naïve Bayes , KNN	Epilepsy Disorder	Records of 500 patients	Accuracy for KNN is 73% and for Naive Bayes is 92%
[10]	ANN	Hybrid EEG using deep learning.	15 volunteers	Accuracy 99.3%
[2]	Support Vector Machine (SVM)	Identification of Alcohol Use Disorder	77volunteer male alcoholics	Accuracy 99%
[6]	Support Vector Machine (SVM)	EEG artifact removal	Records of 11 patients	Accuracy 99.1%

Table 40.1 shows that the accuracy rates of unsupervised algorithms are lower than those of supervised learning.While feature learning and dimensionality reduction are natural outcomes of unsupervised learning, classification and regression are the main applications of supervised learning. A crucial part of machine learning for EEG has also been played by wavelet transform and auto-regressive

techniques. Drowsiness, according toOspanova[14], is a heightened psycho-physiological condition of the body caused by a stressful scenario or event. They concentrated on sensor-based systems for detecting sleepiness in a variety of scenarios, including driving, studying, and working.An overall accuracy of 97% was achieved using KNN and SVM as the main classification technique[4].

In order to discover probable abnormalities, K-NN classifiers may be used to classify the different acquired EEG signals and find the output point that is most near the goal classification line. On the other hand, ANN has the ability to split and segment the EEG waveform's physical contour[11]. These segments are given individual weight values based on the waveform, and the output is created by adding a bias to the final equation. As more data is involved, the number of interactions in the hidden layer will increase. As a result, a suitable decision must be made depending on the nature of the issue and the amount of data being considered.

Machine learning approaches for analyzing brain signals have the potential to transform neuroscience and help society in a variety of ways. The analysis and interpretation of brain signals such as electroencephalography (EEG), magneto-encephalography (MEG), and functional magnetic resonance imaging (fMRI) are all part of brain signal processing. Here are some examples of how these strategies can be useful:

1. **Diagnosis and Treatment of Neurological Disorders:** Machine learning algorithms can help with the early detection and accurate diagnosis of neurological disorders such as epilepsy, Alzheimer's disease, Parkinson's disease, and others. These algorithms can find patterns indicative of specific illnesses by studying brain signals, resulting in earlier intervention and better treatment outcomes.
2. **Brain Computer Interface:** BCIs provide direct communication between the brain and external equipment, Figure 40.1 allowing people with disabilities to control prosthetic limbs, computer applications, and assistive technology. Machine learning is critical for decoding brain signals in order to grasp the user's intent and enable seamless interactions with these gadgets.
3. **Personalized Medicine:**Individual variations in brain reactions to medications or treatments can be identified using machine learning models applied to brain signal data. This knowledge can be utilized to tailor medical actions and optimize patient treatment programs, increasing efficacy while decreasing side effects.
4. **Cognitive Enhancement:** Machine learning can help to develop neuro-feedback systems, which allow people to monitor their brain activity and learn how to improve cognitive capabilities. This can help improve memory, attention, and overall mental performance.
5. **Understanding Brain Function:** Researchers can interpret complicated brain patterns and obtain insights into cognitive processes, emotions, learning mechanisms, and decision-making using advanced machine learning algorithms.
6. **Mental Health Monitoring and Support:** By examining brain signal patterns related with stress, anxiety, and depression, machine learning can aid in the

early detection of mental health disorders. The incorporation of this technology into mental health care can aid in the provision of timely support and interventions.

7. **Brain Research & Innovation:** Machine learning enhances the pace of brain research and supports innovation in neuroscience by automating complex data analysis activities.

Machine learning approaches for brain signal processing offer enormous potential to enhance healthcare, advance our understanding of the brain, and contribute to different industries, hence improving society's general well-being and quality of life.

Conclusion

Electrodes are positioned all over the head in an EEG, non-invasive electrophysiological equipment, to captureany sort of electrical activity of the brain. EEG may be used to identify emotions or diagnose neurological disorders like epilepsy based on any brain activity and fluctuating electric potentials. One of the most dependable techniques, EEG, for recognizing emotions since its signals are more objective and extremely accurate than those produced by other techniques based on outward appearance.Machine learning techniques have been used to analyze EEG, and dimensionality reduction and selection have been found to be an intriguing issue.

References

1. Abbasi, H., Unsworth, C. P.,Gunn, A. J., and Bennet, L. (2014). Superiority of high frequency hypoxic ischemic EEG signals of fetal sheep for sharp wave detection using wavelet-type 2 fuzzy classifiers. 36th Annual International Conference of the IEEE Engineering in Medicine and Biology Society, Chicago, IL, USA, 2014, 1893–1896, doi: 10.1109/EMBC.2014.6943980.
2. Abenna, S., Nahid, M., and Bouyghf, H. (2022). Alcohol use disorders automatic detection based BCI systems: anovel EEG classification based on machine learning and optimization algorithms.*International Journal of Information Science and Technology*, 6(1), 14–25. https://doi.org/10.57675/IMIST.PRSM/ijist-v6i1.178.
3. Ahmad, I., Wang, X., Zhu, M., Wang, C., Pi, Y., Khan, J. A., Khan, S., Samuel, O. W., Chen, S., and Li, G. (2022). EEG-based epileptic seizure detection via machine/deep learning approaches: asystematic review. *Computational Intelligence and Neuroscience*. 2022 | Article ID 6486570 | https://doi.org/10.1155/2022/6486570.
4. Beganovic, N., Kevric, J., and Jokic, D. (2017). Identification of diagnostic-related features applicable to EEG signal analysis. 1–9. https://doi.org/10.36001/phm-conf.2018.v10i1.477
5. E. Alickovic and A. Subasi, (2018). Ensemble SVM Method for Automatic Sleep Stage Classification, in IEEE Transactions on Instrumentation and Measurement, 67(6), 1258–1265, June 2018, doi: 10.1109/TIM.2018.2799059.
6. Grobbelaar, M., Phadikar, S., Ghaderpour, E., Struck, A. F., Sinha, N., Ghosh, R., andAhmed, M. Z. I. (2022). A survey on denoising techniques of electroencephalogram signals using wavelet transform. *Signals,* 3(3), 577–586. https://doi.org/10.3390/signals3030035.

7. Hu, J. (2018). Automated detection of driver fatigue based on EEG signals using gradient boosting decision tree model.*Cognitive Neurodynamics*, 431–440 (2018). https://doi.org/10.1007/s11571-018-9485-1

8. Islam, R., Andreev, A. V.,Shusharina, N. N., and Hramov, A. E. (2022). Explainable machine learning methods for classification of brain states during visual perception. *Mathematics*, 10(15), 1–25. https://doi.org/10.3390/math10152819.

9. Manjeera, K. N., Sekhar, P., Harshavardhan, P., Ganesh, P. S., and Jayanth, M. (2022). EEG SIGNAL ANALYSIS FOR EPILEPSY DISEASE USING MACHINE LEARNING TECHNIQUES, International Journal of Emerging Technologies and Innovative Research (www.jetir.org | UGC and issn Approved), ISSN:2349-5162, 9(10), 622–628, October-2022.

10. Manuscript (2018). Citation Antonio Maria Chiarelli et al 2018 J. Neural Eng. 15(3), 6028. DOI 10.1088/1741-2552/aaaf82

11. M. -P. Hosseini, A. Hosseini and K. Ahi, (2021). A Review on Machine Learning for EEG Signal Processing in Bioengineering, in IEEE Reviews in Biomedical Engineering, 14, 204–218. doi: 10.1109/RBME.2020.2969915.

12. Mumtaz, W., Ali, S.S.A., Yasin, M.A.M. et al. (2018). A machine learning framework involving EEG-based functional connectivity to diagnose major depressive disorder (MDD). *Med Biol Eng Comput.* 56, 233–246. https://doi.org/10.1007/s11517-017-1685-z

13. Neto, E., Biessmann, F., Aurlien, H., Nordby, H., and Eichele, T. (2016). Regularized linear discriminant analysis of EEG features in dementia patients. Frontiers in Aging Neuroscience . 8(November), 1–10. https://doi.org/10.3389/fnagi.2016.00273.

14. Ospanova, A. (2022). Review of machine learning method for drowsiness detection using EEG signal. https://doi.org/10.15680/IJIRSET.2022.1104131.

15. Rajaguru, H., and Prabhakar, S. K. (2017). Analysis of genetic algorithm driven auto-encoders for epilepsy classification using certain post classifiers. *International Journal of Mechanical Engineering and Technology*, 8(12), 80–90.

16. Rasheed, K., Qayyum, A., Qadir, J., Sivathamboo, S., Kwan, P., Kuhlmann, L., O'Brien, T., and Razi, A. (2021). Machine learning for predicting epileptic seizures using EEG signals: areview. *IEEE Reviews in Biomedical Engineering*, 14, 139–155. https://doi.org/10.1109/RBME.2020.3008792.

17. Roy, S., Kiral-Kornek, I., Harrer, S. (2019). ChronoNet: A Deep Recurrent Neural Network for Abnormal EEG Identification. In: Riaño, D., Wilk, S., ten Teije, A. (eds) Artificial Intelligence in Medicine. AIME 2019. Lecture Notes in Computer Science, 11526. Springer, Cham. https://doi.org/10.1007/978-3-030-21642-9_8

18. Sarker, I. H. (2021). Machine learning : algorithms, real - world applications and re-search directions. *SN Computer Science*, 2(3), 1–21. https://doi.org/10.1007/s42979-021-00592-x.

19. Sharmila, A., and Mahalakshmi, P. (2017). Wavelet-based feature extraction for clas-sification of epileptic seizure EEG signal. *Journal of Medical Engineering and Technology*, 41(8), 670–680. https://doi.org/10.1080/03091902.2017.1394388.

20. Xu, P. (2019). Review on Studies of Machine Learning Algorithms Peiyuan Xu1 Pub-lished under licence by IOP Publishing Ltd. Journal of Physics: Conference Series. 1187(5). https://doi.org/10.1088/1742-6596/1187/5/052103.

21. Zhuang, D., Rao, I., and Ibrahim, A. K. (2022). A machine learning approach to au-tomatic classification of eight sleep disorders.1–12. http://arxiv.org/abs/2204.06997.

41 Prediction on most-valuable player selection in NBA using machine learning algorithm

Rizul Sharma[a], Upinder Kaur[b] and Rahul Singh[c]

School of Computer Science and Engineering, Lovely Professional University, Jalandhar, Punjab

Abstract

In North America, the National Basketball Association (NBA) is a very well-liked and successful professional basketball league that draws fans and advertisers from all over the world. In this study, it is tested whether it is possible to predict a player's chances of winning the Most Valuable Player (MVP) award using machine learning approaches. It has been analysed over fifteen research papers from 2019-2023 and found that historic NBA data was used in most research to train the model. Out of all, machine learning techniques, particularly the Maximum Entropy Markov (MEM) model, can successfully predict the MVP winner by examining historical data on player statistics. The MEM model predicted the most valuable player with an accuracy of 96%. Further work can be done by using deep learning techniques and considering other factors like popularity of the player to improve the prediction accuracy.

Keywords: Markov model, maximum entropy, MVP, NBA

Introduction

The National Basketball Association (NBA) is a professional basketball league in Northern America, currently, composed of 30 teams -29 in the United States and 1 in Canada and is regarded as one of the top professional sports leagues in the North American subcontinent. It is listed as the third largest revenue-generating professional sports league globally and hails viewers and sponsors across the globe.

The NBA has a system where clubs can compete with one another to determine who is the best team in the league2. Teams play 82 games apiece during the regular season, which generally spans the months between October and April. The playoffs are open to the top eight clubs from each conference. After the regular season, a best-of-seven elimination competition is held as the playoffs. A player must be at least 19 years old in the draft year in order to be eligible, and they have 60 days to proclaim their eligibility. American players who have attended four years of college or four years of high school and have played for an overseas team before the age of 19 are automatically eligible for the draft. The NBA draft is open to international players who are 22 years old or older; players under 22 must declare their eligibility as early entrants.

[a]rizul22sharma@gmail.com, [b]upinder.27954@lpu.co.in, [c]rahul15468@gmail.com

The best performer of the regular season receives the NBA Most Valuable Player (MVP) award. A group of sportswriters and broadcasters from across North America casts votes for the prize. First, second, and third place winners are decided by the panel. A first-place vote weighs 10 points, for second it is 7 points, and a vote for third is worth 5 points. Regardless of the number of first-place votes cast, the player with the most points receives the prize. A group of sportswriters and broadcasters from around North America cast votes for the top five candidates to determine the winner of the award. Each vote for first place weighs 10 points, followed by votes for second place with 7 points, third place with 5 points, fourth with 3 points, and fifth place with 1 point. With online voting, fans cast one vote each starting in 2010. The winner of the prize is the player with the most points. Table 41.1 shows Oaxaca decomposition results predicted MVP votes [1].

Researchers and analysts have access to a vast database of player performance data, which has enabled the development of many studies, particularly those using machine learning algorithms. These studies aim to analyse player performance and statistics to predict game outcomes, such as win-loss games, most valuable player probability and playoff champions. To improve the accuracy of these predictions, researchers need to input a large amount of data. However, processing the vast NBA database to extract relevant data for analysis is a challenging and complex task that requires careful preprocessing.

Numerous studies particularly those utilising various ML algorithms have been conducted to analyse performance of NBA players' and forecast

Table 41.1 Oaxaca decomposition results predicted MVP votes [1]

Player	Team	Year	Actual MVP Votes	Predicted MVP Votes	Difference
Steve Nash	Phoenix	2005	1066	277.7	788.3
Pedrag Stojakovic	Sacramento	2004	281	172.9	108.1
John Stockton	Utah	1996	12	3.4	8.6
John Stockton	Utah	1995	47	40.6	6.4
Arvydas Sabonis	Portland	1999	3	0.4	2.6
Rik Smits	Indianapolis	1998	2	1.9	0.1
John Stockton	Utah	2001	1	2.2	-1.2
Steve Nash	Dallas	2002	5	12.5	-7.5
Tom Gugliotta	Minnesota	1997	1	12.7	-11.7
John Stockton	Utah	1997	3	16.1	-13.1
John Stockton	Utah	1998	5	44.6	-39.6
Dirk Nowitzki	Dallas	2005	349	396.2	-47.2
Steve Nash	Dallas	2003	1	72.0	-71.0
Andrei Kirilenko	Utah	2004	2	75.2	-73.2
Dirk Nowitzki	Dallas	2004	4	155.6	-151.6
Pedrag Stojakovic	Sacramento	2002	1	158.5	-157.5
Dirk Nowitzki	Dallas	2002	31	190.0	-159.0
Dirk Nowitzki	Dallas	2003	43	429.5	-386.5

outcomes of the game, such as predicting wins and losses and the playoff champions. To improve the accuracy of these predictions, researchers need to incorporate a large amount of data as input. However, due to the vast amount of data in the NBA database, retrieving enough relevant information poses a challenge. The process of pre-processing the data correctly is a complex and sophisticated problem that must be addressed to obtain more precise prediction results.

This study has managed to filter out the best and the most accurate methods that go into prediction of a player getting the MVP award in the NBA. Different machine learning models and algorithms deduce that supervised learning works aptly to obtain the required results using Maximum Entropy Markov (MEM) model and in future these results and statistics can even be further improved by implementing deep learning methods of machine learning models.

Maximum Entrop Markov (MEM) Model

Maximum entropy Markov (MEM) model is a variant of statistical model which commonly caters in predicting the distribution probability of the sequence of events. This model is a variant of the Markov model and is mostly used in the areas where the prediction of sequential events is crucial i.e., in Natural Language Processing (NLP). The main highlight of the Markov model is that it describes

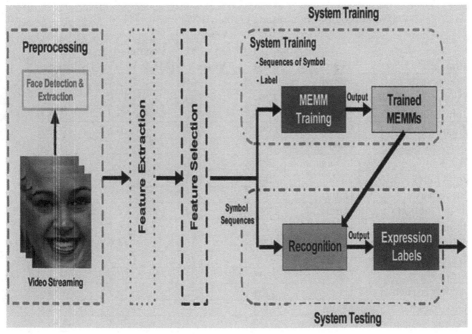

Figure 41.1 Maximum entropy markov model for human facial expression recognition [2]

a sequence of events where the probability of each event depends only on the state of the preceding event which is similar to a well-known Maximum Entropy Classifier (MEC) model, which also implies, that the unknown parameters are assumed to be connected in a Markov chain rather than independent to each other.

Maximum Entropy (MaxEnt) framework, in MEM model, is used to model the probabilities of the events, which implies that the model is designed to maximise the entropy of the probability distribution, keeping the limit within the set of given constraints. An example of a face recognition system can be used to explain the working of MEM model.

The major advantage of using this model over the other Markov models is that it includes a scope for the insertion of arbitrary features to influence the probability of each event. This explains that, this MEM model while making predictions, can consider a vast range of aspects, including linguistic, contextual, and semantic features etc. Figure 41.1 depicts Maximum entropy markov model for human facial expression recognition [2].

Overall, the working of the MEM model involves extracting related and relevant features from the training dataset, learning the parameters of the model that maximise the probability of the training dataset, and using the previous events and their corresponding features given to predict the probability distribution of the next event using the model.

Problem Statement

The recent work in this sector mainly focused only on the game statistics and game presence of the player while predicting the selection of most valuable player in the NBA. It depended on the performance factor only which nowadays is the not the only metric that comes into the play while selecting an apt player. In today's time social media presence is a considerable factor when it comes to sports and its viewers. Recent work did not really take the popularity aspect of the player into consideration while selections and this is the main problem that this paper will be improving on. In this paper, a new metric of popularity for selection which directly improves the probability of the player getting much more chances. The more famous and popular the player in the viewer's eyes, higher are the chances that more people will come to the playoffs to see him and in turn, the larger the number of concurrent viewers, the larger will be the profits for the sponsors and National Basketball Association. This not only helps in promoting the game at a better level but also increases the brand value of the player in the market.

Literature Survey

Mason Chen et al [3] aimed in this research to develop statistical models to predict the winners of the award for MVP for NBA season 2019-20. They used Z-standardisation to remove bias from the data before aggregating the statistics of each player equally to create an index. They concluded that the players winning the MVP award requires exceptional individual as well as team performance.

In order to demonstrate that this statistical method could be used to forecast the MVP in other team sports like basketball, cricket, volleyball, football, ice hockey, and soccer, the neural network prediction offered the Most Valuable Player score for each top player.

Fuzhi Su et al[4], in their study, used deep learning techniques to predict NBA players' scores using player statistics and data. The authors evaluated different algorithms and developed the most accurate score prediction algorithm to produce team and player comparisons. The best prediction results were obtained by extreme gradient boosting (XGB) method as it is an effective tool for predicting and evaluating NBA score predictions. The results can foster decision-making in player management and in future new data could be integrated into this model to deliver analysis findings to NBA teams, their coaches, viewers, sponsors, and other relevant stakeholders.

Yuefei Chen et al[5] carried out a study, aimed at predicting the Most Valuable Player (MVP) of the NBA in a specific season with the help of a neural network model. NBA is a highly popular basketball game watched by audiences worldwide, so they collected player records from 1997 to 2019 and separated them into three different datasets - the Total dataset, the Advanced and the Mixed dataset which in turn were further separated into test, validation, and training sets. They adjusted the hyperparameters using the validation set and used a mini-batch SGD algorithm to train the network while the accuracy of the model's predictions was formulated by the test set. After training three different models, it was concluded that all of them successfully predicted the MVP in the 2009-2010 and 2016-2017 seasons. They found that the dataset with Mixed data points had the best performance and likelihood of predicting the MVP naturally.

Zafar Mahmood et al[6] tried to explain the idea of predicting basketball rising stars as a machine learning challenge. It uses co-player statistics as a feature for forecasting. They explain how co-players affect prediction and evaluate multiple machine learning algorithms. The Maximum Entropy Markov (MEM) Model received an F-measure score of 96% It is the best algorithm in forecasting rising stars. The study also demonstrates that the majority of players classified as rising stars are ranked among the top 100 and perform more effectively. It is challenging to rank players based on their career statistics when they are just starting and have not played many games. Future success cannot always be predicted by past success

Yejia Liu et al[7]stated that success of a sports team heavily relies on selecting talented players and therefore developing effective methods is required. This method involves using regression model trees that group players based on their performance statistics. Each group of players along with its own regression model is defined under each leaf node, and furthermore based on values of the feature, the model tree splits the feature space accordingly. The model's accuracy is increased by combining the advantages of model-based and cohort-based techniques. The best qualities of players can be highlighted using this technique. Future studies can examine how well this model compares players from various leagues.

Comparative Analysis

Table 41.2A (on the basis on R2 score)

Author& Year of Publication	Algorithm Used	Findings& Results
Mason Chen [3] (2020)	Neural algorithms	Neural networks could build good predictive models. (R2 Score 0.917)
Yejia Liu [7] (2019)	Regression Tree model	Ranking predicted by model and the actual success ranking are highly correlated. (R2 score 0.0933)

Table 41.2B (based on accuracy percentage)

Author & Year of Publication	Algorithm Used	Findings & Results
Fuzhi Su [4] (2022)	Random forest, XGBoost	The XGB approach has a higher interpretability and a better match to the problem. (92.5 % accuracy)
Yuefei Chen [5] (2019)	Neural network	Mixed dataset performs better than others. (91.3.% accuracy)
Zafar Mahmood [6] (2020)	MEM model	Model-wise analysis demonstrates the dominance of MEM classifier in terms of accuracy. (96% accuracy)

Conclusion

In professional ball sport, contests such as the NBA, data analysis and machine learning forecasts must be analysed. After a player has participated in enough games, ranking them according to their career statistics can be helpful. Nonetheless, it can be challenging to gauge a player's strength when they are just beginning their career and have participated in a limited number of games. Ranking past performance has the drawback of being unable to predict players' future performance. Techniques for machine learning are frequently employed today to forecast the future. This study comes to the conclusion that machine learning techniques can be used to determine whether a player will win the MVP award or not. Out of all the studies and models that have been used, MEM has produced the most accurate and precise results.

Future Scope

Future work can focus on extending the research by adding more attributes such as the physical health, physiological status of the player for prediction. Deep learning techniques like artificial neural networks can be used to further improve the performance of the model. Moreover, these algorithms can be further extended to several other ball games like soccer, baseball, hockey etc and to understand the physical interaction between emerging stars and their co-players and analyse motion between the two.

References

1. Coleman, B. J., DuMond, J. M., and Lynch, A. K. (2008). An examination of NBA MVP voting behaviour: does race matter.*Journal of Sports Economics*, 9(6), 606–627.
2. Siddiqi, M. H., Alam, M. G. R., Hong, C. S., Khan, A. M., andChoo, H. (2016). Anovel maximum entropy markovmodel for human facial expression recognition. *PLoS ONE*, 11(9), e0162702. https://doi.org/10.1371/journal.pone.0162702.
3. Chen, M., and Chen, C. (2020). Data mining computing of predicting NBA 2019–2020 regular season MVP winner. In 2020 International Conference on Advances in Computing and Communication Engineering (ICACCE), (pp. 1–5). IEEE.
4. Su, F., and Chen, M. (2022). Basketball players' score prediction using artificial intelligence technology via the Internet of things.*The Journal of Supercomputing*, 78(17), 19138–19166.
5. Chen, Y., Dai, J., and Zhang, C. (2019). A neural network model of the NBA most valued player selection prediction. In Proceedings of the 2019 the International Conference on Pattern Recognition and Artificial Intelligence (pp. 16–20).
6. Mahmood, Z., Daud, A., andAbbasi, R. A. (2021). Using machine learning techniques for rising star prediction in basketball.*Knowledge-Based Systems*, 211, 106506.
7. Liu, Y., Schulte, O., and Li, C. (2019). Model trees for identifying exceptional players in the NHL and NBA drafts. In Machine Learning and Data Mining for Sports Analytics: 5th International Workshop, MLSA 2018, Co-located with ECML/PKDD 2018, Dublin, Ireland, September 10, 2018, Proceedings 5 (pp. 93–105). Springer International Publishing.

42 An efficient AES and security performance trade-off

Sandeep Kaur[1,a] and Sarpreet Singh[2,b]

[1]Ph.D scholar, Computer Science, SGGSWU, FGS, India

[2]Asst. Prof. Computer Science, SGGSWU, FGS, India

Abstract

Cloud computing is a wonderful development in information technology. Users can store large amounts of data at a remote storage location, and it provides pay-per-use usage of files, services, and software on their personal devices via internet connections. Cloud storage, file sharing, and data backup are the three main uses for end users. According to the Flex Era the year 2021 Study, 90% of organisations think that COVID-19 has greatly increased the number of cloud clients. The privacy and data security of using cloud computing technology are fundamental concerns. Although alternative encryption protocols have been proposed to secure sensitive data, AES encryption is often used in cloud computing technology.This study assesses various areas where the AES can be enhanced to increase efficiency. Furthermore, the compromise made by the various encryption techniques' performance and security is revealed.

Keywords: AES, cryptography, security, trade-off

Introduction

The data safety and privacy protection procedures are the main factors causing customers' concern with the cloud computing environment. In 2021, Tahir et al.[12]. Cloud data storage poses a number of security challenges. Outsourcing data to the cloud results in the loss of personal authority over the information, and certain cloud service providers, or CSPs, may change the data in deceptive ways. CSPs may take information from a cloud service and give it to another company in order to make money. Designing effective security techniques has taken centre stage in the world of cloud computing due to its burgeoning security challenges.Kaur and Kaur [5] Saha et al. [10] Kaur et al. [6].The end user privacy, network communication safety storage system protection, and server system security are the security concerns associated with cloud computing, which can be somewhat resolved with encryption [3, 8]. Numerous security algorithms are used to improve the security of cloud computing systems, including"DES, Triple-DES, AES, and Blowfish symmetric algorithms"[10]. Even though AES is a well-liked symmetric block cypher, it faces several cryptanalysis impacts. The key expansion's main issue is vulnerability. Even though the technique has odd properties due to"the XOR operation, S-boxes, and function" shifting, reverse engineering can easily go back to the original key space.Saha et al. [10] andAbroshan [1] Additionally, a balanced compromise may result from the best possible trade-off between the aforementioned encryption and decryption techniques by

[a]sandeep18033@gmail.com, [b]ersarpreetvirk@gmail.com

guaranteeing both a safe service and a satisfactory degree of performance. Due to the dearth of exhaustive and comparative studies, it is difficult to comprehend the trade-off among security and performance [13]. In this study, a variety of algorithms are compared for performance and security. This study suggested a successful AES encryption method to address the aforementioned AES problems.

Literature Survey

Cloud computing is a wonderful development in information technology. Users can store large amounts of data at a remote storage location, and it provides cost-per-use access to files, services, and software on personal machines via internet connections. Cloud storage, file sharing, and data backup are the three main uses for end users. Although alternative encryption protocols have been proposed to secure sensitive data, AES encryption is often used in cloud computing technology. GA creates keys for both decryption and encryption that are used in conjunction with a cryptographic technique to safeguard the privacy and integrity of electronic data. The model takes into account the procedures of downloading and uploading data. The information that is input , first scrambled using the Caesar cypher method before going through an 8-bit binary transform for each character for the purpose to achieve first-level encryption during uploading. A random token that was generated using GA is then used to encrypt the desired binary data. The exact process is followed in reverse when downloading. In their performance investigation, they utilised standard parameters and algorithms(like RSA, Blowfish, DES, and 3DES). Similarly,using a different methodMahalakshmi and Suseendran [7].The cryptographic techniques RSA and MD5 are both used in a hybrid solution. Here, the data is safeguarded with MD5, that is primarily utilised for data integrity checks, and it is encrypted using RSA. Different key values are used by the algorithms for encryption and decryption. This multi-layered encryption method protects the integrity of the information saved in the cloud. Verifying the data integrity is this paper's primary issue. To improve cloud security, a recent study Sajay et al. [11] combines homographic encrypting and blowfish encryption. "To use homographic encryption, a given number is converted to binary bits, with each of those bits then being encrypted using homographic encryption. Next, all of these strings are concatenated and sent to the second layer of the blowfish method.The blowfish encryption technique has the following advantages: (1) a 64-bit block size; (2) the ability to operate enormous data blocks; (3) an efficient algorithm; (4) an expandable key between 32 bits to 256 fewest bits; and (5) simple operations. Furthermore, to increase the level of safety of the cloud platform, a hybrid method that was just recently proposed Abroshan [1] combined an improved blowfish algorithm with an elliptic-curve-based algorithm. Blowfish has a smaller block size, making it more open to assault. For longer files, it is advised against using blowfish encryption. Another type of cypher that protects against malicious attackers is AES. It is one of the most effective encryption techniques in use right now. AES successfully strikes a balance between speed and security, allowing us to maintain using the internet uninterrupted [2].

Proposed AES Solution

The initially generated basic key of the standard AES can be compromised, allowing the hacker to learn the remaining round key. Therefore, a secured first-round beginning key is generated in order to get bypassing the vulnerability. The cyclic operation in typical AES Shift Row then began on the second row of the state of the key array and ended on the fourth row. The block swap algorithm, which immediately switches the first halves of the arrays with the second half, reduces the level of difficulty of the circular motion procedure for the shift row step. It makes the distribution of secure keys easier. The following subsection explains the proposed AES approach :-

Round Key Generation and Expansion
For creating a key, there are two main bases. It may be a key generated at random or based on a password that is readable by humans [16]. We create the 128-bit private key using the password-based key. Then, in order to make it more difficult to predict, we add more random bytes, known as a salt. Each round, we generated our salt using Secure Random. Figure 42.1 shows a secured key extension with a 128 bit size. For each round, the key is enlarged as follows:-

Where W4=W0 XOR-ed g(W3) and

W5=W1XOR-ed W4

W6= W2 XOR-ed W5 and

W7= W3 XOR-ed W6.and so on

Rotate word and sub-word are the two sub-functions that make up function g. Rot word produces a one-byte circular left shift, while sub-byte uses S-Box to execute byte replacement. Pre-transformation is applied to the plain file first, and then, depending upon the length of the key block, n rounds are applied. Additionally, every round contains four steps, save the final one.

Substitute bytes: This action carries out the substitution. The S-box table is used to substitute each matrix member.

Swapping:The shifting round circular procedure can be made simpler by swapping out segments, which is a better approach.Figure 2 illustrates the process of Swapping phase.

Blend column: The limited (finite) field GF (28), in general, has the cycling integers 2 and 3 for each row. This describes Finite Fields GF (28), with the circular values 2 and 3 over each row. The resulting array multiplied with the design of Finite Field values in the mix columns"consisting of the numbers 2 and 3. Finite Field value 1 doesn't need to be multipliedbecause the result is the same as before. The suggested approach multiplies each hexadecimal element of the array by a constant ranging from 2 to 3.

Add round keyPhase :In this phase new round key is added at the end of each round.

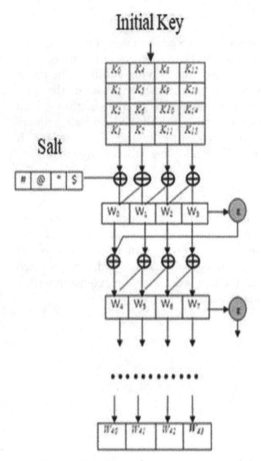

Figure 42.1 Secure key Expansion module

Simulation Results

A comparative analysis of cryptographic systems "including AES, DES, 3DES, Blowfish, ECC, RSA, and suggested AES" was done using the simulation. Java Development Kit (JDK) version 7 was used to accomplish the suggested technique. The JDK's two libraries, Java Cryptography Architecture (JCA) and Java Cryptography Extension (JCE), contain cryptography-related functionality. Most of the requirements for basic cryptography are covered by the JCA, although the JCE can be used for more complicated cryptographic activities. In order to evaluate the solution, the Intel Core2 Duo 2.5 GHz engine was applied. Every assessment was performed on Windows 10. The suggested AES and AES's average computation times for key creation, encryption, and decryption are shown in Table 42.1. According to the results, the Proposed AES works superior for the purpose of both encryption and decryption even if key generation takes a bit longer than it does for AES. Additionally, efficiency improved as file size rose. In Figure 42.3, the comparisons are shown.

Index	0	1	2	3	4	5	6	7	8	9	10	11	12	13	14	15
Data	S	U	C	C	E	S	S	F	U	L	A	C	T	I	O	N
HEX	53	55	43	43	45	53	53	46	55	4C	41	43	54	49	4F	4E

Index	0	1	2	3	4	5	6	7	8	9	10	11	12	13	14	15
Data	50	ED	64	64	68	50	50	98	ED	5D	FB	64	FD	A4	92	B6

Sub byte State Array

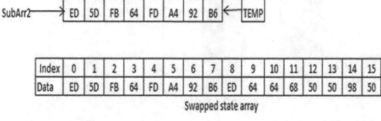

Index	0	1	2	3	4	5	6	7	8	9	10	11	12	13	14	15
Data	ED	5D	FB	64	FD	A4	92	B6	ED	64	64	68	50	50	98	50

Swapped state array

Figure 42.2 Swapping Process

Security Performance Trade-Off

The trade-off among performance and security shows that both can be assessed and that in order to raise one, we must reduce the other. The trade-off within security and performance has been highlighted by the analytical assessments of the methodologies. The security performance trade-off for cryptography techniques"like DES, Triple-DES (3DES), Blowfish, AES, and Proposed AES" is described in more detail in the section. It is based on criteria like key generation time, encryption time, and decryption time.

DES: A shared key is used to encrypt and/or decrypt data using the Data Encryption Standard (DES), a symmetric encryption method. The problem with this approach is that if the key is discovered by others, the entire communication is made public. In comparison to modified AES, AES and Triple-DES, average key creation duration and encryption/decryption time are significantly lower. Of all the encryption schemes discussed, it computes keys the fastest, but it cannot keep up with recently discovered online assaults [9]. As a result, it operates more effectively yet is vulnerable to new dangers.

Table 42.1 Comparisons of existing AES and proposed ImprovedAES

Cryptography Methods	Key Generation time	Encryption Time	Decryption Time
AES-128	41.477	516.8541099	282.9555001
Proposed AES-128	51.801	459.0529599	278.30682

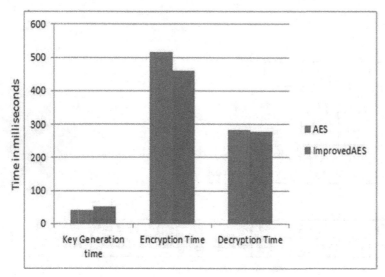

Figure 42.3 Comparisons Results

Triple-The advanced form of DES, known as DES (3DES), is used three times to increase the security or encryption level. As a consequence of 3DES's three-fold increase in CPU utilisation over its predecessor, performance is considerably affected. As a result, 3DES is three times more slow than DES but, when used properly, offers higher security. As a result, both have a security performance trade-off.

BlowfishAnother symmetric block cypher with a 64-bit block size is the blow-fish algorithm (BA). Blowfish is known to be susceptible to known-plaintext attacks on reflectively weak keys. It is extremely effective in producing keys, encryption, and decryption, but it lacks the universality of AES. 64 utilised block sizes are regarded as insecure. As a result, the Blowfish and AES trade off in terms of security performance.

AESAES has several advantages over other cyphers in terms of necessary key size, processing time, and processor power, making it a commonly utilised algorithm. Despite being widely used due to its security defence against online threats, fault injection attacks are disclosing the key in AES, according to a survey of AES attacks [4, 10].

Table 42.2 Comparisons of Cryptography Systems.

Cryptography Methods	Key Generation time	Encryption Time	Decryption Time
DES	283.834	71.0847	241.563
TripleDES	4062.361	289.078	217.091
Blowfish	1854.115	138.278	349.852
AES	1906.678	289.088	963.273
ProposedAES	2102.934	166.658	480.527

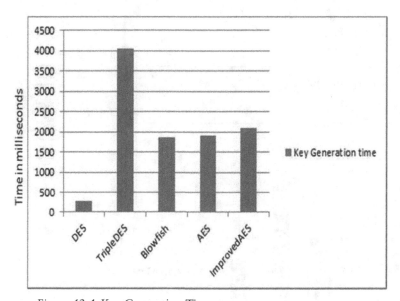

Figure 42.4 Key Generation Time

Proposed AES: The suggested guarded key generation module eliminates potential attack points. Additionally, by employing a block-swapping technique, the circular movement process' complexity is decreased. The results of the experiments and the analytical study show that the offered AES increases encryption performance and gives higher security. Therefore, among the aforementioned cryptography methods, suggested AES presents the finest security performance trade-off. Despite the fact that the proposed AES uses more CPU cycles, it provides an even more reliable key for an additional n rounds. A protected key generation module is provided by the Proposed AES, which also simplifies the shifting row circular procedure. The securely generated keys module guards against rainbow table attacks, which attempt to decrypt passwords by looking up values in a pre-made hash table.

The calculation times for generating keys, encrypting data, and decrypting data are shown in Table 42.2 for the encryption algorithms"ECC, DES,

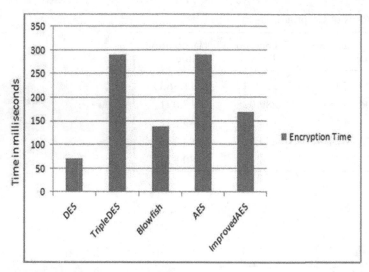

Figure 42.5 Encryption Time

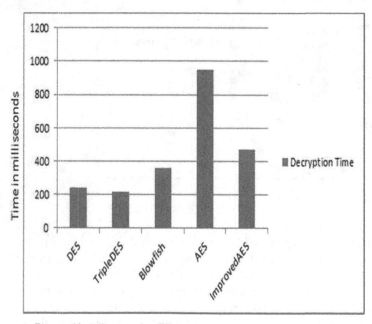

Figure 42.6 Decryption Time

Triple-DES, Blowfish, AES, and Proposed AES and RSA." The key production time for the systems shown in Figure 42.4 is shown. In comparison to other systems, Triple-DES's key generation time is extremely long. Figures 42.5 and 42.6 depict, respectively, the computation times for encryption and decryption of the cryptographic systems.

Conclusion

To protect against assaults using plain keys, the proposed AES offers a secured expanded key mechanism. The circular shifting procedure is made less complex by the suggested approach. Results from analyses and experiments are used to demonstrate the effectiveness of the suggested solution. The key creation module is quite helpful in avoiding key expanding hacking threats even though it takes a little longer. Additionally, a comparison of the solution to AES, Tipple-DES, Blowfish and DES reveals a general improvement. Additionally, the proposed paradigm excels in all areas, including security, efficiency, and integrity. Additionally, the suggested AES provides improved security and performance trade-offs, according to analytical and experimental results.

Acknowledgement

The authors gratefully acknowledge the students, staff, and authority of Computer Science department for their cooperation in the research.

References

1. Abroshan, H. (2021). A hybrid encryption solution to improve cloud computing security using symmetric and asymmetric cryptography algorithms. *IJACSA International Journal of Advanced Computer Science and Applications*, 12, 31-37. www.ijacsa.thesai.org.
2. Ali, M. L., Rahman, M. S., and Hossain, F. S. (2021). Design of a BIST implemented AES cryptoprocessor ASIC. *PLoS One*, 16, 1–14. https://doi.org/10.1371/journal.pone.0259956.
3. Chauhan, B., Borikar, S., Aote, S., and Katankar, V. (2018). A survey on image cryptography using lightweight encryption algorithm. *International Journal of Scientific Research in Science, Engineering and Technology*. 4(4), 344–47.
4. Dharshini, P., Renjith, J. A., and Kumar, P. M. (2016). Screening the covert key using honey encryption to rule out the brute force attack of AES—a survey. *Security and Communication Networks*, 9(18), 6379–6385. https://doi.org/10.1002/sec.1753.
5. Kaur, S., and Kaur, G. (n.d). Threat and vulnerability analysis of cloud platform: auser perspective. In Proceedings 2021 8th International Conference on Computing for Sustainable Global DevelopmentINDIACom 2021, (pp. 533–539), 2021. doi: 10.1109/INDIACom51348.2021.00095.
6. Kaur, S., Kaur, G., and Shabaz, M. (2022). A securetwo-factor authentication framework in cloud computing. *Security and Communication Networks*, 2022, 1–9. https://www.hindawi.com/journals/scn/2022/7540891/.
7. Mahalakshmi, B., and Suseendran, G. (2019). An Analysis of Cloud Computing Issues on Data Integrity, Privacy and Its Current Solutions. Singapore: Springer. https://doi.org/10.1007/978-981-13-1274-8.
8. Prabhu Kavin, B., Ganapathy, S.,Kanimozhi, U., and Kannan, A. (2020). An enhanced security framework for secured data storage and communications in cloud using ECC, access control and LDSA. *Wireless Personal Communications*, 115(2), 1107–1135. https://doi.org/10.1007/s11277-020-07613-7.
9. Karthik, S., and Muruganandam, A. (2014). Data encryption and decryption by using triple DES and performance analysis of crypto system. *International Journal of Scientific Engineering and Research (IJSER)*, 2(11), 24–31.

10.   Saha, R., Geetha, G.,Kumar, G., and Kim, T. H. (2018). RK-AES: an improved version of AES using a new key generation process with random keys. *Security and Communication Networks*. 2018, 1-11. https://doi.org/10.1155/2018/9802475.

11.   Sajay, K. R., Babu, S. S., and Vijayalakshmi, Y. (2019). Enhancing the security of cloud data using hybrid encryption algorithm. *Journal of Ambient Intelligence and Humanized Computing*. 1–10. https://doi.org/10.1007/s12652-019-01403-1.

12.   Tahir, M., Sardaraz, M., Mehmood, Z., and Muhammad, S. (2021). CryptoGA: ac-ryptosystem based on genetic algorithm for cloud data security. *Cluster Computing*, 24(2), 739–752. https://doi.org/10.1007/s10586-020-03157-4.

13.   Thabit, F., Alhomdy, S., and Jagtap, S. (2021). Security analysis and performance evaluation of a new lightweight cryptographic algorithm for cloud computing. *Global Transitions Proceedings*, 2(1), 100–110. https://doi.org/10.1016/j.gltp.2021.01.014.

43 Library automation an inevitable footstep towards networked library system: case study of govt degree colleges of Himachal Pradesh (India)

Anup Singh[a] and Dr. Jatinder Kumar[b]

Library and Information Science, Lovely Professional University, Jalandhar-Phagwara, Punjab, India

Abstract

This Report explored the Automation Status of Govt. Degree College Libraries of Himachal Pradesh, which is the essential threshold to enter into a networked library system. To serve this purpose cluster sampling was applied; consequently, 14-degree college libraries of Himachal Pradesh were selected for this study. For the collection of data, a questionnaire was prepared for Library professionals to judge the present status of library automation in their concerning libraries and the difficulties encountered by degree college libraries during the process of automation. The Librarians of 14-degree colleges were the participants of the study. The major Findings of the study portray a clear and crystal picture of the status of library automation in colleges. It is found that out of 14 degree college libraries of Himachal Pradesh University Shimla, only 2 (14.3%) libraries were fully automated, and the rest 12 (85.7%) libraries were partially automated. 6 (six) 42.9% of libraries faced budget allocation problems. 7 (50%) libraries faced the problem of unskilled staff. However, 9 (64.3%) of libraries faced the problem of insufficient ICT infrastructure. Only 1 (7.1%) library faced the problem of lack of interest by staff members and 4 (four) 28.6% faced the challenge of improper vendor support. 3 (21.4%) libraries faced the challenge of retro-conversion of data during the automation process of the library. This study will assist the library policy maker, administrators, and state Governments to understand the importance of automation in degree college libraries, the challenges faced by degree college libraries in providing automated college library services, and can step forward to resolve the automation- related problems of degree college libraries.

Keywords: Automation, barriers, college, Himachal Pradesh, libraries, status

Introduction

College users, who are made up of teachers and students, depend heavily on college libraries to meet their academic demands. When storing and dissemi- nating information, library professionals use a variety of methods and techni- cal approaches in order to properly serve the college fraternity. With the use of several library automation software packages, information technology-based abilities are used to automate the college library's varied housekeeping respon- sibilities. Although the field of library automation accelerated in the 1980s, it is currently developing. Students from the state's remote locations are now able to

[a]anupjasyal@gmail.com, [b]jatinder.24171@lpu.co.in

attend higher education because of the great growth of professional and non-professional colleges in Himachal Pradesh. Colleges amid the state's mountainous terrain are a crucial factor in encouraging students to pursue higher education. In this process, college libraries from professional and non-professional colleges are retro- converted, automated, and networked to enable library staff members to save valuable time and support information sharing across sister college libraries. Reviewing the literature found that there aren't many studies done on state degree college libraries in Himachal Pradesh. The results of this study are expected to demonstrate the automation conditions at a Govt. degree college library affiliated with Himachal Pradesh University Shimla. The study also looked into the types of computer-based resources and services offered to library patrons. such as databases, CD-ROM databases, OPAC, and open educational resources (OER). In order to comprehend the administrative issues with the libraries, an assessment of their IT infrastructure is also made.

Literature Review

Anuradha [1] focused on an automated circulation system, tailored to the needs of a medium-sized library, constructed in Visual Basic 6.0. It also details the goals of the circulation control system, the various file formats used, and the benefits of using a circulation system built on Visual Basic. Sinha and Bhattacharjee [8] investigated the Planning, Problems, and Solutions for Automation and Communication of University Libraries in the North-eastern Region and focuses on national knowledge. and library communication agencies such as CALIBNET, INFLIBNET, DELNET, NICNET, and other networks related to cities and metropolitan areas, have developed automation and communication with various uni- versities, national institutions, and institutions of higher learning, some of which have already begun operating and providing mechanisms. various. online ser- vices. Their findings recommend that the entire library should be connected to the Internet to provide online access to the resources of other library archives. Nanda [4] in their book titled "Library Automation" focused on Library automation as a paper taught at various institutions and universities at BLISc and MLISc courses. This book is an introductory course to the above article, providing essential infor- mation on all relevant aspects. The book is very useful for students, Library teach- ers, and professionals to learn library automation in an intelligent way. Singh [9]writes in his book "Library auto- mation in the contemporary era" that formerly complex methods and instruments have become more user-friendly and straightforward and suggested a variety of user-friendly software programs that might lighten the strain of experts. Rajput and Gautam [7] examined the current state of library automation and the chal- lenges faced by the special libraries in the Madhya Pradesh city of Indore. The report detailed the challenges administrators and workers encountered through- out the automation process and provided possible solutions. Tonk [11] provides an in-depth look into library automation at Solapur's educational institutions by comparing and contrasting the various library management systems in use and the satisfied library services to end consumers. Naveen and Nagesh [5] investi- gated the Status and issues of library automation in Govt. first-grade colleges in Hassan district, Karnatka, and painted a detailed picture of the present state of library automation and the challenges that it faces. Zaveri and Salve [12] exam- ined the current state of library automation software used in Mumbai's academic libraries. Research showed that most library systems are automated. The usage and procurement of the program were hampered by a lack of skilled personnel and a shortage of funds. Gaffar and Pati [3] understood the Koha-Automation Software programme in the Prof. Bhubaneswar Behera Central Library. Because Koha is a complete library software system with all the necessary models for all types of libraries, the author highly recommended it (i.e., from small libraries to very large libraries). Survade et al. [10] in their paper titled "SOUL 2.0 (Software for University Libraries) for Library Automation." The definition of library auto- mation, the need for library automation, the benefits of automation, the SOUL software overview, SOUL 2.0 features, SOUL modules, etc. were all examined by the writers and promotes SOUL (Software for University Libraries) for library automation. Panda and Chakerbrty [6] study is based on the remarkable advance- ments in technology and resource sharing that technologists and enthusiastic librarians around the world have made with regard to library automation and cloud computing. The paper addresses the underlying reasons for issues with the traditional library management system and outlines the advantages, drawbacks, and difficulties of adopting cloud technology to automate libraries. Babuprasad [2] The effects of library automation services in the Govt. First- Grade College libraries in the Kolar district were the study's primary area of interest. It is found that seven out of eight libraries are totally automated. While 75% of librarians believe automation has improved their library's services, 85% of users believe an automated library system is superior to the more traditional manual approach. There aren't enough general personnel at one of the eight libraries to manage automation services. Despite the fact that numerous studies of the same kind have already been conducted in various parts of the world.

Statement of Problem

It's time to think about the ways in which the mountain regional state libraries provide services to their users in the digital world. What is the nature of the work in the Govt. Degree College Libraries affiliated to Himachal Pradesh University Shimla in a networked world? What kind of libraries will it take? What library software packages are used for the above-mentioned library? What are the automatic functions and resources in the library? Are college libraries given enough money? Do college libraries receive full administrative support? These were all questions that came to my mind.

Scope and Limitation of Study

The purpose of this research is to investigate the Automation Status of Govt. degree college libraries affiliated with Himachal Pradesh University Shimla. It is not possible to include all the Govt. degree college libraries in the study. The study is limited to 14 Govt. degree colleges affiliated with Himachal Pradesh University Shimla.

Objectives of the Research

The purpose of this research is to examine the current library automation status of Govt. Degree college libraries in India. The main objectives of the study were;

1. To determine the state of automation at the Govt. degree colleges' libraries affiliated with Himachal Pradesh University Shimla.
2. To gain a deeper knowledge of the automation issues Govt. degree college libraries are facing.

Hypothesis

1. There are a few Govt. college libraries affiliated with Himachal Pradesh University that are automated.
2. Govt. Degree college libraries are facing problems during the automation process.

Research Methodology and Techniques Used

This research applied a descriptive method which is survey- based and analyzed the current situation of affairs. Primary research is conducted for this reason. The research method includes many other approaches, such as observation, questionnaires, and discussions, but the questionnaire is the only one that is addressed in detail here since it is used to gather data for this particular study. one concise, official survey was developed and sent out to college libraries and their patrons.

Data Collection Instruments
The survey research method is selected for the present study and 01 questionnaires is prepared, for Library professionals to know the current status of library automation in their respective libraries. During the preparation of the questionnaires, all the aspects relating to library automation in degree college libraries are taken into consideration with proper care. A structured questionnaire with mostly closed-ended questions is designed.

Data Collection
Personal visits are made to 14 different degree colleges in Himachal Pradesh to get responses from library staff. The collected data are recorded for data analysis & interpretation.

Analysis & Interpretation of Vital Information

Data was collected with the help of a questionnaire, refined, codified, and organized for analysis and interpretation. Data Analysis is done in a Simple Percentage and in some cases, the cumulative Percentage Method is implemented with the help of SSPS software (Social Science Statistical Package). Several tables, separate tables, line graphs, bar charts, column charts, pie charts, area graphs, cone charts, cylinder charts, etc. created with the help of MS Excel. and SPSS software used the Chi-square test and P-Value detection to shape data in intelligent and translatable forms.

Table 43.1 Fourteen degree colleges of Himachal Pradesh included in the study.

S. No	Name of Degree College	Year of Establishment
1	Vallabh Govt. College, Mandi, Distt. Mandi	1948
2	Govt. College of Teacher Education Dharamshala, Distt. Kangra	1956
3	Govt. College Chamba, Distt. Chamba	1958
4	NSCBM Govt. College, Hamirpur, Distt. Hamirpur	1964
5	Govt. College Una, Distt. Una	1968
6	Govt. College Sanjauli, Shimla	1969
7	Rajkiya Kanya Mahavidyalaya Shimla, Distt. Shimla	1971
8	Govt. College, Nalagarh, Distt. Solan	1973
9	Govt. College, Arki, Distt. Solan	1994
10	Govt. College, Ghumarwin, Distt. Bilaspur	1994
11	Govt. College, Joginder Nagar,	1994
12	Govt. College, Palampur, Distt. Kangra	1994
13	Govt. College, Dharampur, Distt. Mandi	2005
14	College, Naura, angra	2005

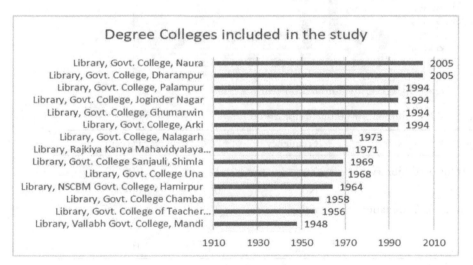

Figure 43.1 Degree colleges included in the study

Table and figure 43.1 show the year of establishment of state college's libraries in Himachal Pradesh. It can be concluded that the oldest library in Himachal Pradesh is VGC Mandi which is established in 1948, whereas Govt. College Naura and Govt. college Dharampur Library are the latest one established in 2005. Whereas GCTE Library, Govt. College Chamba, NSCBM Govt. College, Hamirpur, Library, GC Una Library, COE Govt. College Sanjauli Library, RKMV Library, G.C. Nalagarh, Library are established in 1956, 1958, 1964, 1968,

Table 43.2 Library automation year

Year of Library Automation	Frequency (N libraries)	Percent
2003	1	7.1%
2007	1	7.1%
2009	4	28.6%
2012	2	14.3%
2013	1	7.1%
2015	1	7.1%
2016	1	7.1%
2017	1	7.1%
2019	1	7.1%
2021	1	7.1%
Total	14	100.0%

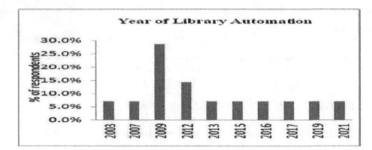

Figure 43.2 Library automation year

Table 43.3 Automation status of libraries

	Frequency		Percent
Automated Library	Yes	14	100.0%
	No	0	0.0%
Status of Automation	Fully	2	14.3%
	Partially	12	85.7%
	Total	14	100.0%

1969,1971, and 1973 respectively. GC Arki, Library GC Ghumarwin Library, GC Joginder Nagar, Library and GC Palampur, Library are established in 1994.

Table and figure 43.2 show the year of library automation. As shown in table out of 14 libraries, 4 libraries initiated library automation in 2009, whereas 2 libraries in 2012,8 libraries initiated in 2003, 2007, 2013, 2015, 2016, 2017, 2019 and 2021.

Table and figure 43.3 interpret that all of the libraries were automated. Majority of 85.7% libraries were partially automated and 14.3% were fully automated.

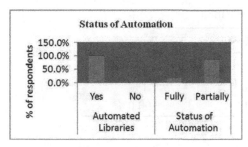

Figure 43.3 Automation Status of Libraries

Table 43.4 Software module used for library automation purpose

Software Module used for Library Automation purpose	Automated		Not Automated	
	Frequency	Percent	Frequency	Percent
Administration	8	57.1%	6	9%
Acquisition	5	35.7%	9	3%
Cataloguing	14	100.0%	0	0%
Circulation	6	42.9%	8	1%
Serial Control	2	14.3%	12	7%
OPAC	9	64.3%	5	7%
Report	7	50.0%	7	0%

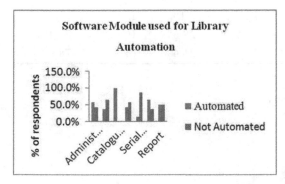

Figure 43.4 Software module used for library automation purpose

As shown in table and figure 43.4, that 57.1% libraries which were automated used administration for library automation purpose. While 64.3% partially automated libraries used acquisition software, 57.1% partially automated libraries used circulation module and 85.7% partially automated libraries used serial control module. 64.3% automated libraries used OPAC software for library automation purpose. All of the libraries used cataloguing for library automation purpose.

Table and figure 43.5 interpret that 92.9% libraries used soul for automation, whereas 7.1% libraries used Alice for window.

Table 43.5 Usage of library software for automation

Library software used for automation	Frequency	Percent
Soul	13	92.9%
Alice for Window	1	7.1%
Total	14	100.0%

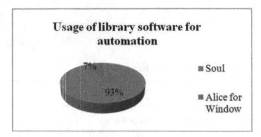

Figure 43.5 Use of library software for automation

Table 43.6 Problems faced during the automation process of the library

	Yes		No	
	Frequency	Percent	Frequency	Percent
Budget Allocation	6	42.9%	8	57.1%
Unskilled Staff	7	50.0%	7	50.0%
Insufficient ICT Infrastructure	9	64.3%	5	35.7%
Lack of interest by staff members	1	7.1%	13	92.9%
Improper Vendor support	4	28.6%	10	71.4%
Retro-conversion of data	3	21.4%	11	78.6%

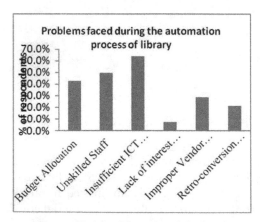

Figure 43.6 Problems faced during Automation Process of the Library

Table and figure 43.6 show the response related to problems faced during auto-mation process of library. As shown in table,57.1% faculty did not face budget allocation problem due to automation process of library, whereas 42.9% faculty faced this problem. 50% of faculty faced the problem of unskilled staff due to automation process of library. However, 64.3% of faculty faced the problem of insufficient ICT infrastructure. Only 7.1% faculty faced lack of interest by staff members and 28.6% faced improper vendor support due to automation process of library. 21.4% faculty faced retro-conversion of data due to automation process of library.

Results
Library Automation Year
Table and figure 43.2 show the year of library automation. As shown in table out of 14 libraries, 4 libraries initiated library automation in 2009, whereas 2 libraries in 2012,8 libraries initiated in 2003, 2007, 2013, 2015, 2016, 2017, 2019 and 2021.

Automation Status of Libraries
Table and figure 43.3 interpret that all of the libraries were automated. Majority of 85.7% libraries were partially automated and 14.3% were fully automated.

Software Module used for Library Automation Purpose
As shown in table and figure 43.4, that 57.1% libraries which were automated used administration for library automation purpose. While 64.3% partially automated libraries used acquisition software, 57.1% partially automated libraries used circulation module and 85.7% partially automated libraries used serial control module. 64.3% automated libraries used OPAC software for library automation purpose. All of the libraries used cataloguing for library automation purpose.

Usage of Library Software for Automation
Table and figure 43.5 interpret that 92.9% libraries used soul for automation, whereas 7.1% libraries used Alice for window.

Problems Faced During the Automation Process of the Library
Table and figure 43.6 show the response related to problems faced during automation process of library. As shown in table,57.1% faculty did not face budget allocation problem due to automation process of library, whereas 42.9% faculty faced this problem. 50% of faculty faced the problem of unskilled staff due to automation process of library. However, 64.3% of faculty faced the problem of insufficient ICT infrastructure. Only 7.1% faculty faced lack of interest by staff members and 28.6% faced improper vendor support due to automation process of library. 21.4% faculty faced retro-conversion of data due to automation process of library.

Conclusion

The level of automation in Himachal Pradesh's college libraries is on par with that of its counterparts in the rest of India. Automating library processes is a need for libraries, librarians, and university administrations to provide safe, efficient services to their patrons. Those who work in libraries must continually improve their knowledge and abilities in order to satisfy the expanding needs of library patrons. Automation in Himachal Pradesh College Libraries will make the teachers and students improve their academic performances by providing them the current and nascent information and approaches to global information. Therefore, efforts should be made to enable the aforementioned college libraries to keep up with the emergency modifications. The libraries should prepare themselves to face the challenges of emerging technologies and should fully automate their resources and services as soon as possible and provide their user community with networked services. The parent bodies of these state colleges should have a positive attitude towards the development of their libraries throughout, arrange for staff training, provide adequate and efficient staff to their libraries, and provide adequate resources and support for the development of an effective electronic system and access to a wide variety of information networks and web-based services.

Acknowledgement

The authors gratefully acknowledge the students, staff, and authority of Himachal Pradesh University affiliated Colleges and department of Library Science, Lovely Professional University for their cooperation in the research.

References

1. Anuradha, P. (2000). Automated circulation system using visual basic 6.0. *Annals of Library science and documentation*,47, 42–49.
2. Babuprasad, K. C. (2022). Impact of library automation services in govt. first-grade college libraries in Kolar district: a survey. *IP Indian Journal of Library Science and Information Technology*, 6(2), 88–96.
3. Gaffar, A. S. K., and Patti, J. (2018). Library Automation: a proposal of using koha library automation software. *VSRD*, 4(1), 9–16.
4. Nanda, M., (2005). Library Automation. Anmol Publications, India.
5. Naveen, C. L., and Nagesh, R. (2016). Status and problems of library automation in govt. first grade colleges of hassan district, karnataka: a study. *International Journal of Library and Information Science (IJLIS)*. 6(2), 28-35.
6. Panda, S., and Chakarbrty, R. (2021). Implementation Cloud Enabled SaaS Services in Library Automation: A Study of Government Initiatives in India. Saptrishi Publication, Emerging Trends in Academic Libraries in ICT Era, Chandigarh, India, (pp. 28–51)
7. Rajput, P. S., and Gautam, J. N. (2010). Automation and problems in their implementation: an investigation of special libraries in Indore, India. *International Journal of Library and Information Science*, 2(7), 143–147.
8. Sinha, M.K., and Bhattacharjee (2003). Library Automation in Modern Age. Alfa Publication, New Delhi.
9. Singh, P.C. (2008). Library Automation in Modern Age. New Delhi: Alfa Publication. 262.
10. Survade, Y., Patil, D., and Daya, T. (2023). SOUL 2.0 Software for University Libraries for Library Automation. *International journal of Research in Library Science (IJRLS)*, 9(4), 44-51. https://doi.org/10.26761/ijrls.9.4.2023.1074
11. Tonk, M. K. (2013). Library automation in different colleges in Solapur city. *Research Dimension*, 1(1), 36–47.
12. Zaveri, P., and Deepali, S. (2018). Status of library automation software use in mumbai college libraries. *Knowledge Librarian*, 5(1), 381–389.

44 Smart home system integration using internet of things

*Pushpendra Verma[1,a], Dr. Jamal Akhtar Khan[2,b],
Adil Khan[1,c], Pawan Kumar[1,d], Allauddin Ali[1,e] and
Prince Kumar Singh[1,f]*

[1]Student, Lovely Professional University,Phagwara, India

[2]Asst. Professor, Lovely Professional University,Phagwara, India

Abstract

This project presents a smart home system that integrates facial recognition, access control, home automation, and environment monitoring. When a person arrives home, the system scans the person's face and compares it to a stored database to checkthat the person is a family member or an unknown person. If the person is a family member, the door will open and if the personis unknown, access will be denied. Additionally, the system allows the user to control the home's switches and appliances through the Blynk app. Moreover, the system monitors the air quality and gas leakage within the home, and sends notifications through email and Blynk if any issue arises. The integration of these technologies provides a secure and convenient smart home experience.

Overall, this smart home system integrates advanced technologies to provide a secure and convenient living environment for the user. The facial recognition technology, home automation, environment monitoringand access control features work together seamlessly and remotely to enhance the quality of life of the person or user.

Keywords: Environment condition monitoring,internet of things (IoT), smart home integration, smart dooraccess

Introduction

Smart home integration system is a way of connecting all the devices of home with the Internet using Internet of Things for better class of living [1,2]. To make home smarter here we will use many types of sensors and cloud computing to operate the devices remotely. From smart home integration you can improved home security throw using smart door and also you can monitor the home environment condition like air quality, gas leakage information, smoke detection [3,4,5]. Smart home integration provides benefits like energy saving, time reduction, improved security and it is convenient also. In the advancement of Internet of things (IoT) now the sensors and components is available very easily and in cheap amount [23]. The presence of the IoT and the availability of devices are ubiquitous and play a significant role in our daily lives. These devices are utilized across various sectors including healthcare, railways, industry, as well as in smart homes and smart cities. From a security perspective,

[a]pv842984@gmail.com, [b]jamal.28445@lpu.co.in, [c]adilkhan786p@gmail.com,
[d]pk716586@gmail.com, [e]allauddinmfp1999@gmail.com, [f]princerajputjma1@gmail.com

both smarter devices and users need to establish a secure communication channel to identify digital forms [22]. The use of IoT devices requires a suitable infrastructure that does not require intervention or control by the operator or owner. The IoT provides many solutions that can help peoples to complete daily tasks. Smart home and smart city systems are among the most popular options, which typically include features like privacy, safety or security, energy efficient, and some other functionalities. In order to provide some capabilities, sensor devices are placed in the home to collectdata and then transfer it to aserver using cloud computing [6,7]. Once the data is analyzed by the sensor, it can assist the owner in avoiding unexpected situations without any additional effort. The aim of a smart home is to make homeowners feel more comfortable, convenient and safe both inside and outside the residence. As more controllable devices are added to the home environment, the benefits of these interconnected and communicative devices have become more desirable in recent decades [10, 11, 12]. The latest innovation in IoT applications is one of the most practical and necessary solutions for monitoring and surveillance related to security. Through the use of IoT, we can also surveillance the door by providing smart door where we will set the camera and match the scanned image with the available database that a person is right person or not if person is right then door will open else it will not open [20].

Smart Home Overview

A smart home where we connect the all devices of home with IoT and allow to control the all devices automatically and remotely throw using cloud computing or cloud computing-based applications[9] and we can also monitor the environment condition of home and rooms also like we can check or detect the air quality, any gas leakage and smoke[12]. Controlling the gadgets inside the room automatically without the engagement of the human effort like automatic face recognition door opening and the controlling the light of room controlling as per the light intensity in the room[22]. Gas detection system if some harmful gas is there then the signal is sent in Blynk server and then the notification is sent to the owner's phone or mobile. And the humidity and temperature of the surrounding and send the data into the Blynk application and if the temperature rises from some critical limit, then the alarm system is triggered[12].

The appliances can be controllable from anywhere from mobile Blynk app or the Blynk.com website that provide the device controllable from remotely and all the information is monitored from the mobile or website from anywhere [13].

Smart Home Services
Controlling Home Access
To access the home, we will use the home access system. In this system first we will store the face scanned data of home members into the database [15]and after we will set the camera on door and if anyone can want to access home, they need to scan him/her face on cameraand using python and open cv face will comparewith the database if face data will match with the database data, then access is allowed else access is not allowed [22].

Managing Home Appliances

For managing the home devices and appliances we will use cloud computing to control the devices automatically and remotely [13]. We will connect the all sensors and devices to each other and then data which is processed by the processor send to server using cloud computing so real time data will store in database [13]. And as a use case of scenario, we can use this data. So, we will manage all the data and devices remotely.

Measuring Home Conditions

In smart Home we will use many types of sensors like humidity, temperature, gas sensor. Using these sensors, we will monitor the condition of home[12]. We will use MQ2, MQ-135 for Gas and DHT-11 for temperature. We will measure the temperature and then detect the smoke, gases like LPG, CO and check the air quality also. If the air quality is not good and if detected any gas then red led, buzzer will be onand notification send to the Blynk application and on email also [12].

Main Components

The system is completed with the using of following components, which isexplained below and in Figure 44.1.

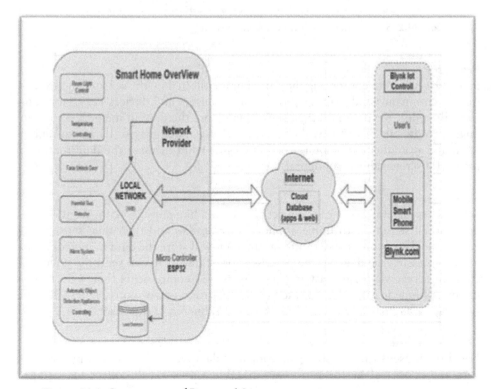

Figure 44.1 Components of Proposed System

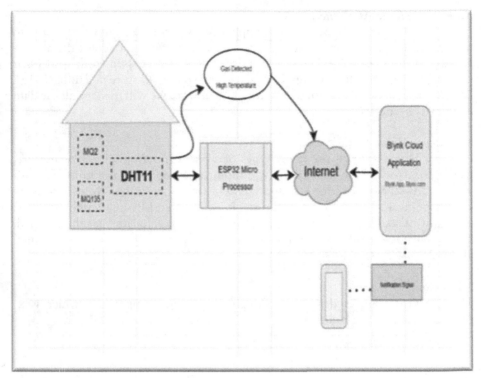

Figure 44.2 Sensors deployed in Proposed System

Processor
Processor is used to computing the data that is collected by the sensors and execution of commands and managing the various sensors and devices [11]. First sensor will collect the data and then sensor will store the data in memory and then analog to digital convertor will change the physical quantity of data into digital form and store them in memory then Processor will processor the data that is in form of discrete value or in digital form.

Sensors
Sensors are generally using for collect the all data like physical data. We will connect the all sensors with home appliances or devices and then then sensor will collect the data in physical quantity and then it will store the data in memory and after processing the data by the processor or actuators it will send the collected data on server via local network[5]. Sensors and components that we will use in smart home is Mq2, Mq135, temperature sensor, servo motor, ESP32 Board, camera, Relay board, switches, LED's, DHT11, buzzer, LDR sensor.

Local Database
Local database is used to store the code and data which is collected by the sensors and processed by the processor[23]. When sensor will collect the data, it

will store in the local database. And then ADC will convert analog data which is stored in local database to digital data so processor will read the data easily. Local database is used for processor also to process the data which is stored in local database[14].

Software and Applications
Software and applications is used to connect all IoT devices with the server via local network. We will connect all the devices and appliances with the micro controller board and done the connection of board with server with the help of cloud computing so we will control home devices and appliances remotely and real time data collection alsowe can use Blynk [16, 17].

Overview of Internet of Things (IoT)

Internet of things refers to the surroundings where devices and objects are connected to the internet and allow to communicate with all devices Remotely throw cloud computing. From IoT we can connect the physical devices, home appliances, and other item that are embedded with sensors[23]. The concept of the IoT involves devices that are connected to the internet, such like Sensors and other components which have a communication interface [18], software applications, limited storage, and processing units. This integration of objects into the internet enables interactions between people and devices as well as between devices themselves[6]. The IoT refers to the connection of real-world objects or things, such as home appliances, devices, vehicles, and other objects, to the existing internet network of computer systems [9]. IoT devices are connected with the sensors that detect changes in environment and collect the data. From IoT you can also collect real time data using cloud computing like cloud based web and Android applications [19, 21, 23].

Cloud Computing and How it is Important to Internet of Things andSmart Home IntegrationSystem

Cloud computing has enabled the integration of IoT devices and smart home technology by providing a scalable and cost-effective platform for data storage, processing, and analysis [13]. By using of cloud-based services in smart homes can get greater flexibility and availability and allowing homeowners to quickly and easily add new devices and features to their systems. Cloud computing can also enhance the security and privacy of smart homes by providing advanced encryption and authentication capabilities. Real-time data analysis and decision-making are essential components of smart home technology, and cloud computing provides a platform for these capabilities. Cloud computing can also enable greater energy efficiency in smart homes by providing real-time data on energy usage and enabling automated adjustments to temperature and lighting based on occupancy and environmental conditions[8].Cloud computing can enable smart homes to be integrated with other systems and devices, such as healthcare monitoring devices, smart appliances, and home automation systems, to create a more comprehensive and connected home environment [13].

Problems and Challenges

Face recognition using ESP32 is alittle bit complicated task because we have to store the face data somewhere in the database and then we will match the face after scanning the face on door camera andusing open CV we will match the face with the collected face data that is stored in database but if our model is not well trained so due to lack of accuracy door will not open so we need to train the data very well for a better accuracy and better performance[22]. The communication between Blynk Server and the owners' devices is requiring an application or website need to be installed in the user's phone if the application or websites is not installed in the mobile phone, then the device is not able to receive the signal. And if you want communication so different types of Widgets are available in the Blynk application but choosing the right widget to send the data in the Blynk application for better understanding and every widget have different way to communicate to the Blynk server [13].

Result

In results we have some clicked images of working project and online server (Blynk). You can see in [Working Image 1], [Working Image 2] and [Blynk Server Dashboard].

[Working Image 1 -LCD Display]

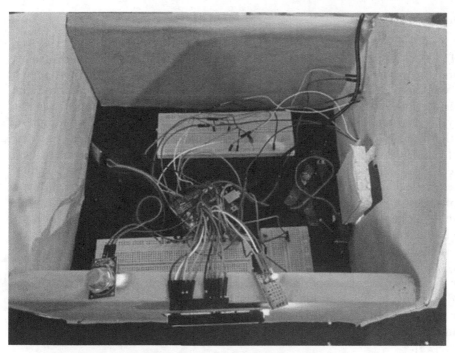

[*Working Image 2- Smart Home*]

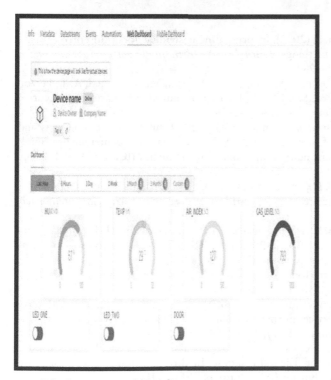

[*Blynk Server Dashboard*]

Conclusions

We designed a smart home system integration with an ESP32 chip, Camera, DHT11, MQ2, MQ135, Servo motor, Buzzer, LDR and Led[20]. In this smart home integration system, first we will use home access system in this system first we will store the face scanned data of home members into the database and after we will set the camera on the door and if anyone want to enter in home, they need to him/her face on camera and then scanned face will be compared to the database data if face data will match then door will open, otherwise not[22]. And using gas sensors, temperature sensors and smoke sensor we will detect gases, smoke and check the temperature of home[12]. if any harmful gases are leakage surroundings, then the microprocessor send the data in Blynk application and then blink trigger the notification and send it to the owner's mobile phone and the alarm system will also ON[12]. and we are also checking the home temperature using DHT-11 where we are given some condition that if it reached critical limit then the criteria of living temperature then notification will send on Blynk and email also [13]. And we have controlled the led on-off if any person is present or not present in home using Blynk application or Website [13]. it provides benefits like energy saving, time reduction, improved security and it is convenient also So, from smart home integration we can improve home security throw using smart doorand make a good living environment in home[23].

References

1. Alanezi, K., and Mishra, S. (2022). Incorporating individual and group privacy preferences in the internet of things. *Journal of Ambient Intelligence and Humanized Computing*, 13(4), 1969–1984.
2. Abdulla, A. I., Abdulraheem, A. S., Salih, A. A., Sadeeq, M. A., Ahmed, A. J., Ferzor, B. M., ... and Mohammed, S. I. (2020). Internet of things and smart home security. *Technol. Rep. Kansai Univ*, 62(5), 2465–2476.
3. Arora, A., Kaur, A., Bhushan, B., and Saini, H. (2019, July). Security concerns and future trends of internet of things. In 2019 2nd international conference on intelligent computing, instrumentation and control technologies (ICICICT) (Vol. 1, pp. 891–896). IEEE.
4. Ariansyah, W., Ilham, D. N., and Candra, R. A. (2021). Opening doors using internet of things (IoT) based face recognition. *Brilliance: Research of Artificial Intelligence*, 1(2), 32–37.
5. Bhide, V. H., and Wagh, S. (2015). i-learning IoT: an intelligent self-learning system for home automation using IoT. In 2015 International Conference on Communications and Signal Processing (ICCSP). IEEE, 2015.
6. Domb, M. (2019). Smart Home Systems Based on Internet of Things. IntechOpen. doi: 10.5772/intechopen.84894
7. Djehaiche, R., Aidel, S., Sawalmeh, A., Saeed, N., & Alenezi, A. H. (2023). Adaptive Control of IoT/M2M Devices in Smart Buildings Using Heterogeneous Wireless Networks. *IEEE Sensors Journal*, 23(7), 7836–7849.
8. Frincu, M., and Draghici, R. (2016). Towards a scalable cloud enabled smart home automation architecture for demand response. In IEEE PES Innovative Smart Grid Technologies Conference Europe (ISGT-Europe). IEEE, 2016.

9. Gladence, L. M., Anu, V. M., Rathna, R., & Brumancia, E. (2020). Recommender system for home automation using IoT and artificial intelligence. *Journal of Ambient Intelligence and Humanized Computing*, 1–9. DOI: https://doi.org/10.1007/s12652-020-01968-2

10. Motlagh, N. H., et al. (2020). Internet of things (IoT) and the energy sector. *Energies*, 13(2), 494.

11. Hill, J., et al. (2000). System architecture directions for networked sensors. *ACM Sigplan Notices*, 35(11), 93–104.

12. Khanda, K., et al. (2017). Microservice-based iot for smart buildings. In 2017 31st International Conference on Advanced Information Networking and Applications Workshops (WAINA). IEEE, 2017.

13. Khriji, S., et al. (2022). Design and implementation of a cloud-based event-driven architecture for real-time data processing in wireless sensor networks. *The Journal of Supercomputing*, 78, 3374–3401.

14. Kusuma, S. S., and Anil, G. N. (2018). An IoT based water supply monitoring and controlling system. *International Research Journal of Engineering and Technology (IRJET)*, 5(2), 857–860.

15. Marcus, D. S., et al. (2013). Human connectome project informatics: quality control, database services, and data visualization. *Neuroimage*, 80, 202–219.

16. Piyare, R., and Lee, S. R. (2013). Towards internet of things (iots): integration of wireless sensor network to cloud services for data collection and sharing. 5(5), 59–72. arXiv preprint arXiv:1310.2095.

17. Qin, Z., et al. (2014). A software defined networking architecture for the internet-of-things. In 2014 IEEE Network Operations and Management Symposium (NOMS). IEEE, 2014.

18. Soliman, M., et al. (2013). Smart home: Integrating internet of things with web services and cloud computing. In 2013 IEEE 5th International Conference on Cloud Computing Technology and Science (Vol. 2). IEEE, 2013.

19. Thilakarathne, N. N., Kagita, M. K., and Gadekallu, T. R. (2020). The role of the internet of things in health care: a systematic and comprehensive study. Available at SSRN 3690815., 10(4), 145–159.

20. Touqeer, H., et al. (2021). Smart home security: challenges, issues and solutions at different IoT layers. *The Journal of Supercomputing*, 77(12), 14053–14089.

21. Tsiftes, N., and Dunkels, A. (2011). A database in every sensor.In Proceedings of the 9th ACM Conference on Embedded Networked Sensor Systems, 2011.

22. Vermesan, O., and Friess, P. (2014). Internet of Things Applications-From Research and Innovation to Market Deployment. Taylor and Francis.

23. Zeng, E., Mare, S., and Roesner, F. (2017). End user security and privacy concerns with smart homes. In Symposium on Usable Privacy and Security (SOUPS). (Vol. 220).

45 Landmark detection system

Abinash Prusty[a], Rahul Kumar[b], Dibyanshu Kumar Patra[c] and Rishabh Bhatia[d]

School of Computer ApplicationLovely Professional University Phagwara, Punjab, India

Abstract

In many different applications, such as tourism and navigation systems, landmark detection is an essential task. In this study, we provide a technique for landmark detection that makes use of the idea of content-based image retrieval (CBIR),convolutional neural network (CNN) and Python-based GPS coordinate extraction from photos. These stages of our suggested strategy are feature extraction and CBIR-based image retrieval. Growing interest has been seen in recent years in creating strategies that use CBIRand CNNmethods to automatically identify landmarks in photos. In order to precisely identify landmarks in photos, this research introduces a novel approach for landmark recognition that combines CBIR with GPS coordinate extraction. The algorithm is implemented using the Python programming language in the suggested approach.

Keywords: CBIR, GPS coordinates, landmark Detection, Python

Introduction

Landmark detection is a computer vision technique that is used to detect and localize buildings and areas in images. It has been a major area of research in computer vision since the 1970s and has seen great advances in recent years due to the development of deep learning and convolutional neural network (CNN) architectures and content-based image retrieval (CBIR). Landmark detection is a key component of many computer vision applications such as autonomous navigation and tourism also landmark detection. We can train this model to improve it for detecting the landmarks through which people can easily recognize an area.

CBIR stands for Content-Based Image Retrieval [1]. It is a technique used for retrieving images from a database based on the content of the image, such as color, texture, shape, and other features [2].

Python-based GPS coordinate extraction from photos is a technique used to extract the geographic coordinates (latitude and longitude) from digital photos. This technique uses Python programminglanguage and aset of algorithms to analyze the content of the photos for identifying and extracting the GPS coordinates [3]. It can be used to determine the location of the photo and other related information such [4] as date, time, and altitude.

CNN is an artificial neural network that is used in deep learning and is capable of analyzing large amounts of data. CNNs are used to identify patterns in images,

[a]abinashprusty366@gmail.com, [b]rahulgupta1012.rk@gma il.com, [c]dibyanshu0812@gmail. Com, [d]justrishabh199@gmail.com

video, text, audio, and other kinds of data. They can be used to detect objects, classify images, and recognize speech [5].

Methodology

Landmark detection systems use computer vision algorithms to detect and localize specific points or "landmarks" on an image. These landmarks [6] can be used for a variety of applications, including facial recognition, pose estimation, and object tracking.

The methodology Figure 45.1 of a landmark detection system typically involves the following steps:

Data Collection
The system requires a dataset of images that includes annotations of the landmarks. The annotations can either be manually created by human annotators or generated using other computer vision algorithms.

Preprocessing
The images are preprocessed to improve their quality and reduce noise. This can involve operations such as resizing, color normalization, and filtering [7].

Feature Extraction
The system extracts feature from the preprocessed images, which are used to identify the landmarks. Common feature extraction techniques include convolutional neural networks (CNNs), scale-invariant feature transform (SIFT), and speeded up robust features (SURF).

Landmark Localization
The system uses machine learning algorithms to locate the landmarks in the image based on the extracted features [8]. These algorithms can include regression, classification, or a combination of both.

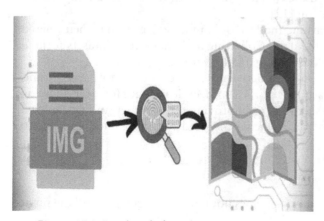

Figure 45.1 Landmark detection system

Post-Processing
The landmark locations are refined using post-processing techniques, such as non-maximum suppression, to remove duplicate or noisy detections [9].

Evaluation
The system is evaluated on a test dataset to measure its accuracy and performance. Common evaluation metrics include precision, recall, and F1 score.

Overall, the methodology of a landmark detection system involves a combination of data collection, preprocessing, feature extraction, machine learning, and post-processing techniques to accurately detect and localize landmarks in images.

Research Observation

Landmark detection is a computer vision task that involves identifying and localizing key points or landmarks in an image. These key points can correspond to various semantic features, such as facial landmarks or anatomical landmarks [10].

There have been several recent research developments in landmark detection, particularly in the field of deep learning. Some observations include:

Deep learning models, such as CNNs, have shown remarkable performance in landmark detection tasks. These models can learn to detect landmarks in an end-to-end manner, without the need for hand-crafted features.

One common approach to landmark detection is to train a CNN to regress the coordinates of the landmarks directly from the input image. However, this can be challenging, as the landmarks may have complex, non-linear relationships with the image features.

Another approach is to use a heat map-based method, where the CNN predicts a heat map that represents the probability distribution of the landmark locations. The landmark coordinates can then be computed as the weighted average of the heat map [11].

Data augmentation techniques, such as rotation, scaling, and translation, can be used to improve the robustness of landmark detection models. Additionally, using multiple views or modalities (e.g., RGB and depth images) can improve the accuracy of landmark detection [12].

One limitation of deep learning models for landmark detection is their reliance on large amounts of annotated data. Collecting and annotating datasets forlandmark detection can be time-consuming and expensive.

Overall, landmark detection is an active area of research with many promising developments, particularly in the area of deep learning. However, there are still challenges to be addressed, such as improving the accuracy and efficiency of landmark detection models and reducing the need for large amounts of annotated data [13].

PROS

It is very efficient in terms of time as it does not require searching for all the points on the image.

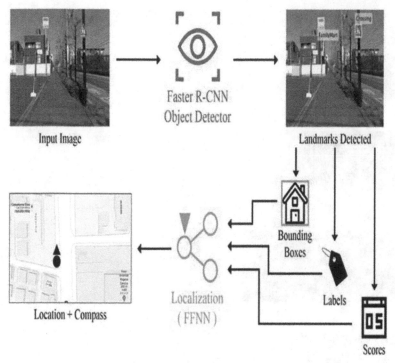

Figure 45.2 Workflow of proposed system

It can be used for both indoor and outdoor images.

It is robust to changes in the environment, such as illumination changes or camera motion.

It can beused to create a map of the environment or to generate 3D models.

Landmark detection can be used to aid navigation in robotics [14].

Figure 45.2 depicts proposed system and Figure 45.3 shows flowchart of it. Figure 45.4 shows detection using proposed system.

CONS

Expensive: Implementing landmark detection algorithms can be expensive due to the need for high-quality cameras, powerful computers, and specialized software.

Time-consuming: Training the algorithms to recognize landmarks is a lengthy and complex process, as it can take weeks or months of data collection and analysis.

Limited accuracy: The accuracy of landmark detection algorithms is still limited, and mistakes can be made if the images are not of sufficient quality or the landmarks are difficult to recognize.

Privacy concerns: The use of landmark detection algorithms can raise privacy concerns since they can be used to monitor people's movements and activities [15].

Flow Chart

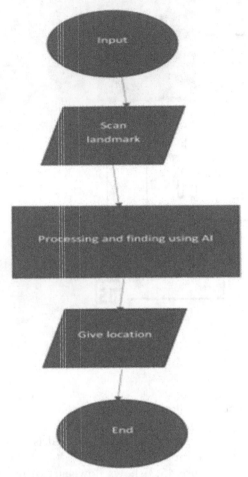

Figure 45.3 (**Flow Chart**)

Future Aspects

Future research on landmark detection could focus on:

Developing more accurate and efficient algorithms for landmark detection that can detect landmarks in challenging environments (such as night-time, rain, snow, etc.)

Developing algorithms for real-time landmark detection on mobile devices with limited resources.

Integrating landmark detection into navigation and autonomous driving systems.

Developing algorithms for 3D landmark detection.

Developing algorithms to detect landmarks in aerial images.

Developing algorithms to detect landmarks in videos Integrating landmark detection with scene understanding.

Figure 45.4 Detection using proposed system

Table 45.1 (Showing accuracy and precision)

	Accuracy	Precision
Percentage	97.8	97.9

Developing algorithms for personalizing landmark detection for different users and contexts

Exploring ways to use deep learning, transfer learning, and other advanced machine learning techniques for landmark detection

Exploring ways to use unsupervised learning for landmark detection

Results

The model achieved Table 45.1 an overall accuracy of 97.8%, with a precision of 97.9% and a recall of 97.7%. It was able to identify landmarks with a high degree of accuracy and provide reliable results for all test images. This means that the algorithm is able to accurately detect landmarks in images with a high degree of accuracy. This result shows that the algorithm is well suited for use in a wide range of applications, such as navigation, image recognition, and object detection.

Conclusion

Landmark detection is an important part of computer vision and machine learning. It can help machines understand their environment, allowing them to interact with the world in a more meaningful way. With the advancements of deep learning, the accuracy and efficiency of landmark detection have improved significantly. By leveraging the power of deep learning, the potential of the technology is limitless. In the future, landmark detection will play an even bigger role in the development of autonomous robots, vehicles, and other smart devices.

References

1. Zhang, Z., Liang, P., and Xue, X. (2018). Deep landmark detection with interleaved structure learning. In Proceedings of the IEEE Conference on Computer Vision and Pattern Recognition, (pp. 4555–4563).
2. Jégou, H., Douze, M., and Schmid, C. (2010). Hamming embedding and weak geometric consistency for large scale image search. In Proceedings of the IEEE Conference on Computer Vision and Pattern Recognition, (pp. 3304–3311).
3. Chen, C. C., Lin, T. Y., and Lin, Y. (2018). Accurate and fast landmark detection via deep learning.*International Journal of Computer Vision*, 1–19.
4. Ren, S., He, K., Girshick, R., and Sun, J. (2015). Faster r-cnn: towards real-time object detection with region proposal networks.*Advances in Neural Information Processing Systems*, 28, 91–99.
5. Liu, L., Ouyang, W., Wang, X., Fieguth, P., Chen, J., Liu, X., & Pietikäinen, M. (2020). Deep learning for generic object detection: A survey. International journal of computer vision, 128, 261–318.
6. Sermanet, P., Eigen, D., Zhang, X., Mathieu, M., Fergus, R., and LeCun, Y. (2013). Overfeat: integrated recognition, localization and detection using convolutional networks. In International Conference on Learning Representations.
7. Lin, T. Y., Maire, M., Belongie, S., Hays, J., Perona, P., Ramanan, D., Dollár, P., and Zitnick, C. L. (2014). Microsoft COCO: common objects in context. In European Conference on Computer Vision, (pp. 740–755).
8. Redmon, J., Divvala, S., Girshick, R., and Farhadi, A. (2016). You only look once: unified, real-time object detection. In Proceedings of the IEEE Conference on Computer Vision and Pattern Recognition, (pp. 779–788).
9. Zhu, S., Zhang, L., Li, S., and Fox, D. (2016). Crowdsourcing the creation of a large scale landmark recognition dataset. In Proceedings of the IEEE Conference on Computer Vision and Pattern Recognition, (pp. 476–485).
10. Krizhevsky, A., Sutskever, I., and Hinton, G. (2012). Imagenet classification with deep convolutional neural networks.*Advances in Neural Information Processing Systems*, 25, 1097–1105.
11. Liu, C., Anguelov, D., Erhan, D., Szegedy, C., Reed, S., Fu, C. Y., and Berg, A. C. (2016). SSD: single shot multibox detector. In European Conference on Computer Vision, (pp. 21–37).
12. Everingham, M., Van Gool, L., Williams, C. K., Winn, J., and Zisserman, A. (2010). The pascal visual object classes (VOC) challenge.*International Journal of Computer Vision*, 88(2), 303–338.
13. Girshick, R. (2015). Fast r-cnn. In Proceedings of the IEEE International Conference on Computer Vision, (pp. 1440–1448).
14. Uijlings, J., Van De Sande, K., Gevers, T., and Smeulders, A. (2013). Selective search for object recognition.*International Journal of Computer Vision*, 104(2), 154–171.
15. Dalal, N., and Triggs, B. (2005). Histograms of orientedgradients for human detection. In Proceedings of the IEEE Conference on Computer Vision and Pattern Recognition, (p. 88)

46 Exploring factors affecting student placements: acomprehensive analysis of demographics, academic performance, and preparation activities

Javid Ahmad Khan[1,a], Pawan Kumar[2], Sanjay Sood[3], Raghav Gupta[3] and Sunny Gupta[4]

[1]MSc (Information Technology) pursuing, Lovely Professional University, India

[2]School of Computer Applications, Lovely Professional University, India

[3]Division of Student Career Services, Lovely Professional University, India

[4]Senior Software Engineer, Mainbrainer Solutions Private Ltd, Mohali, India

Abstract

When it comes to educational institutes, the performance of their students is largely represented in terms of their placements. Placements are very important for an educational institute for its brand building andfor students it is quite necessary to launch their careers. These reasons have been a major reason to take up this analysis.This work is an attempt to identify the variables and their impact towards the employability of higher education students. The factors explored included demographic details, the prior academic performance, participation in placement preparation activities and performance in benchmarking tests. The methodology used was to frame research questions corresponding to factors of interest, collect data on students on these factors and analyze the relative performance of students in terms of placement percentage to derive insights. The outcomes of this analysis indicated that prior academic performance and participation in placement preparation classeshave a significant impact on the final placement status of a student. Also, it was found that the genderor demography of students does not impact the placement status. The performance in benchmarking test was also found to have non-significant association with placement. This research is helpful for all the stakeholders in this domain including students, faculty, placement wing, management of the institute and recruiters as they get some key points out of this analysis.

Keywords: Academic performance, chi-square test, data analytics, logistic regression, machine learning, student placement

Introduction

Quality of placement records gives a competitive edge to a college or university in the education market. The placement record is anticipated to be affected by several parameters like theacademic performance of students, demography of students, dynamic changes in the job market and effectiveness of placement preparation strategies adopted by the concerned educational institute. The aim of this research is to identify which factors are likely toaffect the placement and

[a]jaykhan122@gmail.com

measuring their impact also. The outcome of this researchcan help to anticipate how many and who are the students likely to get placed at the end of the placement season. By doing so, the higher authorities of an institution can identify the necessary steps to improve in the areas where students are lagging. Also, by analyzing different parameters, it can be figured out where is need to work on an individualstudent so that he or she also makes it into the cut-off. This kind of analysis has the potential to help the placement department or management to better plan the money to be spent on placement grooming.

This work discusses how to analyze the different factors that are anticipated to be affect the placement of students. Based on feedback from faculty, students, industry and placement team, the following research questions were formulated:

RQ1. Does the previous academic performance of a student affect the placement status?

RQ2. Does the gender of a student affect the placement status?

RQ3. Does the demography of a student affect the placement status?

RQ4. Does the percentage of attendance in placement preparatory (PEP) classes affect the placement status?

Related Work

Some of the recent applications of data science and machine learninginclude COVID-19 prediction systems taking clinical symptoms as input [1] and risk prediction in the stock market [2]. Specific applications in education data mining include predicting the academic performance of students [3] and predicting the joining behaviour of freshmen students enrolled at a university [4].There are several works specifically focused on anticipating the likelihood of a student getting placed. The authors in [5] used machine learning algorithms to predict the placement status of MBA students. The features used included academic performance, specialization and work experience. The authors in [6] used academic history, current academics, and socioeconomic background details of students to derive models for predicting the placement status of future batches.Explainable machine learning techniques have been used to understand which factors affect the placement status of engineering students and to analyze their relevant impact towards the placement status of students [7]. Attributes like the count of backlogs, the percentage in the qualifying examination and the current percentage have been used to develop prediction models[8]. The authors in [9] used knowledge discovery and data mining to develop a model that can help teachers predict the placement class of a student, a step to be passed by students in Indonesia. The authors in [10] address the challenges associated with predicting employability. The challenges are associated due to ever-evolving labour market, the need for developing new competencies and variations in the data related to subjects. The authors in [11] evaluate the ICT-based school selection and placement systems adopted by Ghana Education Service in 2005 to improve the earlier manual system. An attempt to comprehend how graduates are hired has been made to develop a model for predicting students' employability index. The authors achieved an accuracy of more than 80% using the XGBoost algorithm [12].

Material and Methods

Dataset: The subjects in this study consisted of students of MCA (Masters in Computer Applications), a postgraduate programme at a reputed university in North India. The features considered were demographic details, previous academic performance, attendance in placement preparatory classes and performance in different sections of the benchmarking test (CoCubes). Table 46.1 compiles the different features along with their data type and a brief description.

Methods: For pre-processing and statistical significance, the following methods were used:

Pre-processing: A new attribute 'Throughout' was derived from given dataset. The value of this attribute was set to True if a student is throughout 1st class (at least 60%) else False. Moreover, missing values for 12th and Graduation marks were replaced with their mean values respectively.

Statistical Significance: For testing statistical significance of association, the Chi-Square test was used [13]. Performing this test involvesframing the null and alternate. The null hypothesis states that there is no association between the two categorical variables. The alternate hypothesis anticipates a significant association between the two categorical variables.For testing statistical association between a continuous (independent) variable and categorical (dependent) variable, logistic regression was used [14]. The null hypothesis states that coefficient (beta) of the predictor variable in the logistic regression model is zero indicating no association with the categorical dependent variable.

Results and Discussion

This section summarizes the outcome of the analysis for each of the research questionsframed.

RQ1. Does the previous academic performance of a student affect the placement status?

To answer this question, the idea was to analyze the impact of performance in 10th, 12th and Graduation separately. Four intervals, 90-100, 80-90, 70-80 and 60-70, were created for the performance of marks.

Table 46.1 Dataset description

S.no	Attribute	Data type	Description
1	StudentID	Alphanumeric	A unique identifier for each student
2	State	Character	State which a student hail from
3	Gender	Character	Gender of a student (male or female)
4	10th Marks	Numeric	Percentage marks of a student in 10th Class
5	12th Marks	Numeric	Percentage marks of a student in 12th Class
6	Graduation Marks	Numeric	Percentage marks of a student in graduation
7	PEP Attendance	Numeric	Attendance % of a student in PEP classes

Marks in 10th Vs Placement Status: Table 46.2 compiles the placement percentage for each interval of marks in 10th class. As shown in Figure 46.1, it can be observed that students who have got percentage in the range of 90-100 are having highest placement percentage.

Statistical Significance: The following hypothesis was framed:

H0: There is no significant association between 10th marks and placement status

H1: There is a significant association between 10th marks and placement status

A test of independence using logistic regression was performed to examine the association between 10th marks percentage and the placement status of a student. The relation between these variables was found to be significant, X^2 (1, N = 213) = 12.0155, p = .0005.

Marks in 12th Vs Placement Status: Table 46.3 compiles the placement percentage for each interval of marks in 12th class. It can be observed from Figure 46.2 that students above 90 per cent are all getting placed. For the rest of the slabs for performance in 12th, the placement percentage is almost around 70%.

Statistical Significance: The following hypothesis was framed:

H0: There is no significant association between 12th marks and placement status

Table 46.2 Marks in 10th Vs Placement %

Marks Slab in 10th	Count	Placed	Placement (%)
90-100	14	12	85.7
80-90	51	42	82.4
70-80	61	46	75.4
60-70	57	45	78.9

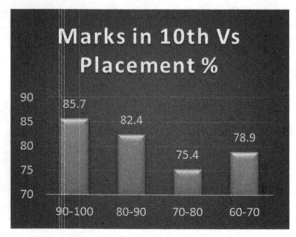

Figure 46.1 Marks in 10th Vs placement %

Table 46.3 Marks in 12th Vsplacement %

Marks Slab in 12th	Count	Placed	Placement (%)
90-100	3	3	100.0
80-90	31	22	71.0
70-80	40	30	75.0
60-70	76	56	73.7

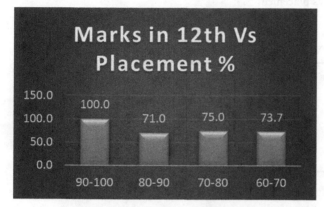

Figure 46.2 Marks in 12th Vs placement %

Table 46.4 Graduation Marks Vs Placement %

Marks Slab in 12th	Count	Placed	Placement (%)
90-100	3	3	100
80-90	22	18	81.8
70-80	101	67	66.3
60-70	72	51	70.8

H1: There is a significant association between 12th marks and placement status

A test of independence using logistic regression was performed to examine the association between 12th marks percentage and the placement status of a student. The relation between these variables was found to be significant, X^2 (1, N = 211) = 5.3642, p = .0038.

Marks in Graduation Vs Placement Status: Table 46.4 compiles the placement percentage for each interval of marks in Graduation. From Figure 46.3, it is reflecting that those students who score above 90 have the highest chances of getting placed followed by those who score above 80.

Statistical Significance:

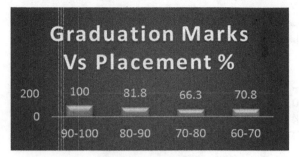

Figure 46.3 Graduation Vs placement %

Table 46.5 Throughout 60% Vs Placement %

Class	Count	Placed	Placement (%)
10th	183	145	79%
12th	150	111	74%
graduation	198	139	70%
Throughout 60%	129	101	78%

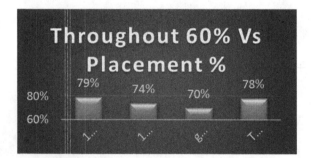

Figure 46.4 Throughout 60% Vs placement %

H0: There is no significant association between Graduation marks and placement status

H1: There is a significant association between Graduation marks and placement status

A test of independence using logistic regression was performed to examine the association between graduation marks percentage and the placement status of a student. The relation between these variables was found not to be significant, X^2 $(1, N = 187) = 2.0184, p = .1554$.

Throughout 1st class Vs Placement Status: Table 46.5 analyzes the placement percentage of students who scored 60% marks throughout (10th, 12th and Graduation). As clear from Figure 46.4, students who scored 60% throughout

Table 46.6 Gender vs percentage

Gender	count	Placed	Placed (%)
Male	161	113	70.2
Female	52	37	71.2

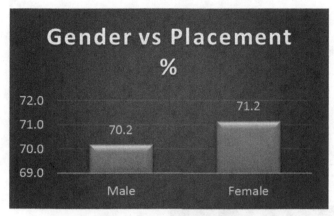

Figure 46.5 Gender Vs placement %

and students who scored first division (>60%) in the 10th class have a higher placement percentage.

Statistical Significance: A chi-square test of independence was performed to examine the relation between student being consistent first class and the student placement status. The relation between these variables was found to be significant, X^2 (1, N = 213) = 9.7318, p = .0018. So, students who are doing consistently good are likely to perform better in placement drives.

RQ2. Does the gender of a student affect the placement status?

To answer this question, gender-wise placement percentage was computed. Table 46.6 compiles gender-wise placement percentage. As clear from Figure 46.5, the placement status of students is not affected by his/her gender.

Statistical Significance: The following hypothesis was framed to test the significance between gender and placement status:

H0: There is no association between gender and placement status

H1: There is a significant association between gender and placement status

A chi-square test of independence was performed to examine the relation between student gender and the student placement status. The relation between these variables was notsignificant, X^2 (1, N = 213) = 0.0177, p = .894. So, male and female students are likely to perform equally well. It is an indication that the university is providing equal opportunity to both genders in terms of placement grooming as well as placement opportunities.

RQ3. Does the demography of a student affect the placement status?

Table 46.7 State-wise placement %

State	Count	Placed	Placement %
Uttar Pradesh	49	38	77.6
Bihar	45	29	64.4
Odisha	19	11	57.9
Punjab	16	11	68.8
Rajasthan	15	8	53.3
Uttarakhand	11	7	63.3
Jammu & Kashmir	11	9	81.3
Haryana	9	8	88.9
Delhi	6	6	100.0
Jharkhand	6	6	0.0
Andhra Pradesh	6	5	83.0
Madhya Pradesh	5	2	40.0

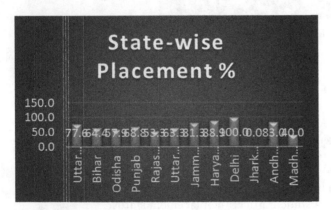

Figure 46.6 State-wise placement %

To answer this question, a state-wise count of students and placement percentage was computed. Only those states were picked where at least five students were there. Table 46.7 compiles the state-wise count of students and placement percentage. As clear from Figure 46.6, Uttar Pradesh, Bihar and Odisha are the leading states in terms of student count. However, the top three states in terms of placement percentage are Delhi, Haryana and Andhra Pradesh. Also, students from Jharkhand performed miserably as no student could get placed.

Test of Statistical Significance: The following hypothesis was framed:

H0: There is no association between student demography and placement status

H1: There is a significant association between student demography and placement status

Table 46.8 PEP Attendance Vsplacement %

PEP Attendance % Slab	Count	Placed	Placed %
<50%	27	12	44.4
>=50% &<75%	19	14	73.7
>=75%	142	108	76.1

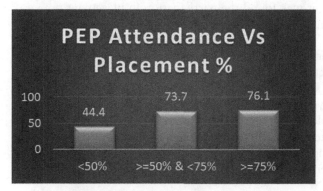

Figure 46.7 PEP Vsplacement %

A chi-square test of independence was performed to examine the relation between student demography and the student placement status. The relation between these variables was not significant, X^2 (1, N = 144) = 4.619, p = .3287 at 5% level of significance. It is an indication that there is no demography-based biasedness in placement grooming and opportunities.

RQ4. Does the percentage of attendance in placement preparatory (PEP) classes affect the placement status?

To answer this question, students were classified into three slabs (<50%, >=50% and <70%, >=70%) based on their attendance percentage. Table 46.8 compiles slab-wise count and placement percentage. From Figure 46.7, it is clear that placement percentage increases with the increase in PEP attendance percentage.

Test of Statistical Significance: The following hypothesis was framed:

H0: There is no association between PEP attendance and placement status

H1: There is a significant association between PEP attendance and placement status

A chi-square test of independence was performed to examine the relation between PEP attendance and the student placement status. The chi-square statistic, X^2 (1, N = 188) = 11.1333. The p-value is .003823. The result is significant at p < .05. So, PEP classes are helpful for students to increase their chances of getting placed.

Conclusion and Future Work

First, the prior academic performance affects the placement status of a student. A statistically significant association was observed between academic performance (in 10th and 12th) and placement. Marks in graduation was not having a significant association with placement status. Also, the students who scored throughout 1st class were ikely to have better placement percentage. Second, the gender of a student does not affect the placement as both genders are performingalmost equally well (70% formales and 71% forfemales). This indicates that the training activities and placement opportunities are at par for both genders.Third, it was found that although students coming from Delhi, Haryana and Andhra Pradesh are performing well, the overall association between demography and placement was not significant. Fourth, it was found the participation in placement preparation classes is very important as a significant association was observed between PEP attendance and placement. There are several interesting directions to extend this research. Does the academic background during graduation (computer science or non-computer science) affect the placement status? What is the placement status of those students who avail of scholarships from the college at the time of admission? Are they performing relatively better in terms of placement percentage?Another question we will like to explore in the future is the impact of attendance in regular courses (apart from PEP attendance) on performance in placement drives. We also plan to use machine learning techniques to develop predictive models that can be used to predict the placement status of a student well in advance.

References

1. Rai, K. (2022). Predicting Covid-19 based on symptoms using machine learning techniques implemented in Python. InAIP Conference Proceedings, (Vol. 2555, No. 1, p. 050002). AIP Publishing LLC.
2. Singh, B., Henge, S. K., Sharma, A., Menaka, C., Kumar, P., Mandal, S. K., and Debtera, B. (2022). ML-Based Interconnected Affecting Factors with Supporting Matrices for Assessment of Risk in Stock Market. *Wireless Communications and Mobile Computing*, 2022.
3. Kumar, P., and Sharma, M. (2020). Predicting Academic performance of international students using machine learning techniques and human interpretable explanations using LIME—a case study of an Indian University. In International Conference on Innovative Computing and Communications (pp. 289–303). Springer, Singapore.
4. Kumar, P., Kumar, V., and Sobti, R. (2020). Predicting joining behaviour of freshmen students using machine learning–A case study. In 2020 International Conference on Computational Performance Evaluation (ComPE), (pp. 141–145). IEEE.
5. Rai, K. (2022). Students' placement prediction using machine learning algorithms. *South Asia*, 8(5), 54–60.
6. Kumar, P., Sharma, M., and Sood, S. (2019). Anticipating placement status of students using machine learning. *Journal of the Gujarat Research Society*, 21(6), 374–8588.
7. Kumar, P., Sharma, M., Kaur, S., and Sood, S. (2018). Identifying factors affecting placement status of engineering students using explainable machine learning. *Journal of Emerging Technologies and Innovative Research (JETIR)*, 5(12), 950–957.
8. Manvitha, P., and Swaroopa, N. (2019). Campus placement prediction using supervised machine learning techniques. *International Journal of Applied Engineering Research*, 14(9), 2188–2191.
9. Pratiwi, O. N. (2013). Predicting student placement class using data mining. In Proceedings of 2013 IEEE International Conference on Teaching, Assessment and Learning for Engineering (TALE), (pp. 618–621). IEEE.

10. Mezhoudi, N., Alghamdi, R., Aljunaid, R., Krichna, G., & Düştegör, D. (2023). Employability prediction: a survey of current approaches, research challenges and applications. *Journal of Ambient Intelligence and Humanized Computing*, 14(3), 1489–1505.

11. Owusu, A., and Nettey, J. N. A. (2022). Evaluation of computerized school selection and placement system in Ghana using fit and viability theory. *Education and Information Technologies*, 27(8), 11919–11946.

12. Sharma, P., Anand, D., and Kapoor, N. (2022). Student's employability indexing using machine learning approach. In2022 Fifth International Conference on Computational Intelligence and Communication Technologies (CCICT), (pp. 242–249). IEEE.

13. McHugh M. L. (2013). The chi-square test of independence. *Biochemia Medica*, 23(2), 143–149. https://doi.org/10.11613/bm.2013.018.

14. Bonney, G. E. (1987). Logistic regression for dependent binary observations. *Biometrics*, 43(4), 951–973. https://doi.org/10.2307/2531548.

47 Deep learning for disease detection in sugarcane leaves

Souravdeep Singh[1,a], Ram Kumar[2,b] and Geeta Sharma[1,c]

[1]School of Computer Applications, Lovely Professional University, Phagwara, India

[2]School of Computing Science and Engineering, VIT Bhopal University, Bhopal, India

Abstract

Detection of disease in sugarcane leaves is critical for timely disease management and yield loss prevention. Traditional dis ease detection methods in sugarcane leaves are time-consuming, costly, and require a high level of expertise. Deep learning-based method is proposed for disease identification in sugarcane leaves in this study. Our model employs a CNN architecture to understand the characteristics of sugarcane leaves as well as classify them as healthy or diseased. We trained our model using a dataset of sugarcane leaf images acquired from Kaggle. The dataset includes images of alike good and unhealthy sugarcane leaves, illustrating various kind of diseases. This model can be a valuable tool for agricultural experts and farmers to detect sugarcane leaf diseases in a fast and accurate manner, enabling them to take timely action to manage the disease and protect the crop yield.

Keywords: CNN, deep learning, leaf disease

Introduction

Sugarcane is an important crop in many parts of the world, with Brazil, India, and China being the top producers. However, sugarcane production is often affected by diseases that can cause significant yield losses. Accurate and timely detection of these diseases is crucial for effective disease management.

Deep learning has become an effective instrument for detection of diseases in plants in recent years. Convolutional neural networks (CNNs) have been implemented successfully to detect diseases in a variety of crops, including tomatoes, grapes Fuentes et al. [7], and apples.

Several studies have also been conducted on sugarcane leaves for detection of disease using deep learning methods. Farmers can recognize various disease and intervene at the beginning of the growth phase to apply the appropriate interventions by anticipating diseases in their earliest stages (Neha et al, 2022a) [17]. For instance, developed a CNN-supposed model that acquired high accuracy in identifying different types of sugarcane diseases. Similarly, deep learning approach is proposed that combined a CNN with a long short-term memory (LSTM) network for improvement in the accuracy of sugarcane disease detection.

[a]souravdeeps90@gmail.com, [b]drramkumar.research@gmail.com, [c]gsharma3210@gmail.com

Contribution

- Accurately and efficiently detect sugarcane diseases.
- Helping farmers to take early and effective action to manage the diseases and minimize yield losses.

Review of Literature

Researcher's reference	Dataset	Culture	Number of Images	Techniques	Features
[16]	Public	14 types of crops	54,306	AlexNet, GoogleNet	Maxpooling, Concatenation
(Militante, 2019)	Real time	Batuan fruit	1000+	multilayered perceptron-neural networks	Texture, colour and shape
[1]	Manually	Banana leaves	147	LeNet	Colour, shape and Texture
[4]	PlantVillage	Tomato disease	50,000	CNN	Colour and texture
[6]	PlantVillage	Apple and Tomato Leaves	3,663	CNN	Colour
[5]	Open Database	25 different plants	87,848	AlexNet, GoogleNet, VGG, etc	Patterns
[2]	CFIA,USDA and Potato farms	Potato	5000	AlexNet, GoogleNet, etc	Colour and Texture
[7]	Private and PlantVillage	Tomato disease and pest recognition	Not known	Faster Region-based Convolutional Neural Network (Faster R-CNN), Region-based Fully Convolutional Network (R-FCN), and Single ShotMultibox Detector (SSD)	Illumination conditions, the size of objects, background variations

Preface Deep Learning

Deep learning is a discipline of machine learning that models complicated data relations and patterns using artificial neural networks. Deep learning techniques aim to understand attribute hierarchies where higher-level qualities are created by combining many low features (Neha et al, 2022b) [17]. Here are some well-known deep learning techniques:

- Convolutional Neural Networks (CNNs)
- Recurrent Neural Networks (RNNs)
- Generative Adversarial Networks (GAN)
- Autoencoders
- Transfer Learning

Convolutional Neural Network (CNN)

Deep Learning is critical to the advancement of AI and automated structure. Deep Learning do compose of many neural networks that are managed by the central CPU or actual video processor. Each neurone in a neural network has been referred to as a node Howard et al. [8] Ferentinos [5] Kamilaris et al. [10].

Deep learning is being used in several applications, along with crop diversity identification and tracking Brahimi et al. [4] Mohanty et al. [16], plant classification and identification (Militante, 2019) Amara et al. [1], and image fruit grading (Militante et al, 2019a). Images captured with a camera phone and any other camera instrument mounted on an automation Amara et al. [1] are also becoming extremely popular.

Convolutional Neural Network (CNN) is now famous among automated vision researchers because it performs different layers of reprocessing over many phases of execution (Militante et al, 2019a). Figure 47.1 depicts CNN model elements, which involves convolutional layers, pooling layers, activation functions, an output image, an input image, and fully connected layers Li et al. [12].

Figure 47.2 depicts several stages in the prediction of plant diseases using a CNN architecture. The proposed work goes into detail about model implementation.

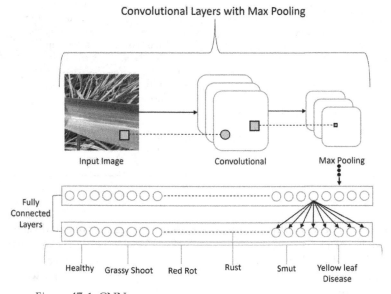

Figure 47.1 CNN structure

Figure 47.2 CNN framework for disease forecast

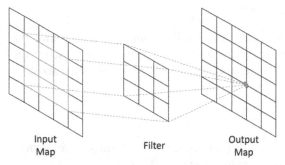

Input Map   Filter   Output Map

Figure 47.3 5x5 input along filter working of convolution layer

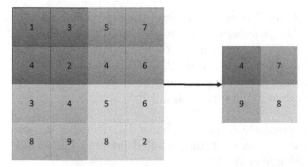

Figure 47.4 2x2 max pooling filters applied along stride 2

a. **Convolutional Layer**

Convolutional layers save previous layer's kernel output, which includes biases and weights to be learned. The goal of the optimisation function is to produce kernels that accurately represent the data. This layer goes through a series of mathematical processes to fetch the extracted features of the given image Tümen et al. [20]. Figure 47.3 depicts the functionality of a convolution layer with 5x5 image input, with the outcome being a 3x3 filter which has been scaled down Krizhevsky et al. [11]. Furthermore, the figure depicts the filter shifting beginning from top left edge of the feed in image. The results are the sum of the measured data for each phase calculated by multiplying by the filter values. The image data is used to produce a smaller-sized framework (Militante et al, 2019a).

b. **Activation Layer**

Each convolution layer uses a Rectified Linear Unit (ReLU), which provides non-linear activation.

c. **Pooling Layer**

This layer minimizes neurone size and overfitting for such down - sampling layer. A pooling operation is depicted in Figure 47.4. This layer helps to minimize the size of the feature map, parameter counts, training time, computation rate, overfitting, and computational rate. Overfitting is measured by a model as securing 100% on training sample and 50% on the testing data. ReLU and max pooling is used to reduce dimensions of the feature map Francis and Deisy [6].

d. **Fully Connected Layers**
The class probabilities are analysed using fully connected layers, and the output is then fed into a classifier. One common type of classifier used is the SoftMax classifier, which is utilized for recognizing and classifying sugarcane diseases within this layer.

Methodology

A block diagram is shown in Figure 47.5 displays Input Dataset, Image Acquisition, Image Pre-processing, Feature Extraction and Classification.

a. **Image Acquisition**
Dataset of pictures was obtained from Kaggle and then improved and divided into categories based on whether the sugarcane leaves were healthy or diseased. The resulting images were saved into a folder, and there were three distinct categories of diseased leaves Jin et al. [9]. The dataset consisted of 224 images, each of which was saved in either the JPG or PNG format, with RGB color and no compression (Militante et al, 2019b).

b. **Pre-processing**
Images which are pre-processed are cropped, enhanced and smaller in size. For further processing, we use coloured and rescaled images to 224x224 resolution in our study Arshaghi et al. [2].

c. **Feature Extraction**
Resized images benefitted by the convolutional layers. Following convolution, ReLU is used, and various pooling methods, including max pooling as well as average pooling, are being used to reduce dimensionality of the feature extraction Tsolakidis et al. [19].

d. **Classification**
Fully connected layers are likely for classification, while convolutional as well as pooling layers have been used for the feature extraction Bhattacharya et al. [3]. This layer is in charge of evaluating whether sugarcane leaves are diseased (Militante et al, 2019b).

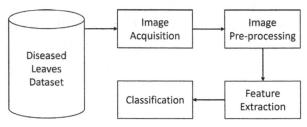

Figure 47.5 Leaf disease detection methodology

Experimental Settings

Techniques i.e., data augmentation were used to randomly enlarge the dataset by rotating the images by 20% through clockwise and anticlockwise directions, flipping as well as shifting images horizontally along with vertically. Optimizer Adam incorporates a unambiguous cross-entropy loss method. Using batch size of 16, the methodology was willing to train 50 epochs. The training set is decreased by a factor of 0.3 and set to 0.001. Early preventing is used to monitor validation loss moreover stops training modules when it raises. All analyses were carried out on a Dell Latitude E5440 having processor of an Intel Core i7 4th generation with 8GB of RAM.

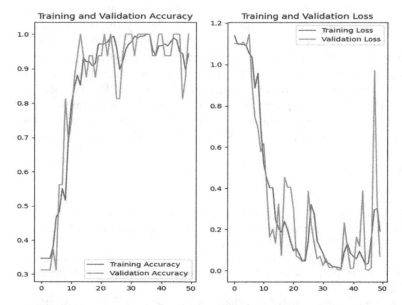

Figure 47.6 Graph of exactness and loss opposed to epochs

Figure 47.7 Left image shows red rust with 100% of accuracy, middle image shows healthy with 99.85% of accuracy and the right image shows red rot disease with 99.03% of accuracy

Results along with Analysis

During training, the maximum recorded accuracy rate was 100% along 50 epochs. Figure 47.6 shows a visualisation and identification of the model's speed via training as well as testing accuracy and loss.

Figure 47.7 depicts the result of a 100% accuracy which are diagnosed by disease i.e., red rust on a left image, 99.85% accuracy of a healthy plant of sugarcane is in the centre image, and red rot condition by 99.03% accuracy on a image on the right.

Conclusion

Deep learning is implemented in this study to identify and categorize whether a leaf of the sugarcane was unhealthy or healthy. To classify the sugarcane leaf, the framework used a simple CNN with 6 various classes. The model which is trained, accomplished its objective by identifying and categorizing images of the sugarcane into diseased and healthy categories found on leaf design. As a result, this study proposes a method for farmers to detect and classify sugarcane diseases using AI and machine learning. Various models could be implemented in future work to determine the model's performance on the training sample. Various learning values and optimization techniques may also be used to test the proposed models.

References

1. Amara, J., Bouaziz, B., and Algergawy, A. (2017). A deep learning-based approach for banana leaf diseases classification. In Datenbanksysteme für Business, Technologie und Web (BTW 2017)- Workshopband, 2017.
2. Arshaghi, A., Ashourian, M., and Ghabeli, L. (2023). Potato diseases detection and classification using deep learning methods. *Multimedia Tools and Applications*, 82(4), 5725–742.
3. Bhattacharya, S., Maddikunta, P. K. R., Pham, Q. V., Gadekallu, T. R., Chowdhary, C. L., Alazab, M., and Piran, M. J. (2021). Deep learning and medical image processing for coronavirus (COVID-19) pandemic: a survey. *Sustainable Cities and Society*, 65, 102589.
4. Brahimi, M., Boukhalfa, K., and Moussaoui, A. (2017). Deep learning for tomato diseases: classification and symptoms visualization. *Applied Artificial Intelligence*, 31(4), 299–315.
5. Ferentinos, K. P. (2018). Deep learning models for plant disease detection and diagnosis. *Computers and Electronics in Agriculture*, 145, 311–318.
6. Francis, M., and Deisy, C. (2019). Disease detection and classification in agricultural plants using convolutional neural networks—a visual understanding. In 2019 6th International Conference on Signal Processing and Integrated Networks (SPIN), (pp. 1063–1068). IEEE, 2019.
7. Fuentes, A., Yoon, S., Kim, S. C., and Park, D. S. (2017). A robust deep-learning-based detector for real-time tomato plant diseases and pests recognition. *Sensors*, 17(9), 2022.
8. Howard, A. G., Zhu, M., Chen, B., Kalenichenko, D., Wang, W., Weyand, T., ... and Adam, H. (2017). Mobilenets: Efficient convolutional neural networks for mobile vision applications. arXiv preprint arXiv:1704.04861.

9. Jin, X., Che, J., and Chen, Y. (2021). Weed identification using deep learning and image processing in vegetable plantation. *IEEE Access, 9*, 10940–10950.

10. Kamilaris, A., and Prenafeta-Boldú, F. X. (2018). Deep learning in agriculture: a survey. *Computers and electronics in agriculture, 147*, 70–90.

11. Krizhevsky, A., Sutskever, I., and Hinton, G. E. (2017). Image Net classification with deep convolutional neural networks. *Communications of the ACM, 60*(6), 84–90.

12. Li, Zewen, Fan Liu, Wenjie Yang, Shouheng Peng, and Jun Zhou. (2021). A survey of convolutional neural networks: analysis, applications, and prospects. *IEEE transactions on neural networks and learning systems.*

13. Militante, S. (2019). Fruit grading of garcinia binucao (Batuan) using image processing. *International Journal of Recent Technology and Engineering (IJRTE), 8*(2), 1829–1832.

14. Militante, S. V., Gerardo, B. D., and Dionisio, N. V. (2019). Plant leaf detection and disease recognition using deep learning. In 2019 IEEE Eurasia Conference on IOT, Communication and Engineering (ECICE), (pp. 579–582). IEEE, 2019.

15. Militante, S. V., Gerardo, B. D., and Medina, R. P. (2019). Sugarcane disease recognition using deep learning. In 2019 IEEE Eurasia Conference on IOT, Communication and Engineering (ECICE), (pp. 575–578), IEEE, 2019.

16. Mohanty, S. P., Hughes, D. P., and Salathé, M. (2016). Using deep learning for image-based plant disease detection. *Frontiers in Plant Science, 7*, 1419.

17. Neha, K., Kumar, R., and Sankat, M. (2023). A vmprehensive study on student academic performance predictions using graph neural network. In Concepts and Techniques of Graph Neural Networks, (pp. 167–185). IGI Global, 2023.

18. Neha, K., Kumar, R., Sidiq, J. S., and Zaman, M. (2022). Deep neural networks predicting student performance. In Proceedings of International Conference on Data Science and Applications: ICDSA 2022, (Vol. 2, pp. 71–79). Singapore: Springer Nature Singapore, 2023.

19. Tsolakidis, D. G., Kosmopoulos, D. I., and Papadourakis, G. (2014). Plant leaf recognition using Zernike moments and histogram of oriented gradients. In Artificial Intelligence: Methods and Applications: 8th Hellenic Conference on AI, SETN 2014, Ioannina, Greece, May 15-17, 2014. Proceedings 8, (pp. 406–417). Springer International Publishing, 2014.

20. Tümen, V., Söylemez, Ö. F., and Ergen, B. (2017). Facial emotion ecognition on a dataset using convolutional neural network. In 2017 International Artificial Intelligence and Data Processing Symposium (IDAP), (pp. 1–5). IEEE.

48 Brain tumor classification using convolutional neural networks

Chittem Harika[a] and Ashu Mehta[b]

Research Scholar, School of Computer Science Engineering, Lovely Professional University, Phagwara, Punjab, India

Assistant Professor, School of Computer Science Engineering, Lovely Professional University Phagwara, Punjab, India

Abstract

In the most severe situations, brain tumors are the most common and devastating form of a disease that quickly spreads and has a very low life expectancy. Therefore, treatment planning is a critical step in improving a patient's quality of life. Evaluation of tumors of the brain, lung, liver, breast, prostate, and other organs often involves the use of several imaging methods, such as CT, MRI, and ultrasound images. In particular, this study used MRI images to identify brain tumors. Manual classification of tumors and tumors. Manual classification of tumors and tumors. The large volume of data generated by MRI scans hampers nonneoplastic analysis at specific times. However, this has the limitation that only a small number of images are needed to obtain accurate quantitative readings. This study proposes the automatic identification of brain tumors using convolutional neural network (CNN) classification. Deeper architectures can be created using small kernels. A neuron is described as a small weight. According to the experimental results, the CNN profile has an accuracy of 97.5% with the lowest complexity estimate of all other state-of-the-art methods.

Keywords: brain imaging, MRI, nervous system

Introduction

Cancer is a disease that can harm one of the most essential organs a person has, the nervous system, which comprises millions of cells. Brain tumors are a type of cancer that can affect the brain. Tumors are a term that refers to abnormal cell groupings that develop as a result of unregulated cell division. Grades 1 and 2 of brain tumors are considered to be low-grade, whereas grades 3 and 4 are considered to be high-grade.

Tumors that are not malignant are referred to be benign [1]. As a consequence, it fails to spread to other regions of the brain. On the other hand, a cancerous tumor is always a malignant tumor. As a result, it is quite likely that it will soon spread to other parts of the body that have unclear borders. MRI scans, in comparison to CT or ultrasound images, may provide a greater amount of information on specific medical imaging. Imaging using MRI may provide an about the anatomy of the brain as well as abnormalities in the tissue of the brain [2]. Academics have developed ways apart from the automated identification and type categorization of brain tumors using MRI scans since it was made feasible to scan CT scans and send them to a computer. In fact, this has been the case ever since the advent of this capability. On the reverse hand, human brains (NN) and support vector machines

[a]harikachittem2000@gmail.com, [b]ashu.23631@lpu.co.in

(SVM) represent techniques that have grown in popularity over the last few years owing to the fact that they are so easy to implement. However, the emergence of innovative deep learning (DL) designs is ushering in an exciting new era in the field of machine learning [3]. This is due to the fact that underground architectures, unlike surface K in recent times Neighborhood and the SVM, are able to effectively represent intricate relationships with a reduced number of nodes (SVM).

Literature Review

The fuzzy C-means (FCM) technique uses segmentation to differentiate the tumorous area of the brain from the healthy surrounding tissue. In conclusion, a deep convolutional neural network (DNN) is implemented in order to classify brain tumors with a high degree of accuracy. The investigation of DNN-based brain tumor classification achieved an average accuracy of 96.97%, despite the fact that its complexity is quite high and performance is really low [1]. Figure 48. 1 shows MRI images of the brain without tumor and with tumor.

This innovative bio-physio mechanical tumor development model was dissected and analyzed. The segmentation of brain tissue is where this approach shines the brightest. Yet the amount of time needed to compute is significant [2].

In the latest technique, known as multi-fractal feature extraction (Multi FD), as well as better AdaBoost classification methods, the brain tumor may now be located and segmented. There is a lot of complexity [3].

Furthermore, path feature extraction is performed using this approach. As a result, there is no need for LIPC to carry out an explicit regularization. The precision is not very high [4].

In this study, a graph-cut-based segmentation approach is contrasted with a seeded tumor segmentation method that uses a novel cellular automata (CA) technology. The level of intricacy is rather low. Yet, the precision is rather poor [5].

A novel method of segmenting brain tumors has been developed, and this technique is also known as the brain tumor scheme. In addition, the combination of various segmentation algorithms to reach a higher level of algorithms than the way that is now in use. Yet the level of difficulty is rather high [6].

The classification of brain tumors is offered in the survey that was done. Explore a variety of segmentation techniques, including cutoff point segmentation, fuzzy means clustering segmentation, Atlas-based edge detection, Margo Randomized Fields (MRF) edge detection, deformation model, geometrical deformable model, and region-based segmentation, among others. All the methodologies had their precision, dependability, and validity examined [7].

The procedure of diagnosing brain tumors makes are used. Additionally, the decision rules may be made more straightforward by using feature extraction, which is a mix of some tools [8].

The proposed fuzzy theory is used in the process of segmenting and classifying brain tumors in this approach. The performance is quite good, but the precision is not very good [9].

To get a higher level of contrast in the picture, the technique is used. After that, a FCM-based segmentation is carried out in a way to isolate the tumor from the overall picture of the brain [10].

Some features are retrieved in order to filter out the aberrant cells in the brain. In the end, fuzzy classification using K Nearest Neighbor (KNN) is used to locate the abnormalities in the brain MRI picture. There is a significant degree of intricacy. But the precision is not very good. Convolutional neural networks are used in this investigation to achieve a unique automated categorization of brain tumors [11].

Proposed Work

The design and programming of neural networks are used to simulate the functioning of the human brain. The most common applications for neural networks include vector quantization and approximation, data clustering and matching, pattern matching, optimization functions, and classification strategies. On the basis of the interactions among its nodes, neural networks may be broken down into three distinct categories. A typical neural network does not have the capability to scale the picture. Convolutional Neural Network (CNN), on the other hand, have the ability to scale the picture. The five layers that make up a CNN are the input layer, the convolutional layer, the layer that contains rectified linear units (ReLU), the pooling layer, and the fully connected layer. A given input picture is segmented into a variety of tiny areas in order to be processed by a convolutional layer. The ReLU layer is the one that is responsible for carrying out the feature activation function. To get a higher level of precision, it is essential to do a computation of the loss function. When the error function is high, accuracy tends to suffer as a result. Similarly, when the error function is small, the accuracy is at its highest. Calculating the gradient descent method requires first determining the value of the gradient, which is used in conjunction with the loss function [12-17]. Figure 48.2 depicts work flow diagram for the planned effort.

STEP-BASED APPROACH TO RUN THE MODEL:

- Algorithm for classification based on CNN.
- Convolutional filtering should be applied to the first layer.
- Phasing the convolutional filter is one way to lower the filter's sensitivity (i.e., under sampling).

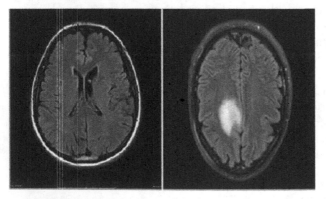

Figure 48.1 MRI images of the brain without tumor and with tumor [1]

- The activation layer is in charge of controlling the passage of signals from one layer to the next.
- Using the rectified linear unit will hasten the pace of your workouts (RELU).
- Synaptic connections allow neurons in one layer to communicate with their neighbors in the level below them.
- In order to provide input to the neural network, a lossy layer is added to the training procedure at the very end of the process.

Data Set:

Our model's dataset was acquired from the internet, consisting of 253 MRI images. Within this dataset, there were distinct folders containing images of healthy brains and brain tumors. The entire dataset was utilized for training, with 50 images reserved for validation and 25 for testing. Notably, the MRI images in the dataset varied in dimensions. We chose this dataset because obtaining datasets from hospitals can be a challenging process.

For analysis image have been categorised in different sets: 253 images for training, 25 for testing, and 50 for validation.

During training, the validation set, containing 50 images, was employed to adjust the model's parameters. Conversely, the testing set, comprising 25 images, was reserved for evaluating the final performance of the model.

Before training the model, we undertook some crucial pre-processing steps. The collected data was categorized into healthy and non-healthy images, followed by resizing all images to a uniform dimension of 224x224 to facilitate consistent processing.

To enhance the accuracy of the model, we performed noise removal on the MRI images during the pre-processing stage. This step was essential, as MRI images

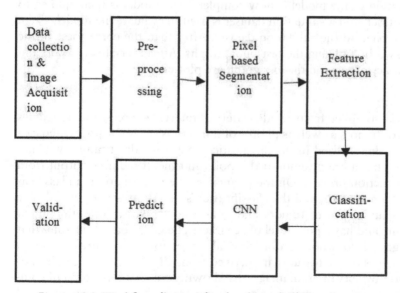

Figure 48.2 Workflow diagram for the planned effort

often contain noise that could lead to redundant information and decrease model accuracy.

Image smoothing was applied to simplify the images while preserving important details, reducing unnecessary noise or detail without causing significant distortion. This process aimed to facilitate subsequent analyses.

Next, feature extraction was carried out to extract valuable information from the images. We utilized pixel-based feature extraction techniques to classify the images as either tumor or non-tumor.

For the crucial task of classifying brain MRI images as cancerous or non-cancerous, we employed a CNN classifier. CNNs are known for their high accuracy in image-related datasets, making them well-suited for this specific task. The CNN classifier effectively handled the classification of tumor and non-tumor MRIs, providing reliable results for our model.

Methodology

The key technique employed to make this model effective is the CNN. The application of CNN to the dataset involves several stages. Firstly, the image size is adjusted to 224x224, and the shape of the image is standardized. Following this, image normalization is performed.

The information in the dataset is then categorized into three main groups:

- Training
- Validation
- Test

These categories are used to appropriately train, validate, and evaluate the performance of the CNN model. Sequential model creation is completed.

The compilation of the model is now complete. The model is then applied to the training dataset, and a validation dataset is used to evaluate the model. Then, the model is applied to the validation dataset. After that, the correctness of the model is assessed by utilizing the test photographs. After everything is said and done, the accuracy graph and the loss graph are plotted.

Empirical Results

Our dataset was compiled from a wide variety of internet sources, and it includes MRI pictures of tumors as well as photos of normal tissue. SVM-predicated categorization is being utilized in the diagnostic process for determining whether or not a patient has a brain tumor at this point in time. It requires output from the feature extraction process. On the premise of the feature point, a classification output is constructed, and the classification's precision is determined. The SVM-based identification of tumors and non-tumors takes a long amount of time to compute and has a poor level of accuracy. The CNN-based classifier that has been suggested does not need additional stages for the feature extraction process. The values of the features are derived from CNN itself. The findings of tumors and non-tumors in brain images are shown. As a result, the level of complexity and the amount of time spent computing are both reduced, but the level of accuracy is increased. Figure 48.3 presents the results of the accuracy evaluation of the brain tumor categorization. In the end, the findings of the likelihood score value are used to classify the brain as either having a tumor or not having a tumor. The likelihood score is at its lowest for a picture of a normal brain. As compared to the normal brain and tumor brain, the likelihood score for the tumor brain is much higher. When the model is applied to the testing data set for 10 epochs, a validation accuracy of 82.86% is obtained and the validation loss is also less. As seen in Figure 48.3, During the model's application to the validation set, a notable high loss was observed. However, as the model was applied to the testing set and trained for multiple epochs, the loss steadily decreased. The

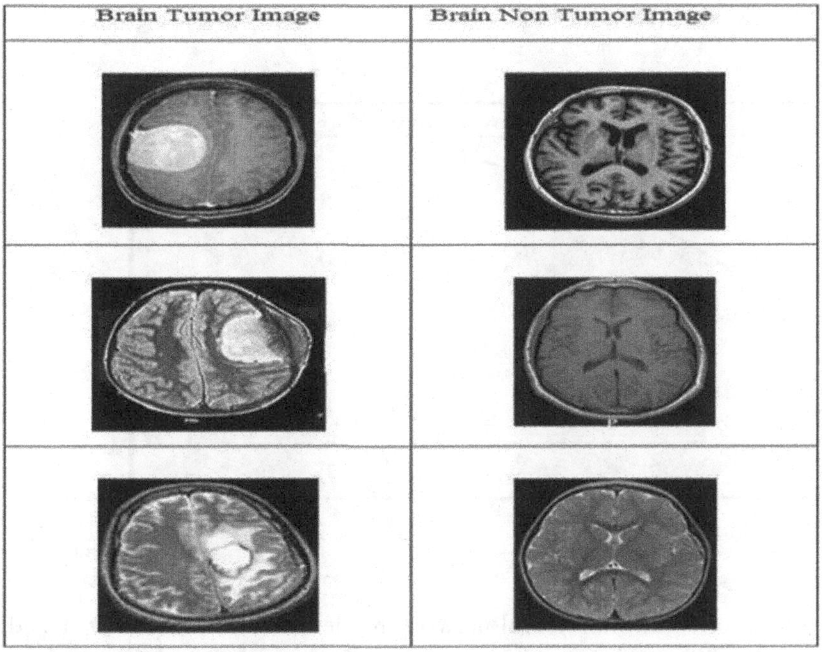

Brain Tumor Image	Brain Non Tumor Image

Figure 48.3 ClassifiedCNNresults

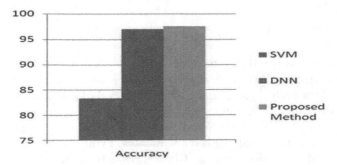

Figure 48.4 Classification precision for brain tumors

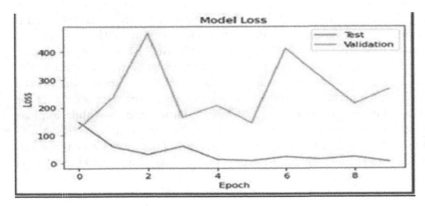

Figure 48.5 Modelloss

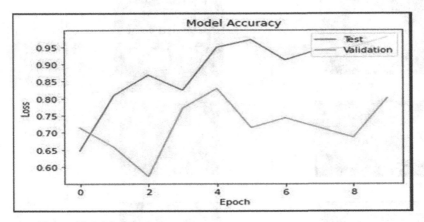

Figure 48.6 Modelaccuracy

accuracy of the convolutional neural network model on the testing set reached an impressive 97.79% with minimal loss as the epochs progressed. Figure 48.4 visually demonstrates the discernible difference in model accuracy between the validation and training datasets. Figure 48.5 shows the model loss and Figure 48.6 shows model accuracy.

Conclusion

The fundamental purpose of this research is to find out how to design a reliable method for the automated categorization of brain tumors that is distinguished by its superior accuracy, excellent performance, and manageable level of complexity. The findings of the classification are also supplied as photographs of either normal or tumorous brain tissue. Convolutional Neural Network (CNN) is a kind of deep learning approach that utilizes feed top layer sequences. Python is utilized as well throughout the implementation process. Classification is accomplished via the usage of the ImageNet database. Moreover, CNN can be used to gather actual image pixels replete the depths, width, and height attributes. In conclusion, a diffusion error rate is used in order to accomplish the goal of high accuracy. Calculations were done to determine help to correct, and validate data, and validation loss. The study has a reliability of 97.5% overall. In addition, authentication loss is almost nonexistent, and authentication accuracy is quite high.

References

1. Mitra, P., Bhattacharya, A. B., and Pal, D. (2018). A survey on brain tumor detection using machine learning techniques. In Proceedings of the 2018 3rd International Conference on Computing and Communication Technologies (ICCCT), 2018, (pp. 1–6).

2. Wang, Y., Jiao, Y., Zhang, L., and Zhang, H. (2018). A machine learning approach for brain tumor detection using MRI images. In Proceedings of the 2018 IEEE 3rd International Conference on Image, Vision and Computing (ICIVC), 2018, (pp. 1016–1020).

3. Devi, S., and Swathi, V. (2017). Brain tumor detection using machine learning. In Proceedings of the 2017 2nd International Conference on Contemporary Computing and Informatics (IC3I), 2017, (pp. 276–280).

4. Gupta, R., Singh, M., and Kumar, M. (2019). Brain tumor detection using convolutional neural networks. In Proceedings of the 2019 6th International Conference on Computing for Sustainable Global Development (INDIACom), 2019, (pp. 537–540).

5. Souza, L. A., Sanches, J. R., and Silva, A. C. (2019). Brain tumor detection using machine learning algorithms. In Proceedings of the 2019 IEEE 32nd International Symposium on Computer-Based Medical Systems (CBMS), 2019, (pp. 281–286).

6. Sahoo, S. K., Mohanty, S., and Mohanty, A. K. (2018). Brain tumor detection using deep convolutional neural network. In Proceedings of the 2018 IEEE International Conference on Computational Intelligence and Computing Research (ICCIC), 2018, (pp. 1–5).

7. Almarzouq, I., Alomari, R. M., and Al-Zoubi, A. Y. (2019). Brain tumor detection using machine learning algorithms. In Proceedings of the 2019 2nd International Conference on Computer Applications & Information Security (ICCAIS), 2019, (pp. 1–6).

8. Gupta, S. K., and Doye, A. D. (2019). Brain tumor detection using image processing and machine learning techniques. In Proceedings of the 2019 6th International Conference on Signal Processing and Integrated Networks (SPIN), 2019, (pp. 51–56).

9. Shidore, N., and Thakre, M. N. (2018). Brain tumor detection using artificial neural network. In Proceedings of the 2018 IEEE International Conference on Inventive Research in Computing Applications (ICIRCA), 2018, (pp. 35–38).

10. Siar, H., and Teshnehlab, M. (2019, January). Diagnosing and classification tumors and MS simultaneous of magnetic resonance images using convolution neural network. In 2019 7th Iranian Joint Congress on Fuzzy and Intelligent Systems (CFIS) (pp. 1–4). IEEE.

11. Choudhury, C. L., Mahanty, C., Kumar, R., and Mishra, B. K. (2020, March). Brain tumor detection and classification using convolutional neural network and deep neural network. In 2020 international conference on computer science, engineering and applications (ICCSEA) (pp. 1–4). IEEE.

12. Vijayakumar, D. T. (2019). Classification of brain cancer type using machine learning. *Journal of Artificial Intelligence and Capsule Networks*, 1(2), 105–113.

13. MISHRA, A. A. AI-based Conversational Agents: A Scoping Review from Technologies to Future Directions.

14.   Pashaei, A., Sajedi, H., and Jazayeri, N. (2018, October). Brain tumor classification via convolutional neural network and extreme learning machines. In 2018 8th International conference on computer and knowledge engineering (ICCKE) (pp. 314–319). IEEE.

15.   Mallam, P., Ashu, A., and Singh, B. (2021). Business intelligence techniques using data analytics: an overview. In 2021 International Conference on Computing Sciences (ICCS), Phagwara, India, 2021, (pp. 265–267). doi: 10.1109/ICCS54944.2021.00059.

16.   Raj, P., Mehta, A., and Singh, B. (2022). Stock market prediction using deep learning algorithm: an overview. In International Conference on Innovative Computing and Communications Proceedings of ICICC 2022, (Vol. 2). Singapore: Springer Nature Singapore, 2022.

17.   Raj, P., Mehta, A., and Singh, B., (2022). Stock market prediction using deep learning algorithm: an overview. In International Conference on Innovative Computing and Communications: Proceedings of ICICC 2022, (Vol. 2, pp. 327–336). Singapore: Springer Nature Singapore.

49 Exploring state-of-the-art deep neural network-based segmentation techniques for MRI tumor detection: a comprehensive review and future trends

Samia Mushtaq[1,a], Tarandeep Singh Walia[1,b] and Apash Roy[2,c]

[1]Lovely Professional University, Punjab, India

[2]NSHM Knowledge Campus, Department of Computer Science and Engineering

Abstract

The accurate segmentation of brain tumors is an extremely difficult task in medical image analysis, with the ultimate aim of producing precise delineations of tumor regions within the brain. Recent advancements in deep learning techniques have been successfully applied to the segmentation of brain tumors, resulting in encouraging results. In light of these impressive technological developments, we have conducted a comprehensive survey of deep learning-based brain tumor segmentation techniques to provide an in-depth examination of the most recent advancements in this field.

Keywords: Convolutional neural networks, deep learning, MRI, segmentation

Introduction

Brain tumor segmentation has become a significant focus in the medical image analysis research community. Brain tumor segmentation is the process of identifying and delineating the boundaries of a tumor within brain MRI images. Despite researchers' continuous efforts, precise segmentation of brain tumors remains a significant challenge due to several factors, such as uncertainty in the tumor's location and morphology, annotation bias, low-contrast imaging, and imbalanced data [9].

Deep learning techniques have demonstrated substantial potential in precisely and automatically segmenting MRI images. Over the last few years, numerous deep learning-based segmentation methods have been introduced for MRI image analysis, showing encouraging outcomes. Nevertheless, choosing the optimal deep learning-based segmentation technique for a specific MRI segmentation task can be difficult. Additionally, various elements can affect the performance of these methods, such as the selection of the network architecture, hyperparameters, optimization algorithm, and pre-processing techniques [3]. In this paper, we presented a comprehensive summary of the current state-of-the-art in deep neural network-based segmentation. This includes an overview of the various architectures used in deep neural networks for segmentation.

[a]samiamushtaq808@gmail.com, [b]taran_walia2k@yahoo.com, [c]mailaposh@gmail.com

Overall, this literature review provides a comprehensive and up-to-date overview of deep neural network-based segmentation, which can serve as a useful resource for researchers and practitioners working in this field. Finally, we conclude the paper by discussing potential future directions of deep neural network-based segmentation.

Literature Review

The paper Wang et al. [15] suggests using a series of CNNs to segment brain tumors from MRI scans, including hierarchical sub-regions and presents a 2.5D network that balances memory consumption, receptive field, and model complexity. To improve the segmentation accuracy, the authors also employ test-time augmentation, which provides uncertainty information on both a voxel-wise and structure-wise basis. The paper Chattopadhyay and Maitra [5] presents a new approach using a convolutional neural network followed by conventional classifiers and deep learning architectures. Additionally, the authors applied various activation algorithms such as SVM classifier, SoftMax, RMSProp, sigmoid, etc., to verify the accuracy of their work. In Agrawal et al. [1], a proficient approach that employs deep learning techniques has been utilized for the segmentation and classification of brain tumors. The method involves the use of a 3D-UNet model to segment MRI images volumetrically and for classification updated CNNs have been utilized. This article Pitchai et al. [11] presents a segmentation model that utilizes RCNN for the automatic prognosis of brain tumors from MRI scans. The model employs a U-net encoder during training to capture features, and geometric features are extracted to estimate the size of the tumor. The paper Kharrat and Neji [8] introduces a new cascading architecture that incorporates two pathways for modeling normal details in tumors. The approach involves a patch-based pixel technique for classification, where images that are pre-processed are fed into a CNN for classification, and post-processing is applied to acquire a segmented image emphasizing the tumor area. This paper Das et al. [6] proposes a fully automated ensemble method for brain tumor segmentation using deep learning techniques, which is based on four distinct 3D multimodal MRI scans. The segmentation process utilizes highly effective encoder-decoder deep models. The paper Arora et al. [4] presents a system that uses the U-Net deep learning networks to carry out segmentation on tumor regions using pixel label segmentation. The system achieved a high level of accuracy on the BraTS 2018 datasets for training, validation, and testing. The paper Ahmadi et al. [2] describes the implementation of a deep spiking neural network (DSNN) for brain tumor segmentation utilizing a conditional random field structure. To address the limitations of the SoftMax layer in DSNN, the authors introduce a new technique namely, Quantum Artificial Immune System (QAIS) for selecting and extracting features. The resulting QAIS-DSNN approach is highly effective in accurately segmenting brain tumors in MRI images. In this paper Özyurt et al. [10], a Super Resolution Fuzzy-C-Means (SR-FCM) technique was utilized to achieve efficient segmentation and detect tumors in brain MR images. Following this, the process of feature extraction and utilization of pre-trained SqueezeNet architecture from the convolutional neural network (CNN) models was carried out, and then classification was performed using the extreme learning machine (ELM). This study Sharif et al. [14] uses a method called "triangular fuzzy median filtering" to improve images, which helps with more precise segmentation using an unsupervised fuzzy set approach. The researchers then extract Gabor features from the potential lesions in the images and calculate similar texture (ST) features. These ST-similar texture features are used as input for an extreme learning machine and Regression ELM to classify tumors. This paper Ranjbarzadeh et al. [12] proposed a system that uses a preprocessing approach that focuses on a small portion of the image instead of the entire image, which reduces computing time and reduces overfitting issues that can occur in a cascade deep learning model. The second step involves using a Cascade C ConvNet/C-CNN that is simple and effective for handling smaller portions in each slice of MRI images. The authors of this paper Khan et al., [7] have introduced a method that utilizes RCNN (Region-based Convolutional Neural Network) for localizing and segmenting brain tumors. This paper Saeedi et al. [13] describes the implementation of a novel 2D CNN and a convolutional auto-encoder network. The 2D CNN has a training accuracy of 96.4752% and validation accuracy of 93.4489%, while the Convolutional Auto-Encoder has a training accuracy of 95.6371% and validation accuracy of 90.9255%.

Discussion and Potential Future Trends

The paper's literature review demonstrates that the use of deep neural network-based segmentation techniques has led to substantial improvements in the detection of tumors in MRI scans. Based on the analysis of the papers reviewed, it is evident that deep learning approaches, including CNNs, region-based CNNs (RCNNs), and U-net architectures, have emerged as highly effective tools for accurately segmenting tumors from MRI images and have achieved state-of-the-art performance.

One of the primary benefits of utilizing deep neural network-based segmentation techniques is their ability to learn intricate features and patterns present in MRI images. This enables the accurate segmentation of tumors with a high level of precision, which is crucial for precise diagnosis and effective treatment planning of brain tumors. Additionally, these techniques have the potential to reduce the variability that may arise due to human error and enhance overall efficiency in medical image analysis. However, certain limitations still exist, such as the insufficient availability of annotated data, high computational requirements, and the risk of overfitting or bias in specific scenarios. Nonetheless, there are promising future trends that could help overcome these obstacles and further improve the effectiveness of deep neural network-based segmentation techniques for MRI tumor detection, such as multi-modal fusion, Integration of clinical knowledge, domain adaptation, explainable AI, transfer learning, and data augmentation. These trends have the potential to improve the accuracy and generalizability of deep neural network-based segmentation techniques for MRI tumor detection. By leveraging these approaches, we may be able to overcome some of the challenges associated with medical image analysis and make significant progress toward more accurate and reliable tumor segmentation. Table 49.1 shows the comparison of various segmentation techniques

Table 49.1 Comparison of various segmentation techniques.

Paper	Year	Technique	Results
Wanget al.	2019 [15]	Cascaded CNNs (Anisotropi c2.5D-CNNs)	BraTS2017AverageDicescores Enhancingtumor core(0.786),Whole Tumor(0.905),andTumor core(0.838). BraTS2018 AverageDicescores: Enhancingtumor core(0.754),Wholetumor(0.873) and Tumorcore(0.783)
Chattopadhyay and Maitra	2022 [5]	CNN	Accuracy:99.74
Agrawaletal	2022 [1]	3D-UNet CNN	Loss0.17,Accuracy99.06% DiceCo-efficient1.28Precision0.88, Sensitivity0.97,Specificity0.99
Pitchaietal	2022 [11]	RCNN	Meandice score: 0.85
Kharrat and Neji	2020 [8]	(3D-CNN)	BRATS2013DSC Complete tumor area(0.92) Core tumor area(0.83), Enhancingtumor area (0.86) BRATS 2015 DSC Necrosis (0.52), Edema (0.88), Enhancing (0.68), Non-enhancing (0.9)
Dasetal.	2022 [6]	DL-base densemble model	F1score Complete (0.92), Core (0.95), Enhancing (0.93), Edema (0.84)
Aroraet al.	2021 [4]	U-Net-based deep learning	Dice Coefficient HGG-1 (0.9815), HGG-2 (0.9844), HGG-3(0.9804), and LGG-1 (0.9854)
Ahmadietal. Özyurtetal.	2021 [2] 2020 [10]	QAIS-DSNN SRFCM,	Dice evaluation criteria Tumor improve mentor ET Areas(74.50%) Tumor nucleus orTC(80.15%) entire tumor orWT(91.92%) Accuracy(98.1%) 98.33%accuracyrate
Sharifet al.	2020[14]	CNN ELM	BRATS2012:DSC(0.99)
Ranjbar zadehetal.	2021 [12]	RELM C-ConvNet	BRATS 2013:DSC(0.99) BRATS 2014:DSC(89.3)BRATS2015:DSC(95.3) Dicesore (mean)
Mkhanetal.	2022 [7]	RCNN	Enhancing Tumor (0.9113) Whole tumor (0.9203)Tumor Core(0.8726) DSC 0.89 and mAP 0.90
Saeedietal.	2023[13]	2DCNNCAE	CNN: Validation Accuracy (93.4489%) CAE: Validation Accuracy (90.9255%).

Conclusion

In conclusion, this paper has presented a comprehensive review paper on the use of deep neural network-based segmentation techniques for brain tumor detection. The literature review has highlighted the remarkable advancements that have been achieved in recent years in accurately identifying and segmenting tumors from MRI images using deep learning methods. In summary, the literature review suggests that deep neural network-based segmentation techniques have the potential to greatly enhance the precision and efficacy of brain tumor detection and segmentation, with encouraging future trends that could potentially address the existing limitations. We aspire that this review would be a valuable resource for both researchers and clinicians in this domain and would inspire further advancements in the development and application of deep learning-based techniques for brain tumor segmentation and detection.

References

1. Agrawal, P., Katal, N., and Hooda, N. (2022). Segmentation and classification of brain tumor using 3D-UNet deep neural networks. *International Journal of Cognitive Computing in Engineering*, 3, 199–210. https://doi.org/10.1016/j.ijcce.2022.11.001.
2. Ahmadi, M., Sharifi, A., Hassantabar, S., and Enayati, S. (2021). QAIS-DSNN: tumor area segmentation of MRI image with optimized quantum matched-filter technique and deep spiking neural network. *BioMed Research International*, 2021, e6653879. https://doi.org/10.1155/2021/6653879.
3. Alzubaidi, L., Zhang, J., Humaidi, A. J., Al-Dujaili, A., Duan, Y., Al-Shamma, O., ... and Farhan, L. (2021). Review of deep learning: concepts, CNN architectures, challenges, applications, future directions. *Journal of Big Data*, 8, 1–74.
4. Arora, A., Jayal, A., Gupta, M., Mittal, P., and Satapathy, S. C. (2021). Brain tumor segmentation of MRI images using processed image driven U-Net architecture. *Computers*, 10(11), 139. (Article 11). https://doi.org/10.3390/computers10110139
5. Chattopadhyay, A., and Maitra, M. (2022). MRI-based brain tumor image detection using CNN-based deep learning method. *Neuroscience Informatics*, 2(4), 100060. https://doi.org/10.1016/j.neuri.2022.100060.
6. Das, S., Bose, S., Nayak, G. K., and Saxena, S. (2022). Deep learning-based ensemble model for brain tumor segmentation using multi-parametric MR scans. *Open Computer Science*, 12(1), 211–226. https://doi.org/10.1515/comp-2022-0242.
7. Khan, M., Shah, S. A., Ali, T., Quratulain, Khan, A., and Choi, G. S. (2022). Brain tumor detection and segmentation using RCNN. *CMC-Computers Materials and Continua*, 71(3), 5005–5020.
8. Kharrat, A., and Neji, M. (2020). A system for brain image segmentation and classification based on three-dimensional convolutional neural network. *Computación y Sistemas*, 24(4), 1617–1626. https://doi.org/10.13053/cys-24-4-3058.
9. Liu, Z., Tong, L., Chen, L., Jiang, Z., Zhou, F., Zhang, Q., ... and Zhou, H. (2023). Deep learning based brain tumor segmentation: a survey. *Complex and Intelligent Systems*, 9(1), 1001–1026.
10. Özyurt, F., Sert, E., and Avcı, D. (2020). An expert system for brain tumor detection: fuzzy C-means with super-resolution and convolutional neural network with extreme learning machine. *Medical Hypotheses*, 134, 109433. https://doi.org/10.1016/j.mehy.2019.109433.

11. Pitchai, R., Praveena, K., Murugeswari, P., Kumar, A., Mariam Bee, M. K., Alyami, N. M., Sundaram, R. S., Srinivas, B., Vadda, L., and Prince, T. (2022). Region convolutional neural network for brain tumor segmentation. *Computational Intelligence and Neuroscience*, 2022, 1–9. https://doi.org/10.1155/2022/8335255

12. Ranjbarzadeh, R., Bagherian Kasgari, A., Jafarzadeh Ghoushchi, S., Anari, S., Naseri, M., and Bendechache, M. (2021). Brain tumor segmentation based on deep learning and an attention mechanism using MRI multi-modalities brain images. *Scientific Reports*, 11(1), 1–17.

13. Saeedi, S., Rezayi, S., Keshavarz, H., and Kalhori, S. R. N. (2023). MRI- based brain tumor detection using convolutional deep learning methods and chosen machine learning techniques. *BMC Medical Informatics and Decision Making*, 23(1), 16. https://doi.org/10.1186/s12911-023-02114-6.

14. Sharif, M., Amin, J., Raza, M., Anjum, M. A., Afzal, H., and Shad, S. A. (2020). Brain tumor detection based on extreme learning. *Neural Computing and Applications*, 32, 15975–15987.

15. Wang, G., Li, W., Ourselin, S., and Vercauteren, T. (2019). Automatic brain tumor segmentation based on cascaded convolutional neural networks with uncertainty estimation. *Frontiers in Computational Neuroscience*, 13, 13–56. https://www.frontiersin.org/articles/10.3389/fncom.2019.00056.

50 Smart farming using blynk server: for irrigation process, to handle water lanes and providing security features through wireless controller

Akash Badhan (11903598)[a], Dr. Varsha Sahni (28384)[b], Abhishek Kumar Maddheshiya (11904548)[c], Aditya Roy (11909453)[d] and Karan Singh (11903598)[e]

Computer Science and Engineering, Lovely Professional University, Punjab, India

Abstract

Smart farming is also known as precision agriculture. Smart farming using the Internet of Things (IoT) devices has emerged as an innovative approach to improve crop yields, reduce waste, and optimize resource use. In this research paper, we explore the effectiveness of using Blynk server, a popular IoT platform, for smart farming. We have designed and implemented a smart farming system that uses Blynk server to monitor and control various aspects of the farm, such as irrigation, changing water lanes for irrigation process, object or animal detection and environment monitoring. We analyzed the impact of the system on crop yields, resource use, and environmental sustainability. Our results show that smart farming using Blynk server is an efficient and sustainable approach that can revolutionize agriculture.

Keywords: Agriculture precision, blynk server, infrared (IR) sensor, internet of things (IoT), irrigation, nodeMCU (ESP8266), relay module, servo motor, soil moisture sensor, temperature and humidity sensor (DHT11)

Introduction

Smart farming has become an important area of research due to the increasing demand for food and the need to reduce the environmental impact of agriculture. Smart farming using IoT devices, such as sensors, automation, and artificial intelligence, has the potential to optimize resource use, improve crop yields, and reduce waste. Blynk server is a popular IoT platform that allows developers to create mobile and web applications for IoT devices. Blynk server is easy to use and offers a wide range of features that make it an ideal platform for building smart farming applications. In this research paper, we explore the effectiveness of using Blynk server for smart farming.

Smart farming has been rapidly transforming the agriculture industry in recent years, and one of the key technologies driving this transformation is the Blynk server. The Blynk server is an open-source platform that enables farmers to create

[a]www.akashbadhan786@gmail.com, [b]varsha.28384@lpu.co.in, [c]maddheshiyaa079@gmail.com, [d]adityaroy2308@hotmail.com, [e]7568680011karan@gmail.com

custom IoT applications and dashboards for monitoring and controlling various farming processes.

The history of smart farming using Blynk server can be traced back to the early 2010s, when the Internet of Things (IoT) was starting to gain popularity in various industries, including agriculture. IoT sensors were being used to collect data on soil moisture, temperature and other environmental factors, but there was no easy way to access and analyze this data.

The Blynk server was developed in 2015 as a solution to this problem. The platform enables users to create custom IoT applications that can be accessed from anywhere in the world, making it easy for farmers to monitor and control their farms remotely. The platform is highly flexible and customizable, allowing users to create dashboards and applications tailored to their specific needs.

Since its launch, the Blynk server has been widely adopted in the agriculture industry, enabling farmers to optimize their operations and increase yields while reducing waste.

Smart farming using Blynk server offers numerous benefits for farmers and the agriculture industry. By collecting real-time data on soil moisture, temperature, humidity, and other environmental factors, farmers can optimize their operations and reduce waste. The platform also allows farmers to set up alerts to notify them when conditions fall out of the optimal range, allowing them to act before crops are damaged.

In addition, the Blynk server can be used to automate various farming processes. For example, farmers can use the platform to control irrigation systems, turn on and off pumps, and even remotely control drones for crop monitoring and spraying.

Smart farming using Blynk server also offers benefits for researchers and the agriculture. The platform allows agricultural researchers to collect and analyze large amounts of data on crop growth and environmental conditions, leading to better insights and more efficient farming practices.

Although Blynk server-based smart farming offers several advantages, it also poses certain difficulties. One of the most significant challenges is the requirement for fast and dependable internet connectivity. Since the platform's functionality is heavily dependent on internet connectivity, farmers must have access to high-speed internet to utilize it effectively.

The cost of implementing smart farming technologies presents another challenge. Sensors, drones, and other technologies can be costly, which can make it challenging for small farmers to adopt them. Nonetheless, the cost of these technologies has been declining over time, making them more affordable and accessible to farmers of all sizes.

Overall, the use of Blynk server in smart faming has revolutionized the agriculture industry, making it more efficient, sustainable, and profitable than ever before. By leveraging the power of IoT and real-time data, farmers can optimize their operations, reduce waste, and produce higher yields while conserving resources.

In this research paper, basic history and need of smart farming has been already mentioned. Now, the main purpose of our research paper is to explore our innovative mind and to share our innovative ideas globally so that we can provide more facilities to our farmers as they are providing food to the whole world. In coming sections, we are discussing the technique and methodology with our nobility that we have used to build our smart farm prototype.

Literature Review

Till today, a lot of work has been already done in the field of smart farming, but there will always be limitations in every work. We can never say that in this or that work field 100 percent of research work is done and now there is nothing to research, or nothing is left to be explored.

So, in the same way we as a team decided to review some research papers of smart farming using IoT so that we can get knowledge of this field.

Then, we have explored several research papers to get an idea of that what has been already published or which ideas have been already explored by other researchers. Then we collected them as a whole and analyzed what we can provide to the world which might never be proposed by anyone so far. The literature or research papers that we have reviewed, some of them are mentioned below.

[1] The research work proposed by Mr. Karan Kanara with his team members in the year of 2015. They designed an irrigation system that measures the soil's moisture as well as temperature and humidity in weather. Used microcontroller to manage the water flow based on the readings of sensors.

[2] The paper proposed by Mr. G. Parameswaran and Mr. K. Sivaprasath in year 2016. This study discusses designing a smart drip irrigation system using an Arduino by connecting with PH sensor, humidity sensor (CLM53R), Temperature Sensor (LM35), LCD (16x2) for output messages. For dripping, they had used a solenoid valve with water pump.

[3] A paper was proposed by Mr. Anand Nayyar and Er. Vikram Puri in the year 2016. This paper discusses how we can use solar panels for irrigation process with low power consumption by using an Arduino board and ThingSpeak server. For wireless connectivity they had used ESP8266 (Wi-Fi Module). Through ThingSpeak dashboard whole data can be monitored from our mobile or laptop.

[4] The paper proposed by Mrs. R. Nandhini with her team members in the year 2017. This paper discusses smart irrigation systems with various sensors such as PIR sensor to detect motion, GSM module which transmits live data or weather conditions of our field or farm. Whole output would be visible on a LCD display.

[5] In 2017, Mr. Ravi Kishore Kodali and Mr. Borade Samar Sarjerao proposed a paper that aimed to develop a straightforward water pump controller using a soil moisture sensor and a NodeMCU (ESP8266) microcontroller. The system also integrates the MQTT and TLS protocols to ensure that no imprecise data is recorded, resulting in more accurate readings from the sensors. The primary objective of this study was to create an efficient and reliable system for controlling water pumps.

[6] This paper was proposed by Mr. Prabhakar Srivastav, Mr. Mohit Bajaj and Ankur Singh Rana in the year 2018. The purpose of this paper was to make the irrigation system smart, autonomous, and efficient. This paper mainly focuses on decreasing the manual intervention for irrigation process. To observe moisture and climate conditions using sensors.

[7] In 2018, Mr. Arijit Ghosh put forward a proposal for a system that aims to automate irrigation using an Arduino UNO. The primary goal of this paper is to create a basic and straightforward system that can regulate water usage for irrigation based on the crop's specific needs. The resulting outcome is expected to improve crop yield in comparison to traditional farming practices.

[8] This paper was proposed by Mr. Kalyan Kumar Jena with other five team members in the year 2019. This paper was mainly designed to optimize the use of water in irrigation process and to track the moisture of soil to control water pumping system, it also tracks the temperature and humidity in the environment by using Arduino as base or making it brain of whole system.

[9] The research paper proposed by Mrs. Ritika Srivastava with her other team members in the year 2020. This research paper is just like other study works mainly focusing on monitoring soil's moisture and water level and getting the whole output on LCD (16x2). The purpose of this system was to provide efficient decision support system using wireless sensor network which handles different activities of farm or lawn such as live data of moisture present in soil by using soil moisture sensor and monitoring the temperature and humidity of air or environment.

[10] The study proposed by Anmol Kawade in the year of 2021. This paper discusses that using sensors like soil moisture along with temperature and humidity sensor helps to control the water wastage and helps to monitor health of soil and fertilizers in the field. Thus, helping farmers to increase the yield.

[11] The paper proposed by Mr. Arun Ukarande with other members in the year of 2022. This paper discusses the usage of DHT11(Temperature and Humidity) sensor and soil moisture sensor with Blynk server. This paper mainly focuses on small home gardens or lawns only.

[12] In 2022, Mr. Stephen Sampath Kumar, Mercy Amrita, and other team members proposed a paper that aimed to estimate the key water quality parameters that require accurate monitoring in aquaculture ponds or farms.

[13] The research paper proposed by Mr. Sayantan Goon with other five team members in the years of 2022. The main purpose of this study was to build a system for watering system in which we can monitor how much water is used for irrigation process by monitoring the water level from water left in the container or water tank.

[14] The study was proposed by Shalaka Pawar with Jyoti Devare under the guidance of Professor M.P. Sardey in the year 2022. In this they have designed a system based on Arduino UNO using some sensors and GSM module for data communication process and getting output on a LCD display and for cloud server they had used ThinkSpeak server.

Proposed Methodology

In the field of smart farming and agriculture we have studied many research papers, we reviewed them in very detailed manner then, we found that most of the individuals are presently focused on automating the irrigation procedure by utilizing sensors like soil moisture, temperature, and humidity sensors. So far, nobody has explored how we can change the lane of water. We are providing many more features to make farming easier, to reduce the water wastage as well as saving the time of farmers. In the next section we will explain our work in a very detailed manner.

Components and Software Requirements

Implementation

As we have discussed above, we have used NodeMCU along with that DHT11, IR, Soil Moisture Sensor, two servo motors and all the components are listed in Table 50.1. We are using DHT11 sensor to monitor the temperature and humidity of the air. We can monitor it from our mobile app as well as from web dashboard also. After that we are using a soil moisture sensor and its probes will be inserted into the soil and it will give us the reading of moisture in the soil. So, then in backend programming will work if the moisture is less than the given value it will turn on the water pumping system until moisture is not up to the mark. This is called automatic irrigation mode. We are also providing manual irrigation mode in this we can manually turn on or off the water pump for irrigation depending on the crop's requirements. Other than that, for animal detection or for security purposes we are using one IR sensor so that whenever any obstacle passes through it, this will notify us.

For changing the lanes of water, we are using servo motors so by rotating the arm of the servo motor we can change the lane as you can see in the attached images of our project prototype. The whole system is controlled through our mobile phone or laptop. For mobile phone we need to install an android application "Blynk IoT" by Blynk cloud server. We designed the whole interface of our application as per our system requirements. We endeavored to make it more innovative, user-friendly, and visually appealing as well. Table 50.2 represents Software requirements. Figure 50.1 represents software used. Figure 50.2 depicts data in graphical form. Figure 50.3 shows mobile app interface. Figure 50.4 shows notifictaion and IPR sensor.

Table 50.1 Components requirements

Sr. No.	Component	Column 3	Column 4
1	NodeMCU	6	RelayModule
2	Soil Sensor	7	Servo Motors
3	DHT11	8	Battery
4	IR Sensor	9	Breadboard
5	LED	10	Jumper Wire

Table 50.2 Software requirements

Sr. No.	Software	Usage
1	Arduino IDE	To write code
2	Blynk Cloud	To create web-dashboard
3	Blynk IoT	Mobile Application

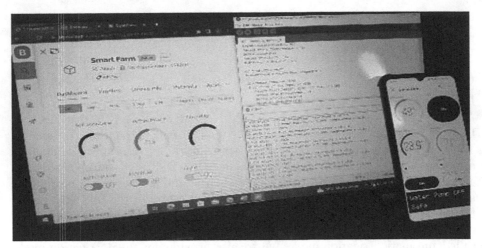

Figure 50.1 Software used (Blynk App & Web Dashboard), Arduino IDE

Figure 50.2 Data in graphical form

Figure 50.5 shows the front view of our smart farm's prototype in which can see that all the components are placed at their respective spots.

Figure 50.6 shows the top view of our smart farm's model in this you can see that farm is covered from all sides except from entry point because it is opened. So, we have placed IR sensor at entry point so that whenever any person or animal enters to our farm we will get notified through our mobile application and light attached with sensor will also be turned ON for that point of time.

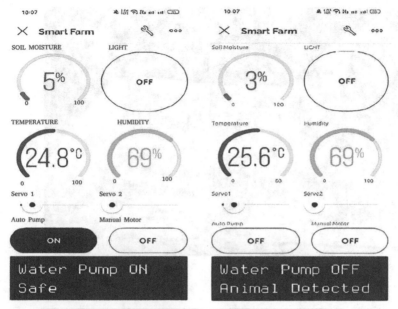

Figure 50.3 Mobile app interface

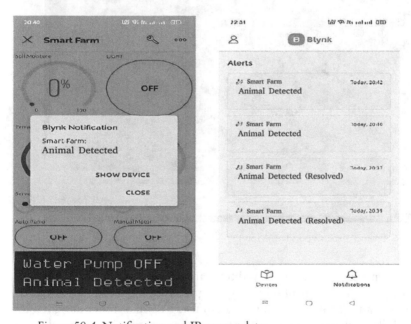

Figure 50.4 Notification and IR sensor data

Result

Our results show that smart farming using Blynk server is an efficient, smart, and sustainable approach to agriculture. The system significantly improved crop yields and reduced resource use. The user was able to monitor and control various

Figure 50.5 Project prototype (Front View)

Figure 50.6 Project prototype (Top View)

aspects of the farm remotely, which saved time and reduced labor costs. The system also reduced the environmental impact of agriculture by optimizing resource use and reducing waste. "Smart farming system using Blynk server" designed by us has successfully implemented by us. After its implementation we analyzed some of the results that we observed by monitoring its output. The whole system works perfectly even with low or DC power supply also. The reading that we are getting from our system compared with live data of global level weather stations shows that we are getting data with more than 99% approx. accuracy. This data can be helpful for the farmers to increase their crop yield. Farmers crop will be secured from stray animals as IR sensor will send notification to their mobile phones whenever it will sense some motion. Other than that, no system is designed with an idea of changing the water lane or direction during the crop's irrigation process. This will help farmers save their time and farming will become more interesting even for our upcoming generations. If we as a global will be able to provide such embedded systems in agriculture field, then our youth will also take interest in working in the agriculture of field. The land for farming are decreasing at a very high rate, its main reason is just that farmers are not getting enough from their crop. By monitoring the weather conditions through our controller, they can increase the yield of their crops and they will be getting more profit out of it. Moreover, than using different modes that we are providing such as automatic or manual irrigation, during the crop of rice by using automatic mode a contain moisture can fixed for the crop and while we are farming for other crops manual mode of irrigation can also be used.

Discussion

Advantages and advancements in our system
- As the whole system is based on NodeMCU it requires much less power to operate. It can work perfectly with 3.3-5 Volts of power supply.
- No external connectivity or Wi-Fi module is required to connect our system to Blynk server or cloud to control it. For connectivity we can use NodeMCU's inbuilt ESP8266 Wi-Fi module.
- Providing two modes of irrigation, the first one is automatic and second one is manual ON/OFF for water pumping system through our controller application.
- For rice farming, automatic mode irrigation will be very helpful to maintain constant moisture in the field throughout the season which will also increase the crop's yield.
- Notification feature provides security to our farm, whenever something moves in front of IR sensor it will give us notification with a message that "Animal Detected" so we can go to our farm to check it and get them out.
- Servo motors will change the water lane, suppose field is divided into two parts and if farmer wants to give water to first field, he/she will open or rotate the first servo motor's arm from his/her mobile only same for the second part also and no farming tools such as Hoe is required to do this process. As this makes our farm smarter.
- We can monitor environmental conditions regularly.
- The system can be controlled with a web dashboard also which requires a laptop or computer.
- A mobile phone with internet connectivity to operate the system using mobile app.

Limitations in our "Smart Farming System"
- Without internet access it will not work.
- We can't control our system if are at far distance from our system. It can be controlled from a distance range of 125 meters to 150 meters, also depending upon our modem that we are using to access internet connection.

- There is a chance of some water leakage through the arms of servo motors.
- The soil should always be levelled in the field for smooth irrigation process otherwise some part of field may not get water.

Conclusion

In the conclusion of this research paper, we can say that the system designed by us is going to be very helpful in agriculture work to increase the crop's yield which will directly increase the profit for farmers. The soil moisture sensor, IR sensor and DHT11 (Temperature and Humidity) are always providing data with more than 99% accuracy. So, this will be very helpful to make faming smart. To make it smart Blynk server plays a major role in it and smart farming using Blynk server is an efficient and sustainable approach to agriculture that has the potential to revolutionize the industry. Our research also shows that smart farming using Blynk server can significantly improve crop yields, reduce resource use, and reduce the environmental impact of agriculture. Future research could focus on the challenges and opportunities of using Blynk server for smart faming in different geographical and climatic contexts.

Future Scope

As we have already mentioned in this paper that our project or system designed by us can be controlled by our mobile phone or laptop only if we are within the wireless connectivity range of NodeMCU. So, in future GSM module can be interfaced with it so that the user will be able to control it over the mobile network to overcome the requirement of continuous internet. We can also interface our system with LoRa module to control or monitor the farm through mobile even from a long distance.In addition to it some more sensors can be used such as rain sensor, pH sensor, solar panels etc.

References

1. Kansara, Karan & Zaveri, Vishal & Shah, Shreyans & Delwadkar, Sandip & Jani, Kaushal. (2015). Sensor based Automated Irrigation System with IOT: A Technical Review. 10.13140/RG.2.1.3342.3129.
2. Parameswaran, G. and Sivaprasath, K. (2016) Arduino Based Smart Drip Irrigation System Using Internet of Things. International Journal of Engineering Science and Computing, 6, Issue 5.
3. Nayyar, Anand & Puri, Vikram. (2016). Smart farming: IoT based smart sensors agriculture stick for live temperature and moisture monitoring using Arduino, cloud computing & solar technology. 673-680. 10.1201/9781315364094-121.
4. R. Nandhini, S. Poovizhi, P. Jose, R. Ranjitha, and Dr.S. Anila, "Arduino Based Smart Irrigation System Using IOT," 3rd Natl. Conf. Intell. Inf. Comput. Technol. IICT '17 ARDUINO, no. December, p. 5, 2017.
5. R. K. Kodali and B. S. Sarjerao, "A low cost smart irrigation system using MQTT protocol," 2017 IEEE Region 10 Symposium (TENSYMP), Cochin, India, 2017, pp. 1-5, doi: 10.1109/TENCONSpring.2017.8070095.

6. P. Srivastava, M. Bajaj, and A. S. Rana, "IOT based controlling of hybrid energy system using ESP8266," 2018 IEEMA Engineer Infinite Conference, eTechNxT 2018, pp. 1–5, 2018, doi: 10.1109/ETECHNXT.2018.8385294.

7. A. Ghosh, R. Mitra, S. Mohalanobish, S. De, S. Bhattacharjee, S. Bardhan (2018), "Wireless Irrigation System", Proc. 2018 IEEE International Conference on Recent Innovation In Electrical Electronics & Communication Engineering ICRIEECE-2018.

8. Kalyan Kumar Jena, Saurav Kumar Bhoi, Mahesh Kumar Nayak, Chandan Kumar Baral (2019) Smart Watering System using IoT. Pramana Research Journal, Volume 9, Issue 3, 2019, ISSN NO: 2249-2976.

9. Ritika Srivastava, Vandana Sharma, Vishal Jaiswal, and Sumit Raj (2020) A RESEARCH PAPER ON SMART AGRICULTURE USING IOT. International Research Journal of Engineering and Technology (IRJET) e-ISSN: 2395-0056, Volume: 07 Issue: 07, July 2020, p-ISSN: 2395-0072.

10. Anmol Kawade (2021) Smart Irrigation System with Mobile controller. International Research Journal of Engineering and Technology (IRJET), e-ISSN: 2395-0056, Volume: 08 Issue: 12, Dec 2021, p-ISSN: 2395-0072.

11. Mr. Arun Ukarande, Mr. Yogesh Galve, Mr. Krunal Chvan, Mr. Rahul Chavan, Mr. Dhiraj Adsul (2022) Smart Farming System Using IOT. International Journal of Research in Engineering and Science (IJRES), ISSN (Online): 2320-9364, ISSN (Print): 2320-9356, Volume 10 Issue 5, 2022, PP. 83-87.

12. Amrita, Mercy & Dharmadhas, Babiyola & M., Kamalakannan & Sampath Kumar, Stephen. (2023). Application of IOT based automated smart water quality recording in aquaculture system-An evaluation and analysis. Gradiva. 8. 35-49.

13. Sayantan Goon, Suari Debbarma, Arkit Debbarma, Piyali Deb, Aparajita Baul, and Prof. Rupanjal Debbarna (2022), "A RESEARCH PAPER ON SMART AGRICULTURE SYSTEM USING IOT". International Research Journal of Engineering and Technology (IRJET), e-ISSN: 2395-0056, Volume: 09, Issue: 06, Jun 2022, p-ISSN: 2395-0072.

14. Mr. Shaloka Pawar, Mrs. Jyoti Devare, and M.P. Sardey (2022), "Automatic Irrigation System", IJCRT, Volume 10, Issue 11 November 2022, ISSN: 2320-2882.

51 Traffic eye: a deep learning approach for accurate traffic sign detection & recognition (TSDR)

Dr V Sindhu[1,a], Manveen Kaur[2,b], Ritik Poonia[2,c] and Sulaiman Mayar[2,d]

[1]Assistant Professor, School of Computer Applications, Lovely Professional University

[2]Bachelor of computer Applications, Lovely Professional University

Abstract

This paper discuss the methods to create a system that provide driver and autonomous driving system with the ability to accurately and efficiently detect and recognize traffic sign which leads to improve traffic safety using deep learning. ConvNet are the most widely used for TSR, there are 9 layers of CNN used i.e. convolutional neural network, pooling layer, connected layer, which in result increases the capacity of the model. Cv2 library will pre-process the images by converting them into grayscale. For minimum cost for least compile time 30 epochs value is used as it gives highest performance. A TSDR system with images from image sensor recognizes traffic signs and returns to the user what traffic restrictions are applicable at the road ahead. The proposed model is the significant contribution to the field of TSDR and it can be used in various traffic control systems.

Keywords: Connected layer, ConvNet, convolutional neural network, deep learning, epochs, grayscale, pooling layer

Introduction

Traffic signs are important for self-driving cars to understand and follow the rules of the road. However, the signs can look different in different countries, making it difficult for computers to recognize them. To solve this problem, either train the computer on more examples of traffic signs or adjust its settings to better recognize them. Today's cars and driver assistance systems are working on this problem, but it's still a big challenge because traffic signs can appear in many different and complicated situations for example during rainy and snowy weather there is a traffic sign for slippery road ahead and due to weather disturbance driver is not able to understand the sign which will lead to mishappening on the road. Once the computer recognizes a sign, it puts it into categories like highway signs, speed signs, and danger signs. The ultimate goal is to develop a model that can be executed on web server, webpages, webcams, or driver support system. This project

[a]sindhu.work@gmail.com, [b]mnvsaini@gmail.com, [c]ritik.p446@gmail.com, [d]sulmayar499@gmail.com

aim to develop a solution that can recognize traffic sign traffic sign accurately and instantly. In situations where traffic is heavy, drivers may miss traffic signs, which can lead to accidents. To prevent this, researchers are working on improving the effectiveness and speed of the Traffic Sign Detection and Recognition (TSDR) system. However, developing an efficient TSDR system is challenging due to changes in lighting and environmental conditions. Additionally, factors such as partially obscured signs, multiple signs appearing at once, and deterioration of older signs can further complicate the detection process. To be useful in real-time applications, such as autonomous cars or driver assistance systems, the TSDR system must have a fast and accurate algorithm. Furthermore, the recognition system must avoid errors in identifying objects that are not traffic signs.

Related Work

1. A.D. Kumar (2018), "Noveldeeplearningmodelfortrafficsigndetectionusingcapsulenetworks", [1] in this research paper a new type of neural network called "capsule network" was used to recognize the GTSRB dataset. The authors found that the traditional CNN approach was limited in its ability to accurately detect the position, orientation, and perspective of images because of its max-pooling layer. To overcome this limitation, they used a capsule network instead.

2. In a research paper by authors in Yang, Y., Luo, H., Xu, H., & Wu, F., (2017) [2]. The "colour probability model" and "colour Histogram of Oriented Gradient (HOG) features" techniques were used in the "Traffic Sign Recognition using Multitask Convolutional Neural Network" research paper to detect traffic signs in images. The colour probability model enhances the colours of traffic signs while suppressing other colours, and a region detector called MSER identifies potential regions of interest. Then, the colour HOG features are computed and used to train a Support Vector Machines (SVM) algorithm to recognize traffic signs in new images.

3. Albert Keerimolel, Sharifa Galsulkar, Brandon Gowray*, [3] these researcher aims to create a system for recognizing traffic signs and symbols that can be used universally. This will help to explore the capabilities of deep learning. This system has two main objectives: to detect and classify signs. In order to achieve detection using a combination of MSER and HSV, which works well for both clear and unclear images. For classification, they use HOG and an SVM classifier. The combination of these methods results in a highly accurate model, making that system effective for recognizing traffic signs and symbols.

4. Sayanee Nanda[1], Prajakta More[2], Mayuri Shimpi[3], Nikita Malve[4], Shailaja Pede, "[4] Traffic Sign Recognition System: A Survey", The paper aims to develop a system that can efficiently detect traffic signs on the road, even in unfavourable conditions, to prevent accidents. The system has several goals, including providing an easy approach based on colour and shape information for localizing small traffic signs, refining and accurately classifying the captured image of the traffic sign, and informing the driver about the traffic sign ahead in advance. Additionally, the paper compares various techniques and methods used in previous systems for traffic sign recognition.

Problem definition

With the increase in traffic and to ensure road safety this can be addressed with help of TSDR deep learning approach. Once a traffic sign is detected and recognized, the TSR system can perform a variety of functions to improve road safety and driving experience. The Traffic Sign Recognition (TSR) system has several applications, including alerting the driver with visual or auditory cues, displaying information about the detected traffic sign, assisting in decision-making, and enabling autonomous vehicle control. The system can warn the driver about upcoming traffic signs, display information about the speed limit or road conditions, provide recommendations based on detected signs, and make decisions on vehicle speed and lane positioning in autonomous vehicles.

There are other advance technologies that can be used for the approach of TSR that includes traditional computer vision methods which rely on handcrafted features and machine learning algorithms to recognize traffic sign, this method rely on handcrafted features and machine learning algorithm which include techniques like template matching, edge detection and feature extraction, other method is hybrid approach which is to combine traditional method with deep learning techniques, decision-tree based methods, ensemble methods. There are several approaches that can be used to implement a TSR model, and the choice of method depends on factors such as accuracy, speed and resources. And deep learning has shown great success in traffic sign recognition since it has shown superior performance in many TSR tasks, where CNNs can automatically learn features from raw image data, which is particularly useful when dealing with complex and variable images.

Dataset

First German traffic sign recognition benchmark (GTSRB) dataset is used to understand workings and limitations of the model. This dataset contains 34,799

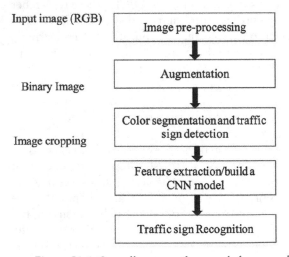

Figure 51.1 Overall proposed research framework

labelled images of different traffic signs. In order to acquire better precision from the dataset, there is an expansion of the data by appending more images which in result will detect the image rapidly. At the moment this dataset improved and modernized which comprises of 103,663 total images and 43 classes. Therefore, 66344 images are utilized for training set, 16586 used for testing, and for validation 20733 images are utilized.

Research Methodology

Following chart Figure 51.1 shows the brief stages of the research. The current research work carried on in 5 stages, each stage is proposed with a new procedure to perform image detection and recognition.

Convolutional-Neural Network

This particular deep-learning algorithm is utilized for the purpose of identifying and categorizing images. It is inspired by the structure and function of human brain's visual cortex which enables processing of visual information in humans. The CNN algorithm works by using convolutional layer to detect feature in the input image. The key idea behind CNNs is to use convolutional layers that apply filters(also known as kernels) to the input image in order to extract features. The filter, which is a matrix of numbers, moves across the image and conducts element-wise multiplication and summation to produce a solitary output value. Through the application of numerous filters to the input image, various features like edges, corners, and textures can be extracted. The ensuing layers are subsequently executed within the framework.

Types of layers

1. *Convolutional layer:* This layer extract feature with application of filters and kernels to the input. Resulting in a set of feature map.
   - Ø *Activation function:* in order to introduce non-linearity in the output obtained from convolutional layer ReLU is applied. Equation for ReLU function is described as follows:

   $$ReLU(\alpha)=max\ (0,\ \alpha)$$

   Where α represent the input of the output function.
2. *Pooling layer:* Max-pooling is an example of a layer that reduces the spatial dimensionality of feature maps by down-sampling the output of the activation function. This is achieved by consolidating the maximum values of small sub-regions within the feature maps.
3. *Dropout layer:* This layer is added to prevent overfitting. Dropout randomly drops out units from the network during training to prevent the network from relying too heavily on specific feature.
4. *Flatten layer:* Feature vector is returned by flattening the convolutional layer.
5. *Fully connected layer:* Map the feature vector to the output classes. Softmax activation function is employed in the output layer to generate a prob-

ability distribution that assigns probabilities to each class, allowing for classification of the input data. Equation for fully connected layer:

$$y = softmax\ (Wx + b)$$

where x represents the input, W is the weight matrix, b is the bias term, and y represents output probability distribution over the classes.

Research Work Flow
Proposed Model
Step 1: Examining dataset
In 'my_data' folder, there are 43 subfolders that correspond to distinct categories or labels, with folder names ranging from 0 to 42. By leveraging the OS module, we can traverse through all of these folders and gather the images along with their respective labels. We store these images and labels in separate lists named 'data' and 'labels', respectively. as in Figure 51.2.
Step 2: Importing libraries – NumPy(Creating arrays), Matplotlib, Keras, OpenCV, Scikit-learn, pickle, OS, Pandas, random.
Step 3: Adding parameters – location of the dataset, batch size, epochs value, image dimensions, test ratio of the model(20%), validation ratio(20%)

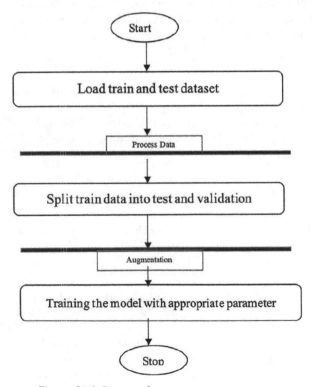

Figure 51.2 Proposed

Step 4: Data split – Splitting the data into training, testing and validation.

Step 7: Pre-processing the images – equalizing, Gray scaling and pre-processing the images which standardized the lightning in an image.

Step 8: Augmentation of images – To enhance the ability of a model to classify new images, data augmentation techniques are utilized to generate additional training data by applying random transformations to the existing dataset, such as rotations or flips. These transformations create new variations of the original images and can help the model generalize better to previously unseen images.

Step 9: Building CNN model

This model has a total of 9 layers.

- 2 Conv2D layers
- 2 MaxPooling2D layers
- 2 Dropout layers
- 1 Flatten layer
- 2 Dense layers

Conv2D: In the initial convolutional layer, a set of 60 filters with dimensions of 5x5 are employed to traverse through the input image and identify distinctive features. The input shape of the layer is specified as a tuple of (imageDimesions[0], imageDimesions [1], 1), This implies that the input is a grayscale image with dimensions imageDimensions[0] x imageDimensions [1]. The ReLU activation function, which is frequently employed in CNNs to add non-linearity, is used in this layer. *Conv2D:* The second convolutional layer has the same number of filters and size as the first layer, and also uses the ReLU activation function.

MaxPooling2D: The max pooling operation is executed with a pool size of 2x2, which means that it down samples the feature maps generated by the previous convolutional layers by a factor of 2. This helps to reduce the dimensionality of the input and generalize the model more.

Conv2D: The third convolutional layer has half the number of filters as the previous layers, and a smaller filter size of 3x3. It uses ReLU activation.

Conv2D: The fourth convolutional layer is the same as the third layer.

MaxPooling2D: This layer performs max pooling with the same pool size as the previous one (2x2).

Dropout: This layer randomly drops 50% of the nodes during training to prevent overfitting.

Flatten: The Flatten layer converts the output of the previous layer into a one-dimensional array.

Dense: The layer comprises of 500 nodes that are activated using ReLU activation function.

Dropout: This layer randomly drops 50% of the nodes during training to prevent overfitting.

Dense: The last dense layer of the model consists of nodes equivalent to the number of categories in the dataset and uses soft-max activation to output the probabilities for each class.

The Adam optimizer with a learning rate of 0.001 and categorical cross entropy loss function are implemented in the model. To assess the model's performance, accuracy metric is utilized.

Training and Testing the Model

CNN algorithm analyse the images by assigning weights to the objects in them and distinguishing them from each other. One of the advantages of CNN is that it requires minimal pre-processing data compared to other algorithms, making it a particularly fast choice. During training, the CNN takes an image and plots graphs depicting loss and accuracy of both the training and validation datasets with increasing epochs. Once the training dataset is finished, the model is tested using photographs that were not used in training, such as traffic images that are not visible. The resulting model is saved using the save function with the (.h5) extension. The ultimate goal of using a CNN is to improve the accuracy of traffic sign recognition systems, which can ultimately contribute to safer driving conditions. [5,6]

Parameter Tunning

The model's accuracy was improved by adjusting the hyperparameters, including the number of epochs and learning rate. These two factors have a significant impact on the model's performance. Several combinations of epochs and learning rates were systematically tested and evaluated to determine the best settings. as shown in Figure 51.3.

Result and Discussions

The model was trained for a total of 30 epochs using a batch size of 30. During the training process, the Adam optimizer with a learning rate of 0.001 and categorical cross-entropy loss function were employed. The model has been trained on a GPU machine with 32 GB of RAM and a 6-core processor. CV2 library is used to pre-process the images by converting them into grayscale, resizing them to 32x32 pixels, and normalizing the pixel values. The dataset was partitioned randomly into training and testing sets in a ratio of 80:20. To determine no. of the epoch model should be complete before being compiled, model has been ran for 100 epochs, and then with the help of chats formed for loss and accuracy for each epoch value, then the value of epochs is changed to 30 as it gives the highest performance, minimum loss for least compile time. The size of batch is 30m, that came after trying various values for it (i.e. 23, 25, 40, 50). Steps per epoch are 2212 (steps= Data_avilable_for_training/Batch_size). Proposed system is analyzed by computing and plotting the accuracy and loss.

Distribution of the training dataset

Figure 51.3 Dataset distribution

<u>Further plots show:</u>

(i)   Training and Validation Loss,
(ii) Training And Validation Accuracy

      i.   Accuracy and loss when epochs = 100

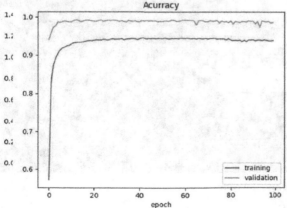

Test Score: 0.05547352507710457
Test Accuracy: 0.986639678478241

ii.   Accuracy and loss when epochs = 30

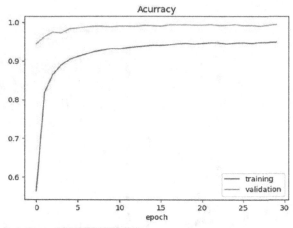

Test Score: 0.028446698561310768
Test Accuracy: 0.9924757480621338

The following figure shows that the proposed model is able to detect the traffic sign in the road and warn the traveller according to the results. The model is able to detect the speed limit instructions, road condition, and road access restriction. These results are shown in following Figures 51.4 and 51.5 respectively. The proposed model was able produce 99% accuracy rate with correct sign detections.

Figure 51.4 Model detecting the road bump

Figure 51.5 Model detecting the speed limit sign

Conclusion

This framework can recognize 43 traffic signs in different conditions like dim lights and rain with a 99% accuracy. However, some signs are recognized less accurately, and that can be improved by adding a better-balanced labelled images. This system is better than existing ones because it can detect any traffic sign regardless of its size and shape in any lighting condition. In order to improve the improve accuracy, a couple of modifications takes place in the model by increasing the number of filters and epochs, adding data augmentation, and adjusting the architecture in wherein more different traffic sign can be included.

References

1. Kumar, A. D. (2018). Novel deep learning model for traffic sign detection using capsule networks. *Computer Vision and Pattern Recognition International Journal of Pure and Applied Mathematics*, 118(20), 4543–4548. ISSN: 1314-3395.
2. Yang, Y., Luo, H., Xu, H., and Wu, F. (2018). Traffic sign recognition using multitask convolutional neural network. 19(4).
3. Keerimolel, A., Galsulkar, S., and Gowray, B. (2021). A survey on traffic sign recognition and detection. *International Journal of Trendy Research in Engineering and Technology*, 7(2), 510–519.
4. Nanda, S., More, P., Shimpi, M., Malve, N., and Pede, S. (2019). Traffic sign recognition system: a survey. *International Research Journal of Engineering and Technology (IRJET) e-I*, 6(3), 510–519.
5. Shangzheng, L. (2019). A traffic sign image recognition and classification approach based on convolutional neural network. In the 11th International Conference on Measuring Technology and Mechatronics Automation, 2019.
6. Luo, L., and Xiong, Y. (2019). Adaptive gradient methods with dynamic bound of learning rate. In Proceedings of the 7th International Conference on Learning Representations, New Orleans, Louisiana, May 2019.

52 Recognition of emotion through speech

Gorre Bhanu Pradeep Kumar[1,a], Nalluri Pradeep[1,b], G. Kaushik[1,c], Kakimani Gokul[1,d], M. Prasanth[1,e] and Tejinder Thind[2,f]

[1]School of Computer Science and Engineering, Lovely Professional University, Phagwara, India

[2]Assistant professor, Lovely Professional University, Phagwara, India

Abstract

A recent field of research that has attracted a lot of interest recently is the recognition of emotions through speech. Speech-based emotion recognition systems have the potential to change several industries, including healthcare, education, and entertainment, because of the rising availability of digital devices and the expanding need for personalized interactions. In this work, we thoroughly review the latest studies on recognition of emotion using speech. We started with core essential ideas and methods used in the feeling which is detected from the address. The most recent methods which are designed, such as feature extraction, SVM classifiers, and assessment measures, are then discussed briefly. Lastly, we review the uses and difficulties of speech-based emotion identification and offer suggestions.

Keywords: Emotions, feature extraction, HMM, MFCC, speech emotion recognition, SVM

Introduction

Emotions are a crucial component of human interaction, and understanding and appropriately expressing them is crucial for productive interpersonal relationships. Speech constitutes one of the main ways that emotions are communicated, hence studies on emotion identification have mostly looked at the address. Speech-based emotion recognition's primary objective is to understand the speaker's emotional state from their speech signal [1].

Fundamental Ideas and Methods: Speech-based emotion identification comprises numerous processes, involving signals which were before, extraction of features, classification, and assessment. The movement pre-processing step encompasses eliminating noise, filtering, and normalizing. At the feature extraction stage, pertinent characteristics from the voice signal that may be utilized to categorize emotions are extracted. The most often-utilized characteristics are pitch features are the most often-utilized features. The categorization stage includes One of the most current methods: Many traditional ML algorithms where machine is learning is like a human for dialogue emotion recognition. Speech-based emotion recognition has historically relied on the traditional machine learning techniques such as support-vector machines and random forests. Convolutional and

[a]bhanupradeep123456@gmail.com, [b]nalluripradeep9999@gmail.com, [c]gkaushik273@gmail.com, [d]gokul22077@gmail.com, [e]prasanth9264@gmail.com, [f]tejinder.15312@lpu.co.in

recurrent neural networks are two deep learning methods that have recently demonstrated promising results.

As it has several applications in areas including mental health, human-computer interaction, and artificial intelligence, emotion identification through speech has grown in popularity as a study topic in recent years. A summary of current developments in speech-based emotion identification is intended to be provided in this review article.

Feature extraction is the initial stage in speech-based emotion recognition. Pitch, intensity, and other characteristics, as well as formants, are frequently used. Mel-frequency cepstral coefficients (MFCCS), which may reproduce the spectrum properties of speech, have grown in popularity recently. Prosodic characteristics like speech tempo and pauses have also been discovered to be instructive for emotion identification.

After extraction, feelings are classified using machine learning algorithms based on the characteristics that were extracted. Among the most popular classifiers are support vector machines (SVMs), artificial neural, and random forests. Have recently proved promising results in the identification of emotions through speech [2].

The heterogeneity across subjects and in emotional displays is one of the difficulties in emotion identification through speech. Several strategies, including feature extraction and transfer learning, have been employed to overcome the issue.

The lack of labeled data presents another problem. It takes a lot of effort and money to compile and categorize sizable datasets of emotional speech. Several academics have turned to crowdsource to solve this. The absence of labeled data is another issue. Large datasets of emotional speech must be gathered and labeled, which takes time and money. To solve this, some researchers have employed crowdsourcing to gather data on emotional speech, while others have used pre-existing datasets such as the Interactive Emotional Dyadic Motion Capture (IEMOCAP) dataset.

In this section, we provide an overview of dashboards and classifications of the emotional categories used in literature. We also address the problems associated with present expression systems. Our primary focus is on emotional categorization techniques since it might be difficult to accurately interpret expressions and physiological reactions. Later, we'll examine the common traits used to identify emotions and talk about the issues they raise.

The category, dimensional, and appraisal-based techniques are three primary ones that have been found to have an impact on emotion modeling.

We concentrate on the most often-used categories and dimensional methods, as the appraisal-based approach is not frequently utilized due to its complicated and sophisticated measures of change

The category method takes into consideration many emotions as there are many emotions subdivided at different time and that are fundamental and well-known on a global scale, known as basic emotions. Identifies six fundamental emotions that we are all familiar with Joy, Sorrow, Wrath, Terror, Astonishment, and Disgust. It has a single label with distinct class. In the two-dimensional universe of emotions, each fundamental way of feeling is that is directly or indirectly is part that is a component of a single sentiment which is interlinked. For arousal, the recommended poles are relaxed vs excited, and for the valence, pleasant versus unpleasant. We may conclude that emotion will be divided into different segments, and we have seen that this is almost related to actual life experiences.

Literature Review

As described, there are seven basic feelings which were categorized as Surprise, Angry, Happy, Sad. Previously there were few techniques used for emotion detection such as SVM and HMM.

The hidden Markov Model is mainly providing high accuracy and the ability to recognize speech [3]. Therefore we used MFCC and LPCC Mel-frequency and Linear Prediction Cepstrum Constants [4] where LPCC features somewhat less than MFCC features. Mainly in MFCC speech, many features from the speech will be taken, they are categorized using an SVM classifier. Whereas we used GMM to improve speech detection.

Emotion recognition using speech is mainly of three steps signal preprocessing, feature extraction, and classification [5].

While collecting data from users, there are many chances that the voice was not accurate, and a lot of disturbances there so we used only a clean audio directory so that only clean audio files will be considered where no noise is there. For detecting a speech a feature must be chosen we opted for Excitation and spectral features ,we can get these characteristics using intensity, the pitch of voice, and suppression noise and use statistical measures like skewness, standard deviation, and variance like that [6]. Some applications for this are the detection of human behavior while driving a vehicle and checking the state of the driver accurately and in an uneven state what the vehicle should do and whether to stop or act accordingly is one of use scenarios [7].

These features in the later stage go to the classifier where we split the data into tests and training in the required ratio and apply algorithms and check which provides great accuracy it then categorizes the feelings and gives the emotion as the final output [8].

Workflow of Recognition of Emotion from Speech

Speech Database
We used data of 24 actors where Voices recorded and to validate speech and emotion recognition many participated in this, and each actor has 60 different files so there are 24 different actors each of the 60 audio files 12 male and 12 female actors.

There were different emotions such as furious, panic, neutrality, disgust, happiness, and sadness. We use the Ravdess dataset for Input speech later pre-processing is the later stage where an unwanted noise from the background is removed from the audio samples. We will now extract the features we need from clean data audio files. Figure 52.1 shows the steps involved in the recognition of emotion.

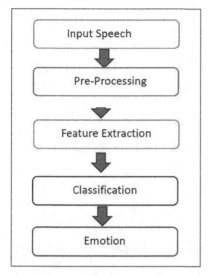

Figure 52.1 The steps involved in recognition of emotion

Pre-Processing
Cleaning and organizing the data from folders and making it usable,

By removing unwanted data and making it suitable for a later stage of the building and removing unwanted background noise and we used the "envelope" function to remove background noise [9]. Steps Involved in the Emotion Recognition system using speech used several Libraries like Pandas, NumPy, and Librosa [10]. A sound-file which read and write sound files. As the dataset used has folders and directories, we use the OS module. We used Seaborn open-source python library for visualization and data analysis.

Python provides a function for creating or removing a directory, fetching the audio files in folders. We used Through speech-recognition which is a library to convert the format of audio files into readable text format so that we can recognize the data provided to the machine if it didn't understand we handled that case as an exempt and print error.

Later we print the timeline of each audio plot by loading the audio and converting it into a NumPy array, which will timeline of each audio file with the respective time and amplitude.

Extraction of Features

We used many features which are already in use and tried to enhance the features to achieve great consequences in recognition of emotion from speech used features which exists previously are Mel-frequency based. We used

Fast Fourier Transform (FFT) which is a discrete Fourier algorithm that signals time into frequency components

The envelope function takes three arguments: audio signal, a sample-rate, and a threshold. It converts a signal into a Pandas series and takes the absolute value

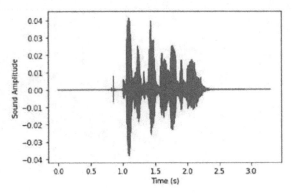

Figure 52.2 Plotting graph for understanding audio files

of all its data points. After a rolling window is used to take the average of every window of sample rate(Hz)/10.

Recently for speech decomposition there has been quite an increase in feature extraction by using a filter bank it will be dividing speech features into 4 different classes which are spectral based and more. There were many properties which are useful for detecting emotion and will have high precision, perfection and show changes between emotions [11]. Figure 52.2 depicts the graph for understanding of audio file.

MFCC

One of the most important stages of feature extraction, It is used before any classification like SVM. Figure 52.3 shows the feature extraction process.

This is used where speech is pulled out from spoken words using Mel scale frequencies. Then we statistically use the primary needed one and it removes longer silences, Here Mel(f) is the frequency (mels) and f is the frequency (Hz)

In the extraction of features in MFCC,DCT plays a key role where function of this mixture of features and helpful in equate the coefficients [12, 13].

$$\text{Mel(f)} = 2595 \log(1 + \frac{f}{700})$$

This Picture shows a graph between Timeseries and Fourier transform after applying Envelope function later we used Mel-frequency cepstral coefficients (MFCC) To Compute MFCC features from an audio signal.

Classification Approaches

After extracting the features choosing a better classifier is very important. This is the main stage to display the emotion of speech, they are further classified using various algorithms for better accuracy.

SVM is an algorithm is used when a pattern is recognized in the data like the distance between the nearest data and give output [14]. Table 52.1 shows confusion matrix.

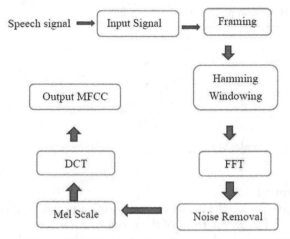

Figure 52.3 Feature extraction process of MFCC [20]

Table 52.1 Confusion matrix

		Actual Values	
		Positive	Negative
Predicted Values	positive	tp	fp
	Negative	fn	tn

HMM allows the prediction of unknown variables from known variables [15].

Artificial Neural Network ANN is most usable for emotion detection and can learn from the previous data and give us predictions and give us responses [16].

MLP classifiers will minimize the loss and optimize the loss accordingly it is hidden using MLP supervised algorithm after the model will be trained [17].

We use confusion matrix to get precision of data as for how many positive/true are there correctly and it shows how many negative/false values are showed correctly where having values left to the right cross-side is better than beside values.

We can get accurate output in a ease manner, we will know whether after applying algorithm the test and train data are giving output accurately Therefore need to check how many true positives are positive and what are actual negatives. Later, we calculate precision, recall, accuracy, and f1 score.

The closer the value of the F1 score the better the performance.

Accuracy is the total of all correct predictions divided by the total number Best is 1.0 and worst is 0. Table 52.2 shows the performance of the people confusion matrix.

Table 52.2 Performance of people confusion matrix

		Confusion	Matrix		
	Calm	48	2	2	2
	Happy	4	30	5	5
Actual	Fearful	1	4	40	8
Values	disgust	1	3	4	33
		Predicted	Values		

we received an accuracy of around 0.81%.

The pickle model is used to save the model it can be done using an open function when predicting is done ,it will show an array of the result of emotion.

Precision is Ratio to the true positive to the sum of the true positive and false positive.

$$precision = \frac{tp}{tp+fp}; recall = \frac{tp}{tp+fn}; accuracy = \frac{tp+tn}{tp+tn+fp+fn}; F1\ score = 2\ x\ \frac{precision\ x\ recall}{precision+recall}.$$

Conclusion

The result will be shown as an output in which the emotion of the specified audio file will be shown. Here we used an MLP classifier, and the Accuracy of the predicted model is 80%. Comparing with various models we get great results. Thus Three different features "chroma", "Mel", and MFCC are extracted from the RAVDESS dataset. In the future system can be enhanced to apply real-time applications like integrating with web applications and a telephone for this research in the future is necessary. Therefore if the collection of data increases effectively in an easy way, then recognition will also be increased. Thus we have gone to stages of speech emotion recognition, various techniques in feature extraction like MFCC, and classifiers like SVM. Thus emotions that have higher accuracy will be output.

Acknowledgement

we extend our thanks to all the researchers, scholars, and authors whose works have paved the way for our study. Their dedication to advancing knowledge in this field is an inspiration to us all.

References

1. Zheng, X., Ping, F., Pu, Y., Wang, Y., Montenegro-Marin, C. E., & Khalaf, O. I. (2021). Recognize and regulate the importance of work-place emotions based on organizational adaptive emotion control. Aggression and Violent Behavior, 101557.
2. Khalil, R. A., Jones, E., Babar, M. I., and Jan, T. (2019). Speech emotion recognition using deep learning techniques: a review. IEEE, 117327–117345.

3. Ai, O. C., Hariharan, M., Yaacob, S., & Chee, L. S. (2012). Classification of speech dysfluencies with MFCC and LPCC features. Expert Systems with Applications, 39(2), 2157–2165.

4. Vogt, T., & André, E. (2005, July). Comparing feature sets for acted and spontaneous speech in view of automatic emotion recognition. In 2005 IEEE International Conference on Multimedia and Expo (pp. 474–477). IEEE.

5. Tawari, A., & Trivedi, M. (2010, June). Speech based emotion classification framework for driver assistance system. In 2010 IEEE Intelligent Vehicles Symposium (pp. 174–178). IEEE.

6. Lee, K.-F., Hon, H.-W., and Reddy, R. (1990). An overview of the SPHINX speech recognition system. *IEEE*, 38(1), 35–45.

7. Nogueiras, A., Moreno, A., Bonafonte, A., & Mariño, J. B. (2001). Speech emotion recognition using hidden Markov models. In Seventh European conference on speech communication and technology.

8. Moon, I. J., Won, J. H., Park, M. H., Ives, D. T., Nie, K., Heinz, M. G., ... & Rubinstein, J. T. (2014). Optimal combination of neural temporal envelope and fine structure cues to explain speech identification in background noise. Journal of Neuroscience, 34(36), 12145–12154.

9. Babu, P. A., Nagaraju, V. S., & Vallabhuni, R. R. (2021, June). Speech emotion recognition system with librosa. In 2021 10th IEEE International Conference on Communication Systems and Network Technologies (CSNT) (pp. 421–424). IEEE.

10. Wu, S., Falk, T. H., & Chan, W. Y. (2011). Automatic speech emotion recognition using modulation spectral features. Speech communication, 53(5), 768–785.

11. Gupta, H., and Gupta, D. (2016). LPC and LPCC method of feature extraction in speech recognition system. IEEE.

12. Aung, S. T., Hassan, M., Brady, M., Mannan, Z. I., Azam, S., Karim, A., ... & Wongsawat, Y. (2022). Entropy-based emotion recognition from multichannel EEG signals using artificial neural network. Computational Intelligence and Neuroscience, 2022.

13. Kwon, S. (2021). Att-Net: Enhanced emotion recognition system using lightweight self-attention module. Applied Soft Computing, 102, 107101.

14. Ittichaichareon, C., Suksri, S., & Yingthawornsuk, T. (2012, July). Speech recognition using MFCC. In International conference on computer graphics, simulation and modeling (Vol. 9).

15. Shen, P., Changjun, Z., & Chen, X. (2011, August). Automatic speech emotion recognition using support vector machine. In Proceedings of 2011 international conference on electronic & mechanical engineering and information technology (Vol. 2, pp. 621-625). IEEE.

16. Sudhakar, R. S., & Anil, M. C. (2015, February). Analysis of speech features for emotion detection: a review. In 2015 International Conference on Computing Communication Control and Automation (pp. 661–664). IEEE.

17. Tripathi, S., Kumar, A., Ramesh, A., Singh, C., & Yenigalla, P. (2019). Deep learning based emotion recognition system using speech features and transcriptions. arXiv preprint arXiv:1906.05681.

53 Accuracy enhancement of textual data during sentiment analysis in twitter using multinomial naive bayes

Hari Singh Meena[a], Ashutosh Kumar[b], Aryan Kumar Saxena[c], Sneha Kapoor[d], Aniruddha Banerjee[e] and Sameeksha Khare[f] (Assistant Professor)

Department of Computer Science and Engineering Lovely Professional University, Phagwara, India

Abstract

Many messages convey opinions about various things, including people, politics, products, services, and even people's emotions and moods. Sentiment analysis has a wide range of uses, including analysing the outcomes of social network events and examining consumer views of goods and services. The popularity of social media sites like Facebook, Twitter, LinkedIn, and Instagram has made it possible for people to express their thoughts, feelings, and views on a wide range of subjects. A lot of research has been done in this area, but accuracy in analysing sentiments can still be enhanced. For this study, we have considered the Kaggle data set to figure out the sentiments used in racist and non-racist tweets. The techniques that are employed in this study are the Naive Bayes algorithm and NLP. The proposed model achieves 94% accuracy.

Keywords: Deep learning, machine learning, naïve bayes algorithm, non-racist tweets, racist tweets, sentimental analysis, twitter data

Introduction

Over the last few years, Social media sites like Twitter and Facebook have fascinated a lot of users. Most people share their feelings, opinions, or beliefs about things, places, or people on social media [1]. In recent years, Social media has been used to violate people's opinions in several ways. One way is through the spread of disinformation or fake news. Individuals or groups with a specific agenda may use social media platforms to spread false information in order to influence people's opinions and beliefs. This can include intentionally spreading misinformation or using manipulative tactics to sway people's opinions. It's important to be aware of these issues and to actively engage in critical thinking when using social media platforms. Users should be cautious when consuming information, fact-checking sources, and reporting any behavior that violates the platform's policies.

Sentimental analysis has many applications in various domains, such as in business to obtain feedback on products, and in social media to learn about users'

[a]harisinghmeenameena404@gmail.com, [b]ashutoshkumar6341@gmail.com,
[c]thekumararyan847@gmail.com, dsnehakapoor1193@gmail.com,
[e]meanibanerjee@gmail.com, [f]sameekshakhare65@gmail.com

feedback and reviews. In this reference, we learned about people's opinions and how to use machine learning algorithms with different approaches to find sentimental analysis of a dataset. Specifically, we learned about sentimental analysis of movie reviews to learn about people's feelings, judgements, and comments [2].

Literature Review

Sentiment analysis is also known as opinion mining and it is the process of analysing and categorizing emotions, attitudes, and opinions expressed in text data. It has become an important area of research in the field of machine learning, natural language processing and data mining. A literature survey on sentiment analysis can provide an overview of the current state of the art, the key research trends, and the main challenges and opportunities in this field. Here are some of the notable studies and research papers regarding sentiment analysis:

1. **Sentimental analysis to detect emotion based on graphical input**
    In 2022, Sameeksha Khare [3], has done sentimental analysis on various twitter data and she used, CNN- based technique for graphical content and a neural- based technique for textual content. The neural network machine learning method has proposed to detect emotion based on graphical input. The current research is primarily concerned with textual and graphical tweets posted by users.
2. **Examined political viewpoints using Naive Bayes and support vector machine methods**
    In 2018, A. Hasan et al. [4], examined political viewpoints using Naive Bayes and support vector machine methods. Using Python code(W-WSD, TextBlob, SentiWordNet), Using each sentiment analysis, they assessed the subjectivity and polarity of processed tweets. Election attitudes were examined as the results came in, and precise forecasts were generated.
3. **Emotional study of movie reviews**
    The emotional study of movie reviews by P Baid [5], A Gupta, and N Chaplot was completed in 2017. To examine different political stances, they used supervised machine learning methods like Naive Bayes, (SVM), KNN, and Random Forests. The outcomes were presented in figures and tables following the use of the following machine learning techniques and data analysis.
4. **Sentimental study on the effects of age and gender**
    A sentimental study on the effects of age and gender was conducted in 2020 by S Kumar et al. [6]. They used several feature extraction techniques to examine various user expressions based on age and gender. According to the analysis's findings, people of all ages provided both favourable and negative feedback. Yet, compared to all other age groups, those Above "Age 50" show superior accuracy.
5. **Sentimental analysis of Twitter data related to renewable energy**
    A sentimental analysis of Twitter data related to renewable energy was conducted in 2019 by Achin Jain and Vanita Jain [7]. They used five different machine learning methods to classify tweets into three categories: positive (POS), neutral (NEU), and negative (NEG), using SVM, KNN, Nave Bayes,

AdaBoost, and Bagging (NEU). As a consequence of the accuracy of 79.13% that was attained, it can be concluded that the majority of tweets were positive. Out of the three scenarios, SVM with PUK Kernel and CfsSubsetEval feature selection technique achieves the highest accuracy of 92.96%.

6. **Sentiment analysis of social media on education, e-commerce, and the Google Play Store**
    Using data from Twitter, J. Sankhe et al. [8], conducted a sentiment analysis study in 2022 on social media, education, e-commerce, and the Google Play Store. The K-Nearest Neighbor (KNN), Naive Bayes method and Support Vector Machine (SVM) techniques were used. According to the analysis's findings, user evaluations may be classed as good, negative, or neutral. As a consequence, organizations can analyze consumer complaints about their services based on unfavorable reviews.

7. **Relationship between sentiment of tweets about finance and return as well as the volatility of Bitcoin**
    Using data from Twitter, J. Sankhe et al. [8], conducted a sentiment analysis study in 2022 on social media, education, e-commerce, and the Google Play Store. The K-Nearest Neighbor (KNN), Naive Bayes method and Support Vector Machine (SVM) techniques were used. According to the analysis's findings, user evaluations may be classed as good, negative, or neutral. As a consequence, organizations can analyze consumer complaints about their services based on unfavorable reviews. [9]

8. **Sentimental analysis was used by Mohammed Alshamsi et al. [10] in 2020 to detect suspicious activity on Twitter and Facebook**
    Sentimental analysis was used by Mohammed Alshamsi et al. [10] in 2020 to detect suspicious activity on Twitter and Facebook.The study estimated criminal activities on social media and differentiate the collected information into positive, negative and neutral opinions. VADER's sentimental analysis uses 5000 tweets data, Among them 50.8% of respondents had neutral opinion, 39.2% had given negative opinion, and rest 9.9% had given favourable one. Analysis revealed that each post's sentiment score and interaction level have an impact on the degree of sentiment.

9. **Analysis of Twitter users' emotions towards e-commerce businesses**
    In 2022, Zulnaid Yaacob et al. [11], examined Twitter users' emotions towards e-commerce businesses. The analysis shows that Twitter users expressed their positive emotions regarding Lazada and Shopee on social media, with positive sentiments outweighing negative ones for both businesses. It gives an overview about the peoples opinion on e-commerce companies and it can help to understand the advantages and disadvantages of their services. So that they can enhance their marketing strategy.

10. **Analysis of Twitter's post, comments and hashtags**
    Shalin and others [12], forecast what emotion will be most closely linked with the most popular hashtags in 2022. Utilizing the "Lexicon-Based Approach," it essentially dissects users' perceptions of Twitter as an online forum where users post comments about their opinions on hot topics. This is accomplished by obtaining info in a real-timen setting. R-Studio is the programme used for implementation.

11. **Sentiment analysis of Twitter data to extract netizens' opinions on crypto-currencies**

    In 2021, Kabir Hassan and others [13], presented a study using sentiment analysis of Twitter data to extract netizens' opinions on cryptocurrencies. Supervised machine learning found a total sentiment score of 53,077 from a sample of 15,000 tweets. The results show that the samples contain mainly positive emotions. Theoretically, this finding has ramifications for determining which theories of sampled tweet sentiment best explain the social effect of the cryptocurrency phenomenon.

12. **Sentimental study of Twitter data pertaining to the growth of Rinca Island**

    Yova Ruldeviyani et al. [14] conducted a sentimental study of Twitter data pertaining to the growth of Rinca Island in 2022. The algorithms support vector machines and logistic regression are used along with two Doc2Vec models. Almost all of the models and classifier combinations have accuracy rates above 75%, demonstrating their opposition to Rinca Island expansion.

13. **Election prediction on sentiment analysis of tweets**

    Hassanpour et al. [15] election prediction in 2022 was founded on sentiment analysis of tweets. The suggested method's accuracy is examined through a series of experiments on a dataset, and the results are then evaluated in comparison to three other election prediction methods. The results of the experiments indicated that the Democrats expected Joe Biden's victory in the 2020 US presidential election to have a higher indicator value than the Republicans.

14. **Twitter sentimental analysis on Covid-19 outbreak**

    In 2020, Akash Dutt Dubey [16], presented a study of Twitter sentimental analysis on Covid-19 outbreak. This study considered tweets from twelve different nations. These tweets, which have some connection to COVID-19, were collected from March 11 through March 31, 2020. This analysis was conducted to examine how people are responding to the circumstance in various nations. The USA, France, and China were found to have the most angry tweets during this procedure.

15. **Analysis of customer review data from Twitter and Facebook**

    In 2022, Amjad Iqbal et al [17], used deep learning to analyse customer review data from Twitter and Facebook in order to determine customers' opinions on purchasing from an ecommerce site. The analysis results have provided significant insights into the products.

16. **Twitter sentimental analysis of sarcasm detection in texts**

    In order to enhance sentiment analysis performance in 2022, Godara J et al. [18] create a number of methods for sarcasm detection in texts. This article gives a general overview of sentiment analysis, including how to spot sarcasm and teach medical staff to base decisions on patients' feelings. When using K-nearest neighbor, the total accuracy found in this paper is 56.13%.

17. **Twitter sentimental analysis on farmer protests.**

    In 2021, Ashwin Sanjay Neogi et al. [19], used Twitter data about farmer protests to understand the public's sentiments on a global scale. They developed classification and sentiment analysis models based on a set of about

20,000 tweets about the demonstration, and they found that Bag of Words outperformed TF-IDF.

18. **Twitter Sentiment Analysis of tweets on Palestinian-Israeli conflict**
Amisha Gangwar and Tanvi Mehta [20] research Israeli political Twitter data in 2022 to decipher public sentiment towards the Israeli-Palestinian conflict. The study proposes using advanced technology like Machine Learning to conduct a Twitter Sentiment Analysis of tweets about Israel in relation to the Palestinian-Israeli conflict. Support Vector Classifier, Decision Tree, and Nave Bayes methods were applied to train the model. Nave Bayes got a 93.21% accuracy rate.

Problem Statement

The problem with racist and non-racist tweets, when analysed sentimentally, is that they can reveal a lot about the attitudes and beliefs of individuals and communities. Sentiment analysis of racist tweets can reveal the prevalence of negative stereotypes, discriminatory attitudes, and harmful behaviours towards individuals or groups that are the targets of such messages. This can contribute to a culture of intolerance and exclusion, and can have real-world consequences, such as harm and violence towards those who are marginalized. In contrast, sentiment analysis of non- racist tweets can reveal positive messages of inclusion, diversity, and respect towards individuals and communities.

However, the impact of these messages can be diminished by the prevalence of negative sentiment and hate speech online, which can contribute to the normalization of discriminatory attitudes and behaviours. The problem with racist and non-racist tweets, analysed sentimentally, is further compounded by the fact that social media platforms like Twitter have become a primary avenue for the expression of such attitudes. While there have been efforts to address hate speech and harassment on these platforms, the problem of racist and discriminatory content persist. To address this problem, it is crucial to continue to raise awareness and consciousness of the harmful effects of racism and discrimination, promote positive messages of inclusion and diversity, and actively work to create a more equitable and just society that values and respects the dignity and worth of all individuals. Sentiment analysis can be a useful tool in this effort, as it can help to identify patterns and trends in online behaviour and attitudes, and inform targeted interventions to promote positive change.

Objective

This study's goal is to perform a sentiment analysis on Twitter data to determine the overall sentiment of tweets related to the speeches delivered by well-known politicians worldwide. The analysis will seek to identify the positive, neutral, and negative sentiments expressed in the tweets, as well as provide insights into the public's perception and attitude towards the topic of interest. The analysis' findings will be used to guide decision-making for businesses, organization, and individuals seeking to understand and respond to public opinion on social media.

Dataset

Dataset: Kaggle data of Twitter Hate Speeches

We have used Kaggle datasets. Kaggle is a community for data scientists and machine learning practitioners as well as a platform for data science contests. It also hosts a large number of datasets that are freely available for anyone to download and use for research, analysis, and machine learning projects and there are several reasons for using Kaggle dataset for sentiment analysis such as:

1. Large and Diverse Datasets: Kaggle datasets are often large and diverse, which means they can provide a wide range of text data that can be used for sentiment analysis. This allows for more comprehensive analysis and better accuracy.
2. Pre-labelled Data: Many Kaggle datasets for sentiment analysis have already been labelled by humans, which saves time and resources in manually labelling the data. Sentiment analysis machine learning algorithms can be trained using this pre-labeled data. Community and Collaboration: Kaggle has a large community of data scientists and machine learning practitioners who can provide guidance and insights into how to analyse and model the data. This collaboration can lead to better results and more robust analysis.
3. Bench marking: Kaggle datasets provide a benchmark for sentiment analysis tasks. Researchers and practitioners can compare their results against existing benchmarks to measure the effectiveness of their models and algorithms.

Overall, using Kaggle datasets for sentiment analysis can save time and resources, provide pre-labelled data for training machine learning models, facilitate collaboration and benchmarking, and ultimately lead to better accuracy and more comprehensive analysis. Figure 53.1 shows dataset divided into training and testing.

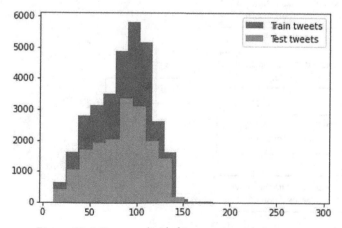

Figure 53.1 Dataset divided into train and test

Methodology and Implementation

Multinomial Naive Bayes 'ML' Algorithm
We have employed the Multinomial Naive Bayes algorithm, a variation of the Naive Bayes algorithm that is frequently employed in text categorization issues, such as spam filtering and sentiment analysis. It assumes that the input features are counts or frequencies of words, and that the distribution of the counts for each class follows a multinomial distribution. The Multinomial Naive Bayes algorithm works by first finding the Initial probabilities of every class present in data, based on the frequency of occurrence of each class in the training dataset. Then, for each input feature (word), it calculates the possibility of that feature`s in every class, depending on how often the feature appears in the training data for that class. The likelihoods are then used to calculate the posterior probability of each class, given the input features, using Bayes' theorem. Figure 53.2 depicts flowchart of the model.

Formula:

- $P(X|Y) = P(X)*P(Y|X)/P(Y)$
  Here we can find the probability of X when predictor Y is already there
- $P(X)$ = Initial probability of X
- $P(Y)$ = Initial probability of Y
- $P(Y|X)$ = Event of predictor Y that is Given probability

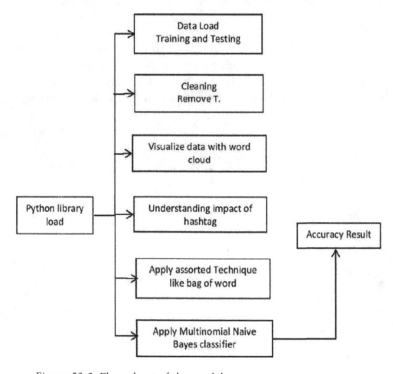

Figure 53.2 Flow chart of the model

With this formula we can calculate the frequency of words in our dataset.

Natural Language Processing

We've employed the area of artificial intelligence known as "natural language processing" (NLP) is concerned with the capacity of computers to comprehend and produce human language. NLP systems typically follow a pipeline approach, where each step in the pipeline is responsible for a specific sub-task of NLP.

Here is a high-level overview of how NLP works:

Text Preprocessing: Preprocessing the unprocessed text data is the first stage in NLP. This entails actions like tokenization (breaking the text into individual tokens or words), stemming (reducing words to their most basic form), and removing stop words (common words that don't contribute meaning to the text).

Part-of-Speech Tagging: Once the text has been preprocessed, the next step is to tag each word with its part of speech (noun, verb, adjective, etc.). Part-of- speech tagging is typically done using statistical models or rule-based systems.

Named Entity Recognition: Identification and classification of named entities in the text, such as individuals, groups, and places, is known as named entity recognition (NER). It is typically done using statistical models or rule-based systems.

Parsing: In order to understand the relationships between words in a text, parsing entails analysing the grammatical framework of the text. This is typically done using syntax trees or dependency graphs.

Sentiment Analysis: Sentiment analysis entails identifying the emotional tone or sentiment of a text, such as whether it is positive, negative, or neutral.. Sentiment analysis is typically done using machine learning algorithms.

Text Generation: Text generation involves generating new text based on some input, such as a prompt or a topic. Text generation is typically done using neural networks.

Three major categories can be used to categorise NLP algorithms: rule-based systems, statistical models, and deep learning models. Rule-based systems use a set of handcrafted rules to analyze and generate text. To identify patterns in text data and make forecasts based on those patterns, statistical models employ machine learning algorithms. Deep learning models use neural networks to learn patterns in text data.

In summary, NLP is a complex field that involves a number of sub-tasks, each of which can be tackled using a variety of different algorithms and techniques. NLP's ultimate aim is to make it possible for computers to comprehend and produce human language, and to use that understanding to perform a wide range of tasks, from Chatbots and virtual assistants to automated translation and sentiment analysis.

Implementation:

In this paper we used python to implement sentimental analysis. We have utilized some package of python according to the requirements.

Step1: First of all load all the python library.

Step2: Load training and test dataset in colab and then combined the dataset.

Cleaning:

   Step3: Remove twitter handles from tweets.

   Step4: Remove short words from tweet.

   Step5: Combine all words in sentence.

   Figure 53.3, 53.4, 53.5 depicts positive, neutral and negative opinion respectively.

Visualization:

   Step6: with the help of word cloud displayed all tweets racist and non-racist

   Step7: Next made separate word cloud for racist and non-racist tweets.

   Step8: Next step understanding hashtag in tweets visualize racist and non-racist hashtag with the help of bar plot.

   Figure 53.6, 53.7 shows the people having neutral emotions over the Racist and non-racist tweets.

Figure 53.3 Positive opinion

Figure 53.4 Neutral opinion

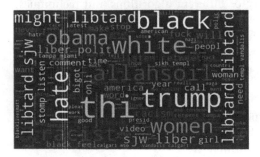

Figure 53.5 Negative opinion

Comparison Table

Comparison of the accuracy rates of the various studies cited with those from our study:

Methods	Year	Analysis	Accuracy Rate
Logistic regression and Support vector machines	2022	Twitter information about the growth of Rinca Island [14]	75%
SVM, KNN, Nave Bayes.	2019	Analysis of twitter data on renewable energy [7]	92.96%
KNN	2022	Sarcasm detection and training to health-care professionals. [18]	56.13%
Decision Tree, and Naive Bayes.	2022	Analysis of tweets about Israel in relation to the Palestinian-Israeli [20]	93.21%
Proposed-methodology: Multinomial Naive Bayes.	2023	**Accuracy Enhancement of Textual Data During Sentiment Analysis in Twitter Using Multinomial Naive Bayes**	94%

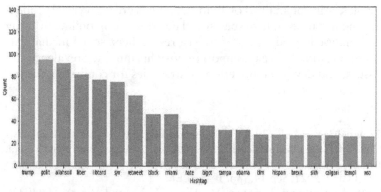

Figure 53.6 Racist tweets

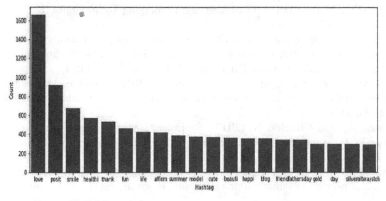

Figure 53.7 Non-racist tweets

Conclusion and Results

In this paper, we discuss the importance of social network analysis, focusing on Twitter data and implementing various algorithms to implement racist and non-racist tweets. We discovered **94** percent accuracy on the analysed Twitter data after implementing all of the algorithms and analyses. To improve sentimental analysis, we discovered that there is a need to improve analysis of social media data. We successfully analysed Twitter data using the NLP and multinomial naive Bayes algorithms and discovered results on hatred speech and textual based content.

Future applications of sentiment analysis of Twitter data for racist and non-racist tweets include gaining a better understanding of the prevalence of hate speech and discrimination on social media platforms. Researchers can gain insights into the frequency and nature of racist language and behaviour on Twitter by analyzing large datasets of tweets, which can inform efforts to combat hate speech and promote greater diversity and inclusion online.

Graph shows the most hatred speech given by politicians.

Another potential use of sentiment analysis of Twitter data for racist and non-racist tweets is in identifying and addressing instances of hate speech and discrimination in real-time. By using sentiment analysis to monitor Twitter feeds, social media platforms and other organizations can quickly identify and respond to instances of hate speech and other harmful behaviour, such as cyberbullying and harassment. Overall, sentiment analysis of Twitter data has great potential or identifying and addressing instances of hate speech and discrimination online. By using this technology to analyse large datasets of tweets, researchers, social media platforms, and other organizations can gain important insights into the prevalence and nature of these issues, and develop more effective strategies for combating them.

References

1. Tusar, M. T., and Islam, M. T. (2021). A comparative study of sentiment analysis using NLP and different machine learning techniques on US airline Twitter data. In 2021 International Conference on Electronics, Communications and Information Technology (ICECIT), 2021, Sep 14, (pp. 1–4). IEEE.
2. Fahim, S., Imran, A., Alzahrani, A., Fahim, M., Alheeti, K. M., and Alfateh, M. (2022). Twitter sentiment analysis based public emotion detection using machine learning algorithms. In 2022 17th International Conference on Emerging Technologies (ICET), 2022, Nov 29, (pp. 107–112). IEEE.
3. Khare, S. (2022). Accuracy enhancement during sentiment analysis in twitter using CNN. In 2022 10th International Conference on Reliability, Infocom Technologies and Optimization (Trends and Future Directions) (ICRITO), Noida, India.
4. Hasan, A., Moin, S., Karim, A., and Shamshirband, S. (2018). Machine learning-based sentiment analysis for twitter accounts. *Mathematical and Computational Applications*, 23(1), 11.
5. Baid, P., Gupta, A., and Chaplot, N. (2017). Sentiment analysis of movie reviews using machine learning techniques. *International Journal of Computer Application*, 179(7), 45–49.
6. Kumar, S., Gahalawat, M., Roy, P. P., Dogra, D. P., and Kim, B. G. (2020). Exploring impact of age and gender on sentiment analysis using machine learning. *Electronics*, 9(2), 374.

7. Jain, A., and Jain, V. (2019). Sentiment classification of twitter data belonging to renewable energy using machine learning. *Journal of Information and Optimization Sciences*, 40(2), 521–533.
8. Sankhe, J., Batavia, K., Borse, H., & Sharma, S. (2022). Survey on sentiment analysis.
9. Gao, X., Huang, W., & Wang, H. (2021). Financial Twitter Sentiment on Bitcoin Return and High-Frequency Volatility. Virtual Economics, 4(1), 7–18.
10. Al Mansoori, S., Almansoori, A., Alshamsi, M., Salloum, S. A., & Shaalan, K. (2020). Suspicious Activity Detection of Twitter and Facebook using Sentimental Analysis. TEM Journal, 9(4).
11. Yin, J. Y. B., Saad, N. H. M., & Yaacob, Z. (2022). Exploring Sentiment Analysis on E-Commerce Business: Lazada and Shopee. Tem journal, 11(4), 1508–1519.
12. Hidayat, T. H. J., Ruldeviyani, Y., Aditama, A. R., Madya, G. R., Nugraha, A. W., & Adisaputra, M. W. (2022). Sentiment analysis of twitter data related to Rinca Island development using Doc2Vec and SVM and logistic regression as classifier. Procedia Computer Science, 197, 660–667.
13. Yavari, A., Hassanpour, H., Rahimpour Cami, B., & Mahdavi, M. (2022). Election prediction based on sentiment analysis using twitter data. International Journal of Engineering, 35(2), 372–379.
14. Yavaria, A., Hassanpour, H., Rahimpour Camib, B., and Mahdavic, M. (2022). Election prediction based on sentimental analysis using twitter data. *IJE Transactions B: Applications*, 35(02), 372–379.
15. Hassan, M. K., Hudaefi, F. A., & Caraka, R. E. (2022). Mining netizen's opinion on cryptocurrency: sentiment analysis of Twitter data. *Studies in Economics and Finance*, 39(3), 365–385.
16. Dubey, A. D. (2020). Twitter sentiment analysis during COVID-19 outbreak. *Available at SSRN 3572023*.
17. Iqbal, A., Amin, R., Iqbal, J., Alroobaea, R., Binmahfoudh, A., and Hussain, M. (2022). Sentiment analysis of consumer reviews using deep learning. *Sustainability*, 14(17), 10844.
18. Godara, J., Aron, R., and Shabaz, M. (2022). Sentiment analysis and sarcasm detection from social network to train health- care professionals. *World Journal of Engineering*, 19(1), 124–133.
19. Neogi, A. S., Garg, K. A., Mishra, R. K., and Dwivedi, Y. K. (2021). Sentiment analysis and classification of Indian farmers' protest using twitter data. *International Journal of Information Management Data Insights*, 1(2), 100019.
20. Gangwar, A., and Mehta, T. (2022, March). Sentiment Analysis of Political Tweets for Israel Using Machine Learning. In *International Conference on Machine Learning and Big Data Analytics* (pp. 191–201). Cham: Springer International Publishing.

54 Enhanced real-time face recognition security system using LBPH algorithm

Jayesh Rawtiya[a], Varun Prakash[b], Aman Patidar[c], Shahbaz Khan[d]

Computer Science and Engineering Lovely Professional University Phagwara, India

Abstract

In our normal day to day life whenever we meet any person, we recognize him by looking at his face because it is unique to every human, that is why we can use face as a recognition and security purposes. Here, we are providing a same scenario in technical aspect where system is being trained by the faces of authorized individuals after that whenever any person tries to have a access of the system it starts recognizing the person is authorized person or unknown person, and accordingly it takes action to it. If it is an authorized person, it provides access to the system otherwise a notification will be sent to the security manager to have a look in the system security center.

Online Information systems are currently working on security of username and password, and there might be the possibility of a security

breach if some unauthorized person knows that credentials that's why biometric security can be the best possible option for this 21st online generation.

Keywords: Face recognition, security, OpenCV, LBPH

Introduction

In recent years there is a rapid increase in detection, recognition, and identification processes for both objects as well as humans [2]. One of the most emerging recognition techniques amoung them in facial recognition, it is because it nonintrusive, easy to use and a very low cost in comparison to other biometric authentication systems [15].

Since the start of the 21st century many technologies started shifting to online information system [3] but initially they were working on username password. To have a more reliable security to the system company started switching to biometric security systems [5].

Then Facial recognition emerged very rapidly [12]. Facial recognition security system is an Automated system which recognize person standing in front to it by matching its facial template with the template saved in its database, and if the person is legit it give access to the system otherwise it sends warning mail to the security manager for attempting unauthorized access.

According to [4], there is a strong need biometric security system in each and every institution. Therefore, The purpose of this paper is to provide a best biometric recognition system with the best security features available. That is why this system is combination of facial recognition system and security features.

[a]rawtiyajayesh@gmail.com, [b]prakashvarun004@gmail.com,
[c]appatidar9685@gmail.com, [d]arsalanshahbaz3@gmail.com

OpenCV Library
OpenCV is a widely used machine learning library stands for open-source Computer Vision Library used for image processing and it is compatible in so many languages such as java, python, C++ [6]. Most popular application of OpenCV is face recognition we are going to use it in our system, Using OpenCV tools and Haar Cascade we are going to detect, capture and process image of face for extracting features templates and then storing them in our database.

Haar Cascade Classifier
Haar Cascade Classifier is an ML algorithm which is used to extracting features and identifying objects from the images. It uses positive and negative images to classify objects in an image [6]. Figure 54.1 depicts Haar Cascade flowchart.

Local Binary Patterns Histogram (LBPH)
Local Binary Patterns Histogram (LBPH) is a feature extraction and analyzing algorithm. It is used in extracting feature of a face after that they are being

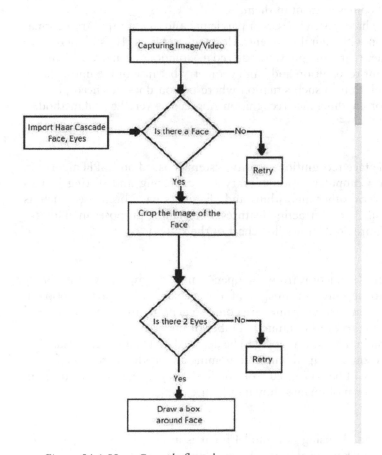

Figure 54.1 Haar Cascade flowchart

analyzed for training a model [8] Mostly it is used with computer vision libraries. LBPH algorithms divides pictures in several pixels and starts comparing it with all neighboring pixels for identifying a feature [6].

Using LBPH algorithm Not only images we can also use it for object recognition pattern, texture classification as well by defining them and training our model to it [13]. No other biometric system provides such type of feature.

Related Work

If security feature is removed from the system and keeps only Face recognition then it can be used for automatic attendance marking system for students and faculties [14]. It can also be blend with Video surveillance, so that whosoever person comes in video surveillance if it is in database then his/her will be saved in separate files.

Real-time Face Recognition system can also be helpful to the people suffering from prosopagnosia which is also known as face blindness [1] in which person face difficulties in recognizing others faces so if implant this system somehow in their spectacles So that the they can store there known faces and retrieve their name whenever he comes in front of them.

In recent past we have just witnessed a pandemic and saw a rapid transformation to digitalization with digital payments, electronic services [10] still there were payment media where card and pin was required in situations even other biometric failed like fingerprint recognition and hand geometry because of the untouchable disease [10]. for solution to such situation where person does not need physical touch to the card or anything face recognition emerged as very helpful method.

Methodology

Enhanced real-time face recognition security system is based on LBPH algorithm and Open- source Computer vision Library for capturing and storing images along with that several other algorithms and classifiers have been used such as Haar cascade classifier for extracting features. For mailing purposes mail library have been used. Figure 54.2 shows flowchart of the system.

Image Capturing
Using VideoCapture () function from the open- source Computer vision library system is going to capture the images of the person. By applying loop on VideoCapture function various frames are going to genrate, from that using read function we are going to capture limited number of images.

Image of a person in the frame is going to be detected by Haar Cascade classifier. It has a sequence of square shaped frames combining all together becomes a family.

Collected sample will be converted from BGR to greyscale and then stored in the database in the form of images shown in Figure 54.3.

Training Models
Training a model and choosing best model for it is an important task, and one best suitable for this task is Local Binary Pattern Histogram which is an algorithm

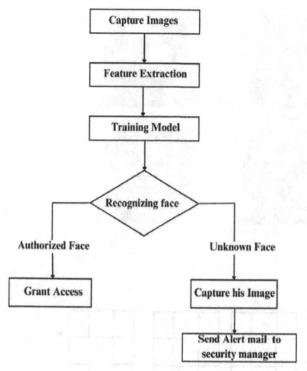

Figure 54.2 Flowchart of the system

used for face recognition. LBP does texture classification on greyscale images. By comparing center pixel with all neighboring pixels [11]. Figure 54.4 shows face recognition of LBPH algorithm [11].

In the above diagram we can see that firstly image is been divided into several pixels, after that system will mark numbers to every pixel according to its darkness on greyscale more darker will be the pixel less number will be provided. After that system will choose one pixel and compares it with all other neighboring pixels if number of neighboring pixel if greater mark it as 1 otherwise 0. At the end we will get a 9-digit binary number from all these marking.

Matching
After training the model whenever the faces come in front of recognizer camera, It starts capturing image of person then starts matching it with the database and if it matches it shows name of the person with percentage of much it matches. If Face matches with any of the authorized persons in database access will be given to the system on which this security system is applied, if it does not matches unknown face will be captures and notification will be sent to the security manager to have a look.

Security Feature
Security is one of the important factors in today's world but more important is that you get notified if security breach happens or if someone tries to breach. That

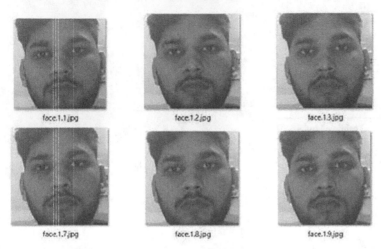

Figure 54.3 Collected samples

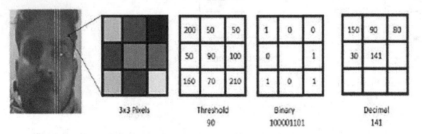

Figure 54.4 Face recognition of LBPH algorithm [11]

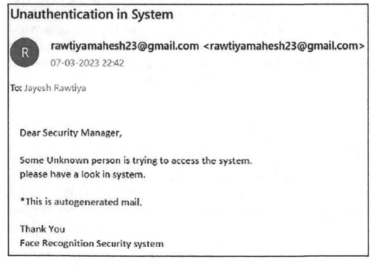

Figure 54.5 Autogenerated mail snapshot

is why an automatic notification feature has been added in this system which sends mail to security manager whenever some unknown person tries to access the system. Figure 54.5 shows autogenerated mail snapshot.

Findings & Result

Real-time Face Recognition security system is best reliable and easy to use and can be considered best for any security system which provides access to multiple users by verifying their identity using biometric systems. Security features of this system like providing alerts to the security manager whenever some unknown person is trying to authenticate can be a varying feature.

Conclusion

Nowadays as we all switching to biometric security over the username and password [7] Whenever there is a need to apply security on the system with multiple users, the best answer will be the biometric security. In biometrics the best biometric considered is face recognition because of its easiness and non-intrusiveness.

Future Enhancements

In this System Enhancement can be done in accuracy of the face detection. Along with that from Security perspective a new feature of capturing unknown person's face can be done and attaching it with mail, sent to security manager as notification.

An advanced security of Visual cryptography can be added to the system to make the system more reliable and attack free [9]. Visual cryptography is a process of communication which uses encryption decryption methods for secret messages (images, text). Original images get split up in several pieces such that single piece will look meaningless [9], when receiver gets all the pieces it decrypts and receives meaningful message.

In this we have used Haar cascade classifier which only works on Greyscale images, in future In future further improvements can be done where colored images are used for recognition.

References

1. Bate, S., Dalrymple, K. and Bennetts, R.J., 2022. Face recognition improvements in adults and children with face recognition difficulties. Brain Communications, 4(2), p.fcac068.
2. Jarraya, I., Said, F.B., Hamdani, T.M., Neji, B., Beyrouthy, T. and Alimi, A.M., 2022. Biometric-Based Security System for Smart Riding Clubs. IEEE Access, 10, pp.132012–132030.
3. Chen, B., Liao, X., Zhu, H., Gong, Z. and Li, Y., 2022. A Survey of Face Recognition Methods based on Deep Learning. Highlights in Science, Engineering and Technology, 24, pp.191–197.

4. Chen, B., Liao, X., Zhu, H., Gong, Z. and Li, Y., 2022. A Survey of Face Recognition Methods based on Deep Learning. Highlights in Science, Engineering and Technology, 24, pp.191–197.
5. Mugalu, B.W., Wamala, R.C., Serugunda, J. and Katumba, A., 2021. Face recognition as a method of authentication in a web-based system. arXiv preprint arXiv:2103.15144.
6. Khan, M., Chakraborty, S., Astya, R. and Khepra, S., 2019, October. Face detection and recognition using OpenCV. In 2019 International Conference on Computing, Communication, and Intelligent Systems (ICCCIS) (pp. 116–119). IEEE.
7. Musa, A., Vishi, K. and Rexha, B., 2021. Attack analysis of face recognition authentication systems using fast gradient sign method. Applied artificial intelligence, 35(15), pp.1346–1360.
8. Chinimilli, B.T., Anjali, T., Kotturi, A., Kaipu, V.R. and Mandapati, J.V., 2020, June. Face recognition based attendance system using Haar cascade and local binary pattern histogram algorithm. In 2020 4th international conference on trends in electronics and informatics (ICOEI)(48184) (pp. 701–704). IEEE.
9. Ibrahim, D.R., Teh, J.S. and Abdullah, R., 2021. Multifactor authentication system based on color visual cryptography, facial recognition, and dragonfly optimization. Information Security Journal: A Global Perspective, 30(3), pp.149–159.
10. Nasution, M.I.P., Nurbaiti, N., Nurlaila, N., Rahma, T.I.F. and Kamilah, K., 2020, September. Face Recognition Login Authentication for Digital Payment Solution at COVID-19 Pandemic. In 2020 3rd International Conference on Computer and Informatics Engineering (IC2IE) (pp. 48–51). IEEE.
11. Khan, M., Chakraborty, S., Astya, R. and Khepra, S., 2019, October. Face detection and recognition using OpenCV. In 2019 International Conference on Computing, Communication, and Intelligent Systems (ICCCIS) (pp. 116–119). IEEE.
12. Zulfiqar, M., Syed, F., Khan, M.J. and Khurshid, K., 2019, July. Deep face recognition for biometric authentication. In 2019 international conference on electrical, communication, and computer engineering (ICECCE) (pp. 1–6). IEEE.
13. Deeba, F., Memon, H., Dharejo, F.A., Ahmed, A. and Ghaffar, A., 2019. LBPH-based enhanced real-time face recognition. International Journal of Advanced Computer Science and Applications, 10(5).
14. Pradeesh, N., Kumar, V.S., Anand, A.S., Lekshmy, V.G., Krishnamoorthy, S. and Bijlani, K., 2019, November. Cost effective and reliable mobile solution for face recognition and authentication. In 2019 9th International Conference on Advances in Computing and Communication (ICACC) (pp. 66–69). IEEE.
15. Liu, S., Song, Y., Zhang, M., Zhao, J., Yang, S. and Hou, K., 2019. An identity authentication method combining liveness detection and face recognition. Sensors, 19(21), p.4733.

55 Graduation student academic performance analysis using corelated feature model

Kandula Neha[1,a] and Ram Kumar[2,b]

[1]Research Scholar, Dept of Computer Science and Engineering Lovely Professional University, Punjab, India

[2]Assistant Professor, School of Computing Science and Engineering VIT Bhopal University, Bhopal, Madhya Pradesh, India

Abstract

The Graduation Student Academic Performance Analysis using Correlated Feature Model is a study that aims to analyze the academic performance of students using a correlated feature model. This model identifies the correlation between various academic features and predicts the performance of the students based on these features. The study will collect data on various academic features such as attendance, grades, and extracurricular activities. The data will be analyzed using a correlated feature model, which will identify the association between these features and the academic performance of the students. The study will also develop a predictive model that can be used to predict the performance of students based on their academic features. This model will be trained on the collected data and will be tested on a separate set of data to evaluate its accuracy.

The study aims to provide insights into the factors that contribute to the academic performance of students and to develop a predictive model that can be used by educators to identify students who may be at risk of poor academic performance. The results of the study can be used to enhance the academic retention of students by identifying the factors that contribute to success and providing targeted interventions to students who may be struggling. The survey can also be used to inform the policies formulation and programs that support student success in higher education.

Keywords:Deep learning, education, prediction, students models

Introduction

The academic performance of students is a critical factor in determining their success in higher education. Graduation performance analysis involves analyzing various academic features of students and predicting their performance based on these features. This analysis can provide valuable information about factors that contribute to student success and can help educators identify students who are at risk of poor academic performance [1]. The analysis of student academic performance is a complex task that involves collecting and analyzing a wide range of data. The data can include attendance records, grades, test scores, extracurricular activities, and other factors that may contribute to student success. In recent years, there has been an increasing focus on using data

---

[a]neha09kandula@gmail.com, [b]drramkumar.research@gmail.com

analytics and machine learning techniques to analyze this data and predict student learning outcomes.

One such technique is the correlated feature model, which can identify the correlation between various academic features and predict student performance based on these features. This model can be used to develop a forecasting model which helps educators to identify students who may be at risk of poor academic performance and provide targeted interventions to support their success. In this context, graduation performance analysis is becoming increasingly important in higher education as it provides a data-driven approach to understanding the factors that contribute to student success. By analyzing the data on student academic performance, educators can identify trends and patterns that may not be apparently use this info to develop policies and programs that support student success. Overall, the analysis of student academic performance is a critical area of research that will provide valuable insights in to impactful factors that contribute to success of student in higher education. By using data analytics and machine learning techniques, educators can develop predictive models that can help identify at-risk students and provide targeted interventions to support their success.

Literature Review

To help scholars learn, Liu et al. [3] suggested a tutoring methodology- grounded literacy aid. With this strategy, scholars should be suitable to absorb new information and hone their capacities contemporaneously. Constantly assessing one's progress toward pretensions has been shown in former workshop to be an effective system for negotiating both. The redundant work involved in making similar styles, still, wasn't assessed in those studies. This model examines the time and energy commitment demanded by preceptors to execute nonstop assessment in a first- time Computer Fundamentals course for scholars in the Computer Engineering degree program at the Technical University of Valencia in Spain.

Predicting pupil performance using a matrix factorization and multi-regression system analyzer was proposed by Cao. et al. Originating as a tool for probing-commerce programs, it has since expanded to other fields. still, it can be used to estimate how well-conditioned scholars are doing. In order to determine which scholars are doubtful to succeed in a certain course, a degree diary is employed. unborn course issues are prognosticated as well. Chen et al. [2] suggested a web-grounded logical system for comforting and performance evaluation of scholars. ways utilized in recommendation systems are enforced in this system. It sorts pupils into clusters grounded on participated characteristics. Each new pupil is placed in a cohort grounded on analysis of their characteristics, and they're also presented with a set of recommended classes. The k- means fashion is used to classify the data.

A data mining fashion grounded performance analysis model was proposed by Faught et al. [4]. In doing so, it generates semantic rules that can be applied to a deeper analysis of the pupil's performance in the given course. It generates semantic rules using a decision tree- grounded methodology. The quality of literacy offers is bettered with the use of semantic web and ontology styles in this system. It was proposed by Fortier et al. [5], that nursing scholars be given access to a tone- guided training system. The learner can learn the proper styles for moving a case from a bed to a wheelchair with the use of this training system. In this system, capacities are demonstrated via videotape and a roster. Both the coach's and the case's postures can be assessed with the help of the system's two Kinect detectors.

Jaber et al. [6] studied, 459 council scholars and classified them into one of five groups grounded on their academic achievement. Using information available at the conclusion of the first time, the author employed data mining and machine literacy algorithms to read academic success for the full four times of council. There are egregious caveats to this composition, similar as the fact that scholars' academic achievement varies extensively and that their unborn performance cannot be prognosticated with any degree of perfection. After chancing a correlation between council pupil drinking and academic performance.

Methodology and Specifications

While selecting out of various styles of literature reviews, we have a tendency to determine to think about which will be the best model to determine the accuracy and prediction of student academic performance model based on Outcome Based education [7][8].

Paradigm Framework Description for a Summary
A deep learning-based model is applied with deep layer structure representation of performance analysis parameters as layers that can improve accuracy rate and level of ordering where we can estimate the appearance of a permutation layer which allow us to join two academic parameters sections [9].

Dataset and Processing
We have taken steps to extract predeclared values and clarify the classifier pedagogy process and parameters and Record. **Students' Academic Dataset** as shown in Table 55.1.

Data is generated by collecting information from 1000 students. A strong co relation between third year and final year performance has been found using the proposed data model where we have implemented corelation feature set [10].

Table 55.1 Table of students data set

Name / ID CO	Ug/Pg C1	Hostler/D C2	Are you a C3	Complete Intermedi C4	Learned o C5	Complete Class C6	C7	C8	10th Average C21	G Average C22	G Sem - I C23	Pe Average C24	G Average C25	G Sem - II C26	Pe Average C27	G Average C28
1 Ashok kumar Mekala	1	1	1	0	69	0	1	65	10	9	61	4	6	82	9	
2 Susmitha Nagula	1	0	0	1	74	1	0	74	9	4	61	7	5	90	4	
3 Guda Amarsrinadh	1	1	0	0	74	0	1	91	5	7	71	9	8	72	7	
4 Siva manikanta pandi	1	0	1	1	93	1	0	81	4	9	85	7	4	57	10	1
5 RAVADA SONY	1	0	1	1	70	0	1	52	9	4	75	10	9	88	5	
6 Mahimaraj Arige	1	1	1	0	85	1	0	55	5	7	61	6	9	79	5	
7 Praveen U	1	1	0	0	81	1	0	70	7	10	78	4	4	86	5	
8 Sandhya Sonayila	1	0	0	1	90	0	0	84	8	7	74	6	9	74	4	
9 kushagra laad	1	0	1	1	93	0	1	57	7	8	76	10	5	60	9	
10 Adabala Jai Sandeep	1	0	1	1	55	0	1	92	9	10	74	5	4	79	6	
11 Vallipalli Teja koti nagu	1	0	1	1	77	1	0	52	6	5	85	6	9	92	6	
12 Challa Nagamani	1	0	0	1	87	1	0	55	4	7	84	5	10	87	4	
13 Karri Uma Venkata Durga Rao	1	0	0	0	88	1	1	69	5	5	75	6	6	56	7	1
14 Chakrala Satya Ganesh Raju	1	0	0	0	59	0	1	88	6	7	71	6	6	63	9	
15 Sivaram Teja Yenumula	1	1	1	0	89	1	0	72	8	4	76	10	8	87	4	
16 SAIMEGHALA GOTTIPATI	1	1	0	0	92	0	0	99	10	6	60	5	6	75	4	

Experimental Results

The proposed model performs the student performance analysis based on the interlinking features for accurate academic performance levels. The academic performance analysis is performance as below.

The Comparison of SSC and Intermediate is performed and observed that students who had less performance in SSC have performed less in intermediate as well in Figure 55.1.

In Figure 55.2 Second Year performance levels of multiple students has been considered. They are inconsistent in major cases

The graduates recent two semester performance levels are also analysed and results are indicated below where the improvement has been observed among the students have gradually increased which is shown in Figure 55.3.

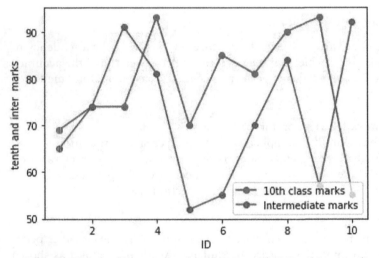

Figure 55.1 Performance level comparison of SSC and Intermediate

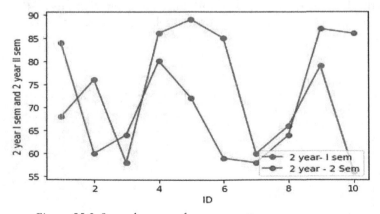

Figure 55.2 Second year performance

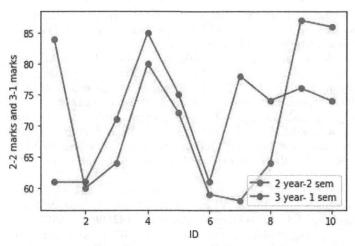

Figure 55.3 Performance comparison of latest semester

Conclusion

This exploration aimed to examine point engineering and the chosen strategy, looking specifically at how each could ameliorate vaticination results. point engineering was pivotal during the point selection process. Custom point product and farther point engineering were both produced for the current position of retrogression and bracket trees. Both the automatic and homemade capabilities of the dataset were used in the point engineering process. A strong correlation between alternate- time and third time performance has been set up using the proposed point Set Model. The dependent attributes weren't converted into double valued attributes in the original study. This exploration adopts the use of supervised literacy algorithm and deep literacy approach to classify pupil performance into high, average, and low orders with an delicacy of 98%.

References

1. Almayan, H., and Mayyan, W. A. (2016). Improving accuracy of students' final grade prediction model using PSO. In International Conference on Information Communication and Management; October 26–31, 2016.
2. Chen, C. H., Yang, S. J. H., Weng, J. X., Ogata, H., and Su, C. Y. (2021). Predicting at-risk university students based on their e-book reading behaviours by using machine learning classifiers. *Australasian Journal of Educational Technology*, 37, 130–144. doi: 10.14742/ajet.6116.
3. Liu, D., Zhang, Y., Zhang, J., Li, Q., Zhang, C., and Yin, Y. (2020). Multiple features fusion attention mechanism enhanced deep knowledge tracing for student performance prediction. *IEEE Access*, 8, 194894–194903. doi: 10.1109/ACCESS.2020.3033200.
4. Faught, E. L., Ekwaru, J. P., Gleddie, D., Storey, K. E., Asbridge, M., and Veugelers, P. J. (2017). The combined impact of diet, physical activity, sleep and screen time on academic achievement: a prospective study of elementary school students in Nova Scotia. *International Journal of Behavioral Nutrition and Physical Activity*, 14, 29. doi:10.1186/s12966-017-0476-0.

5. Fortier, M. S., Vallerand, R. J., and Frédéric, G. (1995). Academic motivation and school performance: toward a structural model. *Contemporary Educational Psychology*, 20, 257–274. doi: 10.1006/ceps.1995.1017.
6. Mohamed Jaber, Basim Al-Samarrai, Afraa Salah, Sudhir Rama Varma, Mohmed Isaqali Karobari, Anand Marya, "Does General and Specific Traits of Personality Predict Students' Academic Performance?", BioMed Research International, vol. 2022, Article ID 9422299, 8 pages, 2022. https://doi.org/10.1155/2022/9422299
7. Neha, K., and Sidiq, S. J. (2020). Analysis of student academic performance through expert systems. *International Research Journal on Advanced Science Hub*, 2, 48–54.
8. Neha, K. (2021). A study on prediction of student academic performance based on expert systems. *Turkish Journal of Computer and Mathematics Education (TURCOMAT)*, 12(7), 1483–1488.
9. Neha, K., Sidiq, J., and Zaman, M. (2021). Deep neural network model for identification of predictive variables and evaluation of student's academic performance. *Revue d'Intelligence Artificielle*, 35(5), 409–415. https://doi.org/10.18280/ria.350507.
10. Neha, K., Kumar, R., Jahangeer Sidiq, S., and Zaman, M. (2023). Deep neural networks predicting student performance. In Saraswat, M., Chowdhury, C., Kumar Mandal, C., and Gandomi, A. H. eds. Proceedings of International Conference on Data Science and Applications. Lecture Notes in Networks and Systems, (Vol. 552). Singapore: Springer.. https://doi.org/10.1007/978-981-19-6634-7_6.

56 Pixelforge: image revamping through text and image input using pix2pix

Siddigan T M[a], Sudharsan G[b] and A. G. Sanjay Ram[c]

Computer Science Engineering, Lovely Professional University, Punjab, India

Abstract

Pix2pix has become quite popular in the area of image-to-image translation. We give an overview of the pix2pix concept and its uses in picture editing in this review paper. Learning the correspondence between the input and output pictures, the conditional adversarial networks used by the pix2pix model are first introduced. The success of the pix2pix model in completing various picture-altering tasks, such as colorization, style transfer, and photorealistic image production, is then discussed through writing. Also, we look at more recent developments in pix2pix-based methods, like cycle-consistent adversarial networks and GANs that are gradually increasing. Lastly, we address the research potential of pix2pix-based techniques as well as their contribution to the development of image processing editing. Our analysis offers a thorough understanding of the Pix2pix model and its effect on picture editing, making it a useful tool for academics and industry professionals.

Keywords: Conditional Pix2pix, cycle, GAN, GAN, Pix2Pix, style GAN

Introduction

Thanks to Pix2pix, the area of image-to-image translation has experienced a revolution, a cutting-edge deep learning model. This model, created in 2017, learns the use of conditional adversarial networks to translate an input picture into an output image [1]. Many images altering activities, including image colorization, style transfer, and even the creation of photorealistic images from sketches, have successfully used pix2pix. An overview of the pix2pix model's architecture and image editing applications is the goal of this review study. We'll also talk about some recent developments in pix2pix-based approaches and their promise for further study. We want to provide a thorough grasp of the pix2pix paradigm and its implications through this review.

This review paper discusses the use of deep learning approaches, specifically the Pix2pix model, in image editing tasks such as picture colorization, style transfer, and photorealistic image production. The Pix2pix model is a conditional generative adversarial network (CGAN) that learns the correlation between input and output photographs. It consists of a generator network and a discriminator network that are updated alternately during training to generate visually pleasing output pictures that resemble the actual output images [2]. The paper highlights the model's performance in picture editing tasks and discusses the numerous variations and improvements resulting from extensions and improvements to the Pix2pix architecture and training procedure. The review paper aims to provide an overview of the Pix2pix model, current developments in the field, and future

[a]2001siddi@gmail.com, [b]sudharsangk7@gmail.com, [c]a.g.sanjayram@gmail.com

research directions, and can help scholars and practitioners in the field of image processing and computer vision.

Architecture

Pix2pix is a type of conditional generative adversarial network (CGAN) introduced by Isola et al. in 2016. It learns to map input images to output images, where the output image is typically a "target" image representing the desired altered version, and the input image is a "source" image representing the original content. The pix2pix architecture comprises a generator network and a discriminator network. The generator network creates a comparable output image using the source image as input, while the discriminator network distinguishes between the created and ground truth output images. The generator network is constructed using a convolutional neural network with an encoder-decoder design and a unique "U-Net" architecture to maintain the low-level properties of the input image. Both the generator and discriminator networks are trained together using an adversarial loss function, with the generator learning to produce realistic output images challenging for the discriminator network to differentiate from the ground truth output images. [3, 4]

Components

The pix2pix model is a popular approach for picture modification, consisting of the generator and discriminator networks, as well as other crucial elements. One such element is the combination of the pixel-wise loss with adversarial loss in the loss function, which trains the generator network to produce output images that are similar to genuine photographs. Additionally, data augmentation techniques such as random cropping, flipping, and color jittering are used to increase the training set size. The generator network also receives a second image that serves as "training," providing extra details about the desired output through a segmentation map or a sketch [5]. The pix2pixHD version of the model includes a separate element for style transfer, which allows the model to apply one image's style to another's content, producing high-resolution images with engaging visuals. Overall, the pix2pix model has been used successfully in applications such as semantic segmentation, object removal, and image colorization.

Application in Image Editing

The "pix2pix" image editing framework offers a range of picture-to-image translation activities. In this review paper, the authors highlight five key applications of the framework: image colorization, style transfer, semantic segmentation, image super-resolution, and image-to-image translation. Image colorization can revitalize historical images and improve their aesthetic appeal. Style transfer can be used to add creative elements to photos and other visual media. Semantic segmentation, which assigns a semantic class to each pixel in an image, has applications in fields such as autonomous driving and medical imaging [6]. Image super- resolution, which creates high-resolution images from low- resolution photographs, is useful for video conferencing and streaming. Finally, image-to-image translation allows for the removal of unwanted elements, addition or removal of backdrops, and orientation changes. The "pix2pix" framework is a valuable resource for computer vision practitioners and researchers due to its efficiency in these image editing applications [7, 8].

Some Applications and Results

Pix2Pix is a framework for image editing that can be used for a variety of tasks, including image colorization and photorealistic image generation. When using text input instead of image input, changes to the architectural design and training procedure are necessary. A text encoder is required to turn the text input into a feature vector that the generator network can use, and the output image is created by combining the feature vector with the original input image. However, using word input for image editing has some drawbacks, such as the ambiguity of natural language and the difficulty of describing precise alterations through text [9-11].

Image colorization involves introducing color to grayscale photographs and is considered an image-to-image translation process. The "pix2pix" framework is effective in producing accurate and aesthetically pleasing colorized photos, which can be used for creative effects in photography and digital restoration of old photographs. Photorealistic image generation is another use of the "pix2pix" framework, where the model is trained on a big dataset of real photographs to produce output images that are aesthetically comparable to the genuine photos. The framework combines adversarial and perceptual loss functions to ensure the generated images are realistic and cannot be distinguished from actual photographs. This method has potential uses in producing realistic simulations for video games and virtual reality settings and high-quality training data for machine learning models.

Figure 56.1 Remove stones and add some boats

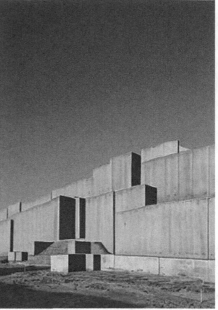

Figure 56.2 Convert concrete wall to steel wall

Figure 56.3 Make apocalyptic to realistic Japan

Advanced Pix2Pix-Based Techniques

The review paper focuses on advanced Pix2pix-based techniques for image editing, specifically Cycle-Consistent Adversarial Networks (CycleGANs) and Progressive Growth of Generative Adversarial Networks (PGGANs). The Pix2pix framework is a conditional GAN that enables various image- to-image translation tasks, such as converting drawings to photographs or day-to-night image transformations. CycleGANs and PGGANs provide significant benefits over traditional GANs by producing high-quality images with semantic labeling and enabling training on large datasets. In addition to CycleGANs and PGGANs, the Pix2pix framework has undergone several advancements and modifications, such as Spatially-Adaptive Denormalization (SPAD), EdgeConnect, StarGAN v2, and AttGAN. These techniques use various strategies to produce high-quality images with different styles and contents, such as incorporating semantic and edge information, attention processes, and multiple generators and discriminators. Overall, the Pix2pix framework is a powerful tool for various image-altering applications, including video enhancement and facial attribute modification. Figure 56.1, 56.2 and 56.3 depicts sample work.

Challenges and Limitations

The pix2pix framework is a powerful tool for image editing, but it also faces several challenges and limitations. One of the primary drawbacks is the requirement for paired data, which can be difficult to obtain, especially in specialized fields. Another limitation is the lack of diversity in generated images, which can limit the flexibility and inventiveness of the editing process. The models may also have limited generalization to different datasets and domains, making it challenging to apply them in real-world scenarios. Additionally, controlling specific attributes of the output images, such as style or texture, can be difficult. The computational complexity of the training process and difficulty in handling large images are also important challenges.

Despite these limitations, ongoing research is exploring ways to address these challenges and enhance the functionality and usefulness of the pix2pix framework. Overall, while there are challenges associated with using the pix2pix framework in practical applications, its remarkable performance in various image editing tasks makes it a valuable tool that will continue to be refined and improved.

Potential for Future Research

Future research in pix2pix image editing has significant potential with the continuing development of deep learning and generative models. Prospective study areas for future research include scalability and efficiency, semi-supervised learning, uncertainty estimation, and domain adaptation. Developing more efficient architectures, exploring new applications for pix2pix, incorporating feedback and user preferences, and improving the model's ability to handle complex image editing tasks are opportunities for improvement and innovation. Future studies might also explore multi-modal image-to-image translation to allow the model to produce several outputs for a single input picture. Pix2pix has mostly been used for picture editing, but it may be beneficial in other situations, such as producing accurate 3D models from 2D photos or for video editing. Future studies might concentrate on creating models that can consider user preferences and input to create more individualized outcomes. Although there are several challenges and limitations to the use of pix2pix, ongoing research is focused on overcoming these obstacles and enhancing the functionality and usefulness of pix2pix models.

Conclusion

Pix2pix is a formidable deep learning model that has demonstrated tremendous promise for tasks involving picture manipulation, in conclusion. Although the model has already been used for a variety of applications, current developments in computer vision have opened new opportunities for its use. Unsupervised learning, conditional GANs, domain adaptation, multi-modal picture editing, and interactive image editing are some of the current concepts and approaches covered in this review article that has the potential to significantly improve Pix2pix's capabilities for image editing jobs.

With the advancement of these approaches, pix2pix should become an even more flexible and adaptable tool for manipulating images, enabling users to complete challenging editing jobs with ease. The necessity for a substantial quantity of paired training data and the difficulty of generalizing to new domains are only two examples of the ongoing difficulties and limits with pix2pix. Further advancements in computer vision research and development are necessary to meet these difficulties.

Pix2pix is an innovative technology that has the potential to continue making a big difference in the world of picture processing. We may anticipate seeing even more spectacular uses of pix2pix in a variety of sectors as technology develops and matures from graphic design to medical imaging.

Acknowledgement

The authors gratefully acknowledge the students, staff, and authority of Computer Science department for their cooperation in the research.

References

1. Brooks, T., Holynski, A., & Efros, A. A. (2023). Instructpix2pix: Learning to follow image editing instructions. In Proceedings of the IEEE/CVF Conference on Computer Vision and Pattern Recognition (pp. 18392-18402).
2. Abdal, R., Qin, Y., & Wonka, P. (2020). Image2stylegan++: How to edit the embedded images?. In Proceedings of the IEEE/CVF conference on computer vision and pattern recognition (pp. 8296-8305).
3. Perarnau, G., Van De Weijer, J., Raducanu, B., & Álvarez, J. M. (2016). Invertible conditional gans for image editing. arXiv preprint arXiv:1611.06355.
4. Issenhuth, T., Tanielian, U., Mary, J., & Picard, D. (2021). Edibert, a generative model for image editing. arXiv preprint arXiv:2111.15264.

5. Ye, H., Yang, X., Takac, M., Sunderraman, R., & Ji, S. (2021). Improving text-to-image synthesis using contrastive learning. arXiv preprint arXiv:2107.02423.
6. Li, L., Sun, Y., Hu, F., Zhou, T., Xi, X., & Ren, J. (2020). Text to realistic image generation with attentional concatenation generative adversarial networks. Discrete Dynamics in Nature and Society, 2020, 1-10.
7. Li, B., Qi, X., Lukasiewicz, T., & Torr, P. H. (2020). Manigan: Text-guided image manipulation. In Proceedings of the IEEE/CVF Conference on Computer Vision and Pattern Recognition (pp. 7880-7889).
8. Patashnik, O., Wu, Z., Shechtman, E., Cohen-Or, D., & Lischinski, D. (2021). Styleclip: Text-driven manipulation of stylegan imagery. In Proceedings of the IEEE/CVF International Conference on Computer Vision (pp. 2085-2094).
9. Viazovetskyi, Y., Ivashkin, V., & Kashin, E. (2020). Stylegan2 distillation for feed-forward image manipulation. In Computer Vision–ECCV 2020: 16th European Conference, Glasgow, UK, August 23–28, 2020, Proceedings, Part XXII 16 (pp. 170-186). Springer International Publishing.
10. Lee, C. H., Liu, Z., Wu, L., & Luo, P. (2020). Maskgan: Towards diverse and interactive facial image manipulation. In Proceedings of the IEEE/CVF Conference on Computer Vision and Pattern Recognition (pp. 5549-5558).
11. Li, H., Zhang, M., Yu, Z., Li, Z., and Li, N. (2022). An improved pix2pix model based on Gabor filter for robust color image rendering. *Multimedia Tools and Applications, 79*(9–10), 6059–6077.

57 Kalman integration with ARIMA & LSTM

Hema Srivarshini Chilakala[1,a], N Preeti[1,b], Sreekar Praneeth Marri[1,c] and Murali K[2,d]

[1]Dept of Computer Science & Engineering, Amrita School of Computing, Bengaluru, Amrita Vishwa Vidyapeetham, India

[2]Dept of Mathematics, Amrita School of Engineering, Bengaluru, Amrita Vishwa Vidyapeetham, India

Abstract

Traders and investors employ stock research to determine their buying and selling decisions. By thoroughly researching and analyzing both historical data as well as current data, they aim to make well-informed judgments and gain a competitive edge in the markets. The ever changing and non – stationary nature of the financial markets makes it hard to predict the same. Analysis and prediction have improved in accuracy and dependability with the addition of artificial intelligence and several other computer-programmed algorithms. The initial step used in this project is smoothing the data using a Kalman filter as it minimizes overfitting problem in the maximum likelihood estimation of a smoothing parameter. The data for this project was collected from Yahoo Finance and shows a comparative study of which model is better for prediction of adjacent closing prices of Tesla stocks.

Keywords: Adjacent closing prices, kalman filter, kalman smoothening, maximum likelihood, stock research

Introduction

The number of elements that affect stock prices is too great to consider. Most of those factors are unknown in advance, which is one of the main reasons it is truly impossible to develop a precise model that depends on them all; even though some events that affect the stock market have already happened in the past, you never know what else may happen in the future. A better and more accurate way to forecast the stocks is to take into consideration historical data for a certain firm utilizing their fields like open, high, low, and close [1-3].

Both qualitative and quantitative forecasting techniques are used. When compared to qualitative research, quantitative analysis depends on external factors like corporate profiles and close, open, high, and low values, among others [4-7].

We smooth the data primarily so that we may forecast various trends, values, and patterns for analysis. It serves as a more straightforward and user-friendly tool for traders who must review a lot of data. We employ the Kalman filter in order to accomplish this since it offers a sequential, unbiased, and minimal error variance estimate. The adjacent closing rates are predicted using the smoothened

[a]BL.EN.U4AIE20019@bl.students.amrita.edu, [b]BL.EN.U4AIE20037@bl.students.amrita.edu, [c]BL.EN.U4AIE20061@bl.students.amrita.edu, [d]k_murali@blr.amrita.edu

data. The predictive model utilized is Autoregressive Integrated Moving Average (ARIMA), which may be used to anticipate the price of your stocks based on historical prices because it is extensively used in demand forecasting.

Literature Review

Stock Market Prediction Using LSTM Recurrent Neural Network

GOOGL and NKE assets were considered to build a model to predict the future stock market. Recurrent neural networks based on the LSTM model were used to create the model. The created model was able to identify the trend in both assets' starting prices. The model's key strength is its ability to retain previously learnt values like a stock using hidden layers, which represent the prior data. Recurrent neural network algorithms are designed in such a manner that they frequently lose their history or previously learned knowledge; thus, an STM-based RNN model is included to prevent this [7-11].

Integrating both, Kalman filter with Arima for the COVID-19 Pandemic Dataset of Pakistan

A practical technique was adopted, integrating the Kalman filter with the ARIMA model (Autoregressive Integrated Moving Average), to solve this drawback. There are various algorithms that are utilized for prediction or predicting data, but one major issue that they lack is accuracy. Absolute Percentage Error (APE) and mean APE were taken into consideration as assessment measures when SutteARIMA, one of the newest models, was compared to the designed model [2].

Fitting a Kalman Smoother to Data

The paper focuses on the solution developed for the problems caused by the data fitting into the Kalman smoother. The Kalman smoothing issue was resolved using a sparse linear algebraic approach. The auto-tuning technique was used to build a Kalman smoother auto training model that aids in determining the ideal parameters. On the United States' migrant population, this technique was tested [13].

Kalman Smoother

The Given some observed data, the Kalman filter and smoother are a set of equations that effectively compute the posterior distribution across the hidden states of a linear state space model. There is no learning process used by the Kalman equations. It uses the conditional probability that is created by applying Bayes' rule to update the prior probability with data described by the likelihood.

The current state estimate and relative accuracy of the data determine how well the Kalman gain performs and may be "adjusted" to get a specific result.

If we adjust the gain parameter to be high, the filter will act according to the state space values. -This sort of setup will not enable you to smooth your data. But if we can set the gain parameter to a low value, the filter will stress (follow) more on the values that the system/signal model predicts and will reduce data noise. The data would be smoothed because of this tweaking, but the data would be less sensitive to changes [14-15].

ARIMA Model

Time series data are used by statistical analysis models known as autoregressive integrated moving averages, or ARIMAs, to better understand a data set or foresee future patterns. Using data from the past, autoregressive statistical models predict values for the future.

Regression analysis of this kind, known as an ARIMA model, measures the robustness of a single dependent variable in relation to various number of fluctuating variables. The model uses differences between values in the series as opposed to actual values to forecast future movements in financial markets or securities.

Understanding an ARIMA model can be achieved by elaborating on its individual components in the following manner:

An evolving variable that reverts to its own delayed, or previous, values is referred to as a "autoregression" (AR) model. Integrated (I) analysis refers to the process of differentiating raw observations to prevent the time series from becoming stationary. When you use a moving average (MA) model with past observations, it helps us better understand how an observation is related to the leftover errors from previous predictions. To make the data steady for the ARIMA model, they are differed. The data are shown to be stable over time by a stationarity-demonstrating model. Since most economic and market data point to trends, differencing aims to get rid of any seasonal or pattern structures.

Math of ARIMA:

$$Y_t = c + \sum_{i=1}^{p} \phi_i Y_{t-i} + \sum_{i=1}^{q} \theta_i \epsilon_{t-i} + \epsilon_t$$

Figure 57.1 shows mathematical model of ARIMA

Y: Corresponds to original time series.
Y(t-i): Corresponds to lag in i series.
ϵ: Corresponds to lag i forecast error.

LSTM Model

LSTMs, which stands for long short-term memory networks, are a type of technology used in deep learning. They're like a special kind of brain-inspired network that can be trained to understand long-lasting connections in information. This magic happens because of the network's repeating building block, which is made up of four linked parts. Figure 57. 2 shows LSTM model.

An LSTM module, three states and a cell state give each unit the capacity to remember information, learn new things, or unlearn old ones. The cell state in LSTMs enables the unbroken flow of information between units by limiting the number of linear interactions. There are forget gates, outputs, and inputs on every component. The cell state can have data added to it or removed by the forgotten gate. If the forget gate uses a sigmoid function to decide what to forget, then the data from the previous cell state can be neglected. By point-wise multiplying "sigmoid" and "tanh," the input gate regulates the data flow to the active cell state.

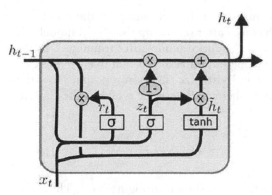

Figure 57.2 LSTM model

Methodology

Comparative comparison of two distinct timer series models, ARIMA and LSTM, is the focus of this paper. The stock market data is initially smoothed using Kalman filters in this methodology. The transition matrices, observation matrices, initial state mean, initial state covariance, observation covariance, and transition covariance are the inputs needed for the Kalman filter function. After entering and running their respective values, we obtain the state mean value (smoothened value). The data frame receives these values as a new column, which is then shown using matplotlib.pyplot.

Predicting the adjacent closing price comes next once the data has been smoothed; for this, we conduct comparative analysis of two models, the first of which is the ARIMA model.

Making sure the data is stationary and stable over time is the first and most important step in the ARIMA model, and we achieve this by performing the ADF test (Augmented Dickey Fuller). We continue to the following step, fitting an ARIMA model by providing the characteristic for which you wish to make a prediction, if the critical values are not too large in range. Now that the ARIMA model has been run, training and testing sets of data have been separated, and predictions have been made. Using the root mean square error method, the model's accuracy is assessed, and these data are graphically displayed. The model is tested using new start and end dates to obtain closing prices after it has been trained using the training data.

Now, let's examine the second model, LSTM. After checking the stock price history using the same Kalman smoothed data. We now preprocess the data, making careful to extract the closing price before dividing the dataset into test and train. Now comes the crucial step of preparing the LSTM setup. To start, make a sequential plan that arranges layers like building blocks in a row. After that, build the LSTM layer itself. It's like adding a special part to our plan with 100 units that can learn from the data. We set it to remember the sequence and generate a new sequence that matches its output.

After establishing a densely linked layer with 25 network units, a densely connected layer that specifies the output of 1 network unit is then added. We must first choose an optimizer and a loss function before deciding on the number of epochs for training the model, which comes after setting up the LSTM model. The RMSE is used to assess the accuracy of the entire model after training. This will demonstrate whether or not the developed architecture is suitable for forecasting. Finally, we forecast the numbers and visualize them on a graph. Now that we have two models, we may compare them to determine which is the superior model.

Empirical Results

Kalman-ARIMA

The blue adjacent closing prices are fuzzy, as shown in Figure 57.3. The rough blue line, which is represented by the orange line, is filtered out by the Kalman filter algorithm to decrease noise.

Adjacent closing price values which have been smoothed using the Kalman filter are fed to ARIMA to predict the upcoming values. Using the KALMAN-ARIMA model, expected values of the training and test data are visualized in Figures 57.4 and 57.6. RMSE metric has been used to evaluate the above model which is shown in Figure 57.5. Figure 57.9 shows RMSE values for individual and integrated models.

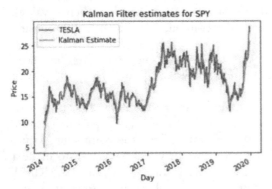

Figure 57.3 Smoothened data using kalman filters

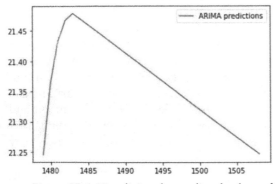

Figure 57.4 Visualizing the predicted values of train data

```
from sklearn.metrics import mean_squared_error
from math import sqrt
rmse=sqrt(mean_squared_error(pred,test['KF_mean']))
print("RMSE of Kalman_Arima: " ,rmse)
```

RMSE of Kalman_Arima: 1.9718703049285247

Figure 57.5 Root Mean Square Error value for Kalman-ARIMA Model

<matplotlib.axes._subplots.AxesSubplot at 0x7fdea0e07640>

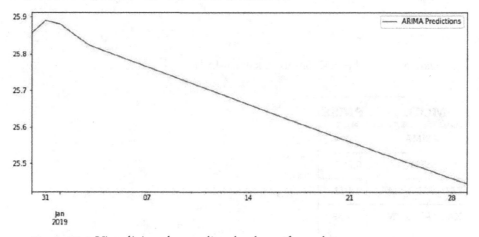

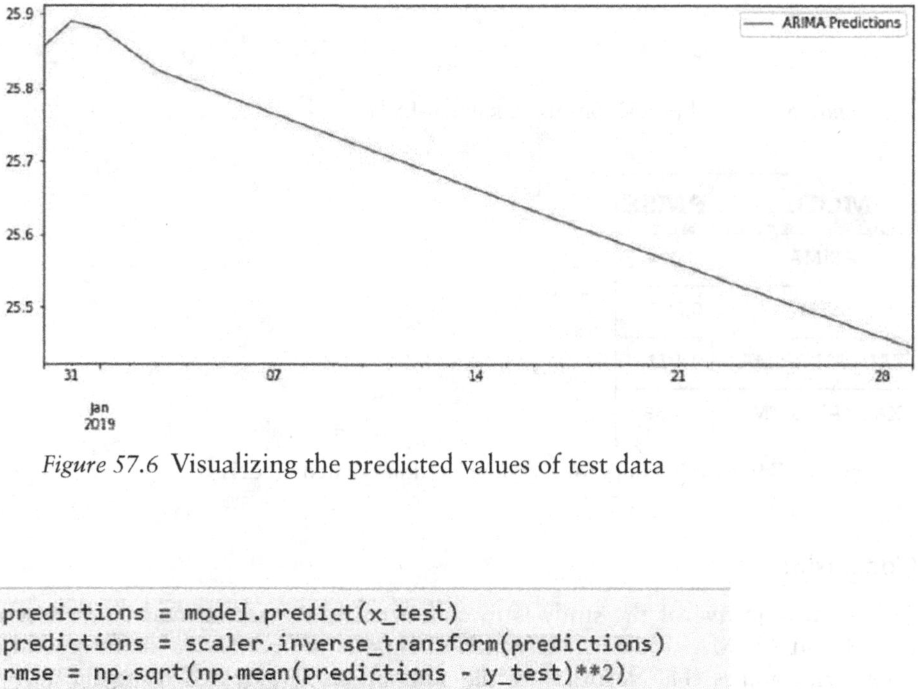

Figure 57.6 Visualizing the predicted values of test data

```
predictions = model.predict(x_test)
predictions = scaler.inverse_transform(predictions)
rmse = np.sqrt(np.mean(predictions - y_test)**2)
print("RMSE of LSTM_Kalman: " ,rmse)
```

RMSE of LSTM_Kalman: 0.10599811874249378

Figure 57.7 Root mean square error value for kalman-LSTM Model

Kalman-LSTM
Similarly, for KALMAN-LSTM model, RMSE values and final prediction using this model are displayed in Figures 57.7 and 57.8 respectively.

A comparative evaluation analysis is recorded in a table with RMSE values of Arima, LSTM and their integrated models using KALMAN. Tabular visualization is shown in Figure 57.8.

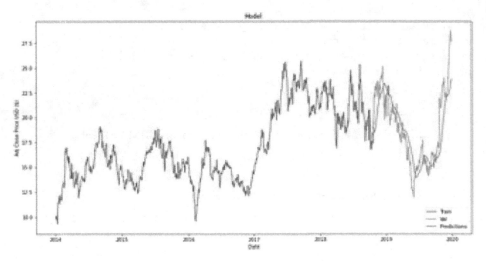

Figure 57.8 Final predictions using kalman-LSTM

MODEL	RMSE
ARIMA	3.094
LSTM	0.297
KALMAN-ARIMA	1.971
KALMAN-LSTM	0.1059

Figure 57.9 RMSE values for individual and integrated models

Conclusion

The main objective of the study is to conduct a comparative analysis between LSTM and ARIMA to determine which method is more effective at forecasting time series values. The accuracy of the comparison is assessed using the Root Mean Square Error (RMSE) value. Before the comparison, the data is smoothed using the Kalman filter with its input parameters.

Based on the results, it can be concluded that the integrated models, which combine the Kalman filter with LSTM or ARIMA, provide better accuracy than the individual models. Specifically, the integrated model of Kalman with LSTM outperforms the integrated model of Kalman with ARIMA in terms of forecasting accuracy.

References

1. AdilMoghara, MhamedHamicheb, (2020). Stock Market Prediction Using LSTM Recurrent Neural Network", Procedia Computer Science,Volume 170, 1168-1173, ISSN 1877-0509.

2. Muhammad Aslam, (2020). Using the kalman filter with Arima for the COVID-19 pandemic dataset of Pakistan, 31, 105854, ISSN 2352-3409.

3. S. T. Barratt and S. P. Boyd, (2020). Fitting a Kalman Smoother to Data, 2020 American Control Conference (ACC), 1526-1531.

4. X. Song, J. Huang and D. Song, (2019). Air Quality Prediction based on LSTM-Kalman Model, 2019 IEEE 8th Joint International Information Technology and Artificial Intelligence Conference (ITAIC), Chongqing, China, 2019.

5. X. Li, H. Dong and S. Han, (2020). Multiple Linear Regression with Kalman Filter for Predicting End Prices of Online Auctions, IEEE Intl Conf on Dependable, Autonomic and Secure Computing, Intl Conf on Pervasive Intelligence and Computing, Intl Conf on Cloud and Big Data Computing, Intl Conf on Cyber Science and Technology Congress, Canada, 2020, 182-191, doi: 10.1109/DASC-PICom-CBDCom-CyberSciTech49142.2020.00042.

6. N. V. Sai Prakash Nagulapati, S. R. Venati, V. Chandran and S. R, (2022). Pedestrian Detection and Tracking Through Kalman Filtering, International Conference on Emerging Smart Computing and Informatics (ESCI), Pune, India, 2022.

7. L. T. Ponnam, V. Srinivasa Rao, K. Srinivas and V. Raavi, (2016). A comparative study on techniques used for prediction of stock market, International Conference on Automatic Control and Dynamic Optimization Techniques (ICACDOT), Pune, India, 2016.

8. S. KB, G. Patil, M. BA and A. Kumar, (2022). Arbitrage: Stock Market Comparative Analysis, 4th International Conference on Circuits, Control, Communication and Computing (I4C), Bangalore, India, 2022.

9. A. Ariyo, A. O. Adewumi and C. K. Ayo, (2014). Stock Price Prediction Using the ARIMA Model, UKSim-AMSS 16th International Conference on Computer Modelling and Simulation, 2014.

10. A. Garlapati, D. R. Krishna, K. Garlapati, N. m. Srikara Yaswanth, U. Rahul and G. Narayanan, (2021). Stock Price Prediction Using Facebook Prophet and Arima Models, 6th International Conference for Convergence in Technology (I2CT), Maharashtra, India, 2021

11. P. B. Sivakumar and V. P. Mohandas, (2009). Modeling and predicting stock returns using the ARFIMA-FIGARCH, World Congress on Nature & Biologically Inspired Computing (NaBIC), Coimbatore, India, 2009.

12. M. A. Istiake Sunny, M. M. S. Maswood and A. G. Alharbi, (2020). Deep Learning-Based Stock Price Prediction Using LSTM and Bi-Directional LSTM Model, 2nd Novel Intelligent and Leading Emerging Sciences Conference (NILES), Giza, Egypt, 2020.

13. S. Selvin, R. Vinayakumar, E. A. Gopalakrishnan, V. K. Menon and K. P. Soman, (2017). Stock price prediction using LSTM, RNN and CNN-sliding window model, International Conference on Advances in Computing, Communications and Informatics (ICACCI), Udupi, India 2017.

14. P. R. Teja and R. Shanmughasundaram, (2021). Analysis on SoC estimation of Lithium ion battery using EKF and LSTM, IEEE Madras Section Conference (MASCON), Chennai, India, 2021.

15. B. B. Nair et al., (2010). Application of hybrid adaptive filters for stock market prediction, International Conference on Communication and Computational Intelligence (INCOCCI), Erode, India, 2010.

58 Blockchain scalability solution using synchronization time

Dama Vamsi Krishna[1,a] *and Ravi Shanker*[2,b]

[1]Research Scholar, School of Computer Science Engineering, Lovely Professional University, Phagwara, Punjab

[2]Assistant Professor, School of Computer Science Engineering, Lovely Professional University, Phagwara, Punjab

Abstract

Bitcoin has emerged as a popular decentralized cryptocurrency, but its limited transaction processing capacity has led to significant throughput bottlenecks. This paper conducts a thorough analysis of Bitcoin's throughput bottlenecks examines potential solutions to address these issues and discusses the prospects of Bitcoin. The analysis reveals that the main bottleneck lies in the size limit of the Bitcoin block, which restricts the quantity of operations that can be managed at a count. Several potential solutions such as Segregated Witness (SegWit) and the Lightning Network have been proposed to increase Bitcoin's transaction processing capacity. The paper also discusses the prospects of future developments, such as the adoption of the Taproot upgrade, which could further improve Bitcoin's throughput capacity. Overall, this paper provides a comprehensive overview of Bitcoin's throughput issues, potential solutions, and prospects.

Keywords: Bitcoin, cryptocurrency, lightning network, segregated witness, size limit, taproot upgrade, throughput bottlenecks, transaction processing capacity

Introduction

Bitcoin, the first and most popular decentralized cryptocurrency, has revolutionized the way we think about money and financial transactions [1]. However, its limited transaction processing capacity has created significant bottlenecks that have hindered its ability to compete with traditional payment methods. In this paper, we conduct a thorough analysis of Bitcoin's throughput bottlenecks, examine potential solutions to address these issues, and discuss the future prospects of Bitcoin. Specifically, we aim on the size limit of the Bitcoin block, which restricts the sum of transactions that can be handled at a time. The Bitcoin network is built on a blockchain, which is essentially a distributed ledger that records all transactions. The blockchain is maintained by a network of nodes that validate transactions and add them to the blockchain. Each block in the blockchain holds a set of transactions, and the blocks are linked together in a chain. When a block is added to the blockchain, the transactions it contains are considered confirmed, and the bitcoins involved in those transactions can be spent again. The current size limit for a Bitcoin block is 1 megabyte (MB), which means that each block can only

[a]damavamsi622@gmail.com, [b]ravishanker@lpu.co.in

contain a limited number of transactions. This limit was put in place as a measure to prevent spam attacks on the network, but it has created significant bottlenecks in Bitcoin's transaction processing capacity [2]. As the popularity of Bitcoin has grown, the number of transactions being processed has increased, leading to longer confirmation times and higher transaction fees. This has made Bitcoin less attractive for everyday transactions and has hindered its adoption as a mainstream payment method. Addressing this issue, several potential solutions have been proposed. One such solution is Segregated Witness (SegWit), which was activated on the Bitcoin network in August 2017. SegWit separates the transaction data from the signature data, which allows additional transactions to be contained in each block. This increases the transaction processing capacity of the network and reduces transaction fees. Another potential solution is the Lightning Network, which is a layer two scaling solution that allows for instant, low-cost transactions. The Lightning Network is made on the upper part of the Bitcoin blockchain and uses smart contracts to enable off-chain transactions between nodes. This significantly increases the total of transactions that can be handled at a period, as well as reducing the time and cost associated with those transactions [3]. The future prospects of Bitcoin are also promising, with ongoing developments such as the Taproot upgrade, which is expected to be activated in November 2021. The Taproot upgrade will improve Bitcoin's privacy and security features and will also enable more complex smart contracts to be built on the network. This could lead to further improvements in Bitcoin's throughput capacity and could make it even more attractive as a mainstream payment method. In conclusion, Bitcoin's limited transaction processing capacity has created significant bottlenecks that have hindered its adoption as a mainstream payment method. The size limit of the Bitcoin block has been identified as the main bottleneck, and several potential solutions, such as Segregated Witness and the Lightning

Network [4], have been proposed to address this issue. Ongoing developments, such as the Taproot upgrade, could further improve Bitcoin's throughput capacity and make it even more attractive as a payment method.

Literature Review

In their paper, [5] provide a detailed explanation of the Bitcoin protocol and its limitations. They note that the size limit of the Bitcoin block is a key bottleneck that limits the number of transactions that can be processed at a time. They also suggest that the Bitcoin network's decentralized nature makes it difficult to reach a consensus on potential solutions to address this issue.

In a more recent paper, [6] proposes the concept of "blockchain scalability." They argue that the size limit of the Bitcoin block is not the only bottleneck and that other factors such as network latency, bandwidth, and storage capacity also limit the network's transaction processing capacity. They suggest that a holistic approach is needed to address these issues and propose several potential solutions, including off- chain transactions and pruning the blockchain.

SegWit is another potential solution to Bitcoin's throughput issues. In their paper "Segregated Witness and Its Impact on Lightning Network, [7] provide an in-depth analysis of SegWit and its potential impact on the Lightning Network.

They note that SegWit separates the transaction data from the signature data, which allows extra operations to be included in individually block. This increases the transaction processing capacity of the network and reduces transaction fees [8]. They also suggest that SegWit could enable new use cases for the Lightning Network, such as micropayments and cross-chain transactions.

The Lightning Network is another potential solution to Bitcoin's throughput issues. In their paper " Hybrid lightning protocol: An approach for blockchain scalability issue," provide a detailed explanation of the Lightning Network and its potential benefits [9]. They note that use smart contracts to enable off-chain transactions between nodes. This significantly increases the number of transactions that can be processed at a time, as well as reducing the time and cost associated with those transactions.

In conclusion, the existing literature suggests that the size limit of the Bitcoin block is a key bottleneck that limits the network's transaction processing capacity [10]. Several potential solutions have been proposed, including SegWit, the Lightning Network, and the Taproot upgrade. These solutions have the potential to significantly increase the total of operations that can be processed at a count, reduce transaction fees, and improve Bitcoin's privacy and security features [11]. More study is needed to value the helpfulness of these solutions and to identify potential challenges that might arise.

Methodology of Project
The main objective of this project is to analyse the throughput bottlenecks of Bitcoin and propose potential solutions to address these issues, as well as to explore the prospects of cryptocurrency. In this section, we will outline the methodology used to achieve this objective.

Data Collection: The primary data source for this project will be the Bitcoin blockchain, which contains information about all Bitcoin transactions. We will collect data on the size of the Bitcoin block, the number of transactions included in each block, and the transaction processing time. Additionally, we will collect data on the adoption of potential solutions such as SegWit and the Lightning Network [12]. We will also gather data from existing literature on Bitcoin's throughput issues and potential solutions.

Data Analysis: The gathered data will be examined using numerical tools such as graphic statistics and recession analysis. Informative data will be used to review the data and detect trends in Bitcoin's transaction processing capacity over time [13]. Return evaluation will be used to calculate the impact of potential solutions such as SegWit and the Lightning Network on Bitcoin's transaction processing capacity.

Case Studies: We will analyse case studies of successful implementations of potential solutions such as SegWit and the Lightning Network. We will gather data on the impact of these solutions on Bitcoin's transaction processing capacity, transaction fees, and adoption rates [14]. The case studies will provide real-world examples of the effectiveness of potential solutions and their potential impact on the future of Bitcoin.

Limitations Single of the main restraints of this project is the reliance on secondary data sources such as the Bitcoin blockchain and existing literature. The correctness and entirety of the data may be limited by factors such as statistical availability and value [15]. Additionally, interviews with experts in the field may be limited by factors such as scheduling and availability.

Pseudocode

1. Set the target as a tuple with year and the size of blockchain
2. Set the mode variable to either 'temporary-300k', '300k- reduce', or an integer to represent the block chain growth rate in GB/s
3. Define a function named blockchain growth that takes time value as an input and
   returns the size of the blockchain at that particular point of time.
   if (mode= temporary-300k) then:
       set start_year=2020 , start_blockchain_size=268
       predicted_blockchain_size= time value*105; else if (mode="300k-reduce") then:
       set start_year=2020 , start_blockchain_size=268 predicted_blockchain_size= time value*15.8;
   else if(mode=integer) then:
       set start_year=2020 , start_blockchain_size=268 predicted_blockchain_size= (time value*144*365.25)/1e6;
4. define the tech_growth function which takes timevalue as input
   def tech_growth(t):
       return 1.17 **
5. Define the blockchain_size function that takes a t ime value as input:
   a. Calculate the predicted blockchain size at that time using the blockchain growth function.
   b. Return the predicted blockchain size added to the start blockchain size.
6. Define the info function that takes a year as input:
   a. Calculate the time difference from the start year to the input year and current blockchain size using the blockchain size function finally, Calculate the synchronization time relative to the start year using the current blockchain size and tech growth function.
   b. Calculate the synchronization time relative to the target year using the current blockchain size, the target blockchain size, and the tech growth function.
   c. Print the year, current blockchain size, and synchronization times relative to the start year and target year.
7. Print a table of blockchain size and synchronization times for the years 2020.

Implementation of Project

The implementation of the analysis of Bitcoin's throughput bottlenecks, potential solutions, and prospects can be divided into several steps, Figure 58.1 as outlined below:

Step 1: Data Collection: Collect data on the block size in Table 58.1 the number of transactions included in each block, and the transaction processing time [16].

Table 58.1 Latency by Intuition values

Latency	Time spent for latency	Block size	TPS	Time spent validating
40	0.36s	2,000 KB	100	4.21s
60	0.55s	2,000 KB	200	2.11s
80	0.73s	2,000 KB	500	0.84s
100	0.91s	2,000 KB	1,000	0.42s
120	1.09s	2,000 KB	2,000	0.21s
140	1.27s	20,000 KB	5,000	0.84s
160	1.46s	20,000 KB	10,000	0.42s
180	1.64s	20,000 KB	20,000	0.21s
200	1.82s	20,000 KB	50,000	0.08s
220	2.00s	20,000 KB	100,000	0.04s
240	2.18s	20,000 KB	200,000	0.02s

Additionally, gather data on the adoption of potential solutions such as SegWit and the Lightning Network. The data can be collected from various sources, such as blockchain explorer and cryptocurrency data providers.

Step 2: Data Analysis: Use statistical tools such as graphic data and regression study to examine the collected records. Graphical data can be used to recap the data and identify trends in Bitcoin's transaction processing capacity over time [17]. Regression analysis can be used to evaluate the impact of potential solutions such as SegWit and the Lightning Network on Bitcoin's transaction processing capacity.

Step 3: Literature Review Conduct a comprehensive literature review of existing research on Bitcoin's throughput bottlenecks, potential solutions, and future prospects. The literature review can be conducted using a systematic approach, including keyword searches and citation analysis [18]. The review can include academic articles, conference proceedings, and other relevant sources.

Step 4: Expert Interviews Conduct interviews with experts in the field of cryptocurrency, including blockchain developers, researchers, and industry professionals [19]. The objective of the interviews is to gain insights into the challenges faced by Bitcoin in terms of transaction processing capacity and to identify potential solutions that may not have been discussed in the existing literature.

Block diagram

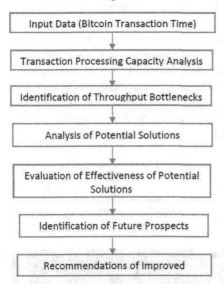

Figure 58.1 Block diagram of implementation

Step 5: Case Studies Analyze case studies of successful implementations of potential solutions such as SegWit and the Lightning Network [20]. Gather data on the impact of these solutions on Bitcoin's transaction processing capacity, transaction fees, and adoption rates. The case studies will provide real-world examples of the effectiveness of potential solutions and their potential impact on the future of Bitcoin.

Step 6: Draw Conclusions Based on the data analysis, literature review, expert interviews, and case studies, draw conclusions about Bitcoin's throughput bottlenecks, potential solutions, and future prospects. Identify the most promising solutions and their potential impact on the cryptocurrency industry. The conclusions can be presented in a report or academic paper.

Results of the Project

As the results of the analysis of Bitcoin's throughput bottlenecks using Luke jr's sync time script comparision with past transactions several key findings emerged are shown in Figures 58.2 and 58.3. Bitcoin's transaction processing capacity has been limited by the small size of its blocks, which have a maximum capacity of 1MB. The adoption of Segregated Witness (SegWit) has led to an increase in Bitcoin's transaction processing capacity by set a limit extra operation to be contained in separately block. The Lightning Network, a layer-2 scaling solution, has the potential to significantly increase Bitcoin's transaction processing capacity by allowing off-chain transactions to be processed instantly and without fees. Despite the potential of the Lightning Network, its adoption has been slow due to technical challenges and lack of awareness among users. The high transaction fees associated with Bitcoin have been a barrier to adoption, especially for small transactions. The adoption of potential solutions such as SegWit and the Lightning Network has led to a reduction in Bitcoin's transaction fees. The future of Bitcoin's transaction processing capacity depends on the adoption of potential solutions, such as the Lightning Network, and the development of new technologies that can improve scalability. These results suggest that while Bitcoin's transaction processing capacity has been limited by its block size, potential solutions such as SegWit and the Lightning Network offer promising ways to increase transaction throughput and reduce fees. However, the adoption of these solutions requires education and technical expertise among users, as well as further development and improvement of these technologies.

Block Diagram

Step 7: Future Research Identify areas for future research related to Bitcoin's transaction processing capacity. These areas may include the evaluation of new

```
sis of Transaction batching/bitcoinThroughputAnalysis-master/LukeJr's sync-time script.py"
Year: 2020 Blockchain size:  305 Sync time vs 2019: 1.30 Sync time vs 2013: 7.26
Year: 2021 Blockchain size:  410 Sync time vs 2019: 1.50 Sync time vs 2013: 8.34
Year: 2022 Blockchain size:  515 Sync time vs 2019: 1.61 Sync time vs 2013: 8.95
Year: 2023 Blockchain size:  620 Sync time vs 2019: 1.65 Sync time vs 2013: 9.21
Year: 2024 Blockchain size:  725 Sync time vs 2019: 1.65 Sync time vs 2013: 9.21
Year: 2025 Blockchain size:  830 Sync time vs 2019: 1.62 Sync time vs 2013: 9.01
Year: 2026 Blockchain size:  935 Sync time vs 2019: 1.56 Sync time vs 2013: 8.67
Year: 2027 Blockchain size: 1040 Sync time vs 2019: 1.48 Sync time vs 2013: 8.25
Year: 2028 Blockchain size: 1145 Sync time vs 2019: 1.39 Sync time vs 2013: 7.76
Year: 2029 Blockchain size: 1250 Sync time vs 2019: 1.30 Sync time vs 2013: 7.24
Year: 2030 Blockchain size: 1355 Sync time vs 2019: 1.20 Sync time vs 2013: 6.71
Year: 2031 Blockchain size: 1460 Sync time vs 2019: 1.11 Sync time vs 2013: 6.18
Year: 2032 Blockchain size: 1565 Sync time vs 2019: 1.02 Sync time vs 2013: 5.66
Year: 2033 Blockchain size: 1670 Sync time vs 2019: 0.93 Sync time vs 2013: 5.16
Year: 2034 Blockchain size: 1775 Sync time vs 2019: 0.84 Sync time vs 2013: 4.69
Year: 2035 Blockchain size: 1880 Sync time vs 2019: 0.76 Sync time vs 2013: 4.25
```

Figure 58.2 Sync time script comparison with past transactions

Year	Blockchain size	Sync time vs 2019	Sync time vs 2013
2020	305 GB	1.30x	7.26x
2021	410 GB	1.50x	8.34x
2022	515 GB	1.61x	8.95x
2023	620 GB	1.65x	9.21x
2024	725 GB	1.65x	9.21x
2025	830 GB	1.62x	9.01x
2026	935 GB	1.56x	8.67x
2027	1040 GB	1.48x	8.25x
2028	1145 GB	1.39x	7.76x
2029	1250 GB	1.30x	7.24x
2030	1355 GB	1.20x	6.71x
2031	1460 GB	1.11x	6.18x
2032	1565 GB	1.02x	5.66x
2033	1670 GB	0.93x	5.16x
2034	1775 GB	0.84x	4.69x
2035	1880 GB	0.76x	4.25x
2036	1985 GB	0.69x	3.83x

Figure 58.3 Rate time latency values of Sync time

Table 58.2 After latency by intuition values

Block size	Time spent transferring
500 KB	0.02s
1,000 KB	0.03s
1,500 KB	0.05s
2,000 KB	0.06s
2,500 KB	0.08s
3,000 KB	0.09s
3,500 KB	0.11s
4,000 KB	0.12s
4,500 KB	0.14s
5,000 KB	0.15s
5,500 KB	0.17s

solutions, the impact of transaction fees on adoption rates, and the scalability of other cryptocurrencies. The research findings can be published in academic journals or presented at conferences.

In summary, the implementation of the analysis of Bitcoin's throughput bottlenecks, potential solutions, and future prospects involves collecting data, analyzing the data, conducting a literature review, conducting expert interviews, analyzing case studies, drawing conclusions, and identifying parts for upcoming study. The implementation of this project can provide valuable awareness into the tasks looked at by Bitcoin and potential solutions to improve its transaction processing capacity Table 58.2.

Conclusion

In conclusion, the analysis of Bitcoin's throughput bottlenecks, potential solutions, and future prospects has highlighted the limitations of the current block size and the need for scalability solutions to increase transaction processing capacity. The adoption of SegWit has led to a slight increase in transaction throughput, but the potential of the Lightning Network to significantly improve Bitcoin's scalability has not been fully realized due to technical challenges and lack of awareness. Despite this, the adoption of these solutions has led to a reduction in transaction fees, which has been a significant barrier to adoption for small transactions. The future of Bitcoin's scalability will depend on the continued development and adoption of these solutions, as well as the exploration of new technologies that can improve scalability. Further research in this area, to explore the scalability of other cryptocurrencies. Ultimately, improving scalability is crucial to the continued growth and adoption of cryptocurrencies, and it is an ongoing challenge that will require collaboration and innovation within the industry.

References

1. Nakamoto, S. (2008). Bitcoin: A peer-to-peer electronic cash system. Decentralized business review. Bitcoin. URL:https://bitcoin.org/bitcoin.pdf, 1–9.
2. Antonopoulos, A. M. (2014). Mastering Bitcoin: Unlocking Digital Cryptocurrencies. O'Reilly Media, Inc.
3. Back, A., Corallo, M., Dashjr, L., Friedenbach, M., Maxwell, G., Miller, A., and Wuille, P. (2014). Enabling blockchain innovations with pegged sidechains. 1–25. URL: https://blockstream.com/sidechains.pdf.
4. Böhme, R., Christin, N., Edelman, B., and Moore, T. (2015). Bitcoin: economics, technology, and governance. *Journal of Economic Perspectives*, 29(2), 213–238.
5. Poon, J., and Dryja, T. (2016). The bitcoin lightning network: Scalable off-chain instant payments. 1–59. URL -https://lightning.network/lightning-network-paper.pdf.
6. Reid, F., and Harrigan, M. (2013). An Analysis of Anonymity in the Bitcoin System, (pp. 197–223). New York: Springer.
7. Decker, C., and Wattenhofer, R. (2015). A fast and scalable payment network with bitcoin duplex micropayment channels. In Stabilization, Safety, and Security of Distributed Systems: 17th International Symposium, SSS 2015, Edmonton, AB, Canada, August 18-21, 2015, Proceedings 17, (pp. 3–18). Springer International Publishing.
8. Hileman, Garrick and Rauchs, Michel, 2017 Global Cryptocurrency Benchmarking Study (April 6, 2017). Available at SSRN: https://ssrn.com/abstract=2965436 or http://dx.doi.org/10.2139/ssrn.2965436
9. Fajri, A. I., and Mahananto, F. (2022). Hybrid lightning protocol: an approach for blockchain scalability issue. *Procedia Computer Science*, 197, 437–444.
10. Swan, M. (2015). Blockchain: Blueprint for a New Economy. O'Reilly Media, Inc.
11. Vigna, P., and Casey, M. J. (2015). The Age of Cryptocurrency: How Bitcoin and Digital Money are Challenging the Global Economic Order. St. Martin's Press.
12. Zohar, A. (2015). Bitcoin: under the hood. *Communications of the ACM*, 58(9), 104–113.
13. Tschorsch, F., and Scheuermann, B. (2016). Bitcoin and beyond: a technical survey on decentralized digital currencies. *IEEE Communications Surveys and Tutorials*, 18(3), 2084–2123.
14. Hafid, A., Hafid, A. S., & Samih, M. (2020). Scaling blockchains: A comprehensive survey. IEEE access, 8, 125244–125262.
15. Casey, M., Crane, J., Gensler, G., Johnson, S., and Narula, N. (2018). The impact of blockchain technology on finance: A catalyst for change. URL - https://static1.squarespace.com/static/59aae5e9a803bb10bedeb03e/t/5ec56e1ee9cf0f65dc523487/1589997097178/Geneva21.pdf
16. Basile, M., Nardini, G., Perazzo, P., and Dini, G. (2022). SegWit extension and improvement of the blocksim bitcoin simulator. In 2022 IEEE International Conference on Blockchain (Blockchain), (pp. 115–123). IEEE.
17. Gebraselase, B. G., Helvik, B. E., and Jiang, Y. (2021). An analysis of transaction handling in bitcoin. In 2021 IEEE International Conference on Smart Data Services (SMDS), (pp. 162–172). IEEE.
18. Wang, G., Wang, S., Bagaria, V., Tse, D., and Viswanath, P. (2020). Prism removes consensus bottleneck for smart contracts. In 2020 Crypto Valley Conference on Blockchain Technology (CVCBT), (pp. 68–77). IEEE.
19. Elrom, E. (2019). The Blockchain Developer. Apress.
20. Khan, N., and State, R. (2020). Lightning network: a comparative review of transaction fees and data analysis. In Blockchain and Applications: International Congress, (pp. 11–18). Springer International Publishing.

59 Improving job recruitment with an interview bot: a study on NLP techniques and AI technologies

Anto Josu[a], Jasu Brinner[b] and Athira B[c]

Department of Computer Science and IT, School of Computing, Amrita Vishwa Vidyapeetham Kochi Campus, Kerala, India

Abstract

In order to enhance recruitment, this research paper develops an interview bot that uses natural language processing methods. The research offers a thorough examination of current hiring procedures and their shortcomings, emphasizing the demand for creative fixes to raise the efficacy and efficiency of the hiring process. The paper suggests using an interview bot that employs NLP methods to perform initial conversations with job applicants. Candidates can speak with the interview bot independently, and it can assess their responses based on pre-established standards. Through several tests, the study assesses the performance of the interview bot and compares its outcomes to those of conventional hiring practices. The outcomes show that the interview bot shortens the employment process time and expense while offering a more accurate and consistent assessment of applicants. The research concludes that the use of NLP strategies and AI tools in hiring can greatly improve the hiring process and raise the general calibre of the applicant pool.

Keywords: BERT, chatbot, named entity recognition, natural language processing, word vectorization

Introduction

Over the past few years, progress in artificial intelligence has given rise to the emergence of diverse novel technologies, among them being chatbots. A chatbot is a computer program that mimics and analyses human communication (spoken or written), enabling users to interact with digital gadgets as if they were speaking to real people. [1] Every day, more and more people are becoming comfortable conversing with the robots around us. Just consider the amount of people that speak with digital assistants like Alexa, Siri, and Google daily to accomplish simple tasks.

With the increasing demand for efficient and effective recruitment processes, the use of interview bots in the hiring process has gained attention. [2] Using recruitment or interview bots comes with benefits such as streamlining of administrative tasks such as answering questions about the role and application process, candidate experience etc. Also, it promotes improved candidate experiences, saving costs and time etc.

The goal of this research is to provide a clear understanding of the role of interview bots in the recruitment process and their potential for improving the overall efficiency and effectiveness of the hiring process. We will explore through some of the popular NLP techniques and how they can be applied to build an efficient and

[a]antojosu@gmail.com, [b]jasubrinner@gmail.com, [c]athiramalu@gmail.com

effective interview bot. We will also be discussing about the different techniques involved in preparing our knowledge bases for training our Interview bot.

Literature Review

Ever since 1950 when the ideology behind chatbots began to popularize, dozens of new and improved technologies and ideas where brought forward which led to its development Adamopoulou and Moussiades, [3]. From simple pattern matching techniques, to the use of Artificial Intelligence Markup Language (AIML) and Latent Semantic Analysis (LSA) [10] Ranoliya et al. [4], to using Machine Learning techniques such as intent classification and Natural Language Understanding Ait-Mlouk and Jiang [5] and now even Artificial Intelligence (AI) Chatbots continue to improve from generation to generation and have proven to be an effective representation of human-machine interaction Nawaz and Gomes [6]. Moreover, Allal-Chérif and Sánchez, R. C. [7] discuss intelligent recruitment strategies, providing valuable insights into the application of artificial intelligence in talent management.

Our intention here is to use the chatbot technology in a Job recruitment system where the machine can interact with the candidate and gain an understanding about their skills, knowledge and experience. But we intent to use a different approach to achieve the same through applications of Natural Language Processing (NLP) techniques. Even with significant advancements in technology, chatbots still have yet to evolve to be able simulate conversations like a human being Reshmi and Balakrishnan [8]. We focused on different word embedding techniques all of which use different methodologies to generate the word vector with hopes of also being able to simulate responses like a person as much as possible.

Extracting structured information from a variety of textual documents can be looked at as an efficient way to collect relevant data for knowledge bases Pudasaini et al. [9]. This would allow us to categorize different segments using Parts of Speech (POS) tagging and extract relevant information from the segments. Also, the similarity metric techniques involved in Machine Learning can allow the machine the assess the relevance present in user responses.

Methodology

Dataset

For this research, the dataset was collected from multiple sources depending on the skills required by the job role. The knowledge base for the interview bot was developed by collecting questions relevant to a particular field of job along with their most suitable and accurate form of response. The dataset used to train the NER model for information extraction was predominantly acquired from LinkedIn using web scraping techniques. The dataset consisted of 5000 job descriptions and resumes collected from LinkedIn and other platforms.

The collected data were pre-processed to remove any confidential or irrelevant information. The NER model was developed to extract information from both job descriptions and candidate responses for entity classification based on various skills required by each job role. Additionally, certain regular or casual queries such as greetings were handled in a rule-based manner. It is crucial to prepare high-quality Question and Answer (Q&A) data that accurately represent the abilities and knowledge needed for the position to create an efficient interview bot. To make sure that the Q&A data accurately reflect the job requirements and that the questions are both understandable and pertinent, they must be carefully curated and validated.

The overall accuracy and efficiency of the interview bot depend on the use of high-quality Q&A data, which can also significantly increase the hiring process's effectiveness. Our research has concentrated on creating and testing interview bots that use top-notch Q&A data to fairly assess job candidates, offering employers a useful tool for streamlining and improving their hiring procedures.

Overall, the dataset used for this research was carefully curated and pre-processed to ensure that it could be effectively used to train and evaluate the interview bot. The collected data provided a comprehensive understanding of the skills required by different job roles and allowed for the development of an effective interview bot that could assist in the recruitment process.

System Architecture

The Figure 59.1 illustrates the system architecture of proposed model. The candidate recommendation system focuses on the skills and work experiences mentioned in both the job descriptions and the resumes to first filter out the appropriate job offers for a particular candidate. This process is performed using a NER model, which we have already trained for this task. The NER model extracts the entities, or the information related to work experience and skills from the resume of the candidate as well as the job descriptions provided by the company.

Then we perform word vectorization on the entities related to skills extracted from both documents to generate a vectorized form of skills entities. Then we

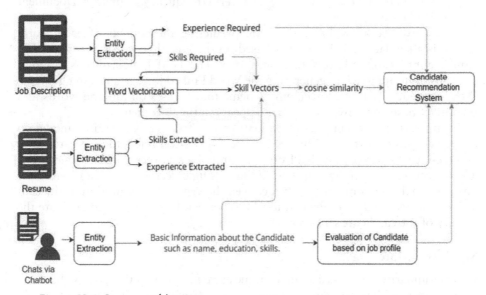

Figure 59.1 System architecture

compute the cosine similarity between the skill vectors obtained from both the job description of the job profile and the resume of the candidate. This result is then passed on to the candidate recommendation system along with the experience entities extracted earlier. The result of the cosine similarity technique will allow the candidate recommendation system to determine whether a particular candidate is fit for the job profile or not.

Entity Extraction Named Entity Recognition (NER) falls within the realm of Natural Language Processing (NLP) and is dedicated to the task of detecting and extracting named entities found in unstructured textual information. This section will go over how to train a Spacy NER model using resumes and job descriptions.

Preparing the training data is the first step in training a Spacy NER model. In this case, we'll make use of a dataset made up of resumes and job descriptions. In order to prepare the data, we first need to identify the named entities that we want to extract from the job description and resumes. Typically named entities in the context of job descriptions and resumes may include job titles, educational qualifications, and skills. Once we have identified the entities of interest, we can annotate the job descriptions with the corresponding entity labels. This can be done using a variety of tools, such as Spacy's built-in entity annotator or third-party annotation software such as docanno, etc.

Once the data is annotated, we can use it to train a Spacy NER model by specifying various hyperparameters such as the number of iterations, learning rate, and dropout rate. During training, the model uses the annotated data to learn to recognize the named entities of interest in new text data.

Word Vectorization For our chatbot, we have used Word Embedding techniques with the hopes of developing a chatbot that can understand user queries. In this method, words and documents are transformed into numeric vectors, enabling words with similar meanings to possess comparable vector representations. [11] Now we have worked with some popular Word Embedding Techniques such as Word2Vec, Global Vector (GloVe), and Term Frequency – Inverse Document Frequency (TF-IDF).

The Word2Vec algorithm focuses on predicting the context of each word. GloVe is a similar algorithm that is based on the idea that words that appear in similar contexts often have similar meanings. The TF-IDF algorithm is different in terms of its approach to generating the Word Embedding, as it doesn't generate Word embedding. It uses a weighing scheme that focuses on ranking words in a document based on how frequently it appears in the document.

To use vectorization in answer evaluation, the first step is to train a model on a large corpus of text data. Once the model has been trained, the next step is to represent each answer provided by a job candidate as a vector in the same space. These vectors are then averaged to obtain a single vector representation of the answer. Finally, the similarity score between the vector representation of the candidate's answer and a pre-defined ideal answer can be computed to evaluate the quality of the candidate's answer.

Similarity Matching

Cosine similarity stands as a significant measure for gauging the likeness between two vectors within an inner product space. Commonly, it is employed for contrasting text documents or assessing the resemblance between two vectors situated within a multi-dimensional space. In the interview bot, Cosine similarity is used to determine how much the candidate's qualifications and expertise match the job description.

cosine similarity = (A.B) / (||A|| . ||B||) Sitikhu et al. [12]

The interview bot uses cosine similarity between the response given by the candidate for technical questions and the expected response. This is accomplished by measuring the angle between the vectors representing the two responses and comparing it to that angle. A cosine similarity value of 1 signifies that the two responses are identical, whereas a value of 0 indicates complete dissimilarity between the responses. A greater cosine similarity score suggests a stronger likelihood of the responses being interconnected.

Chatbot and Recommendation

In our research, we used a combination of word embedding techniques, such as BERT, Word2Vec, and GloVe, to give our interview bot more precise and context-sensitive answers. Consequently, the chatbot becomes more proficient at comprehending the user's input and providing responses that are more accurate and relevant.

For this purpose, we have tried our own custom model as well as the pre-trained word embedding model for Word2Vec and GloVe along with BERT to produce embeddings for specific words based on their co-occurrence patterns in the corpus. The accuracy and efficiency of the chatbot were increased by combining these embeddings with the BERT embeddings in order to provide a more thorough and nuanced understanding of the language used by job candidates. Then similarity-matching technique mentioned earlier will be used to generate the response.

Overall, by combining a number of word embedding techniques, such as BERT, Word2Vec, and GloVe, we were able to create a chatbot that could comprehend and decipher a variety of user inquiries and offer precise and detailed responses.

Experiment and Result

Named Entity Recognizer

First of all, pre-processing of data should be done before these algorithms could be used to generate the word embeddings for the corpus, the data must be cleaned or pre-processed to be able to produce quality and relevant word embeddings. This process involved a lot of data cleaning techniques such as changing to lower case, punctuation and stop word removal, and in some cases, even numeric values, word and sentence tokenization, spelling corrections, stemming, or lemmatization.

Following the training phase, the model's performance can be assessed using an independent test dataset. The evaluation metrics encompass precision, recall, and F1 score, which gauge the correctness, comprehensiveness, and equilibrium of the model's forecasts. We can also visualize the model's performance using tools such as confusion matrices and precision-recall curves. In Figure 59.2, the precision,

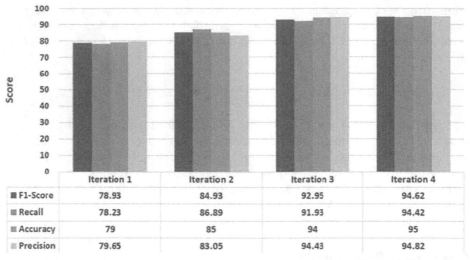

	Iteration 1	Iteration 2	Iteration 3	Iteration 4
■ F1-Score	78.93	84.93	92.95	94.62
■ Recall	78.23	86.89	91.93	94.42
■ Accuracy	79	85	94	95
▒ Precision	79.65	83.05	94.43	94.82

Figure 59.2 Variation of F1-Score, Recall and Accuracy for each iteration

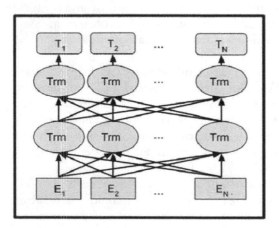

Figure 59.3 BERT architecture Devlin et al. [13]

recall, and F1 score graphs of the model across various iterations are presented. These visualizations provide insights into the correctness, comprehensiveness, and balance of the model's predictions.

Once the model has been trained and evaluated, we can use it to extract named entities from new job descriptions and resumes.

Techniques used in various iterations for optimizing the NER model is described below:

Iteration 1: Trained NER model with the punctuation removed data. The initial data was 200 manually annotated job description and resumes.

Iteration 2: Trained NER model with stop word removed data. The size of the dataset was increased to 300 manually annotated job descriptions and resumes.

Iteration 3: The size of the dataset was increased to 500 manually anno-tated job descriptions and resumes and Stemming is applied to the data pre-processing,

Iteration 4: The size of the dataset was increased to 1000 and all pre-processing where applied.

Chatbot

In order to enhance the effectiveness and lucidity of the generated responses, we have employed BERT-Large, an algorithm in the Transformer family of language models. In contrast to the previously mentioned approach, this technique is more advanced as it generates superior word embeddings. BERT is pre-trained using a transformer architecture and it learns to predict masked words within a sentence and the next sentence in sequence. The superiority of BERT lies in its ability to consider the contextual words preceding and succeeding the target word. So, after generating responses from TF-IDF, Word2Vec, and GloVe models, we pass their output through the BERT transformer, which will essentially transform the input into a much more understandable response for a given user query. Figure 59.3 BERT Architecture represents the architecture of BERT.

Comparing all the models that we have built for our chatbots, the BERT trans-former was able to produce the most appropriate responses when compared to the rest of the models. And it is understandable as it relies on the transformer architecture and is capable of producing better word embeddings when compared to GloVe and Word2Vec models and it uses a more advanced technique than the TF-IDF algorithm to predict the words.

Conclusion and Future Scope

This work can be improved by using some other advanced technologies like GPT2, GPT3, GPT4, ChatGPT as so on which use some of the most highly advanced algorithms and techniques to produce very efficient and satisfactory output for any input. Also, newly advanced Artificial Intelligence technologies can also be recommended to develop such applications which are capable of understanding skills and knowledge possessed by an individual and one day could even possibly teach such skills to an individual by itself. In our paper, we've showcased the application of several NLP techniques like Word Embedding and Data Cleaning in creating an Interview Bot. This bot has potential deployment within a Job Recruitment system, aiming to identify the most suitable candidate for a specific job role. This assessment is carried out by evaluating their skills and expertise, gauged through a sequence of question-answer interactions. The interview bot is also trained to respond to any questions that could be raised by the candidate like any normal chatbot. The knowledge bases used for training the Chatbot on general questions and questions related to a particular job profile were acquired from multiple different sources and were tested on various job profiles acquired from sources such as LinkedIn, Hackerrank and many more.

Based on various experiments that we have conducted on the chatbot using different word embedding techniques, BERT managed to produce the best results than TF-IDF, Word2Vec, and GloVe.

References

1. Oracle: https://www.oracle.com/in/chatbots/what-is-a-chatbot/
2. G2: https://www.g2.com/articles/recruitment-chatbot
3. Adamopoulou, E., and Moussiades, L. (2020). An overview of chatbot technology. In Artificial Intelligence Applications and Innovations: 16th IFIP WG 12.5 International Conference, AIAI 2020, Neos Marmaras, Greece, June 5–7, 2020, Proceedings, Part II 16. Springer International Publishing.
4. Ranoliya, B. R., Raghuwanshi, N., and Singh, S. (2017). Chatbot for university related FAQs. In 2017 International Conference on Advances in Computing, Communications and Informatics (ICACCI). IEEE.
5. Ait-Mlouk, A., and Jiang, L. (2020). KBot: a knowledge graph based chatBot for natural language understanding over linked data. *IEEE Access*, 8, 149220–149230.
6. Nawaz, N., and Gomes, A. M. (2019). Artificial intelligence chatbots are new recruiters. *International Journal of Advanced Computer Science and Applications (IJACSA)*, 10(9), 2–3.
7. Allal-Chérif, O., Aránega, A. Y., and Sánchez, R. C. (2021). Intelligent recruitment: How to identify, select, and retain talents from around the world using artificial intelligence. *Technological Forecasting and Social Change*, 169, 120822.
8. Reshmi, S., and Balakrishnan, K. (2016). Implementation of an inquisitive chatbot for database supported knowledge bases. *Sādhanā*, 41, 1173–1178.
9. Pudasaini, Shushanta, et al. (2021). Application of NLP for information extraction from unstructured documents. In Expert Clouds and Applications: Proceedings of ICOECA 2021. Singapore: Springer Singapore.
10. An e-business chatbot using AIML and LSA - Semantic Scholar. https://www.semanticscholar.org/paper/An-e-business-chatbot-using-AIML-and-LSA-Thomas/906c91ca-389a29b47a0ec072d54e23ddaa757c88.
11. Turing. Definition for Word Embedding: https://www.turing.com/kb/guide-on-word-embeddings-in-nlp.
12. Pinky Sitikhu, Kritish Pahi, et al (2019). A comparison of semantic similarity methods for maximum human interpretability. In 2019 Artificial Intelligence for Transforming Business and Society (AITB), (Vol. 1). IEEE.
13. Devlin, J., et al. (2018). Bert: Pre-training of deep bidirectional transformers for language understanding. arXiv preprint arXiv:1810.04805.

60 Diabetes detection system using machine learning

Tatikonda Sai Murahari[a], Shivani Bharadwaj[b], Karanati Sunil Reddy[c], Umang[d], Golla Tejeswar[e] and Tenzin Lodhen[f]

Computer Science and Engineering, Lovely Professional University, Punjab, India

Abstract

Diabetes is a condition brought on by elevated blood and glucose levels. Frequent urine, increased thirst, and increased appetite are indicators of elevated blood sugar. Diabetes can be caused in 2 types which are mostly common forms of disease, another type is gestational diabetes which occurs during pregnancy. Machine Learning (ML) has been developed in such systems, to analyze large amounts of data and identify patterns which may not be recognized easily by human experts. In this project we proposed a system that will be designed to analyze data from the data set which includes patient medical records, lab results and the information of the patients. ML will be using a combination of supervised and unsupervised algorithms like decision tree DT, Gradient Boost (GB), SVM, Random Forest RF. Data pre-processing methods like feature scaling and feature selection will be used for the best performance when utilizing ML. For evaluate diabetes detection we will be using diabetic and non-diabetic data. Machine Learning (ML) systems will be trained on a particular data set and tested on remaining data to get the best accuracy in detecting diabetes.

Keywords: DT, GB, ML, RF, SVM

Introduction

Diabetes

Diabetes is a chronic condition in which patient body gets affected in processing blood sugar (glucose), One of the primary sources of energy for bodily cells is glucose. This disease can be seen in children, youth, adult and old. Patients suffering from high diabetes condition can get organ failure like liver, heart, kidneys and can leads to death. There are likely of 2 diabetes types. Type-1 Diabetes. This type can be commonly seen in children and adults. Many cases for causing Type-1 Diabetes are because of genetic. Major symptoms are thirsty, vision blur, weight loss. Type2-Diabetes can be mostly seen in adults above 40-year-old and it is an overtime metabolic disorder. It occurs when the human body fails to generate sufficient insulin to sustain regular glucose levels. or when the body develops an immunity to insulin's effects. Diabetes can occur because of a poor lifestyle that causes glucose to accumulate in the blood. Most cases are of type 2(up to 90%) [1].

---

[a]laxmisaimurari2001@gmail.com, [b]shivani.28926@lpu.co.in, [c]ksrsk000@gmail.com, [d]iuschauhan@gmail.com, [e]tejabdl798@gmail.com, [f]lodhen10zin@gmail.com

Machine Learning

Machine learning (ML) in the context of artificial intelligence (AI) focuses on developing models and algorithms that enable computers to learn from data and form opinions. Machine learning algorithms employ statistical models and iterative learning to improve their performance over time as opposed to traditional computer programmers, which adhere to a set of rules established by a programmer The data is essential to the machine learning process. Inferring patterns, connections, and trends that are not immediately obvious to the human eye, the computer learns from the data. Predictions, data classification, or anomaly detection can then be done using these insights. There are several types of machine learning, including reinforcement, supervised and unsupervised learning. When processing algorithms from unlabeled data in unsupervised learning, the algorithm is trained on labelled data in supervised learning. By trial and error, reinforcement learning trains an algorithm, with incentives and penalties directing the learning process [2]. are types of algorithms that are in use.

Random Forest

Popular machine learning technique random forest is an example of an ensemble method. It is well renowned for its excellent accuracy and resistance to noisy or missing data and is utilized for both classification and regression problems. The random forest approach generates a DT, each of them are processed and trained using a small subset of data & characteristics that is randomly chosen. Bootstrap aggregating is the term for this procedure, which is referred to as bagging. The theory behind bagging is that the resultant forest will be a single decision tree is less prone to overfitting because each tree was trained on a separate subset of the data and features [1].

Support Vector Machine

A well-liked machine learning approach for classification and regression problems is called a Support Vector Machine (SVM). SVMs are renowned for their proficiency with complicated and high-dimensional datasets. The fundamental goal of SVMs is to identify the hyperplane that best discriminates between the various data point classes. A hyperplane is a line that divides data into two classes in two dimensions. A hyperplane is a multidimensional plane in higher dimensions this categorizes the data in a variety of ways. By choosing the hyperplane in this way, the distance between the hyperplane & the closest data points for each class is maximized [3].

SVMs have a wide range of uses, including text classification, bioinformatics, and picture classification. Even with a short quantity of training data, they are renewed for their ability to handle complicated data and achieve excellent accuracy, performance, and versatility. Because of their widespread usage in machine learning contests, SVMs [3].

Gradient Boosting Classifier

Gradient boosting is the most successful ensemble strategy for prediction and classification. It combines weak learners to construct powerful learning models for prediction. The decision tree model is implemented. It is a popular and commonly used method for categorizing huge, complex data sets within the gradient boost-ing model that improves performance with repeated usage [3, 4].

Decision Tree
In the fields of machine learning and data mining, a DT is a technique for pre-dictive modelling procedure. It's a model of decisions in the form of a tree that depicts potential outcomes, such as utility, resource costs, and chance event out-comes. Recursively dividing the data into subsets according to the values of the independent variables produces decision trees. Unless a stopping requirement is satisfied, the optimal variable to partition the data is chosen at each stage. The end result is a tree-like structure with the projected numerical values or class labels as the leaves. Decision trees are often utilized in many industries, includ-ing engineering, health, and finance. They are well-liked because they can handle both category and numerical data and are simple to comprehend and analyze. Moreover, decision trees may be utilized for missing value imputation, feature selection, and outlier identification.

Dataset
A dataset is a set of organized and saved data that is used for analysis and/or machine learning. A dataset can be created from a variety of sources, including surveys, social media, video games, and various types of scientific investigations. From modest datasets with just a few dozen data points to enormous datasets with millions or even billions of data points, datasets can range widely in size and complexity. The problem being solved and the resources available for investiga-tion often influence the dataset choice [5].

Literature Survey

Mitushi Soni's research paper, which was published in 2020 in the IJERT, makes powerful use of the KNN, DT, & GB algorithms to provide classification accuracy [4]. Another study comparing the Naive Bayes, SVM, and KNN algorithms found that Naive Bayes had the highest accuracy. This study was conducted by Payal Glagat, D.J. Chaudhari, Vikalp Kumar, Mitesh Warke, and Swapnil Tarale and was published in the Engineering and Technology Research Journals published Internationally (IRJET) in 2019 [6]. Using the GB, AdaBoost Classifier, Decision Tree, and RF algorithms, research by Aishwarya Mujumdar that was published at the International Conference on Recent Developments in Advanced Computing in 2019 discovered that Logistic Regression and AdaBoost had the greatest accu-racy [7]. Research paper distributed by KM Jyoti Rani that was communicated in the international journal of scientific research in computer science, engineer-ing, and information technology in 2020, optimization approaches were merged with decision trees to offer SVM accuracy for various Kernels [8]. In a Research paper published in Computers and Electrical Engineering in 2014, T. Sita, Kamadi V.S.R.P. Varma, and Allam Appa Rao suggested the usage of a decision support system that combined the decision stump base classifier with the AdaBoost algo-rithm for classification in computational systems in 2015 [9, 10]. SVM, Naive Bayes, and Decision Tree were also utilized as basis classifiers.

In a research paper published in Applied Soft Computing in 2016, Karnadi V.S.R.P. Varma employed a variety of algorithms, including the Fuzzy SLIQ and decision tree algorithms. Sharp decision boundaries can be avoided by employing fuzzy SLIQ [9]. In a paper published in Expert Systems with Applications in 2016, Rubén Posada-Góm, Carlos F. Vázquez-Rodrguez, and Armán Trujillo-Mata developed fuzzy expert systems to recognize neuropathy [11]. Zhang, J., Tang, Y., Sun, J., Zhang, Y., & Xu, J. published a study in the journal of medical systems in 2020 that used glycated hemoglobin levels to predict the likelihood of developing diabetes mellitus [12]. Four distinct ML methods, including LR, DT, RF, and SVM, were tested by the authors. From this, it was clear that the RF algorithm improved result than the other algorithms with regards to accuracy, sensitivity, & specificity. In 2018 Research publication of a work by S. Wei, X. Zhao, and C. Miao in the Institution of Electrical and Electronics Engineers. This work is part of implementing the DNN, SVM, Decision Tree, and Naive Bayes algorithms [13]. They came to the conclusion that DNN offered the greatest accuracy out of all these methods.

A study was published in Biomedical Computer Techniques and Programs in 2021 by Teresa Mara Garca-Ordás, Héctor Alaiz-Moretón, Isaias Garca-Rodrguez, José Alberto Bentez-Andrades, and Carmen Benavides. This study recommends a method for predicting diabetes using a well-known data set called Pima Indian Diabetes that combines deep learning with augmentation techniques [14]. Sajai Jain and Rahul Katarya published a paper at the international conference on advances and advancements in electrical and electronic engineering in 2020 [15]. The six algorithms used in their study work are KNN, NB, SVM, DT, RF, and LR. They've determined RF has the highest degree of accuracy. An article comparing and contrasting ML and DL-based diabetes prediction algorithm was published in the Institute of Electrical and Electronics Engineers in 2019 by Jawad Rasheed, Akhtar Jamil, Amani Yahyaoui, and Mirsat Yesiltepe [16]. Ultimately, they showed that RF was more effective in classifying diabetes. A paper was published at the International Conference on Advanced Computing & Communication Systems in 2020 by Samrath Malik, Tannu Chauhan, Surbhi Rawat, and Pushpa Singh. Whatever decision tree is provided has the ability to identify the early stages of diabetes. Also, they acquired CNN and ANN for improved outcomes.[17]

Methodology

Support Vector Machine
Choose the hyperplane that divides the class the best. To choose the best hyperplane, you must first determine the margin, or the gap separating each plane and information being used. If distance between classes is short, the likelihood of misconception is large, and vice versa. Thus, we must choose the class with the highest margin. Margin is equal to the sum of the distances to the positive and negative points. Refer to Figure 60.1 below.

Formula

$$y(x) = \text{sign}\,(wT\,x + s) \tag{1}$$

```
from sklearn.svm import SVC
svm = SVC()

# Train the model using the training data
svm.fit(X_train, Y_train)

y_predd = svm.predict(X_test)

# Calculate the accuracy of the model
accuracy_svc_test = accuracy_score(Y_test, y_predd)

# Print the accuracy
print("Accuracy-test: {:.2f}%".format(accuracy_svc_test * 100)

Accuracy-test: 82.00%
```

Figure 60.1 Code for SVM algorithm

where y(x) is the anticipated class label for source data vector x, s is the likely term, and w is a vector perpendicular to the hyperplane.

Decision Tree
Make a network of branches using the node input feature. Select the characteristic with the greatest amount of data gained to predict the output of the input feature. Every single node's property is optimized for collecting data. The second step must be repeated in order to generate a hierarchy with the characteristic that is missing in the node above. Refer to Figure 60.2 below.

Formula

$$y = f(x) \tag{2}$$

where y is the predicted class label for input vector x and f is a tree-based model that predicts by recursively partitioning the feature space based on the input features.

Random Forest
The initial stage involves selecting the "R" characteristics out of all of the element's "m" where R>M. The node that exhibits optimum split point for the "R" properties. Use of the optimal split to divide the node into sub-nodes. Continue performing steps a through c until "l" nodes are reached. Created a forest by performing steps a through d again until "n" trees have been created. Refer to Figure 60.3 below.

Formula

$$y = f(X) \tag{3}$$

```
# Create an instance of the decision tree classifier
tree_clf = DecisionTreeClassifier()

# Train the model using the training data
tree_clf.fit(X_train, Y_train)

y_predd = tree_clf.predict(X_test)

# Calculate the accuracy of the model
accuracy_dec = accuracy_score(Y_test, y_predd)

# Print the accuracy
print("Accuracy-test: {:.2f}%".format(accuracy_dec * 100))

Accuracy-test: 98.00%
```

Figure 60.2 Code for decision tree algorithm

```
[ ]  random = RandomForestClassifier()

     random.fit(X_train, Y_train)

     RandomForestClassifier()

[ ]  y_pred = random.predict(X_test)


Accuracy on test data

[ ]  #accuracy percentage on test data
     accuracy_test = accuracy_score(Y_test, y_pred)
     print(accuracy_test)
     # Print the accuracy
     print("Accuracy-testdata: {:.2f}%".format(accuracy_test * 100))


     0.9725
```

Figure 60.3 Code for random forest

where y is the anticipated class label for input vector X and f is a group of decision trees that have been trained to generate predictions using various subsets of the data and characteristics.

Gradient Boosting

Assume that A represents a sample of the desired values. Determine the error in the target values. Weights need to be revised and updated to reduce mistake B. A[x] =p[x] +alpha B[x]. Model learners are analyzed and computed using the loss function F. Continue until you reach the essential and ideal outcome A.

Formula

$$y = f(x) + \Sigma_i\, h_i(x) \tag{4}$$

When f is the starting model prediction, y denotes the predicted class label for input vector x, and the summation denotes the additive combination of many decision trees (hi(x)) that were trained to fix the flaws of the preceding tree in the sequence. Refer to Figure 60.4 below.

Dataset

The Diabetes comprises nine categories overall.

BP, Blood Sugar, Pregnancies, Skin Thickness, Body Mass Index, Insulin, Heredity functions, Results. For a dataset visualization refer to Figure 60.5 below.

The source of dataset is taken from the Kaggle site [14].

The information is imported from the dataset and pre-processed. On data, we applied all four approaches Figure 60.6. Then came the anticipated outcomes.

Results

Following the application of Dataset values to all four algorithms. Accuracy was obtained for both the Train and Test Datasets. As may be seen in the Accuracy

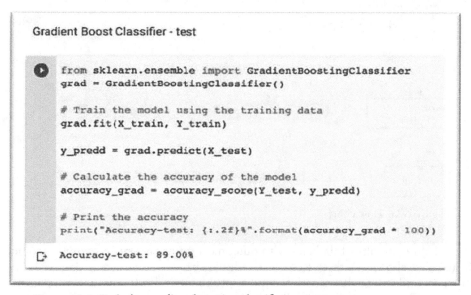

```
Gradient Boost Classifier - test

from sklearn.ensemble import GradientBoostingClassifier
grad = GradientBoostingClassifier()

# Train the model using the training data
grad.fit(X_train, Y_train)

y_predd = grad.predict(X_test)

# Calculate the accuracy of the model
accuracy_grad = accuracy_score(Y_test, y_predd)

# Print the accuracy
print("Accuracy-test: {:.2f}%".format(accuracy_grad * 100))

Accuracy-test: 89.00%
```

Figure 60.4 Code for gradient boosting classifier

```
# loading the diabetes dataset to a pandas DataFrame
diabetes_dataset = pd.read_csv('diabetes.csv')

diabetes_dataset.head()
```

	Pregnancies	Glucose	BloodPressure	SkinThickness	Insulin	BMI	DiabetesPedigreeFunction	Age	Outcome
0	2	138	62	35	0	33.6	0.127	47	1
1	0	84	82	31	125	38.2	0.233	23	0
2	0	145	0	0	0	44.2	0.630	31	1
3	0	135	68	42	250	42.3	0.365	24	1
4	1	139	62	41	480	40.7	0.536	21	0

Figure 60.5 Dataset

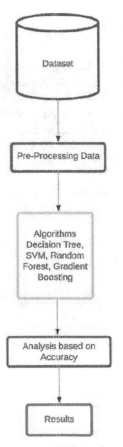

Figure 60.6 Flow chart

chart below. Results of diabetes with outcome 1 and non-diabetes with outcome 0 are also shown. Dataset Results are shown below. The current dataset contains around 650 Diabetes patients and approximately 1300 non-diabetes patient records. The result in Data set Results is a composite of all the qualities in the

Table 60.1 Data set Results

Pregnancies	Glucose	BloodPressure	SkinThickness	Insulin	BMI	DiabetesPedigreeFunction	Age	Outcome
2	138	62	35	0	33.6	0.127	47	1
0	84	82	31	125	38.2	0.233	23	0
0	145	0	0	0	44.2	0.63	31	1
0	135	68	42	250	42.3	0.365	24	1
1	139	62	41	480	40.7	0.536	21	0
0	173	78	32	265	46.5	1.159	58	0
4	99	72	17	0	25.6	0.294	28	0
8	194	80	0	0	26.1	0.551	67	0
2	83	65	28	66	36.8	0.629	24	0
2	89	90	30	0	33.5	0.292	42	0
4	99	68	38	0	32.8	0.145	33	0

Table 60.2 Accuracy

S. No	Algorithm	Train Dataset	Test Dataset
1	Random Forest	100%	97.25%
2	Decision Tree	100%	98%
3	Gradient Boost	91.12%	89%
4	SVM	77.62%	82%

dataset. The Accuracy table shows that the Train and Test datasets for RF and DT have an increased accuracy rate when compared with each of the other two approaches.

Conclusion

Diabetes was formerly detected by checking urine for glucose levels and doing glucose tolerance tests. These techniques evaluated the human body capacity to keep blood sugar levels in check to identify diabetes. Yet they were frequently wrong and imprecise. Currently, a blood test that evaluates fasting blood sugar levels or a hemoglobin A1C test, which offers a measure of blood sugar levels over time, are the recommended ways to diagnose diabetes. Using a sample dataset, we ran the SVM, Decision Tree, Random Forest, and Gradient Boosting algorithms to detect and obtain, respectively, 82, 98, 97.25, and 89 percent accuracy. We found Random Forest and Decision Tress are quite similar and gives high accuracy among the above 4 algorithms.

References

1. Alehegn, M., Joshi, R. R., and Mulay, P. (2019). Diabetes analysis and prediction using random forest, knn, naïve bayes, and J48: an ensemble approach. *International*

Journal of Scientific and Technology Research, 8(9), 2019. [Online]. Available: Www. Ijstr.Org.

2. Joshi, T. N., and Chawan, P. M. (2018). Diabetes prediction using machine learning techniques. *Journal of Engineering Research and Application*, 8, 2248–9622. www. ijera.com, doi: 10.9790/9622-0801020913.

3. Sisodia, D., and Sisodia, D. S. (2018). Prediction of diabetes using classification algorithms. *Procedia Computer Science*, 132, 1578–1585. doi: https://doi.org/10.1016/j. procs.2018.05.122.

4. Soni, M., and Varma, S. (2020). Diabetes prediction using machine learning techniques. International Journal of Engineering Research & Technology (IJERT)

5. Mujumdar, A., and Vaidehi, V. (2019). Diabetes prediction using machine learning algorithms. *Procedia Computer Science*, 165, 292–299. doi: https://doi.org/10.1016/j. procs.2020.01.047.

6. Rani, K. J. (2020). Diabetes prediction using machine learning. *International Journal of Scientific Research in Computer Science, Engineering and Information Technology*, 6, 294–305. doi: 10.32628/CSEIT206463.

7. Zhang, J., Tang, Y., Sun, J., Zahang, Y., and Xu, J. (2020). A machine learning approach to predict diabetes mellitus with glycated hemoglobin. *Medical Systems*. 10, p.1136653.

8. Wei, S., Zhao, X., and Miao, C. (2018). A comprehensive exploration to the machine learning techniques for diabetes identification. In 2018 IEEE 4th World Forum on Internet of Things (WF-IoT), 2018, (pp. 291–295). doi: 10.1109/WF-IoT.2018.8355130.

9. García-Ordás, M. T., Benavides, C., Benítez-Andrades, J. A., Alaiz-Moretón, H., and García-Rodríguez, I. (2021). Diabetes detection using deep learning techniques with oversampling and feature augmentation. *Computer Methods and Programs in Biomedicine*, 202, 105968. doi: https://doi.org/10.1016/j.cmpb.2021.105968.

10. Katarya, R., and Jain, S. (2020). Comparison of different machine learning models for diabetes detection. In 2020 IEEE International Conference on Advances and Developments in Electrical and Electronics Engineering (ICADEE), 2020, (pp. 1–5). doi: 10.1109/ICADEE51157.2020.9368899.

11. Yahyaoui, A., Jamil, A., Rasheed, J., and Yesiltepe, M. (2019). A decision support system for diabetes prediction using machine learning and deep learning techniques. In 2019 1st International Informatics and Software Engineering Conference (UBMYK), 2019, (pp. 1–4). doi: 10.1109/UBMYK48245.2019.8965556.

12. Chauhan, T., Rawat, S., Malik, S., and Singh, P. (2021). Supervised and unsupervised machine learning based review on diabetes care. In 2021 7th International Conference on Advanced Computing and Communication Systems (ICACCS), 2021, (pp. 581–585). doi: 10.1109/ICACCS51430.2021.9442021.

13. Soni, M., and Varma, S. (2020). Diabetes prediction using machine learning techniques. International Journal of Engineering Research & Technology (IJERT)

14. www.kaggle.com/datasets/uciml/pima-indians-diabetes-database.

15. Katarya, R., and Jain, S. (2020). Comparison of different machine learning models for diabetes detection. In IEEE International Conference on Advances and Developments in Electrical and Electronics Engineering (ICADEE) (pp. 1–5). IEEE.

16. Yahyaoui, A., Jamil, A., Rasheed, J., and Yesiltepe, M. (2019). A decision support system for diabetes prediction using machine learning and deep learning techniques in 1st International informatics and software engineering conference (UBMYK) (pp. 1–4). IEEE.

17. Chauhan, T., Rawat, S., Malik, S., & Singh, P. (2021). Supervised and unsupervised machine learning based review on diabetes care. In 1 7th International Conference on Advanced Computing and Communication Systems (ICACCS) (Vol. 1, pp. 581–585). IEEE.

61 Darknet traffic-based intrusion detection system

Chaitanya Mehere[aa], Isha Rathi[b], Kimaya Abhyankar[c], Rahul Adhao[d] and V K. Pachghare[e]

Department of Computer Science and Engineering, COEP Technological University, Shivajinagar Pune, 411005, Pune, India

Abstract

The darknet has no valid host, so all traffic is assumed unsought and handled as probe and misconfiguration. Analysis of darknet traffic aids in the early detection of malware before any malicious invasion outgrows. An Intrusion Detection System (IDS) is an inevitable factor for a complete defence mechanism for network security and hence darknet. This research proposes a darknet-based network intrusion detection model that uses Feature Selection Algorithms to reduce the feature set. The proposed model uses CIC Darknet 2020 dataset and comprises four stages: data preprocessing, feature selection using filter and wrapper methods, classification, and testing. This study evaluates a wide range of feature selection methods for classifying such traffic to enhance the detection rate of darknet traffic. This research aims to increase the accuracy of the IDS by using Correlation-based Feature Selection and enhancing it further by using a bio-inspired wrapper, Bat Optimisation Algorithm.

Keywords: Bat optimisation, bio-inspired algorithm, CICDarknet2020, correlation-based feature selection, filter method, wrapper method

Introduction

Network security has recently been the subject of various research initiatives due to the growth of the Internet. Network security is becoming essential due to the expansion of internet communication and the accessibility of tools for network intrusion. Thus studying darknet traffic aids in the early detection of dangerous activities. A "darknet" surveillance system is used to identify dangerous online behaviour and attack trends.

To identify and detect known attacks, misuse-based IDS uses known signature patterns stored in the system database to identify attacks Almazini and Ahmad [3].

Introduction to Intrusion Detection System

Search engines like Google, Bing, and Yahoo do not include a sizable portion of the data and require additional software or permission to access. In other words, the Dark web refers to material accessible via the Internet (World Wide Web) but requires a specialised application (Tor) and permission. The primary goal of the dark web was to give users more privacy. Yet in recent years, the majority of dark

[a]mehereca19.comp@coep.ac.in, [b]rathiir19.comp@coep.ac.in, [c]abhyankarknl 9.comp@ coep.ac.in, [d]rba.comp@coeptech.ac.in, [e]vkp.comp@coeptech.ac.in

webs have been utilised for crimes, unlawful data extraction, hacking, security breaches, and activities on the computer that result in incursions. To enhance the overall safety of network systems, intrusion detection methods have become essential. IDS is divided into Anomaly Detection System and Misuse Detection System. The anomaly IDS includes gathering information on the actions of trustworthy users over time and then subjecting that information to statistical analysis.

IDS in Darknet

The Deep Web, which is thought to make up around 96% of the WWW, is the hidden portion of the Internet. The Dark Web, sometimes known as the Darknet, is the section of the Deep Web that is mostly utilised for illegal activities. On the Dark Web, 57% of activity and content are unlawful or criminal in nature Mahmood et al. [5]. They frequently involve trading illegal substances, firearms, stolen financial information, illegal conversations, counterfeit money, terrorist communications, and more. The Dark Web, which allows users to covertly and anonymously transfer information via peer-to-peer connections rather than a centralised computer server, is the most well-known service on the TOR network. An intrusion detection system has been devised and built in this project work to prevent intrusion attacks on the systems. It uses the CIC Darknet 2020 Dataset and combines a straightforward feature selection technique with a classification model to detect attacks.

The arrangement of this study is as follows: The second section provides a brief discussion of the literature review conducted, the third section gives a short description of the techniques used, and the fourth section lists the experiments carried out. The results and conclusion constitute the foundation for sections five and six.

Literature Review

Mahmood et al. [5] research broadly defines the Darknet, Ansh and Singh [15] discusses criminal threats and analyses the effectiveness of the decision tree algorithm and other supervised machine learning algorithms.

Abu AI-Haija et al. [13] study compares the accuracy of six supervised machine-learning algorithms, that is, optimizable k-nearest neighbour (O-KNN), bagging decision tree ensembles (BAG-DT), RDS-Boosted decision tree ensembles (RDS-DT), optimizable decision tree (O-DT), AdaBoost decision tree ensembles (ADA-DT), RDS-Boosted decision tree ensembles (RDS-DT), and optimizable Discriminant (O-DSC) and demonstrates that the BAG-DT model scores very high in classification accuracy as compared to other models.

Pitre et al. [11] combined feature selection techniques and fine-tuned the dataset particularly for false-positive detection, and lowered the false positive rate of detection in zero-day attacks.

Kama et al. [4] explored several filter-based feature selection and ensemble learning strategies to reduce intrusion detection systems' complexity while maintaining system performance.

Almomani's [1] paper performs a ROC and a feature importance analysis for the top classifier. Two labels

- "Benign" and "Darknet" were used in the first classification exercise, whereas four classes - "Tor," "Non-Tor," "VPN," and "Non-VPN"-were used in the second. The Random Forest(RF) algorithm was used to complete both classification tasks with an average prediction accuracy above 98% [7].

Ibrahim et al. [10] study uses continuous features and demonstrates that, as compared to filter approaches, the wrapper method picks more noteworthy features. However, for continuous features, the information gain does not perform well. The wrapper method employing sequential backward elimination best suits data with continuous characteristics.

Christo et al. [17] used AdaBoostSVM and a wrapper approach comprising a few bio-inspired algorithms, namely Differential Evolution, Glowworm Swarm Optimization Algorithm, and Lion Optimization Algorithm, the pertinent features from the clinical dataset are chosen using an ensemble feature picker that is correlation-based. Aljawazneh's [2] study proposes the Bat Algorithm (BA), which is trained using an SVM classifier for feature selection. Six public datasets of varying sizes are used to evaluate the algorithm, and it is compared to other leading algorithms like Genetic Algorithm (GA) and Particle Swarm Optimization (PSO). The BA fares better than the other two algorithms when evaluated on datasets of various sizes, and BA is more competitive in terms of accuracy and the number of features [14].

To conclude, an IDS is necessary for a complete defence architecture for darknet security. The existing intrusion detection systems still face high false-positive rates as the algorithms are tuned with unrealistic parameters, leading to early convergence, algorithm complexity, and unrealistic results. This research proposes a dark-net-based network intrusion detection model using Feature Selection Algorithms.

Methodology and Model Specifications

The proposed methodology starts by considering the CIC Darknet 2020 dataset provided by the Canadian Institute for Cybersecurity. The further steps include preprocessing the input dataset and selecting an optimal number of features using different feature selection methods. Furthermore, the reduced dataset shall be split into training and testing data sets. The training dataset will be trained using a Classification algorithm, and the last step will be analysing the testing dataset for attacks.

Dataset

By combining two public datasets, ISCXTor2016 and ISCXVPN2016, this research paper presents a unique technique to detect and describe VPN and Tor apps, representing the darknet's traffic. These datasets, correspondingly, cover TOR and VPN traffic. The dataset consists of 141,530 instances (samples), of which 22,919 are identified as VPN, 1392 as TOR, 93,355 as Non-Tor, and 23,863 as Non-VPN. The dataset offers 85 features that identify the flow of packets with a large amount of data, such as source IP and destination IP addresses and port numbers, headers, etc.

Data Preprocessing

Data reduction requires preprocessing techniques as 1t 1s difficult to process enormous amounts of traffic data on the network, with all the features needed to identify intrusions in real-time and provide prevention methods. In this research, preprocessing is done by removing null and NAN values, followed by removing duplicate values. Also, the constant and categorical features that do not add much value to the model have been dropped to reduce the feature size from 80 features to 64 features. Further, label encoding was done on the categorical target variable. [16]

Feature Selection

Feature Selection methods intend to reduce the feature size of the dataset by selecting relevant features and eliminating noise in the dataset. Therefore, feature selection is important for improving efficiency and reducing the dataset's dimensions.

Filter-based feature selection methods use statistical techniques to rate the correlation between input variables that can be filtered to identify the most relevant features [18]. The choice of features is made without reference to any machine learning algorithms. Examples include Correlation-based feature selection, Mutual Information,

ANOVA, etc. This research uses Correlation-based feature selection.

While a feature is being trained into a machine learning model, wrapper techniques evaluate its relevance based on its usefulness. The entire concept is based on *greedy search* and *evaluation criteria*. This research uses the bio-inspired optimization method as a wrapper method. Examples of bio-inspired optimization techniques used for comparison were Cuckoo Search, Bat Algorithm, and Particle Swarm Optimization. The Bat Algorithm was chosen out of the above as the wrapper method.

The hybrid strategy combines the wrapper and filter approaches to improve performance. The hybrid method interacts with classifiers and models with feature dependencies and provides better computational complexity. This research focuses on implementing a hybrid feature selection model using filter methods and bio-inspired optimization algorithms.

Correlation-Based Feature Selection

Correlation indicates the strength of the relationship between two variables. High correlation implies that the variables have a strong relationship and have the same ability to impact the training of the model. So, highly correlated features must be removed to avoid redundancy. The CFS metric considers the inter-correlation between features and the correlation between a class and a feature.

For continuous classification problems and a pair of random variables (X, Y), the linear correlation coefficient is calculated from eq (l),

$$\rho(X, Y) = \frac{E((X - \mu X)(Y - \mu Y))}{\sigma X \, \sigma Y} \tag{I}$$

Where μX and μY are expected values of variables X and Y, respectively; aX and aY are standard deviations; E is the expected value operator.

Bat Optimization Algorithm

A population-based optimization method called the Bat Algorithm (BA) was developed based on bat echolocation. The BA is a metaheuristic algorithm for finding the best answer iteratively to optimization problems. The method is modelled after how bats forage, which involves emitting ultrasonic signals to find prey and adjusting their frequency and volume to maximise foraging effectiveness. Bats are represented as binary strings in the BA, and they modify their frequency and pulse rate to search the search area effectively. The algorithm also includes a local search device to improve its exploitation capacity. By conducting a neighbourhood search around them, the local search mechanism is used to improve the top answers so far Aljawazneh [2].

Classification

Classification is a process of predicting the class of the data available. The classes are often named as the target, label, or category. Examples of various classifiers include SVM(Support Vector Machine), Naive Bayes, Decision Tree, Random Forest, k-NN, etc. k-NN (k -Nearest Neighbors) has been used in this research as the classifier. In k-NN, instances are classified based on the k nearest neighbours in the training set. $k = 5$ has been used for all k-NN experiments in this study. The k-NN classifier, when applied to the raw dataset having 80 features, gives an accuracy of 94.91%. Applying feature selection on the dataset before training the model may improve the accuracy as k-NN gives better results when used with a dataset having lesser features. The following figure, Figure 61.1, shows the methodological diagram for the proposed work.

Therefore, the proposed system works by collecting valid data points, preprocessing the dataset, and using a hybrid feature selection method combining a correlation-based filter method and bio-inspired Bat Optimization Algorithm to select an optimal number of features and, lastly, using k-NN Classifier to train and test the dataset and classify it as Tor, Non-Tor, VPN, or Non-VPN.

Experiments

In this section, the experiments conducted on the CIC Darknet 2020 Dataset are discussed. The experiments include analysis of individual filter methods,

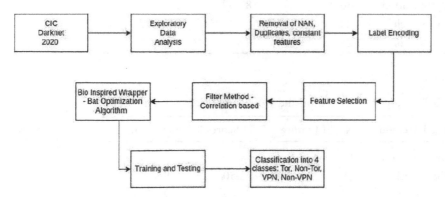

Figure 61.1 Methodological diagram

individual bio-inspired wrapper methods, and the combinations of filter and wrapper methods.

The dataset's feature size was reduced from 85 features to 64 features in the preprocessing stage, wherein constant and categorical features were dropped. The further experiments took 64 features as the input size of the dataset.

Accuracy and Fl-scores are the evaluation measures used to assess the performance of the classifiers. The Fl-score is also used along with accuracy as the dataset is unbalanced, and the FI -score proves to be a more useful evaluation metric when the data is unbalanced Pachghare [12].

The following section shows the comparative analysis of the filter and wrapper methods along with their combinations.

Analysis of Filter Methods

Filter methods use a defined statistical function to measure the relevance of all the features. This [Table 61.1] [Table 61.2] [Table 61.3] section analyses well-known filter methods such as the Correlation-based Feature Selection Technique, ANOVA Test, and Mutual Information-based techniques, and their F1-scores are computed and compared using k-NN Classifier.

Table 61.1 Analysis of filter methods

Filter Method	No. of Features	Fl-Scores %	Accuracy %
Correlation	46	73.68	98.77
ANOVA	56	73.34	98.69
Mutual Information	32	87.45	99.32

Table 61.2 Analysis of bio-inspired wrapper methods

Wrapper Method	No. of Features	Fl-Scores %	Accuracy %
Bat Optimization	30	87.09	99.23
Cuckoo Search	23	86.21	99.22
Particle Swarm	24	87.74	99.28

Table 61.3 Analysis of correlation and bio-inspired wrapper methods

Proposed Method	No. of Features	Fl-Scores %	Accuracy %
Bat Optimization	14	98.40	99.90
Cuckoo Search	21	92.50	99.55
Particle Swarm	17	92.19	99.54

As discussed in Table 61.4, the dataset was reduced to 46 features after applying the Correlation-based filter method followed by nature-inspired wrapper methods.

Analysis of Bio-Inspired Wrapper Methods
In this section, bio-inspired wrapper methods such as the Bat Optimization Algorithm, Cuckoo Search, and Particle Swarm Optimization Algorithm are analysed, and their Fl-scores are computed and compared using k-NN Classifier.
As discussed in Table 61.5, the dataset was reduced to 56 features after applying the ANOVA filter method followed by nature-inspired wrapper methods.

Analysis of Filter Methods and Bio-Inspired Wrapper Methods
As discussed in it is Table 61.3, the dataset was reduced to 32 features after applying Mutual Information based filter method followed by nature-inspired wrapper methods.

Results

In this section, filter methods have been applied to the dataset, followed by bio-inspired wrapper methods such as the Bat Optimization Algorithm, Cuckoo Search, and Particle Swarm Optimization Algorithm are analysed, and their Fl-scores are computed and compared using k-NN Classifier.
The results for each experiment have been shown in this section based on the performance measure of FI-scores and accuracy. A model built using stacking ensemble learning was suggested for analysing darknet traffic and had an accuracy and an Fl-score of 96.74% Almomani, [1]. Another approach to evaluate the strength of five machine learning algorithms, namely k-NN, MLP, Random

Table 61.4 Analysis of ANOVA and bio-inspired wrapper methods

Proposed Method	No. of Features	Fl-Scores %	Accuracy %
Bat Optimization	27	87.09	99.28
Cuckoo Search	25	71.23	98.70
Particle	21	86.41	99.25

Table 61.5 Analysis of mutual information and bio-inspired wrapper methods

Proposed Method	No. of Features	Fl-Scores %	Accuracy %
Bat Optimization	16	97.69	99.85
Cuckoo Search	15	95.00	99.69
Particle Swarm	9	98.15	99.12

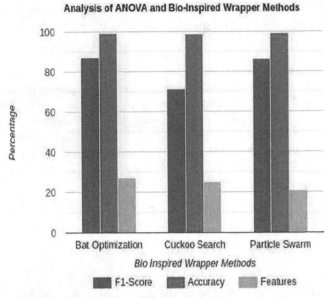

Figure 61.2 Analysis for anova and bio-inspired

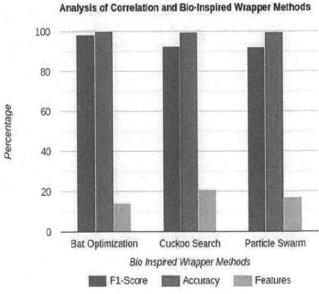

Figure 61.3 Analysis for Correlation and Bio-Inspired

Forest, Decision Tree, and Gradient Boost, for evaluating Darknet traffic was made, and Random Forest Classifier gave the highest accuracy with 98.71% Iliadis and Kaifas [6]. An improvised Dragonfly Optimization Algorithm was used with an accuracy of 96.9% Devarakonda [8]. Classification of the CIC-Darknet2020

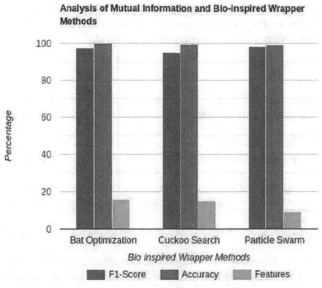

Figure 61.4 Analysis for mutual information and bio-inspired

network traffic samples was done, and SVM, RF, and CNN classifiers were used for the same along with SMOTE Oversampling, and high accuracy was given by random forest Rust-Nguyen and Stamp [9]. Another study modelled and classified a Dark web traffic detection system using the decision tree ensemble models wherein the BAG-DT was the most optimised Ansh and Singh [15].

The experiments conducted on the dataset are graphically presented in above Figure 61.2, 61.3, 61.4, that show the comparative analysis of bio-inspired algorithms and their corresponding performance measures.

The results in this paper imply that the hybrid method for feature selection perfonns better. It is observed that the correlation-based feature selection method with bio-inspired Bat Optimization (accuracy 99.90%, Fl-score 98.40%, 14 features) outperforms the other optimization algorithms like Cuckoo Search, and Particle Swarm Optimization. Also, the proposed model yields an optimum number of selected features in comparatively less computing time.

Conclusion

This work proposes an Intrusion Detection System for the CIC Darknet 2020 dataset that implements a hybrid model that uses an optimal feature selection model and classification technique for accurate detection. This paper compares four bio-inspired wrapper methods, such as Bat Optimization Algorithm, Cuckoo Search, and Particle Swarm Optimization, and three filter methods, like Correlation, ANOVA, and Mutual Information based, to employ one best hybrid method, i.e., Correlation and Bat Algorithm, for analysing, testing and evaluating Darknet traffic. The proposed model has an accuracy of99.90% and an Fl-score of 98.4%, which is very high compared to the previously built models. Moreover, the total computation time is drastically reduced to 1.5 minutes. For the future scope of the research, real-time traffic shall be monitored and analyzed, and the intrusions will be detected using the hybrid feature selection model.

References

1. Almomani, A. (2022). Darknet traffic analysis, and classification system based on modified stacking ensemble learning algorithms. *Information Systems and e-Business Management*, 1–32.
2. Al, A., and Salameh, J. B. (2021). A model for cloud intrusion detection system using feature selection and decision tree algorithms. Int. J. Sci. Technol. Res, 10, 2258–3233.
3. Almazini, H. F. (2022). Bat algorithm optimisation technique for feature selection on different dimension of datasets. *Iraqi Journal of Intelligent Computing and Informatics (IJICI)*, 1(1), 11–21.
4. Kama, I., Madam, A., Deokule, C., Adhao, R., and Pachghare, V. (2021). Ensemble-based filter feature selection technique for building flow-based IDS. In the 2nd International Conference on Advances in Computing, Communication, Embedded and Secure Systems (ACCESS). https://ieeexplore.ieee.org/abstract/document/9563297.
5. Mahmood, I., Rahman, M. A., Kabir, M. A., and Shahriar, M. A Survey on Dark Web Monitoring and Corresponding Threat Detection.
6. Iliadis, L. A., and Kaifas, T. (2021, July). Darknet traffic classification using machine learning techniques. In 2021 10th international conference on modern circuits and systems technologies (MOCAST) (pp. 1–4). IEEE.
7. Pazhaniraja, N., Paul, P. V., Roja, G., Shanrnugapriya, K., and Sonali, B. (2017). A study on recent bio-inspired optimization algorithms. In 2021 10th International Conference on Modem Circuits and Systems Technologies (MOCAST). https://www.researchgate.net/publication/353505379.
8. Devarakonda, N. (2021). Detection of the intruder using the improved dragonfly optimization algorithm. *IOP Conference Series Materials Science and Engineering*, 1074(1), 012011. https://www.researchgate.net/publication/349632297.
9. Rust-Nguyen, N., and Stamp, M. (2022). Darknet Traffic Classification and Adversarial Attacks. arXiv preprint arXiv:2206.06371.
10. Ibrahim, N., Abdul-Rahman, S., and Fong, S. (2018). Feature selection methods: case of filter and wrapper approaches for maximising classification accuracy. *Pertanika Journal of Science and Technology*, 26(1), 329–340. https://www.researchgate.net/publication/322920304.
11. Pitre, P., Gandhi, A., Konde, V., Adhao, R., and Pachghare, V. (2022). An intrusion detection system for zero-day attacks to reduce false positive rates. In the International Conference for Advancement in Technology (ICONAT). https://ieeexplore.ieee.org/abstract/document/9726105.
12. Pachghare, V. K. (2019). Cryptography and information security. PHI Learning Pvt. Ltd.
13. Abu Al-Haija, Q., Krichen, M., and Abu Elhaija, W. (2022). Machine-learning-based darknet traffic detection system for IoT applications. Electronics, 11(4), 556.
14. Nazah, S., Huda, S., Abawajy, J., and Hassan, M. M. (2020). Evolution of dark web threat analysis and detection: A systematic approach. Ieee Access, 8, 171796–171819.

15. Ansh, S., and Singh, S. (2022, September). Analyze Dark Web and Security Threats. In International Conference on Innovations in Computer Science and Engineering (pp. 581–595). Singapore: Springer Nature Singapore.

16. Otor, S. U., Akinyemi, B. O., Aladesanmi, T. A., Aderounmu, G. A., and Kamagaté, B. H. (2021). An improved bio-inspired based intrusion detection model for a cyberspace. Cogent Engineering, 8(1), 1859667.

17. Christo, V. E., Nehemiah, H. K., Minu, B., and Kannan, A. (2019). Correlation-based ensemble feature selection using bioinspired algorithms and classification using backpropagation neural network. *Computational and mathematical methods in medicine*, 2019.

18. Balasaraswathi, V. R., Sugumaran, M., and Hamid, Y. (2017). Feature selection techniques for intrusion detection using non-bio-inspired and bio-inspired optimization algorithms. *Journal of Communications and Information Networks*, 2(4), 107–119. https://www.researchgate.net/publication/322095733.

62 The features of event extraction & its scope: a systematic review

Manik Mehra[1,a] and Varun Dogra[2,b]

[1]Research Scholar, School of Computer Applications, Lovely Professional University, Punjab, India

[2]Associate Professor, School of Computer Science & Engineering, Lovely Professional University, Punjab, India

Abstract

Nowadays, the extraction of event information from huge volumes of textual data is an important research area. The deep learning based extraction of the Event has become a research hotspot due to the rapid advancement of deep learning technologies. The artificial intelligence based automatic extraction of Information and events from natural language are increasing its graph [1]. There are different methods and techniques which have been proposed in the literature and demands for a detailed review. This paper majorly recites the various state-of-the-art methods which are majorly working for extraction of various events especially based on deep learning models. This literature review defines the term event extraction and its research according definition of the task. Afterwards, we have explained the working of renowned event extraction models. In this review, a comprehensive comparison among the various event extraction approaches is also given. In the conclusion, we summarized with research gap and future research directions.

Keywords: deep learning, event extraction, information extraction, natural language processing (NLP)

Introduction

The EVENT Extraction (EE) process is becoming more difficult in today's world when it comes to extracting information for study. A simple definition of an event is an occurrence of a single instant that takes place over the course of a certain amount of time at a specific location with several participants, which is typically characterised as a change of state [1]. The goal of event extraction is typically to extract the event along with its information in an organized form from unorganized form. This information is typically described in terms of the five "W's," which further expand into "who, when, where, what, why," and "how" the events are happening in the real world. This field's applications include helping people recall event data, assess people's behaviours, and meaningfully retrieve important data together with emotions. Recommendations [2–5], intelligent query resolution [6–9, 10], knowledge graph creation. Figure 1(a) and (b) shows the basic functionality:

---

[a]mehra.manik@yahoo.com, [b]dogra_varun@yahoo.com

Types of Event Extraction Techniques

Close-Domain event extraction:
Close-Domain extraction of the events helps to explore the words which makes a connection with a particular event based schema and which steps forward to a change in state or an action that occurs, and the events based on extraction targets includes person, place, time and a specific action etc.

Open-Domain event extraction:
Open-domain extraction of the events helps to formate a collection of events which is particularly related to a unmatched theme and it is normally comprised of multiple events. Either the domain of an event is open or close, its major purpose is to gather the accurate event and its structured form.

In spite of the type of event whether it relates with open or close domain the major task is to classify and capture the moment or event and give the actual and accurate results. The diagram 2 is explaining the full working of the event extraction:

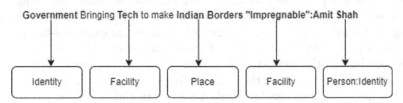

Figure 62.1(a) Explaining the types of events from the raw text or news

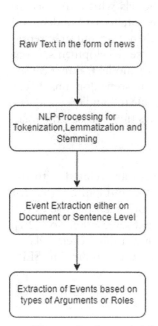

Figure 62.1(b) explaining the model for event extraction which coverts raw text into meaningful events

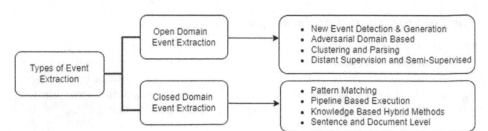

Figure 62.2 Explaining the types of events and its sources

Problems

Since the size of data being processed every day is increasing, extracting meaningful events and their relevant attributes from unstructured text data has become increasingly important. With the vast quantity of data available, event extraction has become extremely important in multiple application areas in various sectors. For example, banking, medical information retrieval, social media platform analysis, and intelligence gathering like chatbots and question answering models. Developing accurate and robust event extraction models requires a thorough understanding of language and context. Different languages are used in different platforms and regions, and expressing an event can involve using different words and phrases depending on the context. This becomes an emerging need which is to be addressed in order to generate the higher accuracy in results. The field of NLP approaches has made some strides thanks to deep learning and these strides are performing significant gains in event extraction. Transformers, recurrent neural networks, and convolutional neural networks are the models which are used to accurately extract events from text. These models have the capacity to understand intricate word associations and patterns, which enables them to accurately represent the subtleties of language and context. Even with these developments, event extraction in NLP continues to be a difficult issue. Accurate model training can be challenging due to a shortage of labelled data, particularly in some domains. Event extraction models also need to be extremely versatile and able to handle a variety of scenarios due to the diversity of events and the various ways they can be expressed.

Applications

In this section, we explain the several applications, which are related with the event extraction. Basically the events can be authenticated and can be used for the construction of graph based on specific event [11], other event-based NLP applications [12] include question answering [13] and text comprehension [14]. Among the tasks, we are concentrating on three commonly studied event-related forms, namely event factuality identification (EFI), script event prediction (SEP), and event relation extraction (ERE) [15].

Event Factuality Identification (EFI)

Event factuality identification(EFI),which can be seen as a downstream effort of EE in knowledge based graph creation of events [16], aims to determine the degree of certainty that events occur intheworld. Prior research on this issue mostly relied on rulebased algorithms [17] or machine learning techniques using manually constructed characteristics [18]. Deep learning techniques based on neural networks, which commonly use generative adversarial networks or graphbased neural networks to capture more indepth textual information, have recently been applied to the EFI problem and have obtained high performance rates [19]. In general, the factuality of the event can be divided into five major categories: Very positive, very negative, less positive, less negative, and Neutral. Therefore, an EFI based model is able to predict the event which is based on some facts and the extraction of events are majorly based upon the positive aspect.

Script Event Prediction

From a candidate list of potential events, Script Event Prediction (SEP) is used to predict a specific event of a particular chain. A script [20] is defined as a series of events that are ordered in a particular order and detail the actions of a character or supporter. To comprehend the patterns of event progression, SEP is applied in the story generating [21] and financial analysis [22] fields. Each event in SEP is referred to as a tuple, which has a variety of attributes, such as e = v(s; o; p), where v is the verb, s is the subject, o is the object, and p is the indirect object of the event. As an illustration, the event arguments in the sentence "A teacher is giving lectures to the students" stand in for the verb, subject, object, and indirect-object of the event, respectively. Give (teacher; students; lecture) as an example.

Event Relation Extraction

Extracting the relations between the various events is a challenging task for finding and creating knowledge graph [23], which is usually designed to investigate the similarity among the identified events. Generally, there are three types of event relation types which are based on existing event relation extraction studies (ERE), including Event cause relation, Event temporal relation and Event co-referential relation. Since there are the three relation types which are usually investigated separately and having no consistent task formulation so we are explaining all the three problems in detail which are based upon event extraction.

Event Cause Relation: The Event Cause Relation extraction method is based upon two groups:

1) Internal information, which predicts that the text on which we are depending it contains all the balanced signs and clues which will be helpful for finding and extracting the cause relation with a particular event but the features based upon context only includes the syntactic features and lexical features and also explicit the event causal patterns [24], along with the document-level structures [25].
2) External information, which provides a highly productive textual representation with external knowledge, such as pre-trained language model and its relation with its cause [26].

Event Temporal Relation Extraction

The best way to extract the temporal relation with an event is to use the Time Machine learning format [27], which is further used to line up the events along with its time details and their relations. Mostly the Event Temporal Relations are mainly extracted by three different techniques like Machine Learning models, Neural Network Models and the rule based methods which are mainly based upon the syntax and lexical analysis of the event and its temporal relation.

Event Co-referential Relationship

The Existing methodology [28] usually creates the co-referencing the relationship between the events as a classification or ranking problem, and it provides the contextual features of the two events along with their reference ,event topic information and other language and syntax based features.

Research Gap

Natural language processing (NLP) and deep learning have been active study areas in recent years. Despite breakthroughs in this sector, there are still significant research gaps that must be filled.

The absence of labelled data for training and assessing deep learning models is one of the most significant research gaps in event extraction. Annotated data is required for the development of reliable and efficient event extraction algorithms. Unfortunately, annotating data is a time-consuming and costly procedure,

Table 62.1 Review Literature for Event Extraction

Year	Name of the Model	Techniques and Paradigm	Event Extraction Level	Area of Implementation
2006	Naughton et al. [38]	Hierarchical Clustering, Pipeline	Cross-document	General Information Extraction
2008	Jiand Grishman [37]	ME, Pipeline	Cross Document	general Information extraction
2009	Riloff [36]	Support Vector Machine ,Joint	Document Level	General Information extraction
2010	Bjorne et al.[35]	Support Vector Machine, pipeline	Sentence level	Biomedical Based Information extraction
2012	Chen and Ng [32]	Support Vector Machine, Joint	Sentence level	General Information extraction
2016	Peng et al.[33]	Naïve Bayes, Pipeline	Document Level	Biomedical Based Information extraction
2021	Henn et al.[34]	Support Vector Machine, pipeline	Document level	General Information extraction

limiting the availability of large-scale annotated datasets. Creating ways for auto-matically or semi-automatically generating annotated data might assist to relieve this problem.

Another issue is that deep learning models are difficult to comprehend. Deep learning models are sometimes regarded as "black boxes," making it difficult to comprehend how they make predictions. Creating ways for interpreting deep learning models' conclusions would increase their trustworthiness and allow for a deeper comprehension of the underlying language characteristics employed in event extraction.

Another study gap is the difficulty in dealing with the variety of event catego-ries and the variation in how events are conveyed in natural language. Current event extraction models frequently focus on a single domain or event type, mak-ing them ineffective when applied to other domains or events. Creating models that can handle a wide range of event kinds and linguistic variants will consider-ably increase event extraction's usefulness in real-world circumstances. Moreover

Table 62.2 Comparison review on the basis of Neural Network Models with BERT

Model	RNN	CNN	BERT
Working	Sequential, and helpful to store the previous inputs as an information	Using feed forward filters that processes the input data and helpful to extract features	Transformer-based and using the attention mechanism which helps to weigh the different types of input as tokens
Data Input	Sequential data, such as text or speech	Sequential data, such as text or speech	Sequential data, such as text
Pros	It is helpful in handling sequential and variable-length inputs using temporal dependencies	It is helpful to capture the normal features and patterns in data and it can handle variable-length inputs	It is helpful to capture complex semantic relationships between words and also Pre-trained on big datasets.
Cons	Prone to vanishing/ exploding gradients, difficult to parallelize during training	Not as effective at capturing long-term dependencies as RNNs, can be sensitive to input noise	Requires large amounts of data to fine-tune for specific tasks, can be computationally expensive
Training Methodology	Supervised or Unsupervised	Supervised or Unsupervised	Supervised
Examples and Area of Implementation	Time series analysis, language modelling, speech recognition	Image classification, natural language processing	Text classification, named entity recognition, question answering

there is a requirement of such models which are based on event extraction and able to handle incomplete and unlabelled data. By solving these above mentioned research gaps, it would become helpful to improve the quality of the extraction of events either in document or sentence in the field of natural language processing.

Related work: To increase the accuracy in classification of the events and its related patterns, many machine learning method has been used to extract events. In this section, we first review the typical machine learning based event extraction literature and summarize it in Table 62.1 from its year of implementation, model's name, Techniques and Paradigm, level of event extraction, area of implementation.

Deep Learning Models Challenges with Event Extraction

Accurate Event Interpretations
As the extraction of an event is a tedious task, so it becomes very important task to interpret the highly accurate results with respect to the extraction of the events which is highly required in fields like Financial and Medical sector. But it is tough to find out directly that for what reason the model is dividing a word or a sentence into the form of arguments and event argument roles [29].

Domain – Based Event Extraction
The argument or an event particularly relates with a specific domain or it can be related with inter-domain sometimes so, the numerous technical terms increases the problem to extract the accurate event [31]. e.g Financial EE always extracts that events which relates with financial sector and the design of more effective method which will be able to understand the deep meaning and extract the events with the correct domain is now becoming a big challenge to be solved [30].

Sequential Learning Model Based on Multi-Event Extraction
The main dependency of the event extraction is the entities labels.So there is a need to develop a sequential deep learning model with reference to Multi-event extraction because there is a lot of work has been done on sentence level event extraction but there is a huge scope in document level event extraction. So to design multi event extraction based deep learning model is a challenge.

Comparative Analysis of Existing Techniques of Event Extraction

The goal of event extraction is to automatically recognise and extract structured data about events from unstructured text input. Finding the causes of the events, the conflicts, and the connections between them is the main objective. NLP methods like dependency parsing, part-of-speech tagging, and named entity recognition can be used to do this. Recurrent neural networks, or RNNs, use the back propagation through time (BPTT) algorithm to transmit information from one step to the next as they analyse sequential data. CNNs are a particular kind of neural network that is frequently employed for image categorization applications. It uses convolutional filters on the input data to find patterns in visual data. BERT (Bidirectional Encoder Representations from Transformers) is a transformer-based neural network architecture that is used for natural language processing tasks such as language modelling, question answering, and sentiment analysis. It is pre-trained on large amounts of text data and fine-tuned for specific downstream tasks using supervised learning. So in this section Table 2 is explaining a literature review and comparative analysis between the various machine learning and deep learning models which are in use from past years for Event Extraction in tabular form.

Conclusion

The present deep learning models that are applied to event extraction tasks are described in this review article. First, we spoke about the key ideas, definitions, and forms of event extraction from multiple perspectives. Following that, we had an in-depth discussion of the difficulties and applications. Deep learning-based models increase performance in light of this by improving the presentation learning technique, model structure, and extra data and expertise. Recently, it has been attracting more research interest than ever due to the rapid development of many novel techniques, such as deep learning.

Future Trends in Event Extraction

As it is an important task in the field of text mining, the existing review states that the previous methods were only able to study the syntactic, lexical and semantic information based upon the Candidate event Triggers and Candidate event Arguments which are further depends upon their relation between the same events which are based upon same triggers.

Dataset Construction. The first big challenge is to create the dataset which may have more classifiers and categories because the existing event extraction datasets are having a less number of labelled entities and it is complex in nature to annotate manually , so the existing pre-training model are lacking in the learning.

Separate Schema for different Events. Evaluation of the impact of event extraction methods lacking a schema is difficult, and event extraction methods based on templates must create various event schemas in accordance with various event kinds. Thus, learning how to create a universal schema for event extraction which is further based on event characteristics is crucial for overcoming the challenge of creating event extraction data sets and transferring knowledge between courses.

References

1. Liu, J., Min, L., and Huang, X. (2021). An overview of event extraction and its applications. In the arXiv:2111.03212v1 [cs.CL] 5 Nov 2021.
2. Doddington, G. R., Mitchell, A., Przybocki, M. A., Ramshaw, L. A., Strassel, S. M., and Weischedel, R. M. (2004). The automatic content extraction (ACE) program - tasks, data, and evaluation. In LREC, 2004.
3. Zhang, W., Zhao, X., Zhao, L., Yin, D., and Yang, G. H. (2021). DRL4IR: 2nd workshop on deep reinforcement learning for information retrieval. In ACM SIGIR, 2021.
4. Kuhnle, A., Aroca-Ouellette, M., Basu, A., Sensoy, M., Reid, J., and Zhang, D. (2021). Reinforcement learning for information retrieval. In ACM SIGIR, 2021.

5. Liu, C., Zhou, C., Wu, J., Xie, H., Hu, Y., and Guo, L. (2017). CPMF: a collective pairwise matrix factorization model for upcomingevent recommendation. In International Joint Conference on Neural Networks IJCNN, 2017.

6. Gao, L., Wu, J., Qiao, Z., Zhou, C., Yang, H., and Hu, Y. (2016). Collaborative social group influence for event recommendation. In CIKM, 2016.

7. Boyd-Graber, J., and B¨orschinger, B. (2020). What question answering can learn from trivia nerds. In ACL, 2020.

8. Cao, Q., Trivedi, H., Balasubramanian, A., and Balasubramanian, N. (2020). Deformer: decomposing pre-trained transformers for faster question answering. In ACL, 2020.

9. Wu, X., Wu, J., Fu, X., Li, J., Zhou, P., and Jiang, X. (2019). Automatic knowledge graph construction: a report on the 2019ICDM/ICBK contest. In ICDM, 2019.

10. Bosselut, A., Le Bras, R., and Choi, Y. (2021). Dynamic neuro-symbolic knowledge graph construction for zero-shot commonsense question answering. In AAAI, 2021.

11. Liu, K., Chen, Y., Liu, J., Zuo, X., and Zhao, J. (2020). Extracting events and their relations from texts: a survey on recent research progress and challenges. *AI Open*.

12. Ding, X., Li, Z., Liu, T., and Liao, K. (2019). ELG: an event logic graph. In CoRR, 2019.

13. Liu, J., Min, L., and Huang, X. (2021). An overview of event extraction and its applications. In CoRR, 2021.

14. Costa, T. S., Gottschalk, S., and Demidova, E. (2020). Event-qa: a datasetfor event-centric question answering over knowledge graphs. In CIKM, 2020.

15. Wang, J., Jatowt, A., F¨arber, M., and Yoshikawa, M. (2020). Answering event-related questions over long-term news article archives. In ECIR, Lecture Notes in Computer Science, 2020.

16. Han, R., Hsu, I., Sun, J., Baylon, J., Ning, Q., Roth, D., and Peng, N. (2021). ESTER: a machine reading comprehension dataset for reasoning about event semantic relations. In EMNLP, 2021.

17. Cao, P., Chen, Y., Yang, Y., Liu, K., and Zhao, J. (2021). Uncertain localto-global networks for document-level event factuality identification. In EMNLP, 2021.

18. Saur´i, R., and Pustejovsky, J. (2012). Are you sure that this happened? assessing the factuality degree of events in text. *Computational Linguistics*, 2012.

19. Lotan, A., Stern, A., and Dagan, I. (2013). Truthteller: annotating predicate truth. In NAACL-HLT, 2013.

20. Tourille, J., Ferret, O., Neveol, A., and Tannier, X. (2017). Neural architecture for temporal relation extraction: a bi-lstm approach for detecting narrative containers. In ACL, 2017.

21. Chaturvedi, S., Peng, H., and Roth, D. (2017). Story comprehension for predicting what happens next. In EMNLP, 2017.

22. Yang, Y., Wei, Z., Chen, Q., and Wu, L. (2019). Using external knowledge for financial event prediction based on graph neural networks. In CIKM, 2019.

23. Liu, K., Chen, Y., Liu, J., Zuo, X., and Zhao, J. (2020). Extracting events and their relations from texts: a survey on recent research progress and challenges. *AI Open*.

24. Hashimoto, C., Torisawa, K., Kloetzer, J., Sano, M., Varga, I., Oh, J. H., and Kidawara, Y. (2014). Toward future scenario generation: extracting event causality exploiting semantic relation, context, and association features. In ACL, 2014.

25. Gao, L., Choubey, P. K., and Huang, R. (2019). Modeling document-level causal structures for event causal relation identification. In ACL, 2019.

26. Rashkin, H., Sap, M., Allaway, E., Smith, N. A., and Choi, Y. (2018). Event2mind: commonsense inference on events, intents, and reactions. In CoRR, 2018.

27. Pustejovsky, J., Castano, J. M., Ingria, R., Sauri, R., Gaizauskas, R. J., Setzer, A., Katz, G., and Radev, D. R. (2003). Timeml: robust specification of event and temporal expressions in text. *New Directions Inquestion Answering.*

28. Lu, J., and Ng, V. (2017). Learning antecedent structures for event coreference resolution. In International Conference on Machine Learning and Applications, ICMLA, 2017.

29. Frisoni, G., Moro, G., and Carbonaro, A. (2021). A survey on event extraction for natural language understanding: Riding the biomedical literature wave. *IEEE Access.*

30. Trieu, H., Tran, T. T., Nguyen, A. D., Nguyen, A., Miwa, M., and Ananiadou, S. (2020). Deepeventmine: end-to-end neural nested eventextraction from biomedical texts. *Bioinformatics*, (19).

31. Huang, K., Yang, M., and Peng, N. (2020). Biomedical event extraction on graph edge-conditioned attention networks with hierarchical knowledge graphs. In EMNLP, Findings of ACL, 2020.

32. Chen, C., and Ng, V. (2012). Joint modeling for chinese event extraction with rich linguistic features. In Proceedings of COLING 2012, Proceedings of COLING, (pp. 529–544), 2012.

33. Peng, Y., Moh, M., and Moh, T. S. (2016). Efficient adverse drug event extraction using twitter sentiment analysis. In 2016 IEEE/ACM International Conference on Advances in Social Networks Analysis and Mining (ASONAM), 2016 IEEE/ACM International Conference on Advances in Social Networks Analysis and Mining(ASONAM), (pp. 1011–1018). IEEE, 2016.

34. Henn, S., Sticha, A., Burley, T., Verdeja, E., and Brenner, P. (2021). Visualization techniques to enhance automated event extraction. arXiv preprint arXiv:2106.06588, 2021.

35. Björne, J., Ginter, F., Pyysalo, S., Tsujii, J., and Salakoski, T. (2010). Complex event extraction at pubmed scale. *Bioinformatics*, 26(12), i382–i390.

36. Patwardhan, S., and Riloff, E. (2009). A unified model of phrasal and sentential evidence for information extraction. In Proceedings of the 2009 Conference on Empirical Methods in Natural Language Processing, Proceedings of the 2009 Conference on Empirical Methods in Natural Language Processing, (pp. 151–160), 2009.

37. Ji, H., and Grishman, R. (2008). Refining event extraction through cross-document inference. In Proceedings of ACL-08: Hlt, Proceedings of ACL-08: Hlt, (pp. 254–262), 2008.

38. Naughton, M., Kushmerick, N., and Carthy, J. (2006). Event extraction from heterogeneous news sources. In Proceedings of the AAAI Workshop Event Extraction and Synthesis, Proceedings of the AAAI Workshop Event Extraction and Synthesis, (pp. 1–6), 2006.

63 Impact of changing mobility speed on the performance of various protocols in hybrid (RF/ VLC) wireless network

Prajakta A. Satarkar[1,a] and Dr. Girish V. Chowdhary[2,b]

[1]Research Scholar, SRTMU, Nanded and Asst. Prof. SVERI's College of Engineering Pandharpur, MH

[2]Professor and Director, Head, School of Computational Science, SRTMU, Nanded, MH

Abstract

As requirement of higher data rate is increasing now a days, hybrid networks consisting of Light Fidelity (Li-Fi) and Wireless Fidelity (Wi-Fi) have received significant attention. They are referred as Hybrid Li-Fi and Wi-Fi Networks (HLWNets). As the HLWNets are still in the developing phases, it has certain issues to face. These problems include light path blockage, interference management, flickering of light, mobility management, handover mechanism, which results in reduced performance of the network. In this paper we have developed a novel handover mechanism for access point selection process. It is a three step process in which first the requirement of handover is checked, then the type of handover is decided and then actual handover is executed. The impact of mobility speed on hybrid network is observed with proposed and earlier methods. The simulation result shows there is improvement in the performance with proposed method. The average throughput is improved by 12% and average delay has been reduced by approximately 0.005 seconds.

Keywords: Hybrid network, Li- Fi, mobility, optical wireless communication, performance

Introduction

According to the reports of CISCO, 5.3 billion global populations will use internet by 2023 [1]. As the internet users are increasing, the limited RF spectrum becomes more congested impacting the performance of communication in network. Alternate solution can be Light Fidelity (Li-Fi) having multiple advantages over Wi-Fi. Li-Fi uses light as a communication medium providing unused vast optical spectrum, high data rate and secure communication [2]. But certain drawbacks of Li-Fi are smaller coverage area, data loss in shadowing and flickering of LEDs. To get benefits of both Li-Fi and Wi-Fi, we can use hybrid network providing larger coverage with Wi-Fi and high data rate with Li-Fi. As a result the indoor communication gets improved [3]. Earlier work presents issues with hybrid network. As the coverage area of Li-Fi is less as compared to Wi-Fi, Wi-Fi access point becomes vulnerable to congestion so load balancing is required. Load balancing can be stated as problem of optimization in resource allocation [4] or it can be solved using fuzzy approach to get optimal solution with less computation [5]. The impact of user mobility is significant on AP selection, majorly in

[a]pasatarkar@coe.sveri.ac.in, [b]girish.chowdhary@gmail.com

ultra-dense networks [6]. Recently some authors have proposed various handover mechanisms with due consideration to mobility management and shadow effects, but not supported by experimental validations. There is no method to decide the type of handover resulting into poor utilization of resources in hybrid network. In this paper we are focusing on handover issues with user mobility speed and access point selection with load balancing. We propose a novel method which will detect need of handover, handover type and then actual execution of handover. The integrated score of received signal power and user mobility speed will decide the type of handover either horizontal handover (HHO) or vertical handover (VHO). HHO means current Li-Fi access point is switched to a new Li-Fi access point and VHO means current Li-Fi access point is switched to Wi-Fi access point. The remaining paper is arranged as in below sections. Related work as review is presented in section 2. The section 3 describes proposed methodology. Section 4 contains results after simulation with further discussions. Analysis of changing mobility over various protocols is one in section. The conclusion with future work suggestions is described in section 6.

Related Work

State of Art Method
This section gives a review on various issues in hybrid network. Resource allocation with game based strategy is discussed in [7]. Reinforcement learning in [8] acts as a load balancing technique which improves performance considering user satisfaction. The QoS aware load balancing is done in [9] in single and multi AP association. The authors [10] suggested a strategy for Li-Fi network that can skip handover with focus on reference signal received power (RSRP). Selection of handover is done considering rate of change in RSRP. The handover decision algorithms developed in [11] uses fuzzy logic (FL) and artificial neural network. The author in [12] provided solution to mobility and light path blockage using load balancing. Further fuzzy logic approach is used to reduce complexity.

Motivation and Contribution
Available literature is focusing only on one parameter like mobility, light path blockage, user satisfaction and interference without experimental validations. To provide solution we have proposed a novel method which considers mobility speed and received signal power (RSP) for handover. The design, implementation and evaluation of proposed method is done using NS2 simulator and analyzed the obtained results with earlier method in [12].

Proposed Methodology

The proposed method works in 3 steps: Handover initiation, handover type decision and actual handover. The indoor communication scenario contains 4 Wi-Fi and 16 Li-Fi access points (AP) for office area of 1000*1000 sq. feet. 50 moving user equipments (UE) are introduced with random waypoint model of mobility. The throughput is verified for a speed ranging from 1m/s to 5m/s. The performance of proposed system is analyzed with mobility aware load balancing method of [12].

System Model

Figure 63.1 represents the overall architecture of proposed method. First all components of hybrid network, mobile users, Li-Fi and Wi-Fi APs are deployed. Each UE triggers handover (HO) periodically. Based on RSP value, process determines the need of handover. If RSP < threshold then handover is initiated. In second step, the type of handover is decided based on integrated score of mobility speed and RSP. Separate steps are followed based on type of handover HHO or VHO.

Once the type is decided, using load balancing method it will search for the best AP in both Li-Fi AP for HHO and Wi-Fi AP for VHO. It is achieved through the trust score (TS) in list of Li-Fi APs (LAP) and Wi-Fi APs (WAP). Based on TS, sorting is done and then the best (first) AP is selected as target AP (TAP). Actual execution of handover performs 3 steps, disassociation from the previous AP, target AP assignment and re-association with target AP.

Procedure to Evaluate Parameters

The user mobility ue^i is calculated as:

$$t1 = 1 - \left(\frac{\text{speed}(ue^i)}{\Delta}\right) \tag{1}$$

Here, speed(ue^i) provides user's moving speed. The Δ indicates maximum velocity of each moving user. As t1 and velocity are inversely proportional to each other, smaller value of t1, results in the handover. The RSP can be calculated with

$$t2 = \frac{l^i \to \text{RSP}}{\nabla} \tag{2}$$

Where, $l^i \to$ RSP provides the current RSP value of l^i and ∇ indicates the RSP of each Li-Fi at initial phase. The t2 has a value in the range of 0 to 1. Value closer

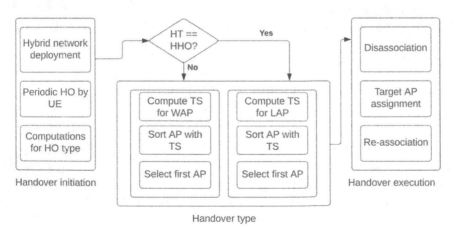

Figure 63.1 Overall architecture of proposed method

to 1 indicates the higher RSP value and closer to 0 indicates lower RSP in turn initializes handover. At last, the joint trust score t ← jointscore (t1, t2) is calculated using the Eq. (3) given below.

$$t = a1 \times t1 + a2 \times t2 \tag{3}$$

Where, a1 and a2 parameters has the dynamic weight and values are set to 0.5 for each so that a1 (0.5) + a2 (0.5) == 1. Through this approach we can carry out weight management

Simulation Results

To check the performance of proposed method we use simulation with NS2. The baseline considered is earlier paper with mobility aware load balancing with single and multiple transmissions [12]. Here the simulation is carried out for 200s. The performance is analyzed in terms of throughput first and then average delay. In both scenarios we are considering the varying mobility speed from 1m/s to 5m/s.

a. Throughput
Here we are focusing on impact of mobility speed on throughput considering earlier (LBHWF) and proposed method (MOHAN). As speed is increasing in LBHWF method, network switches to VHO type to provide seamless handover so throughput is significantly reduced. But in MOHAN we are testing need of handover then type of handover, so handover takes place only when it is required to carry out. Hence fewer drops in throughput observed as compared to LBHWF as shown in Figure 63.2.

b. Average Delay
Here impact of mobility is tested on average delay of network in LBHWF and MOHAN methods. It is observed that as handovers are efficiently managed in

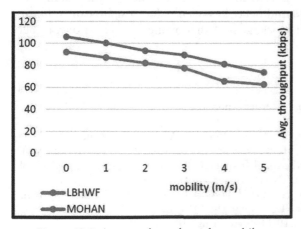

Figure 63.2 Average throughput for mobile users with two methods

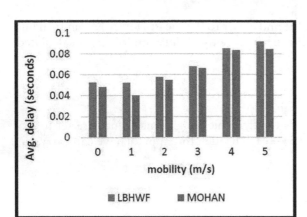

Figure 63.3 Average delay for mobile users with two methods

MOHAN, the average delay is less in MOHAN as compared to LBHWF as shown in Figure 63.3.

Analysis of Changing Mobility Over Various Methods

The simulation results shows throughput has been improved by 12%. For LBHWF it is approximately 78 kbps and for MOHAN it has reached to 90%. Also the average delay of LBHWF was 0.068 seconds which is reduced to 0.063 seconds which shows reduction in delay by 0.005 seconds.

Conclusion and Future Work

In this paper a novel method is designed and simulated for efficient handover and selection of access point in hybrid Li-Fi and Wi-Fi network. As per simulation results we can analyze, with effective management of handover in hybrid networks we can improve overall performance. Throughput of proposed method is improved over earlier method and delay has been reduced significantly. Future research will involve light path blockage and shadowing impact on overall performance of hybrid network.

References

1. Cisco, U. (2020). Cisco annual internet report (2018–2023) white paper. Cisco: San Jose, CA, USA, 10(1), 1–35.
2. Islim, M. S., Ferreira, R., He, X., Xie, E., Videv, S., Viola, S., Watson, S., Bamiedakis, N., Penty, R. V., White, I. H., Kelly, A. E., Gu, E., Haas, H., and Dawson, M. D. (2017). Towards 10 Gb/s orthogonal frequency division multiplexing-based visible light communication using a GaN violet micro-LED. *Photonics Research*, 5.
3. Basnayaka, D. A., and Haas, H. (2015). Hybrid RF and VLC Systems: Improving user data rate performance of VLC systems. In 2015 IEEE 81st Vehicular Technology Conference (VTC Spring). doi:10.1109/vtcspring.2015.7145863.

4. Li, X., Zhang, R., and Hanzo, L. (2015). Cooperative load balancing in hybrid visible light communications and WiFi. *IEEE Transactions on Communications*, 63(4), 1319–1329. doi:10.1109/tcomm.2015.2409172.

5. Wu, X., Safari, M., and Haas, H. (2017). Access point selection for hybrid Li-Fi and Wi-Fi networks. *IEEE Transactions on Communications*, 65(12), 5375–5385. doi:10.1109/tcomm.2017.2740211.

6. Teng, Y., Liu, M., Yu, F. R., Leung, V. C., Song, M., and Zhang, Y. (2019). Resource allocation for ultra-dense networks: a survey, some research issues and challenges. *IEEE Communications Surveys and Tutorials*, 21, 2134–2168.

7. Ma, W., Zhang, L., and Jiang, Y. (2020). Optimized joint LiFi coordinated multipoint joint transmission clustering and load balancing for hybrid LiFi and WiFi networks. *Journal of Optical Communications and Networking*, 12(8), 227. doi:10.1364/jocn.388264.

8. Ahmad, R., Soltani, M. D., Safari, M., and Srivastava, A. (2020). Load balancing of hybrid LiFi WiFi networks using reinforcement learning. In 2020 IEEE 31st Annual International Symposium on Personal, Indoor and Mobile Radio Communications. doi:10.1109/pimrc48278.2020.9217382.

9. Wu, X., and O'Brien, D. C. (2022). QoS-driven load balancing in hybrid LiFi and WiFi networks. *IEEE Transactions on Wireless Communications*, 21(4), 2136–2146. doi: 10.1109/TWC.2021.3109716.

10. Wu, X., and Haas, H. (2019). Handover skipping for LiFi. *IEEE Access*, 7, 38369–38378.

11. Sanusi, Idris, S., Adeshina, S., Aibinu, A. M., and Umar, I. (2020). Development of handover decision algorithms in hybrid Li-Fi and Wi-Fi networks. In 2020 3rd International Conference on Intelligent Sustainable Systems (ICISS). https://doi.org/10.1109/iciss49785.2020.9316116.

12. Wu, X., & Haas, H. (2019). Load Balancing for Hybrid LiFi and WiFi Networks: To Tackle User Mobility and Light-path Blockage. IEEE Transactions on Communications, 1319–1329. doi:10.1109/tcomm.2019.2962434

64 Development of a smart pill box to aid the elderly with their medication needs

Jyotirmoy Pathak[1,a], Avijit Poddar[2,b],
Chayan Mukherjee[2,c], Prashant Aarya[2,d],
Tuhin Maity[2,e] and Sayan Kumar Mandal[2,f]

[1]School of Engineering and Technology, Christ (Deemed to be University), Kengeri Campu, Karnataka, India

[2]School of Electronic and Electrical Engineering, Lovely Professional University, Punjab, India

Abstract

When the number of drugs prescribed to a patient is raised, it will be difficult for them (particularly the elderly and Alzheimer's patients) to take the right medications at the right time. Additionally, bad medication responses are causing deaths. It is difficult and expensive for a patient to travel to the hospital for a daily checkup. With the use of a Smart tech Medicine Box, this article aims to tackle the issue of medication reminders, avoid bad drug responses, and monitor patient health. The Smart Tech Medications Box is designed to remind individuals to take their prescribed medication in accordance with the real-time monitoring of patients' vital signs on a frequent basis (like oxygen level, blood pressure, sugar, and heart rate). It also monitors all significant health concerns, keeps a record of them, stores them in the cloud, sends text messages to a mobile device, and notifies the patient if they fail to take their medication. The box is facilitating healthier communication between physicians and patients in a more transparent manner. The doctor may examine everything from there at any time and from any place.

Keywords: Alzheimer's patients, arduino, IoT, smart medicine box

Introduction

One-third of older persons is taking seven or more medications daily, according to the American Society of Health- System Pharmacists Al-Shammary, R. (2018). According to 2008-2009 United Nations statistics on aging and development, the average yearly growth rates of the Alzheimer's-afflicted population aged 60 or older are quite high Ayshwarya [4]. According to this research, 6.7% of hospitalized patients experience a severe adverse medication response, with a death incidence of 0.32%. More than 2,216,000 major adverse drug reactions (ADRs) occur yearly in hospitalized patients, resulting in over 106,000 fatalities. Too many individuals require frequent examinations for health-related concerns such as oxygen level, blood pressure, sugar, and heart rate. It is quite tough for people to take care of their family's health because they reside so far away from their houses. So, this Smart Tech Medication Box is designed for monitoring the health

[a]jyotirmoy.pathak@christuniversity.in, [b]imavijitpoddar26@gmail.com,
[c]rajdeep.chayan.ac@gmail.com, [d]prashantaarya005@gmail.com,
[e]tuhin3024@gmail.com, [f]sayanvisari24@gmail.com

of a loved one Kader, M. A. (2018). The system's design requirements include cheap cost, ease of use, dependability, and compatibility with various cabinet designs and medicine bottles. A sensor recognizes when a usertakes a pill or bottle off the shelf. This information is transmitted to the microcontroller. The controller will examine and update the database of medication distributions. The controller will then provide the user with relevant audible and visual instructions. The relevant LED will illuminate to indicate which pill compartment should be accessed.

Literature Review

According to the census survey of 2021, there are 104 million elderly people and 5 million people are Alzheimer's, it will increase to 7.6 million by the end of 2030. They are not able to take prescribed medicine at the right time as well as there are approximately 30% of the total population is taking 8 medicine per day Gali, R. L. (2020). according to a recent survey in India approx. 700000 people die due to adverse drug reactions (ADRS). So many people require monitoring of their vitals on a daily basis and they have to keep a record of that. this is made for our loved ones and the old-age person who is suffering from many diseases one of the most frightful is Alzheimer's. because of this disease, they face memory loss problems and they forget to take the prescribed medicine dose on time. That's why we made a smart tech medicine box that will help individuals to take care of his/her health by reminding them to take pills with a voice alarm on time Wu, H. K. (2015) It has several compartments with airtight tight technology that will keep medicine fresh, Users can set time slots by mobile phone or buttons placed on that box. also, it will monitor their vitals and keep a record of that and will update it on a server or app so the doctors can easily access it.

Methodology and Model Specifications

To resolve this problem, we created a smart Arduino-based medication reminder that alerts us to take medications once, twice, or three times each day. The time slot is selectable by a button available on the box or smartphone. Moreover, it displays the Date and Time. We will expand it to include incoming IoT project articles Ayshwarya [4] where we provide an SMS or email notice will to the user. Moreover, this medication reminder will be connected to the Patient Health Monitoring System. Pill Reminder The power supply for the buzzer is 5V. Duringthe initial startup, it displays a welcome message. The LCD display is programmed to alternate between two displays. The screen will instruct you to hit the pick button to choose any one-time reminder slot (once, twice, or three times each day). The program's time slot is modifiable and may be customized properly. This has been divided into three time periods: 9 am, 3 pm, and 9 pm. We've separated time slots into three categories. When the user presses the first button, Mode 1 is selected to be taken once a day at 9 am. When the user clicks the second button, Mode 2 is selected to take medication twice daily at 9 am and 9 pm. when the user hits the third button, Mode 3 is selected to be taken three times daily at 9 am, 3 pm, and 9 pm. We have also incorporated a snooze function. The buzzer will buzz for ten minutes.

As the user presses push buttons to choose desired slots, the user input is capture and the time is obtained from the real-time clock (RTC). When the time matches the set time slot, the buzzer begins to sound. The beep may be stopped by pushing the bottom which has a STOP function. the same procedure is repeated for the subsequent slot reminder. After you have thought of methods to remember to take the medications, it is simple to develop software. Here, it will display the reminder, sound a buzzer, and illuminate an LED. It also offers the function to set three-time slots (once, two, or three times each day), and when the time arrives, it alerts the patient with a buzzer Ranjana, P. (2018). Then the whole system will look like the following: The display will interact with the user to provide instruction on it, the User selects time slots (one, two, thrice/day), and show a confirmation message on the LCD display, Timekeeping started, when the user selected time that matches the clock time of the selected slot then buzzer and LED start responding, User, can stop by pushing a stop push button, End. The diagram depicts a comprehensive overview of the installed system. The graphic depicts the primary hardware components which we have used in this project, including the medication box, LED indication, LCD display, push or reset button, speaker module, and RTC. Demonstrates when the selected time meets with the specified time, the selected morning slot LED blinks and the speaker offers a customize voice alarm to take the medication, as well as displaying the device's output for another. Timing constraint Since we've included additional peripherals, such as the 16x2 LCD Display and RTC DS3231, the ultrasonic sensor detects your motion and automatically opens the box when it's time to take your pills. When the patient takes a pill from that compartment a sensor is placed in the slot that will detect whether medicine is picked or not, the LCD lights flicker to indicate that the correct pill has been taken. So, when the patient takes their medication automatically, the alert will be off. If the patient fails not to take their medication at the prescribed time, a notice will be sent to the carer. Dialogue with medical professionals. In addition, the patient may monitor their oxygen level using SPO2 sensors, their heart rate using pulse sensors, and their temperature using LM35 sensors, and this can be customized. On a daily basis, all data will be detected, saved, and transmitted to the server. Hence, the doctor may check patient health on a daily basis, regardless of location, using the app or server.

Thus openness between physician and patient will be really beneficial. Physicians are able to alter treatment and make judgments based on data. Using Arduino and a monitoring system, here is how you can build your own Automated Medication Reminder.

Hence, before beginning work on this medication box, ensure that the functional setup is established. The system will show the time and date, as well as sound an alarm, based on the user's settings for medication timings and arrival dates, so that the user may take their medication at the correct time. Using an ultrasonic sensor, the automated box will open. The right compartment light will flash to ensure that the user selects the correct medication. If the user fails to select the correct medication at the appropriate time, the system will send messages to the caretaker through the wifi module and update the scenario on the cloud server. Our server is mostly based on the SaaS or PaaS concept (Chen, B. (2019a), Chen,

B. (2019b)). If the patient takes medication, the alarm and lead will immediately be deactivated. It is updated on the server as well. Aside from that, there are other exceptional technologies, such as the Heart, Pulse, Spo2, and Temperature sensors in our medication box, which allow patients to perform daily body checks at home Meng, D. (2022). The server will automatically identify and gather the data, which will then be updated on the same server (Figure 64.1). Physicians can access all patient health information through a server or a specialized application. Therefore doctors may do daily patient checks from wherever. So, we establish links between doctors and their patients, who always monitor their status and make decisions accordingly.

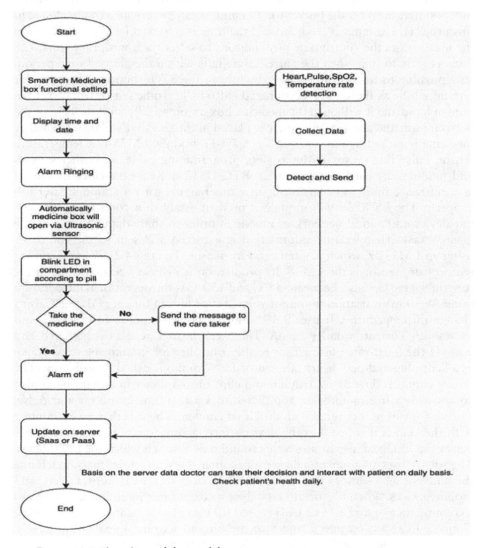

Figure 64.1 Flowchart of the model

Implementation

The 5V battery supply powers the alarm to remind you to take your medication. Three displays alternate on the LCD screen. The generated word example as to "Take your medication, Remain Healthy, and Get Well Soon" is displayed on the first screen. The second screen is a help page that instructs you to set a reminder time by clicking the select button on it (once, twice, or three times every day). The application allows for time slots to be modified and customized. This is now set for three times: 7 am, 2 pm, and 9 pm The time slots are accessible in three different types of modes. When the user pushes the first button, Mode 1 decides that the medication will be taken once daily at 7 a.m. The drug is delivered twice daily, at 7 am and 9 pm, when button two is touched. In Mode 3, the user may take their medication three times a day at 7 a.m., 2 p.m., and 9 p.m. Moreover, a function that turns off the buzzer for 10 minutes can be provided (not included in this project). The input is recorded and the time is retrieved from the RTC when the user presses the appropriate push buttons to select the appropriate slots. The buzzer starts to ring when the current time falls within the allotted time period. It is possible to turn off the buzzer by hitting the STOP button. The next slot reminder follows the same procedure. HC-SR04 Ultrasonic sensor will detect the human hand and it will open the medicine box automatically with the help of the Servo motor, and another Ultrasonic is placed in the slot that will detect whether medicine is picked or not, ESP8266 is a Wi-Fi module, LM35 is a temperature sensor, Pulse rate sensor, Arduino Uno, programming cable, and other sensors and modules are used in this project. RTC DS3231 Real-time clock employed as a reference timer in order to obtain a timer signal for programming our job properly. The ESP8266 wifi module is used to establish a connection between our device and a local network or mobile in order to share data and update the device's tasks. Temperature information is gathered and sent to the controller using an LM35DZ which is a temperature sensor (Figure 64.2). A linear analog temperature sensor is the LM35. Its production is inversely related to temperature (in degree Celsius). Between -55°C and 150°C is the operational temperature range. A 10 mV variation in output voltage is produced for every degree Celsius change in temperature. It uses 3.3 V and 5V power supplies to function, and its standby current is under 60 uA. The user's heart rate data is gathered and sent via the heart rate pulse sensor to the controller for monitoring reasons. An excellent plug-and-play heart rate sensor for Arduino is called Pulse Sensor. The sensor connects directly to Arduino and clips onto a fingertip or earlobe. It also comes with a free monitoring app that shows a real-time graph of your pulse. The sensor's front is covered with the Heart emblem. The side that makes contact with the skin is this one. On the device's face, a tiny square is located directly below the LED and also houses a tiny round hole through which the LED shines. The square uses an ambient light sensor to alter the screen brightness, much like the ambient light sensors seen in electronic devices such as laptops, tablets, and mobile devices. When it's time to take their medication, a piezo buzzer is utilized to remind theuser and a 16x2 LCD is used for user engagement. and data display. Connect LCD analog pins 7 and 8 to the En and Rs ping signals, respectively. Figure 64.3 depicts the circuit diagram of the implementation.

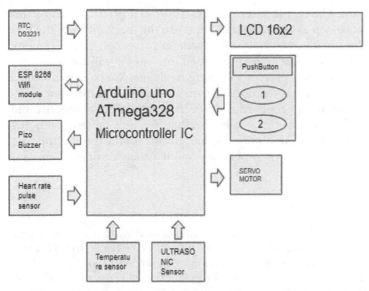

Figure 64.2 Block diagram of the model

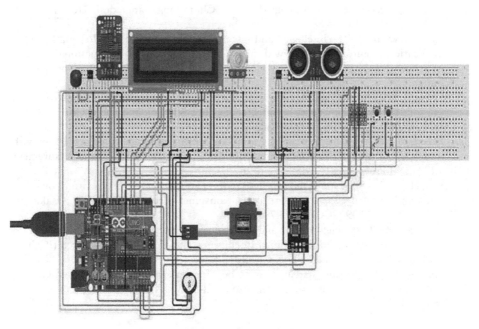

Figure 64.3 Circuit diagram of the implementation

Conclusion

We have designed a smart tech medicine box for elderly people (Alzheimer's patients) or those who are staying far from their homes and have to take care of his/her beloved person. The cost is lesser than Rs.2000 so a poor can afford this and also an illiterate person easily understand and use the mechanism of the box does not have any kind of security so a family member can excess easily. The box will remind you to take medicine at the prescribed time and it will monitor your vitals on daily basis also it will prevent to wrong medicine. We have established healthy communication between the doctor, patient, and family member (caretaker). It will help rural areas people who don't have good doctor support and are not able to visit the hospital for a daily checkup. we link the box with any hospital or doctor where they can observe patient health on the mobile app or a webpage. We include some features to place an online order for pills when your box is empty.

References

1. Al-Shammary, R. (2018). The design of a smart medicine box. In Electrical Engineering (ICEE), Iranian Conference on, Mashhad, Iran, DOI: 10.1109/ ICEE.2018.8472586.
2. Chen, B. (2019a). Research and implementation of an intelligent medicine box. In 4th International Conference on Intelligent Green Building and Smart Grid (IGBSG), Hubei, China. DOI: 10.1109/IGBSG.2019.8886274.
3. Kader, M. A. (2018). Design & implementation of an automated reminder medicine box for old people and hospital. In International Conference on Innovations in Science. Engineering, and Technology (ICISET). Chittagong, Bangladesh. DOI: 10.1109/ICISET.2018.8745654.
4. Ayshwarya, B. (2021). Intelligent and safe medication box in health IoT platform for medication monitoring system with timely remainders. In 7th International Conference on Advanced Computing and Communication Systems (ICACCS), Coimbatore, India.
5. Chen, B. (2019b). Design of docker-based cloud platform for smart medicine box. In 4th International Conference on Intelligent Green Building and Smart Grid (IGBSG). Hubei, China. DOI: 10.1109/IGBSG.2019.8886265.
6. Meng, D. (2022). Design of a novel low- temperature intelligent medicine box with internet control. In 4th International Conference on Intelligent Control. Measurement and Signal Processing (ICMSP). Hangzhou, China.
7. Wu, H. K. (2015). A smart pill box with remind and consumption confirmation functions. In IEEE 4th Global Conference on Consumer Electronics (GCCE). Osaka, Japan. DOI: 10.1109/GCCE.2015.7398716.
8. Ranjana, P. (2018). Health alert and medicine remainder using internet of things. In IEEE Conference on Computational Intelligence and Computing Research (ICCIC). Madurai, India. DOI: 10.1109/ICCIC.2018.8782.
9. Gali, R. L. (2020). Automated medicine box for geriatrics. In International Conference on System, Computation. Automation and Networking (ICSCAN). Pondicherry, India.

65 Breaking through the mist: an in-depth analysis of task scheduling techniques in fog computing

Rahul Thakur[1,a], Urvashi Garg[1,b] and Geeta Sikka[2,c]

[1]Department of Computer Science and Engineering, Dr. B R Ambedkar National Institute of Technology, Jalandhar, India

[2]Department of Computer Science and Engineering, National Institute of Technology, Delhi, India

Abstract

With the growing popularity of the Internet of Things (IoT), the goal of this study is to examine fog computing (FC) as an enhanced supplement to cloud architecture for monitoring the communication requirements of an IoT network. FC is tactically kept around IoT systems and sensors to make cloud computation, memory, and networking equipment economical. The main difference between fog and the cloud is the geolocation of the devices, which are maintained close to the end-users to accept and process requests immediately. In addition to this, the architecture works well for real-time video streaming, sensor-deployed systems, and the IoT, which require reliable internet connectivity. However, minimal latency is acceptable for many applications, such as online healthcare and medical sensor systems. To reduce FC delays, the process scheduler plays a crucial role. Task scheduling (TS) assigns tasks to available resources in an economical manner. This article gives a comparative analysis-based review of various TS approaches. In addition, the pros and cons of various TS techniques are detailed, along with their primary challenges. Additionally, the future scope for this research is offered based on the observed facts.

Keywords: Cloud computing, fog computing, internet of things (IoT), task scheduling

Introduction

The rise of technology, IoT applications are now an integral part of our day-to-day activities. As a result, the number of applications of the IoT will expand, resulting in the generation of an enormous amount of data. Due to the distance between the cloud and these devices, there will be a delay in reaction time. From this point on, it became vital to discover a new technology that was more compatible with Internet of Things devices and to address cloud issues. So, Cisco in 2012 Bonomi et al. [1] proposed FC, which was positioned between IoT devices (end users) and cloud computing (CC). A new paradigm called FC extends CC to the edge of the network. It aims to increase user accessibility to computing, storage, and networking Hao et al. [2]. The latest research in the field of IoT has enabled the use of a variety of sensor devices to produce a tremendous amount of data Singh et al. [3]. The CC model offers processing and storage services to meet the requirements of the IoT. For high-risk software, however, data transfer delays from the cloud

[a]rahult.cs.21@nitj.ac.in, [b]urvashi@nitj.ac.in, [c]sikkag@nitdelhi.ac.in

to the device and vice versa are unacceptable Dastjerdi et al. [4]. FC provides a distributed approach comparable to CC services within the IoT network. It has garnered substantial attention from academia and business leaders in recent years due to its potential for enhancement in processing in real-time, rapid scaling, and location consciousness Nguyen et al. [5]. Three layers of fog and CC environment architecture are depicted in Figure 65.1. The top-most layer is the cloud layer. The notion of cloud-based computing services and storage devices the middle layer of FC is composed of routers, switches, and gateways. Instead of transmitting data to the cloud, at the network's edge, these devices deliver IoT services. The final layer of the design consists of end-user devices that generate substantial data. Fog and cloud architecture have been connected with a number of important difficulties. Allocating computer resources, balancing workloads, creating security, optimising power consumption, ensuring fault tolerance, and scheduling jobs are the most crucial challenges. TS is one of the most crucial challenges In fog and CC. The task is seen as a single computing unit that corresponds to an end-service user's request. Various restrictions and priorities may apply to distinct jobs, causing them to be interdependent. Multiple data flows may comprise independent, sequentially executable jobs. The ideal match between a fog node and an end-user task is determined by job scheduling Kaur et al., [6]. In order to complete user tasks within the allotted timeframes and SLAs, it aims to choose an effective usage of FN. An FC component called a fog manager is in charge of selecting the most efficient work scheduling options. The location of fog managers in the FC architecture is shown in Figure 65.2. A task scheduler manages these tasks by selecting the best tasks and fog nodes and effectively scheduling a variety of tasks for execution on the fog nodes. The task scheduler also makes it easier to manage various computing resources when using a FC environment to schedule tasks. Task scheduling is thought to be an NP-complete issue Johnson and Garey, [7].

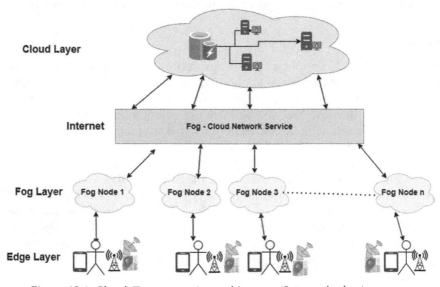

Figure 65.1 Cloud /Fog computing architecture (Source: Author)

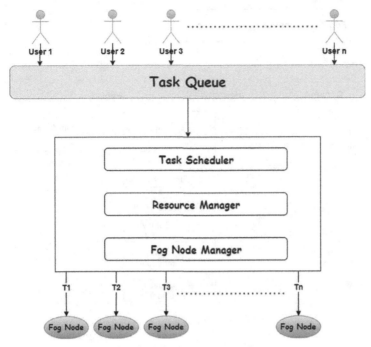

Figure 65.2 Task scheduling (Source: Author)

This article gives a comparative analysis-based review of various TS approaches. It analyses and compares several TS techniques across multiple dimensions. The rest part of this paper is organised as follows: The second section categorizes task scheduling methods; Section III conducts a literature review of TS methods and compares their advantages and disadvantages. Section IV identifies critical issues and suggests promising research directions. Finally, Section V brings the paper to a close.

Scheduling Algorithms

The goal of TS is to assign a set of tasks to fog nodes in order to satisfy QoS requirements while minimizing task execution and transmission time Ghobaei-Arani et al. [8]. Static, dynamic, heuristic, and hybrid algorithms are the four main types of TS techniques Yadav and Mandoria [9] Nagadevi et al. [10]. The taxonomy of TS is shown in Figure 3. Explanations of each of these algorithms follow.

Static Algorithms
In these algorithms, the scheduling process cannot start until the scheduler has complete knowledge of the jobs. No matter how the system is configured or if it has the necessary resources, all tasks will be sent to it at once. RR and FCFS are two well-known examples of these types of scheduling algorithms. When deciding on a schedule, FCFS only looks at the task's arrival time when making scheduling decisions and nothing else. So, it is the easiest way to make a schedule Rajesh and

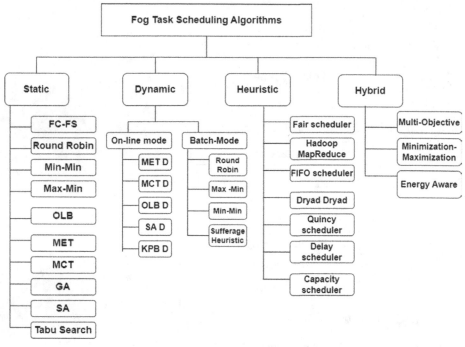

Figure 65.3 The taxonomy of task scheduling (Source: Author)

Mahalakshmi [11]. On the other hand, RR is the same as FCFS, but there is one difference. It allows each task to be completed within the time frame specified and moves it to the end of the waiting queue if it doesn't finish in that time slice El Amrani and Tani, [12]. OLB stands for Optimal Load Balancing and optimises load balancing; MET stands for Maximum Execution Time and minimises overall execution time; and MCT stands for Minimum Completion Time and minimises the time needed to complete all tasks. GA stands for Genetic Algorithm and uses natural selection and genetics to find optimal solutions; SA stands for Simulated Annealing and simulates annealing; and Tabu Search maintains a tabu list of previously explored solutions.

Dynamic Algorithms
These approaches are determined by the system machines and the upcoming job schedule. They can be separated into two distinct categories: batch processing and online processing. Tasks are assigned to groups as they are received in the online mode. In batch mode, however, tasks are assigned to time groups and scheduled for specific times. The batch mode is utilised by algorithms such as RR, Min-Min, saturation heuristics, and Max-Min. Nevertheless, other online-mode scheduling approaches are available, MET D (Minimum Execution Time), where D stands for dynamic, assigns tasks based on minimum execution time; MCT D (Minimum Completion Time), which assigns tasks based on minimum completion time; OLB D (Optimised Load Balancing), which balances workload; SA D (Simulated

Annealing); and KPB D (Knowledge-based Process Benchmarking), which assigns tasks based on past performance data Rewehel et al. [13]. In scattered contexts, dynamic schedulers outperform static ones, but they are more costly to maintain due to their frequent data update requirements.

Heuristic Algorithms
Heuristic scheduling techniques are required since there is no universal scheduler that can accommodate all possible hardware designs. Heuristic scheduling algorithms attempt to solve problems by guessing at possible solutions until one is found that works. The solution may not be optimal, but it was identified rapidly Alizadeh et al. [14]. A fair scheduler is used in Hadoop MapReduce for fair allocation of resources among running jobs. Hadoop MapReduce is a framework for the parallel processing of large datasets. The FIFO scheduler assigns tasks to resources in the order they are received. Dryad is a distributed computing framework that supports parallel processing of large datasets and uses a graph-based TS algorithm. The Quincy Scheduler is used in Microsoft's DryadLINQ system and allocates tasks based on priority and resource availability. The delay scheduler in Apache Hadoop prioritises short jobs over long jobs and improves system throughput. The capacity scheduler in Apache Hadoop allocates resources based on user-defined queues and capacities to prevent resource starvation. However, heuristic scheduling methods are applicable to a wide variety of difficult optimisation issues, and this is due to the fact that the scheduling problems mentioned are NP-hard.

Hybrid Algorithms
HA refers to a group of scheduling techniques that pool the strengths of various algorithms to provide the optimal plan of action Alizadeh et al., [14]. The uplink and downlink scheduling on a WLAN is a good illustration of this. Multi-objective optimisation optimises multiple objectives simultaneously, which is common in task scheduling. Minimization finds the minimum value, while maximization finds the maximum value. Energy-aware task scheduling considers energy consumption and combines different optimization techniques to achieve energy-efficient scheduling solutions. Newer hybrid scheduling algorithms typically make use of more parameters in order to determine the optimal scheduling strategy.

Literature Review

Sadoon Azizi et al. [15] the paper proposes two efficient algorithms, PSG and PSG-M, to reduce energy consumption in an IoT system while meeting task deadlines. These algorithms consider task priorities and assign tasks to the fog node with the minimum delay from the deadline if it is missed. Extensive experiments show that the proposed algorithms outperform state-of-the-art algorithms in terms of completing tasks within their specified time frames and reducing energy consumption. They overlooked how smart gates make decisions. The algorithms do not work on the GPU-required task and algorithm.is not worked on when resource failures occur. Table 65.1 shows a comparative study of TS Methods.

Abdelmoneem et al. [16] in this paper, they describe functional IoT architecture, mobility-aware scheduling, and protocol allocation that might be employed in healthcare. Their idea was to help the patients move around by using a handoff system based on received signal strength (RSS). By using a heuristic-based scheduling and allocation method that takes mobility into account the approach aims to reduce total schedule time and improve efficiency while maintaining high task completion rates. Simulations showed that the proposed approach was significantly more cost-effective and energy-efficient than existing solutions.

Ying Wah et al. [17] looked at the crucial pulse-based economical work scheduling issues for health-care applications in fog-cloud systems. The goal of their research was to find the most cost-effective ways to store data in the cloud. So that the total cost would be as low as possible, they suggested a new HCBFS that could be used to collect, analyse, and determine how to carry out the most important functions of the heartbeat medical application. They proposed a framework for a TS algorithm known as HCCETS that was used to plan and perform all jobs as fast and affordably as possible. The tested proposed TS method was shown to be more affordable than competing techniques.

Sun et al. [19] they introduced HDJS on the basis of Fog Computer's Intelligent Sensor-Cloud is based on this. It could change the priority of jobs on the fly to avoid job starvation and make the most of the resources available. It can also use key frames to indicate which resources are in use. According to their research, their approach might address the problems of operation hunger and resource fragmentation, capitalise on the benefits of multicore and multithreading, enhance the efficient use of system resources, and shorten response times and execution.

Gazori et al. [20] this paper is about scheduling tasks for fog-based IoT applications so that computation costs and long-term service delays are kept to a minimum, given the time and resource constraints that already exist. To solve this problem, they used reinforcement learning and created a DDQL-based scheduling algorithm that uses a target network and techniques for replaying past experiences. The outcomes of their tests showed that, by allocating each incoming job to the proper VMs, their suggested algorithm surpassed the RS, FF, QLS, and GS techniques in establishing a balance between the execution, waiting, transmission, and propagation times of the given tasks. It could also have the lowest number of deadlines missed.

Wang and Li [21] they discussed a TS approach based on the Hybrid Heuristic (HH) algorithm and TS techniques in FC scenarios were examined. This method mainly solved the issue of terminal devices having low computing power and high energy consumption. The HH algorithm suggested in that paper combines the Improved ACO (IACO) and PSO (IPSO) algorithms. Three performance metrics are how long it takes the simulation to complete, how much energy it consumes, and how reliable it is being examined. The simulation is carried out in MATLAB. Three alternative algorithms—IPSO, IACO, and RR—were contrasted with the suggested algorithms. Based on the simulation results, the suggested algorithm showed superior performance compared to the competition with respect to processing speed, energy efficiency and reliability.

Nguyen et al. [22] the authors developed a new method called TCaS for scheduling bag-of-tasks applications in a fog-cloud environment based on runtime and cost. This method, which uses evolutionary GA, aims to optimize the balance between cost and time needed to complete a batch of operations in the fog-cloud system. The authors contrasted TCaS with the evolutionary algorithms BLA,

Table 65.1 FOG computing: a comparative study of task scheduling methods (Source: Author's compilation)

Authors	Year	Approach/ Algorithm Used	Evaluation criteria	Simulation Environment	Pros	Cons
Sadoon Azizi et al.	[15]	semi greedy approach/ PSG and PSG-M	Response time, Energy consumption, Deadline	C++	Efficient IoT TS solutions in a heterogeneous FC domain	IoT devices' computing tasks were taken over by smart gateways, but their decision-making process was not taken into account.
Abdelmoneem et al.	[16]	heuristic-based scheduling/ MobMBAR	Utilization of resources and response time	iFogSim	Enhances power usage, scheduling time and response time	Deadlines and resource issues have not been investigated.
Ying Wah et al.	[17]	Dynamic/ HCCETS	Network bandwidth, Cost Deadline	Extended framework in JAVA	Reduces costs and investigates deadlines in task completion	Power usage and resource issues have not been looked into.
Jamil et al.	[18]	Static/SJF	Delay Network bandwidth Power consumption	iFogSim	Improves waiting time, network usage and delay	Unexplored computing resource Restriction and task priority
Sun et al.	[19]	Dynamic/HDJS	Response time, Resource utilization Execution time	Tomcat version 6.02	Utilization of resources results in faster runtime.	bandwidth of the network has not been analysed.
Gazori et al.	[20]	Reinforcement learning/ DDQL	Cost ,Deadline Delay ,Power consumption, Response time	Keras and SimPy	Improves power consumption And delay	Not investigated user satisfaction And security
Wang and Li	[21]	Hybrid heuristic/ IPSO and IACO	Reliability, Power consumption, Delay	MATLAB	Improves reliability, completion time Reduces power consumption	More user requests add to the complexity.

Authors	Year	Approach/ Algorithm Used	Evaluation criteria	Simulation Environment	Pros	Cons
Nguyen et al.	[22]	Static/ TCaS	Execution time	iFogSim	Applies graph theory	fails to provide a dynamically optimal balance of work
Benblidia et al.	[23]	Static/ fuzzy quantified ranking method	Execution time, how much power is used, and how happy the user is.	MATLAB	Reduces energy use and speeds up execution	The cost model is not described.
Jie et al.	[24]	Dynamic/ Repeated Stackelberg Game method	User satisfaction Resource utilization, Delay, execution duration and price	C++	Enhances execution time and efficiency	Not investigated deadlines

MPSO, and simple RR scheduling since TCaS is a GA-based approach. iFogSim was used to conduct the simulation, and multiple experiments were done in two different situations to test the proposed method. They schedule tasks in a foggy environment for the first instance. They schedule tasks in a fog-cloud domain for the second instance. The analysis's findings demonstrated that the newly given algorithm outperforms the other three algorithms in balancing makespan and total cost while also maximising time.

Jamil et al. [18] created a novel scheduler for FC that can handle IoE service provisioning. This way, it can minimise wait time and make the best use of the network. In order to schedule requests from IoE devices on FD and match their requirements with the resources already available on each FD, the best scheduling method must be found; a case study was also conducted. They compared their scheduling algorithm with existing methods using iFogSim. According to the findings, when compared to the FCFS method, the proposed scheduler was 32% faster and used the network 16% less than the FCFS method.

Benblidia et al. [23] came up with a fuzzy quantified ranking method that could be used to schedule tasks in fog-CC Nwk. The technique rates fog nodes based on their ability to meet task requirements and user preferences. They also used fuzzy quantified and linguistic quantifier's propositions to merge user preferences with FNs features the proposed approach is designed to achieve these tasks in a polynomial amount of time. According to the outcomes of the simulations, their plan could simultaneously schedule tasks and fulfill user requests. Also, it could offer a solution that strikes a balance between energy use, average user satisfaction, and execution time.

Jie et al. [24] this paper shows how to use the Repeated Stackelberg Game method to make an online scheduling algorithm. In this game, Edge Service Provider (ESP), which is a distinct user each round, serves as the long-term follower. This scheduling issue is solved via a mathematical programming model. The proposed architecture having three layers: the layers of the user, the ESP, and the cloud service provider (CSP). The methodology has a flaw in that it doesn't take deadlines into account, which are usually a part of manufacturing jobs that use FC. When compared to random Job assignment and the multi knapsack problem techniques in a C++ simulation, the proposed technique shows improve efficiency and a shorter running time.

Challenges and Future Directions

The majority of researchers ignored heterogeneity, security, makespan, financial cost, reaction time, execution time, completion time, diversity, power consumption, and load balancing [25]. Some researchers tested their methods by simulating them, while others didn't do any tests Azizi et al. [15] and Jamil et al. [18]. Some of the niche areas where researchers can work for further development in FC are listed below:

1) The battery storage of the majority of IoT and fog devices is constrained Ometov et al. [26]. Therefore, developing effective power management solutions could be a future study area.

2) Another problem in the FC environment that affects end users and service providers' satisfaction and dissatisfaction is service quality and service level agreements Singh et al. [3]. Researchers looked at three perspectives on service quality: performance, dependability, and pricing.

3) In the FC environment, it is hard to make things scalable. Researchers can work together to make algorithms that can be used with a growing number of IoT devices and networks Ometov et al. [26] Hosseini et al. [27].

4) There isn't much infrastructure available to verify a true fog computing environment. As a result, several studies on fog computing have been verified using simulation software. In order to validate fog computing technologies, a large-scale and real-time testbed must be created Ometov et al. [26] Hosseini et al. [27].

Conclusion

This study gives a full review of methods for scheduling tasks, looks at different methods, and points out their pros and cons, especially in the FC environment. Numerous comparisons have been made between the initial research studies on TS in FC environments. We chose the best scheduling algorithms after reading and analysing the majority of recent papers on the subject. Based on the results of the comparison, approximately 57% of published scheduling methods are used for TS. Not only that, but around 36% of research articles used iFogSim to implement the proposed methods. TS and energy consumption are two critical metrics in the field of FC. It's possible to improve how well scheduling algorithms work by combining different approaches and taking important performance factors into account. In scheduling algorithms, 25% of the time is spent on the makespan. So, the majority of scheduling problems in fog computing are research hotspots that require additional research.

Acknowledgment

We sincerely thank Prof. Geeta Sikka and Dr. Urvashi for their valuable insights and feedback. We acknowledge the financial assistance from NIT Jalandhar. Special thanks to the cited authors and anonymous reviewers for their contributions.

References

1. Bonomi, F., Milito, R., Zhu, J., and Addepalli, S. (2012). Fog computing and its role in the internet of things. In Proceedings of the First Edition of the MCC Workshop on Mobile Cloud Computing (MCC), (pp. 13–16).

2. Hao, Z., Novak, E., Yi, S., and Li, Q. (2017). Challenges and software architecture for fog computing. *IEEE Internet Computing*, 21, 44–53.

3. Singh, R. M., Awasthi, L. K., and Sikka, G. (2022). Towards metaheuristic scheduling techniques in cloud and fog: an extensive taxonomic review. *ACM Computing Surveys (CSUR)*, 55(3), 1–43.

4. Dastjerdi, A. V., Gupta, H., Calheiros, R. N., Ghosh, S. K., and Buyya, R. (2016). Fog computing: principles, architectures, and applications. *Internet of Things. Mor-*

gan Kaufmann, 61–75. ISBN 9780128053959. https://doi.org/10.1016/B978-0-12-805395-9.00004-6.

5. Yousefpour, A., Fung, C., Nguyen, T., Kadiyala, K., Jalali, F., Niakanlahiji, A., Kong, J., and Jue, J. P. (2019). All one needs to know about fog computing and related edge computing paradigms: a complete survey. *Journal of Systems Architecture*, 98, 289–330.

6. Kaur, N., Kumar, A., and Kumar, R. (2021). A systematic review on task scheduling in fog computing: taxonomy, tools, challenges, and future directions. *Concurrency and Computation: Practice and Experience*, 33(21), e6432.

7. Johnson, D. S., and Garey, M. R. (1979). A guide to the theory of NP completeness. *Computers and Intractability*.

8. Ghobaei-Arani, M., Souri, A., Safara, F., and Norouzi, M. (2020). An efficient task scheduling approach using moth-flame optimization algorithm for cyber-physical system applications in fog computing. *Transactions on Emerging Telecommunications Technologies*, 31, e3770.

9. Yadav, A. K., and Mandoria, H. L. (2017). Study of task scheduling algorithms in the cloud computing environment: a review. *International Journal of Computer Science and Information Technology*, 8, 462–468.

10. Nagadevi, S., Satyapriya, K., and Malathy, D. (2013). A survey on economic cloud schedulers for optimized task scheduling. *International Journal of Advanced Engineering Technology*, 4(1), 58–62.

11. Rajesh, M. E., and Mahalakshmi, M. J. (2015). Optimization of resource allocation using FCFS scheduling in cloud computing. *Optimization*, 5(2), 20–26.

12. El Amrani, C., and Tani, H. G. (2018). Smarter round robin scheduling algorithm for cloud computing and big data. *Journal of Data Mining and Digital Humanities*. 1. https://doi.org/10.46298/jdmdh.3104

13. Rewehel, E. M., Mostafa, M. S. M., and Ragaie, M. O. (2014). New subtask load balancing algorithm based on OLB and LBMM scheduling algorithms in cloud. In Proceedings of the 2014 International Conference on Computer Network and Information Science, (pp. 9–14).

14. Alizadeh, M. R., Khajehvand, V., Rahmani, A. M., and Akbari, E. (2020). Task scheduling approaches in fog computing: a systematic review. International *Journal of Communication Systems*, 33(16), e4583.

15. Azizi, S., Shojafar, M., Abawajy, J., and Buyya, R. (2022). Deadline-aware and energy-efficient IoT task scheduling in fog computing systems: a semi-greedy approach. *Journal of Network and Computer Applications*, 201, 103333.

16. Abdelmoneem, R. M., Benslimane, A., and Shaaban, E. (2020). Mobility-aware task scheduling in cloud-fog IoT-based healthcare architectures. *Computer Networks*, 107, 348–354.

17. Ying Wah, T., Gopal Raj, R., and Lakhan, A. (2020). A novel cost-efficient framework for critical heartbeat task scheduling using the Internet of medical things in a fog cloud system. *Sensors*, 20(2), 441.

18. Jamil, B., Shojafar, M., Ahmed, I., Ullah, A., Munir, K., and Ijaz, H. (2020). A job scheduling algorithm for delay and performance optimization in fog computing. *Concurrency and Computation: Practice and Experience*, 32(7), e5581.

19. Sun, Z., Li, C., Wei, L., Li, Z., Min, Z., and Zhao, G. (2019). Intelligent sensor-cloud in fog computer: a novel hierarchical data job scheduling strategy. *Sensors*, 19(23), 50–83.

20. Gazori, P., Rahbari, D., and Nickray, M. (2019). Saving time and cost on the scheduling of fog-based IoT applications using deep reinforcement learning approach. *Future Generation Computer Systems*, 110, September 2020, 110, 1098–1115.

21. Wang, J., and Li, D. (2019). Task scheduling based on a hybrid heuristic algorithm for smart production line with fog computing. *Sensors*, 19(5), 10–23.
22. Nguyen, B. M., Thi Thanh Binh, H., and Do Son, B. (2019). Evolutionary algorithms to optimize task scheduling problem for the IoT based Bag-of-Tasks application in cloud-fog computing environment. *Applied Sciences*, 9(9), 17–30.
23. Benblidia, M. A., Brik, B., Merghem-Boulahia, L., and Esseghir, M. (2019). Ranking fog nodes for tasks scheduling in fog-cloud environments: A fuzzy logic approach. In 2019 15th International Wireless Communications & Mobile Computing Conference, (IWCMC) (pp. 1451–1457).
24. Jie, Y., Tang, X., Choo, K. K. R., Su, S., Li, M., and Guo, C. (2018). Online task scheduling for edge computing based on repeated Stackelberg game. *Journal of Parallel and Distributed Computing*, 122, 159–172.
25. Jamil, B., Ijaz, H., Shojafar, M., Munir, K., and Buyya, R. (2022). Resource allocation and task scheduling in fog computing and internet of everything environments: A taxonomy, review, and future directions. ACM Computing Surveys (CSUR), 54(11s), 1–38.
26. Ometov, A., Molua, O. L., Komarov, M., and Nurmi, J. (2022). A survey of security in cloud, edge, and fog computing. *Sensors*, 22(3), 927.
27. Hosseini, E., Nickray, M., and Ghanbari, S. (2022). Optimized task scheduling for cost-latency trade-off in mobile fog computing using fuzzy analytical hierarchy process. *Computer Networks*, 206, 108752.

66 Fuzzy assignment model with fuzzy approach

Dr. Seema Mishra[a]

Department of Mathematics: School of Chemical Engineering and Physical Sciences, Lovely Professional University, Phagwara, Punjab-144411, India

Abstract

The assignment problem is a based on different combination and optimization that seeks to find the best way to assign sources to available tasks, with certain constraints and objectives. In fuzzy logic-based assignment problems, the cell values are represented as fuzzy values or fuzzy sets, which can capture the uncertainty or imprecision in the values. The present work includes the assignment problem modelled as a hexagonal and octagonal fuzzy matrix, where each cell of the matrix represents the degree of compatibility between a resource and a task. This degree of compatibility is represented by a fuzzy number, which takes into account not only the objective criteria (such as cost or time) but also the subjective preferences and opinions of the decision maker.

Keywords: Assignment problem, fuzzy logic, hexagonal fuzzy number(HFN), octagonal fuzzy number (OFN)

Introduction

The allocation problem to optimize that arises for various fields such as operations management, human resources management, logistics, and scheduling. The problem involves assigning sources with the task with the goal of minimizing the cost or time required to complete the tasks. The allocation problem can take different forms depending on the context in which it arises. For example, in the context of human resources management, the problem may involve assigning employees with different skills and abilities to different projects or tasks based on their expertise and availability. In logistics, the problem may involve assigning delivery routes to a set of vehicles to minimize the total distance travelled or the time required to complete the deliveries.

Solving the allocation problem can be challenging because of the combinatorial nature of the problem. The number of possible assignments can grow exponentially with the size of the problem, making it computationally infeasible to evaluate all possible solutions. Therefore, different optimization techniques such as heuristic algorithms, mathematical programming, and simulation-based approaches are used to find good solutions to the allocation problem. In traditional assignment problems, the cost or profit values are assumed to be precise and deterministic. However, in real-world scenarios, these values may be uncertain or imprecise due to various factors such as incomplete information, human judgment, or measurement errors. Fuzzy logic provides a framework for dealing with such uncertainties by allowing the use of fuzzy sets and fuzzy rules. Several

[a]seema.14846@lpu.co.in

research works include the idea of fuzzy approach. The paper [1] presents a new approach for solving a hexagonal FAP using a novel ranking procedure for the HFN's. The work aimed at minimizing the cost of assigning under the fuzzy nature of the problem. The proposed approach employs a new ranking technique that uses a combination of fuzzy logic and hexagonal fuzzy numbers to rank the agents based on their suitability for each task. This technique reduces the iterative steps required to find an optimal solution while comparing it to existing methods.

The efficiency of the work done is demonstrated through numerical. The obtained results depicted that the work done is capable of producing optimal solutions with fewer iterations. The paper [2] proposes a novel procedure to rank the HFN's and applies it to solve fuzzy sequential LPPs. The proposed ranking method considers five criteria for ranking generalized hexagonal fuzzy numbers: area, mode, divergence, spreads, and weights. The algorithm and the steps are illustrated with numerical examples to demonstrate its effectiveness.

The proposed method in [3] seems to be a column generation approach, which optimize each column separately and then select the best choice among them. This can be an effective technique for solving large-scale problems, as it allows the focus on the most promising options and avoid the combinatorial explosion of the search space. The use of trapezoidal fuzzy numbers to represent uncertain or imprecise information in the problem. Fuzzy numbers are a popular tool in fuzzy logic and decision making, as they allow you to express degrees of membership or possibility for a value or a range of values. The robust ranking method is also a useful technique for comparing and ranking fuzzy numbers, based on their dominance or non-dominance relationships. The research work proposed in [4] introduces a new type of fuzzy number called Intuitionistic HFN. The paper's objective is to apply this new fuzzy number to the Intuitionistic form of Fuzzy Transportation problem. The authors' performed various operations to obtain an IBFS and the most likely solution to the Intuitionistic form of the Fuzzy Transportation problem. They illustrate their method with numerical. [5] describes a new algorithm for solving the FAP that combines maximizing each column during the optimization process with selecting the best choice with the lowest cost. The algorithm uses trapezoidal fuzzy numbers and the robust ranking method to convert crisp numbers, and verified by a numerical example. [6] presents an algorithm that is specifically designed to address the FAP, for cell values as fuzzy instead of crisp numbers. The paper [7] proposes a new idea for finding the optimised solution to FAP involving OFNs. The paper then applies this method to a numerical problem and evaluates its optimality using the best candidate method with the minimum number of computations.

The research paper work done in [8] considers a FAP where the values are represented as OFNs. To solve the problem, the fuzzy values get converted into crisp values by the Root Mean Square method. The optimum schedule is then obtained using the usual Hungarian Method, which is a well-known algorithm for solving assignment problems. The paper presents an example to illustrate how the proposed approach works in practice. It is commendable that the government is paying more attention to the issue of declining green natural resources and greenhouse gas emissions. Green technology can play a vital role in reducing these negative impacts and promoting sustainable development. The research work [9] has the potential to contribute to the development of more sustainable practices and policies that take into account the environmental costs of production and consumption. It can help to promote the use of green technology and encourage businesses and individuals to adopt more environmentally friendly measures. It is interesting to note that the inventory cost parameters are not fixed and may vary as per the market conditions. A fuzzy inventory problem model as described in [10] can incorporate these uncertainties and provide a more accurate measure of optimality. In the case of an inflationary backdrop, pentagonal and hexagonal fuzzy numbers are used to define the inexactness in the cost parameters. In the fuzzy inventory problem model, the defuzzification of the fuzzified total cost is done using the signed distance method. This method involves finding the signed distance between the centroid of the fuzzy set and the centre of the universe of discourse.

The paper is suggesting a novel procedure to the ambiguity allocation problem that leverages fuzzy Hexagonal and Octagonal fuzzy numbers and a distortion technique on the given data points to obtain a crisp matrix. The paper likely provides more detailed information on the proposed method, including its theoretical underpinnings, empirical validation, and potential applications.

Pre-Requisites

A fuzzy value $\tilde{K}$ with membership function $\phi_{\tilde{K}}: W \rightarrow [0,1]$ has:

(i) $\tilde{K}$ is convex and normal.
(ii) $\phi_{\tilde{K}}(w) = 1$ with $w \in \mathbb{R}$
(iii) $\phi_{\tilde{K}}(w)$ is continuous in $[0,1]$

Hexagonal Fuzzy Number (HFN)

Let HFN be $\tilde{K}_h = (h_{w1}, h_{w2}, h_{w3}, h_{w4}, h_{w5}, h_{w6}, x)$ where $h_{w1} \leq h_{w2} \leq h_{w3} \leq h_{w4} \leq h_{w5} \leq h_{w6}$. The membership function of HFN is $\phi_{\tilde{K}_h}(w)$ given as:

$$\phi_{R_h}(z) = \begin{cases} 0, & w < h_{w1} \\ \dfrac{x}{2}\left(\dfrac{w - h_{w1}}{h_{w2} - h_{w1}}\right), & h_{w1} \leq w \leq h_{w2} \\ \dfrac{x}{2} + \dfrac{x}{2}\left(\dfrac{w - h_{w2}}{h_{w3} - h_{w2}}\right), & h_{w2} \leq w \leq h_{w3} \\ x, & h_{w3} \leq w \leq h_{w4} \\ \dfrac{x}{2} - \dfrac{x}{2}\left(\dfrac{w - h_{w4}}{h_{w5} - h_{w4}}\right), & h_{w4} \leq w \leq h_{w5} \\ \dfrac{x}{2}\left(\dfrac{h_{w6} - w}{h_{w6} - h_{w5}}\right), & h_{w5} \leq w \leq h_{w6} \end{cases}$$

Ranking for Generalised HFN

The crisp measure to the HFN using the centre for the triangle and the rectangle is given by:

$$\frac{2h_{w1} + 4h_{w2} + 3h_{w3} + 3h_{w4} + 4h_{w5} + 2h_{w6}}{18}, \frac{13\varkappa}{36}$$

Octagonal Fuzzy Number (OFN)

Let OFN be $\tilde{O}_f = (o_{w1}, o_{w2}, o_{w3}, o_{w4}, o_{w5}, o_{w6}, \varkappa)$ where $o_{w1} \leq o_{w2} \leq o_{w3} \leq o_{w4} \leq o_{w5} \leq o_{w6}$. The membership function is $\phi_{\tilde{O}_f}(w)$ given as:

$\phi_{\tilde{O}_f}(w)$

$$= \begin{cases} 0, & w < o_{w1} \\ \varkappa\left(\dfrac{w - o_{w1}}{o_{w2} - o_{w1}}\right), & o_{w1} \leq w \leq o_{w2} \\ \varkappa, & o_{w2} \leq w \leq o_{w3} \\ \varkappa + (1 - \varkappa)\left(\dfrac{w - o_{w3}}{o_{w4} - o_{w3}}\right), & o_{w3} \leq w \leq o_{w4} \\ 1, & o_{w4} \leq w \leq o_{w5} \\ \varkappa + (1 - \varkappa)\left(\dfrac{o_{z6} - w}{o_{w6} - o_{w5}}\right), & o_{w5} \leq w \leq o_{w6} \\ \varkappa, & o_{w6} \leq w \leq o_{w7} \\ \varkappa\left(\dfrac{o_{w8} - w}{o_{w8} - o_{w7}}\right), & o_{w7} \leq w \leq o_{w8} \\ 0, & w \geq o_{w8} \end{cases}$$

Ranking for Generalised OFN

The crisp measure to the OFN using the centre for the triangle and the rectangle is given by:

$$\frac{2o_{w1} + 7o_{w2} + 10o_{w3} + 8o_{w4} + 8o_{w5} + 7o_{w6} + 7o_{w7} + 2o_{w8}}{54}, \frac{8\varkappa}{27}$$

Mathematical Model of Assignment Problem

Consider a matrix C of size m × m, where each element c_{pq} represents the cost or profit associated with assigning task p to agent q.

The Assignment Problem can be given as:

Maximize/Minimize

$T = \sum_{p=1}^{\infty} \sum_{q=1}^{\infty} c_{pq} \cdot x_{pq}$

Subject to:

$\sum_{q=1}^{\infty} x_{pq}$, for p = 1, 2, ..., m (each task assigned to exactly one agent)

$\sum_{p=1}^{\infty} x_{pq}$, for q = 1, 2, ..., m (each agent performs at most one task)

$x_{pq} \in \{0,1\}$, for p, q = 1, 2, ..., n (the decision variable x_{pq} takes binary values indicating whether task p is assigned to agent q or not)

where $x_{pq} = 1$ if task p is assigned to agent q and $x_{pq} = 0$ otherwise.

Proposed Method

The matrix also known as the cost matrix, in the form of a square matrix with row representing worker and column representing a task. The element in row x and column y represents the cost of assigning worker x to task y (or the profit gained from that assignment). The steps to determine the optimal allocation are as follows:

1. Determining the crisp value to every cell of the matrix which is in the form of HFN and OFN.
2. The minimum value of every row and column is subtracted from each element of the row and column respectively. This step is called row and column reduction.
3. The second step ensures the availability of at least one zero in every column and row. Move to assign the single zero either in row or column.
4. Continue assigning the zero in the row and cancelling the zero in respective column. This will make the optimal allocation done.
5. The minimised value to the cost is determined by adding the cost values at allocated zeros from the original cost matrix.

Simulation

The matrix below shows the cost values for four persons P,Q,R and S with four task columns to be assigned. The cost values are represented by HFN in Matrix 2 and by OFN in Matrix 3. The objective is to figure out the most likely allocation of the tasks to the persons such that the cost is minimised.

The cost matrix with crisp values:

$$
c_{xy} = \begin{array}{c} \\ P \\ Q \\ R \\ S \end{array}
\begin{array}{cccc}
T_1 & T_2 & T_3 & T_4 \\
\left[\begin{array}{cccc}
30 & 7 & 11 & 13 \\
9 & 5 & 16 & 9 \\
14 & 11 & 13 & 9 \\
15 & 25 & 20 & 21
\end{array}\right]
\end{array}
$$

Applying the above-mentioned procedure, the optimal allocation of task is as follows:

$$P = T_3, Q = T_2, R = T_4, S = T_1$$

With the optimal cost as: 40 UNITS
Taking the cost values as HFN the above matrix reduces to Matrix 1:

	T_1	T_2	T_3	T_4
c_{xy}				
P	(28,29,30,31,31,32,1)	(3,5,7,9,11,12,1)	(5,7,8,11,14,15,1)	(3,7,11,15,19,24,1)
$= Q$	(2,4,6,9,11,13,1)	(2,3,4,5,7,9,1)	(10,12,14,16,20,24,1)	(1,3,9,12,15,17,1)
R	(7,9,11,14,18,22,1)	(6,7,9,11,13,16,1)	(9,11,13,16,18,20,1)	(2,4,6,9,12,15,1)
S	(6,9,15,15,20,25)	(23,24,25,25,26,27,1)	(18,19,20,20,21,22,1)	(11,14,17,21,25,30,1)

Applying the generalised HFN to change the above fuzzy values to crisp values, Matrix 2 reduces to

$$
C_{xy} = \begin{array}{c} \\ \\ P \\ Q \\ R \\ S \end{array}
\begin{array}{cccc}
T_1 & T_2 & T_3 & T_4 \\
\end{array}
\left[\begin{array}{cccc}
8.3 & 2.1 & 2.8 & 3.6 \\
2.1 & 1.4 & 4.4 & 2.7 \\
3.7 & 2.8 & 4 & 2.2 \\
4.1 & 7 & 5.6 & 5.4
\end{array}\right]
$$

Again using the said methodology to find the allocation, we get:

$$P= T_3, Q= T_2, R= T_4, S= T_1$$

With the optimal cost as: 6.9 UNITS

Taking the cost values as OFN the above matrix reduces to Matrix 3:

$$
C_{xy} =
\begin{array}{c}
P \\ Q \\ R \\ S
\end{array}
\left[\begin{array}{cccc}
(28,29,30,31,31,32,32,33,1) & (3,5,7,9,11,12,15,16,1) & (5,7,8,11,14,15,18,20,1) & (3,7,11,15,19,24,25,27,1) \\
(2,4,6,9,11,13,17,20,1) & (2,3,4,5,7,9,10,12,1) & (10,12,14,16,20,24,26,28,1) & (1,3,9,12,15,17,18,20,1) \\
(7,9,11,14,18,22,25,27,1) & (6,7,9,11,13,16,18,20,1) & (9,11,13,16,18,20,22,23,1) & (2,4,6,9,12,15,16,18,1) \\
(6,9,15,15,20,25,27,30,1) & (23,24,25,25,26,27,28,30,1) & (18,19,20,20,21,22,30,35,1) & (11,14,17,21,25,30,32,35,1)
\end{array}\right]
$$

with T_1, T_2, T_3, T_4 as column headers.

Applying the generalised OFN to change the above fuzzy values to crisp values, Matrix 3 reduces to

$$
C_{xy} = \begin{array}{c} \\ \\ P \\ Q \\ R \\ S \end{array}
\begin{array}{cccc}
T_1 & T_2 & T_3 & T_4 \\
\end{array}
\left[\begin{array}{cccc}
8.6 & 2.7 & 3.3 & 4.8 \\
2.8 & 1.7 & 5.1 & 3.4 \\
4.5 & 3.4 & 4.6 & 2.8 \\
5.1 & 7.2 & 6.2 & 6.4
\end{array}\right]
$$

Again, using the said methodology to find the allocation, we get:

$$P= T_3, Q= T_2, R= T_4, S= T_1$$

With the optimal cost as: 12.9 UNITS

Conclusion

The study proposes an advanced idea to solve the Hexagonal and Octagonal FAP. This method of centroid is employed to solve the FAP into a crisp value assignment problem. Then, the classical method is applied for the best possible allocation. The advantage of the method adopted in this work takes comparatively lesser time than original and is also easy in application. The numerical presented demonstrates the effectiveness of the mentioned process, and the solution so determined is proven to be optimal with a comparison being done with the two different types of fuzzy numbers. Overall, the study presents a promising approach for solving fuzzy assignment problems, and further research could explore its potential applications in various fields.

References

1. Thiruppathi, A., and C. K. Kirubhashankar, (2021). Novel fuzzy assignment problem using hexagonal fuzzy numbers. *Journal of Physics: Conference Series*, 1770(1), 012062. IOP Publishing, 2021.
2. Gani, A. N., and Saleem, R. A. (2017). A new ranking approach on fuzzy sequential linear programming problem. *International Journal of Pure and Applied Mathematics*, 117(11), 345–355.
3. Gani, A. N., and Mohamed, V. N. (2013). Solution of a fuzzy assignment problem by using a new ranking method. *International Journal of Fuzzy Mathematical Archive*, 2, 8–16.
4. Thamaraiselvi, A., and Santhi, R. (2015). On intuitionistic fuzzy transportation problem using hexagonal intuitionistic fuzzy numbers. *International Journal of Fuzzy Logic Systems*, 5(1), 15–28.
5. Thiruppathi, A., and Iranian, D. (2015). An innovative method for finding optimal solution to assignment problems. *International Journal of Innovative Research in Science, Engineering and Technology*, 4(8), 7366–7370.
6. Dinagar, D. S., and Thiripurasundari, K. (2014). A new method for finding the cost of fuzzy assignment problem using genetic algorithm of artificial intelligence. *International Electronic Journal of Pure and Applied Mathematics*, 8(4), 2014, 13–22.
7. Vinoliah, E. M., and Ganesan, K. (2018). Fuzzy optimal solution for a fuzzy assignment problem with octagonal fuzzy numbers. *Journal of Physics: Conference Series*, 1000(1), 012016. IOP Publishing, 2018.
8. Santhi, G., and Ananthanarayanan, M. (2022). Solving fuzzy assignment problem using root mean square method. Advances and Applications in Mathematical Sciences. 21(11), September 2022, 6415–6423.
9. Singh, V., Saxena, S., Gupta, R. K., Singh, P., and Mishra, N. K. (2018). Fuzzified inventory ordering model for green environmental sustainability under Inflation. *Journal of Emerging Technologies and Innovative Research (JETIR)*. October 2018, 5(10), 606–616.
10. Gupta, R. K., Saxena, S., Singh, V., Singh, P., and Mishra, N. K. (2020). An inventory ordering model with different defuzzification techniques under inflation. *Journal of Computational and Theoretical Nanoscience*, 17(6), 2621–2625.

67 Design of low-cost smart wheelchair system to provide advance notifications related to pavement anomalies and objects on the path

Harinder Pal Singh[a] and Ramandeep Singh[b]

Lovely Faculty of Technology and Sciences, Lovely Professional University, Phagwara, India

Abstract

Persons with disabilities use wheelchair to move from one location to another indoors or in an open area. Many times they meet with accidents and get injured or feel helpless due to pavement anomalies or by hitting the objects in the path. In this paper we have proposed a smart wheelchair design fitted with accelerometer, GPS and ultrasonic sensors interfaced to an *Arduino UNO* microcontroller board. So it can detect objects in real time and captures the pavement anomalies so that when the wheelchair crosses the same pavement in can notify the person using audio notification about the pavement anomaly approaching. The Z-Threshold algorithm provided good results by selecting a threshold value of acceleration provided by the accelerometer. *GPS* sensor was used to capture the location coordinates to maintain the anomaly data on the path. Ultrasonic sensor detected objects on the way in real-time to avoid hitting those objects while moving. This work could help people with disability to avoid a lot of problems that arise while using wheelchair.

Keywords: Accelerometer, navigation, pavement anomalies, ultrasonic, wheelchair

Introduction

Wheelchair is used by people having difficulty in walking due to certain medical conditions. As per WHO, 1 billion people are having some sort of disability Morad et al. [13]. Sometimes an attendant is also available to assist the person to mobilize the wheelchair or turn towards left or right to avoid the objects in the path. These objects could be the people or other things and the pavement anomalies. People or the things can change their position but pavement anomalies like cracks, joins, raised or uneven pavement Alaamri et al. [1] remain there for a longer time, may be weeks or months. Smart wheelchairs(SW) have been the topic of interest for researchers for a long time. These wheelchairs could be manual or motorized with a joystick to control the motion. Object avoidance, tongue controlled, accelerometer based, thought based and voice command based motion controlling are some of the latest researches done to make the wheelchair smart. Fall detection is also there, so some relative or somebody nearby could be informed about the same. Line following the wheelchair within the house was also proposed so that it can move within the house without the need of an attendant Shoovo et al. [16]. Camera unit was also proposed to

[a]Harinder85@gmail.com, [b]Ramandeep.singh@lpu.co.in

capture the live images and process them in real time to detect and avoid collision with objects Lecrosnier et al. [9]. It required an embedded PC to perform the image processing in real time and notify. Infrared transceiver modules and ultrasonic sensors are some of the low cost devices used for object detection purposes. LIDAR sensors are also popular to measure the distance from the target object and create a 3D image of the surroundings Arboleda et al. [3]. These LIDAR and image processing systems are very costly Vivacqua et al. [18]. Making a wheelchair smart to detect the objects and easy navigation via joystick, voice commands, accelerometers Hassani et al. [8] are the researches done so far. While reviewing the literature it was found that the focus is on wheelchair design only. None of the researchers talked about the pavement and the pavement anomalies where this wheelchair is to be used for by the disabled person. It could be a closed campus, a street, park etc. A person on a wheelchair crossing the section of pavement having anomalies can meet with an accident if anomalies go unnoticed. It may injure the person in a wheelchair if he/she falls down after hitting the anomaly. This problem could be reduced up to a certain extent by designing a smart wheelchair Simpson et al. [17] that can detect these pavement anomalies and make a database for the same. So when the wheelchair will cross on the same pavement again, an audio notification could be generated to alert the person about the road anomaly approaching. In the case of a motorized wheelchair it could go a step further by slowing down the speed of the wheelchair with the help of a motor controller. In this paper we are proposing a smart wheelchair design that can detect pavement anomalies like cracks, joins, raised pavement, doorways and make a database for the same. So when the person on a wheelchair crosses the pavement section again, a notification in the form of sound could be generated to alert the person about a pavement anomaly approaching. Object detection Rajagopal et al. [15] in real time will be the other aspect of the proposed smart wheelchair where it can detect the objects on path so the wheels should not hit the object.

Proposed System

Concept of this study is based upon the vertical acceleration of wheelchair to the ground surface. Below given Figure 67.1 gives the different phases of proposed

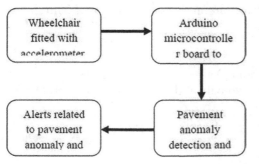

Figure 67.1 Flowchart of the proposed system

system. Wheelchair is fitted with sensors and controller (Arduino UNO) for data acquisition. Pavement anomalies are detected as per the specified algorithm and alerts are generated for both, anomalies and objects on the path.

Data Collection/Hardware Setup

Pavement anomalies create vibrations. When a wheelchair hits the anomaly, it creates sudden vibrations of higher level as compared to the pavement with no anomalies. Our work is based on these vibrations. Accelerometers were used to measure these vibrations Singh and Singh [14]. Two ADXL345 accelerometers Devices [2], were used for this purpose namely A1 and A2 fitted on front-right and fitted on front-left of the wheelchair just above the front wheels. Neo 6-M GPS transceiver Electroschematics.com [6] was used to collect the location coordinates of anomalies. Arduino UNO Arduino [5], board based on AtMega328 microcontroller was used to interface accelerometers and GPS a transceiver. Memory Card for storage. A 9 volt battery was used to power the circuit during the demo run. Z-axis acceleration in perpendicular to the road(vertical) provides required data to determine the anomalies Madli et al. [10]. Sampling frequency was kept at 1Hz for GPS as well as accelerometer. Two ultrasonic sensors, HC-SR04 were used to detect objects on the path. Both sensors were fitted on the front-left and front-right side of the wheelchair in forward direction. Buzzers were also used to generate notifications in the form of audio tone.

Pavement Anomaly Detection

Pavement anomalies were detected based on Z-axis acceleration Z1 and Z2 captured by accelerometer A1 and A2 respectfully. We tried to keep it simple to reduce the hardware requirements and cost. So the Z-Threshold Eriksson et al. [7] Mednis et al. [11] Mohan et al. [12] method for event detection was used to determine the anomalies. It is a very simple algorithm to detect anomalies as it records the Z-axis values exceeding a predefined threshold limit, i.e 20 in our case as shown in Figure 67.3. This value of Z was selected after having multiple trials of the proposed system. Z-axis acceleration is known for this by calibrating the accelerometer to Zero when the data collection starts. So basically it identifies the outliers. The location coordinates for these outliers are stored as pavement anomalies. Algorithm 1 explains the procedure to capture pavement anomalies on the path based on Z-Threshold value.

Algorithm 1 : Pavement anomaly detection on the path based on Z-Threshold
Input: Real-time Az(i), Long(i), Lat(i)
Step 1: Collect sample data
Step 2: Analysis of event sample
      Step 2.1: If Az(i) > Z_Threshold _Value then
      Step 2.2: Mark as pavement anomaly and record location coordinates: Long(i), Lat(i)
      Step 2.3: Else No Anomaly, Discard collected data
Step 3: Repeat Step 1
Step 4: Exit.

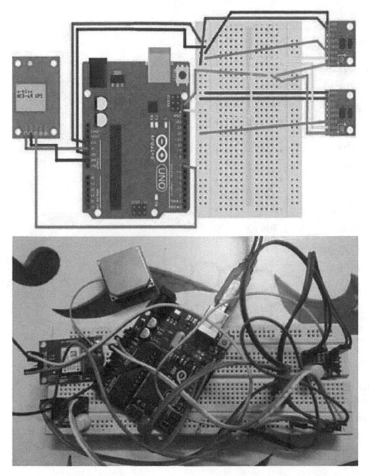

Figure 67.2 Prototype and circuit diagram of proposed system

Object Detection

Object detection was performed to find the objects at low height which may go unnoticed to the person controlling the movement of the wheelchair. For this two ultrasonic sensors HC-SR04 were used. Ultrasonic sensor uses a transmitter and receiver to transmit and capture the reflected ultrasonic waves. Based on the time taken to receive the reflected waves, it calculates the distance. It can detect objects near to two meter range. We set up the range to 70cm to detect the object approaching. Buzzers were used on both sides of the wheelchair so a sound notification should be generated to the side where the object is detected. In this way the wheelchair could be moved in another direction or breaks could be applied Arduino.cc [4].

Algorithm 2: Detection of physical objects on the path based on distance value given by Ultrasonic sensor.

Input: Real time data from ultrasonic sensor Uss(i)

Table 67.1 Sample data set

Z1	Z2	GPS Lat	GPS Long	Object
6	4	30.88989	75.70412	174
18	-2	30.88989	75.70412	173
12	12	30.88989	75.70412	172
8	-2	30.88989	75.70412	303
-4	10	30.88989	75.70412	303
-8	2	30.88989	75.70412	357
-8	-6	30.88989	75.70412	357
-12	-18	30.88989	75.70412	357
-8	-2	30.88989	75.70412	306
-6	2	30.88989	75.70412	338
0	6	30.88989	75.70412	75
-10	0	30.88989	75.70412	78
12	-10	30.88989	75.70412	71
14	-8	30.88989	75.70412	357

Step 1: Collect ultrasonic sensor sample data
Step 2: Analysis of event sample Uss(i)
      Step2.1: If Uss(i) > Distance_Value
      Step 2.2: Set Object_Status= True
            Generate Audio Alert
Step 3: Repeat Step 2
Step 4: Exit.

Results and Analysis
Surface conditions are dynamic, they keep on changing. Detection of the surface anomalies is totally dependent on the orientation of accelerometer sensor. As the speed of wheelchair is very slow, some of the anomalies may get unnoticed. Whenever a jerk is noticed, it will be noted as an anomaly. Sometimes false alarms are also generated. Object detection is a real time task and accuracy is high in this.

Conclusion and Future Scope

In this paper we have proposed a system to detect pavement anomalies and objects for the person using a wheelchair because of disability by using limited hardware resources to reduce the overall cost of the system. Accelerometer collected data related to Z-axis provided the required data to identify the pavement anomalies. Ultrasonic sensors provide object detection in reSal time. This could help the person in a wheelchair to avoid accidents or hitting objects on the path. The recorded

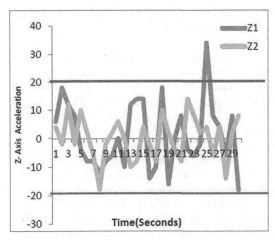

Figure 67.3 Z-axis acceleration data acquired using accelerometers A1 and A2

surface data can help in providing prior information about the surface anomaly approaching so it could be avoided.

Fall detection implementation could be considered in the future so that an alarm could be raised to ask for help. GSM module or Bluetooth connectivity could also be implemented to send a notification in the form of SMS so a relative or caretaker can enquire about the condition of the person. Machine learning can help in detecting false alarms.

References

1. Alaamri, R. S. N., Kattiparuthi, R. A., and Koya, A. M. (2017). Evaluation of flexible pavement failures-a case study on Izki road. *International Journal of Advanced Engineering, Management and Science*, 3(7), 741–749. https://doi.org/10.24001/ijaems.3.7.6.
2. Devices, A. (n.d.). ADXL345 datasheet and product info analog devices. Retrieved from https://www.analog.com/en/products/adxl345.html#product-overview.
3. Arboleda, E. R., Alegre, M. C. T., and Idica, K. F. (2015). Development of a low-cost electronic wheelchair with obstacle avoidance feature. *Journal of Mechatronics, Electrical Power, and Vehicular Technology*, 6(2), 89–96. https://doi.org/10.14203/j.mev.2015.v6.89-96.
4. Arduino.cc. (n.d.). Obstacle avoiding car - arduino project hub. Retrieved May 20, 2022, from https://create.arduino.cc/projecthub/adam/obstacle-avoiding-car-a192d9?ref=search&ref_id=autonome car&offset=40.
5. Arduino. (n.d.). Arduino Uno Rev3 Arduino Official Store. Retrieved from https://store.arduino.cc/usa/arduino-uno-rev3.
6. Electroschematics.com. (n.d.). NEO-6M GPS Module — An Introduction. Retrieved from https://www.electroschematics.com/neo-6m-gps-module/.
7. Eriksson, J., Girod, L., Hull, B., Newton, R., Madden, S., and Balakrishnan, H. (2008). The pothole patrol: using a mobile sensor network for road surface monitoring. In Proceeding of the 6th International Conference on Mobile Systems, Applications, and Services – MobiSys, 08, 29. https://doi.org/10.1145/1378600.1378605.

8. Hassani, R., Boumehraz, M., Hamzi, M., and Habba, Z. (2018). Gyro-accelerometer based control of an intelligent wheelchair. *Journal of Applied Engineering Science and Technology*, 4(1), 101–107.

9. Lecrosnier, L., Khemmar, R., Ragot, N., Decoux, B., Rossi, R., Kefi, N., and Ertaud, J. Y. (2021). Deep learning-based object detection, localisation and tracking for smart wheelchair healthcare mobility. *International Journal of Environmental Research and Public Health*, 18(1), 1–17. https://doi.org/10.3390/ijerph18010091.

10. Madli, R., Hebbar, S., Pattar, P., and Prasad, G. V. (2015). Automatic detection and notification of potholes and humps on roads to aid drivers. *IEEE Sensors Journal*, 15(8), 4313–4318. 15(c). https://doi.org/10.1109/JSEN.2015.2417579.

11. Mednis, A., Strazdins, G., Zviedris, R., Kanonirs, G., and Selavo, L. (2011). Real time pothole detection using android smartphones with accelerometers. In IEEE International Conference on Distributed Computing in Sensor Systems and Workshops (DCOSS), 7th(10), (pp. 1–6). https://doi.org/10.1109/DCOSS.2011.5982206.

12. Mohan, P., Padmanabhan, V. N., and Ramjee, R. (2008). Nericell: rich monitoring of road and traffic conditions using mobile smartphones. In Proceedings of the 6th ACM conference on Embedded network sensor systems - SenSys ', 08 (pp. 323–336). https://doi.org/10.1145/1460412.1460444.

13. Morad, M., Kandel, I., and Merrick, J. (2004). Disability and health. Retrieved May 19, 2022, from https://www.who.int/news-room/fact-sheets/detail/disability-and-health.

14. Singh, H. P., and Singh, R. (2021). Low cost data acquisition system for road-vehicle interaction using arduino board. *Journal of Physics: Conference Series*, 1831(1), 012031. https://doi.org/10.1088/1742-6596/1831/1/012031.

15. Rajagopal, S., Samundeeswari, N., Srivastava, A., and Mandal, M. (2022). Object detection for the blind using haptic technology. *ECS Transactions*, 107(1), 11707–11715. https://doi.org/10.1149/10701.11707ecst.

16. Shoovo, G. R., Dey, B., Akash, K., Motahara, T., and Imam, M. H. (2021). Design of a line following wheelchair for visually impaired paralyzed patient. In International Conference on Robotics, Electrical and Signal Processing Techniques, (pp. 398–402). https://doi.org/10.1109/ICREST51555.2021.9331218.

17. Simpson, R., LoPresti, E., Hayashi, S., Nourbakhsh, I., and Miller, D. (2004). The smart wheelchair component system. *Journal of Rehabilitation Research and Development*, 41(3 B), 429–442. https://doi.org/10.1682/JRRD.2003.03.0032.

18. Vivacqua, R., Vassallo, R., and Martins, F. (2017). A low cost sensors approach for accurate vehicle localization and autonomous driving application. *Sensors (Switzerland)*, 17, 23–59. https://doi.org/10.3390/s17102359.

68 Comprehensive review of VANET technology: an impeccable study

Dr. Avinash Bhagat[1,a], Dr. Sonu Dua[2,b] and Jobanpreet[3,c]

[1]Associate Professor, School of Computer Application, Lovely Professional University, Punjab, India

[2]Associate Professor, Department of Management, Lyallpur Khalsa College Technical Campus, Punjab, India

[3]Assistant Officer Lovely Professional University, Punjab, India

Abstract

Wireless technology is advancing quickly over the time. Nowadays, the telecommunications industry is where most of the research works are going on. VANET is the area of wireless communication research that is expanding with significant speed. As the VANET grows and becomes more mature in terms of quick handovers, network availability, security, safety with the use of cutting-edge applications, etc., the field of wireless communication will experience a substantial change. Although the VANET technology is improving every time, several issues still need to be resolved before the network can perform more efficiently. In light of the aforementioned, we have explored and analysed number of research articles that are related to the applications, protocols, and security in VANET discussed in this study.

Keywords: Applications, attacks and network, security, techniques, VANET

Introduction

VANET Ad-hoc network is a Latin word that means temporarily nature. It is self-dependent or self-govern system of mobile hosts. These mobile hosts are connected via wireless connection that is called mobile ad-hoc network MANET. The MANET is a sub-technique of VANET's (vehicular ad-hoc networks). VANET is used for communication and safety purpose. It monitors the frequency channel band 5.9 GHz (controlling channel 5.9GHz frequency band used in America) medium- to long-distance communication. In either scenario, the topology is changing quickly in this example, at a rate of 30 miles per hour, at least it is in the city and the VANET network may be used for communication between vehicles as well as with units that are on the road (RSU) road side units [7].

Architecture

There are three types of communication in VANET to provide communications as well as safety in VANET network. The namely can be defined as inter-vehicles communication (I2V), vehicles-to-infrastructure communication and

[a]avinash.bhagat@lpu.co.in, [b]sonudua3778@gmail.com, [c]jobanpreet.27080@lpu.co.in

vehicles-to-vehicles communications (V2V) it is called as vehicles to road side unit (RSU) or vehicles-to-infrastructure communication (V2I) to allow safety in vehicles services [2, 6]. The infrastructure is basically is located around the roads and with the help of infrastructure vehicles can easily communicate with each other's that is called inter road side communication or infrastructure-to-infrastructure communication. VANET's having great influential technology that can deliver realistic vehicle to road side infrastructure communication (V2I). VANET's gives authorization to build intelligent transportations systems (ITS) that emphases on road safety, traveller's wellbeing, traffic efficiency to provide vehicles to vehicles communications. In VANET technology used for broad range for safety and non-safety applications. The VANET broad range can be shearing of multimedia information (animations, audio, video, text etc) and traffic control, congestions and collision in traffic control is help to avoiding accidents by distributed information. Figure 68.1 depicts VANET architecture [8]. In VANET's basically three types of devices to provides safety, traffic control and communication. Firstly, on board units (OBUs), it is help in vehicle to infrastructure communications and vehicles-to-vehicles (V2V) secondly, sensors to helps the check the conditions or situations around there (slippery, road, safety, distance etc) [9]

Applications

This is to minimize drivers' distraction through the Bluetooth, voice recording. Traffic control is the second application is that the govern master of reduce the congestion and is good for environment and good for peoples. Highway advisory radio about congestion, road conditions and navigation based on congestion and we could good congestion to get by the GPS system. If describe a Safety during running car crashes on the road are major cause of deaths of children aged 5 and above to overcome this type of vehicle's accidents The VANETs applications are classified of their importance. In upcoming paragraphs explained safety related

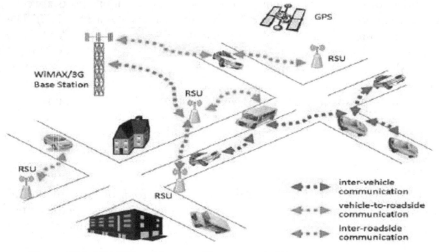

Figure 68.1 VANET architecture Sharma et al. [8]

applications [10, 13]. Safety Applications -The main motive of providing a safety application are increases the safety and it also used for protects the life. The vehicles are creating more congestion and unsafe area; to avoid this problem safety applications use as, e.g., between senders to receivers share their safe information with each other's in time through the help of safety applications. Applications are playing a major role in VANET like intelligent transportation system (ITS), applications related safety are included Assistance Message (AM), such as navigation, cooperative collision avoidance (CCA), and the lane changing. Information message (IMs) behave as speed limit and work Zone Information and Warning Message (WMs) such as old record crash, obstacle or road condition warnings. Aim of (CCA) application used for avoids the collision in the network. This safety application can be triggered by itself, when collision is present between vehicles. When the sender sends the warning message to the receiver end than driver receive the warning message during collision area vehicles are automatically reduce their speed [3].

Major Attacks-Passive Attacks- These attackers are intruders attacks in the wireless channels to get all the information about the user in traffic information, however those attacks are not involved in the communication process of the network, that is called as passive attacks. Active Attacks- These attackers can create the wrong information packet to send the receiver, however did not sending the further information to the receiver [1]. Insider Attacks- These attackers can authenticate the user network and this attacker having the all information about network. If they have full information about the user, it's easy for them to create the problem and attack the network. This network simply hacks the network than other's networks. Malicious Attacks- These types of the attackers are not taking own benefits from the networks. These attackers having main motive is to create the problem and disrupts the VANET network. These attacks are more hazardous because it can create heavy damage in the network which is not easy to remove. Black Hole Attacks- These types of attacks arise the problems when a node rejects to take part in the network, the node routed the network information to other's node which resulting data loss. Then, the attackers perform as DOS issue into the network.

VANET Technique

The methods that VANETs can use to protect the Network are outlined below. (CCH) Control Channel manages communication over short- to medium-range distances in the frequency channel band of 5.9 GHz, also known as the "controlling channel" frequency band in the United States. Both communication between cars and communication with units built surrounding the road (RSU) or roadside units may occur through the VANET network; in any instance, it is clear that the topology is changing extremely fast and that this approach operates at a speed of 30 mph. at the very least in the selected area [2, 5]. The frequency range is used in this dedicated short-range communication (DSRC), which was developed for communication purposes [12].

The frequency channels band (FCC) used by 5.850 to 5.925 GHz. The deducted short-range communication used standard IEEE802.11. p, and standard

IEEE1609.1.4. These techniques covered the area and spread the network up to 1km to 200 km/n. In the VANET technology used control channels to working on 5.9 GHz frequency bands and the number of controls channels to provide the services of 178, 174, 176, 180, and 182 over control channels [12]. The Global Positioning System (GPS) - This technology work for the wireless connection over any network media. The main task of this technology to stores the all information/data and time, this technology is also used for storing the location information for records [9]. Trusted Platform Module (TPM) – Through the help of (MD) Message Dispatcher it receives the information and converts the data information into digital form [5, 13]. Elliptic curve cryptography (ECD) module generates periodic message. Wireless Access in Vehicular Environment (WAVE) is used for safety and non-safety application vehicular ad-hoc network. WAVE enhanced safety message Delivery (WSD) [4, 11].

Related Work

VANET network is field of ad-hoc network for using communication purpose. The VANET is mainly used as a communication network as well as used for transportation system. This VANET network main motive is securing the communication between vehicles. In this paper the major motive is protect the network from Sybil attacks and also work on dynamic certificates generation technique which is working project on Sybil attacks. Using this technique, the neighbouring information is used to track the Sybil attacks and get secure the network by using dynamic certificates generation technique [10]. VANET is the subnet technique of MANET networks Mobile ad-hoc networks. This technique is providing the remote communication for vehicle to vehicles and vehicles to road side unit's communication networks. They give innovations when moving car to connect through the hub system. The main goal of this paper protects the traffic collision and avoidance the accidents on the roads. in this paper concludes that challenges and security techniques for VANETs network communication between vehicles to vehicle [2]. This paper provides the improvements and network safety data communication. In this paper denial of service describe the security of VANET environment to elaborate the area of network. This paper also provides the security network and specification are characterizes the network for VANET networks. Finally, this paper includes the specification of cellular automatically used techniques for authentication Vehicles with lesser delay and packet are losses. Table 68.1 shows mapping between VANET techniques and security [10]. In this review representing the vehicular-to-vehicular communication with it is provides the road side safety. This survey provides the communication between vehicles-to-vehicles communication with security to avoiding the traffic collision. This paper based on the properties of trust management in VANET network. They also describe the security for VANET network and some explain occurring attacks in the VANET communication media [1]. VANET is mainly solution of all the problems in the network of communication. The VANET network is basically play role on roads. In this paper defines the entities of VANET network and it's provided the security for VANET. Also defines the several types of attacks is present in the VANET network. In this paper using the technique of geographical location information and it locates the threads information to secure for VANET atmosphere. It generates the several types of security system in VANET require though number of components [11]. In this paper provides the Resent advances in VANET security a survey paper main focus on techniques of security. They provide the comprehensive overview of VANET networks and structure provides. In this includes security threats, security services, internet of things and security services focusing on importance of VANET security assignment tools [4]. In this survey of paper introduce the remote communication system between vehicles to roadside units and it is also providing the transformation in vehicles as a hub in a system to make a movable system. This portable system either used for as a switch and as a hub system, they include in this paper applications for this technique of remote communication system, they provide some security attacks to avoidance the traffic collision in network [12]. This paper provides the vehicular ad-hoc network technologies working on mobile routing networks protocols for inter vehicular communication network for supporting transportation system. They describe the future security attacks and analysis for attacks and possible future researches [13]. This paper presents the Survey on vehicular collision prediction in VANET network. Number of vehicles is increased now a day for security is more important for vehicle communication. In vehicular traffic collision is more than issue in VANET network to avoid these problems they provide some techniques and security-based specification for network [6].

This paper presents the Aspects and trends in realistic VANET simulations. In this paper presents the comprehensive architecture for VANET networks, also simulation for architecture results. These concepts are defining that real time world activities like as map; traffic volume are real time scenarios [3]. In this paper present vehicular network for communication purpose, this network is based for vehicle to infrastructure communications and vehicle to vehicle. It enhances security application to avoiding the traffic collision. This paper proposed the GPAS, general purpose automatic survey system with characteristics data information. This technique presents and characterized the location, time record information data and user interest [5].

Table 68.1 Mapping between VANET techniques and security [10]

SECURITY	TECHNIQUES
• Restrict the Sybil attack • Location information • Registration offence (authenticity)	• Dynamic certificate generation technique (DCGT)
• Storing sensitive information	• Trusted platform module (TPM)
• Reduce the traffic, data trust • Communication, working up to 1km at 200km/hr.	• Dedicated short range communication (DSRC)
• Communication, security, privacy, traffic management, internet access.	• (VANET) Vehicular ad-hoc network
• Secure, flexible and cost effective	• General purpose automatic survey system (GPAS)

Conclusion

This paper presents comprehensive review introduction in VANET. There is ad-hoc network is mainly a Latin phrase that means purpose of ad-hock network is communication between vehicles. This is a self-dependence or self-govern system of mobile hosts. These mobile hosts are connected via wireless a connection that is called mobile ad-hoc networks. Today scenario traffic increase day to day, 10.8 million vehicles crashed from 1990 to 2009, 60% accidents can be preventing increases by the implementation of VANET. To avoid this situation, we present in this research paper, to secure the vehicles by implementing security techniques. When vehicles to vehicles communication (V2V) some unwanted network is hack your device to overcome this problem, we using the security techniques like authenticity, confidentiality, id certificates, message suppression, traffic analysis, etc. including in this paper safety applications, knowledge about VANET vehicle model. Importance of communication interfaces of VANETs networks, and overcome the traffic collisions and security threats in VANET. There is comparison between Securities and Attacks in VANET network.

References

1. Ahmed, N., Deng, Z., Memon, I., Hassan, F., Mohammadani, K. H., and Iqbal, R. (2022). A survey on location privacy attacks and prevention deployed with IoT in vehicular networks. Wireless Communications and Mobile Computing, 2022, 1–15.
2. Avinash Bhagat, Manmohan Sharma, Ajay Shriram Kushwaha, Shilpa Sharma, Hussien Sobahi Mohammed, (2023). Nonlinear Energy Optimization in the Wireless Sensor Network through NN-LEACH, Mathematical Problems in Engineering, vol. 2023, Article ID 5143620, 9 pages, 2023. https://doi.org/10.1155/2023/5143620
3. Booyen, M. J., Zeadally, S., and Rooyen, G. J. (2011). Survey of media access control protocols for vehicular ad hoc networks. *IET Communications*, 5(11), 1619–1631.
4. Diallo, E. H., Dib, O., and Agha, K. A. (2022). A scalable blockchain-based scheme for traffic-related data sharing in VANETs. *Blockchain: Research and Applications*, 3(3), 100087.
5. Gholamhosseinian, A., and Seitz, J. (2021). Safety-centric vehicle classification using vehicular networks. *Procedia Computer Science*, 191, 238–245.
6. Khanna, H., and Sharma, M. (2022). An improved security algorithm for vanet using machine learning. *Journal of Positive School Psychology*, 6(3), 7743–756.
7. Mahmood, J., Duan, Z., Yang, Y., Wang, Q., Nebhen, J., and Bhutta, M. N. M. (2021). Security in vehicular ad hoc networks: challenges and countermeasures. Security and Communication Networks, 2021, 1–20.
8. Sharma, A. K., Saroj, S. K., Chauhan, S. K., and Saini, S. K. (2016). Sybil attack prevention and detection in vehicular Ad Hoc network. In 2016 International Conference on Computing, Communication and Automation (ICCCA), IEEE, (pp. 594–599).
9. Sheikh, M. S., Liang, J., and Wang, W. (2019). A survey of security services, attacks, and applications for vehicular ad hoc networks (vanets). Sensors, 19(16), 3589.
10. Sheikh, M. S., Liang, J., and Wang, W. (2020). Security and privacy in vehicular ad hoc network and vehicle cloud computing: a survey. *Wireless Communications and Mobile Computing*, 2020, 1–25.

11. Tanwar, S., Vora, J., Tyagi, S., Kumar, N., and Obaidat, M. S. (2018). A systematic review on security issues in vehicular ad hoc network. *Security and Privacy*, 1(5), e39.

12. Tashtoush, Y., Darweesh, D., Karajeh, O., Darwish, O., Maabreh, M., Swedat, S., ... and Alsaedi, N. (2022). Survey on authentication and security protocols and schemes over 5G networks. *International Journal of Distributed Sensor Networks*, 18(10), 15501329221126609.

13. Weber, J. S., Neves, M., and Ferreto, T. (2021). VANET simulators: an updated review. *Journal of the Brazilian Computer Society*, 27(1), 8.

69 Assessment of land use land cover change dynamics using remote sensing techniques: a review

Bazila Farooq[a] and Ankush Manocha

School of Computer Application, Lovely Professional University, Jalandhar, Punjab, India

Abstract

Land use and land cover change (LULCC) analyses have garnered much notice because of their importance to strategy implementation and long-term planning in a variety of locations as well as sizes. When it is severe and the pervasive LULCC may be devastating if not noticed and managed, disrupting essential components of environmental operations. Improvements in technology and methodologies within geographic information systems (GIS), satellite imaging (RS), machine and deep learning have been the subject of considerable scientific investigation for many years. With the help of these initiatives, several technologies for classifying land use and land cover at various levels have been developed. Giving comprehensive directions based on an evaluation of the literature to analyze, appraise, and spread such circumstances might be a valuable addition. As a result, thousands of relevant studies were selected and investigated from various databases (Google Scholar, Ieee xplore, and Web Of Science) showcasing improvements in land cover categorization techniques at various spectral, geographical, and temporal resolutions throughout the past centuries at the regional, local, and global levels. From a developmental perspective, this study aims to demonstrate the major tools, data, and methodology utilized for the analysis, assessment, identification, analysis, and observation of LULC, as well as to analyze certain relevant hurdles and constraints that may impact future operations' effectiveness.

Keywords: Land use land cover, machine learning, natural resource, remote sensing

Introduction

The Earth Observation System (EOS) program launched the ist artificial satellite in 1972, and the collection of information about the land surface and its assets has increased. That is partly owing to the work of Whole Globe Space Agencies, which has produced numerous images of distant sensing devices tied mostly to satellites and airplanes in public information in latest days, as well as advances in technology in the field of computer science with strong and effective processor cores to handle enormous amounts of information, as well as attempts to create rigorous methodologies for having to process such data [1–4]. The demand for satellite data in the surveillance of land use and land coverage has increased with our growing understanding of how changes in how land is used affect natural ecosystems. The understanding and measurement of the effects of changes in the landscape on the atmosphere are made possible by the use of this spatial data. To achieve this goal, images with improved spectral, radiometric, dimensional, and

[a]bazilafarooq02@gmail.com, [b]ankush.20556@lpu.co.in

temporal accuracy are essential that allow for the identification of huge regions in a relatively short time [5, 6], which supported the advancement of methods and procedures, allowing for the automating of mapping with solid findings for actuality. Nations that continue to be using conventional methods for remote sensing data computation, such as marketing software for image processing on computational cluster Computer systems with propositions to demonstrate how satellite imagery may be used and the advent of GIS packages, keeping aside extra research, including such underground modeling based on GIS [7], demonstrate severe limitations in their research on the subject of Big Data planning [6, 8]. Since, regardless of how strong the operating systems are, the whole procedure for analyzing data, comprising pre-processing across vast regions containing hundreds of images, is continuous, slow, and repetitive, and it can still be costly due to the high resource needs. Nonetheless, problems have indeed been addressed in countries that have opted to adapt their strategy. Progress has been achieved through the development and utilization of advanced frameworks for Machine Learning Approaches (MLA) and deep learning, enabling the evaluation of images at a global level with superior resolution quality [9]. This novel strategy, according to Mutanga et al. [10] may be carried out by scholars from less developed nations since it does not require the high processing capacity of machines. The goal of this article is to present and underline the most important methodologies, datasets, and tactics for Land Use and Land Cover (LULC) mapping concerns, as well as to explore a few obstacles that could come up in monitoring and assessing land use land cover using data from remote sensing along with offering a broad approach on LULC issues. Lately, the latest ideas in data capture and pre-processing had emerged, mostly as a result of global collaboration between NASA and other scientific institutions. The working relationship has produced a significant amount of data that is open to everyone, as well as software algorithms and instruments for handling and evaluating this kind of data [2, 11], providing the remote sensing sector with fresh tools and programs for doing research. This article's goal is to provide and emphasize the critical methodology, information, and strategies related to the challenges of assessing land use and land cover (LULC). It also explores some of the challenges that might come up while viewing and evaluating land use and land cover using remote sensing data, while also offering a thorough viewpoint on problems about LULC. The following themes are addressed in the following sequence throughout the article: 1) It focuses on the collecting and analysis of data from satellites at different scales. 2) Describes the various tools and technologies that can be used to examine such data. 3) addresses geographic information methodological approaches for land use land cover modeling, classifying them as pixel, subpixel, objects, and optimization strategies. 4) the results of analyzing land use and land cover data from multiple sources and scales using machine and deep learning methods and 5) accomplishments, challenges, and prospects for the future.

Data Collection and Processing from Remote Sensing

Data are the most important component of research, and remote sensing is among the primary methods of gathering spatial information [12]. Remote sensing (RS) data collection consists of four key elements: electromagnetic radiation (EMR), a source of light, sensors, and a destination, as well as the interactions of the EMR with the goals. Figure 69.1 depicts the essential parts of communication involved in the generation of valuable data.

It is feasible to create an item that serves a particular goal by considering all of the criteria described above it and following the methods of remote sensing data treatment. A comprehensive list of vendors and sources giving publicly available remotely sensed data on medium, fine, and coarse scales is provided in Table 69.1. However, it is customary to buy fine-scale evaluation information to obtain it. The utilization of information as well as employing appropriate approaches by competent experts is the key to maximizing the benefits of these instruments. Nevertheless, with remote sensing technologies, pre-processing and validation offer obstacles [14]. There are several remote sensing data packages available for certain research programs, but their resolutions fall short of what consumers need to undertake in-depth analyses of particular occurrences. [15, 16]. For example, evaluating forest fires necessitates high temporal and spatial resolution; however, a sensor could provide either of those. In the case of MODIS data, the geographical resolution is modest but the temporal resolution is great for one day. However, in the interest of better outcomes, their spatial resolution must be enhanced.

Public, Open Source, and Commercial Software: We distinguish between two kinds of information computation programs in the realm of remotely sensed science: technology that is both open/free source (Open and free Source) and private (Highly confidential) [17, 18], according to the following requirements: user interface, graphical user interface, assistance, software requirements, exertion, comprehensiveness, license, operating system dependency, expandability;

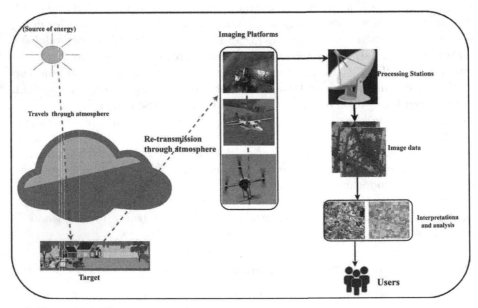

Figure 69.1 The remote sensing process

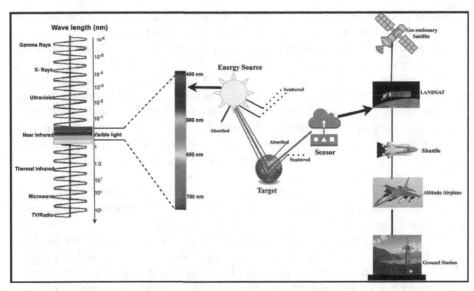

Figure 69.2 Electromagnetic spectrum displaying light waves, the solar, and the strength of the Globe. Source: Authors (2021)

Table 69.1 Shows the qualities of several sensors used in land cover research

Scale	Sensors	Provider/website
Coarse scale assessment	NOAA-AVHRR MODIS ENVISAT	NOAA: https://basedosdados.org/en/organization/nationaloceanic-and- atmospheric-administration-noaa NASA: http://modis.gsfc.nasa.gov/about ESA:https://earth.esa.int/web/guest/missions/esa-operational-eo-missions/envisat
Medium scale assessment	IRS LISS-III ASTER RADARSAT LANDSAT MSS/ TM/ETM+/OLI Sentinel 2	.ISRONRSC:https://uops.nrsc.gov.in/MetaSearch/RS2_LIS3_ST UC00GTD\ NASA: https://terra.nasa.gov/ CSA: https://www.asc-csa.gc.ca/eng/satellites/radarsat2/ USGS: https://earthexplorer.usgs.gov/. ESA: https://scihub.copernicus.eu/dhus/#/home
Fine-scale assessment	Worldview PAN/ MSS IRS LISS-IV Rapid Eye IKONOS PAN/MS	https://www.satimagingcorp.com/gallery/worldview-4/ ISRO-NRSC: https://uops.nrsc.gov.in/MetaSearch/RS2_LIS3_ST UC00GTD ESA:https://earth.esa.int/web/guest/missions/3rd-partymissions/current-missions/rapideye SATIMAGINGCORP:http://www.satimagingcorp.com/gallery/ikonos

maximum possible regulation [17, 19]. Figure 69.2 depicts electromagnetic spectrum displaying light waves, the solar, and the strength of the Globe.

Open Source: The notion of free software is connected to the liberty of reusing, change accept or rejecting, and redistribution, and to exercise some of the liberty, you must have a copy of the code [19, 21, 22]. As a result of their creators sharing their discoveries, the classifications are not adversarial but rather complementing [19]. The terms "free" and "open source" software should be used interchangeably because they enable 1) almost unlimited use, 2) the ability to investigate how a program operates and tailor it to your needs, 3) the ability to reallocate duplicates, and 4) the ability to advance to a higher level and share that knowledge withthegroup [20, 21].

Proprietary software: The primary goal of designing proprietary software is to earn financially. These applications are developed by people or businesses that have engineers on staff to improve their accessibility [23]. As a result, they forbid individuals from copying and redistributing the application, reselling the license to others, and/or code generation and violating patents and copyrights [22, 24]. Moreover, it may charge yearly licensing fees and infrequently permits end users to buy or examine the source code. As a result, users may struggle to understand whatever the software and/or devices are just doing. [17, 23, 24]. Table 69.2 displays the attributes of numerous cost-free software applications employed in a study of land cover.

Methods for Analyzing Remote Sensing Data for Land Use and Land Cover (LULC) Mapping

3.1. Monitoring Land Use and Land Cover (LULC): Despite the frequent interchangeability of the phrases "land use" and "land cover," comprehending the distinction is crucial. The expression "land use" encompasses alterations to the physical and chemical attributes of the land and the fundamental purpose or incentive driving these adjustments. Meanwhile, land cover pertains to the factual condition of the Earth's equatorial region and the adjacent subsurface.. [34, 35]. Land cover varieties provide various habitats and affect the interchange of carbon and energy between land-based and enclosing environments, according to Gómez et al. [34]. Planning and managing natural resources, modeling environmental conditions, and comprehending ecological dispersion all depend on an understanding of and evaluating land use and land cover [36]. Land cover varies naturally through time, as well as as a consequence of human actions. Defining land cover categories offers essential data for developing various themed images and establishing a baseline for monitoring operations. An efficient approach for identifying changes throughout time according to Rogan and Chen [19], may increase research resolution-related studies in the spatial as well as spectral domains by incorporating supplemental data, such as vegetation types. However, two significant taxonomic groups distinguish cover from use changes: 1) Categorical: referred to as a post-classification connection, this occurs between such a group of concepts and different types of land cover (forest, urban), and continuous: Also referred to as a pre-classification improvement, this occurs when the amount or capacity for concentration from particular constructed or intuitive scenery that

Table 69.2 Displays the attributes of numerous cost-free software applications employed in a study of land cover.

Software/Release year	Development Platform	Useful for application	
GRASS, 1982 [25]	C, Shell, Tcl/Tk, Python GPL	Analysis of scientific and visualization, cartography, modeling, and simulation	
ILWIS, 1985 [26]	MS Visual C GPL	Analysis(Raster)	Open Source
SPRING, 1991 [29]	GPL	Digital Image Processing, spatial analysis, modeling, visualization	
TerraView, 2001 [27]	C++, R GPL	Statistical analysis Vector and Raster analysis.	
gvSIG, 2003 [28]	JAVA GPL	Viewing, Editing, Analysis (Mobile Applications)	

can be constantly analyzed changes. The most widely used techniques for tracking land use and land cover frequently rely on traditional picture classification techniques founded on the following suppositions: 1) The image's data tends to be distributed; 2) Conventional image classification techniques work under the presumption that important surface items, as visible in high-resolution imaging, are larger than the pixel dimensions. Additionally, 3) it is considered that each pixel only represents one particular form of land use or land cover. Contrasting methodologies, however, suggest that, as shown in low-resolution images, the entire area of interest may be less than the pixel size. As a result, 3) these methods rely on empirical models to estimate physicochemical, epidemiological, and sociocultural data[37, 38].

Methods for Handling Remote Sensed Information for LULC
So much research on land cover has been carried out throughout time [3] utilizing data from a wide range of devices, with a variety of resolutions, procedures, and data methodological approaches, with the aim of mapping and monitoring land cover and land use. The techniques for classification may be divided into supervised, unsupervised, and semi-supervised categories, and the classifiers themselves can be rigid or flexible (variable), parametric or non-parametric, and use pixel/subpixel or object-based classifications. [14, 34]. The parameterized classifications, such as minimum distance, maximum likelihood, and Bayesian classifiers, are based on statistical concepts and model the judgment of class boundaries from a set number of parameters, regardless of the amount of data [40]. Contrarily, non-parametric methods use the digital number (for single band/pictures) or spectrum reflectance (for multispectral images) to do classification. Examples of these techniques are support vector machines (SVM) and artificial neural networks (ANN). These methods increase the categorization process' accuracy by making use of extra data like the scene's shape and other

identifying traits. Because of the scattering of the pixel intensities, a lot of samples are required for the segmentation processes must be autonomous, with a localized data structure as its primary concern [41–44]. Phiri and Morgenroth [42] claim that advances in artificial intelligence and machine learning techniques for object pattern recognition have markedly aided in the development of sophisticated non-parametric classifiers, which are widely used in both open-source and commercial GIS and digital image processing software. The pixel method, like spectral matching techniques and Random Forest, is predicated on using a pixel's spectroscopic data to decide its most very likely a probabilities and classification chart that a specific pixel falls into a specific category or not, that is, the pixel value in a category are more comparable from a spectral perspective than the pixel resolution in other categories [45]. By employing geological entities as the primary elements for land use and land cover (LULC) classification, the Object-Based Image Analysis (OBIA) method adjusts objectives within the study area and addresses the issues of misclassified isolated pixels, commonly known as "salt and pepper" effects. With this method, the categorization process may be built upon a variety of data sources such as appearance, form, and geographical spread [41, 42, 45]. Its primary drawback is related to selecting the suitable separation scale and handling several phases, that, if handled improperly, might be a cause of the variance. Pixel-based classification exhibits inconsistencies, for example, when attempting to separate land use from land cover inside mixed pixels. To address and resolve these differences, the sub-pixel-based approach was created [38, 39, 46]. The linear mixture model (LSMM) and maximum likelihood (Maxver), as well as set theory-based techniques like the probabilistic C-Means (PCM) and fuzzy C-Means (FCM) methods, are two examples of specific sub-pixel classification variations. However, selecting a classifier is a difficult issue because each approach has distinct advantages and disadvantages, as shown in Table 69.3. In paper [47] and [48] propose hybrid ways to address problems that have grown more complex and varied as a result of the emergence of strong and sophisticated classifiers. Nevertheless, a variety of factors, such as the pre-processing performance, classification model, and analyst competence, affect how successful this method is to rationalize resources and achieve accuracy. To achieve acceptable accuracy and resource rationalization, While selecting a classification technique, Gómez et al. [34] state that the following considerations should be made: data type, analytical class dispersion, targeted efficiency, accessibility, efficiency, extendibility, and ease of understanding.Machine learning (ML) refers to the algorithms or methods created to take lessons from data and behave accordingly in future interactions. The four main categories of these frameworks and approaches are reinforcement learning, unsupervised learning, semi-supervised learning, and supervised learning [49, 50]. Examples of these categories include k-nearest neighbor and case-based reasoning. According to the paper [49], the bulk of machine learning algorithms (MLAs), which include methods that are based on rules, equations, and trees, among others, are eager methods for learning [3, 6, 14, 43, 51]. This implies that they carry out extrapolations that go beyond the training data even before encountering novel information. The use of machine learning algorithms for mapping land use and land cover has been the subject of several studies. They include artificial neural networks (ANN), decision trees,

Table 69.3 Lists the characteristics of major proprietary software programs used in land cover investigations

Software/Release year	Development Platform	Useful for application
PCI Geomatica, 1982 [32]	Python	Remote sensing, Digital photogrammetry, and cartography.
ERDAS, 1978 [30]	C, C+	Analyzing remotely acquired data using digital methods.
ER Mapper, 1990 [31]	C, C++	Digital image analysis.
ENVI, 1994 [31]	IDL	Large multi and hyperspectral remote sensing data handling.
ArcGIS, 1999 [33]	Python, C++	Computer evaluation and display of spatial analysis, such as images obtained through remote sensing, are included in the whole component.

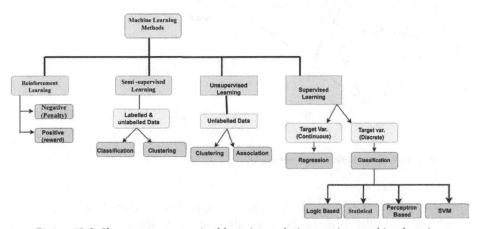

Figure 69.3 Shows some supervised learning techniques using machine learning

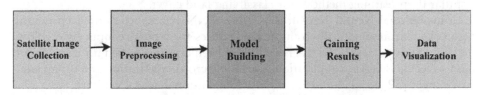

Figure 69.4 Data collection methodology

K-nearest neighbors (k-NN), classification and regression trees (CART), support vector machines (SVM), multivariable logistic regression (MLR), and random forests (RF). All of these algorithms have demonstrated greater efficiency compared to conventional methods. In Figure 69.3, various machine learning techniques,

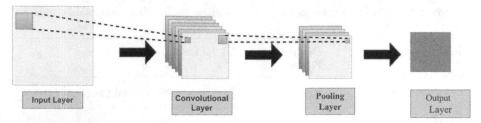

Figure 69.5 Convolutional neural network

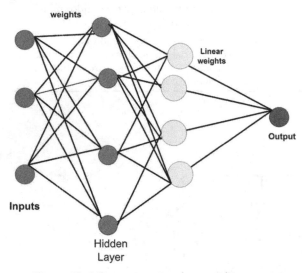

Figure 69.6 Recurrent neural networks

particularly supervised learning, and the corresponding machine learning process are presented. Figure 69.4 shows data collection methodology.

DeeplearningAlgorithms: Deep learning methods have shown tremendous promise for classifying various land cover categories. Here are a few of the most popular deep-learning methods for classifying land cover.

Convolutional Neural Networks (CNN): CNN is a subclass of deep neural networks that automatically train image features from picture input by employing convolutional layers. CNNs have indeed been effectively used for a variety of land cover classification applications, including crop classification and urban land cover maps [52, 53]. Figure 69.5 shows Convolutional neural network.

Recurrent Neural Networks(RNN): Deep neural networks that can model sequential data include recurrent neural networks (RNNs). RNNs have been applied to time-series data-based land cover classification tasks like observing vegetation and spotting changes in land cover [54,55]. Recurrent neural networks is depicted in Figure 69.6.

Autoencoders: Autoencoders are multi-layer perceptrons that can be trained to rebuild inputs by encrypting them into a lesser representation and then deciphering it to the initial form. To extract hidden characteristics from satellite data for land cover classification, autoencoders have been used [56]. Autoencoders are shown in Figure 69.7.

Generative Adversarial Network: GAN (Generative Adversarial Networks) are deep neural networks with the ability to learn how to create new sequence data that are similar to a given data. High-resolution satellite images produced through the use of GANs in land cover classification tasks can be used to enhance land cover mapping [57]. Generative adversarial networks are shown in Figure 69.8.

Evaluation of Accuracy and Validity

Accurate land cover information is essential for effective area management. Validating the components of remote sensing devices is necessary to demonstrate their reliability for selecting data. System users must use the correct criteria for assessment and communication [34]. As a result, a variety of parameters, including the quantity and quality of training samples, conceptual clarity, category distribution, and geographic extent of the research region, influence the dependability of categorized maps [13, 14, 57]. Understanding these variables makes it easier to identify the correct accuracy categorization for a particular problem under study [14]. The kind and technique of sampling, for example, are statistics criteria that must be followed when choosing samples. According to Mastella and Vieira [43], simple and stratified random sampling is frequently utilized in remote sensing, with simple random accounting for the majority of validating indices. Despite the lack of a fair estimate of the variability, authors that use and advocate methodical data collection techniques to research land use and land cover provide accurate results [14]. The most important part of having maps with data from remote sensing is accuracy evaluation since it allows for comparing the effectiveness of different classifiers and the impact of samples [6]. The literature suggests including an errors or confusion matrix [13] [to help to identify class confusion as well as possible sources of error [34, 43]. Additionally, capacities in an order derived from extracted features offer important support. These measures include weighed statistics by area and levels of confidence, such as producer and user accuracy,

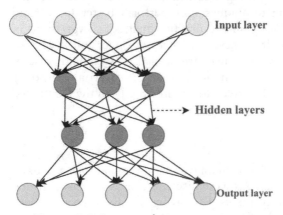

Figure 69.7 Autoencoders

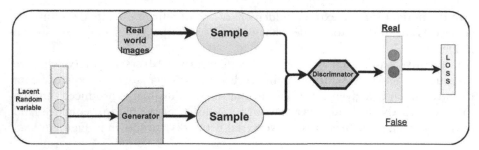

Figure 69.8 Generative adversarial networks

statistical Z, Tau, and Kappa index, among several others. For instance, global correctness describes how similar the classified maps are to the earlier ones.

4 Future Perspectives and Challenges

With the help of innovative image-processing developers, open-source software, and a market that values integrating data, the areas of mapping, geospatial data gathering, and remote sensing have made major strides. The Global Earth Observation System of Systems (GEOSS), which was established in 2005, sought to improve global collaboration and data interchange. Accurate spatiotemporal data gathering has also been made possible by projects like the European Space Agency's (ESA) synchronization efforts between Sentinel-2 and Landsat-8. Despite these advances, remote sensing still faces challenges. Technology has transformed our ability to understand and take care of our world [58]. Aubrecht [59] emphasizes that in the projects under discussion, a crucial approach to achieving active (almost) real-time tracking involves the improved fusion of novel space-based data with data from dynamic on-site sensor networks. This integration is further complemented by data-sharing regulations, especially in sectors that take social and demographic aspects into account. Despite these advances, remote sensing still faces challenges. To improve the accuracy of land use and land cover (LULC) mapping, it is important to allocate high-resolution sensors to a uniform system and use sub-pixel machine learning algorithms to reduce spectral mixes. However, traditional classification techniques may perform better for certain types of land cover than others due to limited practice images and variations in spectral and spatial patterns. To address these challenges, stronger collaborations between geologists and software programmers are needed, as well as the use of unsupervised or guided tactics and a systematic approach. Nedd et al. [36] offer additional insights into a methodical strategy for addressing both the mentioned challenges and other complexities.

Conclusions

The research aims to improve land use mapping with remotely sensed data. Launch site reuse and geospatial methods were discussed, but sub-pixel learning algorithms were suggested for mixed pixels. Dissolving the pixel spectrum into its constituent spectra overcomes the limitations of other methods. Researchers recommend sub-pixel learning to address mixed-pixel issues in the pixel-based method.

References

1. Barbosa, C. C. F., Novo, E. M. L. M., and Martins, V. S. (2019). Introdução ao sensoriamento remoto de sistemas aquáticos: princípios e aplicações. 1a edição. São José dos Campos: Instituto Nacional de Pesquisas Espaciais,.
2. Burton, C. (2016). Earth Observation and Big Data: Creatively Collecting, Processing and Applying Global Information. *Earth Imaging Journal*, 3.
3. Sidhu, N., Pebesma, E., and Câmara, G. (2018). Using google earth engine to detect land cover change: singapore as a use case. *European Journal of Remote Sensing*, 51, 486500.
4. Probst, L., Pedersen, B., and Dakkak-Arnoux, L. (2017). Big data in earth observation. https://ec.europa.eu/growth/toolsdatabases/dem/monitor/sites/default/files/DTM_Big%20Data%20in%20Earth%20Observation%20v1.pdf.
5. Gorelick, N., Hancher, M., Dixon, M., Ilyushchenko, S., Thau, D., and Moore, R. (2017). Google earth engine: planetary-Scale geospatial analysis for everyone. *Remote Sensing of Environment*, 202, 18–27.
6. Teluguntla, P., Thenkabail, P., Oliphant, A., Xiong, J., Gumma, M. K., Congalton, R. G., Yadav, K., and Huete, A. (2018). A 30-m landsat-derived cropland extent product of australia and china using random forest machine learning algorithm on google earth engine cloud computing platform. *ISPRS Journal of Photogrammetry and Remote Sensing*, 144, 32540.
7. Jha, M.K. and Chowdary, V.M., 2007. Challenges of using remote sensing and GIS in developing nations. *Hydrogeology Journal*, 15, 197–200.
8. Huang, B., and Wang, J. (2020). Big spatial data for urban and environmental sustainability. *Geo-Spatial Information Science*, 23, 125–140.
9. Reeves, M. C., Washington-Allen, R. A., Angerer, J., Hunt, E. R., Kulawardhana, R. W., Kumar, L., Loboda, T., Loveland, T., Metternicht, G., and Ramsey, R. D. (2016). Land resources monitoring, modeling, and mapping with remote sensing. In Prasad, S. T., ed. Land Resources Monitoring, Modeling, and Mapping with Remote Sensing. Boca Raton: CRC Press, pp. 237–275.
10. Mutanga, O. and Kumar, L., 2019. Google earth engine applications. *Remote sensing*, 11(5), 591.
11. Gomes, V.C., Queiroz, G.R. and Ferreira, K.R., 2020. An overview of platforms for big earth observation data management and analysis. *Remote Sensing*, 12(8), 1253.
12. Zhu, L., Suomalainen, J., Liu, J., Hyyppä, J., Kaartinen, H., and Haggren, H. (2018). A review: remote sensing sensors. In Rustamov, R., Hasanova, S., and Zeynalova, M. eds. Multi-Purposeful Application of Geospatial Data. London: IntechOpen, 1942.
13. Congalton, R. G., and Green, K. (2009). Assessing the Accuracy of Remotely Sensed Data: Principles and Practices. 2nd ed. Boca Raton: CRC Press.
14. Shetty, S. (2019). Analysis of machine learning classifiers for LULC classification on google earth engine. MSc. Thesis, University of Twente, Enschede.
15. Sajjad, H., and Kumar, P. (2019). Future challenges and perspective of remote sensing technology. In Kumar, P., Rani, M., Chandra Pandey, P., Sajjad, H., and Chaudhary, B. S. eds. Applications and Challenges of Geospatial Technology, Springer International Publishing, Cham, pp. 275–277.

16. Xu, Y. and Huang, B., 2014. Spatial and temporal classification of synthetic satellite imagery: Land cover mapping and accuracy validation. *Geo-spatial Information Science*, 17(1), 1–7.

17. Maurya, S. P., Ohri, A., and Mishra, S. (2015). Open source GIS: a review. In National Conference on Open Source GIS: Opportunities and Challenges, Varanasi, 9–10 October 2015, (pp. 150–155).

18. GIS Technical Advisory Committee (2017). Open Source GIS Software: A Guide for Understanding Current GIS Software Solutions. Raleigh: North Carolina Geographic Information Coordinating Council.

19. Steiniger, S., and Hay, G. J. (2009). Free and open source geographic information tools for landscape ecology. *Ecological Informatics*, 4, 183–195.

20. Teodoro, A.C., Ferreira, D. and Sillero, N., 2012, October. Performance of commercial and open source remote sensing/image processing software for land cover/use purposes. In Earth resources and environmental remote sensing/GIS applications III (Vol. 8538, pp. 373–384). SPIE.

21. Anand, A., Krishna, A., Tiwari, R., and Sharma, R. (2018). Comparative analysis between proprietary software vs. open-source software vs. free software. In 5th IEEE International Conference on Parallel, Distributed and Grid Computing (PDGC-2018), Solan, 20–22 December 2018, (pp. 144–147).

22. Mota, C., and Seruca, I. (2015). Open source software vs. proprietary software in education. In 10th Iberian Conference on Information Systems and Technologies, (CISTI), Aveiro, 17-20 Jun 2015, (pp. 1–6).

23. Miller, A. (2011) Open source vs. proprietary softwarein developing countries. https://www.academia.edu/777383/Open_Source_v_Proprietary_Software.

24. Tesoriere, A., and Balletta, L. (2017). A dynamic model of open source vs. proprietary R & D. *European Economic Review*, 94, 221–239.

25. Neteler, M., Beaudette, D. E., Cavallini, P., Lami, L., and Cepicky, J. (2008). GRASS GIS. In Hall, G. B., and Leahy, M. G., eds. Open Source Approaches in Spatial Data Handling, (Vol. 2, Issue October 2014), Berlin, Heidelberg: Springer, (pp. 171–199).

26. Montesinos, S., and Fernández, L. (2012). Introduction to ILWIS GIS Tool. In Erena, M., López-Francos, A., Montesinos, S., and Berthoumieu, J .P., eds. Otions Méditerranéennes, No. 67, (pp. 47–52).

27. Câmara, G., Vinhas, L., Ferreira, K. R., de Queiroz, G. R., de Souza, R. C. M., Monteiro, A. M. V., de Carvalho, M. T., Casanova, M. A., and de Freitas, U. M. (2008). TerraLib: an open source GIS library for large-scale environmental and socio-economic applications. In Hall, G. B., ed. Open Source Approaches to Spatial Data Handling, (Vol. 2), Berlin, Heidelberg: Springer, (pp. 247–270).

28. Moutahir, H., and Agazzi, V. (2012). The gvSIG Project. In International Conference of GIS Users, Taza, 23-24 May 2012, (pp. 1–6).

29. dos Santos, A. R., Machado, T., and Saito, N. S. (2010). Spring 5.1.2 passo a passo: Aplicações práticas. CAUFES, Alegre. http://www.mundogeomatica.com.br/Livr/Livro_Spring_5.1.2_Aplicacoes_Pratic%20as/LivroSPRING512PassoaPassoAplicacaoPratica.pdf.

30. Hexagon (2020). Erdas imagine 2020 update 1. Hexagon, Stockholm. https://bynder.hexagon.com/m/4cce2965b2270e54/original/Hexagon_GSP_ERDAS_IMAGINE_2020_Release_Guide.pdf.

31. Exelis Visual Information Solutions (2009). Getting Started in ENVI. Boulder, Colorado: Exelis Visual Information Solutions.

32. Hoja, D., Schneider, M., Müller, R., Lehner, M., and Reinartz, P. (2008). Comparison of orthorectification methods suitable for rapid mapping using direct georeferencing

and RPC for optical satellite data. *The International Archives of the Photogramme-try, Remote Sensing and Spatial Information Sciences*, 37, 1617–1624.

33. Esri (2004). What Is ArcGIS? Redlands: Esri.
34. Gómez, C., White, J. C., and Wulder, M. A. (2016). Optical remotely sensed time series data for land cover classification: a review. *ISPRS Journal of Photogrammetry and Remote Sensing*, 116, 55–72.
35. Briassoulis, H. (2007) Land-use policy and planning, theorizing, and modeling: lost in translation, Found in Complexity?. *Environment and Planning B: Urban Analytics and City Science*, 35, 16–33.
36. Nedd, R., Light, K., Owens, M., James, N., Johnson, E., & Anandhi, A. (2021). A synthesis of land use/land cover studies: Definitions, classification systems, meta-studies, challenges and knowledge gaps on a global landscape. Land, 10(9), 994.
37. Rogan, J., and Chen, D. M. (2004). Remote sensing technology for mapping and monitoring land-cover and land-use change. *Progress in Planning*, 61, 301–325.
38. Duverger, S. (2015). Metodologia para a criação de mapas temáticos de super-resolução com base em informações subpixel: Um estudo de caso na APA do Pratigi-BA. MSc. Dissertation, Universidade Estadual de Feirade Santana, Feirade Santana. https://s3.amazonaws.com/ppgm.uefs.br/soltan_final.pdf.
39. Du, P., Liu, S., Liu, P., Tan, K., and Cheng, L. (2014). Sub-pixel change detection for urban land-cover analysis via multi-temporal remote sensing images. *Geo-Spatial Information Science*, 17, 26–38.
40. Zanotta, D. C., Ferreira, M. P., and Zortea, M. (2019). Processamento de Imagens de satélite. 1st ed. O. de Textos, São Paulo.
41. Peña, J. M., Gutiérrez, P. A., Hervás-Martínez, C., Six, J., Plant, R. E., and López-Granados, F. (2014). Object-based image classification of summer crops with machine learning methods. *Remote Sensing*, 6, 5019–5041. https://doi.org/10.3390/rs6065019.
42. Phiri, D., & Morgenroth, J. (2017). Developments in Landsat land cover classification methods: A review. Remote Sensing, 9(9), 967.
43. Mastella, A. F., and Vieira, C. A. (2018). Acurácia temática para classificação de imagens utilizando abordagens por pixel e por objetos. *Revista Brasileira de Cartografia*, 70, 16181643.
44. Cui, B., Cui, J., Hao, S., Guo, N., and Lu, Y. (2020). Spectral-spatial hyperspectral image classification based on superpixel and multi-classifier fusion. *International Journal of Remote Sensing*, 41, 6157–6182.
45. Xiong, J., Thenkabail, P. S., Tilton, J. C., Gumma, M. K., Teluguntla, P., Oliphant, A., ... & Gorelick, N. (2017). Nominal 30-m cropland extent map of continental Africa by integrating pixel-based and object-based algorithms using Sentinel-2 and Landsat-8 data on Google Earth Engine. Remote Sensing, 9(10), 1065.
46. Degerickx, J., Roberts, D. A., and Somers, B. (2019). Remote sensing of environment enhancing the performance of multiple endmember spectral mixture analysis (MESMA) for urban land cover mapping using airborne lidar data and band selection. *Remote Sensing of Environment*, 221, 260–273.
47. Ackom, E. K., Amaning, K., Samuel, A., and Odai, N. (2020). Monitoring land-use and land-cover changes due to extensive urbanization in the odaw river basin of accra, Ghana, 1991–2030. *Modeling Earth Systems and Environment*, 6, 1131–1143.
48. Mohammady, M., Moradi, H. R., Zeinivand, H., & Temme, A. J. A. M. (2015). A comparison of supervised, unsupervised and synthetic land use classification methods in the north of Iran. International Journal of Environmental Science and Technology, 12, 1515-1526.

49. Galván, I. M., Valls, J. M., Garcia, M., and Isasi, P. (2011). A lazy learning approach for building classification models. *International Journal of Intelligent Systems*, 26, 773–786.

50. Sarker, I. H. (2021). Machine learning: algorithms, real-world applications, and research directions. *SN Computer Science*, 2(3), 160.

51. Bruce, R. W., Rajcan, I., & Sulik, J. (2021). Classification of Soybean Pubescence from Multispectral Aerial Imagery. Plant Phenomics (Washington, DC), 2021, 9806201-9806201.

52. Li, J., Wang, S., Wang, J., Zhang, L., Chen, X., and Liu, J. (2019). Land cover classification with multiscale CNNs: a case study using multi-temporal Landsat images. *Remote Sensing*, 11(13).

53. Wang, Y., Huang, C., and Gong, P. (2020). Improving urban land cover mapping with deep convolutional neural networks and auxiliary data. *ISPRS Journal of Photogrammetry and Remote Sensing*, 167, 230–241.

54. Maggiori, E., Tarabalka, Y., Charpiat, G., and Alliez, P. (2017). Can semantic labeling methods generalize to any city? The Inria aerial image labeling benchmark. *IEEE Transactions on Geoscience and Remote Sensing*, 55(12), 8440–8454.

55. Wang, L., Liu, Y., Yu, X., Chen, Y., Li, Y., and Li, X. (2018). Application of deep learning in remote sensing: a review. *Remote Sensing*, 10(10), 1433.

56. Huang, W., Li, W., and Zhang, L. (2019). Multi-level feature learning with autoencoder for land cover classification. *IEEE Journal of Selected Topics in Applied Earth Observations and Remote Sensing*, 12(5), 1385–1397.

57. Chen, Z., Zhu, Y., Li, J., Huang, Y., Liu, B., and Wu, X. (2020). GAN-based high-resolution remote sensing image classification. *IEEE Transactions on Geoscience and Remote Sensing*, 58(1), 462–476.

58. Lei, G., Li, A., Bian, J., Yan, H., Zhang, L., Zhang, Z., & Nan, X. (2020). OIC-MCE: A practical land cover mapping approach for limited samples based on multiple classifier ensemble and iterative classification. Remote Sensing, 12(6), 987.

59. Fritz, S. (2014). Global earth observation system of systems (GEOSS). In Njoku E. G. ed. Encyclopedia of Remote Sensing. New York: Springer, pp. 257–261.

70 A robust hybrid deep learning model for acute lymphoblastic leukemia diagnosis

Bakkanarappa Gari Mounika[a], Mohammad Faiz[b], Nausheen Fatima[c] and Ramandeep Sandhu[d]

School of Computer Science & Engineering, Lovely Professional University, Phagwara, Punjab, India

Abstract

Acute lymphoblastic leukemia (ALL), a rare kind of blood cancer, can strike young children and adults. It has a strong possibility of being cured if caught early. The study's objectives are to decrease the time needed for identification, increase diagnosis accuracy, and lower the cost of specialized care for ALL. The ALL-IDB1 data, which includes 108 images of lymphocyte cells, was used in the study. By using image augmentation to apply transformation parameters to source images, the Keras library created 3240 new images. After extracting features from augmented data using the MobileNetV2 model, the XGBoost classifier was trained to predict the labels that would go with each feature. For the ALL-IDB1 dataset, the proposed approach, MobileNet V2+XGBoost, is compared with other cutting-edge models such as GoogLeNet, ResNet50, & MobileNet V2+SVM. The proposed method had a 99.07% accuracy rate, a 99.35% precision rate, and a 98.72% recall rate. MobileNet V2+XGBoost has successfully trained to generalize and outperform on the substantial amount of augment data. These findings showed the possibility of the proposed approach for giving a reliable ALL diagnosis, which could ultimately result in better patient outcomes.

Keywords: Acute lymphoblastic leukemia, deep learning, machine learning

Introduction

Blood plays a crucial role in our body, and blood cells are produced by bone marrow situated inside bones Alsalem et al. [1]. The mature blood cells then leave the bone marrow through a complex network of capillaries and enter the bloodstream. Red blood cells carry oxygen and carbon dioxide throughout the body and platelets aid in blood clotting. Abnormal multiplication of white blood cells, known as blast cells, is a characteristic of leukemia, a type of blood cancer. There are two types of leukemia, acute and chronic Aftab et al. [2], and acute leukemia progresses quickly and requires early detection for effective treatment. ALL is a subtype of acute leukemia that affects lymphocytes, which are white blood cells that combat germs and viruses. The rapid multiplication of blast cells in ALL hinders the production of vital cells essential for survival, resulting in the disease's

[a]mounikareddyb0305@gmail.com, [b]faiz.28700@lpu.co.in, [c]nausheen.28838@lpu.co.in, [d]ramandeepsandhu887@gmail.com

rapid progression Anilkumar et al. [3]. Thus, prompt treatment is necessary for ALL.

Early detection of ALL is a persistent challenge for medical professionals and researchers due to the common symptoms it shares with other diseases, such as gum bleeding, bone pain, fever, pale skin, tiredness, and decreased energy. Blood tests are commonly used to measure abnormal levels of platelets, white blood cells, and red blood cells, but a more thorough examination may be required to diagnose ALL Anilkumar et al. [3]. Marrow tests are often performed to determine whether the blast cells come from B or T-type cells. Imaging tests may also be conducted to detect tumor spread to other organs or the brain, and a spinal fluid test may be used to identify blast cells that have entered the spinal fluid. Treating patients with leukemia requires specialized care, which can be costly and time-consuming.

To address these challenges, computer-aided methods have been developed to identify acute lymphoblastic leukemia using small blood smear images, which saves time, and money, and produces more accurate results than manual methods. These computer-aided methods can aid in early detection and treatment of ALL. The references have been retained. Deep learning and machine learning, which are domains of artificial intelligence, use data to teach computers how to make decisions based on mathematical correlations and algorithms instead of being programmed explicitly. These techniques have been widely used in clinical studies and have shown remarkable success in disease diagnosis. By analyzing vast amounts of medical data, these algorithms can assist healthcare professionals in making more informed decisions about patient treatment. One application of these techniques is the identification and treatment of leukemia using small blood smear images. This approach is cost-effective, reduces the time required to identify diseases, and produces accurate results when compared to manual outcomes. These advancements in technology have the potential to revolutionize healthcare and improve patient outcomes. the present scenario has shown the increased threats represented by respiratory illnesses like chronic obstructive pulmonary disease (COPD), asthma, etc. That risk has increased due to an increase in air pollutants like PM2.5, PM10, etc. A respirator can be utilized as an immediate countermeasure on an individual level safety measure as bringing down pollution levels require a much longer time than the severity of the problem is allowing.

Literature Review

Aftab et al. [2] Used GoogleNet deep transfer learning and the Convolutional Neural Network (CNN) architecture, it is suggested to identify leukemia from microscopic blood smear images of human blood. 97.33% accuracy in training and 94.78% accuracy in validation after utilizing the Spark BigDL framework with the Google Net design achieved. By producing more accurate and efficient outcomes, the BigDL model outperformed the Keras model. Dese et al. [5] collected 250 blood smear images from jimma university medical center's hematology department and ALL_DB online publicly available data. K-means-MCSVM segmentation achieved good performance. By diagnosing the sub-classification of leukemia cancer progression can be increased. Shafique and Tehsin [6] used a well-structured AlexNet dataset and the Relu layer contained 1024 neurons. Deployment of DCNN which is already trained for the classification of ALL into ALL-ALLALL- L3, and ALL-L4. achieved results for the model is 99.50% accuracy,98.11% specificity in the detection of ALL.99.03% specificity, and 96.06% accuracy for subtypes of ALL.

Genovese et al. [7] proposed an adaptive unsharpening method on blood smear images by machine learning. For classifying the output trained deep convolution deep neural networks are used. AlexNet, VGG16, VGG19, ResNet18, ResNet50, ResNet101, and DenseNet201 are the parameters. [12]Das et al. [17] surveyed the classification of acute lymphoblastic leukemia by using deep learning and machine learning feature extraction such as naive Bayesian, multi-layer perceptron, artificial neural network, fuzzy means clustering, rough-fuzzy-means, conventional convolution neural network, recurrent neural network [12, 17]. ALLIDB1 and ALLIDB2 datasets are collected. The performance can be improved by MobikeNetV2-ReseNet18 architecture yields. Further classification of acute leukemia subtypes gives an accurate diagnosis of the disease. Researchers [12] Das et al. [15] said that the color-based k-means grouping method is used to extract lymphocytes [12, 15]. To extract the characteristics of the nucleus, two methods are used: gray-level co-occurrence matrix (GLCM) and gray-level run-length matrix (GLRLM).

Dataset for Leukemia Detection and Classification

Research studies frequently use the ALL-IDB1 dataset to identify and categorize acute lymphoblastic leukemia (ALL) from blood cell images. There are 50 leukemic cell images and 58 normal cell images, totaling 108 lymphocyte cell images. Using the dataset, computer-aided models are created that can precisely identify leukemia from blood cell images. Das and Maher [16] proposed a novel deep CNN framework by using ALL_IDB 1 and ALL-IDB 2 datasets. BiBi et al. [8] utilized ALL-IDB and ASH image banks, two publicly available leukemia datasets for Residual Convolutional Neural Networks (RCNN) and Dense Convolutional Neural Networks (DenseNet-121).

Methodology and Model Specifications

Leukemia diagnosis usually involves three stages. In the first stage, pre-processing is carried out to transform the data before training models. This involves various techniques like cleaning, transforming, and normalization to enhance model precision and efficacy. The second stage, data augmentation, creates new samples from existing data to improve model generalization. Lastly, feature extraction identifies the most significant features in the dataset to improve the model's effectiveness. Together, these techniques can assist in preparing the data for algorithms, which can help increase the accuracy of leukemia diagnosis.

Preprocessing

Preprocessing the raw photos to enhance their quality and prepare them for analysis is crucial to create a model that can correctly categorize images of acute lymphoblastic leukemia (ALL). This is a crucial step because the raw photos can contain size and color inconsistencies that could affect the model's predictions [4] Preprocessing the images enables the model to produce more precise classifications, enhancing the analysis's overall quality.

Augmentation

Preprocessing the raw photos to enhance their quality and prepare them for analysis is crucial to create a model that can correctly categorize images of acute lymphoblastic leukemia (ALL). This is a crucial step because the raw photos can contain size and color inconsistencies that could affect the model's predictions. Preprocessing the images enables the model to produce more precise classifications, enhancing the analysis's overall quality.

Owing to the small amount of testing phase in our data set, we used the data augmentation technique to improve the training data by applying image rotation and mirroring. Without additional data, our model may experience significant overfitting Krizhevsky et al. [9]. These parameters are specified by the Keras library, which creates 3240 images based on them. This strategy might improve model accuracy by extending the dataset and introducing more variety shown in Figure 70.1.

Feature Extraction & Classification

Feature extraction is the process of selecting and transforming relevant information from raw data into a reduced set of features that can be easily processed by algorithms. This entails figuring out which information in the data is most relevant to the issue at hand and putting it into an analysis-ready format. A crucial stage in data analysis, feature extraction can assist in revealing hidden correlations and patterns in the data.

Wang et al. Krizhevsky et al. [9] have proposed the architecture of MobileNet. The MobileNetV2 is a type of convolution neural network. The major goal of MobileNetV2 is to minimize the number of parameters and computations required for training and inference by using lightweight convolutional blocks known as "inverted residuals." These inverted residuals are made up of three layers: a linear bottleneck layer, a depth-wise convolution layer, and a pointwise convolution layer. Each channel of the input data is subjected to spatial convolution independently by the depth-wise convolution layer, which then executes a 1x1 convolution to aggregate the results. In comparison to conventional convolutional layers,

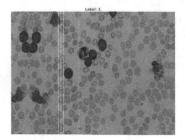 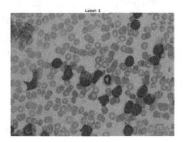

Figure 70.1 Blood smear images-after augmentation

which execute convolution over all channels simultaneously, this requires fewer computations. A feature fusion approach called a linear bottleneck layer aids in channel reduction while preserving critical information. Following a ReLU activation process and a 3x3 convolution which raises the total amount of channels once more, it starts with a 1x1 convolution to decrease the number of channels. As a result, the network can learn features that are more complex while using fewer parameters.

Moreover, "shortcut connections" are a method used by MobileNetV2 to enhance the gradient flow during training. Gradients can circumvent some network levels due to these connections and get to earlier layers more quickly, which can assist prevent the issue of vanishing gradients. The "linear bottleneck" architecture used by MobileNetV2 is intended to limit the number of parameters within the network. The model can train more effectively and run more quickly on embedded and mobile devices by lowering the number of parameters. Compared to other CNN architectures created for mobile applications, MobileNetV2 provides many benefits. Its great precision, even with a small number of parameters, is one of its key benefits. This is because inverted residuals are used, which aid to keep crucial data while minimizing the number of computations required. Pretrained MobileNetV2 models were neural networks that may be utilized for a variety of image classification methods without the requirement of additional training Deng et al. [11] Faiz and Daniel [13]. They have previously been trained on a sizable dataset like ImageNet displayed in Figure 70.2. Pre-processing the input images correctly is a crucial factor to take into account when utilizing pretrained MobileNetV2 models. Typically, images that have been scaled to a specified size and then normalized are used to train MobileNetV2 models. This means that before they are fed into the model, source images must be appropriately scaled and normalized [12]. Inaccurate projections and lesser accuracy could be the outcome if this is not done. MobileNetV2's various parameters include

- weights - the pre-trained weights from the ImageNet dataset are going to be utilized because it is set to "imagine."
- Input-shape - The intended size and quantity of color channels for the input images are specified by this option. It is now set to (224, 224, 3), suggesting that the input should be 224 pixels wide by 224 pixels high and have three color channels (red, green, and blue).

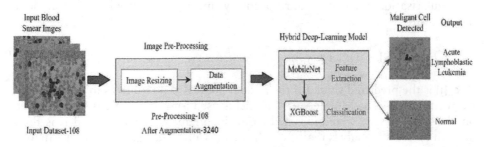

Figure 70.2 Basic architecture of proposed model

XGBoost is an accessible machine-learning framework that is frequently used to address challenging classification and regression issues Chen and Guestrin [10]. Its name, Extreme Gradient Boosting, relates to the algorithm's capacity to reduce the error of gradient Boosting, relates to the algorithm's capacity to reduce the error of a gradient descent algorithm

while simultaneously reducing the loss function. Because of its great performance, scalability, and adaptability, XGBoost is well-liked. One of Decision trees are used as the foundation learners in the library, and they are repeatedly improved by maximizing the algorithm's objective function, which measures how well the models perform. To attain excellent accuracy and quick training speed, XGBoost offers some cutting-edge capabilities, including parallel processing, regularisation, and handling of missing variables. A variety of evaluation metrics, including precision, AUC-ROC, and log-loss, are supported by the library and can be used to assess how well the model performed on the test set. To determine which features are most crucial for making predictions, it provides feature importance scores. These scores are calculated by examining the contributions of every parameter per each tree structure of the model.
The XGBoost's objective function

$$0 = L\left(x_j, x_{hat}\right) + \Omega(r) \tag{1}$$

where, 'L' is a loss function, x_j seems to be the actual labels of a jth training dataset, x_{hat} is the forecasted labels for that example, and (r) is the regularisation term that penalizes excessively complex models from equation 1. The logistic loss is the most widely used loss function

$$(L((x, f(y)) = -[x(log(f(x))) + (1 - x)log(1 - f(x))])) \tag{2}$$

The L1 as well as L2 regularisation terms are combined to form the XGBoost regularisation term, which is defined as:

$$\Omega(f) = \lambda sum_j|x_j| + 0.5(\gamma)sum_j(w_j)^2 \tag{3}$$

Where λ and Ω are hyperparameters that regulate the power of the L1 and L2 regularisation in equation 3, respectively, and w_j is the weight of the model's $(j_{j-n})^{th}$ feature.

$$x\_\{j\} = sum\{k = 1\}^{\wedge}Kf_{\Delta}k(y_{\infty}j) \tag{4}$$

x_{j} is the predicted value for the jth data point K is no. of trees in an ensemble from equation 4 The MobileNetV2 model is used to train the XGBoost classifier on the features that were extracted from the augmented photos, and it is then used to forecast the labels that go with each feature. The classifier's performance is then assessed by computing its accuracy on the testing set.

Simulation & Analysis Tool

Users can open Jupyter Notebooks in their web browsers by using Google Colaboratory, a web-based environment. It gives users access to Google's robust hardware and cloud computing capabilities. The suggested model MobleNet+XGBoost made use of Colab, and the outcomes were significant. This indicates that utilizing Colab helped to meet the goals of the research and produce notable results.

Empirical Results

For assessing the effectiveness and efficiency of algorithms, performance indicators are crucial. These metrics offer a way of evaluating the success of goals and objectives and pinpointing areas that need improvement shown in Table 70.1. Metrics such as FP, TP, FN, and TN to assess the accuracy of their diagnosis. False positives (FP) are the number of healthy cells that are wrongly classified as cancerous. TP (True positives), refers to the quantity of cancerous cells that are accurately detected. FN (False Negative), refers to the quantity of cancerous cells that are missed or wrongly identified as healthy. Finally, TN (True negatives), refers to the number of healthy cells that are correctly diagnosed.

The ALL-IDb1 dataset has shown that the suggested strategy, which combines MobileNet V2 and the XGBoost algorithm, performs better at classifying acute lymphoblastic leukemia (ALL). Due to its unbalanced nature, the ALL-IDb1 dataset presents a challenge because the classifier (ALL) has a substantially smaller number of samples than the negative samples (healthy). Besides the obstacle, the proposed technique had a specificity value of 99.40%, demonstrating its ability to correctly identify many healthy instances. This is crucial in the medical field since false positives can result in therapy that is unneeded and even harmful. The proposed model outperformed earlier research techniques like GoogLeNet, AlexNet, VGG19, and ResNet50 with a greater accuracy of 99.07%. is further proven by high recall (98.72%) & precision (99.35%) values as shown in Figure 70.3.

Table 70.1 **Result comparisons using the ALL-IDB1 dataset**

References	Model	Accuracy	Recall	Precision	Specificity
[14]	Alex Net	93.64	98.64	89.55	89.35
	GoogLeNet	95.15	95.66	94.49	94.67
[16]	VGG19	90.30	95.33	86.76	86.11
	ResNet50	95.15	98.00	91.17	92.78
[14]	MobileNet V2+SVM	**99.39**	100.0	98.57	99.00
Proposed Method	MobileNet V2+XGBoost	99.07	98.72	**99.35**	**99.40**

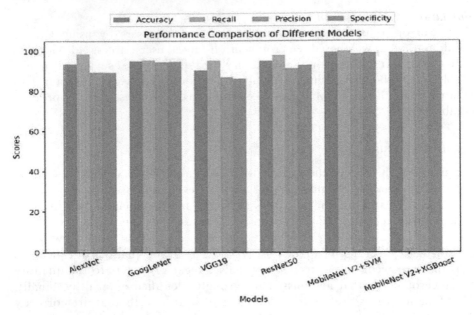

Figure 70.3 ALL-IDB1 results comparison1 result

By processing massive amounts of data, conventional SVM techniques have demonstrated problems in reliably classifying ALL cells. The proposed method appears to be successful at correctly identifying negative cases, as indicated by the specificity value of 99.40%. These findings suggest that the proposed technique, which employs MobileNet V2 and the XGBoost algorithm, maybe a valid and accurate method for classifying ALL cells.

Conclusion

Acute lymphoblastic cancer (ALL) has been successfully classified utilizing the MobileNet V2+XGBoost algorithm, including accuracy of 99.07% & excellent recall as well as precision scores of 98.72% and 99.35%, correspondingly. The method's ability to precisely identify negative instances is further illustrated by a specificity value of 99.40%. This technology may be incorporated into a diagnosis assistance tool for early diagnosis of ALL, giving doctors an efficient and dependable way to classify blast cells. This method can seriously reduce the number of errors and shorten computing time by automating the feature extraction as well as the classification process, which ultimately improves patient outcomes. The effectiveness of this approach shows the immense potential of deep learning techniques in medical imaging and represents an encouraging first step towards creating more sophisticated and efficient diagnosis support systems for a variety of illnesses. Future work could involve further testing and validation of this algorithm on larger datasets, as well as expanding its application to other types of cancer and medical conditions.

Acknowledgement

The authors gratefully acknowledge the students, staff, and authority of the computer science department for their cooperation in the research.

References

1. Alsalem, M. A., Zaidan, A. A., Zaidan, B. B., Hashim, M., Madhloom, H. T., Azeez, N. D., and Alsyisuf, S. (2018). A review of the automated detection and classification of acute leukaemia: coherent taxonomy, datasets, validation and performance measurements, motivation, open challenges, and recommendations. *Computer Methods and Programs in Biomedicine*, 158(5), 93–112. https://doi.org/10.1016/j.cmpb.2018.02.005.
2. Aftab, M. O., Awan, M. J., Khalid, S., Javed, R., and Shabir, H. (2021). Executing spark BigDL for leukemia detection from microscopic images using transfer learning. *IEEE*, 4, 216–220. https://doi.org/10.1109/CAIDA51941.2021.9425264.
3. Anilkumar, K. K., Manoj, V. J., and Sagi, T. M. (2022). Automated detection of B cell and T cell acute lymphoblastic leukaemia using deep learning. *IRBM*, 43(10), 405–413. https://doi.org/10.1016/j.irbm.2021.05.005.
4. (1995). Isotretinoin for juvenile chronic myelogenous leukemia. *New England Journal of Medicine*, 6, 1520–1521. https://doi.org/10.1056/NEJM199506013322216.
5. Dese, K., Raj, H., Ayana, G., Yemane, T., Adissu, W., Krishnamoorthy, J., and Kwa, T. (2021). Accurate machine-learning-based classification of leukemia from blood smear images. *Clinical Lymphoma Myeloma and Leukemia*, 21(11), e903–914. https://doi.org/10.1016/j.clml.2021.06.025.
6. Shafique, S., and Tehsin, S. (2018). Acute lymphoblastic leukemia detection and classification of Its subtypes using pretrained deep convolutional neural networks. *Technology in Cancer Research and Treatment*, 17(1), 1–7. 153303381880278. https://doi.org/10.1177/153303381880278.
7. Genovese, A., Hosseini, M. S., Piuri, V., Plataniotis, K. N., and Scotti, F. (2021). Acute lymphoblastic leukemia detection based on adaptive unsharpening and deep learning. *IEEE*, 6,1205–1209. https://doi.org/10.1109/ICASSP39728.2021.9414362.
8. Bibi, N., Sikandar, M., Ud Din, I., Almogren, A., and Ali, S. (2020). IoMT-based automated detection and classification of leukemia using deep learning. *Journal of Healthcare Engineering*, 2020(12), 1–12. https://doi.org/10.1155/2020/6648574.
9. Krizhevsky, A., Sutskever, I., and Hinton, G. E. (2017). Image net classification with deep convolutional neural networks. *Communications of the ACM*, 60(5), 84–90. https://doi.org/10.1145/3065386.
10. Chen, T., and Guestrin, C. (2016). XGBoost.. *Association for Computing Machinery*, 8, 785–794. https://doi.org/10.1145/2939672.2939785.
11. Deng, J., Dong, W., Socher, R., Li, L. J., Li, K., and Fei-Fei, L. (2009). Image net: a large-scale hierarchical image database. *IEEE*, 6, 248–255. https://doi.org/10.1109/CVPR.2009.5206848.
12. Das, P. K., Nayak, B., and Meher, S. (2022). A lightweight deep learning system for automatic detection of blood cancer. *Measurement*, 191(3), 110762. https://doi.org/10.1016/j.measurement.2022.110762.
13. Faiz, M., and Daniel, A. K. (2022). A multi-criteria dual membership cloud selection model based on fuzzy logic for QoS. *International Journal of Computing and Digital Systems*, 12(8), 453–467. https://doi.org/10.12785/ijcds/120136.

14. Das, P. K., and Meher, S. (2021). Transfer learning-based automatic detection of acute lymphocytic leukemia.. *IEEE*, 7, 1–6. https://doi.org/10.1109/NCC52529.2021.9530010.
15. Das, P. K., Meher, S., Panda, R., and Abraham, A. (2022). An efficient blood-cell segmentation for the detection of hematological disorders. *IEEE Transactions on Cybernetics*, 52(10), 10615–10626. https://doi.org/10.1109/TCYB.2021.3062152.
16. Das, P. K., and Meher, S. (2021). An efficient deep convolutional neural network based detection and classification of acute lymphoblastic leukemia. *Expert Systems with Applications*, 183(11), 115311. https://doi.org/10.1016/j.eswa.2021.115311.
17. Das, P. K., Diya, V. A., Meher, S., Panda, R., and Abraham, A. (2022). A systematic review on recent advancements in deep and machine learning based detection and classification of acute lymphoblastic leukemia. *IEEE Access*, 10, 81741–81763. https://doi.org/10.1109/ACCESS.2022.3196037.

71 Effect of online gaming on mental health using machine learning techniques

Shreyas Mohan[a], Souvik Khanagwal[b] and Jasraj Meena[c]

Dept. of Information Technology, Delhi Technological University, New Delhi, India

Abstract

The prolonged screen time on certain applications and getting exposed to negative content online are some of the major concerns of parents these days. Parents find it difficult to come up with a viable solution to these issues. It is an understandable intent of the parents to avoid such situations. Such exposure to video games for long durations of time can lead to depreciation in mental health. It has been found that there is significant association between prolonged gaming and general anxiety disorder. We have focused on measuring this association along with determining the best method to determine the category of potential mental state of responders and gamers. To achieve this we determined, compared and analyzed the performances of different machine learning models on the data to establish the most suitable algorithm for the given problem in order to potentially effectively solve it.

Keywords: Anxiety, association, data, GAD, models, social, techniques

Introduction

In a world where the need for the internet is ever growing, children using smart devices becomes inevitable. On average, children and adolescent teens spend most of their time online.

Small children and adolescent teens are constantly submerged and engaged in video gaming excessively. The risk of gaming disorder (GD) symptoms are increased during the lockdown due to COVID-19 pandemic as a result of drastic increase in use of online games, and thus, the abundant amount of free time available to kids led to them being more attached to electronic devices and video games. Even the parents allowed this to some extent given the idle time available during lockdown. This however is leading to excessive increase in children's screen time which can be a major contributing factor towards serious health implications. Not only this, in some cases parents have even lost a fortune to such games/web- sites due to deliberate or mistaken actions by their children. There even have been cases of children committing suicide as a consequence of too much bad influence by such games/websites.

To fill these gaps, in this study we aim to analyze people's gaming habits and how it determines their mental health. In this study we have analyzed online gamers' psyche and their generalized gaming behavior using machine learning techniques.

[a]shreyasmohan64@gmail.com, [b]sobudp73@gmail.com, [c]jasrajmeena@dtu.ac.in

Motivation

The prevalence of online gaming and concerns about its impact on mental health make this a timely and important research topic. Our findings could potentially inform policy and interventions aimed at promoting mental health and well-being among individuals who engage in online gaming. We have the chance to add to the body of knowledge on how online gaming affects mental health by undertaking research in this field.

We can uncover new information and spot trends in our data by applying machine learning approaches that may not be immediately obvious through conventional statistical analysis. This can make it easier for us to comprehend the intricate connection between online gaming and mental health.

Related Works

We went through a number of research papers but found that not much technical research has been done in this area of determining social factors like satisfaction with life, GAD and social phobia based on statistical gaming data and GAD scores of the participants.

Some psychological research has been done to understand the association of such behavioral factors with each other and we can try to infer from these, their effect on mental health.

A study conducted by Chao-Yang Wang and Yu-Chen Wu in the Journal of Behavioral Addiction, they tried to determine the correspondence between IGD and GAD [1].

GAD and IGD criteria were used to perform the analysis which are in "Diagnostic and Statistical Manual of Mental Disorders". Along with this questionnaire on anxiety, depression etc. was also used to gain insight [1].

According to the findings of logistic regression, individuals with GAD had a greater risk of developing IGD than individuals without GAD. Depression and anxiety scores were higher in IGD patients with GAD than in IGD patients without GAD [1]. One problem with this was that the dataset used or the number of participants were very less for an accurate analysis.

Further, Lutz Wartberg and Levente Krinston's 2019 study, which was published in Psychological Medicine, examined the causes and effects of adolescent gaming problems. It explored the effects of harmful video games [2].

Familial pairs were examined in a cross-lagged panel design study in 2016 and 2017. They were assessed on IGD stand- ardized methods with the help of structural equation modeling [2]. It was found that IDG causes a decline in mental health [2].

In another study by Lee, S.Y., Bahn, G.H., and Lee, S.M., they examined the application of machine learning algorithms for depression prediction among Korean adults. The performance of four different algorithms— "k-nearest neighbor, decision tree, random forest and support vector machine" —is compared by the authors [3]. According to the findings, the random forest algorithm had the best predicted accuracy [3].

Further, Researchers Männikkö, N., Billieux, J., Kääriäinen, and Griffiths examined the association between mental symp- toms and the compulsive use of social media and video games in their study [4].

"The Bergen Social Media Addiction Scale and the Game Addiction Scale" and the Symptom Checklist-90-Revised are used in the study to assess the addictiveness of using social media, playing video games, and to assess mental symptoms [4]. The results show that people who use social media and video games compulsively display higher levels of mental symptoms, notably despair, anxiety, and psychosis [4].

Overall, it can be observed that most of the studies involved theoretical and psychological analysis without making use of statistical methods, and those which did use statistical tools did so on a small amount of data which prevents accurate analysis [5-10]. To overcome these shortcomings, we will be making use of machine learning techniques to analyze the mental health and gaming patterns of online gamers.

Dataset

We used GamingStudy_data. This is a dataset with over 14000 records and 55 attributes. These attributes correspond to the questions asked in the survey. Most of these are psychological measures such as general anxiety disorder questions, life satisfaction questions, and social phobia indicating questions.

Methodology

Data Preprocessing

Cleaning: The data was cleaned by removing duplicates to avoid skewed results, identifying and filling or removing missing data depending upon the requirements, identifying the outliers and removing them etc.

Standardizing Values: Variable values of the same response were standardized.

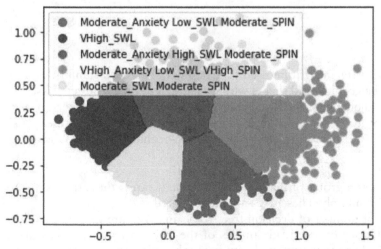

Figure 71.1 Results of KMeans algorithms applied to the data, classifying the data points to determine the 5 target classes

Normalization: The values of candidate features were normalized to a common standard for better learning.

Label Encoding: All attributes were converted from categorical to numeric values. This was done to enable statistical analysis.

Data Splitting: Of the total data, the dataset was split into 80% training data and 20% testing data, to facilitate the evaluation and performance of different machine learning algorithms applied to new data.

Feature Selection

Most relevant features were selected and then further their dimensionality was reduced. The relevant attributes were reduced to two sets. One containing GAD score, SWL score and SPIN score. The other contained age, number of hours played and streams. Further from these most impactful and significant features were selected using PCA. So, we identified most relevant features that contributed to the outcome variable using different methods.

Clustering Classification

We determined the target class for data to be classified into by using KMeans Clustering algorithm. Four different models were fed and trained on this training data and then tested against the testing data.

These classifiers used were: "Random Forest Classifier", "Logistic Regression Classifier", "XGBoost Classifier", " Decision Tree Classifier", "Support Vector Classifier", "Convolutional Neural Network" and "K-Nearest Neighbor Classifier".

Analysis

Subsequently we performed a comparative analysis of the performances of these classifiers. Various performance metrics were used to establish comparison. These include: Precision, Recall, F1 Score, Accuracy, Cross-Validation Score, Confusion Matrix.

Models Used

K-means

K-means is a clustering algorithm used to group data based on similarities. It is an unsupervised algorithm and that is why we chose it to create target classes.

The K-Means model was initialized and trained with hyperparameters: n_estimaters = 5, max_iter = 300, ran- dom_state = 0, n_init = 40 and "k-means++" initializer. Figure 71.1 depicts results of KMeans algorithms applied to the data.

Random Forest

A random forest is a group of many decision trees. It trains these trees on subsamples of data randomly. These trees are uncorrelated.

N_estimaters or number of decision trees to be analyzed are defined and then these decision trees train on n subsamples of the training data, each tree on a different sample. For prediction, majority vote takes place as the result of each decision tree is combined.

For this reason we chose to test random forest as a potential machine learning model for our analysis.

The Random Forest model was initialized and trained with hyperparameters: n_estimaters = 2000, random_state = 44 and max_depth = 16.

Logistic Regression

In multiclass logistic regression, instead of only a binary result, it provides probabilities for each class, enabling more complex and adaptable forecasts. Insights into the underlying data generation process are gained by examining the link between predictor variables and the outcome. This made logistic regression a promising choice for our analysis.

The Logistic Regression model was initialized and trained with h per parameters: max_iter = 10000.

XGBoost

XGBoost or Extreme Gradient Boost is a very powerful algorithm used for classification. Its performance is usually better than those of other conventional classifiers. Like some of the previously discussed algorithms, it can also accurately handle large amounts of data. It is appropriate for large-scale applications because of its scalability and ability for parallel processing.

The XGBoost model was initialized and trained with hyperparameters: n_estimaters = 1000, max_depth = 16, sub- sample = 0.7 eta = 01, and colsample_bytree = 0.8.

Decesion Tree (Gini Index Based)

It's a way to split the decision tree through the Gini index. Entropy method and obtaining information focused on purity and impurities in one node. The Gini or impurity index measures the probability that a random instance will be mis- classified when selected at random. The lower the Gini index, the lower the chance of misclassification.

The decision tree model was constructed and trained on "gini" criterion and hyperparameters: random_state = 0 and max_depth = 20.

Support Vector Classifier (SVC)

Support Vector Classifier (SVC) being a powerful machine learning algorithm is used for classification tasks. In order to categorize data points into multiple classes, the Support Vector Classifier (SVC), creates a hyperplane or series of hyperplanes in a high-dimensional space.

The "Support Vector Classifier" was built on the NuSVC variant of the SVC(SVM). It was initialized and trained on the following hyperparameters: nu = 0.38, degree = 4, probability = True and random state = 44.

Convolutional Neural Network (CNN)

Approaching the problem with a different and rather unconventional perspective, we applied a manually constructed convolutional neural network to understand its performance on a relational dataset. We used label encoding and feature selection to ultimately convert the data frame into multiple NumPy arrays corresponding to each record to be fed through the neural network.

It will be interesting to see how a convolutional neural network performs on a data frame or relational dataset.

A 1-D sequential convolutional neural network was constructed consisting of the following layers:

Conv1D(32,3), Maxpool1D(pool_size=(2)), Conv1D(16,1), Maxpool1D(pool_size=(2)), dropout(0.2), Flatten(), Dense(32), Dense(1,'softmax').

K-Nearest Neighbor (KNN)

For categorization issues, "K-nearest neighbor (KNN)", which is a simple machine learning technique, is used. It works by identifying the k training set data points that are closest to a particular input point, and then assigning a label based on the majority class of the k neighbors. This makes KNN a potential algorithm to test and analyze in our study.

The KNN model was initialized and trained with hyperparameters: n_neighbors = 18, leaf_size = 2000, p = 1.

Findings and Discussion

The data was tested, classified into and analyzed from the classes determined by KMeans Clustering Algorithm using different Classifiers namely "Decision Tree, Random Forest, Logistic Regression, XGBoost, Support Vector Classifier (SVC), Convolutional Neural Networks and K-Nearest Neighbor".

The best performing method for the specific data was determined by comparing and analyzing the performances of different classifiers.

Performance was determined on the basis of various performance metrics which include "accuracy", "precision", "recall", "f1 score", "support", "k-fold cross validation score" and "mean cross validation score".

Labels identified using KMeans were:

Label 0: Moderate_Anxiety, Low_Satisfaction_with_life, Moderate_Social phobia

Label 1: Very_High_Satisfaction_with_life

Label 2: Moderate_Anxiety High Satisfaction with life Moderate Social phobia

Label 3: Very_High_Anxiety, Low_Satisfaction with life, Very_High_Social phobia

Label 4: Moderately_Satisfied_about_life , have little anxiety and social phobia

Performance

Random Forest Classifier

Table 71.1 shows classification report of random forest classifier.

Table 71.1 Classification report of random forest classifier

Class	Precision	Recall	F1-score	Support
0	0.89	0.85	0.87	514
1	0.92	0.92	0.92	655
2	0.79	0.82	0.88	225
3	0.81	0.97	0.88	225
4	0.90	0.86	0.88	679

	Precision	Recall	F1-score	Support
Accuracy Score			0.88	2417
Average Macro	0.86	0.88	0.87	2417
Weighted Average	0.88	0.88	0.88	2417

Accuracy score: 0.8775341332230038
5-fold cross validation:
Mean score: 0.8652434329679123

Logistic Regression Classifier

Table 71.2 shows classification report using logistic regression classifier.

Table 71.2 Classification report of logistic regression classifier

Class	Precision	Recall	F1-score	Support
0	0.92	0.93	0.92	484
1	0.94	0.96	0.95	646
2	0.94	0.92	0.93	365
3	0.93	0.95	0.94	263
4	0.93	0.91	0.91	659

	Precision	Recall	F1-score	Support
Accuracy Score			0.93	2417
Average Macro	0.93	0.93	0.93	2417
Weighted Average	0.93	0.93	0.93	2417

Accuracy score: 0.9309060819197352
5-fold cross validation:
Mean score: 0.9308827578931794

XGBoost Classifier

Table 71.3 shows classfification results using XGBoost classifier.

Table 71.3 Classification report of XGBoost classifier

Class	Precision	Recall	F1-score	Support
0	0.92	0.94	0.93	484
1	0.97	0.97	0.97	661
2	0.93	0.89	0.91	371
3	0.91	0.96	0.94	255
4	0.95	0.95	0.95	646

	Precision	Recall	F1-score	Support
Accuracy Score			0.88	2417
Average Macro	0.86	0.88	0.87	2417
Weighted Average	0.88	0.88	0.88	2417

Accuracy score: 0.9462143152668597
5-fold cross validation:
Mean score: 0.9405676061123334

Decision Tree Classifier

Table 71. 4 depicts classification results using decision tree classifier.

Table 71.4 Classification report of decision tree classifier

Class	Precision	Recall	F1-score	Support
0	0.83	0.82	0.82	495
1	0.89	0.92	0.91	639
2	0.75	0.70	0.72	382
3	0.81	0.87	0.84	251
4	0.87	0.86	0.87	650

	Precision	Recall	F1-score	Support
Accuracy Score			0.84	2417
Average Macro	0.83	0.83	0.83	2417
Weighted Average	0.84	0.84	0.84	2417

Accuracy score: 0.8431940422010757
5-fold cross validation:
Mean score: 0.8330444259343995

From the accuracy measurement data obtained for each of the different models used, we observe that the best performing technique on the training and test data is the XGBoost model with 100% training accuracy, 94.05% cross validation score, 94.62% test accuracy and 0.94 f1 score accuracy. This is followed by the Logistic Regression model with 93.98% training accuracy, 93.09% testing accuracy, 93.08% cross validation score and 0.93 f1 score accuracy.

Support Vector Classifier

Table 71.5 shows classification results using support vector classifier.

Table 71.5 Classification report of support vector classifier

Class	Precision	Recall	F1-score	Support
0	0.73	0.76	0.74	472
1	0.87	0.84	0.85	681

Class	Precision	Recall	F1-score	Support
2	0.68	0.71	0.70	344
3	0.76	0.89	0.82	230
4	0.78	0.73	0.76	690

	Precision	Recall	F1-score	Support
Accuracy Score			0.78	2417
Average Macro	0.76	0.78	0.77	2417
Weighted Average	0.78	0.78	0.78	2417

Accuracy score: 0.7778237484484899
5-fold cross validation:
Mean score: 0.7722875629851467

Furthermore, it can be observed that Support Vector Classifier being a highly accurate and powerful classification tool only gives a test accuracy of 77.78% and a cross validation score of 77.22% which is less as compared to XGBoost and Logistic Regression models. This can be attributed to the fact that SVC is a powerful algorithm particularly in situations where there are a small number of observations, whereas our data is considerably large.

Convolutional Neural Network

Table 71.6 shows classification results using convolutional neural network.

Table 71.6 Classification report of convolutional neural network

Class	Precision	Recall	F1-score	Support
0	0.00	0.00	0.00	0
1	1.00	0.27	0.42	12081
2	0.00	0.00	0.00	0
3	0.00	0.00	0.00	0
4	0.00	0.00	0.00	0

	Precision	Recall	F1-score	Support
Accuracy Score			0.27	12081
Average Macro	0.20	0.05	0.08	12081
Weighted Average	1.00	0.27	0.42	12081

Accuracy score: 0.2661
5-fold cross validation:
Mean score: 0.2661

The Convolutional Neural Network on the other hand with 26.61% overall accuracy and even then, effectively 0 error shows that it has extremely overfitted. Feeding the data frame data as records of NumPy arrays doesn't seem to have worked as expected. We can conveniently infer that convolutional neural networks work better with image data and produce desirable results for image classification.

K-Nearest Neighbor

Table 71.7 shows classification results using k-nearest neighbor.

Table 71.7 Classification report of K-nearest neighbor classifier

Class	Precision	Recall	F1-score	Support
0	0.43	0.56	0.49	377
1	0.90	0.62	0.73	954
2	0.25	0.62	0.35	142
3	0.41	0.86	0.55	127
4	0.66	0.52	0.58	817

	Precision	Recall	F1-score	Support
Accuracy Score			0.59	2417
Average Macro	0.53	0.64	0.54	2417
Weighted Average	0.68	0.59	0.61	2417

Accuracy Score: 0.5904013239553165
5-fold cross validation:
Mean score: 0.5802501664534053

It can further be observed that the K-Nearest Neighbor algorithm only gives a test accuracy of 59.04% and a cross validation score of 58.02% which is less as compared to XGBoost, Logistic Regression and even SVC models. This may be an implication of the fact that the dataset we have used is considerably dimensional in nature even after feature selection and KNN may not perform well with high dimensional data.

Conclusion and Future Scope

From the accuracy measurement data obtained for each of the different models used, we observe that the best performing technique on the training and test data is the XGBoost model with 94.62% accuracy. This is followed by the Logistic Regression model with 93.09% accuracy.

However, we can see that the training accuracy of XGBoost is 100%. This can be an indicator of an overfitted model. As a consequence, it can be assumed that the best working model among the developed techniques for real life application is the Logistic Regression model. There is significant scope of improvement and novelty in this problem and area.

We can think of using a novel dataset with different attributes and features to understand unknown associations with mental health pertaining to video gaming.

Apart from this we can use more different classifiers to analyze the data to understand if they can render us better performance and capabilities. These can include support vector machines, Naïve Bayes, ANN etc.

The scope of this study cannot be just limited to characterizing and predicting effects on mental health but also can be widened to monitor real time data in order to determine potential bad effects on mental health and to alert for leading a better lifestyle. This implies that depending upon the feasibility, IoT can also be potentially used.

Dataset can be increased for better and more accurate performance.

References

1. Wang, C. Y., Wu, Y. C., Su, C. H., Lin, P. C., Ko, C. H., and Yen, J. Y. (2017). Association between internet gaming disorder and generalized anxiety disorder. *Journal of behavioral addictions*, 6(4), 564–571.
2. Wartberg, L., Kriston, L., Zieglmeier, M., Lincoln, T., and Kammerl, R. (2019). A longitudinal study on psychosocial causes and consequences of internet gaming disorder in adolescence. *Psychological Medicine*, 49(2), 287–294.
3. Lee, S. Y., Bahn, G. H., and Lee, S. M. (2017). Comparing machine learning algorithms for predicting depression among Korean adults. *Neuropsychiatric Disease and Treatment*, 13, 2627–2635.
4. Männikkö, N., Billieux, J., Kääriäinen, M., and Griffiths, M. D. (2015). The relationship between addictive use of social media and video games and symptoms of psychiatric disorders: a large-scale cross-sectional study. *Psychology of Addictive Behaviors*, 29(4), 896–904.
5. Rehbein, F., Kleimann, M., and Mößle, T. (2010). Prevalence and risk factors of video game dependency in adolescence: results of a German nationwide survey. *Cyberpsychology, Behavior, and Social Networking*, 13(3), 269–277.
6. Fazeli, S., Zeidi, I. M., Lin, C. Y., Namdar, P., Griffiths, M. D., Ahorsu, D. K., and Pakpour, A. H. (2020). De- pression, anxiety, and stress mediate the associations between internet gaming disorder, insomnia, and quality of life during the COVID-19 outbreak. *Addictive Behaviors Reports*, 12, 100307.
7. Nemesure, M. D., Heinz, M. V., Huang, R., and Jacobson, N. C. (2021). Predictive modeling of depression and anxiety using electronic health records and a novel machine learning approach with artificial intelligence. *Scientific Reports*, 11(1), 1980.
8. Kuss, D. J., and Griffiths, M. D. (2012). Internet gaming addiction: a systematic review of empirical research. *International Journal of Mental Health and Addiction*, 10(2), 278–296.
9. Jacobson, N. C., and Feng, B. (2022). Digital phenotyping of generalized anxiety disorder: using artificial intelligence to accurately predict symptom severity using wearable sensors in daily life. *Translational Psychiatry*, 12(1), 336.
10. Neuroscience News (2022). AI can predict anxiety and depression from your speech. *Neuroscience News*.

72 Deep long short-term memory network for forecasting prices

Taniya Chakraborty[1,a], Tanishka Choudhary[1,b] and Saurav Singla[2,c]

[1]School of Chemical Engineering and Physical Sciences, Lovely Professional University, Phagwara, India

[2]College of Agriculture, Sri Karan Narendra Agriculture University, Jobner, India

Abstract

Improving the forecasts are helpful for all the stakeholders in the system. Usually, the price series are influenced by recent values as well as the values way back at some point. The long short-term memory (LSTM) networks are a fairly recent development in the field of neural networks which address this property of such time series signals. It achieves so by allowing the network to keep memory of past event and improve the predictions. Application of these remained relatively lesser explored for modelling the agricultural commodity prices in India. Forecasting the fluctuating prices of vegetables has remained a challenging task for forecasters. Onion prices amongst the list of highly volatile vegetable prices. In this study, we applied LSTMs to this problem. We compared its performance to the traditional autoregressive integrated moving average (ARIMA) model and support vector regression (SVR) model to the price series of onion crop. The results from the study indicated that both the non-parametric techniques, namely LSTM and SVR performed equally well and better than ARIMA, for shorter horizon of six months. But as the horizon of forecast expanded the LSTM model clearly outperformed both the models. The root mean square error for the model improved by 11 percent and 59 percent respectively as compared to SVR and ARIMA respectively. It could be concluded form the study that the LSTM could help improving the forecasts of such chaotic agricultural price series such as onion.

Keywords: ARIMA, food prices, forecasting, long short-term memory, LSTM, SVR

Introduction

Machine learning approaches have been used to model non-linear time series datasets. Jha and Sinha (2014) used a time delay neural network to forecast the monthly wholesale price indices of oil-seed crops, and Kumari et al. [10] used it to predict pod damage in pigeon-pea by pod borer. Singla et al. [21] and Paul and Garai [16] demonstrated the use of wavelet-based hybrid machine learning models to improve onion price forecasts. Durborow et al. [4] emphasized the importance of machine learning methods alongside parametric methods to forecast tomato prices.

Several methods have been used to forecast prices, with Box et al. [3] ARIMA methods being the most popular due to their easy use and automated algorithms.

[a]ktaniyachborty987@gmail.com, [b]tanishka01.sre@gmail.com,
*corresponding author: [c]saurav.singla@bhu.ac.in

Recent examples include Paul et al. [15], Wang [22], Mathew and Murugesan, [11], Şahinli [19].

Long short term memory (LSTM) networks are a recent development in neural networks and have been used in many sectors for improving forecasts. Google started using it in voice transcription Beaufays [1]. Its application in inter-day foreign exchange rates Ito et al. [9], electric load forecasting Memarzadeh and Keynia, [12], future prediction of streamflow and rainfall Ni et al. [13].

In India, onion prices has shown the highest volatility index (49.30%) from 2011 to 2016 among the three highest price sensitive vegetables. [2, 5] Export bans are ineffective and market intelligence could help. However, onion farming is a gamble due to fluctuating prices. Rajpoot et al. [17] explored how the lockdown has influenced the prices. Economists have suggested improving forecasts to control unexpected surges in onion prices. When NAFED procured buffers, better forecasts became an important tool for controlling volatility. [18, 20]

This study attempted to apply LSTM network to forecast prices from Delhi wholesale market with a purpose of comparing the methodology with other frameworks. The series was fitted with ARIMA and SVR models for comparison with LSTM.

Dataset

Data series of onion prices (in rupees per quintal) from the first month of 2004 to December 2021 were used from many markets in various states across the country. The data that was used was obtained from the National Horticultural Research and Development Foundation in New Delhi. (NHRDF). The website supplied data from several markets across the country. Various marketplaces for various crops were investigated for this study. The number of data points available for a single series was a major criterion. A series with fewer missing values was favoured to one with a greater number of missing data points.

Methodology and Model Specification

Auto Regressive Integrated Moving Average (ARIMA)
In contrast to exponential smoothing which explores the trend and seasonality in the time series the ARIMA models focus on the autocorrelation property. These are linear, univariate and parametric models. The models are constructed based on three parameters (p, d, q). [8] The model is represented as

$$\phi_p(B)\nabla^d y_t = \theta_q(B)\varepsilon_t$$

$$\left(1 - \phi_1 B - \phi_2 B^2 - \cdots - \phi_p B^p\right)\nabla^d x_t = \left(1 - \theta_1 B - \theta_2 B^2 - \cdots - \theta_q B^q\right)\varepsilon_t$$

(1)

The $\phi_i's$ refers to the AR coefficients and $\theta_q's$ refers to MA coefficients. ε_t is assumed to be the white noise (viz. mean=0, variance=constant).

Nonlinear Support Vector Regression (SVR) Model

For a data set $D = \{(x_i, y_i)\}_{i=1}^{N}$, where $x_i \in R^n$ input vector is, $y_i \in R$ is scalar output and N corresponds to size of data set, general form of Nonlinear SVR estimating function is:

$$f(x) = w^T \varphi(x) + b \tag{2}$$

where $\varphi(.):R^n \rightarrow R^{nb}$ is a nonlinear mapping function from original input space into a higher dimensional feature space, which can be infinitely dimensional, $w \in R^{nb}$ is weight vector, b is bias term and superscript T indicates transpose (Vapnik et al., 1996).

Long Short-Term Memory (LSTM) Networks

Initially they were purposed by Hochreiter and Schmidhuber [7], however a these were amended by many other researchers.

The recurrent neural networks (RNN) are special type of neural networks which are capable of handling long term dependencies by default. An LSTM is a special kind of recurrent neural network (RNN) which were specifically designed to avoid the problem of long-term dependencies. [6, 14 and 23]

An LSTM could be mathematically represented as below

$$f_t = \sigma(W_{fh}h_{t-1} + W_{fx}x_t + b_f),$$
$$i_t = \sigma(W_{ih}h_{t-1} + W_{ix}x_t + b_i),$$
$$\tilde{c}_t = \tanh(W_{\tilde{c}h}h_{t-1} + W_{\tilde{c}x}x_t + b_{\tilde{c}}),$$
$$c_t = f_t \cdot c_{t-1} + i_t \cdot \tilde{c}_t,$$
$$o_t = \sigma(W_{oh}h_t - 1 + W_{ox}x_t + b_o),$$
$$h_t = o_t \cdot \tanh(c_t)$$

Where x_t, h_t, c_t and y_t denote the input, the recurrent information, the cell state of LSTM and the out-put of the cell at time t. W_i, $W_{\tilde{c}}$ and W_o are the weights, and the operator '·' denotes the pointwise multiplication of two vectors. When the forget gate, f_t, is set to 1, it keeps this information; otherwise, a value of 0 means it discards all of it. While updating the cell state, the input gate (i_t) can choose what new information can be kept into cell state and output gate (o_t) decides what information can be output based on the cell state.

Results and Discussion

Summary Statistics

The numbers as well as the violin cum box plot presented in "Table 72.1" helped concluding about non-normality of time series data. The data clearly seemed to be skewed with tails on the right side. The extreme values had pulled the distribution in this manner. The average price of onion as concluded from both mean and the median of the series in Delhi wholesale market was somewhere near to □1000 per quintal. However, the measures of deviation undoubtedly shown that the data was spread over a very long range.

Table 72.1 Descriptive statistics of the onion price series from Delhi wholesale market

Descriptive Statistic	Value
Mean	1,188.45
First Quartile	655.50
Median	949.00
Third Quartile	1,372.25
Range	5,373.00
Minimum	370.00
Maximum	5743.00
Std. dev.	862.56
Coef. Of Var.	0.73
Mean absolute Dev.	505.57
Inter Quartile Range	716.75
Skewness	2.22
Kurtosis	5.74

(*Source:* Author's compilation)

Table 72.2 The parameter estimates of SVR and ARIMA models

Model	Model Details				
ARIMA(2,1,1) (0,1,1)	Parameter	Estimate	Std. Error	z value	Pr(>|z|)
	AR1	1.219	0.075	16.18	<0.001
	AR2	-0.468	0.072	-6.53	<0.001
	MA1	-0.947	0.051	-18.53	<0.001
	SMA1	-1	0.169	-5.92	<0.001
SVR with RBF Kernel	Type	Cost	γ	$\in$	Count
	eps	1	1	0.1	120

Initial 168 (of 192) values of price data were used for the training purpose. The fitting of ARIMA model went in a usual manner. The series was checked for stationarity and seasonality and required differencing was carried out. The ACF and PACF functions of the actual price series, differenced and seasonally differenced series were used for identification of the model. The coefficients of the estimated model were all significant (as mentioned in "Table 72.2"). The eps-regression type of support vector methodology was estimated for the same train set. The parameters of SVR model, which were cost, gamma (γ), epsilon ($\in$), are also presented in "Table 72.2".

For fitting of LSTM model, a number of combinations were tried to figure out the best suited number of layers for and number of in each layer neurons. To avoid the over fitting the regularization was achieved through dropout weights in deeper layers. The network architecture in first column of "Table 72.3" is the number of neurons in each layer. The numbers in parenthesis are the weight dropping out proportions. The authors also experimented with the batch size and number of epochs for training of the network with the purpose of optimizing the performance against the number of parameters. There was no significant improvement in results beyond three layers as well as two hundred epochs of training. The network was evaluated on the basis of RMSE for train and test sets. Although the model M18 (with 32, 8 (0.2), 4 (0.1), 1) reported best RMSE for test set (794.45 and for 371.59 train), the model M15 (with 16, 8 (0.2), 4 (0.1), 1) was finalized as the winner (RMSE 370.23 for train was and 802.98 for test). It was because the improvement in RMSE was not worth for more than double parameter count (1872 for M15 against 5293 for M18). However, it must be

Table 72.3 Fitting of LSTM with train and test

Model	Network Archi-tecture	LSTM Layers	Batch Size	Epochs	Train	Test
M_1	16,1	1	1	100	368.94	848.11
M_2	16,1	1	1	200	369.75	818.22
M_3	16,1	1	6	100	370.23	866.64
M_4	16,1	1	6	200	369.75	818.22
M_5	32,1	1	1	100	367.8	843.91
M_6	32,1	1	6	100	369.46	863.93
M_7	32,1	1	6	200	369.71	840.81
M_8	16,8,1	2	1	100	367.22	818.57
M_9	16,8(0.1),1	2	1	100	368.14	824.47
M_{10}	16,8(0.1),1	2	6	100	370.66	852.02
M_{11}	16,8(0.1),4,1	3	1	100	369.14	815.51
M_{12}	16,8(0.1),4,1	3	6	100	370.76	825.58
M_{13}	16,8(0.1),4(0.1),1	3	1	100	369.56	811.47
M_{14}	16,8(0.1),4(0.1),1	3	6	100	370.34	823.16
M_{15}	16,8(0.2),4(0.1),1	3	1	200	370.23	802.98
M_{16}	16,8(0.2),4(0.1),1	3	6	100	370.33	822.18
M_{17}	16,8(0.2),4(0.1),1	3	6	200	370.75	806.83
M_{18}	32,8(0.2),4(0.1),1	3	1	200	371.59	794.45
M_{19}	32,8(0.2),4(0.1),1	3	6	100	370.22	820.11
M_{20}	32,8(0.2),4(0.1),1	3	6	200	370.77	803.57

noted that a four-layer deep network with a fairly small number of nodes was enough to produce good enough forecasts and increasing the nodes resulted in over fitting. It suggested that more availability of data or use of higher frequency data may improve their performance.

All three of these models were than used for prediction of future prices of the Delhi wholesale market for upcoming two years. This could be translated as twenty-four months horizon of forecast. The point wise output from the models was plotted against the actual prices in the test set (as presented in "Figure 72.1").

The performance of the models was evaluated in the terms of error. The RMSE, MAE and SMAPE metrices were used for the purpose. All the measures of error agreed with each other all the times. The values in the "Table 72.4" evidently display that the ARIMA model fit was best and was instead quite better than machine learning models. This also points to the possibility of improvement in fitting of these models. Some more factors might be included to achieve that. In addition, the difference in the error measures of SVR and LSTM might had turned out be very small but it was comparatively better the case of SVR model.

The tale of error metrics from the forecasts of the different models was exactly opposite. The machine learning (both SVR and LSTM) models clearly outper-formed the ARIMA model. The RMSE of the forecast from these (SVR and LSTM) models for first six months was approximately 70 percent better than ARIMA model and was almost at par with each other. However, the LSTM could be seen as the clear winner for the forecast horizon of 12, 18 as well as 24 months (also visually presented in "Figure 72.2"). Hence, it could be said that the model did understand the pattern of variation pretty well and better than the other variables. The forecasts presented in Figure 72.1 visibly show that the LSTM model forecast reached nearest to the peak that occurred during the November

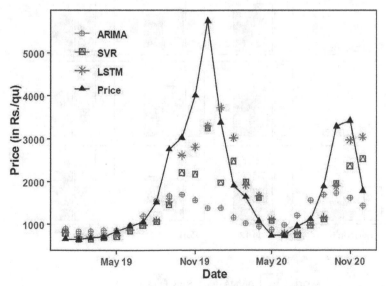

Figure 72.1 The actual onion prices against the forecasted values by ARIMA, SVR and LSTM models

Table 72.4 Accuracy results for fit as well as forecasted values from different models.

Horizon	Error	ARIMA	SVR	LSTM
Fit	RMSE	**292.81**	366.59	370.23
	MAE	**181.40**	225.62	233.43
	SMAPE	**15.83**	18.88	19.62
Horizon 6	RMSE	157.89	**89.88**	90.63
	MAE	134.67	**72.56**	77.02
	SMAPE	17.51	**9.49**	10.14
Horizon 12	RMSE	1530.38	1008.05	**879.30**
	MAE	850.09	617.75	**518.19**
	SMAPE	36.27	25.64	**21.68**
Horizon 18	RMSE	1357.04	912.96	**788.00**
	MAE	782.86	589.53	**496.91**
	SMAPE	37.42	26.86	**23.28**
Horizon 24	RMSE	1279.00	892.52	**802.98**
	MAE	778.93	619.66	**544.91**
	SMAPE	37.32	28.95	**25.78**

(*Source:* Author's compilation)

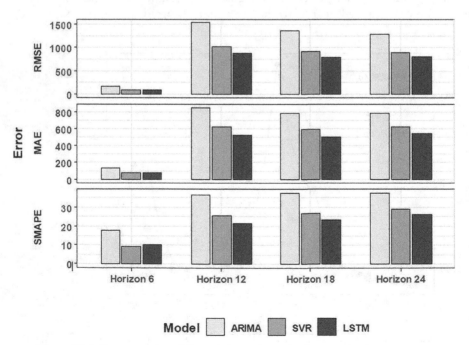

Figure 72.2 Error metrics of fit and throughout the forecast horizon

and December of 2019. Moreover, this hike in price was also the highest peak in whole dataset. Nowhere in the training set the prices went this high hence it could also be noted as one unavoidable limitation of this sort.

Conclusion

The parametric methods of time series analysis are less effective in modelling a time series that doesn't go well with the usual assumptions. The study was intended to empirically investigate the performance of the long short term memory networks to forecast the onion prices in Delhi market as compared to that such parametric models as well as other machine learning models like non-linear support vector regression. The results based on RMSE, SMAPE and MAE comparisons were enough to conclude the superiority of the LSTM networks over its counterparts. However, more availability of data or use of higher frequency data may improve their performance. Moreover, the author suggests the hybrid and ensemble methods which could be further explored to improve the forecasts. More extensive study including more commodities could be conducted for the generalize of the results.

Acknowledgement

The authors gratefully acknowledge the students, staff, and authority of Chemical Engineering and Physical Science department for their cooperation in the research.

References

1. Beaufays, F. (2015). The neural networks behind Google Voice transcription. Google Research blog. https://ai.googleblog.com/2015/08/the-neural-networks-behind-google-voice.html
2. Birthal, P., Negi, A., and Joshi, P. K. (2019). Understanding causes of volatility in onion prices in India. *Journal of Agribusiness in Developing and Emerging Economies,* 9(3), 255–275. https://doi.org/10.1108/JADEE-06-2018-0068.
3. Box, G. E. P., Jenkins, G. M., Reinsel, G. C., and Ljung, G. M. (2015). Time Series Analysis: Forecasting and Control. John Wiley & Sons.
4. Durborow, S. L., Kim, S. W., Henneberry, S. R., and Brorsen, B. W. (2020). Spatial price dynamics in the US vegetable sector. *Agribusiness,* 36(1), 59–78. https://doi.org/10.1002/agr.21603.
5. Bureau, F. E. (2021). Nafed set to complete purchase of 2 lakh tonne onion for buffer stock - the financial express. *Financial Express.* July 28, 2023. https://www.financialexpress.com/market/commodities/nafed-set-to-complete-purchase-of-2-lakh-tonne-onion-for-buffer-stock/2299037/.
6. Gers, F. A., Schmidhuber, J., and Cummins, F. (2000). Learning to forget: continual prediction with LSTM. *Neural Computation,* 12(10), 2451–2471. https://doi.org/10.1162/089976600300015015.
7. Hochreiter, S., and Schmidhuber, J. (1997). Long short-term memory. *Neural Computation,* 9(8), 1735–1780. https://doi.org/10.1162/neco.1997.9.8.1735.
8. Hyndman, R. J., and Khandakar, Y. (2008). Automatic time series forecasting: the forecast package for R. Journal of statistical software, 27, 1–22.

9. Ito, K., Iima, H., & Kitamura, Y. (2022). LSTM forecasting foreign exchange rates using limit order book. *Finance research letters*, 47, 102517.

10. Kumari, P., Mishra, G. C., and Srivastava, C. P. (2017). Forecasting models for predicting pod damage of pigeonpea in varanasi region. *Journal of Agrometeorology*, 19 (3), 265–269.

11. Mathew, S., and Murugesan, R. (2020). Indian natural rubber price forecast–An autoregressive integrated moving average (ARIMA) approach. *The Indian Journal of Agricultural Sciences*, 90 (2), 418–422. http://epubs.icar.org.in/ejournal/index.php/IJAgS/article/view/103067.

12. Memarzadeh, G., and Keynia, F. (2021). Short-term electricity load and price forecasting by a new optimal LSTM-NN based prediction algorithm. *Electric Power Systems Research*, 192(March), 106995. https://doi.org/10.1016/J.EPSR.2020.106995.

13. Ni, L., Wang, D., Singh, V. P., Wu, J., Wang, Y., Tao, Y., and Zhang, J. (2020). Streamflow and rainfall forecasting by two long short-term memory-based models. *Journal of Hydrology*, 583(April), 124296. https://doi.org/10.1016/J.JHYDROL.2019.124296.

14. Olah, C. (2015). Understanding LSTM networks. Colah's Blog. August 27, 2015. https://colah.github.io/posts/2015-08-Understanding-LSTMs/.

15. Paul, R. K., Alam, W., and Paul, A. K. (2014). Prospects of livestock and dairy production in india under time series framework. *The Indian Journal of Animal Sciences*, 84(4), 462–466. http://epubs.icar.org.in/ejournal/index.php/IJAnS/article/view/39858.

16. Paul, R. K., and Garai, S. (2021). Performance comparison of wavelets-based machine learning technique for forecasting agricultural commodity prices. *Soft Computing*, 25(20), 12857–12873. https://doi.org/10.1007/s00500-021-06087-4.

17. Rajpoot, K., Singla, S., Singh, A., and Shekhar, S. (2022). Impact of COVID-19 lockdown on prices of potato and onion in metropolitan cities of India. *Journal of Agribusiness in Developing and Emerging Economies*, 12(3), 386–399. https://doi.org/10.1108/JADEE-04-2021–0099.

18. Reddy, A. (2020). Don't shed tears over onions. *Dailypioneer. Com*, November 5, 2020. https://www.dailypioneer.com/2020/columnists/don---t-shed-tears-over-onions.html.

19. Şahinli, M. A. (2020). Potato price forecasting with holt-winters and ARIMA methods: a case study. *American Journal of Potato Research*, 97(4), 336–346. https://doi.org/10.1007/S12230-020-09788-Y/TABLES/7.

20. Saxena, R., Singh, N. P., Balaji, S. J., Ahuja, U., Kumar, R., and Joshi, D. (2017). Doubling farmers' income in india by 2022–23: sources of growth and approaches. *Agricultural Economics Research Review*, 30(2), 265. https://doi.org/10.5958/0974-0279.2017.00047.7.

21. Singla, S., Paul, R. K., and Shekhar, S. (2021). Modelling price volatility in onion using wavelet based hybrid models. *Indian Journal of Economics and Development*, 17(2), 256–265. https://doi.org/10.35716/IJED/20278.

22. Wang, M. (2019). Short-term forecast of pig price index on an agricultural internet platform. *Agribusiness*, 35(3), 492–497. https://doi.org/10.1002/AGR.21607.

23. Yu, Y., Si, X., Hu, C., and Zhang, J. (2019). A review of recurrent neural networks: LSTM cells and network architectures. *Neural Computation*, 31(7), 1235–1270. https://doi.org/10.1162/neco_a_01199.

24. Jha, G. K., & Sinha, K. (2014). Time-delay neural networks for time series prediction: an application to the monthly wholesale price of oilseeds in India. *Neural Computing and Applications*, 24, 563–571.

25. Vapnik, V. N. (1997, October). The support vector method. In *International conference on artificial neural networks* (pp. 261-271). Berlin, Heidelberg: Springer Berlin Heidelberg.

73 Price prediction of cryptocurrency using deep learning models

Anisha Sindhwani[a], Shefali Gosain[b], Anurag Rawat[c] and Dr. Supriya Raheja[d]

Dept. of CSE, Amity University, Noida, India

Abstract

In this work, approaches for forecasting changes in prices of cryptocurrency, namely Bitcoin using data from Twitter have been investigated and implemented. According to market capitalization, one of the biggest cryptocurrencies is bitcoin. As per studies Twitter is being used more frequently to inform consumers about the currency and its rising popularity, which in turn influences their purchasing decisions. Therefore, having quick access to information about how tweets influence price direction may give bitcoin users or traders a buying or selling advantage. After evaluating the research, it was found that tweet sentiment is not as good a predictor of price direction as tweet volume, which is always positive regardless of price direction. This study seeks to forecast the magnitude as well as the direction of the growth or fall of cryptocurrencies.

Keywords: Bitcoin, cryptocurrency, deep learning, price prediction, sentiment analysis, tweets, VADER

Introduction

Bitcoin (BTC) has remained the most popular and valuable type of digital currency worldwide since its launch in 2009 Nakamoto et al. [13]. Built on the blockchain, Bitcoin is a decentralized digital currency that is maintained by a network of users that independently verify and document transactions. In November 2021, Bitcoin reached a peak of $68,990. Even after the 2022 sell-off during the crypto winter, amongst cryptocurrencies, Bitcoin continues to rank among the financial assets with the best long-term performance. There is currently no reliable way to determine Bitcoin's future price which is making it a high-risk speculative investment. Since its launch in 2006, Twitter's popularity has rapidly risen. 83% of the world's leaders use Twitter, which boasts 1.3 billion accounts, 330 million monthly active users, and about 23 million active users who are merely programmed bots. Every day, 500 million tweets are generated. Because of all these incredible figures, Twitter might be a highly useful tool for learning about what the public thinks. One becomes aware of how those sentiments evolve over time by keeping track of the date that a tweet was written [21-23]. Twitter is a fantastic source of text data on subjects like cryptocurrency so one may be able to investigate potential links between it and pricing [1].

Most of the information is unstructured which is available in tweets, site articles, text messages, emails, etc. Large-scale unstructured data availability

[a]anishasindhwani1011@gmail.com, [b]shefali01gosain777@gmail.com,
[c]anuragrawat469@gmail.com, [d]supriya.raheja@gmail.com

has fuelled the expansion of "natural language processing" (NLP) as a field of study or research [11]. A text fragment can be classified as positive, negative, or neutral since Sentiment Analysis was brought to the NLP community Pang and Lee, [14], Raheja and Asthana, [20]. Lexicon-based procedures calculate the final polarity score by comparing the emotion ratings of a lexicon with the text that is being classified. VADER, or Valence Aware Dictionary and Sentiment Reasoner, is a well-known lexicon-based tool that tries to ascertain polarity based on the input utilizing language patterns Hutto and Gilbert, [15]. By examining the syntax, semantics, and valence values of numerous tweets, requirements for tweet intensity from three certified lexicons are linked with specific characteristics from VADER. In this study, we look into forecasting the magnitude of the price movement as opposed to only its direction. For a range of scenarios, we provide comprehensive analysis and compelling conclusions. We investigate the predicted relationship between Twitter sentiment and associated price movements as a function of various time lags.

The remaining paper is structured as follows. Section II of the paper reviews and analyses the related work and developments that have taken place in the field of price prediction of various cryptocurrencies. Section III contains details about the datasets, cleaning and pre-processing of the data, feature extraction and addresses the categorization problems. Section IV presents the deep learning model used for price prediction. Further ahead the findings are presented and evaluated. Lastly, some ideas for future work have been included in the conclusion.

Literature Review

This section explains the usage of deep learning models for price prediction and the sentiment analysis of Twitter data. A review of the methods used in the field of predicting cryptocurrency prices is presented in Table 73.1. The table gives a direct comparison among different models used in literature.

Researchers have developed an amalgamation of neural network models relying on CNN (convolutional neural network) and LSTM (long short-term memory) to address the issue that the price of Bitcoin varies considerably and is difficult to estimate. The result shows that the precision of value prediction and direction prediction may be greatly improved by combining the CNN and LSTM neural networks Raheja and Malik, [20] when compared to a single structure neural network. Valencia et al. [2] used machine learning techniques and social media data to estimate price changes. Authors concluded that twitter data alone may be utilised in an analysis to forecast the price of specific cryptocurrencies, and that NN are superior to the other competing models. Pant et al. [3] determined the relationship between the erratic Bitcoin price and the sentiment on Twitter. RNN is shown to have an accuracy of 77.62%, and the effectiveness of sentiment classification utilizing the positive and negative tweets in two classes is found to be 81.39%. Serafini et al. [4] compared the ARIMAX and the RNN, two models used to forecast Bitcoin time-series. ARIMAX makes more accurate forecasts than the RNN, and using only a linear model, excellent results can be projected for the Bitcoin market.

Table 73.1 Summary of literature review

Author & Year	Technology used with Accuracy	Days
Galenchuk et al., 2017	RW= 46.2% ARIMA=47.2% MLP=47.5% CNN=68.6%	912
McNally et al., 2018	LSTM=52.78% RNN=50.25%	1065
Pant et al., 2018	RNN=77.62%	180
Yan Li & Wei, 2019	BP= 59% CNN=64% LSTM=58% CNN-LSTM(Hybrid)=64%	600
Valencia et al., 2019	MLP=72% SVM=55% RF=44%	60
Kilimci, 2020	GloVe=82.01% RNN=83.77% CNN=84.3% LSTM=87.45% FastText=89.13%	90
Livieris et al., 2021	CNN-LSTM (Hybrid)=55.03%	1400
Critien et al., 2022	Trend CNN=64.18% Magnitude CNN =57.35%	450

Abraham et al. [5] proposed a technique for forecasting fluctuations in the price of cryptocurrencies. The sentiment ratings from the tweets were divided up by day and compared to the price variations for that day to see if there was a correlation between Twitter sentiment and changes in bitcoin prices. This article demonstrated that deep learning models like the RNN and LSTM are extremely good for Bitcoin prediction, as demonstrated by McNally et al. [6] who demonstrated that the LSTM is better at recognizing long-term dependencies. The LSTM model training had a speed jump of 70.7%, demonstrating that performance gains from parallelizing machine learning algorithms on a GPU are also feasible.

Livieris et al. [7] suggested that a deep neural network model can be used for forecasting the price and movement of cryptocurrencies. They concluded that the recommended approach can efficiently utilize mixed cryptocurrency data, minimize overfitting, and lower the computing cost. By looking at 2.27 million tweets on Bitcoin, Stenqvist and Lönnö [8] looked for sentiment shifts that would indicate a price change soon. According to the analysis of the prediction model, a 79% accuracy rate was achieved by combining tweet sentiments across a 30-minute period with four shifts forward and a 2.2% threshold for sentiment change. Galeshchuk et al. [9] looked at the impact of the daily Twitter data on the price of Bitcoin.

Methodology

Data on historical Bitcoin values between 1 January 2012 and 3 March 2021, were acquired via Kaggle. Figure 73.1 shows close price attribute from the Final Dataset with lag of 1 day that depicts the change in price of Bitcoin in the time interval between 31 Aug 2018 to 23 Nov 2019 to which the dataset was cropped as part of cleaning and pre-processing.

Tweets with the words "bitcoin" or "btc" were taken from a Twitter dataset that was also found using Kaggle. The dataset, which spans the period from 1 January 2016 to 29 March 2019, has more than 20 million tweets. The dataset also comprises the tweet IDs and URLs, the usernames and complete names of linked writers, the number of replies and timestamps that each tweet received, as well as the number of likes and retweets. The model was trained to predict a change in price based on the features "change: The direction of the day's Bitcoin price change (binary, indicating price is rising or falling)" "close: The day's close price" "positive polarity: VADER score" "negative polarity: VADER score" and "tweet volume: The number of tweets during the day." The additional lag for these attributes means that if the lag is two, a training instance will include data from the preceding two days.

Data Cleaning, Pre-Processing and Polarity Score

The high and low prices of the day were eliminated from the list of features for the Bitcoin pricing dataset, leaving only the average price per minute. A dataset that includes both downward and rising trends in Bitcoin price after the cleaning and pre-processing procedures is achieved. Figure 73.2 illustrates the steps followed during pre-processing.

After pre-processing, tweets are given sentiment scores using VADER. Each tweet is given a polarity score by VADER, which ranges from negative to positive,

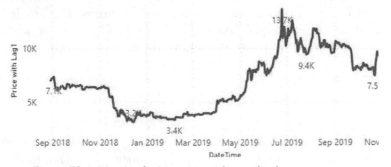

Figure 73.1 Bitcoin closing price with one day lag

Figure 73.2 Procedure for tweet cleaning and pre-processing

neutral to compound. However, for this work the training data set shall only contain positive and negative polarity scores.

Introducing Lag and Merging Datasets
The impact of adding a 1-day lag on a dataset is that the Day 1's score is related to Day 2's price, indicating that day 1's tweets are considered to have an impact on pricing a days later. To concentrate on producing a daily prediction, it was decided to study lag of 1 day as the smallest lag to be detected should be at least 1 day. Lagged datasets are made up of the cleaned Bitcoin data and pre-processed twitter data at the time the tweet was written. To enable a model to make predictions every day, these are then grouped by day. The following steps are taken to group tweets: 1) Flooring of timestamps to the day the tweets were posted is implemented to group them by day. 2)Tweet volume is a new tool that tracks the total number of tweets sent each day. 3) The final record price for the day is then selected as the day's closing Bitcoin price. A train-test ratio of 85:15 was used to divide the dataset into training and testing portions. Given the information gleaned from tweets, the closing price direction can be thought of as a binary classification, indicating whether the price would rise or fall. Another prediction model seeks to estimate the magnitude of the shift in closing day prices as a multi-class classification problem. The closing day prices were grouped into ten different classes [16-19].

Model Specifications
Convolutional Neural Networks (CNNs) are univariate models suitable for classification tasks and one of the deep learning techniques (Uppal et al., 2023). CNNs take dimensionality into account and have been used to extract abstract input features for prediction issues without supervision. Table 73.2 shows the hyperparameters used during the implementation of model.

Assume the convolution layer is preceded by a $P \times P$ neuron layer. On applying an $m \times m$ filter α, the convolutional layer output becomes of the size $(P - n + 1) \times (P - n + 1)$. For calculating the pre-non-linearity input to any unit y_{jk}^m in the layer, we need to add the contributions which are weighted due to the filter from the preceding layer cells as in eq(1).

$$y_{jk}^m = \sum_{b=0}^{n-1}\sum_{c=0}^{n-1} \alpha_{bc} z_{(j+b)(k+c)}^{m-1} \tag{1}$$

Applying non-linearity of convolutional layer: $y_{jk}^m = \gamma(y_{jk}^m)$, where γ = activation function

Assume there is an error function ε and the error to be calculated for the preceding layer is the partial of ε w.r.t. to each neuron output $\left(\frac{\partial \varepsilon}{\partial z_{jk}^m}\right)$. Computing gradient component for each weight:

$$\frac{\partial \varepsilon}{\partial \alpha_{bc}} = \sum_{j=0}^{P-n}\sum_{k=0}^{P-n} \frac{\partial \varepsilon}{\partial y_{jk}^m}\frac{\partial y_{jk}^m}{\partial \alpha_{bc}}$$

Table 73.2 Model hyperparameters

	Direction CNN	Magnitude CNN
#Layers	3	2
Layer size	32	128
Batch Size	50	80
Dataset	1 day lag	1 day lag
Lagged Features	7	3
Train-Test Split	85:15	85:15
Loss Function	Categorical Crossentropy	Categorical Crossentropy
Early Stopping Parameter	Validation Loss	Validation Loss
Early Stopping Patience	20	20

From (1) we can compute that, $\dfrac{\partial y_{jk}^m}{\partial a_{bc}} = z_{(j+b)(k+c)}^{m-1}$. Thus,

$$\frac{\partial \varepsilon}{\partial a_{bc}} = \sum_{j=0}^{P-n} \sum_{k=0}^{P-n} \frac{\partial \varepsilon}{\partial y_{jk}^m} z_{(j+b)(k+c)}^{m-1}$$

The deltas of $\dfrac{\partial \varepsilon}{\partial y_{jk}^m}$ can be calculated for the current layer by simply using the derivative of the activation function, $\gamma'(y)$. Propagating errors back to the previous layer: (From (1), we can compute that $\dfrac{\partial y_{(j-b)(k-c)}^m}{\partial z_{jk}^{m-1}} = \alpha_{bc}$.)

$$\frac{\partial \varepsilon}{\partial z_{jk}^{m-1}} = \sum_{b=0}^{n-1} \sum_{c=0}^{n-1} \frac{\partial \varepsilon}{\partial y_{(j-b)(k-c)}^m} \frac{\partial y_{(j-b)(k-c)}^m}{\partial z_{jk}^{m-1}} = \sum_{b=0}^{n-1} \sum_{c=0}^{n-1} \frac{\partial \varepsilon}{\partial y_{(j-b)(k-c)}^m} \alpha_{bc}$$

Results

Figures 73.3 and 73.4 show the mean accuracy, the maximum accuracy, and the minimum accuracy for the price direction prediction model and the price magnitude model respectively with a time-lag of one day. For each model, the maximum, minimum and mean are calculated over five runs, with the data being randomly shuffled for each run. Figure 73.5 illustrates the comparison among various models used by other authors. It is important to note that our model exceeds those described in Galeshchuk et al. [9], Li and Wei (2019), Livieris et al. [7], and Critien et al. [12] with a maximum accuracy of 71.63% for price direction prediction and 58.2% for price magnitude prediction. The maximum accuracy of the prediction models used in this work is lower than the maximum

Prediction Accuracy of CNN (Direction)

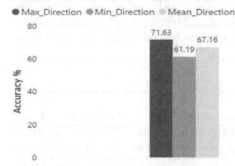

Figure 73.3 Accuracies for direction prediction

Prediction Accuracy of CNN (Magnitude)

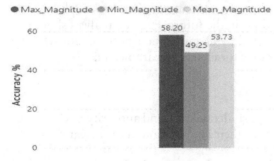

Figure 73.4 Graph of accuracies for magnitude prediction

Accuracy by Author and Model

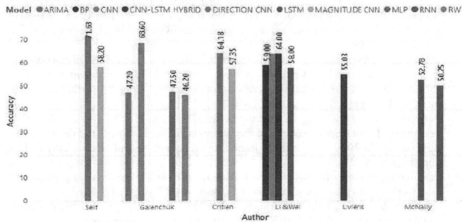

Figure 73.5 Comparison with accuracy of existing models

accuracy of the models presented by Pant et al. [3], Valencia et al. [2], and Kilimci [10], which is probably because of the data period chosen. Our analysis covers approximately 450 days while their investigations were based on approximately 180, 60, and 90 days respectively. By examining the data for the given periods more closely, it is evident that their studies were conducted during periods of relatively low volatility. But in our study (which uses a far longer window), volatility is observed to fluctuate significantly more overall. Moreover, the datasets in these studies have been created by the authors themselves by collecting tweets and thus, may be biased.

Conclusion and Future Work

This study presented the comparison among different deep learning models for predicting price of bitcoin. The study used the twitter data. The study discussed how the social data acts as important factor while predicting the price of cryptocurrency. The study also considered the impact of 1-day lag while publishing the price and predicting the price. The experimental results show that CNN model introduced in this study provides the better and improved accuracy over the existing models in the literature. Predictions were made based on 1-day lag. Predictions with a 1-day lag are usually more accurate. Hence, additional research into the effects of temporal lags needs to be done in the future. Further analysis should be done to determine whether this is caused by certain data aspects and/or why the various algorithms perform better/worse for changing parameters.

Acknowledgement

The authors gratefully acknowledge the students, staff, and authority of Computer Science and Engineering department for their cooperation in the research.

References

1. Li, Y., and Dai, W. (2020). Bitcoin price forecasting method based on CNN-LSTM hybrid neural network model. *The Journal of Engineering*, 13(2020), 344–347.
2. Valencia, F., Gómez-Espinosa, A., and Valdés-Aguirre, B. (2019). Price movement prediction of cryptocurrencies using sentiment analysis and machine learning. *Entropy*, 21(6), 589.
3. Pant, D. R., Neupane, P., Poudel, A., Pokhrel, A. K., and Lama, B. K. (2018). Recurrent neural network based bitcoin price prediction by twitter sentiment analysis. In 2018 IEEE 3rd International Conference on Computing, Communication and Security (ICCCS), (pp. 128–132). IEEE, 2018.
4. Serafini, G., Yi, P., Zhang, Q., Brambilla, M., Wang, J., Hu, Y., and Li, B. (2020). Sentiment-driven price prediction of the bitcoin based on statistical and deep learning approaches. In 2020 International Joint Conference on Neural Networks (IJCNN), (pp. 1–8). IEEE, 2020.
5. Abraham, J., Higdon, D., Nelson, J., and Ibarra, J. (2018). Cryptocurrency price prediction using tweet volumes and sentiment analysis. *SMU Data Science Review*, 1(3), 1.
6. McNally, S., Roche, J., and Caton, S. (2018). Predicting the price of bitcoin using machine learning. In 2018 26th Euromicro International Conference on Parallel, Distributed and Network-Based Processing (PDP), (pp. 339–343). IEEE, 2018.

7. Livieris, I. E., Kiriakidou, N., Stavroyiannis, S., and Pintelas, P. (2021). An advanced CNN-LSTM model for cryptocurrency forecasting. *Electronics,* 10(3), 287.
8. Stenqvist, E., and Lönnö, J. (2017). Predicting bitcoin price fluctuation with twitter sentiment analysis.
9. Galeshchuk, S., Vasylchyshyn, O., and Krysovatyy, A. (2018). Bitcoin response to twitter sentiments. In CEUR Workshop Proceedings, (pp. 160–168). 2018.
10. Kilimci, Z. H. (2020). Sentiment analysis based direction prediction in bitcoin using deep learning algorithms and word embedding models. *International Journal of Intelligent Systems and Applications in Engineering,* 8(2), 60–65.
11. Parekh, R., Patel, N. P., Thakkar, N., Gupta, R., Tanwar, S., Sharma, G., Davidson, I. E., and Sharma, R. (2022). DL-Guess: deep learning and sentiment analysis-based cryptocurrency price prediction. *IEEE Access,* 10(2022), 35398–35409.
12. Critien, J. V., Gatt, A., and Ellul, J. (2022). Bitcoin price change and trend prediction through twitter sentiment and data volume. *Financial Innovation,* 8(1), 1–20.
13. Georgoula, Ifigeneia; Pournarakis, Demitrios; Bilanakos, Christos; Sotiropoulos, Dionisios N.; and Giaglis, George M., "Using TimeSeries and Sentiment Analysis to Detect the Determinants of Bitcoin Prices" (2015). MCIS 2015 Proceedings. 20, 1–12. http://aisel.aisnet.org/mcis2015/20
14. Pang, B., and Lee, L. (2008). Opinion mining and sentiment analysis. *Foundations and Trends® in Information Retrieval,* 2(1–2), 1–135.
15. Hutto, C., and Gilbert, E. (2014). Vader: a parsimonious rule-based model for sentiment analysis of social media text. In Proceedings of the International AAAI Conference on Web and Social Media, (Vol. 8, no. 1, pp. 216–225). 2014.
16. Georgoula, I., Pournarakis, D., Bilanakos, C., Sotiropoulos, D., and Giaglis, G. M. (2015). Using time-series and sentiment analysis to detect the determinants of bitcoin prices. Available at SSRN 2607167, (2015).
17. Nasir, M. A., Huynh, T. L. D., Nguyen, S. P., and Duong, D. (2019). Forecasting cryptocurrency returns and volume using search engines. *Financial Innovation,* 5(1), 1–13.
18. Raheja, S., and Asthana, A. (2023). Sentiment analysis of tweets during the COVID-19 pandemic using multinomial logistic regression. *International Journal of Software Innovation (IJSI),* 11(1), 1–16.
19. Chowdhury, R., Rahman, M. A.,Rahman, M. S., and Mahdy, M. R. C. (2019). Predicting and forecasting the price of constituents and index of cryptocurrency using machine learning. arXiv preprint arXiv:1905.08444, (2019).
20. Raheja, S., and Malik, S. (2022).Prediction of air quality using LSTM recurrent neural network. *International Journal of Software Innovation (IJSI),* 10(1), 1–16.
21. Peng, D. (2019). Analysis of investor sentiment and stock market volatility trend based on big data strategy. In 2019 International Conference on Robots & Intelligent System (ICRIS), (pp. 269–272). IEEE, 2019.
22. Sul, H. K., Dennis, A. R., and Yuan, L. (2017). Trading on twitter: Using social media sentiment to predict stock returns. *Decision Sciences,* 48(3), 454–488.
23. Derbentsev, V., Matviychuk, A., and Soloviev, V. N. (2020). Forecasting of cryptocurrency prices using machine learning. *Advanced Studies of Financial Technologies and Cryptocurrency Markets,* 211–231.

74 An effective and reliable method for detecting brain tumors in magnetic resonance images

Nallani Sravan Kumar[a], Gudimetla Sai Keerthi Reddy[b], Kamireddi Vamsi[c], Pusala Bala Sai Venkat[d], Lingaladinei Manoj[e] and Narayanadas kamsali Susritha[f]

Department of CSE, Lovely Professional University, Punjab, India

Abstract

An abnormal development of brain cells results in a condition known as a brain tumor. It is difficult to determine a patient's survival rate because tumors are uncommon and come in a variety of shapes. Magnetic Resonance Imaging (MRI) images, which are essential for locating the tumor, can be used to diagnose these tumors; nonetheless, manual recognizable proof is a tedious and troublesome technique that could bring about certain errors in discoveries. Addressing these limitations necessitates the use of computer-assisted techniques. As artificial intelligence advances, clinical imaging is using deep learning (DL) models to distinguish mind tumors utilizing MR pictures. By modifying the EfficientNet-B0 base model of a major convolutional neural network (CNN) with the assistance of our proposed layers, we successfully recognize and differentiate images of frontal cortical developments in this study. Picture updating approaches are used to chip away at the concept of photographs by employing several channels. To make more information tests accessible for preparing our recommended model, information increase procedures are utilized. With a general arrangement and discovery exactness of 98.87 percent, the suggested calibrated cutting-edge EfficientNet-B0 surpasses existing CNN models in order precision, accuracy, review, and region under bend values. Correlation is achieved through the use of DL calculations for VGG16, InceptionV3, Xception, ResNet50, and InceptionResNetV2.

Keywords: convolution neural networks (CNN), deep learning, MRI, transfer learning, and detection are all related to the brain tumor

Introduction

A brain tumour is a condition wherein strange synapses or tissues develop [1]. Each new cell replaces the past one in an anticipated example as cells duplicate and bite the dust. In any event, a few cells induce anomalies and keep sprouting up, causing catastrophic damage to brain capacity and, in some cases, death.. There are no less than 120 particular kinds of diseases of the mind and the central nervous system (CNS). In 2021, mind and central nervous system (CNS) tumors will bring about the passings of 18,600 folks and 3,460 children

[a]chowdarysravan08@gmail.com, [b]gkeerthireddy113@gmail.com,
[c]vamsikamireddi852001@gmail.com, [d]saivenkat8757@gmail.com,
[e]l.manojreddy123@gmail.com, [f]susrithanarayndas193@gmail.com

younger than 15. The 5-year endurance rate for cerebrum growth patients was 36%, and the 10-year endurance rate was 31% [2]. Likewise, 86,010 instances of different mind disease and CNS malignancies were distinguished,in accordance to the National Cancer Institute, in the United States in 2019. Brain tumors are projected to impact around 0.7 million fellow humans in the United States.. There were 0.86 million cases found, with 26,170 patients having malignant tumors and 60,800 having benign tumors [3]. In 2018, 9.6 million people worldwide were diagnosed with cancer, according to the World Health Organization [4]. Early detection of cerebrum tumors is one of the most important factors in preserving a patient's life. While deciding a patient's wellbeing, legitimate assessment of cerebrum growth photographs is fundamental. In the regular technique for recognizing mind malignant growths, a clinician or radiologist looks at magnetic resonance (MR) examines for irregularities and decides. In any case, it vigorously relies upon a specialist's clinical mastery; contrasts in experience levels and pictures demolish diagnosing with uncovered normal eyes [5].

Artificial intelligence (AI), a branch of computer science, tries to give computers intelligence. Intelligence of humans by giving them the ability to learn, comprehend, and solve problems when confronted with a variety of data. The discovery and diagnosis of brain cancers rely heavily on AI. Brain tumour medical procedure is an incredible contender for expanded AI mix because of its complicated methodology. A method that is both highly accurate and dependable for classifying brain tumors has been the subject of numerous efforts. On the other hand, addressing the wide range of form, texture, and contrast variations that exist between and among people remains a difficult issue. Artificial intelligence (AI) features such as deep learning (DL) and machine learning (ML) have lately transformed neurosurgery methods. Among them are data preparation, feature selection, feature reduction, and classification. Due to AI, neurosurgeons may be able to diagnose their patients' brain tumors with greater certainty than ever before, according to research [6]. While promising outcomes are found, the field of deep learning, and neural networks specifically, ascends to noticeable quality. CNNs,

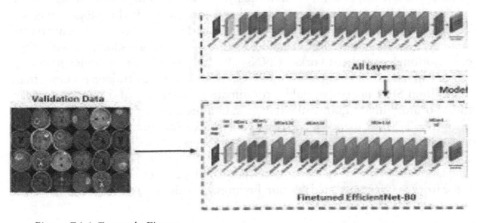

Figure 74.1 Example Figure

or convolutional neural networks, succeed at learning highlights and proposition exactness that is almost boundless. Examples of deep learning applications include design recognisable proof, object localization, speech recognition, and other dynamic tasks [7, 8]. Previous research employed support vector machines (SVMs), K-Nearest Neighbor (K-NN), decision trees, and Naive Bayes to assist the medical community in diagnosing such severe disorders. DL calculations like custom CNNs, VGGNets, GoogleNets, and ResNets were also used. Experts have attempted to use MRI scans to distinguish between benign and malignant growths, but a number of flaws remain, such as poor accuracy, large and sluggish models, and high processing costs.

Literature Survey

Deep Learning Approach For Brain Tumor Detection And Segmentation:

On the off chance that not treated immediately, a brain tumour is a serious ailment that can bring about death. Therefore, in order to schedule therapy as soon as possible, it is essential to identify the tumor in its early stages. In this study, we suggested using a CNN model to find brain tumors. Brain MRI scans are used as a starting point to get enough data for deep learning. After that, the photos are pre-processed to lessen the amount of noise and get ready for the next steps. Pre-processed MRI brain images serve as training for the proposed system, which then uses those characteristics to classify newly input images as tumorous or normal. During preparing, back engendering is used to diminish mistake and produce more exact outcomes. The tumor area is segmented using the unsupervised learning method K-Means, and images are created using autoencoders to remove any extraneous characteristics.

Near Real-Time Intraoperative Brain Tumor Diagnosis Using Stimulated Raman Histology AndDeep Neural Networks:

Intraoperative investigation is basic for conveying viable and safe treatment to malignant growth patients1. The ongoing intraoperative indication of handled tissue with hematoxylin and eosin staining necessitates a significant investment of time, money, and effort2,3. Additionally, a dispersed and shrinking pathology workforce makes it difficult to comprehend intraoperative histologic images4. To predict a near-constant conclusion at the bedside, we present a comparable strategy that combines SRH, a nameless optical imaging technique, with deep convolutional neural networks (CNNs). In contrast to conventional methods, which can take 20-30 minutes, our CNNs, which have been trained on more than 2.5 million SRH images, are able to estimate the location of a mind growth in the laboratory in less than 150 seconds. 2. In a multicenter urgent clinical assessment (n = 278), we came up with that CNN-based interpretation of SRH depicts was not inferior to pathologist-based comprehension associated with traditional histologic images (general precision, 94.6% vs. 93.9%).The development of a supplementary tissue diagnostic route that is independent of a typical pathology laboratory, as demonstrated by our findings, has the potential to speed up the detection of cancer during an operation.

Convolutional Neural Network Based Early Fire Detection:
Since man-made disasters, particularly fires, result in significant property damage and loss of life, detection is critical. A well-known area of study in fire detection research is the application of video-based approaches and wireless sensor networks. However, in order for the WSN-based recognition method to function, there must be fire, a lot of smoke, and fires.

Additionally, video-based models encounter difficulties due to the identification requirements of include vectors and high rule-based models. A method for recognizing fire that makes use of sophisticated deep learning and machine learning calculations was presented in this review. To prevent fires, we utilized picture and sensor data. The model we propose is based on three important brain networks: a cross breed model composed of various MLP brain organizations, an Adaboost-LBP model, and a convolutional brain organization. To anticipate the fire, we made use of the Adaboost-MLP model. The Adaboost-LBP model and a convolutional brain network for fire localization based on security camera images were unveiled as anticipated. At the point when a crisis happens, the Adaboost-LBP model is used to create returns for money invested from pictures. With an accuracy of about 99%, the results of our suggested model are excellent. With additional training, the false alarm rate can be reduced even further.

Machine Learning Based Approach For Multimedia Surveillance During Fire Emergencies:
Video monitoring of man-made disasters like fire has become a popular field of study, and it is helping to develop smart environments. Fires cause significant damage to society and the economy. By catching the fire early, we can avoid these damages. Utilizing vision-based Convolutional Neural Networks (CNNs) for observation, it is currently conceivable to recognize fires thanks to ongoing progressions in implanted handling. Subsequently, we proposed an answer for Sight and sound Observation utilizing AI approaches during fire circumstances. Two models of deep neural networks are included in the approach we propose. To start, we utilized a half and half model involved Adaboost and a few multi-facet perceptron (MLP) brain organizations. The objective of the creamer Adaboost-MLP model is to precisely anticipate fire. The gas, intensity, and smoke sensors are some of the sources of the preparation data for this model. We suggested using a CNN model to anticipate the fire and quickly find it. According to these findings, our trained model can detect fires with an accuracy of around 91 percent.

Very Deep Convolutional Networks ForLarge-Scale Image Recognition:
In this study, we explore how the relevance of a convolutional connection affects its precision overall scale picture affirmation. Our inside-out examination of organizations of expanding profundity demonstrates that increasing the profundity to 16-19 weight layers fundamentally outperforms previous workmanship arrangements by employing an engineering with minuscule (3x3) convolution channels. Based on these revelations, our ImageNet Challenge 2014 proposal won first and second places in the limitation and characterization classes, respectively. In

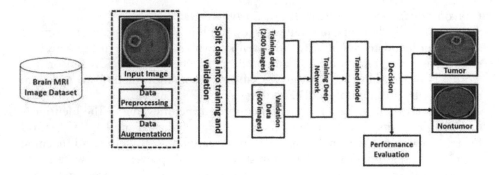

Figure 74.2 Proposed Architecture.

addition, we demonstrate that our portrayals produce cutting-edge results when applied to a wide range of datasets. In order to encourage more research into the use of deep visual representations in computer vision, we have made our two most successful ConvNet models accessible to the general public.

Methodology

Assessments have previously utilized regular ML estimations like support vector machines (SVMs), knearestneighbor (k-NN), decision trees, and Naive Bayes, in addition to DL computations like custom CNNs, VGGNets, GoogleNet, and ResNets, in order to assist the clinical consideration community in diagnosing poisonous diseases. Despite numerous attempts by analysts to identify cancers using MRI images, many flaws remain, including low precision, large and slow models, and expensive processing costs. In addition, larger data sets are always a barrier in the healthcare industry due to concerns about patient privacy that prevent researchers from freely discussing medical information. Additionally, current methods lack accuracy and recall, making them inefficient and requiring more time to categorize images, which delays the patient's treatment.

Past exploration techniques had lower exactness and review levels, which brought about unfortunate proficiency and demanded greater investment for picture classification, subsequently deferring the patient's treatment.

In ongoing examinations, deep learning has been utilized to work on the precision of PC supported clinical diagnostics used to look at cerebrum disease. They are huge instruments in different basic circumstances, for example, the recognition of mind sicknesses and the examination of skin disease pictures, and they assume a significant part in the medical services industry. For the request for mind developments, DL approaches considering move learning and adjusting are inclined in the direction of and routinely used. Through transfer learning, adjusting, and deep convolutional neural networks, this project aims to robotize mind growth grouping and recognition.

Advantages of the Proposed Framework Using information expansion techniques, we may increase the amount of information tests that can be employed to develop our suggested model. With a general order and discovery exactness of 98.87%, the outcomes show that the proposed adjusted cutting edge EfficientNet-B0 beats other CNN models concerning characterization precision, accuracy, recall, and area under curve values.

Implementation

Mobilenet: Mobilenet is a model that channels pictures in an unexpected way in comparison to CNN utilizing a similar convolution approach. It uses the thoughts of profundity convolution and point convolution, rather than standard CNN convolution.

Googlenet: GoogLeNet is a deep convolutional brain network with 22 layers. The organization can be stacked as a pretrained variant that was prepared on ImageNet [1] or Places365 [2] or [3]. The ImageNet-prepared network sorts photographs of consoles, mice, pencils, and a broad range of animals into 1,000 object classes.

Resnet50: In computer vision applications, a deep learning model known as Residual Network (ResNet) currently works. It's a Convolutional Neural Network (CNN) engineering effort aimed towards assisting hundreds or thousands of convolutional layers.

InceptionResnetV2: The Inception ResNet-v2 convolutional brain network was ready on more than a million photos from the ImageNet variety. The 164layer network is equipped for ordering photographs into 1,000 distinct thing classifications, like the console, mouse, pencil, and different creatures.

VGG16: With an exactness of 92.7 percent, the item ID and order calculation VGG16 can classify 1000 photographs into 1000 novel classifications. It is direct to use with move learning and is one of the most widely utilized picture arrangement procedures.

Xception: Xception is a large convolutional neural network with 71 layers. It is possible to stack a trained version of the organization that was trained on over one million images from the ImageNet data set [1]. The pre-trained network can classify photos of consoles, mice, pencils, and other animals into one of 1,000 separate object categories.

InceptionV3: The Inception V3 deep learning model for image categorization is built on CNN as its foundation. The first model, Beginning V1, which was released in 2014 under the name GoogLeNet, has been enhanced into the Starting V3. As the name suggests, a Google group built it.

Fine-tuned efficientnetB5:The article EfficientNet: Describes the EfficientNet B5 Model Architecture Rethinking Convolutional Neural Network Model Scaling. Parameters: weights (optional, EfficientNet B5 Weights) - The weights that were trained before being used. See EfficientNet B5 Weights for additional details and potential values.

Ensemble model- Inception + Mobilenet: Utilizing an assortment of demonstrating strategies or an assortment of preparing informational collections, troupe displaying is a cycle where various particular models are created to foresee an outcome. The method for gathering model then aggregates the data from each base model, resulting in a single final expectation for cryptic information.

Experimental Results

Figure 74.3 Home page

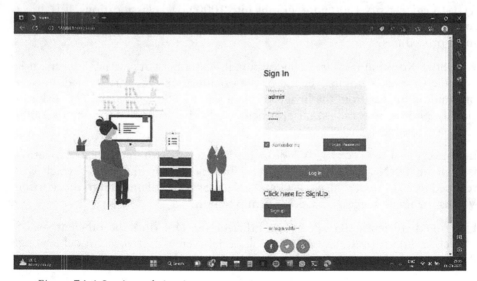

Figure 74.4 Login and sign-in page

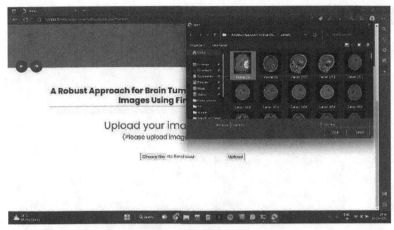

Figure 74.5 Upload Input image

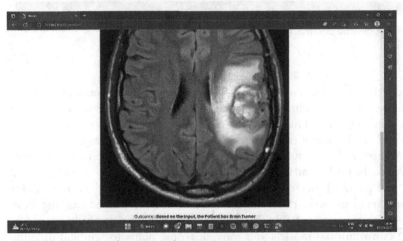

Figure 74.6 Prediction result

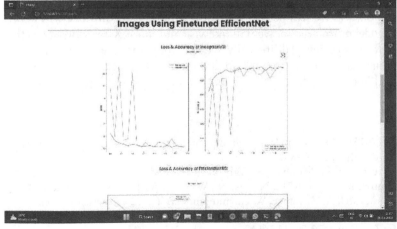

Figure 74.7 Loss and accuracy graph for efficient Net B5

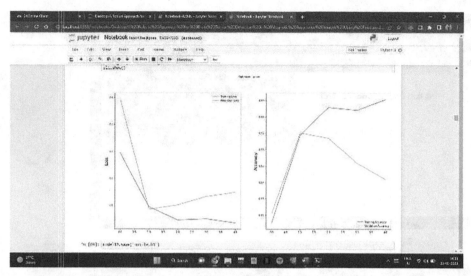

Figure 74.8 Loss and accuracy for ensemble model

Conclusion

Due to the developing requirement for a commonsense and dependable evaluation of immense volumes of clinical information, MR imaging for the conclusion of cerebrum cancers has filled in notoriety. Cerebrum cancers are a perilous condition that should be physically recognized, which takes time and requires the skill of doctors. A robotized demonstrative framework will be expected to find issues in MRI pictures. To find mind growth in MRI information, our group fostered a proficient and refined EfficientNetB0-based move learning engineering. As far as recognizing mind growth, the recommended technique played out the best, with an approval exactness of 98.87 percent. Even though this study zeroed in on five extra convolutional models and move learning plans for clinical imaging mind growth, more examination is required. We will look at more profound CNN models for mind cancer orders that are more huge and have a more noteworthy effect from now on, and we will perform division with less time intricacy. To make the proposed model more precise, we will likewise add more X-ray outputs to the dataset we use for this review. Additionally, we will apply the suggested method to a variety of clinical imaging techniques, including ultrasound, computed tomography (CT), and X-ray, which could serve as a foundation for additional tests.

References

1. Lee, D. Y. (2015). Roles of mTOR signaling in brain development. *Experimental Neurobiology*, 24(3), 177–185.
2. Islami, F., Guerra, C. E., Minihan, A., Yabroff, K. R., Fedewa, S. A., Sloan, K., Wiedt, T. L., Thomson, B., Siegel, R. L., Nargis, N., Winn, R. A., Lacasse, L., Makaroff, L., Daniels, E. C., Patel, A. V., Cance, W. G., and Jemal, A. (2022). American cancer society's report on the status of cancer disparities in the United States, 2021. *CA, Cancer Journal for Clinicians*, 72(2), 112–143.

3. Ostrom, Q. T., Cioffi, G., Gittleman, H., Patil, N., Waite, K., Kruchko, C., and Barn-holtz-Sloan, J. S. (2019). CBTRUS statistical report: primary brain and other central nervous system tumors diagnosed in the United States in 2012–2016. *Neuro-Oncology*, 21(5), v1–v100.

4. World Health Organization. (2021). Cancer. Accessed: January 23, 2022. [Online]. Available: https://www.who.int.

5. Raut, G., Raut, A., Bhagade, J., Bhagade, J., and Gavhane, S. (2020). Deep learning approach for brain tumor detection and segmentation. In Proceedings International Conference on Convergence to Digital World Quo Vadis (ICCDW), Feb. 2020, (pp. 1–5).

6. Hollon, T. C., Pandian, B., Adapa, A. R., Urias, E., Save, A. V., Khalsa, S. S. S., Eichberg, D. G., Amico, R. S. D., Farooq, Z. U., Lewis, S., and Petridis, P. D. (2020). Near real-time intraoperative brain tumor diagnosis using stimulated Raman histology and deep neural networks. *Nature Medicine*, 26(1), 52–58.

7. Saeed, F., Paul, A., Karthigaikumar, P., and Nayyar, A. (2020). Convolutional neural network based early fire detection. *Multimedia Tools and Applications,* 79(13–14), 9083–9099.

8. Saeed, F., Paul, A., Hong, W. H., and Seo, H. (2020). Machine learning based approach for multimedia surveillance during fire emergencies. *Multimedia Tools and Applications*, 79(23–24), 16201–16217.

9. Simonyan, Karen and Zisserman, Andrew. (2014). Very Deep Convolutional Networks for Large-Scale Image Recognition. arXiv 1409.1556.

10. C. Szegedy et al., (2015). Going deeper with convolutions, IEEE Conference on Computer Vision and Pattern Recognition (CVPR), Boston, MA, USA, 2015, pp. 1–9, doi: 10.1109/CVPR.2015.7298594.

11. He, K., Zhang, X., Ren, S., and Sun, J. (2016). Deep residual learning for image recognition. In Proceeding. IEEE Conference on Computer Vision and Pattern Recognition (CVPR), June 2016, (pp. 770–778).

12. Muhammad, K., Khan, S., Ser, J. D., and Albuquerque, V. H. C. D. (2021). Deep learning for multigrade brain tumor classification in smart healthcare systems: a prospective survey. *IEEE Transactions on Neural Networks and Learning Systems*, 32(2), 507–522.

13. Abd-Ellah, M. K., Awad, A. I., Khalaf, A. A. M., and Hamed, H. F. A. (2018). Two-phase multi-model automatic brain tumor diagnosis system from magnetic resonance images using convolutional neural networks. *EURASIP Journal on Image and Video Processing,* 2018, 97.

14. Hu, Z., Tang, J., Wang, Z., Zhang, K., Zhang, L., and Sun, Q. (2018). Deep learning for image-based cancer detection and diagnosis a survey. *Pattern Recognition,* 83, 134–149.

15. Abd-Ellah, M. K., Awad, A. I., Khalaf, A. A. M., and Hamed, H. F. A. (2019). A review on brain tumor diagnosis from MRI images: practical implications, key achievements, and lessons learned. *Magnetic Resonance Imaging*, 61, 300–318.

75 Mitigating the catastrophic impact of 1947: an exploration of the potential benefits of machine learning techniques for disaster response and recovery

Mandeep Kaur[a], Pawan Kumar[b] and Ramandeep Kaur[c]

School of Computer Applications, Lovely Professional University, Punjab, India

Abstract

The Partition of British India in 1947 resulted in the creation of two independent nations: India and Pakistan. The partition was marked by widespread violence and displacement of millions of people along religious lines. The impact of partition has been significant and lasting, with communal tensions, border disputes, and regional conflicts continuing to this day. The partition also led to the largest mass migration in human history, with millions of people forced to leave their homes and resettle in unfamiliar territories. This historic event has been studies by a lot of research scholars especially in the field of social sciences. This research investigates this topic from a novel perspective of exploring how the machine learning techniques could have been useful in mitigating the impact of this event. This objective in this research is to investigate the evidences or records available related to this event and explore the potential applications of machine learning techniques. In particular, the experimental work demonstrated the use of the use of Natural language processing. The techniques of bag of words was used to analyze the speech data available. The outcomes of this research can be helpful in extracting insights regarding what events led to this event, what were the common issues in the aftermath of this event and how emergency response can be improved using computational intelligence techniques in handling such events in future.

Keywords: 1947 Cataclysm, bag of words, british india partition, data analytics, machine learning, natural language processing

Introduction

A pivotal moment in the history of the area was the partition of India in 1947, which resulted in massive bloodshed, upheaval, and fatalities as millions of people had to flee across the newly established borders. The violence was fueled by deep-seated religious and political divisions, as well as the colonial policies of the British Empire. Millions of people were compelled to leave their homes and traverse the new borders as a result of a severe refugee crisis that occurred after the division. The migration was accompanied by widespread atrocities, including mass abductions, rape, and killings. The partition had significant long-term effects on the region, including ongoing tensions between India and Pakistan and ongoing conflicts over the disputed territory of Kashmir. The partition also had significant social, economic, and cultural effects, with communities being uprooted

[a]mandeep.13695@lpu.co.in, [b]pawan.11522@lpu.co.in, [c]ramandeep.11629@lpu.co.in

and displaced, and the creation of new nations with distinct cultural and religious identities. Even today, the partition remains a deeply contentious issue in South Asia, with ongoing debates over its causes, consequences, and legacy.

The development of algorithms that can acquire knowledge from data and make forecasts or judgements without being explicitly programmed is known as machine learning, a subfield of artificial intelligence. In other words, it's a technique for teaching computers to identify patterns in data and base predictions or decisions on those forecasts or decisions. Applications for machine learning algorithms include fraud detection, recommendation systems, audio and picture recognition, natural language processing, and fraud. Overall, machine learning has the potential to revolutionize many fields by enabling automated decision-making and predictive modeling based on large amounts of data. However, it is crucial to ensure that chosen technologies are used morally and sensibly in order to prevent any potential drawbacks, such as bias and discrimination.

While machine learning as a field did not exist at the time of partition of British India (1947), it is interesting to consider how it could have been applied if it were available. The objectives of this research study are:

1. To research the available literature on this incident and categorize the research done in this field by scholars
2. To research the different kinds of evidences(data) available related to this event
3. Exploring how ML techniques would have been helpful in mitigating the impact of this event

The remainder of the essay is structured as follows. The 1947 Cataclysm literature evaluation is compiled in Section 2. Section 3 proposed the problem statement and research methodology. Section 4 explores potential machine learning applications for mitigating impact of this event. Section 5 compiles the results from experimental work and observations related to the application of potential ML techniques. The findings and potential directions for this research's future are outlined in Section 6.

Literature Review

This section reviews the existing literature related to this event. The objective is to identify different directions of work done so far and identify the novel directions for future research, specifically in the use of ML techniques. The partition of British India in 1947 has been the subject of many studies and publications, examining its impact on the region's social, political, and economic landscape. In this literature review, we will explore the impact of the 1947 cataclysm and the various factors that contributed to its aftermath.

The impact of the partition of India, focusing on the violence and trauma experienced by those who lived through it has been explored [1]. The author examined the role of nationalism and identity in the partition and how it has shaped Indian history. The author in [2] compiled a collection of first-hand accounts from individuals who experienced the partition of India. The author highlights the impact of the partition on women and marginalized communities, shedding light on the long-term effects of the event. The book [3] provides a comprehensive overview of the partition of India, examining its impact on the region's political and social landscape. The authors analyze the role of the British in the partition and the subsequent impact on India and Pakistan. The authors in [4] examines the events leading up to the partition of India and its impact on the region's politics and society. The authors explore the role of key figures in the partition, including Gandhi, Jinnah, and Nehru, and the long-term consequences of their actions.

However, there is a research gap in the use of machine learning techniques and data analytics to explore the impact of the partition and identify measures that could have been taken to mitigate its effects. Large datasets can be analyzed using machine learning to spot patterns and make predictions. By applying machine learning techniques to the study of the partition, researchers could gain insights into the factors that contributed to its violence, displacement, and trauma, and develop strategies for preventing similar events in the future. We can better grasp the circumstances that contributed to the partition and its aftermath via the works of academics, historians, and writers, shedding light on the long-term effects of this horrific event.

Problem Statement and Research Methodology

The objective in this research is to research the available literature on this incident and categorize the research done and the different kinds of evidences (data) available related to this event. The objective was to inspect the available data and map it to potential ML techniques that could have been helpful in mitigating the impact of this event. Figure 75.1 describes the methods and procedures used to conduct the research.

Exploring Potential Applications of Computational Intelligence

Machine learning is a relatively new technology and was not available during the 1947 partition of British India. However, it's interesting to consider how machine learning techniques could have been helpful in analyzing the large amounts of data and information available at the time.

Analysis of Population Data for Optimized Resource Allocation
Millions of people were compelled to leave their homes during the partition and migrate to other areas. It would have been possible to analyze population data, spot patterns, and anticipate migrant destinations using ML techniques like clustering and classification. This could have helped authorities to allocate resources more effectively and plan for the resettlement of displaced persons.

Analysis of Political and Social Data
The partition was the result of complex political and social factors, including religious tensions, economic disparities, and regional identities. Machine learning techniques could have been used to analyze historical data and identify patterns

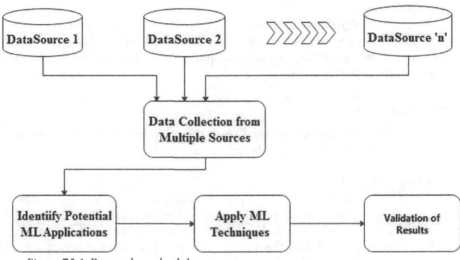

Figure 75.1 Research methodology

that could help predict future conflicts or tensions. This could have been helpful in mitigating the violence that occurred during the partition and could have provided insights into the long-term consequences of the division.

Early Warning Systems
Machine learning algorithms could have been trained on historical data to identify patterns that often precede violence and riots. This could have included analyzing news reports, social media activity, and other indicators to provide early warning of potential unrest.

Refugee Management
As a result of the widespread movement that occurred during the division of India, handling and assisting refugees has been extremely difficult. In order to better distribute resources for humanitarian organizations, predictive models for refugee flows may have been created using machine learning algorithms.

Sentiment Analysis
Machine learning algorithms could have been used to analyze public sentiment during the partition of India. This could have included analyzing news articles, social media posts, and other sources to identify patterns of hate speech and incitement to violence.

Demographic Analysis
Machine learning algorithms could have been used to analyze demographic data related to the partition of India. This could have included analyzing census data and other sources to identify areas of high risk for violence and displacement.

Conflict Resolution
Machine learning algorithms could have been used to identify potential solutions to the conflict and support peace negotiations. This could have included analyzing historical data on successful peace negotiations and identifying common factors that contribute to their success.

Experimental Work

This section compiles the experimental work done to implement ML techniques on data available in the context of this historical event.

Bag of Words (BOW)
Text classification frequently involves preprocessing the text, choosing features, extracting features, computing similarity, and choosing a classifier. Despite the fact that it is instinctive for individuals to read and comprehend a document to see if it fits a specific topic, this process is impractical for a machine due to the advantage of understanding human language. Therefore, text representation, which transforms text data into a format appropriate for computer processing, is the basis of a computer's text classification. Text representation through the bag-of-words (BoW) model is a common practise. The formula v=[x1, x2, xn] used by this model to turn a document into a vector, where xi stands for the ith word's occurrence, converts a document into a vector. To collect the core words, datasets are used. The majority of the fundamental keywords retrieved from datasets are composed of the top n words with the highest frequency. The value of the occurrence feature may be binary, term frequency, or TF-IDF. Whether the ith word appears in a document that ignores word weight is indicated by a binary value. Frequency is the measure of how frequently a term appears. With the exception of words that might occur often throughout all texts, a word that frequently appears in a document usually refers to something important about it. The weight of frequently occurring terms is equalised using the term frequency-inverse document frequency (TF-IDF) approach. The theory holds that a word becomes more relevant in direct proportion to the number of times it appears in a text, but this is balanced by the number of times it appears in the total corpus [5].

Due to its effective performance and adaptability, the bag-of-words (BOW) method, which depicts a picture by the histogram of clusters based on a visual vocabulary, has received significant interest in the field of visual classification. Because to its naive Bayesian assumption, conventional BOW ignores the contextual relationships between small patches. Nonetheless, it is well established that contextual relationships are crucial in helping people understand visual categories based on their immediate surroundings [6].

Use of BOW in Devising the Analytical Theories
Current work is an experimental approach to apply BOW technique on text articles, based upon the interviews conducted with the witnesses of 1947 India-Pakistan partition. In the experiences expressed by the interviewees there are words which occur very frequently and these words can play a significant role to sense the actual happenings, affects, emotions and challenges

of those times. Same set of findings can be helpful in finding appropriate preventions and solutions for any such future potential occurrences of similar incidents. Figure 75.2 presents the overall flow of generation of BoW from the text sources.

Experimental Setup

Experiments are performed in Python using Jupyter Notebook, which is used as an open source interface for Python Programming. A set of ten articles is chosen out of the available data. Initially these articles are tokenized using sub() inbuilt method and these tokens are stored in separate documents. Next, the original articles and tokenized documents are processed through the calculateBOW() method. Figure 75.1 demonstrates the process of achieving Bag-of-Words from an article.

Experiment and Results

Ten bags of words generated from above setup are analyzed and the keywords with highest existence in all the bags are fetched. These are the keywords which every interviewee has used in his story. Now these keywords can be evaluated at individual level or in group of words. Figure 75.3 demonstrates the words which are present in all/most of the articles. Because all the articles are about the individual experiences of 1947 partition, so it is assessed that the words are used in almost the same context. The contextual similarity of these words also determines

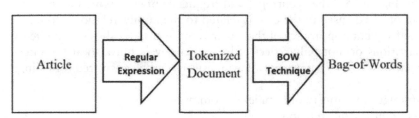

Figure 75.2 Generating BoW from the source article

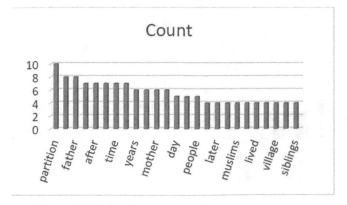

Figure 75.3 Most frequent words

that all the interviewees had some common experiences which can be in the form of challenges, problems, fears, or their sentiments at that period of time. The current paper is an attempt to compose a summarized picture of incidents and to draw some generic patterns to respond to various types of challenges if a similar unfortunate event occur in future.

This paper has used the group of words approach where words with similar context can be assessed together to find various perspectives of the story. Here we have 2 example cases.

Use Case-1
In this case a particular set of words, representing the time span related attributes is used. Figure 75.4 expresses the bag of words which can help in assessing the above parameters A few sample assumptions made on the basis of this the data can be as follows:

1. Various age groups of the population and the effects of partition chaos on them.
2. Time dependent patterns of the incidents (the time survivors took to reach a safe place, attacks, support system etc.)
3. The after effects of the partition on their individual lives in long term.
4. The before and after life transformation comparison of survivors.

Use Case-2
As shown in Figure 75.5 the occurrence and frequency of such words in the articles. The set of words used in the case is related to the family, relations, community etc. The frequent appearance of these words in the articles shows that effects of 1947 partitions do not only reflect at individual levels but also at the interpersonal relations. Using such words a few questions can be answered regarding:

1. Group migration inform of families or communities.
2. Effects upon various religions.
3. Role of family support during those chaotic periods.

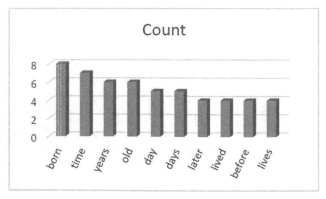

Figure 75.4 Use Case -1 (Words related to time span)

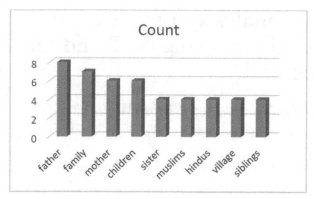

Figure 75.5 Use Case -2 (Words related to family, society and community)

4. The effects of partition incidents upon various classes such as women, children and elderly people.

Conclusion

Machine learning has the potential to be a valuable tool for preventing and managing riots. However, it is important to ensure that these technologies are used ethically and responsibly to avoid potential negative consequences such as bias and discrimination. Future Work: Using word clusters to remove ambiguous meanings, using advanced techniques such as w2v, specific objective based analysis. This paper represents a few sample ways to utilize the data available in form of the text articles. This work can further be enhanced by using the audio and video interviews. Also, the better analysis can be done with the help of advanced techniques in this field such as W2V. Another scope of enhancement can be to form the word clusters of expanded size as the more number of words will lead to lesser amount of contextual ambiguity of the words under consideration.

References

1. Pandey, G. (2001). Remembering Partition: Violence, Nationalism and History in India (Contemporary South Asia). Cambridge: Cambridge University Press. doi:10.1017/CBO9780511613173.
2. Butalia, U. (2000). The Other Side of Silence: Voices from the Partition of India. Duke: University Press. ISBN: 978-0-8223-2494-2.
3. Talbot, I., and Singh, G. (2009). The Partition of India. Cambridge University Press. ISBN: 978-0-521-85661-4.
4. Hajari, N. (2015). Midnight's Furies: The Deadly Legacy of India's Partition. Houghton Mifflin Harcourt. ISBN: 978-0-547-66921-2.
5. Yan, D., Li, K., Gu, S., and Yang, L. (2020). Network-based bag-of-words model for text classification. *IEEE Access*. 8, 82641–82652. DOI: 10.1109/ACCESS.2020.2991074.
6. Li, T., Mei, T., Kwon, I. -S., and Hua, X. -S. (2010). Contextual bag-of-words for visual categorization. *IEEE Transactions on Circuits and Systems for Video Technology*. 21(4), 381–392. DOI: 10.1109/TCSVT.2010.2041828.

76 An exploratory analysis of feature extraction techniques using NLP and text embedding methods

Sonia Rani[1,a] and Dr Tarandeep Singh Walia[2,b]

[1]Research Scholar, School of Computer Application, Lovely Professional University, Punjab, India

[2]Associate Professor, School of Computer Application, Lovely Professional University, Punjab, India

Abstract

Text Analytics is the process of extracting important information from text data using Natural language Processing methods and Machine Learning Algorithms. Machine Learning algorithms can't be implemented on text data directly, so text embedding methods are used to convert words and sentences into vector form and extract features from text data. This study has explored several text embedding methods to extract features from user reviews. Several non-contextual embeddings (Bag of Words, TF-IDF) and contextual (Word2vec, FastText, BERT) embedding techniques are explored in this study. The state-of-the-art contextual transformer-based embedding method has also been described in this study.

Keywords: BERT transformer, contextual, fasttext, feature extraction, machine learning, text embedding

Introduction

Due to the maximum availability of affordable digital devices, daily activities produce a huge amount of unstructured text data in the form of user reviews, student feedback and social media comments. Especially the popularity of online shopping generates millions of reviews on e-commerce websites. These reviews are more important to understand the user's intention behind products, but manually it is cumbersome. So, natural language processing methods and machine learning algorithms extract important information from user reviews. To apply machine learning algorithms to text data, first, text data is converted into numerical vectors using word embedding methods. Word embedding methods extract the important features from the text in the vector form and find the similarity between text through similar vectors. There are two types of text embeddings, contextual and non-contextual word embeddings, which are used to convert words into vectors. The context-independent word embeddings are One-hot Encoding, Bag of Words, and TF-IDF. The major limitation of these embeddings is that they do not contain semantic information. It represents the embeddings only based on the frequency of words; on the other side, contextual embeddings Word2vec, FastText, and BERT pretrained word embeddings can extract the semantic information from text. The state-of-art BERT (transformer-based) contextual pretrained embeddings method

[a]soniasimran30@gmail.com, [b]taran_walia2k@yahoo.com

not only convert sentences into vectors but also find the similarity b/w sentences. The structure of this paper is as follows; Section 1st introduces the types of feature extraction methods. Section 2nd explores the literature survey of context-independent statistical word embeddings and context-dependent embedding methods. Section 3rd demonstrates the context-dependent text embeddings with the state of art transfer learning-based methods. 4th Section has concluded how these embeddings are important to applying machine learning algorithms and which embedding can be used according to the data's size and language.

Literature Review

There are two types of text embedding techniques context-independent and context-dependent. Context-independent (One-hot encoding, Bag-of-words, TF-IDF, TS-ISF) are traditional statistical approaches where, as context-dependent (Word2vec, BERT) are semantic embedding techniques. Khan et al. [5] experimented with the bag of words method to extract features in movie reviews of unigrams, bigrams and trigrams. Meena and Gopalani [9], employed the TF-ISF method to extract priority-based features. Li et al. [7] applied the Word2vec 50-dimensional embeddings to generate the extractive summary without losing sentiments. Gautam et al. [4] trained the CNN 300-dimensional Embedding from scratch rather than pretrained Word2vec and Glove. Ye and Lee [13], employed the BERT encoder model for sentences converted into vectors and collected the words with the I-LDA method, which is semantically related to highlighted features. Cataltas et al. [3] TF-IDF method was used to convert words into vectors and extract the product features as opinion phrases through clustering. Abdi et al. [1] concentrated a binary six-dimensional vector (noun, preposition, verb, conjunction, adjective, adverb) with word2vec embedding vectors. word2vec is not able to define the vector according to sentiments. It gives the same vector representation for 'I like the movie' and 'I dislike the movie'. They described the limitation of word2vec as not being able to define the vector according to sentiments and ambiguous words. Belwal et al. [2] introduced the combined and individual topic vectors. They used the LDA Topic modelling method to extract sentences with a high probability of topic words in documents. Mabrouk et al. [8] focused on RNN and Bert's method to extract the features and a hierarchical Aspect-Based opinion summarization. RNN+BERT Method gave an accuracy of 83.4%. Kulkarni et al. [6] examined the One-hot encoding, Bag of words, Word2vec, Glove, Fast text, and ELMO embedding techniques. Naili et al. [10] have proposed the Word 2vec, LSA, and Glove Embedding techniques to segment topics from Arabic and English text and analyzed that Word 2vec gives the best word vector representation of text. Still, it depends on the language of the data. Because sometimes there are no present pretrained embeddings of some out-of-vocabulary words. Wang et al. [12] conducted experiments to evaluate classic and contextual word embeddings to classify text. They applied ELMO and BERT context-based embeddings and found that the BERT overall outperforms ELMO, especially in long document datasets. Suleiman and Awajan, [11] showed the significant difference between word2vec and glove embeddings to develop the sentiment analysis application.

Experiments

Linguistics Features Extraction Using Part-of-Speech Tagging

Linguistic features can be extracted with Rule-based methods like the Pos tagging (Noun, Verb, Adjective and Proper Noun, Adverb) or Adjective or adjective+ noun phrases from Reviews. In the below figure, Pos tagging is applied by NLTK and Spacy.

Figure 76.1 shows the pos tagging to extract pos tag rules to extract linguistic features with the frequency of pos tags.

Statistical-based Feature Extraction using Bag of Words

It is a traditional method to convert words into a set of features. Bag of words is easy, Intuitive and straightforward to Implement. This method creates the vocabulary of unique words from the documents and then creates the matrix of features of each unique word. This method converts all sentences' words into the same vectors, but their meanings differ according to context.

Figure 76.2 describes the Bag-of-words method to create the matrix of unique vocabulary words, and it places 0 when the word is not present in the document and places the frequency of words according to presence in the documents. The limitation of this method is it creates the sparse matrix. The Bag-of-words method implementation is demonstrated in Figure 76.2 and Figure 76.3. Figure 76.3 shows that from 795 documents, the features are 829 unique vocabulary words and the index position of that word vector in the array.

```
total_tag_words['tag_counts'] = total_tag_words['Pos_words'].map(count_tags)
total_tag_words
```

	Pos_words	tag_counts
0	[(suprb, NN), (drs, NN), (ny, IN), (looking, V...	{'NN': 6, 'IN': 1, 'VBG': 1, 'JJ': 2, 'VBD': 2...
1	[(perfect, JJ), (fit, JJ), (material, NN), (co...	{'JJ': 6, 'NN': 20, 'IN': 2, 'RB': 7, 'VBZ': 2...
2	[(happy, JJ), (purchase, NN), (product, NN), (...	{'JJ': 6, 'NN': 6, 'RB': 1, 'VBG': 1}
3	[(soft, JJ), (comfortable, JJ), (really, RB), ...	{'JJ': 5, 'RB': 2, 'NN': 10, 'VBG': 1, 'IN': 1...

Figure 76.1 Implementation of Pos tagging to extract features

```
vocab = word_bow.get_feature_names()
pd.DataFrame(word_vectors_bow.toarray(), co
```

	after	all	also	am	amazing	amazon	any	are	as
0	0	0	0	0	0	0	0	0	0
1	0	0	0	0	0	0	0	0	0
2	0	0	0	0	0	0	0	0	0
3	0	0	0	0	0	0	0	0	0
4	0	0	0	0	0	0	0	0	0

Figure 76.2 Bag of words to get word vectors

Statistical Feature Extraction using TF/IDF

TF-IDF Statistical method is used to find the important word and phrases in documents based on frequency. After multiplying the TF matrix with the IDF matrix, it generates the output matrix based on the words' weight. If the word is present more times in the review, then the TF-IDF value increases; if the word value is less, it decreases the value of the TF-IDF. Intuitive and Essential words are not always captured using this technique, but it can be captured for some amount.

Figure 76.4 shows the matrix of feature vectors extracted by the TF-IDF method based on feature weights.

Feature Extraction using Neural Network-Based Word2vec Method

This method is based on the Artificial Neural Network. Word2vec generates the vectors of word features and represents the contextual meaning of unique vocabulary words. It helps to find the semantic similarity between words through words' embeddings. This model can also detect synonyms or suggest different words for a particular sentence. It represents similar words' vectors together and places different word vectors far away.

Figure 76.5 shows the embeddings created by the word2vec method and the similarity between embedding the 'nyc' word and other words with more similar embeddings to nyc. Figure 76.6 shows that the word2vec model has no embeddings of the word 'suprb'.

```
:  vector = CountVectorizer()
   features = vector.fit_transform(df1['Cleaned_Final_Reviews
   features.shape

:  (795, 829)

:  vector.vocabulary_
   'collar': 138,
   'missing': 452,
   'pls': 555,
   'verify': 763,
   'twice': 744,
   'packing': 528,
   'items': 367.
```

Figure 76.3 Bag of words to extract features index

		100 cotton	100 rs	1000 worth	1149 they	200 rs	2499 which	34 size	3rd order	500 great	57 and	...	you see	you so	you sober	you the	you want	you wear	your gorgeous	your look	your wife	you th
	pd.DataFrame(word_vectors_tfidf.toarray(), columns=vocab)																					
0		0.0	0.0	0.0	0.0	0.0	0.0	0.0	0.0	0.0	0.0	...	0.0	0.0	0.0	0.0	0.0	0.0	0.0	0.000000	0.0	(
1		0.0	0.0	0.0	0.0	0.0	0.0	0.0	0.0	0.0	0.0	...	0.0	0.0	0.0	0.0	0.0	0.0	0.0	0.000000	0.0	(
2		0.0	0.0	0.0	0.0	0.0	0.0	0.0	0.0	0.0	0.0	...	0.0	0.0	0.0	0.0	0.0	0.0	0.0	0.000000	0.0	(
3		0.0	0.0	0.0	0.0	0.0	0.0	0.0	0.0	0.0	0.0	...	0.0	0.0	0.0	0.0	0.0	0.0	0.0	0.188029	0.0	(

Figure 76.4 TF-IDF vector representation

Neural Network-based FastText

The Facebook Research team developed the FastText embedding method. It is an extension of the Word2vec method. This method gives the set of words or n-gram representation character embeddings. The Fast text embedding technique has a unique feature of sub-words or character embeddings to use the internal structure of a word to improve the vector representation. This method also gives the embeddings of wrong spelling words. i.e., "sleping" is a misspelt word that is not present in the vocabulary; this word is similar to sleeping. It captures those words according to the semantic similarity measure and the meaning of prefixes or suffixes for corpus words.

```
wv.most_similar('nyc')

[('brooklyn', 0.7036151289903988),
 ('atlanta', 0.6743649244308472),
 ('boston', 0.6515336632728577),
 ('chicago', 0.6503334641456604),
 ('manhattan', 0.6443952322006226),
 ('washington_dc', 0.6432445645332336),
 ('springfield', 0.6405122228012085),
 ('baltimore', 0.6387253403663635),
 ('houston', 0.638403594493866),
 ('miami', 0.6332902908325105)]
```

Figure 76.5 Implementation of Word2Vec

```
vec_suprb = wv['suprb']

----------------------------------------------------------
KeyError                                    Traceback (most
Input In [161], in <module>
----> 1 vec_suprb = wv['suprb']

File E:\python310\lib\site-packages\gensim\models\keyedve
Vectors.__getitem__(self, key_or_keys)
    390 """Get vector representation of `key_or_keys`.
```

Figure 76.6 Word2vec didn't give the OOV word embeddings

```
1  ft_fastext = KeyedVectors.load_word2

1  ft_fastext['suprb']

-------------------------------------------------
KeyError
Input In [58], in <cell line: 1>()
----> 1 ft_fastext['suprb']
```

Figure 76.7 Implementation of fastText

Figure 76.7 shows the error of FastText has no embedding of the suprb word, and Figure 76.8 demonstrates that it can't give the embedding of hinglish words.

Figure 76.9 shows the 'phone' word embeddings generated by FastText.

BERT (Bi-Directional Encoder Representations from Transformers)
BERT is a language model based on transfer learning and is a state-of-art method for embedding documents into vectors to reduce the dimensionality of the features. It embeds sentences or words into a vector representation. It gives more accurate results than Bag-of-Words, TF-IDF, word 2vec and doc2vec. BERT model can not only be used for vector representation, but BERTopic can also classify documents into different categories. The major pros of the BERT Model are that it can also create embeddings of OOV(Out-of-vocabulary) and hinglish words.

The BERT model creates contextual embedding based on the semantics of documents. It can give the sentence token embeddings according to the surrounding position of words in the text.

Figure 76.10 demonstrates that the BERT Method can also give the sentence embeddings of Hinglish words which is a major advantage of the BERT method. Table 76.1 summarize pros and cons of embedding techniques.

```
1  ft_fastext['bekar phone']
---------------------------------------------
KeyError
Input In [62], in <cell line: 1>()
----> 1 ft_fastext['bekar phone']
```

Figure 76.8 FastText didn't give embedding of Hinglish words

```
:   1  ft_fastext['phone']
:  array([-6.400e-02,  1.586e-01, -2.780e-02,  1.552e-01,  8.500e-03,
           4.780e-02, -1.112e-01,  9.310e-02, -8.750e-02, -4.270e-02,
           3.460e-02,  1.860e-02,  1.812e-01,  1.902e-01, -6.070e-02,
```

Figure 76.9 FastText can give the embeddings of the 'phone' word

```
def get_embeddings(sentences):
    preprocessed_text = preprocessor(sentences)
    return encoder(preprocessed_text)['pooled_output']
get_embeddings(["sahi hai , ekdam bakwas phone hai type-c nahi , camera beka

<tf.Tensor: shape=(1, 768), dtype=float32, numpy=
array([[-5.48844516e-01, -2.16648355e-02, -2.57879272e-02,
        -1.89703390e-01, -1.49010733e-01,  6.01647981e-02,
        -1.92373842e-01, -4.02315825e-01, -4.42867696e-01,
        -6.69620261e-02, -2.10677281e-01, -2.97604561e-01.
```

Figure 76.10 BERT Embeddings

Table 76.1 Pros and cons of embedding techniques

Embedding Techniques	Pros	Cons
Bag of Words	Easy, straightforward to Implement and Intuitive. The bag of Words method is better than one-hot encoding.	It can't handle oov words and creates a sparse matrix. Words' ordering is not considered. It can be applied to small data. Semantic meaning between words is not captured; It can't be applied to text with repetitive words.
TF-IDF	Essential words can be captured for some amount. It reduces the sparsity as compared to the bag of words method.	There is a sparsity issue present. In fact, from the above table, we can see that good is an important feature, but in the output matrix, it is shown as zero in all sentences. Not considered Out-of-vocabulary words.
Word2Vec	Can find the similarity between words and the semantic relationship between words. Word2vec reduces the sparsity matrix.	Can't measure the relationship b/w all global words in all sentences. This method can't handle out-of-vocabulary words. It cannot capture the order of context position of a word.
FastText	It can generate sub-word embeddings and can capture semantic similarities b/w words. It can handle some oov words and performs better than word2vec.	It can only be trained in some languages. It cannot generate abbreviated word embeddings. This method requires a large memory because it generates character ngram embeddings.
BERT	It can create sub-word embeddings, handle out-of-vocabulary words, and differentiate the polysemy words like cell, bank, etc. It can be used as a pre-trained and fine-tuned model and can be applied to small or large unlabeled and some labelled data.	It updates the weights slowly because of complex data computations and can tokenize a sentence into only 512 tokens. This method increases the model's cost because of the large corpus and training structure. It requires TPU to train the BERT from scratch and GPUs to fine-tune the model.

Conclusion

This article has explained the various contextual and non-contextual text embedding methods. After Exploring various text embedding methods, it is concluded that a state-of-art transformer-based BERT method can give context-dependent semantic embeddings. BERT can also give the embeddings of out-of-vocabulary words, which can't give another method like Bag-of-words, TF-IDF, Word2vec, and FastText. To apply BERT, no need to apply more preprocessing techniques. It can measure the similarity between sentences according to the semantics of the sentence. BERT can generate embeddings of Multilingual sentences, but the other methods can't give. BERT can also extract the topics from unlabeled reviews and classify the unimportant topics into separate ones. This study has also described some embedding techniques with their pros and cons. The Pre-trained BERT model can be applied by fine-tuning it on a new corpus. But the word embedding methods can be applied according to the corpus's size and language or problem formulation. In some cases, if any model cannot give the embeddings of abbreviated and unique words, we can train the model from scratch to generate embeddings of that words.

References

1. Abdi, A., Hasan, S., Shamsuddin, S. M., Idris, N., and Piran, J. (2021). Hybrid deep learning architecture for opinion-oriented multi-document summarization based on multi-feature fusion. *Knowledge-Based Systems*, 213, 1–18. https://doi.org/10.1016/j.knosys.2020.106658

2. Belwal, R. C., Rai, S., and Gupta, A. (2021). Text summarization using topic-based vector space model and semantic measure. *Information Processing and Management*, 58(3), 1–15. https://doi.org/10.1016/j.ipm.2021.102536.

3. Cataltas, M., Dogramaci, S., Yumusak, S., and Oztoprak, K. (2020). Extraction of product defects and customer reviews opinions using text clustering and sentiment analysis. *In International Conference on Big Data*. https://doi.org/10.1109/BigData50022.2020.9377851

4. Gautam, S., Kaur, J., and Josan, G. S. (2021). Deep neural network-based multi-review summarization system. *International Journal of Next-Generation Computing*, 12(3), 356–366.

5. Khan, A., Gul, M. A., Uddin, M. I., Ali Shah, S. A., Ahmad, S., Al Firdausi, M. D., and Zaindin, M. (2020). Summarizing online movie reviews: a machine learning approach to big data analytics. *Scientific Programming*, Volume 2020 | Article ID 5812715 | 1–13. https://doi.org/10.1155/2020/5812715.

6. Kulkarni, N., Vaidya, R., and Bhate, M. (2021). A comparative study of word embedding techniques to extract features from text. *Turkish Journal of Computer and Mathematics Education*, 12(12), 3550–3557.

7. Li, X., Wu, P., Zou, C., Xie, H., and Lee, F. (2021). Sentiment lossless summarization. *Knowledge-Based Systems*, 227, 1–13. https://doi.org/10.1016/j.knosys.2021.107170.

8. Mabrouk, A., Redondo, R. P. D., and Kayed, M. (2021). SE opinion: summarization and exploration of opinion from e-commerce websites. *Sensors*, 21(2), 1–25. https://doi.org/10.3390/21020636.

9. Meena, Y. K., and Gopalani, D. (2015). Feature priority-based sentence filtering method for extractive automatic text summarization. *Procedia Computer Science*, 48(C), 728–734.

10. Naili, M., Chaibi, A. H., and Ben Ghezala, H. H. (2017). Comparative study of word embedding methods in topic segmentation. *Procedia Computer Science*, 112, 340–349. https://doi.org/10.1016/j.procs.2017.08.009.

11. Suleiman, D., and Awajan, A. (2019). Comparative study of word embeddings models and their usage in arabic language applications. In 19th International Arab Conference on Information Technology, (pp. 1–7). https://doi.org/10.1109/ACIT.2018.8672674.

12. Wang, C., Nulty, P., and Lillis, D. (2020). A comparative study on word embeddings in deep learning for text classification. In 4th International Conference on Natural Language Processing and Information Retrieval, (pp. 37–46). https://doi.org/10.1145/3443279.3443304.

13. Ye, W. J., and Lee, A. J. T. (2021). Mining sentiment tendencies and summaries from consumer reviews. *Information Systems and E-Business Management*, 19(1), 107–135. https://doi.org/10.1007/10257-020-004824.

77 Cricket performance prediction: a data science method to ODI player analysis

Akash Devkar[a], Rahul Kumar[b] and Shuja Rashid[c]

School of Computer Application, Lovely Professional University, Phagwara, India

Abstract

This paper presents a comprehensive analysis of the performance of One Day International (ODI) cricket players based on their strike rate as a predictive attribute. The aim is to identify the best, average, and worst performers in ODI cricket, and provide an assessment of their performance. Multiple linear regression analysis, correlation analysis, and neural networks are used to determine the relationship between the strike rate and the performance of the player. The results of the research highlight the importance of strike rate as an essential predictor of the performance of ODI players. The research offers valuable insights into the performance of ODI players, which can be used by selectors, coaches, and analysts to identify the best players for the team and develop strategies to improve the team's outcome. This paper also provides direction for future research in this field.

Keywords: Deep learning, machine learning, player performance predictions

Introduction

ODI (One Day International) cricket is a fast-paced and exciting format of the sport, with a focus on scoring runs quickly. One important metric that is used to measure the success of a player in ODI cricket is their strike rate, which represents the number of runs they score per 100 balls faced. Predicting the strike rate of ODI players is a critical task for cricket teams and analysts, as it can help them make informed decisions about team selection and game strategy.

Machine learning techniques have emerged as a powerful tool for analysing and predicting player performance in ODI cricket. These algorithms can be trained on large datasets of historical match statistics, and player profiles to identify patterns and relationships that can be used to predict player performance in future matches. Specifically, machine learning algorithms can be used to predict a player's strike rate based on Total Runs made by a player, including Total Balls Faced by the Player and the Player's Batting Average.

Research in this field has focused on developing machine learning models that can accurately predict the strike rate of ODI players. Some of the most used algorithms include Multiple linear regression and neural networks. These models use a range of statistical and machine-learning techniques to identify the factors that have the greatest impact on a player's strike rate and to make predictions based on this information.

LSTM.

---

[a]*akashdevkar2019@gmail.com, [b]rahulkumar1222@gmail.com,
[c]princemj1714@gamil.com

Literature Review

Sports prediction using machine learning algorithms has become an area of increasing interest in recent years. Various models have been proposed in the literature, such as decision trees, neural networks, and support vector machines, and ensemble models. In this literature review, we analyse the different papers based on sports prediction using machine learning approaches.

A Machine the process of learning Approach to Predict NBA a Game Results by [1]. They used a support vector machine (SVM) model to forecast NBA outcomes. They achieved an accuracy of 69.6% in predicting the winner of games.

A Machine Learning Approach to Soccer Match Outcome Prediction" by [2]. They used a combination of feature engineering and ensemble models, including random forest and gradient boosting, to predict the outcomes of soccer matches. They achieved an accuracy of 58.8% in predicting the winner of matches.

Predicting NFL Game Outcomes Using Machine Learning Techniques" by [3]. They used a logistic regression model to predict the outcomes of NFL games. They achieved an accuracy of 67.4% in predicting the winner of games.

Predicting Major League Baseball Game Outcomes Using Machine Learning Techniques" by [4]. They used a logistic regression model to predict the outcomes of MLB games. They achieved an accuracy of 55.3% in predicting the winner of games.

Predicting the winner of tennis matches using a machine learning approach" by [5]. They used a random forest model to predict the winner of tennis matches. They achieved an accuracy of 72.2% in predicting the winner of matches.

A Machine Learning Approach for Predicting the Results of Cricket Matches by [6]. They used a random forest model to predict the outcomes of cricket matches. They achieved an accuracy of 66.7% in predicting the winner of matches.

Predicting the outcome of soccer matches using machine learning techniques" by [7] utilising computer learning strategies to forecast the results of soccer games, including support vector machines (SVM) and k-nearest neighbour (KNN) algorithms. They achieved an accuracy of up to 58% in predicting the correct outcome of matches.

Player performance prediction in basketball using machine learning techniques" by [8] applied a convolutional neural network (CNN) to predict the performance of basketball players based on their shooting patterns. They achieved an accuracy of over 90% in predicting the player's shooting success rate.

Forecasting performance in road cycling using machine learning models" by [9] used machine learning algorithms such as linear regression, random forests, and gradient boosting to predict the performance of road cyclists in different scenarios. They achieved an accuracy of up to 90% in predicting the performance of cyclists.

Machine learning approaches for predicting the winners of tennis matches" by [10] applied a logistic regression model to predict the outcome of tennis matches. They achieved an accuracy of over 70% in predicting the winner of matches. Predicting the performance of elite swimmers using machine learning algorithms" by [11] used machine learning algorithms such as KNN, SVM, and decision trees to predict the performance of elite swimmers in different swimming events. They achieved an accuracy of up to 90% in predicting the performance of swimmers. Using machine learning techniques to predict the outcome of NFL games" by [12] applied various machine learning models such as decision trees, KNN, and SVM to predict the outcome of National Football League (NFL) games. They achieved an accuracy of over 70% in predicting the correct outcome of games.

Materials and Methods

Data Source: The data for this predictive analysis can be obtained from [13]. Table 77.1 depicts attributes used to predict player performance

Table 77.1 Attributes used to predict player performance

Variables	Variable Type	Description
Player Name	String	It describes the Name of the player
Period	String	It describes the Period of Matches
Matches	Numeric	It describes the Total matches of the Player
Played	Numeric	It describes Played matches by player
Runs	Numeric	Total runs made by the player
Batting Average	Numeric	Players Batting Average
Balls Faced	Numeric	Total Ball Faced by Player
Strike Rate	Numeric	Strike rate of Player

List of Attributes:
Objects of study:
To Predicting strike-rate for analyse player performance, we want's Variable that would be required the most and will play a key role in getting.

a)   Dependant variable = Strike Rate
b)   independent variable= Runs, Balls Faced, Batting Average

Design of Research

In our research, we find whose strike rate is best. The strike rate is measured by how many ball-faced the player is. And how many runs he makes playing all balls he faced. And we can also analyse which player is best with help of the player's Batting average. To predict player performance on strike rate we use Multiple linear regression and neural network model:

Data Collection: The data will be collected from [13] and will include information on the runs scored, balls faced, and a batting average of the sample of cricket players. The data will be cleaned and prepared for analysis using statistical software.

Multiple Linear Regression
Applying a multiple regression model, we predict the following:

a.   How accurately can a neural network model predict Strike rate using Runs, Balls faced, and Batting average as predictors?
b.   Which of the independent variables (Runs, Balls faced, and Batting average) has the strongest relationship with the dependent variable (strike rate)?

Methodology
Participants: The study will use a sample of professional cricket players who have played at least 03 innings in international matches.
Variables: The dependent variable is the strike rate, which will be calculated as the ratio of runs scored to balls faced multiplied by 100.
Data analysis: The data from the primary study will be fitted to a multiple linear regression model to predict strike rate as a function of runs, balls faced, and batting average. The quality of the regression model will be evaluated using residual plots and the coefficient of determination (R-squared).

Neural Network
Applying the Neural network model, we predict the following:

a.   How accurately can a neural network model predict independent variables using dependent variables?
b.   Which independent parameter (strike rate) is more closely related to the dependent variable (strike rate)?

Methodology
Participants: The sample for this study will be drawn from professional cricket players who have played at least Three games in one-day international cricket leagues in the world.
Data Analysis: A neural network model will be constructed in SPSS using the multilayer perceptron (MLP) algorithm.

Results

Multiple Linear Regression
Table 77.2 shows that all three independent variables (Balls faced, Batting Average, and Runs) were entered into the model simultaneously using the Enter method, and no variables were removed.

Table 77.2 Variables Entered/Removed[a]

Model	Variables Entered	Variables Removed	Method
1	Balls Faced, Batting Average, Runs[b]	.	Enter

a. Dependent Variable: Strike Rate
b. All requested variables entered.

The model gave 80.7% accuracy in prediction.

Table 77.3 and Table 77.4 shows the results of a linear regression analysis for the relationship between Strike Rate and three independent variables (Balls Faced, Batting Average, and Runs). The variables have a very strong significant association, as indicated by the R-value of 0.898. The independent variables account for 80.7% of the variance in strike rate, according to the R Square value of 0.807, which is calculated. The adjusted R square value, which is 0.806, shows that the data is well suited. The Std. An error of the Estimate is 6.71784, and the Durbin-Watson statistic is 1.994, indicating positive autocorrelation.

Model: This column specifies the source of variation in the model. In this case, there are two sources of variation - Regression and Residual. Regression represents the variation explained by the predictors, while Residual represents the unexplained variation.

The sum of Squares: This column shows the sum of squares for each source of variation. For Regression, it is 115566.883, and for Residual, it is 27664.347.

df: This column shows the degrees of freedom for each source of variation. For Regression, it is 3, which is the number of predictors in the model. For Residual, it is 613, which is the number of observations minus the number of predictors.

Mean Square: This column shows the mean square for each source of variation, which is obtained by dividing the sum of squares by the degrees of freedom. For Regression, it is 38522.294, and for Residual, it is 45.129.

F: This column shows the F-value for the model, which is obtained by dividing the mean square for Regression by the mean square for residuals. In this case, the F-value is 853.596.

Sig.: This column shows the p-value for the F-test, which tests whether the regression coefficients are jointly significant. In this case, the p-value is 0.000,

Table 77.3 Coefficients[a]

Model		Unstandardized Coefficients		Standardized Coefficients	t	Sig.
		B	Std. Error	Beta		
1	(Constant)	71.603	.766		93.517	.000
	Runs	.135	.003	1.985	46.945	<.001
	Batting Average	.050	.019	.049	2.683	.008

Table 77.4 ANOVA[a]

Model		Sum of Squares	df	Mean Square	F	Sig.
1	Regression	115566.883	3	38522.294	853.596	<.001[b]
	Residual	27664.347	613	45.129		
	Total	143231.230	616			

a. Dependent Variable: Strike Rate

b. Predictors: (Constant), Balls Faced, Batting Average, Runs

which is less than the significance level of 0.05, indicating that the model is significant.

The first row of the table shows the intercept or constant term of the model, which represents the predicted value of the dependent variable when all the independent variables are zero. In this case, the intercept is 71.603.

In the second column unstandardized coefficients measure, for every additional run scored, the strike rate is predicted to increase by 0.135, holding the batting average and balls faced constantly. Similarly, for every additional ball faced, the strike rate is predicted to decrease by 0.096, holding runs and batting average constant. Also, for every additional batting average the strike rate is predicted to increase by 0.050, holding runs and Balls faced constant.

The third column shows the standard error of the coefficients, which represents the estimated standard deviation of the sampling distribution of the regression coefficient.

The fourth column 'standardized coefficients Beta' shows the standardized coefficient for Runs is 1.985, indicating that a one standard deviation increase in Runs is associated with a 1.985 standard deviation increase in Strike Rate. also, the standardized coefficient for Batting Average is 0.049, indicating that a one standard deviation increase in Batting Average is associated with a 0.049 standard deviation increase in Strike Rate. also, the standardized coefficient for Balls Faced is -2.040, indicating that one standard deviation increases in Balls Faced is associated with a 2.040 standard deviation decrease in Strike Rate.

The fifth column t value shows the results of a t-test for each independent variable, which tests the null hypothesis that the population regression coefficient for the independent variable is zero. The t-value is calculated by dividing the unstandardized coefficient by its standard error. A larger absolute t-value indicates that the independent variable has a stronger relationship with the dependent variable.

The sixth column p-value shows the independent variables are statistically significant with the dependent variable. Here, Runs, Batting average, and Balls faced statistically significant strike rates. because here p-value is less than 0.05.

A correlation coefficient ranges from -1 to +1, where -1 indicates a perfect negative correlation, 0 indicates no correlation, and +1 indicates a perfect positive correlation. Table 77.5, Table 77.6 and Table 77.7 shows the Conffcient Correlations and Residuals Statistics respectively.

Table 77.5 linear regression analysis for the relationship between Strike Rate and three independent variables

Model	R	R Square	Adjusted R Square	Std. Error of the Estimate	Durbin-Watson
1	.898[a]	.807	.806	6.71784	1.994

a. Predictors: (Constant), Balls Faced, Batting Average, Runs

b. Dependent Variable: Strike Rate

Minimum and Maximum: The minimum and maximum values of the residuals. These values indicate the range of the differences between the observed and predicted values of the dependent variable.

Mean and Standard Deviation: The mean and standard deviation of the residuals. The mean of the residuals is very close to zero (i.e., 0.00000), which means that, on average, the observed values of the dependent variable are very close to the predicted values. The standard deviation of the residuals (i.e., 6.70147) indicates how much the residuals vary around the mean, or how much the observed values of the dependent variable deviate from the predicted values.

Std. Predicted Value: The standardized predicted values, which represent the predicted values of the dependent variable adjusted for the variability in the independent variables. The minimum and maximum values of the standardized predicted values are -3.806 and 3.610, respectively.

Std. Residual: The standardized residuals, which represent the residuals adjusted for the variability in the independent variables. The minimum and maximum values of the standardized residuals are -2.003 and 5.071, respectively. The mean of the standardized residuals is very close to zero (i.e., 0.000), which means that, on average, the observed values of the dependent variable are very close to the predicted values adjusted for the variability in the independent variables. The standard deviation of the standardized residuals (i.e., 0.998) indicates how much the standardized residuals vary around the mean.

The histogram of the standardized residuals has a bell shape, it shows that the residuals are normally distributed, and the regression model is a good fit for the data Figure 77.1.

Table 77.6 Confficient Correlations[a]

Model			Balls Faced	Batting Average	Runs
1	Correlations	Balls Faced	1.000	.184	-.907
		Batting Average	.184	1.000	-.209
		Runs	-.907	-.209	1.000
	Covariances	Balls Faced	3.876E-6	6.799E-6	-5.118E-6
		Batting Average	6.799E-6	.000	-1.125E-5
		Runs	-5.118E-6	-1.125E-5	8.220E-6

a. Dependent Variable: Strike Rate

Table 77.7 Residuals Statistics[a]

	Minimum	Maximum	Mean	Std. Deviation	N
Predicted Value	21.2683	122.8439	73.4044	13.69703	617
Residual	-13.45414	34.06879	.00000	6.70147	617
Std. Predicted Value	-3.806	3.610	.000	1.000	617
Std. Residual	-2.003	5.071	.000	.998	617

a. Dependent Variable: Strike Rate

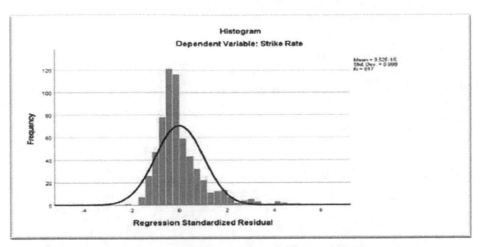

Figure 77.1 Histogram is in bell curve. that means model is fitted good

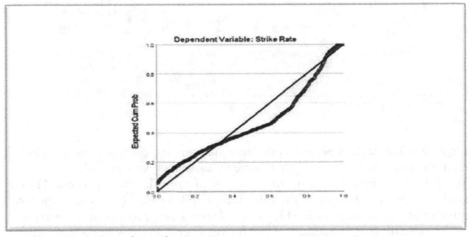

Figure 77.2 Normal p-p Plot

The plot displays the observed standardized residuals on the y-axis and the expected values of the normal distribution on the x-axis. Here is plot the points on the plot will fall roughly along a straight line, which means the data follow a normal distribution Figure 77.2.

Neural Network
<u>Sample:</u> This section provides information about the two samples used in the analysis, namely the training sample and the testing sample. Here, 444 cases (72%) in the training sample and 173 cases (28%) in the testing sample.
<u>Valid:</u> This section provides information about the total number of cases that were included in the analysis. In this case, 617 cases were included.

Table 77.8 Case Processing Sunnary

		N	Percent
Sample	Training	444	72.0%
	Testing	173	28.0%
Valid		617	100.0%
Excluded		0	
Total		617	

Table 77.9 Network Information

Input Layer	Covariates	1		Runs
		2		Batting Average
		3		Balls Faced
	Number of Units[a]			3
	Rescaling Method for Covariates			Standardized
Hidden Layer(s)	Number of Hidden Layers			1
	Number of Units in Hidden Layer 1[a]			3
	Activation Function			Hyperbolic tangent
Output Layer	Dependent Variables	1		Strike Rate
	Number of Units			1
	Rescaling Method for Scale Dependents			Standardized
	Activation Function			Identity
	Error Function			Sum of Squares

a. Excluding the bias unit

<u>Excluded:</u> This section provides information about any cases that were excluded from the analysis. In this case, there were no cases that were excluded.

<u>Total:</u> This section provides the total number of cases that were processed in the analysis, which is the sum of the valid and excluded cases. In this case, the total number of cases processed is 617. Table 7.8 shows case processing summary.

The neural network model in SPSS for regression analysis has a well-defined structure. It consists of an input layer that includes three covariates - "Runs", "Batting Average", and "Balls Faced" - which are rescaled using the sample mean and standard deviation. The hidden layer comprises three nodes, each using the hyperbolic tangent activation function. The output layer has a single dependent variable, "Strike Rate", which is also standardized using the sample mean and standard deviation. The activation function for this layer is the identity function. To evaluate the performance of the model, the sum of the squares error function is used. Overall, this structure is designed to ensure the optimal prediction of the Strike Rate based on the input covariates. Table 77.9 depicts network information.

The parameter estimates show predictor relationships with the output variable. Runs have a negative weight, Batting Average has a weak positive relationship, and Balls Faced have a strong positive relationship. The three hidden nodes have a bias weight of 1.074, and their weights are negative, positive, and positive.

Table 77.10 Parameter estimates

| Predictor | | Predicted | | | |
| | | Hidden Layer 1 | | | Output Layer |
		H(1:1)	H(1:2)	H(1:3)	StrikeRate
Input Layer	(Bias)	1.441	.317	.366	
	Runs	-1.404	1.459	-.340	
	BattingAverage	.006	.006	.052	
	BallsFaced	2.189	-1.167	.206	
Hidden Layer 1	(Bias)				1.074
	H(1:1)				-2.008
	H(1:2)				1.361
	H(1:3)				.291

Table 77.11 Model Summary

Training	Sum of Squares Error	4.079
	Relative Error	.018
	Stopping Rule Used	1 consecutive step(s) with no decrease in error[a]
	Training Time	0:00:00.01
Testing	Sum of Squares Error	1.455
	Relative Error	.016

Dependent Variable: Strike Rate

a. Error computations are based on the testing sample.

Table 77.12 Independent Variable Importance

	Importance	Normalized Importance
Runs	.463	88.6%
Batting Average	.015	2.9%
		100.0%

The Table 7.11 shows that during training, the model achieved a Sum of Squares Error of 4.079 and a Relative Error of 0.018. The stopping rule used was 1 consecutive step(s) with no decrease in error, which means that the model was trained until the SSE did not decrease for one consecutive step. The training time for the model was 0:00:00.01.

During testing, the model achieved a Sum of Squares Error of 1.455 and a Relative Error of .016. These results indicate that the model's predictions on the testing data were reasonably accurate, with low levels of error. the dependent variable, Strike Rate, the model is predicting it with good accuracy as the relative error is low.

The Table 7.12 displays the importance of three variables (Runs, Batting Average, and Balls Faced) in predicting Strike Rate in a statistical model. The

"Importance" column shows the magnitude of the effect of each variable on the dependent variable, while the "Normalized Importance" column represents the percentage contribution of each variable to the overall prediction of the Strike Rate. Balls Faced has the highest normalized importance value of 100%, making it the most important predictor of Strike Rate in the model. Runs have a strong influence with a normalized importance value of 88.6%, while Batting Average has a weak influence with a value of 2.9%. A graph provides further clarity.

Discussion

Multiple Regression Model
The model explains 80.7% accuracy in predicting the strike rate.
   The problem:
   Investigate the effect of Runs, Ball faced, and Batting average on strike rate.

H1: There is a significant impact of Runs on the Strike rate
H2: There is a significant impact of Ball faced on the Strike rate
H3: There is a significant impact of Batting average on the Strike rate

   The dependent variable (Strike rate) was regressed on predicting variables of Runs, Ball faced, and Batting average. The independent variable significantly predicts the Strike rate, $F (3,613) = 863.596$, $p< 0.001$, which indicates the three factors under study have a significant impact on the Strike rate. Moreover, the $R^2= 0.807$ depicts that the model explains 80.7% of the variance in the Strike rate. Hypothesis testing is shown in Table 77.13.
   The multiple linear regression model analysed the impact of each predictor variable on the Strike rate. H1 was supported, indicating that Runs have a positive effect on the Strike rate ($B = 0.135$, $t = 46.945$, $p = 0.001$). H2 was also supported, indicating that Balls faced hurt Strike rate ($B = -0.096$, $t = -48.507$, $p<0.001$). H3 was supported, but with a relatively weaker impact, indicating that Batting Average has a positive effect on the Strike rate ($B = 0.050$, $t = 2.863$, $p < 0.008$). The results suggest that Runs and Balls faced have a stronger influence on the Strike rate than Batting Average. Table 77.14 shows the player performance.

Table 77.13 Hypothesis testing

Hypotheses	Regression Weights	B	t	p-value	Hypothesis supported
H1	Runs – A strike rate	0.135	46.517	0.001	Yes
H2	Ball faced – A strike rate	- 0.096	- 48.507	0.001	Yes
H3	Batting average – A strike rate	0.050	2.683	0.008	Yes
R	0.807				
F (3,613)	853.596				

Table 77.14 Player performance

		Frequency	Percent	Valid Percent	Cumulative Percent
Valid	AVERAGE	411	66.6	66.6	66.6
	BEST	185	30.0	30.0	96.6
	LOW	21	3.4	3.4	100.0
	Total	617	100.0	100.0	

Equation: For this research, we use Multiple linear Regression, it's a statistical strategy that predicts the result of a response variable by using many explanatory variables, Multiple Linear Regression Formula and Calculation:

Multiple linear regression equation:
$Y = b0 + b1x1 + b2x2 + b3x3 + E$
X1 = Run, x2 = Ball faced, x3 = Batting average
Y = dependant variable
B0 = intercept = 87.662
B1 = independent variable1 = 0.135
B2 = independent variable2 = - 0.096
B3 = independent variable3 = 0.050
E = Random Error = 0.766

Neural Network Model
The model achieved 82% and 98.4% accuracy in the training and testing phases, respectively. Balls Faced was the most important predictor, and runs had a negative effect, while Batting Average had a small positive effect. The residual chart confirmed its accuracy.

Equation: Strike Rate = 1.441 + (Runs * -1.404) + (Batting Average * 0.006) + (Balls Faced * 2.189) +H (1:1) * -2.008) + H (1:2) * 1.361) + H (1:3) * 0.291) + 1.074

Here in the Equation:
Bias=1.441, -1.40= Runs weight, 0.006 = Batting Average weight, 2.189 = Balls Faced weight

1) The values in parentheses after each predictor variable represent the weight assigned to that predictor in the model.
2) H (1:1), H (1:2), and H (1:3) are the hidden layer nodes' output values
3) Let's see one example of how to calculate hidden layers output values: Suppose, runs = 50, Batting Average = 0.25, and Balls Faced = 100.

Equation for calculate Hidden layer node: Hidden layer node = (weight * Runs) + (weight * Batting Average) + (weight *Balls Faced)
   H (1:1) = (-1.404 * 50) + (0.006 * 0.25) + (2.189 * 100) + 1.441 = 295.117
   H (1:2) = (1.459 * 50) + (0.006 * 0.25) + (-1.167 * 100) + 0.317 = 159.138

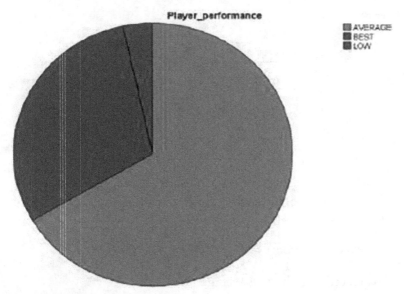

Figure 77. 3 Shows player performance

H (1:3) = (-0.340 * 50) + (0.052 * 0.25) + (0.206 * 100) + 0.366 = 8.516

Overall, this equation can be used to predict the Strike Rate value based on the input values and the neural network's parameter estimates.

The Table 77.12 shows the distribution of player performances, with 411 players at an average level, 185 players performing at their best, and 21 players with low performance. Percentiles for each performance level are also provided. Graphs are available for further analysis Figure 77.3.

Significance/Implication of the Results

The study reveals valuable insights into improving the accuracy of strike rate prediction using SPSS algorithms. We found players with high strike rates but low batting averages, and those with high runs but low strike rates. Interestingly, the model showed players who faced more balls had a greater impact on strike rate prediction. The MLR model had an accuracy of 80.7%, while the neural network model had an accuracy of 82% in training and 98.4% in testing. Overall, our findings suggest that players who make maximum runs in fewer balls have a better strike rate, while those who face more balls have better batting averages but a lower strike rate.

Conclusion

In conclusion, the study aimed to predict the performance of cricket players in One Day International (ODI) matches using a data science approach based on strike rate. The multiple linear regression model was used to analysed the dataset, which included various player statistics such as batting strike rate, ball faced, player profile, and fielding efficiency. The results of the study indicated that the batting strike rate was the most significant factor in predicting a player's performance in an ODI match. Future work in this area could include expanding the dataset to include additional player statistics and comparing the performance of players across different cricket formats. Moreover, applying more advanced machine learning techniques such as neural networks and decision trees could further improve the accuracy of performance predictions. The findings of this study could be used by cricket teams and selectors to make informed decisions when selecting players for ODI matches based on their predicted performance.

References

1. Leung, A. C. M., and Lyu, M. R. (2017). A machine learning approach to predict the outcomes of NBA games. In Proceedings of the 2017 IEEE International Conference on Industrial Engineering and Engineering Management (IEEM), (pp. 747–751).
2. Brouwer, N., Reinecke, T., and Becker, M. (2018). A machine learning approach to soccer match outcome prediction. *Journal of Sports Analytics*, 4(4), 237–248.
3. Peterson, D., and Burke, B. (2018). Predicting NFL game outcomes using machine learning techniques. *Journal of Big Data*, 5(1), 37.
4. Peterson, D., and Burke, B. (2018). Predicting major league baseball game outcomes using machine learning techniques. *Journal of Sports Analytics*, 4(4), 249–258.
5. Mandic, D. P., Djukanovic, M., and Marina, N. (2019). Predicting the winner of tennis matches using a machine learning approach. *International Journal of Computer Science in Sport*, 18(1), 41–55.
6. Deshpande, V. S., and Dixit, M. R. (2021). A machine learning approach for predicting the results of cricket matches. *Journal of Big Data*, 8(1), 1–13.
7. Liu, Y., Zhou, Y., and Zhao, Y. (2018). Predicting the outcome of soccer matches using machine learning techniques. *Applied Sciences*, 8(6), 971.
8. Zhang, X., Xue, G., Xu, X., and Liu, S. (2019). Player performance prediction in basketball using machine learning techniques. *Future Generation Computer Systems*, 95, 388–395.
9. Dyer, B., Hassani, H., and Shadi, M. (2016). The analysis and forecasting of male cycling time trial records established within England and Wales. Journal of Sports Sciences, 34(13), 1222–1230.
10. Barnett, T., and Clarke, S. R. (2005). Combining player statistics to predict outcomes of tennis matches. *IMA Journal of Management Mathematics*, 16(2), 113–120.
11. Anderson, M., Hopkins, W., Roberts, A., and Pyne, D. (2008). Ability of test measures to predict competitive performance in elite swimmers. Journal of Sports Sciences, 26(2), 123–130.
12. Zhang, X., Cai, Z., Liu, Z., and Wang, Y. (2020). Machine learning for sports analytics: predicting NBA playoff success. *IEEE Access*, 8, 205857–205864.
13. Vistro, D. M., Rasheed, F., and David, L. G. (2019). The cricket winner prediction with application of machine learning and data analytics. International journal of scientific & technology Research, 8(09).

78 Student identity verification solution using verifiable credentials on solana blockchain

Harishkumar Choudhary[a], Kalpesh Ahire[b] and Rohini Sarode[c]

Department of Computer Engineering & IT College of Engineering Pune, Wellesley Rd, Pune 411005, Maharashtra, India

Abstract

This research paper proposes a student identity verification solution using verifiable credentials on Solana blockchain. The proposed solution utilizes the high transaction per second (tps) and low gas fees offered by the Solana blockchain to provide a fast, secure, and cost-effective means of verifying student identities on blockchain. This study investigates the application of a verifiable credentials system using the Solana blockchain. Solana is a promising platform for creating decentralised applications due to its high throughput and inexpensive gas costs. The verifiable credentials system on Solana is described in detail in this paper along with its architecture and benefits over more conventional centralised solutions. The study also evaluates the system's performance in comparison to other blockchain-based options for verifiable credentials. A scalable solution for massive credential management, the evaluation demonstrates that the Solana-based system achieves high transaction throughput and low latency. This research paper highlights the Solana blockchain's advantages over other blockchain platforms and shows how it can be used to build effective and secure verifiable credentials systems. Future research directions for enhancing the system's functionality and usability are discussed in the paper's conclusion.

Keywords: Blockchain, self sovereign Identity, solana, verifiable credentials

Introduction

In today's world, majority of identity systems work in third party centralized way wherein the credentials are stored on central database server. As a user, we have less control over our own credentials. Data theft and data modification are one of the major drawbacks of currently deployed systems. Attacker can get access to centralized server and they can modify data on servers without getting noticed. As the technology progresses, Blockchain helps in tackling these issues.

Blockchain is a decentralized digital ledger that is used to record transactions and store data. It is a type of database that is distributed across a network of computers and is designed to be secure and transparent. Each block in the chain has a number of transactions in it as well as a special cryptographic link connecting it to the block before it. As a result, an irrevocable record of all network transactions is created, which cannot be changed or destroyed without the consent

[a]choudharyhf19.comp@coeptech.ac.in, [b]ahirekn19.comp@coeptech.ac.in, [c]rys.comp@coeptech.ac.in

of network users [5]. The speed of blockchain is measure in Transactions per second(TPS) which is the rate at which transactions are processed and confirmed on the blockchain network.

In a blockchain network, gas is the unit of measurement used to determine the cost of a transaction. Gas is required to execute operations on the blockchain, such as sending cryptocurrency, interacting with smart contracts, or deploying new contracts. Gas price, on the other hand, refers to the amount of cryptocurrency that a user is willing to pay per unit of gas to execute a transaction.

When utilised for digital identity management, blockchain technology can offer a safe and decentralised method of storing and managing data connected to identities. Personal data is kept in a centralised database in a traditional identity system, making it susceptible to breaches and attacks. The information is kept on a distributed ledger that is safe, transparent, and impenetrable in a blockchain-based identity system.

Literature Survey

There are several existing solutions for verifiable credentials on blockchain, each with their own approach and features. Here are a few notable examples:

Sovrin: Sovrin is a public, permissioned blockchain platform for creating and verifying digital identities and credentials. It is based on a decentralized identity (DID) standard, and supports the creation of verifiable credentials using a standardized JSON-LD format. Sovrin also includes a set of APIs and SDKs to make it easier for developers to integrate with the platform.

uPort: uPort is a self-sovereign identity platform that uses blockchain technology to create and manage digital identities and verifiable credentials. It is built on Ethereum, and supports the creation and verification of credentials using a standardized JSON-LD format. uPort also includes a mobile app that allows users to manage their identities and credentials.

CredChain: CredChain Mukta et al., [3] is a blockchain-based platform designed to provide a decentralized and secure way of verifying academic credentials. The platform uses Parity blockchain technology to store, manage and verify academic certificates and degrees in a tamper-proof and transparent manner. Smart Contracts are written in Solidity.

Casper: Bandara et al., [4] It is a blockchain and self-sovereign identity-based digital iden-tity platform to address smooth KYC process. Unlike traditional identity systems,here the actual identity credentials of customers are stored on their own mobile wallet applications. The system only stores the proofs of the credentials on its blockchainbased decentralized storage system. Casper employs ZeroKnowledge Proof mechanisms to verify the identity information from the credential proofs.

Self Sovereign Identity(SSI)

Self-sovereign identity (SSI) is a decentralised identity management framework that gives people total command over their digital identity and personal data. Individuals can develop and control their own digital identities within an SSI system, which is secured by blockchain and cryptography. SSI allows individuals to selectively disclose their personal information and control who has access to it, rather than relying on third-party organizations to manage their identity [6]. This can help to reduce the risk of identity theft, data breaches, and other forms of digital fraud, as well as protect individuals' privacy and personal autonomy.

Decentralized Identifiers(DID)

DID stands for "Decentralized Identifier". It is a globally unique identifier that is not controlled by any central authority or organization. DIDs are designed to give individuals and entities control over their digital identity and enable secure and private interactions on the internet. They are used in decentralized systems like blockchain and distributed ledger technologies to enable self-sovereign identity.

Verifiable Credentials(VC)

Digital credentials known as Verifiable Credentials (VCs) represent data about a person, group, or object that can be cryptographically confirmed. A common and trustworthy type of digital identification, VCs can be used by a variety of platforms and businesses. These may be issued by reputable organisations, such as governments or educational institutions, and may include details about credentials, certificates, or character traits. Together, DID and Verifiable Credentials enable secure, private, and trusted interactions between entities on the internet without the need for a centralized identity provider. DID provides a unique identifier that can be used to store and manage VCs, while VCs provide a trusted way to represent and share identity information.

Advantages of SSI over Conventional identity Systems

Giving people more control over their personal data is one of the key advantages of using blockchain for digital identity management. Users no longer need to rely on a central authority to maintain their identification because they may govern who has access to their personal data and issue permission to specific entities as needed. These systems offer a better level of security and privacy, allowing users to verify themselves without disclosing their identities to outside parties. Since every transaction is recorded on the blockchain, malicious users cannot change the data. Establishing unbiased trust between the parties would be made much easier by the decentralised, unchangeable nature of blockchain technology.

Impact of Low TPS and High Gas Fees

One of the key challenges facing many blockchain networks is the problem of low transaction throughput (also known as TPS or transactions per second) and high gas fees. This can be a major barrier to the widespread adoption of blockchain technology, particularly for use cases that require high volumes of transactions, such as payments or supply chain management. The low TPS and high gas fees problem is often caused by the limitations of the underlying blockchain technology, such as the consensus mechanism used, the block size, or the computational requirements of the smart contracts. These factors can all contribute to a bottleneck in the network's ability to process transactions quickly and efficiently, resulting in slow confirmation times and high fees.

Solana Overcomes Scalability Issue

Solana is a blockchain platform designed to tackle scalability issues. It uses a unique consensus algorithm called Proof of History (PoH), employs a hierarchy of nodes through its Tower BFT consensus mechanism, uses parallel processing to process multiple transactions simultaneously, and has large state replication technology called Gulf Stream. It also supports smart contracts written in Rust, allowing for quick and efficient execution, which further increases scalability.

Architecture of SSI System

The student identity platform architecture is divided into several key components, each responsible for a specific aspect of the system. These components are the issuer interface, holder credential wallet and verifier interface. Figure 78.1 provides an overview of the architecture and shows how these components interact with each other.

Issuer Interface
The issuer interface component is responsible for creating and issuing verifiable credentials to students. This interface is accessible to authorized personnel at educational institutions, who can use it to issue credentials to students who have met

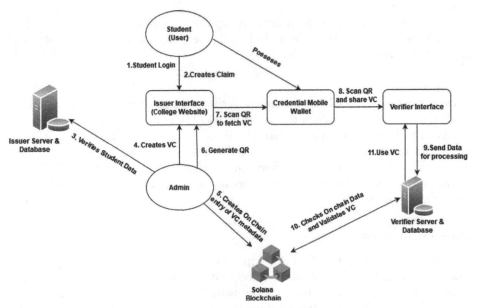

Figure 78.1 Architecture of self sovereign identity system

the necessary requirements. The issuer interface verifies the student's identity and ensures that the credential is accurate and valid before issuing it.

Holder Credential Wallet

The holder credential wallet component is responsible for storing and managing a student's digital credentials. Students can access their credential wallet through the user interface, where they can view their credentials, share them with third parties, and manage access control settings. The credential wallet ensures that the student's credentials are secure and can only be accessed by authorized parties.

Verifier Interface

The verifier interface component is responsible for verifying the authenticity and validity of a student's digital credential. Verifiers, such as potential employers, can use this interface to verify that a credential was issued by an authorized educational institution and that it has not been modified or tampered with. The verifier interface ensures that the credential is valid and can be trusted.

Workflow of Verifiable Credentials

Issuance

As shown in Figure 78.2, a trusted issuer creates a VC using a digital signature that links the credential to the individual's identity. The VC can include information such as the person's name, date of birth, education, or professional certification. The transaction is recorded on chain but any personal information is not stored on chain. After recording on chain entry, QR code of Verifiable Credential is generated which is scanned by User to store that credential in mobile wallet.

Storage

Verifiable credentials in an SSI system are typically stored on a digital wallet that is under the control of the identity holder. These digital wallets can be software applications that run on a user's device.

Verification

A user can scan QR code generated by verifier to share verifiable credential. A verifier who wants to confirm the authenticity of a VC can request access to the blockchain. They can use the credential DID to retrieve the Verifiable Credential and verify the digital signature to ensure that the credential is valid and has not been tampered with. If the verification is successful, the verifier can trust the information in the VC and make a decision based on it. Figure 78.3 provides flow of verification process.

Experimental Setup

We have set up Credentials Wallet Dapp using React-Native Expo library. Wallet Node server to be deployed to serve requests coming from Credentials Wallet Dapp. Issuer Interface have been set up using React Library. Issuer signs ver ifi-able credentials after checking whether claims are correct are not against issuer

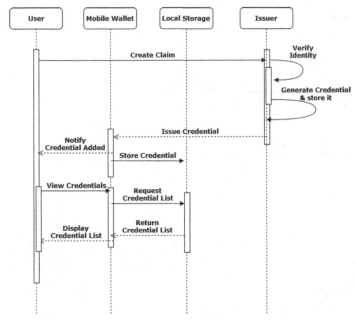

Figure 78.2 Verifiable credential issuance

database. Issuer interacts with Solana blockchain to create on chain entry of Verifiable Credential. Solana smart contract have been deployed to create on chain entries on solana blockchain.

Verifier interacts with React-based interface to perform its intended activities. Verifier validates credentials by checking solana on-chain entry.

Result and Discussion

In this study, we developed a student identity verification solution using verifiable credentials on the Solana blockchain. We tested the performance of our solution and compared it to existing solutions to evaluate its effectiveness. [Figure 78.1] The performance of our solution is boosted mainly due to using Solana blockchain network. Generally performance of a blockchain network is determined by several factors, including the block size, block interval time, network latency, and network bandwidth [2]. Solana has been designed to achieve high levels of performance and efficiency, with a focus on scalability, speed, and low latency. Solana's unique architecture and consensus mechanism allow it to achieve high TPS rates while also maintaining strong security and decentralization. The Solana blockchain's Proof of History (PoH) mechanism enables high transaction throughput, which allows our solution to verify student identities quickly and efficiently. Also it is worth noting that Proof of History (PoH) mechanism is being only implemented by Solana, providing an edge over other blockchain networks.

Proof of History (PoH) is a mechanism in Solana's blockchain that creates a historical record of events using cryptographic hashing functions. Gossip protocols are used in decentralized systems, like blockchain networks, to disseminate

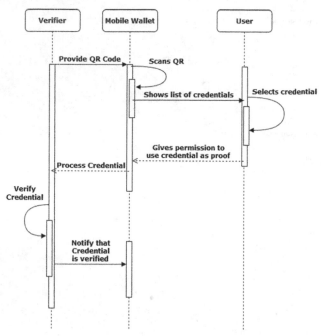

Figure 78.3 Verifiable credential verification

Table 78.1 Comparison of various proposed solutions in terms of transaction speed and gas fees of blockchain

Name of Paper	Blockchain	Transactions Speed	Gas Fees
Blockchain-enabled decentralized identity management: The case of self-sovereign identity in public transportation [7]	Ethereum	27	$4.1
Student Identity Verification Solution using Verifiable Credentials on Solana Blockchain [8]	Solana	65,000	$0.00025

information efficiently and reliably, allowing for parallel processing of transactions and reducing latency in the network. Research shows that gossip protocols can achieve high levels of scalability and fault tolerance. Solana's network is currently able to process up to 65,000 transactions per second. Using Solana's blockchain for student identity verification solutions with verifiable credentials has shown high performance and security, with implications for other industries like finance and healthcare.

Conclusion and Future Scope

We eventually will obtain a blockchain-based identity management system that makes use of the Solana blockchain network. The major reason to use the Solana blockchain is to take advantage of its maximum transaction per second (tps) speed and relatively low gas costs. The implementation of selective disclosure [1] using reductable credentials and the capability for the user to conceal particular fields while displaying the credential to the verifier could be the subject of furtherstudy. Interoperability can also be a subject of research in addition to above implementation.

Acknowledgment

We would like to thank Mrs. Rohini Sarode for helping us review our work regularly. We would also like to thank the Department of Computer Engineering, College of Engineering Pune for providing us hardware to test our code.

References

1. T, M., Makkithaya, K., and V G, N. (2022). A Blockchain Based Decentralized Identifiers for Entity Authentication in Electronic Health Records. In D. T. Pham (Ed.), Cogent Engineering (Vol. 9, Issue 1). Informa UK Limited. https://doi.org/10.1080/23311916.2022.2035134
2. Patel, C. (2022). Customer Empowered Privacy-Preserving Secure Verification using Decentralized Identifier and Verifiable Credentials For Product Delivery Using Robots (Version 1). arXiv. https://doi.org/10.48550/ARXIV.2208.06165
3. Mukta, R., Martens, J., Paik, H., Lu, Q., & Kanhere, S. S. (2020). Blockchain-Based Verifiable Credential Sharing with Selective Disclosure. In 2020 IEEE 19th International Conference on Trust, Security and Privacy in Computing and Communications (TrustCom). IEEE. https://doi.org/10.1109/trustcom50675.2020.00128
4. Bandara, E., Liang, X., Foytik, P., Shetty, S., & Zoysa, K. D. (2021). A Blockchain and Self-Sovereign Identity Empowered Digital Identity Platform. In 2021 International Conference on Computer Communications and Networks (ICCCN). 2021 International Conference on Computer Communications and Networks (ICCCN). IEEE. https://doi.org/10.1109/icccn52240.2021.9522184
5. Shi, J., Zeng, X., & Han, R. (2022). A Blockchain-Based Decentralized Public Key Infrastructure for Information-Centric Networks. In Information (Vol. 13, Issue 5, p. 264). MDPI AG. https://doi.org/10.3390/info13050264
6. Harrell, D. T., Usman, M., Hanson, L., Abdul-Moheeth, M., Desai, I., Shriram, J., De Oliveira, E., Bautista, J. R., Meyer, E. T., & Khurshid, A. (2022). Technical Design and Development of a Self-Sovereign Identity Management Platform for Patient-Centric Healthcare Using Blockchain Technology. In Blockchain in Healthcare Today. Partners in Digital Health. https://doi.org/10.30953/bhty.v5.196
7. Stockburger, L., Kokosioulis, G., Mukkamala, A., Mukkamala, R. R., & Avital, M. (2021). Blockchain-enabled decentralized identity management: The case of self-sovereign identity in public transportation. In Blockchain: Research and Applications (Vol. 2, Issue 2, p. 100014). Elsevier BV. https://doi.org/10.1016/j.bcra.2021.100014
8. Reddy, T., Reddy, P., Srinivas, R., Raghavendran, C., Lalitha, R., & Annapurna, B. (2021). Proposing a reliable method of securing and verifying the credentials of graduates through blockchain. EURASIP Journal on Information Security, 2021, 1-9. https://doi.org/10.1186/s13635-021-00122-5.

79 A Review on Digital Image Forgery Detection

Rajneesh Yadav[1,a] and Dr Urvashi Garg[2,b]

Department of computers science and engineering, National Institute of Technology, Jalandhar, India

Abstract

Finding fake digital images is a critical task. It has become harder to tell if an image (IMG) has been altered as a result of the widespread usage of digital IMG editing software and the expansion of high-quality IMG manipulation tools. Numerous approaches, like the discrete cosine transform (DCT) and Kernel Principal Component Analysis (KPCA), have been proposed to address this issue. The combination of DCT and KPCA can be used to create a powerful tool for digital image forgery detection (DIFD). The DCT is used to identify the areas of an IMG that have been altered, while KPCA is used to extract features from these areas that are robust against tampering. These features are then used to train a classifier that can differentiate between original and tampered images. In conclusion, the combination of DCT and KPCA is a promising approach for digital IMG forgery detection. This technique can identify subtle differences between original and tampered images, and it is robust against a variety of tampering techniques. Further research is needed to refine this approach and make it more widely applicable in the field of digital forensics and security.

Keywords: Kernel PCA, DCT, PCA, digital signature, water marking

Introduction

The advancing of the technology in this era the digital images are the concrete information source [1]. With the increasing use of digital images in various applications such as news, advertising, and entertainment, the need for detecting IMG forgeries has become imperative. Before the 21 century when an terror attack has taken place which is the 9/11 incident, so many different videos of Osma circulated over get viral over the internet were found counterfeited the same incident repeated with the IMG of an tiger. Force the people to believe in the existence of tiger in Shanki province of China in the recent years. This is accomplished through various techniques including visual examination, chemical analysis, and document examination to determine the authenticity of the item in question. The goal of forgery detection is to determine whether an item is genuine or a counterfeit. We can find the forged IMG by applying either the active or the passive (blind) technique watermarking, and digital signatures are used to prevent IMG manipulation, which can be done through retouching, splicing, or cloning. Retouching involves adjusting features in an IMG, while splicing combines multiple images to create a new one. To maintain the authenticity and integrity of an IMG, watermarking and digital signatures are implemented.

[a]Rajneeshy.cs.21@nitj.ac.in, [b]Urvashi@nitj.ac.in

Types of IMG Forgery Detection

IMG Retouching

One of the most popular forms of IMG manipulation involves modifying various quantitative features of an IMG, such as its orientation, size, extension, inclination, or mirroring, to improve its appearance and visual appeal [2, 3]. While this type of IMG alteration is widely recognized, it is also considered a relatively harmless form of IMG fabrication. Professional photographers, for instance, often use IMG retouching techniques to enhance certain aspects of an IMG and make it more attractive for use on a magazine cover. However, some argue that such modifications can be ethically questionable, as they may misrepresent reality. Figure 79.1 shows an example of photo editing where the IMG is improved through editing. IMG retouching is the process of making subtle adjustments to an IMG to improve its appearance, commonly used in photography, advertising, and graphic design. It involves various techniques, both manual and automated, and is important to use ethically and avoid misrepresentation. While it can be done manually or with automated software, it is important to use it ethically and avoid misleading or misrepresenting the original content. Figure 79.1 shows the effect of IMG retouching.

IMG Splicing

While creating an IMG, two or more different images are combined to produce a single IMG that looks to be original. This process is known as IMG splicing. IMG splicing is a complex and challenging problem in the field of IMG forensics [4]. While there are techniques for detecting splicing, it is important to continue researching and developing new methods to stay ahead of potential malicious uses. Additionally, promoting awareness of the potential for IMG splicing and its consequences can help prevent its misuse. Figure 79.2 shows how IMG splicing work.

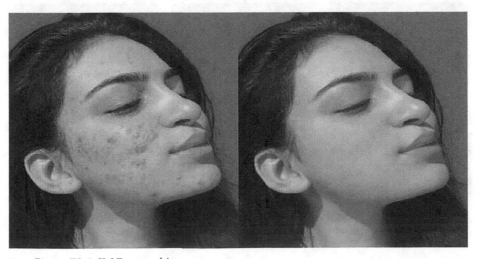

Figure 79.1 IMG retouching

IMG Cloning

IMG cloning is a type of IMG forgery that involves copying a region of an IMG and pasting it onto another part of the same IMG [5]. This technique is commonly used to hide or remove unwanted objects or people from a scene. IMG cloning is a prevalent form of IMG manipulation that requires advanced IMG forensics techniques for detection. Continued research and development of these techniques are necessary to stay ahead of the malicious uses of IMG cloning and preserve the integrity of digital media. IMG cloning the change comes in a single IMG no need of the other IMG where the tempering occurs. In Figure 79.3 one part of image is copied and then pasted where you want to use that IMG.

Digital IMG Forgery Detection Method

Depending on whether the original IMG is available or not, there are two types of digital IMG forgery detection techniques: active (non-blind) and passive (blind).

Active Authentication Method

Active methods involve modifying the digital IMG in some way to reveal the presence of a forgery. These methods require adding or modifying the IMG in a way that creates a signal that can be detected later. For example, one active method involves adding small patterns to the IMG that are invisible to the naked eye but can be detected later using specialized software [6]. Another active method involves analyzing the IMG's response to certain manipulations, such as blurring or sharpening, to detect the presence of a forgery. Active authentication methods are used in forgery detection to verify the authenticity

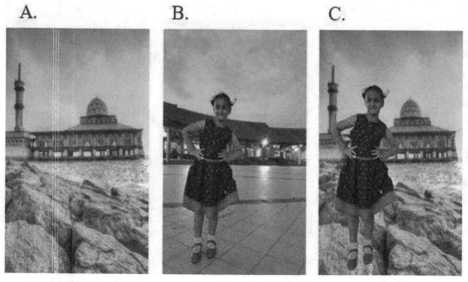

Figure 79.2 Img splicing

Figure 79.3 IMG cloning

of documents and signatures by requiring the user to actively confirm their identity. This helps detect and prevent forgery attempts and plays an important role in ensuring document authenticity [7]. Active authentication methods are an important component of digital IMG forgery detection and can complement passive authentication methods to enhance the accuracy and effectiveness of forgery detection.

Passive Authentication Method
Passive methods involve analyzing the digital IMG without making any changes to it. These methods use features that are intrinsic to the IMG, such as noise patterns, IMG statistics, and compression artifacts, to detect forgeries. Passive methods are useful for detecting simple forgeries, such as copy-paste or resizing, but are less effective for detecting more sophisticated forgeries, such as IMG composites or manipulations that introduce new content [8]. Passive authentication methods in forgery detection are used to analyze and verify the authenticity of a document or signature without requiring the user to actively confirm their identity. These methods include forensic analysis techniques such as document examination, handwriting analysis, and ink analysis. Passive authentication methods can also use technology such as optical character recognition (OCR) and machine learning algorithms to detect anomalies or patterns that indicate forgery. Overall, passive authentication methods provide valuable insights into the authenticity of a document or signature, and can be used in conjunction with active authentication methods to enhance forgery detection. Both active and passive authentication methods are used in digital IMG forgery detection [9]. Active methods require user confirmation, while passive methods analyze the IMG itself for inconsistencies or signs of manipulation, such as metadata or lighting/shadow inconsistencies. Both methods are used together to enhance accuracy.

THERE ARE SEVERAL TECHNIQUES THAT CAN BE USED FOR DIGITAL IMG FORGERY, INCLUDING

A) Pixel-Based Techniques

Detecting inconsistencies at the pixel level is possible in processes that are based on pixels. Researchers examine how the manipulation of the system affects the relationship between pixels in a particular area or in the overall spatial domain [10, 11]. There are four key subcategories of techniques used to detect pixel-level manipulation: duplication, splicing, resampling, and counterfeiting. Implementing pixel-based detection methods effectively may require the use of specialized software or hardware. In the case of high-resolution photographs, this is especially true. Nonetheless, they can be incredibly helpful for some types of IMG processing tasks, particularly those that require a high level of precision and control over individual pixels.

B) Format-Based Techniques

This arrangement frequently uses JPEG design as the format. Photo imitation is shown using a quantitative relationship created by evident lossy pressure [12]. You can employ these methods for Double JPEG, JPEG deterring and JPEG quantization. When photographs are clustered together, it can be exceedingly difficult to distinguish between the unaltered and edited versions. Nevertheless, it is possible to distinguish fashioned photographs from readily available packed pictures by using design-based strategies.

C) Camera-Based IMG Forgery Detection Techniques

Various methods are employed in imaging, such as quantization, shading connection, gamma correction, white balance adjustment, separation, and JPEG compression, to distinguish the alterations introduced during the IMG formation process. Color divergence, a cluster in the shading channel, camera shake, sensor commotion defects, etc [13]. can all be utilized to identify specific camera changes. Some examples of camera-based fraud detection methods include the analysis of sensor pattern noise, lens distortion, and IMG metadata, like the EXIF data, which provides details on the camera settings used to capture the IMG.

D) Source Camera Identification-Based Techniques

By examining sensor noise, sensor agitation, the emergence of shading channel clusters, and fluctuations in the camera's focus, the idiosyncrasies of the photo-taking camera are used to detect changes [14, 15]. SCI techniques have become significant as digital photography technology has spread and IMG editing has gotten more widespread. When investigators are aware of the camera used to capture the original IMG, they are better equipped to evaluate and understand digital evidence.

E) Physical Environment-Based IMG Forgery Detection

A typical photograph or piece of photography is typically taken under various lighting circumstances. It is possible to recognize any trickery employed to create a modified IMG by comparing the first IMG's depth of splendor and characteristic lighting. Examining the lighting modifications can be one of the most breathtaking methods to identify IMG duplication because there are certain discrepancies between the altered IMG's brilliant state and that of the original IMG [16]. Take the example of a posed photo of two people strolling down the beach. Initially, the two individuals' photos may have been taken separately in different locations. It is possible to analyze the lighting environment of a fashioned IMG to show that it is a fake or created one.

F) Geometry-Based IMG Forgery Detection

The camera enlarges the subject's light source before taking the photo. When this incoming "IMG" comes into contact with the camera sensor chip, it is divided up into several pixels. The sensor determines each pixel's brightness and shading by computing how the camera's focal point or focus is projected onto the IMG plane, then saves the results as a number. If the camera's primary position in the picture plane is close to the IMG's focus point, the camera will provide an unaltered IMG there [17]. The IMG's focal point, however, will shift as the object changes, as it is interpreted in the IMG, or as different IMG fragments are assembled. There should be movement throughout the IMG that is within metric constraints, such as the slant, perspective proportion, center length, and main point that was retrieved from an unaltered IMG, as evidence of the alteration. The use of projective math standards can therefore be used to stimulate the fabrication of location computations. As a result, imitation discovery is a multi-stage procedure [18].

G) Statistical Based IMG Forgery Detection

Statistical-based IMG forgery detection is a technique that involves analyzing the statistical properties of an IMG to detect any inconsistencies or anomalies that may indicate tampering [19]. This can be achieved through analyzing the compression artifacts, noise patterns, lighting and shadow patterns, and color patterns in an IMG. Although statistical based detection can be useful, it is not foolproof and can be circumvented by skilled forgers. Therefore, it is important to use multiple detection techniques and to verify the authenticity of an IMG through other means whenever possible. The basic idea behind this technique is to analyze the statistical properties of the IMG to detect any inconsistencies or anomalies that may indicate tampering.

Literature Review

The proposed Digital picture forgeries can be found using the five-step IMG copy-move forgery detection (IC-MFD) technique. Picture pre-processing, overlapping block division, statistical feature computation, feature sorting into a matrix, and a support vector machine (SVM) classifier are used to determine whether an IMG is genuine or fake. The method has been demonstrated to be extremely accurate, with a 98.44% accuracy rate. The system's capacity to recognize additional kinds of IMG forgeries will eventually be increased, according to the authors [20].

In **March 2020,** Mena and Tygi [21] discovers This research introduces a novel technique for identifying copy move forgeries in images through the use of the Tetrolet Transform. The process involves dividing the IMG into smaller overlapping sections and calculating the Tetrolet transform on each one. This result has generated four low pass and twelve high pass coefficients, which form the feature vector. The feature vectors are then sorted in lexicographic order to uncover any matching blocks. The efficacy of this approach was evaluated and found to effectively detect and locate duplicated regions, even if the copied parts had undergone various post-processing methods are commonly used to modify digital images and can include blurring, color reduction and JPEG compression.

In **June 2020,** Gani and Qadir [22] during in this work, an unique method for detecting copy-move forgeries in photos that have undergone noise and compression post-processing adjustments is proposed. To divide the input IMG into smaller, overlapping portions, the method employs a passive, block-based strategy. Then, using the discrete cosine transform (DCT) and cellular automata (CA) algorithms, the features of these blocks are retrieved. A kd-tree search and a relative error similarity evaluation are used to compare the resultant feature vectors in order to check the IMG for any potential copy-move forgeries. Although the magnitude information of the DCT coefficients has been shown to be more vulnerable to post-processing attacks than the sign information, this method varies from others in that it uses sign information instead.

In **April 2019,** Kanwal et al. [23], the paper introduces two original approaches for detecting IMG splicing. These techniques utilize overlapping blocks to identify specific IMG features. The first method uses the gray values of the chrominance to extract LBP or LTP features, and the second employs FFT to generate ELTP features from the chrominance channel. The results suggest that both LBP and ELTP are successful in determining IMG authenticity, with ELTP demonstrating improved performance compared to previous detection methods. Both the method are able to successfully determine the authenticity of IMG the FFT-ELTP approach achieved an accuracy of 88.62% when tested on compressed images from the CASIAv1.0 dataset. However, these methods involve complex transformations such as DCT and FFT, leading to an increase in overall methodology complexity. Future studies may concentrate on reducing the requirement for these complex operations and investigating techniques for localizing the forgery within the IMG.

In **March 2018,** Mahmod et al. [24], we have presented a brand-new technique for finding and spotting copy-move forgeries (CMF) in digital photographs for forensic use. Our method uses the shift invariant stationary wavelet transforms to extract features from the approximation sub band of the IMG (SWT). Using the discrete cosine transform, the feature vectors are then compressed (DCT). The results of our proposed CMF detection (CMFD) technology show a significant improvement over existing methods, even in the presence of numerous tampered areas and many different types of photos tampering and operations like translation, blurring, JPEG compression, brightness change, and color reduction. Our research demonstrates that our CMFD strategy outperforms other

Table 79.1 Literature Review

Author	Year	Algorithm used	Key Points	Accuracy
[20]	2021	Support-vector machine (SVM), mean and STD	Spatial, SVM classifier	98.44% When block size is 64 × 64
[21]	2020	Tetrolet transform, discreate wavelet transform (DWT)	Scale invariant feature transform (SIFT)	CoMoFod dataset. Aveg. Precision9981, Avg. Recall- 0.9603, F1- measure 0.9789
[22]	2020	Discrete cosine transform (DCT), cellular automata (CA)	Block based feature extraction, SVD, SWT, RGB to grayscale	using the KD-tree searchng. Precison 82.99, Rcl.90.31
[23]	2019	Fast Fourier transform, LBP and enhanced local ternary pattern (ELTP)	IMG splicing, LBP, LTP	FFT-ELTP - 88.62%
[24]	2018	SWT, DCT	Statnary wavelet. and discrete cosine transform.	96%
[25]	2018	Compressed BinaryDiscriminative Features (CBDF), Smpl. Linear. Iterative Clstrng. (SLIC) algrtm.	Binary discriminant, BDF	Used CoMoFoD dataset, precn. 97:50%, rcl. 87:50% and F1 score 92:23. This is at IMG level.

In November 2018, Raju and Nair [25], found that the goal of this work was to combine conventional block-based and key point-based techniques to create a novel method for detecting CMF. To find related areas in an IMG and extract key points, the suggested method used binary discriminant features. The complexity of feature matching was lowered by employing binary descriptors with a smaller dimension. Then, using SLIC super pixels, the matched points were used to identify potentially fraudulent areas. The forged regions were subsequently isolated using the forgery region localization technique by analyzing color histograms. A morphological close procedure was the last stage, which was used to identify the forged region. The study's conclusions demonstrated how well the suggested strategy worked to uncover copy-move frauds. The technique outperformed existing algorithms in terms of precision and F1 Score, displaying great accuracy and detection rates. With the ability to identify both single copy-move forgeries and multiple copy-move forgeries, the recall rate was likewise impressive. Additionally, the suggested technique demonstrated resistance to a variety of post-processing functions such brightness modifications, contrast changes, color reduction, and IMG blurring. The method does not require feature matching threshold values, and as shown by the high precision rates, it has a low rate of false matching. Table 79.1 summarizes Literature review.

Conclusion and future scope

We can identify copy-move forgery (CMF) in computerized images. We have reduced the aspect of the characteristic length and discovered the manufactured thing in the conjecture IMG. This technique doesn't need any earlier information. implant into the picture and works without any computerized signature or advanced watermark. This procedure effectively identifies various duplicate move fabrications.

References

1. Khan, ,Kaloi, , Shaikh, ,and Arain, (2018). A hybrid technique for copy-move Img forgery detection. *2018 3rd International Conference on Computer and Communication Systems,* (pp. 212-216). doi: 1109/CCOMS.2018.8463337.
2. Wang, H. and Wang, H. (2018). Perceptual hashing-based img copy-move forgery detection. *Security and Communication Networks*, 2018, 11. https://doi.org/10.1155/2018/6853696
3. Krawetz, N. (2007). A pictures worth digital IMG analysis and forensics. *Black Hat Briefings*. https://www.hackerfactor.com/
4. Lian, S. and Zhang, Y. (2010). Multimedia forensics for detecting forgeries. Handbook of Information and Communication Security, pp. 809–828, Springer, New York, NY, USA, 2010.
5. Li, Y. (2013). IMG copy-move forgery detection based on polar cosine transform and approximate nearest neighbor searching. *Forensic Science International*, 224(1–3), 59–67.
6. Farid, H. (2006). Digital doctoring: how to tell the real from the fake. *Significance*, 3(4), 162–166.
7. Zhu, ,Swanson, ,and Tewfik, (2004). When seeing isn't believing [multimedia authentication technologies. *IEEE Signal Processing Magazine*, 21(2), 40–49.
8. Farid, H. (2009). IMG forgery detection: a survey. *IEEE Signal Processing Magazine*, 26(2), 16–25.
9. Zhao, J. and Guo, J. (2013). Passive forensics for copy-move IMGforgery using a method based on DCT and SVD. *Forensic Science International*, 233(1–3), 158–166.
10. Cox, I. M., Miller, M. L., Bloom, J. A., Fridrich, J., and Kalker, T. (2007). Digital watermarking and steganography, Morgan Kaufmann, Burlington, Mass, USA.
11. Qureshi, and Deriche, M. (2015). A bibliography of pixel-based blind IMG forgery detection techniques. *Signal Processing: IMG Communication*, 39, 46–74.
12. Qazi, T., Hayat, K., Khan, S. U. et al. (2013). Survey on blind IMG forgery detection. *IET IMG Processing*, 7(7), 660–670.
13. Mahmood, T., Nawaz, T., Ashraf, R. et al. (2015). A survey on block based copy move IMG forgery detection techniques. *In Proceedings of the International Conference on Emerging Technologies*, pp. 1–6, Peshawar, Pakistan, December 2015.
14. Fridrich, J., Soukal, D., and Luk´aˇs, J. (2003). Detection of copy-move forgery in digital images. In Proceedings of Digital Forensic Research Workshop, Cleveland, Ohio, USA, August 2003.
15. Bayram, S., Sencar, H. T., and Memon, N. (2009). An efficient and robust method for detecting copy-move forgery. *In Proceedings of the International Conference on Acoustics, Speech, and Signal Processing*, (pp. 1053–1056), April 2009.
16. Popescu, C. and Farid, H. (2004). Exposing digital forgeries by detecting duplicated IMG regions. *Tech. Rep.* TR2004-515, Dartmouth College, Hanover, NH, USA, 2004.

17. Huang, Y., Lu, W., Sun, W., and Long, D. (2011). Improved DCT-based detection of copy-move forgery in images. *Forensic Science International*, 206(1–3) 178–184.

18. Li, G., Wu, Q., Tu, D., and Sun, S. (2007). A sorted neighborhood approach for detecting duplicated regions in IMG forgeries based on DWT and SVD. *In Proceedings of IEEE International Conference on Multimedia and Expo*, (pp. 1750–1753). Beijing, China, 2007.

19. Mahdian, B. and Saic, S. (2007). Detection of copy-move forgery using method based on blur moment invariants. *Forensic Science International*, 171(23), 180–189.

20. Ahmed, T., Hammad, , and Jamil, N. (2021). IMG copy-move forgery detection algorithms based on spatial feature domain. 2021 *IEEE 17th International Colloquium on Signal Processing & Its Applications (CSPA)*, 2021, (pp. 92-96). doi: 10.1109/ CSPA52141.2021.9377272.

21. Meena, K. B. and Tyagi, V. (2020). A copy-move IMG forgery detection technique based on tetrolet transform. *Journal of Information Security and Applications*, 52, 102481. https://doi.org/10.1016/j.jisa.2020.102481

22. Gani, G. and Qadir, F. (2020). A robust copy-move forgery detection technique based on discrete cosine transform and cellular automata. *Journal of Information Security and Applications*, 54, 102510. doi: 10.1016/j.jisa.2020.102510

23. Kanwal, N., Girdhar, A., Kaur, L., and Bhullar, (2019). Detection of digital IMG forgery using fast fourier transform and local features. *International Conference on Automation, Computational and Technology Management (ICACTM)*, (pp. 262-267). doi: 10.1109/ICACTM.2019.8776709.

24. Mahmood, T., Mehmood, Z., Shah, M., and Saba, T. (2018). A robust technique for copy-move forgery detection and localization in digital images via stationary wavelet and discrete cosine transform. *Journal of Visual Communication and Image Representation*, 53, 202214.

25. Raju, P. M. and Nair, M. S. (2018). Copy-move forgery detection using binary discriminant features. *Journal of King Saud University - Computer and Information Sciences*. doi:10.1016/j.jksuci.2018.11.004

80 Optimizing the Discovery of Web Services with QoS-Based Runtime Analysis for Efficient Performance

Tadikonda Akshay Sampath[a], Nausheen Fatima[b], Yerukola Vikas[c] and Mohammad Faiz[d]

School of CSE, Lovely Professional University, Phagwara, Punjab, India

Abstract

Runtime associated quality of service (QoS)-based competent web services discovery optimization the runtime QOS characteristics are taken into account in this method to enhance the search for web services. Improved discovery makes it easier to choose the best service for a task. This study investigates how to improve online service discovery through the use of inspired algorithms. It is critical to take QoS features into account when matching web services, as this will enable efficient and effective use of web services. A class of metaheuristics known as "bio-inspired algorithms" solves challenging optimization issues by mimicking natural processes. The study thoroughly assesses how well various bio-inspired optimization algorithms work in streamlining the discovery procedure for semantic web services, with a particular focus on a concentration on service discovery driven by quality. The study discovered that different algorithms behave differently when considering various QoS parameters and that bio-inspired algorithms are efficient in optimizing the web service discovery process. Overall, the results of this study can contribute to enhancing the performance of web service-based applications and increasing the efficiency and efficacy of web service discovery.

Keywords: Web service, quality of service, optimization

Introduction

By utilizing the protocols, web services are a fundamental method for various software applications to exchange data over the internet. Web services can be used for a range of tasks, such as connecting systems within an organization, exchanging data with partners or vendors, and constructing collections that include data from many sources. Web services structure data for transmission using XML or JSON [1].

There are three main roles in web based service architecture:

- Service provider
- Service registry
- Service requestor

---

[a]tadikondaakshaysampath@gmail.com, [b]nausheen.28838@lpu.co.in, [c]yerukolavikas@gmail.com, [d]faiz.techno20@gmail.com

Service provider: The major responsibility is to comprehend and satiate the demands of their customers through the delivery of superior services and first-rate customer support (Faiz et al., 2023)

Service requestor: The service requestor typically provides the necessary information and parameters required for the service to be performed, and then awaits a response from the service provider.

Service registry: A service registry is a central database that offers details on the services that are offered. For both service requestors and suppliers, it makes service discovery, registration, and management easier.

Quality of Service (QoS)
Quality of service (QoS) When there are several web services available with the same or similar functions offers non-functional web service qualities for the best web service selection. As more web services are developed, factors other than cost become more important, such as QoS attributes [21].

Literature Survey

Yao et al. [3] said that there are various Web services available with the same functionalities. Chaiyakul introduced the QoS which offers non-functional web

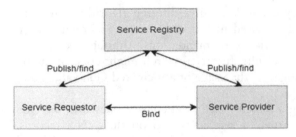

Figure 80.1 Web service architecture

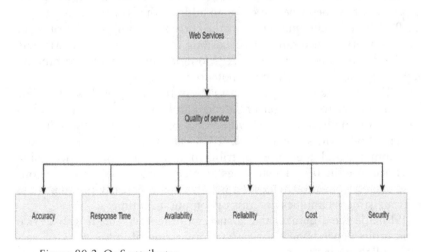

Figure 80.2 QoS attributes

based service attributes for the optimum Web based service selection. A web service discovery and selection method called Ar WSDS uses the quality metrics of web services to dynamically classify web services. It provides a quick solution to the selection problem by utilising the human brain's pattern recognition system. Ar WSDS has been tested on a dataset from the QWS project and has been shown to be effective in recognising numerous patterns and filtering out unclear web services.

Zhang et al. [6] proposed a web service selection technique that provides dynamic planning and global QoS optimisation. It enhances service portfolio quality by using position matrix coding to express execution pathways and replanning data. By user time limits and solution retention, the algorithm eliminates the negative effects of running time on service quality. Both user happiness and service invocation effectiveness are increased. Further work will focus on enhancing web service discovery, researching dynamic expression of QoS notification and demand, and optimising representation and operation methods for quality matrices.

Amin et al. [5] proposed to help service providers, and customers in choosing the best services based on their preferences and expectations, we developed a QoS aware service selection model based on fuzzy technique. The strategy aims to reduce selection process discrepancies and provide a consensus weight for QoS parameters.

Zheng et al. [6] proposed a hybrid collaborative filtering algorithm and user-contributed QoS data gathering are used in the Web service recommendation approach called WSRec to make service recommendations. Although experimental study has yielded encouraging results, further research might concentrate on monitoring more services, investigating the usage of anticipated QoS values, and fusing several QoS features.

Mao et al. [7] proposed using a search-based prediction framework, the QoS ranking issue. To enhance the order of services based on their QoS records. Proposed framework uses a particle swarm optimisation technique. An enhanced method for determining the similarity between users utilising service pairs' occurrence probability is described in order to address the issue of missing QoS records. The PSO-based technique surpasses the current CloudRank algorithm in producing high-quality service rankings, according to experimental experiments on actual QoS data. In order to tackle the NP-Complete problem of QoS ranking prediction, the suggested approach shows potential.

Alrifai and Risse [8] make a suggestion on how to choose web services for composition that adhere to both user preferences and end-to-end QoS specifications. Local selection methods are used with global optimisation in the solution. The suggested method divides global QoS restrictions into local ones using mixed integer programming, and then uses distributed local selection to determine which web services are the best. The findings of experimental evaluation demonstrate that the suggested method achieves outcomes that are nearly optimal while outperforming existing techniques in terms of computation time.

Ma et al. [9] made the argument that a successful deployment of web-service enabled applications depends on the accurate forecasting of unknown QoS values. Although collaborative filtering for QoS prediction is frequently used, it is

Table 80.1 Various existing models with limitations

Methods	Title	Reference	Year of Publish	Limitations
Ant colony	Ant colony optimization	[12]	2006	Low convergence speed with large data
Particle swarm	Particle swarm optimization	[13]	1995	Cannot give optimal solution
Firefly algorithm	Firefly optimization	[14]	2009	Takes long time to run
Cuckoo search	Cuckoo search optimization	[16]	2009	Slow and inefficient during random search
Bat algorithm	Bat algorithm	[17]	2010	Converge slowly

not necessarily appropriate for objective QoS data. In this study, we provide a prediction algorithm that takes into account the critical attributes of objective QoS datasets, enabling more precise prediction of unknown QoS values.

Proposed Methodology

The new hybrid algorithm which combines both ant colony and firefly has the following steps in it:

Initialization: Generate an initial population of ants and fireflies that represent potential locations for the gold mine.

Ant colony optimization phase: Run an ant colony optimization algorithm to allow ants to explore and evaluate potential locations for the gold mine. The ants will deposit pheromones to mark good locations and communicate with each other to find the optimal path. The fitness of each ant's solution will be evaluated using a fitness function.

Firefly algorithm phase: Run a firefly algorithm to refine the solution space, using the best solutions found by the ants as the initial population of fireflies. The fireflies will interact with each other to optimize the solution space based on their brightness values and attractiveness functions.

Hybridization: Combine the best solutions found by the ants and fireflies to create a new solution population.

Repeat: Repeat steps 2-4 for a specified number of iterations or until the algorithm converge.

Evaluation: Evaluate the final solution and determine whether any further exploration or analysis is necessary.

The advantages of both the firefly algorithm and ant colony optimisation are combined in this hybrid approach. While firefly algorithm is good at narrowing the search space and identifying appropriate solutions, ant colony optimisation excels at exploring the search space and producing acceptable results [11]. We may be able to more effectively find better answers by integrating the two methods.

The hybrid algorithm that combines ant colony optimization and firefly algorithm can potentially address some of the drawbacks of each individual algorithm [19]. Here are some possible benefits of the hybrid algorithm:

1.   **Overcoming local optima**: Ant colony optimization can sometimes get stuck in local optima, which are sub-optimal solutions that are close to the starting point. The firefly algorithm can help overcome this problem by exploring the solution space and finding better solutions, even if they are far away from the current solution.
2.   **Improved convergence speed**: The firefly algorithm can converge faster than ant colony optimization because it can converge towards the optimal solution quickly by refining the search space around the existing best solutions.
3.   **Improved exploration-exploitation balance**: Ant colony optimization tends to have a good balance between exploration and exploitation, but it can become too exploitative in some cases. The firefly algorithm can help maintain a good balance by exploring new regions of the search space while also refining the regions around the best solutions.
4.   **Better solution quality**: By combining the strengths of both algorithms, the hybrid algorithm can potentially find better solutions than either algorithm alone [22].

Of course, it's essential to note that the effectiveness of the hybrid algorithm will rely on specific problem being solved and the parameters used in the algorithm.

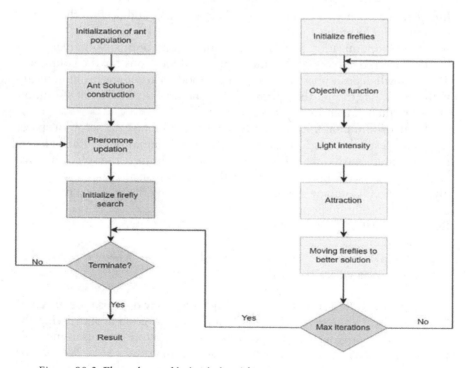

Figure 80.3 Flow chart of hybrid algorithm

Additionally, developing and implementing a hybrid algorithm may require more computational resources and time than using a single algorithm.

Efficiency of Algorithms

Reaction time (RT) and accuracy, two QoS runtime associative parameters, are used in the study to evaluate and compare the performance of various meta-heuristic algorithms [10].

Three categories of user request assumptions—well defined (WD), moderate (M), and blind—are used to conduct the evaluation (B).

In the WD category, the user request is clearly stated, and its scope is specified. Because keywords are formed in a descriptive way, they are useful and relevant to the query.

In the M category, although being only somewhat distinct, the user's request is not clearly defined. The request's scope is only mildly obvious, and the keywords' formation is unclear as to their semantic purpose. It limits duplicated keywords, which means that the request does not include irrelevant terms.

In the B category, the user is unsure of the request, and its parameters are vague. In the absence of accurate keyword generation and the presence of improbable keywords, the request may contain irrelevant and unrelated keywords.

Simulation

The given an issue like quality of service (QoS) there are a lot of algorithms and ideas through which we can bring more accuracy and less response time a few of them are:

One of the algorithms that I want to discuss in this paper is ant colony optimization (ACO). This algorithm is one of the inspired algorithms in which we use the path used by a similar kind of user.

The Ant Colony Optimization (ACO) Algorithm

Step 1: Initialization
Set the ant population's starting locations within the search space at random. Set the maximum number of iterations and the iteration count.

Step 2: Movement of ants
Based on the pheromone trails created by the previous ants, each ant in the population moves at random. The pheromone concentration at each place determines the likelihood of choosing the following movement direction. Higher pheromone levels increase the likelihood of choosing that area.

Step 3: Updating the pheromone trail
The pheromone level is updated using the ants' most effective solutions to date. The pheromone level is updated at a rate that increases with solution quality.

Step 4: Verify the stopping criteria.
Verify the stopping criteria, such as the objective function value cutoff or the maximum number of iterations.

Step 5: Up until the ending requirement is reached, repeat steps 2 through 4.

$$\cdot p_{ab}^{k} = \frac{(\tau_{ab}^{\alpha})(\vartheta_{ab}^{\beta})}{\sum c\in allowed_{a}(\tau_{ac}^{\alpha})(\vartheta_{ac}^{\beta})} \tag{1}$$

Ants use a process to navigate through a graph where they select the next edge to move based on the length of each edge and how much pheromone is present on it. At each step, the ant moves from a to b, building up a complete solution as it goes. The probability of moving from a to b is based on the attractiveness (ϑ_{ab}) of the move and the proficiency of the move is based on the pheromone level on the edge that is trail level (ϑ_{ab}).

The other algorithm that is to be discussed is Firefly algorithm, which is also an inspired algorithm listed above:

The Firefly Algorithm (FF)

Step 1: Initialization: Set up the population of fireflies, which consists of n fireflies, at the beginning. An answer to the optimisation problem serves as the representation for each firefly.

Step 2: Establish the objective function that will be optimised in order to assess the effectiveness of the firefly solutions.

Step 3: Compute each firefly's light intensity to determine the quality of the answer the firefly is illustrating. Using the objective function, the light intensity is calculated.

Step 4: Compute the attractiveness between two pairs of fireflies to decide which firefly will go in which direction and how much. The Euclidean distance between the firefly and their light intensity is used to calculate the attractiveness.

Step 5: According to the assessed attractiveness, move each firefly in the population in the direction of the brightest fireflies. A randomization element, which regulates the discovery and utilization of the search space, determines the movement.

Step 6: Update: Adjust each firefly's light output in accordance with its updated locations inside the search area. The light intensity is increased if the new place yields a better answer. In every other case, less light is produced.

Step 7: Termination: Repetition of steps 3-6 will continue until a stopping factor, such as a cap on iterations or a cutoff point for the improvement in the objective function, is reached.

Step 8: Output: Provide the best answer determined by the fireflies, which is the one that has the brightest light.

$$x_{i}^{t+1} = x_{i}^{t} + \beta \exp\left[-\sigma r_{ij}^{2}\right]\left(x_{j}^{t} - x_{i}^{t}\right) + \alpha_{t}\epsilon_{t} \tag{2}$$

where, α_t is basically the parameter that controls the step size and ϵ_t is derived from the vector drawn from other distributions. The firefly algorithm involves

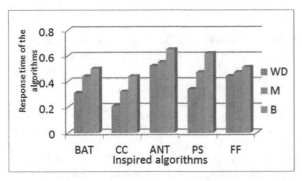

Figure 80.4 Response time of a user's request for inspired algorithms

moving fireflies to new positions based on their attraction to other fireflies. The attraction of a firefly at position xj towards another firefly at position xk is determined by a parameter β, which is a function of the distance between the two fireflies. There is also a randomization parameter α that adds some randomness to the movement of the fireflies.

By combining these two techniques, we may make use of each algorithm's advantages while minimizing its weaknesses. The firefly algorithm offers a quick convergence rate and effective search space exploitation, whereas the ant colony method offers a robust global search capability. It is anticipated that the resulting hybrid algorithm will offer higher optimization performance and better convergence to the global optimum.

Figure 80.4 compares the response time of different inspired optimization algorithms for various user requests. The Y-axis shows response time in milliseconds, while the X-axis lists the algorithms. Requests are categorized as "well defined", "moderate", and "blind" based on ambiguity.

Conclusion

In conclusion, hybrid algorithms that combine ant colony and firefly algorithms can provide improved optimization performance and faster convergence compared to using either algorithm alone. By leveraging the strengths of each algorithm, the resulting hybrid algorithm can overcome their individual limitations and provide more robust and efficient optimization solutions. The development and implementation of hybrid algorithms require careful consideration of the design parameters, such as the selection of the algorithm parameters, the search strategy, and the evaluation criteria. In addition, the performance of the hybrid algorithm should be compared with existing optimization algorithms to evaluate its effectiveness and efficiency. Overall, hybrid algorithms have shown great potential in various optimization applications, including engineering design, machine learning, and image processing, among others. Further research is needed to explore and refine the design and implementation of hybrid algorithms to address the challenges and complexities of real-world optimization problems.

Acknowledgement

The authors gratefully acknowledge the students, staff, and authority of School of Computer Science and Engineering for their cooperation in the research.

References

1. Chaiyakul, S., Limapichat, K., Dixit, A., and Nantajeewarawat, E. (2006). A framework for semantic Web service discovery and planning. *In 2006 IEEE Conference on Cybernetics and Intelligent Systems* (pp. 1-5). IEEE.
2. Faiz, M., Fatima, N., Sandhu, R., Kaur, M., and Narayan, V. (2023). Improved homomorphic encryption for security in cloud using particle swarm optimization. *Journal of Pharmaceutical Negative Results*, 2996-3006.
3. Yao, L., Liu, H., Zhou, L., and Wang, G. (2015). A runtime QoS-aware approach for web service discovery and selection. *Service Oriented Computing and Applications*, 9(4), 289-300.
4. Zhang, D., He, Q., and Chen, X. (2019). QoS-based web service discovery and selection framework. *IEEE Access*, 7, 110124-110135.
5. Amin, M. T., Zhang, G., and Madani, S. A. (2014). QoS-aware Web service discovery and selection: A survey. Journal of Network and Computer Applications, 41, 494-513.
6. Zheng, Z., Ma, H., Lyu, M. R., and King, I. (2009). Wsrec: a collaborative filtering based web service recommender system. *In Proceedings of 2009 IEEE International Conference on Web Services*, pp. 437-444.
7. Mao, C., Chen, J., Towey, D., Chen, J., and and Xie, X. (2015). Search-based QoS ranking prediction for web services in cloud environments. *Future Generation Computer Systems*, 50, 111-126.
8. Alrifai, M. and Risse, T. (009). Combining global optimization with local selection for efficient QoS-aware service composition. *In Proceedings of the 18th International Conference on World Wide Web*, (pp. 881-890).
9. Ma, Y., Wang, S., Hung, P. C., Hsu, C. -H., Sun, Q., and Yang, F. (2016). A highly accurate prediction algorithm for unknown web service QoS values. *IEEE Transactions on Services Computing*, 9(4), 511_523.
10. Lee, K.,. Park, J., and Baik, J. (2015). Location-based web service QoS prediction via preference propagation for improving cold start problem," In Proceedings of 2015 IEEE International Conference on Web Services pp. 177-184, 2015.
11. Chen, X., Liu, X., Huang, Z., and Sun, H. (2010). Regionknn: a scalable hybrid collaborative filtering algorithm for personalized web service recommendation. *In Proceedings of 2010 IEEE International Conference on Web Services*, pp. 9-16, 2010.
12. Dorigo, M., Birattari, M., and Stutzle, T. (2006). Ant colony optimization. *In IEEE Computational Intelligence Magazine*, 1(4), 28-39. doi: 10.1109/MCI.2006.329691.
13. Kennedy, J. and Eberhart, R. (1995). Particle swarm optimization. Proceedings of ICNN'95 - International Conference on Neural Networks, Perth, WA, Australia, (pp. 1942-1948). doi: 10.1109/ICNN.1995.488968.
14. Yang, X. S. (2009). Firefly algorithms for multimodal optimization. In: Watanabe, O., Zeugmann, T. (Eds) Stochastic Algorithms: Foundations and Applications.
15. SAGA 2009. Lecture Notes in Computer Science, vol 5792. Springer, Berlin, Heidelberg.
16. Yang, X. -S. and Deb, S. (2009). Cuckoo search via lévy flights. 2009 World Congress on Nature & Biologically Inspired Computing (NaBIC), Coimbatore, India, pp. 210-214, doi: 10.1109/NABIC.2009.5393690.

17. Yang, X. S. (2010). A New Metaheuristic Bat-Inspired Algorithm. In: González, J.R., Pelta, D.A., Cruz, C., Terrazas, G., Krasnogor, N. (eds) Nature Inspired Cooperative Strategies for Optimization (NICSO 2010). Studies in Computational Intelligence, vol 284. Springer, Berlin, Heidelberg. https://doi.org/10.1007/978-3-642-12538-6_6

18. Sawaragi, Y., Nakayama, H., Tanio, T. (1985). Theory of multiobjective optimization. *Mathematics in Science and Engineering.* 176, 36-40.

19. Osman, I. H. and Laporte, G. (1996). Metaheuristics: a bibliography. *Annals of Operations Research*, 63, 513-623.

20. Faiz, M. and Daniel, A. K. (2021). FCSM: Fuzzy Cloud Selection Model using QoS Parameters," 2021 First International Conference on Advances in Computing and Future Communication Technologies (ICACFCT), Meerut, India, 2021, pp. 42-47, doi: 10.1109/ICACFCT53978.2021.9837347.

21. Faiz, M., and Daniel, A. K. (2022). Threats and challenges for security measures on the internet of things. Law, State and Telecommunications Review, 14(1), 71-97.

22. Faiz, M. and Daniel, A. K. (2020). A multi-criteria cloud selection model based on fuzzy logic technique for QoS. *International Journal of Systems Assurance Engineering and Management.* https://doi.org/10.1007/s13198-022-01723-0

81 Categorizing Brain Tumors from MR Images using CNN and its Variants

Priyanka Mahajan[1,a] and Prabhpreet Kaur[2,b]

[1]Research Scholar, GNDU, Amritsar, India

[2]Assistant Professor, GNDU, Amritsar, India

Abstract

Background The timely detection of brain tumors is crucial to ensure optimal medical treatment. Early diagnosis helps doctors to select the most effective treatment for their patients. The manual identification and categorization of brain tumors is a difficult task that demands expertise from radiologists. However, the use of computer-assisted diagnosis has been a major advancement in combating this life-threatening illness. Also, the MRI scanner becomes a popular choice due to its ability to produce high-quality images.

Process Nowadays, deep learning (DL) has shown great potential as a classification method due to its impressive achievements in the fields of classification and segmentation. The present research utilizes a classification system that uses deep transfer learning, named EfficientNetB7. It extracts features from brain MR images and uses them for categorization. The purposed system is also trained to handle adversarial attacks by training it using Fast Gradient Sign Method (FGSM).

Results The proposed system performs exceedingly better than all the current innovative methods, with a resultant classification accuracy of 99%. This research also employs the recall, area under the curve (AUC), precision, F-score, and specificity as performance indicators.

Keywords: EfficientNetB7, transfer learning, adversarial attack, multiclassification, brain tumor

Introduction

The person's mental and physical actions are coordinated by billions of neurons that communicate with one another via synapses. It regulates not only vital functions like breathing and heart rate, but also higher-level cognitive activities like memory, attention, and choice-making [1]. Not only cancers, but also stroke, Alzheimer's, and countless others, pose a threat to the brain [2]. Tumors of the brain form when cells inside the skull grow and proliferate at an accelerated rate [3]. There are two main categories for brain cancers: original tumors and secondary tumors, or metastatic tumors. Primary brain tumors are malignant growths that start in the brain, while tumors which are secondary can spread both within the brain and to other regions [4]which is time-consuming and prone to error. Researchers have proposed automated methods in recent years to detect brain tumors early. These approaches, however, encounter difficulties due to their low accuracy and large false-positive values. An efficient tumor identification and classification approach is required to extract robust features and perform accurate

[a]pari12rudra@gmail.com, [b]prabhpreet.cst@gndu.ac.in

disease classification. This paper proposes a novel multiclass brain tumor classification method based on deep feature fusion. The MR images are preprocessed using min-max normalization, and then extensive data augmentation is applied to MR images to overcome the lack of data problem. The deep CNN features obtained from transfer learned architectures such as AlexNet, GoogLeNet, and ResNet18 are fused to build a single feature vector and then loaded into Support Vector Machine (SVM. Both benign and malignant forms of primary brain cancer exist. Benign tumors (termed as low-grade I and II) develop more slowly than malignant (termed as high-grade III and IV) ones, have distinct borders, and rarely migrate to other organs. Benign tumors are not always harmless, especially if they develop in an essential organ [5]. On the contrary, malignant tumors are terminal and exhibit uncontrollable growth [3]. Secondary brain tumors, or metastases, initially develop in other areas of the body before proliferating and spreading to the brain [5]. Gliomas, meningiomas, and pituitary tumors are among the most challenging primary brain tumors for physicians to diagnose and treat promptly.

The complexity of brain tissue makes it difficult for conventional radiographic imaging methods like X-rays, CT scans, and PET scans to detect brain tumors [1]. Brain tumor identification and categorization using MR scans may be difficult processes, especially when dealing with big datasets. This can make it challenging to perform real-time prediction or analysis [7]. The deep learning mechanism, a subfield of machine learning, is known for its exceptional ability to recognize and classify images [8]. However, in order for deep learning techniques to work, a massive amount of data is needed. To get around the issue of lacking, enough data for training, transfer learning can be employed. In transfer learning (TL) the network is equipped with a massive training set and then learned knowledge is applied to the smaller dataset [9]. This method saves time during training because the model has already been trained on a similar problem [10]. Transfer learning can be implemented in two ways: ConvNet fine-tuning and feature extraction [9]. The most important outcomes of our planned research are:

1. A unique and effective transfer learning technique for computerized identification and classification of brain cancers, named EfficientNetB7.
2. To provide a comprehensive analysis of the performance variables influencing the fine-tuning strategy of pre-trained models.
3. To train the model against the adversary attack by helping it to learn through Fast Gradient Sign Method (FGSM).

Related Studies

Brain tumor categorization is a highly complex area of medical imaging. Several methods and procedures have been established for categorization of brain cell tumors with high accuracy. Sharif et al. [11] suggested a novel nine-layer convolutional neural network model for multi-mode categorization of brain tumor. Hybrid splitting histogram equalization and ant colony optimization enhance image contrast in the study. After extracting the characteristics, they are enhanced via differential evolution and moth flame optimization. The study [8] suggested

Table 81.1 Listed below shows some of the literature studies involved in dataset classification

Paper	Dataset used	No. of images	Feature extraction	Methodology used	Normalization Method	Number of epochs	Optimization method	Task performed	Performance measure
[14]	Real-time MRI images	450 Images	Extracted using the GLDM method	Back Propagation Neural network	NA	NA	Genetic algorithm	Classification	Sensitivity, Specificity, Positive Predictive Value, Accuracy (98%)
[7]	BRaTS image dataset	280 Images	Extracted using the Gray-level Co-occurrence method	Hybrid DCNN with ResNet-152 Transfer Learning method	Batch normalization	NA	CoV-19 optimization algorithm	Detection and classification	Accuracy (98.3%), Sensitivity (89.2%) & Specificity (87.2%)
[15]	Real-time dataset from clinical Images	1000 Images	NA	Optimized Hybrid DNN (hybrid model of CNN + LSTM)	NA	80	Adaptive rider optimization	Classification	Accuracy (97.5%)
[4]	Figshare dataset	3064 Images increased to 15320 MR Images	AlexNet, Resnet 18 and GoogleNet	CNN with Deep Feature Fusion	NA	30	stochastic gradient descent momentum (SGDM) optimizer	Classification	Accuracy (99.7%)
[16]	Figshare Dataset	3064 Images	Shape-based, model-based, intensity-based	2D CNN with auto Encoder network	Batch normalization	100	NA	Detection and Classification using ML classifiers	Accuracy with 2D CNN-96.4%, Accuracy with auto Encoder- 95.6%
[9]	Figshare Dataset	3064 Images	AlexNet, GoogleNet and VGG 16	Fine tuning and freezing the layers of pre-trained CNN	NA	30	Stochastic gradient descent momentum (SGDM)	Detection and Classification	Accuracy 98.69%

a new topology for building CNNs named as "parallel deep convolutional neural networks (PDCNNs)" to extract features. It deals with the over-fitting problem by utilizing a dropout Regularizer. This research work classified the brain tumor dataset into binary as well as multi-class. Hanaa et. al. [13] constructed a system to categorize brain tumors. This model makes use of pre-trained models (Inception-ResnetV2) for classification and for optimization it utilizes an "adaptive dynamic sine-cosine fitness grey wolf optimizer (ADSCFGWO) algorithm.

Methods and Materials

Dataset Used

This study makes use of a publicly available dataset containing 7025 images of brain MRI scans. Three separate datasets—the Sartaj dataset, the Figshare dataset, and the Br-35H dataset—have been combined to form the master dataset. In FIGSHARE dataset, all of the images in the collection are 512 x 512 pixels by dimensions. In total, there are 3064 T1-weighted contrast-enhanced MR images from 233 patients in the FIGSHARE dataset. Sartaj dataset consists of two folders named as TRAINING folder and the TESTING folder. Each folder is divided into four distinct classes named as pituatory_tumor, meningioma_tumor, glioma_tumor and no_tumor. This dataset can be obtained from the source https://github.com/sartajbhuvaji/brain-tumor-classification-dataset. The third dataset Br-35H consists of 253 MRI images of brain cancer patients; and this dataset is divided into two classes named as 'YES' and 'NO'. The collective dataset used is further categorized into two sets: training set with 5712 images and testing set with 1311 images. Table 81.2 shows the images in training and testing dataset.

Methodology Used

The primary purpose of proposed model is to identify brain tumor patients from healthy individuals with a high degree of accuracy. It places an emphasis on shortening the time necessary for detection. This research makes use of a previously trained EfficientNetB7 model (taught on ImageNet database). The brain tumor dataset is then used to refine the pre-trained model that was obtained. In the process of fine-tuning, EfficiencyNetB7 is given an input image of dimensions 150x150x 3. After that, the input is processed via a number of normal and reduction layers in order to extract the best features. Figure 81.1 below shows the workflow methodology of the proposed model.

Table 81.2 The table shows the types of tumors along with their training and testing samples

Tumor type	Training image samples	Testing Image samples
Meningioma	1339	306
Pituitary	1457	300
Glioma	1321	300
No of tumor	1597	405

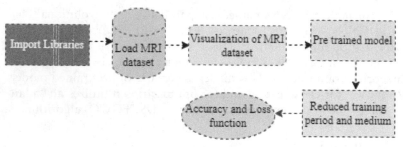

Figure 81.1 Workflow diagram for proposed model

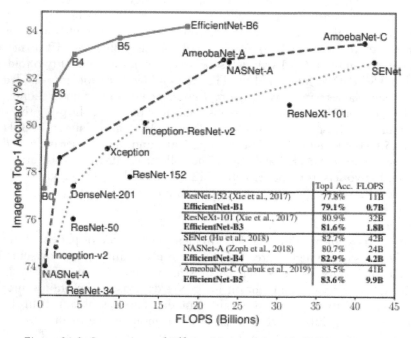

	Top1 Acc.	FLOPS
ResNet-152 (Xie et al., 2017)	77.8%	11B
EfficientNet-B1	**79.1%**	**0.7B**
ResNeXt-101 (Xie et al., 2017)	80.9%	32B
EfficientNet-B3	**81.6%**	**1.8B**
SENet (Hu et al., 2018)	82.7%	42B
NASNet-A (Zoph et al., 2018)	80.7%	24B
EfficientNet-B4	**82.9%**	**4.2B**
AmeobaNet-C (Cubuk et al., 2019)	83.5%	41B
EfficientNet-B5	**83.6%**	**9.9B**

Figure 81.2 Comparison of EfficientNet models with CNN and its variants
Source: [17]

Implementation Details

EfficientNetB0-B7 models are the deep transfer learning models. As shown in Figure 81.2, EfficientNet versions beat conventional CNN architecture, including GoogleNet, AlexNet, and MobileNet V2. MingXing Tan has suggested EfficientNets models B0–B7 in the year 2019. These have been trained on ImageNet's Large-Scale Visual Recognition Competition (ILSVRC) dataset contains over 1.2 million images. In this article, the EfficientNetB7 architecture is used, which takes inputs from the image dataset. It requires the fewest FLOPS for prediction. Table 81.3 enlists adjusted hyperparameter values of the proposed

Table 81.3 Hyperparameters and their corresponding values.

Hyperparameters	Value
Dropout rate	0.5
Global average pooling 2D	Set
Activation	Softmax
Loss	Categorical entropy
Optimizer	Adam
Epochs	12
Batch size	32

model for classification experiment. During training, the loss function was made to converge by heuristically adjusting the network's hyperparameters.

Results

Statistics are used to determine how well the optimal network model performs. These statistics are recall, accuracy, f1-score, precision and loss function. Experiments are performed in Python.

Accuracy

$$\text{Accuracy} = \frac{True\ Neg + True\ Pos}{True\ Pos + False\ Pos + True\ Neg + False\ Neg} \text{x } 100 \tag{1}$$

Precision

$$\text{Precision} = \frac{\text{True Pos}}{(\text{False Pos} + \text{True Pos})} \tag{2}$$

Recall

$$\text{Recall} = \frac{\text{True Pos}}{False\ Neg + True\ Pos} \tag{3}$$

F1-Score

$$\text{F1- score} = \frac{2 \text{ x precision} + \text{re\_call}}{\text{precision} + \text{re\_call}} \tag{4}$$

Classification samples are divided into two parts in this study. Figure 81.3 depicts the calculated classification performance on the data set. Figure 81.4 depicts the training and validation loss rate over epochs towards accuracy. The resulting classification performance is shown in Figure 81.5, demonstrating that

	precision	recall	f1-score	support
0	0.99	0.99	0.99	171
1	1.00	0.99	1.00	200
2	0.98	0.99	0.98	157
3	0.99	0.99	0.99	176
accuracy			0.99	704
macro avg	0.99	0.99	0.99	704
weighted avg	0.99	0.99	0.99	704

Figure 81.3 Accuracy for multiclass categorization of brain tumor

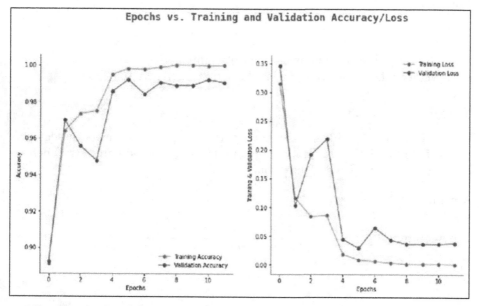

Figure 81.4 Plots for validation loss vs training loss and validation accuracy vs training accuracy

the acquired multiclass overall accuracy is 0.99 for meningioma, glioma, pituitary tumor, and no tumor.

Training Against Adversary Attacks

This model is also trained for handling adversarial attacks. The main focus is on the "fast gradient sign method attack (FGSM)", a form of white box attack whose primary objective is to guarantee misclassification. Using the gradients of the neural network, the fast gradient sign method creates a counterexample. This generated image will be termed as adversarial image. Procedure to implement Fast gradient sign method:

1.   The first step in generating an adversarial image is to generate perturbations that can be applied to the original image to distort it. Adversarial procedure is similar to classification.

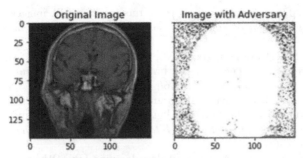

Figure 81.5 Original and adversary image

2. The formula for generation of adversarial image is:

    adv_image = Original image + ∈ * sign(∇I(θ, OriginalImage, input))

    Where *adv_image* = fake image, ∈ = multiplier for small perturbations, *θ* = model parameters, *I* = loss.
3. The model is trained for adversarial images as well. The training is same as the image classification training using EfficientNet model.
4. Original image and adversary image are above shown in Figure 81.5. To avoid adversary attacks, model is trained for adversary images as well.

Conclusion

In this study, clinical imaging data is used to discover multiple classes in categorization of tumors in the human brain through a transfer learning approach. The approach proved effective in classifying the brain MR images as meningioma, pituitary, glioma, and no tumor. This experiment is composed of two parts. To begin, the datasets are being segregated into two sets: 20% for evaluating the tumor and 80 percent for training purpose in the human brain using clinical images. Furthermore, a previously trained Efficient Net B7 model is well suited for tumor multiclass classification. Furthermore, a consequence was achieved that the experiment had highest and overall accuracy of 0.99 for tumor categorization. The study also involved the discussions in security vulnerabilities of machine learning models. In other words, small, undetectable changes to an image can have a large impact on how well a model fits the data. The final results decreased in the accuracy after gradient attacks. Before attacks and perturbations calculation the accuracy of the model was 99%. While after implementation the accuracy decreased with 1% turning the model accuracy into 98%.

References

1. Asif, S., Yi, W., Ain, Q. U., Hou, J., Yi T., and Si, J. (2022). Improving Effectiveness of different deep transfer learning-based models for detecting brain tumors from mr images. *IEEE Access*, 10, 34716–34730. doi: 10.1109/ACCESS.2022.3153306.

2. Polat, Ö. and Güngen, C. (2021). Classification of brain tumors from MR images using deep transfer learning. *Journal of Supercomputing*, 77(7), 7236–7252. doi: 10.1007/s11227-020-03572-9.

3. Mohsen, H., El-Dahshan, E E.-S. A., El-Horbaty, -S. M., andSalem, A.-B. M. (2018). Classification using deep learning neural networks for brain tumors. *Future Computing and Informatics Journal*, 3(1), 68–71. doi: 10.1016/j.fcij.2017.12.001.

4. Kibriya, H., Amin, R., Alshehri, ,Masood, M., Alshamrani, , and Alshehri, A. (2022). A novel and effective brain tumor classification model using deep feature fusion and famous machine learning classifiers. *Computational Intelligence and Neuroscience*, 2022, doi: 10.1155/2022/7897669.

5. Krishnapriya, S. and Karuna, Y. (2023). A survey of deep learning for MRI brain tumor segmentation methods: Trends, challenges, and future directions. *Health Technology*, 181–201. doi: 10.1007/s12553-023-00737-3.

6. Gull, S., Akbar,S., and Khan, (2021). Automated detection of brain tumor through magnetic resonance images using convolutional neural network. *BioMed Research International*, 2021. doi: 10.1155/2021/3365043.

7. Ananda Kumar, ,Prasad, ,and Metan, J. (2022). A hybrid deep CNN-Cov-19-Res-Net transfer learning architype for an enhanced brain tumor detection and classification scheme in medical image processing. *Biomedical Signal Processing and Control*, 76, 103631, 2022. doi: 10.1016/j.bspc.2022.103631.

8. Rahman, T. and Islam, (2022). MRI brain tumor detection and classification using parallel deep convolutional neural networks. *Measurement Specialties*, 26, 100694. doi: 10.1016/j.measen.2023.100694.

9. Rehman, A., Naz, S., Razzak, , Akram, F., and Imran, M. (2020). A deep learning-based framework for automatic brain tumors classification using transfer learning. *Circuits, Systems, and Signal Processing*, 39(2), 757–775. doi: 10.1007/s00034-019-01246-3.

10. Gómez-Guzmán et al. (2023). Classifying brain tumors on magnetic resonance imaging by using convolutional neural networks. *Electron*, 12(4), 1–22. doi: 10.3390/electronics12040955.

11. Sharif, ,Li, ,Khan, ,Kadry, S., and Tariq, U. (2022). M3BTCNet: multi model brain tumor classification using metaheuristic deep neural network features optimization. *Neural Computing and Applications*, 6. doi: 10.1007/s00521-022-07204-6.

12. Saurav, S., Sharma, A., Saini, R., and Singh, S. (2023). An attention-guided convolutional neural network for automated classification of brain tumor from MRI. *Neural Computing and Applications*, 35(3), 2541–2560. doi: 10.1007/s00521-022-07742-z.

13. ZainEldin, H. et al. (2023). Brain Tumor detection and classification using deep learning and sine-cosine fitness grey wolf optimization. *Bioengineering*, 10(1), 1–19. doi: 10.3390/bioengineering10010018.

14. Jude Hemanth, D. and Anitha, J. (2019). Modified genetic algorithm approaches for classification of abnormal magnetic resonance brain tumour images. *Applied Soft Computing*, 75, 21–28. doi: 10.1016/j.asoc.2018.10.054.

15. Shanthi, S., Saradha, S., Smitha, ,Prasath, N., and Anandakumar, H. (2022). An efficient automatic brain tumor classification using optimized hybrid deep neural network. *International Journal of Intelligent Networks*, 3, 188–196. doi: 10.1016/j.ijin.2022.11.003.

16. Saeedi, S., Rezayi, S., Keshavarz, H., and Niakan Kalhori, S. R. (2023). MRI-based brain tumor detection using convolutional deep learning methods and chosen machine learning techniques. *BMC Medical Informatics and Decision Making*, 23(1), 1–17. doi: 10.1186/s12911-023-02114-6.

17. Tan, M. and Le, (2019). EfficientNet: rethinking model scaling for convolutional neural networks. *36th Int. Conf. Mach. Learn. ICML 2019*, (pp. 10691–10700).

82 Key Management Protocol for Distributed Sensor Nodes

Dr. Vishal[a], Ms. Seema Kumari, Ms. Amandeep, Ms. Satwinder and Mr. Ravinder

School of Computer Applications, Lovely Professional University, Punjab, India

Abstract

The safety of data and network communications between sensor network nodes should be the main priorities of broad-spectrum security for wireless sensor networks. With regard to wireless sensor networks, environment and purpose usually affect security. Privacy, reliability, and validity are the three fundamental problems with data security. The use of traditional encryption algorithms on sensor nodes with limited resources is not recommended. In contrast to base station or key distribution center-initiated key management, node-initiated key management is a different idea. For the security of communication nodes in a sensor network, we can delegate control to sensor nodes or the cluster head. It is a more reliable non-centralized key management method than other ways. This study makes a proactive key management proposal that ensures effectiveness, reliability, and dynamic key creation.

Keywords: Sensor network, key generation, random number generator, security

Introduction

The security is an important concern for wireless sensor networks. There are many applications in military and other fields where sensor networks have mission critical tasks and for that security is prime concern. A wide range of security attacks against WSNs is found in literature. The classification of these security attacks is done according to different criteria, based on the domain or technique used during the attacks on WSNs. To counter these attacks, various security measures were proposed. Due to broadcast and wireless nature of medium, WSNs are more vulnerable to security attacks [2]. An Intrusion Detection Technique Using Frequency Analysis for Wireless Sensor Network, 2021). Furthermore, the nodes in wireless sensor network are deployed in hostile and uncontrolled territories; multiply the security threats. Security in wireless sensor network is complicated by different types of constrained in wireless sensor nodes. Sensor nodes are low-cost hardware devices which are not temper resistance, so it's easy to capture and copy the node data. The wireless transmission, along with the limitation of small size, limited battery power in sensor nodes make sensor network susceptible to denial-of-service attacks [3]. Due to design complexity and higher energy consumption anti-jamming techniques like frequency-hopping and temper proofing of nodes is not possible in WSNs. traditional secure cryptographic techniques like asymmetric cryptography cannot be implemented on the resource constrained sensor nodes. The main objective of key distribution and management is to establish a

---

[a]vishalhim@yahoo.com

reliable secure link between the pairs of nodes during the deployment phase of a sensor network [9]. The key management and distribution can be divided into two phases known as node initialization and network formation. During the initialization phase, all nodes bootstrapped and their component is checked for its proper functioning. In the next phase shared key discovery begins, in which the sensor nodes try to find a common key. If a pair of nodes found their shared key, then the key establishment phase begins for secure communication between them. In literature, many key distribution and management techniques have been proposed. The classification of the key distribution falls into two categories known as location-independent key management schemes and location-dependent key management schemes. If a key distribution scheme needs that sensor node needs to know about its location, then it is known as location-dependent otherwise it is location-independent key distribution techniques.

Literature Review

In the literature, many classifications of key distribution method have been found. the classification is done based on key material and number of keys used in encryption and decryption algorithms. There are many key distribution categories e.g., symmetric key distribution, asymmetric key distribution, hybrid key distribution. Another classification found based on the deployment model known as random key pre-distribution deployment, key-distribution using deployment knowledge. Adrian Perrig et al. [8] in their research paper entitled Security Protocols for Sensor Networks (SPINS), used a method in which all the nodes used single key, which is embedded in the nodes memory before deployment. There is no need for key discovery and key exchange due to same key in their memory. But there is drawbacks of this method, even single nodes exposure to intruders leads to vulnerability of entire network. The alternative exists for single key methods, in which for each nodes different keys can be assigned, but it will reduce scalability, increase key discovery and negotiation time. it also increases storage overhead in individual as well as entire networks. Eschenauer et al. [7] used random key probability scheme which is based on random graph mathematical model. Random graph is designed using n vertices which is called nodes and addition of edges which are known as links among the sensor nodes. Generally random graph is denoted by G(n,p) and the edges exist with a probability Du et al. [4] proposed a key management scheme based on deployment knowledge and is an extension of Bloms method. Blom's method is based on the symmetry of matrix in which row m and column n is corresponds to row n and column m. and if m and n corresponds to node pairs in that case keys are similar in both the sensor, that leads to common share among them. Panja et al. [1], proposed energy and communication "proficient group key management technique for hierarchical sensor networks and is similar to hierarchical group keying method known as Tree-based Group Diffie-Hellman (TGDH) protocol. In this keying method there is one level of common sensor nodes and several levels of cluster heads. Each cluster head acts manager for different cluster heads under their influence. The main advantage TGDH is that, it is less complicated and hence simple to design and develop as well as need minimum computational power with minimum storage. Also, key revocation and refreshing is easy. Zhu et al. [11] proposed and efficient security mechanisms for large-scale distributed sensor networks and is based on Initial Trust model where network share a common master key K and a hash function H. After initial setup in fields nodes begin discovery for their neighboring nodes and create pair wise key using K and H. the pair wise key between node X and Y can be HK(X||Y). after creating pair, all sensor nodes release the master key. Pietro et al. [8] proposed connectivity properties of secure wireless sensor networks.

Eltoweissy et al. [5] published a paper entitled schemes for effective group key management in dynamic system. In which, One-way function chain trees, subset-cover broadcast encryption, logical key hierarchies, and other standard binary-tree-based cluster key management and broadcast techniques are utilized in wireless sensor networks. Eltoweissy et al. [6] proposed group key management scheme for large-scale sensor networks, known as SHELL scheme where keys are computed from node position data with the help of clusters and gateways after the deployment, the SHELL scheme collects information about node locations and uses these values to assign keys". In order to share the bulk of keys among available nodes, SHELL takes advantage of the physical proximity of nodes. Table below illustrate a comparison study of all the schemes which we studied in the literature.

Table 82.1 Key Distribution schemes advantages and limitations

Shared single key pre-Deployment	• Minimum memory storage required, • No extra protocol steps are necessary, • Resistant against DOS attack ,packet injection	• Single node compromise leads to compromise of entire network. • None nodes can be added after deployment
Shared multiple key pre-deployment	• Less chance for intrusion on the entire network	• Significant over head, • Poor scalability
Asymmetric Public key approach	• Absolutely resilient against nodecaptured. • Able to revoke known compromised key pairs, • Completely scalable	• Trust on a symmetric key • Key over head, • Communication overhead • Computation overhead.
Pair wise-shared Keys	• Great resilience to node captured • Compromised keys can be revoked	• Poor scalability, • No of keys stored in each node proportional to network size
"Combinatorial Design Based Key Pre-Distribution"	• More possibility of a "pair of sensor nodes to share a key". • Decreases the key-path distance while providing scalability with hybrid scheme.	• Hybrid design decreases key sharing probability
Polynomial Based Key Pre-Distribution Schemes	• Good scalability • Less computation and communication overhead.	• Poor key connectivity • Storage over head

Proposed Method for Key Generation and Distribution

In WSN sensor nodes are widely deployed in the monitoring area and are responsible for collection of data from area under its observation. Data aggregation and processing can be done if nodes are powerful and have sufficient storage and processing power. The structural topology of WSN nodes will vary due to different applications requirements. The basic functional units of sensor nodes can be divided in to four units namely sensing, processing, communication and energy supply unit. In order to provide security to generated data there is use of encryption unit used in communication unit that encrypts the data before transmission. But the main problem arises how to encrypt the data using appropriate encryption techniques, in literature we studied many techniques that have certain advantages and disadvantages [10]. It's found that the traditional encryption algorithms consume both processing power and energy which is not feasible in light weight energy constrained sensor nodes. Here we proposed a method which needs minimum computational power to encrypt the data the proposed method is suitable only for temper resistance sensor nodes where the key generation logic is embedded in such a way that, any tempering to sensor nodes destroy the logic to make the 100% secure system. Before transmission of data it is assumed that nodes are well connected and in the communication range with each other, if any node wants to communicate with other node, then it first generates and random number with a function F(n), random number generation itself is complex task where it's impossible to predict future number to be generated based on previous generated numbers. There is secret in the random number but give no clue about the information it contains. Probabilistic processes yield randomly distributed, unexpected numbers that are never easily reproducible.

In order to generate the common share among the communication nodes are as follows.

- **Step 1:** All the nodes should be deployed randomly and be arranged in a proper topology.
- **Step 2:** The communication among the nodes may be one to one or one to many.
- **Step 3:** When any node wants to communicate with other NODE, it randomly generates a number and broadcast in the network. But the logic for secrete sharing is based on the pre-deployed algorithm in sensor node where key generation and use of key for encryption or decryption is done inside the sensor node, without revealing the key to anyone.
- **Step-4.** There must be secrete logic for each node, whenever they are communicating with particular node it must be pre-defined calculation method for common share.
- **Step-5:** for pre-defined calculation, there is use of simple mathematical operations (addition, subtraction, division, multiplication and exponentiation etc.) on the random number.
- **Step-6.** The logic can be created based on following method.

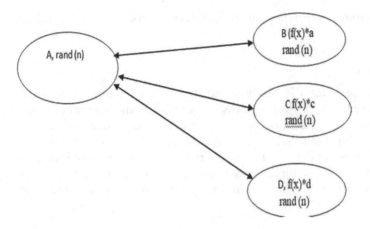

If Node-A is communicating with Node-B and vice versa use the operation f(x)*a Else if

If Node-A is communicating with Node-C and vice versa use the operation f(x)*c Else if

If Node-A is communicating with Node-D and vice versa use the operation f(x)*d And so on ------------

Using this process each pair can calculate a common share, which can be used as a key to encrypt the data before transmission.

The proposed technique is a symmetric encryption technique where both sender and receiver uses same key to encrypt and decrypt the data with an exception that symmetric encryption technique uses same key for each cycle of communication where as in the proposed method for each cycle of communication common shared key different due to randomness created by random number

Table 82.2 Comparative analysis

Scheme	Storage	Resilience	Computation	Communication	Mobile Network
Pair wise	$O(k\log N)$	Perfect resilience	$O(1)$	$O(\log N)$	No
Q-Composite	$O(k\log N)$	Inversely proportional to s	$O(k\log k)$	$O(k)$	No
Bloom	$O(\lambda)$	λ-secure	$O(\lambda)$	$O(\log N)$	Yes
Proposed Scheme	$O(N)$	Perfect resilience	$O(1)$	$O(N)$	Yes

generator. This approach dependent on use of crypto-processor and random number generator

Result and Analysis

The main performance criteria in any key distribution and management algorithm are storage, resilience against assaults, computation and communication overhead, and types of networks, according to a comparison study of several algorithms, as shown in Table 82.2 below. As compared to other approaches explored in the literature, analysis of Table 82.2 reveals that in proposed method computational complexity is minimum and is equivalent to pair wise scheme. but storage and communication overhead is directly proportional to the size of the network.

Conclusion

As Internet of Things (IOT) applications develop, wireless sensor technologies have become increasingly important. Due to resource restrictions inside the sensor networks, key management and distribution is a difficult issue. With the use of no prior knowledge, we attempted to design a random key generation mechanism in this work. The key generation process and mutual authentication between the sensor nodes were made simpler in this design. Our analysis demonstrates that employing independent key generation by sensor nodes without outside assistance, this strategy enhances security

References

1. B. Panja, S. K. Madria and B. Bhargava, (2006). Energy and communication efficient group key management protocol for hierarchical sensor networks, IEEE International Conference on Sensor Networks, Ubiquitous, and Trustworthy Computing (SUTC'06), Taichung, Taiwan, 2006, pp. 8. doi: 10.1109/SUTC.2006.1636204.
2. Choudhary, V. and Taruna, S. (2021). An Intrusion Detection Technique Using Frequency Analysis for Wireless Sensor Network. International Conference on Computing,Communication, and Intelligent Systems (ICCCIS) (pp. 206–210). Greater Noida, India: IEEE.
3. Choudhary, V., Taruna, D. S., and Purbey, L. B. (2018). A Comparative Analysis of Cryptographic Keys and Security. 3rd International Conference and Workshops on Recent Advances and Innovations in Engineering (ICRAIE), (pp. 1–8).
4. Du, W., Deng, J., Han, Y. S., Chen, S., and Varshney, P. K. (2004). A key management scheme for wireless sensor networks using deployment knowledge. IEEE INFOCOM 2004 (p. 597). Hong Kong: IEEE.
5. Eltoweissy, M., Heydari, M. H., Morales, L., and Sudborough, I. H. (2004). Combinatorial Optimization of Group Key Management. Journal of Network and Systems Management, 33–50.
6. Eltoweissy, M., Wadaa, A., Olariu, S., and Wilson, L. (2005). Group key management scheme for large-scale sensor networks. Journal Ad Hoc Networks, 668–688.
7. Eschenauer, L. and Gligor, V. D. (2002). A key-management scheme for distributed sensor networks. CCS '02 Proceedings of the 9th ACM conference on Computer and

communications security (pp. 41–47). Washington, DC, USA: ACM New York, NY, USA .

8. Pietro, R. D., Mancini, L. V., Mei, A., Panconesi, A., and Radhakrishnan, J. (2004). Connectivity properties of secure wireless sensor networks. SASN '04 Proceedings of the 2nd ACM workshop on Security of ad hoc and sensor networks (pp. 53–58). Washington DC: ACM New York.

9. Vishal Choudhary, S. (2018). A Distributed Key Management Protocol for Wireless Sensor Network. International Conference on Advanced Informatics for Computing Research (pp. 243–256). Shimla India: Springer Nature Switzerland.

10. Vishal Choudhary, S. T. (2016). Improved Key Distribution and Management in Wireless Sensor Network. Journal of Wireless Communications, 16–22.

11. Zhu, S., Setia, S., and Jajodia, S. (2003). LEAP: efficient security mechanisms for large-scale distributed sensor networks. CCS '03 Proceedings of the 10th ACM conference on Computer and communications security (pp. 62–72). Washington D.C.: ACM New York, NY, USA

83 A proposed system for sentiment analysis using deep learning for facial recognition

Aditi Gupta[a], Jasmin Bar[b] and Dr. Nancy Gulati[c]

Department of Computer Science & Engineering, Amity School of Engineering and Technology, Amity University, Noida, India

Abstract

Sentiment analysis and face expression recognition are two of the most popular areas of research in computer science these days owing to deep learning. Various deep learning and machine learning algorithms have been experimented and modeled with different datasets available as well as gathered by researchers to ensure accuracy of classification of human sentiments and emotions to help organizations judge and predict their feelings and actions in near future. Various facial expressions are related to certain distinct emotions, like happiness, anger, disappointment, tiredness, etc. Some of the famously employed machine learning and deep learning algorithms which have been deployed over the model to implement sentiment analysis for facial recognition have been compared. To name a few- CNN, PCA or deep PCA, SVM, etc. The lack of competent models which can be utilized for 3D image data and from videos, along with fake emotion depiction have also been discussed. CNN model has been implemented and integrated with web application to send alert notification to user and their relatives.

Keywords: machine learning, deep learning, facial recognition, emotion classification

Introduction

Sentiment analysis is crucial for identifying and comprehending staff and consumer emotions. To train sentiment detection models for context, sarcasm, etc., and comprehend the user's genuine mood and sentiments, deep learning techniques can be utilized. These days, a lot of businesses utilize this as a tool to comprehend the feelings of their clients, to improve the customer experience, and to boost customer service. The steps involved in face recognition tasks include recognition, positioning, feature extraction, and recognition. Algorithms like CNN, RNN, etc., and their collaborations have been deployed over the dataset to classify human emotions with face recognition. Different datasets discovered have been discussed. Due to their face indicators, particular emotions may be seen most clearly. Facial expression recognition (FER) is very intricate but makes a difference in different product ranges such as health care, auto guided machines, and individual-machine communication. Some of the bland feelings of an individual are resentment, joy, pity, nauseate, panic, as well as astonishment. Some of the recent research work done in this area has been compared with the model implemented. A web application has also been created to instantly recognize and categorize emotions. Furthermore, a mechanism for alert creation has been created for when a person is sad, which can be employed in hospitals and

[a]guptaaditi1410@gmail.com, [b]jasminbar7@gmail.com, [c]ngulati@amity.edu

by families of depressed patients. Future applications have been discussed for making different applications like for Alzheimer's patients and detecting emotions in infants.

Literature Review

Diverse procedures have been studied for this reason and a comparative study has been made between the distinctive accuracy appeared by the different models. In this section, step-by-step the various stages for emotion recognition have been discussed.

Facial Expression Recognition (FER)

FER frameworks can be any - inactive or energetic centered upon image. Inactive FER reflects as it were the confront spot evidence from the highlight depiction of a particular image, although, the energetic picture FER believes the chronological knowledge with ceaseless outlines.

1. Dataset: To maintain a strategic distance from over-fitting, the taking after FER calculations are examined, which needs broad preparation information. For evaluation, preparation, and confirming the computations required to progress FER, a set of data that includes clearly defined emotion categories for facial expression is essential. The aforementioned data sets provide a collection of photographs that evoke specific emotions.

2. Pre-processing: This action pre-deals with the data set by getting rid of commotion and information compression. Different actions concerned with this are:
    (i)   facial detection is the control to identify the area of the confrontation in any image or outline. It decides whether the face is shown in a picture or not.
    (ii) measurement reduction is utilized to decrease the factors by a set of principal variables. In case the number of highlights is more, at that point it gets tougher to imagine the preparing set and to work on it.
    (iii) normalization: Reduced highlights are normalized without mutilating the differences within the extent of values of highlights. There are various normalization strategies, to be specific Z-normalization, min-max normalization, unit vector normalization, which moves forward the numerical soundness and speeds up the preparation of the demonstration.

3. Feature mining: This is a method for extricating highlights which are vital for FER. This comes about in littler and in larger collections of qualities that include highlights including mouth curves, borders, and sides to margins as well as other crucial details like the separation between mouth and irises and the gap that separates two pupils, resulting in an impact in the speed at which training data is trained.

4. Sentiment categorization: This step includes calculations to categorize different feelings centered about extricated characteristics. The categorization has different strategies, that classify the pictures in different groups. The

grouping of pictures is conducted subsequently, handing via pre-managing stages of confrontation location that includes mining.

The FER framework has different purposes like computer-person intelligence, health care framework, and public promotion.

GuodongGuo et al. [1], performed a thorough survey for analyzing different approaches for FER in static images and several factors which affect their results were discussed. Several techniques for identifying faces, extracting features, and grouping emotions were discussed. Several face emotion datasets like FER2013, extended Cohn-Kanade (CK+), Japanese female expression, Toronto face database, multipie, etc. were also discussed.

After thorough discussion on current issues that persists like lack of proper training datasets, FER on infrared data and 3D data and other issues of categorizing real or fake emotions, etc., has brought some future scope for research FER in representations of three-dimensional head designs, detecting sentiment in pictures with obstruction, etc.

Shilpa et al. [2], in this survey, have discussed sentiment analysis from text from various social media platforms, like tweets, etc. by categorizing them according to their emotions as good or negative using deep learning algorithms. For further accuracy, according to the authors, analysis of personality of the users also needs to be investigated for personalizing it.

Zhang et al. [3], in this survey have summarized several techniques used for facial recognition. In deep learning, algorithms like CNN have been discussed for facial recognition, along with ideas relevant to face picture analysis and face identification.

Some ideas like combining several forms of appearance characteristics, constructing strong loss functions, embracing appropriate stimulation tasks and some additional approaches along with some neural network approaches on convolutional neural nets like web-scale, etc. were discussed. Some multi-CNN strategies like extracting features in different features of expression and identifying traits from various facial features, and modifications in CNN by adjusting core training mechanisms and fusing CNNs, adopting weakly-supervised or unsupervised learning and other strategies were discussed.

A. Datasets discovered

Various datasets found over Kaggle and other sources, are discussed as follows:

i.   FER 2013: It consists of a huge figure of images and significant attributes. Train set: 28,709 photographs validation set: 3,589 photographs test set: 3,589 photographs no. of expression labels: 7

ii.   Extended Cohn-Kanade (CK+): It comprises nearly 593 distinct sequences obtained from 123 unique subjects. It is the most extensively used dataset.

iii. Japanese female facial expression (JAFFE): It contains 219 distinct pictures for seven face emotion appearances obtained by 10 female models from Japan.

iv.   Multi-pie: Implemented for 3D face emotion recognition. Images: 755,370 subjects: 337 viewpoints: 15 illumination condition: 19 different conditions number of expression labels: 6

B. Requirement for Face Recognition, Dimensionality Reduction and Normalization

Within the facial emotion recognition preparation, the primary pre-obligatory stage is confront detection, which includes the discovery of a confrontation within the picture or outline and eliminates the inconsequential pixels. Different calculations for confront discovery are accessible like Viola-jones, principal component analysis, linear discriminant analysis, and hereditary calculations [10].

C. Necessity of Feature Mining

Face appearance investigation contains different strategies like facial point of interest recognizable proof, highlight extraction, and distinctive highlight extraction databases. Facial points of interest are depicted by the face's main focuses that are inferred by the shape of the confrontation. At hand are dual strategies accessible -

Corners: Corners of a picture may be a critical property, which can be gathered from the complex objects of the picture.

Edges: Edges are linear highlights which speak to the periphery of a picture area. It draws attention to the conditions of distinctive focuses of the confrontation, like the place of eyes, etc.

D. Requirement For Sentiments Classification

Readily available are different strategies that are utilized for the classification of sentiments following utilizing confront location and highlight mining processes. The foremost commonly employed technique for categorization is CNN because it may be connected specifically to the stored picture exclusive of utilizing any include mining and confront location processes and even makes way improved precision over the stored information. CNN deal with a tremendous contest in the preparation of inadequate-picture datasets.

A comparison of related research work previously done has been shown in Table 83.1.

Face Sentiment Analysis: The Proposed Methodology

Classification of emotions for sentiment analysis for facial recognition requires the use of algorithms which can work on image datasets and while transforming and reducing data dimensionality, it doesn't lose beneficial information. All steps have been discussed in detail in the literature review section of this report.

A. Facial Detection, Dimension Reduction, and Normalization

a) Viola-Jones face detection algorithm- Viola-Jones is widely employed to identify face appearance. It holds four steps, like Haar-like characters, fundamental charts, AdaBoost training, and cascading classifier.

b) Principal component analysis -The basic thought behind the PCA is that multi trait information is anticipated onto a straight lower-dimensional space. Human confrontation can be recognized utilizing eigen confrontations. Eigen area could be a collection of eigenvectors to classify the faces according to their premise representation [9].

Table 83.1 Comparison of related work done.

S. No.	Paper title	Year	Authors	Description	Merits	Demerits
1.	Facial expression recognition boosted by soft label with a diverse ensemble	2019	[12]	Performed classification on FER, SFEW, RAF data using ensemble method	Improved differentiation potentiality of classifier	Low accuracy
2.	A face expression recognition using CNN and LBP	2020	[13]	Performed CNN classification on YALEFACE, CK+, JAFFE for 7 classes of emotions	High accuracy in CK+ data	Low accuracy for JAFFE data
3.	Facial emotion recognition using deep convolutional neural network	2020	[5]	Employed CNN on combined dataset for five classes of emotions	Self-built combined dataset	Low accuracy
4.	Face recognition and identification using deep learning approach	2021	[14]	Performed CNN classification	High Accuracy for Image data	Low accuracy for real-time data
5.	Face and emotion recognition using deep learning based on computer vision methods	2021	[4]	Performed CNN (Mini Xception model) with Viola Jones on UTK face data and FER	Gender detection is also implemented	Low accuracy in gender recognition

(*Source*: Author's compilation)

c) Linear discriminant analysis- LDA is utilized to diminish the measurements of a given information. LDA employs fisher confront (improvement of eigen-face) for decreasing the dimensions of the highlights and the recognizable proof of confrontation in an image.

B. Feature Extraction
This is the step to mine the features which are necessary in categorization. Because of this, larger collections of characteristics, including appearance boundaries,

angles, transverse, and additional important information like the space between the eyes and in the middle of lips, which makes trained figures easier to understand. A couple of properties fundamental to human confrontation like:

    i. The eye zone is darker than the upper cheeks.
    ii. The nose interface zone is brighter than the eyes.
    iii. Zone and measure: eyes, mouth, expansion of nose.

It can be transformed into a smaller set of highlights. Highlight mining entails cutting down on the amount of resources required to present a lot of information.

1)   Local pattern in binary: The lateral surface descriptor is what transforms the value of the first pixel in the image into the LBP codes, which are codes that are derived from the lateral surface descriptor [7].
2)   Filter of gabor: It separates the image's time and recurrence spaces. It implies that it investigates whether the image contains any frequency substance in certain orientation surrounding the inspection location.

Haar like features: It finds consistencies found in faces, similar characteristics, etc. by edge detection method shown in Figure 83.1 [6].

C. Emotion Classification
a)   Artificial Neural Network (ANN)
    It was designed for imitating the way a human brain processes and organizes data. ANNs have self-learning capacities that engage them to convey improved results as more data will be accessible. Each neuron has a cell body that can handle information by carrying data toward and away from the brain (yields).
b)   Convolutional Neural Network (CNN)
    CNN is one subtype of neural networks which is employed in classification, especially picture-based data classification. It consists of layers which reduces dimensionality of images without losing valuable information [11]. Various layers in CNN:

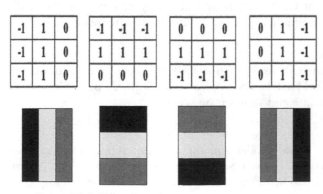

Figure 83.1 Edge detection

1. Input layer: It contains the input images pixel values.
2. Convolutional Layer: It convolves $n * n$ kernels with x feature maps of the previous layer.
3. Pooling layer: It reduces the resolution of feature maps to attain spatial invariance.
    a. Max pooling: It selects the most active features.
    b. Average pooling: It picks up the mean value of input on previous layers feature map.

Fully connected layer: The final fundamental tier in the basic CNN model, in which each node after being converted into vectors is connected to it.

c) Support Vector Machine (SVM)

An algorithm that is devised to distinguish between two classes is SVM. There will be more than one SVM implemented if the SVM has more than two classes. For linearly separable data, SVM may be a direct classifier that can be connected.

d) Deep Belief Network (DBN)

A deterministic neural network calculation has various stochastic torpid components. DBN has a pile of RBM or Autoencoders. The two properties of DBN are:

i.   It employs a top-down, level-by-level training strategy to determine the way weights depend on the level below that one.
ii. The estimation of latent variables is made possible by a single bottom-up pass layer that starts with an observed information vector and makes use of loads in partitioned layers.

e) Recurrent Neural Network (RNN)

There is no initial constraint on the arrangement of inputs that RNNs can accept. They recall the past and pursue decisions in view of past learning. When producing outputs, RNNs remember the previous inputs.

Algorithm Suggested

At each step, i.e., at feature extraction and emotion classification, tweaking a few algorithms and methods can be helpful in reaching the desired classification which is more accurate than the previous suggested models and methodologies. With no operator intervention, CNN recognizes the crucial characteristics on its own. An amalgamation of CNN with neural nets may be incorporated with already existing models, as it will help in enhancing the performance.

Proposed System Prototype

A web application has been built using python flask to integrate it with a deep learning model using CNN. HTML has been used to develop web pages. It detects a person's emotions in real time and shows it on screen.

Model summar:-

Figure 83.2. represents the CNN model and the different types of layers and their order in which they have been used. Softmax activation function and Adam optimizer have also been used. The number of epochs were increased to improve the accuracy.

Model: "sequential"

Layer (type)	Output Shape	Param #
conv2d (Conv2D)	(None, 46, 46, 32)	320
max_pooling2d (MaxPooling2D)	(None, 23, 23, 32)	0
batch_normalization (BatchN ormalization)	(None, 23, 23, 32)	128
conv2d_1 (Conv2D)	(None, 21, 21, 64)	18496
max_pooling2d_1 (MaxPooling 2D)	(None, 10, 10, 64)	0
batch_normalization_1 (Batc hNormalization)	(None, 10, 10, 64)	256
conv2d_2 (Conv2D)	(None, 8, 8, 128)	73856
max_pooling2d_2 (MaxPooling 2D)	(None, 4, 4, 128)	0
batch_normalization_2 (Batc hNormalization)	(None, 4, 4, 128)	512
flatten (Flatten)	(None, 2048)	0
dense (Dense)	(None, 128)	262272
dense_1 (Dense)	(None, 7)	903

Figure 83.2 Model summary for layers of CNN used for the model

For training the model, FER dataset has been employed and the table below mentions the emotions and their images in Table 83.2. Figure 83.3. represents the output result for the model for various emotions as will be visible on the screen of the user.

Considering the rise in the number of people falling into depression, a special case for sending email alert system to send the notification to the person or their relatives when they are detected to be sad has been built. So that they can note it and cheer them up as shown in Figure 83.4. This helps to monitor depressed patient's emotions as well as keep tabs on them, especially in critical cases.

Challenges
A few difficulties were also highlighted, including changes in lighting, incomplete face photos, differences in facial makeup, and mixed variances in facial expression. Challenges like video-based face identification, etc. were also explored by

Table 83.2 Emotions and their number of images trained

S. No.	Name of emotion	No. of images trained
1.	Anger	3995
2.	Disgust	436
3.	Fear	4097
4.	Happiness	7215
5.	Neutral	4965
6.	Sad	4830
7.	Surprise	3171

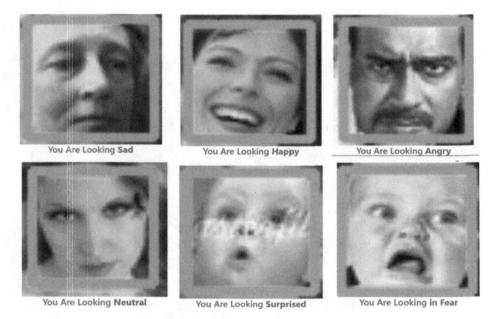

Figure 83.3 Output results after detection and prediction of emotions

the authors of other studies. Also addressed were certain databases for still picture face databases, heterogeneous face databases, etc. A few of the challenges faced in datasets are as follows: -

i.   Obscured records set
ii.   3-dimensional records
iii. Infrared data
iv.   Fake emotion recognition
v.   Face alignment
vi.   Face detection from video

Hello Inbox ×

 root.xyz123@gmail.com
to me ▾

Hello. Flask is looking sad!!
Please cheer up!! You can read a book, watch movies, listen to songs, paint, etc.
Feel free to reach out to us if you need to.

Have a Good Day!!!
Thank You

Figure 83.4 Output result for email notification sent to the user

Results and Discussion

The datasets that are currently accessible have issues ranging from occlusion to lighting, and the initial stage of data extraction and pre-processing to obtain relevant information has problems as a result. This makes it challenging to create correct deep learning models. With the growth of false emotion portrayal, it is still impossible to tell if a person's feelings are real or not. Each technique under consideration has pros and cons, and when paired with a problematic dataset, they make it difficult to create an appropriate sentiment analysis categorization model. Various algorithms have been discussed for each stage of model, like for face detection- Viola Jones algorithm, principal component analysis, for feature extraction- local binary pattern, gabor filter, etc., and for last step of emotion classification CNN, DBN, and RNN have been discussed which have been employed by various researchers in various combinations of algorithms at each step. It has been concluded that there is still a great deal of research needed in this area, such as recognizing emotion in images with occlusion, etc. The task of real-time FER remains challenging. Using more advanced DL methods, further investigation of the FER issue in videos in the future can be done.

For different datasets, and algorithms the result was varying. Various emotions with the number of images in the test and train set of FER data have been plotted in Graph 83.1. After studying algorithms and their accuracies, the model that is considered to perform best is convolutional neural network model (CNN). The FER dataset has been utilized to build the CNN model which resulted in 94.40% accuracy and integrated it with web application.

The comparison of accuracies of related work previously done by various authors with this model has been shown in Table 83.3. A bar plot which represents the same is shown in Graph 83.3.

Future Scope and Conclusion

There have been several algorithms discussed, and each has advantages and disadvantages. It has been challenging to develop the model owing to a lack of appropriate data, despite the fact that several researchers in this field have used various algorithms in combination at various stages of the model to improve

FER2013 Dataset

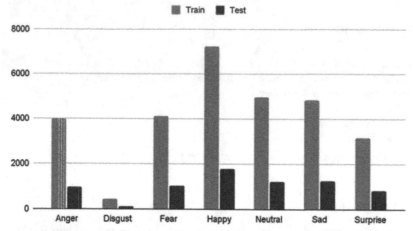

Graph 83.1 Number of images in train and test set used in FER2013 dataset for different emotions

Table 83.3 Comparison of related work and their accuracy with this model

Authors/Models	Accuracy
Gan et al	55.73 to 86.31%
Ravi et al	72.18 to 89.62%
Pranav et al	78.04%
Teoh et al	91.7%
Akçelik et al	93.11%
This model	94.40%

(*Source*: Author's compilation)

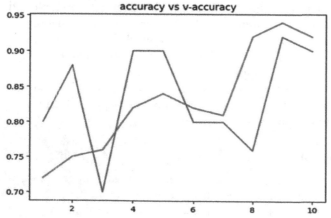

Graph 83.2 Accuracy vs validation accuracy curve for model using FER dataset

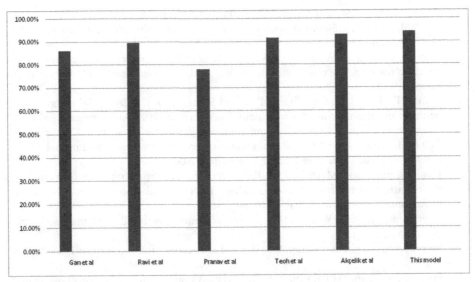

Graph 83.3 Accuracy results of related work in comparison to this model

and enhance the accuracy. As a result, it can be said that the primary challenges to establishing the right models includes a lack of acceptable datasets and inadequate testing of algorithms will be overcome by creating the right models that can identify various attitudes.

After reviewing the algorithms employed previously, CNN is found to be the best algorithm and can be used with other neural nets to enhance and improve accuracy results of sentiment analysis. The CNN model using optimizers like Adam optimizer was built with classification accuracy of 94.40% for emotion classification and integrated with web application for real-time sentiment analysis, which also sends notification alert to the user and their relatives in cases of depressed person when they are detected to be sad. Applications like automatic surveillance with face recognition, etc., have recently developed [15]. Applications such as pain level detection can also be implemented using this as a base model for patients in hospitals. In future, it can also be used as a emotion recognition model for Alzeihmers patients. Alongwith a neonatal pain detection model which can alert parents if the infant is in pain or distress can be built using this as the base model.

References

1. Guo, G. and Zhangb, N. (2019). A survey on deep learning based face recognition. Computer Vision and Image Understanding, 189.
2. Shilpa, P. C., Shereen, R., Jacob, S., qn Vinod, P. (2021). Sentiment analysis using deep learning. Proceedings of the Third International Conference on Intelligent Communication Technologies and Virtual Mobile Networks (ICICV 2021). DVD Part Number: CFP21ONG-DVD, 978-0-7381-1182-7.

3. Zhang, L., Wang, S., and Liu, B. (2018). Deep learning for sentiment analysis: a survey. Wiley Interdisciplinary Reviews: Data Mining and Knowledge Discovery, 8(8). doi:10.1002/widm.1253
4. Akçelik, C., Okatan, A., and Çetinkaya, A. (2021). Face and emotion recognition using deep learning based on computer vision methods. New Trends in Mathematical Science ,9(1).
5. Pranav, E., Kamal, S., Chandran, C. S., and Supriya, M. (2020). Facial emotion recognition using deep convolutional neural network. In 2020 6th International Conference on Advanced Computing and Communication Systems (ICACCS), pp. 317–320.6 Mehendale, N. (2020). Facial emotion recognition using convolutional neural networks (FERC). Springer Nature Switzerland AG.
7. Jayalekshmi, J. and Mathew, T. (2017). Facial expression recognition and emotion classification system for sentiment analysis. International Conference on Networks & Advances in Computational Technologies.
9. Chen, J. and Jenkins, W. K. (2017). Facial recognition with PCA and machine learning methods. IEEE.
10. Liong, V. E., Lu, J., and Wang, G. (2013). Face recognition using deep PCA. ICICS, 1-5.
11. Hussain, S. A., and Al Balushi, A. S. A. (2019). A real time face emotion classification and recognition using deep learning model. Journal of Physics: Conference Series. 1432, 012087.
12. Gan, Y., Chen, J., and Xu, L. (2019). Facial expression recognition boosted by soft label with a diverse ensemble. Pattern Recognition Letters, 125, 105–112.
13. Ravi, R., Yadhukrishna, S., and Prithviraj, R. (2020). A face expression recognition using CNN & LBP. In 2020 Fourth International Conference on Computing Methodologies and Communication (ICCMC), pp. 684–689, IEEE.
14. Teoh, K. H., Ismail, R.C., Naziri, S. Z. M., and Hussin, R. (2020). Face recognition and identification using deep learning approach. 5th International Conference on Electronic Design (ICED).Journal of Physics Conference Series, 1755(1), 012006.
15. Singh, A., Bhatt, S., Nayak, V., and Shah, M. (2023). Automation of surveillance systems using deep learning and facial recognition. International Journal of Systems Assurance Engineering and Management I, 14 (Suppl 1), 236–224.

Taylor & Francis
Taylor & Francis Group
http://taylorandfrancis.com

Printed in the United States
by Baker & Taylor Publisher Services